Michael Noel
Colin Spence

SharePoint® 2013

UNLEASHED

SAMS | 800 East 96th Street, Indianapolis, Indiana 46240 USA

Microsoft® SharePoint® 2013 Unleashed

ISBN-13: 978-0-672-33733-8

ISBN-10: 0-672-33733-9

Library of Congress Control Number: 2013937704

Printed in the United States of America

First Printing August 2013

Trademarks

All terms mentioned in this book that are known to be trademarks or service marks have been appropriately capitalized. Sams Publishing cannot attest to the accuracy of this information. Use of a term in this book should not be regarded as affecting the validity of any trademark or service mark.

Warning and Disclaimer

Every effort has been made to make this book as complete and as accurate as possible, but no warranty or fitness is implied. The information provided is on an "as is" basis. The author(s) and the publisher shall have neither liability nor responsibility to any person or entity with respect to any loss or damages arising from the information contained in this book or from the use of the programs accompanying it.

Bulk Sales

Sams Publishing offers excellent discounts on this book when ordered in quantity for bulk purchases or special sales. For more information, please contact

U.S. Corporate and Government Sales
1-800-382-3419
corpsales@pearsontechgroup.com

For sales outside the United States, please contact

International Sales
international@pearsoned.com

Editor-in-Chief
Greg Wiegand

Executive Editor
Neil Rowe

Development Editor
Mark Renfrow

Managing Editor
Kristy Hart

Project Editor
Elaine Wiley

Copy Editor
Keith Cline

Indexer
Tim Warner

Proofreader
Anne Goebel

Technical Editor
Jonathan Chen

Contributing Writers
Anthony Adona
Agnes Molnar
Alex Kirchmann
Alpesh Nakar
Ayman El-Hattab
Ben Nadler
Eric Harlan
Jonathan Chen
Ken Lo
Mark Rhodes
Mona Zhao
Toni Frankola
Ulysses Ludwig

Publishing Coordinator
Cindy Teeters

Book Designer
Mark Shirar

Composition
Nonie Ratcliff

Contents at a Glance

Table of Contents

About the Authors

Michael Noel, MVP, MCITP, is an internationally recognized technology expert, bestselling author, and well known public speaker on a broad range of IT topics. He has authored several major industry books that have been translated into more than a dozen languages worldwide. Currently a partner at Convergent Computing (www.cco.com) in the San Francisco Bay Area, Michael's writings and extensive public speaking experience across all seven continents leverage his real-world expertise helping organizations realize business value from Information Technology infrastructure.

Colin Spence, MCP, MCTS SharePoint, is a partner at Convergent Computing (www.cco.com) and manages the SharePoint practice for the organization. He has worked with SharePoint technologies for more than a decade and has worked with hundreds of clients architecting, implementing, configuring, and supporting SharePoint solutions that meet their unique business requirements. Colin has authored several best-selling books on SharePoint products for the Sams Publishing Unleashed series, including *SharePoint 2003*, *2007*, *2010*, and now *2013*. He presents regularly on SharePoint technologies, and frequently writes white papers and articles for a wide range of clients.

Dedications

I dedicate this book to my daughter Julia: my angel, my inspiration, and my greatest source of pride. Papa loves you very much.
—Michael Noel

My work is dedicated to my wonderful wife Nancy, and our bundle of joy: Logan Christopher Jonathan Spence.

—Colin Spence

Acknowledgments

Michael Noel: It's almost become cliché for me to swear off writing these books and, at the exhaustive end of each one of them, harbor fantasies of disappearing into the woods to live in a cave in the companion of various woodland creatures. But inevitably time passes, a new version of SharePoint is released, and I get the crazy idea to torture myself once again with the bleary late-night lab work, marathon writing sessions, and subsequent tearing of hair and wringing of hands. So once again here I stand at the end of this process, bloodied and bruised, glancing furtively back at the carnage behind me and reflecting on the madness of it all. In this moment of clarity, I can see clearly that I could never have made it to this point without the help of the phenomenal team I have helping me along the way.

First and foremost, the biggest inspiration and help to me along the way is provided by my wonderful family. To my wife Marina: You are my reason for living, my muse, my love, and my best friend. I could not have gotten to where I am without your help and your unconditional love. To my daughter Julia: You are an inspiration to me and I know you will accomplish great things in life! And to some of the most amazing in-laws a man could ask for: Val and Elizabeth Ulanovsky. Я вас люблю! And of course to my parents, George and Mary: Thank you for a childhood of happy memories and great opportunities!

On a professional level, big thanks to Rand Morimoto, a great inspiration to me who has worked with me on many of these books over the years. And thanks as well to the other consultants and engineers at Convergent Computing whom I've had the distinct pleasure of working with all these years. At the same time, special professional thanks to my coauthor Colin Spence, a brilliant writer without whom I wouldn't have been able to even think about finishing this book.

Extra helpings of praise and thanks must also go out to the many great SharePoint folks I've met all around the world, in every continent and from every walk of life. This crazy tool brings the most amazing people together, and I am truly lucky to have had the chance to meet all of you, commiserate with you about technology, and get to know you all on a personal level. Way too many people to list here, and I apologize in advance for leaving so many of you out, but I must at least personally thank: Abir Yahyaoui, Agnes Molnar, Alexander Romanov, Alistair Pugin, Alyona Diachenko, Amina Idigova, Andrew Connell, Anton Vityaz, Asif Rehmani, Baraah Omari, Betim Drenica, Bil Simser, Bramley Maetsa, Brian Farnhill, Brian McElhinney, Bjørn Furuknap, Chandima Kulathilake, Chris Givens, Dan Holme, Dan McPherson, Debbie Ireland, Dmitri Plotnikov, Dux Sy, Elaine Van Bergen, Elias Mereb, Eric Harlan, Gavin Barron, Gus Fraser, Hélio Sá, Huthaifa Afanah, Ilia Sotnikov, Ivan Pabaded, Jeremy Thake, Joel Oleson, Jose Francisco Rossi, Laura Rogers, Mai Desouki, Mark Miller, Mark Rackley, Mark Rhodes, Mohammed Zayed, Muhanad Omar, Nadya Belousova, Nick Hadlee, Oksana Prostakova, Paul Culmsee, Paul Swider, Ricardo Munoz, Rob LaMear, Roux Visser, Saed Shela, Salman Ahmad, Sefora Toumi, Serge Tremblay, Sergey Slukin, Todd Baginski, Todd Klindt, Toni Frankola, Veronique Palmer, Wictor Wilén, Yulia Belyanina, Zlatan Dzinic, and of course all the wonderful folks who have attended my sessions over the years!

Last but not least, thanks to one of the best editors anyone could ask for, Neil Rowe: You are not only a classy editor, I can honestly count you as a good friend. Thanks for putting up with us once more on one of these crazy tomes!

Colin Spence: My father wrote a book called *The Memory Palace of Matteo Ricci* that I read a long time ago. It is a historical account of a Jesuit priest who visited China in the 16th century and taught young students tricks to increase their memory skills. This process involved the creating of virtual rooms in a mental construct (a "memory palace") as a means of remembering and organizing large amounts of information. The concept has stuck with me over the years and I find is applicable to the process of writing something as complex as a 1,000-page technology book. Each chapter is a room of sorts that contains information on a focused topic, and these rooms need to form a structure which needs to be "stable" and complete for the book to have integrity. I'll end the metaphor there (since I tend to stretch metaphors too far), but looking back over the writing process over the last decade, I can definitely see the evolution of the book into an entity that will hopefully meet the expectations of its readers.

I have found that once the structure of the SharePoint Unleashed book was fully vetted, which to me took place in the last edition on SharePoint 2010, the project became a lot less daunting. It was, however, still a massive, yearlong undertaking, even with the structure in place and the "veteran's" perspective of having worked with the material previously. The challenge became one of ensuring value in every chapter, focusing on what "really matters" to a very diverse audience.

Fortunately, I've worked with hundreds of companies interested in SharePoint products over the years, and have seen many different sizes and shapes of SharePoint environments. Increasingly, I've been involved in more projects that use SharePoint as a development platform for workflows, forms, full blown applications, business intelligence, and many other purposes. These continuing experiences from my "day job" have assisted immensely in the tuning of the content contained in this Unleashed book. A key learning point for me has been the importance of "right-sizing" the SharePoint solution to an organization's unique needs and internal resources. It doesn't help a company by selling them on the most complex features in SharePoint that are clearly beyond their ability to develop, let alone support.

It also helps that I've had a lot of assistance in the process of writing this fifth book in the series. At the beginning of the timeline, I have to thank Rand Morimoto, who got me involved in the writing process all those years ago, and understands the impact on my "day job" as one of his partners and practice leads. Tremendous thanks to Michael Noel, who has gone through this process with me numerous times now and who understands the functionality and integration points of SharePoint at a level that I never will.

Neil Rowe at Sams Publishing continues to make the process a breeze logistically as we moved through the process of creating an Unleashed tome yet again. Many thanks also to the team at Sams Publishing/Pearson Education who assisted with the editing, formatting, and fine-tuning of the content.

In addition, I'd like to thank my loving wife Nancy and our toddler Logan for their support. Because all this work needed to be done after hours from my home office ("the cave"), my wife needed the patience of a saint to deal with my permanent status of unavailability for normal activities (such as walking the dog and eating dinner), and assorted mood swings, rants, and diatribes. Often, I think, the writing process is tougher for her than me, so I thank her from the bottom of my heart! I could tell that Logan understood as well, when I patted him on the head and slunk off to the cave.

There are also several contributing writers who assisted with a number of the chapters in my half of the book. These include: Ulysses Ludwig, Ben Nadler, Anthony Adona, Alex Kirchmann, Ken Lo, and Mona Zhao. Their individual experiences, skill sets, and insights on what was most important in different topic areas were invaluable:

Ulysses Ludwig and Ben Nadler enabled me to confidently expand the scope of the book to cover the topics of application development and business intelligence in more detail. I consider Ulysses to be my right-hand man in the day-to-day delivery of services to clients and can confidently say he is the most accomplished SharePoint developer and expert I know. Ben's expertise with PerformancePoint and Business Connectivity Services was once again very welcome. Jonathan Chen played double duty as both technical editor and contributing writer as we wrapped up the book, for which I am grateful.

Anthony Adona assisted with ensuring the Using Libraries and Lists in SharePoint 2013 chapter truly met the needs of end users and administrators alike, while Alex Kirchmann provided his experience with metadata and content types. Ken Lo and Mona Zhao assisted with some of the finer points of Office applications' integration with SharePoint and SkyDrive Pro. I can't list all the other friends, clients, and sources of knowledge that assisted in this final product, but my thanks go out to you as well!

We Want to Hear from You!

As the reader of this book, *you* are our most important critic and commentator. We value your opinion and want to know what we're doing right, what we could do better, what areas you'd like to see us publish in, and any other words of wisdom you're willing to pass our way.

You can email or write me directly to let me know what you did or didn't like about this book—as well as what we can do to make our books stronger.

Please note that I cannot help you with technical problems related to the topic of this book, and that due to the high volume of mail I receive, I might not be able to reply to every message.

When you write, please be sure to include this book's title and author as well as your name and phone or email address. I will carefully review your comments and share them with the authors and editors who worked on the book.

E-mail: feedback@samspublishing.com

Mail: Neil Rowe
Executive Editor
Sams Publishing
800 East 96th Street
Indianapolis, IN 46240 USA

Reader Services

Visit our website and register this book at informit.com/register for convenient access to any updates, downloads, or errata that might be available for this book.

Introduction

When we sat down to write the original *SharePoint 2003 Unleashed* book more than a decade ago, we had a hunch that the technology would be popular, but did not anticipate how quickly the product would take off and how much interest the IT industry would end up taking in SharePoint products and technologies. In the interim years, as we worked with implementing the product in companies of all sizes, we learned what the product did well and what it didn't do so well, and further refined our knowledge of SharePoint best practice design, deployment, and administration.

Our exposure to the latest version of SharePoint started well before its release when SharePoint v15 was still being developed. We developed experience through our company, Convergent Computing (CCO), deploying it for early adopters through our close relationship with Microsoft as a Gold Partner. In addition, we collaborated with and provided input to the SharePoint development team and the broader SharePoint community through Microsoft's Most Valuable Professional (MVP) program. The richness of features and the capabilities of what became the SharePoint 2013 version became evident to us during this time, and we used our hands-on experience with the early stages of the product to begin designing this book, which provides a comprehensive look at SharePoint 2013 functionality, administration, and infrastructure.

A major challenge of this book was trying to identify and cover the most important tools, topics, practices, and skills that the range of our readers will find valuable in their interactions with SharePoint 2013. To do this, we drew upon our experiences over the last decade with hundreds of different organizations and distilled out the most common requirements in the areas of design, architecture, integration, and customization.

We endeavored to provide value to readers who may never have used SharePoint products before and those who are well versed with the products and may currently be using SharePoint. You might be an IT manager, IT architect, SharePoint administrator, SharePoint power user, developer, and, of course, a SharePoint end user. Therefore, we carefully crafted the book to cover what we felt would add the most value to our audience. A key piece of this strategy is to expand beyond the out-of-the-box features of SharePoint 2013 and share our experience on some of the most common integration points of SharePoint 2013, such as SQL Server 2012; Exchange Server 2010 or 2013; Edge Security products; and tools such as SharePoint Designer, Visual Studio, and PerformancePoint. Since SharePoint is such a powerful development platform, we made sure to include content that educates readers on a number of development processes and best practices. In this way, the book becomes more than a treatise on what SharePoint 2013 can do in a vacuum, but what it can do in a complex technology ecosystem.

This book is the result of our experience and the experiences of our colleagues at CCO and our clients in working with SharePoint 2013 products and technologies, both in the beta stages and in production deployments. We wrote this book to be topical so that you can quickly browse to a particular section and follow easy-to-understand, step-by-step scenarios. These exercises, instead of just giving simple examples of a feature, are designed to give examples of real-world applications of the technologies and tools that provide you with business value. In addition, if you need a comprehensive overview on SharePoint 2013, the book can be read in sequence to give you a solid understanding of the higher levels of security and functionality SharePoint can provide. Topics in the book are divided into six sections, each with topics in similar categories.

How This Book Is Organized

This book is organized into the following sections:

- Part I, "Planning for and Deploying SharePoint Server 2013," provides an introduction to the products in the SharePoint 2013 stack and includes prescriptive advice for how to architect and implement them. In addition, it covers upgrade advice from legacy versions of SharePoint and also details advanced installation scenarios with SharePoint 2013.
- Part II, "Administering and Maintaining SharePoint Server 2013," focuses on the day-to-day administration and monitoring required for a SharePoint back-end environment. It details how to use new tools, including Windows PowerShell for SharePoint 2013 Administration, and covers backup and restore. It also focuses in particular detail on how to administer and maintain the SQL databases used by SharePoint.
- Part III, "Securing, Protecting, and Optimizing SharePoint Architecture," covers security concepts in detail that focus on edge, transport, and content security. Topics such as SQL Transparent Data Encryption, Secure Sockets Layer (SSL) Certificates, Internet Protocol Security (IPsec) encryption, Active Directory Rights Management Services, Edge Security, and more are detailed. In addition, this part includes information on how to virtualize a SharePoint 2013 farm using server virtualization technology.
- Part IV, "Using SharePoint 2013 Technologies for Collaboration and Document Management," starts with a comparison of SharePoint Foundation and SharePoint Server 2013, then moves to the tools and capabilities provided by libraries and lists, customization of libraries and lists, and then to managing the sites and pages that house these components. One chapter is dedicated to metadata and content types; another chapter focuses on the greatly improved social networking tools; and another covers the process of SharePoint 2013 governance.

- Part V, "Leveraging Office Applications with SharePoint," focuses on key features in Office 2013 applications that power users and administrators should be familiar with, including protecting documents, document versions, and coauthoring. The SkyDrive Pro product line is demystified, and Outlook connectivity is reviewed. Next, topics including Excel Services, Access Services, Visio Graphics Services, the new and improved Office Web Apps 2013 product, and out-of-the-box as well as SharePoint Designer 2013 workflows are covered.
- Part VI, "Extending the SharePoint Environment," dedicates one chapter to the topic of application development with SharePoint Designer 2013 and Visual Studio 2013, one chapter to PerformancePoint Services, and one chapter to Business Connectivity Services. This part is written with power users and developers in mind, and contains more complex exercises and examples that will be of great value to these readers.

If you, like many out there, were recently tasked with administering a SharePoint environment, or are looking for ways to bring document management and collaboration to the next level and need to understand how SharePoint 2013 can fit into your IT ecosystem, this book is for you. We hope you enjoy reading it as much as we've enjoyed creating it and working with the product.

CHAPTER 1

Introducing SharePoint 2013

IN THIS CHAPTER

- Understanding the Capabilities of SharePoint 2013
- Using SharePoint for Collaboration and Document Management
- Outlining Improvements in SharePoint 2013
- Securing SharePoint 2013 with New Security Enhancements
- Leveraging Metadata and Content Types
- Social Networking Tool Advances
- Working with Office Web Apps
- Creating Powerful and Flexible Workflows
- Developing Applications Using Visual Studio
- Leveraging Business Intelligence Tools in SharePoint 2013
- Governing the SharePoint Environment

SharePoint has grown up over the past decade in terms of features and stability, and the user base has grown slowly and steadily. Whereas 10 years ago, it was a novelty and appealed to a small number of adventurous organizations, it is now a "version 5" product from Microsoft and has grown much the way a business might: through maturation of its "moving parts" and acquisition of new "talent." Statistics found from Gartner, Forrester, and other industry-leading analysts show SharePoint leading in many technology areas, with more than three-quarters of Fortune 500 companies using it and well over 100,000,000 licenses sold.

This is no fluke. SharePoint is popular because of its integration into the Office product line, its relative affordability, and capacity to provide a platform for the creation of flexible, powerful, and intelligent business solutions. It provides for comprehensive document and records management, team collaboration, web content management, and extranet capabilities, all from an easy-to-understand and customizable interface. It has also evolved and matured as a development platform, where applications that provide solutions to very specific business needs can be added (for example, to provide flexible workflows, customized web parts for presenting data, and data analysis tools such as dashboards).

Microsoft has further upped the ante with this latest release of SharePoint products and technologies, collectively referred to as SharePoint 2013. New features are included, such as a redesigned and streamlined tablet-friendly interface, an improved set of search tools, rich business data visualization, and much more. Microsoft has listened to customer feedback and improved the platform significantly, providing for an intelligent platform that can grow with all types of organizations.

This chapter introduces the SharePoint 2013 products, giving a high-level overview of the features and functions in the platform. It summarizes key changes and features in SharePoint 2013 and serves as a jumping-off point to the other chapters in this book, indicating which particular areas of the book give more information about individual features and technologies.

Understanding the Capabilities of SharePoint 2013

Answering the question "What is SharePoint 2013?" is not an easy task. This is primarily because, unlike many of the other Microsoft tools on the market, SharePoint is designed to be a platform that can be molded and shaped to fit the needs of nearly any organization. One SharePoint environment might look drastically different from another SharePoint environment and might be used for completely different tasks.

Indeed, SharePoint is designed to be customized to solve individual business problems and to satisfy specific organizational needs. It is built to serve as a full-fledged document management solution, collaboration portal, team site workspace, public-facing website, extranet partner collaboration environment, or all these things at the same time.

SharePoint 2013 has evolved over the years from a disparate set of small-scale tools into a complex and capable tool in use at a large proportion of organizations in the world. But where did SharePoint 2013 come from? Before understanding what this version is, it is first important to gain a better understanding of the history of SharePoint products and technologies and how we got where we are today.

Exploring the SharePoint 1.0 Wave: SharePoint Team Services and SharePoint Portal Server 2001

SharePoint as we know it today had its roots in two distinct products developed by two different teams at Microsoft. These products overlapped in many areas, but during the development phases, they were seen as completely different products and were expected to have different names upon release. It was only as the release date approached that Microsoft decided to give each the name SharePoint, even though they were different in many ways.

The first of these two products became SharePoint Team Services (STS) and was seen as a team collaboration product with limited document management functionality. This product was released as an add-on to the FrontPage media, which is how many administrators stumbled upon it eventually. Although unique in approach, it wasn't very scalable and was limited in functionality. The letters *STS* still can be found in today's product line, such as in the STSADM tool.

The second product developed by Microsoft eventually became SharePoint Portal Server (SPS) 2001 and was seen as an extension to public folder functionality in Microsoft Exchange Server. The storage engine for SPS 2001 was the Microsoft Exchange jet engine database, which was completely different from the SQL Server-based back end of SharePoint Team Services.

Although innovative and providing some interesting and powerful features, these two versions of SharePoint did not see too much use in most organizations, aside for the occasional team site put together by scattered departments and an occasional portal.

Exploring the SharePoint 2.0 Wave: Windows SharePoint Services 2.0 and SharePoint Portal Server 2003

Microsoft's first real attempt to marry these two tools into a single product line and create a true collaboration environment was borne out of the second wave of SharePoint technologies, SharePoint 2003, as shown in Figure 1.1. SharePoint Team Services was rebranded as Windows SharePoint Services (WSS) 2.0, and the portal product became SharePoint Portal Server 2003. Both products were built on the same SQL Server database engine, and Microsoft positioned the features to be an extension of each other. WSS was the "free" product, available with every license of Windows Server, whereas the SPS 2003 product became the fully featured portal that incorporated WSS sites into its topology.

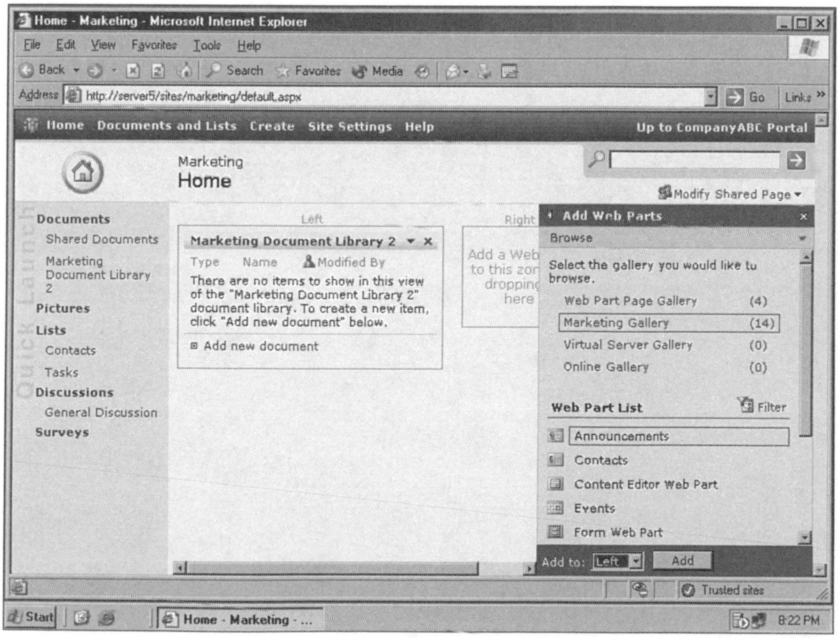

FIGURE 1.1 Viewing a legacy SharePoint 2003 environment.

Although it was a great effort, and a much more mature product than the 2001 line of SharePoint products, growing pains were still visible in the software. For many people, it wasn't quite clear whether to use SPS 2003 Areas or WSS Sites, and the integration was loose. This wave saw the first strong adoption of SharePoint, however, as many organizations deployed it for the first time.

Exploring the SharePoint 3.0 Wave: Windows SharePoint Services 3.0 and Microsoft Office SharePoint Server 2007

The point at which Microsoft SharePoint products and technologies really took off was the 3.0 wave. This wave saw the tightest integration between the new versions of the two products. WSS became WSS 3.0, and SPS 2003 was renamed Microsoft Office SharePoint Server (MOSS) 2007. In addition, Microsoft combined its Content Management Server product with SharePoint, integrating it into MOSS 2007.

MOSS 2007 and WSS 3.0, as shown in Figure 1.2, saw massive adoption across the board, and many organizations started to deploy for collaboration, document management, intranets, and extranets. In addition, major industry websites started to move to SharePoint 2007, with tens of thousands of public-facing sites deployed on SharePoint within the first few years. This version saw true comprehensive document management, enterprise search, and collaboration capabilities as well, and many organizations deployed it to improve their efficiency and communications capabilities.

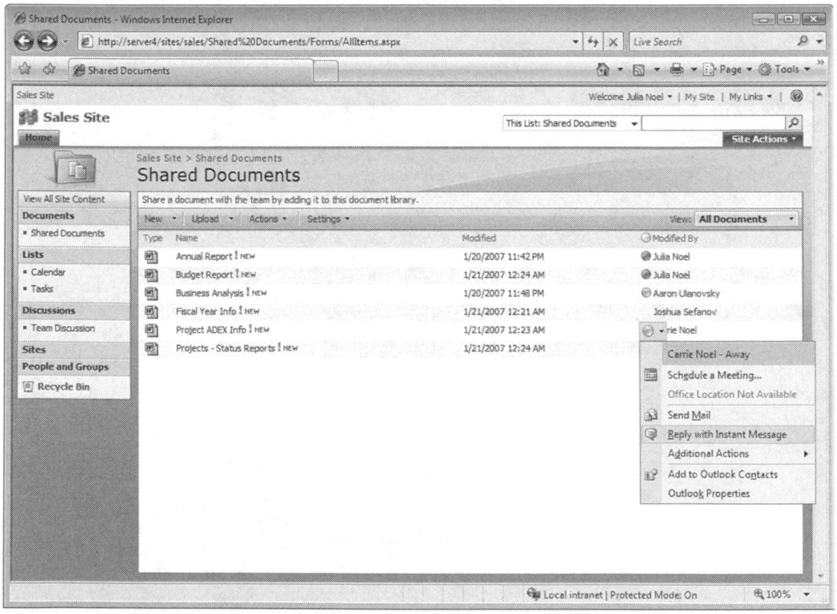

FIGURE 1.2 Viewing a legacy SharePoint 2007 document library.

SharePoint 2007's success was one of its disadvantages as well, unfortunately, as the growth of SharePoint sites led in some cases to a proliferation of siloed SharePoint farms and sites in many spots across organizations. There was a general lack of governance of the SharePoint environments, and this ended up hurting many companies as it created redundancy of data and inefficiencies. In addition, certain features were asked for that were not part of the product, and people complained about other annoyances that Microsoft sought to fix. Organizations looked to Microsoft to further improve its product, and Microsoft busily gathered information on what people liked and didn't like to improve the next release of the product.

Exploring the SharePoint 4.0 Wave: SharePoint Foundation Server and Microsoft SharePoint Server 2010

Early in 2010, Microsoft released its next wave of SharePoint products: SharePoint 2010. WSS was renamed once again, this time to SharePoint Foundation Server, and the Office in MOSS was dropped, with the product simply renamed Microsoft SharePoint Server 2010. A significant number of new features found their way into these two products, including the introduction of the Managed Metadata Service, greater scalability, and inclusion of the Office ribbon into the collaboration space, as illustrated in Figure 1.3.

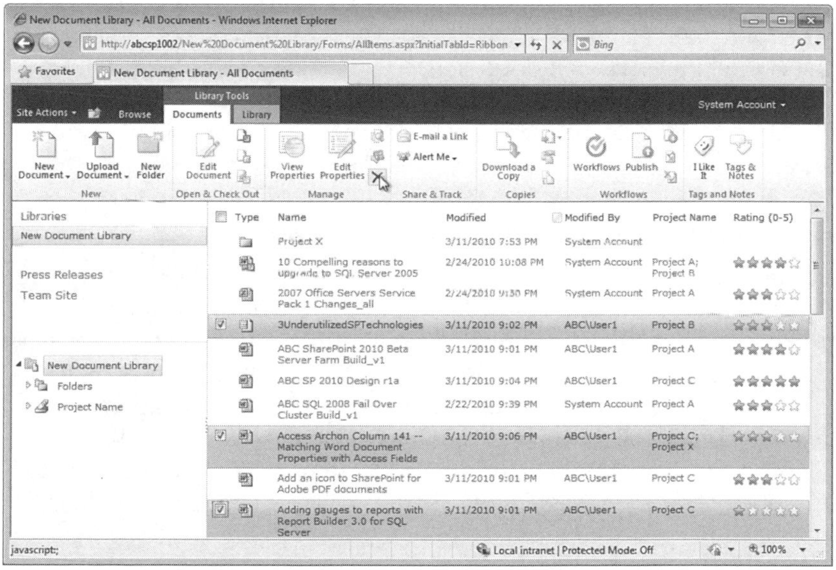

FIGURE 1.3 Examining a legacy SharePoint 2010 Site.

Exploring the SharePoint 5.0 Wave: SharePoint Foundation 2013 and Microsoft SharePoint Server 2013

Late in 2012, Microsoft released its latest wave of SharePoint products: SharePoint 2013. SharePoint Foundation retained the same name, and SharePoint Server 2010 simply became SharePoint Server 2013. This latest version retooled the default user interface (UI) again, this time making it more "contemporary" and mobile device and tablet "friendly" as well as tweaking and tuning the different components that enable the platform to deliver its wide range of tools and capabilities. These features are discussed in depth throughout the rest of this book, and are covered from a high level in the rest of this chapter.

Using SharePoint for Collaboration and Document Management

SharePoint 2013 is many things to many people, so it is difficult to narrow the focus to specific features and functionality. Two areas that are usually focused on, and help business decision makers better understand how SharePoint 2013 can be used, are in the areas of collaboration and document management functionality. SharePoint 2013 integrates extensively with the Office 2013 product line, so it becomes an extension of the business productivity tools that knowledge workers already know like the backs of their hands and therefore enhances collaboration between employees. SharePoint 2013 provides for road-tested and robust enterprise content management, document management, and records management for organizations of all different shapes and sizes. Organizations can store their documents within SharePoint document libraries and take advantage of version control, check-in/check-out, and features such as the Managed Metadata Service, which can help control the type of metadata that documents in SharePoint have. SharePoint lists store rows of data rather than files and can be leveraged in many ways, because each is a self-contained "database" that can be used in many of the same ways that a spreadsheet can.

Integrating Deeply with Microsoft Office Applications

Digging deeper into the concepts of collaboration and document management, SharePoint 2013 provides the highest level of integration with Office 2013 products but supports users of Office 2010 and, to some extent, Office 2007 applications. The integration is most extensive with Word, Excel, Outlook, Access, PowerPoint, Visio, and the tool essentially designed for using with SharePoint 2013: SharePoint Designer 2013. This integration serves as the cornerstone for the collaborative capabilities of SharePoint 2013. Chapter 25, "Using Word, Excel, PowerPoint with SharePoint 2013," digs deeper into the topic of Office integration, as does Chapter 26, "Extending SharePoint 2013 with Excel Services, Visio Graphics Services, and Access Services."

An example of enhanced collaboration that many organizations are seeking is to reduce reliance on email as a primary collaboration tool. SharePoint offers an ideal solution because it enables users to simply email a URL that is a link to a SharePoint document in a document library instead of emailing the entire document. Then users can access the document in the document library, check out the document, make changes, and check the document back in. SharePoint can create a new version of the document to allow for access to the historical versions of the document. And the end result is one document title and one URL for the document, as opposed to the "old way of doing things" in which users had to try to locate the document on a file share or in a public folder, and then locate the proper document while trying to figure out why "ABC Proposal v1.0csmn NEW.docx" was newer than "ABC Proposal v2.0mncs.docx."

Libraries and Lists as Data Management and Collaboration Tools

It is revealing to understand how SharePoint 2013 stores data; the main repositories are libraries and lists. Some of the advantages provided by a SharePoint document library include the tools provided to the library administrator to control "who can do what" within the library, in terms of adding, deleting, editing, or just reading documents. In addition, versioning tools are available to track major and minor versions of files, as are alerts that inform users of changes, check-in and check-out controls, document templates available from the library, and powerful tools to create metadata that is added to the documents stored in the libraries.

Libraries are used for many purposes, one of which is to reduce reliance on file shares, which only offer a small subset of the features of SharePoint libraries. SharePoint libraries are usually managed by power users and IT staff, so more control can be put in the hands of the people using the tools every day. In addition, any text-based, Office, or index-supported file uploaded to a SharePoint library is crawled and indexed, making the contents available for searching, while still maintaining security trimming on the file. Many other features are available in libraries, such as enhanced navigation tools, workflows, and the ability to add tags and notes, which greatly enhance collaboration within the libraries.

Alerts in SharePoint libraries and lists generate informative emails to users when certain types of changes occur, which means users don't have to religiously visit their lists and libraries every day to see what has changed, because SharePoint is "smart" enough to let them know. Workflows can be triggered manually or automatically when certain conditions are met, such as a user indicating that a document should be published to a major version, which sends an email with instructions to a manager to review and approve a document, for example.

Document libraries are one set of repositories in SharePoint 2013, and the other main set of repositories is called lists, which store data in rows and columns much like Excel spreadsheets or databases. Most organizations immediately start moving data from Excel spreadsheets to SharePoint lists when the product is available. Consider the example of the spreadsheet used by sales for forecasting. Historically, each salesperson updates it the night before team meetings. The manager must then frantically collate the information into a "single source of the truth." When this manager moves the data to a SharePoint list, he can retire the spreadsheet, and each user simply adds or modifies rows of data in the list, and multiple users can access the list at the same time. Even better, the list tracks versions of the data in each row (a feature not offered by Excel) and time stamps each change and the identity of the user that made it for powerful auditing capabilities. SharePoint lists enable users to export data to Excel or Access, edit data in the user-friendly datasheet view, and create different views to show subsets of the total data.

Several chapters explore these subjects and provide step-by-step examples to help new and experienced SharePoint users put concepts into action in small amounts of time. Chapter 19, "Using Libraries and Lists in SharePoint 2013," starts with a ground-up approach to inform users, managers, designers, and architects about the range of capabilities in these repositories. Chapter 20, "Customizing and Managing Libraries and Lists to Meet Business

Requirements," addresses the tools that power users and SharePoint site administrators will want to understand more fully to better meet end-user requirements. Chapter 22, "Managing Metadata and Content Types in SharePoint 2013," covers the vitally important topic of metadata and how it can be leveraged within the SharePoint ecosystem to help organizations better manage their data and provide value to knowledge workers.

Organizing Collaborating with SharePoint Site Collections and Sites

Building upon the power of lists and libraries, SharePoint 2013 provides a powerful framework of sites and site collections to manage these repositories and provides additional management tools. The sites and site collections enable IT to build a framework that provides working spaces for departments, groups, teams, programs, divisions, offices, and any other type of business grouping. These sites can be branded with appropriate logos and color schemes and have web parts added to .aspx pages that perform many tasks, from simply displaying rich text, graphics, and charts to stock tickers, information about the weather, or data pulled directly from corporate databases.

Site collections are hierarchical groups of sites that can be managed as a unit. A wide range of templates are available that make it quick and easy to create functionally specific site collections, such as the following:

- Team Site
- Blog
- Developer Site
- Project Site
- Community Site
- Basic Search Center
- Document Center
- eDiscovery Center
- Records Center
- Business Intelligence Center
- Enterprise Search Center
- My Site Host
- Community Portal
- Visio Process Repository
- Publishing Portal
- Enterprise Wiki
- Product Catalog

Chapter 21, "Designing and Managing Pages and Sites for Knowledge Workers," focuses on other templates, tools, and capabilities of sites and site collections.

These features help departments, collaborative teams, and other business units (even unstructured ad hoc groups which can be referred to as communities) work more efficiently and share data better. In addition, you can use extranet capabilities, such as the ones discussed in Chapter 13, "Deploying SharePoint for Extranets and Alternate Authentication Scenarios," to collaborate with remote partners.

Deploying SharePoint Websites with Comprehensive Web Content Management

In addition to the document management and collaboration features in SharePoint, SharePoint 2013 is also ideally positioned to allow for web content management capabilities, enabling for complex and useful public-facing websites to be created that are very Web 2.0 in nature. Because SharePoint is a platform, these websites can take multiple forms and be customized visually, allowing for a large degree of personalization to suit the needs of the organization. Microsoft has also improved its Internet-facing licensing model for SharePoint 2013, making it a more attractive candidate for web content management.

Outlining Improvements in SharePoint 2013

Microsoft has spent considerable time gathering input from customers on previous versions of SharePoint. This input was directly used by the development team to create new functionality and features in this version of SharePoint. The product team delivered a huge range of services and functionality. For SharePoint administrators familiar with SharePoint 2010, it is important to gain a better understanding of what those changes are and how they can be used to build a better collaboration environment for your organization.

Understanding the Scalable Service Application Model in SharePoint 2013

The overall service application architectural model that was introduced in SharePoint 2010 has been maintained and expanded in SharePoint 2013. Service applications in SharePoint 2013 are independent services that can be shared across web applications or across farms.

New service applications in SharePoint 2013 include Machine Translation Services, which allow for cloud-based translation of documents by sending them to Microsoft's Bing Translation Services. Other new service applications include the App Management Service, which manages the SharePoint App Store and the Work Management Service, which keeps alert status in sync across Exchange, SharePoint, and Project Server.

Most service applications that existed in SharePoint 2010 are still around today, with the exception of the Web Analytics service application, which was retired in favor of similar functionality embedded in SharePoint 2013's Search.

Other familiar service applications are available, such as the Business Data Connectivity Service, which allows for connection to an external data source; the Managed Metadata Service, which enforces common metadata across a farm; and the Search Service, which is critical for Enterprise Search functionality. In total, more than a dozen service applications are available out-of-the-box in SharePoint 2013, and Microsoft enables third-party service applications to be created as well.

Service applications enable a SharePoint 2013 environment to be more scalable because they can be easily shared across multiple servers. SharePoint architects can define which servers run which service applications, and which service applications apply to what farms. By separating the functionality in SharePoint onto this highly flexible service application tier, it becomes easier to scale up the environment with the needs of the individual environment. For example, Figure 1.4 illustrates a very large farm with multiple servers running individual service applications. Although most organizations are served by smaller farms, it shows the scalability of the service application model. Chapter 2, "Architecting a SharePoint 2013 Deployment," covers service applications in more detail.

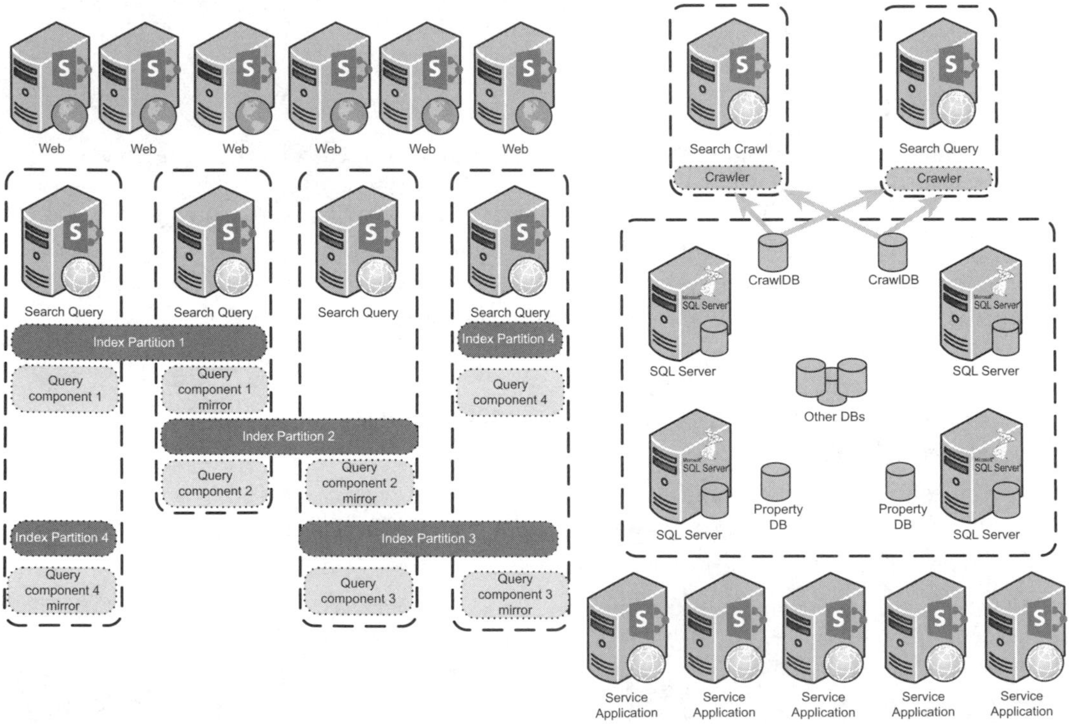

FIGURE 1.4 Viewing a large distributed SharePoint 2013 farm.

Outlining Search Improvements in SharePoint 2013

Another area of significant improvement in SharePoint 2013 is SharePoint's built-in Enterprise Search functionality. This functionality can prove extremely valuable to organizations struggling to provide a central search engine to enhance knowledge workers' efficiency and their ability to simply "find what they're looking for." SharePoint's native search tool has been re-architected to include native FAST Search functionality, which includes the following features:

- Document thumbnail-preview capabilities
- Massive scalability across index partitions
- Click-through relevance
- Automatic metadata tagging

This is an example of growth through acquisition within the SharePoint product line, since Microsoft acquired the FAST ESP product in 2008, and then provided a FAST Search add-on to SharePoint 2010, which has now been incorporated into the standard search tools in SharePoint 2013. Chapter 8, "Leveraging and Optimizing Search in SharePoint 2013," provides more details on SharePoint 2013's search capabilities.

Accessing the Improved Administration, Monitoring, and Backup Tools

There are two major improvements in the area of administration for SharePoint. The first comes in a revamped SharePoint Central Administration tool, shown in Figure 1.5. The second comes with an increased reliance on Microsoft PowerShell as a scripting administration interface.

Administrators familiar with earlier versions of SharePoint will recall the SharePoint Central Administration tool, a web-based interface used to administer SharePoint functionality. SharePoint 2013 improves this interface, organizing functional tasks within specific pages, continuing support for the SharePoint ribbon to make tasks easier to perform, and adding new functionality that previously was unavailable. You can find more information about the use of the SharePoint Central Administration Tool in Chapter 6, "Managing and Administering SharePoint 2013 Infrastructure."

The addition of Microsoft PowerShell as a SharePoint administration tool in earlier versions of SharePoint enabled administrators to have a robust and comprehensive scripting interface that allows for automation of manual tasks, scripted installations, and remote administration support. Microsoft has continued this support in SharePoint 2013 and has added multiple new commandlets (cmdlets) for PowerShell specific to SharePoint, some of which are shown in Figure 1.6. You can find detailed information about PowerShell administration for SharePoint in Chapter 7, "Leveraging PowerShell for Command-Line SharePoint Administration and Automation."

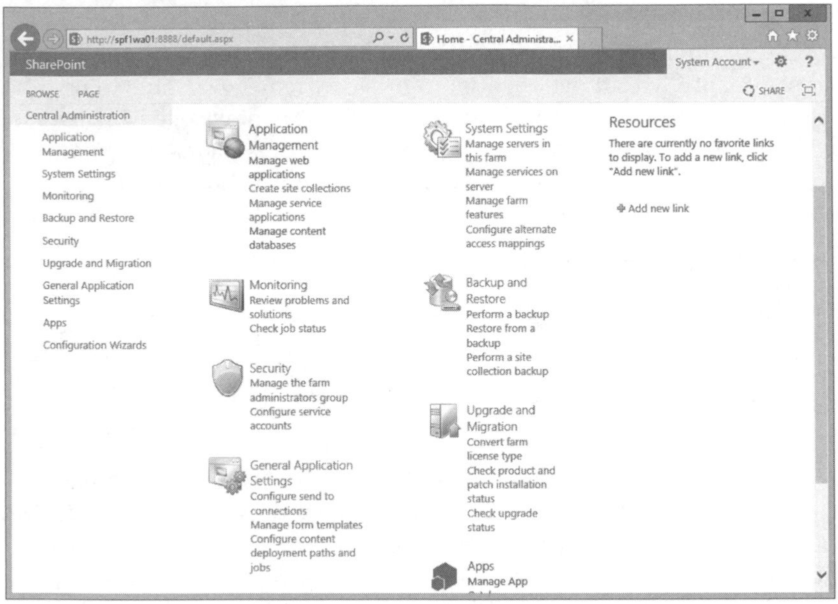

FIGURE 1.5 Examining the revamped SharePoint Central Administration tool.

FIGURE 1.6 Using PowerShell for SharePoint 2013 administration.

Using the Improved Backup and Restore Tools

Backup and Restore in the SharePoint admin interfaces in SharePoint 2013, shown in Figure 1.7, has been streamlined. Features include progress bar indicators, granular site recovery options, and the capability to recover data out of unattached content databases.

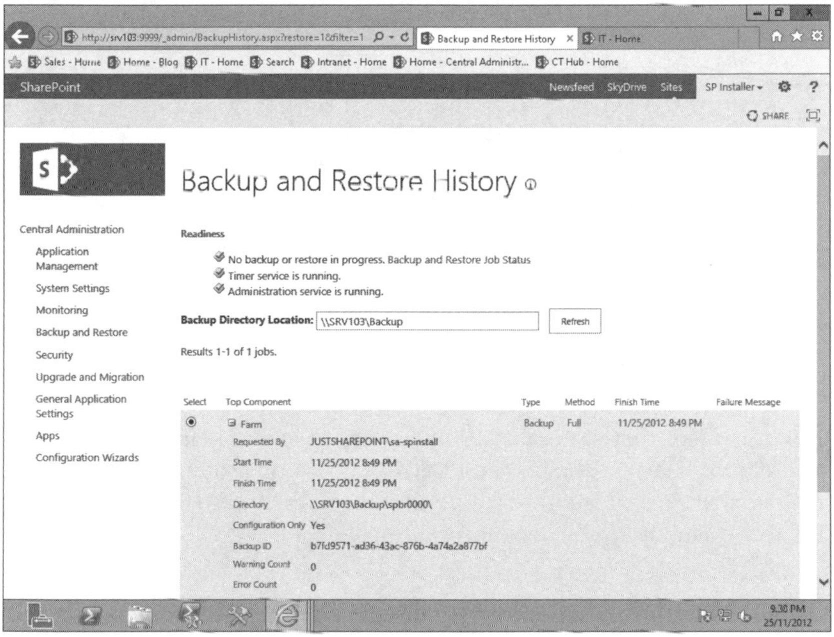

FIGURE 1.7 Using SharePoint Central Admin's backup interface.

Although these tools improve the administration available in SharePoint 2013, they do not necessarily provide comprehensive enterprise backup and restore capabilities. In certain cases, it may become necessary to use a third-party product or an enhanced Microsoft tool such as System Center Data Protection Manager. Chapter 10, "Backing Up and Restoring a SharePoint Environment," discusses these options in more detail.

Shredded Storage and the Remote BLOB Storage Option

SharePoint 2013 introduces the concept of shredded storage, which promises to reduce the overall size of SharePoint content databases. Shredded storage takes the BLOBs (binary large objects)—essentially the actual documents in the database—and allows multiple versions of the same file to be stored as delta versions. This differs from the way that it was in earlier versions of SharePoint, in which all versions of documents were stored as full BLOBs, as illustrated in Figure 1.8.

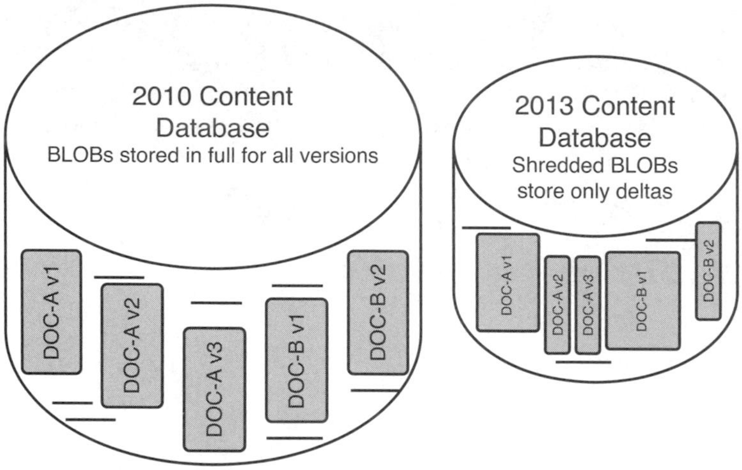

FIGURE 1.8 Understanding the difference in how SharePoint 2013 and SharePoint 2010 store documents in BLOBs.

For example, a 50MB document that maintains 10 older versions would take up approximately 500MB in SharePoint 2010. With SharePoint 2013, assuming around 1MB of changes in each version, that same document would only take up around 59MB of space in the database. This technology is on by default for all new documents in SharePoint 2013.

SharePoint 2013 also allows for utilization of the BLOB externalization technology known as Remote BLOB Storage (RBS). RBS allows for the BLOBs to be stored outside the SharePoint content database. Because the space consumed within the SharePoint content database is approximately 95% to 98% BLOB content, using RBS can have a significant effect on the size and maintenance of content databases. You can find more information on configuring RBS for SharePoint 2013 in Chapter 9, "Managing and Maintaining SQL Server in a SharePoint Environment."

Securing SharePoint 2013 with New Security Enhancements

Out-of-the-box, SharePoint provides for a secure interface, restricting access to documents and sites with comprehensive security down to the item level. In addition, SharePoint Search is security trimmed, enabling users to see search results only from files to which they have access.

Although these security measures are robust, several layers of security aren't configured by default in a SharePoint farm, including transport security, storage-level encryption, or rights management. Fortunately, it is not too difficult to configure these items, and this book covers each topic in step-by-step detail.

Protecting SharePoint 2013 with Transport Security Options

A SharePoint environment provides two types of transport-level encryption. The first and most critical are Secure Sockets Layer (SSL) certificates. These certificates protect the traffic between clients and the servers by encrypting the packets using Public Key Infrastructure (PKI) encryption. The second type of transport-level encryption useful for SharePoint 2013 is Internet Protocol Security (IPsec) encryption between servers in a SharePoint farm, such as between a SharePoint role server and the SQL database server. Chapter 17, "Safeguarding Confidential Data in SharePoint 2013," discusses both these options in more detail.

Protecting SharePoint Data with Storage Security Options

By default, SharePoint databases that store all content are not encrypted. The data within them is stored in a format that can be viewed if an administrator or backup operator has access to them. Indeed, if a content database is taken to a different farm, all content can be easily viewed simply by the administrator resetting the security credentials for the site collections.

This presents a challenge for many organizations that need to demonstrate that the data stored within SharePoint is properly secured and encrypted, and that if backup tapes are lost or stolen, the data will not be at risk of compromise. For these types of scenarios, Microsoft provides for an SQL encryption option known as Transparent Data Encryption (TDE), which allows for the databases to be fully encrypted on the SQL server without the application—in this case, SharePoint—being aware that there is any encryption at all. TDE is covered in more detail in Chapter 17.

Protecting SharePoint Web Access on the Edge Using Advanced Tools

Providing access to a SharePoint 2013 environment is not a task you should take lightly. Multiple security exploits and viruses on the web are constantly attacking web-based servers. Although SharePoint 2013 is built to be secure, it is not specifically designed to fend off these types of attacks. Subsequently, a more effective application layer inspection utility such as those provided by Microsoft's Forefront Edge line is ideal for securing a SharePoint 2013 environment. Chapter 14, "Protecting SharePoint with Advanced Edge Security Solutions," covers this topic in detail.

Leveraging Metadata and Content Types

Simply stated, metadata is data about data, and it plays a vital role in the SharePoint 2013 ecosystem. First introduced in SharePoint 2010, managed metadata allows IT and power users to create term sets which contain terms, which are then available for use in libraries and lists. For organizations interested in creating taxonomies for organizing their documents, this is a critical tool, and it also facilitates the search and retrieval process for users of the system.

If a term set is then made available in a document library, when a SharePoint user adds a document, she can easily choose the metadata from the managed metadata panel as shown in Figure 1.9. In this example, the organization has defined a number of terms in a managed metadata term set that describe the subject matter of a document. By establishing a basic taxonomy of subject matter, document types, or other categories, the organization provides standards that help users quickly find the specific type of document they are looking for.

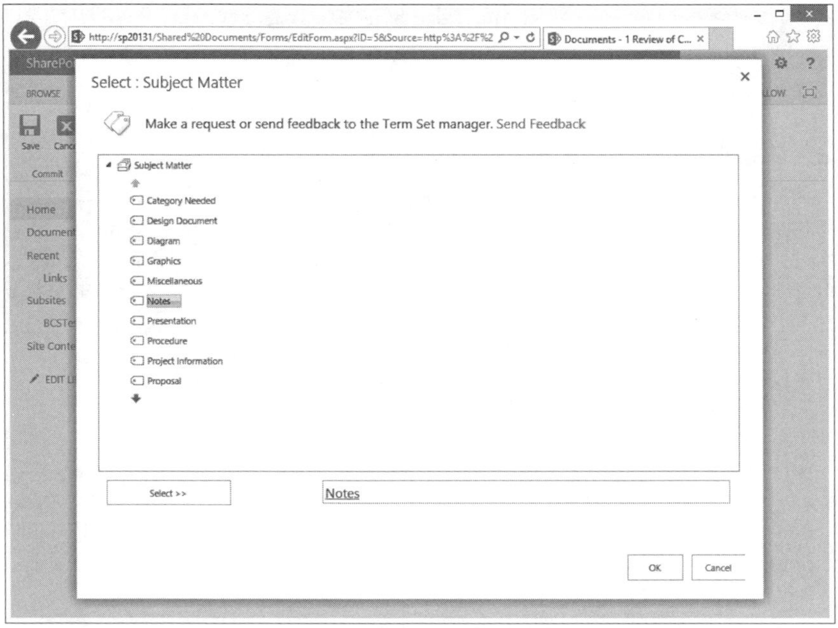

FIGURE 1.9 Choosing a managed metadata value for a document.

Content types are essentially "wrappers" that are applied to a list or library item that then bring tools and functionality with them. For example, a content type can have metadata columns associated with it (such as the document type managed metadata just discussed) and a document template, workflow settings, information management policy settings, and other settings. Although these might seem confusing initially, with some testing and experience, their value becomes very apparent. Chapter 22 discusses both metadata and content types in more detail and covers some of the new managed metadata features, including the use of managed metadata for navigation.

Social Networking Tool Advances

My Site personal websites have often been derided for not providing particularly useful tools and features while also potentially being distracting for employees, which made IT generally reluctant to fully deploy them. Microsoft has revamped My Site websites and the social networking tools in SharePoint 2010, and has now done so again in SharePoint 2013. Initial adopters of SharePoint 2013 have found that My Sites seem to have finally reached a point where they offer sufficient benefits that most organizations are now rolling them out. In addition, the power of social networking tools is no longer a debate in most larger organizations, so the business landscape is more accepting of these sorts of tools now, compared to 3 to 5 years ago.

Figure 1.10 shows an example of the About Me page on a My Site, which shows the new, "more contemporary" look and feel of the personal site. My Sites still enable users to edit their profiles, to a degree that can be controlled by the farm administrator, encouraging users to add information that better shares their experiences and abilities. Organizations that have a distributed workforce are finding great value in this data, as it can greatly increase the efficiency of collaboration between employees. Users can track sites, communities, and individuals, and the new microblogging tool set in SharePoint 2013 makes data available to individuals tracking sites or other users. Users also have a "diary" of their activities in their activity feed, as shown in Figure 1.10. Clearly, Microsoft has learned from the success of other social networking tools, and has built upon the foundation of My Sites in earlier versions of SharePoint. Chapter 22 and Chapter 23, "Leveraging Social Networking Tools in SharePoint 2013," provide additional insights into the value of these enhanced tools to the organization.

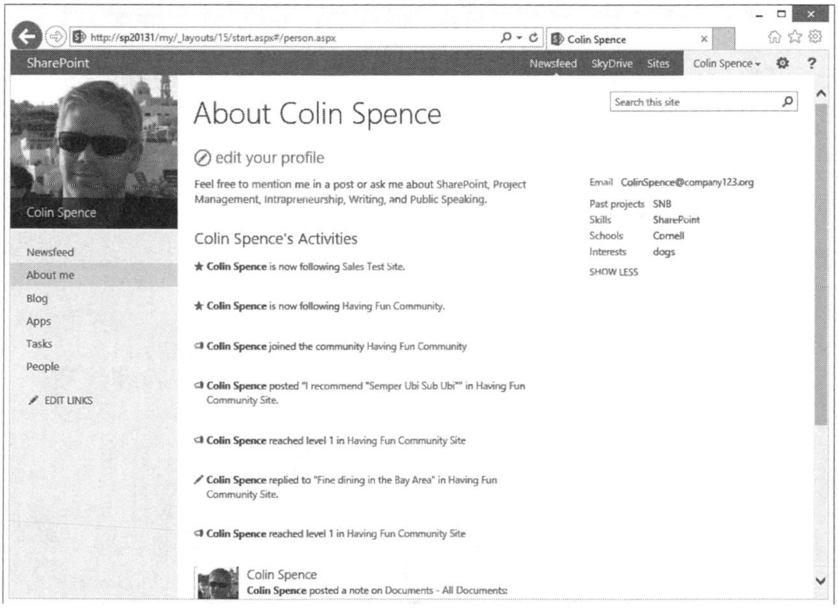

FIGURE 1.10 About Me page in a My Site in SharePoint 2013.

Working with Office Web Apps

The Office Web Apps service application was introduced in SharePoint 2010 to provide a browser-based viewing and editing experience for SharePoint 2010 users who need to collaborate on Word, Excel, PowerPoint, or OneNote documents. Office Web Apps provided a subset of functionality of the full client applications but helped organizations offer a browser-based method of accessing certain file types in SharePoint libraries, which has become more important with the proliferation of tablets and smartphones. Office Web Apps in SharePoint 2013 has evolved into a standalone product that is completely separate from SharePoint Central Administration. Chapter 27, "Office Web Apps 2013 Integration with SharePoint 2013," covers Office Web Apps Server 2013.

Creating Powerful and Flexible Workflows

Workflows are another feature in the SharePoint family that appeals to many organizations on many different levels. Most organizations still struggle with manual workflows, where a document is moved around the organization via email or manually for signatures or reviews. Another typical challenge is that of onboarding a new employee, where multiple departments must perform a variety of tasks to ensure the new employee has a place to sit, a computer to work on, Active Directory account, and the like.

SharePoint 2013 supports legacy SharePoint 2010 workflows (and uses the Windows Workflow Foundation 3), while introducing new capabilities that require the installation of the Workflow Manager product (which uses the Windows Workflow Foundation 4). It is important for an organization interested in implementing SharePoint-based workflows to gain a better understanding for the moving parts of a workflow, and what can be done with out-of-the-box workflows, in SharePoint Designer 2013 and in Visual Studio.

A number of the workflows available in SharePoint 2013 are covered in Chapter 28, "Out-of-the-Box Workflows and Designer 2013 Workflows," and Chapter 29, "Application Development with SharePoint Designer 2013 and Visual Studio," continues on the topic by covering more complex workflow development options. Basic out-of-the-box workflows such as document approval workflows provide solutions to the most basic document review and approval needs, while SharePoint Designer 2013 allows power users to expand upon these basic capabilities, and Visual Studio 2012 allows experienced developers to accomplish "anything" the organization might need for the most complex workflows.

Developing Applications Using Visual Studio

One appealing feature of SharePoint is that it supports application development in many shapes and forms. Because SharePoint is built on the .NET platform, developers can create applications to perform any set of functions required by the organization. SharePoint 2013 is intended to partner with SharePoint Designer 2013 and Visual Studio 2012 to make it even easier for developers to create powerful and stable applications. Additional enhancements in the development arena include the following:

- Several new client objects models allowing interaction with SharePoint objects, methods, lists, libraries, and even service applications
- The addition of the SharePoint 2013 Workflow Manager, which is Azure-based and cloud-enabled

- Updated Visual Studio 2012 templates for site definitions, business data connectivity model, event receivers, and modules
- A new App Catalog in Visual Studio 2012 allowing for developers to develop, package, and deploy Apps that integrate with SharePoint both directly and remotely
- REST application programming interfaces (APIs) allowing for standards-based Extensible Markup Language (XML) over Hypertext Transport Protocol (HTTP) communication with SharePoint
- Language-Integrated Query (LINQ) support allowing for integrated, object-like access to SharePoint data from familiar .NET languages such as C# and VB.NET

Chapter 29 provides step-by-step instructions on how to create a Designer 2013 workflow that interacts with multiple SharePoint lists when items are created and modified, as well as create an app in Visual Studio 2012 that renders a SharePoint announcements list in a custom format using the JavaScript Client Object Model (CSOM).

Leveraging Business Intelligence Tools in SharePoint 2013

The business intelligence tools in SharePoint 2013 are complex enough and powerful enough that two full chapters are dedicated to the concept: Chapter 30, "Business Intelligence in SharePoint 2013 with PerformancePoint Services," illustrates the capabilities of the PerformancePoint service application, and Chapter 31, "Business Intelligence in SharePoint 2013 with Business Connectivity Services," delves into the capabilities of Business Connectivity Services. Excel Services, which enables end users to publish content to SharePoint libraries that can be exposed via the Excel Web Access web part, is covered in Chapter 26. Figure 1.11 gives an example of a dashboard that Chapter 30 provides full instructions for creating.

Governing the SharePoint Environment

An overarching concern for IT has always been answering the question, "Now that we have SharePoint and people are using it, how do we govern it?" Chapter 24, "Governing the SharePoint 2013 Ecosystem," provides insight and recommendations on the steps needed to ensure that the SharePoint 2013 environment meets the goals and vision set forth by IT and the needs of the end users. Although every organization is unique, and its goals and purposes for deploying SharePoint 2013 also unique, the range of tools and processes discussed in this chapter can have value for all different types of organizations and businesses.

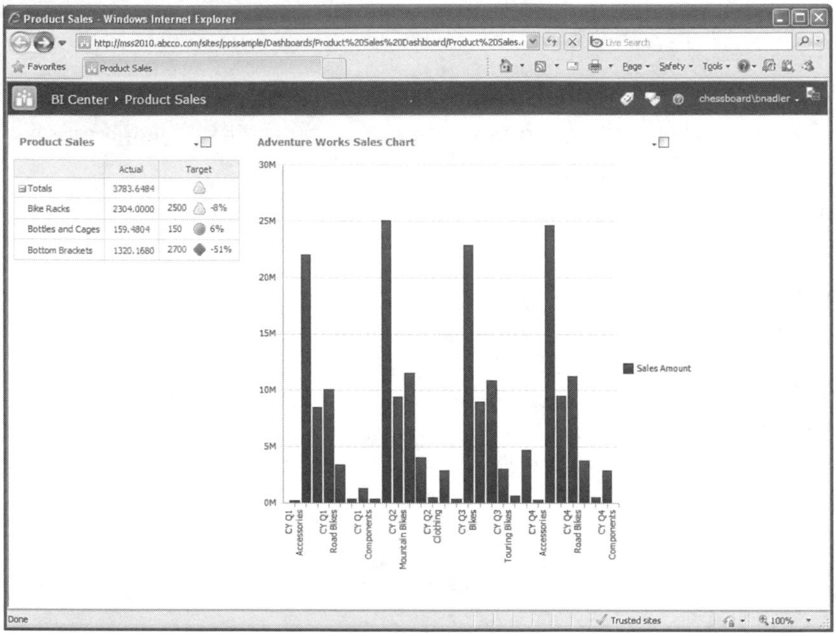

FIGURE 1.11 PerformancePoint dashboard.

Summary

SharePoint 2013 provides for comprehensive document management, collaboration, web content management, and extranet capabilities in a powerful and capable set of products. SharePoint 2010 was essentially a complete redesign of the product, but SharePoint 2013 improves upon the SharePoint 2010 platform in many ways, both by introducing new capabilities and improving upon existing capabilities. As discussed in this chapter, these improvements come in the areas of user interface, document management tools, server management tools, search tools, workflow, and business intelligence and development tools.

Each of these improvements and the core capabilities are discussed in detail throughout this book. Refer to the table of contents or the index to locate a specific topic, tool, or concept.

Best Practices

The following are best practices from this chapter:

- SharePoint 2013 is a complex product line that can be many things to many different companies, and IT should have a clear understanding of how SharePoint will be leveraged and which tools will be provided to the user community.

- A general best practice is to create a design and deployment plan for SharePoint 2013 and "right size" the server farms to meet these requirements, only configuring the tools (such as service applications) that are required to meet the requirements.
- Help leverage SharePoint 2013 in your organization by understanding the integration points with the Office products, especially the most often used applications such as Word, Excel, and Outlook.
- Become familiar with the range of SharePoint 2013 administration tools available for site collections and the farm, as well as PowerShell cmdlets that are critical for administration of a SharePoint environment.
- Familiarize yourself with the incredible range of tools and capabilities in SharePoint 2013 by reviewing the topics covered in this book and by following the step-by-step exercises to learn how to leverage the technologies.
- Learn how key technologies in SharePoint 2013, such as the Managed Metadata Service, search, workflows, and business intelligence tools, can help meet business challenges and requirements.

CHAPTER 2

Architecting a SharePoint 2013 Deployment

IN THIS CHAPTER

- Understanding the SharePoint Server Roles
- Understanding the Reasons for Deploying Multiple Farms
- Choosing the Right Hardware for SharePoint
- Determining Optimal Operating System Configuration
- Planning for Database and Additional Software
- Examining Real-World SharePoint 2013 Deployments
- Addressing Common Business Issues with SharePoint Features
- Deploying a Team Collaboration Solution with SharePoint
- Deploying a Corporate Intranet Solution with SharePoint
- Deploying a Customer Extranet Solution with SharePoint

Many organizations have made the decision to use SharePoint for one or more reasons but are not sure how to start deploying the infrastructure needed by the platform. There are many misconceptions about SharePoint, and further confusing the issue is that the architecture and terminology of SharePoint 2013 has changed over the years.

Many SharePoint 2013 products and technologies are extremely powerful and scalable, but it is critical to properly match the needs of the organizations to a design plan. Matching these needs with a properly planned and implemented SharePoint farm is highly recommended and will go far toward ensuring that deployment of SharePoint is a success.

This chapter covers SharePoint 2013 design and architecture. The structural components of SharePoint are explained and compared. Server roles, database design decisions, and application server placement are discussed. This chapter focuses specifically on physical SharePoint infrastructure and design. Logical design of SharePoint user components, such as site layout and structure, are covered in the chapters in Part IV, "Using SharePoint 2013 Technologies for Collaboration and Document Management."

Understanding the SharePoint Server Roles

What an end user of a SharePoint environment sees on a SharePoint page is the result of a complex interaction that occurs on one or more servers performing varying tasks. Information is stored in complex databases, web rendering is displayed courtesy of the web role, and searches and processes are driven by the Search service application role on servers.

Depending on the size of the environment, these roles may be on one or many servers. In very small environments, all roles may exist on a single server, whereas in very large-scale farms, the roles may be spread across tens or even hundreds of servers. These server roles are the base architectural elements in a SharePoint farm, or collection, of servers that provide for SharePoint services in an environment. It is subsequently critical to understand what these server roles are and how they are used in a SharePoint farm.

NOTE

There may be more than one SharePoint farm per organization. Best practices stipulate that there should be at least one farm used for testing in any environment. Chapter 4, "Advanced SharePoint 2013 Installation and Scalability," deals with scenarios in which more than one farm is deployed.

Understanding the Three Tiers of SharePoint Architecture

One of the most important points to understand about SharePoint architecture is that it is fundamentally a three-tiered application, as illustrated in Figure 2.1. The Web tier is composed of a server or servers running Windows Server's Internet Information Services (IIS) that respond directly to end user requests for information and deliver the content to the user.

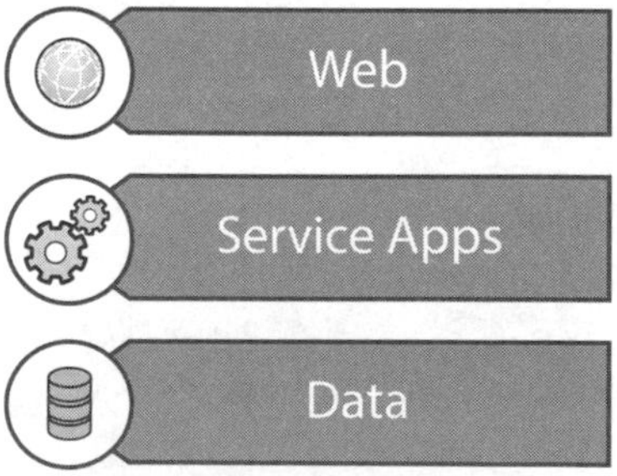

FIGURE 2.1 Understanding the three tiers of SharePoint architecture.

The second tier of SharePoint architecture is the Service Application tier, which includes a list of what Microsoft calls service applications that run various services that are shared between farm members. This includes obvious services such as Search, but also includes an entire list of additional service applications such as the Managed Metadata Service, the

User Profile Synchronization Service, and others. More information on this tier is provided in later sections of this chapter.

The third tier of SharePoint is the Database tier, a critical tier that runs on Microsoft's SQL Server and that stores all content within a SharePoint environment, as well as serving as a location for shared data for service applications. Each of these tiers has unique architectural and functional requirements, and it is subsequently critical to understand these three layers before beginning design of a SharePoint farm.

Understanding the Database Server Role

Nearly all SharePoint content is stored in databases, including all document library content, list items, document metadata, and web parts. There are only two exceptions to this. The first is if the database server uses a concept known as Remote BLOB Storage (RBS), which allows for the storage of the documents, or BLOBs (Binary Large OBjects), in another storage medium such as a file server or an archive. This concept is discussed in detail in Chapter 9, "Managing and Maintaining SQL Server in a SharePoint Environment." The other exception to this rule is the full-text search index, which is stored in flat-file format. (See the following sections on the Search service application role.) In some rare cases, certain web part solutions may store flat files on web front ends as well, which is a good idea in any case, but in reality the vast majority of SharePoint content is stored on the database server role, making it highly critical both for high availability (HA) and for disaster recovery (DR).

The only supported database format for SharePoint is Microsoft SQL Server, and at least one SQL Server database role server must exist in a farm for SharePoint to function.

Supported versions of SQL Server for SharePoint 2013 are as follows:

- SQL Server 2008 R2 x64
- SQL Server 2012 x64

CAUTION

Although SQL Server Express is supported, it is not recommended for most modern SharePoint environments because it does not scale well. Any production SharePoint environment should consider using either the full Standard or Enterprise Editions of SQL Server.

There may be more than one database server role in a SharePoint farm, because a SharePoint administrator can define where a particular SharePoint database resides. In large environments, for example, there may be multiple SharePoint database role servers, each serving multiple databases as part of the farm. You can find more detailed information about the Database tier in SharePoint, including how to enable new features such as SQL Server 2012 AlwaysOn Availability Groups (AOAGs) for SharePoint farms, in Chapters 4 and 9.

Understanding the Web Server Role

The Web Server role is the most obvious of the SharePoint roles, as most people understand the concept of a server running an application that serves up web pages to users that request them. In SharePoint's case, that application is Windows Server's IIS application. A SharePoint farm member running the Web Server role is responsible for rendering SharePoint content, including web parts, page layout, and all other information displayed to the user.

A SharePoint Web Server role runs on either Windows Server 2008 R2 IIS 7.0 or, preferably, Windows Server 2012 IIS. In both cases, SharePoint 2013 requires specific roles to be installed in advance of installation, including the following components:

- Web server (IIS) role
- Application server role
- Windows .NET Framework version 4.5
- SQL Server 2008 R2 SP1 Native Client
- Microsoft WCF Data Services 5.0
- Microsoft Information Protection and Control Client (MSIPC)
- Microsoft Sync Framework Runtime v1.0 SP1 (x64)
- Windows Management Framework 3.0 (includes Windows PowerShell 3.0)
- Windows Identity Foundation (WIF) 1.0 and Microsoft Identity Extensions
- Windows Server AppFabric
- Cumulative Update Package 1 for Microsoft AppFabric 1.1 for Windows Server (KB 2671763)

Each of these components can be installed using the SharePoint 2013 media by clicking the Install Prerequisites link on the initial splash screen. This operation requires Internet connectivity. If Internet access is not available, each individual component needs to be manually installed.

TIP

Multiple web role servers may be set up in a SharePoint environment to scale out the number of users that can use the platform or to provide for HA access to the environment. In this case, load balancing of the connections made to a SharePoint environment allows for a larger number of users to access the content. Load balancing can be either hardware based or software based using Windows Network Load Balancing (NLB), fully supported for SharePoint web role servers.

Service Application Roles

The most significant architectural change that was introduced originally with SharePoint 2010 was the addition of service applications, which replaced the SharePoint 2007 concept of shared services providers (SSPs). Service applications, which are still a critical element in SharePoint 2013, are independent services that can be shared across web applications or, in some cases, across farms.

Table 2.1 lists the service applications available with SharePoint 2013 and which version of SharePoint 2013 software they are available in.

TABLE 2.1 SharePoint 2013 Service Applications

	SharePoint Foundation 2013	**SharePoint Server 2013 Standard Edition**	**SharePoint Server 2013 Enterprise Edition**	**Can Be Consumed Cross-Farm**
Machine Translation Service	X	X	X	X
Managed Metadata service application	X	X	X	X
Search service application	X (non-FAST, limited)	X	X	X
Business Data Connectivity Service	X	X	X	X (Caution cross-WAN)
Secure Store Service	X	X	X	X (Not cross-WAN)
User Profile service application	X	X	X	X (Not cross-WAN)
App Management Service	X	X	X	
Work Management service application	X	X	X	
State Service		X	X	
Web Analytics Service		X	X	
Word Automation Services		X	X	
PowerPoint Automation Services		X	X	
Access Services			X	
Excel Services Application			X	
PerformancePoint service application			X	
Visio Graphics Service			X	

In addition, because the service application framework is extensible, it is possible to install third-party applications that have their own service applications. Indeed, developers themselves can also design and deploy their own applications, a concept which is beyond the scope of this book.

Service applications can be resource intensive and are often deployed on their own dedicated servers to separate their impact from the web role servers. This allows for the service application tier to run within its own contained space, rather than sharing memory, processor, and disk input/output (I/O) with the web/database roles.

NOTE

Just because you've purchased access to a service application does not mean that you should turn it on. Every service application running on a server consumes a significant percentage of that server's resources, and turning on all the available service applications is a bad idea unless you've planned accordingly. Turn on only those service applications that need to run a service that satisfies a specific business need.

Search Service Application Role

One of the most commonly used service application roles in SharePoint 2013 is the Search service application role, because it is responsible for running the Enterprise Search functionality that enables you to search both within and outside of SharePoint.

The Search service application differs from the way it was in SharePoint 2010, and drastically differs from what was provided in SharePoint 2007. SharePoint 2013 retains the capability to have multiple redundant indexes, something that was not possible in SharePoint 2007. In addition, the major change made from SharePoint 2010 was the addition of FAST Search functionality directly in all SharePoint Search engines except for SharePoint Foundation Search. FAST Search, previously a separate licensed engine, allows for new features such as thumbnail views for search results, automatic metadata tagging, and other improvements.

Notice a few key things when architecting for the SharePoint Search service application role. First, the index corpus used to store the full-text copy of all documents crawled can grow large in size based on the amount of content being indexed. The size of the corpus is directly related to the size of the actual document data being crawled. Depending on what is being indexed, and how much actual text is included in that data, the index corpus can range from 5% to 30% of the size of content being indexed, so be sure to include a large enough index disk drive for your index server.

Note a few things about SharePoint search:

- Search in SharePoint is security-trimmed for supported content, excluding some external content sources. This means that end users get search results only from content that they have rights to access. This is a highly useful feature that prevents users from seeing content to which they don't have access.

- Although search is security-trimmed, the permissions are reevaluated only after performing a full crawl of content. Subsequently, if someone is removed from having permissions to a document, she can still see the text of that document as part of a search until a full, not an incremental, crawl has been performed.
- Because SharePoint 2013 allows for redundant search and indexing capability, any one server being down does not take down the entire environment, assuming the Search service application is running on more than one server.

For detailed information on configuring search in SharePoint 2013, see Chapter 8, "Leveraging and Optimizing Search in SharePoint 2013."

Inbound Email Server Role and Team Mailboxes

For scenarios where SharePoint is configured to be email enabled, various SharePoint servers can be assigned to the inbound email server role. Servers with this role have the Simple Mail Transfer Protocol (SMTP) service installed directly on them and are configured to enable inbound emails to be sent directly into SharePoint document libraries and lists. This functionality is critical for an environment looking to use SharePoint for records management or enterprise content management.

TIP

Don't forget to load balance the SMTP service across multiple inbound email role servers in environments with HA requirements! If this is not done, inbound email functionality will not be redundant and will be down for users if an outage of the primary server occurs.

SharePoint 2013 also introduces team mailbox functionality for environments running both SharePoint 2013 and Exchange 2013. The team mailboxes concept takes collaboration with email mailboxes to the next level, allowing for communications to be archived within SharePoint sites that are represented by mailboxes that adhere to the security of the site itself. For more information on how to configure SharePoint for inbound email functionality and team mailbox functionality, see Chapter 16, "Configuring Email-Enabled Content, Site Mailboxes, and Exchange Server Integration."

SharePoint Central Admin Server Role

The server or servers that hold the SharePoint Central Administration service, the main management application for SharePoint, is also considered a server role. In some large environments, this role may be separated onto dedicated servers to provide for Central Administration functionality without affecting existing server functionality.

TIP

It is best practice to make the Central Administration role highly available by installing it on multiple servers, usually on multiple servers that also run the web role. Not doing this runs the risk of a server outage causing a loss of access to the tools necessary to troubleshoot the outage. Although PowerShell can still be used for administration in the event of an outage, it is still useful to have redundancy built in for this role, despite guidance on the Internet that may tell you to install this role on a single server.

Understanding the Reasons for Deploying Multiple Farms

A SharePoint farm is fundamentally a collection of SharePoint role servers that provide for the base infrastructure required to house SharePoint sites and provide for other services, such as Enterprise Search. The farm level is the highest level of SharePoint architecture, providing a distinct operational boundary for a SharePoint environment. Each farm in an environment is a self-encompassing unit made up of one or more servers, such as web role servers, service application role servers, and SharePoint database servers.

In many cases, a single SharePoint farm is not enough to provide for all the needs of an organization. Some deploy multiple SharePoint farms to provide for test environments, farms where development can occur, or farms for extranet users or Internet use. In addition, other farms may be created to provide for centralized services for other farms within the organization. You need to define how many farms are required for an organization when beginning the design process, because the number of farms created can directly reflect on the physical architecture of the servers in a SharePoint environment. Of course, the more farms required, the more hardware is needed, so a full understanding of what can be gained by deploying multiple farms is first required.

Deploying Test Farms

Any production SharePoint environment should have a test environment in which new SharePoint web parts, solutions, service packs, patches, and add-ons can be tested. This applies to all organizations, regardless of size. It is critical to deploy test farms, because many SharePoint add-ons could potentially disrupt or corrupt the formatting or structure of a production environment, and trying to test these new solutions on site collections or different web applications is not enough because the solutions often install directly on the SharePoint servers themselves. If there is an issue, the issue is reflected in the entire farm.

Because of these reasons, many organizations create a smaller SharePoint farm just for testing. The farm should be similar to the existing environments, with the same add-ons and solutions installed and should ideally include restores of production site collections to make it as similar as possible to the existing production environment. All changes and new products or solutions installed into an environment should subsequently be tested first in this environment.

NOTE

The SharePoint server or servers used for a test farm or even a production farm do not necessarily need to be installed on physical hardware; many scenarios with SharePoint servers installed on virtual server infrastructure are possible. See Chapter 12, "Virtualizing SharePoint Components," for more information on this topic.

Deploying Development Farms

Developers in an organization that makes heavy use of SharePoint often need environments to test new applications, web parts, solutions, and other SharePoint customization. These developers often need a sandbox area where these solutions can be tested, and potentially one with different characteristics from production. These environments are also usually quickly provisioned and deprovisioned, so test environments are not the best location for them.

For these organizations, it might make sense to deploy one or more development farms so that developers have the opportunity to run their tests and develop software for SharePoint independent of the existing production environment. When developed, these applications can first be tested in the test farm and then finally deployed into production. For information on automating the creating of test farms using virtual host management software, see Chapter 12.

Deploying Extranet or Intranet Farms

Another reason to deploy multiple farms is for security. For security reasons, it is not generally recommended to have an internal SharePoint document management or intranet environment directly accessible from the Internet unless it is secured by an advanced reverse proxy platform such as Microsoft's Forefront Unified Access Gateway (UAG).

Even for environments properly secured for inbound access, there may be scenarios in which SharePoint content needs to be made accessible by external users, such as in anonymous Internet portal scenarios or for extranet partner scenarios. Because a SharePoint farm requires high connectivity between farms members, it subsequently becomes necessary in these cases to deploy dedicated SharePoint environments in the demilitarized zone (DMZ) of a firewall or in another isolated network. For an in-depth look at SharePoint extranets, including step-by-step guidance for how to set them up using claims-based authentication using various authentication providers, see Chapter 13, "Deploying SharePoint for Extranets and Alternate Authentication Scenarios."

NOTE

SharePoint content deployment can be used to push site content from one farm to another (for example, when content from an internal farm is pushed to an external extranet farm on a regular basis). The extranet farm remains secure and cannot access content on the internal farm, but users can still access required content that has selectively been chosen for publishing.

Deploying Global or Distributed Multifarm Environments

For environments with multiple geographic locations, it might make sense to deploy multiple farms in different geographic locations. This enables SharePoint content to be consumed locally and is what is recommended in scenarios in which WAN links are not as robust. Consider several key points before deciding where to deploy geographic farms:

- A single SharePoint farm should not span a WAN link and should ideally be limited to one geographic location. In some organizations, in which the definition of WAN includes at least 1Gb of bandwidth with less than 10ms of latency between offices located relatively close to one another, it may be possible to stretch a farm across locations, but this is the only scenario in which this would be supported. If you need to consume content locally, it must be part of a separate farm.
- There is no native way to do two-way replication of content between farms with SharePoint 2013. However, several third-party companies on the market enable this type of functionality, which can be advantageous in disaster recovery scenarios in which content is replicated to multiple farms.
- For many organizations, it might make more sense to deploy a single, centralized SharePoint farm in one location rather than to deploy siloed SharePoint farms in multiple locations. Clients access SharePoint using the latency tolerant Hypertext Transport Protocol (HTTP)/HTTPS protocols, so access to a centralized infrastructure might make sense. In addition, SharePoint 2013 has new minimal download features that allow a page to render much more quickly across slower WAN links. This means that centralizing SharePoint becomes much easier, and it also has the advantages of providing a single URL to access SharePoint and keeps data in one location. Organizations need to decide if the level of service accessing SharePoint across a WAN is sufficient for this to be a possibility.

Planning for Multiple Farms

Consider several key points when designing a SharePoint environment to include multiple farms:

- All SharePoint server roles, with the exception of the database role, can only be members of a single farm. You cannot have a SharePoint server reside in more than one farm at a time.
- A single database server can contain databases from multiple farms, dependent on the available capacity of the SQL instance.
- If deploying multiple farms on a single SQL server, be sure to use a common naming convention for each farm database so they can be logically organized on the SQL server. For example, naming all databases with the prefix SP_Farm1, SP_Farm2, and so on can help identify which databases belong to which farm.
- All farm members must have near-full network connectivity (1Gb+ bandwidth, <10ms latency) to all other farm members, with a large number of open ports with nearly all of them open. This effectively limits scenarios in which firewalls separate farm members, unless the proper ports are open between hosts.
- Although not required to have a test environment exactly match production in terms of the number of servers or the type of server roles, it is critical that the web role servers in each environment match each other so that more effective testing can take place.

Choosing the Right Hardware for SharePoint

When farm architecture has been outlined, it is critical to properly size the hardware environment that makes up your SharePoint farm. As illustrated in Table 2.2, the hardware requirements for SharePoint 2013 servers are much higher than earlier versions required.

TABLE 2.2 Hardware Requirements for the Various Server Roles of SharePoint 2013

Type	Memory	Processor
Dev/stage/test server	8GB RAM	4 CPU
All-in-one Database/Web/Service Application	24GB RAM	4 CPU
Web/SA server	12GB RAM	4 CPU
DB server (medium environments)	16GB RAM	8 CPU
DB server (small environments)	8GB RAM	4 CPU

In addition, each SharePoint server role has different hardware requirements, so it is important to first understand those requirements before beginning the procurement process.

Hardware Requirements for the SQL Database Role Servers

The heaviest hitter of all the SharePoint roles is the SQL database server role. This server role houses the SharePoint databases, where nearly all content in a SharePoint environment is stored. The databases house document libraries, documents, lists, sites, site collections, and their contents. For obvious reasons, this server role is highly critical for SharePoint and requires a significant amount of hardware resources. Following are several key hardware requirements for the SQL database role:

- **Disk space:** Because SharePoint content is stored in the databases, the SQL database role server requires a large amount of disk space. How much disk space depends on how much content is stored in SharePoint, but assume the worst: When document versioning is turned on, SharePoint can consume much more space than people realize, even with new features in SharePoint 2013 such as Shredded Storage.
- **Disk performance:** The amount of disk I/O power required can be fairly substantial. Microsoft requires at least 0.25 input/output operations per second (IOPS) per gigabyte (GB) of storage, and recommends around 2.0 IOPS per GB for optimal performance.
- **Processor:** The SQL database role works best when multiple processor cores are allocated to the database role. SQL Server is built to be multithreaded and can use whatever you give it. Today's multicore processors and virtualization platforms that provide for up to eight cores to be allocated (such as Hyper-V 2012) are the perfect fit for SharePoint.

- **Memory:** Server memory requirements are also high for the database role. The same general rule of thumb applies: The more memory allocated, the better an SQL server performs. The total amount of memory recommended varies depending on how heavily utilized the server is, but it is common to have SQL servers with 24GB, 32GB, 64GB, or more.

Hardware Requirements for Service Application Roles

The service application roles, depending on how many run on an individual server, can have serious hardware requirements. The Search service application role, for example, which is responsible for creating a full-text searchable index for search, is the heaviest hitting of the SharePoint roles, excluding, of course, the database role. Search service application servers usually consume more memory and processor capacity because they are constantly engaged in the process of crawling content and making it searchable. Depending on the number of content sources crawled, there can be significant memory requirements, and index servers have been known to use at least 12GB, 16GB, or 24GB of memory and take advantage of multiple processor cores as well.

Other service application role servers may require an equal amount of memory and processor cores allocated as well. It's a general rule of thumb that SharePoint 2013 memory and processor requirements are much higher than for SharePoint 2007 and SharePoint 2010, and many people underestimate the required resources.

In addition to its processor and memory requirements, the Search service application role requires enough drive space to physically store the index files, which are essentially copies of all text that has been crawled across all data sources. The size of this index can range from 5% to 20% of the total size of the searchable content being crawled. For example, if SharePoint is configured to search a file share, and that file share contains 1TB of office documents, the index size may total between 50GB and 200GB, depending on how much actual text is stored in the documents. Large graphical documents with little text do not bloat the index by much, but simple text files can consume a much larger percentage.

NOTE

Remember to calculate your index size based on the total size of all crawled content. Because SharePoint is an Enterprise Search application, the total size of all content may include not only documents in SharePoint, but also file servers and external websites that are crawled.

Hardware Requirements for Web Role Servers

The web role server is the most utilitarian role, requiring a reasonable amount of memory and processor power, but nothing excessive. Indeed, better performance can often be gained by adding additional web role servers to a farm rather than by increasing the size of memory and processor power added to a system. Web role servers usually have between 12GB and 16GB RAM in most cases, and at least two cores allocated to it.

Determining Optimal Operating System Configuration

The core of a functioning SharePoint environment is the operating system that SharePoint runs on. All servers in a SharePoint farm require the Windows Server operating system. The following versions of Windows Server are supported:

- ▶ Windows Server 2008 R2, Standard, Enterprise, or Datacenter, x64 with Service Pack 1
- ▶ Windows Server 2012, Standard or Datacenter, x64

Windows Server 2012 Operating System for SharePoint

The most optimal, secure, and performance-tuned operating system for SharePoint is Windows Server 2012, which has built-in security enhancements to Kerberos and also handles client/server communications traffic better than earlier versions of Windows, making it ideal to host SharePoint servers. For any new SharePoint farm deployments, you should highly consider the use of Windows Server 2012 for these reasons where possible. An alternative to Windows Server 2012 is Windows Server 2008 R2 w/SP1.

Planning for Database and Additional Software

In addition to the operating system, a SharePoint farm requires software for the database, and preferably other add-ons such as backup and antivirus software. Although these are the most common software add-ons, there can be multiple third-party and other add-ons installed into SharePoint, depending on the needs and scale of the deployment. Consult with third-party vendors to determine any potential needs for your farm.

Database Software

The only supported database for SharePoint is Microsoft SQL Server. SharePoint databases must be installed on 64-bit SQL servers, and they can be successfully installed on the following types of SQL servers:

- ▶ SQL Server 2008 R2 x64 with SP1, Standard or Enterprise
- ▶ SQL Server 2012 x64, Standard or Enterprise

It is highly recommended to consider SQL Server 2012 for the SharePoint database role because it provides for the most robust, capable, and secure platform for SharePoint. In addition, it includes features that are useful for SharePoint, such as AOAGs, PowerPivot, and Transparent Data Encryption (TDE), which enables the SharePoint databases to be stored in encrypted format. You can find information about these features in Chapter 9.

With so many new features to discuss and so little space, this section focuses on a number of different components that, together, make up the entire new SQL Server product. This discussion introduces SQL's many components and purpose. The components consist of the following:

- **Database engine:** The database engine component is the heart of SQL Server. It is responsible for storing data, databases, stored procedures, security, and many more functions, such as full-text search, replication, and HA.
- **Analysis services:** Analysis services delivers online analytical processing (OLAP) and data mining functionality for business intelligence applications. Analysis services allows organizations to aggregate data from multiple heterogeneous environments, and transform this data into meaningful information that can then be analyzed and leveraged to gain a competitive advantage in the industry.
- **Integration services:** Provides businesses the opportunity to integrate and transform data. Businesses can extract data from different locations, transform data that may include merging data together, and move data to different locations, such as relational databases, data warehouses, and data marts. Integration services is the official SQL server extract, transform, and load (ETL) tool.
- **Reporting services:** Includes tools such as Report Manager and Report Server. This component is built on standard IIS and .NET technology and enables businesses to design report solutions, extract report data from different areas, customize reports in different formats, manage security, and distribute reports.
- **Notification services:** Consists of a notification engine and client components meant for developing and deploying applications that generate and send notifications to subscribers. Notifications are generated when they are either prompted by an event or triggered by a predefined or fixed schedule. Notifications can be sent to email addresses or mobile devices.

Backup Software

Although SharePoint 2013 products include built-in backup capability, the tools used are not enterprise level and do not have built-in scheduling, item-level restore, or robust alerting capabilities. It is subsequently recommended to purchase and install enterprise backup software. This may include software from a number of third-party vendors, or it may include a solution from Microsoft such as System Center Data Protection Manager (DPM) 2012. Backup and restore is discussed in more detail in Chapter 10, "Backing Up and Restoring a SharePoint Environment."

Antivirus Software

SharePoint 2013 includes an antivirus application programming interface (API) that enables all documents to be scanned for viruses by a compliant antivirus engine. It is highly recommended to include SharePoint-specific antivirus as part of a SharePoint deployment, because client-specific antivirus cannot disinfect documents in SharePoint, and alternatively, viruses could be uploaded into SharePoint if the client antivirus is missing or out of date.

There are multiple third-party antivirus vendors in the SharePoint space. For more information on antivirus products for SharePoint, see Chapter 14, "Protecting SharePoint with Advanced Edge Security Solutions."

Index iFilters

The most common add-on for SharePoint search are iFilters. Index iFilters provide specific knowledge for the SharePoint indexer on how to break open specific file types and index the text content within them. The most common iFilter in earlier versions of SharePoint was the PDF iFilter, which is fortunately included in the FAST Search engine that is used in SharePoint search in SharePoint 2013. Other iFilters may be needed, however, so it is subsequently important to determine which file types will be stored in SharePoint and to determine whether iFilters are available for those file types so that the files can be properly indexed.

Examining Real-World SharePoint 2013 Deployments

Conceptually speaking about a SharePoint environment is not the same as actually viewing some real-design scenarios with the product. Therefore, the last section of this chapter focuses on viewing some sample real-world deployment scenarios that are supported and give insight into the architecture and design concepts surrounding SharePoint 2013.

Deploying Single-Server SharePoint

The most straightforward deployment of SharePoint 2013 is one that involves a single all-in-one server that runs the database components and the web and all service application roles. This type of server deployment, shown in Figure 2.2, has the distinct advantage of being simple to deploy and administer.

FIGURE 2.2 Viewing a sample single-server SharePoint farm.

In this type of deployment, the server takes on all the roles of the environment, including the following:

- SharePoint Central Administration tool
- Content databases and other SharePoint databases

- All site collections and sites
- All service application roles

This environment works well for those environments with a small number of users. Its biggest disadvantage is that there is a great deal of contention between the database role and the SharePoint roles, which can cause performance constraints.

Deploying Small SharePoint Farms

For those organizations with a greater number of users or whose users are more active and require a separate server, the next step up in SharePoint design is a small farm model, as shown in Figure 2.3.

FIGURE 2.3 Viewing a sample small SharePoint farm.

In this type of deployment, two servers are set up. The first holds all the databases and is essentially a dedicated SQL server box for SharePoint. The second server runs the SharePoint roles. By separating the database role from the SharePoint roles, significant performance increases can be obtained.

Deploying Mid-Sized SharePoint Farms

As an organization's document management and collaboration needs to grow, the SharePoint farm needs to grow with it. Figure 2.4 illustrates a mid-sized SharePoint farm with four total servers, which is the minimal number of servers that can be deployed to provide for full HA of all SharePoint components.

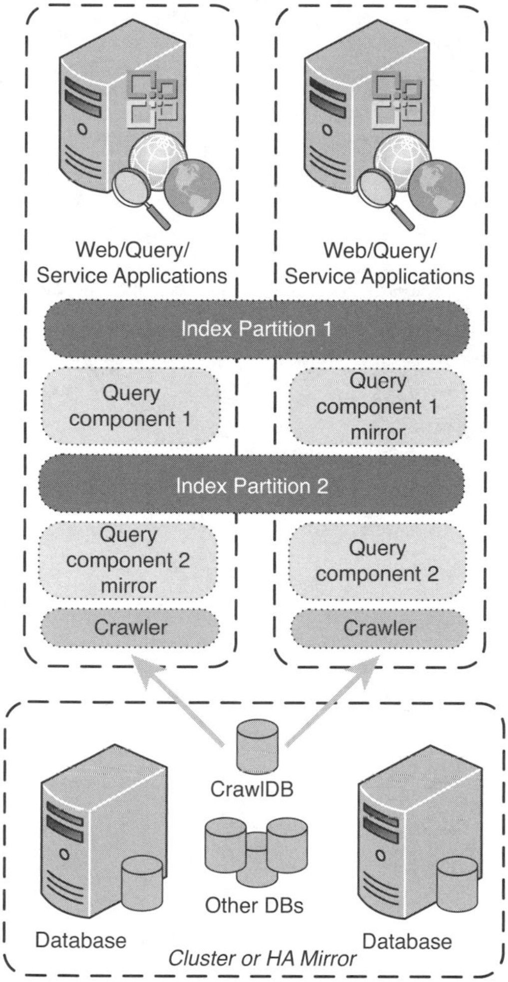

FIGURE 2.4 A four-server mid-sized SharePoint farm.

For best performance and scalability, however, many organizations may choose instead to separate the web and service application tiers of SharePoint and deploy a mid-sized six-server environment, such as what is shown in Figure 2.5.

In this configuration, the web role is now separate from the service application roles, which increases performance. In addition, NLB is used between the web role servers to provide for availability, and the SQL servers are clustered using either AlwaysOn Failover Cluster Instances (FCIs) or AOAGs to provide for HA and DR of the database tier. This type of environment can easily scale into the tens of thousands of users.

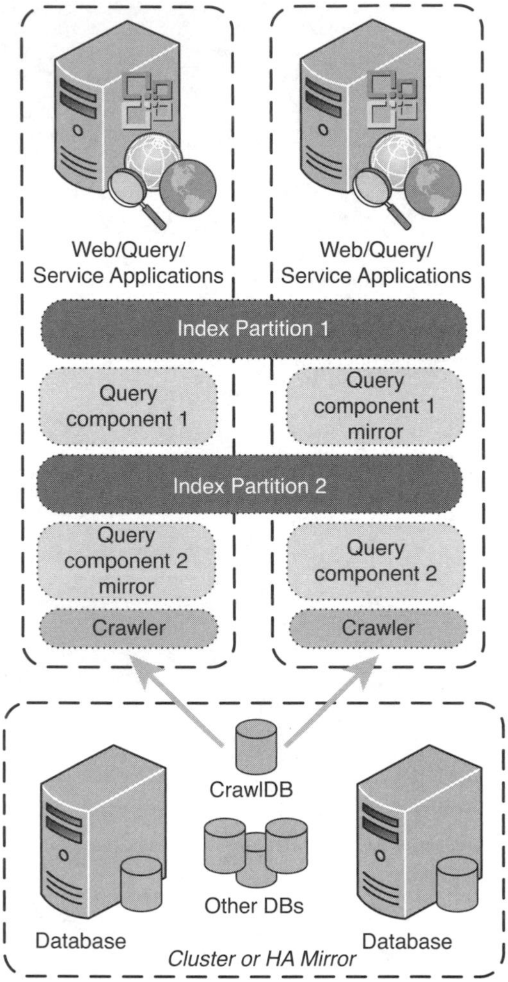

FIGURE 2.5 A six-server mid-sized SharePoint farm.

Taking a look at one final mid-sized design (see Figure 2.6), some organizations may instead choose to separate those six servers into two separate farms, one for the service applications and the other for the content. This has the advantage of keeping the two farms completely independent of each other for patching and maintenance, and the content farm (or farms) can consume services provided on the services farm, such as Search and the Managed Metadata Service.

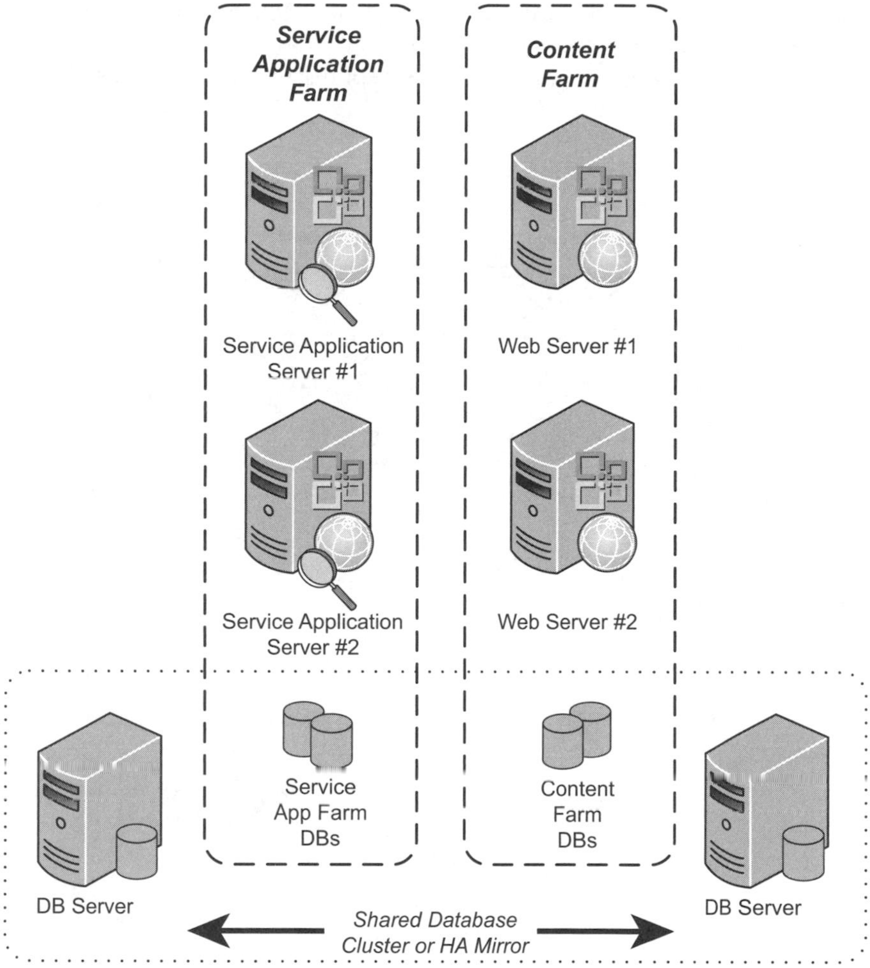

FIGURE 2.6 A six-server mid-sized SharePoint multifarm environment.

Deploying Large SharePoint Farms

SharePoint operates under design principles that are massively scalable if needed. Using redundancy and load-balancing techniques such as the SQL AlwaysOn and NLB, you can obtain more performance from an environment simply through the addition of other servers to provide redundancy and load balancing to specific roles. For example, in a large farm, such as the one shown in Figure 2.7, multiple servers in cluster and NLB configurations enable the environment to be scaled into a large numbers of users. In addition, multiple Search service servers and striped index partitions enable the Search infrastructure to scale into the tens of millions of documents indexed. New features such as SharePoint 2013 Resource Management (RM) automatically allow for content to be intelligently distributed between web servers. RM is a concept discussed in more detail in Chapter 4.

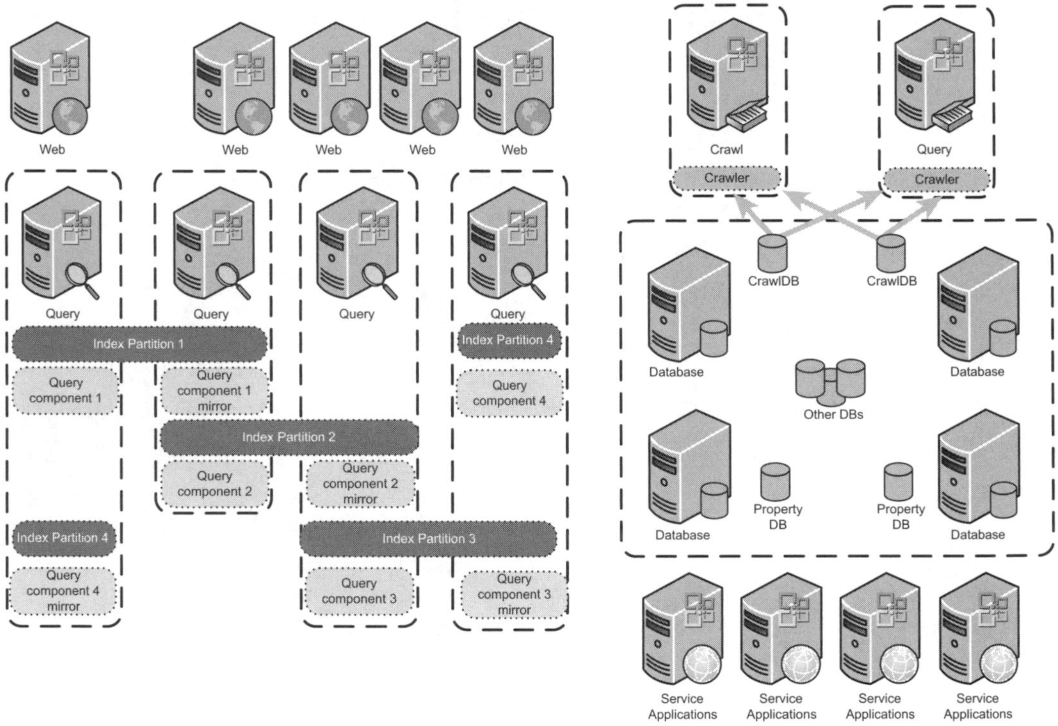

FIGURE 2.7 Deploying a large multiple-farm SharePoint environment.

Addressing Common Business Issues with SharePoint Features

SharePoint 2013 was designed to address business needs and issues that commonly arise in organizations. This section pulls together the information about SharePoint features described in other chapters of this book to summarize some of the common business issues and how features of SharePoint can address those issues. Scenarios that represent these issues are described, along with the specific SharePoint technologies that can address the issues.

Addressing the Redundant Re-Creation of Documents with SharePoint

In many organizations, users duplicate efforts or reinvent the wheel creating documents or gathering information previously used by someone else in the organization either because they didn't know the information existed or couldn't find it. This results in an inefficient use of time.

> **SharePoint solution:** Full-text indexing and search of SharePoint document libraries, workspaces, metadata information, and lists.

SharePoint Search service application indexing of SharePoint 2013 sites enables indexing and searching site content so that users can quickly find the documents or information they need.

Addressing the Inability to Efficiently Search Across Different Types of Content

Users need information, and often the only way they can get it is to perform multiple different types of searches on multiple content sources and then manually consolidate the results. This results in the possibility of content not being searched (either because it is overlooked or just takes too much time) and an inefficient use of time.

> **SharePoint solution:** SharePoint 2013 content sources that can be indexed and searched.

Adding frequently used sources of information as content sources in a SharePoint 2013 environment provides a means for users to perform one search request and have the results from many different content sources displayed together. For example, a single SharePoint search request could span other SharePoint sites, websites external to the organization, file shares, and Microsoft Exchange public folders. This enables users to easily search across many sources to find the information they need.

Addressing Inefficient Means of Document Collaboration with SharePoint Document Libraries

A team of people need to collaborate on a project and produce a set of documents to be sent to a client. User A works on the first document and saves it as Doc1. User A emails User B to let User B know the document is available for review. User B makes changes and additions and saves the document as Doc1 R1. User B creates an email with a list of ideas about additional changes that could be made and emails User A and User C. User C replies to User A and User B about User B's email about proposed changes, makes her own changes, saves it as Doc1 R2, and emails Users A and B to let them know changes have been made. User A also replies about the proposed changes, makes "final" changes to the document, saves it as Doc1 Final, and emails the document to the client. Two days later, the client emails back with the list of changes the client wants to see in the document. User A edits the document again and saves it as Doc1 Final R1. The process continues until there are suddenly 10 versions of the document and 16 emails floating around about what should be in the document. At this point, the team isn't sure what changes have been made; the folder where the document is stored is cluttered with various versions of the document (and taking up a lot of space), and nobody knows which versions were sent to the client.

SharePoint solution: SharePoint team site with a shared document library, document-versioning enabled, and document discussions.

Instead of having multiple versions of multiple documents floating around with different names, a team site for the project with a shared document library could be used. Each client document would be stored in the library, and by using versions and entering version comments, the team would know who made changes, be provided with a brief overview of what or why changes were made, and know which one was sent to the client. By using document discussions in place of emails to have an online discussion of the document, all comments are stored in one place, with the document right there for easy access as opposed to sifting through multiple emails.

Addressing the Excessive Use of Email Attachments/Ability to Know When Documents Have Been Modified

A user emails an attachment to a group, revises the attachment, and then emails it to the group again, and so on. This results in excess email traffic, excess storage, and the potential that recipients won't see the current version of the attachment if it is modified after the email is sent.

SharePoint solution: Document workspaces/libraries and alerts.

Use document workspaces and libraries storing documents in a centralized document library, accessible by all team members. Alerts set up by team members notify them when the document changes. Team members know where the most current version of the document is located and are notified automatically when the document changes.

Addressing Difficulty Organizing or Classifying Content

In a traditional file system environment, a user creates a document. For future reference, should the document be stored in a folder based on the subject of the document, in a folder based on document type, in a folder based on the client the document was created for, or in all three places? Decisions of this type need to be made all the time, weighing the consequences of storing the document in one place versus another versus storing multiple copies of the document.

SharePoint solution: Use of topics and global document metadata using the Managed Metadata Service search.

When using SharePoint, using document metadata and topics prevents the document creator from having to worry about where the document is stored. Metadata or specific fields of information that can be stored with the document can be used for information such as subject, client, and document type. Metadata can be enforced across all documents in a farm using the Managed Metadata Service available in SharePoint 2013. Because these fields are searchable, a document can be easily found regardless of what folder it is in.

Addressing Access to Line-of-Business Application Information

An organization may use a business application such as SAP or Microsoft Dynamics. Some individuals in the organization need to access information stored in these applications, but it would be costly to install and maintain the application on each desktop and to train all the users.

SharePoint solution: ASP.NET web parts and single sign-on.

ASP.NET web parts can be developed and used to access and display information from other applications and data sources. Single sign-on can also be enabled to provide seamless integration with the application. This provides the user with an easy, usable method for accessing information, and the IT department can maintain the code centrally and not have to worry about desktop deployment and specific training for the line-of-business applications. SharePoint 2013 also supports web parts, which opens it to the ability to view content from multiple third-party software and web part vendors.

Using SharePoint for Sharing Information with Partners, Vendors, and Clients

An organization needs to collaborate with another organization (for example, a marketing company doing research and developing collateral for the organization, or a client that the organization is working with on a specific project). The users from both organizations email documents and other information back and forth. Usually, these emails are sent to *all* people involved with the project so as to not leave anyone out. This can result in excess email traffic and emails being sent to users that they may not need (or want) to see.

SharePoint solution: Team site with extranet access.

The SharePoint team site template fits the needs of groups of people working collaboratively. The site can be set up for extranet access, enabling outside parties to participate as team members. Using a team site over a traditional email-based method of communication provides all kinds of benefits, including giving people the ability to review only what they want to review, set up alerts to be notified when specific information changes, set up a process for approving final documents, participate in online real-time discussions, and look at earlier document versions.

Deploying a Team Collaboration Solution with SharePoint

A team collaboration site is used by a group of people working together for a common end result, or to complete a project. The success of the team or project depends on the effectiveness of the team and its ability to efficiently collaborate to complete the project. Therefore, the site is designed to facilitate team communications and sharing project information.

Usually, a team collaboration site is an internal, decentralized site that has a relatively small number of members. However, it can be configured to provide access for members external to the organization. When the site is implemented, it replaces the traditional file share-based storage, use of email, and use of other traditional applications the organization may have for storing and accessing documents and other information.

Outlining Business Needs for the Team Collaboration Solution

The general categories of business needs for this group are communications, project management, and document management. These needs can be mapped to SharePoint features, as presented in this section:

- **Communications:** Interacting with other team members electronically using workspace instant-messaging capabilities. Finding out when information has changed through the use of alerts. Having discussions on issues or documents using the general or document discussion components.
- **Project management:** Assigning major project tasks to individuals using a tasks list. Tracking and following up on tasks using a tasks list and various views of the list. Centralizing and distributing information such as objectives, agendas, and decisions for project meetings in one place using meeting workspaces. Providing status reports to management based on information in task items.
- **Document management:** Having a common place for storing documents by using shared document libraries. Managing document revisions using the check-in/check-out and version retention features. Controlling document publication using content approval. Enhancing the ability to find and feature specific documents by assigning them to topics and best-bets classifying documents for retrieval using metadata attached to the document.

Implementing a Team Collaboration Solution with SharePoint

The team collaboration site is implemented using a SharePoint team site. A shared document library is created in the team site for document management and a tasks list for assigning responsibilities. Content approval is enabled for the document library with the project manager assigned the role of approver. Document workspaces are also used for individual documents to incorporate direct access from SharePoint 2013 applications. The team uses document discussions to communicate ideas about document contents and a general discussion for items relating to the project. The team site is part of a SharePoint implementation that has content sources defined for searching relevant information and archived documents.

Outlining Ideas for Using the Team Collaboration Solution

This section includes some ideas to incorporate into the team site solution with the elements previously discussed. The major project milestone tasks can be entered into a tasks list, assigned to individual team members, and then tracked by the project manager. The tasks list can also be used for status reporting.

Users can initially create documents using Microsoft Office 2007/2013 applications and then save them to a document workspace. The document workspace can be used by the team members as a conduit for instant messaging on project-related issues. Discussions within the document can be used for providing feedback and recommendations for document content.

When the document is ready for publishing, it can be moved to the shared library where it is reviewed by the approver. The approver can set up an alert to be notified when the new documents are added or modified within the library.

Deploying a Corporate Intranet Solution with SharePoint

The corporate intranet is used for communicating information to employees and providing them with access to corporate line-of-business applications. The primary goals of a corporate intranet are to provide resources to employees that can help improve performance and to provide employees with centralized electronic access to corporate-based information for things such as policies, procedures, and roles and responsibilities. The benefits of the corporate intranet include providing an electronic means of accessing information as opposed to reliance on human intervention, providing an easier way of finding information, automating processes, and eliminating duplication of effort. The end result is a reduction in operational costs.

Meeting Business Needs with the Corporate Intranet Solution

The general business needs of this group include searching for information, corporate communications, workflow processing, management of web-based content, and application integration. These needs can be mapped to SharePoint features as presented in this section.

Corporate communications:

- Notifying employees about company events using an events list
- Notifying employees about changes in policies and procedures using announcements
- Obtaining feedback from employees using discussion boards and surveys
- Providing access to company policies, procedures, and forms through shared document libraries
- Providing access to company-maintained information, such as employee directories, using lists such as the contacts list

Searching:

- Finding location-specific information by having the ability to search across local sites, division-based sites, and the corporate portal

- Having a means for searching content external to the SharePoint infrastructure, such as external websites, file systems, and other internal application databases, and SharePoint-based information and displaying the results together by using content sources and source groups

Workflow processing:

- Requiring documents to be approved before publishing using content approval
- Notification of outstanding items using alerts
- Simplifying processing using approve/reject views

Managing web content:

- Providing non-IT staff with the ability to create team-based sites when necessary through the self-service site creation
- Standardizing the look and feel of sites by creating site templates
- Enabling users to create a place for collaboration when needed through the use of shared document workspaces
- Providing a way to make meetings more effective and meaningful by using meeting workspaces
- Removing the dependency on IT departments for updating sites and site content by using the web-based customization features and document library concept
- Enabling users to tailor the view of the intranet to accommodate their specific needs using personal sites

Application integration:

- Providing a single interface for intranet capabilities and access to applications by using link lists
- Providing a way for users to view application data without having to load the application on the desktop by creating web parts that retrieve and display application data
- Minimizing the problems associated with providing multiple user accounts and passwords for various applications by using single sign-on for application access

Implementing the Corporate Intranet Solution

The corporate intranet site is implemented using SharePoint 2013 sites. Features used on the site home page include announcements, links (to other major corporate sites and applications), search, events, and discussions. In the quick launch area are links to lists such as the corporate directory and to shared libraries including policies and procedures, newsletters, training, and benefits. Areas can be configured for operational groups within the organization and geographic groups within the organization, depending on the organizational requirements. Content sources that contain information useful to employees for doing their job can be added for indexing and search. Security and content approval can be implemented to enable controlled creation of sites and site content by a wide group of users. Integration can be provided for SharePoint-compatible applications by using preexisting integration web parts and developing custom web parts. Single sign-on can also be used for making it easier for users to access applications from within the site collection.

Ideas for Using the Corporate Intranet Solution

This section includes some ideas to incorporate into the corporate intranet site solution with the elements previously discussed.

Disseminate important corporatewide information such as policy and procedure changes using announcements. Put an expiration date on the announcements. If users see the same ones day in and day out, they have a tendency to ignore them.

Use a general discussion for obtaining employee feedback on policies, procedures, events, and other items of interest to employees. Moderate the discussion; have the human resources department or legal department responsible for approving all items submitted to the discussion group to ensure they are appropriate. Maintain a separate discussion forum for non-company-related items, such as employees selling candy for their children's youth groups. This type of discussion should not take up valuable home page space but provide a link to it from the home page. Surveys can also be used to get specific input on a topic.

Maintain a corporate events list in a calendar view to provide visual impact for upcoming events. Depending on the corporate climate, things such as birthdays and vacations can be maintained on the corporate calendar as well as company events and holidays.

Store company policies, procedures, and forms in shared document libraries for ease of maintenance and accessibility. The department responsible for maintaining the documents should also be responsible for the publishing of documents (approve contents) and read access provided to other users.

Create content source groups for logical breakdown of content for searching to prevent an inordinate amount of time from being spent performing searches.

Using Active Directory as the basis for the company directory assists in keeping the SharePoint-viewed company directory synchronized with it. A customized view of the directory can be created that filters and displays only relevant columns of information.

Using an application such as InfoPath 2013 or InfoPath Forms Services, InfoPath forms can be created, filled out, and stored in document libraries for access and processing. Alerts can be set up in the library for people who need to process the documents so that when something is submitted, they are notified and can review the items. Approval processing can also be used to approve and reject the documents. This concept could be used for things such as expense reports and other workflow documents. For an end-to-end solution, application code can be developed to feed the data from the form documents into the appropriate external application (for example, the accounting system) for final processing.

Because there is generally a great deal of information on a corporate intranet, users should take advantage of the ability to create and customize their own personal sites to include information they find useful. By using web parts that interface with Microsoft Outlook 2007/2013, the Windows SharePoint Services (WSS) personal site can become the primary user interface.

Deploying a Customer Extranet Solution with SharePoint

The primary purpose of the customer extranet portal is to service the needs of customers. The customer extranet enables customers to find information about products and services, and place help desk calls. In some customer extranets, client access is provided for things such as invoice payment and viewing account status and payment history. The customer extranet can also be used for document collaboration and managing joint projects with the customer. The content for this type of portal can originate from internal and external sources.

Meeting the Business Needs of the Customer Extranet Solution

The business needs of this group include searching for information, aggregating content from multiple sources, providing a dynamic view of relevant business information, collaborating on documents, sharing documents, managing joint projects, resolving issues, and providing a means for business transactions. The SharePoint features used to meet these needs are outlined as follows:

Searching:

- Providing customers with a means for viewing information about their account by using web parts that access line-of-business applications to retrieve and display customer-related information
- Enabling customers to find product/service information using the search features of SharePoint without having to speak with a service representative
- In addition to searching, providing the ability to view the results in a variety of ways depending on the needs using the filtering and sorting features of SharePoint

Content aggregation:

- Combining information from various sources into a single source for searching using content sources
- Accessing information from multiple business applications into one view using web parts

Dynamic views:

- Using filters to display subsets of information such as product-specific or location-specific data
- Using sort capabilities to present the information in a different order

Document collaboration:

- Sharing documents with clients using shared document libraries
- Controlling publication of documents using content approval
- Categorizing documents so that they can be easily found using document metadata
- Finding documents on a specific subject by searching the document text or the metadata attached to the document

Working on joint projects:

- Assigning/delegating tasks between parties using a tasks list
- Following up on overdue tasks by using views such as the Due Today view
- Sharing project-related information using a team site
- Discussing and resolving project issues using discussion boards
- Managing the overall project and reporting on status using a recurring event or multiple meeting workspace site

Resolving issues:

- Submitting issues/questions to a help desk using the issues list
- Responding to issues in a timely manner by using the alert feature on the issues list
- Having the ability to check the status of outstanding issues by using the My Issues view
- Managing and tracking issue resolution using views of the issues list

Business interaction:

- Providing clients with access to business information such as invoice/payment status using customized web parts
- Enabling clients to perform business transactions by providing links to web-based application interfaces or customized web parts

Implementing the Customer Extranet Solution

The customer extranet site is implemented using SharePoint 2013 Sites. In addition, integration for SharePoint-compatible applications can be provided using existing web parts, developing custom web parts, and providing links to web-based front ends to business applications. Single sign-on can also be implemented to make it easier for users to access applications.

Features available on the extranet portal home page include a links list, announcements, discussion board, and search. The quick launch area can contain links to lists such as a limited corporate directory (with the listings for the salespeople and other people who customers usually deal with, such as accounting personnel) and frequently accessed shared libraries such as newsletters, training documents, and product information. Areas can be configured for support, product/service information, and billing information. A content source group can be created for the content in each area to make searches more targeted.

Document workspaces can be used to collaborate on documents. Team sites can be used when working with the customer on a joint project. Content sources can be created for product/service documentation and historical accounting information.

Security needs to be tight to ensure the integrity of customer-specific information. Restrictions need to be in place to prevent one customer from obtaining access to another customer's data.

Outlining Ideas for Using the Corporate Extranet Solution

This section includes some ideas to incorporate into the customer extranet site solution with the elements previously discussed. In addition to providing standard content, use audiences to target specific content to an individual or group of users.

Use the support area for linking to an issues list and a document library containing technical information. Links to supporting websites could also be in this area. Other possibilities would be to include a top 10 issues list and a download library.

Include a shared library with documents relating to products and services offered and links to corporate or other websites that have this information in the product/service information area. There could also be a discussion board on this area page so that clients could submit product- or service-related questions or requests and provide their ideas and feedback on products and services. When there is a need to get specific client feedback, a survey can be used.

Use team sites when working on projects with the customer. Include a tasks list to document division of responsibility, a contacts list for maintaining the contact information for members from both sides of the team, a custom punch list to document items yet to be completed, a general discussion area as an alternative to email for documenting project-related correspondence in a central location, and create a weekly status meeting event or use a multiple meeting workspace for tracking and managing project status.

Summary

Microsoft SharePoint Server 2013 is a powerful tool that can enable knowledge workers to become more productive with a wide array of built-in tools and web parts. To take advantage of these features, however, the SharePoint environment must be properly designed and all the SharePoint components fully understood by the administrator in charge of designing the environment.

With SharePoint 2013 design knowledge, an administrator can properly scope and scale the infrastructure to handle anywhere from a handful of users to a large, distributed deployment of hundreds of thousands of users, enabling those users to take full advantage of the productivity gains that can be realized from the platform.

Best Practices

The following are best practices from this chapter:

- Become familiar with SharePoint 2013 design terminology, particularly in how it relates to service application architecture.
- Use the latest version of SQL Server, SQL Server 2012, whenever possible, particularly to take advantage of features such as SQL AlwaysOn, Transparent Data Encryption, and PowerPivot.
- Consider separating the service application roles from the web role servers to improve performance.
- Separate the database role from the SharePoint roles whenever possible to improve performance.
- Take an in-depth look at virtualization technologies, at a minimum for development and test farms, and potentially for production farms.
- Consider best-practice security approaches such as SQL Server TDE for storage security, IPsec and Secure Sockets Layer (SSL) certificates for transport security, and Active Directory Rights Management Services (AD RMS) for data loss prevention.
- Consider database mirroring for the content databases to provide for both high availability and disaster recovery of SharePoint content.
- Remember to purchase and install any necessary third-party web parts, iFilters, backup, and antivirus software, or use some of the Microsoft offerings such as System Center DPM 2013.
- Allocate a significant amount of memory and processor cores to SharePoint servers because they are resource intensive. SharePoint 2013's resource requirements are much higher than in earlier versions of SharePoint. Start with 12GB RAM and two CPUs for a simple web server.

- Be sure to allocate enough hard drive space for the Search service application roles for the index corpus; allocate 5% to 30% of the size of the data being indexed.
- Use SQL AlwaysOn technologies and network load balancing to scale the SharePoint server environment and provide redundancy.

CHAPTER 3

Installing a Simple SharePoint Server 2013 Farm

IN THIS CHAPTER

- Examining SharePoint Installation Prerequisites
- Installing the SharePoint Server Operating System
- Installing SQL Server 2012
- Installing Microsoft SharePoint Server 2013

After SharePoint architecture has been established, the actual SharePoint infrastructure must be installed, and servers must be deployed. For the most part, installation of SharePoint 2013 can be straightforward for smaller environments, particularly when using SharePoint Foundation Server. The full Microsoft SharePoint Server 2013 product, however, requires more thought and involves the installation of more components.

This chapter covers the specifics of how SharePoint 2013 is installed for a simple single-server farm. Although these examples outline a simple farm, the concepts can be extended to multiserver farm deployments. After reading this chapter, see Chapter 4, "Advanced SharePoint 2013 Installation and Scalability," for more complex farm configurations.

Review Chapter 2, "Architecting a SharePoint 2013 Deployment," (the design chapter) before beginning installation of a production environment. However, you can easily install a SharePoint server for testing with only this chapter as a guide.

Examining SharePoint Installation Prerequisites

Before installing SharePoint 2013, several prerequisites must first be satisfied, including both hardware and software prerequisites.

Defining Hardware Prerequisites for SharePoint 2013

SharePoint 2013 has some stringent installation requirements in terms of how much memory and processor power to allocate to the servers in a farm. Table 3.1 describes the amount of memory and processor to allocate.

TABLE 3.1 Hardware Requirements for SharePoint Server Roles

SharePoint Role	Memory (min)	Processor (min)
Dev/stage/test server (SharePoint-only)	8GB RAM	4 cores
All-in-one Database/Web/Service Application (SA)	24GB RAM	4–8 cores
Web/SA server	12GB RAM	4 cores
DB server (medium-large environments)	16GB RAM	8 cores
DB server (small environments)	8GB RAM	4 cores

In addition, at least 100GB is required on the system drive for the operating system, plus enough space for twice the amount of memory on the system. For example, if you have 24GB RAM, set aside 148GB (100GB + (2 x 24GB)) for the operating system (OS) drive. SharePoint also requires significant drive space for the database and logs volume, in the range of hundreds of gigabytes to terabytes for the database volume depending on the amount of documents you anticipate storing in SharePoint.

From a drive performance perspective, ensure that the database volume used for SharePoint has at least 0.25 input/output operations per second (IOPS) per gigabyte of content and ideally around 2.0 IOPS per gigabyte of content for maximum performance. For example, if you anticipate 400GB of data to be stored in SharePoint, be sure that the database volume provides at least 100 IOPS of performance at a minimum, and ideally around 800 IOPS for maximum performance.

NOTE

The move toward virtualization of servers has been gaining strength in recent years, and SharePoint server roles can all be virtualized using certain guidelines. See Chapter 12, "Virtualizing SharePoint Components," for specific guidance on designing and deploying SharePoint using server virtualization technologies.

The server that holds the SharePoint database, whether on the same box (an all-in-one server) or on a dedicated server or existing SQL Server implementation, should generally be designed toward the high level on the hardware scale, because some of the more intensive activity is centralized on that server role.

As a rule of thumb, it is always recommended to deploy SharePoint on multiple servers, and at a minimum to deploy SharePoint on at least two servers: one for the database and one for the other SharePoint-specific roles. For more information on supported farm topologies, see Chapter 2. For the sake of simplicity, however, the remainder of this chapter assumes that SharePoint is installed on a single all-in-one server.

Examining Software Requirements for SharePoint 2013

SharePoint 2013 requires either Windows Server 2008 R2 SP1 or Windows Server 2012. More specifically, the following Windows OS editions are supported:

- Windows Server 2008 R2 with SP1 Standard, Enterprise, or Datacenter Editions
- Windows Server 2012 Standard or Datacenter Editions

In nearly all scenarios, it is recommend to use the latest version of the Windows Server OS (in this case, the 2012 edition), though some organizations might not be ready for the new tile-based Modern User Interface and will opt for Windows Server 2008 R2. For most deployments, the Standard Edition of Windows Server suffices, except in certain scenarios when the Enterprise/Datacenter Edition is required for those environments that need to run the Enterprise Edition of SQL Server.

Service Account Requirements

It is strongly recommended that you create multiple service accounts for SharePoint. Although doing so might seem tedious, SharePoint is not secure unless multiple service accounts are used. And in any situation, do *not* use a domain admin account for any SharePoint service.

You should create the following recommended list of service accounts. This should not be considered an exhaustive list; more might be needed depending on the requirements of the individual deployment:

- **SQL admin account:** SQL Server should be administered with a separate set of credentials than those used for SharePoint.
- **Installation account:** Used to install the SharePoint binaries on the SharePoint role servers. This account requires local admin rights on each SharePoint server and DBCreator and SecurityAdmin rights on the SQL Server.
- **SharePoint farm admins:** Used to administer the farm; should be configured. Usually one account for each physical admin is created.
- **Application pool identity accounts:** Needed for each app pool. Generally speaking, it is good practice to have a separate app pool for each application. These accounts must be separate from farm admin accounts.
- **Default content access account:** The default account used to crawl SharePoint and other content. It must not be a farm admin; otherwise, the search results will include unpublished data in the results. There may be additional content access accounts created for other data sources that are crawled as well.
- **Search service application account:** This account is used to run the search service application.
- **Additional service application accounts as needed:** May require a separate service application account in certain scenarios.

Table 3.2 provides a default list of service accounts required for a standard installation of SharePoint and illustrates what (if any) additional rights each account needs.

TABLE 3.2 Sample Service Accounts for a Default SharePoint Install

Service Account Name	Role of Service Account	Special Permissions
COMPANYABC\SRV-SP-Setup	SharePoint installation account.	Local admin on all SP servers (for installs).
COMPANYABC\SRV-SP-SQL	SQL service accounts (should be separate admin accounts from SP accounts).	Local Admin on database servers. (Generally, some exceptions apply.)
COMPANYABC\SRV-SP-Farm	SharePoint farm accounts (can also be standard admin accounts).	N/A
COMPANYABC\SRV-SP-Search	Search account.	N/A
COMPANYABC\SRV-SP-Content	Default content access account.	Read rights to any external data sources to be crawled.
COMPANYABC\SRV-SP-Prof	Default profiles access account.	Member of Domain Users (to be able to read attributes from users in domain) and Replicate Directory Changes rights in Active Directory (AD).
COMPANYABC\SRV-SP-AP-SPCA	Application pool identity account for SharePoint Central Admin (SPCA).	DBCreator and SecurityAdmin on SQL, create and modify contacts rights in organizational unit (OU) used for mail.
COMPANYABC\SRV-SP-AP-Data	Application pool identity account for the content-related app pool (portal, My Sites, and so on). Additional as needed for security.	N/A

Database Role Prerequisites

For the database role, you should deploy the latest version of SQL Server, SQL 2012. The following versions of SQL Server are directly supported:

- SQL Server 2012, Standard or Enterprise Editions
- SQL Server 2008 R2 with SP1, Standard or Enterprise Editions

Installing the SharePoint Server Operating System

After choosing the edition of the server OS, you must install it on the SharePoint server. As previously mentioned, this step by step assumes that a single all-in-one SharePoint server is set up and deployed.

The Windows Server 2012 OS encompasses a myriad of new technologies and functionality, more than can be covered in this book. If you want to learn more about the capabilities of the operating system, see *Windows Server 2012 Unleashed* (Sams Publishing).

NOTE

It is highly recommended to install SharePoint 2013 on a clean, freshly built OS on a reformatted hard drive. If the server used for SharePoint was previously running in a different capacity, the most secure and robust solution would be to completely reinstall the OS using the procedure outlined in this section.

Installing Windows Server 2012

This chapter assumes installation of SharePoint on the latest version of Windows Server, the 2012 version. The steps for installation on Windows Server 2008 R2 are very similar, and architects can follow the same approximate steps of installation outlined here.

Installation of Windows Server 2012 is extremely straightforward and takes approximately 30 minutes to 1 hour to complete. Microsoft has built the installation process to be nearly touch-free. Simply accept the defaults for any SharePoint server; there is no need to choose any custom installation settings. The high-level steps involved are as follows:

1. Install Windows Server 2012 with the defaults.
2. Activate the server.
3. Install any server-specific tools required.
4. Patch and update the OS.
5. Add the server to an Active Directory domain.
6. Copy the SharePoint 2013 binaries locally to the server (recommended).
7. Copy the SQL Server 2012 binaries locally (if installing the database role).

Installing SQL Server 2012

The SharePoint databases need to reside in an SQL Server implementation. The version of SQL must be either SQL Server 2008 R2 with SP1 or SQL Server 2012. The SQL server component can either reside on a separate server or installed on the SharePoint server itself for smaller single-server deployments.

NOTE

For testing or development, you can use the Express version of SQL Server, which is included in a standalone installation option of SharePoint. The standalone version of SharePoint and the Express version of SQL are *not* recommended for production environments.

This chapter assumes that the full SQL Server 2012 product will be installed on a single SharePoint all-in-one server. Installation steps are subsequently illustrated for this scenario. The same concepts can be used for installing a two-server farm, as well, with SQL Server on a single server and all SharePoint roles on another server. For more advanced installation scenarios, including scenarios where SharePoint is installed from PowerShell, see Chapter 4.

Installing SQL Server 2012

From the SQL 2012 binaries, complete the following steps to install:

1. Run setup.exe from the SQL binaries.
2. From the SQL installation center, shown in Figure 3.1, click the installation link on the navigation bar, and choose the link for new installation or add features to an existing installation.

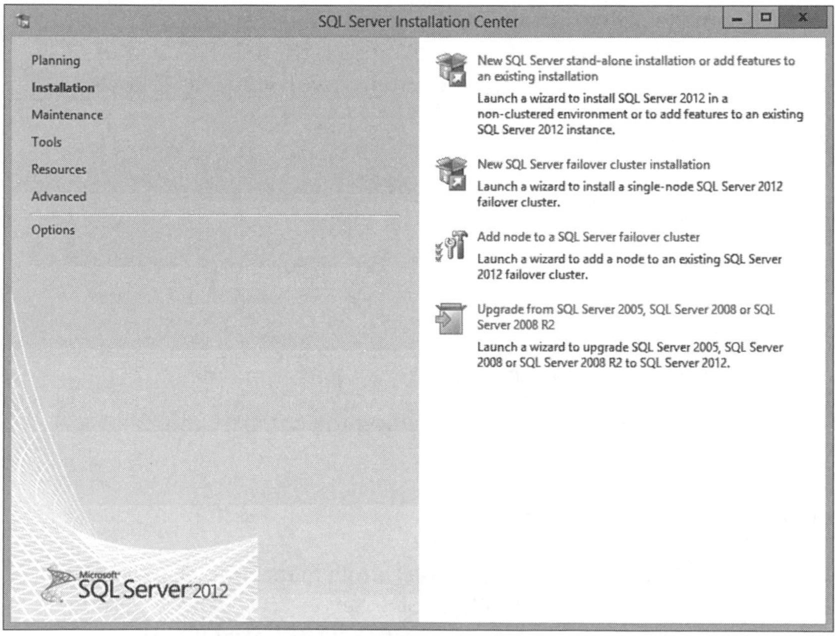

FIGURE 3.1 Starting an SQL Server 2012 install.

3. From the dialog box specifying the edition to install, enter a valid product key, and click Next to continue.

4. Check the box to accept the license terms, and click Next to continue.

5. Review the report generated, as shown in Figure 3.2, and click Next to continue.

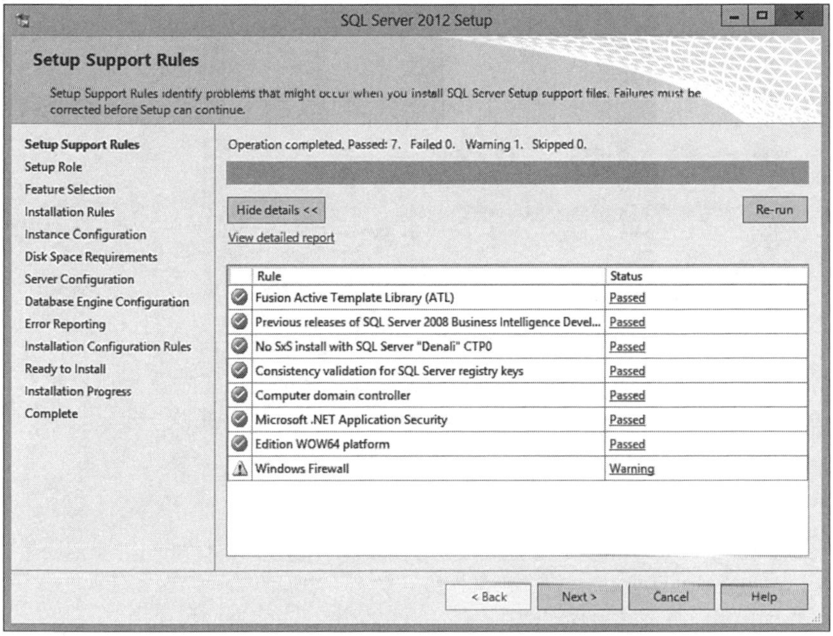

FIGURE 3.2 Reviewing setup warnings from SQL Server.

6. Select SQL Server Feature Installation from the Setup Role dialog box; then click Next to continue.

7. From the Feature Selection dialog box, select Database Engine Services, and click Next to continue. (Reporting Services and Analysis Services might be required for advanced business intelligence features of SharePoint, a topic not covered in this basic install chapter.)

8. Choose to install the Default instance, and click Next to continue.

9. Review disk space requirements, and click Next to continue.

10. From the Server Configuration dialog box, choose Service Accounts for each service. In most cases, you want to use a dedicated SQL service account. After setting the service accounts, click Next to continue.

11. Under the Database Engine Configuration, choose Windows Authentication Mode. Click the Add Current User button to add the installation account as an SQL administrator, as shown in Figure 3.3. (Or add an account that will be logged in later.)

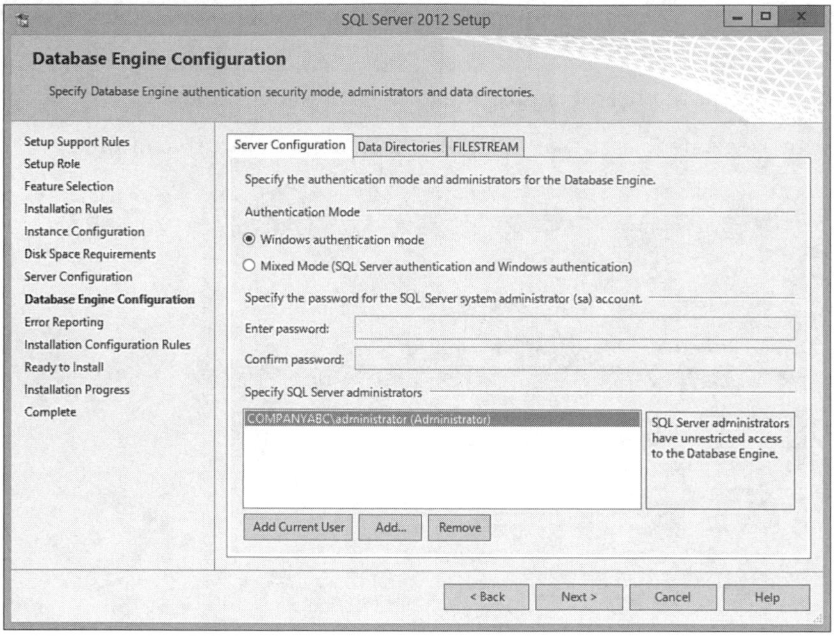

FIGURE 3.3 Designating SQL administrator accounts.

12. Click the Data Directories tab, and choose default installation directories for logs, database files, and backup files. It is recommended to do this in advance and to separate SQL Logs from the databases from the beginning. Click Next to continue.
13. Accept the defaults for Error Reporting, and click Next to continue.
14. After the installation configuration rules have run, click Next to continue.
15. At the summary page, review the settings and click Install.
16. When the install is complete, review the summary log file and click Close to finish.

Post-installation tasks should be conducted after SQL Server has been installed. Some of these post-installation tasks validate whether the installation was successful, whereas other tasks are required to ensure that the server is secure and operational. The post-installation tasks include the following:

1. Review installation logs.
2. Review event logs.
3. Obtain and apply the latest SQL Server service packs and critical updates.
4. Verify the server components that were installed.

It is also critical to rerun Microsoft Update to apply any necessary SQL Server patches. Running Microsoft Update displays the patches necessary for SQL.

NOTE

Remember to use Microsoft Update, and not the default Windows Update, because only Microsoft Update can detect the non-Windows patches, including SQL Server and SharePoint patches.

Creating a Windows Firewall Port Exception for SQL Server

The Windows firewall is highly recommended for security reasons, and you should not simply turn it off. By default, however, to get SQL services to run, you must create a manual Windows firewall port rule that enables port 1433, the SQL port, to be open on the server, as shown in Figure 3.4. If this port is not open, SharePoint cannot connect to the SQL server if it is installed on a separate server from the SharePoint server.

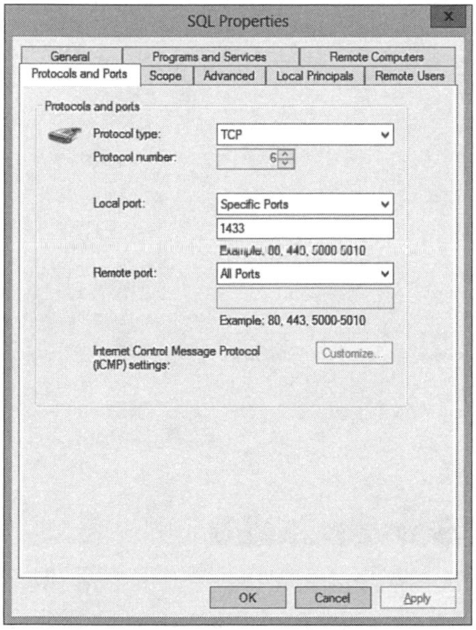

FIGURE 3.4 Creating an SQL port exception for the Windows firewall.

In addition to port 1433, you may also want to create a Windows firewall port exception for port 5022, the endpoint mapping service, particularly if you need to configure SQL for AlwaysOn Availability Groups (AOAGs), a concept covered in Chapter 17, "Safeguarding Confidential Data in SharePoint 2013."

Enabling TCP/IP in SQL Configuration Manager

By default, some SQL Server installations do not have TCP/IP enabled for remote access. However, TCP/IP is required for use by a remote SharePoint server. To enable TCP/IP, open SQL Server Configuration Manager (Microsoft SQL Server 2012—Configuration Tools, SQL Server Configuration Manager) and navigate to SQL Server Network Configuration, Protocols for <INSTANCENAME>. Change the TCP/IP to Enabled, as shown in Figure 3.5. If you do not do this, SharePoint cannot connect to the SQL Server.

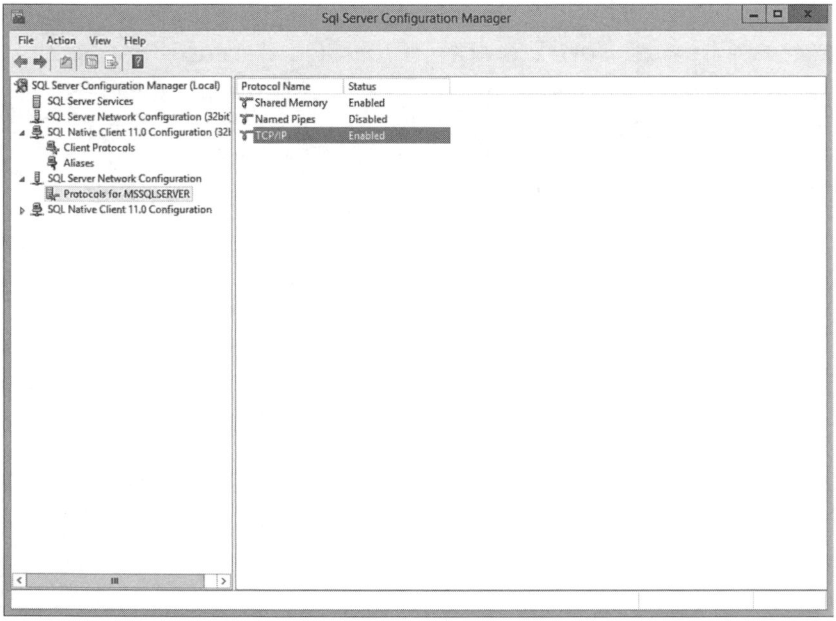

FIGURE 3.5 Enabling TCP/IP support in SQL Configuration Manager.

Installing Microsoft SharePoint Server 2013

Installation of SharePoint 2013 is deceivingly simple, but be sure that you understand the process. Be sure you log in as the SharePoint setup account before beginning the process.

Running the Prerequisite Check for SharePoint 2013

The SharePoint team at Microsoft has done an excellent job in creating a prerequisite check and installation utility that can be run in advance of a SharePoint installation to turn on all server roles required and install all prerequisites automatically. Simply by running a wizard, SharePoint administrators can automate the installation of the SharePoint binaries and position the server to be ready to join or create a new farm.

You can run the prerequisite check directly from the splash screen displayed when running the setup from the SharePoint binaries. Click Install Software prerequisites, accept the license terms, and follow the prompts to install all necessary components.

When the prerequisite check is complete and the roles and hotfixes required are installed, click Finish to reboot the server. The server is now ready for installation of the SharePoint 2013 binaries.

Installing the SharePoint 2013 Binaries

To install the SharePoint 2013 binaries after the prerequisite checks have been run and all necessary software components have been installed, follow these steps:

1. While logged in as the Install account, run Setup.exe, and from the splash screen, click Install SharePoint Server.
2. Enter a valid SharePoint 2013 license key. Note that the Standard and Enterprise Edition license keys are separate, and installing a Standard license key only turns on Standard Edition services.
3. Accept the license terms and click Continue.
4. From the Server Type dialog box, as shown in Figure 3.6, choose Complete as the type of installation. Do *not* select Standalone, unless the server is only used as a demo box. The Standalone version installs a copy of SQL Server Express and should not be used in production.

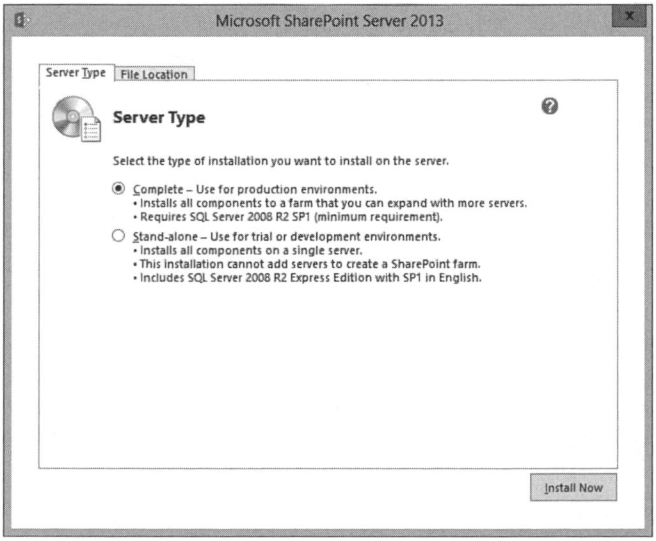

FIGURE 3.6 Installing SharePoint 2013 using the Complete option.

5. Select the File Location tab and specify a location for index files, as shown in Figure 3.7. Ideally, these files will be stored on a separate drive than the OS and SharePoint binaries. If you choose this option now, you won't have to go through the complex process of moving the index later. Click Install Now to start the installation process.

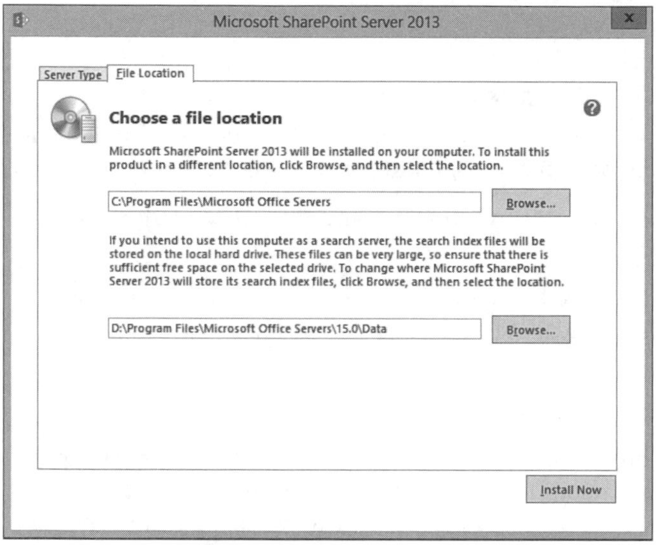

FIGURE 3.7 Choosing a location for the Index files.

6. After the installation has completed, you can choose to run the Configuration Wizard now or later, as shown in Figure 3.8. It is recommended to not run the Configuration Wizard immediately but to first exit the application and check for any updates or patches before proceeding.

Patch SharePoint 2013 with any necessary patches, bearing in mind that there may be cumulative updates that are not reflected in Microsoft Update. It is important to install any service packs and cumulative updates first before continuing with the SharePoint installation, because it is much easier to patch now rather than when farm components are already configured.

NOTE

This point in the installation process, after the binaries have been installed and the system patched, is an ideal spot to create server templates from, for use in virtual server environments. These templates can be used to quickly provision SharePoint farm members, allowing for the creation of new SharePoint farms in a matter of minutes. For more information on this concept, see Chapter 12.

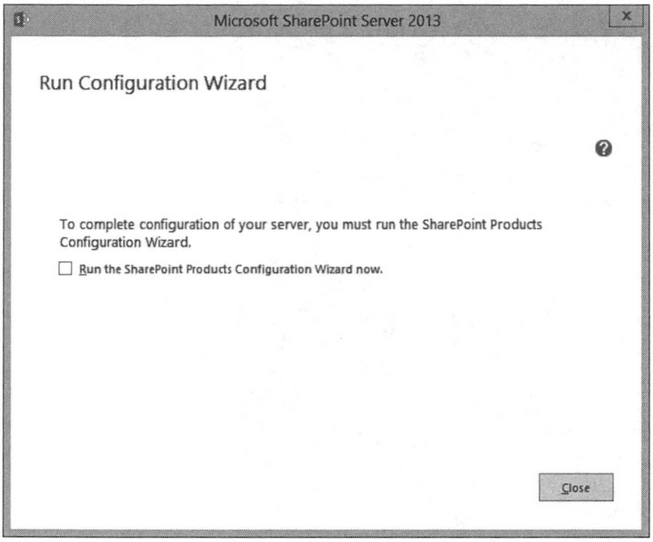

FIGURE 3.8 Deciding whether to run the Configuration Wizard during setup.

Running the SharePoint 2013 Configuration Wizard

The SharePoint 2013 Configuration Wizard is the component that enables a server to either be added to an existing SharePoint 2013 farm or to create a new SharePoint farm from scratch.

NOTE

You can use Windows PowerShell to run the Configuration Wizard, using your own PowerShell scripts or the ones provided by the authors of this book at http://tinyurl.com/SP2013-Config and illustrated in Figure 3.9. Indeed, PowerShell is the only supported method of provisioning SharePoint with custom database names for some of the databases, so it is recommended for many scenarios. Installation using PowerShell is covered in Chapter 4.

If choosing to configure SharePoint using the graphical user interface (GUI) process, complete the following steps:

1. Start the Configuration Wizard (Start, All Programs, Microsoft SharePoint 2013 Products, SharePoint 2013 Configuration Wizard).
2. Click Next at the Welcome screen, and click Yes to acknowledge that Internet Information Services (IIS) will be reset during the process.
3. Select to Create a New Server Farm, and click Next to continue.

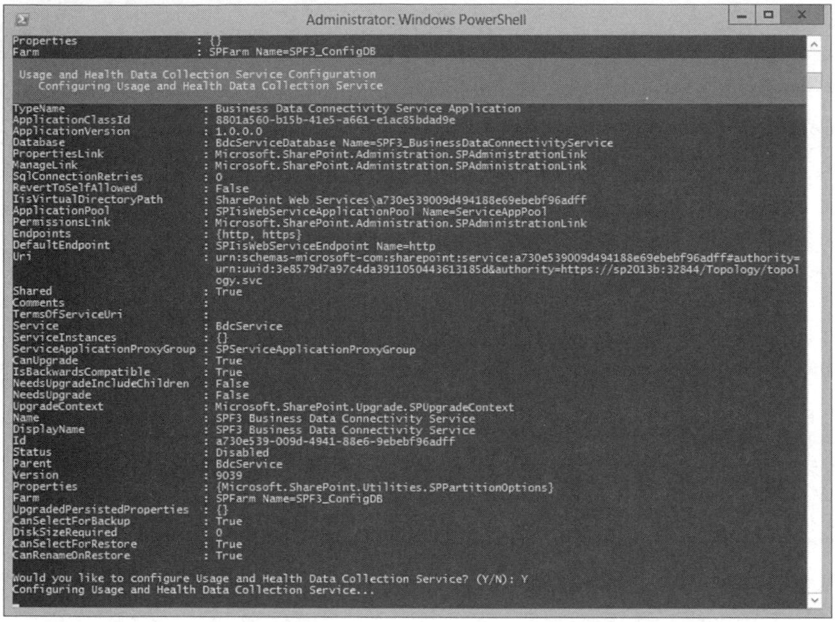

FIGURE 3.9 Configuring SharePoint using the author-supplied PowerShell scripts.

4. For the Configuration Database settings, enter the name of the database server and select a name for the Config database. Consider the use of an SQL alias for the database server name so that it can be easily changed in the future. If the database server is the same as the one that is used for SharePoint, enter the local server name. Enter a Database Access Account that has DBCreator and SecurityAdmin rights on the SQL instance. Click Next to continue.

5. Enter a farm passphrase into the subsequent dialog box. Keep this passphrase in a safe place; it is needed to add any additional servers to the farm in the future. Click Next to continue.

6. Specify a port for the SharePoint Central Administration web application. It is recommended to choose an easily remembered port name initially. You also have the opportunity to choose NT LAN Manager (NTLM) or Kerberos. Kerberos is the recommended setting for the long term, but for the initial installation, choose NTLM to ensure that you can gain access initially. For long-term production support, however, Kerberos, Secure Sockets Layer (SSL), and a default port of 443 are highly recommended for the SharePoint Central Administration web application. More information on changing to Kerberos and configuring SSL and a default port for the central web application can be found in Chapter 4. Click Next to continue.

7. Review the settings and click Next to start the Configuration Wizard.

8. Click Finish when the wizard is complete.

Running the Initial Farm Configuration Wizard

After the Configuration Wizard has run, the newly provisioned SharePoint Central Administration web application starts automatically. You may need to provide credentials to the site; use the farm installation credentials to start the application.

By default, SharePoint is configured to run the initial farm Configuration Wizard upon the first time using the Central Administration web application. This wizard will complete most other farm tasks, including installing and configuring service applications. As mentioned earlier, however, it is highly preferential to install SharePoint using PowerShell, instead of these GUIs. For simpler environments, this wizard can be used to get SharePoint to a condition where it is more or less ready for use. For more complex provisioning scenarios, see Chapter 4.

To run the initial farm Configuration Wizard, follow these steps:

1. Select whether to join the Customer Experience Improvement Program from the initial dialog box and click OK.
2. From the wizard introduction screen, select whether to run the wizard. If it is not run, you need to manually configure each service application component and manually provision web applications and site collections. In this scenario, we use the wizard to provision the components. Click Start the Wizard.
3. From the subsequent screen, enter a service account that will become a managed service account for the farm. This should differ from the farm account.
4. Check the service applications that will be installed. Only install those service applications that supply required functionality for the site, because each service application uses a significant amount of resources on the server.
5. After selecting which service applications to install, click Next to start the provisioning process. This process may take a while to complete, depending on the resources of the server.
6. After the service application provisioning process has completed, the wizard prompts you to create a web application and root site collection as the main site collection for the portal. You can skip this step or have the wizard provision it for you. Enter a title and choose a template. Click OK to continue.
7. Click Finish to close the wizard. You now should have a fully provisioned SharePoint 2013 environment.

SharePoint Central Administration, as shown in Figure 3.10, will open and allow for additional configuration. For more information on additional configuration and how to administer a SharePoint farm using SharePoint Central Administration, see Chapter 6, "Managing and Administering SharePoint 2013 Infrastructure."

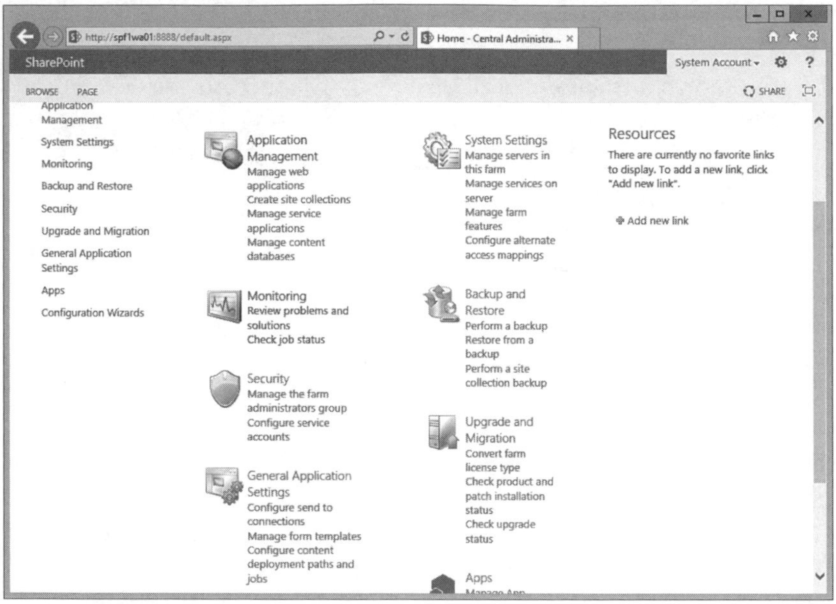

FIGURE 3.10 Running SharePoint Central Administration for the first time.

Summary

Installation of SharePoint 2013 products and technologies has been streamlined and is fairly straightforward, as long as necessary prerequisites are met and attention to detail is observed. With the proper precautions in place and the scenarios in this chapter followed, administrators can immediately take advantage of the advanced feature set available in SharePoint 2013.

Best Practices

The following are best practices from this chapter:

- Review Chapter 2 before installing SharePoint 2013 into a production environment.
- Create multiple service accounts for use by SharePoint. Do not use a single service account, and do not use any domain admin accounts for SharePoint.
- Do not use any of the standalone installation options for a production environment.
- Use the latest version of Windows Server and SQL Server whenever possible. At the time of publishing, this included Windows Server 2012 and SQL Server 2012.
- Highly consider deploying SQL Server on a separate server from SharePoint. Review the supported farm topologies from Chapter 2.
- Patch the OS with all critical updates before installing SharePoint.

- Patch SharePoint 2013 with all the latest service packs and cumulative update patches before running the Configuration Wizard.
- Enable only those service applications that supply required functionality for the farm.
- Review Chapter 4 for more complex installation scenarios, including scenarios involving provisioning using PowerShell.
- Highly consider installation of SharePoint via PowerShell, rather than the default Configuration Wizards. For sample PowerShell scripts written by the authors of this book, visit http://tinyurl.com/SP2013-Config.

CHAPTER 4

Advanced SharePoint 2013 Installation and Scalability

IN THIS CHAPTER

- Creating an Installation Checklist
- Installing SharePoint 2013 Using PowerShell
- Understanding Scalability for SharePoint
- Scaling Logical SharePoint Components

The needs of most organizations are not going to be met by a simple single-server SharePoint farm. Indeed, the power of SharePoint 2013 is in its scalability, and the majority of organizations are going to want to take SharePoint to the next level in terms of functionality.

This chapter covers the more advanced installation scenarios that aren't covered in Chapter 3, "Installing a Simple SharePoint Server 2013 Farm." It is meant to build upon the simple farm deployment examples illustrated in the previous chapter, but take you into the realm of tasks that are often performed during the installation of larger and more complex environments, including Kerberos, Secure Sockets Layer (SSL) configuration, and scripted installations of an entire farm using PowerShell.

In addition, this chapter focuses on techniques and information necessary to scale a SharePoint implementation to organizations of varying sizes. Specific components that can be scaled are described and contrasted. In addition, examples of scalability in organizations of different sizes are presented.

Creating an Installation Checklist

Installation of a large and complex SharePoint environment can be a complicated task, and various subtasks and routines must be run before the environment is production ready. It is subsequently important to create a mental and physical checklist of the types of tasks required for rollout of a farm.

The following list of tasks represents a common large farm deployment routine and can be used as a starting point for determining the task list that is required for installation of your specific environment. It is not a definitive list of all tasks, and the order of tasks performed might vary depending on the environment.

Conceptualizing and Architecting a SharePoint Farm

The following list denotes the high-level steps that should be followed before architecting a SharePoint environment:

1. Define the business needs that should ideally be met by the project.
2. Map business needs to technical solutions in SharePoint 2013.
3. Define the number of farms required to satisfy business and technical needs and to provide for publishing and other features.
4. Define the number and scale of intranet versus extranet environments, using guidelines from Chapter 13, "Deploying SharePoint for Extranets and Alternate Authentication Scenarios."
5. Define the physical architecture required to deploy the technical solutions.
6. Define the security requirements, including number of service accounts and the rights they require.
7. Define the number of third-party and other Microsoft solutions to properly secure and deploy.

See Chapter 2, "Architecting a SharePoint 2013 Deployment," for more information on these tasks.

Installing SharePoint 2013

Most SharePoint environments follow the same general process for the installation of a farm. Use the following high-level checklist for advanced SharePoint installations:

1. Build the SQL Server Database environment for SharePoint.
2. Build the SharePoint Server environment, including all role servers, from an operating system (OS) perspective and also by installing the SharePoint binaries.
3. Create the SharePoint farms using the Configuration Wizard or (preferably) using PowerShell (as demonstrated in this chapter).

See Chapter 3 for more information on these tasks.

Configuring SharePoint 2013

Following the creation of the farm itself, use the following high-level checklist to continue the installation of an advanced SharePoint environment:

1. Create Web Applications required, configuring them for Kerberos, SSL, and load balancing (all best practices).
2. Configure the managed paths and content database structure, based on the parameters defined during the design phase.
3. Configure the SharePoint Central Administration web application as a load-balanced, SSL, and Kerberos-enabled web application for performance, security, and high availability.
4. Configure all service applications required for the farm, using either the web-based wizard or (preferably), PowerShell, as demonstrated in this chapter.
5. Configure the User Profile Service to pull information into user profiles. This can also be scripted, but requires very specific settings and configuration. Namely, it requires the account used for the service to be both a local admin on the server it is installed on as well as a farm admin in the forest. (These rights can be later modified after provisioning.) The account also needs Replicating Directory Changes rights within Active Directory.
6. Configure inbound mail settings, and configure them to be load balanced for availability of the service.
7. Configure outbound mail settings for alerts and other messages to be sent from SharePoint.
8. Create and configure My Sites personal sites.
9. Configure search (covered in more detail in Chapter 8, "Leveraging and Optimizing Search in SharePoint 2013," including third-party iFilters, such as PDF iFilters, and FAST Search if needed.
10. Configure backup (third-party, Microsoft Data Protection Manager [DPM], or integrated backup). See Chapter 10, "Backing Up and Restoring a SharePoint Environment," for more details.
11. Configure edge security (covered in Chapter 14, "Protecting SharePoint with Advanced Edge Security Solutions").
12. Configure data and transport security options (covered in Chapter 17, "Safeguarding Confidential Data in SharePoint 2013").
13. Configure SQL maintenance and optimization, using concepts defined in Chapter 9, "Managing and Maintaining SQL Server in a SharePoint Environment."
14. Configure third-party product functionality as necessary.
15. Test, test, and retest before deploying into production.
16. Migrate content into SharePoint using third-party tools (if necessary).

Installing SharePoint 2013 Using PowerShell

PowerShell is a critical tool for SharePoint administrators that actually allows for options not available in the standard SharePoint Central Administration graphical user interface (GUI). For example, PowerShell is the only method that enables the creation of custom names for many of the databases created by SharePoint during the installation. In addition, creating a custom PowerShell script for installation of a new farm enables that farm to be repeatedly created, such as in the case of development farms.

Examining a PowerShell Script for Provisioning a Farm

When SharePoint binaries are installed in an environment, PowerShell can be used to provision any farm. Listing 4.1 illustrates a way to have PowerShell create a new farm based on input from the end user and have all databases from that farm use the name of the farm in the database name, to enable multiple farms to be created in a single environment.

NOTE

You can download this script and all scripts listed in this chapter at http://tinyurl.com/SP2013-Config.

LISTING 4.1 PowerShell Farm Provisioning Script

```
---------------------------------------
#
# SharePoint 2013 Unleashed - PowerShell farm config script
# http://www.amazon.com/Microsoft-SharePoint-2013-Unleashed-Michael/dp/0672337339
# Copyright: Toni Frankola, Michael Noel
# Version: 2.0, Jan 2013.
#
# Source: http://tinyurl.com/SP2013-Config
# Licensed under the MIT License:
# http://www.opensource.org/licenses/mit-license.php
#

$path = Get-Location
[xml]$settings = Get-Content ($path.Path + "\settings.xml") -ErrorAction
SilentlyContinue

Function Get-SettingValue
{
       param([xml]$Xml,
                [string]$XPath,
                [string]$Prompt)
```

```
        if($Xml -ne $null -and $Xml.SelectSingleNode($XPath) -ne $null -and $Xml.
SelectSingleNode($XPath).InnerXml -ne "")
        {
                return $Xml.SelectSingleNode($XPath).InnerXml
        }
        else
        {
                $value = Read-Host $Prompt;
                return $value;
        }
}

$configType = Get-SettingValue -Xml $settings -XPath "/settings/NewFarm" -
Prompt "Do you wish to create a new farm? (Y/N)"
if ($ConfigType -eq "N") {
    $DatabaseServer = Get-SettingValue -Xml $settings -XPath
"/settings/DatabaseServer" -Prompt "Preparing to join existing farm. Please
specify the name of your SQL Server";
    $ConfigDB = Get-SettingValue -Xml $settings -XPath "/settings/ConfigDB"
-Prompt "Next, specify the name of your Farm Configuration Database";
    $Passphrase = Get-SettingValue -Xml $settings -XPath
"/settings/Passphrase" -Prompt "Finally, please enter your Farm passphrase"
} else {
    $DatabaseServer = Get-SettingValue -Xml $settings -XPath
"/settings/DatabaseServer" -Prompt "Preparing to create a new Farm. Please
specify the name of your SQL Server (ex SERVER or SERVER\INSTANCE[,PORT])";
    $FarmName = Get-SettingValue -Xml $settings -XPath "/settings/FarmName"
-Prompt "Please specify a name for your Farm (ex. SP2013Dev)";
    $ConfigDB = $FarmName+"_ConfigDB";
    $AdminContentDB = $FarmName+"_CentralAdminContent";
    Write-Host "Please enter the credentials for your Farm Account (ex.
COMPANYABC\SP_Farm)";
    $FarmAcct = Get-Credential -Message "Please enter the credentials for
your Farm Account (ex. COMPANYABC\SP_Farm)";
    $Passphrase = Get-SettingValue -Xml $settings -XPath
"/settings/Passphrase" -Prompt "Enter a secure Farm passphrase (must meet
password complexity requirements)";
    $Port = Get-SettingValue -Xml $settings -XPath
"/settings/CentralAdminPort" -Prompt "Enter a port number for the Central
Administration Web App";
    $Authentication = Get-SettingValue -Xml $settings -XPath
"/settings/CentralAdminAuthentication" -Prompt "Finally, specify your
authentication provider (NTLM/Kerberos)";
}
```

```
$Passphrase = convertto-securestring $Passphrase -asplaintext -force

 if((Get-PSSnapin | Where {$_.Name -eq "Microsoft.SharePoint.PowerShell"}) -eq
$null) {
       Add-PSSnapin Microsoft.SharePoint.PowerShell;
}

$ErrorActionPreference = "Stop"

if ($ConfigType -eq "N") {
    Connect-SPConfigurationDatabase -DatabaseName $ConfigDB -DatabaseServer
$DatabaseServer -Passphrase $Passphrase
} else {
    Write-Host "Your SharePoint Farm is being configured..."

       New-SPConfigurationDatabase -DatabaseName $ConfigDB -DatabaseServer
$DatabaseServer -AdministrationContentDatabaseName $AdminContentDB
-Passphrase $Passphrase -FarmCredentials $FarmAcct
}

Initialize-SPResourceSecurity
Install-SPService
Install-SPFeature -AllExistingFeatures
New-SPCentralAdministration -Port $Port -WindowsAuthProvider $Authentication
Install-SPHelpCollection -All
Install-SPApplicationContent
Write-Host "Your SharePoint 2013 Farm has been created!"
if ($ConfigType -eq "Y") {
    $WebAppCreation = Get-SettingValue -Xml $settings -XPath
"/settings/WebApp" -Prompt "Would you like to provision a Web Application
using the default Team Site Template? (Y/N)";
    if ($WebAppCreation -eq "Y") {
        $HostHeaderQ = Get-SettingValue -Xml $settings -XPath
"/settings/WebAppHostHeaderQ" -Prompt "Would you like to specify a host
header? (Y/N)";
        if ($HostHeaderQ -eq "Y") {
            $HostHeader = Get-SettingValue -Xml $settings -XPath
"/settings/WebAppHostHeader" -Prompt "Please specify a host header for your
Web Application (ex. intranet.contoso.com)";
                     $URL = "http://"+$HostHeader;
              }
              else {
                     $URL = "http://"+$env:COMPUTERNAME;
              }
```

```
            Write-Host "Creating your Web Application...";
            $ap = New-SPAuthenticationProvider
            New-SPWebApplication -Name "SharePoint 2013 Team Site" -Port
80 -Url $URL -ApplicationPool "Content_AppPool" -ApplicationPoolAccount
(Get-SPManagedAccount $FarmAcct.UserName) -DatabaseServer $DatabaseServer -
DatabaseName ($FarmName + "_TeamSite_ContentDB_01") -AuthenticationProvider
$ap;
            New-SPSite $URL -OwnerAlias $FarmAcct.UserName -Language 1033
-Template "STS#0" -Name "Team Site";
            Write-Host "Configuration completed.";
    }
    else {
        Write-Host "Configuration completed.";
    }
}

$serviceAppsConfig = Get-SettingValue -Xml $settings -XPath
"/settings/Services/ServiceAppsConfig" -Prompt "Do you wish to configure
Service Applications? (Y/N)"

if($serviceAppsConfig -eq "Y") {
       PowerShell -File "Configure-ServiceApps.ps1" $FarmName
}
else {
       Write-Host "Press any key to continue..."
       $x = $host.UI.RawUI.ReadKey("NoEcho,IncludeKeyDown")
}
--------------------------------------
```

Using concepts such as those demonstrated in this script, you can automate the creation of an entire custom farm and have more control over the entire farm creation process. This particular script utilizes a variables file (settings.xml) that allows for the input of variables. Customizing the commandlets illustrated in the script can enable further customization.

PowerShell for Provisioning Service Applications

Service application provisioning is a much more complex process than the installation of a single farm. Consequently, a PowerShell script to provision all service applications in a farm can be much longer and more complex. You can use the following script, available at the same http://tinyurl.com/SP2013-Config link, to provision nearly all available SharePoint 2013 service applications, and it walks the end user through the process and enables them to choose which service applications they want to install (as shown in Listing 4.2).

LISTING 4.2 SharePoint Installation PowerShell Script

```
---------------------------------------
#
# SharePoint 2013 Unleased - PowerShell farm config script
# Copyright: Toni Frankola, Michael Noel
# Version: 2.0, Jan 2013.
#
# Source: http://tinyurl.com/SP2013-Config
# Licensed under the MIT License:
# http://www.opensource.org/licenses/mit-license.php
#

cls
Remove-PSSnapin Microsoft.SharePoint.PowerShell -ErrorAction SilentlyContinue
if((Get-PSSnapin | Where {$_.Name -eq "Microsoft.SharePoint.PowerShell"}) -eq $null)
{
       Add-PSSnapin Microsoft.SharePoint.PowerShell;
}

$path = Get-Location
[xml]$settings = Get-Content ($path.Path + "\settings.xml") -ErrorAction
SilentlyContinue

Function Get-SettingValue
{
       param([xml]$Xml,
                  [string]$XPath,
                  [string]$Prompt)

       if($Xml -ne $null -and $Xml.SelectSingleNode($XPath) -ne $null -and $Xml.
SelectSingleNode($XPath).InnerXml -ne "")
       {
              return $Xml.SelectSingleNode($XPath).InnerXml
       }
       else
       {
              $value = Read-Host $Prompt;
              return $value;
       }
}

function Start-SPService($ServiceInstanceTypeName) {
       $ServiceInstance = (Get-SPServiceInstance | Where {$_.TypeName -eq
$ServiceInstanceTypeName})
```

```
        if($ServiceInstance -ne $null -and $ServiceInstance.Status -ne "Online" -and
$ServiceInstance.Status -ne "Provisioning") {
                $ServiceInstance | Start-SPServiceInstance
        }

        $i = 0;
        while(-not ($ServiceInstance.Status -eq "Online") -and $i -lt 10) {
                Write-Host -ForegroundColor Yellow "Waiting for the
$ServiceInstanceTypeName service to provision...";
                sleep 100;
                $ServiceInstance = (Get-SPServiceInstance | Where {$_.TypeName -eq
$ServiceInstanceTypeName})

                $i += 1;

                if($i -eq 10) {
                        $continue = Read-Host "Service $ServiceInstanceTypeName has not
yet been provisioned. Would you like to wait? (Y/N)"

                        if($continue -eq "Y") {
                              $i = 0;
                        }
                }
        }
}

Function Configure-SPSearch  {
        PARAM($AppPool, $FarmName, $SearchServiceAccount)

        $searchServiceInstance = Get-SPEnterpriseSearchServiceInstance -local
        Start-SPEnterpriseSearchServiceInstance -Identity $searchServiceInstance

        $dbName = $FarmName + "_SearchServiceApplication"

        $searchApplication = New-SPEnterpriseSearchServiceApplication -Name
"$FarmName Search Service Application" -ApplicationPool $AppPool -DatabaseName
$dbName
        $searchApplicationProxy = New-SPEnterpriseSearchServiceApplicationProxy -name
"$FarmName Search Service
Application Proxy" -SearchApplication $searchApplication

        Set-SPEnterpriseSearchAdministrationComponent -SearchApplication
$searchApplication  -SearchServiceInstance $searchServiceInstance

        $crawlTopology = New-SPEnterpriseSearchCrawlTopology -
```

```
SearchApplication $searchApplication
        $crawlDatabase = Get-SPEnterpriseSearchCrawlDatabase -
SearchApplication $searchApplication

        New-SPEnterpriseSearchCrawlComponent -CrawlTopology $crawlTopology -
CrawlDatabase $crawlDatabase -SearchServiceInstance $searchServiceInstance

        while($crawlTopology.State -ne "Active")
        {
                $crawlTopology | Set-SPEnterpriseSearchCrawlTopology -Active
-ErrorAction SilentlyContinue
                if ($crawlTopology.State -ne "Active")
                {
                        Start-Sleep -Seconds 10
                }
        }

        $queryTopology = New-SPenterpriseSerchQueryTopology -
SearchApplication $searchApplication -partitions 1
        $searchIndexPartition = Get-SPEnterpriseSearchIndexPartition -
QueryTopology $queryTopology
        New-SPEnterpriseSearchQueryComponent -indexpartition
$searchIndexPartition -QueryTopology $queryTopology -SearchServiceInstance
$searchServiceInstance

        $propertyDB = Get-SPEnterpriseSearchPropertyDatabase -
SearchApplication $searchApplication

        Set-SPEnterpriseSearchIndexPartition $searchIndexPartition -
PropertyDatabase $propertyDB

        while ($queryTopology.State -ne "Active")
        {
                $queryTopology | Set-SPEnterpriseSearchQueryTopology -Active
-ErrorAction SilentlyContinue

                if ($queryTopology.State -ne "Active")
                {
                        Start-Sleep -Seconds 10
                }
        }
}

function Start-SPTimer {
        $spTimerService = Get-Service "SPTimerV4"
```

```
        if($spTimerService.Status -ne "Running") {
                Write-Host -ForegroundColor Yellow "SharePoint 2013 Timer Service is
not running. Atempting to start the timer."
                Start-Service "SPTimerV4"
                $spTimerService = Get-Service "SPTimerV4"

                while($spTimerService.Status -ne "Running") {
                        Start-Sleep -Seconds 10
                        Start-Service "SPTimerV4"
                        $spTimerService = Get-Service "SPTimerV4"
                }

                Write-Host -ForegroundColor Green "SharePoint 2013 Timer Service is
running."
        }
        else {
                Write-Host -ForegroundColor Green "SharePoint 2013 Timer Service is
running."
        }
}

Function Get-SPServiceApplicationPoolByName($SPApplicationPoolName, $ManagedAccount)
{

        $appPool = Get-SPServiceApplicationPool | Where {$_.Name -eq
$SPApplicationPoolName}

        if($appPool -eq $null) {
                $appPool = New-SPServiceApplicationPool -Name $SPApplicationPoolName
-Account $ManagedAccount
        }

        Return $appPool
}

Function Get-SPManagedAccountByName($AccountName) {
        $managedAccount = Get-SPManagedAccount | Where {$_.Username -eq
$AccountName}

        if($managedAccount -eq $null) {
                Write-Host "Please enter the credentials for your Managed
Account ($AccountName)";
        $managedAccountCredential = Get-Credential $AccountName -Message
"Please enter the credentials for your Managed Account ($AccountName)";
                $managedAccount = New-SPManagedAccount $managedAccountCredential
        }
```

4

```
        Return $managedAccount
}

Function Get-SPServiceApplicationByType($TypeName) {
        $serviceApplications = Get-SPServiceApplication | Where  {$_.TypeName -eq
$TypeName}

        if($serviceApplications -ne $null) {
                $true;
        }
        else {
                $false;
        }
}

Function New-SPUsageApplicationAndProxy($FarmName) {
        Write-Host -ForegroundColor Yellow "Configuring Usage and Health Data
Collection Service..."

        $dbName = $FarmName + "_UsageandHealthDataCollectionService"
        New-SPUsageApplication "$FarmName Usage and Health Data Collection
Service" -DatabaseName $dbName
        $usageApplicationProxy = Get-SPServiceApplicationProxy |
where{$_.Name -eq "$FarmName Usage and Health Data Collection Service"}

        if($usageApplicationProxy.Status -eq "Disabled") {
                $usageApplicationProxy.Status = "Online";
                $usageApplicationProxy.Update();
        }

        Write-Host -ForegroundColor Green "Installing Usage and Health Data
Collection Service installed."
}

Function New-SPStateServiceApplicationGroup($FarmName){
                $dbName = $FarmName + "_StateService"

                Write-Host -ForegroundColor Yellow "Installing State Service
Application..."

                New-SPStateServiceDatabase $dbName | New-
SPStateServiceApplication -Name "$FarmName State Service Application" | New-
SPStateServiceApplicationProxy -Name "$FarmName State Service Application
Proxy" -DefaultProxyGroup
                sleep 10;
```

```
            Write-Host -ForegroundColor Green "State Service Application
installed..."
}

#arguments from Config-Farm script
$FarmName=$args[0];

# Starting SP Timer Service
Start-SPTimer

if($appPoolName -eq $null -or $appPoolName -eq "") {
       $appPoolName = Get-SettingValue -Xml $settings -XPath
"/settings/Services/ServiceAppPool" -Prompt "Please specify a name for the
ServiceApp Application Pool (eg. ServiceAppPool)"
}

if($managedAccountName -eq $null -or $managedAccountName -eq "") {
       $managedAccountName = Get-SettingValue -Xml $settings -XPath
"/settings/Services/ManagedAccountName" -Prompt "Please enter service
account (eg. CompanyABC\sp_serviceapps)"
}

if($FarmName -eq $null -or $FarmName -eq "") {
       $FarmName =  Get-SettingValue -Xml $settings -XPath "/settings/FarmName"
-Prompt "Please enter your farm name";
}

$managedAccount = Get-SPManagedAccountByName $managedAccountName
$appPool = Get-SPServiceApplicationPoolByName $appPoolName $managedAccount

$decision = Get-SettingValue -Xml $settings -XPath
"/settings/Services/StateServiceApplication" -Prompt "Would you like to
install State Service Application? (Y/N)"
if ($decision -eq "Y") {
       New-SPStateServiceApplicationGroup $FarmName
}

$decision = Get-SettingValue -Xml $settings -XPath
"/settings/Services/Access2010" -Prompt "Would you like to install Access
Services 2010? (Y/N)"
if ($decision -eq "Y") {
       Write-Progress -Activity "Access Service 2010 Service Installation"
-Status "Starting Access Database Service 2010 Service"
       Start-SPService("Access Database Service 2010")

       Write-Progress -Activity "Access Service 2010 Service Installation"
```

4

```
-Status "Creating Access Service 2010 Application"
       New-SPAccessServiceApplication -Name "$FarmName Access Services
2010" -ApplicationPool $appPool -Default

       Write-Progress -Activity "Access Service 2010 Service Installation"
-Status "Completed" -Completed $true
}

$decision = Get-SettingValue -Xml $settings -XPath "/settings/Services/BCS" -Prompt
"Would you like to install Business Data Connectivity Service? (Y/N)"
if ($decision -eq "Y") {
       Write-Progress -Activity "Business Data Connectivity Service Installation"
-Status "Starting Business Data Connectivity Service"
       Start-SPService("Business Data Connectivity Service")

       $dbName = $FarmName + "_BusinessDataConnectivityService"

       Write-Progress -Activity "Business Data Connectivity Service Installation"
-Status "Creating Business Data Connectivity Service Application"
       New-SPBusinessDataCatalogServiceApplication -Name "$FarmName Business Data
Connectivity Service" -ApplicationPool $appPool -databaseName $dbName

       Write-Progress -Activity "Business Data Connectivity Service Installation"
-Status "Completed" -Completed $true
}

$decision = Get-SettingValue -Xml $settings -XPath "/settings/Services/
UsageAndHealth" -Prompt "Would you like to configure Usage and Health Data
Collection Service? (Y/N)"
if ($decision -eq "Y") {
       Write-Progress -Activity "Usage and Health Data Collection Service
Configuration" -Status "Configuring Usage and Health Data Collection Service"
       New-SPUsageApplicationAndProxy $FarmName
       Write-Progress -Activity "Usage and Health Data Collection Service
Configuration" -Status "Completed" -Completed $true
}

$decision = Get-SettingValue -Xml $settings -XPath "/settings/Services/Excel"
-Prompt "Would you like to install Excel Services? (Y/N)"
if ($decision -eq "Y") {
       Write-Progress -Activity "Excel Services Installation" -Status "Starting
Excel Calculation Services"
       Start-SPService("Excel Calculation Services")

       Write-Progress -Activity "Excel Services Installation" -Status "Creating
Excel Service Application"
```

```
        New-SPExcelServiceApplication -Name "$FarmName Excel Services"
-ApplicationPool $appPool -Default
        Write-Host -ForegroundColor Green "Excel Services installed."

        Write-Progress -Activity "Excel Services Installation" -Status "Completed"
-Completed $true
}

$decision = Get-SettingValue -Xml $settings -XPath "/settings/Services/
ManagedMetadata" -Prompt "Would you like to install Managed Metadata Service? (Y/N)"
if ($decision -eq "Y") {
        Write-Progress -Activity "Managed Metadata Service Application
Installation" -Status "Starting Managed Metadata Web Service"
        Start-SPService("Managed Metadata Web Service")

        $dbName = $FarmName + "_ManagedMetadataService"

        Write-Progress -Activity "Managed Metadata Service Application Installation"
-Status "Creating Managed Metadata Service Application"
        $MetaDataServiceApp = New-SPMetadataServiceApplication -Name "$FarmName
Managed Metadata Service" -ApplicationPool $appPool -DatabaseName $dbName
        $MetaDataServiceAppProxy = New-SPMetadataServiceApplicationProxy -Name
"$FarmName Managed Metadata Service Proxy" -ServiceApplication $MetaDataServiceApp
-DefaultProxyGroup

        Write-Progress -Activity "Managed Metadata Service Application
Installation" -Status "Completed" -Completed $true
}

$decision = Get-SettingValue -Xml $settings -XPath
"/settings/Services/SecureStore" -Prompt "Would you like to install Secure
Store Service? (Y/N)"
if ($decision -eq "Y") {
        Write-Progress -Activity "Secure Store Service Application Installation"
-Status "Starting Secure Store Service"
        Start-SPService("Secure Store Service")

        $dbName = $FarmName + "_SecureStore"

        Write-Progress -Activity "Secure Store Service Application
Installation" -Status "Creating Secure Store Service Application"
        $secureStoreServiceApp = New-SPSecureStoreServiceApplication -Name
"$FarmName Secure Store Service Application" -ApplicationPool $appPool
-DatabaseName $dbName -AuditingEnabled:$true
        New-SPSecureStoreServiceApplicationProxy -ServiceApplication
```

```
$secureStoreServiceApp -Name "$FarmName Secure Store Service Application
Proxy" -DefaultProxyGroup

       Write-Progress -Activity "Secure Store Service Application Installation"
-Status "Completed" -Completed $true
}

$decision = Get-SettingValue -Xml $settings -XPath "/settings/Services/Visio"
-Prompt "Would you like to install Visio Graphics Service? (Y/N)"
if ($decision -eq "Y") {
       Write-Progress -Activity "Visio Graphics Service Application Installation"
-Status "Starting Visio Graphics Service"
       Start-SPService("Visio Graphics Service")

       Write-Progress -Activity "Visio Graphics Service Application Installation"
-Status "Creating Visio Graphics Service Application"
       New-SPVisioServiceApplication -Name "$FarmName Visio Graphics Service"
-ApplicationPool $appPool

       Write-Progress -Activity "Visio Graphics Service Application Installation"
-Status "Creating Visio Graphics Service Application Proxy"
       New-SPVisioServiceApplicationProxy -Name "$FarmName Visio Graphics Service
Proxy" -ServiceApplication "$FarmName Visio Graphics Service"

       Write-Progress -Activity "Visio Graphics Service Application Installation"
-Status "Completed" -Completed $true
}

$decision = Get-SettingValue -Xml $settings -XPath
"/settings/Services/Word" -Prompt "Would you like to install Word Automation
Services? (Y/N)"
if ($decision -eq "Y") {
       Write-Progress -Activity "Word Automation Services Application
Installation" -Status "Starting Word Automation Services"
       Start-SPService("Word Automation Services")

       $dbName = $FarmName + "_WordAutomationService"

       Write-Progress -Activity "Word Automation Services Application
Installation" -Status "Creating Word Automation Service Application"
       New-SPWordConversionServiceApplication -Name "$FarmName Word
Automation Service" -ApplicationPool $appPool -DatabaseName $dbName -Default

       Write-Progress -Activity "Word Automation Services Application
Installation" -Status "Completed" -Completed $true
}
```

```
$decision = Get-SettingValue -Xml $settings -XPath
"/settings/Services/MachineTranslation" -Prompt "Would you like to install
Machine Translation Service Application? (Y/N)"
if ($decision -eq "Y") {
       $dbName = $FarmName + "_MachineTranslationService"

       Write-Progress -Activity "Machine Translation Service Application
Installation" -Status "Starting Machine Translation Service"
       Start-SPService("Machine Translation Service")
       Write-Progress -Activity "Machine Translation Service Application
Installation" -Status "Creating Machine Translation Service Application"
       New-SPTranslationServiceApplication -Name "$FarmName Machine Translation
Service" -ApplicationPool $appPool -DatabaseName $dbName
       Write-Progress -Activity "Machine Translation Service Application
Installation" -Status "Completed" -Completed $true
}

$decision = Get-SettingValue -Xml $settings -XPath "/settings/Services/
PerformancePoint" -Prompt "Would you like to install PerformancePoint Service
Application? (Y/N)"
if ($decision -eq "Y") {
       $dbName = $FarmName + "_PerformancePoint"

       Write-Progress -Activity "PerformancePoint Service Application Installation"
-Status "Starting PerformancePoint Service"
       Start-SPService("PerformancePoint Service")
       Write-Progress -Activity "PerformancePoint Service Application Installation"
-Status "Creating PerformancePoint Service Application"
       New-SPPerformancePointServiceApplication -Name "$FarmName PerformancePoint
Service" -ApplicationPool $appPool -DatabaseName $dbName
       Write-Progress -Activity "PerformancePoint Service Application Installation"
-Status "Completed" -Completed $true
}

$decision = Get-SettingValue -Xml $settings -XPath "/settings/Services/Search"
-Prompt "Would you like to install Search Service? (Y/N)"
if ($decision -eq "Y") {
       Write-Progress -Activity "Search Service Application Installation" -Status
"Starting Search Service Application"

       $hostname = (Get-ChildItem env:computername).Value
       Start-SPEnterpriseSearchServiceInstance $hostname
       Start-SPEnterpriseSearchQueryAndSiteSettingsServiceInstance $hostname

       $dbName = $FarmName + "_SearchService"
```

4

```
    Write-Progress -Activity "Search Service Application Installation" -Status
"Creating Search Service Application"
    $SearchServiceApp = New-SPEnterpriseSearchServiceApplication -Name "$FarmName
Search Service Application" -ApplicationPool $appPool -DatabaseName $dbName
    $SearchServiceAppProxy = New-SPEnterpriseSearchServiceApplicationProxy
-Name "$FarmName Search Service Proxy" -ServiceApplication $SearchServiceApp
-DefaultProxyGroup

    Write-Progress -Activity "Search Service Application Installation" -Status
"Configuring Topology"
    $clone = $searchServiceApp.ActiveTopology.Clone()
    $searchServiceInstance = Get-SPEnterpriseSearchServiceInstance
    New-SPEnterpriseSearchAdminComponent -SearchTopology $clone
-SearchServiceInstance $searchServiceInstance
    New-SPEnterpriseSearchContentProcessingComponent -SearchTopology $clone
-SearchServiceInstance $searchServiceInstance
    New-SPEnterpriseSearchAnalyticsProcessingComponent -SearchTopology $clone
-SearchServiceInstance $searchServiceInstance
    New-SPEnterpriseSearchCrawlComponent -SearchTopology $clone
-SearchServiceInstance $searchServiceInstance
    New-SPEnterpriseSearchIndexComponent -SearchTopology $clone
-SearchServiceInstance $searchServiceInstance
    New-SPEnterpriseSearchQueryProcessingComponent -SearchTopology $clone
-SearchServiceInstance $searchServiceInstance
    $clone.Activate()

    Write-Progress -Activity "Search Service Application Installation" -Status
"Completed" -Completed $true
}

$decision = Get-SettingValue -Xml $settings -XPath "/settings/Services/
WorkManagement" -Prompt "Would you like to install Work Management Service
Application? (Y/N)"
if ($decision -eq "Y") {
    $dbName = $FarmName + "_WorkManagement"

    Write-Progress -Activity "Work Management Service Application Installation"
-Status "Starting Work Management Service"
    Start-SPService("Work Management Service")
    Write-Progress -Activity "Work Management Service Application Installation"
-Status "Creating Work Management Service Application"
    New-SPWorkManagementServiceApplication -Name "$FarmName Work Management
Service" -ApplicationPool $appPool
    Write-Progress -Activity "Work Management Service Application Installation"
-Status "Completed" -Completed $true
}
```

```
$decision = Get-SettingValue -Xml $settings -XPath "/settings/Services/UPA"
-Prompt "Would you like to install User Profile Service Application? (Y/N)"
if ($decision -eq "Y") {
       Write-Host -ForegroundColor Yellow "WARNING: This part of the script
needs to run under Farm account with elevated privileges. Farm admin must be
local admin while UPA is provisioning."
       $decision = Read-Host "Please confirm: SharePoint Farm admin account
is local admin and I want to proceed with UPA provisioning (Y/N)?"
       if ($decision -eq "Y") {

              Restart-Service SPTimerV4

              Write-Progress -Activity "User Profile Service Application
Installation" -Status "Starting User Profile Service"
              Start-SPService "User Profile Service"

              $username = ((Get-SPFarm).DefaultServiceAccount).Name;
              $farmAccount = Get-Credential $username;

              Start-Process $PSHOME\powershell.exe -Credential $farmAccount
-ArgumentList "-Command Start-Process $PSHOME\powershell.exe -ArgumentList
'$path\Provision-UPA.ps1',$farmName,$appPoolName -Verb Runas" -Wait

              $upa = Get-SPServiceApplication | Where TypeName -eq "User Profile
Service Application"
              $ups = Get-SPServiceInstance | Where TypeName -eq "User Profile
Synchronization Service"
              $hostname = (Get-ChildItem env:computername).Value
              $upa.SetSynchronizationMachine($hostname, $ups.ID, $username,
$farmAccount.GetNetworkCredential().password)

              Write-Progress -Activity "User Profile Service Application
Installation" -Status "Starting User Profile Synchronization Service"
              Start-SPService "User Profile Synchronization Service"

              Write-Host "Please remove your farm account from local admins."
       }
}

iisreset

Write-Host -ForegroundColor Green "Installation completed."
---------------------------------------
```

Scripts such as these can be modified by administrators and customized as needed. The power of PowerShell is in this flexibility, because custom scripts can be used by administrators to build entire farms from scratch or simply perform everyday tasks.

For more information on using PowerShell with SharePoint 2013, see Chapter 7, "Leveraging PowerShell for Command-Line SharePoint Administration and Automation."

Understanding Scalability for SharePoint

The first step in scaling a SharePoint environment is to understand the level of usage it will receive, both presently and in the future. After the level of usage is determined, understanding which specific components can be extended is vital to structuring the system to match the desired user load. The key is to match SharePoint functionality to the specific identified need.

Mapping SharePoint Functionality to Business Needs

When deploying SharePoint, the primary concern for scalability is how many users will use the system. For departmental collaboration, the numbers may be small. For large, publicly accessible portals, however, the numbers could scale up quickly. Scaling a SharePoint implementation based on the number of users is simple, but can be used as a starting point. In addition to total number of users, the following factors should be identified to more fully understand the load placed on a SharePoint server:

- Number of users
- Pages per user per work day
- Length of work day (hours)
- Type of work performed and level of office integration
- Size of document repositories

Collecting this information and understanding who will be accessing a SharePoint environment is the first step toward properly scaling the environment.

Gauging Content Growth

In addition to the amount of data that initially is loaded into SharePoint, an understanding of how fast that content will grow is critical toward properly scaling an environment. Running out of storage space a year into a SharePoint deployment is not an ideal situation. You need to understand how quickly content can grow and how to control this inevitable growth.

Proper use of site quotas in SharePoint is an effective way to maintain control over the size that a SharePoint database can grow to. Implementing site quotas as they are created is a recommended best-practice approach and should be considered in most situations. It is easy to bloat SharePoint with unnecessary data, and site quotas help local site administrators make judicious use of their available space.

SharePoint's SQL database can grow in size dramatically, depending on how heavily it is used and what type of content is included in it. Use of the Remote Binary Large OBject (BLOB) Storage application programming interface (API), covered extensively in Chapter 9, can help to keep the size of content databases under control by taking documents out of the database and storing them in other file formats.

Scaling Logical SharePoint Components

The key to SharePoint's success is its capability to intelligently present information needed for each individual user, giving them quick and easy access to that information. SharePoint accomplishes this through various logical mechanisms that exist to help organize this content, structuring it in a way that pulls unstructured data together and presents it to the user. For example, a file server simply holds together a jumbling of documents in a simple file structure. Multiple versions of those documents further confuse the issue. SharePoint contains mechanisms to organize those documents into logical document libraries, categorized by metadata, which can be searched for and presented by the latest version.

In addition to the most obvious logical components, SharePoint enables sets of data to be scaled out to support groups of users. For example, by using different site collections with their own unique sets of permissions, you can configure SharePoint to host different groups of users on the same set of machines, increasing flexibility.

Scaling Out with Site Collections

Building on the success of previous versions of SharePoint, SharePoint sites in SharePoint Foundation enable various teams or groups of users to have access to particular information relevant to them. For example, sites can be set up for each department of a company to enable them to have access to information pertinent to their groups.

Sites can be scaled out to support various site collections for each group of users. This enables the data to be distributed across a SharePoint environment logically, allowing a much larger population of users to be distributed across a SharePoint server environment. Each site collection can be administered by a unique owner designated within the site structure, similar to the one shown in Figure 4.1. This allows for security to be scaled out across a SharePoint site.

Scaling Out with Web Applications

SharePoint stores its data in SQL content databases but serves up access to that data via HTML and web services. The access to this data is served up to the user via the Windows Server Internet Information Services (IIS) service. IIS is composed of various logical structures known as *websites*, which are entry points to web content. Each website can be configured to point to various sets of information located on the web server or extended via SharePoint to be unique SharePoint web applications.

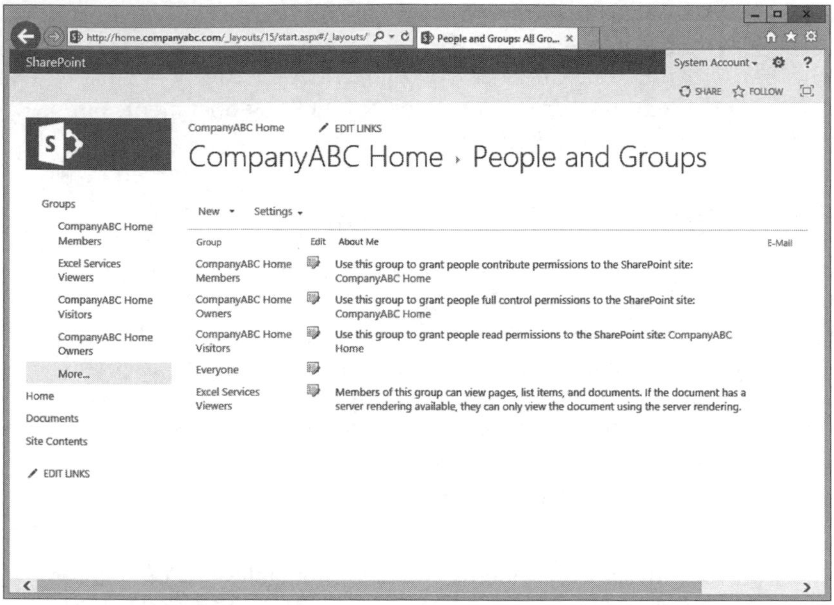

FIGURE 4.1 Examining the security options of a SharePoint site.

Utilizing unique web applications with SharePoint can help to further scale the functionality of an environment, allowing the flexibility to grant access to SharePoint using SSL encryption, or across different ports. In addition, deploying multiple virtual servers enables the use of multiple host headers for a SharePoint organization, such as sharepoint.companyabc.com, docs.companyabc.com, info.companyabc.com, sp.organizationa.com, and so on.

Summary

Although SharePoint 2013 is deceptively easy to install, it is also a sophisticated product that can be complex to install and configure. Using techniques such as scripted installations using PowerShell, installation checklists, and scalability options can help to ensure the longevity of SharePoint architecture and can make it easier to grow a SharePoint 2013 environment.

Best Practices

The following are best practices from this chapter:

- ▶ Create installation checklists to manage the installation process for a complex SharePoint 2013 environment.
- ▶ Use best practices for web applications, including configuring web applications for Kerberos security, SSL encryption, and load balancing using Windows Network Load Balancing (NLB) or hardware-based load balancers.

- Manage content growth through site quotas and monitoring solutions, such as System Center or third-party products.
- Use site collections to scale SharePoint to varying groups with different security needs.
- Use IIS websites mapped to SharePoint web applications to manage varying types of web-based access to SharePoint sites, such as SSL-encryption or different host headers.
- Use a different SharePoint farm for the ultimate layer of security for a SharePoint environment, beyond what is provided by different site collections or web applications.
- Map SharePoint's functionality with the specific user needs of the organization.

CHAPTER 5

Migrating from SharePoint 2010 to SharePoint 2013

IN THIS CHAPTER

- Understanding Key Differences in the SharePoint 2013 Upgrade Process
- Content Considerations
- Planning for an Upgrade to SharePoint 2013
- Performing a Database-Attach Upgrade
- Performing a Site Collection Upgrade
- Performing a Service Application Upgrade
- SharePoint 2010 (14) Mode and SharePoint 2013 (15) Mode

Organizations that have invested in SharePoint technologies over the years and are looking to take advantage of some of the new capabilities of SharePoint 2010 will eventually find themselves considering an upgrade of their content and their services over to the new SharePoint 2013 platform.

Fortunately, the story for upgrading content databases in SharePoint 2013 hasn't changed much from its 2010 predecessor. That said, planning for upgrade to SharePoint 2013, particularly at the service application level, can be complex, with new PowerShell switches, service application databases, and deprecated options.

This chapter covers upgrade from SharePoint 2010 to SharePoint 2013, discussing content database upgrades and procedures for upgrading service applications as well. Upgrades from earlier versions of SharePoint to SharePoint 2013 are not natively supported, and organizations must first upgrade to SharePoint 2010 before beginning on the 2010 to 2013 upgrade path.

Understanding Key Differences in the SharePoint 2013 Upgrade Process

The migration paths to SharePoint 2013 have become much more streamlined than in earlier versions. In SharePoint 2010, three options for upgrade were available: in place, database-attach and hybrid. In SharePoint 2013, we still have database attach for normal and large-scale deployments, but we have lost the ability to do in-place upgrades, as most have found that most organizations were performing the database-attach upgrade and determined that it was a safer approach as well.

With the introduction of SharePoint 2010 and the service application model, SharePoint 2013 enables you to upgrade these features sets, which can complicate a migration process, so you want to closely examine whether service application functionality is required for migration. In other words, if you don't have any customizations that you need to keep in SharePoint 2010 service applications, you should instead simply focus on migrating content, because service application migration is the most complex part of the upgrade process.

NOTE

There is no direct supported upgrade path to SharePoint 2013 from the 1.0, 2.0, or 3.0 versions of SharePoint technologies. The only way to upgrade these environments to 2013 using Microsoft techniques is to first upgrade the servers and sites to SharePoint 2010 and then follow the upgrade path demonstrated in this chapter.

Microsoft has deprecated NT LAN Manager (NTLM) authentication for use in content web applications for SharePoint 2013. This means that all web application authentication models must be made claims aware in order to take advantage of all the features in SharePoint 2013. This is an extra step of preparation for many organizations that are planning their upgrade and extra effort needed on the source SharePoint farm. There is also full support available for converting web applications in SharePoint 2010 to claims.

It is best practice to create a new web application using windows classic mode in the new SharePoint 2013 environment. After this is done it is possible to attach a windows classic mode content database directly to SharePoint 2013. It is also possible to carry on using this authentication model; however, sites in this content database will not be able to take full advantage of all features in SharePoint 2013, most notably the App Management Service (APPS). When this content database is mounted and tested, it is then possible to go through the steps of converting the content database base to claims-based.

NOTE

Microsoft has provided full documentation on how to migrate from classic mode to claims-based authentication at http://technet.microsoft.com/en-us/library/gg251985.aspx.

Visual Upgrade in SharePoint 2010 allowed organizations to keep the SharePoint 2007 look and feel during a migration. This model had a few drawbacks, however, as it only simulated a 2007 environment and many branding, features, and solutions that were deployed in SharePoint 2007 would not be compatible in the Visual Upgrade view. With SharePoint 2013, we have SharePoint 2010 mode (14 mode) in addition to the new SharePoint 2013 mode (15 mode). The SharePoint 2010 mode keeps many of the core

SharePoint 2010 source files in the environment. As a result, many of the branding and feature solutions that were built for a SharePoint 2010 environment work in SharePoint 2010 mode for SharePoint 2013.

Examining the Database-Attach Scenario

The database-attach scenario is a supported upgrade scenario that involves a new SharePoint 2013 farm being built, followed by a restore of the SharePoint 2010 content databases directly attached to this farm and upgraded in place. The biggest drawback to using this method is that all configurations that need to match the source environment must be reconfigured in the destination environment because upgrade of the configuration database is not supported.

The types of settings that you must configure in advance of a database-attach scenario include the following:

- Internet Information Services (IIS) and domain name server (DNS) settings
- Host headers
- Alternate access mappings
- Managed Paths

The benefit of using the database-attach method is the ability to strictly control the content that gets populated into the destination environment. In addition, it gives the enterprise the flexibility to systematically "roll in" content databases and their site collections as needed.

The story as it pertains to content database upgrade has not changed at all in 2013 except in the case of scheduling individual site upgrades via PowerShell, as discussed later in this chapter.

Examining Alternative Approaches and Third-Party Migrations

Although the database-attach upgrade approach is the only Microsoft-supported migration scenario, you can use various other approaches, including the following:

- **Third-party migration tools:** These tools usually do not have limitations as to what versions can be migrated from and also allow for splicing and splitting of site collections and content databases, something not supported in the Microsoft approaches. They also usually handle exceptions better.
- **STSADM/PowerShell exports or backups/restores:** Although STSADM, the command-line tool, can only export or backup/restore to the same version, you can use it to export SharePoint content to a farm of the same version level and then run the upgrade process on that farm. You can use this same concept with database restores as well. Keep in mind that STSADM has been deprecated, but PowerShell commandlets (cmdlets) that allow for backups/restores and exports are also available.

- **Manual content move:** Some organizations simply prefer to build a new SharePoint 2013 environment and then show their users how to move content from the old farm to the new farm. This proves particularly useful if there is a great deal of abandoned or useless data in the older farms.

Determining which approach to use is critical during the planning phase of an upgrade or migration project.

Content Considerations

Prior to upgrade and as part of the planning process, it is wise to undergo an extensive view of the content in the environment that will be upgraded to SharePoint 2013. Many organizations choose to give power to site owners to archive, delete, or mark for upgrade the site content to the new environment. There are many ways to do this, and many administrators decide to enact a series of categorization either using content types deployed to all items or some other method of manually marking content.

Ultimately, regardless of the method, it is important to upgrade only the content that is actually needed in the new environment. The process of simply removing unnecessary versions of documents could potentially save hours in the upgrade process. Taking the time upfront to determine actual valuable content can save hours of upgrade time as well as resource costs and so on.

Creating a Prototype Test Environment

When installing and configuring a SharePoint 2013 test environment, it is important to replicate what the production environment was in SharePoint 2010 (to a degree) and what the end result in production will be.

The hardware requirements in SharePoint 2013 for standalone servers have increased and, as a result, administrators must take into account greater demand on physical and virtual resources. Creating an environment to test your final production upgrade is critical for many reasons. The most important reason is timing out the duration of your overall upgrade process.

No two content databases are created equally, a concept that comes into play with upgrades. For example, a content database that is exactly 50GB, has 20 site collections with 50 subsites each, and has a document library for each subsite with 100 items in each one takes exponentially longer to upgrade than a content database that is 50GB, has 1 site collection and 1 document library, and only a handful of items in that library.

The SharePoint upgrade process must iterate through all these sublevels of the content database and process each item for upgrade. As a result, there is no set way to determine the length of time an upgrade of a content database will take.

This also comes into play when the environment's available resources differ from one environment to another. If during the upgrade testing process the environment used has less computing power or less RAM available, the time to upgrade a given database is affected. Therefore, when it becomes crucial to know exactly how long a given content database will take to upgrade (for example, a large database must be upgraded and traffic pointing to it before the 8 a.m. workday starts), it is imperative to test on hardware/resources as close as possible to final production.

NOTE

Many administrators work from a single set of hardware (virtual host) that has multiple servers provisioned virtually on that hardware. As servers are provisioned, snapshots of each major milestone are taken of the environment. All considerations are taken into account, and the upgrade process is tested and vetted out. When it is time to provision a new production SharePoint 2013 environment, you can use those snapshots to roll back the environment so that the same resources are consumed and timing can be estimated very closely.

SQL Server Upgrade Considerations

With the introduction of more features and more caching in SharePoint 2013, the demand on physical resources in the SharePoint 2013 server farm has increased as well. SQL servers now demand 8GB for small farms and 16GB for larger farms. They also require four cores and eight cores, respectively, for each type of farm. Administrators should keep in mind that this is for each node of a cluster if redundancy is built in to a given SharePoint 2013 environment.

The major software requirements are SQL Server 2012 x64 or SQL Server 2008 R2 x64 with Service Pack 1. Although some organizations might stay with SQL 2008 R2 SP1, the introduction of Microsoft SQL Server 2012 has many enterprises weighing the option of upgrading to this latest version because it provides some significant high-availability (HA) improvements, outlined in Chapter 9, "Managing and Maintaining SQL Server in a SharePoint Environment."

Installing SharePoint 2013 Prerequisites

As in earlier versions of SharePoint, the prerequisites install portion of the install process can be handled through the PrerequisiteInstaller.exe before you install SharePoint. Alternatively, administrators may script out the download and install of the prerequisites. In addition, you can download all the prerequisites and store them on network or local storage for the prerequisite installer to execute these files with no Internet connectivity. This comes in handy when environments are in secure setups and are not permitted to access external networks.

If you need to manually install prerequisites, such as when there is no Internet access to the system, or you choose to install via a PowerShell script, the following roles and tools are required:

- Application server role
- Web server (IIS) role

- Microsoft .NET Framework version 4.5 Release Candidate (RC)
- SQL Server 2008 R2 SP1 Native Client
- Microsoft WCF Data Services 5.0
- Microsoft Information Protection and Control Client (MSIPC)
- Microsoft Sync Framework Runtime v1.0 SP1 (x64)
- Windows Management Framework 3.0 RC, which includes Windows PowerShell 3.0
- Windows Identity Foundation (WIF) 1.0 and Microsoft Identity Extensions
- Windows Server AppFabric
- Cumulative Update Package 1 for Microsoft AppFabric 1.1 for Windows Server (KB 2671763)

NOTE

By altering the PrerequisiteInstaller.Arguments.txt file, administrators can "tell" SharePoint's prerequisite installer to look for files located on a network or local drive location instead of going out to the Internet for the file downloads.

Planning for an Upgrade to SharePoint 2013

In Service Pack 2 for SharePoint 2007, Microsoft added a new Pre Upgrade Checker command-line tool. This tool enables the examination of a SharePoint 2007 environment and reports back on possible issues that would either limit or altogether block an upgrade to SharePoint 2010.

In SharePoint 2010, the Pre Upgrade Checker tool was deprecated and administrators were left with relying on the tools in PowerShell 2.0. Using PowerShell is the best way to shed light on possible issues that may arise in an upgrade from SharePoint 2010 to SharePoint 2013. If you use the `Test-SPContentDatabase` cmdlet, PowerShell simulates the result of actually mounting the database to a given web application and reports back any issues that would limit or block an upgrade, as shown in Figure 5.1.

After opening up SharePoint Management Shell (PowerShell for SharePoint) as Administrator, run `Test-SPContentDatabase -Name` *`DBNAME`* `-WebApplication` *`http://domain`*. In this example, *`DBName`* is the name of the database you want to test and is currently in SQL, and *`http://domain`* is the web application that currently exists in SharePoint.

Planning an upgrade requires the most upfront work in the overall upgrade process. Running through various test mounts, clearing issues in the source database, and running more test database mounts will result in an overall smooth upgrade when it comes time to actually perform the upgrade in production. Note that ignoring errors during the test mount of a database results in greater work after the mount is actually performed. After a database has been populated with references to site definitions that do not exist or solution packages that are not deployed to the new environment, cleaning these references while the site is live carries many risks as well as time restrictions.

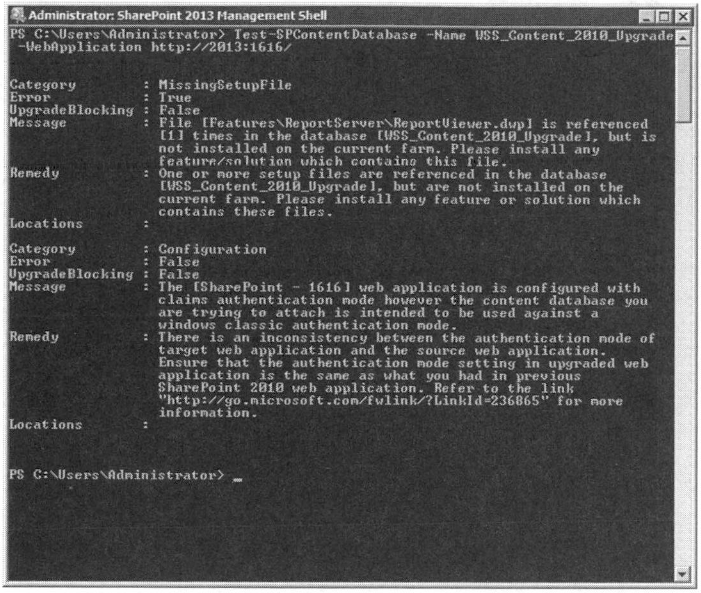

FIGURE 5.1 Using the `Test-SPContentDatabase` cmdlet to view any pre-upgrade issues. As shown, a web application hasn't been converted to claims, and there are some other artifacts.

One of the most common issues that administrators face when attempting to upgrade their content databases to SharePoint 2013 is the lack of claims-enabled databases in existence, because many organizations have opted instead to deploy SharePoint 2010 using the default, which is non-claims based. Microsoft has subsequently provided guidance on how to convert SharePoint 2010 web applications to claims.

Which method you use to "clean up" the database before the upgrade depends significantly on the issue that is showing in the `Test-SPContentDatabase` report. How to physically clean these issues out of a content database is entirely specific to each issue that the report identifies. Currently, you cannot successfully clean all potential issues in a few simple quick steps.

Performing the mount is as simple as replacing `Test` with `Mount` in the `SPContentDatabase` cmdlet. Doing so tells SharePoint to start the mount and upgrade process of the database specified. During the mount, SharePoint 2013 provides a percentage complete status indicator. After a successful or unsuccessful database mount, the final output is shown after the process has failed or succeeded, as shown in Figure 5.2.

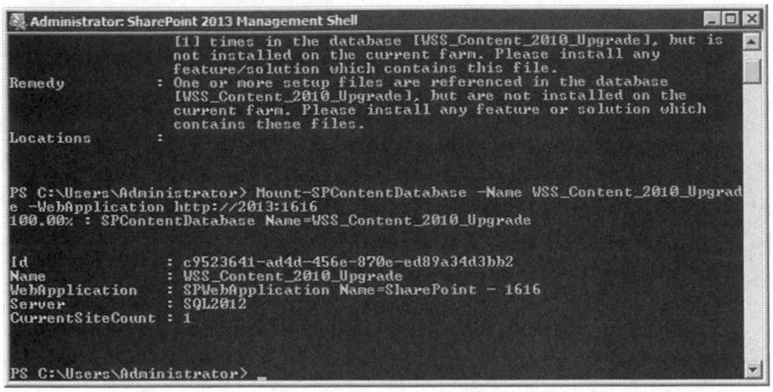

FIGURE 5.2 Running a `Mount-SPContentDatabase` cmdlet.

NOTE

Missing web parts, solutions, features, site definitions, and the like are what are to be expected in artifacts displaced in the new SharePoint 2013 environment. Focus on one reported issue at a time and the process to scrub the database of that issue.

Performing a Database-Attach Upgrade

The database-attach process is a much more risk-averse upgrade process and is subsequently more likely to be used for most environments. It has the significant advantage of enabling SharePoint administrators to create new best-practice SharePoint 2010 environments and simply move the databases to a new farm and upgrade them there.

In SharePoint 2013, site collections are not upgraded when a content database is upgraded. This process is sectioned into two parts to allow site owners to decide whether and when to upgrade their site collections, as covered later in this chapter.

Content Database-Attach Upgrade Guide

The high-level steps involved with a database-attach upgrade are as follows:

1. Create a new destination SharePoint 2013 farm complete with all configurations made before attaching any databases. Remember that you need to configure any operational settings such as URLs or host headers as well.

2. Create a web application where the newly upgraded database will reside.

3. Perform an SQL backup of the content database you want to upgrade by going into the SQL instance that supports the 2010 environment, highlighting the database, and right-clicking and selecting Tasks > Backup.

4. When ready to do the actual upgrade, set the database in question to Read-Only in SQL. This allows for the SharePoint 2010 sites that are in that content database to be accessed but not written to or changed in any way.

5. Within SQL, restore the content database you backed up to the SQL instance.
6. Assuming that adequate test mounts have been done to clear any issues that would block a successful and clean upgrade, run the following PowerShell command `Mount-SPContentDatabase -Name` *`UnleashedDB`* `-WebApplication` *`http://SharePointUnleashed`*, where *`UnleashedDB`* is the backed-up content database and *`http://SharePointUnleased`* is the fully qualified domain name (FQDN) of the web application created in step 2.

NOTE

When creating a new web application, administrators must create a content database that under normal operation contains the site collections. However, when creating a web application for an upgraded content database, there is no need for this extra database, and it is later discarded. Be sure to name the database something relevant that ensures easy identification for later deletion.

In addition, you can append many parameters to `Mount-SPContentDatabase`.

5

Performing a Site Collection Upgrade

In SharePoint 2013, site collection owners now have the option of when to upgrade their sites from the SharePoint 2010 "mode" to the SharePoint 2013 "mode"; more on modes later in this chapter. The database upgrade process actually handles the upgrade in two components, database schema and site collections, and they are not mutually exclusive as they were in SharePoint 2010.

Site owners can use the preview mode and view how the SharePoint 2013 mode looks and, more important, how it functions with their site collection. Farm administrators can set the time limit and exceptions on matters that relate to when and by whom the site collection must be upgraded. These parameters include whether the site collection is allowed to be upgraded (if this is disabled, the farm administrator must perform the upgrade) and when reminders and notifications are sent to site owners.

Farm administrators may also choose to perform site collection upgrades immediately after schema upgrade, but a certain amount of risk that is associated with this must be taken into account, such as incompatible features, resource-intensive draw on servers, and so on.

Farm administrators may also control how frequently requested site collections can be upgraded. This is a valuable asset when resources are limited and during peak operation hours.

Here are a few script examples for site collection upgrade.

To upgrade an entire content database and all its site collections, use the following syntax, as shown in Figure 5.3:

```
Get-SPSite -ContentDatabase DBNAMEHERE -Limit All | Upgrade-SPSite -VersionUpgrade
```

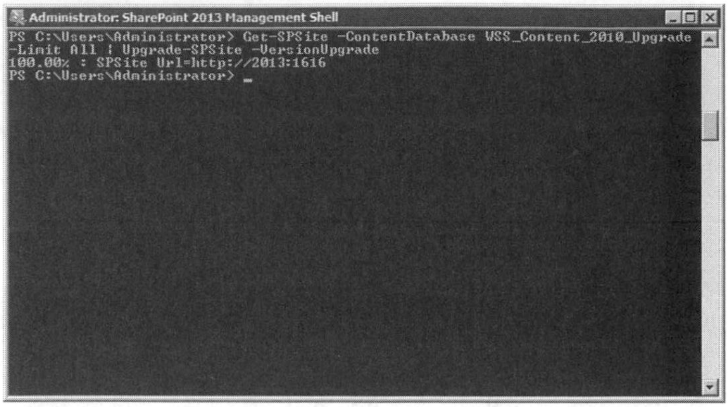

FIGURE 5.3 PowerShell command to upgrade the site collection.

To view upgrades that have completed, use the following syntax, as shown in Figure 5.4:

```
Get-SPSiteUpgradeSessionInfo -ContentDatabase -DBNAMEHERE -ShowInProgress
-ShowCompleted -ShowFailed
```

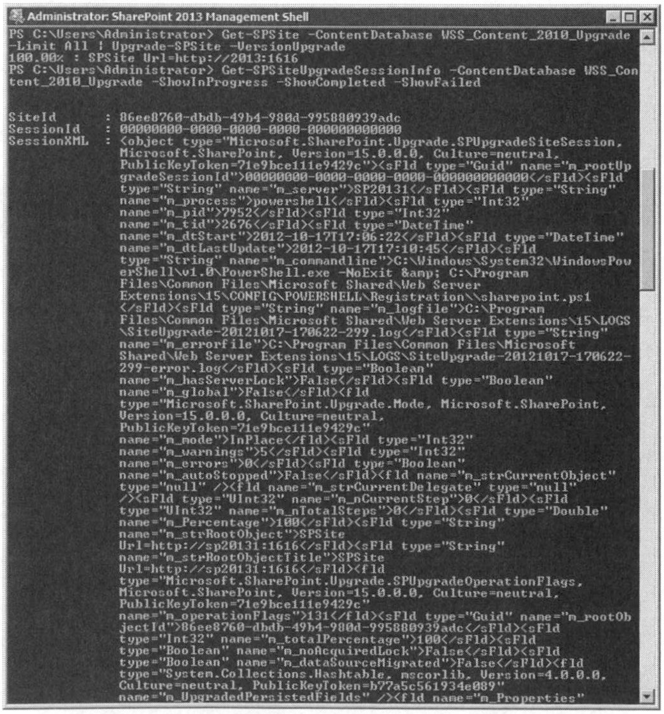

FIGURE 5.4 PowerShell command to get sites previously upgraded.

To add a site collection to the upgrade queue, use the following syntax:

```
Upgrade-SPSite http://URLHere -VersionUpgrade -QueueOnly
```

Performing a Service Application Upgrade

In SharePoint 2013, administrators now need to also be concerned about data stores in the service application databases. As a result of this added model in SharePoint 2010, a path for upgrading many service application databases has been made available in SharePoint 2013.

The following databases are supported for upgrade:

- Content databases
- Sync database
- Social database
- User profile database
- Project databases (All four databases get merged into one in SharePoint 2013.)
- Secure store database
- Social database
- Search admin database
- Managed metadata database

Each service application differs slightly depending on which dependencies they have, in addition to their database and their proxy. For most of the service applications, however, the upgrade process is as follows:

1. Create an application pool or declare an existing application pool for the service application.
2. Restore the service application database.
3. Create the service application proxy.

NOTE

If upgrading the My Site host, you must upgrade the User Profile Service (UPS) and the Managed Metadata Service (MMS) first.

Managed Metadata Upgrade

Upgrade of the MMS involves multiple steps. For the MMS application, you must complete the additional steps of reconfiguring the content type hub and starting the MMS, as shown in the following screenshots. The content type hub should be changed because the old hub URL is still present in the content database. Changing the content type hub causes all the content types to be redistributed to the new 2013 farm.

The first step in creating/associating the Managed Metadata application pool consists of running the `New-SPServiceApplication Pool` cmdlet, as shown in Figure 5.5. This creates a new application pool in your SharePoint 2013 environment.

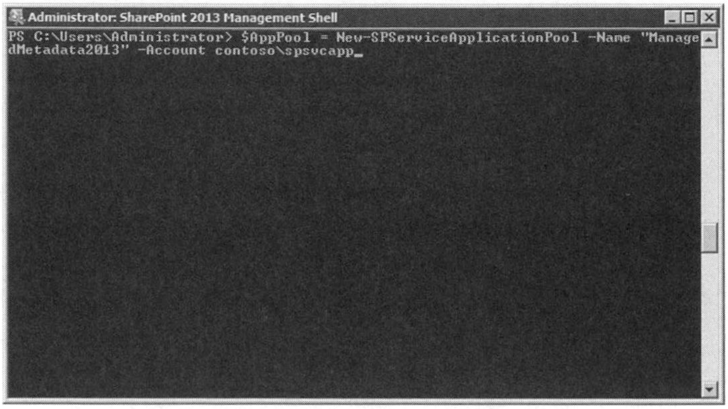

FIGURE 5.5 Creating a new application pool for the upgraded MMS application.

If you choose to use an application pool currently in use, utilize the following PowerShell script:

```
"$AppPool = Get-SPServiceApplicationPool -Identity "Application Pool Name"
```

The next step, illustrated in Figure 5.6, is to create the MMS application and restore the managed metadata database (from SharePoint 2010) to the new application pool. Note that if you reference the restored (to SQL) database within the `New-SPMetadataServiceApplication` cmdlet, the cmdlet automatically uses the 2010 database to build the new service application and upgrade it in the process.

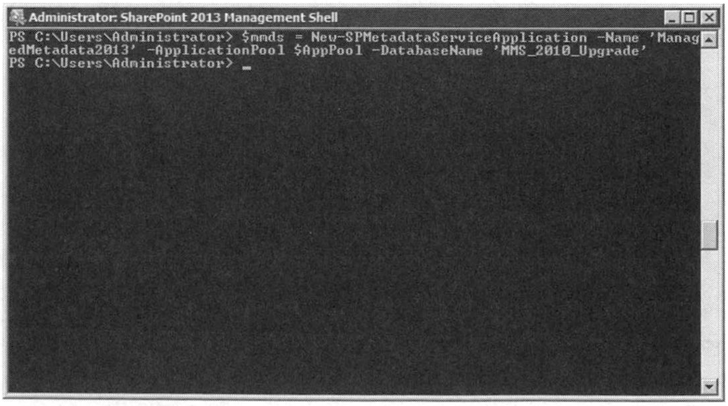

FIGURE 5.6 Referencing the old 2010 managed metadata database.

At this point, the newly created MMS application can be seen in Central Administration. We now have to create the proxy for our newly created service application.

Creating the Managed Metadata application proxy is as simple as running the `New-SPMetadataServiceApplicationProxy` cmdlet. This cmdlet name speaks for itself and does exactly that: creates the MMS proxy. By entering a few required parameters, such as name and service application, you can bind it to the proxy, as shown in Figure 5.7.

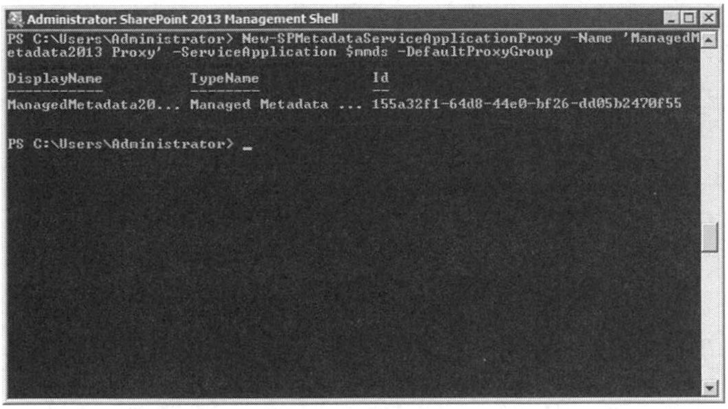

FIGURE 5.7 Creating the Managed Metadata application proxy.

After the proxy creation has been completed, navigating through Central Administration displays the newly created MMS application proxy, as shown in Figure 5.8.

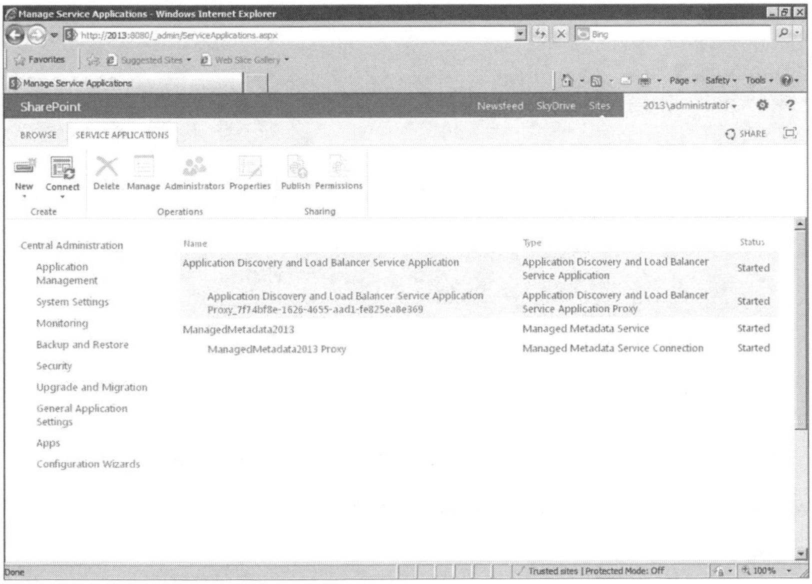

FIGURE 5.8 Viewing the new service application and service application proxy in Central Administration.

In addition, after the service application has been created, the administrator should then be able to navigate the MMS, as shown in Figure 5.9. Upon a successful upgrade, all the content from the previous SharePoint 2010 environment should be available in this structure.

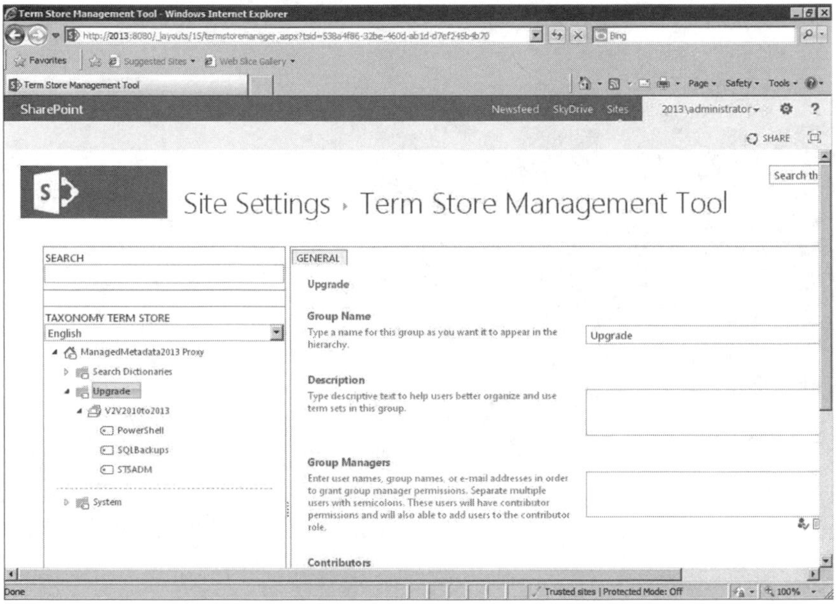

FIGURE 5.9 Navigating the upgraded Managed Metadata Store.

NOTE

If a red error alert states that the MMS is unavailable, ensure that the service is started in Services on Server in Central Administration.

The final step in the process is to change the content type hub URL using the cmdlet shown in Figure 5.10. Note that the cmdlet is showing uri rather than what might seem logical (url).

User Profile Service Upgrade

You can upgrade the UPS application if you want, but you must give careful attention to the process. The high-level steps for upgrading the UPS application are as follows:

1. Export the Microsoft Identity Integration Services (MIIS) encryption key (optional).
2. Create the web application for the UPS.
3. Create the UPS.

4. Restore user profile databases to the new SharePoint 2013 farm (sync optional).
5. Import the MIIS encryption key (optional).

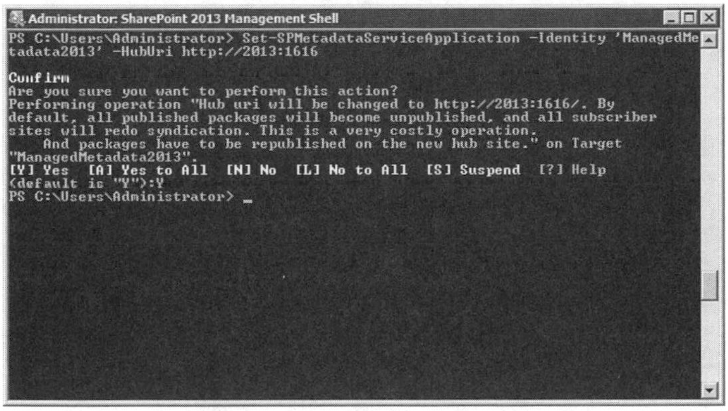

FIGURE 5.10 Changing the content type hub URL.

Exporting the MIIS Encryption Key

The UPS application depends on the MIIS key to authenticate its processes against Active Directory. To upgrade the user profile sync database, this key must be exported from its location at 14\Synchronization Service\Bin and imported into the new SharePoint 2013 environment. The sync database stores configuration and staging data for use when profile data is being synchronized with directory services such as Active Directory.

It is possible to upgrade the UPS without exporting/importing the encryption key, but the administrator must re-create the sync database manually. This method is much easier and cleaner overall. However, if you choose to use the existing sync database and the resulting encrypting key, you need to complete some preliminary steps to extract this key:

1. To export the existing encryption key, navigate to <root directory drive>\Program Files\Microsoft Office Servers\14.0\Synchronization Service\Bin on the SharePoint 2010 Server that hosts the Synchronization Service and locate the miiskmu.exe application. Run the miiskmu.exe application and choose the option to export the key set by filling out the credentials that are used to currently run the Synchronization Service and the desired location to save the key to. After doing this, review the summary and finalize the export with the Close button.
2. Navigate to <root directory drive>\Program Files\Microsoft Office Servers\14\Synchronization Service\Bin and execute miiskmu.exe, as shown in Figure 5.11.
3. Select Export Key Set, as shown in Figure 5.12. This process exports the encryption key currently being used for synchronization.

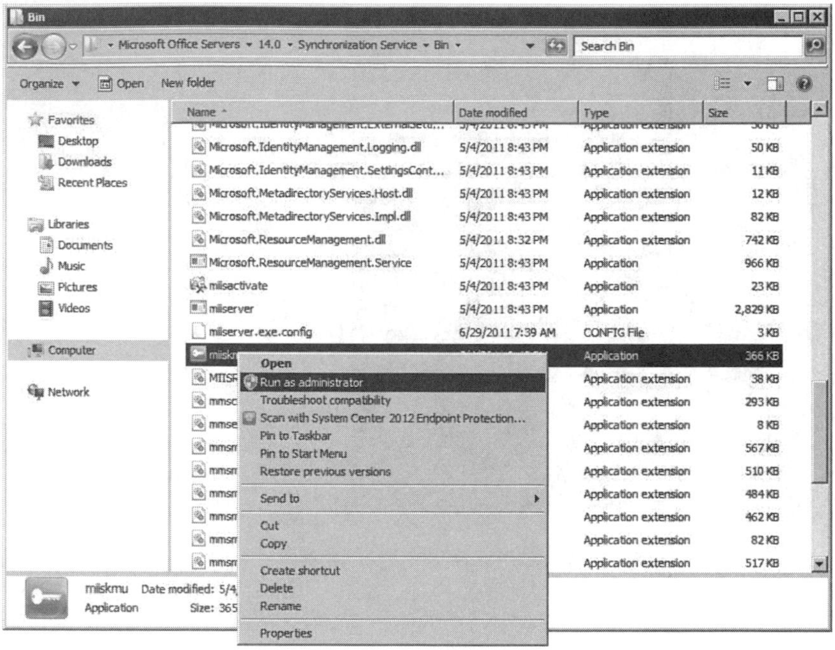

FIGURE 5.11 Executing the MIISKMU utility to export the UPS application key.

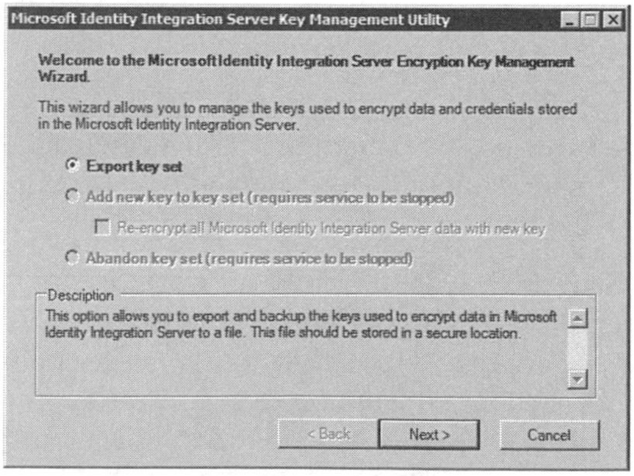

FIGURE 5.12 Exporting the UPA key using the MIISKMU utility.

4. Enter the credentials that run the current 2010 UPS when prompted, as shown in Figure 5.13. This is usually the farm account that was originally used to start the User Profile Synchronization Service.

5. Choose the path to save the file, click Next, and then click Close when the operation completes successfully. The file exports as a .bin file, and it makes no difference where the file is exported to. However, it saves you work later if the file is exported

to the new SharePoint 2013 server that runs the UPS and places the file at <Root>\Program Files\Microsoft Office Servers\15.0\Synchronization Service\Bin.

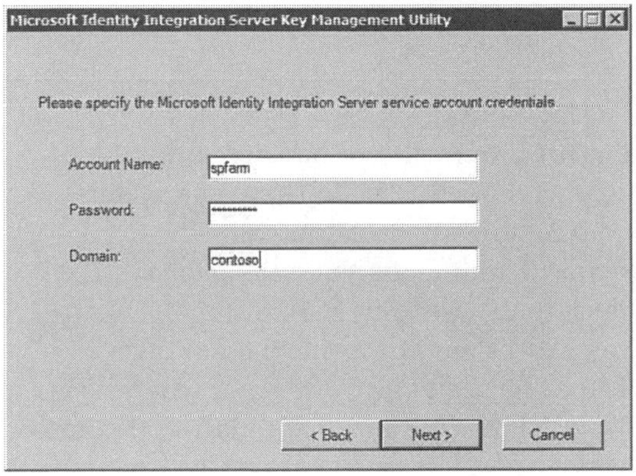

FIGURE 5.13 Entering credentials into the MIISKMU utility.

We cover adding this key back to the new environment later in this section; you should do that last.

Creating the New User Profile Synchronization Service Application

Just as before with the MMS application, the second process that is used to upgrade the UPS application is to create a new application pool to create the new service application and attach the previous SharePoint 2010 UPS database to it.

Before creating the application pool and UPS, start the UPS in Services on Server. Make sure that you select the server drop-down appropriate for the server on which the UPS will run and where you have set permissions. Then create the new application pool using the `New-SPServiceApplicationPool` cmdlet, as illustrated in Figure 5.14.

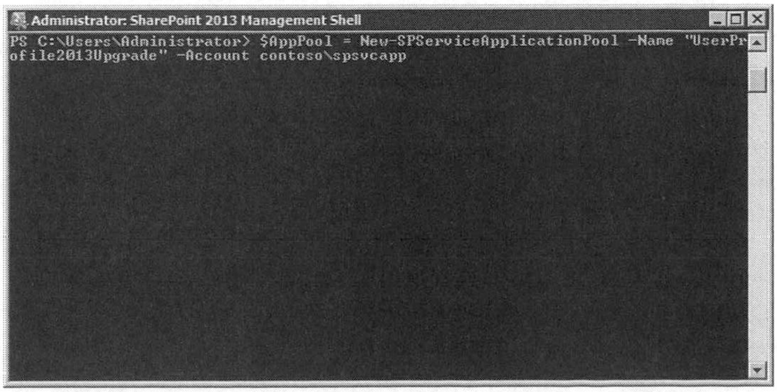

FIGURE 5.14 Creating a new application pool for the UPS application.

NOTE

You must still complete all steps to provision a UPS application before restoring the service application. You must complete all the procedures to prepare the environment to accept a UPS application (for example, setting permissions correctly for the UPS accounts on the servers running the services).

During the creation of the new UPS application, the administrator has the option of defining specific parameters in the cmdlet, as shown in Figure 5.15. These parameters are optional, but in most cases, all are used in a normal upgrade situation, with the exception of `-ProfileSyncDBName`. If administrators choose to include the sync database, the `ProfileSyncDBName` parameter is used to reference the SharePoint 2010 SyncDB. When restoring the sync database to the new SharePoint 2013 environment, the build version of the database does not change from when it lived in SharePoint 2010 and when it gets "upgraded" in SharePoint 2013. The upgrade only serves the purpose of placing the database into the farm and making it usable.

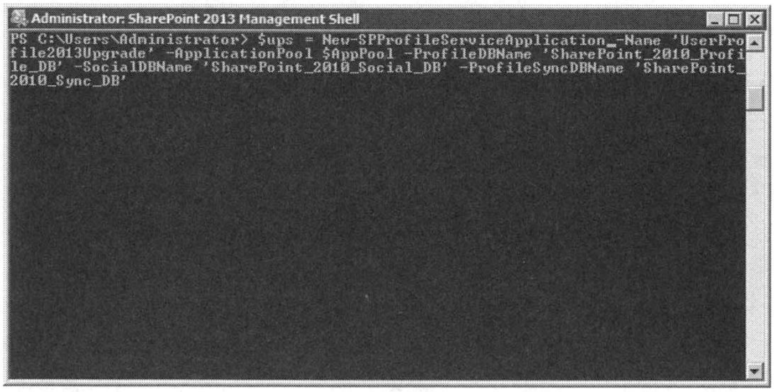

FIGURE 5.15 Defining additional parameters when creating a new UPS application.

After you create it, the new UPS application appears within SharePoint Central Administration.

In PowerShell, the administrator may use piping to insert the output value of a previously run cmdlet. However, if piping is not used in this process, the administrator must directly reference the service application that was created earlier (by globally unique identifier [GUID]) when creating the proxy for that service application. To acquire this GUID, just run the SQL query shown in Figure 5.16, which exposes the GUID needed in the `-ServiceApplication` parameter.

After recovering the GUID for the UPS application, creating the proxy is similar to creating the proxy for the MMS. However, the Profile Service is referenced in the cmdlet. Figure 5.17 shows a script example for creating a UPS application proxy with the GUID reference previously acquired.

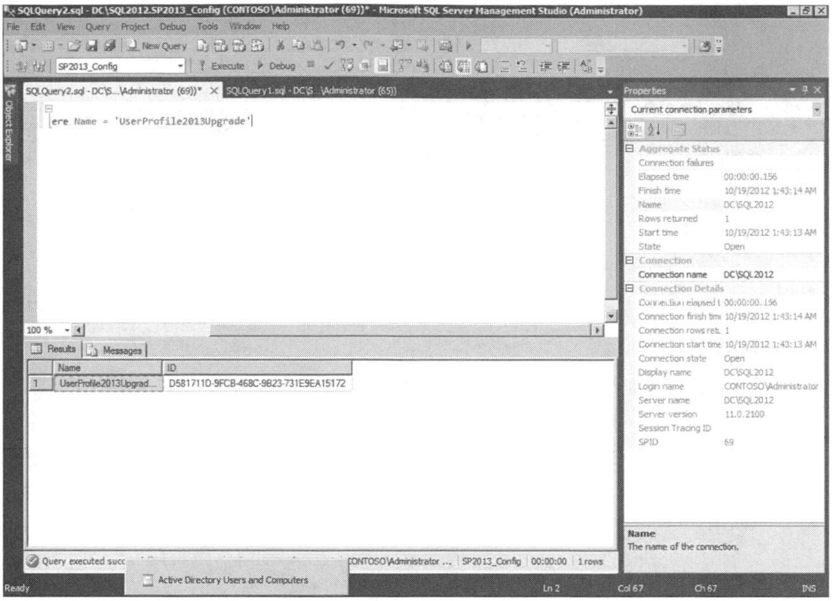

FIGURE 5.16 Capturing the UPA GUID.

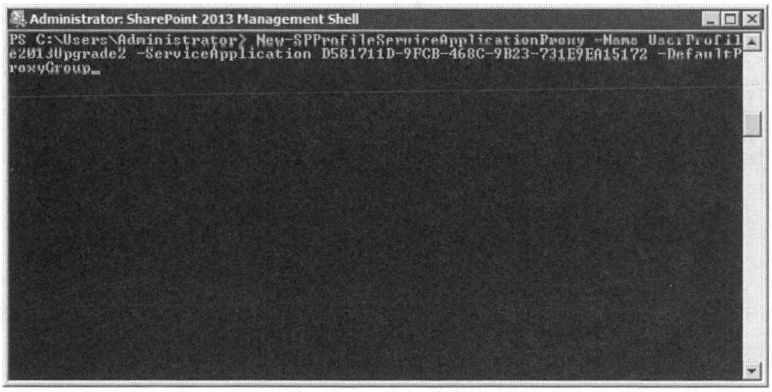

FIGURE 5.17 Entering the UPA GUID.

After the service application and proxy has been created, the administrator can view the UPS application proxy, as shown in Figure 5.18.

NOTE

Unfortunately, no percentage status indicator appears during service application database upgrades.

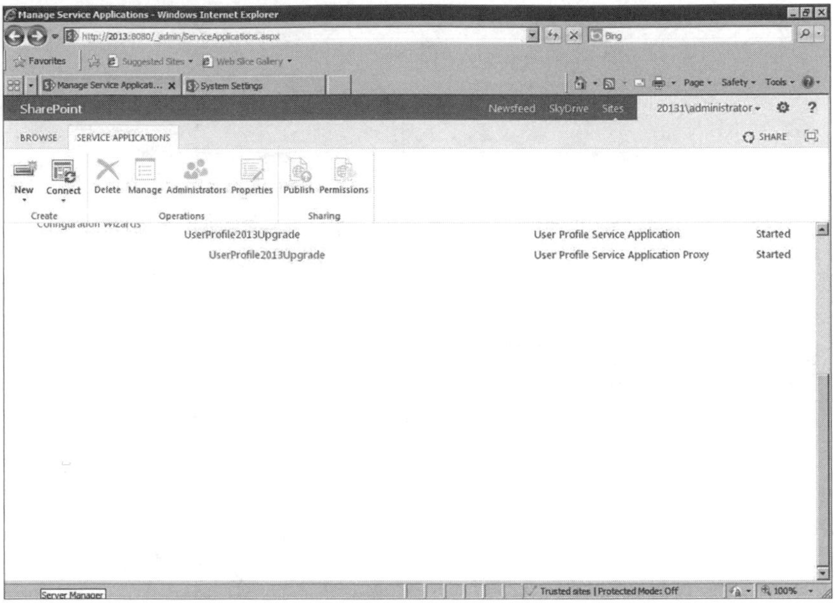

FIGURE 5.18 Viewing the newly created UPS application proxy in SharePoint Central Administration.

Note that when you are restoring the MIIS encryption key, this process must be done last, because when declaring the location in which to associate the key, the key assumes that there is a sync database to connect to. If this process is done before restoring (or creating) a sync database, you receive this error: "The operation encountered an error and cannot be completed."

The next step is to import and connect the encryption key that was previously exported (if you are restoring the sync database) from the SharePoint 2010 environment to the SharePoint 2013 environment. The first step in this process is to copy the key to <Root>\Program Files\Microsoft Office Servers\15.0\Synchronization Service\Bin.

To do this, open the command prompt and change directory (cd) to the <Root>\Program Files\Microsoft Office Servers\15.0\Synchronization Service\Bin directory and press Enter. After the directory has been changed, enter the following:

```
miiskmu.exe /I Path {GUID}
```

If you do not know the GUID of the encryption key, you can query this in the SharePoint 2010 environment; they are identical when imported into the SharePoint 2013 environment.

Figure 5.19 shows the command-line query used on the SharePoint 2010 server to acquire the GUID of the MIIS encryption key. By pressing Ctrl+C directly within this alert box, the administrator can copy all the text, including the MIIS database key, to the Clipboard for easy extraction in the next step in the process of importing the key.

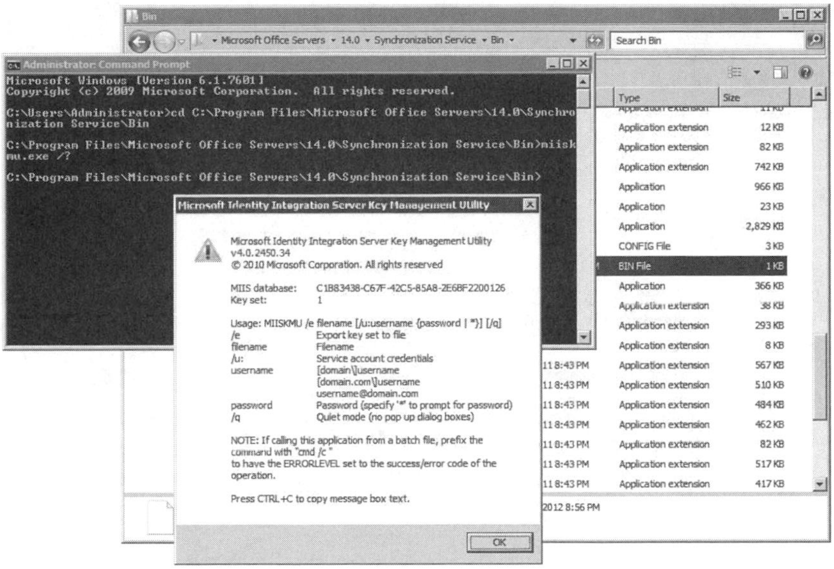

FIGURE 5.19 Acquiring the GUID of the MIIS encryption key.

From the command-line tool on the SharePoint 2013 server, change the directory line to `<Root>\Program Files\Microsoft Office Servers\15.0\Synchronization Service\Bin`. `miiskmu.exe /I Path` *{GUID}* is being run to inject the key, as shown in Figure 5.20.

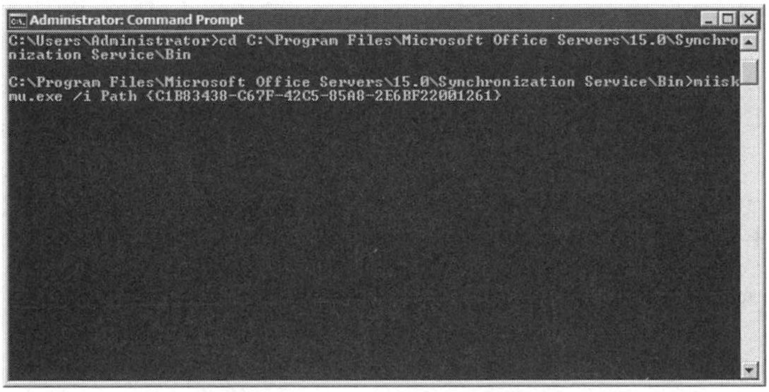

FIGURE 5.20 Injecting the MIIS encryption key.

After completing these steps, proceed to Services on Server in Central Administration and start the User Profile Synchronization Service.

Figure 5.21 shows the restored SharePoint 2013 UPS application synchronization statistics and information. The last crawl shows from the last successful run when the database lived in the SharePoint 2010 environment.

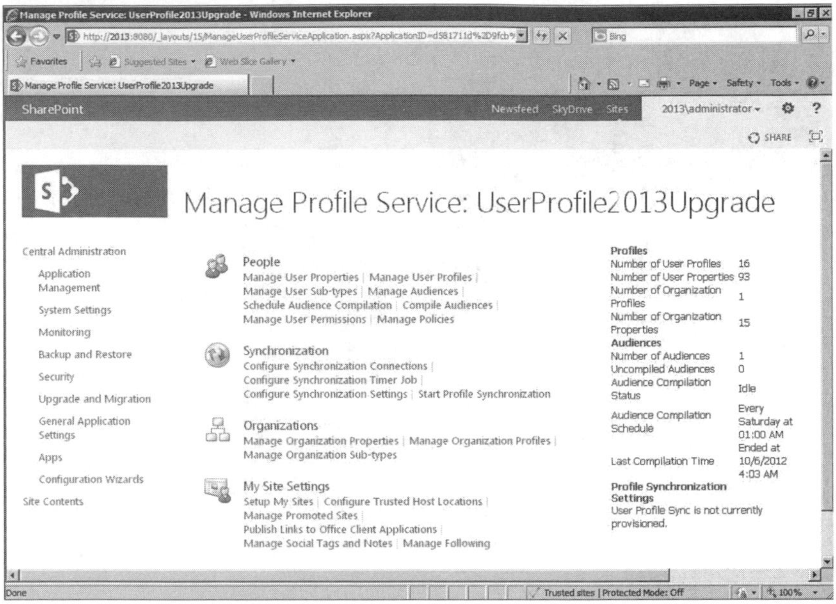

FIGURE 5.21 Viewing the restored UPS application.

Search Service Application

When restoring the Search service application, remember that only the Search administration database is restored. Any indexes must be re-created by running a new full crawl. This means that the only items that are upgradable from SharePoint 2010 Search to SharePoint 2013 Search are content sources, federated locations, crawl rules, schedules, best bets, and search scopes (and search results pages, web parts, and settings that come bundled with the content database of a site collection).

If the enterprise environment consists of multiple SharePoint 2010 farms where a designated farm serves as the search instance for multiple child instances, each child instance must be reconfigured to point to the new SharePoint 2013 search instance.

In SharePoint 2010, Microsoft included the FAST for SharePoint service application as part of the service application model. In SharePoint 2013, FAST has been integrated directly into SharePoint Server 2013.

Because site collections are upgraded at different times from when a content database is mounted to a web application, the Search service application can be upgraded before site collection-level search centers are fully upgraded. This scenario is known as mixed mode, and until the site collection is fully upgraded to 15 mode, some content features might not be available on the search center.

SharePoint 2010 (14) Mode and 2013 (15) Mode

By default, all upgraded content databases show as if they resided in SharePoint 2010. The SharePoint 2010 mode, as stated earlier, has taken the place of the Visual Upgrade in SharePoint 2013. Virtual directories in IIS control the management and routing of the bits that get used to drive the look and feel of the site as it renders in a given mode (for example, _layouts/_controltemplates in 14 hive or the same in the 15 hive). Solutions deployed originally to the 14\Templates directly still have this directory on the environment to point to and thus still function correctly. After the upgrade of a database, unless otherwise instructed to do so, the SharePoint 2013 site collection shows up in 14 mode, meaning it will have the look, feel, and functionality of a site that is still in the SharePoint 2010 environment.

Having the 14 mode available during the upgrade makes it easier to complete the upgrade. The 14 mode files allow for site functionality to be more or less identical to the way it was in SharePoint 2010, and allows organizations the luxury of indefinitely keeping a site or its features as if they were still native to SharePoint 2010.

Two types of notifications are available when a mode event is triggered (read-only, upgraded, reminder to upgrade, and so on): An email can be sent out, or a dynamic status bar is shown on top of a site in a given mode.

Summary

With proper planning and risk management, upgrade from SharePoint 2010 can be a seamless and stress-free exercise. Planning is always the key, and key factors from this chapter should be taken into account when planning for an upgrade. Administrators need to take into account the need for a claims-based authentication upgrade as well as a content upgrade. In addition, organizations need to decide whether or not they will be upgrading their service applications, or whether or not those service applications will be recreated from scratch.

Best Practices

The following are best practices from this chapter:

- Planning is always overstated, but it really is the best defense against problematic upgrades. As a general rule of thumb, planning should take three times as long as the actual upgrade process itself.
- Encourage content owners to review old and stale content. Upgrading data irrelevant or outdated data and archiving such add exponential time to the upgrade process.
- Do not assume that upgrading old content (and more specifically, service applications) is the best method. Often, it is much more efficient to reprovision content or service applications.
- Reset unghosted sites to standard SharePoint site definitions where possible to ensure consistency across sites.

- It is much easier to upgrade the profile and social database for UPS and simply re-create the sync database than it is to restore the sync database to the new SharePoint 2013 environment.
- Use 14 mode wisely; it can be a simple and easy transition from SharePoint 2010 to SharePoint 2013. Because of the 14 bits on the server, most customizations work inside the 2013 environment.

CHAPTER 6

Managing and Administering SharePoint 2013 Infrastructure

IN THIS CHAPTER

- Operations Management with the SharePoint Central Administration Tool
- Administering Site Collections and Sites
- Using Additional Administration Tools for SharePoint

Administration of a SharePoint 2013 infrastructure can be complex and intimidating, because multiple running parts and tools can be used. The most important tool is the web-based SharePoint Central Administration (SPCA) tool, which is built in to the infrastructure of a farm itself. Aside from PowerShell, the SPCA is the most critical component to understand for a SharePoint administrator. PowerShell itself is covered in detail in Chapter 7, "Leveraging PowerShell for Command-Line SharePoint Administration and Automation," and SPCA and other admin tools are covered in this chapter.

This chapter gives an overview of the SharePoint administrative tools, including a step-by-step look at all the major links and tasks included in the SharePoint Central Administration tool. Considerable emphasis is placed on common tasks performed by administrators using the SharePoint Central Administration tool. In addition, this chapter takes a look at the other administration interfaces a SharePoint administrator may run into, such as the developer dashboard, SQL Server Management Studio, and Internet Information Services (IIS) Manager.

Operations Management with the SharePoint Central Administration Tool

The single most important tool to a SharePoint administrator is the SPCA, shown in Figure 6.1. This tool runs on a dedicated SharePoint site collection within a dedicated web application and is initially installed on the first server in a farm. You can invoke the tool from the server console from the Start menu or, because it is web based and is effectively just a SharePoint site collection within a dedicated web application, you can invoke it from any workstation. It is actually preferable from a security perspective to access the SPCA tool from a different workstation. If doing so, note what the hostname and port are for the SharePoint central web application when created.

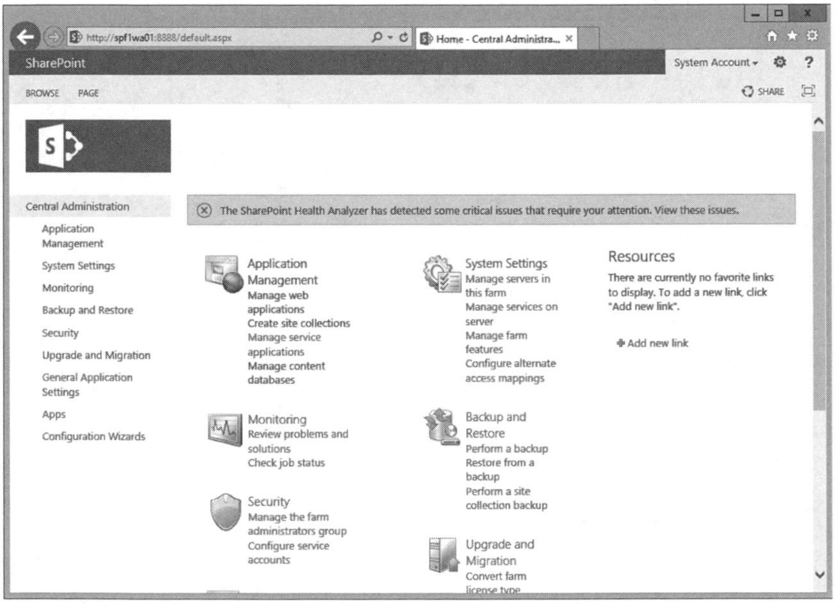

FIGURE 6.1 Using the SPCA tool.

NOTE

Although the default is to choose a custom port for the SPCA tool, it is recommended to instead change this to the default Hypertext Transport Protocol Secure (HTTPS) port of 443 so that a Secure Sockets Layer (SSL) certificate can be easily added and a unique name for the SPCA tool can be used. For example, https://spca.companyabc.com is an example of a best-practice way of accessing the SPCA tool from another workstation. This has the added advantage of enabling SPCA to be easily load balanced using network load balancing (NLB), either hardware based or software based, between two servers running the SPCA service.

The SPCA tool's home page, shown in Figure 6.1, provides a launching point for some of the most commonly used tasks in SPCA. You can launch more detailed sets of tasks by clicking the links listed in the left pane of the page. These links take you to specific pages for each category of administration, including the following:

- Application Management
- System Settings
- Monitoring
- Backup and Restore
- Security
- Upgrade and Migration
- General Application Settings
- Apps
- Configuration Wizards

Each of these categories and the tasks that can be performed within them are listed in subsequent sections of this chapter.

Administering Application Management Tasks in SPCA

The Application Management page, shown in Figure 6.2, contains those tasks directly related to the management of site collections, sites, content databases, web applications, and service applications. It is therefore a page where an administrator can spend a great deal of time during the initial configuration of SharePoint 2013.

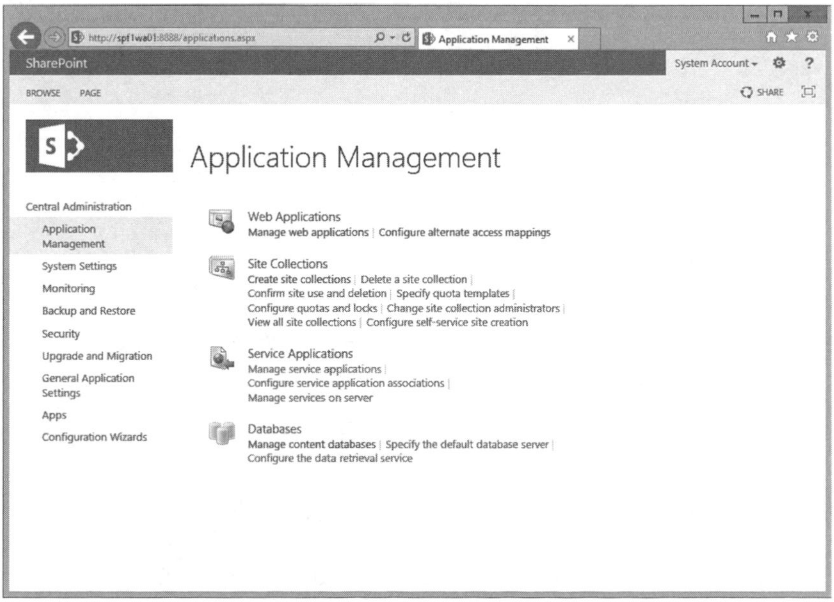

FIGURE 6.2 Exploring SPCA options on the Application Management page.

Web Applications

The first category on the page deals specifically with web applications and includes the following links:

- **Manage Web Applications:** Simply lists the web applications in the farm and their URLs and port. This area also enables the configuration of various web application settings.
- **Configure Alternate Access Mappings:** This highly important area controls Alternate Access Mappings (AAMs), shown in Figure 6.3. AAMs are needed to indicate different server host header values for the machine. If an AAM is configured, SharePoint automatically translates all links to the host header value used by the client to access site content. This reduces the chance of links not working externally. For more information on configuring AAMs for remote access, see Chapter 14, "Protecting SharePoint with Advanced Edge Security Solutions."

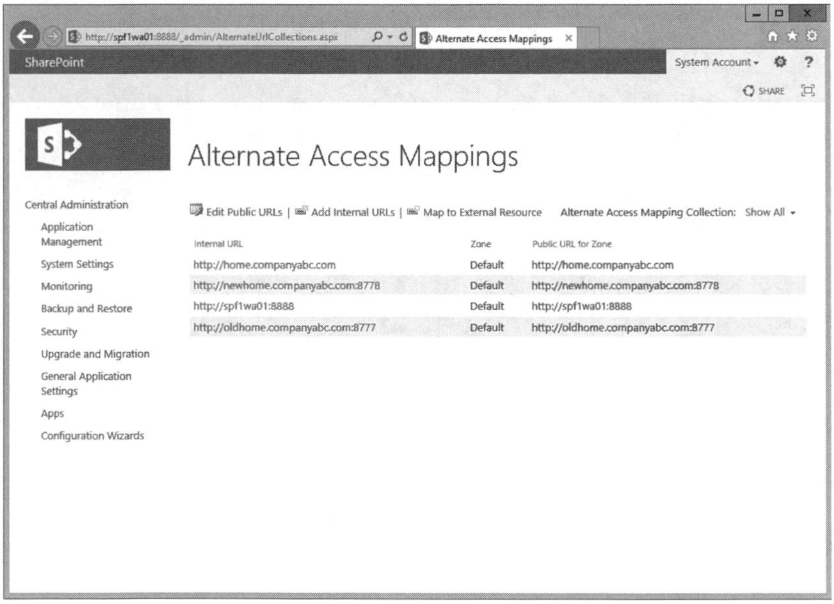

FIGURE 6.3 Using AAMs.

Site Collections

Within the second category on the Application Management page, labeled Site Collections, all the options for creating, deleting, and managing individual site collections are listed. Site collections provide the highest level administrative object entity within SharePoint, with the exception of web applications and the farm. The links provided within the Site Collections category include the following:

- **Create Site Collections:** This link allows for the creation of new site collections from within SPCA, as shown in Figure 6.4. Site collections can be created from a default list of templates, or via custom templates created by the organization and added into SPCA using PowerShell or the STSADM command-line tool.

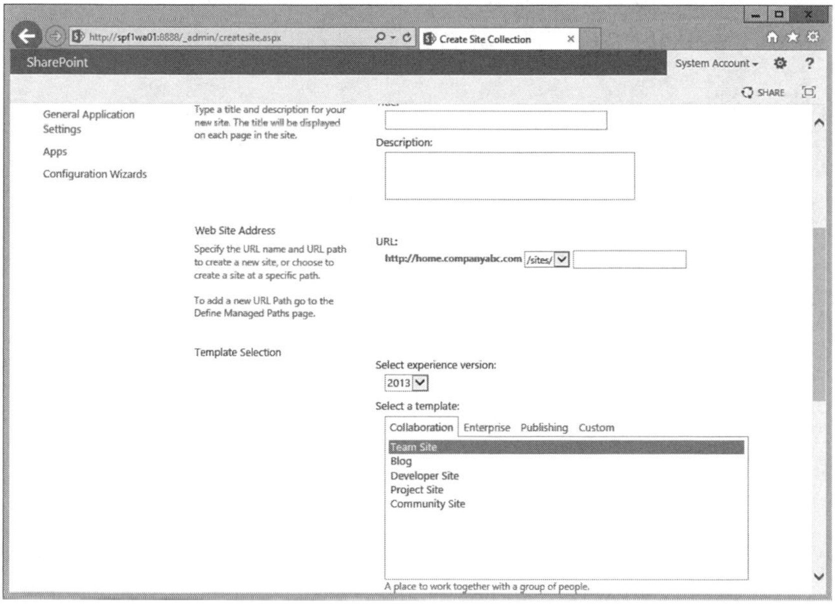

FIGURE 6.4 Creating new site collections.

- **Delete a Site Collection:** Enables an administrator to delete specific site collections. Note that when deleted, it is not easy to recover an entire site collection.
- **Confirm Site Use and Deletion:** Leads to a page that enables the configuration of automatic site collection deletion of unused sites. This functionality is meant to help control the growth of SharePoint content by removing site collections no longer in use and enables administrators to define warnings that are sent to site collection administrators.
- **Specify Quota Templates:** Enables administrators to create and modify quota templates for site collections. Individual size limits can be defined for site collections and applied to the individual site collections as they are created or at a later time. Site collection administrators are notified if their sites grow above a warning limit or if they are above the maximum size limit, which results in new content not being added to the site.
- **Configure Quotas and Locks:** Takes the administrator to settings shown in Figure 6.5 that define whether a site collection is locked, effectively not allowing any content to be added because of the result of exceeding a template or simply because the content was locked into read-only mode for one reason or another.

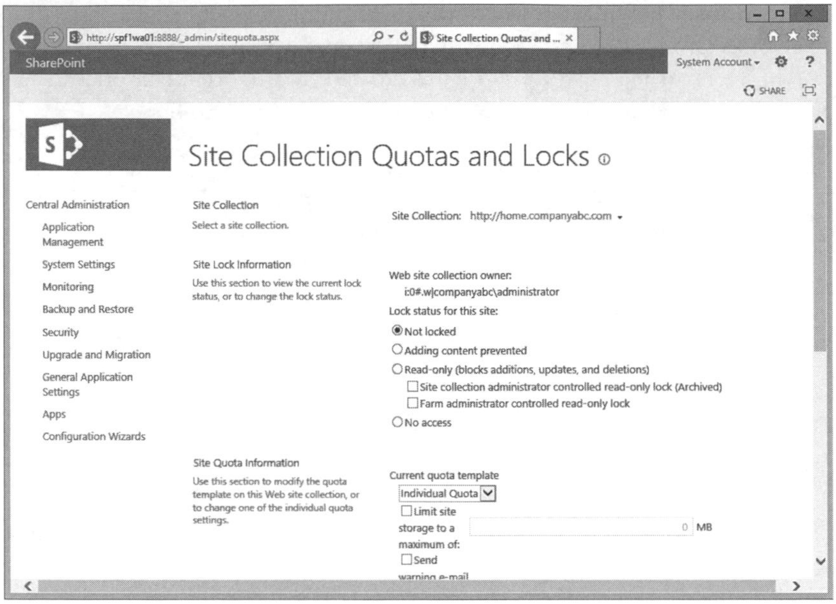

FIGURE 6.5 Viewing site quotas and locks.

- **Change Site Collection Administrators:** Clicking this link in SPCA enables administrators to define who the primary and secondary site collection administrators are for a site collection.
- **View All Site Collections:** All site collections within a specific content database can be viewed from within this link.
- **Configure Self-Service Site Creation:** Enables administrators to turn Self-Service Site Creation on or off for a web application. This concept enables users with the Use Self-Service Site Creation permission to create sites in defined URL namespaces. Be cautious when enabling this; it can lead to a proliferation of sites within a site collection very quickly.

Service Applications

Within the third category on the Application Management page, labeled Service Applications, the tasks related to the critical service applications in SharePoint 2013 can be modified. For more detailed information about individual service applications, see the chapters in which they are discussed. For example, for the Managed Metadata Service (MMS), see Chapter 22, "Managing Metadata and Content Types in SharePoint 2013," and for many other service apps, see Chapter 26, "Extending SharePoint 2013 with Excel Services, Visio Graphics Services, and Access Services."

- **Manage Service Applications:** This link takes administrators to the Service Applications page, shown in Figure 6.6. This page is the main administrative point to all the service applications, such as the MMS, PerformancePoint, Excel Services, and others.

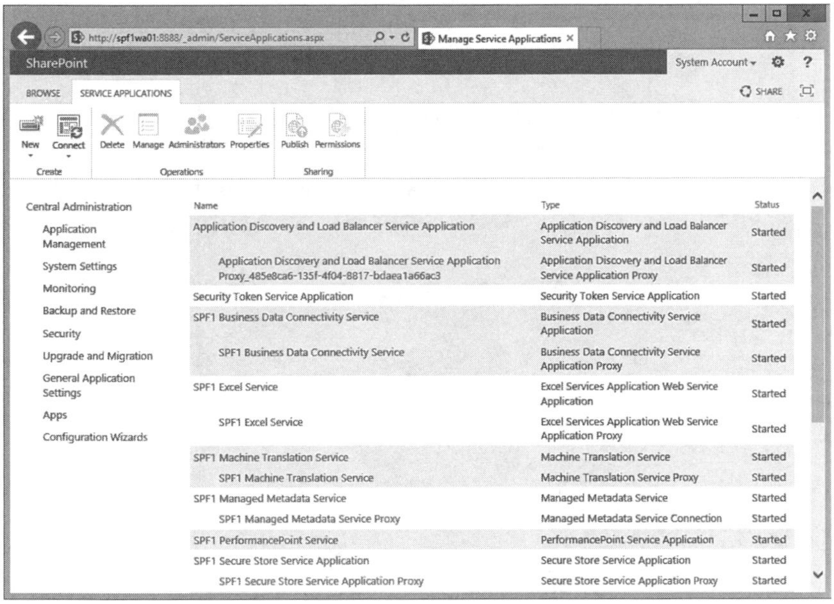

FIGURE 6.6 Viewing service applications within SPCA.

- **Configure Service Application Associations:** Configuring service application associations enables them to be "tied" to an individual web application so that they can be used by the site collections within those web applications. Administrators can modify which web applications these service applications are tied to from within this interface.
- **Manage Services on Server:** This link takes administrators to the page shown in Figure 6.7, which enables individual services to be started or stopped on servers. Configuration information for those specific services can be accessed by clicking the blue links for services that enable settings to be modified.

Databases

Within the fourth category on the Application Management page, labeled Databases, all the tasks associated with SharePoint content databases are made accessible. This includes the following links:

- **Manage Content Databases:** This link presents a list of all content databases, similar to what is shown in Figure 6.8. As a side note, by modifying the maximum number of sites that can be created within a content database, you can control which content database a site collection is installed in. This can also be controlled from within PowerShell when creating a site collection.

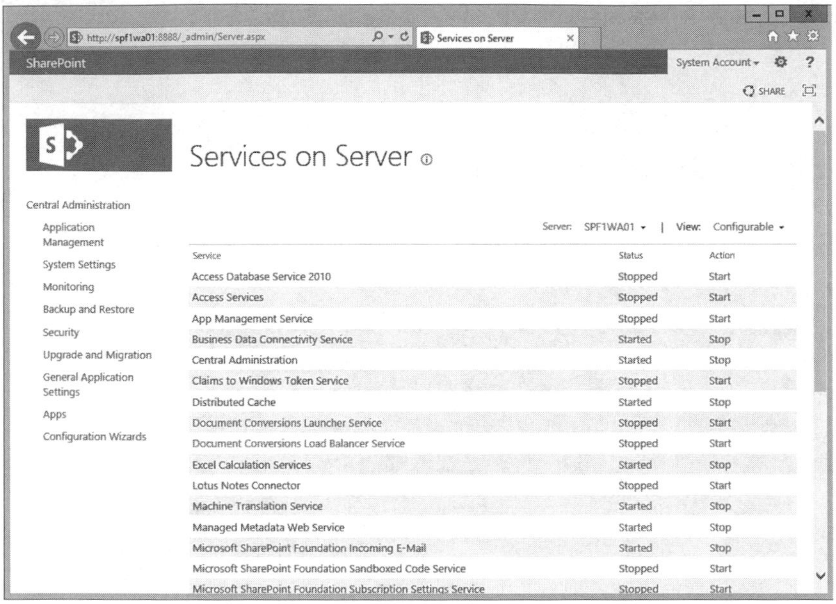

FIGURE 6.7 Modifying services on servers.

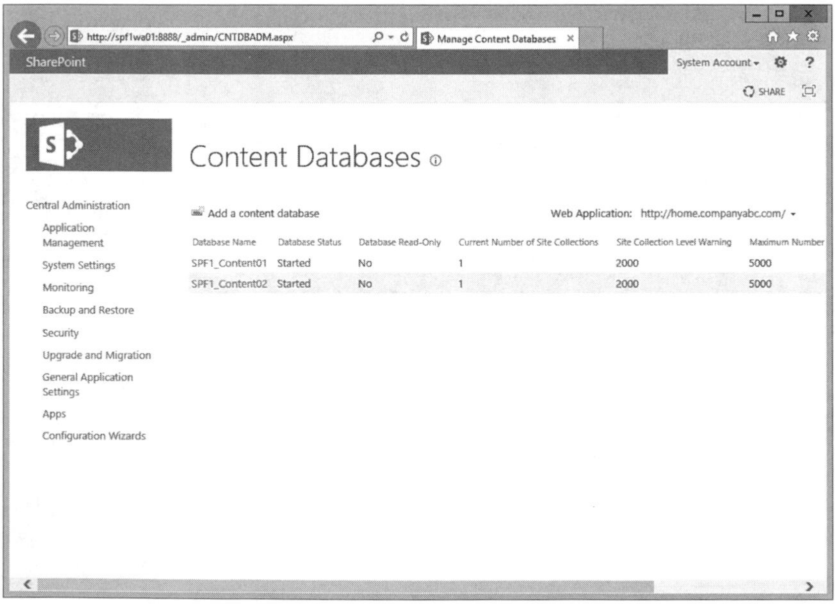

FIGURE 6.8 Administering content databases.

- **Specify the Default Database Server:** The default database server used for all new databases can be specified in this section of SPCA. In addition, if using SQL Server authentication (not recommended) to connect to the SQL Server, the Service Account account and password can be designated here.
- **Configure the Data Retrieval Service:** Data retrieval services such as Object Linking and Embedding Database (OLEDB), Simple Object Access Protocol (SOAP) Passthrough, CML-URL, or SharePoint Foundation can be enabled or disabled on individual web applications in this area of SPCA.

Administering System Settings Tasks in SPCA

The System Settings page, shown in Figure 6.9, consolidates tasks related to servers and the farm. This page is often referenced while setting up the infrastructure components of a farm during the initial configuration.

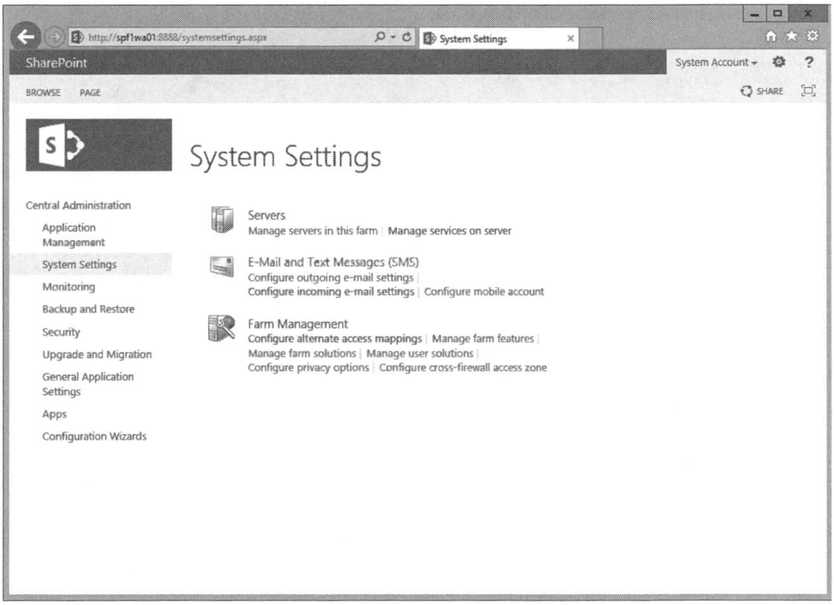

FIGURE 6.9 Viewing the System Settings area of SPCA.

Servers

The first category on the page deals specifically with the servers used by SharePoint and includes the following links:

- **Manage Servers in This Farm:** Simply lists the servers in the farm, as shown in Figure 6.10, and which services they have running. This area also enables the removal of a specific server from the farm.

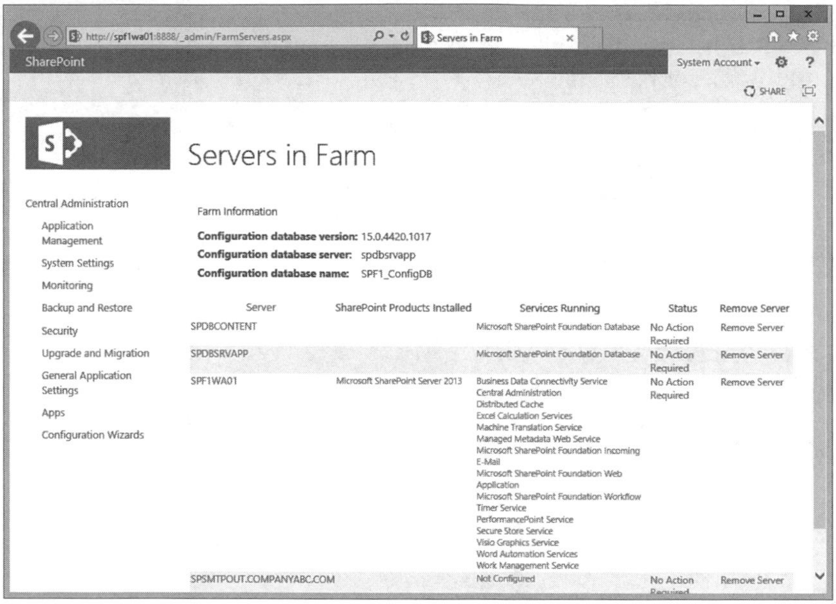

FIGURE 6.10 Managing servers in a farm.

- **Manage Services on Server:** This link takes you to the same services view as is linked to from the Application Management area of SPCA. It enables modification of individual service settings, and for starting and stopping services on individual servers.

E-Mail and Text Messages (SMS)

Within the second category on the System Settings page, labeled E-Mail and Text Messages (SMS), all tasks related to messaging in the new environment, including outbound and inbound email to SharePoint, are displayed. For more detailed information on this area, including steps for enabling messaging functionality, see Chapter 16, "Configuring Email-Enabled Content, Site Mailboxes, and Exchange Server Integration." This particular area includes the following links:

- **Configure Outgoing Email Settings:** Enable a Simple Mail Transfer Protocol (SMTP) server to be defined that will be used to forward alerts and other emails to end users. The SMTP server must be configured to accept connections and allow relaying from the SharePoint server.

- **Configure Incoming Email Settings:** Enables mail to be received directly by the SharePoint server and delivered into email-enabled distribution lists and email-enabled discussion groups. This powerful piece of functionality that integrates SharePoint with email platforms is also covered in detail in Chapter 16.

- **Configure Mobile Account:** If using a web-based text messaging service, it can be configured within this area of SPCA. This allows for monitoring alerts to be generated even if an outage in the email platform occurs.

Farm Management

Within the third category on the System Settings page, labeled Farm Management, tasks related to functions that apply to all servers in the farm are listed. These include the following:

- **Configure Alternate Access Mappings:** Link to the same AAM list that the Application Management area linked to. AAMs define how links are translated when users access SharePoint using a specific fully qualified domain name (FQDN), such as https://sharepoint.companyabc.com or http://sharepoint.
- **Manage Farm Features:** Enables specific farm features, such as the ones shown in Figure 6.11, to be turned on or off. It is the first area that should be referenced when trying to determine why a feature doesn't show up as an available option within a SharePoint site.

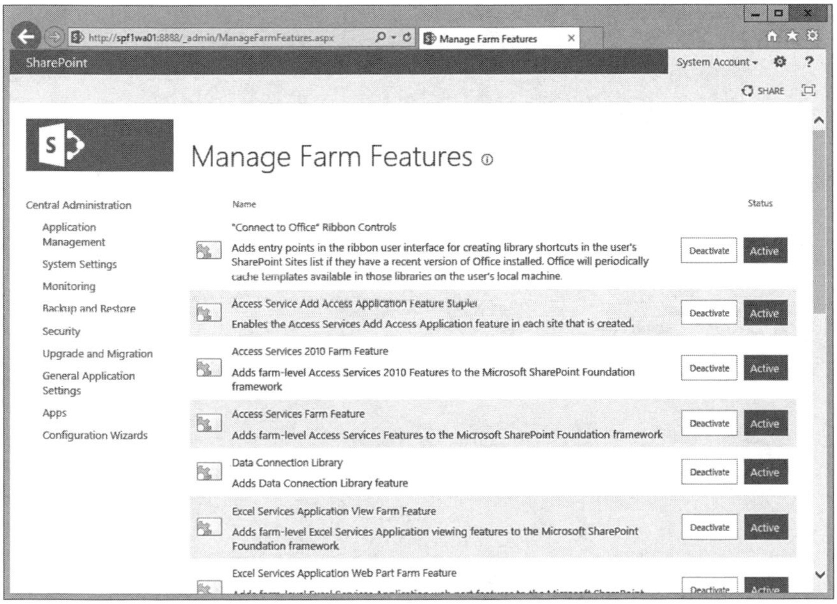

FIGURE 6.11 Managing farm features.

- **Manage Farm Solutions:** List any custom solutions, such as third-party products, which are added into the farm.
- **Manage User Solutions:** Although not obvious from the title of its link, this area allows management of sandbox solutions and enables administrators to define whether specific solutions are blocked for end users.
- **Configure Privacy Options:** Private settings, such as whether to sign up for the Customer Experience Improvement Program (CEIP) or error reporting that is sent to

Microsoft, are defined in this area of SPCA. This area also enables administrators to define whether external web-based help is available for users within sites.

- **Configure Cross-Firewall Access Zone:** Defines which zone generates URLs that are generated when alerts and other messages are sent from the web application. For example, any administrator can define that all URLs are generated from the Internet zone settings, which have a URL of https://sharepoint.companyabc.com.

Administering Monitoring Tasks in SPCA

The Monitoring page in SPCA, as shown in Figure 6.12, deals with all built-in monitoring tools and concepts in SharePoint 2013. For more detailed information on configuring monitoring with SharePoint 2013, see Chapter 11, "Monitoring a SharePoint 2013 Environment."

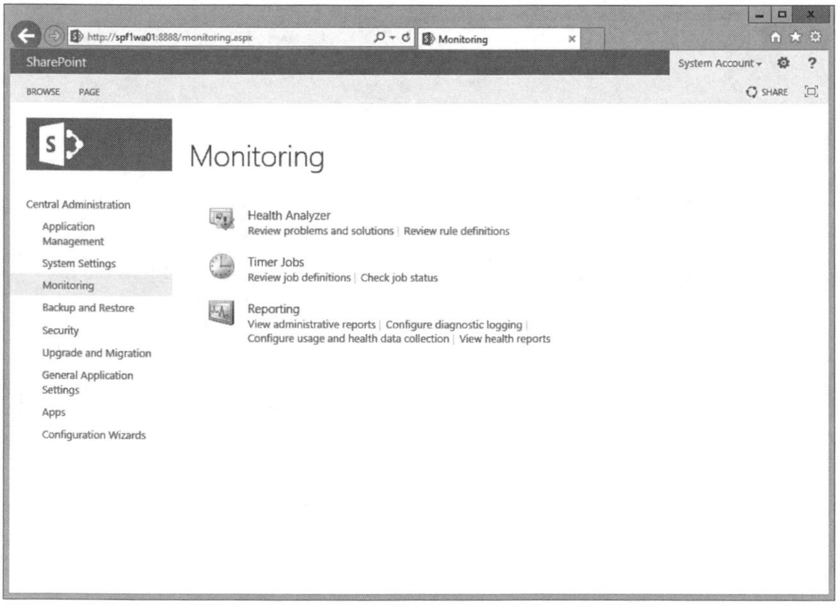

FIGURE 6.12 Exploring the monitoring options in SPCA.

Health Analyzer

The first category on the page deals specifically with the Health Analyzer, which determines the overall health of the SharePoint farm. This section includes the following links:

- **Review Problems and Solutions:** Takes the administrator directly to a list of configuration issues that exist in the farm based on the rules that are set up by the Health Analyzer.

- **Review Rule Definitions:** The rules that are run by the Health Analyzer can be modified in this area, as shown in Figure 6.13.

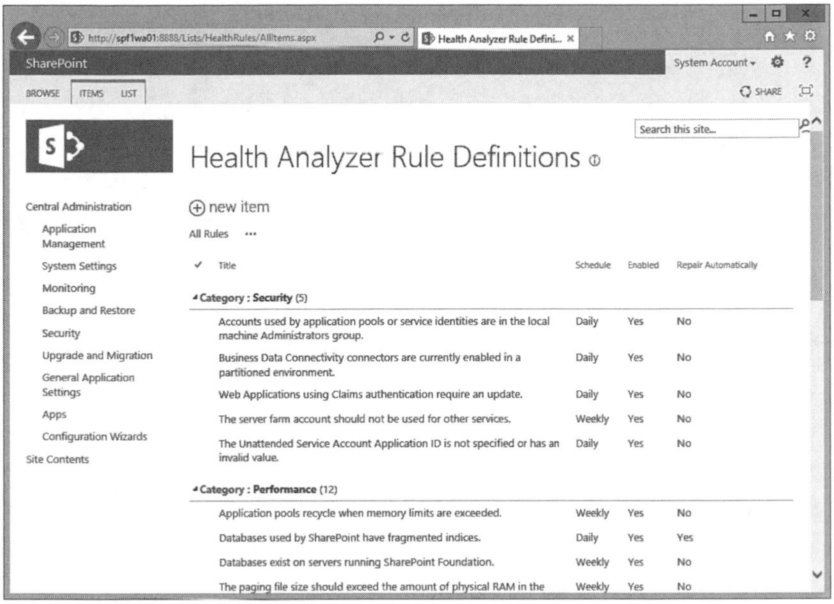

FIGURE 6.13 Modifying Health Analyzer rules.

Timer Jobs

Within the second category on the System Settings page are the tasks related to timer jobs. Timer jobs, as shown in Figure 6.14, are extremely important services that run on a regularly scheduled basis to perform specific tasks, such as maintenance, analysis, synchronization, and other farm-critical tasks that must be performed on a regular basis. The links available within this field include the following:

- **Review Job Definitions:** This area of SPCA, as shown in Figure 6.14, enables the current timer job settings to be viewed and their schedules to be modified, if necessary.

- **Check Job Status:** The job status area of SPCA, shown in Figure 6.15, is where administrators should go to check on the status of current timer jobs and see the next time they are scheduled to run.

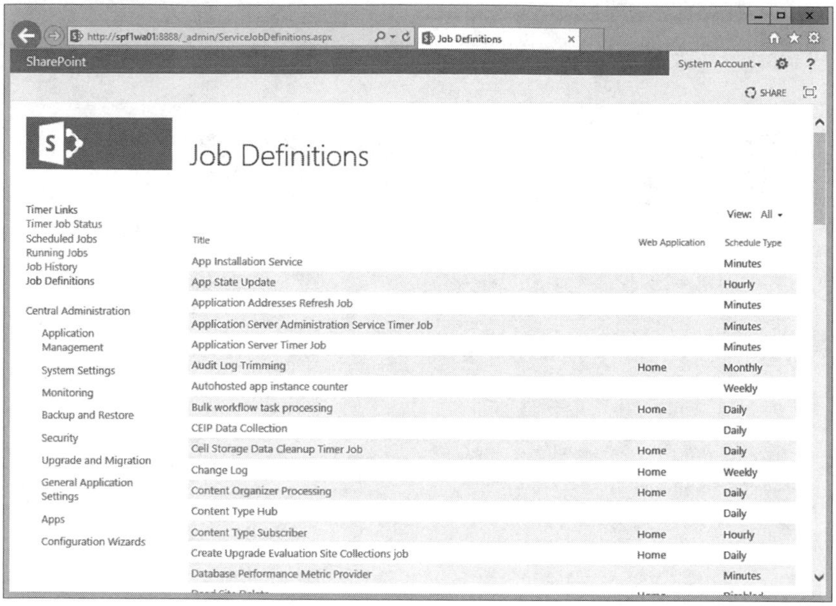

FIGURE 6.14 Exploring timer jobs.

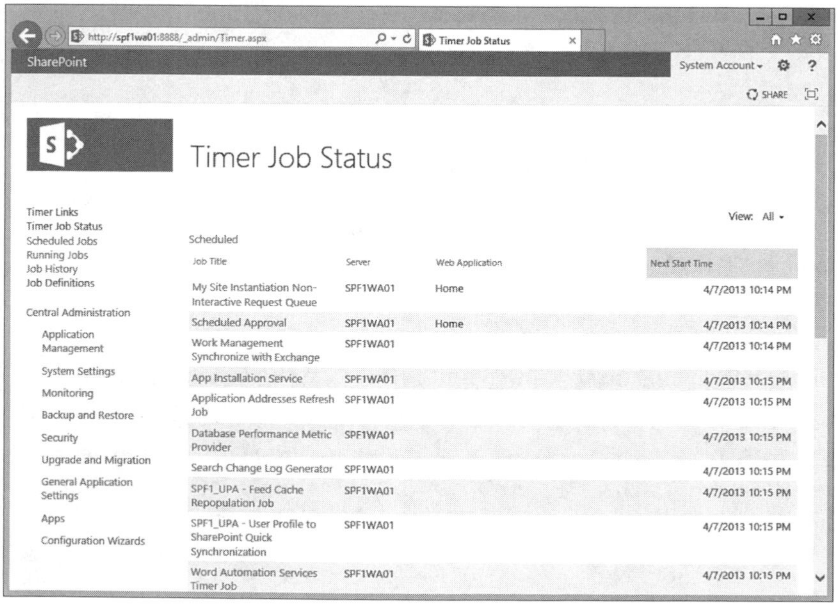

FIGURE 6.15 Reviewing timer job status.

Reporting

Within the third category on the Monitoring page, labeled Reporting, are links to all those administrative areas directly related to reporting, including diagnostic logs, usage reports, and health reports. The following key links are included in this area:

- **View Administrative Reports:** This area focuses on those reports that are related to administrative tasks.
- **Configure Diagnostic Logging:** Diagnostic logs are not turned on by default in SharePoint 2013, but can be enabled from within this area of SPCA. Logs can be generated for each category of service, as shown in Figure 6.16. In addition, settings related to event log flood protection and trace logs can be modified in this area. It is highly recommended to place all logs on a separate volume from the drive where SharePoint installation files and the operating system (OS) are installed to avoid running out of disk space.

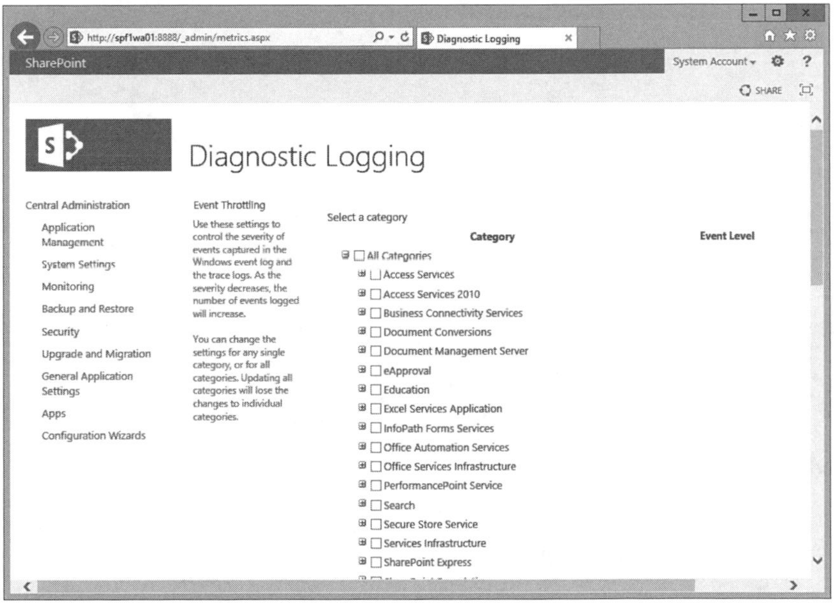

FIGURE 6.16 Configuring diagnostic logging.

- **Review Information Management Policy Usage Reports:** These types of reports are used for information management policy reports, which are related to Information Rights Management and Data Leak Prevention (DLP), concepts discussed in more detail in Chapter 17, "Safeguarding Confidential Data in SharePoint 2013."

- **View Health Reports:** Health reports provide information such as what pages are the slowest, and who are the top active users in a site.
- **Configure Usage and Health Data Collection:** This area, shown in Figure 6.17, is critical because it allows for the configuration of the usage data logs, which can determine what areas of SharePoint are being used. It also enables the location of the usage logs to be set. As with all logs in SharePoint, it is highly recommended to store these on a separate data partition than SharePoint and the OS are installed on. Usage job definitions, shown in Figure 6.18, can also be modified from this area.

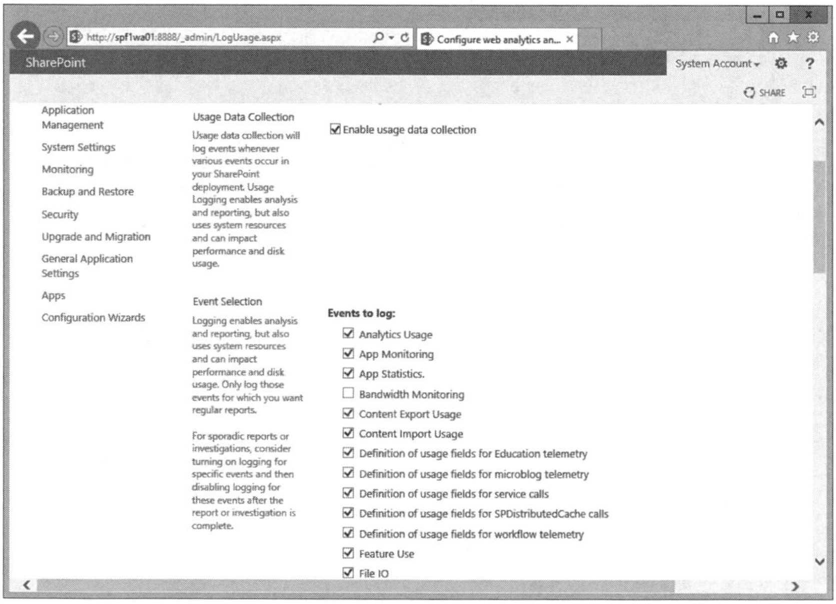

FIGURE 6.17 Modifying usage logs settings.

- **View Web Analytics Reports:** Web analytics reports can determine top visitors to pages, number of page views, and other useful metrics in the SharePoint environment.

Reviewing Backup and Restore Settings in SPCA

The Backup and Restore page in SPCA, as shown in Figure 6.19, contains all relevant links that provide for integrated backup and restore functionality. This includes old options such as farm backup and restore, and new options such as granular backups. For detailed information on these options, see Chapter 10, "Backing Up and Restoring a SharePoint Environment."

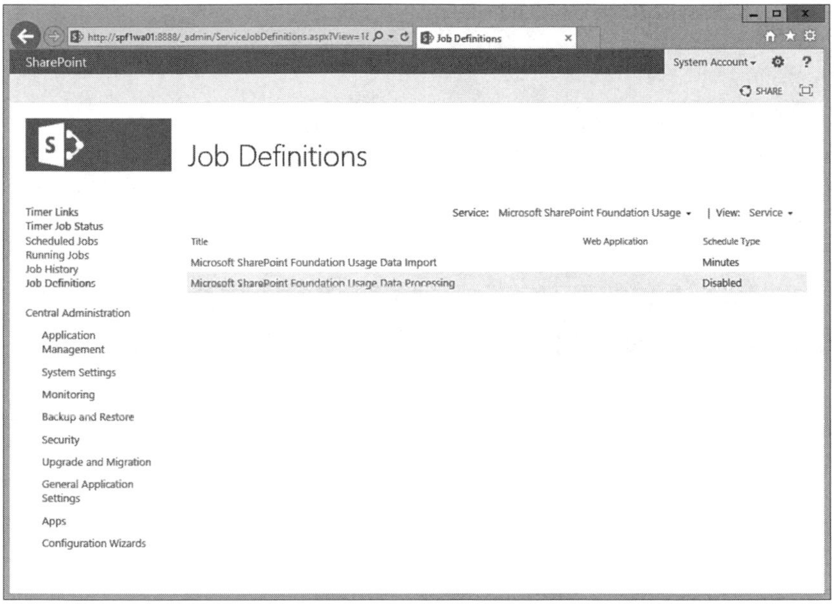

FIGURE 6.18 Modifying usage data import logs.

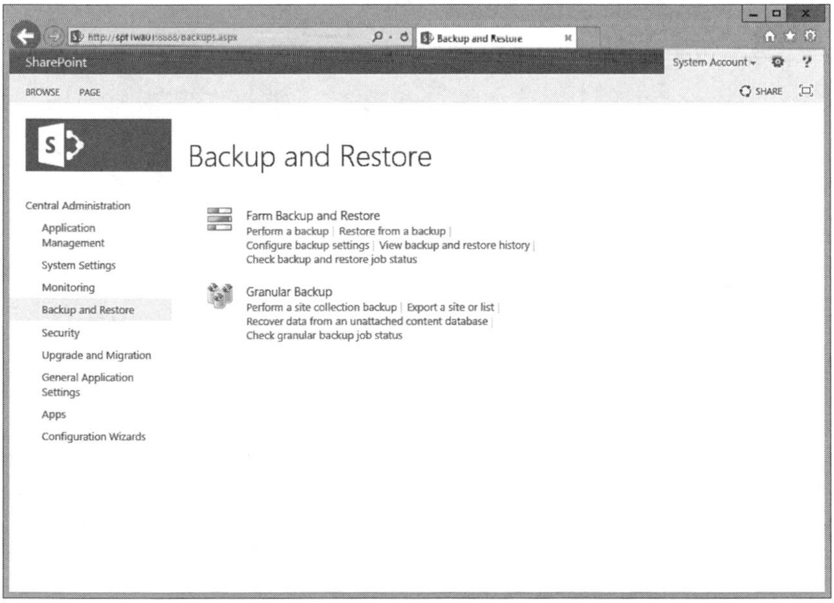

FIGURE 6.19 Viewing the Backup and Restore page in SPCA.

Farm Backup and Restore

Within the first category on the Backup and Restore page, labeled Farm Backup and Restore, the following links are included:

- **Perform a Backup:** Enables administrators to perform a full farm backup or a backup of individual components in a farm using the wizard shown in Figure 6.20. This can back up all components needed to restore a farm, including content databases and indexes.

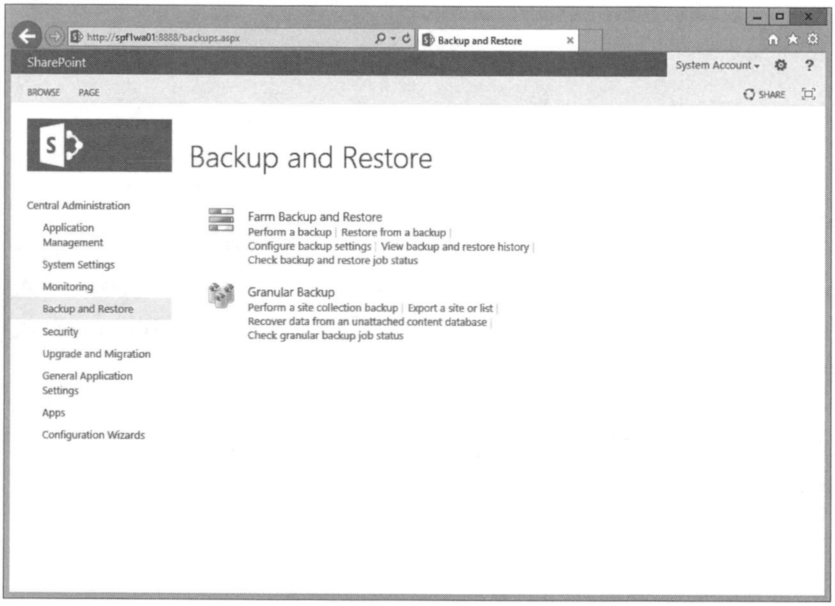

FIGURE 6.20 Backing up the farm using SPCA.

- **Restore from a Backup:** Enables restores of the farm or farm components from the backups performed using the previous area of SPCA.
- **Configure Backup Settings:** Enables the number of backup and restore threads to be chosen and a default backup file location to be set.
- **View Backup and Restore History:** History of backup and restore jobs can be viewed in this area of SPCA.
- **Check Backup and Restore Job Status:** Enables currently running backup and restore jobs to be viewed in real time.

Granular Backup

Within the second category on the Backup and Restore page, labeled Granular Backup, the options to back up individual site collections or subcomponents to site collections are provided:

- **Perform a Site Collection Backup:** Enables an entire site collection to be exported to a full-fidelity flat file copy that can be exported to a different location within the farm, to the same location, or to a new location in a different farm.
- **Export a Site or List:** Enables content within a site collection to be exported using the settings shown in Figure 6.21. Note that these types of exports are not full fidelity, and some settings such as individual document permissions can be lost using the export option.

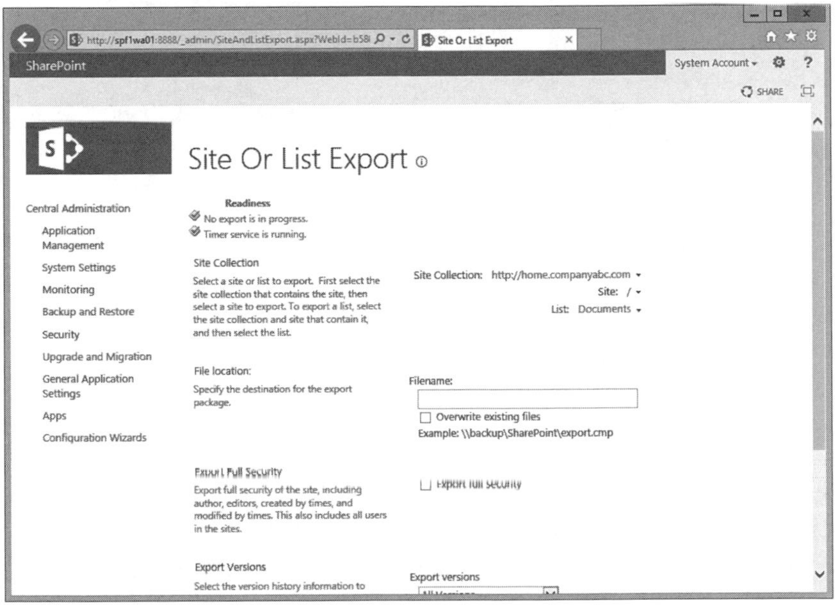

FIGURE 6.21 Exporting content using SPCA.

- **Recover Data from an Unattached Content Database:** This option, new in SharePoint 2013, is powerful, because it enables content to be recovered out of databases that are not attached to a SharePoint farm, although they do need to be attached to an SQL Server.
- **Check Granular Backup Job Status:** Enables administration to check on the status of an existing granular backup job.

Reviewing Security Settings in SPCA

The Security page in SPCA, as shown in Figure 6.22, contains all security-related items available for configuration in SPCA. For a detailed discussion on security in SharePoint 2013, see Chapter 15, "Implementing and Validating SharePoint Security."

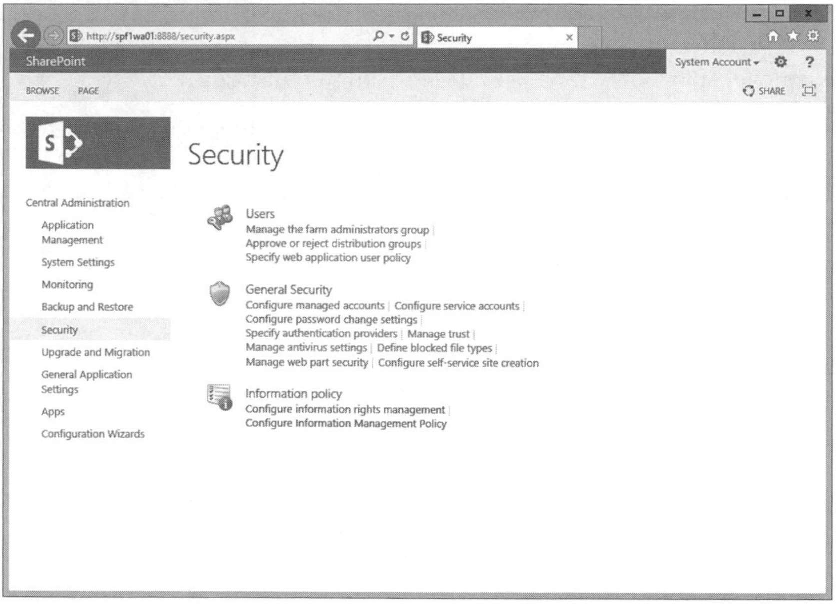

FIGURE 6.22 Viewing the security items in SPCA.

Users

Within the first category on the Security page, labeled Users, all security settings related to not only users, but also specific user groups, are listed. This includes the following:

- **Manage the Farm Administrators Group:** Enables full farm administrators to be defined.
- **Approve or Reject Distribution Groups:** Distribution groups automatically added by the Directory Management Service are listed in this area if the farm is configured to require administrator approval for new distribution groups. The Directory Management Service is enabled from within the incoming email settings in SPCA.
- **Specify Web Application User Policy:** Permission for an individual user or group to override security within a web application can be set in this area. For example, the Search Crawling Account can be configured to have read access to all content within the entire web application to enable it to be crawled.

General Security

Within the second category on the Security page, labeled General Security, all other security settings that don't fit into either the first or third category are listed, including the following:

- **Configure Managed Accounts:** This area is highly useful for SharePoint admins, because it allows for the concept of a managed account to be configured. A managed account is a service account that can be set to automatically have its password changed, as shown in Figure 6.23. Managed accounts can be set for all SharePoint service accounts, such as the Crawl account, Search account, accounts for service applications, and application pool identity accounts.

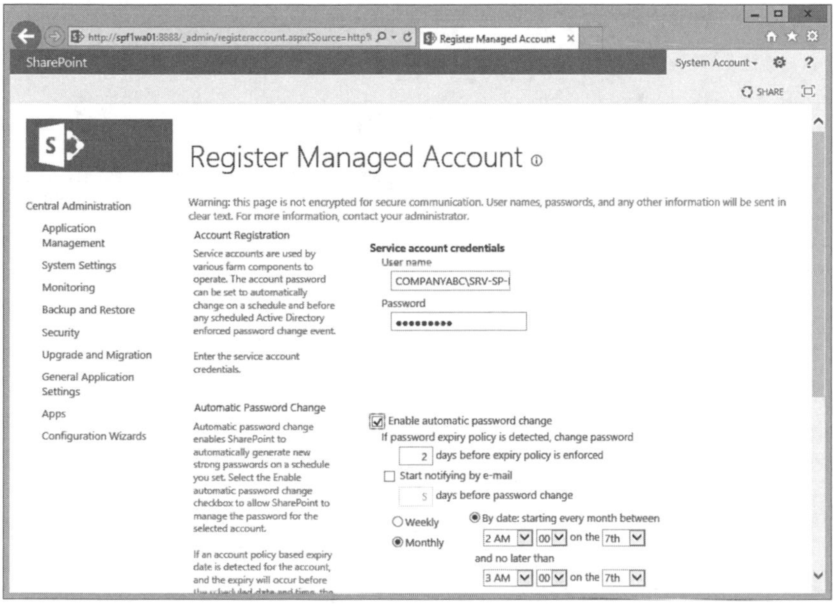

FIGURE 6.23 Creating a new managed account in SPCA.

- **Configure Service Accounts:** Enables specific services in Windows Server to be updated with the credentials of a specific managed account used as the service account. This enables services that run with the credentials of a user to be automatically updated per best practices.

- **Configure Password Change Settings:** Enables administrators to determine what the individual settings for password changes are, such as who is notified via email of the changes and how many seconds to wait before notifying services of the change.

- **Specify Authentication Providers:** Enable administrators to define more than one authentication directory to use to gain access to SharePoint content, as shown in Figure 6.24. This complex topic is covered in great detail in Chapter 13, "Deploying SharePoint for Extranets and Alternative Authentication Scenarios."

- **Manage Trust:** Within this area, different farms can be "trusted," allowing for their content to be intermingled with the farm and allowing for sharing of information between the farms. The trust relationships to other farms must be set up using Public Key Infrastructure (PKI) certificates and requires a common trusted root certificate when creating the trust, as shown in Figure 6.25. Trusts are required to consume information from another farm.

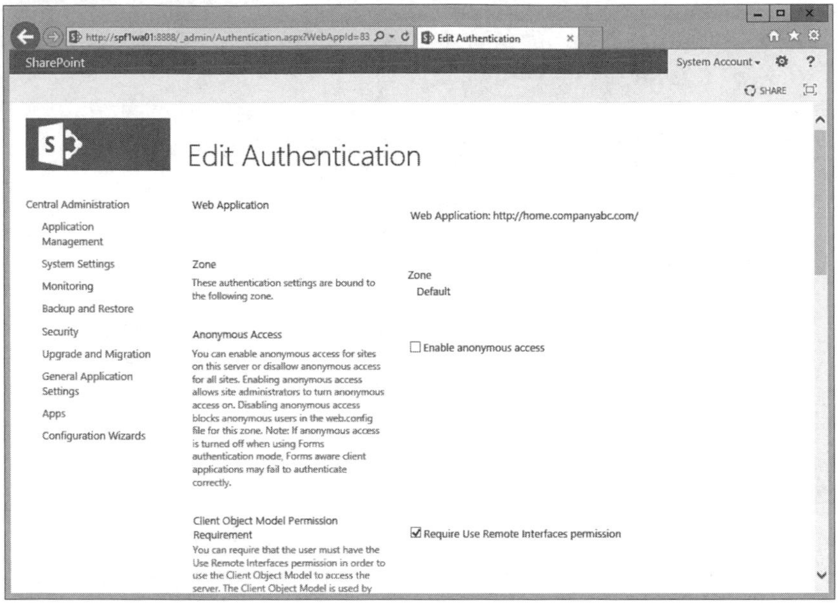

FIGURE 6.24 Modifying authentication providers.

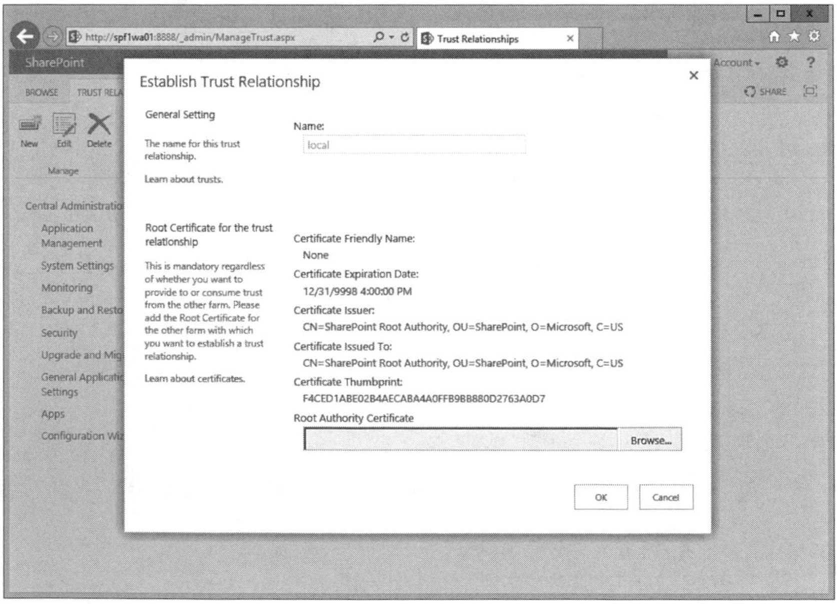

FIGURE 6.25 Adding a trust to a different farm.

- **Manage Antivirus Settings:** Antivirus settings are provided in SPCA as part of the built-in antivirus application programming interface (API). Note that just because the API is there does not mean that antivirus functionality is available out-of-the-box. To enable antivirus, a supported antivirus product must be installed. For more information on the antivirus settings in SharePoint and using antivirus products for SharePoint, see Chapter 14.
- **Define Blocked File Types:** The default list of file type extensions that are blocked in SharePoint is defined in this area. You can modify this as necessary.
- **Manage Web Part Security:** The security settings related to web parts, such as whether users can create connections between web parts, are listed in this area.
- **Configure Self-Service Site Creation:** Also linked to from the Application Management area of SPCA, this enables specific users with the proper rights to create their own subsites.

Information Policy

Within the third category on the Security page, labeled Information Policy, information about enabling Information Rights Management (IRM) to enable document libraries to be secured using Active Directory Rights Management Services (AD RMS) is provided. For more information on IRM in SharePoint and AD RMS, see Chapter 17.

- **Configure Information Rights Management:** Enables IRM settings to be enabled or disabled within SharePoint, depending on whether AD RMS is already deployed within the AD forest or whether SharePoint should manually address the server or get the information from a published service connection point (SCP) in AD, as shown in Figure 6.26.
- **Configure Information Management Policy:** You can define individual IRM policies for SharePoint, such as policies for labels, barcodes, auditing, and retention, within this area.

Reviewing Upgrade and Migration Settings in SPCA

The Upgrade and Migration page in SPCA, as shown in Figure 6.27, contains all settings related to an upgrade of SharePoint and also includes some links to useful information such as the patch status of systems in a farm. For detailed information on upgrading or migrating to SharePoint 2013, see Chapter 5, "Migrating from SharePoint 2010 to SharePoint 2013."

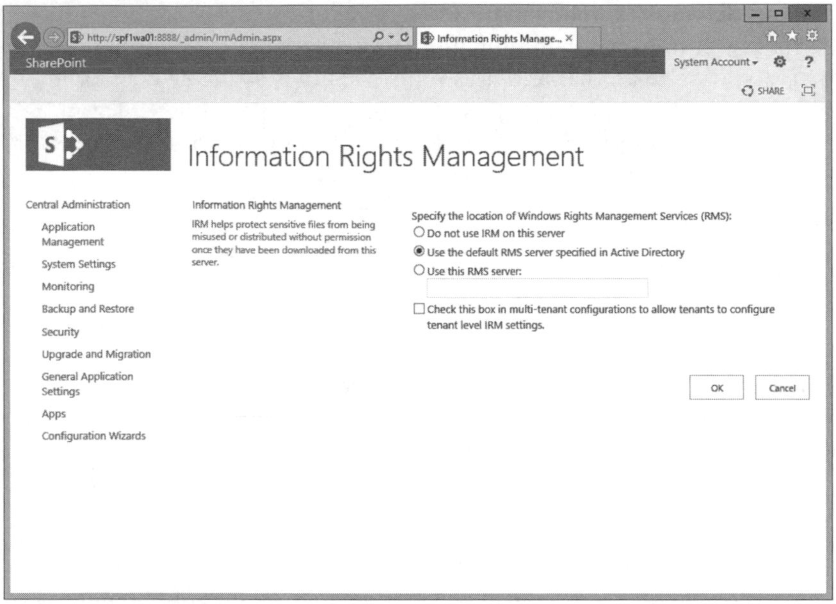

FIGURE 6.26 Configuring IRM settings in SPCA.

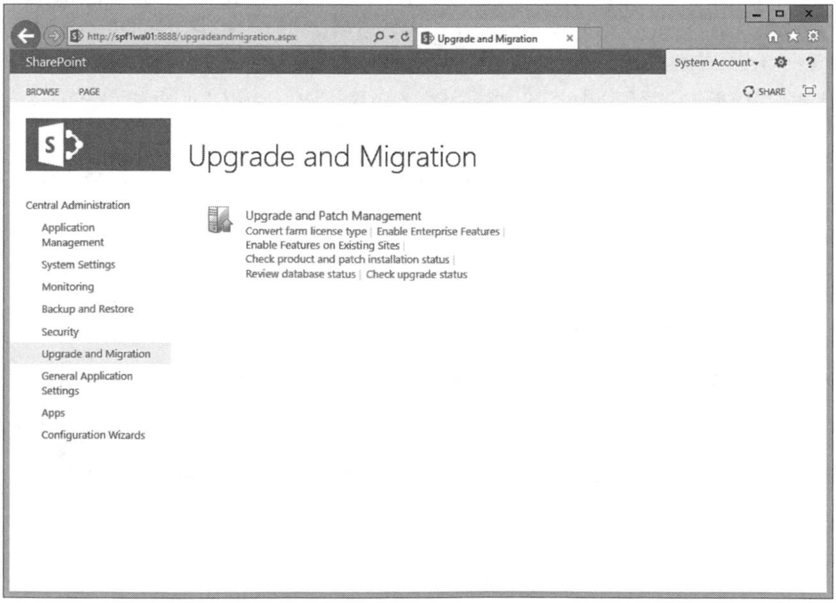

FIGURE 6.27 Viewing the upgrade and migration options in SPCA.

Upgrade and Patch Management

Within the only category on the Upgrade and Migration page, labeled Upgrade and Patch Management, the following links are included:

- **Convert Farm License Type:** Enables sites to input a license key to upgrade them from a standard license key to an enterprise license key, which would give them access to enterprise features in SharePoint 2013.
- **Enable Enterprise Features:** When an enterprise key has been enabled, enterprise features can be enabled from within this area. For a farm with an enterprise key enabled from the beginning, these settings are grayed out (dimmed).
- **Enable Features on Existing Sites:** For sites that were provisioned with standard edition features, the enterprise feature set can be enabled on them from within this area.
- **Check Product and Patch Installation Status:** This area, shown in Figure 6.28, provides useful information on the exact version number of all components on individual servers.

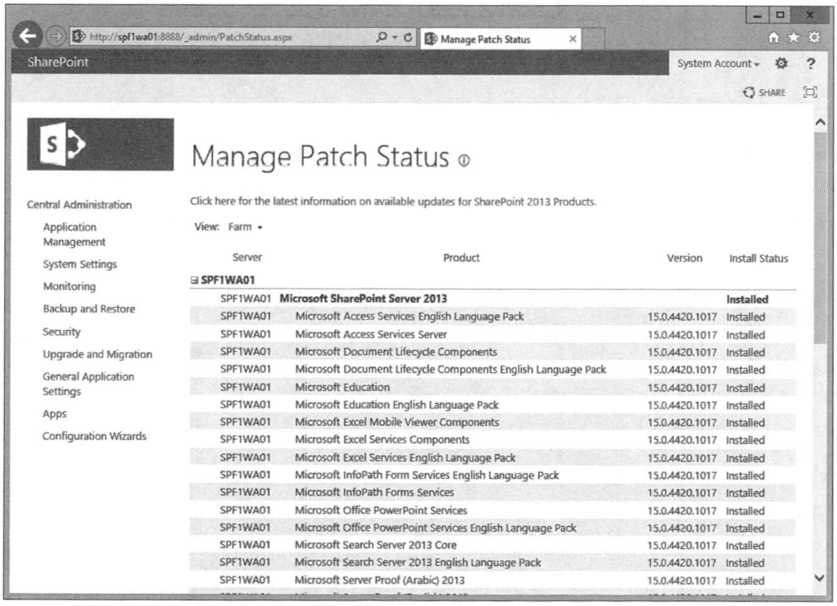

FIGURE 6.28 Checking patch status in SPCA.

- **Review Database Status:** This area, useful only during a database-attach upgrade, enables administrators to check on the upgrade status of individual databases.
- **Check Upgrade Status:** This final area is only used during an upgrade and is used to monitor the status of existing upgrade sessions.

Reviewing General Application Settings in SPCA

The General Application Settings page in SPCA, as shown in Figure 6.29, is perhaps the most complex of the various areas within SPCA. It includes all other settings in SPCA that didn't fit well into other categories, such as Content Deployment, Site Directory, InfoPath Forms Services, and others.

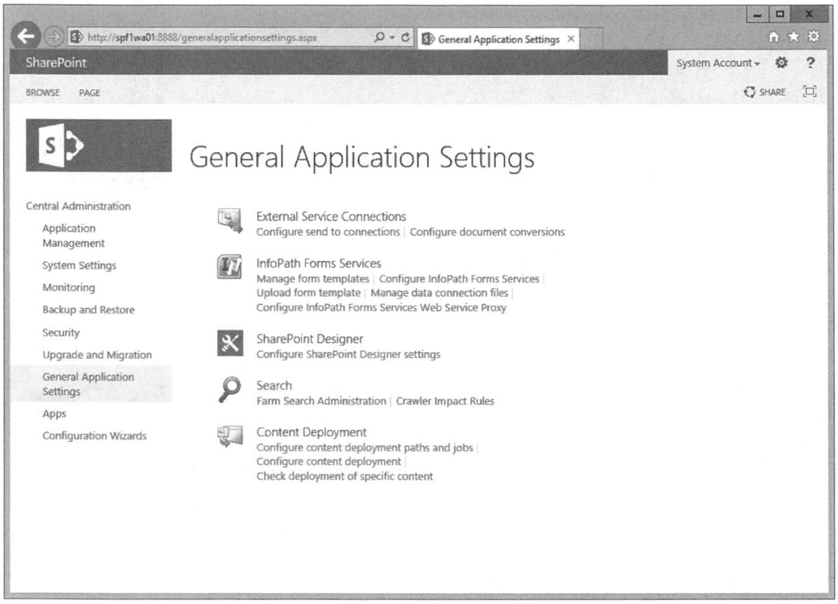

FIGURE 6.29 Viewing the general application settings in SPCA.

External Service Connections

Within the first category on the General Application Settings page, labeled External Service Connections, the following links are included:

- **Configure Send to Connections:** Enables administrators to choose whether to allow hosted site subscriptions to set up connections to sites outside their subscription. These settings are done on a per web application basis.
- **Configure Document Conversions:** As shown in Figure 6.30, enables administrators to define whether documents such as InfoPath forms, Word documents, or XML pages can be converted to HTML pages so that they can be viewed by browsers. A document conversions server must first be set up from within the Services on Servers area of SPCA for this to work properly.

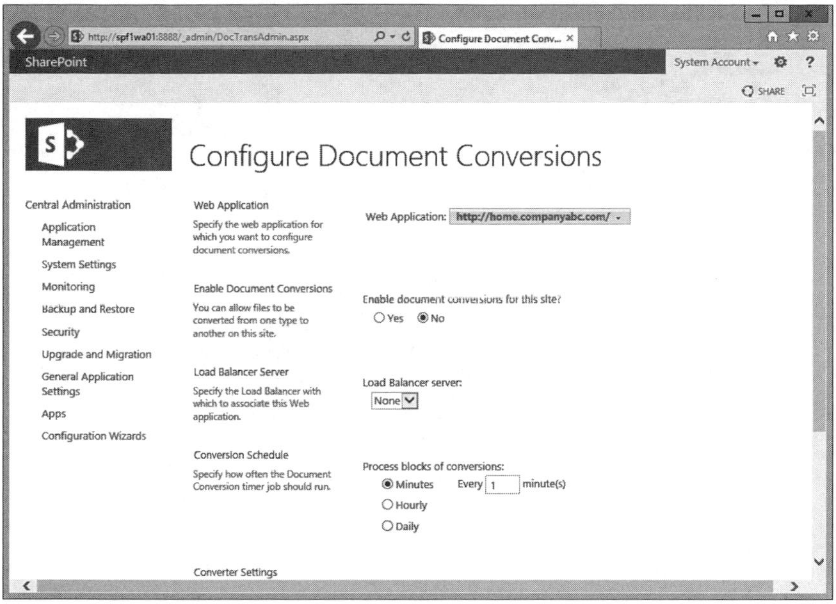

FIGURE 6.30 Configuring the document conversions service.

InfoPath Forms Services

Within the second category on the General Application Settings page, labeled InfoPath Forms Services, all settings related to InfoPath Forms Services, a valuable tool that allows for custom forms to be created and used in SharePoint, are discussed. This includes the following settings:

- **Manage Form Templates:** Displays the default form templates used by InfoPath Forms Services, such as the ones shown in Figure 6.31.
- **Configure InfoPath Forms Services:** Settings unique to InfoPath Forms Services can be configured from within this area of SPCA, including whether the service is enabled for use by users within the farm.
- **Upload Form Template:** New form templates can be uploaded using this area of SPCA.
- **Manage Data Connection Files:** Data connection files used with InfoPath can be uploaded using this interface.
- **Configure InfoPath Forms Services Web Service Proxy:** If a proxy is used between InfoPath Forms Services forms and web services, this functionality can be enabled in this area.

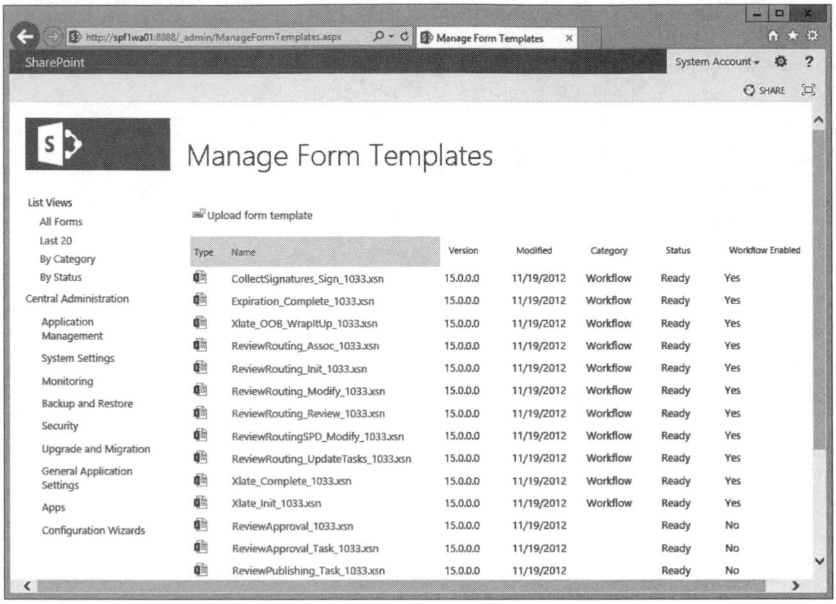

FIGURE 6.31 Using default form templates for InfoPath Forms Services.

SharePoint Designer

Within the third category on the General Application Settings page, labeled SharePoint Designer, a single link is included, as follows:

- **Configure SharePoint Designer Settings:** This area, shown in Figure 6.32, allows for SharePoint Designer access to be turned on or off for an individual site collection. Because SharePoint Designer is quite powerful and can cause problems for the uninitiated, some administrators turn it off, at least initially.

Search

Within the next category on the General Application Settings page, simply labeled Search, Search administration settings can be accessed, including the following:

- **Farm Search Administration:** Focuses on setting up the individual content deployment jobs and paths used by those jobs.
- **Crawler Impact Rules:** This setting takes administrators to a page shown in Figure 6.33, where content deployment can be enabled or disabled for the farm.

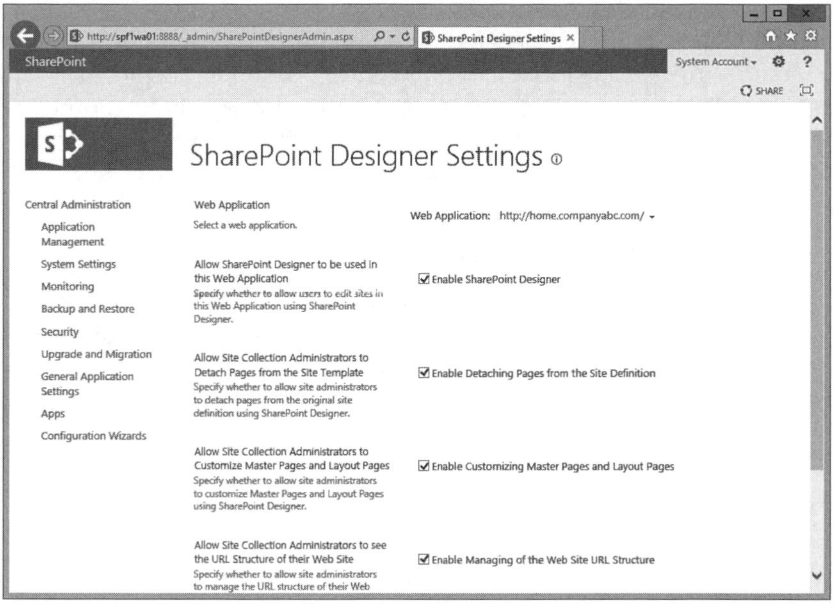

FIGURE 6.32 Enabling SharePoint Designer access within a web application.

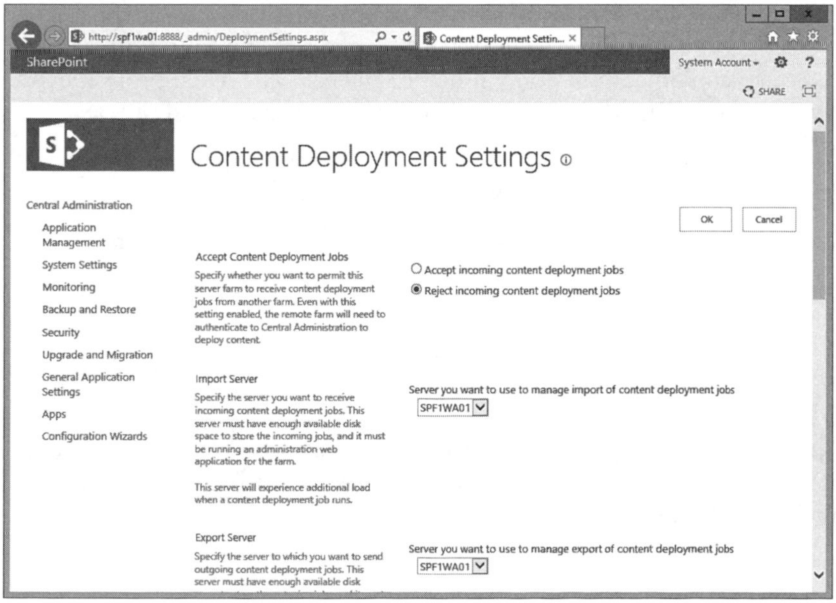

FIGURE 6.33 Enabling content deployment.

Content Deployments

Within the fifth and final category on the General Application Settings page, labeled Content Deployment, all settings related to Microsoft's concept of content deployment are listed. Content deployment is a one-way push of site content from one farm to another, usually done to publish content from internal farms to extranet farms or to push content out to remote locations. The settings related to content deployment in SPCA include the following:

- **Configure Content Deployment Paths and Jobs:** Focuses on setting up the individual content deployment jobs and paths used by those jobs.
- **Configure Content Deployment:** This setting takes administrators to a page shown in Figure 6.33, where content deployment can be enabled or disabled for the farm.
- **Check Deployment of Specific Content:** Used to check on the status of content deployment jobs.

Managing SharePoint Apps in SPCA

A new administrative page that has been added in SharePoint 2013 is the Apps page; now administrators can allow for SharePoint apps to be installed into a site to provide for specific functionality, much in the way that mobile device app stores allow isolated apps to be installed on devices.

SharePoint apps in a farm rely on configuration and customization of both an App Management service application and the Subscription Settings service application, as well as creation of a dedicated app domain in domain name server (DNS). When provisioned, the SharePoint app settings can be administered from SharePoint Central Admin, as shown in Figure 6.34.

You can find the following settings related to SharePoint apps on this page:

- **Purchase Apps:** This setting allows for new apps to be purchased in the farm.
- **Manage App Licenses:** Takes administrators to a page that allows for management of the licenses for each app.
- **Configure Store Settings:** This setting allows administrators to determine what apps users can purchase/request.
- **Manage App Catalog:** The App Catalog is a SharePoint site that can be created that allows users to browse the app store and request specific apps to be installed. It can be created from the Manage App Catalog link, as shown in Figure 6.35.
- **Monitor Apps:** This area of SPCA relies on the Search service and allows for the SharePoint app store to be monitored.
- **Configure App URLs:** This area allows for the URLs associated with the SharePoint app domain to be specified/modified.
- **App Permissions:** The App Permissions page allows administrators to define which users have rights to which SharePoint apps.

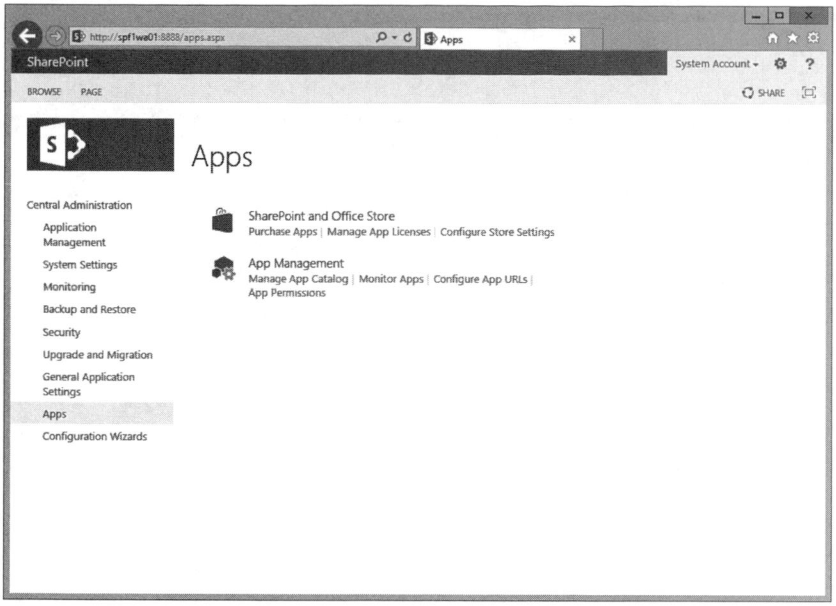

FIGURE 6.34 Administering SharePoint apps in SPCA.

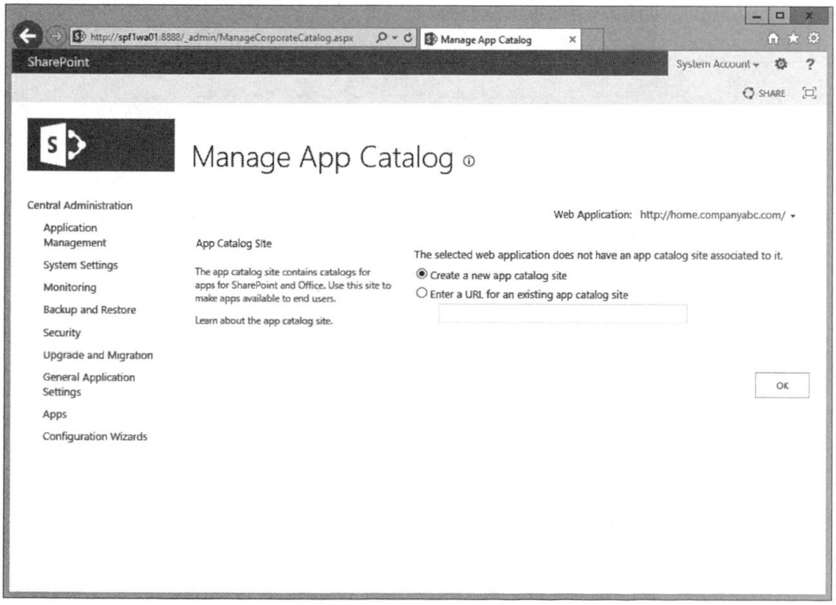

FIGURE 6.35 Creating a new App Catalog site.

Using the Configuration Wizards' Page in SPCA

The final page in SPCA, as shown in Figure 6.36, has one link, which takes administrators to the wizard they can use to configure the SharePoint farm for the first time or to enable individual service applications. This wizard is covered in more detail in Chapter 3, "Installing a Simple SharePoint Server 2013 Farm."

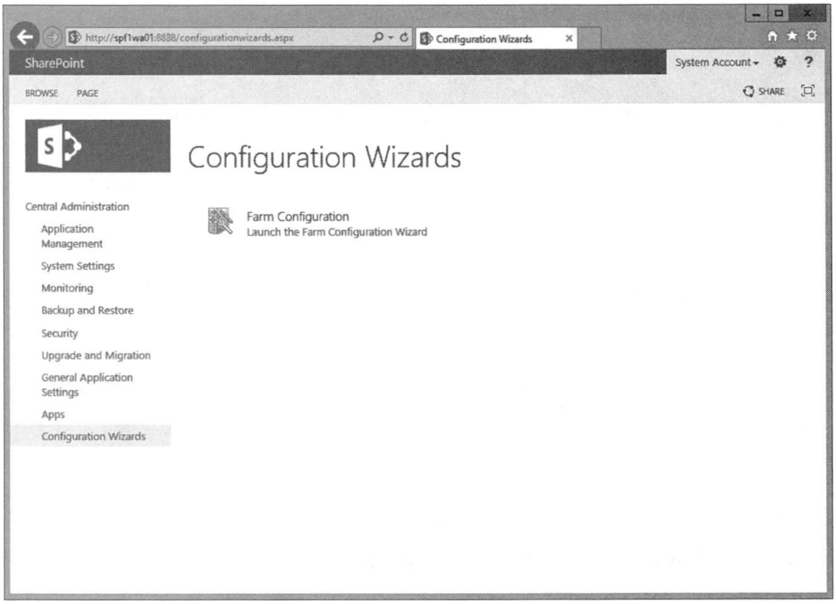

FIGURE 6.36 Viewing the SPCA launch link for the Farm Configuration Wizard.

Generally speaking, you should avoid the use of this Farm Configuration Wizard and instead use PowerShell scripting to create farm elements, a concept explored in more detail in Chapter 4, "Advanced SharePoint 2013 Installation and Scalability."

Administering Site Collections and Sites

Administration of individual site collections differs from administration of the back end of SharePoint. Indeed, Microsoft broke these two administrative tasks into two areas to enable the site collections to be administered by the people "closer to the ground" with SharePoint, usually the ones who use it on a regular basis for document management and collaboration.

These administrators can perform their own set of administration tasks that affects only their specific site collections. The administrative tasks that they can perform are outlined in the next section of the chapter and apply to site collections created within SharePoint Foundation or full SharePoint Server 2013. These sets of administration options, as shown in Figure 6.37, are not visible to standard site members who do not have admin access to the site but are available to each site administrator, by clicking the Settings Gear and selecting Site Settings.

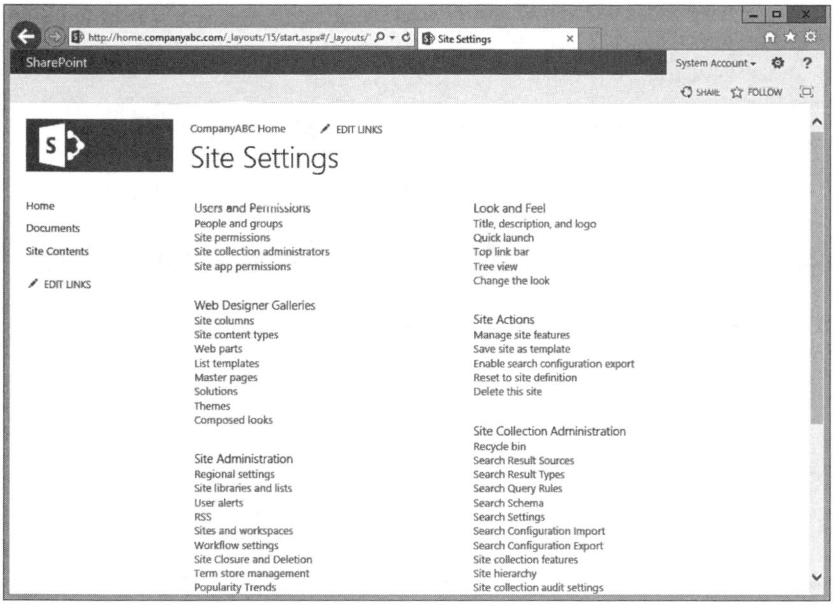

FIGURE 6.37 Administering SharePoint sites.

Each administrative task is organized within the Site Settings tool by category, with categories such as Users and Permissions and Look and Feel. For more information on administration of site collections and site settings, see Chapter 21, "Designing and Managing Pages and Sites for Knowledge Workers."

Using Additional Administration Tools for SharePoint

Although the vast number of administrative tools are stored within either the SharePoint Central Admin tool or individual site settings administration, SharePoint administrators can use some additional tools to fully administer a SharePoint environment. These include the critical PowerShell scripting tool, the legacy command-line STSADM tool, and specialty admin tools such as the IIS Manager and SQL Server Management Studio.

Command-Line Administration of SharePoint Using the STSADM Tool

The STSADM tool has a long history with SharePoint products and technologies. Indeed, the acronym itself refers to SharePoint Team Services (STS) administration, which was the 1.0 version name of the SharePoint Foundation product, originally released with an older version of the FrontPage (now SharePoint Designer) web authoring tool.

With SharePoint 2013, the STSADM tool is still used and supported, but Microsoft is switching focus of command-line administration to its PowerShell tool, which now supports hundreds of commandlets specifically built just for SharePoint. Administrators should first learn how to use PowerShell before using STSADM because it is the preferred method of administering SharePoint. You can find more information on PowerShell administration for SharePoint in Chapter 7.

It's not intuitive to find the STSADM tool, unfortunately, because it is buried in the C:\Program Files\Common Files\Microsoft Shared\web server extensions\15\BIN folder on a SharePoint server, where C:\ is the drive where SharePoint was installed.

TIP

It is convenient to add the C:\Program Files\Common Files\Microsoft Shared\web server extensions\15\BIN folder to the `PATH` statement on a SharePoint server so that STSADM can be run from any location in the command prompt window.

STSADM can create sites, delete sites, back up sites, restore sites, add users, remove users, change timer job intervals, change roles, and perform many other tasks. You should review the entire list of options available.

Working with the Internet Information Services Manager Tool

Occasionally, some administration of the IIS application is required that cannot be performed using the SharePoint Central Admin tool. This includes installing the SSL certificates and changing authentication settings. The IIS Manager tool, as shown in Figure 6.38, can be used for this functionality and can be invoked by clicking Start, All Programs, Administrative Tools, and Internet Information Services (IIS) Manager.

Some SharePoint administration tasks can be performed only from within IIS Manager, including IP address assignment for web applications, SSL certificates, bindings, and some authentication settings. Therefore, it is critical to become familiar with this tool for administration of a SharePoint 2013 environment.

SQL Server Administration for SharePoint

Administration of the SharePoint databases needs to be performed using SQL Server Management Studio with SQL Server 2008 R2 or SQL Server 2012. The SQL Server Management Studio, shown in Figure 6.39, is discussed in more detail in Chapter 9, "Managing and Maintaining SQL Server in a SharePoint Environment."

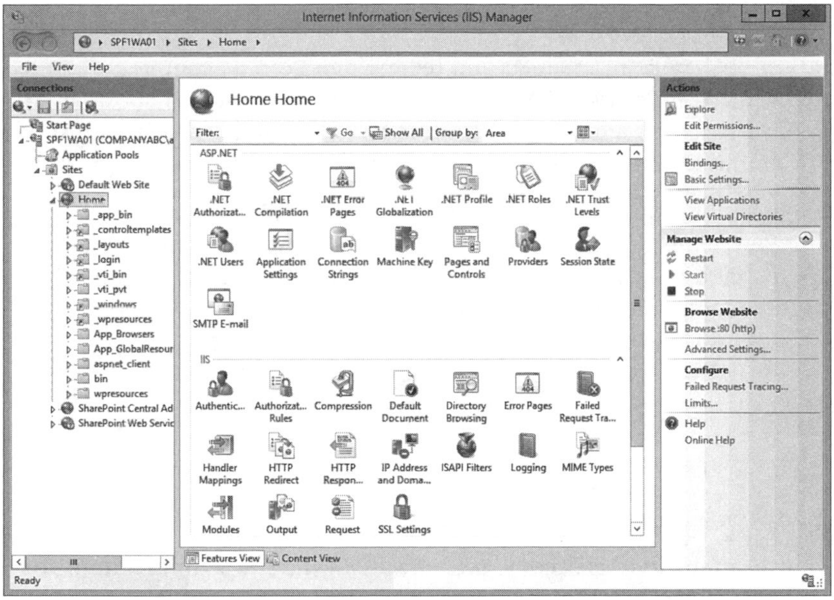

FIGURE 6.38 Administering SharePoint using IIS Manager.

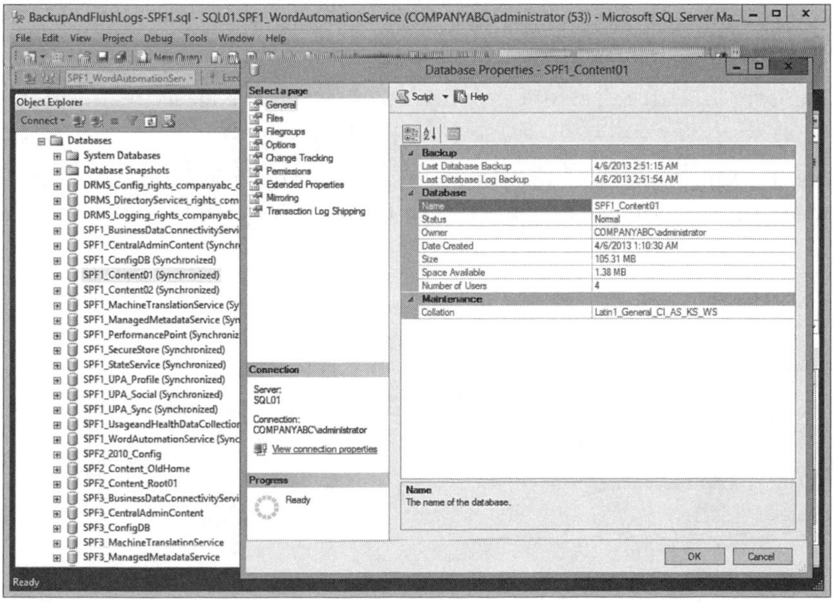

FIGURE 6.39 Administering SharePoint using SQL Server Management Studio.

Summary

Because administration of SharePoint products and technologies can be complex, Microsoft has centralized a vast number of administrative functions into a small number of highly powerful tools. Familiarity with these tools, and in particular with the SharePoint Central Administration tool, is therefore a must for a SharePoint administrator.

In addition to the SharePoint Central Administration tool, powerful command-line administration using PowerShell and the legacy STSADM tool is available, and database and IIS-specific administration tools provide for additional administrative functionality. Through the use of these tools, administration of a SharePoint environment becomes more streamlined and capable.

Best Practices

The following are best practices from this chapter:

- Become familiar with all the tasks in the SharePoint Central Administration tool.
- Let individual site administrators become more aware of the site settings administration options available in each site.
- Become very familiar with PowerShell; many administrative tasks can only be performed with it.
- Consider the use of auto-site deletion for stale sites to reduce the overhead on the environment generated by unused sites.
- Use the IIS Manager tool for SSL certificate generation and to change authentication settings on individual IIS websites used by web applications in SharePoint.
- Use PowerShell for command-line administration, and use the legacy STSADM tool only for specific scenarios when legacy command-line functionality is needed.

CHAPTER 7

Leveraging PowerShell for Command-Line SharePoint Administration and Automation

IN THIS CHAPTER

- Understanding Windows PowerShell
- SharePoint Administration with PowerShell
- Using Scripts to Automate SharePoint Administration
- Understanding Advanced PowerShell Topics
- Beyond Built-In SharePoint PowerShell Cmdlets
- Tools for PowerAdmins

Microsoft originally developed Windows PowerShell in 2003 as an automation-scripting engine to help administrators use various products across the Microsoft stack. Unlike other command-line tools that accept and return text, PowerShell works with .NET Framework objects, which enables it to be more flexible for administration of bulk changes and automation.

With the release of SharePoint 2010, Microsoft released 500+ PowerShell commandlets (cmdlets) designed to help automate and administrate SharePoint environments. Microsoft has added further emphasis on PowerShell in SharePoint 2013 as well, adding additional cmdlets that provide for enhanced command-line administration of a SharePoint environment. Indeed, SharePoint 2013 administration is positioned as PowerShell-first rather than graphical user interface (GUI)-first, and many tasks can only be performed from the command line. It is subsequently critical that SharePoint administrators have at least a basic understanding of PowerShell and how to use it to administer a SharePoint farm.

This chapter introduces PowerShell to SharePoint administrators. It focuses first on a general overview of how PowerShell works, and then branches off to demonstrate how specific PowerShell cmdlets can automate and administer SharePoint. Specific examples of common SharePoint administration tasks in PowerShell are included, and download links for the examples are provided.

Understanding Windows PowerShell

Before understanding how to use PowerShell to manage SharePoint, an administrator must first understand how PowerShell functions and must conceptualize the concepts used with PowerShell.

Getting Started with Windows PowerShell

PowerShell is available on all new Microsoft operating systems, and administrators can begin learning PowerShell even when SharePoint 2013 is not installed. To make sure that the latest version of PowerShell is installed, check the Microsoft PowerShell scripting center (http://technet.microsoft.com/en-us/scriptcenter/default.aspx). All the examples in this book were written with PowerShell 3.0.

To start working with PowerShell, just click the PowerShell icon on the taskbar. This starts the PowerShell shell that you can use for typing PowerShell commands and executing scripts. Figure 7.1 shows the default PowerShell shell.

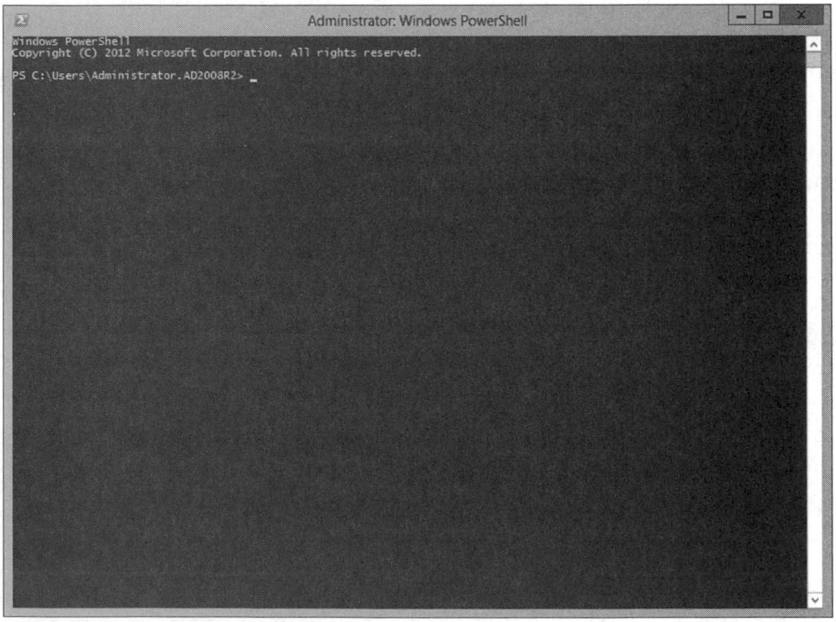

FIGURE 7.1 Viewing the default PowerShell shell on Windows Server 2012.

On a computer with SharePoint installed, a SharePoint 2013-branded PowerShell shell with preloaded SharePoint cmdlets is installed. To start this shell, do the following:

- On Windows 2008 R2, go to Start, All Programs, Microsoft SharePoint 2013 Products, SharePoint 2013 Management Shell.
- On Windows 2012, type **SharePoint 2013 Management Shell** to start the shell from the Start menu.

Using PowerShell to Display "Hello Shell!"

A common task performed when learning a new language is how to display "Hello World!" Creating such an application with PowerShell is simple. Type the following into a shell (You can omit lines starting with #. Everything after # is a comment.) and press Enter:

```
# To comment in PowerShell use a Hash tag followed by your comments.
Write-Host "Hello Shell!" # you can also put comments after your command
```

PowerShell scripts can also be saved to a file and executed. Save this Hello Shell example to HelloShell.ps1. Use the standard command-line `cd` command to navigate to the folder in which HelloWorld.ps1 is saved. To execute the script, type the following to the shell:

```
.\HelloShell.ps1
```

Using the Integrated Scripting Environment

PowerShell comes with an integrated scripting environment to ease the creation and testing of scripts and functions. The scripting environment is available in Start, All Programs, Windows PowerShell 3.0, Windows PowerShell ISE (Integrated Scripting Environment; search from Start menu on Windows 2012). PowerShell ISE is shown in Figure 7.2. This newly updated tool color codes your scripts, includes integrated debugger and IntelliSense, and has a Help Wizard to help construct scripts.

Before running any PowerShell cmdlets, make sure that you have loaded the appropriate snap-in (not required if you start SharePoint 2013 Management Shell). The following code checks if SnapIn has been loaded and loads it if necessary:

```
if((Get-PSSnapin | Where {$_.Name -eq "Microsoft.SharePoint.PowerShell"})
 -eq $null) {
Add-PSSnapin Microsoft.SharePoint.PowerShell;
}
```

Site Collections, Sites, and Webs

Cmdlets for SharePoint implement a different naming convention from the one used in the user interface (UI). Table 7.1 shows the names of the most important SharePoint user UI objects and the names of their respective GUI objects. The naming conventions in the PowerShell are the same as in server-side application programming interfaces (APIs).

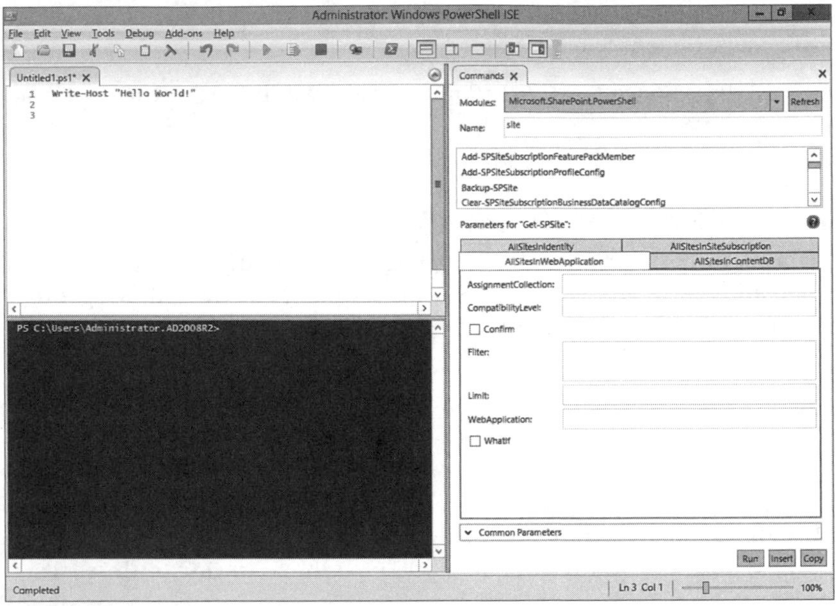

FIGURE 7.2 Viewing the Hello World example from within the PowerShell-integrated scripting environment. The Commands Help Wizard is located on the right side of the screen, and it lists all the SharePoint-related cmdlets.

TABLE 7.1 Overview of the Most Important SharePoint Objects Naming Conventions

Object Name in UI	Object Name in PowerShell
Farm	`SPFarm`
Web Application	`SPWebApplication`
Site Collection	`SPSite`
Site	`SPWeb`

Most of the examples in this chapter reference the preceding given objects, and you need to understand the difference between the two naming conventions.

The SharePoint Software Development Kit

PowerShell is a technology designed for IT professionals managing IT systems. However, the management of SharePoint is much easier if administrators are familiar with the SharePoint 2013 software development kit (SDK): Administrators should understand how SharePoint functions under the hood so that they know which objects enable them to retrieve certain properties.

`Get-Command` and `Get-Help`

PowerShell comes with numerous cmdlets. Microsoft released more than 800 just for SharePoint, and this number grows with each new release or service pack. Memorizing all these commands would be a challenge.

Two cmdlets come to the rescue and help administrators understand what the individual cmdlets are. Type the following in your SharePoint PowerShell shell:

```
Get-Command
```

This command lists all available SharePoint commands. Because there are so many cmdlets, they cannot fit on one screen. To check only specific sets of commands related with one object—for example, `Site`—type the following:

```
Get-Command *Site*
```

The preceding command lists all SharePoint cmdlets that have `Site` in their name. Depending on your SharePoint version, you will probably get the results shown in Figure 7.3 (or similar results).

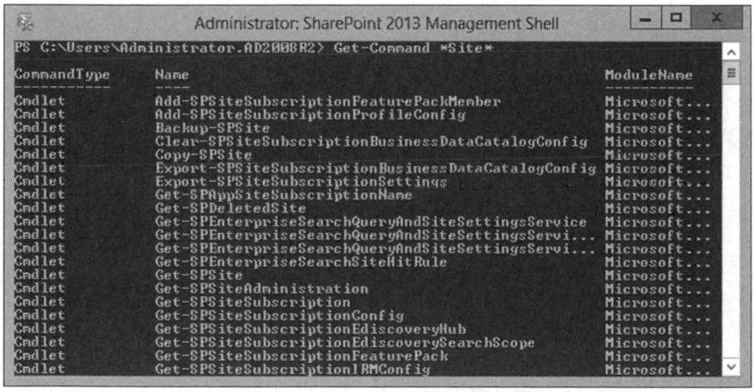

FIGURE 7.3 Viewing the results of `Get-Command` cmdlet in SharePoint 2013 Management Shell.

As you can see, commands usually start with a verb (`get`, `set`, `backup`, and so on) and end with a noun. All the commands listed in Figure 7.3 enable you to work with SharePoint sites collections either for retrieving properties (`Get-` commands) or modifying site collection properties with `Set-` commands.

Most SharePoint commands require input before you can run them. If you run a command without all the required properties, you are prompted to enter these. To familiarize yourself with a PowerShell cmdlet, type the following:

```
Get-Help Get-SPSite
```

This command can give you detailed help for the `Get-SPSite` cmdlet. You can also type the preceding command with the following `-examples` or `-detailed` parameters to check out more info on this command. These SharePoint cmdlets are well documented and provide a great learning starting point.

If you already have different scripts written for SharePoint 2010, in most cases, these will work with SharePoint 2013. However, Microsoft removed a number of cmdlets for these services that were ether re-architected (Search) or removed (Web Analytics), so double-check old scripts against a SharePoint 2013 test farm.

The First SharePoint Cmdlet

The easiest way to start working with SharePoint cmdlets is to start the SharePoint 2013 Management Shell. On a computer with SharePoint 2013 installed, go to Start, All Programs, Microsoft SharePoint 2013 Products, SharePoint 2013 Management Shell. After the shell loads, type the following command into the command prompt:

```
Get-SPSite
```

The preceding command lists all site collections in the current SharePoint farm. Figure 7.4 shows sample results.

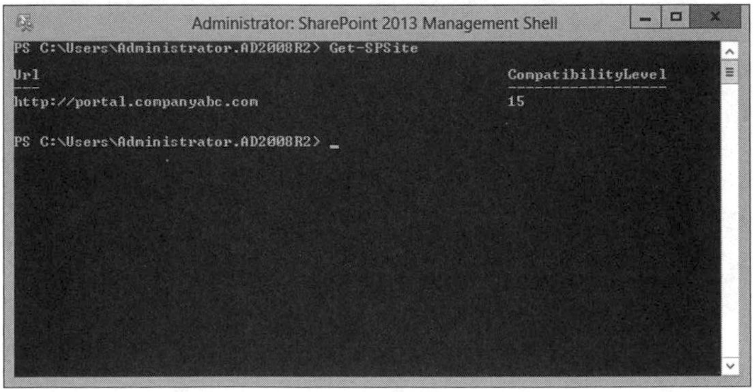

FIGURE 7.4 `Get-SPSite` cmdlet displays a list of SharePoint site collection URLs.

Verbs and Nouns

Every built-in PowerShell cmdlet is composed of a verb and noun (Verb-Noun)—for example, `Get-SPSite`. The verb part of a cmdlet indicates an operation that will be performed, and the noun indicates the object on which the operation will be performed. The `Get-SPSite` command gets an `SPSite` object (SharePoint site collection object).

The other common PowerShell operations (verbs) are `Set-` (modifies object), `Remove-` (deletes object), and `New-` (creates a new object).

Most SharePoint cmdlets come with these four verb-noun combinations. However, some objects might have more or fewer cmdlets depending on the object type—for example, the `SPSite` object also comes with `Backup-`, `Move-`, `Restore-`, `Test-`, `Copy-`, `Repair`, and `Upgrade` cmdlets.

Working with Variables, Function, and Cmdlets

You can use PowerShell variables to store results from any executed command. The following example demonstrates how to use variables:

```
$SiteCollection = Get-SPSite "http://portal.companyabc.com"
$SiteCollection.Url
$SiteCollection.Owner
```

The preceding given command saves site collection (from http://portal.companyabc.com) to a variable `$SiteCollection`; the variable can then be used to retrieve properties. The preceding example shows how to retrieve `Url` and `Owner` properties and display them in the shell.

The value stored to `$SiteCollection` is a SharePoint-specific .NET Framework object (SPSite) and exposes all available properties as in any other .NET language.

PowerShell Command Piping

In real life, people use pipes to transfer goods (for example, oil) from one end to another. PowerShell pipes are similar because they enable you to easily transform, modify, or pass the result of one cmdlet to another.

Suppose, for example, that we want to list all site collections in a SharePoint farm. The `Get-SPSite` cmdlet displays all the site collections, but in large farms it might return hundreds or thousands of results. If `Get-SPSite` is combined with a filter command (over pipe), it returns only specific site collections that require attention:

```
Get-SPSite | Where {$_.Url -eq "http://portal.companyabc.com"}
```

By using the pipe (|), we see results (all site collections) of the `Get-SPSite` cmdlet that are passed to the `Where` pipe, which dictates that only site collections whose URL equals (operator `-eq`) to http://portal.companyabc.com are released to the next cmdlet in the pipeline.

The preceding example has only one pipe, but additional pipes could be used:

```
Get-SPSite | Where {$_.Url -like "*portal*"} | Sort RootWeb | Select
RootWeb, Url
```

The preceding command lists all the site collections that contain (operator `-like`) the word `portal` in their URL and then sorts them by `RootWeb` property and displays the results in table format with two columns, `RootWeb` and `Url`.

Figure 7.5 shows the results of running the preceding code in the SharePoint 2013 Management Shell.

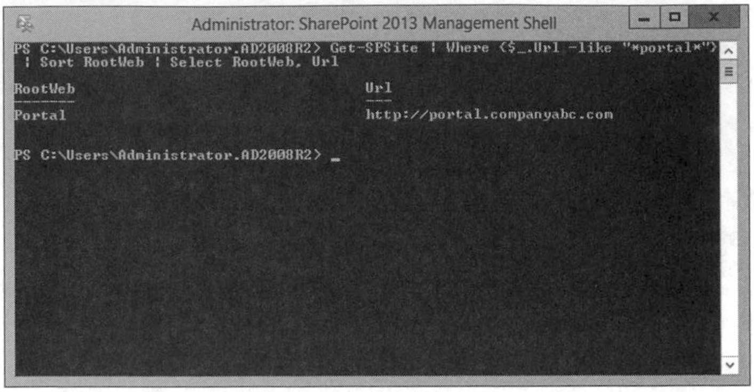

FIGURE 7.5 Examining a PowerShell statement that returns a list of site collections with the word `portal` in the URL.

Formatting Results

Results retrieved from PowerShell cmdlets are usually displayed in a tabular form but can be further customized by adding the `format` command. Typical `format` commands are `Format-List`, `Format-Table`, and `Format-Wide`:

```
Get-SPSite | Select RootWeb, Url, Owner | Format-Table
```

The preceding command lists all the site collections and displays results in table format. (We selected `RootWeb`, `Url`, and `Owner` properties of site collection to be displayed in the table.)

In addition to formatting results, you can choose a different output destination than a default one (shell screen). One of the useful output destinations is `GridView`. (A PowerShell-integrated scripting environment must be installed to use it.)

```
Get-SPSolution | Select * | Out-GridView
```

The preceding command displays all installed SharePoint solutions in a `GridView` format, as shown in Figure 7.6. If you do not have installed solutions, you could combine `Out-GridView` with other cmdlets, such as `Get-SPSite`.

What's New in PowerShell 3.0

SharePoint 2013 Management Shell works on top of PowerShell 3.0, an enhanced version of PowerShell. The benefits introduced in the new version are general, but SharePoint admins will benefit because day-to-day operations should be easier.

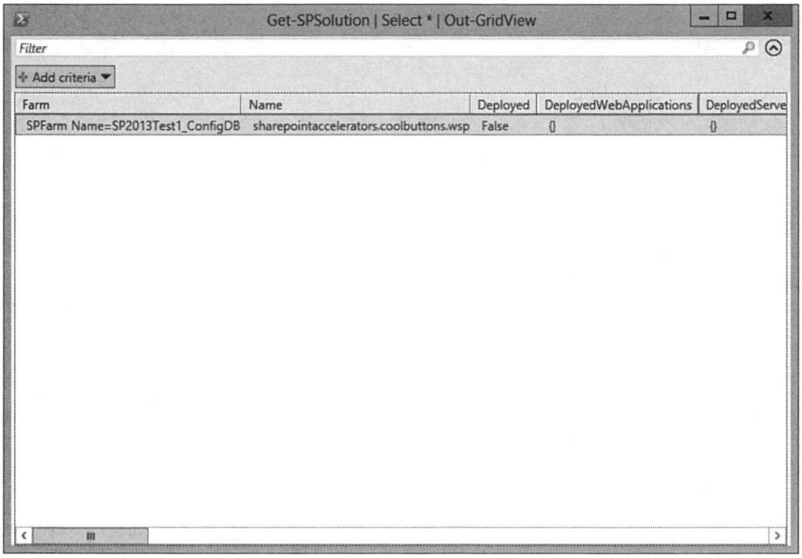

FIGURE 7.6 Displaying results of PowerShell cmdlet in a `GridView` format.

The most important new features in PowerShell 3.0 include the following:

- **Simplified syntax for `Where-Object` and `ForEach-Object`:** Writing PowerShell syntax can be challenging for a novice administrator, so Microsoft introduced changes that allow administrators to write more "natural" commands. The following example shows how to list all the site collections with SharePoint 2013 (v15) compatibility level:

```
Get-SPSite | Where CompatibilityLevel -eq 15
```

- **The `Get-Help` cmdlet:** This help cmdlet can now download help updates from the Web, and you can also use the `-Online` switch to directly query the Microsoft knowledge base.

- **Enhanced remoting in Windows Server 2012:** With the release of Windows Server 2012, PowerShell becomes one of the most important tools in a toolbox of any Windows admin. Remoting is enabled by default in Windows 2012 and enables administrators to control remote servers even when these are in core mode (that is, when the UI has been turned off). If you are running a multiserver farm, this can prove handy for changes that need to be performed on any server in the SharePoint farm. Scripting various procedures can save you time when dealing with large farms or when environments need to be rebuilt on a regular basis (for example, a test or dev farm).

- **`Show-Command`:** This newly introduced cmdlet is a visual enhancement of `Get-Help`, assisting when one is not sure about the proper choice of parameters and outcomes, as shown in Figure 7.7.

FIGURE 7.7 Displaying the results of running `Show-Command` for `Get-SPSite`.

PowerShell-integrated scripting has been improved with IntelliSense and other features that can help administrators to be more efficient when writing scripts.

Introducing PowerShell: The SharePoint Admin's Best Friend

With the release of SharePoint 2010, Microsoft decided to slowly replace STSADM with PowerShell. In SharePoint 2013, STSADM is still around, but only a few features can be exclusively managed (for example, People Picker) with STSADM. Everything else is available via PowerShell, and it becomes the most important tool for SharePoint administration automation. With the 2013 release, a number of new features can only be administrated with PowerShell because there is no UI in Central Admin. These include multitenancy administration (as in 2010), configuring infrastructure for apps and marketplace, configuring licensing options, managing integration with Office Web Apps Server 2013, and so on.

Administrators can still use various tools to administer SharePoint. An administrator who only periodically needs to create a single site collection should probably still use Central Administration, but PowerShell should be the first choice when one wants to fully automate SharePoint solutions. PowerShell is an important resource when it comes to building scripted environments like dev environments or test farms. Administrators running System Center Virtual Machine Manager 2012 can leverage PowerShell to script entire multiserver farms to be built from machine templates.

SharePoint Administration with PowerShell

This section covers some of the common PowerShell usage scenarios.

The Naming of PowerShell Cmdlets

As previously mentioned, the naming of PowerShell cmdlets differs from the ones you got used to in the SharePoint Central Administration interface and is similar to the SharePoint server object model. Here are the most commonly used cmdlets in this chapter:

- **`Get-SPFarm`**: Returns a SharePoint farm object (unique per farm)
- **`Get-SPWebApplication`**: Returns all SharePoint web applications
- **`Get-SPSite`**: Returns all site collections
- **`Get-SPWeb`**: Returns all SharePoint sites in a given site collection

Retrieving Site Collections and Sites with PowerShell

One of the most common scenarios when you use PowerShell is retrieving site collections and sites. To retrieve the list of site collections, simply type **Get-SPSite** in the shell.

To retrieve the list of all SharePoint sites in a site collection, `Get-SPSite` needs to be combined (piping) with `Get-SPWeb`. For example, type the following:

```
Get-SPSite | Get-SPWeb
```

This command lists all site collections in a SharePoint farm and then lists all the websites in each site collection.

If you need to list format or all object properties, type the following:

```
Get-SPSite | Select *
```

Your PowerShell shell lists all the site collections with all the associated properties. A special cmdlet, `Get-SPSiteAdministration`, enables farm administrators to view certain information (for example, owner, usage) about site collections to which they might not have access. The following example lists all site collections along with their primary and secondary admins:

```
Get-SPSiteAdministration | Select -Property Url, OwnerLoginName,
SecondaryContactLoginName
```

Modifying Site Collection Properties with PowerShell

Administrators can use PowerShell to easily modify all the properties of any PowerShell object.

Consider the following scenario. An administrator needs to add user CompanyABC.com\John as a secondary administrator for all site collections. This is an ideal example of how PowerShell can help to automate SharePoint administration. To achieve the goal, type the following command:

```
Get-SPSite | Set-SPSite -SecondaryOwnerAlias "CompanyABC.com\John"
```

In the preceding example, we use `Get-SPSite` to get the list of all the site collections and then combine that with the `Set-SPSite` cmdlet that sets a `Secondary Owner` value to `"CompanyABC.com\John"`.

To verify that the cmdlet completed successfully, run the following command to display the owner and secondary owner for each site collection:

```
Get-SPSite | Select RootWeb, Url, Owner, SecondaryContact
```

Working with Solutions and Features

One of the most common tasks that administrators perform on SharePoint farms is solution and feature management. Previously, in SharePoint 2007, administrators couldn't install solutions without calling STSADM commands. In SharePoint 2013, this has not changed much; you still can use STSADM to install custom solutions, but dedicated PowerShell cmdlets now can help you further automate this procedure.

Deploying a Custom Solution with Features

Consider the following scenario. A custom solution needs to be deployed to the CompanyABC SharePoint portal. The solution has two features, as shown in Figure 7.8: a content type and custom web part.

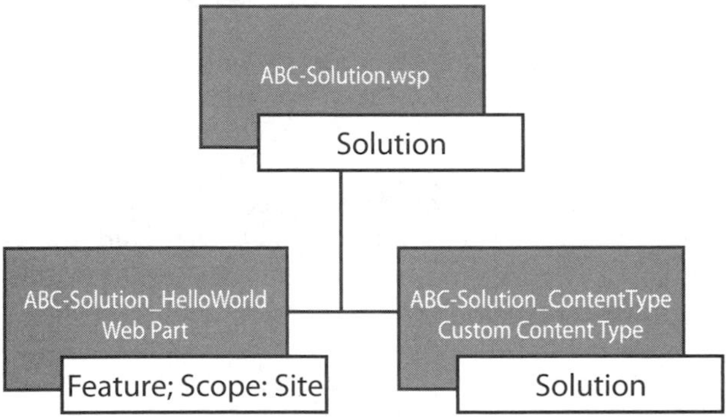

FIGURE 7.8 Examining the structure of custom ABC-Solution, which contains two features: a web part `HelloWorld` and a custom content type.

Here are the steps you need to complete to install the ABC feature to a SharePoint environment.

The first step of this procedure is to upload the solution from the file system to the central solution farm store. Use this command (use the path where you have a .wsp file):

```
Add-SPSolution "C:\My-Solutions\ABC-Solution.wsp"
```

When the command uploads the solution, it is visible in the Central Administration, Solution Management. You need to deploy the solution via the Central Administration UI or with the following PowerShell code:

```
Install-SPSolution "CompanyABC_Solution.wsp" -AllWebApplications
 -GACDeployment -Force
```

The preceding command deploys solutions to all web applications (`-AllWebApplications` parameter) and also enables custom code to be deployed to Global Assembly Cache (GAC) via the `-GACDeployment` parameter. If the solution already exists, it is overwritten (`-Force`).

To activate features on individual site collection, use the following code. The ABC solution has two features, and each needs to be enabled individually:

```
Enable-SPFeature "ABC-Solution_HelloWorld" -Url "http://portal.companyABC.com"
Enable-SPFeature "ABC-Solution_ContentType" -Url "http://portal.companyABC.com"
```

In the custom `ABC-Solution`, the `HelloWorld` web part is scoped as a site collection (Site) feature, and the `ContentType` is scoped as a site-level (Web) feature. To activate it on every site in your site collection, run the following command:

```
Get-SPSite "http://portal.companyABC.com" | Get-SPWeb | ForEach-Object
{Enable-SPFeature "ABC-Solution_ContentType" -Url $_.Url}
```

To remove these features and solutions, you must call commands in reverse order: First, deactivate the feature, uninstall the solution, and then remove it. To perform these operations, type the following:

```
Disable-SPFeature "ABC-Solution_HelloWorld" -Url "http://portal.companyABC.com"
-confirm:$false
Disable-SPFeature "CompanyABC-Solution_ContentType" -Url "http://portal.companyABC.
com" -confirm:$false

Uninstall-SPSolution "ABC-Solution.wsp" -confirm:$false -AllWebApplications:$true
Remove-SPSolution "ABC-Solution.wsp" -confirm:$false
```

PowerShell Backup and Restore Options

Backups can now be completely controlled via a series of cmdlets that perform backups of the SharePoint farm, site collection, and configuration database.

Every cmdlet comes with a `restore` command. SharePoint 2013 also maintained cmdlets from SharePoint 2010 that provide the ability to export and import site collections, web applications, sites, or lists.

Automating Site Collection Backup and Restore

To perform a backup of an individual site collection, type the following:

```
Backup-SPSite "http://portal.companyABC.com" -path "C:\Backups\portal.bak" -force
```

The command in the preceding example backs up a site collection at the given URL to the designated path. Before running this cmdlet, make sure that this path (for example, C:\Backup\) exists. If there is a previous backup file at this location, use the `-force` parameter to overwrite an existing backup file. Additional backup cmdlets include `Backup-SPConfigurationDatabase` (creates a backup of SharePoint Config database), `Backup-SPEnterpriseSearchServiceApplicationIndex` (new in 2013, creates a backup of search index), and the overall `Backup-SPFarm` that creates a backup of the entire farm or an individual web application.

To restore the site collection, type the following:

```
Get-SPSite "http://portal.companyABC.com" | Get-SPWeb | ForEach-Object
{Enable-SPFeature "ABC-Solution_ContentType" -Url $_.Url}
```

Two parameters must be used for silent site collection restore. `-force` ensures any existing site collection at http://portal.comapanyabc.com will be overwritten; and `-confirm:$false` suppresses the overwrite confirmation dialog. By suppressing the confirmation, you can easily automate a restore operation.

Exporting SharePoint Sites and Content

In SharePoint 2013, Microsoft introduced a new capability to export and import SharePoint objects. These new operations enable administrators to more easily move content between different site collections. During import and export operations, administrators can control which content is transferred and how versions are affected by the move.

Here is an example for exporting a site:

```
Export-SPWeb "http://portal.companyABC.com/Team-Site" -path "C:\Exports\
Team-Site.bak"
```

The syntax to export a list is similar, but the list path, relative to the site path, must be passed as `-ItemUrl` parameter:

```
Export-SPWeb "http://portal.companyABC.com/Team-Site" -path "C:\Exports\Doc-Lib.bak"
-ItemUrl "/Doc-Lib"
```

When exporting lists and libraries, associated workflows and alerts are not exported along with the content. In addition, item-level permissions are not maintained.

Sometimes a business might ask for a snapshot of SharePoint for archiving or compliance purposes, which PowerShell can easily handle. The cmdlet `Export-SPWeb` enables administrators to control versions that are exported to an export file.

To export content of a document library, use the same code as previously given. By using optional parameter `-IncludeVersions`, you can choose to export: `LastMajor`, `CurrentVersion`, `LastMajorAndMinor`, or `All`.

Importing Exported Content

Export operations can be performed via Central Administration, but import is available only via PowerShell. Before importing, you need to create an empty site in your site collection. A new site can be created via UI or PowerShell, but make sure you use the same site template as the site that was exported.

The following command lists all installed site templates:

```
Get-SPWebTemplate
```

To create a site with a desired template, use the following cmdlet (in this case, a site based on a blank site template is created):

```
New-SPWeb -url "http://portal.companyABC.com/New-Site" -Template "STS#1"
```

To import a document library, type the following:

```
Get-SPSite "http://portal.companyABC.com/New-Site" | Import-SPWeb -path
"C:\Exports\Doc-Lib.dat" -force -UpdateVersions Overwrite
```

The preceding example imports a document library that was previously exported to a file. The `-Force` parameter ensures that existing data is overwritten, and `-UpdateVersions` instructs the command to overwrite all existing versions. There is also an append switch. (Versions are appended to existing versions.)

Monitoring SharePoint Databases and Site Collection Usage

To monitor SharePoint databases, first use the following cmdlet to retrieve the list of databases:

```
Get-SPWebApplication | Get-SPContentDatabase | Select WebApplication, Name, Server |
Format-Table
```

The preceding command displays all SharePoint web applications available in this farm, along with their respective database names and SQL server name.

To check the current size (in bytes) of each site collection, use the following cmdlet:

```
Get-SPSite | Select RootWeb, Url,
@{Name="Size"; Expression={"{0:N2} GB" -f ($_.Usage.Storage/1E9)}},
@{Name="Storage Warning"; Expression={"{0:N2} GB" -f
($_.Quota.StorageWarningLevel/1E9)}},
@{Name ="Storage Max"; Expression={"{0:N2} GB" -f
($_.Quota.StorageMaximumLevel/1E9)}} | ConvertTo-HTML | Out-File
"C:\Temp\SiteUsage.html"
```

The example might look complicated, but it gets all the site collections and formats the output in any easy-to-read fashion. Here are a few notes:

7

- `SPSite.Usage` property is a complex object, and to retrieve storage usage, we had to construct an expression.
- A similar expression was used to retrieve quota properties.
- An expression also demonstrates PowerShell's capability to convert results to HTML and save it to a file (`ConvertTo-HTML | Out - File`).

Figure 7.9 shows results that could be retrieved by running such a command in CompanyABC's farm.

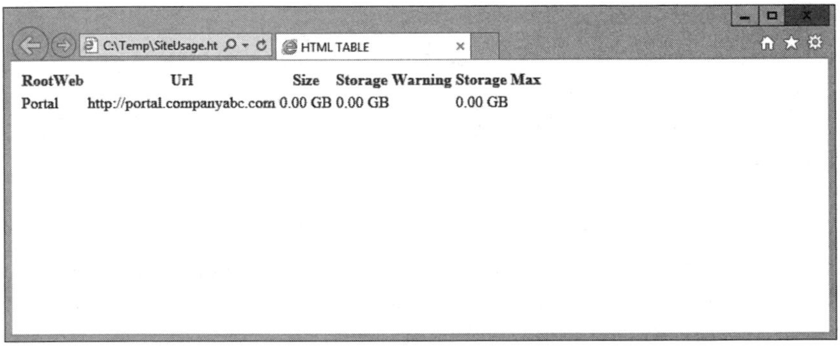

C:\Temp\SiteUsage.ht
HTML TABLE
RootWeb Url Size Storage Warning Storage Max
Portal http://portal.companyabc.com 0.00 GB 0.00 GB 0.00 GB

FIGURE 7.9 Understanding the displayed results of PowerShell cmdlet in a `GridView` format.

`Set-SPSite` enables you to change quotas for a site collection via PowerShell. To change a quota for a site collection, type the following, and note that `"My Quota Template"` uses the name of an existing quota template available in your farm. A new template can be created via Central Administration:

```
Set-SPSite "http://portal.companyABC.com" -QuotaTemplate "My Quota Template"
(if Comment [JPC33] is applicable)
```

Managing Content Databases and Site Collections

The built-in cmdlets enable you to manage content databases. If a SharePoint farm is not adequately planned, one of your content databases might grow too large. In such scenarios, you can rely on PowerShell to fix the problem. Type the following command to create a new database:

```
$webApplication = Get-SPWebApplication "http://portal.companyABC.com"
New-SPContentDatabase -Name "WSS_Portal_Content_New" -WebApplication $webApplication
```

The preceding command creates a new content database for the portal web application. All the other database settings (for example, database server, warning site count, and maximum site count) can be changed at a later stage with the `Set-SPContentDatabase` cmdlet.

The following example demonstrates how warning and maximum site levels can be changed via PowerShell. Type the following to change the warning and maximum site count to 1000 and 2000, respectively:

```
Set-SPContentDatabase "WSS_Portal_Content_New" -WarningSiteCount 1000 -MaxSiteCount
2000
```

With multiple databases per web application, you can now easily move site collections between databases. Use the following code, but make sure that you already have `"WSS_Portal_Content_New"` in place:

```
Move-SPSite "http://portal.companyABC.com/sites/sub-site-collection" -
DestinationDatabase "WSS_Portal_Content_New" -confirm:$false
```

The preceding command moves the site collection at the given URL (`"http://portal.companyABC.com/sites/sub-site-collection"`) to the new database. If you omit the `-confirm` parameter, you are prompted to confirm this operation. As noted in the warning, Internet Information Services (IIS) must be restarted to complete the move. You can accomplish this by using the `iisreset` command.

Enabling and Managing Per-User Licensing Models with PowerShell

Ever since three editions of SharePoint were introduced back in SharePoint 2007, customers have wanted to be able to mix users with Standard and Enterprise client access licenses (CALs) within the same SharePoint farm. In earlier versions, this was impossible to achieve without installing multiple farms. In 2013, however, Microsoft now allows for per-user licensing models within a single farm. These licensing models can be enabled with the following "licensing" PowerShell cmdlets to control the state of licensing enforcement (turned off by default):

- `Disable-SPUserLicensing`
- `Enable-SPUserLicensing`
- `Get-SPUserLicensing`

The following commands are related to user objects:

- `Get-SPUserLicense`
- `Get-SPUserLicenseMapping`
- `Add-SPUserLicenseMapping`
- `New-SPUserLicenseMapping`
- `Remove-SPUserLicenseMapping`

Administrators can use `*-SPUserLicensing` cmdlets to enable or disable licensing engines. When enabled `*-SPUserLicenseMapping` cmdlets help to assign licenses to individual users (claims based), Active Directory (AD) security groups, or roles. The following example shows how to assign an Enterprise license to a user:

```
$user = New-SPClaimsPrincipal -identity "CompanyABC\BobSmith" -IdentityType
"WindowsSamAccountName"
$userMapping = New-SPUserLicenseMapping -Claim $user -License Enterprise
$userMapping | Add-SPUserLicenseMapping
```

Configuring New Service Applications and Features in SharePoint 2013

In SharePoint 2013, Microsoft introduced new offerings related to apps. To configure these administrators, use PowerShell cmdlets. This section provides an overview of these new cmdlets. To see these cmdlets in action, you can use the PowerShell script written to allow for automated farm provisioning and provided in Chapter 4, "Advanced SharePoint 2013 Installation and Scalability." These scripts are also available for download at the following URL: http://tinyurl.com/SP2013-Config.

The Office Web Apps component is now a standalone server called Office Web Apps Server. Administrators should follow this guide to configure these servers to work together: http://technet.microsoft.com/en-us/library/ff431687(v=office.15).aspx. This article includes a couple of new cmdlets used to integrate these two servers: `New-SPWOPIBinding` and `Set-SPWopiZone`.

The same approach applies if you plan to use new SharePoint apps in your on-premises farm. The article http://technet.microsoft.com/en-us/library/fp161236(v=office.15).aspx explains this procedure in more detail. There are a few prerequisite steps like configuring domain name system (DNS) and obtaining a Secure Sockets Layer (SSL) certificate. SharePoint configuration needs to be performed via PowerShell. This includes the following:

- Starting the AppManagementServiceInstance with the `Start-SPService` cmdlet
- Creating an application pool with `New-SPServiceApplicationPool`
- Creating a new SharePoint 2013 application Subscription Settings service application using the cmdlets `New-SPSubscriptionSettingsServiceApplication` and `New-SPSubscriptionSettingsServiceApplicationProxy`
- Creating an instance of Application Management service application using the cmdlets `New-SPAppManagementServiceApplication` instance and `New-SPAppManagementServiceApplicationProxy`
- Configuring the domain for apps via `Set-SPAppDomain` and `Set-SPAppSiteSubscriptionName`

Administrators can use PowerShell to control marketplace settings. For some on-premises deployments, administrators can choose to completely block the marketplace feature or to redirect users to a different marketplace (for example, internal).

PowerShell is used to control these settings via `Set-SPAppMarketplaceSettings` and `Get-SPAppMarketplaceSettings`.

One interesting new app in SharePoint is the Work Management service application. The application is in charge of integrating users' tasks across the entire stack of Microsoft products, including SharePoint, Exchange, Project, and so on. The application can be created using the PowerShell cmdlets `New-SPWorkManagementServiceApplication` and `New-SPWorkManagementServiceApplicationProxy`.

Using Scripts to Automate SharePoint Administration

This section examines some of the most useful scripts you can use to automate a SharePoint farm. These scripts automate common SharePoint tasks, and in many cases, greatly improve the control administrators have over their SharePoint farms. You can download all these scripts from http://tinyurl.com/SP2013-Config.

Automating the Creation of Web Applications and Site Collections

PowerShell can help administrators when they need to create a number of site collections. This often happens when administrating large SharePoint farms or providing hosting services.

Site collection creation operations consists of the following three steps:

1. Create an IIS web application and application pool.
2. Create a site collection.
3. Choose a template for the site collection.

These operations can be performed via Central Administration or easily automated via PowerShell. The following example combines all three steps as a single cmdlet:

```
Function New-SPSiteSet
{
    param(
        [Parameter(Mandatory=$true)]
        [string]$SiteName,
        [int]$Port = 80,
        [string]$HostHeader = "",
        [string]$URL = "",
        [Parameter(Mandatory=$true)]
        [string]$ApplicationPool,
        [Parameter(Mandatory=$true)]
        [string]$ApplicationPoolAccount,
        [string]$SiteCollectionOwner = $ApplicationPoolAccount,
        [string]$TemplateName = "Blank Site"
    )
```

7

```
   $ap = New-SPAuthenticationProvider

    if($URL -ne "")
    {
        New-SPWebApplication -Name $SiteName -Port $Port -HostHeader
$HostHeader -URL $Url -ApplicationPool $ApplicationPool -
ApplicationPoolAccount (Get-SPManagedAccount $ApplicationPoolAccount) -
AuthenticationProvider $ap
    }
    else
    {
        New-SPWebApplication -Name $SiteName -Port $Port -HostHeader
$HostHeader -ApplicationPool $ApplicationPool -ApplicationPoolAccount (Get-
SPManagedAccount $ApplicationPoolAccount) -AuthenticationProvider $ap
    }

    $webApplication = Get-SPWebApplication $SiteName
    $currentUserAlias = "{0}\{1}" -f $Env:USERDOMAIN, $Env:USERNAME

    $templates = Get-SPWebTemplate | Where {$_.Name -eq $TemplateName -or $_.Title
-eq $TemplateName}
    if($templates.Length -eq $null)
    {
        $template = $templates.Name
    }
    else
    {
        $template = $templates[0].Name
    }

    if($template -eq $null)
    {
        $templates = Get-SPWebTemplate | where {$_.IsHidden -eq $false -and
$_.IsRootWebOnly -eq $false}
        $template = $templates[0].Name
    }


    New-SPSite -Name "SiteName" -Url $webApplication.Url -OwnerAlias
$SiteCollectionOwner -SecondaryOwnerAlias $currentUserAlias
    Get-SPWeb $webApplication.Url | Set-SPWeb -Template $template

}
```

To execute this function, type the following into the PowerShell shell:

```
New-SPSiteSet -SiteName "NewSiteCollection" -Port 8080 -ApplicationPool
"ApplicationPool-NewSiteCollection" -ApplicationPoolAccount
"companyABC.com\SPServiceAccount"
```

The script calls all necessary cmdlets and enables you to create a new site collection with a single call. In the previous example, a site collection with the associated pool is created, and it is available at port 8080 with the default template (Blank Site).

The function can be further customized with additional site collection parameters as needed. Default parameters include the following:

- **`SiteName`**: Name for your site collection and web application.
- **`Port`**: Port used for your site collection URL; the default port is 80.
- **`HostHeader`**: Optional host header (for example, portal.companyABC.com). If the host header is not provided, the site collection is available as http://SP_Server_Name:Port.
- **`URL`**: Custom URL for your site collection.
- **`ApplicationPool`**: Name of application pool used.
- **`ApplicationPoolAccount`**: Account used as application pool account (must be managed account).
- **`SiteCollectionOwner`**: Account that is primary site collection administrator. If a value is not provided, `ApplicationPoolAccount` is used instead.
- **`TemplateName`**: Template applied to newly created site collection. If a value is not provided, the Blank Site template is used.

Customers upgrading from SharePoint 2010 should note that the default authentication mode for web applications in SharePoint 2013 is now claims-based authentication. To be able to use all the SharePoint 2013 features, all existing web applications should be converted to claims authentication using the `Convert-SPWebApplication` cmdlet. You can find detailed information about upgrade procedures in Chapter 5, "Migrating from SharePoint 2010 to SharePoint 2013." You can also find more information at http://technet.microsoft.com/en-us/library/gg251985(v=office.15).aspx.

To use the previously mentioned cmdlet, type the following:

```
Convert-SPWebApplication -Identity "http://portal.companyabc.com" -To Claims
-RetainPermissions -Force
```

Creating Site Structures On-the-Fly

SharePoint comes with many built-in templates that you can customize to match your needs. With PowerShell, you can streamline site creation for any purpose you need. You can leverage the built-in cmdlets to create and tear up site structures.

The following example shows how you can use PowerShell to automate the creation of a site structure. It combines the abilities to list templates and to create a new site. The script first lists all available site templates. Hidden templates designed for root sites and templates with more complicated setup routines (for example, business intelligence [BI]) are omitted to retain simplicity of this script. For each site in that collection, a new site based on that template is created.

Here is the example:

```
Function Create-SPMockupSites($Path)
{
    $webTemplates = Get-SPWebTemplate | Where{$_.IsHidden -eq $false -and
$_.IsRootWebOnly -eq $false -and $_.CompatibilityLevel -eq 15 -and $_.Name -ne
"BICenterSite#0" -and $_.Name -ne "EDISC#1"}
    New-SPWeb -url ($Path + "/templates") -Template "STS#1" -Name "Templates"
    $rootWeb = Get-SPWeb ($Path + "/templates")

    ForEach($webTemplate in $webTemplates)
    {
            $templateName = ($webTemplate.Title -replace '\s', '')
        New-SPWeb -url ($rootWeb.Url + "/" + $templateName) -Template $webTemplate.
Name -Name $webTemplate.Title -Description $webTemplate.Description
    }
}
```

To use the preceding code, type the following:

```
$siteUrl = Read-Host "Hello, please enter your site collection URL"
Create-SPMockupSites $siteUrl
```

The script creates a blank site at http://portal.companyABC.com/Templates and then a subsite below it for each template available.

In out-of-the-box SharePoint installation (Enterprise Edition), this command creates approximately 20 new sites. Use this script when you are preparing presentations, building demo sites, or preparing educational sites for end users.

Administrators can create a similar example when you need to create a number of sandbox sites for an upcoming educational course. All these sites could use the same template but have a different site owner.

Automating Site Collection Backups with PowerShell

In the original SharePoint 2003 and 2007 Unleashed books, the script to back up site collections was one of the most asked-for scripts because it enabled administrators to back up individual site collections to flat files on a nightly basis. In the SharePoint 2010 and 2013 Unleashed books, we upgraded this script to PowerShell, and the same script is available as part of this chapter.

The script enables the following:

- You can back up all site collections in your server farm.
- The backup filename is a combination of the site collection name and date when the backup was created.
- Users running this script can specify the number of previous backups they want to retain.
- When the backup finishes, a notification is sent to a specified email address.

Here is the script listing:

```
Function Backup-SPSiteCollections ()
{
        param(
                [Parameter(
                        Position=0,
                        Mandatory=$true
                )]
                [Guid]$SPSiteID,
                [Parameter(
                        Position=0,
                        Mandatory=$true
                )]
                [string]$BackupFolder,
                [Parameter(
                        Position=0,
                        Mandatory=$true
                )]
                [string]$RootWeb,
                [Parameter(
                        Position=0,
                        Mandatory=$true
                )]
                [int]$BackupFilesLimit,
                [Parameter(
                        Position=0,
                        Mandatory=$false
                )]
```

```
            [string]$Email = "",
            [Parameter(
                    Position=0,
                    Mandatory=$false
            )]
            [string]$SmtpServer = ""
    )

    # Test if backup folder exists
    if (Test-Path $BackupFolder)
    {
            # Retrieve previous backup files, sorted by last write time (last
modified)
    $files = Get-Childitem $BackupFolder | where {$_.Name -like ("*" + $RootWeb +
"*.dat")} | Sort $_.LastWriteTime
    $filesCount = @($files).Count

            # If there are more files in directory than backupFilesLimit
    if($filesCount -ge $BackupFilesLimit)
    {
                    # Delete all older files
            for ( $i=0; $i -lt $filesCount-$BackupFilesLimit+1; $i++)
            {
            Remove-Item ($BackupFolder + $files[$i].Name)
            }
    }
    }
    # If backup folder does not exist it will be created
    else
    {
            New-Item $BackupFolder -type directory
    }

  $backupFileName = ("" + $RootWeb + "_" + (Get-Date -Format yyyy-MM-ddThh-mm-ss)
+ ".dat")
  $backupFilePath = $BackupFolder + $backupFileName
  $startTime = Get-Date
  Backup-SPSite -identity $_.ID -path ($backupFilePath) -force
  $endTime = Get-Date

    # Checking if Email and SmtpServer values have been defined
    if($Email -ne "" -and $SmtpServer -ne "")
    {
            $subject = "SharePoint Site Collection Backup Completed!"
            $body = "The following site collection was backuped: " + $RootWeb +
"`n"
```

```
            $body += "Site collection was backuped to: " + $backupFileName + "`n"
            $body += "Backup started on: " + $startTime + ", and ended on: " +
$endTime + "`n`n"
            # Retrieving Site Collection size
            $SiteCollectionSize = Get-SPSite | Where {$_.ID -eq $SPSiteID} |
Select @{Expression={$_.Usage.Storage/1MB}}
            # Retrieving backup file size
            $backupFileSize = Get-ChildItem $backupFilePath | Select {$_.
Length/1MB}
            $body += "Site collection size on SharePoint system is: " +
$SiteCollectionSize + " MB`n"
            $body += "Backup file size: " + $backupFileSize + " MB"
            $smtp = new-object Net.Mail.SmtpClient($SmtpServer)
            # Sending email
            $smtp.Send($Email, $Email, $subject, $body)
      }
}
```

You can execute this script by using the following code snippets:

```
# Back up all site collections in your farm
Get-SPSite | ForEach-Object {Backup-SPSiteCollections -SPSiteID $_.ID -
BackupFolder "C:\Backups\" -RootWeb $_.RootWeb -BackupFilesLimit 5}
# Back up all site collections in your farm and send an email
Get-SPSite | ForEach-Object {Backup-SPSiteCollections -SPSiteID $_.ID -
BackupFolder "C:\Backups\" -RootWeb $_.RootWeb -BackupFilesLimit 5 -Email
"administrator@companyABC.com" -SmtpServer "mail.companyabc.com"}
# Back up a site collection whose URL equals http://portal.companyABC.com
Get-SPSite | Where {$_.ID -eq "http://portal.companyABC.com"} | ForEach-
Object {Backup-SPSiteCollections -SPSiteID $_.ID -BackupFolder "C:\Backups\"
-RootWeb $_.RootWeb -BackupFilesLimit 5}
# Back up all site collections whose URL is not equal to
http://no-backup.companyABC.com
Get-SPSite | where {$_.ID -ne "http://no-backup.companyABC.com"} | ForEach-
Object {Backup-SPSiteCollections -SPSiteID $_.ID -BackupFolder "C:\Backups\"
-RootWeb $_.RootWeb -BackupFilesLimit 5}
```

The preceding three examples show you how you can execute your script in various scenarios. A backup script has six parameters:

- **`SPSiteID`:** A globally unique identifier (GUID) that uniquely identifies a site collection. In the earlier examples, we pass the ID value from the `ForEach-Object` loop.
- **`BackupFolder`:** The Backup folder on a local drive. Leave the trailing backslash (\.) If this folder does not exist, it is automatically created.
- **`RootWeb`:** Value of site collection `RootWeb` property. The value being used forms the backup filename (for example, RootWeb-BackupTime.dat).

- **`BackupFilesLimit`:** The number of previous backup files to retain at `BackupFolder` location. If this number is five, only the last five backups are left in the Backup folder, and all previous files are deleted.
- **`Email`:** The email value used as a To and From email address. This value is optional. If a value is not provided, a notification email is not sent.
- **`SmtpServer`:** The address of the Simple Mail Transfer Protocol (SMTP) server to send the notification email to. If this value is not provided, an email is not sent.

Automatic Solution Installation

When administrators need to prepare a new SharePoint environment, a number of features must sometimes be installed and deployed. New solutions cannot be added from the UI, only with STSADM or PowerShell. Third-party solutions usually have a built-in installer, but most free solutions or in-house solutions do not come with one. To install and deploy these features, you need to run a few cmdlets. The following script eases that procedure for you.

The following example "connects" a number of built-in cmdlets and creates a single function that streamlines the installation process. The script is listed here:

```
Function Install-SPFeatures ($Path)
{
    $files = get-childitem $Path | where {$_.Name -like "*.wsp"}

    ForEach($file in $files)
    {
        $existingSolution = Get-SPSolution | Where{$_.Name -eq $file.Name}
        # check if this solution already exists
        if($existingSolution -eq $null)
        {
            Add-SPSolution -LiteralPath ($Path + "\" + $file.Name)
        }
        # upgrade existing solution
        else
        {
            # if solution is deployed we will update it with new version
            if($existingSolution.Deployed -eq $true)
            {
                Update-SPSolution -identity $existingSolution.SolutionId
-LiteralPath ($Path + "\" + $file.Name) -GACDeployment
            }
            # non-deployed solution needs to be removed and installed
            else
            {
```

```
                Remove-SPSolution -identity $existingSolution.SolutionId
-confirm:$false
                Add-SPSolution -LiteralPath ($Path + "\" + $file.Name)
            }
        }

        $existingSolution = Get-SPSolution | Where {$_.Name -eq $file.Name}

        if($existingSolution -ne $null)
        {
            Install-SPSolution -identity $existingSolution.SolutionId -GACDeployment
-force
        }

    }


}
```

To execute this script, call it with the following:

```
Install-SPFeatures "C:\Installation-Store\"
```

`Installation-Store` in the preceding example is the folder on your local drive (or network drive) that contains a number of .wsp files. The script iterates through .wsp files in this folder and tries to add and deploy each solution.

There are some limitations in the script. If there is a solution with the same name, it is upgraded. During deployment, GAC deployments are allowed, so use these scripts only with trusted solutions. Solutions are deployed to all sites.

7

Understanding Advanced PowerShell Topics

All administrators will eventually reach the point when their PowerShell skills are robust enough to do basic administration of SharePoint. At that point, it becomes valuable to understand how to take your PowerShell skills to the next level.

Remote SharePoint Administration with PowerShell

PowerShell 2.0 introduced an interesting feature: the ability to execute PowerShell cmdlets remotely from a client machine without having to be at the console of a server or use a server control tool such as the Remote Desktop Protocol (RDP). To run a cmdlet from a remote location, make sure that every server has an identical version of PowerShell.

The following code demonstrates how to execute `Get-SPSite` on a remote computer. During its execution, users are prompted for the SharePoint administration credentials. Replace `SPServer` with the actual SharePoint server name:

```
$administrator = Get-Credential
Invoke-Command -Computername SPServer -Credential $administrator -
ScriptBlock {Add-PSSnapin Microsoft.SharePoint.PowerShell; Get-SPSite |
Select Url}
```

Beyond Built-In SharePoint PowerShell Cmdlets

The set of 800+ PowerShell cmdlets that come with SharePoint enable you to perform a wide range of SharePoint administration tasks. But for complete automation of SharePoint administration, some areas are not covered via built-in cmdlets. This section explores how you can extend PowerShell beyond its original programming.

Creating Custom Functions with PowerShell

Custom functions in PowerShell enable developers to easily group sections of code together for easier and repeated usage.

Here is a simple `HelloWorld` function:

```
Function HelloWorld()
{
    Write-Host "Hello World! "
}
```

To execute this function, type the following:

```
HelloWorld
```

The easiest way to get started with functions is with PowerShell ISE and by executing the code directly from the ISE. If the ISE is not available, save the code to a .ps1 file with any text editor, such as Notepad. Execute it from a PowerShell shell by typing the following:

```
\HelloWorld.ps1
```

Functions and Parameters

When creating a PowerShell function, you can define a number of parameters that need to be passed when a function is called from the code. The simplest version of a PowerShell function with parameters is the following:

```
Function HelloWorld($YourName)
```

For more flexibility with parameter properties, use the `Param` syntax:

```
Function HelloWorld
{
    Param (
        [Parameter(Mandatory=$true)]
        [string]$YourName ="John Smith",
```

```
        [int]$YourAge = 0
    )
    Write-Host "$YourName ($YourAge)"
}
```

With the preceding syntax function, an author can define which parameters are required, variable types for each variable, and default values. Functions with parameters can be called as shown next. When passed, parameters are separated with spaces only; commas are not used:

```
HelloWorld "John Smith" 47
HelloWorld -YourAge 47 -YourName "John Smith"
```

Using the SharePoint .NET API to Extend PowerShell

The built-in SharePoint PowerShell cmdlets enable you to manage your SharePoint farm, all the features, site collections, and sites. These cmdlets do not give you access to SharePoint lists, pages, workflows, and so on. You can easily overcome this limitation by using the existing SharePoint .NET API.

To use the additional API (SharePoint, in this example) functions, the API must be referenced before using its objects and functions:

```
[System.Reflection.Assembly]::LoadWithPartialName("Microsoft.SharePoint")
```

Retrieving SharePoint Lists with PowerShell

The following example shows how to get a list of SharePoint lists and libraries on a SharePoint site. To display such a list, a custom function is needed:

```
function Get-SPList
{
    param(
        [Parameter(
            Position=0,
            Mandatory=$true,
            ValueFromPipeline=$true
        )]
        [Microsoft.SharePoint.SPWeb]$CurrentWeb,
        [Parameter(
            Position=1,
            Mandatory=$false
        )]
        [string]$Title = $null

    )
```

7

```
    foreach($list in $CurrentWeb.Lists)
    {
        if($list.Hidden -eq $false -and ($Title -eq $null -or $Title -eq ""))
        {
            Write-Output $list
        }
        elseif($list.Title -eq $Title)
        {
            Write-Output $list
        }
    }
}
```

The preceding function receives `SPWeb` as the object and then invokes the appropriate functions from SharePoint API to retrieve lists (only those available on the Quick Launch menu).

To call this function, type the following:

```
Get-SPSite | Get-SPWeb -Limit ALL | ForEach-Object {Get-SPList -CurrentWeb
$_} | Select ParentWeb, ParentWebUrl, Title, DefaultViewUrl
```

The `Get-SPSite` cmdlet lists all site collections (`SPSite`) and pipes the results to `Get-SPWeb` that lists every site (`SPWeb`) within the site collection. Finally, `Get-SPList` lists every list (only visible lists; system lists are usually hidden) in each of the sites found. The `"-Limit ALL"` parameter is optional and should not be switched on for large farms. To display only lists within a single site, use the following code:

```
Get-SPWeb "http://portal.companyABC.com/A-Project-Site" | ForEach-Object
{Get-SPList $_} | Select ParentWeb, ParentWebUrl, Title, DefaultViewUrl
```

Creating New Lists and Document Libraries

Administrators can combine the built-in PowerShell cmdlets with the SharePoint .NET APIs to create lists and document libraries on-the-fly. Use the following code:

```
function New-SPList()
{
    param(
        [Parameter(
            Position=0,
            Mandatory=$true,
            ValueFromPipeline=$true
        )]
        [Microsoft.SharePoint.SPWeb]$SPWeb,
        [Parameter(
            Position=1,
            Mandatory=$true
```

```
        )]
        [string]$Title,
        [Parameter(
            Position=2,
            Mandatory=$false
        )]
        [string]$Description = "",
        [Parameter(
            Position=3,
            Mandatory=$false
        )]
        [string]$ListTemplateType = "DocumentLibrary"
        )

        $SPWeb.Lists.Add($Title, $Description, $ListTemplateType)
}
```

To call the above given function, type the following:

```
Get-SPWeb "http://portal.companyABC.com/A-Project-Site" | New-SPList -Title
"Sample Doc. Lib" -Description "Doc. Lib. Sample"
Get-SPWeb " http://portal.companyABC.com/A-Project-Site" | New-SPList -Title
"Sample Custom List" -Description "Custom List Sample" -ListTemplateType
"GenericList"
Get-SPWeb "http://portal.companyABC.com/A-Project-Site" | New-SPList -Title
"Sample Calendar" -Description "Calendar Sample" -ListTemplateType "Events"
```


The preceding example creates three lists on a SharePoint site (`"http://portal.companyABC.com/A-Project-Site"`). The function `New-SPList` takes three parameters: `Title`, `Description`, and `ListTemplateType`. You must supply a unique title for a list within one site to pass an appropriate template value, such as those listed by `SPListTemplateType`. For more information, refer to http://msdn.microsoft.com/en-us/library/microsoft.sharepoint.splisttemplatetype(office.15).aspx.

Modify List Properties

Consider the following scenario. A site owner wants uniform versioning settings for all lists and libraries in the site farm. A combination of PowerShell and API comes to the rescue in such a scenario. To achieve that, we can combine existing `Get-SPSite` and `Get-SPWeb` cmdlets with a custom function:

```
function Set-SPList()
{
    param(
        [Parameter(
            Position=0,
            Mandatory=$true,
```

```
            ValueFromPipeline=$true
        )]
        [Microsoft.SharePoint.SPList]$SPList,
        [Parameter(Mandatory=$false)]
        [bool]$EnableVersioning = $null,
        [Parameter(Mandatory=$false)]
        [bool]$EnableMinorVersions = $null,
        [Parameter(Mandatory=$false)]
        [int]$MajorVersionLimit = -1,
        [Parameter(Mandatory=$false)]
        [int]$MajorWithMinorVersionsLimit = -1
    )

    if($SPList -ne $null)
    {
        if($EnableVersioning -ne $null)
        {
            $SPList.EnableVersioning = $EnableVersioning
        }
        if($MajorVersionLimit -gt -1)
        {
            $SPList.MajorVersionLimit = $MajorVersionLimit
        }

        if($SPList.BaseType -eq "DocumentLibrary")
        {
            if($EnableMinorVersions -ne $null)
            {
                $SPList.EnableMinorVersions = $EnableMinorVersions
            }

            if($MajorWithMinorVersionsLimit -gt -1)
            {
                $SPList.MajorWithMinorVersionsLimit = $MajorWithMinorVersionsLimit
            }
        }
        $SPList.Update()
    }
}
```

If an administrator needs to enable five major versions and keep minor versions for the three last major versions, the function needs to be called like this:

```
Get-SPSite | Get-SPWeb -Limit All | ForEach-Object {Get-SPList $_ | ForEach-
Object {Set-SPList $_ -EnableMinorVersions $true -EnableVersioning $true -
MajorVersionLimit 5 -MajorWithMinorVersionsLimit 3}}
```

Creating List Items On-the-Fly

When building demonstration and presentation sites, a function that might come in handy is the PowerShell function for creating items in a list. The following example shows how you could build such a function. It creates a list item in a custom list and assigns only a title for the list item, but it could be extended to create more complex items:

```
Function New-SPListItem()
{
    param(
        [Parameter(
            Position=0,
            Mandatory=$true,
            ValueFromPipeline=$true
        )]
        [Microsoft.SharePoint.SPList]$SPList,
        [Parameter(
            Position=1,
            Mandatory=$true
        )]
        [string]$Title
        )

        [Microsoft.SharePoint.SPListItem] $listItem = $SPList.Items.Add();

        $listItem["Title"] = $Title
        $listItem.Update()
}
```


You can use the preceding function by typing the following:

```
Get-SPWeb "http://portal.companyABC.com/A-Project-Site" | Get-SPList -Title
"The Team" | New-SPListItem -Title "John White"
Get-SPWeb "http://portal.companyABC.com/A-Project-Site" | Get-SPList -Title
"The Team" | New-SPListItem -Title "Ann Green"
Get-SPWeb "http://portal.companyABC.com/A-Project-Site" | Get-SPList -Title
"The Team" | New-SPListItem -Title "Zoey Gray"
```

The preceding code creates three new items (`John White`, `Ann Green`, `Zoey Gray`) in the list `"The Team"` located on the site `"http://portal.companyABC.com/A-Project-Site"`.

Managing Back-End Systems with PowerShell

PowerShell can also manage back-end systems in the SharePoint environment. Microsoft and third-party vendors released numerous packs to manage various systems, and the most important ones for SharePoint environment are management packs for IIS, Windows Server, and Active Directory.

IIS Management with PowerShell

The IIS PowerShell management module built into Windows 2008 R2 and Windows 2012 can help administrators automate most common operations with IIS sites and pools. SharePoint administrators in complex environments can benefit from the ability to automatically reset individual websites, recycle application pools, back up IIS configuration, and so on.

To use this module, it must be imported; type the following:

```
Import-Module WebAdministration
```

This snap-in is no different from the SharePoint one; use `Get-Command` and `Get-Help` to learn more about cmdlets. Use the following code to list all web applications and pools:

```
# Lists all web applications (sites and pools) on IIS
Get-WebApplication
# Lists names of all websites that are stopped
Get-WebSite | Where State -eq "Stopped" | Select Name with "Started"
```

Commands with `Start`, `Stop`, and `Restart` verbs enable administrators to perform those actions against websites and pools. To reset a SharePoint central administration pool, type the following:

```
# Restarts the Central Administration application pool
Restart-WebAppPool "SharePoint Central Administration v4"
```

Windows Server PowerShell Cmdlets

PowerShell cmdlets for managing Windows servers are built into the PowerShell core and do not need to be loaded separately. In SharePoint environments, you can use them to control, for example, SharePoint-related Windows Services and file systems.

The following command lists all SharePoint and ForeFront services currently stopped (ForeFront services are used to sync user accounts):

```
Get-Service | Where {($_.DisplayName -like "*SharePoint*" -or $_.DisplayName
-like "*ForeFront*") -and $_.Status -eq "Stopped"}
```

To start a service, type the following:

```
Start-Service -name "SharePoint Timer Service"
```

Automate User Provisioning with PowerShell

The built-in SharePoint PowerShell cmdlets enable you to easily manage users across site collections, but the real power of PowerShell is revealed when you combine these with AD management cmdlets.

The most common usage scenario for user provisioning occurs when a new user needs to have an AD user account provisioned and then needs access to a SharePoint site. In this scenario, each new employee must be given contributor rights to the SharePoint site at http://portal.companyABC.com.

Here is how a new employee procedure could be automated with PowerShell. Use the following sample code to create a new AD account:

```
Import-Module ActiveDirectory
New-ADUser -Name "JohnS" -GivenName "John" -Surname "Smith" -DisplayName
"John Smith" -AccountPassword (ConvertTo-SecureString "pass@word1" -
AsPlainText -force) -Enabled $true
```

To completely automate importing from PowerShell, use the `Import-CSV` cmdlet that enables automatic imports to be done from a CSV file. `New-ADUser` has more parameters that you can specify on account creation, but these are beyond the scope of this book.

When you have a new user created in AD, you can use existing SharePoint cmdlets to assign proper user privileges:

```
New-SPUser -UserAlias "companyABC.com\JohnS" -Web "http://portal.companyABC.com"
```

PowerShell also enables you to implement a similar procedure for disabling employee access to a particular site and removing it from AD. The following example shows how to disable and remove a user:

```
# Removes a User from a SharePoint Site
Remove-SPUser -Web "http://portal.companyABC.com" -UserAlias "companyABC.com\JohnS"
Import-Module ActiveDirectory
# Disables AD User
Set-ADUser "JohnS" -Enabled $false
# Removes AD User
Remove-ADUser "JohnS" -confirm $false
```

If you have multiple site collections, you can combine `Remove-SPUser` with results from `Get-SPSite | Get-SPWeb` cmdlets.

Tools for PowerAdmins

Microsoft has made substantial effort to make SharePoint administration with PowerShell as easy as possible. Still, an administrator who has never worked with PowerShell needs to invest some time to grasp the important concepts and then improve on these to be able to truly unleash PowerShell potential. You can use a number of resources to help you better utilize SharePoint:

- **PowerGUI:** Free PowerShell integrated development environment (IDE) from Quest that includes support for color coding, IntelliSense, debugging, and much more: http://www.powergui.org.

- **SharePoint Downloads & Scripts:** A large repository with a number of different SharePoint PowerShell scripts: http://gallery.technet.microsoft.com/sharepoint.
- **AutoSPInstaller:** Community-driven project that fully automates the installation and configuration of a SharePoint 2010/2013 farm: http://autospinstaller.codeplex.com/.
- **Windows PowerShell for SharePoint Server 2010:** Microsoft tool that helps administrators to create scripts with a GUI: http://technet.microsoft.com/en-us/sharepoint/ff603532.aspx.

Summary

Changes to PowerShell in SharePoint 2013 are not dramatic and represent a continuous investment made by Microsoft that started with the introduction of Windows PowerShell as a SharePoint management and administration tool in SharePoint 2010. All skills that SharePoint 2010 administrators had can be easily transferred to SharePoint 2013 farms. A number of new features introduced in SharePoint 2013 can be properly managed only via PowerShell, and PowerShell is the only option to fully automate farm and services provisioning in multiserver or multitenant environments.

SharePoint 2013 administrators need to have at least a basic knowledge of PowerShell to properly maintain and administrate SharePoint 2013, so it is subsequently critical that they learn how to leverage the tool. This chapter provides a good first step for understanding PowerShell and includes PowerShell script examples that you can use to immediately administrate a SharePoint 2013 environment.

Best Practices

The following are best practices from this chapter:

- Become familiar with Windows PowerShell for SharePoint 2013 administration.
- Understand the concept of piping commands from one cmdlet to another to automate processes.
- Learn how to write functions in PowerShell and how to use .NET object properties and methods.
- Script SharePoint farm installs.
- Use PowerShell for remote administration of SharePoint farm servers and for automation of tasks.
- Download the script from this chapter from http://tinyurl.com/SP2013-Config and use them as a template to start building your own scripts.

CHAPTER 8

Leveraging and Optimizing Search in SharePoint 2013

IN THIS CHAPTER

- Outlining the Capabilities of SharePoint 2013 Search
- SharePoint 2013 Search Architecture
- Deploying a Native SharePoint 2013 Search Service Application
- Capturing Content

One of the core strengths with SharePoint 2010 was its Enterprise Search capabilities—and this is ever more remarkable in SharePoint 2013. A considerable investment has been made by Microsoft into the native search capabilities within the tool, and new features and functionalities have positioned SharePoint's Search as a robust and comprehensive search application for organizations of all sizes.

As the main step on this way of improvements, Microsoft has fully integrated the former FAST Search core into SharePoint, so that there's one search core we have in SharePoint 2013, making the installation, administration, and maintenance much easier.

This chapter covers all the main deployment and configuration topics related to SharePoint 2013 Search. Discussed are the various options in each search component and how to configure and set up the optimal search solution. In addition, advanced customization and configuration scenarios are discussed.

Outlining the Capabilities of SharePoint 2013 Search

SharePoint has always been strong in its search capabilities, and SharePoint 2013 Search features improve the situation even more, both from an end-user perspective and for administrators.

The first and most important architectural change is that there's only one single search core in SharePoint 2013: The separated product FAST Search for SharePoint does not exist anymore; it has been fully integrated into the SharePoint core. This means much easier installation, deployment, and administration and much less confusion on the end-user side. Powerful indexing, linguistics, extraction, and query expressiveness that are the heritage of FAST are now available as a part of SharePoint search, as shown in Figure 8.1.

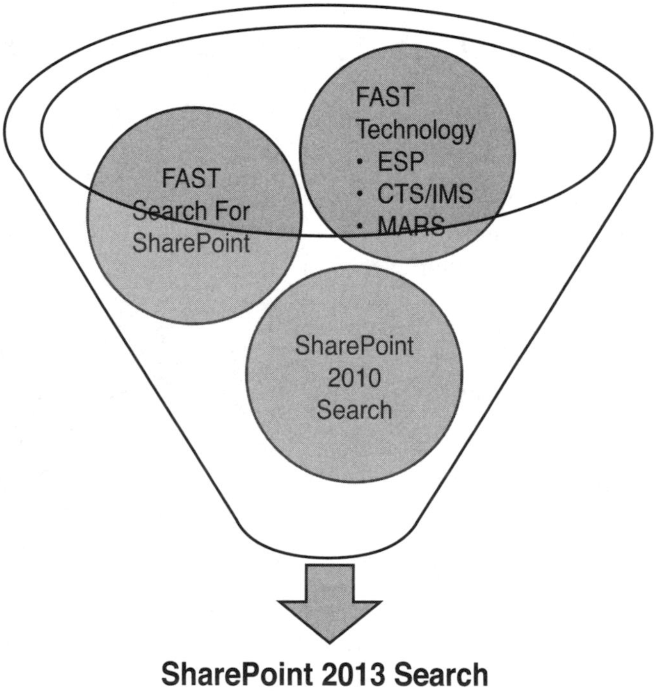

FIGURE 8.1 Single search core in SharePoint 2013.

Of course, these architectural changes lead to a lot of functional changes and new capabilities:

- User experience (UX) is totally renewed—not just because of general changes in SharePoint UX, but with deep refiners everywhere, display templates, better display results using result blocks, a hover panel with document previews, and much more.
- On the query side, search scopes, federated locations, and best bets are now deprecated in favor of result sources, query rules, and result templates. As a result, we get much more effective query processing and search result presentation.
- As for crawling, continuous crawling is a very important enhancement to get better content freshness. Also, content processing and linguistic capabilities are now very strong and extensible.

- As a result of the changes in the general development model of SharePoint 2013, extending Search is much easier now.

SharePoint 2013 Search Architecture

Thanks to the new model, there's one core and one integrated administration of Search in SharePoint 2013. This means a lot of improvements:

- Search is fully integrated into SharePoint; there is no longer a separate FAST Search for SharePoint, and there is no longer a separate Search Server. To get a "Search Server" functionality, simply create a service farm on SharePoint 2013 that is used for search only.
- There are four databases (DBs) for Search, each dependent on each other:

  Crawl DB: Tracking information and details about crawled items.

  Link DB: Information extracted by the content processing component. It also stores information about the number of times people have clicked a search result.

  Analytics Reporting DB: The results of usage analytics and extracted information from the link database.

  Search Administration DB: Search configuration data and the access control list (ACL) for the crawl component.
- Every component can be scaled out for capacity and fault tolerance.
- Search is multitenant and much more administration can be done at site, site collection, and tenant level.

You can see the components in Figure 8.2:

- **Crawler:** This is the least changed component of SharePoint 2013 Search.
- **Content Processing:** Processes crawled items (for example, document parsing, property mapping, language detection, entity extraction) and sends these items to the index component.
- **Index:** A brand new next-generation search core. This receives processed items from the content processing component and writes those items to an index file stored on a disk.

  Also receives queries from the query processing component and returns result sets.

  The search index can be divided onto discrete partitions. Each index partition holds one or more index replicas. The search index is the aggregation of all index partitions.
- **Query Processing:** Analyzes and processes queries and results to optimize precision, recall, and relevance. The processed query is submitted to the index component.

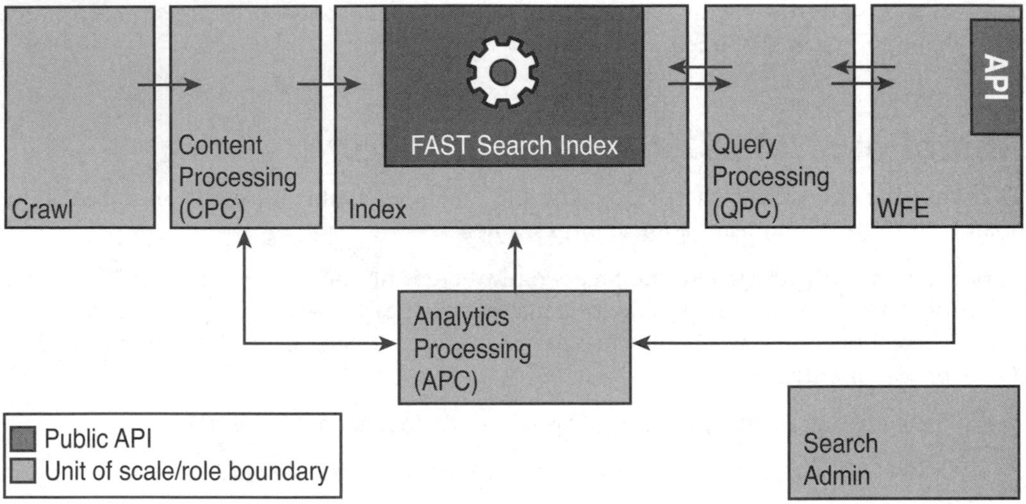

FIGURE 8.2 SharePoint 2013 Search architecture.

- **Analytics Processing:** Analyzes crawled items (search analytics) and how users interact with search (usage analytics).
- **Search Administration:** Runs the system processes for Search.

Deploying a Native SharePoint 2013 Search Service Application

In SharePoint 2013, Search is deployed as a service application, similar to the SharePoint 2010 services. The most important difference is that there is no option to choose the type of search service application (SharePoint Search, FAST Content, FAST Query) because of the architectural changes described earlier.

During the post-installation configuration steps, you can choose to use the automated wizard to deploy farm components. It automatically configures native SharePoint 2013 Search for you. Although this can be convenient, it doesn't allow for control of the process, so it is recommended to deploy Search manually. To do this, you need to create a new Search Service Application, as follows:

1. Go to the SharePoint 2013 Central Administration site and choose Application Management, Service Applications, Manage Service Applications.
2. In the next dialog box, as shown in Figure 8.3, you can find the list of deployed service applications, modify their settings, or add a new one.
3. If you want to add a new search service application, choose the menu New, Search Service Application. You get a pop-up window with the required settings for your search service.

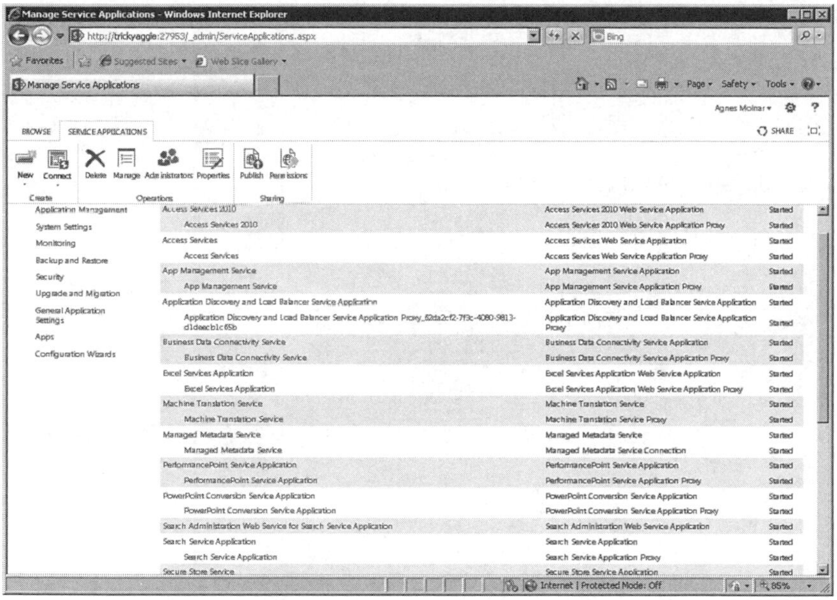

FIGURE 8.3 Service application management.

4. Give a name to your service—in this example, Search Service Application.

5. Select the search service account, a managed account for running the search service on your farm. It is highly recommended to use a dedicated user instead of the default one with high farm administration privileges.

6. Select or create a new application pool for the Search Admin web service.

7. Select or create a new application pool for the Search Query and Site Settings web service.

After completing these steps, your search service application is ready to be used in your web applications. But before starting to use that, you need to associate the proper search service application to your web applications. To do so, complete the following steps:

1. Go to the SharePoint 2010 Central Administration site. Open Application Management, Service Applications, Configure Service Application Associations.

2. On this page, you can find the web applications with the associated service applications. Click the name of the web application; you then see the list of all associated and disassociated services. If you want to change the associations, change the group default to custom.

3. Select the service applications you want to associate with the web application, as shown in Figure 8.4. Choose the one created earlier—in this example, the one named SharePoint Search Service.

FIGURE 8.4 Configuring service application associations.

Capturing Content

Capturing content is fundamental to search; if it's not crawled and indexed, you can't find it. The process of connecting to content sources, crawling them to get content, and making that content searchable is much more complex than most people realize.

The functions of crawler are as follows:

- ▶ Connects to the content source
- ▶ Maps the content
- ▶ Feeds the Indexing engine
- ▶ Finds any changes

Similar to SharePoint 2010, SharePoint 2013 can crawl and index various types of contents. The crawled content sources can include the following types of sources:

- ▶ SharePoint
- ▶ HTTP (web crawler)
- ▶ Business Data Connectivity (BDC) Framework, including (all built on the BDC Framework)
    - ▶ Exchange Public Folders Connector
    - ▶ Lotus Notes Connector

- Documentum Connector
- Taxonomy Connector: connects to the Managed Metadata Service (MMS)
- People Profile Connector

Most parts and functions of the crawler component have been taken directly from SharePoint 2010, so they have few changes. However, these changes are still notable and important:

- Anonymous crawl for HTTP
- Asynchronous web part crawl
- Continuous crawl (as discussed in the next section)

Continuous Crawl

Continuous crawl is a new way of crawling, which makes possible to have the most current data in your index. When you enable continuous crawls, a crawl schedule no longer applies; you are running crawls in parallel, and the crawler gets changes from SharePoint sites every *N* minutes. (By default, this interval is set to 15 minutes by default, but you can change this parameter by using PowerShell.) Continuous crawls do not stop for errors, but rather note the error and continue to crawl content. Continuous crawls can occur while other crawls are active or starting. With this capability, you can now keep content fresh and won't experience mysterious delays when additional content sources are added.

NOTE

Continuous crawl is available for SharePoint content only.

Content Sources

One of the first steps is to get SharePoint Search to index the local SharePoint sites. To do so, complete the following steps:

1. From SharePoint Central Administration, navigate to the administration page of your search service application and choose Content Sources from the Crawling group of the Quick Launch navigation bar.
2. Click New Content Source.
3. Enter a name for the new content source and choose SharePoint Sites as the type of the content source.

4. Type the start addresses for the SharePoint sites. By default, you have to type the following URLs. (In this example, the URL of the main SharePoint site is https://home.companyabc.com, and the My Site web application is https://mysite.companyabc.com.)

   `https://home.companyabc.com`: for crawling the content

   `sps3://mysite.companyabc.com`: for crawling people content

5. Choose one of the following options: Crawl Everything Under the Hostname for Each Start Address or Only Crawl the Site Collection of Each Start Address.

6. Define full crawl scheduling for the content source crawling. During the full crawling, all items of content source are crawled from scratch.

   Also, select if you want to define a schedule for incremental crawl or if you prefer to enable continuous crawl, as in Figure 8.5.

   Schedules can be daily, weekly, or monthly; each of them can be configured granularly.

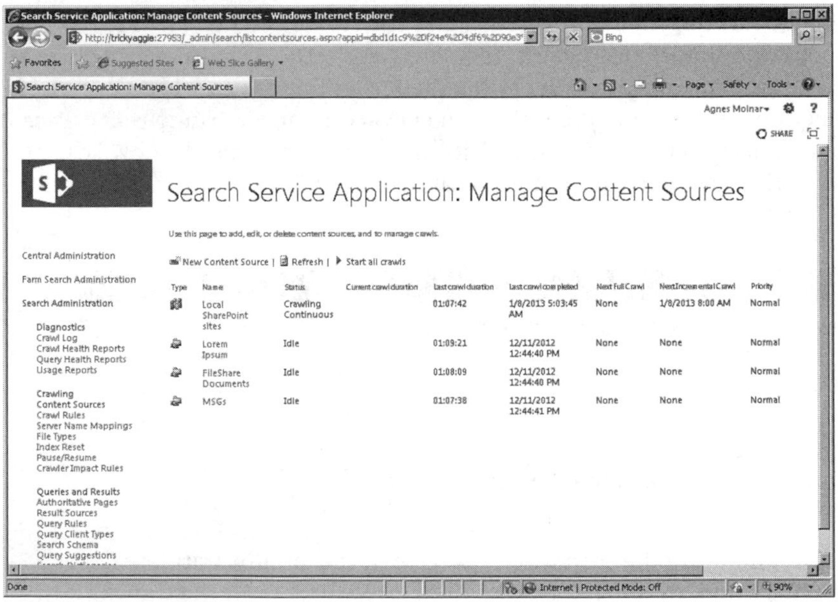

FIGURE 8.5 Managing crawl schedules.

7. Select the priority of this content source. Content sources with high priority are processed over the content sources with normal priority during the crawling.

The settings of content sources can be modified later. Just click the name of the content source and select Edit Operation from its context menu, and you get the same configuration page.

Content Processing

The Content Processing component is brand new with SharePoint 2013. It takes content from the crawler and prepares it for indexing, as shown in Figure 8.6. With SharePoint 2013, there is also a new Analytics Processing component that feeds information into Content Processing.

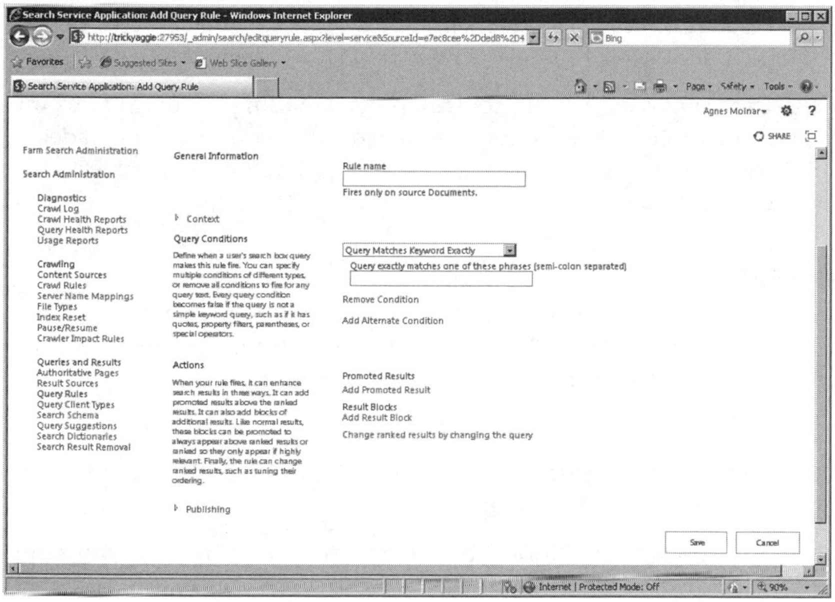

FIGURE 8.6 Adding a new query rule.

The most important new features of Content Processing are as follows:

- Linguistics (improved phonetic search for people names, cross-lingual name search, and so on)
- Entity extraction (moved to the Term Store)
- New format handlers in document parsing
- Higher throughput
- Automatic content-based file format detection, eliminating dependencies on file extensions
- Improved content processing and error reporting

Result Sources and Federation

Federation is the ability to query remote indexes and present the results together with the local results. As a result, users don't have to be aware of and use multiple search centers to search all content available in their organizations.

Federation has been available since Microsoft Office SharePoint Server (MOSS) 2007 SP2, but SharePoint 2013 improved the federation capabilities. Besides Open Search protocol, you can now federate results from remote SharePoint farms via result sources. This is a big help for distributed organizations.

Some limitations apply to using remote result sources. If you are using remote SharePoint protocol, it's limited to SharePoint 2013 and requires all federated farms to be upgraded to SharePoint 2013. Results are still not interleaved; they're displayed in result blocks. Refiners are also not combined.

Query Processing

In SharePoint 2013, by understanding the intent of the query, you can use a lot of techniques to reformulate the query (for example, where the query is from, who initiated the query, what concepts or entities can be recognized in the query).

Query Rules

Query rules are designed to provide control and configurability based on the intent of the query. Each query rule is defined by three features:

- **Query conditions:** Define the conditions that fire this rule. Multiple conditions of different types can be defined for the same rule.

> **NOTE**
>
> Every condition becomes false if the query is not a simple keyword query. (For example, it has quotes, property filters, parentheses, or special operators.)

  Query Matches Keyword Exactly

  Query Matches Action Term

  Query Matches Dictionary Exactly

  Query Commonly Used on Source

  Result Type Commonly Clicked

  Advanced Query Text Match

  The queries also can be restricted on specific result sources (for example, media files or conversations).

- **Query actions:** When a query rule fires, it can enhance search results in three ways. It can do the following:

  Add promoted results above the ranked results.

Add blocks of additional results. Like normal results, these blocks can be promoted to always appear above ranked results or ranked so they only appear if highly relevant.

Change ranked results, such as tuning their ordering.

- **Publishing options:** These settings control when the rule can fire. If the rule is not active, it never fires. The start date is when you want it to start firing. The end date is when you want it to stop firing. The review date is when you want the contact to review the rule.

Query Suggestions

Query suggestions enable users to ask better questions and make it simpler to search for information. Query suggestions now take on two forms, both helping the users to ask better questions by showing what others have asked before:

- **Pre-query suggestions:** Includes a list of queries from other users and a list of items the current user has clicked before. Pre-query suggestions are displayed while typing the query, before it gets executed.

NOTE

Suggestions with zero results are never provided by this feature.

- **Post-query suggestions:** Are provided after a query is executed and results are displayed. They are based on the results that you have clicked at least twice. These suggestions can be tuned (inclusions, exclusions) on the search service application level.

Query Spell Correction

Query Spell Correction is a useful and needed feature because people have a habit of misspelling and fat-fingering. It's managed in the Term Store, including both inclusions and exclusions.

Result Types

A result type is a set of rules that describe which of the items in the search results match that result type. When a user runs a query, the results come back and each result is evaluated against the rules in the result types. Then a display template (as discussed later in this chapter) is applied to the result based on the type that it matches.

Features in result types include the following:

- Specify a rule based on a criterion.
- Specify the managed properties to have returned when the rule conditions are met.
- Specify the rendering template to be used. With this, you can define the display of requested properties, by using HTML and JavaScript.

Query Client Types

Client type identifies an application from which a search query is sent (for example, user interface [UI], ObjectModel, Alert). Applications are prioritized by tiers. The top tier has the highest priority. When the resource limit is reached, query throttling turns on and the search system processes the queries from top tier to bottom tier.

Delegated Administration

In SharePoint 2013, there's an option to delegate some search administration tasks to site collection or even to site level. This feature can prove very useful because it makes the central search administrator's life much easier and requires the local (site collection or site) administrators to take more responsibility for their search solutions.

Tasks that can be delegated to site collection and site admins include the following, as shown in Figure 8.7:

- Create/override query rules, including promoted results
- Create/override result types and display templates
- Create/override result sources, either for remote locations or as a custom search "vertical"
- Create managed properties in search schema (site collection level only!)
- Create refiners
- Start a local crawl (can even be done down to the list level)

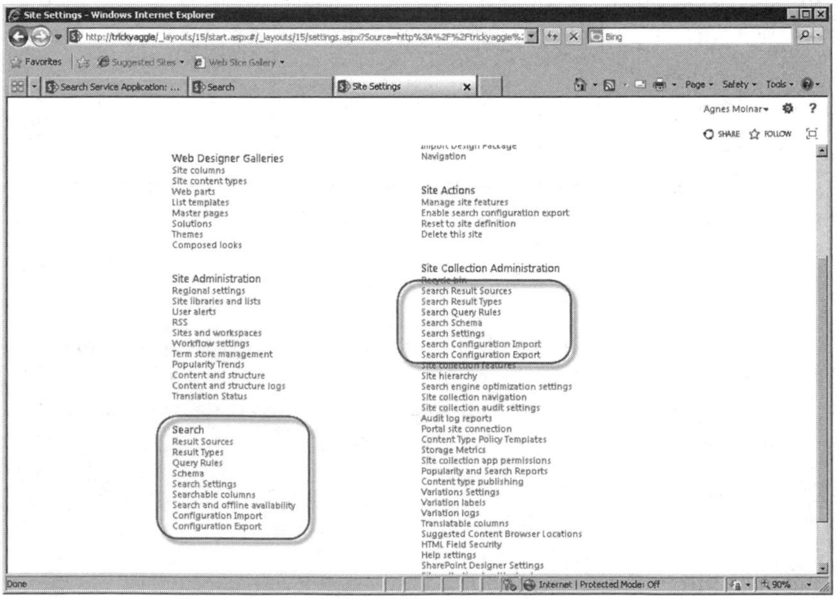

FIGURE 8.7 Site and site collection level administration.

User Experience

SharePoint 2013 has a lot of overall UI enhancements and improvements provided via HTML, JavaScript, and AJAX style interactions. The same applies in terms of search experience: You now have a modern, cleaner, and more user friendly UI, as shown in Figure 8.8:

- Hover panel for all types of results.
- Document previews for Office documents.
- Enhanced refiners and faceted navigation, with deep refiners everywhere.
- Display templates offer control over many aspects of the Search UI: result types, refiners, hover panels, and so on. For example, if you want to extend your Contract search experience, you could create a refiner for Contractors Bar Graph template. Or, you could create a custom hover panel that surfaces even more properties that are specific to your Contracts.

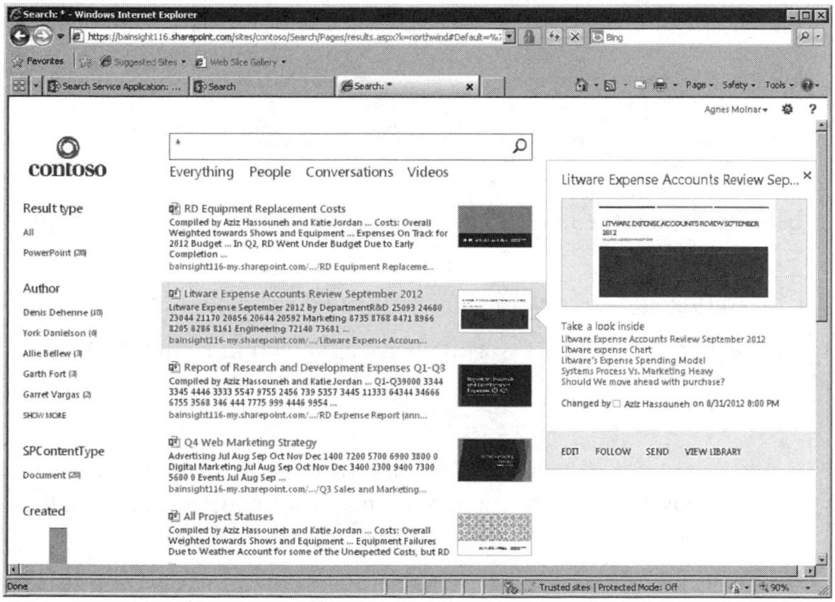

FIGURE 8.8 Search user experience.

Deep Refiners and Item Counts

As an inheritance of FAST Search for SharePoint 2010, all refiners used in SharePoint 2013's faceted navigation are deep refiners, so there are no gaps caused by a missed item in the deeper result set.

But the refiner UI might be surprising at first sight because we don't have the item counts displayed, despite the deep refiners, as shown in Figure 8.9.

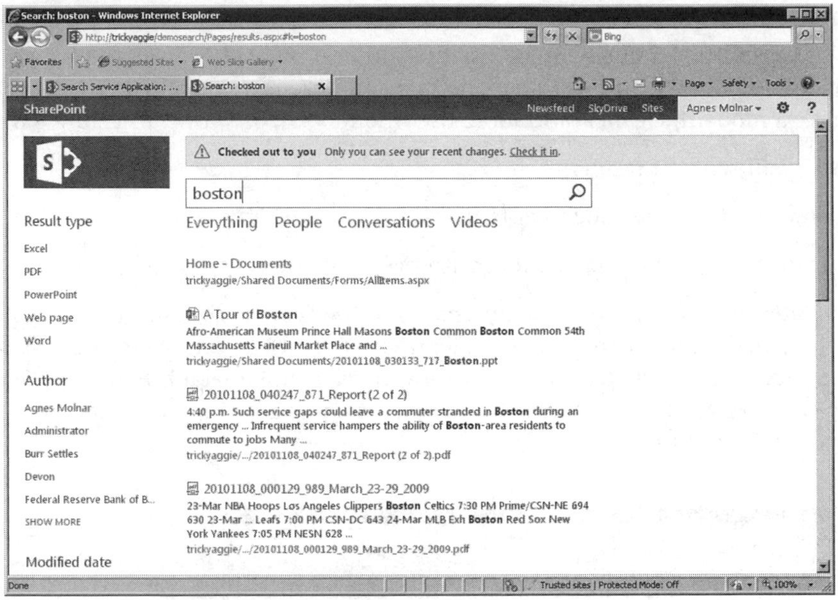

FIGURE 8.9 Out-of-the-box search refiners.

The reason for this behavior is that the item count is simply hidden by default. To display it, complete these steps:

1. Open the page for editing and go to the Refinement Panel web part's properties.
2. Click the Choose Refiners button. This wizard opens, as shown in Figure 8.10.

What we have here are the following:

- The top half of this wizard is a visual control for selecting the refiners you need on your Search page. You don't need to do more XSLT magic for configuring the refinement panel.
- On the left side, there's the list of available refiners (managed properties). On the right side, you can see your current selections. Of course, you can add and remove as well as reorder the refiners here.

When you select a refiner in the list, you see its configuration in the bottom half of the screen. You can configure the following here:

- Display name
- Display template (as discussed later)
- Sort by

- Sort direction (ASC/DESC)
- Max number of refiner values

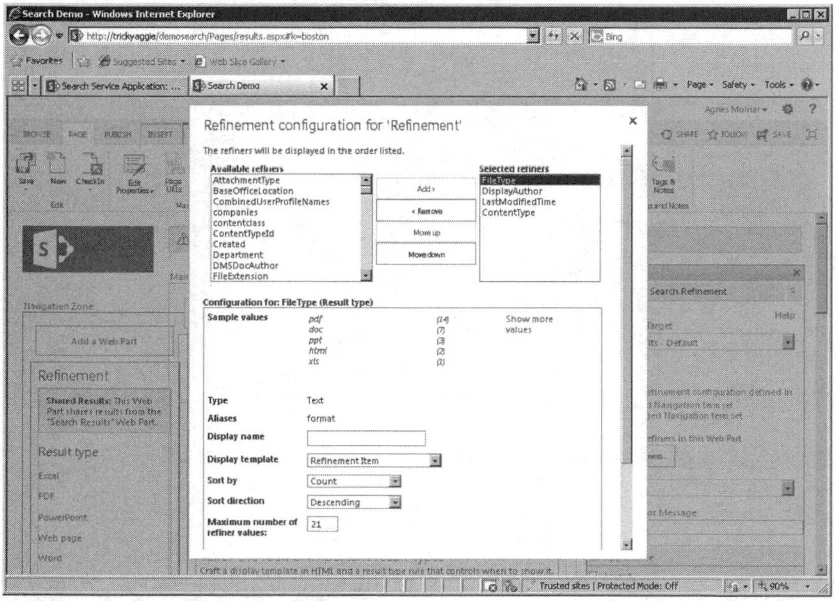

FIGURE 8.10 Refinement configuration.

By default, there are two display templates defined for refiners: Refinement Item and Multi-value Refinement Item, but the item counts are hidden in both cases.

If you want to display the item counts, you have two options:

- Modify the existing Refiner Item display template.
- Create a custom display template.

In the first case, you modify the default behavior of your refiners. In the second case, you have the option to choose whether to display the item counts.

To create a new display template or modify the existing one, follow these steps:

1. Open Design Manager from the Site Settings menu.
2. Select Upload Design Files from the left-side navigation.
3. On this page, you can map the Master Page gallery as a network drive, where the display templates are. It looks like Figure 8.11.
4. When you have the Windows Explorer opened with your Master Page gallery, open the Display Templates/Filters folder.

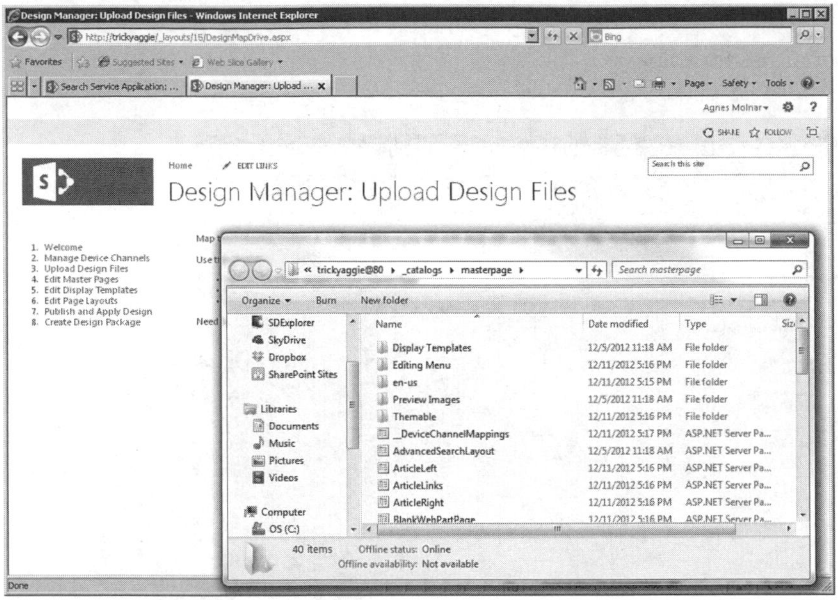

FIGURE 8.11 Design Manager.

NOTE

It's worth mapping this location as a network drive, to make the navigation easier in the future.

5. Locate the file named Filter_Default.html. This file contains the display template named Refiner Item we found in the Refiner Wizard earlier.

NOTE

To figure out which file contains what kind of display template, open the Design Manager and select Edit Display Templates from the left-side navigation. This opens the list of existing display templates with both titles and filenames. You can also do some operations here, like download the files (for further processing) and so on.

6. If you want to modify the default behavior of your refiners, open the file Filter_Default.html.

7. If you want to create your own display template for refiners with item counts, copy the file Filter_Default.html and give it a name like Filter_Default_with_ItemCounts.html.

8. Open the file with any HTML editor and locate these lines:

```
this.Options = {
ShowClientPeoplePicker: false,
```

```
ShowCounts: false
};
```

Here, note the parameter `ShowCounts`. This is what you have to change to `true`.

NOTE

If you're going to create a new display template instead of modifying the existing one, it's better to change its title too, in order to give it a unique name (for example, <title>Refinement Item with Counts</title>).

9. Save your file to the Master Page gallery.

NOTE

There's a .js file for each design template HTML file. At this moment, don't worry about it even if you're going to create your new custom display template; this JavaScript is created when you create (or upload) the HTML file.

That's it. Just go back to your Search page. If you have just modified the default display template, you should see the item counts for each refiner. Anyway, if you created a new display template, open the Refiner Panel's properties and go back to the Display Template drop-down. At this point, you'll see the third one with the title Refiner Items with Counts (see Figure 8.12).

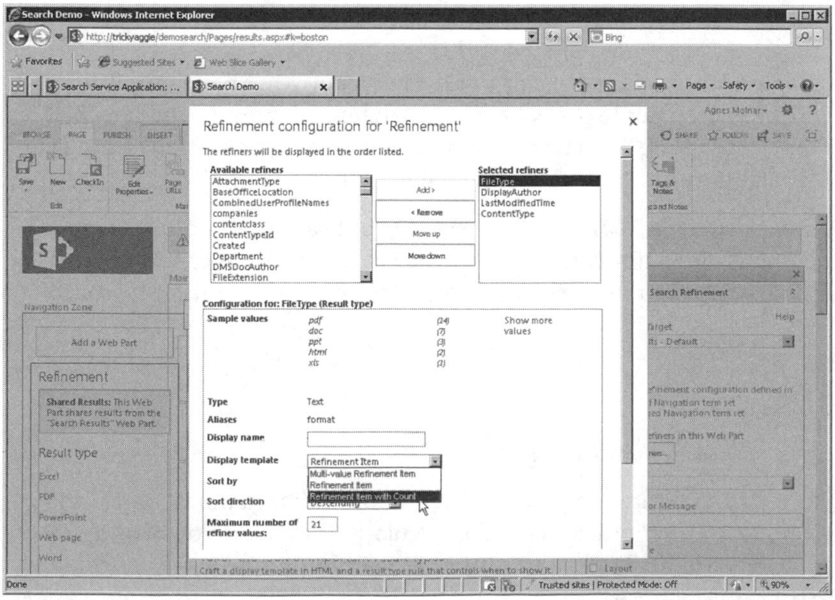

FIGURE 8.12 Using the new display template.

After you select the proper display template here, you're done. Save your settings; the item counts are displayed with the refiners, as shown in Figure 8.13.

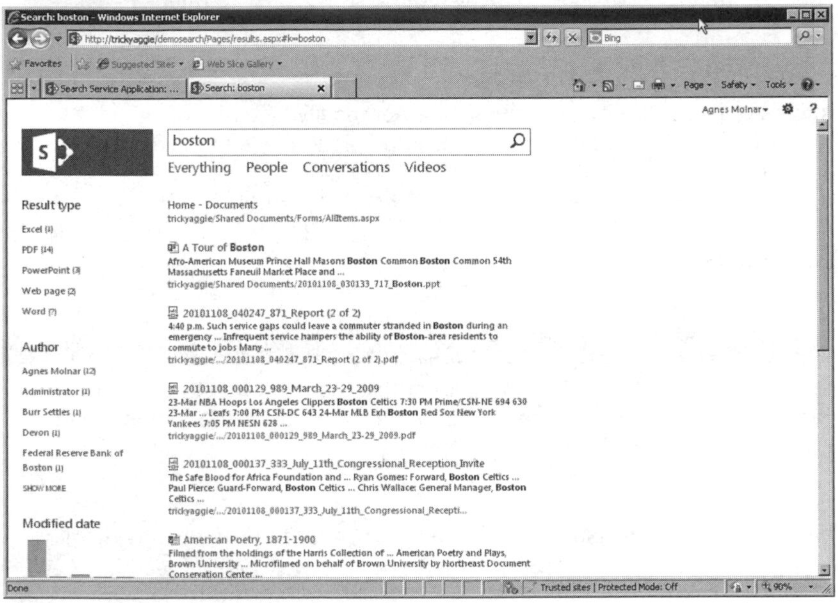

FIGURE 8.13 Deep refiners with item counts.

Summary

As shown in this chapter, Search has been improved significantly in SharePoint 2013 with features such as Crawl, Query, User Experience, and Analytics. As a result, the new platform is clean, fast, and easy to use. It makes creating search-based applications simpler than ever. It's also straightforward to install, administer, and scale.

If you want to leverage SharePoint 2013 Search's benefits but cannot or do not want to migrate your full SharePoint infrastructure to the new version, consider setting up a service farm first that hosts Search only and provides a "search first" solution to your users.

Best Practices

The following are best practices from this chapter:

- Consider the use of a dedicated Service Application farm that handles Search and that content farms can then utilize. This is particularly the case if you want to take advantage of SharePoint 2013's Search capabilities without immediately upgrading a SharePoint 2010 Farm.

- Manually install the Search Service Application, either via PowerShell or via SharePoint Central Administration. Do not rely on the Automated Wizard to perform the process.
- Utilize continuous crawl for SharePoint content to maintain fresh search results.

CHAPTER 9

Managing and Maintaining SQL Server in a SharePoint Environment

IN THIS CHAPTER

- Monitoring SQL Server in a SharePoint Environment
- Maintaining SQL Server in a SharePoint Environment
- Managing SharePoint Content Databases
- Externalizing BLOB Storage in SharePoint 2013

SharePoint 2013 introduces multiple new Structured Query Language (SQL) Server databases and, subsequently, more SQL Server resources are needed. SQL Server databases are the heart of every SharePoint farm; they are the back-end repository for all SharePoint data and provide for critical architectural elements. To achieve maximum stability of a SharePoint farm, administrators must monitor and maintain SQL Server's storage and performance on a regular basis because heavy stress on an SQL Server can ultimately degrade the end-user experience.

This chapter covers the most important SQL Server administration concepts and techniques useful for administrators. It focuses on specifics for monitoring, maintaining, and managing SharePoint databases; discusses the essential monitoring and maintenance tools; and presents guidelines for improving the performance and storage of SharePoint Server solutions running on Microsoft SQL Server.

In addition, at the end of this chapter, administrators learn how to solve the storage, performance, and manageability issues associated with huge SharePoint content databases by making use of the powerful storage externalization capabilities of SQL Server 2012 with the Remote Binary Large Objects Storage (RBS) feature.

The new high availability features of SQL 2012 that involve the use of SQL Server 2012 AlwaysOn Availability Groups (AOAGs) are covered in Chapter 4, "Advanced SharePoint 2013 Installation and Scalability."

Monitoring SQL Server in a SharePoint Environment

SharePoint administrators need to know how to proficiently monitor SQL Server performance and storage in SharePoint environments. Understanding monitoring strategies and tools enables administrators to shift from reactively dealing with issues to proactively troubleshooting and fixing problems before the server gets to the point where end users are impacted. This section walks administrators though a range of monitoring tools they should be aware of to efficiently and powerfully monitor, maintain, and troubleshoot SQL Server in SharePoint environments. Topics include Windows Management Instrumentation (WMI), event logs, dynamic management views, Reliability and Performance Monitor, Activity Monitor, Management Data Warehouse, and SQL Server Profiler. With a vast range of monitoring tools available, choosing the right tool for the job is an important skill.

Windows Management Instrumentation

WMI is a Microsoft implementation of Web-Based Enterprise Management (WBEM), an industry initiative that establishes management infrastructure standards. WMI supplies administrators with the tools to explore, understand, and use various system devices, resources, and applications of Microsoft operating systems and servers. WMI includes a rich infrastructure that enables efficient and scalable monitoring, data collection, and problem recognition. Think of WMI as a set of functionalities embedded into Microsoft operating systems and servers, including SQL Server, that enables local and remote monitoring and management.

WMI is a huge initiative and certainly deserves an entire book of its own. However, what administrators need to know is that the architecture of WMI enables extensibility through the use of *providers*, which are dynamic link library files that interface between WMI and software or hardware components.

Each provider contains a set of WMI classes. Each WMI class represents a manageable entity, exposes information through properties, and enables the execution of some actions via methods. Because a provider is designed to access some specific management information, the WMI repository is logically divided into several areas called *namespaces*. Each namespace contains a set of providers with their related classes specific to a management area.

Administrators should also know that SQL Server, as part of its installation process, adds two providers to the WMI repository (WMI Provider for Configuration Management and WMI Provider for Server Events):

- The **WMI Provider for Configuration Management** enables administrators to use WMI to manage SQL Server services, SQL Server client and server network settings, and server aliases. For example, after a connection is established with the WMI provider on a remote computer, not only is it possible to retrieve information about SQL Server instances, but it's also possible to perform actions on them such as starting and stopping the instances.

- The **WMI Provider for Server Events** enables administrators to use WMI to monitor events in SQL Server. Included are Data Definition Language (DDL) events that occur when databases are created, altered, or dropped and when tables are created, altered, or dropped, for example. In addition, software developers can write code that responds to these events, and they can even author their own set of monitoring tools. Administrators can also create an SQL Server Agent alert that is raised when a specific SQL Server event occurs that is monitored by the WMI Provider for Server Events.

It's worth mentioning that WMI enables scripting languages such as VBScript or Windows PowerShell or even the WMI command-line utility (Wmic.exe) to manage local and remote servers. This enables administrators to query this huge amount of management information through an SQL-like language called the WMI Query Language (WQL).

To explore the available namespaces, classes, and events, administrators can use a downloadable tool such as the WMI Explorer shown in Figure 9.1.

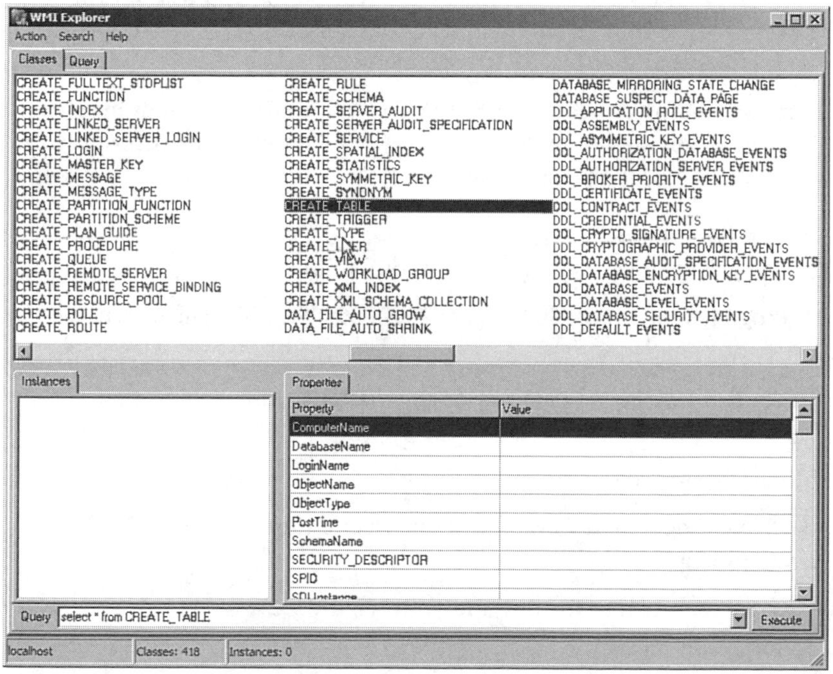

FIGURE 9.1 Using WMI Explorer.

Event Logs

An additional aspect of monitoring often disregarded by some administrators is monitoring the various log files available. SQL Server logs certain system events and user-defined events to the SQL Server error log and the Microsoft Windows application log.

Administrators can use information in the SQL Server error log to troubleshoot problems related to SQL Server. Browsing the SQL Server logs for irregular entries is an essential administration task; preferably, it should be carried out on a daily basis to help administrators spot any current or potential problem areas. An application-aware solution such as Microsoft's System Center Operations Manager (SCOM) can help to automate the process of monitoring SQL (and SharePoint) logs.

SQL Server error log files are simple text files stored on disk, but it is good practice to examine them by using SQL Server Management Studio or by executing the xp_readerrorlog extended stored procedure to prevent any SQL operations from being blocked by opening one of these files in a text editor.

A new error log file is created each time an instance of SQL Server is started; however, the sp_cycle_errorlog system stored procedure can be used to cycle the error log files without having to restart the instance of SQL Server.

The Windows application log describes events that occur on the Windows operating system and other events related to SQL Server and SQL Server Agent. Administrators can use the Windows Event Viewer to view the Windows application log and to filter the information. These event logs should be another place that administrators go to look for information about any issues that take place with SQL Server.

In the past, administrators had to view the SQL Server and Windows event logs independently; however, the SQL Server Management Studio Log File Viewer makes it possible for administrators to combine both sets of logs into a united view.

Using the SQL Server Log File Viewer

To view the log files using SQL Server Management Studio, follow these steps:

1. Click Start, All Programs, Microsoft SQL Server 2012, SQL Server Management Studio.
2. Connect to the desired SQL Server database engine instance and expand that instance.
3. In Object Explorer, expand Management.
4. Right-click SQL Server Logs, click View, and then select either SQL Server Log or SQL Server and Windows Log.
5. Double-click any log file, such as the one shown in Figure 9.2.

Log File Cycling

One thing administrators should keep in mind is that in production environments, log files can get quite large and take a long time to open. To avoid huge log files, it is a good idea to cycle them on a regular basis. Restarting the SQL Server service is not good practice. Alternatively, the log file can be automatically cycled using the sp_cycle_errorlog system stored procedure. The more entries written to the error log, the more often it should be cycled. To automate the log cycling process, administrators can utilize the SQL Server Agent to create a new agent job with a single T-SQL task to execute the stored procedure, or they can include it in a regular daily or weekly maintenance plan. Maintenance plans are covered in depth later in this chapter.

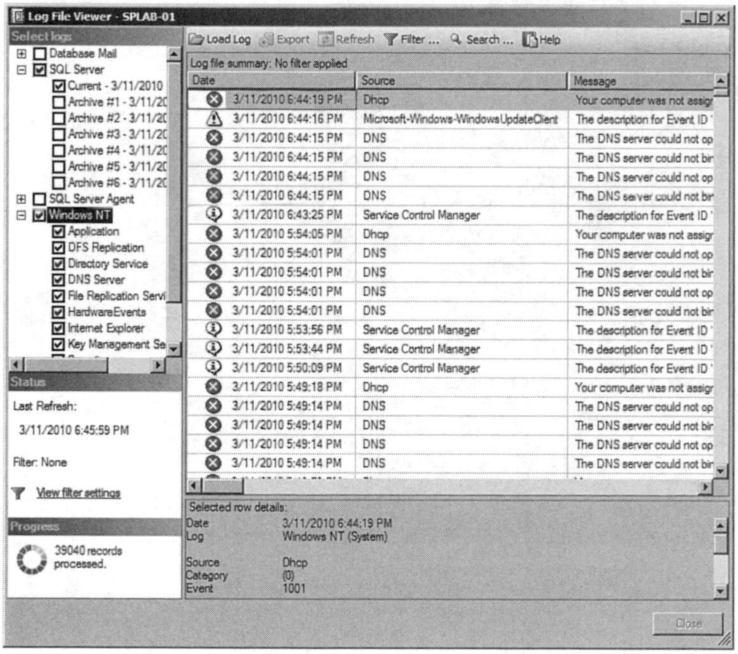

FIGURE 9.2 Using the SQL Server Log File Viewer.

Number of Log Files to Maintain

To keep as much historical information as possible, it is recommended that administrators configure the number of log files to be retained; this number depends on the amount of disk space available and the amount of activity on the server.

To configure the number of log files to be retained, follow these steps:

1. Click Start, All Programs, Microsoft SQL Server 2012, SQL Server Management Studio.
2. Connect to the desired SQL Server database engine instance and expand that instance.
3. In Object Explorer, expand Management.
4. Right-click SQL Server Logs, and click Configure.
5. As shown in Figure 9.3, check the box to limit the number of error logs created before they are recycled. SQL Server retains backups of the previous six logs, unless this option is checked and a different maximum number of error log files specified.
6. Specify a different maximum number of error log files and click OK.

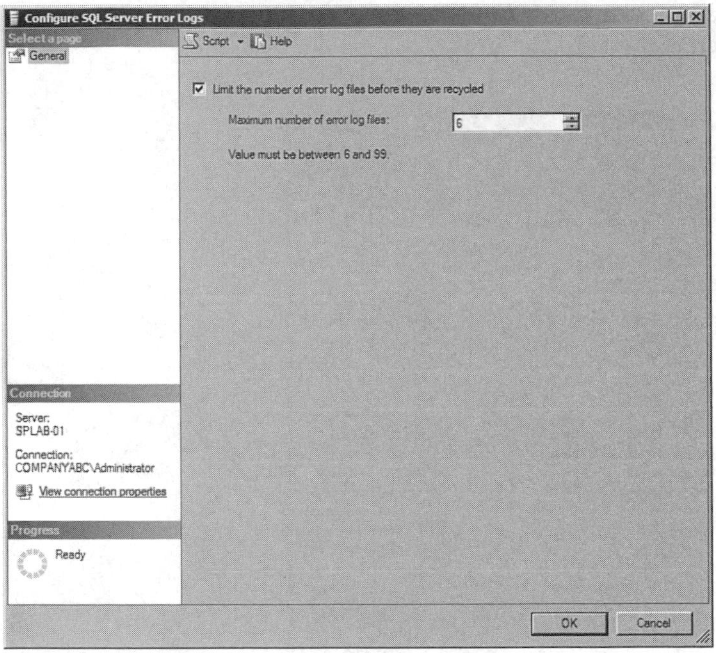

FIGURE 9.3 Configuring the number of log files to be retained.

Dynamic Management Views

Another area to retrieve monitoring information is the Master database; this is where SQL Server stores most of its configuration information. It is not a good idea to directly query the Master database, because Microsoft could change the structure of the Master database from version to version or even in service pack releases. Rather than developers building solutions that rely on the Master database schema and risking any changes in a service pack messing up the solution, Microsoft instead has created a set of dynamic management views (DMVs) and functions.

DMVs and functions return valuable information that can be used to monitor the health of a server instance, diagnose problems, and tune performance. They give administrators an easy way to monitor what SQL Servers are doing and how they are performing by providing a snapshot of the exact state of the SQL Servers at the point they are queried. They replace the need to query the system tables or to use other inconvenient methods of retrieving system information in use prior to SQL Server 2005. SQL Server 2005 introduced DMVs, and the latest release, SQL Server 2012, includes additional useful DMVs.

Whenever an instance is started, SQL Server starts saving state and diagnostic data into DMVs. When an instance is restarted, the information is flushed from the views, and new data begins to be loaded.

DMVs and functions are part of the sys schema in the Master database. Administrators can find a list of dynamic views in SQL Server Management Studio under Master/Views/System Views, and the dynamic functions are located under Master/Programmability/Functions/System Functions/Table-valued Functions. Each dynamic object's name has a dm_ prefix.

For example, later in this chapter, the `sys.dm_db_index_physical_stats` dynamic management function is used to determine the fragmentation percentage of the indexes for efficient database maintenance.

Reliability and Performance Monitor

One of the Windows tools administrators should be skilled at using is the Reliability and Performance Monitor. Administrators who used `perfmon` in Windows Server 2003 may find the Reliability and Performance Monitor in Windows Server 2008/R2/2012 a bit confusing when they first explore it. However, in addition to all the features included in previous versions, it now presents some new functionality that can make performance troubleshooting much easier and powerful because it provides a more detailed view of Windows server performance and per-instance SQL Server-specific counters.

The Reliability and Performance Monitor can monitor resource usage for the server and provide information specific to SQL Server either locally or for a remote server. It provides a massive set of counters that can be used to capture a baseline of server resource usage, and it can monitor over longer periods to help discover trends. It can also detect abnormal values at a glance for key performance counters on critical SQL Server instances. In addition, administrators can configure it to produce alerts when preset thresholds are surpassed.

After opening the Reliability and Performance Monitor, as shown in Figure 9.4, the % Processor Time counter from the Processor object is automatically monitored in real time with a 1-second refresh interval. Additional counters can be appended to the graph by clicking the green plus icon on the toolbar and navigating through objects, which classify the counters into groups. When an SQL Server instance is installed on a server, it adds more than 1,000 new performance counters to the Performance Monitor section of the Reliability and Performance Monitor. Of the many performance counters that can be selected when troubleshooting an SQL Server instance, choosing the appropriate key indicators can significantly help administrators quickly isolate bottlenecks and direct their investigation to the appropriate resources for corrective actions.

In addition, administrators can capture performance counters to log files for long-term analysis by creating data collector sets. Creating data collector sets is beyond the scope of this chapter.

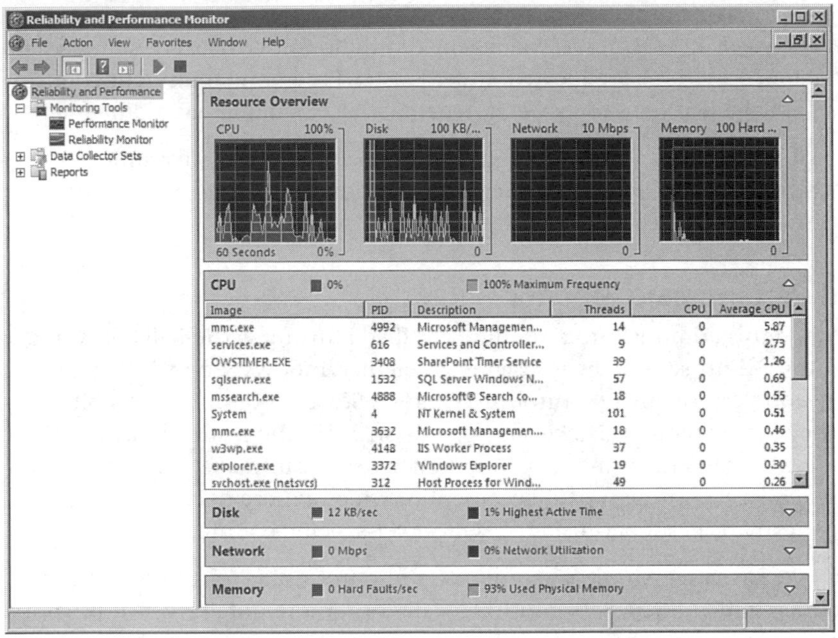

FIGURE 9.4 Reliability and Performance Monitor.

Activity Monitor

Undoubtedly, the Reliability and Performance Monitor is a great tool for administrators to monitor resource usage. However, an administrator should first leverage the SQL Server Activity Monitor, as shown in Figure 9.5, when needing to gain some quick insight into an SQL Server system's performance. Starting in SQL Server 2008, the Activity Monitor introduced a new performance dashboard with intuitive graphs and performance gauges with drill-down and filtering capabilities. The new tool's look and feel is similar to the Reliability and Performance Monitor, but the information captured is broken down into five main sections dedicated to SQL Server performance monitoring.

The sections are Overview, Processes, Resource Waits, Data File Input/Output (I/O), and Recent Expensive Queries. In SQL Server 2012, right-clicking an SQL Server instance within Object Explorer and specifying the Activity Monitor launches the tool, as shown in Figure 9.5.

- **Overview:** Shows the graphical display of Processor Time (%), Number of Waiting Tasks, Database I/O (MB/Sec), and the Number of Batch Requests/second.
- **Processes:** Lists all the active users who are connected to the SQL Server database engine. This is beneficial for administrators because they can click any of the session IDs, run an SQL Server Profiler trace to capture all its activities, or even kill a specific process.

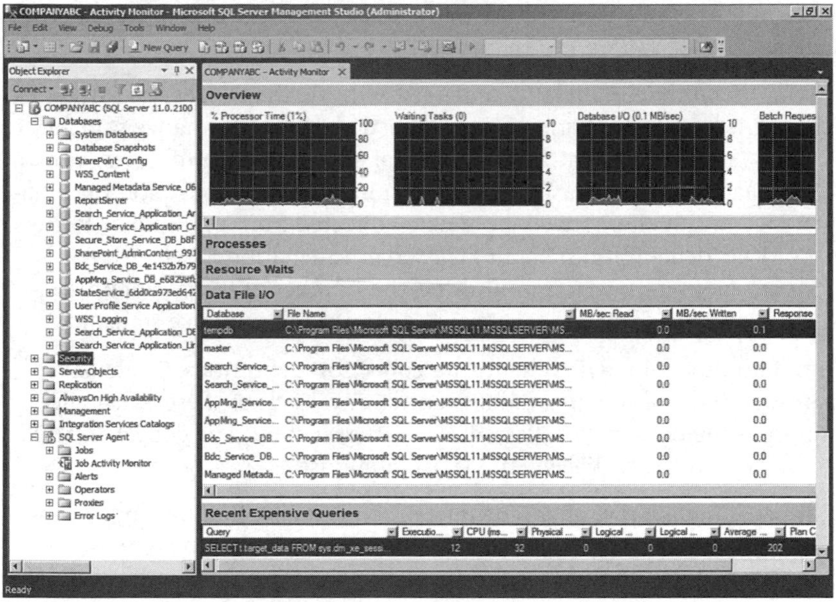

FIGURE 9.5 Activity Monitor in SQL Server 2012.

- **Resource Waits:** Displays resource waits vertically based on the following wait categories: CPU, SQL Common Language Runtime (SQLCLR), Network I/O, Latch, Lock, Logging, Memory, Buffer I/O, Buffer Latch, and Compilation. From a horizontal perspective, the Wait Time, Recent Wait Time, Average Waiter Counter, and Cumulative Wait Time metrics are published for each Wait category. Analogous to the Processes section, data can be filtered based on items within a column.

- **Data File I/O:** Displays disk-level I/O information related to all the data and log files of user and system databases. Administrators can use this to rapidly recognize databases that are performing badly because of disk bottlenecks.

- **Recent Expensive Queries:** The last section in Activity Monitor is Recent Expensive Queries. This section gives administrators the opportunity to capture the queries that are performing the worst and negatively influencing an SQL Server instance. Approximately 10 to 15 of the worst and most expensive queries are displayed in the performance dashboard. The actual query is displayed with augmenting metrics such as Execution in Minutes, CPU ms/sec, Physical Reads/sec, Logical Write/sec, Logical Reads/sec, Average Duration in ms, and Plan Count. It is also possible to right-click the most expensive query and show the execution plan.

Data Collectors

The Management Data Warehouse provides administrators with a simple mechanism to track statistics over time. By implementing the Management Data Warehouse, administrators can monitor performance and do trend analysis for the SQL Server 2012 instances they manage.

The Management Data Warehouse is a relational database inside the SQL Server 2012 instance that holds a variety of performance-related statistics. The performance statistics in the Management Data Warehouse are gathered via special data-gathering routines, known as *data collections*. The Management Data Warehouse can include data collection information from a sole instance or can alternatively hold data collected from multiple instances. The data collection process depends on prebuilt SQL Server Integration Services (SSIS) routines and SQL Server Agent jobs, which diminishes the number of things administrators need to do to build and maintain a database that contains performance statistics.

SQL Server 2012 provides three different system data collection definitions. These data collections are Disk Usage, Query Activity, and Server Activity. Each of these data collection definitions identifies the data to be collected, how often it should be collected, and how long it should be kept in the Management Data Warehouse.

Data collections can be run manually, on a schedule, or continually. Manual and scheduled data collections collect and upload data into the Management Data Warehouse on the same schedule. These types of data collections are known as *noncached* collections. When a data collection runs continually, data is cached in a directory and then uploaded to the Management Data Warehouse from time to time. These are known as *cached collections*.

It is also worth mentioning that Microsoft has also provided standard reports to enable administrators to drill down into data gathered for each of these collections using SQL Server Management Studio.

SQL Server Profiler

Microsoft SQL Server Profiler is a graphical user interface to SQL Trace for monitoring an instance of the Database Engine or Analysis Services. Administrators can capture and save data about each event to a file or table to analyze later. For example, administrators can monitor a production environment to tell which stored procedures are affecting the overall performance. SQL Server Profiler is used for activities such as the following:

- Stepping through problematic queries to find the cause of a problem.
- Finding and diagnosing bad-performing queries.
- Capturing the series of T-SQL statements that lead to a problem. Saved traces can then be used to replicate the problem on test servers for later diagnostics.
- Monitoring the performance of SQL Server to tune architecture.
- Correlating performance-collected counters to diagnose problems.

To use SQL Server Profiler, an administrator needs to understand the terms that describe the way the tool functions.

Event

An *event* is an action that is generated within an instance of SQL Server Database Engine. These actions are used to perform specific tasks such as the following:

- Login connections and disconnections
- T-SQL `SELECT`, `INSERT`, `UPDATE`, and `DELETE` statements
- Remote procedure call (RPC) batch status
- The start or end of a stored procedure
- The start or end of statements within stored procedures
- The start or end of an SQL batch
- An error written to the SQL Server error log
- Lock-related actions on a database object
- Security permission checks

All the data generated by an event is displayed in the trace in a single row. This row is intersected by data columns that describe the event in detail.

Event Class

An *event class* is a type of event that can be traced. The event class contains all the data that can be reported by an event, like the following:

- SQL:BatchCompleted
- Audit Login
- Audit Logout
- Lock:Acquired
- Lock:Released

Event Category

An *event category* defines the way events are grouped within SQL Server Profiler. For example, all lock events classes are grouped within the Locks event category. However, this grouping is only related to SQL Server Profiler, not the database engine.

Data Column

A *data column* is an attribute of an event class captured in the trace. Because the event class determines the type of data that can be collected, not all data columns are applicable to all event classes. For example, in a trace that captures the Lock:Acquired event class, the BinaryData data column contains the value of the locked page ID or row, but the Integer Data data column does not contain any value because it is not applicable to the event class being captured.

Template

A *template* defines the default configuration for a trace. Specifically, it includes the event classes an administrator wants to monitor with SQL Server Profiler. For example, an administrator can create a template that specifies the events, data columns, and filters to use. A template is saved as a file which controls the trace data that is captured when a trace based on the template is launched. This is useful for quick look and diagnostics in search for common known issues.

Trace

A *trace* captures data based on selected event classes, data columns, and filters. For example, an administrator can create a trace to monitor exception errors or to monitor what is being currently executed on the server, how long it takes, who is executing the statement, and all the different data columns.

Filter

Criteria can be defined to *filter* the data collected by an event. To avoid large traces, an administrator can limit the Microsoft Windows usernames in the trace to specific users, thereby reducing the output data.

If a filter is not set, all events of the selected event classes are returned in the trace output.

Using SQL Server Profiler

1. Click Start, All Programs, SQL Server 2012, Performance Tools, SQL Server Profiles.
2. Click File, New Trace, and then log in to the desired server.
3. The Create Trace window pops up, as shown in Figure 9.6.

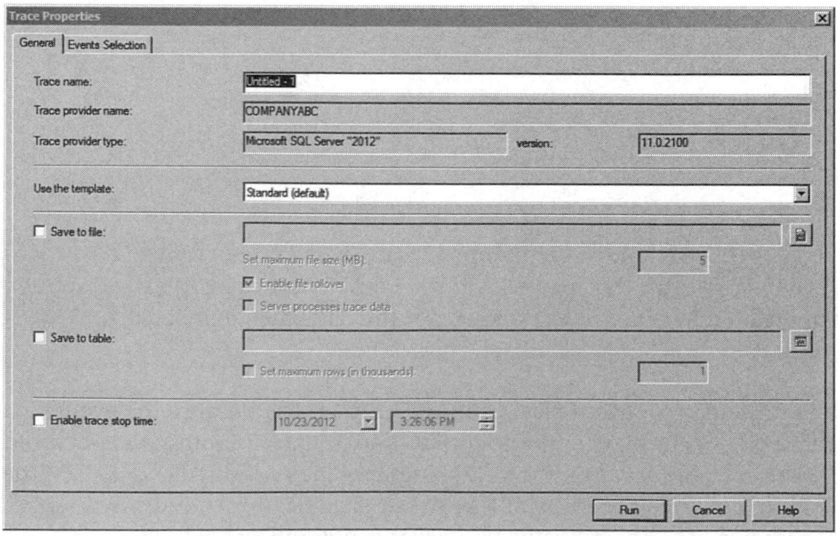

FIGURE 9.6 New profiler trace.

4. Administrators can provide the trace name and choose a template for tracking some events or filters in addition to the way to store the trace. This can be an SQL Server table or a simple file.

5. By clicking the second tab, the event selection opens as shown in Figure 9.7.

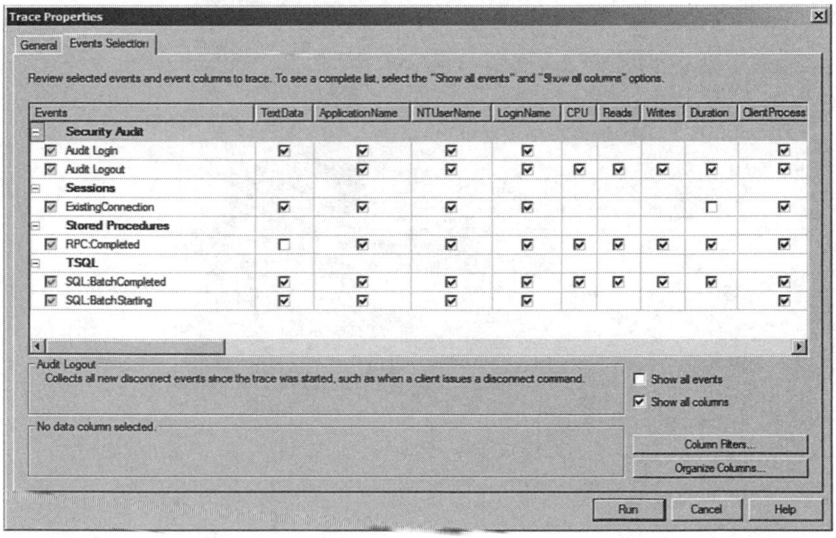

FIGURE 9.7 Profiler trace events and columns.

6. Administrators can select the events to trace, to view the query and its execution parameters; the info will reside in SQL:BatchCompleted because this event occurs when a query is fired to the database. In this event, the actual query appears, who fired it, and how long it took to execute.

7. Figure 9.8 shows the trace that starts listing all events requested in the previous window and the actual statement that's being executed on the database. Stopping or erasing the trace for better readability options exist, and filteration in the previous window is very useful to query down all the rows with useful information about the desired database.

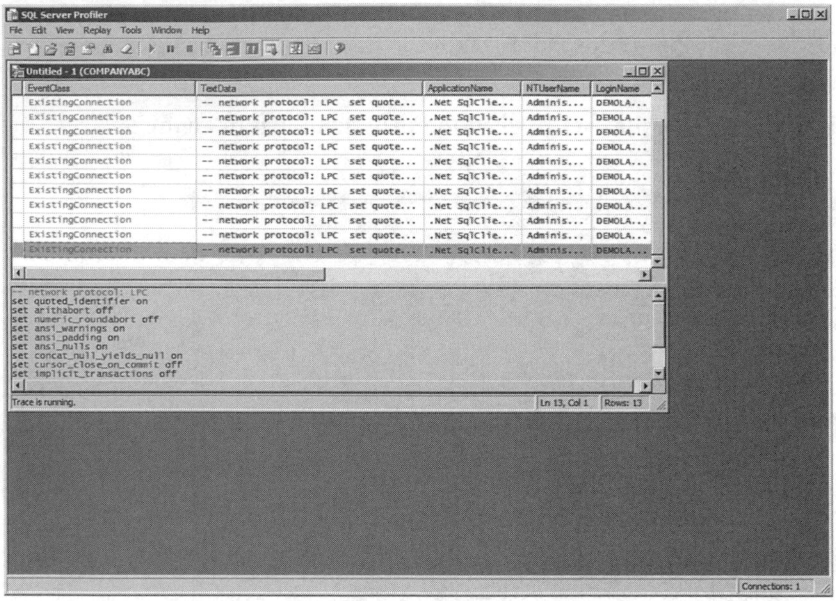

FIGURE 9.8 Running trace in profiler.

Maintaining SQL Server in a SharePoint Environment

To keep SharePoint operating smoothly and with optimal performance, it is highly recommended that SharePoint administrators conduct regular maintenance on each SQL Server database. Such maintenance tasks include rebuilding indexes, checking database integrity, encrypting the databases, updating index statistics, and performing internal consistency checks and backups. Administrators can perform database maintenance tasks either by executing T-SQL commands or by running the Database Maintenance Wizard. This section provides information and recommendations for maintaining the databases that host SharePoint data and configurations. Later in this section, administrators learn how to automate and schedule the major maintenance tasks by creating database maintenance plans via SQL Server Database Maintenance Wizard.

Checking and Repairing Database Integrity

`DBCC CHECKDB` is the most often used validation command for checking the logical and physical integrity of the whole database. Essentially, `DBCC CHECKDB` is a superset command that actually runs `CHECKALLOC`, `CHECKTABLE`, and `CHECKCATALOG`.

Here are some recommendations for using `DBCC CHECKDB`:

- Administrators should run `DBCC CHECKDB` rather than the individual operations because it identifies most of the errors and is generally safe to run in a production environment.

- After running `DBCC CHECKDB`, administrators should run it again with the `REPAIR` argument to repair any reported errors.
- `DBCC CHECKDB` can be time-consuming, and it requires schema locks that prevent metadata changes; therefore, it is highly recommended that administrators run it during nonproduction hours.
- The command should be run on a table-by-table basis if it is used to perform consistency checks on large databases.

Monitoring and Reducing Fragmentation

Although indexes can speed up the execution of queries, some overhead is associated with them. Indexes consume extra disk space and involve additional time to update themselves any time data is updated, deleted, or inserted in a table.

When indexes are first built, little or no fragmentation should be present. Over time, as data is inserted, updated, and deleted, fragmentation levels on the underlying indexes might begin to increase.

When a page of data is completely full and further data must be added to it, a page split occurs. To make room for the new arriving data, SQL Server creates another data page somewhere else in the database (not necessarily in a contiguous location) and moves some of the data from the full page to the newly created one. The effect of this is that the blocks of data are logically linear but physically nonlinear. Therefore, when searching for data, SQL Server has to jump from one page to somewhere else in the database looking for the next page it needs instead of going directly from one page to the next. This results in performance degradation and inefficient space utilization.

Monitoring Fragmentation

The fragmentation level of an index is the percentage of blocks that are logically linear and physically nonlinear. In SQL Server 2012 and SQL Server 2008 R2, administrators can use the sys.dm_db_index_physical_stats dynamic management function and keep an eye on the avg_fragmentation_in_percent column to monitor and measure the fragmentation level. The value for avg_fragmentation_in_percent should be as close to zero as possible for maximum performance. However, values from 0% percent through 10% may be acceptable.

Reducing Fragmentation

In the previous version of SharePoint, it was recommended to track and reduce the fragmentation level by running the database statistics timer job, which in turn updates the query optimization statistics and rebuilds all indexes in the content databases every time it runs. Another option was reorganizing or rebuilding the indexes on a regular basis using the SQL Server 2012 or SQL Server 2008 R2 Maintenance Wizard.

In SharePoint 2013, administrators no longer need to worry about fragmentation because SharePoint can do that on their behalf via the health analyzer. The health analyzer performs "health checks" based on timer jobs and self-heals the database index fragmentation automatically.

Shrinking Data Files

In SQL Server 2012 and SQL Server 2008 R2, administrators can reclaim free space from the end of data files to remove unused pages and recover disk space.

However, shrinking data files is not recommended unless the content database has lost at least half its content. This usually happens after some activities create white space in the content database, such as moving a site collection from a content database to another one or deleting a massive amount of data. Shrinking SharePoint databases other than content databases is not recommended, because they do not generally experience as many necessary deletions to contain considerable free space.

Shrinking a Database by Using SQL Server 2012 Management Studio

To shrink a database by using SQL Server 2012 Management Studio, follow these steps:

1. Click Start, All Programs, Microsoft SQL Server 2012, SQL Server Management Studio.
2. Connect to the desired SQL Server database engine instance and expand that instance.
3. Expand Databases, right-click the database to be shrunk, click Tasks, click Shrink, and click Files.
4. Select the file type and filename from the dialog box shown in Figure 9.9.

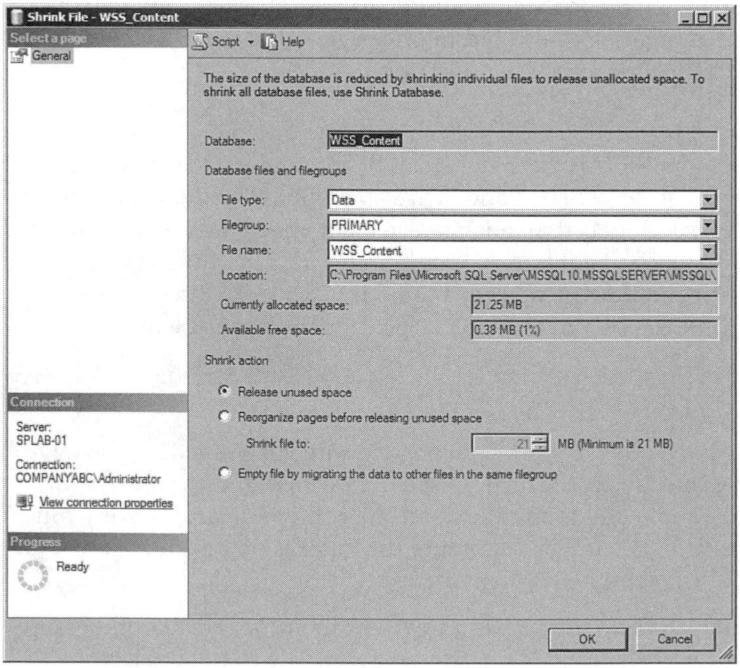

FIGURE 9.9 Shrinking a database using SQL Server 2012.

5. (Optional) Select Release Unused Space. Selecting this option causes any unused space in the file to be released to the operating system and shrinks the file to the last allocated extent. This reduces the file size without moving any data.

6. (Optional) Select Reorganize Pages Before Releasing Unused Space. If this option is selected, the Shrink File To option must be set to value. Selecting this option causes any unused space in the file to be released to the operating system and tries to relocate rows to unallocated pages.

7. (Optional) Select Empty File by Migrating the Data to Other Files in the Same Filegroup. Selecting this option moves all data from the specified file to other files in the filegroup. The empty file can then be deleted. This option is the same as executing `DBCC SHRINKFILE` with the `EMPTYFILE` option.

8. Click OK.

Creating SQL Server Maintenance Plans

Maintaining SharePoint back-end databases can significantly improve the health and performance of SharePoint servers. Unfortunately, administrators often do not perform regular database maintenance because maintaining SharePoint 2013 environments involves a huge set of maintenance tasks.

Fortunately, Microsoft has provided *maintenance plans* as a way to automate these tasks. A maintenance plan performs a comprehensive set of SQL Server jobs that run at scheduled intervals. Specifically, the maintenance plan conducts scheduled SQL Server maintenance tasks to ensure that databases are performing optimally, are regularly backed up, and are checked for anomalies. Administrators can use the Maintenance Plan Wizard (included with SQL Server) to create and schedule these daily tasks. In addition, the wizard can configure database and transaction log backups.

It is also worth mentioning that administrators should set any maintenance operations or maintenance plans to run during off-hours to minimize the performance impact on users.

Configuring an SQL Server 2012 Database Maintenance Plan

To configure an SQL Server 2012 database maintenance plan, follow these steps:

1. Click Start, All Programs, Microsoft SQL Server 2012, SQL Server Management Studio.

2. Connect to the desired SQL Server database engine instance.

3. Click Management, right-click Maintenance Plans, and click Maintenance Plan Wizard. (The SQL Server Agent Service should be running.)

4. On the Welcome to the Database Maintenance Plan Wizard screen, click Next to continue.

5. On the Select Plan Properties screen, as shown in Figure 9.10, enter a name and description for the maintenance plan.

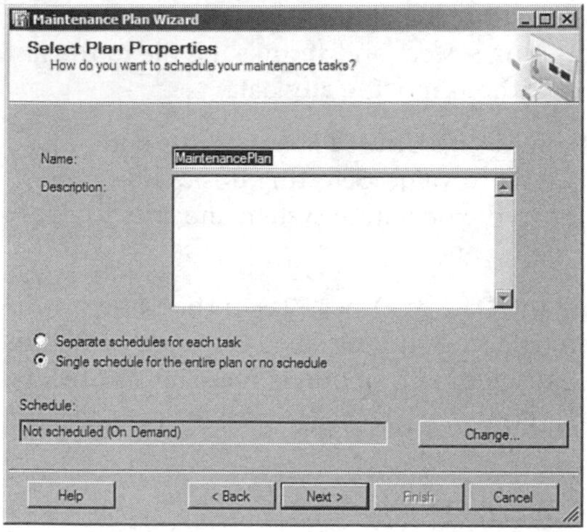

FIGURE 9.10 Creating a database maintenance plan.

6. Decide whether to configure one or more maintenance plans.

   To configure a single maintenance plan, select Single Schedule for the Entire Plan or No Schedule. This option is chosen in the example in Figure 9.10.

   To configure multiple maintenance plans with specific tasks, select Separate Schedules for Each Task.

7. Click Change to set a schedule for the plan. The Job Schedule Properties dialog box appears, as shown in Figure 9.11.

8. Complete the schedule, click OK, and then click Next to continue.

9. On the Select Maintenance Tasks screen (see Figure 9.12), select the maintenance tasks to include in the plan, and then click Next to continue.

10. In the Select Maintenance Task Order page, change or review the order that the tasks will be executed in, select a task, and then click Move Up or Move Down. When tasks are in the desired order, click Next. The wizard helps you through setting the details for each task. For example, Figure 9.13 shows the configuration of the Database Check Integrity Task.

11. On the Select Report Options page, select Write a Report to a Text File, select a location for the files, as shown in Figure 9.14, and then click Next until the wizard is completed.

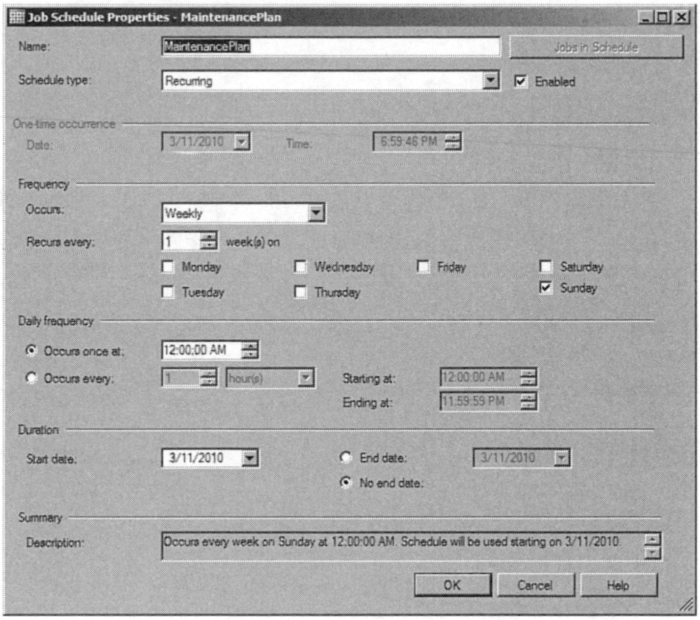

FIGURE 9.11 Scheduling a database maintenance plan.

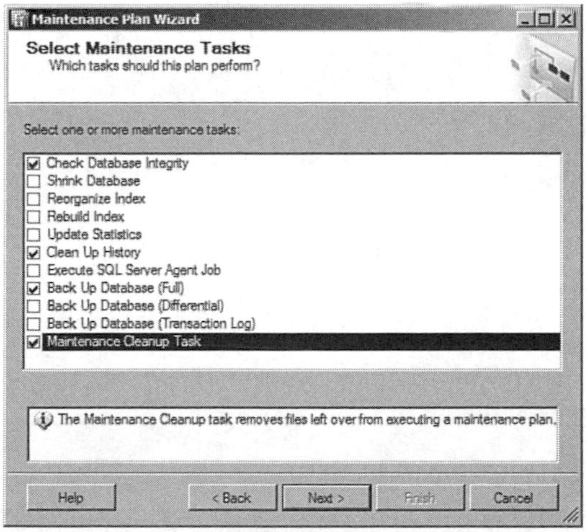

FIGURE 9.12 Selecting database maintenance tasks.

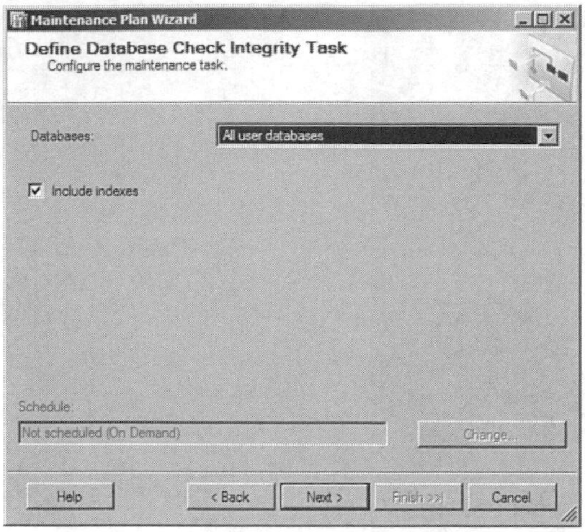

FIGURE 9.13 Configuring database maintenance tasks.

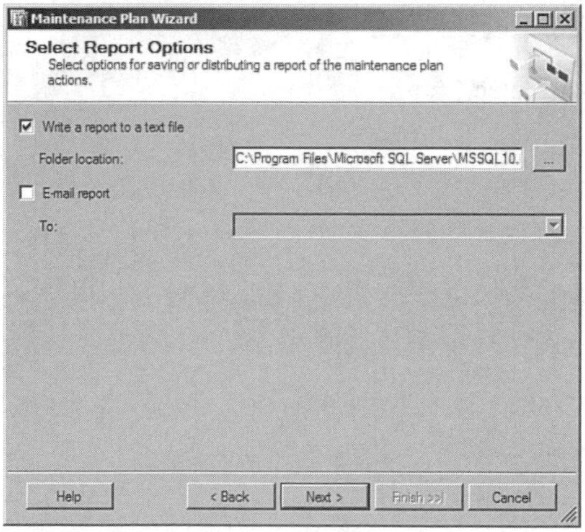

FIGURE 9.14 Saving and emailing maintenance plan reports.

NOTE

It is highly recommended that administrators include the Check Database Integrity maintenance task for all SharePoint databases and the Maintenance Cleanup Task maintenance task in their plans. It is also recommended not to select the option to shrink the database, primarily because automatically shrinking databases on a periodic basis leads to excessive fragmentation and produces I/O activity, which can negatively influence the performance of SharePoint.

Using SQL Server Transparent Data Encryption

Transparent Data Encryption (TDE) was first introduced in SQL Server 2008 to provide a real-time encryption and decryption for the database data and log files. This feature can be used to encrypt SharePoint content databases at the SQL level, without the need to modify any settings in the SharePoint farm. This type of transparent encryption allows organizations to comply with governmental and industry regulations that require content to be stored in encrypted format, but does not present any new complications to a SharePoint environment, as the application itself is unaware that any encryption is happening. Stolen SharePoint database backups or data files are useless since the database will not be restored on any other server without the master certificate or the encrypting key. TDE uses a database encryption key (DEK), which is a symmetric key secured by a certificate in the Master database or an asymmetric key stored in Enterprise Knowledge Management (EKM) module. The encryption process is very easy, and the first thing an administrator should do after encrypting the database is to back up the certificate. Otherwise, the database will not be readable on any another server without the master key.

To enable TDE encryption on a SharePoint database, follow these steps:

1. Open SQL Server Management Studio by clicking Start, All Programs, Microsoft SQL Server 2012, SQL Server Management Studio. Connect to the desired SQL Server database engine instance, and then create a master key and a certificate in the master database by executing the following T-SQL commands:

```
USE master;
GO
CREATE MASTER KEY ENCRYPTION BY PASSWORD = '<CERTIFICATEPASSWORD>';
go
CREATE CERTIFICATE MyServerCert WITH SUBJECT = ENCRYPTION_CERTIFICATE';
go
```

2. Create the encryption key that will encrypt the database with the pre-created certificate by executing the following T-SQL commands:

```
USE WSS_Content;
GO
CREATE DATABASE ENCRYPTION KEY
WITH ALGORITHM = AES_128
ENCRYPTION BY SERVER CERTIFICATE MyServerCert;
GO
ALTER DATABASE WSS_Content
SET ENCRYPTION ON;
GO
```

3. The process runs and starts encrypting the database. An administrator can check the status of the encryption process by executing the following T-SQL command:

```
SELECT *
FROM sys.dm_database_encryption_keys
WHERE encryption_state = 3;
```

3 is the status for an encrypted database.

4. Back up the encryption certificate to restore it on other servers:

```
BACKUP CERTIFICATE sales05 TO FILE = 'c:\storedcerts\MyServerCert'
  WITH PRIVATE KEY (FILE = 'c:\storedkeys\MyServerCertKey',
  ENCRYPTION BY PASSWORD = 'STRONGPASSWORD');
```

5. Before restoring the database on other servers, restoring the certificate is mandatory by using the following T-SQL command:

```
USE master;
GO
CREATE MASTER KEY ENCRYPTION BY PASSWORD = 'STRONGPASSWORD';
GO

CREATE CERTIFICATE MyServerCert
FROM FILE = 'c:\storedkeys\MyServerCert'
WITH PRIVATE KEY
(
    FILE = 'c:\storedkeys\MyServerCertKey',
    DECRYPTION BY PASSWORD = 'STRONGPASSWORD'
);
GO
```

An administrator can now guarantee the security of the database files with an encryption standard that is compliant with most of the different security standards.

Managing SharePoint Content Databases

As previously explained in the “Monitoring SQL Server in a SharePoint Environment” section, administrators should always keep an eye on the performance and storage of SharePoint back-end databases. In response to the data they gather from the vast range of monitoring tools, administrators should also know how to manage SharePoint content databases, how to manually add a content database to a web application, how to move a site collection between content databases, and how to move content databases between servers that are running SQL Server, between instances of SQL Server, or from one SharePoint 2013 web application to another. Some of these tasks can be completed directly from Central Administration; others can be done only via PowerShell or the deprecated STSADM command-line utility. These different tasks and techniques are explained in detail in this section.

Adding a Content Database

Creating a new content database does not mean that any new content will be stored in it, because a site collection cannot span content databases. However, by creating a new content database and following some extra steps, administrators can instruct SharePoint where to create new site collections.

Adding a Content Database Using Central Administration

To create a new content database and attach it to the specified web application, follow these steps:

1. Click Start, All Programs, Microsoft SharePoint 2013 Products, SharePoint 2013 Central Administration.
2. On the SharePoint Central Administration (SPCA) website, click Application Management.
3. In the Databases section, click Manage Content Databases.
4. On the Manage Content Databases page, as shown in Figure 9.15, click Add a Content Database.

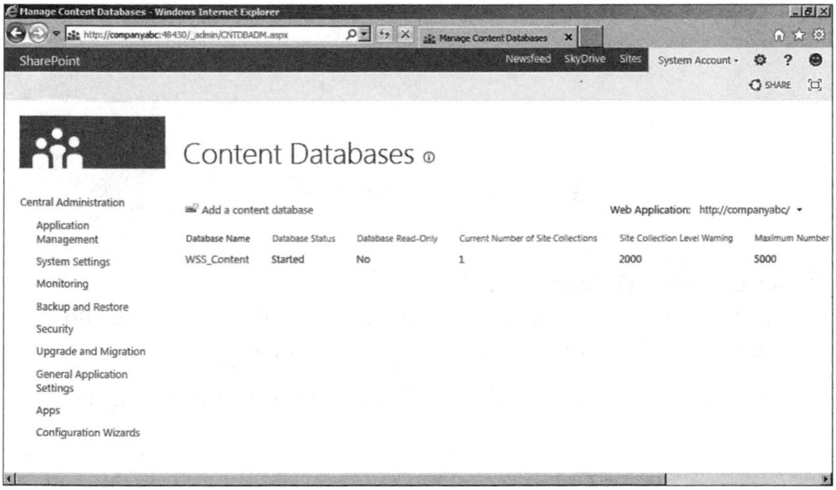

FIGURE 9.15 Manage Content Databases page in Central Administration.

5. On the Add Content Database page, as shown in Figure 9.16, do the following:
   A. Select a web application for the new database.
   B. Select a database server to host the new database.
   C. Specify the authentication method that the new database will use, and supply an account name and password, if they are necessary.

D. Specify both the total number of top-level sites that can be created in the database and the number at which a warning will be issued.

6. Click OK.

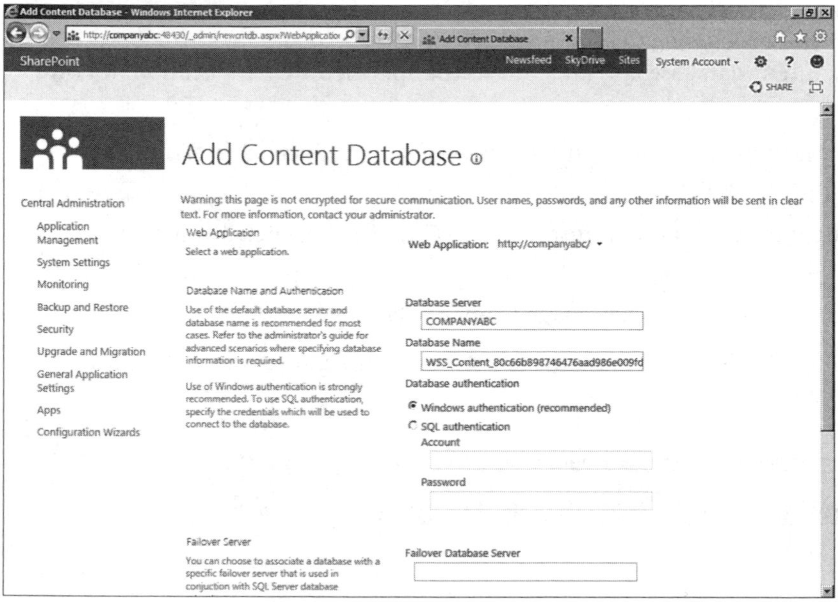

FIGURE 9.16 Add Content Database page in Central Administration.

Adding a Content Database Using Windows PowerShell

Administrators can use the following procedure to create a new content database and attach it to the specified web application using Windows PowerShell:

1. Click Start, All Programs, Microsoft SharePoint 2013 Products, SharePoint 2013 Management Shell.

2. At the Windows PowerShell command prompt (PS C:\>), type the following command, and then press Enter:

```
New-SPContentDatabase -Name <String> -WebApplication <SPWebApplicationPipeBind>
```

The `-Name` parameter specifies the name of the content database to be created. The `-WebApplication` parameter specifies the web application to which the new database is to be attached.

Creating a Site Collection in a Specific Content Database

In SharePoint 2010 days, to force SharePoint to create new site collections in a specific content database, the target database should have been the only one with the Ready status; all the other databases associated with the web application should have been set Offline. In SharePoint 2013, this is no longer the case; administrators can now directly use the `New-SPSite` PowerShell commandlet (cmdlet) to create a new Site Collection in a specific content database.

Creating a Site Collection in a Specific Content Database Using Windows PowerShell

To directly use the content database for a new collection using PowerShell, follow these steps:

1. Click Start, All Programs, Microsoft SharePoint 2013 Products, SharePoint 2013 Management Shell.
2. At the Windows PowerShell command prompt (PS C:\>), type the following command, and then press Enter:

```
New-SPSite -Url <String> -OwnerAlias <String> [-ContentDatabase
<SPContentDatabasePipeBind>]
```

Moving Site Collections Between Content Databases

There might be some situations when a site collection hosted within a content database is unexpectedly growing, and the database is approaching the 100GB limit recommended by Microsoft. At such times, administrators should manually move the growing site collections from the larger content database to another smaller one.

Determining the Size of the Source Site Collection Using Windows PowerShell

Administrators should always double-check that the destination hard disk can comfortably store the site collection data by determining the size of the site collection that is to be moved. To determine the size of a site collection, follow these steps:

1. Click Start, All Programs, Microsoft SharePoint 2013 Products, SharePoint 2013 Management Shell.
2. At the Windows PowerShell command prompt (PS C:\>), type the following command, and then press Enter:

```
Get-SPSiteAdministration -Identity http://ServerName/Sites/SiteName| ft
Url,DiskUsed
```

   Replace `http://ServerName/Sites/SiteName` with the name of the site collection.

Moving Site Collections Between Content Databases Using Windows PowerShell

Administrators can use the Windows PowerShell command `Move-SPSite` to move site collections between content databases:

1. Click Start, All Programs, Microsoft SharePoint 2013 Products, SharePoint 2013 Management Shell.

2. At the Windows PowerShell command prompt (PS C:\>), type the following command, and then press Enter:

```
Move-SPSite <http://ServerName/Sites/SiteName> -DestinationDatabase
<DestinationContentDb>
```

Replace `http://ServerName/Sites/SiteName` with the name of the site collection, and replace *`<DestinationContentDb>`* with the name of the destination content database.

Moving Content Databases in SharePoint 2013

Administrators might sometimes need to move content databases between servers that are running SQL Server, between instances of SQL Server, or from one SharePoint 2013 web application to another. This can be completed using SharePoint 2013 Central Administration or using Windows PowerShell. In both cases, you follow these steps:

1. Pause any service applications and services that might run against the desired content database.
2. Remove the content database from the SharePoint web application.
3. Detach the database from the source SQL Server instance.
4. Move the database files to the target location.
5. Attach the database files to the destination SQL Server instance.
6. Add the content database to the destination SharePoint web application.

Moving Content Databases Using Central Administration

1. Click Start, All Programs, Microsoft SharePoint 2013 Products, SharePoint 2013 Central Administration.
2. On the SPCA website, click Monitoring, and then click Check Job Status, as shown in Figure 9.17.
3. For each Timer Job running for the target database, click Edit Job, Disable, and then click OK, as shown in Figure 9.18.
4. On the SPCA website, click Application Management.
5. In the Databases section, click Manage Content Databases.
6. On the Manage Content Databases page, choose the desired content database.
7. In the Remove Content Database section, as shown in Figure 9.19, click Remove Content Database, and then click OK.
8. Open SQL Server Management Studio by clicking Start, All Programs, Microsoft SQL Server 2012, SQL Server Management Studio.

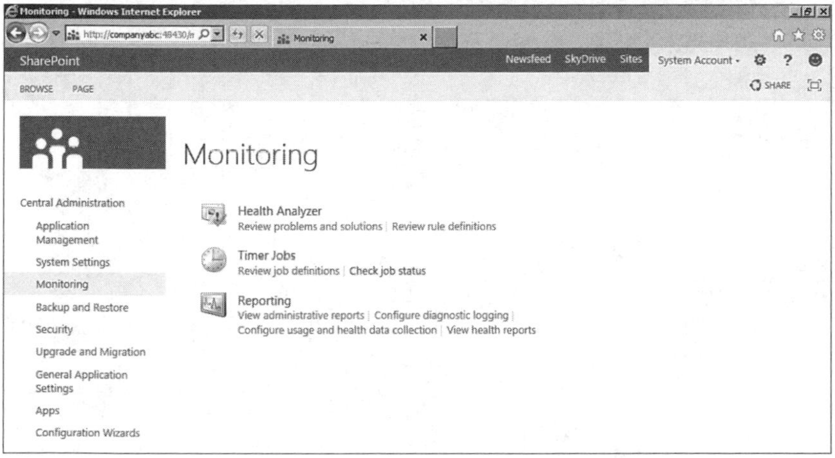

FIGURE 9.17 Viewing the Monitoring page in SPCA.

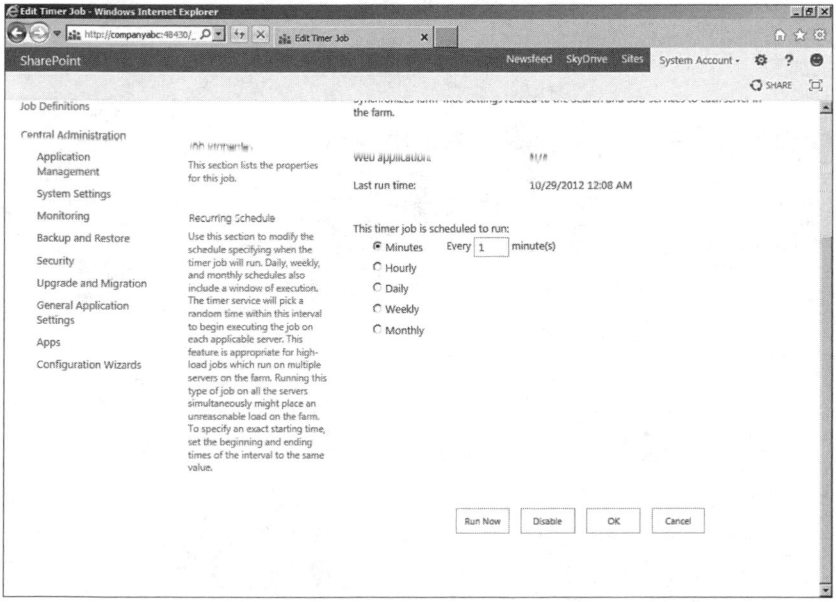

FIGURE 9.18 Disabling the Timer Jobs.

9. Connect to the desired SQL Server database engine instance and expand that instance.

10. Right-click the content database, point to Tasks, and then click Detach, as shown in Figure 9.20.

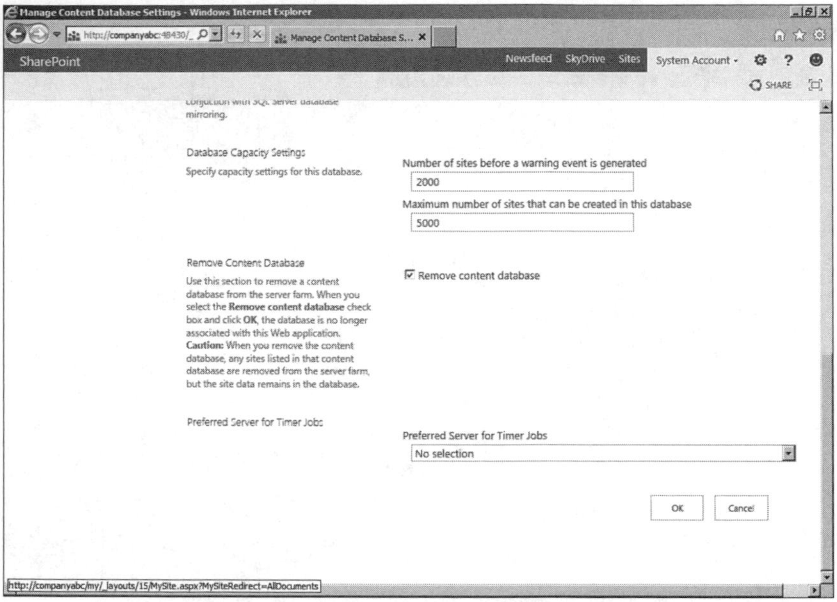

FIGURE 9.19 Removing a content database from Central Administration.

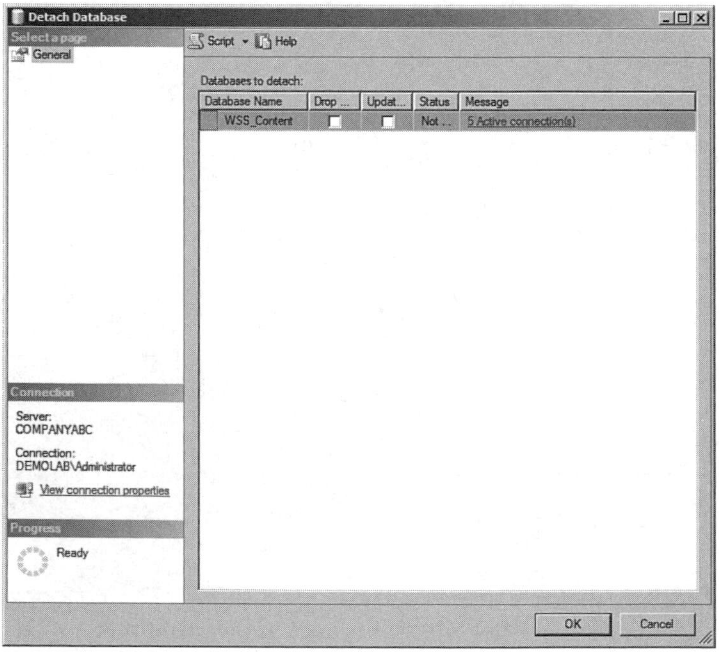

FIGURE 9.20 Detaching a content database using SQL Server 2012.

11. Using Windows Explorer, move all database files (.mdf, .ldf, and .ndf) to the desired location in the other server.
12. In the destination server, open SQL Server Management Studio and connect to the desired SQL Server instance.
13. Right-click the destination instance in Object Explorer, point to Tasks, and then click Attach, as shown in Figure 9.21.

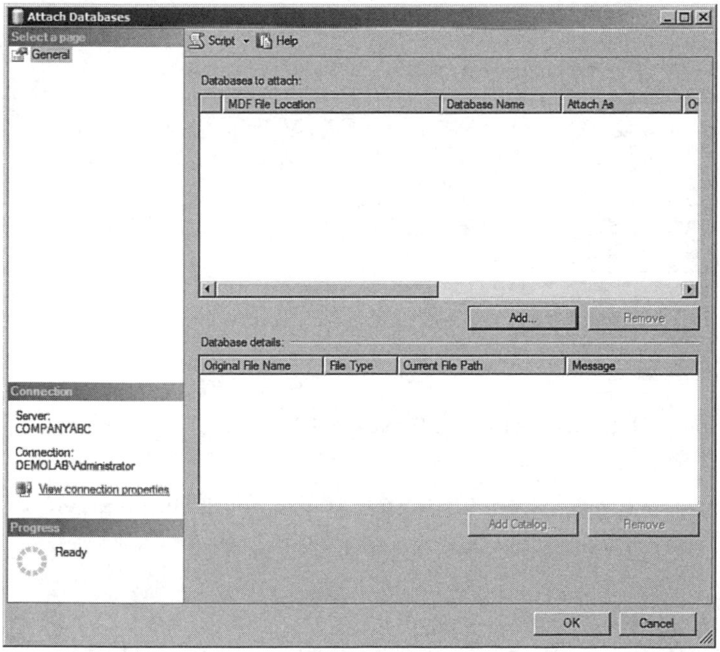

FIGURE 9.21 Attaching a content database using SQL Server 2012.

14. In the Attach Databases dialog box, point to the database files that were just moved, choose the .mdf file, and then click OK, as shown in Figure 9.22.
15. On the SPCA website, click Application Management.
16. In the Databases section, click Manage Content Databases.
17. On the Manage Content Databases page, click Add a Content Database while verifying that the target web application is selected.
18. Type the exact name in the Database Name field while specifying the required authentication.
19. On the SPCA website, click Monitoring, and then click Check Job status.

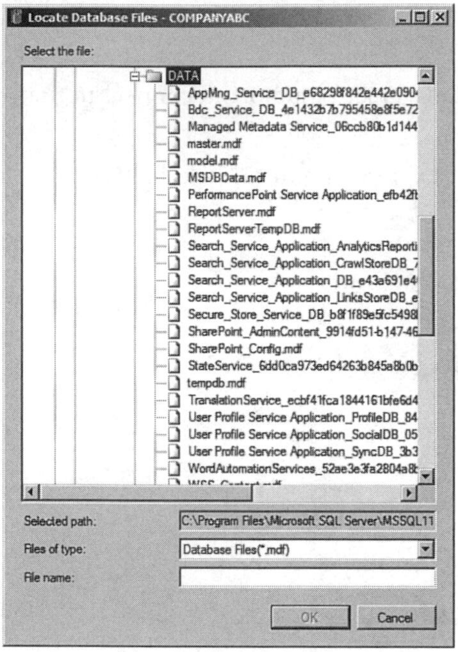

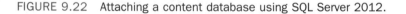

FIGURE 9.22 Attaching a content database using SQL Server 2012.

20. Start the paused services by clicking Edit Job and then starting back all the previously paused services.

Moving Content Databases Using Windows PowerShell

The previous SharePoint-related steps can be completed using Windows PowerShell as follows:

1. Click Start, All Programs, Microsoft SharePoint 2013 Products, SharePoint 2013 Management Shell.

2. At the Windows PowerShell command prompt (PS C:\>), to stop all associated services to the database, type the following command, and then press Enter:

   ```
   Get-SPTimerJob -webapplication <http://WebApplicationURL> | select name |
   Out-File <c:\timerjob.txt> -Append -Encoding ascii
   ForEach($tmrjob in (Get-Content <c:\timerjob.txt>)) { Get-SPTimerJob -Identity
   $tmrjob | Disable-SPTimerjob }
   ```

   The `-webapplication` is the URL of the desired web application and the `c:\timerjob.txt` is the location of the file that will contain all timer jobs associated with this database.

3. Detach the desired content database using the following cmdlet:

```
Dismount-SPContentDatabase "<ContentDB>"
```

   where `ContentDB` is the name of the desired database.

4. Detach the content database from the source SQL Server and reattach it again on the destination server by following steps 8 to 14.

5. Reattach the content database to the destination SharePoint web application using the following cmdlet:

```
Mount-SPContentDatabase "<ContentDb>" -DatabaseServer "<DbServer>"
-WebApplication <http://SiteName>
```

   The `-Name` parameter specifies the name of the content database to be created. The `-DatabaseServer` specifies the database server where the database resides to be mounted. The `-WebApplication` parameter specifies the web application to which the new database will be attached.

6. To start back all the paused services, execute the following command:

```
ForEach($tmrjob in (Get-Content <c:\timerjob.txt>)) {Get-SPTimerJob -Identity
$tmrjob | Enable-SPTimerjob}
```

   The `c:\timerjob.txt` is the location of the file that contains all timer jobs associated with this database.

Externalizing BLOB Storage in SharePoint 2013

By default, SharePoint stores all the uploaded documents and files in its content databases. This has always led to storage, performance, and manageability issues, especially for large SharePoint deployments in SharePoint 2003 and the early days of SharePoint 2007. In SharePoint 2007 SP1, Microsoft made its first attempt to store documents and files out of SQL Server; however, the implementation was difficult and came with many limitations. In SharePoint 2010 and SharePoint 2013, Microsoft took this to a completely new level by making use of the powerful storage externalization capabilities of SQL Server 2008 R2 and SQL Server 2012. This section explains what Binary Large Objects (BLOBs) are, how they are stored in SharePoint, and how Microsoft made use of the RBS technology in SharePoint 2013 to move the storage of large documents and files from SQL Server to remote stores. At the end of this section, administrators learn how to install and configure RBS in SharePoint 2013 environments and how to migrate and move data between different stores.

Understanding BLOBs

Most of the values stored in SQL Server consist of ASCII (American Standard Code for Information Interchange) characters. A basic explanation of ASCII characters is that they are the letters, numbers, and symbols found on the keyboard. A text editor such as Notepad can alter a file holding only ASCII characters without any consequences. However, data is not limited to strings and numbers; it is always a common requirement to store a large amount of binary data in an SQL Server table along with other ASCII data; Word documents, XML documents, and images are some examples. Binary files contain ASCII characters, special control characters, and byte combinations not found on the keyboard. Opening a Microsoft Word document inside Notepad and modifying it would result in the file being corrupted and not readable, because Notepad cannot correctly interpret or create binary bits. BLOBs, then, are binary files that are large, or Binary Large Objects (BLOBs).

SQL Server provides special data types for dealing with such large volumes of binary data. These various data types have changed over time.

In SQL 2000, there were two different families of data type options for this type of data: binary and image. The binary family included two different data types: the binary data type and the VARBINARY data type. The VAR in VARBINARY means that the size is variable rather than fixed, as in the case of the standard binary data type. However, it still has a maximum length of 8,000 bytes.

The image data type family was used to store BLOBs that are greater than 8,000 bytes. This data type is still present in newer versions, but it is deprecated. Microsoft recommends avoiding using these data types in new development work and recommends modifying applications that currently use them.

Starting in SQL Server 2005, Microsoft included the VARBINARY(MAX) data type to the binary data type family. This variation extends the usual limit of around 8,000 bytes and allows storage up to 2GB of data.

Later, in SQL Server 2008, Microsoft introduced the FILESTREAM option for VARBINARY(MAX) fields. This enables storage, efficient streaming, and integrated management of large BLOBs in an SQL database by using the underlying New Technology File System (NTFS) for BLOB storage/streaming, while managing and accessing it directly within the context of the database.

Instead of being a completely new data type, FILESTREAM is a storage attribute of the existing VARBINARY(MAX) data type. FILESTREAM alters how the BLOB data is stored—in the file system rather than in the SQL Server data files. Because FILESTREAM is implemented as a VARBINARY(MAX) column and integrated directly into the database engine, most SQL Server management tools and functions work without modification for FILESTREAM data.

It is also worth mentioning that the behavior of the regular VARBINARY(MAX) data type remains entirely unchanged in SQL Server 2008/R2/2012, including the 2GB size limit. The addition of the FILESTREAM attribute means a VARBINARY(MAX) column can essentially be unlimited in size. (In reality, the size is limited to that of the underlying NTFS volume.)

BLOB Storage in SharePoint

In SharePoint 2003 and the early days of SharePoint 2007, Microsoft SQL Server stored BLOB data in its databases as a rule, as illustrated in Figure 9.23. As a database's usage increased, the total size of its BLOB data could quickly grow larger than the total size of the document metadata and the other structured data stored in the database. There were no exceptions for this; content metadata and BLOBs had to go into content databases. This was not efficient because Microsoft estimates that as much as 80% of the data stored in SharePoint content databases is nonrelational BLOB data, such as Microsoft Office Word documents, Microsoft Office Excel spreadsheets, and Microsoft Office PowerPoint presentations. Only 20% is relational metadata, and this caused storage, performance, and manageability issues, especially for large SharePoint deployments.

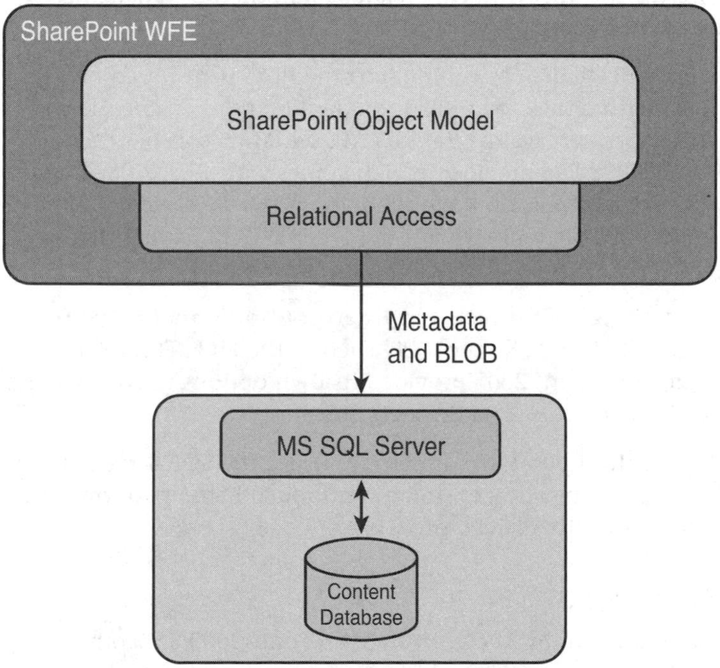

FIGURE 9.23 BLOB storage in previous versions of SharePoint.

In May 2007, Microsoft released a hotfix for Windows SharePoint Services 3.0 and Microsoft Office SharePoint Server 2007 that was later rolled into Service Pack 1. The hotfix exposed an External BLOB Storage (EBS) application programming interface (API), which enabled the storage of BLOBs outside content databases by implementing a set of interfaces. This seemed revolutionary, but EBS was difficult to implement because it exposed an unmanaged interface. Accordingly, this part had to be handled by third parties, or independent software vendors (ISVs). In addition, EBS had some limitations; for example, it could be enabled only on the farm level and not on the content database level.

Starting in SharePoint 2010, Microsoft heard its customers' feedback loud and clear and decided to fix the BLOB storage pain points. In SharePoint 2013, it is possible to move the storage of BLOBs from database servers to commodity storage solutions by using RBS technology, which was first introduced in SQL Server 2008.

Introducing Remote BLOB Storage

RBS is a library API set designed to move storage of BLOBs from Microsoft SQL Server to external storage solutions.

Using RBS, applications can store large amounts of unstructured data (such as Office documents, PDF files, or videos) and enjoy both the relational capabilities of SQL Server and the scalability of a dedicated BLOB store. Best of all, developers do not have to write the code to handle the job of tying together the SQL metadata and the BLOB data. RBS handles the transactional consistency completely.

An application stores and accesses BLOB data by calling into the RBS client library. ISVs and storage solution vendors can create their own RBS provider library to enable the use of custom stores with applications written against the RBS API set. Microsoft has even created a provider named FILESTREAM RBS provider, which comes with RBS 2008 R2 and RBS 2012, and can be used for storing BLOBs on the underlying NTFS file system. The FILESTREAM RBS provider ties the RBS technology with the FILESTREAM feature that was first introduced in SQL Server 2008.

SharePoint 2007 did not take advantage of the recent SQL Server features that Microsoft first introduced for unstructured data in SQL Server 2008, such as the FILESTREAM attribute or RBS technology; instead, SharePoint 2007 provided its own options to enhance the storage efficiency and manageability of huge data through EBS.

SharePoint 2010 and SharePoint 2013 support RBS and can leverage the SQL Server FILESTREAM RBS provider, thus providing cheaper storage and much better performance. Figure 9.24 illustrates how RBS works with SharePoint 2013.

EBS Support in SharePoint 2013

As mentioned, EBS was an earlier attempt by Microsoft in SharePoint 2007 SP1 to help customers externalize their BLOBs. However, EBS was hard to implement and had some limitations. Microsoft introduced EBS as an immediate help, and it was designed in a way that make it an evolutionary approach in that administrators can move to RBS later. Although EBS was supported for SharePoint 2010, its support was completely removed from SharePoint 2013.

Installing and Configuring RBS

Administrators can use the following procedure to install and configure the BLOB externalization in SharePoint 2013 using RBS and the RBS FILESTREAM provider. Each step in the following procedure is explained in detail in the following subsections:

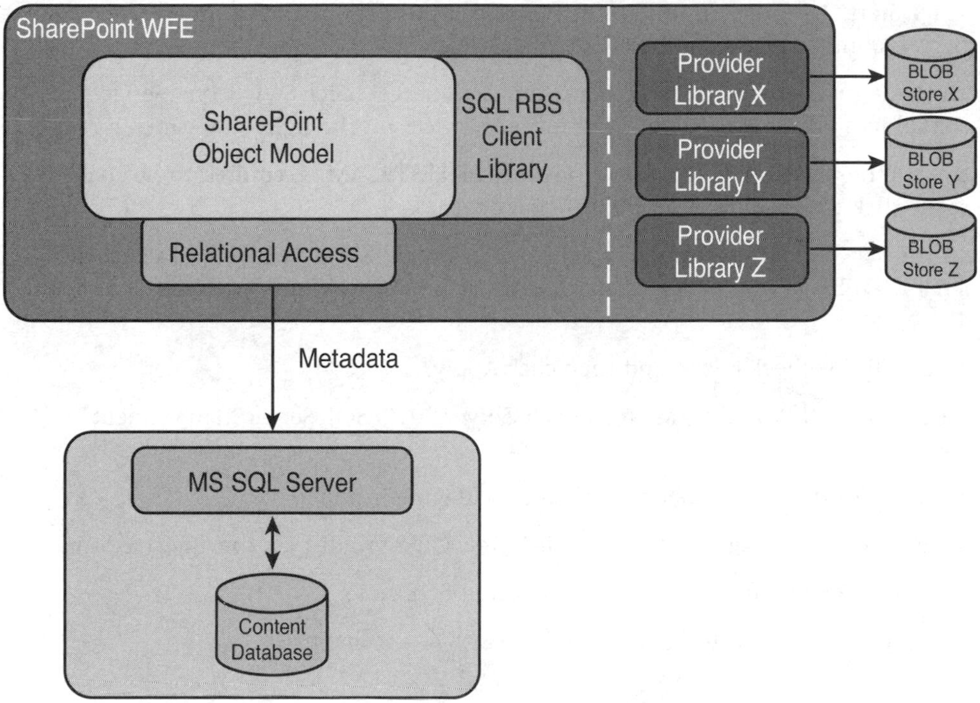

FIGURE 9.24 Externalizing BLOB storage using RBS.

1. Enable FILESTREAM on SQL Server.
2. Prepare the database, and create a BLOB store.
3. Install the RBS client.
4. Enable RBS using Windows PowerShell.

NOTE

For SQL Server 2008 R2, RBS is incorporated as an add-on feature pack and can be downloaded from http://go.microsoft.com/fwlink/?LinkID=165839&clcid=0x409. For SQL Server 2012, RBS is included on the installation media but is not installed by the SQL Server Setup program. It is also available as a separate download from www.microsoft.com/en-us/download/details.aspx?id=29065.

9

Enable FILESTREAM on SQL Server

Administrators must enable and configure FILESTREAM on the computer running SQL Server 2008 R2 or SQL Server 2012 that hosts the SharePoint Server 2013 databases, as follows:

1. Click Start, All Programs, Microsoft SQL Server 2012, Configuration Tools, SQL Server Configuration Manager.
2. In the left panel of SQL Server Configuration Manger, click SQL Server Services, which lists all the SQL Server 2012-related services on the right-side panel.
3. Locate the instance of SQL Server on which FILESTREAM is required to be enabled, right-click the instance, and then click Properties.
4. In the SQL Server Properties dialog box, click the FILESTREAM tab and select the Enable FILESTREAM for Transact-SQL Access check box, which enables the rest of the options.
5. Select all the check boxes, and then click Apply.
6. Click Start, All Programs, Microsoft SQL Server 2012, SQL Server Management Studio.
7. Connect to the desired SQL Server database engine instance.
8. In SQL Server Management Studio, click New Query to display the Query Editor.
9. In Query Editor, enter the following Transact-SQL code:

```
EXEC sp_configure filestream_access_level, 2; RECONFIGURE
```

10. Click Execute.

Prepare the Database and Create a BLOB Store

To prepare the database and create a BLOB store, follow these steps:

1. Click Start, All Programs, Microsoft SQL Server 2012, SQL Server Management Studio.
2. Connect to the desired SQL Server database engine instance and expand that instance.
3. Expand the databases, select the content database for which a BLOB store will be created, click New Query, and then execute the following commands:

```
use [ContentDatabaseName]
if not exists (select * from sys.symmetric_keys where name = N'##MS_
DatabaseMasterKey##')create master key encryption by password = N'Admin Key
Password !2#4'
use [ContentDatabaseName]
if not exists (select groupname from sysfilegroups where groupname=
N'RBSFilestreamProvider')alter database [ContentDatabaseName] add filegroup
RBSFilestreamProvider contains filestream
use [ContentDatabaseName]
alter database [ContentDatabaseName] add file (name = RBSFilestreamFile,
filename = 'c:\RemoteBlobStore') to filegroup RBSFilestreamProvider
```

Install RBS

To install RBS, follow these steps:

1. Launch SQL Server 2012 RBS with the FILESTREAM provider (RBS.msi) on the database server (RBS.msi must first be downloaded from Microsoft), all the web front ends, and all the application servers.

2. On the database server, run the following commands from the location of the RBS.msi file using the command prompt:

```
msiexec /qn /lvx* rbs_install_log.txt /i RBS.msi TRUSTSERVERCERTIFICATE=true
FILEGROUP=PRIMARY DBNAME="ContentDatabaseName" DBINSTANCE=
"DatabaseInstanceName" FILESTREAMFILEGROUP=RBSFilestreamProvider
FILESTREAMSTORENAME=FilestreamProvider_1
msiexec /qn /lvx* rbs_install_log.txt /i RBS.msi DBNAME=
"ContentDatabaseName" DBINSTANCE="DatabaseInstanceName" ADDLOCAL="Client,Docs,
Maintainer,ServerScript,FilestreamClient,FilestreamServer"
```

   This should be run against each content database that should support RBS.

3. On all the web front ends and all the application servers, run the following command from the location of the RBS.msi file using the command prompt:

```
msiexec /qn /lvx* rbs_install_log.txt /i RBS.msi DBNAME="ContentDatabaseName"
DBINSTANCE="DatabaseInstanceName" ADDLOCAL="Client,Docs,Maintainer,ServerScrip
t,FilestreamClient,FilestreamServer"
```

   These commands kick off an msiexec service that runs in a silent mode, not providing any feedback about their success or failure. Administrators can monitor the service in the Task Manager to ensure that they are finished.

4. Administrators can confirm the RBS installation by looking for the text Product: SQL Remote Blob Storage—Configuration Completed Successfully in the RBS log file. The previous installation commands create a log file named rbs_install_log.txt in the same location as the RBS.msi file. The installation also creates several tables in the specified content database with names that are preceded by mssqlrbs. Administrators can also look for these tables to confirm the installation.

Enable RBS Using Windows PowerShell

To enable RBS using Windows PowerShell, follow these steps:

1. Click Start, All Programs, Microsoft SharePoint 2013 Products, SharePoint 2013 Management Shell.

2. At the Windows PowerShell command prompt (PS C:\>), type each of the following commands and press Enter after each one:

```
$cdb = Get-SPContentDatabase ContentDatabaseName
$blobstoragesettings = $cdb.RemoteBlobStorageSettings
```

```
$blobstoragesettings.Enable()
$blobstoragesettings.SetActiveProviderName($blobstoragesettings.
GetProviderNames()[0])
```

The `Enable` cmdlet enables the usage of RSB for a certain content database. When RBS is enabled, BLOBs get stored in the active BLOB store. When the active BLOB store is disabled through the `Disable` cmdlet, the BLOBs get stored back in the content database.

The `GetProviderNames` cmdlet can be used to list all the registered providers in the farm, and the names are retrieved from the configuration database.

The `SetActiveProviderName` cmdlet is used to activate a certain provider for a certain content database. A farm can have multiple RBS providers, but only one of them can be active at a time for a given content database.

Another useful cmdlet that was not used previously is the `MinimumBlobStorageSize` cmdlet. This cmdlet can be used to set a size threshold. For example, an administrator can decide to store files smaller than 1MB in the content database and larger ones in the BLOB store.

3. Now, all the uploaded documents should go to the BLOB store (c:\RemoteBlobStore) rather than being saved in the specified content database. Figure 9.25 illustrates the upload operation workflow in SharePoint 2013 after enabling RBS.

Migrating and Moving BLOBs Between BLOB Stores

SharePoint 2013 ships with a powerful PowerShell cmdlet named `Migrate` that administrators can use to move BLOBs from their current locations to the current active RBS provider store. This implies that administrators can use the cmdlet to move data from SQL Server to another remote BLOB store and vice versa. Moving BLOBs from a content database is a typical requirement after installing and configuring RBS on already running SharePoint systems.

It is also worth mentioning that the `Migrate` cmdlet performs a deep copy of the BLOBs one BLOB at a time, and there is no downtime required for moving all the BLOBs. The migration process also can be paused and resumed at any time, which means that at a point, part of the BLOBs can be in SQL Server, and the other part can reside in another BLOB store.

This cmdlet can even be used to move BLOBs from one BLOB store to another one by moving them back to SQL Server and then migrating them to another store.

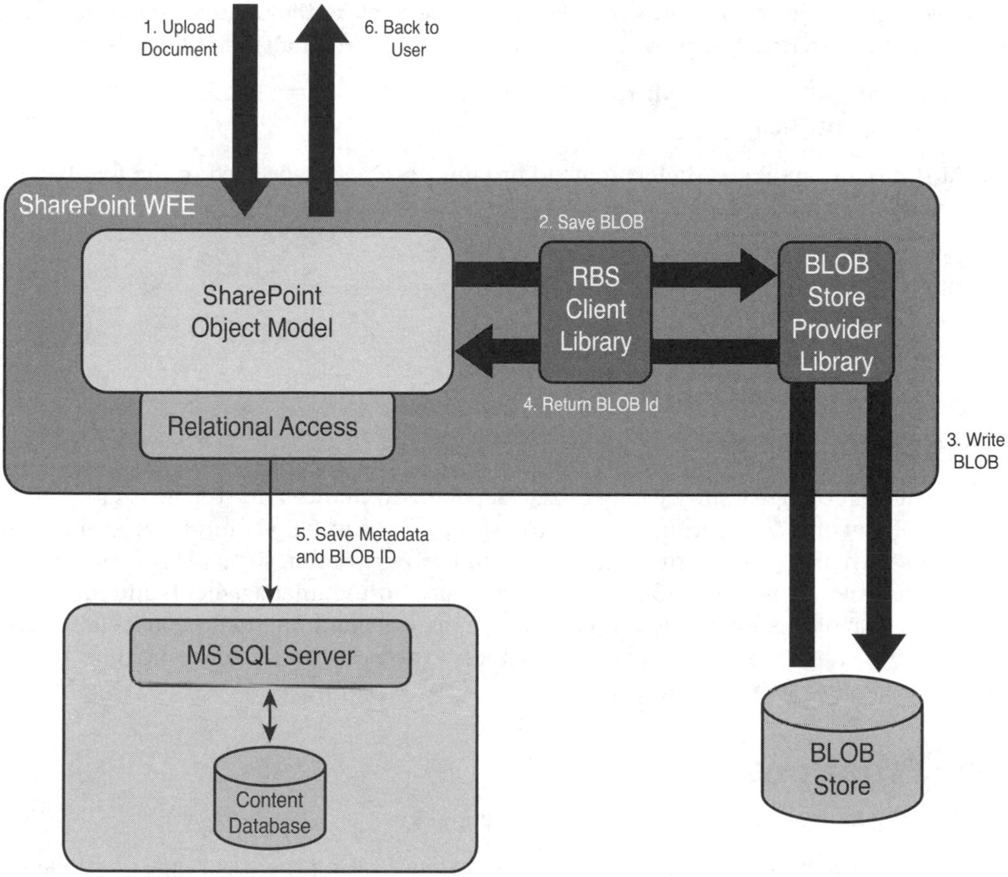

FIGURE 9.25 The upload operation workflow in SharePoint 2013 and RBS.

Migrating BLOBs from a Content Database to the Current Active Provider Store

To migrate BLOBs from a content database to the current active provider store, follow these steps:

1. Click Start, All Programs, Microsoft SharePoint 2013 Products, SharePoint 2013 Management Shell.

2. At the Windows PowerShell command prompt (PS C:\>), type each of the following commands and press Enter after each one:

```
$cdb = Get-SPContentDatabase ContentDatabaseName
$blobstoragesettings = $cdb.RemoteBlobStorageSettings
$blobstoragesettings.Migrate()
```

9

Migrating BLOBs from the Current Active Provider Store Back to the Content Database

To migrate the current active provider store back to a content database, follow these steps:

1. Click Start, All Programs, Microsoft SharePoint 2013 Products, SharePoint 2013 Management Shell.

2. At the Windows PowerShell command prompt (PS C:\>), type each of the following commands and press Enter after each one:

```
$cdb = Get-SPContentDatabase ContentDatabaseName
$blobstoragesettings = $cdb.RemoteBlobStorageSettings
$blobstoragesettings.Disable()
$blobstoragesettings.Migrate()
```

Summary

The proficient and regular monitoring of SQL Server performance and storage is vital to keeping a SharePoint farm running optimally. Monitoring can help administrators manage and maintain their environments as they grow and can help them proactively deal with catastrophic issues. It is crucial to plan SQL Server monitoring, management, and maintenance to help avoid redundant effort. Following a management and maintenance regimen reduces administration, maintenance, and business expenses while at the same time increases reliability, stability, and performance.

Best Practices

The following are best practices from this chapter:

- Keep an eye on SQL Server performance and storage using the vast range of available monitoring tools.
- Use the SQL Server Management Studio Log File Viewer to monitor both SQL Server and Windows event logs. It is highly recommended to look through the logs on a daily basis to detect any existing or possible issues.
- Use the SQL Server Maintenance Plan Wizard to set up SQL maintenance plans.
- Do not include the option to shrink the database when creating SQL Server maintenance plans; this should be run manually only if the content database has lost at least half its content.
- Set the maintenance plans in production environments to run during off hours.
- Ensure that the health analyzer is configured to automatically self-heal the database's index fragmentation.
- Saving the TDE certificate in a secured place is very important and the first action to be done after encrypting the database.
- To enhance the performance of SharePoint implementations, try not to let content databases grow larger than 100GB.

- Create new site collections in new content databases; this enhances the performance, simplifies the manageability, and provides flexibility for disaster recovery strategies.
- Move the storage of BLOBs from content databases to commodity storage solutions by using the RBS technology to avoid storage and performance issues.
- Highly consider the use of SQL Server 2012 AOAGs for high availability and disaster tolerance of your data. This concept is covered in Chapter 4.

CHAPTER 10

Backing Up and Restoring a SharePoint Environment

IN THIS CHAPTER

- Backing Up and Recovering SharePoint Components
- Using the Recycle Bin for Recovery
- Using SharePoint Central Administration for Backup and Restore
- Performing Granular Backup Using the SharePoint Central Administration
- Restoring SharePoint Using SharePoint Central Administration
- Using SharePoint 2013 Management PowerShell for Backup and Restore
- Backing Up Internet Information Services v7 Configuration
- SQL Backup Tools

A SharePoint document management and collaboration environment is a critical component, on par with mail in terms of criticality for many organizations. The ability to perform comprehensive backup and restore of a SharePoint 2013 environment is subsequently a critical requirement as part of an enterprise disaster recovery strategy.

SharePoint 2013 includes a wide variety of tools that provide for backup and restore, which can sometimes be confusing. These tools are powerful, but in many cases overlap, and it is not immediately obvious how to use them.

This chapter focuses on the built-in tools provided for backup and restore of a SharePoint 2013 environment. Specific guidance around usage of these tools is given, and recommended backup routines are provided.

Backing Up and Recovering SharePoint Components

Backup options in SharePoint 2013 have been scoped across wider areas in comparison to SharePoint 2010 RTM (release to manufacturing). SharePoint 2013 administrators have an array of options to choose from and combine, per best practices outlined in this chapter, to back up and restore SharePoint 2013 content.

In comparison to earlier versions, SharePoint 2013 administrators can now back up the farm configuration, complete farm and site collection only, do a granular level of backup and restore, and connect to an unattached content database and restore content from it. In addition to this,

SharePoint 2013 administrators can now restore a site from the Recycle Bin and site collection using Windows PowerShell.

The tools covered in this chapter for backup and restore are the following:

- **Recycle Bin:** This tool has been very popular since it was introduced in SharePoint 2007, and is widely used by end users and SharePoint administrators. Because the data can be restored by the end user within 30 days of deletion and thereafter by the site collection administrators, it has led to reduced IT overheads in data restoration.
- **Central Administration:** The Central Administration graphical user interface (GUI) is one of the tools that can be used to back up and restore the SharePoint environment. However, not all backup and restore options are available when using the Central Administration site.
- **SharePoint 2013 Management Shell:** The SharePoint Management Shell, introduced in the SharePoint 2010 version, now leverages on Windows PowerShell 3.0. Windows PowerShell is a command-line tool that SharePoint administrators can use to administer the SharePoint environment. Windows PowerShell provides additional options for the SharePoint administrators that are not available to execute using the Central Administration GUI.
- **STSADM:** STSADM is still available in SharePoint 2013; it remains deprecated and is provided only to support backward compatibility. SharePoint 2013 Management Shell remains a preferred option for managing the SharePoint 2013 environment. In certain situations, SharePoint 2013 Management Shell is the only option to administer SharePoint 2013 environment.
- **Internet Information Services (IIS) backup:** IIS 7 configuration on Windows Server 2008 can now be backed up using the appcmd executable file. The IIS 7 configuration file is composed of web.config files and applicationHost.config files. In a situation in which a system failure occurs, systems administrators can restore the IIS 7 configuration from the backup file.
- **Structured Query Language (SQL) backup:** SharePoint configuration and content databases stored in SQL Server can be backed up using built-in backup functionality, either by the database administrator's initiating this as a one-time task or scheduling tasks to do a full backup. SQL database backup can be combined with other SharePoint backup options, such as Central Administration or SharePoint 2013 Management Shell. Unlike SharePoint restore procedures, SQL restore procedures cannot restore item-level objects, only complete database restores.
- **Microsoft System Center 2012 Data Protection Manager (DPM) 2010:** DPM 2010 is Microsoft's enterprise backup tool. DPM does snapshot-level backup and restore of SharePoint content, providing for full farm or individual item-level recovery. DPM is a separate component and is not included with SharePoint 2013.
- **Third-party backup tools:** Vendors such as Quest, Idera, and AvePoint already have backup tools for SharePoint 2010 that facilitate item-level restores. These vendors are currently working on releasing backup tools for SharePoint 2013.

Using the Recycle Bin for Recovery

Recycle Bin introduced in SharePoint 2007 is available in SharePoint 2013 with significant improvements since SharePoint 2010 RTM. This functionality is the first line of defense for restores, enabling end users and administrators to restore deleted items and deleted sites easily and reduce overheads associated with restore operations and loss of productivity.

Understanding the Two Stages of the Recycle Bin

The Recycle Bin in SharePoint 2013 retains the two-stage functionality, but with an added level of functionality: restoring deleted sites, which was introduced in Service Pack (SP) 1 for SharePoint 2010.

When an item is deleted, it goes through both Recycle Bins before being deleted completely from the database.

The first Recycle Bin, shown in Figure 10.1, is at the site level. This Recycle Bin is available and managed by the users of the site.

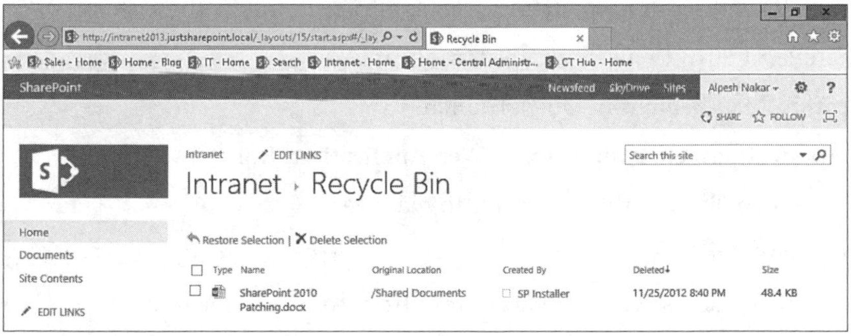

FIGURE 10.1 Viewing a team site first-stage Recycle Bin.

To restore deleted items from the Recycle Bin, the user needs to click the Site Content link in the quick launch (left-side navigation in the SharePoint team site), and then click the Recycle Bin link on the right side of the page, select the deleted items to restore, and click Restore Selection. This restores the deleted items to the original location.

NOTE

Users see only the items that have been deleted by them. They do not see items that other users have deleted.

If the users have not restored the deleted items from the site Recycle Bin within the retention period (default is 30 days), or have deleted the items from the Recycle Bin, the items are moved to the secondary Recycle Bin. This Recycle Bin is at the site collection level, and only site collection administrators have access to this Recycle Bin to restore items and deleted sites for the end users, as shown in Figure 10.2.

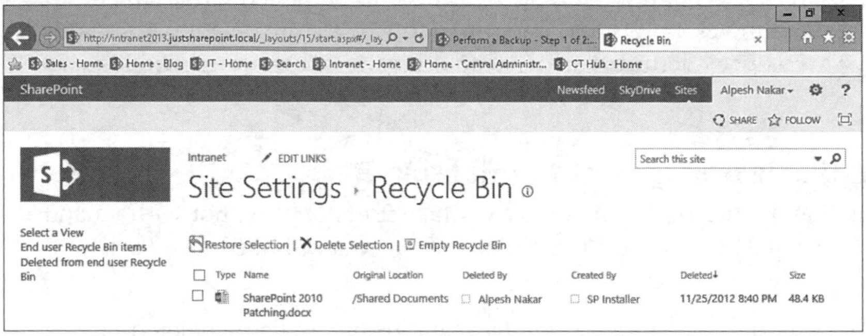

FIGURE 10.2 Viewing a site collection second-stage Recycle Bin.

Enabling Recycle Bin Functionality in SharePoint

To access the Recycle Bin settings for a particular web application, follow these steps:

1. Open the SharePoint 2013 Central Administration site.
2. Select Application Management in Quick Launch.
3. Under Web Applications, click the Manage Web Applications link.
4. Highlight the web application that you want to manage.
5. The ribbon is highlighted.
6. Click General Settings and select General Settings from the drop-down menu.
7. Scroll down to the Recycle Bin options, modify the settings, and click OK to save these changes.

The Recycle Bin settings listed, shown in Figure 10.3, provide the following options:

- **Recycle Bin Status:** This setting enables the entire web application Recycle Bin, including both stages, to be toggled on or off.
- **Delete Items in the Recycle Bin:** This option sets the number of days before items are removed from the end-user Recycle Bin. The default value is 30 days. This setting can be altered with a number of days of your choice, or it can be toggled to never delete items from the Recycle Bin.
- **Second-Stage Recycle Bin:** The Site Collection Recycle Bin, also known as the second-stage Recycle Bin, can be either turned off or configured to be emptied after it reaches the specified percentage of the web application's quota. For example, if the web application has a quota of 500MB, a setting of 50% enables up to 250MB of data to be stored in the second-stage Recycle Bin, increasing the effective quota of

the web application to 750MB. This setting can be changed to a different number up to 100% or can be toggled off.

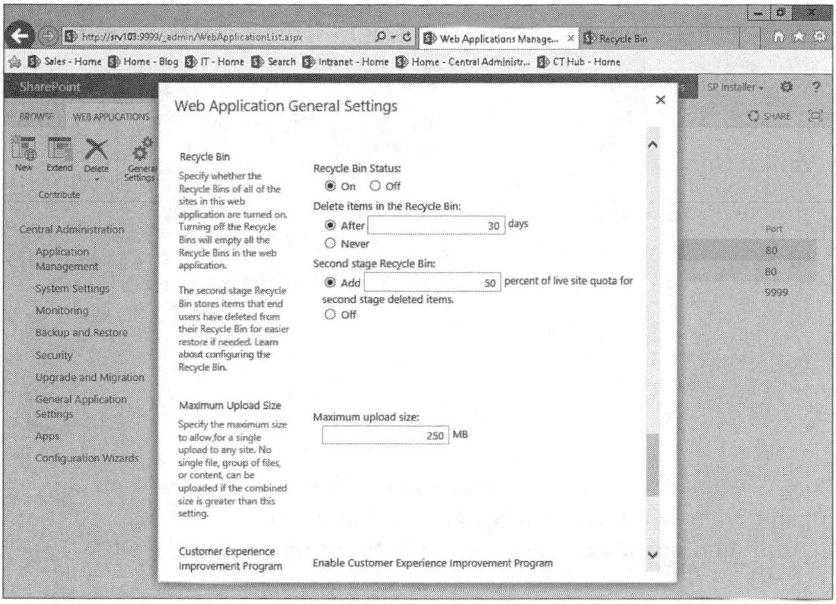

FIGURE 10.3 Recycle Bin settings for a web application.

CAUTION

These settings should be altered only after analyzing the usage pattern of the Recycle Bin at the site level, the number of requests received for second-stage Recycle Bin restore, and the type of restore requests received by the SharePoint administrators. Items retained in the site Recycle Bin count toward the quota of a site collection, so this setting has to strike a balance between the number of days and the site collection quota. Similarly, settings of 100% for the second-stage Recycle Bin would mean that the size of site collection would be twice as much in the content databases.

Site restoration, introduced in SP 1 for SharePoint 2010, has proven valuable not only for SharePoint administrators but also for users. The Recycle Bin helps reduce SharePoint restore operations, helps to improve business continuity, and reduces overall IT overhead. Users should be trained in the use of the Recycle Bin.

Using SharePoint Central Administration for Backup and Restore

The SharePoint 2013 Central Administration Backup and Restore page introduced in SharePoint 2010 remains unchanged in SharePoint 2013. The Backup and Restore page has two options for backup and restore:

- Farm Backup and Restore
- Granular Backup

Using the Farm Backup and Restore option, SharePoint administrators can back up the following:

- Complete Farm
- Farm Configuration Only
- Individual Components in a Farm

The Granular Backup and Restore section enables SharePoint administrators to do the following:

- Back Up Site Collection
- Export Site or List

Ideally, the SharePoint Central Administration tool would be used to do a one-time backup or restore operation. As with earlier versions, scheduling backups via the SharePoint 2013 Central Administration tool is not an option from within the GUI.

Back Up Using Central Administration

Before backing up using the SharePoint Central Administration tool, the backup location needs to be configured. The backup location can be a local drive on the server or a network share.

Farm Configuration Backup

To back up farm configuration using the SharePoint Central Administration tool, follow these steps:

1. Open the SharePoint Central Administration site on a SharePoint server (Start, All Programs, Microsoft SharePoint 2013 Products, SharePoint 2013 Central Administration).
2. Select Backup and Restore in quick launch.
3. Under the Farm Backup and Restore section, select Perform a Backup.
4. From the Select Component to Backup page, select the Farm component, as shown in Figure 10.4.
5. Click Next at the bottom of the page.
6. In the Select Backup Options page, select Full Backup, as shown in Figure 10.5. (When performing a backup of the component for the first time, Differential Backup should not be selected because the backup operation will fail.)

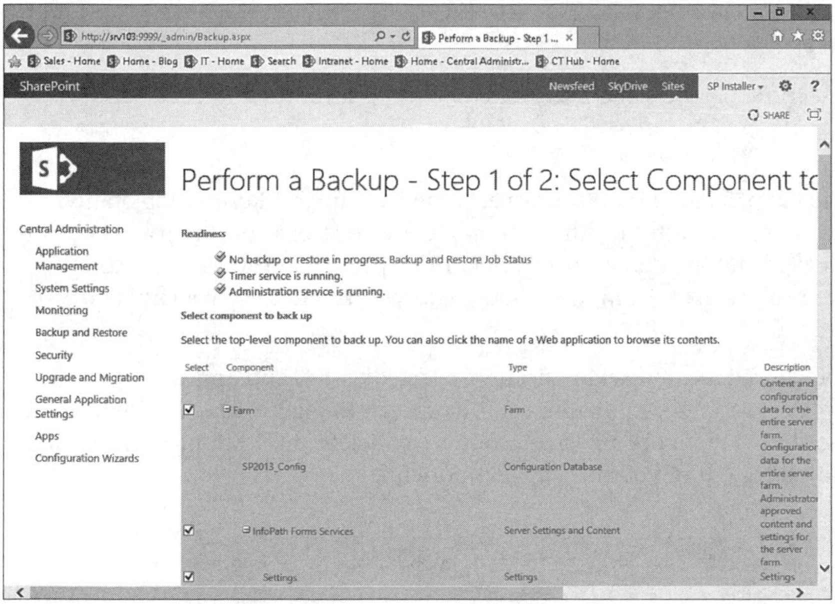

FIGURE 10.4 Backing up a farm from the Central Administration tool.

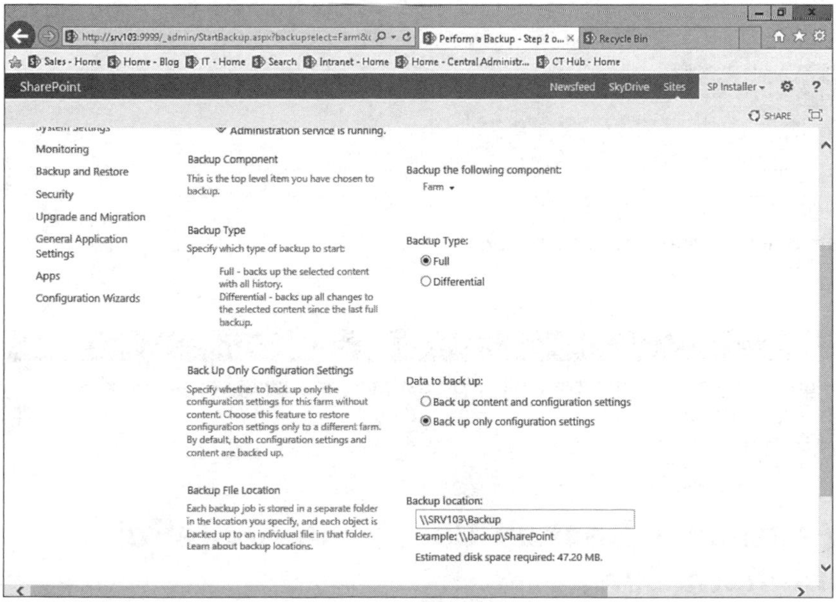

FIGURE 10.5 Choosing backup options in the Central Administration tool.

7. In the next section, on the same page, select Back Up Only Configuration Settings, and then click Next.
8. In the next section, on the same page, enter a backup location and click Start Backup.

After starting the backup, SharePoint 2013 displays the Backup and Restore Job Status page. It might take several minutes for the backup process to appear on the page, depending on the backup type and the data to back up. On this page, you can monitor the backup and restore progress by clicking the View History link, View the Backup, and Restore History.

Backup files can be viewed in the Backup location selected earlier and appear as an Extensible Markup Language (XML) manifest file, as shown in Figure 10.6, and as a folder full of .bak files, as shown in Figure 10.7. You should *not* delete the XML manifest file in the root; it is required to restore your backup components.

FIGURE 10.6 Examining a SharePoint backup manifest file.

NOTE

When doing configuration backup, service application settings, including service proxies, are not included in the backup.

Performing Granular Backup Using the SharePoint Central Administration

Granular backup of SharePoint 2013, previously available only from the STSADM command-line tool, is available from within the GUI.

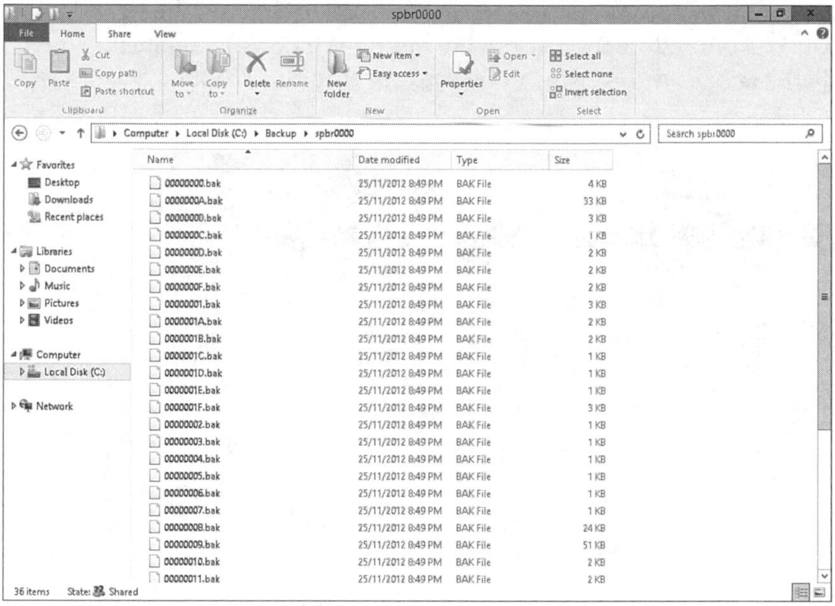

FIGURE 10.7 Viewing a site backup file location.

Backing Up a Site Collection

To back up a site collection using the SharePoint Central Administration tool, follow these steps:

1. Open the SharePoint Central Administration site on a SharePoint server (Start, All Programs, Microsoft SharePoint 2013 Products, SharePoint 2013 Central Administration).
2. Select Backup and Restore in quick launch.
3. Select Perform a Site Collection Backup, under the Granular Backup section.
4. On the Site Collection Backup page, select a site collection to back up from the drop-down menu, as shown in Figure 10.8.
5. Enter the backup location and the filename ending with extension .bak in the Filename box. Select Overwrite Existing File if you want to overwrite, and then click Start Backup.

After starting the backup, SharePoint 2013 displays the Granular Backup Job Status page. On this page, you can monitor the granular backup progress; it also displays site collection backup status and content export status (discussed later in this chapter).

Unlike the farm backup and restore operation, a detailed history of the granular backup operations cannot be viewed. In addition, a backup of the site collection done using

SharePoint Central Administration cannot be restored via the SharePoint Central Administration GUI. You can restore this backup only using Windows PowerShell commandlet (cmdlet) `Restore-SPSite`, which is covered later in this chapter.

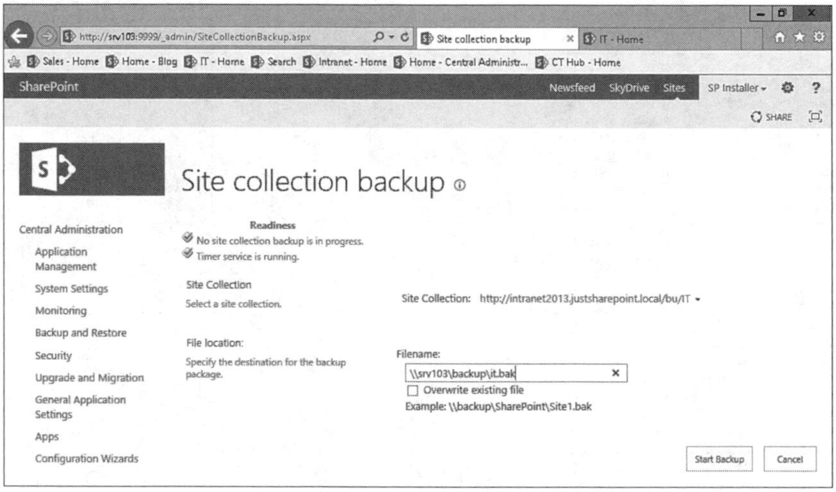

FIGURE 10.8 Performing a granular SharePoint site backup.

This method is recommended when a one-time backup of a site collection is required, perhaps because the site collection content needs to be archived or because the site collection needs to move so that it is under a different web application.

NOTE

Granular backup and export is a processor-intensive function in comparison to a farm backup operation.

Export a Site or List Using the Central Admin Console

To export a site or a list using the SharePoint Central Administration, follow these steps:

1. Open the SharePoint Central Administration site on a SharePoint server (Start, All Programs, Microsoft SharePoint 2013 Products, SharePoint 2013 Central Administration).
2. Select Backup and Restore in quick launch.
3. Select Export a Site or List, under Granular Backup section.
4. On the Site or List Export page, select a site collection, select the site, and then select the list to export from the drop-down menu, as shown in Figure 10.9.

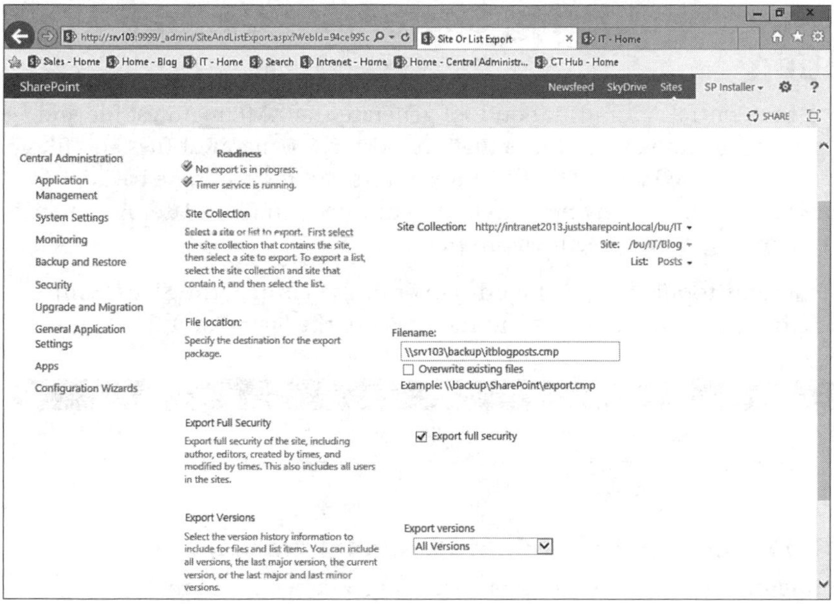

FIGURE 10.9 Exporting a list using Central Admin backup.

5. Enter a backup location and the filename ending with extension .cmp in the Filename box. Select Overwrite Existing Files if you want to overwrite.

6. The next toggle gives an option to export full security, including author, editors, created by times, and modified times. If the selection is not at the list level but at the site level (that is, exporting a site), then Export Full Security will include all users in the site. Select this option if required.

7. The next drop-down menu gives options to export the version history for files and list items. The options are All Versions, Last Major, Current Version, and Minor Versions. Select the desired choice from the drop-down menu, as shown in Figure 10.9, and then click Start Export.

After starting the export, SharePoint 2013 displays the Granular Backup Job Status page. On this page, you can monitor the granular backup progress; the page also displays the content export and site collection backup status (discussed earlier in this chapter).

Unlike the farm backup and restore operation, a detailed history of the granular backup operations cannot be viewed. In addition, content export done using SharePoint Central Administration cannot be imported via the SharePoint Central Administration GUI. The import operation can be done only using Windows PowerShell cmdlet `Import-SPWeb`, which is covered later in this chapter.

This method is recommended for when a site needs to be moved to a different site collection or (as is more common) when moving a SharePoint list to a different site.

Restoring SharePoint Using SharePoint Central Administration

Backups done using the Central Administration tool generate the XML manifest file and files with .bak extensions. In case of a restore situation, both XML manifest files and files with .bak extensions are required. SharePoint administrators can restore these backups to the same environment or to an entirely new environment (for example, a User Acceptance Test [UAT] environment or a development environment).

Similarly, in case of a catastrophic failure of hardware or of the entire farm, SharePoint administrators can rebuild the environment and then restore the SharePoint 2013 farm.

NOTE

Only site collections can be recovered from a site collection backup.

Restore Farm Configuration Using Central Administration

To restore farm configuration and other components using SharePoint Central Administration, follow these steps:

1. Open the SharePoint Central Administration site on a SharePoint server (Start, All Programs, Microsoft SharePoint 2013 Products, SharePoint 2013 Central Administration).
2. Select Backup and Restore in quick launch.
3. Under the Farm Backup and Restore section, select Restore from a Backup.
4. On the Backup and Restore History page, enter the backup directory location.
5. Select the farm component that you want to restore, as shown in Figure 10.10, and click Next.
6. It takes a few minutes before the Select Component to Restore page displays. On this page, select the SharePoint component to restore, as shown in Figure 10.11, and then click Next.
7. On the Select Restore Options page, select New Configuration to restore a farm with different computer names, web application names, or database servers, or select Same Configuration to restore a farm with the same computer names, web application names, and database servers, as shown in Figure 10.12. Click Start Restore to begin the restore process.

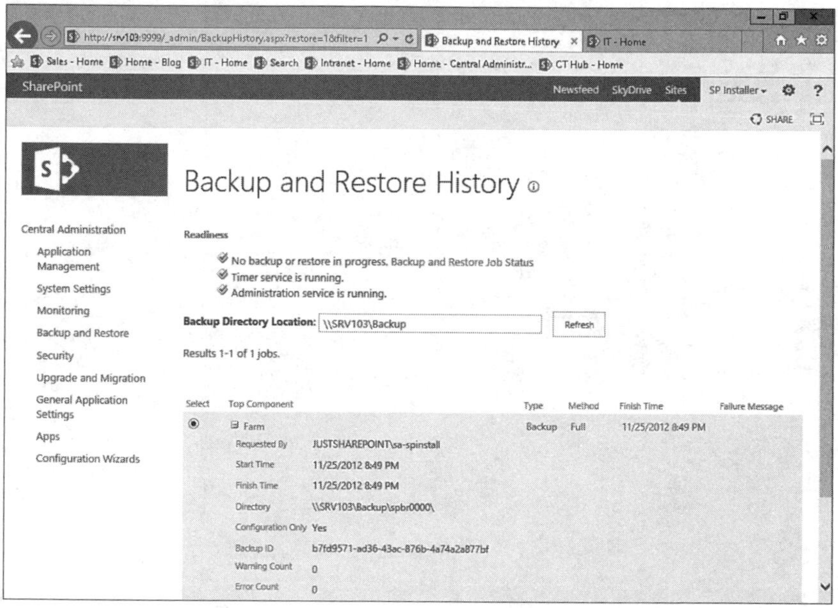

FIGURE 10.10 Restoring a SharePoint farm using SharePoint Central Administration.

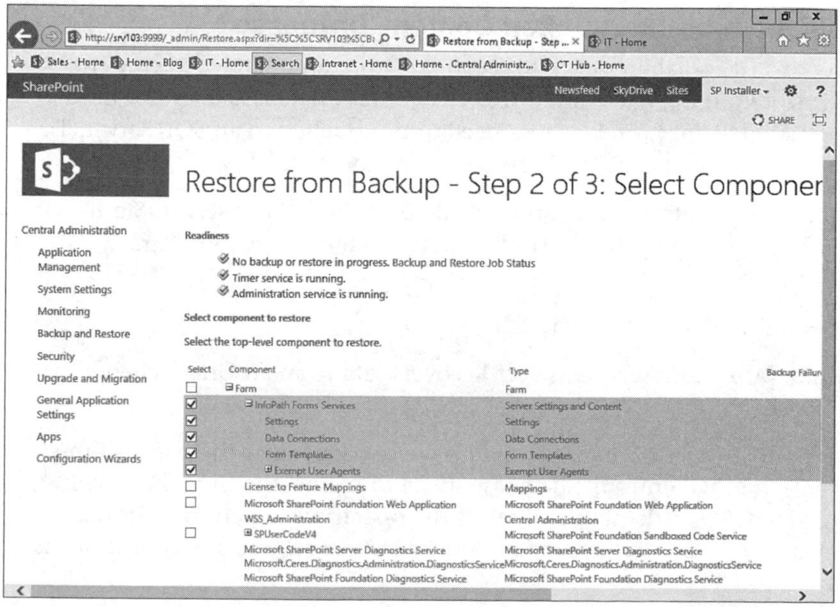

FIGURE 10.11 Selecting components to restore.

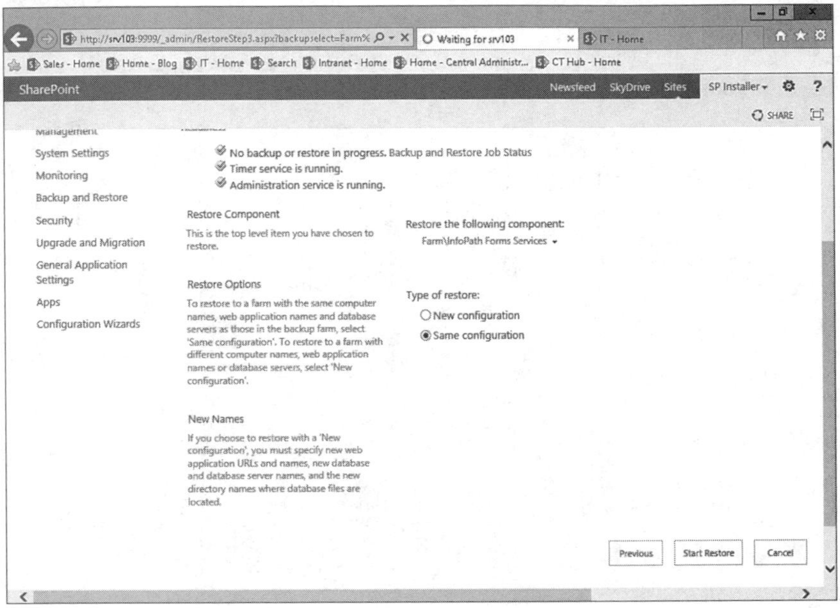

FIGURE 10.12 Finalizing settings for a farm restore.

Recovering Data from an Unattached Content Database

SharePoint 2013 retains the capability to restore content from an unattached content database that was introduced in SharePoint 2010. The content database does not need to be "attached" to a SharePoint farm but does need to be attached to an SQL Server. To recover data from an unattached content database, follow these steps:

1. Open the SharePoint Central Administration site on a SharePoint server (Start, All Programs, Microsoft SharePoint 2013 Products, SharePoint 2013 Central Administration).

2. Select Backup and Restore in quick launch.

3. Under the Granular Backup section, select Recover Data from an Unattached Content Database.

4. On the Unattached Content Database Data Recovery page, enter the name of the database server, and then enter the database name to connect to. If you use SQL authentication, provide credentials and select the operation to perform (Browse Content, Backup Site Collection, or Export Site or List) to select a site collection, as shown in Figure 10.13.

5. On the Browse Content page, select the site collection from the drop-down menu. On the site collection dialog page, check the name of the content database, and then select the site collection to back up from the unattached content database. Click OK to return to the Browse Content page.

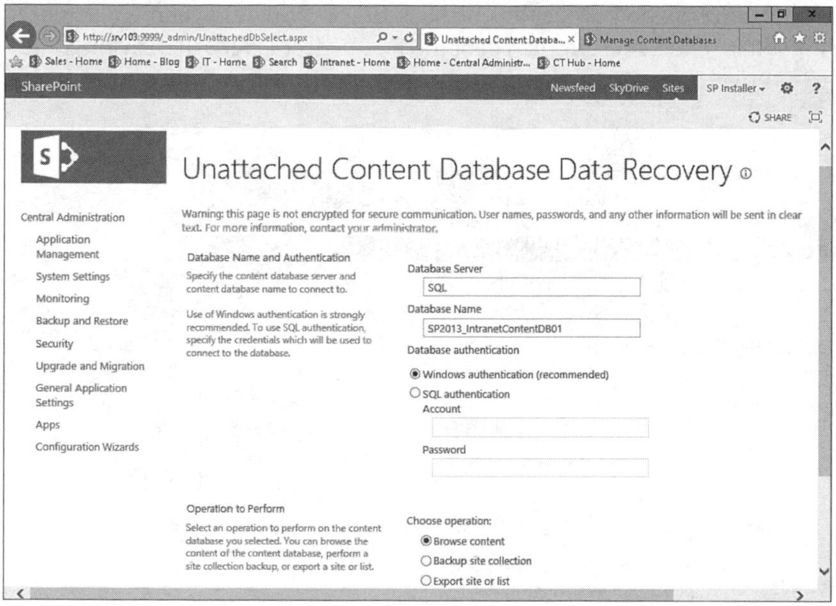

FIGURE 10.13 Recovering data from an unattached content database.

6. The Browse Content page looks like Figure 10.14. Select Backup Site Collection operation and click next.

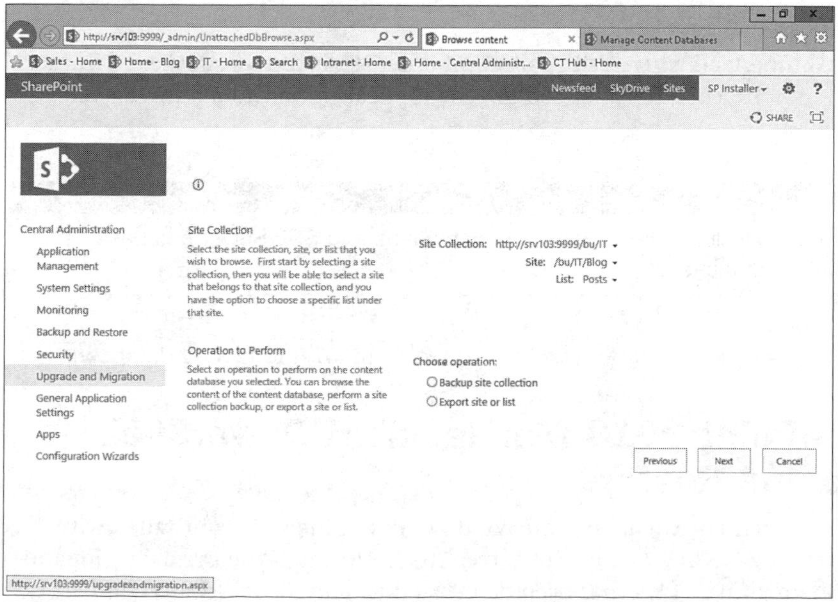

FIGURE 10.14 Browsing for content to restore in an unattached content database.

7. On the Site Collection Backup page, enter the backup location, and then enter the filename (using a .bak extension) in the Filename box. Select Overwrite Existing File if you want to overwrite, and then click Start Backup, as shown in Figure 10.15.

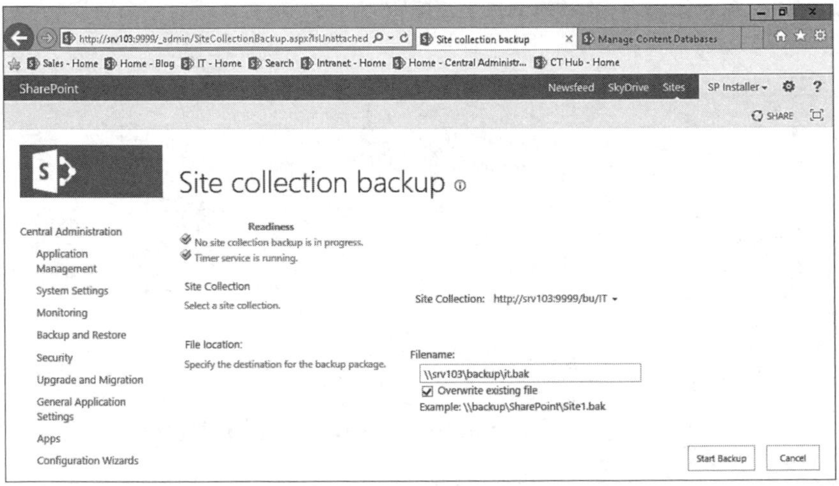

FIGURE 10.15 Extracting content from an unattached content database by backing it up.

After starting the backup, SharePoint 2013 displays the Granular Backup Job Status page. On this page, you can monitor the granular backup progress; the page also displays site collection backup status.

This method is recommended when a site collection or a list needs to be retrieved from a content database not attached to a SharePoint web application but to an SQL Server instance.

NOTE

Unattached databases include read-only content databases and SQL Server database snapshots of content databases.

Site collections, sites, lists, and libraries can be restored from an unattached database.

Using SharePoint 2013 Management PowerShell for Backup and Restore

SharePoint 2013 Management Shell, built on Windows PowerShell v3, is installed with SharePoint Foundation 2013 and SharePoint Server 2013. Although the `STSADM` command is available with SharePoint 2013, it has been deprecated to provide backward compatibility with earlier versions. SharePoint 2013 administrators have been armed with a powerful management shell to administer SharePoint 2013 environments. SharePoint 2013 Management Shell is much more powerful than SharePoint Central Administration and STSADM combined. SharePoint Central Administration is limited in functionality to what is represented in the GUI, whereas SharePoint 2013 Management Shell is highly extensible, with more than 800 prebuilt cmdlets available (in addition to support for creating custom cmdlets).

NOTE

Sample backup and restore scripts are included in Chapter 7, "Leveraging PowerShell for Command-Line SharePoint Administration and Automation."

Backing Up the Farm Configuration Using PowerShell

To back up farm configuration using the SharePoint 2013 Management Shell, execute the following command from within the PowerShell shell, as shown in Figure 10.16:

```
Backup-SPFarm -BackupMethod Full -Directory \\srv03\backup\  -ConfigurationOnly
```

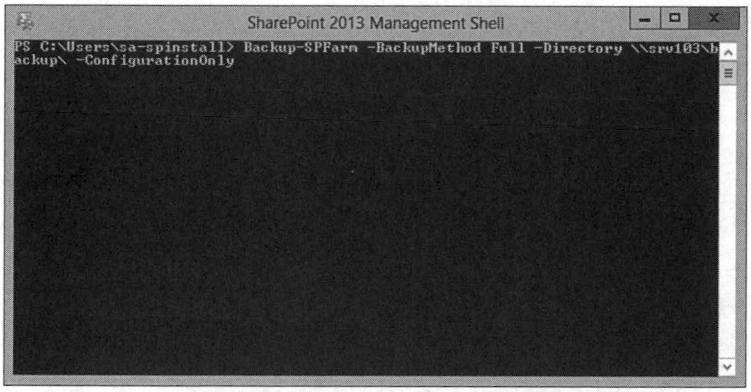

FIGURE 10.16 Backing up the farm using PowerShell.

Backing Up an Entire Web Application

To back up a single web application using the SharePoint 2013 Management Shell, execute the following command, as shown in Figure 10.17:

```
Backup-SPFarm -BackupMethod Full -Directory \\srv03\backup\ -Item <web application name>
```

10

NOTE

<web application name> is the name of the web application to be backed up using the Full method. If the web application is being backed up for the first time, it has to be full backup; otherwise, the backup will fail if it is a first-time differential backup.

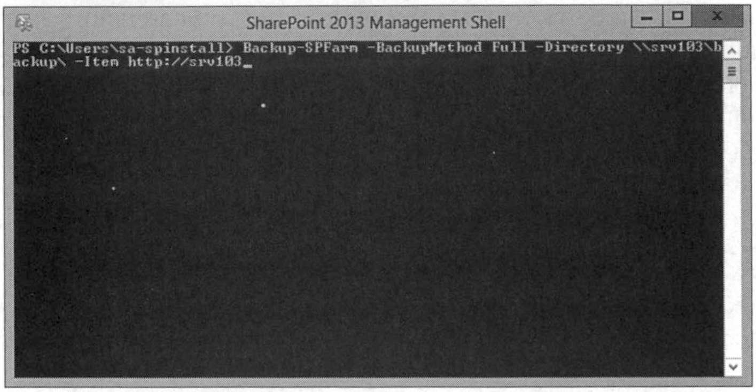

FIGURE 10.17 Backing up a web application using PowerShell.

The advantage of using Windows PowerShell is in executing multiple instances of Windows PowerShell scripts to back up site collections using the `BackUpThreads` parameter in `backup-spfarm`. The recommended value for SharePoint is three threads.

Restoring a Site Collection from Backup

To restore a single site collection using the SharePoint 2013 Management Shell, execute the following command, as shown in Figure 10.18:

```
Restore-SPSite -Identity http://intranet2013.justsharepoint.local/bu/it -Path \\
srv03\backup\IT.bak -force
```

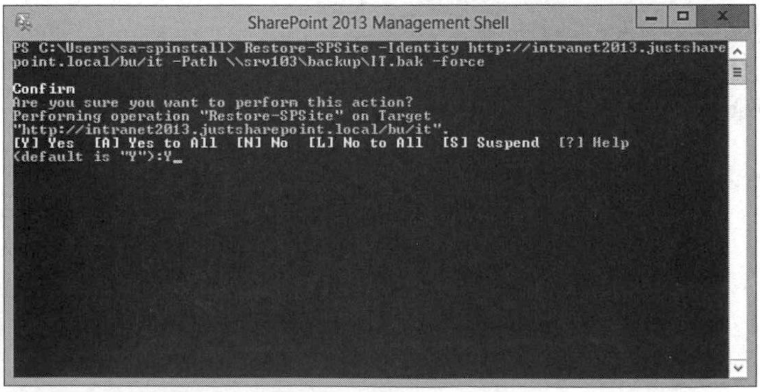

FIGURE 10.18 Restoring a site collection using PowerShell.

NOTE

We have used force to overwrite the site collection in the web application.

Restoring a Site Collection from the Recycle Bin

This feature was introduced in SP 1 of SharePoint 2010 and is available in SharePoint 2013. The deleted site collection can be restored from the secondary-stage Recycle Bin using the SharePoint 2013 Management Shell. You cannot restore a deleted site collection from the SharePoint 2013 GUI.

To restore a site collection from the Recycle Bin using the SharePoint 2013 Management Shell, execute the following command from within the PowerShell shell, as shown in Figure 10.19:

```
Get-SPDeletedSite
```

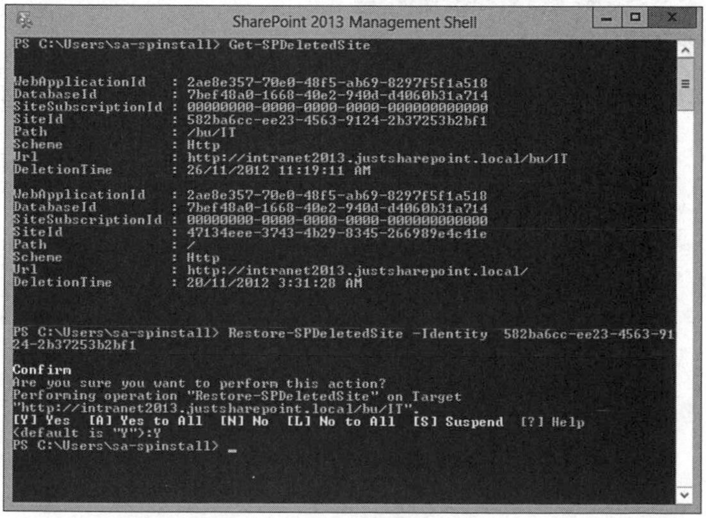

FIGURE 10.19 Restoring a deleted site collection from Recycle Bin.

NOTE

Identity GUID (globally unique identifier) of the Site Collection - SiteID must be noted for the next command:

```
Restore-SPDeletedSite -Identity <siteid guid>
```

Import Site or List

To import a list within a site using the SharePoint 2013 Management Shell, execute the following command from within the PowerShell shell:

```
Import-SPWeb -Identity http://intranet2013.justsharepoint.local/bu/it/Announcements/
-Path \\srv03\Backup\IT\Announcements.cmp -IncludeUserSecurity
```

10

Figure 10.20 shows the syntax for the `Import-SPWeb` command.

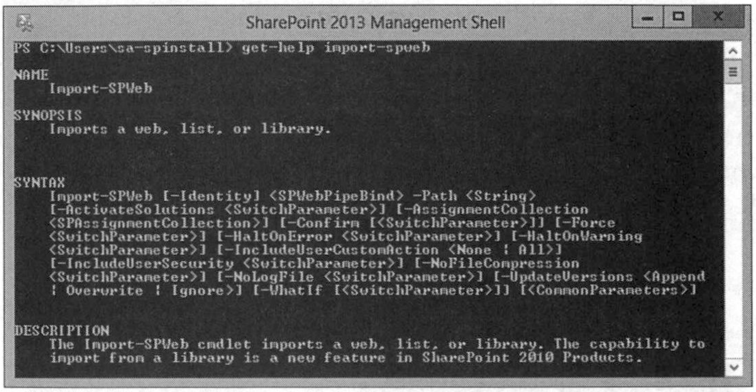

FIGURE 10.20 Examining the syntax for the `Import-SPWeb` cmdlet.

Importing a Site

Before you can import your web, you need to create the site. To create a site using the SharePoint 2013 Management Shell, execute the following command from within the PowerShell shell:

```
New-SPWeb -URL http://intranet2013.justsharepoint.local/bu/it/blog/ -Verbose
```

The `Verbose` parameter has been used to see how this cmdlet executes and creates a new site, as shown in Figure 10.21. After the site has been created, it can be overwritten with the backup as described next.

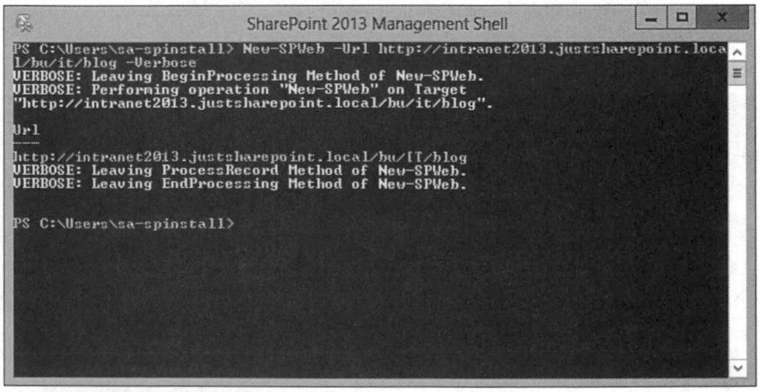

FIGURE 10.21 Creating a new site using the `New-SPWeb` cmdlet.

To import a site using the SharePoint 2013 Management Shell, execute the following command, as shown in Figure 10.22:

```
Import-SPWeb -Identity http://intranet2013.justsharepoint.local/bu/it/blog -Path \\
srv03\backup\itblogposts.cmp -IncludeUserSecurity -UpdateVersions Overwrite
```

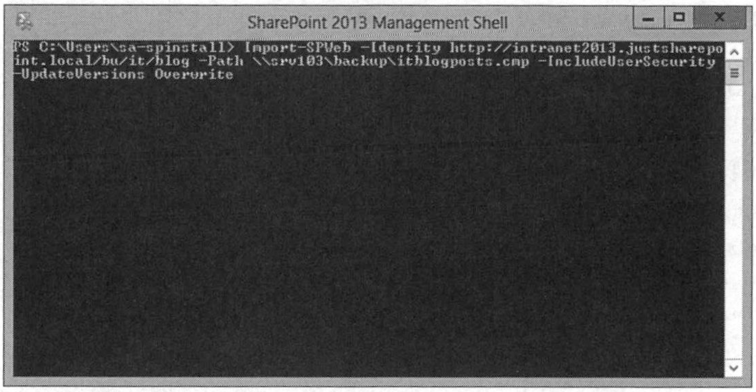

FIGURE 10.22 Importing a site using PowerShell.

With SharePoint 2013, backup and restore of site collections, sites, or lists can now be easily done with the Central Administration tool or SharePoint 2013 Management Shell. This functionality was removed from SharePoint Designer 2010 and is also not available in SharePoint Designer 2013.

Backing Up Internet Information Services v7 Configuration

You can use the appcmd.exe executable to back up IIS configuration in Windows 2008 R2; none of the other methods previously discussed enable you to do this.

The IIS 7 configuration is split between the web.config files and the applicationHost.config files. The applicationHost.config files include configuration information for the sites, applications, virtual directories, application pool definitions, and the default configuration settings for all sites on the web server.

To back up the IIS 7 configuration from a command prompt, follow these steps:

1. Log in to the Windows Server 2008 R2 computer with an account that has administrator rights.
2. Open a command prompt by using the Run as Administrator option and change the directory to %windir%\system32\inetsrv.
3. At the command prompt, type **appcmd add backup *<backupname>***. If you do not include the name of the backup, the system will name it for you by using a date, time format.

SQL Backup Tools

Fully loaded and deployed with Office Web Application Server 2013, all SharePoint 2013 Server service applications, the logging database, content databases, and configuration databases, SharePoint 2013 will have approximately 25 databases stored in SQL Server 2008 R2 SP1. That is a huge number of databases to maintain, and there is certainly a lot of content in these databases! To minimize the loss of content, it is crucial to incorporate a solid SQL database backup plan to back up all these databases.

Many options are available to back up SharePoint databases in SQL Server. In addition to Central Administration and SharePoint 2013 Management Shell, SQL Server facilitates the backup and restore of SharePoint 2013 databases with the SQL Server Management Studio, SQL Server Maintenance Plans, or Transact-SQL scripts that can be executed from within SQL Server. Further, you can use a third-party SQL backup engine to back up these SharePoint 2013 databases.

The backup options out-of-the-box in SharePoint give an array of tools to back up the configuration and the content databases, but critical SQL Server databases such as Master, MSDB, and TempDB cannot be backed up by these tools from within SharePoint. If a catastrophic event or hardware failure occurs, restoring the full SQL Server installation to the point of failure is not possible unless there is a strategic plan to do a backup and recovery of SQL Server databases.

In addition to the standard backup features in SQL Server 2008 R2 SP1, backup compression has been introduced.

SQL Server Backup Methods

SQL Server offers a wide range of options to back up databases, including the following:

- **Full:** Complete database backup that includes transaction logs.
- **Differential:** All data changes since the last full backup are backed up.
- **Transaction Log Backup:** All transactions performed against the database since the last full backup or transaction log backup are backed up.
- **File and File Group Backup:** A portion of the database is backed up.
- **Partial Backup:** All data in the primary group, every read-write file group, and any specified files are backed up. File groups marked read-only are skipped.
- **Differential Partial Backup:** Although similar to partial backup, this backup records only changes to the data in the file groups since the previous partial backup.
- **Copy-Only Backup:** This backup enables a backup of any type to be taken without affecting any other backups. Normally, a database backup is recorded in the database and is identified as part of a chain that can be used for restoration.

To do a full backup of an individual database via the SQL Server Management Studio, follow these steps:

1. Open the SQL Server Management Studio (Start, All Programs, Microsoft SQL Server 2008, SQL Server Management Studio).
2. In the Connect to Server dialog box, select the database server name to connect to and click Connect.
3. In the left pane of the Object Explorer, expand the server and the database folder.
4. Select the desired SharePoint Database to back up.
5. Right-click the database, select Tasks, and then click Backup.
6. On the General Settings page in the Backup Database window, review the name of the databases to be backed up and confirm that the Backup Type option is set to Full.
7. For the Backup Component option, select a Database option.
8. In the Backup set, enter the name and the description for the database backup.
9. In the next Destination section, the Tape option is grayed out if no tape devices are attached to the database server. In such a scenario, the only option available is to back up to disk. Click Add to add up to 64 disk devices that will contain the backup information. The same limit applies to tape media. If multiple devices are specified, the backup information will be spread across those devices. All the devices must be present to restore the database.
10. In the Select Backup Destination dialog box, enter the path and the backup filename in the destinations on the disk where the database is to be backed up. Click OK if the backup is to be initiated, or select Options in the Select a Page pane to configure advanced backup options.

In the Overwrite Media section, you have an array of options to choose from: Append to the Existing Backup Set or Overwrite All Existing Backup Sets. Backup sets can be added to an existing media, in which case you select Append to the Existing Backup Set. If you want to overwrite the backup sets with the latest backup on the media, select the Overwrite All Existing Backup Sets option.

NOTE

SQL Server 2008 R2 Enterprise Edition supports compression. Note, however, that compressed and uncompressed database backups cannot co-exist on the same media set. Also note that the Overwriting Backup Sets feature will be removed from the next version of Microsoft SQL Server; therefore, you should avoid using this feature for any new development instances and modify any existing applications that currently use this feature.

In the Reliability section, you can choose from among the following options:

- **Verify Backup When Finished:** Recommended to select because it verifies the database backup, but it does extend the time it takes to complete the database backup.

- **Perform Checksum Before Writing to Media:** Ensures that the database backup is completed without any errors. However, selecting this option adds to the time it takes to complete the database backup.
- **Continue on Error:** Database backup continues even if an error has been encountered. Selecting this option has an impact on the performance of the server because it increases the CPU overheads.

The Transaction Log section is available only if the Transaction Log backup type is selected on the General page. The Truncate the Transaction Log option removes any inactive portion of the transaction log after the database backup is complete. This is the default option and helps keep the size of your transaction log manageable. The Backup the Tail of the Log option relates to point-in-time restores and is discussed in more detail later in this chapter.

The options in the Tape Drive section are enabled only when Tape has been selected for the destination media. The Unload the Tape After Backup option ejects the media tape after the backup completes. This can help identify the end of the backup and prevents the tape from being overwritten the next time the backup runs. The Rewind the Tape Before Unloading option causes the tape to be released and rewound prior to unloading the tape.

New in SQL Server 2008 R2 is the backup compression feature. This is the last option in the Backup Database Option section. This feature is a Microsoft proprietary formula that may shrink the size of the database backup down to 20% of the original size (depending on the value specified in the Backup-Compression Default Server Configuration option).

CAUTION

Using the compression option can increase the load on the CPU and negatively affect processing power.

Continue with the process as follows:

1. On the Options page, in the Overwrite Media section, maintain the default settings Back Up to the Existing Media Set and Append to the Existing Backup Set.
2. In the Reliability section, choose Verify Backup When Finished, Perform Checksum Before Writing Media, and Continue On Error Options. Click OK to execute the backup.
3. Review the success or failure error messages and click OK to finalize.
4. Repeat for additional SharePoint databases.

Understanding the SQL Server Recover Models

You can choose from three recovery models: Simple, Full, and Bulk-Logged. The choice of the model depends on various factors that you need to consider, such as the extent to which data loss is acceptable, performance of the SQL server, and database recovery to the point of failure.

The simple recovery model recovers the database only to the point of the last successful full or differential backup. Content added to the database after the backup cannot be recovered with this model.

The full recovery model recovers the entire database to any point in time, because transaction logs are maintained. It must be noted that because all transactions to the database are logged, SQL Server database performance tends to degrade. For performance enhancement and recovery, you should store transaction logs and the database files on separate hard disks.

The bulk-logged recovery model is similar to the full recovery model because it maintains a transaction log; however, this model should be used only when large amounts of data are written to the database. To improve performance of the database server in such situations of bulk insertion or indexing, you should temporarily switch the recovery model to the bulk-logged model.

Business requirements define the disaster recovery strategies and drive the database administrator's decision as to the appropriate recovery model for the database. By default, the SharePoint configuration, AdminContent, and site content databases' recovery model is set to Full. As a result, these databases can be restored to the point of failure.

To set the recovery model on a SharePoint content database, follow these steps:

1. Open the SQL Server Management Studio (Start, All Programs, Microsoft SQL Server 2008, SQL Server Management Studio).
2. On the screen, select the database server to connect to the SQL database.
3. In the left pane of the Object Explorer, expand the server and then the database folder.
4. Select the desired SharePoint database to back up. Right-click the database, and select Properties.
5. In the Database Properties dialog box, select the Options node.
6. In the Recovery Mode dialog box, select Full, Bulk-Logged, or Simple from the drop-down list. Full is usually selected in most cases. Click OK to save the changes.

Summary

For SharePoint 2013 administrators, the wide array of options to back up content and configuration can be quite daunting. However, with the correct mix of these options, based on the business requirements, SharePoint configuration and content can be backed up and restored effectively without any loss to the business. Although backup and restore functionality has been removed from SharePoint Designer 2013, granular backup and restore via Central Administration or SharePoint 2013 Management Shell is a more effective and efficient mechanism in situations that require content recovery.

Best Practices

The following are best practices from this chapter:

- Implement external vendors' SharePoint backup and restore solutions or Microsoft's System Center DPM 2010 to enable enterprise-wide automation of backup and restore capabilities.
- For one-time backup and restore, SharePoint 2013 administrators have a choice of either using Central Administration tool or SharePoint 2013 Management PowerShell.
- Consider regular scripted backups using SharePoint 2013 Management Shell and SQL Server 2008 built-in tools.
- Perform regular scripted backups of IIS 7 configuration.
- Confirm that the SQL recovery model is set to Full on SharePoint databases to allow for full restores of SQL data.
- SharePoint 2013 Management Shell can be used to back up the entire farm or only business-critical site collections or sites via either one-time backups or scheduled scripts. However, if the content is business critical, SQL Server tools can be used to back up the content database or, using SQL snapshots options, to back up against the SQL snapshot.
- Simulation of recovery on regular intervals is highly recommended. This can help in plugging any shortcomings in the backup strategies and plans.

CHAPTER 11

Monitoring a SharePoint 2013 Environment

IN THIS CHAPTER

- Using the SharePoint Health Analyzer
- Using SharePoint Native Reporting Capabilities
- Understanding Timer Jobs for SharePoint 2013
- Using System Center Operations Manager to Simplify Management of SharePoint 2013
- Establishing Maintenance Schedules for SharePoint

A SharePoint farm is complex, with many moving parts contributing to the functionality of the entire platform. Therefore, the farm components need to be well maintained and monitored on a regular basis to ensure the smooth functioning of the environment. Of particular emphasis are the SQL databases that SharePoint runs on, which are often neglected but require regular maintenance and monitoring.

Fortunately for the SharePoint administrator, Microsoft has revamped SharePoint 2013 to include robust monitoring capabilities and features, including an optimized Health Monitor that automatically determines whether issues exist that affect SharePoint health. The SharePoint team has also built in advanced reporting capabilities natively in SharePoint and improved timer jobs.

In addition to the internal tools, outside of SharePoint, applications such as Microsoft's System Center Operations Manager (SCOM) 2012 provide for SharePoint-aware management capabilities that exceed those of the internal tools.

This chapter focuses on the specifics for monitoring and maintaining SharePoint, including an analysis of the native tools, the SharePoint Health Analyzer, and a discussion of System Center Operations Manager 2012 monitoring for a SharePoint 2013 environment. In addition, practical guidance for daily, weekly, monthly, quarterly, and yearly maintenance is provided.

Using the SharePoint Health Analyzer

Earlier versions of SharePoint did not include many integrated tools to help with monitoring the health of the SharePoint environment. SharePoint 2013 was built with a native SharePoint Health Analyzer, shown in Figure 11.1, which greatly improves the ability of SharePoint administrators to quickly detect issues within the farm.

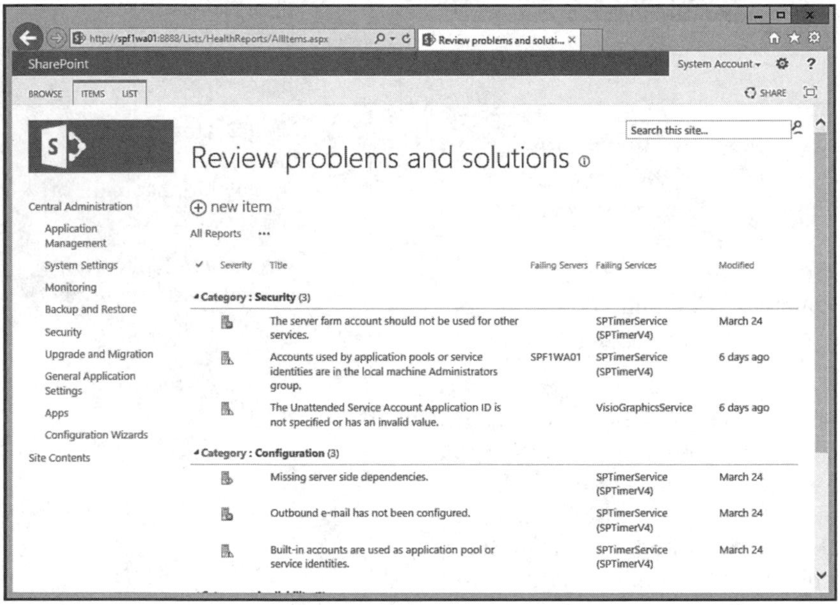

FIGURE 11.1 Viewing the SharePoint Health Analyzer.

Reviewing SharePoint Health Analyzer Settings

The SharePoint Health Analyzer is essentially a SharePoint list, as shown in Figure 11.2, that is driven by timer jobs that run on a regular basis. The list settings are Extensible Markup Language (XML) driven and can be configured to automatically resolve SharePoint health issues in certain cases.

In a default installation, there are more than 60 preconfigured rule definitions, in 4 different categories: Availability, Configuration, Performance, and Security. Each list item is configured to be checked on a regular basis. The following is a list of some of the default rules created in SharePoint 2013:

Accounts used by application pools or service identities are in the local machine Administrators group.

Business Data Connectivity connectors are currently enabled in a partitioned environment.

Web applications using claims authentication require an update.

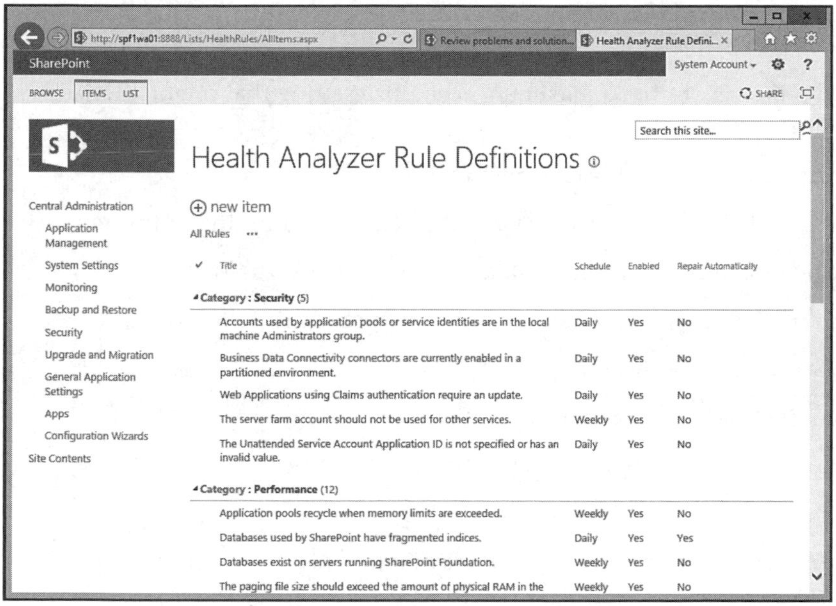

FIGURE 11.2 Examining Health Analyzer rule definitions.

The server farm account should not be used for other services.

The Unattended Service Account application ID is not specified or has an invalid value.

Application pools recycle when memory limits are exceeded.

Databases used by SharePoint have fragmented indices.

Databases exist on servers running SharePoint Foundation.

The paging file size should exceed the amount of physical memory in the system.

Databases used by SharePoint have outdated index statistics.

The timer service failed to recycle.

The Visio Graphics Service has a maximum cache age setting that adversely impacts performance.

The Visio Graphics Service has a maximum web drawing size setting that adversely impacts performance.

The Visio Graphics Service has a maximum recalculation setting that adversely impacts performance.

The Visio Graphics Service has a minimum cache age setting that adversely impacts performance.

The Visio Graphics Service has a minimum cache age setting that might cause a security issue.

The Visio Graphics Service has a maximum cache size setting that might adversely impact performance.

Alternate access URLs have not been configured.

The Application Discovery and Load Balancer Service is not running in this farm.

Automatic Update setting is inconsistent across farm servers.

Built-in accounts are used as application pool or service identities.

Missing server-side dependencies.

Databases require upgrade or are not supported.

Databases running in compatibility range, upgrade recommended.

Outbound email has not been configured.

Product/patch installation or server upgrade required.

Databases within this farm are set to read-only and fail to upgrade unless it is set to a read-write state.

Web.config file has incorrect settings for the `requestFiltering` element.

The number of distributed cache hosts in the farm exceeds the recommended value.

This distributed cache host might cause cache reliability problems.

Firewall client settings on the cache host are incorrect.

More cache hosts are running in this deployment than are registered with SharePoint.

Distributed cache service is not enabled in this deployment.

Web.config files are not identical on all machines in the farm.

One or more web applications are configured to use Windows classic authentication.

Dedicated crawl target configuration has one or more invalid servers.

The InfoPath Forms Services Maintenance timer job is not enabled.

InfoPath form library forms cannot be filled out in a web browser.

InfoPath Forms Services forms cannot be filled out in a web browser because no State Service connection is configured.

Expired sessions are not being deleted from the ASP.NET session state database.

The State Service Delete Expired Sessions timer job is not enabled.

Verify each User Profile Service application has an associated Managed Metadata Service connection.

Verify each User Profile Service application has an associated Search service connection.

Verify each User Profile Service application has a My Site host configured.

Verify that the critical User Profile Application and User Profile Proxy Application timer jobs are available and have not been mistakenly deleted.

Validate the My Site host and individual My Sites are on a dedicated web application and separate URL domain.

Verify that the Activity Feed timer job is enabled.

People search relevance is not optimized when the Active Directory has errors in the manager reporting structure.

The settings for the Machine Translation Service are not within the recommended limits.

Verify that OAuth is configured correctly for the Machine Translation Service application proxy.

Verify that OAuth is configured correctly for the Machine Translation Service application.

Immediate translations for the Machine Translation Service are disabled.

The Machine Translation Service is not running when it should be running.

XLIFF translation for the Machine Translation Service is disabled.

Content databases contain orphaned apps.

Drives are running out of free space.

Drives are at risk of running out of free space.

Content databases contain orphaned items.

Some content databases are growing too large.

Database has large amounts of unused space.

The Security Token Service is not available.

One or more servers are not responding.

One or more services have started or stopped unexpectedly.

One of the cache hosts in the cluster is down.

Cached objects have been evicted.

The current server is running low on memory.

Drives used for SQL databases are running out of free space.

All State Service databases are paused for a State Service application.

A State Service application has no database defined.

The settings for Word Automation Services are not within the recommended limits.

Critical state of this rule indicates that the Word Automation Services is not running when it should be running.

Modifying Health Analyzer Job Definitions

You can modify the default SharePoint Health Analyzer rules directly from within Central Admin or from PowerShell. In addition, the rules can be easily extended by third-party tools or add-ons to SharePoint. Developers or administrators can also write their own custom rules to look for specific criteria.

Custom rules can be created through creation of code that uses either the `SPHealthAnalysisRule` or `SPRepairableHealthAnalysisRule` classes. Rules are compiled and registered with the Health Analyzer and, when created, are allocated an associated timer job created to run the rule.

For SharePoint administrators, the default content rules can be modified to change how often they run and whether the rule will attempt to automatically fix the problem associated with the rule. Clicking the rule and then clicking Edit Item pulls up a dialog box similar to the one shown in Figure 11.3, which enables for customization of the rule.

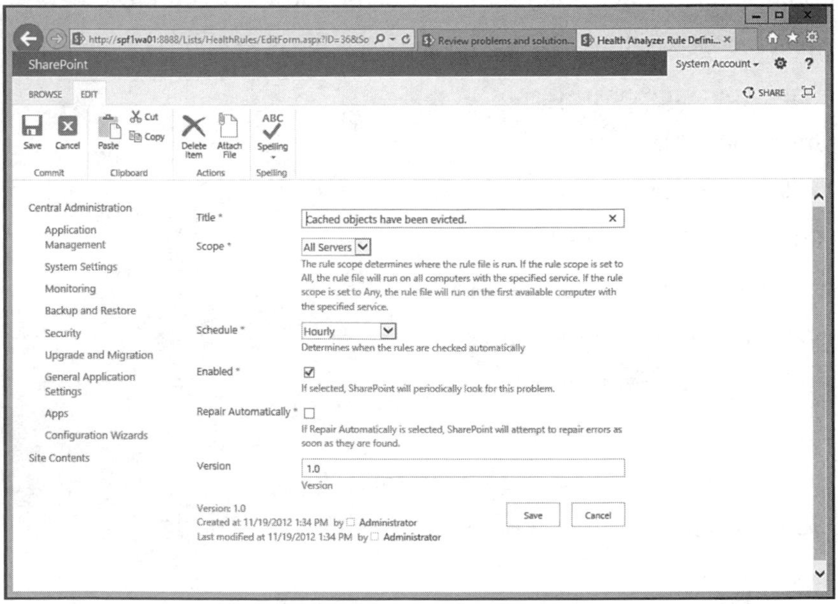

FIGURE 11.3 Modifying SharePoint Health Analyzer rule definitions.

Using SharePoint Native Reporting Capabilities

Out-of-the-box, SharePoint 2013 gives administrators access to a default set of reports that can analyze traffic patterns or perform diagnostics on an environment.

The default set of reports can also be extended by third-party utilities or with custom-created reports. In addition, SharePoint administrators can customize individual reports to fit their own specific needs.

NOTE

SharePoint reporting can be further extended using SQL Server Reporting Services running in SharePoint integration mode.

Optimizing Usage Data Collection Log Settings

By default, usage data collection logs, which are used to analyze traffic patterns on SharePoint sites, are stored on the default system volume with the rest of the SharePoint data. Because these files can grow quite large, you should move them to their own volume or limit their growth. To modify these settings for the farm, click the Configure Usage and Health Data Collection link under the Monitoring section of SharePoint Central Admin, and modify the settings, as shown in Figure 11.4.

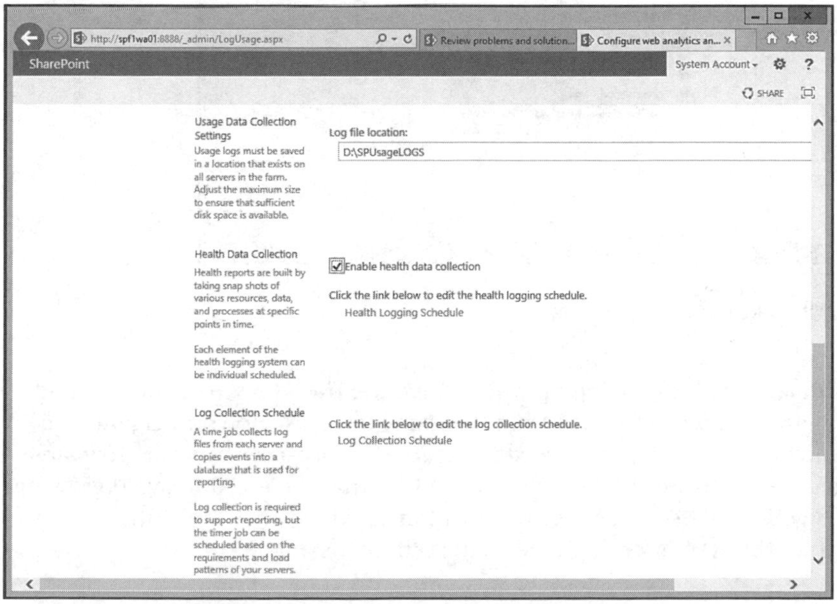

FIGURE 11.4 Modifying the usage data collection log location.

NOTE

The location for the usage collection logs must exist on all SharePoint servers in the farm. This note applies to any other log location setting defined, because these settings apply to every server within the farm.

Modifying Diagnostic Log Settings

You can use diagnostic logs to determine whether issues exist with individual services in SharePoint 2013. You can turn on (or off) logging for individual services in the Diagnostic Logging dialog box, as shown in Figure 11.5.

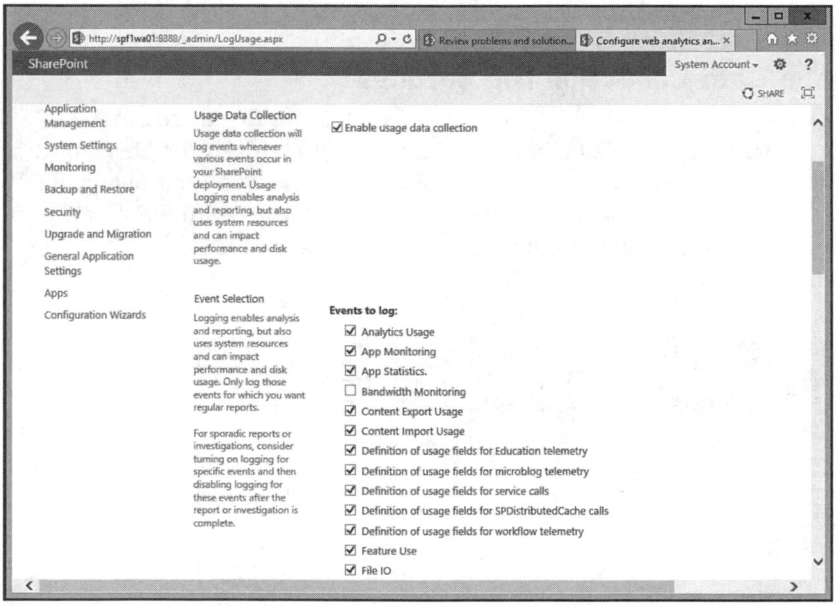

FIGURE 11.5 Viewing diagnostic log settings.

Other settings for diagnostic logs, including which drive the trace files are stored on and how large they can grow, can be modified from this same page, as shown in Figure 11.6. It is highly recommended to control the growth of trace files because they can grow large very quickly. In general, enable only those diagnostic files that you need to avoid growing out of control. It is good practice to change the location to which they are written to something other than the system drive where SharePoint is installed.

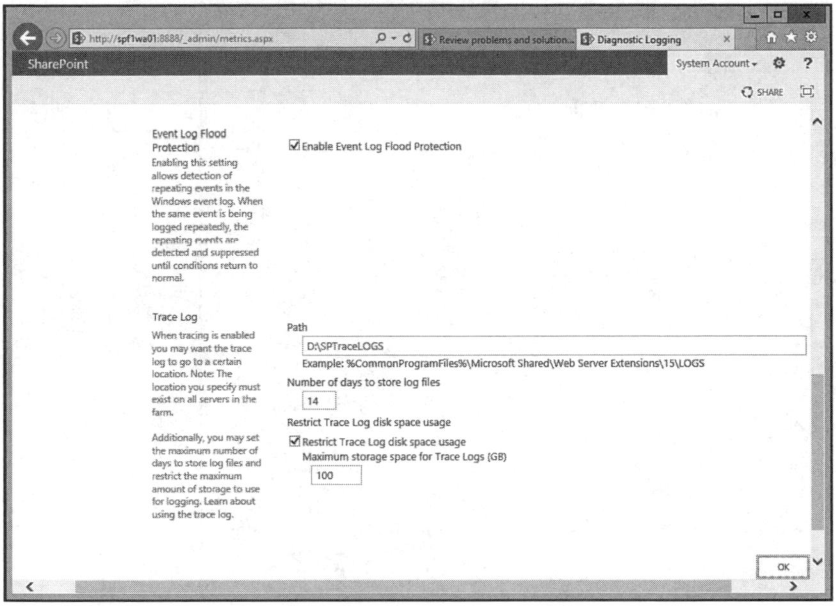

FIGURE 11.6 Modifying the trace log default location.

Understanding Timer Jobs for SharePoint 2013

Timer jobs, as shown in Figure 11.7, are critical components in SharePoint jobs. They are used to fire off tasks on a scheduled basis and are critical to the smooth operation of a farm. It is critical to understand which timer jobs are configured and how to modify them to understand how to administer a SharePoint environment.

Modifying Timer Jobs

The schedule for individual timer jobs can be modified by clicking the name of the timer job from within the Timer Job page, located within the Monitoring area of SharePoint Central Admin. Jobs can be modified to occur as often as every minute or as seldom as monthly, as shown in Figure 11.8. In addition, you can kick off individual timer jobs by clicking the Run Now button.

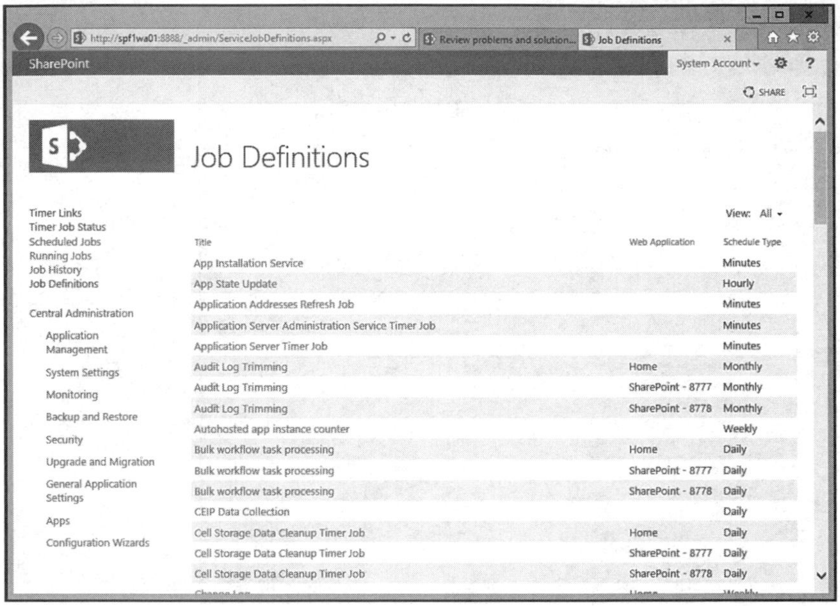

FIGURE 11.7 Viewing timer jobs.

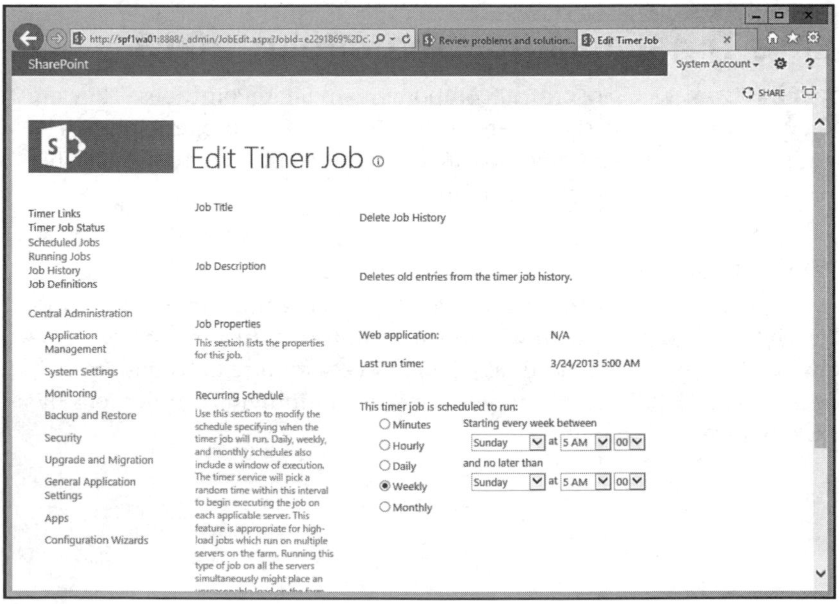

FIGURE 11.8 Modifying the schedule for individual timer jobs.

Monitoring Timer Jobs

The status for any one timer job can also be easily monitored, this time by clicking the Timer Job Status link within the Monitoring page of SharePoint Central Admin (see Figure 11.9). The job schedule is shown at the top of the page, and job status is shown at the bottom.

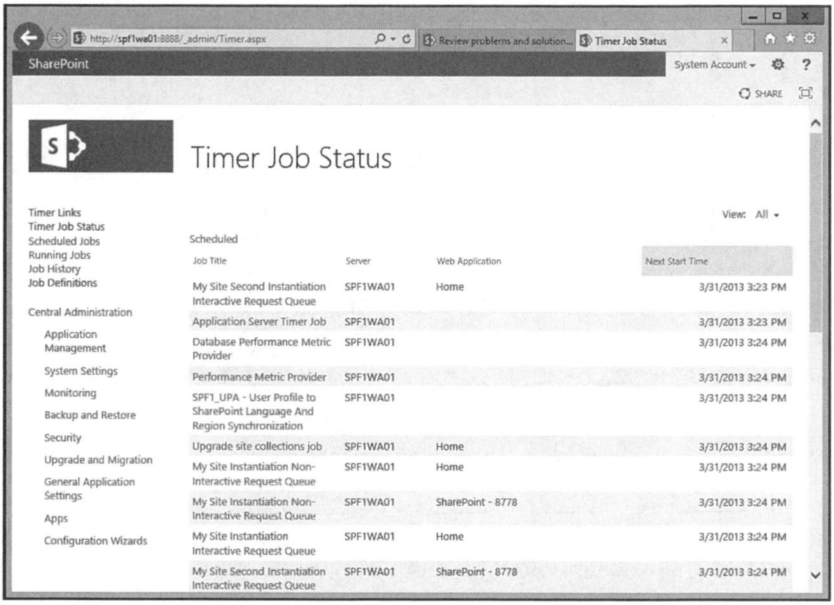

FIGURE 11.9 Monitoring timer job status.

In addition to the SharePoint Central Admin tool, you can use the PowerShell scripting interface to administer timer jobs. Enter `Get-Command *SPTimerJob` from PowerShell to get a list of commands that you can use to administer timer jobs from the command line.

Using System Center Operations Manager to Simplify Management of SharePoint 2013

SCOM is an enterprise-class monitoring and management solution for Windows environments. It is designed to simplify SharePoint server management by consolidating events, performance data, alerts, and more into a centralized repository. Reports on this information can then be tailored depending on the environment and the level of detail needed and extrapolated. This information can assist administrators and decision makers in proactively addressing SharePoint server operation and any problems that exist or may occur.

The latest version of SCOM, System Center Operations Manager 2012, can be further extended through the addition of management packs for SharePoint Foundation and SharePoint Server, which contain built-in event and performance analysis tools specifically written to ensure smooth functionality of a SharePoint environment. Deployment of a SCOM solution in a SharePoint environment would not be complete without installation of this tool.

Many other intrinsic benefits are gained by using SCOM, including the following:

- Event log monitoring and consolidation
- Monitoring of various applications, including those provided by third parties
- Enhanced alerting capabilities
- Assistance with capacity-planning efforts
- A customizable knowledge base of Microsoft product knowledge and best practices
- Web-based interface for reporting and monitoring

Taking a Closer Look at System Center Operations Manager

SCOM 2012 is the latest version of Microsoft's enterprise monitoring product. Previously owned by NetIQ and then sold to Microsoft, the product has evolved from a product known as Microsoft Operations Manager (MOM) to the latest generation.

SCOM provides for several major pieces of functionality, as follows:

- **Event log consolidation:** SCOM agents, deployed on managed systems, forward all event log information to a central SCOM SQL Server database, which is managed and groomed by SCOM. This data is used for reporting, auditing, and monitoring the specific events.
- **Advanced alerting capabilities:** SCOM provides advanced alerting functionality by enabling email alerts, paging, and functional alerting roles to be defined.
- **Performance monitoring:** SCOM collects performance statistics that can let an administrator know whether a server is being overloaded or is close to running out of disk space, among other things.
- **Built-in application-specific intelligence:** SCOM management packs are packages of information about a particular application or service, such as domain name server (DNS), Dynamic Host Configuration Protocol (DHCP), Exchange Server, or SharePoint Server. The Microsoft management packs are written by the design teams for each individual product and are loaded with the intelligence and information necessary to properly troubleshoot and identify problems. For example, the SharePoint management pack automatically knows which event IDs indicate configuration errors in the software and specifically directs an administrator to the proper location on the Web where Microsoft Knowledge Base articles can be used for troubleshooting.

SCOM architecture can be complex, but often it is as simple as an SQL database running on a server, with another server providing the management server functions of SCOM. This type of server is also known as an SCOM management server.

Installing SCOM Management Packs for SharePoint 2013

As previously mentioned, management packs contain intelligence about specific applications and services and include troubleshooting information specific to those services. Microsoft has released two management packs for SharePoint 2013. The first is the management pack for SharePoint Foundation 2013; the second is for the full SharePoint 2013 suite. It is recommended to deploy those management packs that are used within your environment.

To download these management packs, go to http://pinpoint.microsoft.com and search for "SharePoint 2013 management pack." Within the Search results, you should see the following available for download:

- System Center Monitoring Pack for SharePoint Server 2013
- System Center Monitoring Pack for SharePoint Foundation 2013

Install and import each management pack individually into SCOM 2012 via the Import/Export Management Packs link to enable them in the environment. When installed, they intelligently sense which servers are SharePoint servers and deploy scripts and event viewer monitors to those systems.

Installing Additional Management Packs for SharePoint Farms

In addition to the SharePoint 2013-specific management packs, a SharePoint environment should leverage additional management packs installed on SCOM to monitor the other non-SharePoint components:

- Microsoft SQL Server Management Pack for Operations Manager 2012
- Windows Server Internet Information Services (IIS) for System Center Operations Manager 2012
- Windows Server Operating System (OS) Management Pack for Operations Manager 2012
- Active Directory Management Pack for System Center Operations Manager 2012 (for the domain controllers)

Review the list of components used within the SharePoint environment and compare that list with the list of management packs provided. This might mean that additional management packs are needed. For example, if Forefront Threat Management Gateway or Forefront Unified Access Gateway are used to secure inbound Hypertext Transport Protocol Secure (HTTPS) access to SharePoint, those management packs may be required.

Monitoring SharePoint Functionality and Performance with SCOM

After the management pack is installed for SharePoint and the agent has been installed and is communicating, SCOM consolidates and reacts to every event and performance counter sent to it from the SharePoint server. This information is reflected in the SCOM operations console.

Performance data for SharePoint can also be displayed in SCOM. This enables reports and performance metrics to be obtained from the farm. For more information on SCOM 2012, refer to www.microsoft.com/SystemCenter.

Establishing Maintenance Schedules for SharePoint

Maintaining a SharePoint farm is not an easy task for administrators. They must find time in their firefighting efforts to focus and plan for maintenance on the server systems. When maintenance tasks are common in an environment, they can alleviate many of the common firefighting tasks.

The processes and procedures for maintaining Windows Server systems can be separated based on the appropriate time to maintain a particular aspect of SharePoint. Some maintenance procedures require daily attention, whereas others may require only yearly checkups. The maintenance processes and procedures that an organization follows depend strictly on the organization; however, the categories described in the following sections and their corresponding procedures are best practices for organizations of all sizes and varying IT infrastructures.

Outlining Daily Maintenance Tasks

Certain maintenance procedures require more attention than others. The procedures that require the most attention are categorized as daily procedures. A SharePoint administrator should review these procedures each day to ensure system reliability, availability, performance, and security. These procedures are examined in the following three sections.

Checking Overall SharePoint Server Functionality

Although checking the overall server health and functionality may seem redundant or elementary, this procedure is critical to keeping the system environment and users working productively.

Questions that should be addressed during the checking and verification process include the following:

- Can users access data in SharePoint document libraries?
- Can remote users access SharePoint via Secure Sockets Layer (SSL) if configured?
- Is there an exceptionally long wait to access the portal (that is, longer than normal)?
- Do Simple Mail Transfer Protocol (SMTP) alerts function properly?
- Are searches properly locating newly created or modified content?

Verifying That Backups Are Successful

To provide a secure and fault-tolerant organization, it is imperative that a successful backup be performed every night. If a server failure occurs, the administrator may be required to perform a restore from tape. Without a backup each night, the IT organization is forced to rely on rebuilding the SharePoint server without the data. Therefore, the administrator should always back up servers so that the IT organization can restore them with minimum downtime if a disaster occurs. Because of the importance of the tape backups, the first priority of the administrator each day needs to be verifying and maintaining the backup sets.

If disaster ever strikes, the administrators want to be confident that a system or entire farm can be recovered as quickly as possible. Successful backup mechanisms are imperative to the recovery operation; recoveries are only as good as the most recent backups.

Although Windows Server's or SharePoint's backup programs do not offer alerting mechanisms for bringing attention to unsuccessful backups, many third-party programs do. In addition, many of these third-party backup programs can send emails or pages if backups are successful or unsuccessful. For more information on backing up and restoring SharePoint, see Chapter 10, "Backing Up and Restoring a SharePoint Environment."

Monitoring the Event Viewer

The Windows Event Viewer is used to check the system, security, application, and other logs on a local or remote system. These logs are an invaluable source of information regarding the system. The following event logs are present for SharePoint servers running on Windows Server:

- **Security:** Captures all security-related events being audited on a system. Auditing is turned on by default to record success and failure of security events.
- **Application:** Stores specific application information. This information includes services and any applications running on the server.
- **System:** Stores Windows Server-specific information.

All Event Viewer events are categorized as informational, warning, or error.

NOTE

Checking these logs often helps to understand them. Some events constantly appear but aren't significant. Events will begin to look familiar, so it will be noticeable when something is new or amiss in event logs. It is for this reason that an intelligent log filter such as SCOM 2012 is a welcome addition to a SharePoint environment.

Best practices for monitoring event logs include the following:

- Understand the events being reported.
- Set up a database for archived event logs.

- Archive event logs often.
- Use an automatic log parsing and alerting tool, such as SCOM.

To simplify monitoring hundreds or thousands of generated events each day, the administrator should use the filtering mechanism provided in the Event Viewer. Although warnings and errors should take priority, the informational events should be reviewed to track what was happening before the problem occurred. After the administrator reviews the informational events, he/she can filter out the informational events and view only the warnings and errors.

To filter events, follow these steps:

1. Start the Event Viewer by choosing Start, All Programs, Administrative Tools, Event Viewer.
2. Select the log from which you want to filter events.
3. Right-click the log and select Filter Current Log.
4. In the Filter Current Log window, select the types of events to filter.
5. (Optional) Select the time frame in which the events occurred, event source, category, event ID, or other options that will narrow down the search. Click OK when finished.

Some warnings and errors are normal because of bandwidth constraints or other environmental issues. The more logs are monitored, the more familiar an administrator should be with the messages and therefore will spot a problem before it affects the user community.

NOTE

You might need to increase the size of the log files in the Event Viewer to accommodate an increase in logging activity.

Performing Weekly SharePoint Maintenance

Maintenance procedures that require slightly less attention than daily checking are categorized in a weekly routine and are examined in the following sections.

Checking Disk Space

Disk space is a precious commodity. Although the disk capacity of a Windows Server system can seem virtually endless, the amount of free space on all drives should be checked daily. Serious problems can occur if there isn't enough disk space.

One of the most common disk space problems occurs on database drives where all SQL SharePoint data is held. Other volumes such as the system drive and partitions with logging data can also quickly fill up.

As mentioned earlier, lack of free disk space can cause a multitude of problems, including the following:

- SharePoint application failures
- System crashes
- Unsuccessful backup jobs
- Service failures
- Inability to audit
- Degradation of performance

To prevent these problems from occurring, administrators should keep the amount of free space to at least 25%.

CAUTION

If needing to free disk space, move or delete files and folders with caution. System files are automatically protected by Windows Server, but data files are not.

Verifying SharePoint Hardware Components

Hardware components supported by Windows Server are reliable, but this doesn't mean that they'll always run continuously without failure. Hardware availability is measured in terms of mean time between failures (MTBF) and mean time to repair (MTTR). This includes downtime for both planned and unplanned events. These measurements provided by the manufacturer are good guidelines to follow; however, mechanical parts are bound to fail at one time or another. As a result, hardware should be monitored weekly to ensure efficient operation.

Hardware can be monitored in many different ways. For example, server systems may have internal checks and logging functionality to warn against possible failure, Windows Server's System Monitor might bring light to a hardware failure, and a physical hardware check can help to determine whether the system is about to experience a problem with the hardware.

If a failure occurs or is about to occur on a SharePoint server, having an inventory of spare hardware can significantly improve the chances and timing of recoverability. Checking system hardware on a weekly basis provides the opportunity to correct the issue before it becomes a problem.

Archiving Event Logs

The three event logs on all servers can be archived manually, or a script can be written to automate the task. You should archive the event logs to a central location for ease of management and retrieval.

The specific amount of time to keep archived log files varies on a per-organization basis. For example, banks or other high-security organizations might be required to keep event logs up to a few years. As a best practice, organizations should keep event logs for at least three months.

TIP

Organizations that deploy SCOM with SharePoint can take advantage of SCOM's capability to automatically archive event log information, providing for a significant improvement to monitoring and reporting of SharePoint.

Performing Monthly Maintenance Tasks

When you determine the maintenance required for SharePoint, it is vital to formalize the procedures into documented steps. A maintenance plan can contain information on what tasks to perform at different intervals. You should perform the tasks examined in the following sections on a monthly basis.

Maintaining File System Integrity

CHKDSK scans for file system integrity and can check for lost clusters, cross-linked files, and more. If Windows Server senses a problem, it runs CHKDSK automatically at startup.

Administrators can maintain FAT, FAT32, and NTFS file system integrity by running CHKDSK once a month. To run CHKDSK, follow these steps:

1. At the command prompt, change to the partition that you want to check.
2. Type **CHKDSK** without any parameters to check only for file system errors.
3. If any errors are found, run the CHKDSK utility with the `/f` parameter to attempt to correct the errors found.

Testing the UPS Battery

You can use an uninterruptible power supply (UPS) to protect the system or group of systems from power failures (such as spikes and surges) and keep the system running long enough after a power outage so that an administrator can gracefully shut down the system. A SharePoint administrator should follow the UPS guidelines provided by the manufacturer at least once a month. Also, monthly scheduled battery tests should be performed.

Validating Backups

Once a month, an administrator should validate backups by restoring the backups to a server located in a lab environment. This is in addition to verifying that backups were successful from log files or the backup program's management interface. A restore enables the administrator to verify the backups and to practice the restore procedures that would be used when recovering the server during a disaster. In addition, this procedure tests the state of the backup media to ensure that it is in working order and builds administrator confidence for recovering from a true disaster.

Updating Documentation

An integral part of managing and maintaining any IT environment is to document the network infrastructure and procedures. The following are just a few of the documents you should consider having on hand:

- SharePoint Server build guides
- Disaster recovery guides and procedures
- Maintenance checklists
- Configuration settings
- Change control logs
- Historical performance data
- Special user rights assignments
- SharePoint site configuration settings
- Special application settings

As systems and services are built and procedures are decided upon, document these facts to reduce learning curves, administration, and maintenance.

It is not only important to adequately document the IT environment, but it's also often even more important to keep those documents up-to-date. Otherwise, documents can quickly become outdated as the environment, processes, and procedures change as the business changes.

Performing Quarterly Maintenance Tasks

As the term implies, quarterly maintenance is performed four times a year. Areas to maintain and manage on a quarterly basis are usually self-sufficient and self-sustaining. Infrequent maintenance is required to keep the system healthy. This doesn't mean, however, that the tasks are simple or that they aren't as critical as those tasks that require more frequent maintenance.

Checking Storage Limits

Storage capacity on all volumes should be checked to ensure that all volumes have ample free space. Keep approximately 25% free space on all volumes.

Running low or completely out of disk space creates unnecessary risk for any system. Services can fail, applications can stop responding, and systems can even crash if there isn't plenty of disk space.

Keeping SQL database disk space consumption to a minimum can be accomplished through a combination of limiting document library versioning or implementing site quotas.

Changing Administrator Passwords

Administrator passwords should, at a minimum, be changed every quarter (90 days). Changing these passwords strengthens security measures so that systems can't easily be compromised. In addition to changing passwords, other password requirements such as password age, history, length, and strength should be reviewed.

Summary of Maintenance Tasks and Recommendations

Table 11.1 summarizes some of the maintenance tasks and recommendations examined in this chapter.

TABLE 11.1 Maintenance Tasks for SharePoint Servers

Daily	Weekly	Monthly	Quarterly	Task
X				Check overall server functionality, including the SharePoint Health Analyzer.
X				Verify backups.
X				Monitor Event Viewer.
X	X			Check disk space.
X	X			Verify hardware.
	X			Archive event logs.
	X			Check SharePoint logs.
	X			Test the UPS.
		X		Check SQL maintenance plans.
		X		Run CHKDSK.
			X	Update documentation.
			X	Change administrator passwords.
			X	Test farm restores.

Summary

Although SharePoint administrators can easily get caught up in daily administration and firefighting, it's important to structure system management and maintenance to help prevent unnecessary amounts of effort. Following a management and maintenance regimen reduces administration, maintenance, and business expenses, while at the same time increasing reliability, stability, and security.

SharePoint 2013 includes built-in monitoring capabilities using tools such as the SharePoint Health Analyzer, enhanced timer job capabilities, and enhanced logging that can help SharePoint administrators have better control over their SharePoint environment. Combined with an enterprise tool, such as System Center Operations Manager, and together with a comprehensive maintenance schedule composed of daily, weekly, monthly, and quarterly tasks, a SharePoint 2013 farm can be properly monitored and controlled.

Best Practices

The following are best practices from this chapter:

- Use the SharePoint Health Analyzer to proactively identify health issues in a SharePoint 2013 farm.
- Understand how to modify timer job schedules and to run timer jobs manually.
- Move the trace and usage logs to a dedicated drive that exists on all SharePoint farm members.
- Use SCOM 2012 to proactively manage SharePoint Server 2007 systems.
- Download all relevant SCOM management packs, including SQL, IIS, and Windows OS management packs, in addition to the two SharePoint 2013-specific ones.
- Identify tasks important to the system's overall health and security.
- Thoroughly test and evaluate service packs and updates in a lab environment before installing them on production servers and client machines.
- Install the appropriate service packs and updates on each production SharePoint server and client machine to keep all systems consistent.
- Categorize and document daily, weekly, monthly, and quarterly tasks required to monitor SharePoint farm servers.

CHAPTER 12

Virtualizing SharePoint Components

IN THIS CHAPTER

- Microsoft's Virtualization Support Story
- Virtualization Infrastructure Requirements and Recommendations
- Software Recommendations and Licensing Notes
- Virtualization of SharePoint Roles
- Exploring Sample Virtualized SharePoint 2013 Architecture
- Virtual Machine Management with System Center Virtual Machine Manager

Server virtualization technologies have become so common that they are the de facto standard for server deployment in many organizations. It's becoming more and more common to run into data center environments that operate with the assumption that all new servers will be deployed as virtual machines (VMs) unless there's some specific reason not to virtualize. This is a significant change from even just a few years ago when the situation was reversed and servers were deployed on physical equipment unless there was a specific reason to virtualize.

So, what about Microsoft SharePoint? Should you virtualize some or all of a SharePoint environment and take advantage of the consolidation, optimization, and flexibility options that virtualization infrastructure provides? The reality is that SharePoint environments, particularly those running SharePoint Server 2013, can be robustly deployed on virtual servers as long as sufficient resources are allocated to virtual guests and the virtual hosts are scaled correctly. Deploying SharePoint improperly in a virtual environment can lead to slowness and other performance problems and can decrease management confidence in virtualization as a whole, so it's vital to review virtualization design criteria for SharePoint in advance.

Microsoft's Virtualization Support Story

The support story for Microsoft products running on virtualization hardware is long and complicated. Until several years ago, Microsoft offered limited support for its flagship server products, such as SQL Server, Exchange Server, and SharePoint Server. Microsoft even left open the option that a support problem might need to be duplicated on physical hardware if support technicians couldn't determine the nature of the problem in a virtual environment. Adding to Microsoft's weak support story was the fact that Virtual Server 2005 R2 was its virtualization product during the early days of Microsoft Office SharePoint Server (MOSS) 2007. Virtual Server 2005 R2 wasn't a hypervisor-based product and couldn't virtualize 64-bit guests, which limited supported environments to those running the 32-bit versions of MOSS 2007. This greatly curtailed the performance that could be achieved, particularly for the database role, which was the most resource intensive and could take advantage of the 64-bit architecture the most. In addition, web front ends usually required significantly more memory than a 32-bit platform.

Two significant developments changed this story. The first was Microsoft's release of a 64-bit-capable hypervisor named Hyper-V. The second was the development of a program called the Server Virtualization Validation Program (SVVP), which outlined Microsoft's official support stance on running its products on third-party hypervisor virtualization platforms. This program, outlined in the Microsoft article "Support Policy for Microsoft Software Running in Non-Microsoft Hardware Virtualization Software" (http://support.microsoft.com/kb/897615), allowed for support of Microsoft products on third-party virtualization products that were validated by Microsoft and complied with certain criteria, namely the ability to give guest sessions direct access to hardware resources via a virtualization hypervisor. These two developments opened the doors for Microsoft servers running on VMs and gave peace of mind to organizations that needed to deploy supported virtualized solutions.

SharePoint Virtualization Support

The 2007 wave of SharePoint products—which includes Windows SharePoint Services 3.0 (WSS 3.0) and MOSS 2007—was the first to gain broad virtualization support from Microsoft. However, in production, most clients opted to virtualize only the web role and sometimes the search query role. Other roles weren't usually implemented, for various reasons. For example, the index role was often implemented only on physical hardware because of heavy processor and memory constraints and the limitation in SharePoint 2007 of one index server per shared services provider.

With SharePoint 2010 and then later SharePoint 2013, Microsoft's official support stance is that any SharePoint role or service is supported for hardware virtualization. SharePoint 2013 is positioned as an excellent virtualization candidate because of virtualization technology advances. In addition, advances in hardware virtualization make it easier to virtualize I/O-intensive applications such as SQL Server. As a result, many organizations are looking at virtualizing their new SharePoint 2013 farms.

Virtualization Infrastructure Requirements and Recommendations

The key to a stable and high-performance virtualized SharePoint environment is using the proper architecture in the virtualization hosts. Out-of-the-box settings and slow disks might work for a test environment, but specific requirements need to be met when building the host system for proper performance to be achieved. Therefore, be sure to follow these minimum requirements when you design the virtualization host infrastructure:

- The processors must support hardware-assisted virtualization, which is available in processors that include a virtualization option. Specifically, this means processors with Intel Virtualization Technology (Intel VT) or AMD Virtualization (AMD-V) technology.
- Hardware-enforced data execution prevention (DEP) must be available and enabled.

  SharePoint guests must be deployed on a Hyper-V hypervisor or a third-party hypervisor that is part of the SVVP, which include popular hypervisors such as VMware ESX and Citrix XenServer.
- Sufficient memory must be allocated for the host operating system (OS). If you're using Hyper-V, you need to reserve at least 1GB of RAM for use by the Hyper-V host. If you're using a third-party hypervisor, check with the individual provider to determine the minimum amount of memory required.
- A dedicated network interface card (NIC) must be allocated for host management. This NIC must be separate from the NICs used by the VMs.
- Use multiple independent drive arrays of disk spindles. Best practice is to allocate a dedicated set of disk spindles or storage array for the host OS, another for the guest OS virtual disks, and at least two more (logs and database volumes) for virtualized SQL Server sessions. Be sure to allocate the required amount of disk input/output operations per second (IOPS) values for the SharePoint databases, including a recommended 2.0 IOPS per gigabyte for the content databases.
- Fixed-size or pass-through (raw device mapping) virtual hard disks (VHDs) can be used for best guest disk performance. Pass-through disks give you the fastest performance. Fixed-size disks are also faster than dynamically expanding disks, which can suffer performance hits when they're resizing.
- Consider pass-through (raw device mapping) NICs for the best network performance or, at minimum, configure virtual NICs to use a single virtual switch for SharePoint servers.
- A 2:1 ratio for the number of virtual processors to physical cores is the maximum that should be used in a production environment. A virtual host that has too many allocated virtual CPUs can be overloaded and perform poorly. Therefore, you need to have a 2:1 ratio (or less) for the virtual processor-to-physical core ratio. For example, if your host is a 2-processor 12-core system (24 cores total), the maximum number of virtual processors that can be allocated and running at any one time is 48. If each VM is allocated eight virtual processors, the number of running VMs is capped at six on that host. Highest performance environments limit the ratio to 1:1.

In addition to these technical requirements for the virtualization host, keep in mind these recommendations when you set up your virtual environment:

- You should allocate a dedicated NIC for failover, such as in the scenario when you use virtual host failover software such as Hyper-V Live Migration.
- You should give as much memory and as many processor cores to your virtual hosts as your budget allows. Virtual hosts with multiple multicore processors and large amounts of RAM (256GB or more) are becoming commonplace because of the virtual host software's ability to take advantage of the additional resources, and because host failover solutions require additional resources. When it comes to sizing virtualization hosts, there's a sweet spot that balances the cost of the additional components against the need to have fewer hosts. Generally, the virtualization overhead required to run virtual servers is only 5%, so the cost of adding memory and processor cores is more than made up by the advantages of having those additional resources.
- You should run only the virtualization software and the virtualization role on the virtual hosts. (The two exceptions are antivirus and backup software.) Overloading a virtual host with other software or other server roles can significantly degrade guest performance. In addition, from a Windows Server licensing perspective, running any roles other than the virtualization role on a Windows Server requires one additional license. However, if the host runs only virtualization host software, the host OS isn't counted when determining the number of Windows licenses used as part of Microsoft's virtualization licensing program.
- For performance reasons, you shouldn't install all the SharePoint roles and the SQL Server role on the same VM. Even small environments should use at least two VMs—one for the SQL Server database role and the other for the SharePoint front-end and application roles.

Software Recommendations and Licensing Notes

It's highly recommended that you use the latest virtualization host software from your particular vendor. For example, the latest version of Hyper-V is included with Windows Server 2012. Hyper-V 3.0, included in Windows Server 2012, has significant performance improvements over the early versions Hyper-V, such as I/O improvements for fixed-size VHDs and support for up to eight processors on virtual guests. Hyper-V 2.0, included in Windows Server 2008 R2, introduced new features such as Core Parking, Live Migration, TCP Offload, the Jumbo Frames feature, and support for Second-Level Address Translation (SLAT)-enabled processors. If you're virtualizing SharePoint on Hyper-V, also consider deploying the virtual host on Server Core to minimize its security footprint, OS disk overhead (2GB versus 10GB), and memory use.

Microsoft provides cost-effective virtualization licensing options for Windows Server, which lets organizations save significantly on Windows Server licenses when virtualizing servers. The three types of virtualization server licensing are as follows:

- Windows Server Standard Edition, which allows a single physical OS environment (POSE) or up to two virtual OS environment (VOSE) licenses with each Standard Edition license. Note that a virtualization host that's dedicated to virtualization tasks doesn't consume a license, regardless if it's running Windows Server (such as in the case of Hyper-V). Note that Windows Server 2008 R2 only supports a single VOSE per Standard Edition license.
- Windows Server Enterprise Edition, which allows for up to four VOSEs to be run at any one time on the host. Note that only running VMs are counted. So, if a VM is shut down, it doesn't count against the four concurrent VOSEs permitted by the Enterprise Edition license. Note that Enterprise Edition is only supported by Windows Server 2008 R2, and there is no equivalent edition available with Windows Server 2012.
- Windows Server Datacenter Edition, which is a per-processor (not per core) license for the virtual host (for example, a dual quad-core server would require two licenses) that grants you the right to run an unlimited number of VMs on the host.

These licensing options apply not only to Hyper-V but also to any hypervisor that is part of the SVVP. For organizations with a significant investment in virtualization infrastructure, buying the appropriate number of Datacenter Edition licenses to cover all your virtual hosts is the most cost-effective.

Virtualization of SharePoint Roles

Virtualization requirements vary by server role. It is subsequently important when designing that you understand the individual requirements of each role.

Virtualization of the Web Role

The best candidate for virtualization is the SharePoint server that has the web role, which means it runs Microsoft Internet Information Services (IIS) and handles all web requests sent to SharePoint. Table 12.1 shows resource guidelines for virtualized SharePoint servers that have the web and other roles.

TABLE 12.1 SharePoint Server Role Resource Guidelines

Roles	Virtual Processors	Minimum RAM	Recommended RAM
Web role only	2	12GB	16GB+
Service application role only	2	12GB	16GB+
Search role only	4	12GB	16GB+
Combined web, service application, and search roles	8	12GB	20GB+
Database role	4	16GB	24GB+

As you can see in Table 12.1, a SharePoint server that holds only the web role (otherwise known as the web server) should be allocated at least two virtual processors and a minimum of 12GB RAM (preferably at least 16GB RAM), along with a single VHD for the OS. If a web server needs to handle more web traffic, you can simply allocate additional web servers that have the same specifications. The size of the host OS disk should be at least 12GB plus three times the total amount of memory allocated to the VM, but it's good practice to size this volume larger (usually around 50GB to 100GB) to allow the host OS to grow in size.

Virtualization of the Application Roles

The next likely candidates for virtualization include the SharePoint server with one or more service application roles (otherwise known as the application server). Application servers can include various service applications, such as Access Services, PerformancePoint Services, Machine Translation Services, or the Managed Metadata Service. For purposes of design, this excludes the search services, which are technically service applications, but for architectural purposes are usually classified as part of a different server role.

As Table 12.1 shows, the typical virtualized application server consists of a VM with two virtual processors and a minimum of 12GB RAM allocated to it. It needs a single VHD that's presized in the 50GB to 100GB range for the guest OS. Note that these numbers can vary, depending on how many service applications are installed on a single machine and how many people use the applications.

In smaller organizations, the application role and the web role are often combined onto a single SharePoint server. Combining the roles increases the memory and processor requirements of the guest session.

Virtualization of the Search Role

Third in line for virtualization is the SharePoint server or servers that hold the search role (otherwise known as the search server), which provide SharePoint's indexing and querying functionality. SharePoint 2013 doesn't have the same single-index restrictions that SharePoint 2007 did, which makes this role more scalable and allows for more distributed deployment models.

The typical virtualized search server consists of a VM with four virtual processors and 12GB RAM allocated to it (see Table 12.1), assuming that SharePoint 2013's out-of-the-box search functionality is being used. Like the application server numbers, the search server numbers can vary, depending on how many items are being indexed and how heavy the search requirements are.

The search server needs a single VHD that's presized in the 50GB to 100GB range for the guest OS and another VHD for the index and query corpus. The size of this VHD varies, depending on how much full text is indexed from various sources.

The crawler component is used by SharePoint to crawl documents for search purposes. Multiple crawl components can be created on different servers for redundancy.

In smaller organizations, the search role is often combined with the web role. Combining these roles can increase the memory and processor requirements of the guest session.

Virtualization of a Server with All Three Roles

Many organizations combine the web, application, and search roles on a single virtualized SharePoint server. This is often the case in smaller organizations that want to deploy SharePoint across two guest sessions to be highly available but have a smaller number of guests.

Although combining the three roles results in additional load on an individual server session, many of the same processor and memory guidelines that apply to a dedicated web role server apply to a combined server, as Table 12.1 shows.

The typical virtual web/query/search server role system consists of a VM with eight virtual processors and 12GB to 20GB RAM allocated to it, depending on how many users the system supports. It has a single VHD presized in the 50GB to 100GB range for the guest OS and another VHD for the index and query corpus.

SharePoint administrators familiar with earlier versions of SharePoint might be dismayed at the memory requirements of SharePoint 2013, but the fact is that SharePoint 2013 requires much more memory than earlier versions. RAM requirements can be lessened, however, by turning off nonessential service applications. In general, to reduce the overall requirements of the SharePoint servers, it is recommended to turn on only those service applications required by the business.

Virtualization of the Database Role

The SQL Server database role is the last but most challenging server role to virtualize. The server with the database role (otherwise known as the database server) needs the lion's share of RAM and processor allocation. A minimum of eight virtual processors and 16GB RAM should be allocated to the database server. For best performance, though, at least 24GB RAM should be allocated.

Like SharePoint VMs, SQL Server VMs require either fixed-sized or pass-through VHDs. The same disk considerations that apply to physical SQL Server machines apply to virtual SQL Server machines. So, be sure to allocate enough disk spindles for the database and logs volumes. In addition, be sure to follow standard best practices for SharePoint-SQL Server optimization, such as presizing the tempdb and moving it to fast disk volumes.

Keep in mind that these guidelines are simply guidelines. Actual performance is dictated by the type of disk, hardware architecture, and other factors. Some organizations calculate their hardware requirements and then just add RAM or reduce the number of databases on a single SQL Server session.

Microsoft supports both forms of SQL mirroring, SQL AlwaysOn Availability Groups (AOAGs), and clustering as high-availability (HA) options in a virtualized SQL Server environment. In addition, host failover options such as Hyper-V Live Migration are supported for SQL Server VMs. One fact to note, however, is that all SQL Server databases within a SharePoint farm need to be restored from the same point in time as the other databases.

This applies to virtualization snapshot technology or storage area network (SAN)-based snapshots of SQL Server databases.

Exploring Sample Virtualized SharePoint 2013 Architecture

There are many ways to deploy SharePoint 2013 in a virtualized environment. However, some designs are more widespread than others and reflect common needs across many organizations. For example, high availability is becoming a must for the critical document management and collaboration functionality in SharePoint. All the new high-availability options in SharePoint 2013 are available for virtual environments and can actually be easier to deploy because of the flexibility that virtualization provides.

Figure 12.1 illustrates a small virtualized SharePoint 2013 environment with all components running on a single virtual host. This type of deployment doesn't have any built-in high availability or disaster recovery (DR), but it's the simplest environment to set up, and it can still take advantage of virtualization benefits and scalability. In addition, architects can install multiple farms into the same environment, as shown in Figure 12.1. Table 12.2 shows sample server specifications for an environment of this size. These specifications assume 500 active users in the environment.

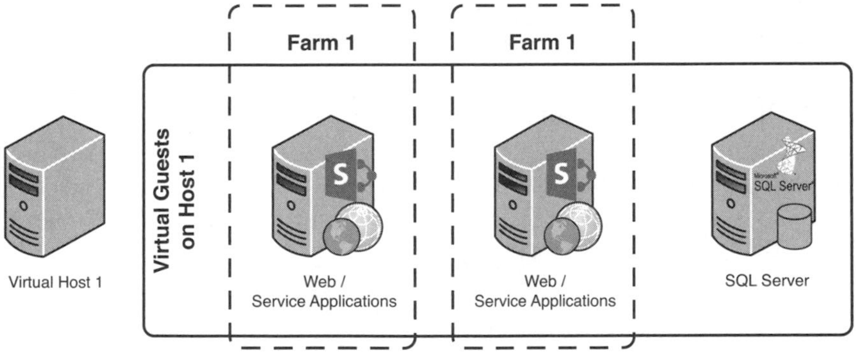

FIGURE 12.1 Conceptualizing a small virtualized SharePoint farm.

TABLE 12.2 Sample Small Virtual SharePoint Environment Deployment Specifications

Server	Memory	Processors	Disk
Virtual host	48GB+ RAM	2 8-core+ (16 cores)	C: drive—OS, Windows Server 2012 with Hyper-V, 50GB+ dedicated volume D: drive—Dedicated volume for OS VHDs E: drive—500GB+ dedicated volume for SQL Server database VHDs F: drive—100GB+ dedicated volume for SQL Server log VHDs

Server	Memory	Processors	Disk
SQL Server server	22GB RAM	8 virtual processors	C: drive—OS, fixed-size VHD (100GB) D: drive—Fixed-size VHD (100GB) for the SQL Server logs E: drive—Fixed-size VHD (500GB) for the SQL Server data
SharePoint web/query/app (Farm1)	12GB RAM	4 virtual processors	C: drive—OS and transport queue logs, fixed-size VHD (100GB+) E: drive—Fixed-size VHD (100GB+) for indexing and querying
SharePoint web/query/app (Farm2)	12GB RAM	4 virtual processors	C: drive—OS and transport queue logs, fixed-size VHD (100GB+) E: drive—Fixed-size VHD (100GB+) for indexing and querying

The next design, illustrated in Figure 12.2, provides a virtualization architecture that provides a high level of availability, disaster tolerance, and scalability for an environment with 2,000 active users. The entire SharePoint environment is deployed across two virtual hosts, which provides for high availability of the environment. SQL Server databases are replicated between two SQL servers using SQL 2012 AOAGs, providing for automatic failover in the event the virtual host or virtual guest fails. For more information about using SQL AOAGs for high availability, see Chapter 17, "Safeguarding Confidential Data in SharePoint 2013."

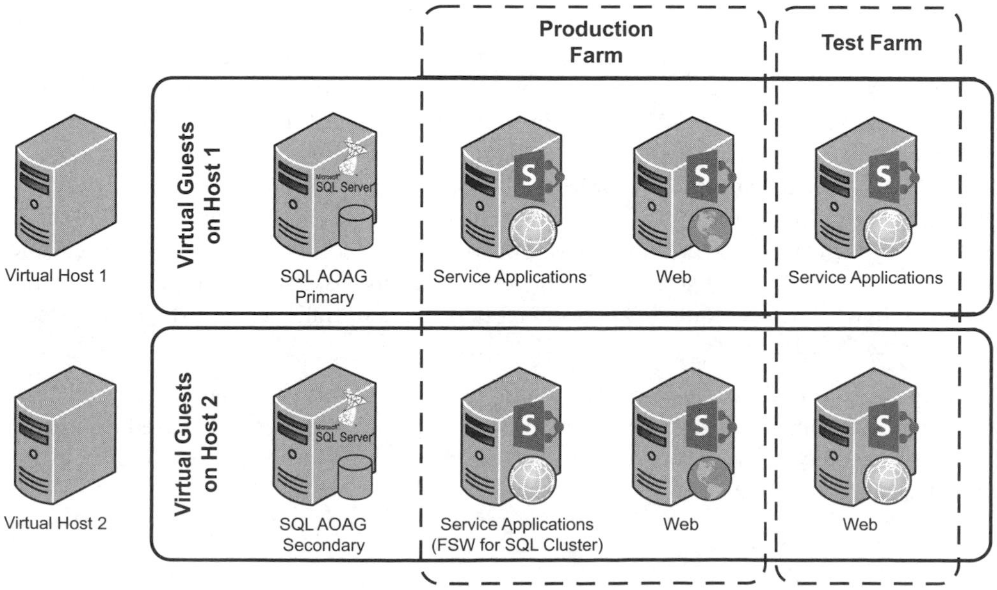

FIGURE 12.2 Conceptualizing a medium-sized SharePoint farm.

These high-availability and disaster-recovery options are possible without the need for shared storage, a SAN, or host availability solutions. Table 12.3 lists the sample virtual host and guest architecture guidelines for the solution in Figure 12.2.

TABLE 12.3 Sample Medium-Sized Virtual SharePoint Environment Deployment Specifications

Server	**Memory**	**Processor**	**Disk**
Virtual hosts	64GB+ RAM	2 8-core (16 cores)	C: drive—OS, Windows Server 2012 with Hyper-V, 50GB+ dedicated logical unit number (LUN) D: drive—Dedicated LUN for VHDs Raw volume—100GB+ dedicated LUN for SQL Server logs Raw volume—2TB+ dedicated LUN for SQL Server databases
SQL Server servers	24GB RAM	8 virtual processors	C: drive—OS, fixed-size VHD (50GB+) D: drive—Pass-through dedicated LUN (100GB+) for SQL Server logs E: drive—Pass-through dedicated LUN (2TB+) for SQL Server data
SharePoint web role	12GB RAM	4 virtual processors	C: drive—OS, fixed-size VHD (100GB+)
SharePoint service application	16GB RAM	4 virtual processors	C: drive—OS, fixed-size VHD (100GB+) D: drive—Fixed-size VHD (200GB+) for indexing and querying

Virtualization technologies allow for a high degree of scalability and aren't limited to small and mid-sized organizations. For example, the architecture that Figure 12.3 shows provides for tens of thousands of SharePoint users, full disaster tolerance, and high availability, all with the high performance expected from SharePoint. In this particular model, multiple SQL Server instances hold copies of the databases in SQL AOAGs. In addition, workload is streamlined and spread out using server groups to divide tasks for different SharePoint server roles, and the web tier is broken into two components: one for users and another for crawl and administration. In this example, host-based failover solutions such as Hyper-V Live Migration could also conceivably provide for failover of individual guest sessions between failed hosts.

These three examples illustrate some of the potential design options available for a virtual SharePoint environment. Every environment is unique, and specifics vary based on business and technology needs. However, you can use these architecture examples as a starting point for developing a high-performance virtualized SharePoint 2013 environment.

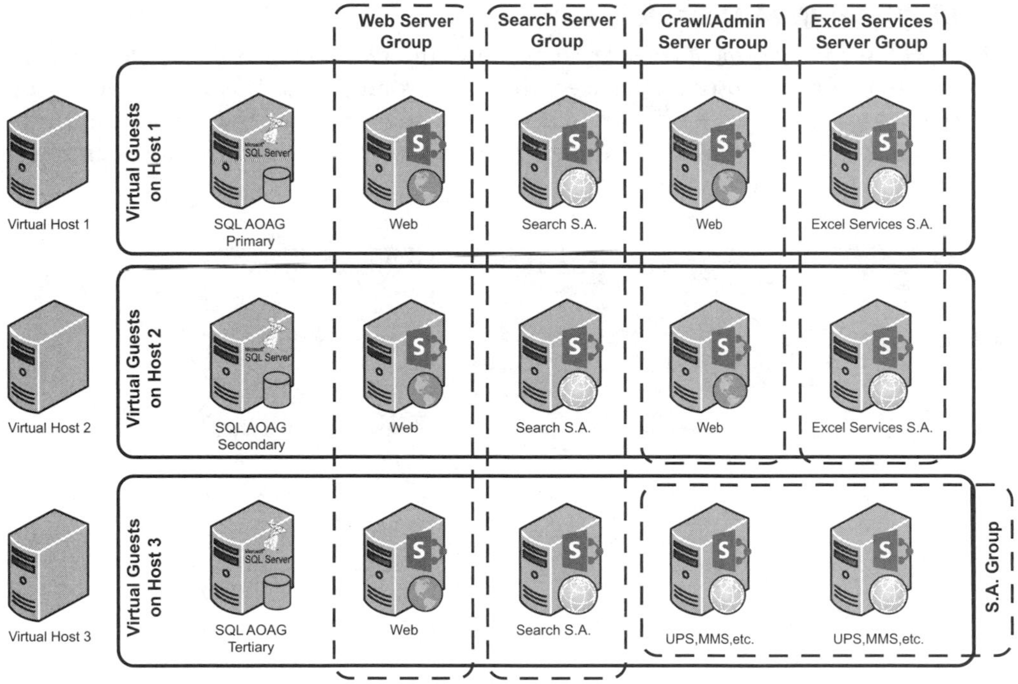

FIGURE 12.3 Conceptualizing a large virtualized SharePoint 2013 environment.

Virtual Machine Management with System Center Virtual Machine Manager

If managing multiple virtual host machines, centralized management software is also highly recommended. Microsoft has released its own product for VM management and is positioning it as an enterprise utility that allows for centralized control over a broader virtualization environment. This tool, part of the System Center line of products, is known as System Center Virtual Machine Manager (VMM). The latest version of VMM, the 2012 SP1 edition, has the following tools and capabilities:

- **P2V and V2V:** VMM allows for physical-to-virtual (P2V) or virtual-to-virtual (V2V) migration capabilities, allowing existing physical systems or VMware guests to be migrated to an equivalent Hyper-V guest session.
- **Hyper-V, VMware, and Citrix XenServer management support:** VMM provides for the ability to manage Microsoft Hyper-V, VMware, and XenServer hosts and guests through the interface.
- **Creation of template servers:** VMM supports the creation of server templates, which can be used to automate the creation of virtual guests, including SharePoint role servers, a concept explored in subsequent sections of this chapter.

Exploring the VMM Console

VMM 2012 SP1's management console, shown in Figure 12.4, provides a wide degree of functionality that can be used to manage virtual SharePoint guests. This console allows a distributed virtualized SharePoint farm to be more tightly managed, and gives administrators a tool they can use to easily move guest sessions between one or more hosts (and to perform other virtualization tasks).

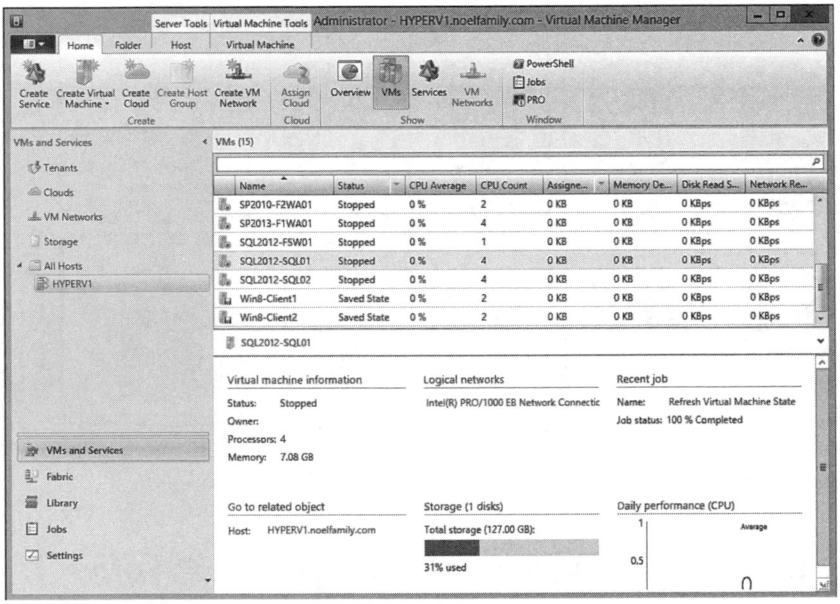

FIGURE 12.4 Using the VMM console.

Provisioning Farm Members from Virtual Server Templates

VMM allows SharePoint administrators to define a library of templates and VMs that can be used to provision new SharePoint sessions. For example, a Windows Server 2012 server template could be created with the right amount of memory and virtual processors, plus a pair of virtual hard drives for the OS and index files. With SharePoint 2013 binaries installed on that system, it can then be turned into a template that can be used to provision new SharePoint farm members or even entirely new farms.

VMM Template Options, shown in Figure 12.5, allow administrators to modify the type of disks that are installed, set different memory options, and also specific OS options such as those that allow the server to be automatically added to a domain, be validated with a valid server key, and also to have a script run after first login. For example, a custom PowerShell script could be run automatically after login that joins the SharePoint template server to an existing farm or creates a new farm from scratch.

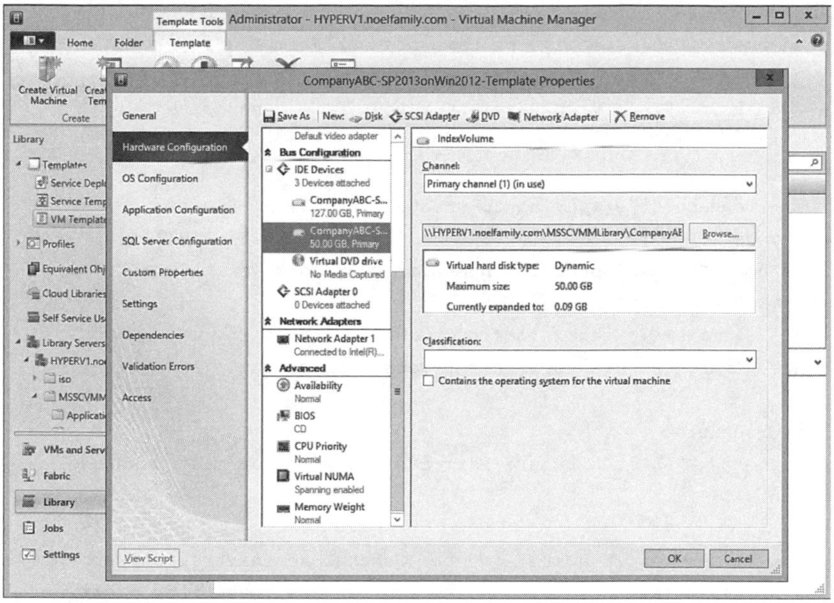

FIGURE 12.5 Creating a VM template.

Using this concept, an organization could easily set up a scenario where developers are given the rights, through the self-service portal, to provision a new SharePoint guest session. After provisioning the server, they could then log in to that session and have it automatically run a PowerShell script that would create a new farm. With the proper hardware, developers could provision an entirely new SharePoint environment within 10 to 15 minutes and have that farm completely independent from other farms.

For this scenario to work, the SQL server used must be on a different system, because SQL doesn't lend well to name changes after it has been installed. In this scenario, a single SQL instance can hold the databases from multiple farms. Commonly, a single SQL guest session would be used for all development farms created in this manner.

A farm provisioning script (ProvisionFarm.ps1) is provided here as an example of the type of script that can be configured to run automatically upon login to the virtual session provisioned. For more complex scripts, see Chapter 4, "Advanced SharePoint 2013 Installation and Scalability," which contains new service application provisioning scripts which can be automated. You can download these scripts from http://tinyurl.com/SPFarm-Config:

```
PROVISIONFARM.PS1
$configType = read-host "Do you wish to create a new farm? (Y/N)"
if ($ConfigType -eq "N") {
    $DatabaseServer = read-host "Preparing to join existing farm. Please specify the
```

```
name of your SQL Server";
    $ConfigDB = read-host "Next, specify the name of your Farm Configuration
Database";
    $Passphrase = read-host "Finally, please enter your Farm passphrase"
-assecurestring
} else {
    $DatabaseServer = read-host "Preparing to create a new Farm. Please
specify the name of your SQL Server (ex SERVER or SERVER\INSTANCE[,PORT])";
    $FarmName = read-host "Please specify a name for your Farm (ex. SP2013Dev)";
    $ConfigDB = $FarmName+"_ConfigDB";
    $AdminContentDB = $FarmName+"_CentralAdminContent";
    Write-Host "Please enter the credentials for your Farm Account (ex. COMPANYABC\
SP_Farm)";
    $FarmAcct = Get-Credential;
    $Passphrase = read-host "Enter a secure Farm passphrase (must meet password
complexity requirements)" -
assecurestring;
    $Port = read-host "Enter a port number for the Central Administration Web App";
    $Authentication = read-host "Finally, specify your authentication provider
(NTLM/Kerberos)";
}
if ($ConfigType -eq "N") {
    if((Get-PSSnapin | Where {$_.Name -eq "Microsoft.SharePoint.PowerShell"}) -eq
$null) {
              Add-PSSnapin Microsoft.SharePoint.PowerShell;
    }
    Connect-SPConfigurationDatabase -DatabaseName $ConfigDB -DatabaseServer
$DatabaseServer -Passphrase $Passphrase
} else {
    if((Get-PSSnapin | Where {$_.Name -eq "Microsoft.SharePoint.PowerShell"}) -eq
$null) {
              Add-PSSnapin Microsoft.SharePoint.PowerShell;
    }
    Write-Host "Your SharePoint Farm is being configured..."
    New-SPConfigurationDatabase -DatabaseName $ConfigDB -DatabaseServer
$DatabaseServer -AdministrationContentDatabaseName `
$AdminContentDB -Passphrase $Passphrase -FarmCredentials $FarmAcct
}
Initialize-SPResourceSecurity
Install-SPService
Install-SPFeature -AllExistingFeatures
New-SPCentralAdministration -Port $Port -WindowsAuthProvider $Authentication
Install-SPHelpCollection -All
Install-SPApplicationContent
Write-Host "Your SharePoint 2013 Farm has been created!"
if ($ConfigType -eq "Y") {
```

```
    $WebAppCreation = read-host "Would you like to provision a Web Application using
the default Team Site Template? (Y/N)";
    if ($WebAppCreation -eq "Y") {
        $HostHeaderQ = read-host "Would you like to specify a host header? (Y/N)";
        if ($HostHeaderQ -eq "Y") {
            $HostHeader = read-host "Please specify a host header for your Web
Application (ex. intranet.contoso.com)";
            $URL = "http://"+$HostHeader;
            Write-Host "Creating your Web Application...";
                     $ap = New-SPAuthenticationProvider
            New-SPWebApplication -Name "SharePoint 2013 Team Site" -Port 80
-HostHeader $FQDN -Url $URL -ApplicationPool
"Content_AppPool" -ApplicationPoolAccount (Get-SPManagedAccount $FarmAcct.UserName)
-DatabaseServer $DatabaseServer -
DatabaseName $FarmName + "_TeamSite_ContentDB_01" -AuthenticationProvider $ap;
            New-SPSite $URL -OwnerAlias $FarmAcct.UserName -Language 1033 -Template
"STS#0" -Name "Team Site";
            Write-Host "Configuration completed.";
        }
        else {
        Write-Host "Creating a Web Application using the default Team Site
Template..."
        }
    }
    else {
        Write-Host "Configuration completed.";
    }
}
$serviceAppsConfig = read-host "Do you wish to configure Service Applications?
(Y/N)"
if($serviceAppsConfig -eq "Y") {
       PowerShell -File "Configure-ServiceApps.ps1" $appPoolName $managedAccountName
$FarmName
}
else {
       Write-Host "Press any key to continue..."
       $x = $host.UI.RawUI.ReadKey("NoEcho,IncludeKeyDown")
}
```

The high-level steps involved in running this scenario are as follows:

1. Create a new Windows Server 2012 guest session in VMM with at least 12GB RAM and four virtual CPUs allocated to it. (Remember that SharePoint 2013 has large resource requirements.) Give the session two virtual hard drives: one for the OS and another for the index.

2. Install the SharePoint 2013 binaries on the guest session but don't run the Config Wizard. Copy the Provisioning Farm PowerShell script into a directory on the server, such as C:\Scripts. See step 3 for the syntax of the script name.

3. Using VMM, turn the guest session into a server template. Specify within the server template to automatically add the machine into a domain and to run `powershell.exe -noexit C:\scripts\ProvisionFarm.ps1`.

4. Use the self-service portal to provision a new server based off the template. After the session has been created and added to the domain, log in to the system and walk through the farm provisioning script. Because the SharePoint 2013 binaries are already installed, the script can provision a new farm or add the server into an existing farm.

Within approximately 15 minutes, a new SharePoint farm can be provisioned with running web applications and services. Using this approach, modifications can also be made to the PowerShell script to expand the functionality of the script, such as by adding the ability to provision service applications. In addition, it can be made to run completely without user input, providing for a 100% automated farm provisioning solution.

This same process can be used with other virtualization management software, such as the third-party VMware VirtualCenter. The concepts still apply: Just install the SharePoint 2013 binaries, and then create a server template. Using a provisioning script, you can then automatically create a new virtual farm or add additional members to it.

Summary

Server virtualization can provide significant advantages and can let SharePoint architects design highly available and disaster-tolerant environments more easily than could be done solely on physical hardware. In addition, virtualized environments have consolidation, optimization, and cost-saving benefits that make them ideal for many organizations. With proper thought into host and guest virtualization architecture, you can deploy a fault-tolerant and high-performance SharePoint environment that lets you fully capture the benefits of virtualization for your organization.

Use of a virtualization management tool such as System Center VMM can be particularly advantageous because it allows for scenarios such as the one described in this chapter, where a virtualized SharePoint 2013 farm can be automatically provisioned from templates in a matter of minutes, thus enabling developers and farm architects to provision quality-controlled SharePoint farms on an as-needed basis.

Best Practices

The following are best practices from this chapter:

- Do not over-allocate memory or processor resources; maintain a maximum of a 2:1 ratio between the number of allocated virtual CPUs on guests and the number of cores on the host.

- Use an approved hypervisor for virtualization, such as Microsoft's Hyper-V on Windows Server 2012 or a third-party hypervisor that is part of the SVVP such as VMware ESX or Citrix XenServer.
- Allocate up to 1GB of the memory of the virtual host to running the virtualization host software.
- Highly consider pass-through (raw device mapping) NICs and pass-through disks rather than virtual NICs or virtual hard drives; the best performance can be achieved with them. This is particularly true for virtual SQL database servers.
- If using Microsoft's Hyper-V hypervisor, use the latest version included with Windows Server 2012; it has significant performance improvements over the initial versions of Hyper-V.
- Do not install anything other than virtualization software on the host sessions. Exceptions to this rule may include backup or antivirus software, although you should avoid these if possible.
- Consider the use of Server Core for the host OS session if using Microsoft's Hyper-V hypervisor for virtualization. This cuts down on the overall system requirements and provides a more streamlined host.
- Consider the use of a tool such as Microsoft's System Center VMM for virtualization guest and host management and for scenarios such as those where farm members need to be provisioned quickly and reliably.

CHAPTER 13

Deploying SharePoint for Extranets and Alternative Authentication Scenarios

IN THIS CHAPTER

- Outlining Common Extranet Scenarios and Topologies
- Configuring Google as an Identity Provider in Azure Access Control Services
- Enabling Facebook Authentication to Azure Control Services

A useful but difficult-to-implement usage of a SharePoint environment is the extranet. An *extranet* is an extension of the intranet to users who exist outside the direct environment of the provider, allowing access to required services without exposing an entire intranet to the outside world.

The two key properties of an extranet are accessibility over the Internet and mandatory authentication. From a SharePoint perspective, an extranet is easy to implement because it is just another web application on a SharePoint farm that has been created so that it is accessible via the Internet after a user has authenticated.

The more challenging aspect of an extranet deployment is in the authentication. A user account must exist somewhere to be utilized by SharePoint; traditionally, this would be an Active Directory (AD). Maintaining AD accounts requires a large amount of work to create and support user accounts; for instance, if a user forgets his password, manual intervention is required. This scenario happens much more often for extranet users than for intranet users, because accounts are less likely to be used on a regular basis, and therefore users are more likely to forget their login details between login attempts.

This particular problem was resolved in SharePoint 2007 by utilizing forms-based authentication. This method involved modifying the SharePoint web applications to leverage a *membership provider*; this is a Dot Net terminology that reflects a source of user authentication, such as a Structured Query Language (SQL) database or AD.

In most scenarios, an SQL database membership provider was used to allow user login based on details contained within the database. This method was quite popular because it allowed vendor solutions to assist with the user management, incorporating functions such as reset lost password and create new account. With SharePoint 2010, however, the addition of a claims-based authentication and a Security Token Service meant that understanding and deploying a forms-based authentication approach was more difficult and that troubleshooting was much more complex.

Fortunately, the addition of the claims-based authentication has larger implications in that it enables us to use authentication sources outside our established identity sources, which totally eliminates the headaches of implementing and troubleshooting membership-based forms authentication and also has the benefit of completely externalizing sources of user authentication so that there is never any need to reset passwords or assist users with their authentication. Furthermore, we can use sources of authentication that the users most likely already have, such as a Facebook account, a Windows Live account, or a Google account.

SharePoint 2013 builds upon the platform provided by SharePoint 2010 by now having claims-based authentication as the default and supported option on web applications.

This chapter explains and demonstrates how to leverage three different external identity sources, coupled with the Windows Azure Access Control Services (ACS), to create a framework for extranet authentication. This cloud-based approach gives tremendous flexibility while reducing the complexity of extranet authentication significantly. The end goal of this is, of course, to use LiveID, Google, or Facebook accounts to log in to the SharePoint extranet site.

Outlining Common Extranet Scenarios and Topologies

To allow SharePoint 2013 to be used for alternative authentication scenarios and to perform the steps outlined in this chapter, you need the following:

- **A SharePoint 2013 web application:** In this case, you want extranet.contoso.com.
- **An Azure subscription:** You can obtain this from www.windowsazure.com.
- **A Windows Live, Google, or Facebook account:** You can obtain these from www.live.com, www.google.com, and www.facebook.com, respectively.

When obtained, complete the steps outlined in this chapter.

Creating an Access Control Services Namespace

To leverage Azure ACS, you must first create a namespace. A *namespace* is just a partition within Azure that acts as a container for settings. In this case, the namespace is used to partition authentication information for just this farm.

Visit www.windowsazure.com and sign in. If you do not have an account, you can sign up for a free trial or create a new account.

The Azure Management Portal, shown in Figure 13.1, is used to create the custom authentication provider.

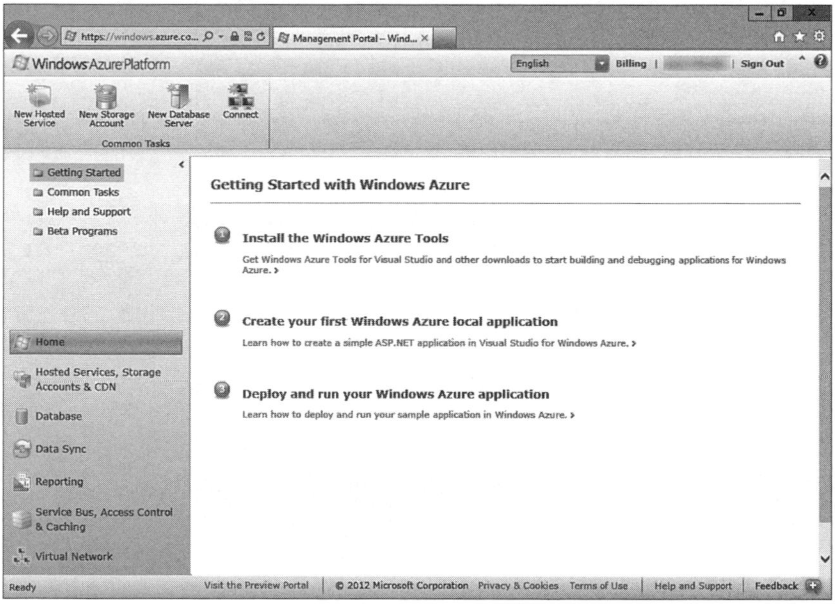

FIGURE 13.1 Viewing the Azure Management Portal.

For the duration of this exercise, the focus is on ACS, which you can find under Service Bus, Access Control & Caching. You can access this area by clicking Service Bus, Access Control & Caching and then selecting Access Control from the Services tree that appears, as shown in Figure 13.2.

You now need to create a new namespace. So, click New to bring up a new form that you can complete.

When a namespace is created, it is across the entirety of Azure and therefore must be unique. The name of the namespace has no bearing on the implementation, so choose a name that helps identify your environment while still being unique. For demonstration purposes, the namespace created here is ContosoExtranet. A geographic region must also be selected, and for this it makes sense to pick the closest geographic region to the location of your SharePoint environment, as shown in Figure 13.3.

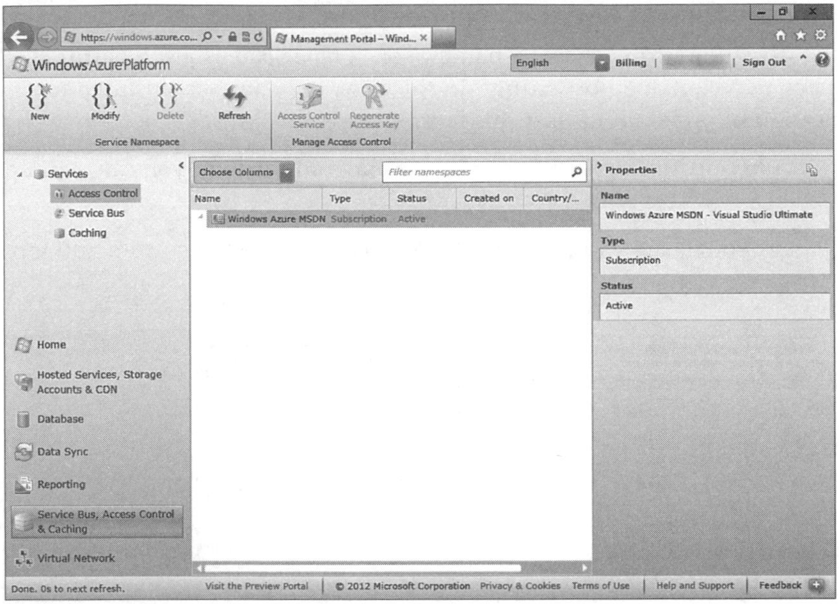

FIGURE 13.2 Configuring ACS in the Azure Management Portal.

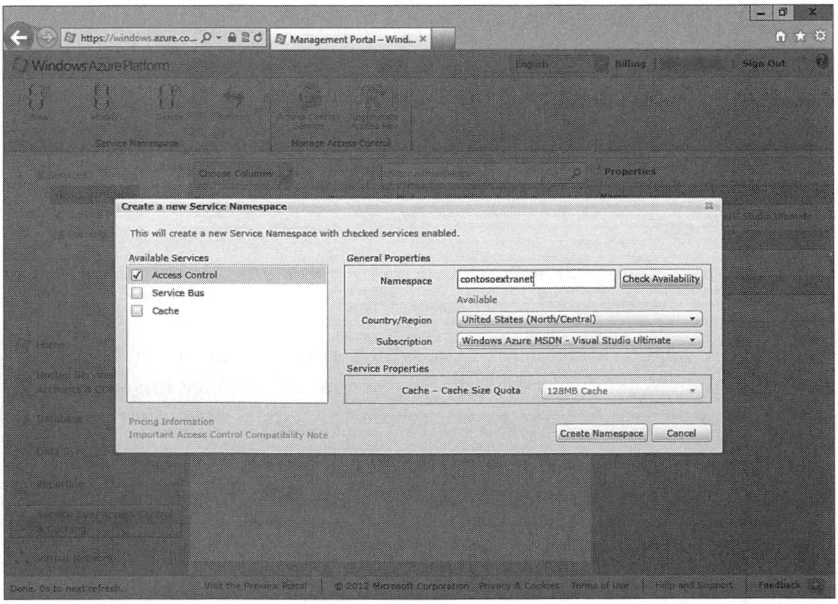

FIGURE 13.3 Creating a new service namespace.

After you click Create Namespace, it might be several minutes before the namespace is available for use, as indicated in the Azure Management Portal by the namespace showing a status of Activating.

When the namespace is created, this status changes to Active, and at that point the namespace is ready for use, as shown in Figure 13.4.

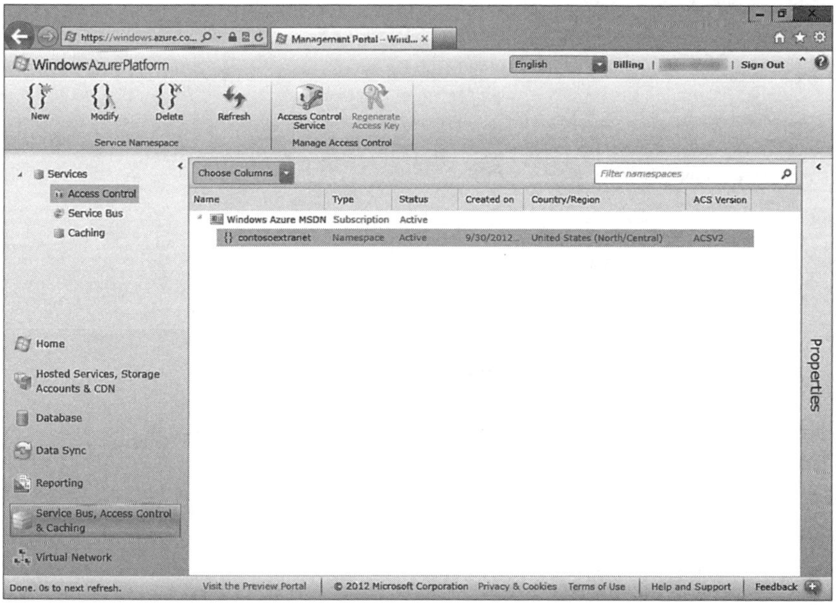

FIGURE 13.4 Viewing the newly created namespace.

You can access the namespace from the Manage Access Control area on the Windows Azure Management Portal's ribbon. To access this area, click Access Control Service while the new Namespace is selected. Clicking this redirects the browser to a new address (in this case, https://contosoextranet.accesscontrol.windows.net/v2/mgmt/web), as shown in Figure 13.5.

As the Getting Started page indicates, four activities need to take place to set up ACS for this new namespace:

- Configuring an identity provider or multiple identity providers
- Configuring a relying party application
- Configuring the appropriate rules for the relying party to function
- Configuring integration with the namespace

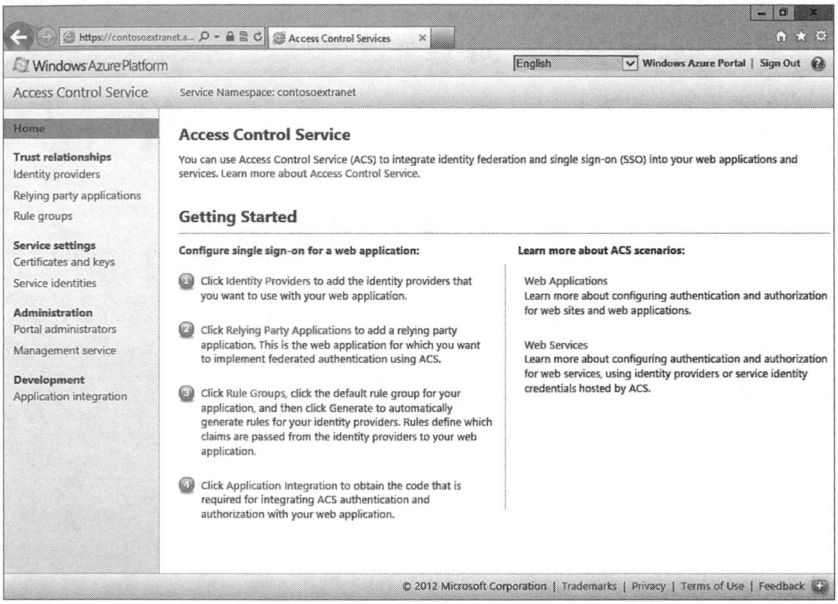

FIGURE 13.5 Accessing the ACS page within the Azure Management Platform.

While these entities might be difficult to understand at first glance, they are quite easy to configure, and when these are configured do not generally need to be modified unless significant changes occur to your farm.

Prior to these four options being configured, you need to complete some work on your SharePoint farm. On your SharePoint farm, you need to create a new certificate. This is used to establish a trust between the SharePoint farm and the Azure ACS namespace.

Log in to your SharePoint farm's server to begin.

Creating and Exporting Certificates

Before you can create a trust between the new Azure ACS namespace and your SharePoint farm, a self-signed (or Enterprise Certificate Authority created) certificate must be generated and uploaded to Azure. This certificate is also uploaded into the SharePoint certificate authority.

To create this certificate, open a command prompt as an administrator and issue the following commands, as shown in Figure 13.6:

1. `CD "C:\Program Files\Microsoft Office Servers\15.0\Tools"`
2. `makecert.exe -r -pe -n "CN=extranet.contoso.com" -sky exchange -ss my`

NOTE

Do not use `"CN=extranet.contoso.com"`. For ease of identification, you should use anything that will easily identify your certificate, such as the URL of your extranet or a simple short designator.

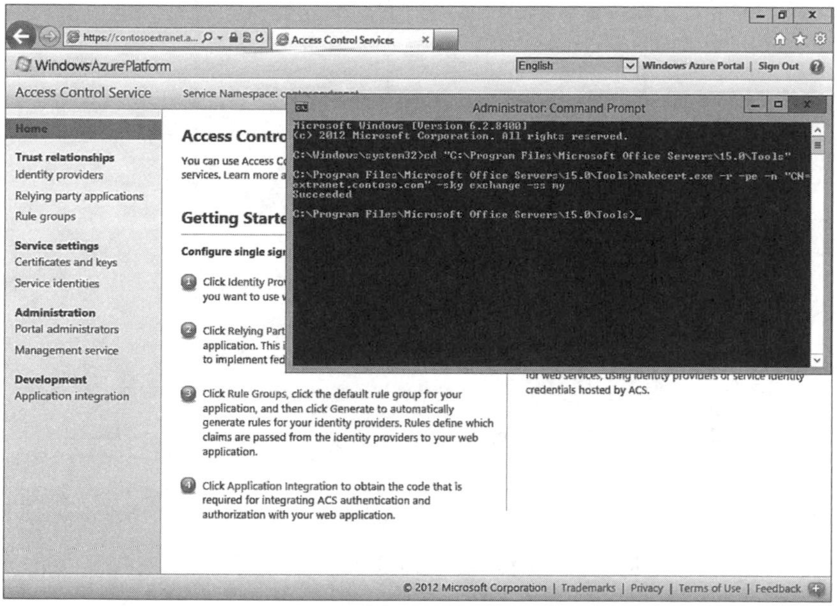

FIGURE 13.6 Creating a certificate for the Azure trust.

The command prompt can now be closed. The command that was issued to it created a new certificate with the name of Contoso.extranet.com that was stored in the certificate store of the user that executed it. To be of use in this exercise, this certificate now needs to be exported in two formats.

To export the certificate, follow these steps:

1. Type **MMC**.
2. Select File, Add/Remove Snapins.
3. Select Certificates from Available Snapins and click Add.
4. Select My User Account.
5. Click Finish.
6. Click OK. The Microsoft Management Console (MMC) should then display the Certificates snap-in, as shown in Figure 13.7.

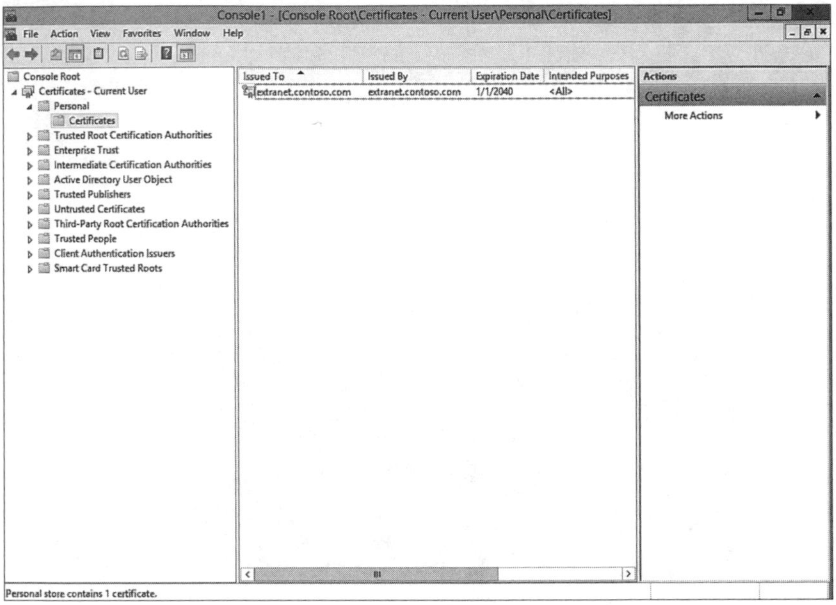

FIGURE 13.7 Opening the Certificates MMC snap-in.

7. Expand Certificates—Current User, Personal and click Certificates.

   The certificate that was previously generated should now be visible.

8. Right-click the certificate and select All Tasks, Export.
9. Click Next to skip the welcome message on the Certificate Export Wizard.
10. Select Yes, Export the Private Key and then click Next.
11. Leave all the default values on this screen and click Next again.
12. Enter a password. This can be any password. However, do not lose this password; otherwise, the exported certificate will not be of any use. Click Next.
13. Click Browse and create a new directory on C:\ called Certificates.
14. Save the certificate on the local file system. Save this in C:\Certificates (for example, C:\Certificates\extranet.contoso.com.pfx).
15. Click Next.
16. Click Finish.
17. Click OK.

The Azure ACS namespace requires a .pfx format for certificate import, but for import into the SharePoint certificate authority, we use a .cer with no private key. To generate a .cer format certificate, follow these steps:

1. Right-click the certificate and select All Tasks, Export.
2. Click Next to skip the welcome message on the Certificate Export Wizard.
3. Select No, Do Not Export the Private Key and then click Next.
4. Leave all the default values on this screen and click Next again.
5. Click Browse and select the C:\Certificates directory.
6. Save the certificate on the local file system. Save this in C:\Certificates (for example, C:\Certificates\extranet.contoso.com.cer).
7. Click Next.
8. Click Finish.
9. Click OK.

If you now browse to C:\Certificates, there should be two files present. The file named Extranet.Contoso.com.pfx is now uploaded to Azure ACS.

Configuring Google as an Identity Provider in Azure Access Control Services

An identity provider is the source of identity that is being provided to Azure ACS. In this chapter, three sources are used: LiveID, Google, and Facebook. An identity provider for each of these needs to be configured.

Return to the web browser and the Azure Management Portal and the namespace's ACS page for this step. Click Identity Provider to bring up a screen similar to the one shown in Figure 13.8.

An identity provider for Windows LiveID has already been created, but providers for Google and Facebook integration do not yet exist:

1. Click Add to create an identity provider entry for Google accounts.
2. Select Google, as shown in Figure 13.9.
3. Click Next.
4. Click Save.

Because ACS already has the built-in functionality to leverage Google accounts, you need to do very little to add the identity provider.

Now that the identity providers have been created, you need to configure the relying party applications.

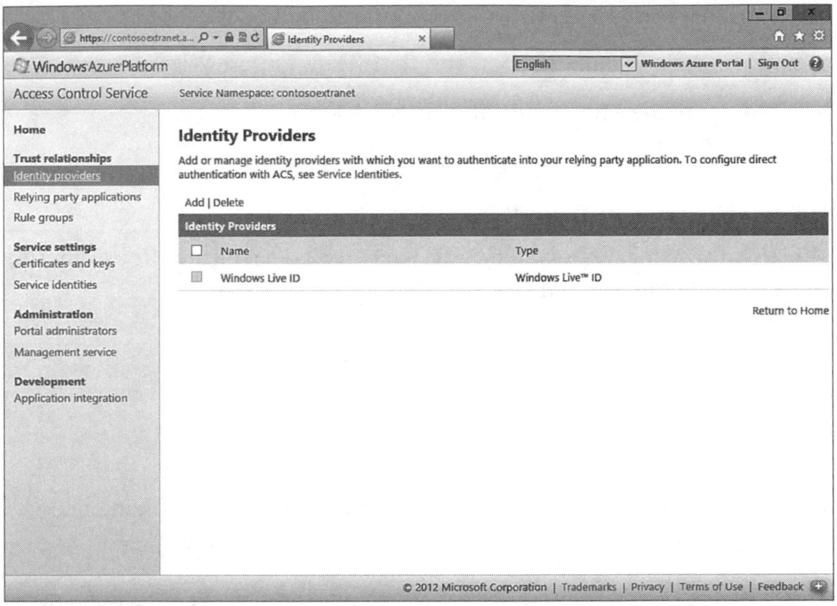

FIGURE 13.8 Viewing the identity providers in the Azure Management Platform.

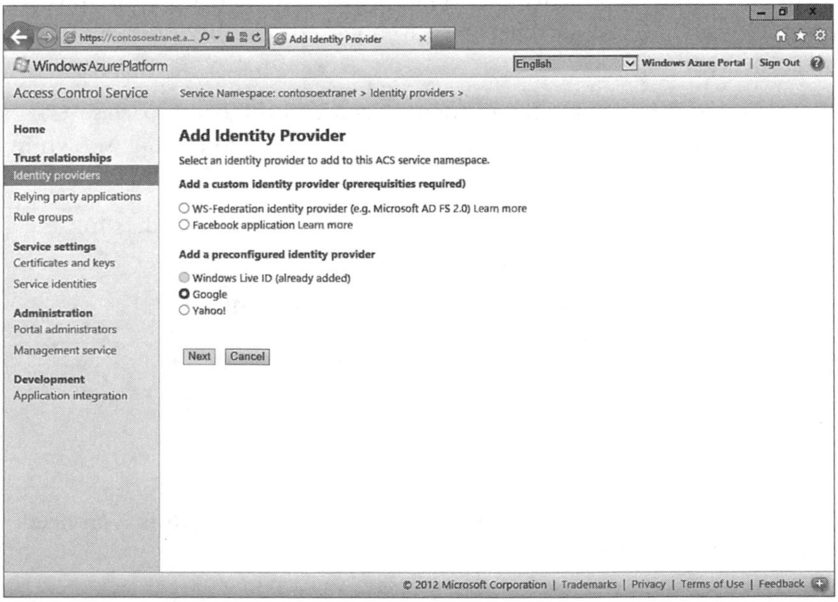

FIGURE 13.9 Adding Google as an identity provider.

Configuring the Relying Party Applications

Relying parties are services that consume the authentication from identity providers to allow federated sign in. In this case, the relying party is the Contoso extranet site, which needs to be created.

Click Relying Party Applications to begin, as shown in Figure 13.10.

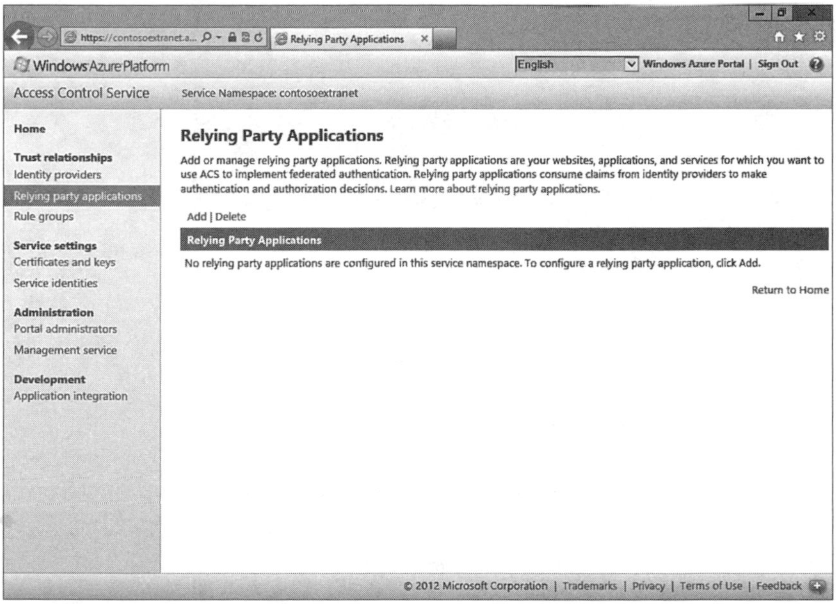

FIGURE 13.10 Configuring relying party applications.

Because no relying party has been created, click Add to begin the process of creating a relying party application for the Contoso extranet, and then complete the following steps:

1. Enter a name. For simplicity, it is easiest to use the URL for the extranet (in this case, extranet.contoso.com).
2. Enter the full URL for the realm (in this case, http://extranet.contoso.com).
3. Enter the full URL for the return URL, suffixed with /_trust/ (in this case, http://extranet.contoso.com/_trust/), as shown in Figure 13.11.
4. Ensure that the token format is set to Security Assertion Markup Language (SAML) 1.1.
5. Ensure that the token lifetime is set to a value greater than 600, because 600 is the same value that will be set in SharePoint and can cause unpredictable behavior. In this case, the value of 1,800 has been used to give a 30-minute timeout.
6. Ensure that both Google and LiveID options are checked for the identity providers to be used with this relying party, as shown in Figure 13.12.

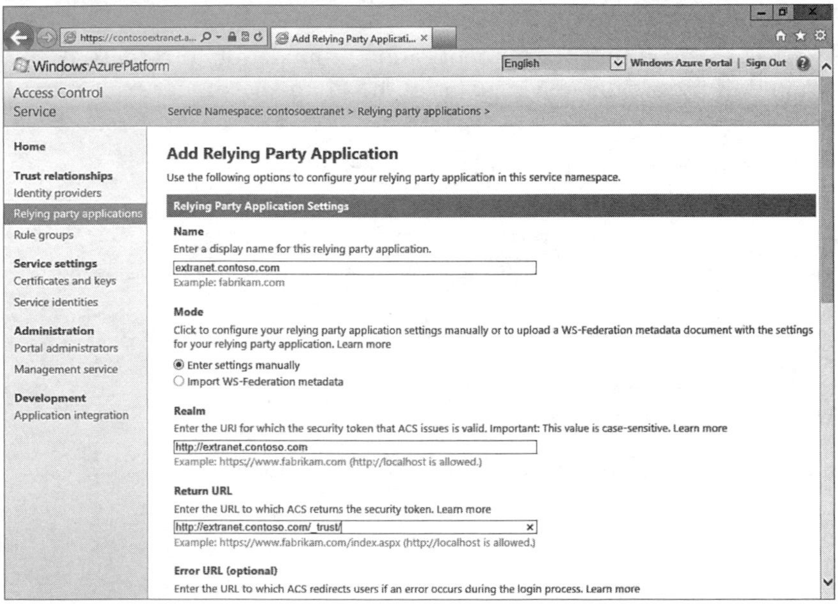

FIGURE 13.11 Adding a relying party application.

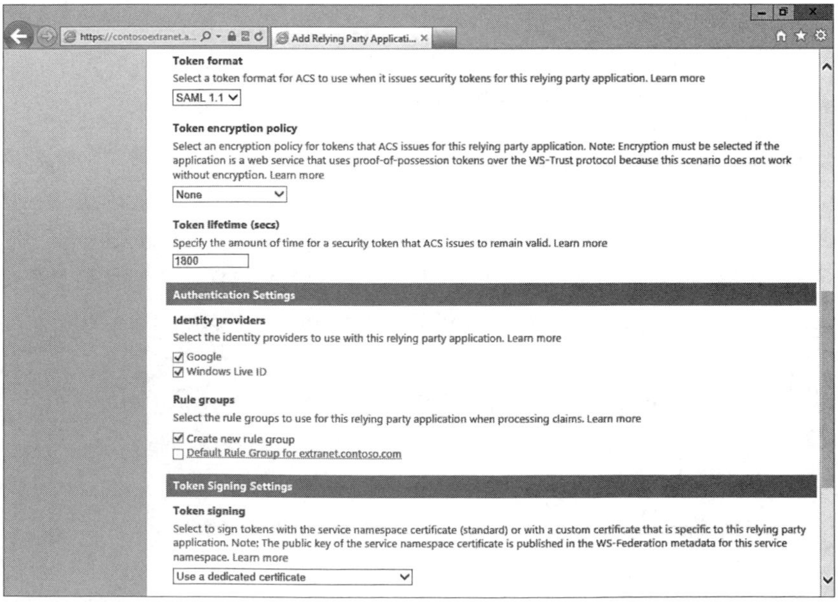

FIGURE 13.12 Configuring authentication settings for Google auth integration.

7. Ensure that Create New Rule Group is ticked.
8. Select Use a Dedicated Certificate from the Token Signing area.
9. Click Browse to select a certificate to upload. Ensure that the .pfx certificate is uploaded (in this case, C:\Certificates\extranet.contoso.com.pfx).
10. Enter the password that was associated with this certificate from the earlier steps, as shown in Figure 13.13.

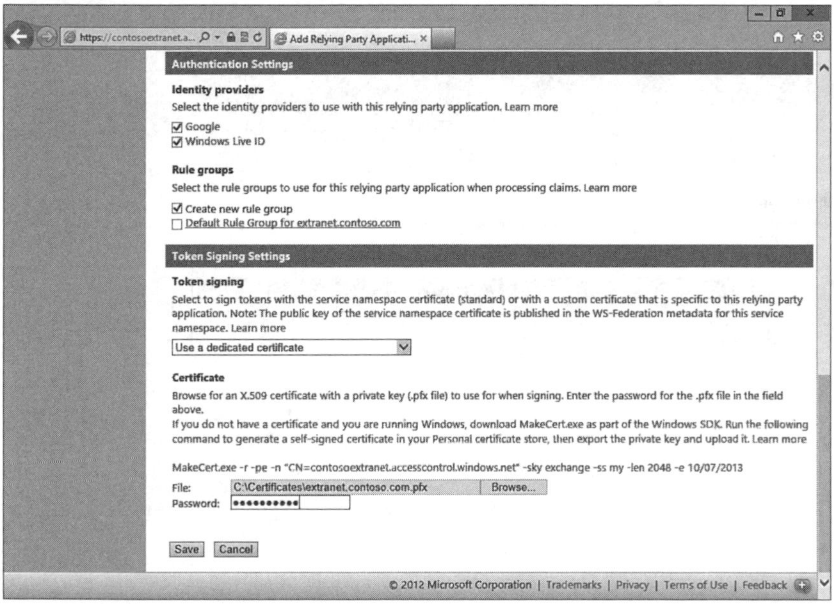

FIGURE 13.13 Entering the PFX password when creating an authentication provider.

11. Click Save to complete the creation of the relying party application.

Configuring Rule Groups for the Relying Party Application

Before the identity providers will work with the relying party applications, you need to create a set of rules to govern how the identity providers interact with the relying party applications.

These rules allow the association of inbound and outbound claims to be mapped against specific properties, which in turn facilitates the ability to log in to the sites. Examples of these claims include values such as email address, first name, last name, or a unique identifier.

SharePoint requires very few claims that are needed to establish authentication, but these are often not enough to be useful within the SharePoint site. It is much easier to share with John Smith than it is with a long unique identifier string such as User 57439772-3dfd-4fc8-aa5e-a47f3dfda13b.

To begin the creation of these rules that will translate the identifier strings to names, click the Rule Groups area of Azure ACS.

A default rule should be visible on this page, and as in the previous step, the Create New Rule Group option should be checked.

Click the Default Rule Group link, as shown in Figure 13.14, and then complete the following steps:

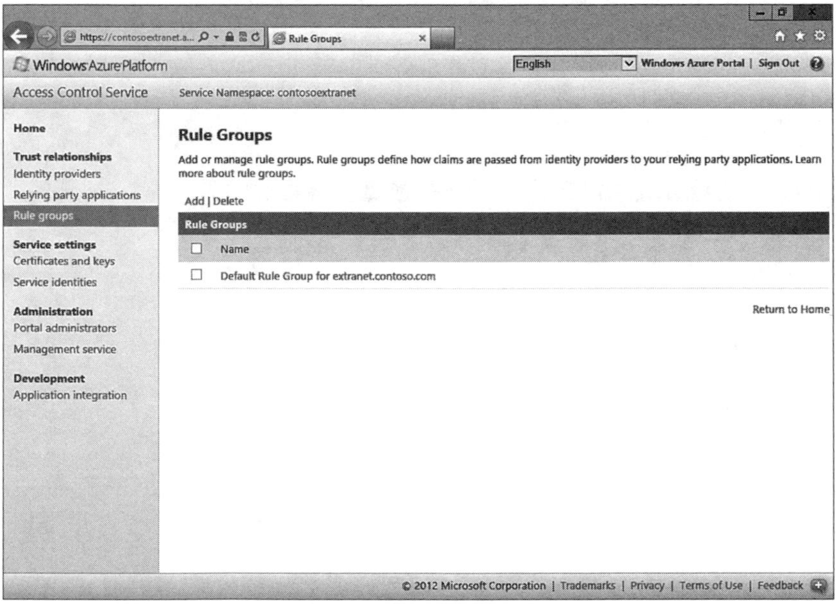

FIGURE 13.14 Creating a rule group.

1. Click Generate on the page displayed in Figure 13.15. This generates a setup of default rules that Azure ACS is already aware of for the in-built identity providers that are utilized here.
2. Ensure that both Windows LiveID and Google are ticked.
3. Click Generate.

A set of basic rules has been generated by these steps. By default, though, these rules are insufficient to allow SharePoint access, because the minimum requirement for an account to sign in to SharePoint is an email address.

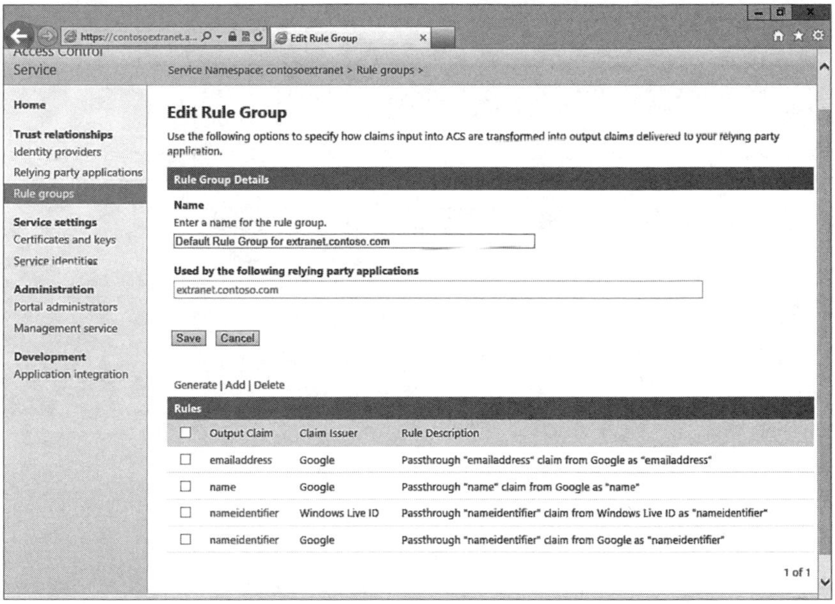

FIGURE 13.15 Editing the rule group being created.

Note that this is conspicuously absent for the LiveID identity provider (listed as a claim issuer on this page). This is due to LiveID only providing a `NameIdentifier` attribute as a consumable property or claim.

Because the `EmailAddress` property must be present, but only the `NameIdentifier` property is available, you must create an additional rule mapping the incoming attribute of `NameIdentifier` to the outgoing attribute of `EmailAddress`.

To create this additional rule, follow these steps:

1. Click Add.
2. Ensure that the identity provider is set to Windows LiveID.
3. Select http://schemas.xmlsoap.org/ws/2005/05/identity/claims/nameidentifier as the input claim type. This should be the only option that is available for selection, as shown in Figure 13.16.
4. Select http://schemas.xmlsoap.org/ws/2005/05/identity/claims/emailaddress as the outgoing claim type, as shown in Figure 13.17.
5. Click Save.

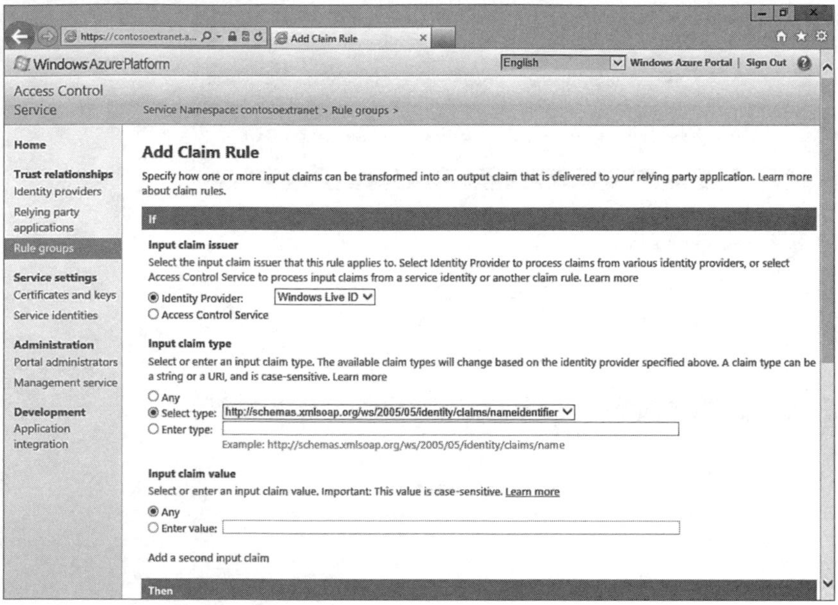

FIGURE 13.16 Adding a claim rule.

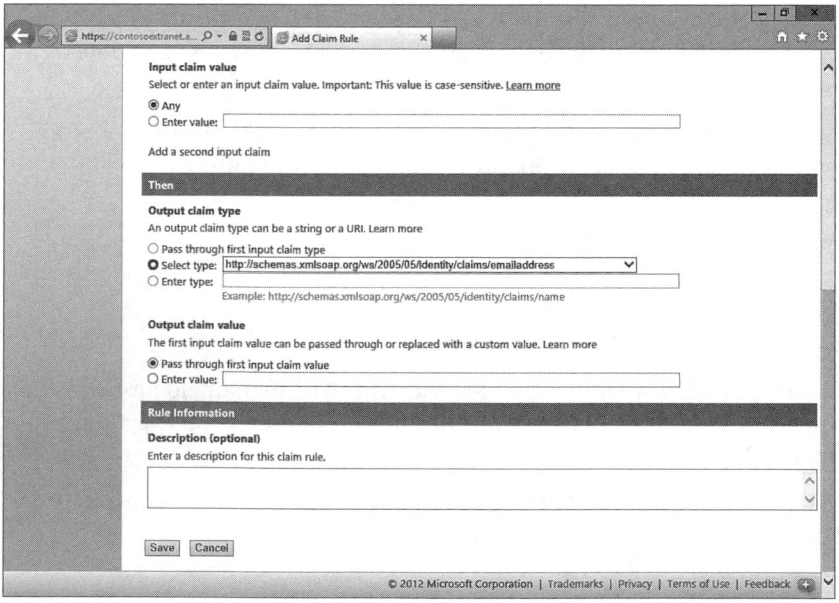

FIGURE 13.17 Setting the output claim type.

Adding a Trusted Identity Provider in SharePoint

Azure ACS has been configured to allow sign-in from both Google and Windows LiveID, and a relying party application has been created. However, you still need to complete a few more steps to configure SharePoint to leverage this external identity source.

This configuration must be done via PowerShell utilizing the SharePoint snap-ins provided. Start PowerShell by navigating to the Start menu and selecting the SharePoint 2013 Management Shell. Ensure that this PowerShell session is run as an administrator (otherwise the steps will most likely fail).

To configure SharePoint to leverage this external identity source, follow these steps:

1. Change directory to C:\Certificates by issuing `"CD \Certificates"`.
2. Create a new object called `$trustCert` and import the certificate to this object `"$trustCert = Get-PFXCertificate C:\Certificates\extranet.contoso.com.cer"`. Ensure that the .cer file is used rather than the .pfx file for this operation.
3. Create a new trusted root authority within SharePoint by issuing `New-SPTrustedRootAuthority "Azure ACS" -Certificate $trustCert`, as shown in Figure 13.18.

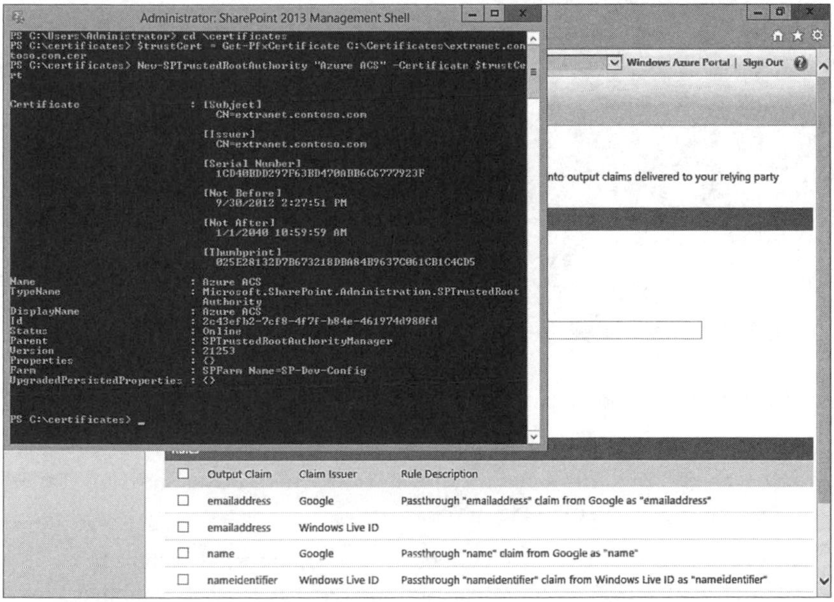

FIGURE 13.18 Using PowerShell to add a trusted identity provider in SharePoint.

4. Issue the following command to create a `ClaimTypeMapping` object:

```
$ClaimTypeMapping = New-SPClaimTypeMapping
"http://schemas.xmlsoap.org/ws/2005/05/identity/claims/emailaddress" -
IncomingClaimTypeDisplayName "Email" -SameAsIncoming
```

5. Issue the following command to create a new trusted identity token issuer, as illustrated in Figure 13.19. Be sure to replace `http://extranet.contoso.com` with the appropriate URL. This is https://<yournamespace>.accesscontrol.windows.net:443/v2/wsfederation. If in doubt, you can retrieve this from the Azure ACS portal under the Application Integration area:

```
New-SPTrustedIdentityTokenIssuer -Name "ACS" -Description "Windows Azure
ACS" -Realm "http://extranet.contoso.com" -SignInUrl
"https://contosoextranet.accesscontrol.windows.net:443/v2/wsfederation" -
ImportTrustCertificate $trustCert -ClaimsMappings $ClaimTypeMapping -
IdentifierClaim $ClaimTypeMapping.InputClaimType
```

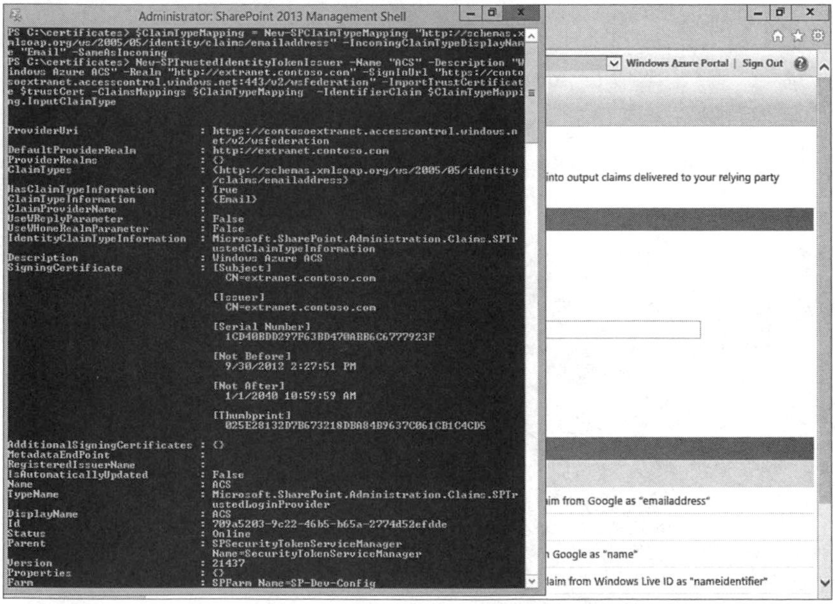

FIGURE 13.19 Using PowerShell to add a trusted identity provider in SharePoint.

Step 4 creates a mapping on the incoming claim types so that when a user signs in, it will utilize the `EmailAddress` claim as the email claim.

Step 5 then creates a new trusted identity token issuer; this is an external system that SharePoint trusts for authentication. The mapping used in step 4 is used to establish which claim is used as the unique identifier for each account that signs in to SharePoint.

The core configuration is now complete for this system, and you can now use it to add additional authentication providers to each SharePoint application. Step 5, in particular, added a new authentication provider named ACS to the SharePoint farm.

Using the Authentication Provider

Now that you have finished the work in PowerShell, you can complete the rest from within a web browser from Central Administration. One big advantage of using this method is that zero configuration files have to be modified, and the most complicated part of the entire exercise is now behind us with the PowerShell completed.

To configure authentication for web applications, follow these steps:

1. Open Central Administration and navigate to Managed Web Applications, as shown in Figure 13.20.

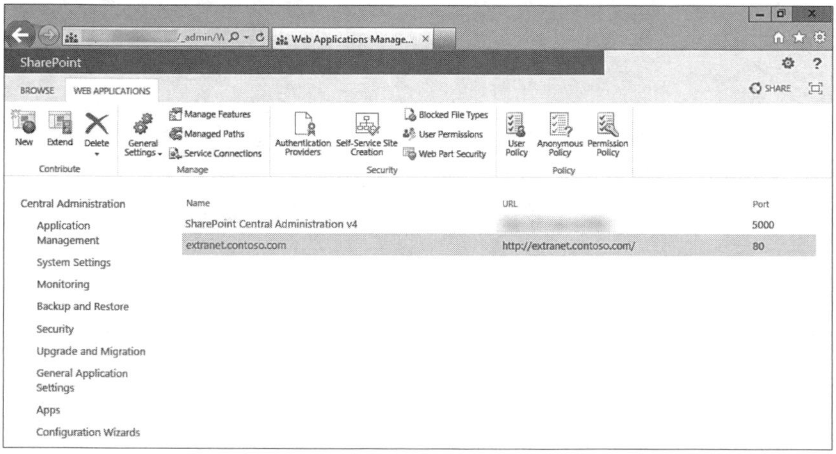

FIGURE 13.20 Configuring web application settings for authentication.

2. Select the appropriate web application and click Authentication Providers.

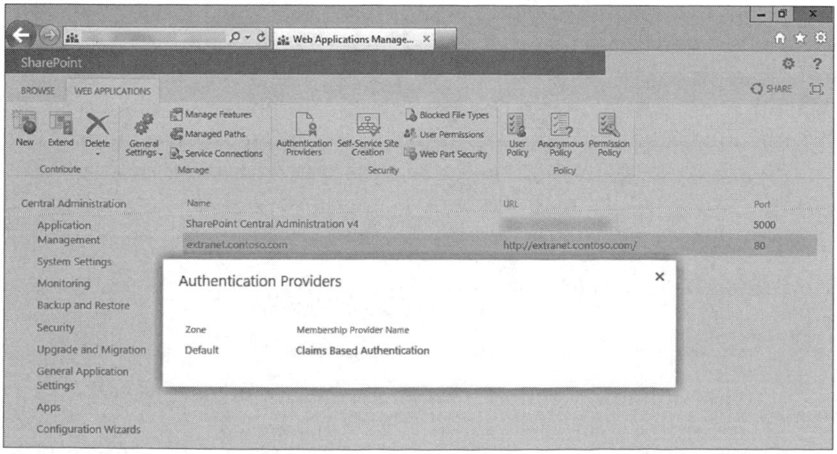

FIGURE 13.21 Configuring web application settings for authentication.

3. Click Default to open the settings for the default zone.
4. Scroll down through the authentication provider settings until you reach the Claims Authentication Types area.
5. Unselect the Enable Windows Authentication option, and then select Trusted Identity Provider and ACS, as shown in Figure 13.22. This activates the ACS authentication and sets it is as the default authentication for this zone.

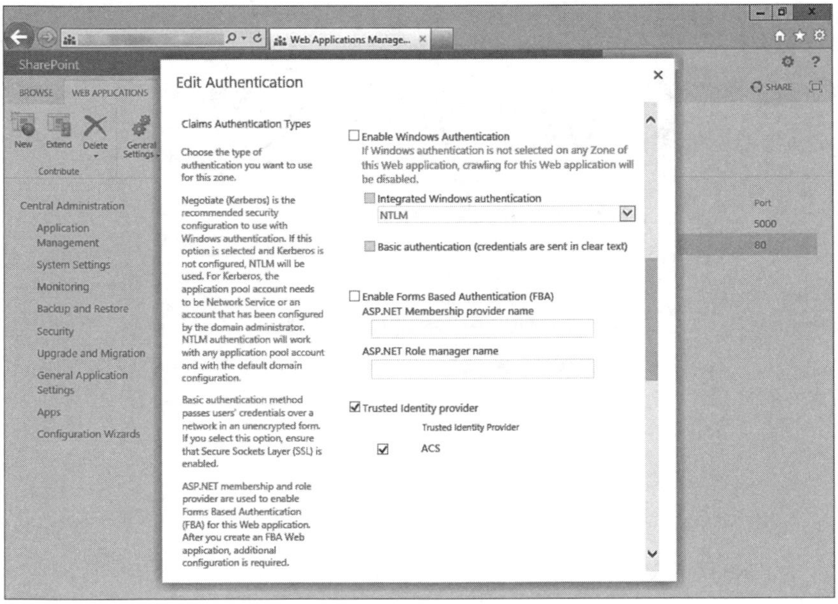

FIGURE 13.22 Configuring web application settings for authentication.

You may note a warning: If Windows authentication is not selected on any Zone of this web application, crawling for this web application will be disabled. If Windows Authentication is left ticked, your users are given a selection box to choose between Windows authentication and ACS, which might cause confusion. The solution to this issue is to extend an additional zone to the web application and use this for crawling. If another zone is extended, users are not prompted for the type of authentication to be used, which will dramatically reduce the number of confused users calling your help desk.

6. Scroll to the very bottom of the page and click Save.

This completes the configuration of the web application, but there is a problem: No ACS users currently have access to the site, and Windows authentication has been disabled.

The easiest way to deal with this problem is to edit the site collection administration to be a Google or LiveID account. For this step, you should use a Google account because producing the unique identifier on a LiveID account can prove difficult.

Setting a New Site Collection Administrator

To set a new site collection administrator, follow these steps:

1. From Central Administration, browse to Application Management and then Change Site Collection Administrators.
2. In the Primary Site Collection Administrator field, there is an account that is no longer valid, because the Windows authentication provider has been removed.
3. Clear this field and enter a correct address as the site collection administrator. Then click the icon that resembles a person with a tick. This should validate the user account and put an underline under it, as shown in Figure 13.23.

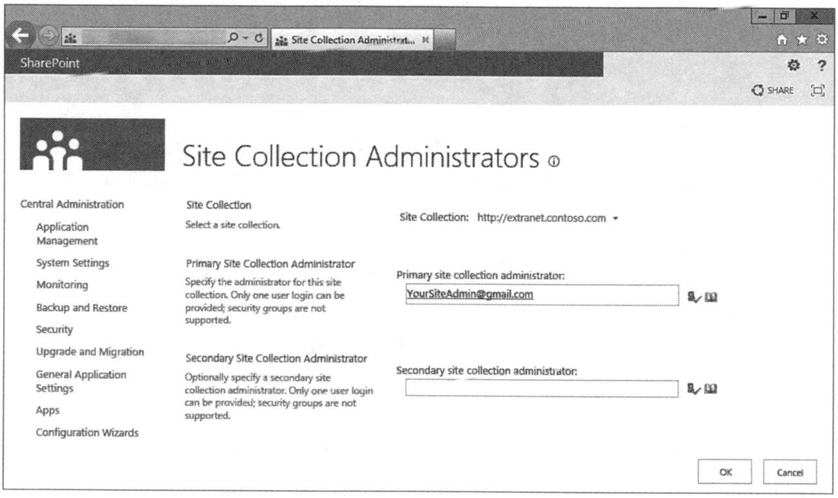

FIGURE 13.23 Changing the site collection admin to a Google ID.

Note that all accounts return a successful validation regardless of the account name; this is due to SharePoint being unable to poll the remote directory to approve the account. This is not a concern; however, it is behavior that most users do not expect.

4. Click OK to save the new site collection administrator.

Testing the New Authentication Type

With all these steps complete, it is now time to test the authentication. Browse to the URL of your web application to begin this process.

The browser should redirect to Azure and display the form shown in Figure 13.24.

This is the default Azure sign-in form. Should the form require modification, this is possible but is not covered in this chapter.

Click Google to sign in with your Google account.

FIGURE 13.24 Testing login with a Google auth provider.

The browser should be redirected to a standard Google login, where username and password can be entered. Do this to complete the sign in. A page similar to one displayed in Figure 13.25 will open.

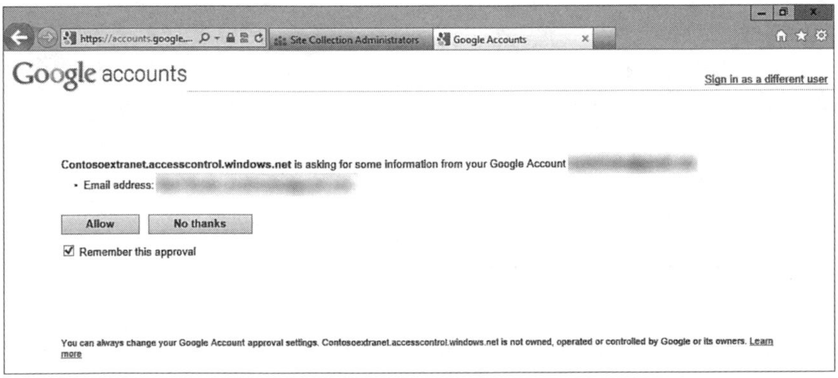

FIGURE 13.25 Authentication with a Google ID.

This is Google Accounts asking for your permission for the Contosoextranet.accesscontrol.windows.net application to access your Google account. In particular, Google is being asked permission for your email address. Click Allow to continue.

The browser should now be redirected back to SharePoint and access should be granted to the site, as shown in Figure 13.26.

Adding additional users is as easy as adding in their Google address or LiveID.

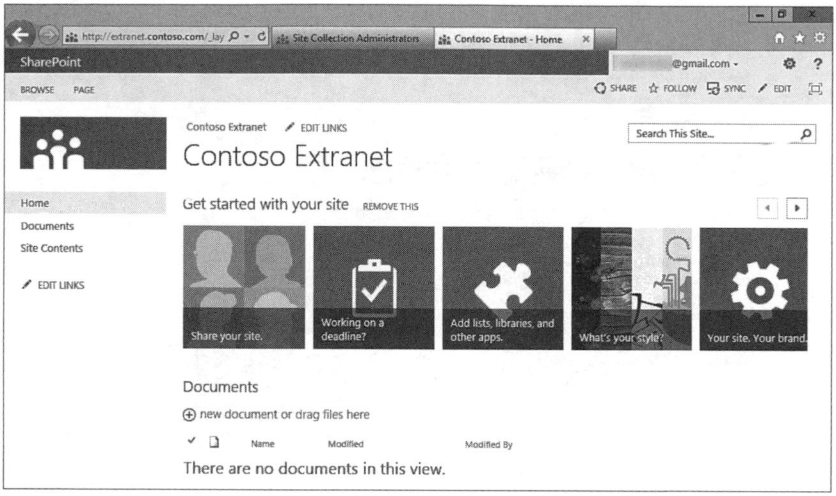

FIGURE 13.26 Logging in to a SharePoint site using a Google ID.

Discovering a Windows LiveID Unique Identifier

Unfortunately, utilizing the Windows LiveID system is a little more difficult because each account does not have an easy-to-use identifier like Google and Facebook have. The best scenario to allow this is to have a landing page with anonymous access where users can sign in and then discover their unique identifier.

For this reason, most users of this authentication method prefer to stick to Google and Facebook accounts, for their ease of use.

Enabling Facebook Authentication to Azure Control Services

Because a trust has been established with Azure ACS from SharePoint, any modifications or enhancements to the sign-in process are now done completely outside SharePoint and are handled within Azure ACS.

This simplifies the addition of identity providers, and in this exercise, that simplicity is exploited to add in Facebook authentication.

Before Azure ACS can leverage Facebook authentication, you need to create a new Facebook app. This is much simpler than it sounds. Just follow these steps:

1. Visit http://developers.facebook.com and sign in. After you have signed in, click Apps from the top menu, and then the Create a New App button, as shown in Figure 13.27.

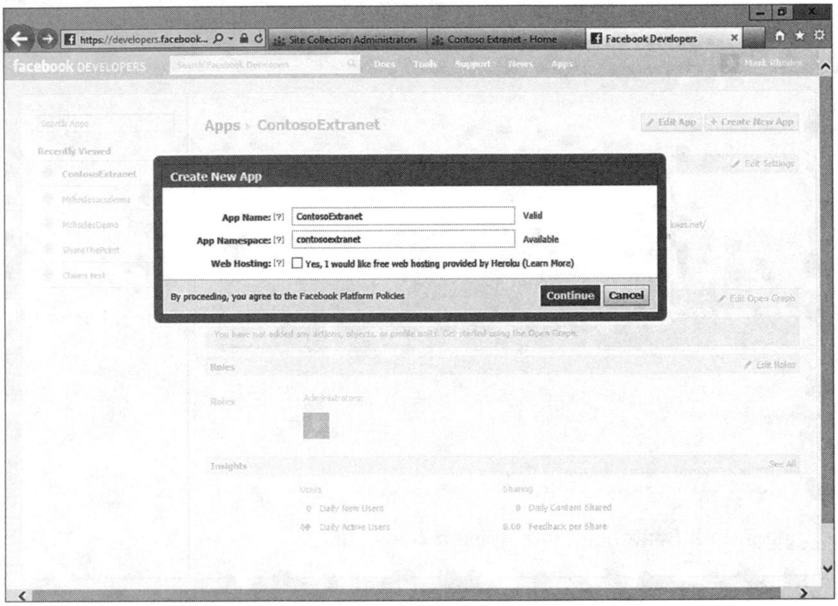

FIGURE 13.27 Creating a new app in Facebook for SharePoint authentication.

2. Enter a valid app name and namespace, and then click Continue.

   The screen shown in Figure 13.28 appears.

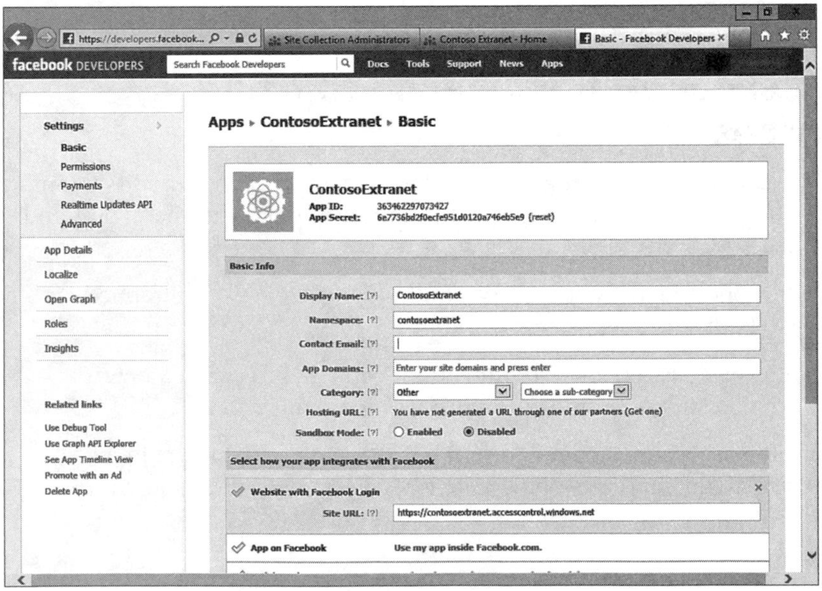

FIGURE 13.28 Configuring the Settings of the Facebook App.

3. Take note of both the app ID and app secret. These are used to establish a trust between Facebook and Azure ACS.

4. Scroll down until you reach the Select How Your App Integrates with Facebook section. Select Website with Facebook Login. You are now prompted for a site URL. Enter the URL for your Azure ACS namespace. This will always be https://<yournamespace>.accesscontrol.windows.net, as shown in Figure 13.29.

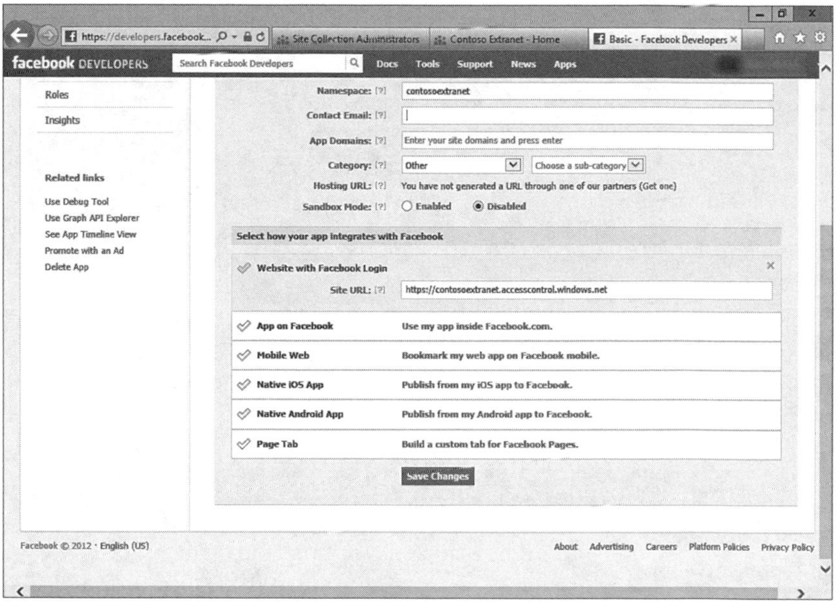

FIGURE 13.29 Configuring the settings of the Facebook app.

5. Click Save Changes.

Completing Facebook Integration with Azure Control Services

Return to Azure ACS to complete the integration with Facebook. Then complete the following steps:

1. After you have returned to the Azure ACS namespace, click Identity Providers and then Add.

2. Select Facebook Application from the list of custom identity providers and click Next, as shown in Figure 13.30.

3. Enter the app ID and app secret that were created in the previous step on Facebook, as shown in Figure 13.31, and then scroll down and click Save.

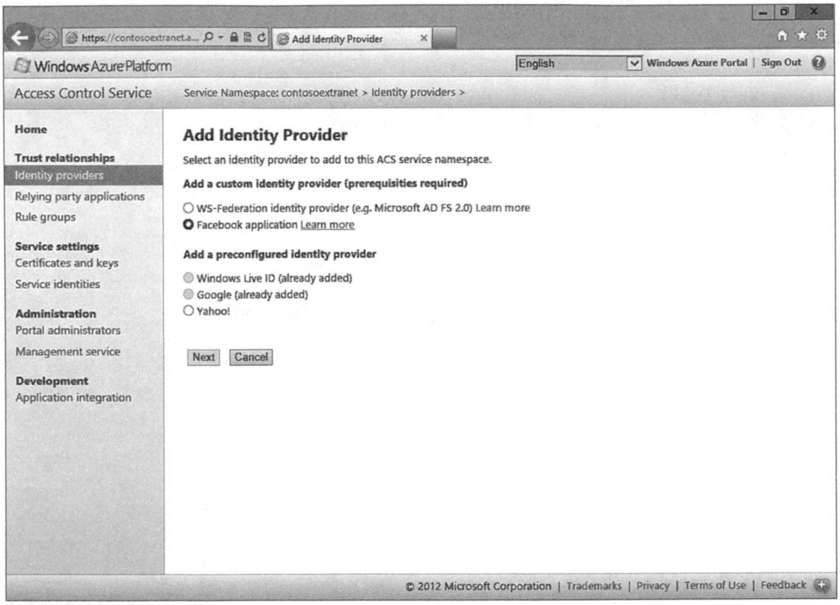

FIGURE 13.30 Continuing identity provider configuration for Facebook.

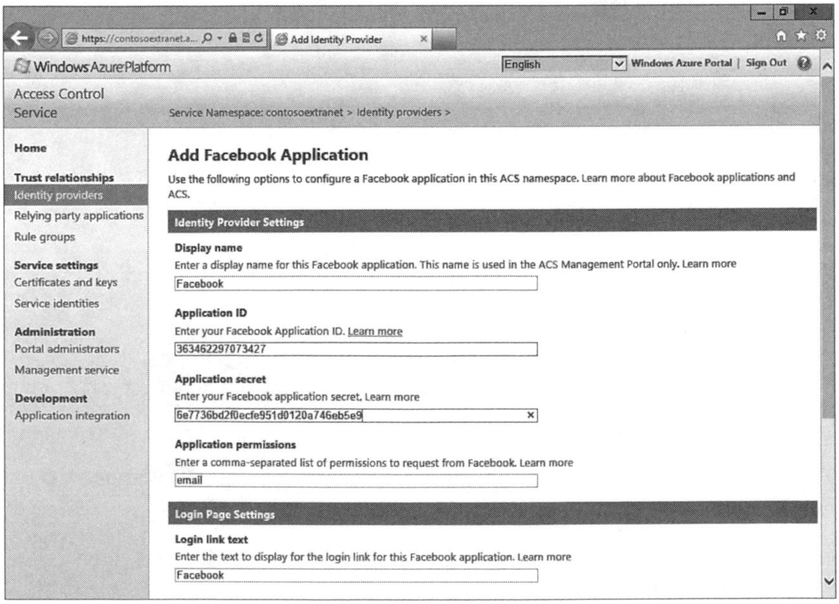

FIGURE 13.31 Entering the app ID and app secret.

The only thing that now remains to ensure Facebook users can authenticate to SharePoint is to generate the appropriate rules for the account. To do this, follow these steps:

1. Click Rule Groups, and then select the default rule group for your namespace. Click the Generate link shown in Figure 13.32.

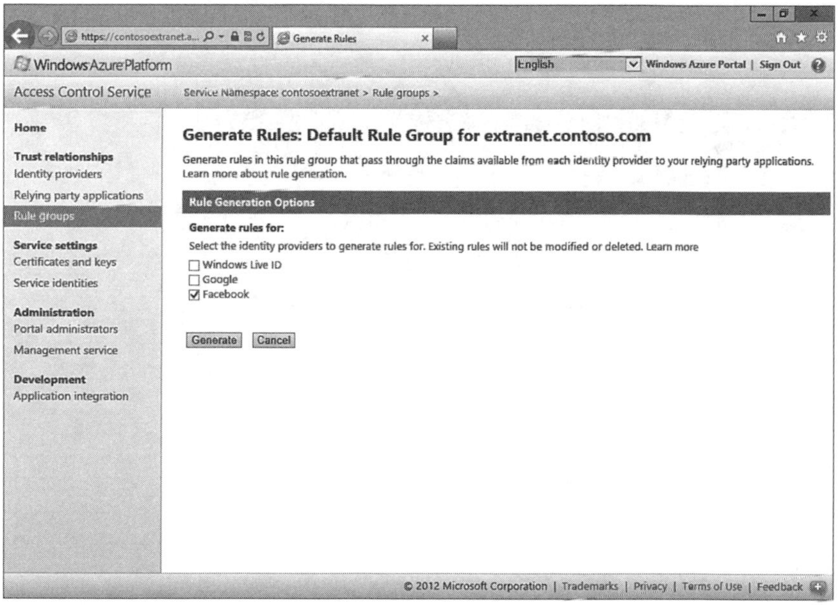

FIGURE 13.32 Generating the rule for the Facebook auth provider.

2. Ensure that only Facebook is ticked, and then click the Generate button.

There should now be rules for Facebook, LiveID, and Google identity providers, as shown in Figure 13.33.

The addition of Facebook as an identity provider is now complete.

Testing Authentication with Facebook

To test authentication with Facebook, open a new browser and browse to the URL of your web application.

NOTE

Prior to testing, it is recommended to wait at least 15 minutes for Facebook to replicate the changes made to the new Facebook app.

Facebook should now be an option on the Azure ACS login page, as shown in Figure 13.34.

13

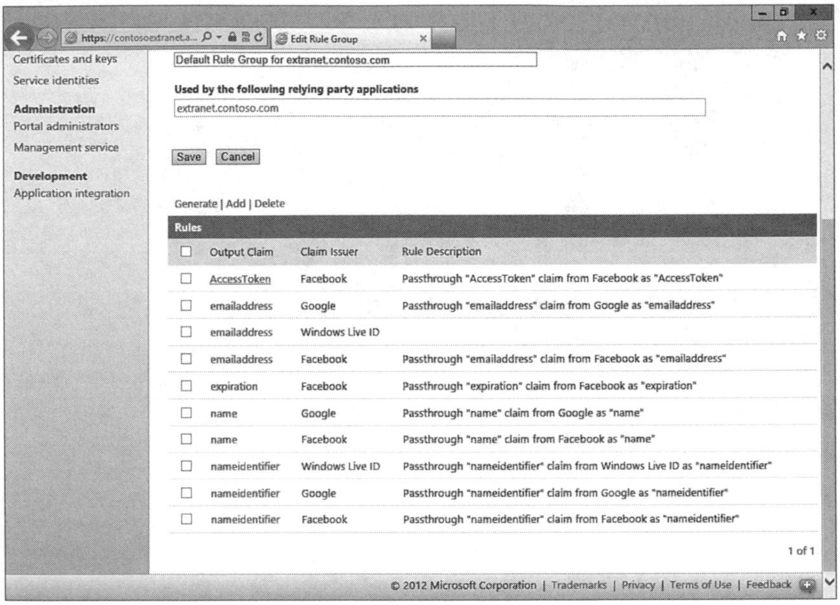

FIGURE 13.33 Reviewing the rules for Facebook.

FIGURE 13.34 Authenticating to a SharePoint site with a Facebook account.

When you click Facebook, the browser is directed to a Facebook login page. Enter your account details to sign in.

After sign-in, the browser redirects to a page prompting for acceptance of your account logging in to the new Facebook app. Click Go to App to confirm, as shown in Figure 13.35.

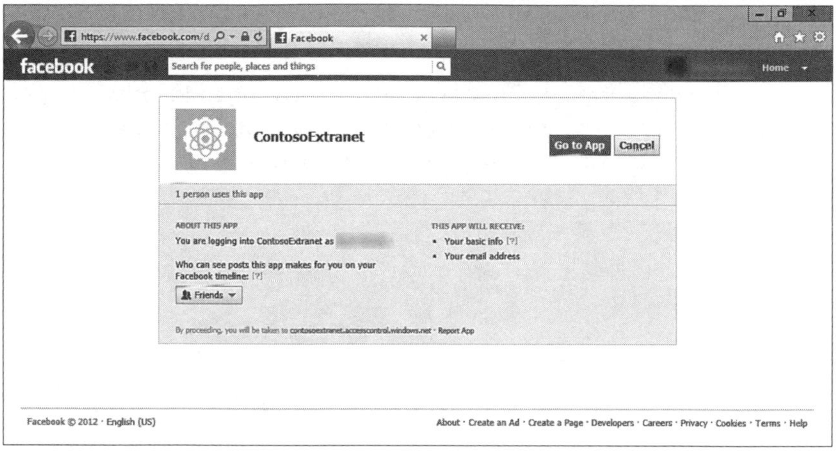

FIGURE 13.35 Confirming the Facebook app to allow access to SharePoint.

Congratulations, you have successfully authenticated to SharePoint using a Facebook account!

If you receive an access denied message, ensure that your Facebook email address is added into the Site Collection Administrator fields or that an administrator has added your Facebook email address as a user in the site collection.

Summary

SharePoint 2013 offers many new features and enhancements that improve extranet scenarios for collaboration with partners, vendors, and customers. Most notable, the ability to easily use external authentication providers such as Google, LiveID, and Facebook accounts allows for simplified management of extranet accounts. In addition, improved Office client integration with forms-based authentication and other authentication providers make SharePoint 2013 a better extranet solution platform.

Best Practices

The following are best practices from this chapter:

- ▶ Secure your extranet with Secure Sockets Layer (SSL) encryption and always use port 443 inbound only. Using nonstandard ports does not improve security and only complicates the farm configuration. Some services do not work on nonstandard ports.
- ▶ Avoid storing confidential and secure data in an extranet.
- ▶ External-facing web front end (WFE) servers should always be in a secured network. Seek to reduce the vulnerability surface area.

- Use external authentication providers such as Facebook, Google, or LiveID to provide for extranet access to simplify the management of extranet accounts.
- If an external auth provider is not an option, consider the use of an identity management tool such as Forefront Identity Manager (FIM) 2010 R2 to manage the accounts and automate the provisioning/deprovisioning process.

CHAPTER 14

Protecting SharePoint with Advanced Edge Security Solutions

IN THIS CHAPTER

- Understanding the Forefront Edge Line of Products
- Outlining the Need for the Forefront Edge Line for SharePoint Environments
- Outlining the Inherent Threat in SharePoint Web Traffic
- Securing SharePoint Sites with Forefront TMG 2010
- Securing SharePoint Sites Using Forefront UAG

In today's risk-fraught computing environment, any exposed service is subject to frequent attack from the Internet. This is particularly true for web services, including those offered by SharePoint 2013. Exploits using the Hypertext Transport Protocol (HTTP) that these services use are becoming very common, and it is not considered best practice to make a SharePoint server directly accessible via the Internet.

Fortunately, the productivity gains in SharePoint 2013 can still be utilized and made more accessible by securing them behind a reverse-proxy server such as Microsoft's Forefront Threat Management Gateway (Forefront TMG) 2010 or Forefront Unified Access Gateway (Forefront UAG) 2010. These tools, part of the Forefront Edge line, allow for advanced application layer filtering of network traffic, greatly securing the overall SharePoint environment.

This chapter details the ways that SharePoint 2013 sites can be secured using the Forefront TMG 2010 and Forefront UAG 2010 products. Deployment scenarios for securing SharePoint-related services with Forefront TMG/UAG are outlined, and specific step-by-step guides are illustrated.

Note that Microsoft has started to deprecate the TMG product, but TMG functionality can still be found in Forefront UAG and administrators can still use existing supported TMG environments to secure SharePoint 2013 sites as described in this chapter.

Understanding the Forefront Edge Line of Products

The rise in the prevalence of computer viruses, threats, and exploits on the Internet has made it necessary for organizations of all shapes and sizes to reevaluate their protection strategies for edge services such as SharePoint Server. No longer is it possible to ignore or minimize these threats as the damage they can cause can cripple a company's business functions. A solution to the increased sophistication and pervasiveness of these viruses and exploits is becoming increasingly necessary.

Corresponding with the growth of these threats has been the development of Microsoft's Forefront Edge line of products, including Forefront TMG and Forefront UAG products from Microsoft. These products are fast becoming a business-critical component of many organizations, who are finding that many of the traditional packet-filtering firewalls and technologies don't necessarily stand up to the modern threats of today. The Forefront Edge products provide for that higher level of application security required, particularly for tools such as SharePoint sites and other web services.

NOTE

Microsoft has begun the process of deprecating Forefront TMG, so environments looking at new solutions for security SharePoint should look instead at Forefront UAG. That said, existing Forefront TMG environments can still publish SharePoint 2013 sites with TMG.

Understanding the Difference Between Forefront UAG and Forefront TMG

The first important distinction that needs to be made is the difference between the two products in the Forefront Edge line. Forefront TMG is the direct replacement for the Internet Security and Acceleration (ISA) Server 2006 product and is positioned by Microsoft as the preferred product for outbound security filtering of web and other traffic. Forefront UAG, however, is a full-function Secure Sockets Layer/Virtual Private Network (SSL/VPN), and is positioned by Microsoft as the preferred solution for inbound security filtering of traffic destined for SharePoint and other internal published resources.

So, in a perfect world, SharePoint administrators would use the full Forefront UAG product for securing access to a SharePoint site. Indeed, Forefront UAG has a Forefront TMG engine within it, so there is no loss of functionality using the Forefront UAG line. Forefront TMG, however, has fewer overall features and is not a true SSL/VPN, and is primarily positioned as a forward proxy solution rather than a reverse-proxy one, which is what is needed for securing SharePoint.

That said, Forefront TMG does not lose any of its reverse proxy capabilities that it inherited from the older ISA 2006 product, so it can still be used for reverse-proxy securing of inbound SharePoint traffic. Either solution can be used for properly securing critical SharePoint traffic, and both solutions are outlined in this book. This chapter points out instances when there are differences between the two tools, but also assumes that either tool may be used.

At a minimum, it is highly recommended to use an application layer-aware security solution for inbound traffic to SharePoint sites, whether that is the Forefront Edge line or whether it is another third-party solution. Exposing a SharePoint site to direct uninspected access from the Internet is highly discouraged.

Outlining the Need for the Forefront Edge Line for SharePoint Environments

A great deal of confusion exists about the role that the Forefront Edge line can play in a SharePoint environment. Much of that confusion stems from the misconception that Forefront TMG or Forefront UAG are only proxy server products. Both Forefront Edge products are, on the contrary, fully functional firewalls, VPN servers, web caching proxies, and application reverse-proxy solutions. In addition, the Forefront Edge line addresses specific business needs to provide a secured infrastructure and improve productivity through the proper application of its built-in functionality. Determining how these features can help to improve the security and productivity of a SharePoint environment is subsequently of key importance.

In addition to the built-in functionality available within the Forefront Edge line, a whole host of third-party integration solutions provide additional levels of security and functionality. Enhanced intrusion detection support, content filtering, web surfing restriction tools, and customized application filters all extend the capabilities of the Forefront Edge line and position it as a solution to a wide variety of security needs within organizations of many sizes.

Outlining the High Cost of Security Breaches

It is rare when a week goes by without a high-profile security breach, denial-of-service (DoS) attack, exploit, virus, or worm appearing in the news. The risks inherent in modern computing have been increasing exponentially, and effective countermeasures are required in any organization that expects to do business across the Internet.

It has become impossible to turn a blind eye toward these security threats. On the contrary, even organizations that would normally not be obvious candidates for attack from the Internet must secure their services, as the vast majority of modern attacks do not focus on any one particular target, but sweep the Internet for any destination host, looking for vulnerabilities to exploit. Infection or exploitation of critical business infrastructure can be extremely costly for an organization. Many of the productivity gains in business recently have been attributed to advances in information technology functionality, including SharePoint-related gains, and the loss of this functionality can severely impact the bottom line.

In addition to productivity losses, the legal environment for businesses has changed significantly in recent years. Regulations such as Sarbanes-Oxley (SOX), Health Insurance Portability and Accountability Act (HIPAA), and Gramm-Leach-Bliley have changed the playing field by requiring a certain level of security and validation of private customer data. Organizations can now be sued or fined for substantial sums if proper security precautions are not taken to protect client data. The atmosphere surrounding these concerns provides the backdrop for the evolution and acceptance of the Forefront Edge line of products.

Outlining the Critical Role of Firewall Technology in a Modern Connected Infrastructure

It is widely understood today that valuable corporate assets such as SharePoint sites cannot be exposed to direct access to the world's users on the Internet. In the beginning, however, the Internet was built on the concept that all connected networks could be trusted. It was not originally designed to provide robust security between networks, so security concepts needed to be developed to secure access between entities on the Internet. Special devices known as firewalls were created to block access to internal network resources for specific companies.

Originally, many organizations were not directly connected to the Internet. Often, even when a connection was created, no type of firewall was put into place because the perception was that only government or high-security organizations required protection.

With the explosion of viruses, hacking attempts, and worms that began to proliferate, organizations soon began to understand that some type of firewall solution was required to block access to specific "dangerous" TCP or UDP ports that were used by the Internet's TCP/IP protocol. This type of firewall technology would inspect each arriving packet and accept or reject it based on the TCP or UDP port specified in the packet of information received.

Some of these firewalls were ASIC-based firewalls, which employed the use of solid-state microchips, with built-in packet-filtering technology. These firewalls, many of which are still used and deployed today, provided organizations with a quick-and-dirty way to filter Internet traffic, but did not allow for a high degree of customization because of their static nature.

The development of software-based firewalls coincided with the need for simpler management interfaces and the ability to make software changes to firewalls quickly and easily. The most popular firewall brand in organizations today, CheckPoint, falls into this category, as do other popular firewalls such as SonicWall and Cisco PIX. The Forefront Edge line was built and developed as a software-based firewall, and provides the same degree of packet-filtering technology that has become a virtual necessity on the Internet today.

More recently, holes in the capabilities of simple packet-based filtering technology has made a more sophisticated approach to filtering traffic for malicious or spurious content a necessity. The Forefront Edge line responds to these needs with the capabilities to perform application layer filtering on Internet traffic.

Understanding the Growing Need for Application Layer Filtering

Nearly all organizations with a presence on the Internet have put some type of packet-filtering firewall technology into place to protect the internal network resources from attack. These types of packet-filter firewall technologies were useful in blocking specific types of network traffic, such as vulnerabilities that utilize the RPC protocol, by simply blocking TCP and UDP ports that the RPC protocol would use. Other ports, however, were often left wide open to support certain functionality, such as the TCP 80 or 443 ports, utilized for HTTP and HTTPS web browsing and for access to SharePoint. As previously mentioned, a packet-filter firewall is only able to inspect the header of a packet, simply understanding which port the data is meant to utilize, but unable to actually read the content. A good analogy to this would be if a border guard were instructed to only allow citizens with specific passports to enter the country but had no way of inspecting their luggage for contraband or illegal substances.

The problems that are becoming more evident, however, is that the viruses, exploits, and attacks have adjusted to conform to this new landscape, and have started to realize that they can conceal the true malicious nature of their payload within the identity of an allowed port. For example, they can "piggy-back" their destructive payload over a known "good" port that is open on a packet-filter firewall. Many modern exploits, viruses, and "scumware," such as illegal file-sharing applications, piggy-back off the TCP 80 or 443 ports, for example. Using the border guard analogy to illustrate, the smugglers realized that if they put their contraband in the luggage of a citizen from a country on the border guard's allowed list, they could smuggle it into the country without worrying that the guard will inspect the package. These types of exploits and attacks are not uncommon, and the list of known application-level attacks continues to grow.

In the past, when an organization realized that they had been compromised through their traditional packet-filter firewall, the common knee-jerk reaction was to lock down access from the Internet in response to threats. For example, an exploit that would arrive over HTTP ports 80 or 443 might prompt an organization to completely close access to that port for a temporary or semi-permanent basis. This approach can greatly impact productivity as SharePoint access would be affected. This is especially true in a modern connected infrastructure that relies heavily on communications and collaboration with outside vendors and customers. Traditional security techniques would involve a trade-off between security and productivity. The tighter a firewall was locked down, for example, the less functional and productive an end user could be.

In direct response to the need to maintain and increase levels of productivity without compromising security, application layer "stateful inspection" capabilities were built into the Forefront Edge line that could intelligently determine whether particular web traffic is legitimate. To illustrate, the Forefront Edge line inspects a packet using TCP Port 80 to determine if it is a properly formatted HTTP request. Looking back to the analogy we have been using, the Forefront Edge line is like a border guard who not only checks the passports, but is also given an x-ray machine to check the luggage of each person crossing the border.

The more sophisticated application layer attacks become, the greater the need becomes for a security solution that can allow for a greater degree of productivity while reducing the type of risks which can exist in an environment that relies on simple packet-based filtering techniques.

Outlining the Inherent Threat in SharePoint Web Traffic

The Internet provides somewhat of a catch-22 when it comes to its goal and purpose. On one hand, the Internet is designed to allow anywhere, anytime access to information, linking systems around the world together and providing for that information to be freely exchanged. On the other hand, this type of transparency comes with a great deal of risk because it effectively means that any one system can be exposed to every connected computer, either friendly or malicious, in the world.

Often, this inherent risk of compromising systems or information through their exposure to the Internet has led to locking down access to that information with firewalls. Of course, this limits the capabilities and usefulness of a free information exchange system such as what web traffic provides. Many of the web servers need to be made available to anonymous access by the general public, which causes the dilemma, as organizations need to place that information online without putting the servers it is placed on at undue risk.

Fortunately, the Forefront Edge line provides for robust and capable tools to secure web traffic, making it available for remote access but also securing it against attack and exploit. To understand how it does this, it is first necessary to examine how web traffic can be exploited.

Understanding Web (HTTP) Exploits

It is an understatement to say that the computing world was not adequately prepared for the release of the Code Red virus. The Microsoft Internet Information Services (IIS) exploit that Code Red took advantage of was already known, and a patch was made available from Microsoft for several weeks before the release of the virus. In those days, however, less emphasis was placed on patching and updating systems on a regular basis, because it was generally believed that it was best to wait for the bugs to get worked out of the patches first.

So, what happened is that a large number of websites were completely unprepared for the huge onslaught of exploits that occurred with the Code Red virus, which sent specially formatted HTTP requests to a web server to attempt to take control of a system. For example, the following URL lists the type of exploits that were performed:

http://sharepoint.companyabc.com/scripts/..%5c../winnt/system32/ cmd.exe?/c+dir+c:\

This one in particular attempts to launch the command prompt on a web server. Through the proper manipulation, viruses such as Code Red found the method for taking over web servers and using them as drones to attack other web servers.

These types of web-based attacks were a wakeup call to the broader security community. It became apparent that packet-layer filter firewalls that could simply open or close a port were worthless against the threat of an exploit that packages its traffic over a legitimately allowed port such as HTTP or HTTPS.

Web-based filtering and securing, fortunately, is something that the Forefront Edge line does extremely well and offers a large number of customization options that enable administrators to have control over the traffic and security of the web server.

Securing Encrypted (SSL) Web Traffic

As the World Wide Web was maturing, organizations realized that if they encrypted the HTTP packets that were transmitted between a website and a client, it would make it nearly unreadable to anyone who would potentially intercept those packets. This led to the adoption of SSL encryption for HTTP traffic.

Of course, encrypted packets also create somewhat of a dilemma from an intrusion detection and analysis perspective because it is impossible to read the content of the packet to determine what it is trying to do. Indeed, many HTTP exploits in the wild today can be transmitted over secure SSL-encrypted channels. This poses a dangerous situation for organizations that must secure the traffic against interception but must also proactively monitor and secure their web servers against attack.

The Forefront Edge line is uniquely positioned to solve this problem, fortunately, because it includes the ability to perform end-to-end SSL bridging. By installing the SSL certificate from the SharePoint web front-end server on either the Forefront UAG or Forefront TMG servers, along with a copy of the private key, the server is able to decrypt the traffic, scan it for exploits, and then reencrypt it before sending it to the SharePoint server. Very few products on the market do this type of end-to-end encryption of the packets for this level of security other than the two Forefront Edge line products. Before Forefront UAG or Forefront TMG can secure SharePoint SSL traffic, however, an SSL certificate must be placed on the SharePoint server.

Securing SharePoint Traffic with SSL Encryption

By default, SharePoint is configured to use integrated Windows authentication. This form of authentication works fine if access to the server is over a trusted internal network, but is not feasible for access over the Internet.

Because of this limitation, a form of authentication that can be sent across the Internet must be used. This effectively limits the SharePoint server to using basic authentication, which is supported by most web browsers and devices. The problem with basic authentication, however, is that the username and password that the user sends is effectively sent in clear text and can be intercepted and stolen in transit. In addition, documents and other confidential information are transmitted in clear text, a huge security issue.

The solution to this problem is to use what is known as SSL encryption on the traffic. SSL encryption is performed using Public Key Infrastructure (PKI) certificates, which work through the principle of shared-key encryption. PKI SSL certificates are widely used on the Internet today; any website starting with an https:// uses them, and the entire online merchant community depends on the security of the system.

For SharePoint, the key is to install a certificate on the server so that the traffic between the device and the server is protected from prying eyes. There are effectively two options to this approach, as follows:

- **Use a third-party certificate authority:** A common option for many organizations is to purchase a certificate for SharePoint from a third-party trusted certificate authority (CA), such as VeriSign, Thawte, or others. These CAs are already trusted by a vast number of devices, so no additional configuration is required. The downside to this option is that the certificates must be purchased and the organization doesn't have as much flexibility to change certificate options.
- **Install and use your own CA:** Another common approach is to install and configure Windows Server 2008 R2 Active Directory Certificate Services (AD CS) to create your own CA within an organization. This gives you the flexibility to create new certificates, revoke existing ones, and not have to pay immediate costs. The downside to this approach is that no browsers will trust the certificate by default, and error messages to that effect will be encountered on the devices unless the certificates are manually trusted or forced out to client domain members via Active Directory Group Policy Objects.

Securing SharePoint Sites with Forefront TMG 2010

SharePoint sites comprise one of the more common types of content that are secured by the Forefront Edge line. This stems from the critical need to provide remote document management while at the same time securing that access. Although Forefront UAG is the preferred solution for reverse proxy of a SharePoint environment, the Forefront TMG product is also a highly capable product that allows for reverse proxy functionality. Both products are covered in this chapter, but this section illustrates the creation of a Forefront TMG publishing rule for a SharePoint site for clients with an investment in Forefront TMG but without a Forefront UAG environment.

Forefront TMG can be used to secure a SharePoint implementation and can be deployed in multiple scenarios, such as an edge firewall, an inline firewall, or a dedicated reverse-proxy server. In all these scenarios, Forefront TMG secures SharePoint traffic by "pretending" to be the SharePoint server itself, scanning the traffic that is destined for the SharePoint server for exploits, and then repackaging that traffic and sending it on, such as what is illustrated in Figure 14.1.

Forefront TMG performs this type of securing through a SharePoint site publishing rule, which automatically sets up and configures a listener on the Forefront TMG server. A listener is a Forefront TMG component that listens to specifically defined IP traffic and processes that traffic for the requesting client as if it were the actual server itself. For example, a SharePoint listener on Forefront TMG would respond to SharePoint HTTP/HTTPS requests made to it by scanning them for exploits and then repackaging them and forwarding them on to the SharePoint server itself. Using listeners, the client cannot tell the difference between the Forefront TMG server and the SharePoint server itself.

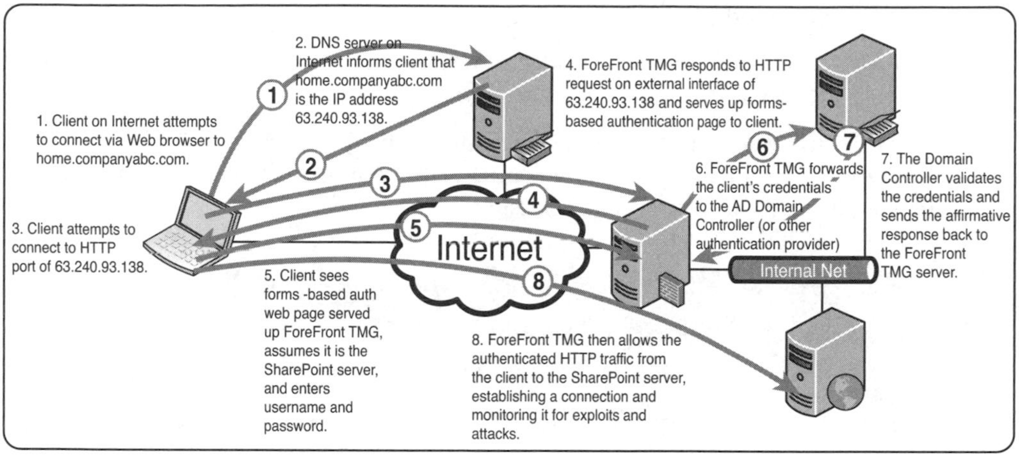

FIGURE 14.1 Conceptualizing the process of securing a SharePoint site using Forefront TMG.

Forefront TMG is also one of the few products, along with Forefront UAG, that can secure web traffic with SSL encryption from end to end. It does this by using the SharePoint server's own certificate to reencrypt the traffic before sending it on its way. This also allows for the "black box" of SSL traffic to be examined for exploits and viruses at the application layer, and then reencrypted to reduce the chance of unauthorized viewing of the traffic. Without the capability to scan this SSL traffic, exploits bound for a SharePoint server could simply hide themselves in the encrypted traffic and pass right through traditional firewalls.

This chapter covers one common scenario that the Forefront TMG server is used for: securing a SharePoint site collection (in this example, home.companyabc.com) using Forefront TMG. The steps outlined here describe this particular scenario, although Forefront TMG can also be used for multiple other securing scenarios as necessary.

Configuring the Alternate Access Mapping Setting for the External URL

Before external access can be granted to a site, an alternate access mapping (AAM) must be established for the particular web application. An AAM is a host header value (such as https://portal.companyabc.com, http://server4, https://home.companyabc.com, and so on) that must be consistently applied to the site across all links. If it is not put into place, external clients are not able to access internal links.

To configure the AAM in this scenario, home.companyabc.com, on a web application, follow these steps:

1. Open the SharePoint Central Administration tool.
2. Click the System Settings area, and then click the Alternate Access Mappings link in the links provided on the left of the screen.

3. Click Edit Public URLs.
4. Under Alternate Access Mapping Collection, select the AAM Collection that corresponds to the web application for home.companyabc.com.
5. Enter the https:// AAM needed under the Internet box, as shown in Figure 14.2. In this example, we enter https://home.companyabc.com. If the web application will be addressed by other names, enter all possible names here. Click Save.

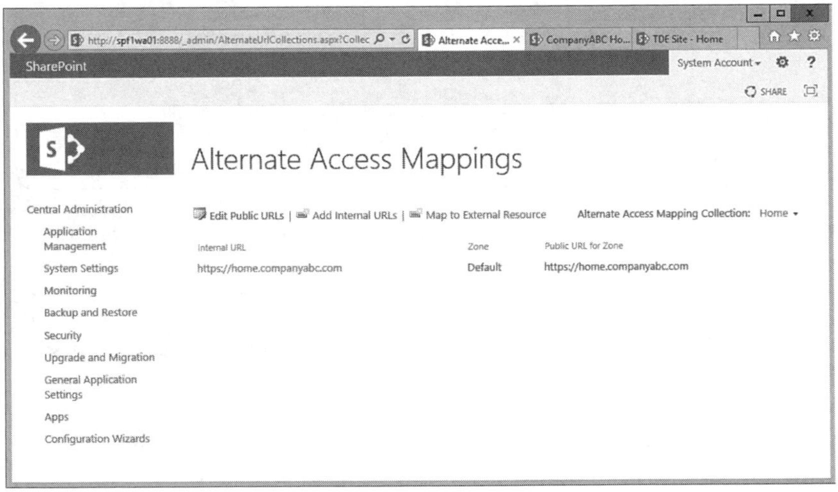

FIGURE 14.2 Creating an AAM for external published use.

6. Review the AAMs listed on the page for accuracy, and then close the SharePoint Central Admin tool.

Creating a SharePoint Publishing Rule Using Forefront TMG

After an SSL Certificate from the SharePoint server has been installed onto the Forefront TMG server, the actual Forefront TMG SharePoint publishing rule can be generated to secure SharePoint via the following procedure:

NOTE

The procedure outlined here illustrates the Forefront Edge line SharePoint publishing rule that uses forms-based authentication (FBA) for the site, which allows for a landing page to be generated on the Forefront Edge line to pre-authenticate user connections to SharePoint.

1. From the Forefront TMG console, click once on the Firewall Policy node from the console tree.

2. Click the link in the Tasks tab of the Tasks pane labeled Publish SharePoint Sites.
3. Enter a descriptive name for the publishing rule, such as SharePoint Publishing Rule.
4. Select whether to publish a single website, multiple websites, or a farm of load-balanced servers, as illustrated in Figure 14.3. In this example, we choose to publish a simple single website. Click Next to continue.

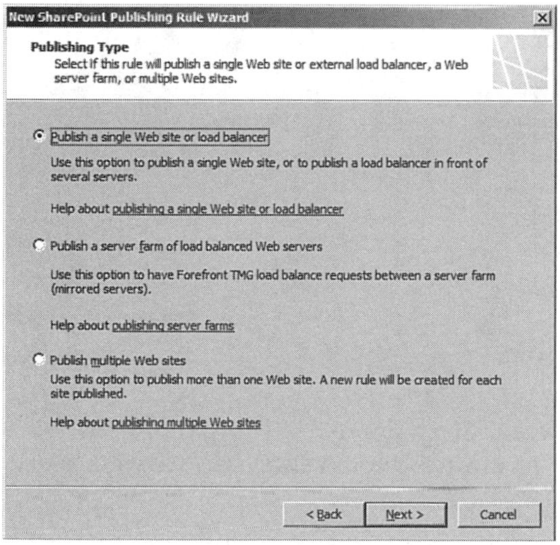

FIGURE 14.3 Creating a Forefront TMG publishing rule for SharePoint sites.

5. Choose whether to require SSL from the Forefront Edge line server to the SharePoint server, as shown in Figure 14.4. It is recommended to provide end-to-end SSL support for the Forefront Edge line, although it will require a copy of the SSL certificate with the private key exported to the TMG server for this to be set up properly. Click Next to continue.
6. In the Internal Publishing Details dialog box, enter the site name that internal users use to access the SharePoint server. Examine the options to connect to an IP address or computer name; this gives additional flexibility to the rule. Click Next to continue.
7. Under the subsequent dialog box, enter to accept requests for This Domain Name (type below): and enter the fully qualified domain name (FQDN) of the server, such as **home.companyabc.com**. This will restrict the rule to requests that are destined for the proper FQDN. Click Next to continue.
8. Under Web Listener, click New.
9. At the start of the Web Listener Wizard, enter a descriptive name for the listener, such as **SharePoint HTTP/HTTPS Listener**, and click Next to continue.

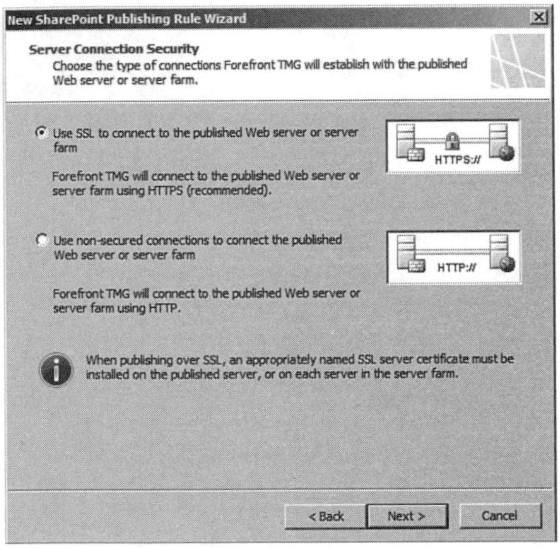

FIGURE 14.4 Configuring SSL for publishing rule.

10. Again, a prompt is given to choose between SSL and non-SSL. This prompt refers to the traffic between client and SharePoint, which should always be SSL whenever possible. Click Next to continue.

11. Under Web Listener IP addresses, select the External network and leave it at All IP Addresses. Click Next to continue.

12. Under Listener SSL Certificates (if creating an SSL-based rule; if not, you are not prompted for this), click Select Certificate.

13. Select the previously installed certificate (if using SSL) and click the Select button.

14. Click Next to continue.

15. For the type of authentication, choose HTML Form Authentication, as shown in Figure 14.5. Leave Windows (Active Directory) selected and click Next.

16. The Single Sign-On (SSO) Settings dialog box is powerful; it allows all authentication traffic through a single listener to be processed only once. After the user has authenticated, he can access any other service, be it an Exchange Outlook Web App (OWA) server, web server, or other web-based service that uses the same domain name for credentials. In this example, we enter **.companyabc.com** into the SSO domain name. Click Next to continue.

17. Click Finish to end the Web Listener Wizard.

18. Click Next after the new listener is displayed in the Web Listener dialog box.

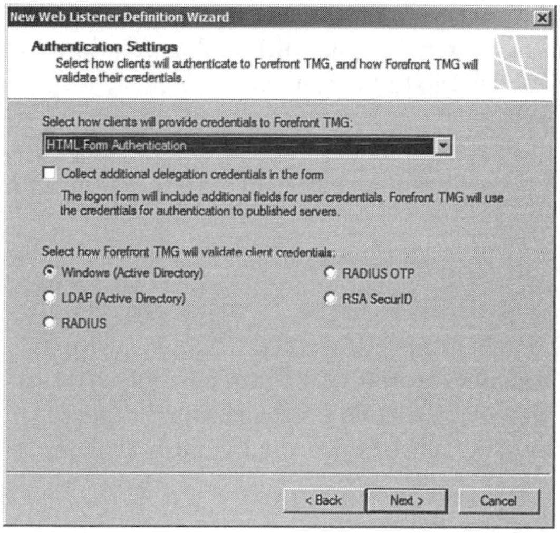

FIGURE 14.5 Selecting to use forms-based authentication for a Forefront TMG publishing rule.

19. Under Authentication Delegation, choose Basic from the drop-down box. Basic Authentication is used if SSL is the transport mechanism chosen. If using HTTP only, it is recommended to use NTLM authentication to avoid the passwords being sent in clear text. Click Next to continue.

20. At the Alternate Access Mapping Configuration dialog box, shown in Figure 14.6, select that SharePoint AAM is already configured, as we configured the Alternate Access Mapping on the SharePoint server in previous steps.

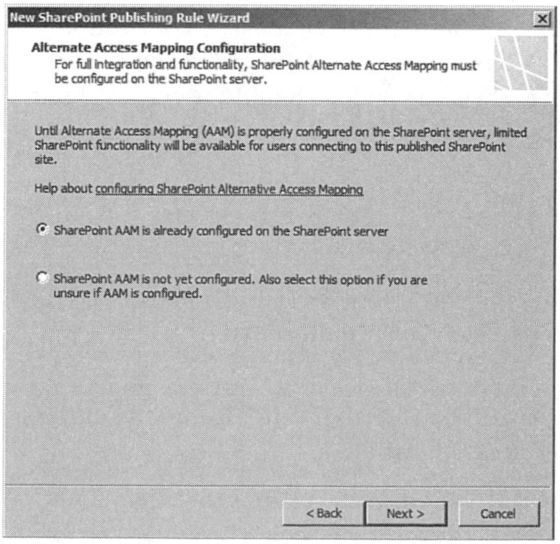

FIGURE 14.6 Creating a Forefront TMG publishing rule for a SharePoint site with AAM already configured.

21. Under User Sets, leave All Authenticated Users selected. In stricter scenarios, only specific AD groups can be granted rights to SharePoint using this dialog box. In this example, the default setting is sufficient. Click Next to continue.
22. Click Finish to end the wizard.
23. Click Apply in the details pane, and then complete the change management options and click Apply again.
24. Click OK when finished to commit the changes.

The rule now appears in the details pane of the Forefront TMG server. Double-clicking the rule brings up the settings. Tabs can be used to navigate around the different rule settings. The rule itself can be configured with additional settings based on the configuration desired. For example, the following rule information is used to configure our basic FBA web publishing rule for SharePoint:

- **General tab:** Name: SharePoint; Enabled = checked.
- **Action tab:** Action to take = Allow; Log requests matching this rule = checked.
- **From tab:** This rule applies to traffic from these sources = Anywhere.
- **To tab:** This rule applies to this published site = home.companyabc.com; Computer name or IP address = 10.10.10.105 (internal IP address of SharePoint server). Forward the original host header instead of the actual one (specified in the Internal Site Name field) = checked; Specify how the firewall proxies requests to the published server = Requests appear to come from the Forefront TMG computer.
- **Traffic tab:** This rule applies to traffic of the following protocols = HTTPS.
- **Listener tab, Properties button:** Networks tab = External, All IP addresses; Connections tab—Enabled HTTP connections on port 80, Enable SSL connections on port 443; HTTP to HTTPS Redirection = Redirect authenticated traffic from HTTP to HTTPS; Forms tab = Allow users to change their passwords, Remind users that their password will expire in this number of days = 15; SSO tab = Enable Single Sign-On, SSO Domains = .companyabc.com.
- **Public Name tab:** This rule applies to requests for the following websites = home.companyabc.com.
- **Paths tab:** External paths = All are set to <same as internal> Internal paths = /_vti_inf.html*, /_vti_bin/*, /_upresources/*, /_layouts/*, /* (as illustrated in Figure 14.7).
- **Authentication Delegation tab:** Method used by the Forefront Edge line to authenticate to the published web server = Basic authentication.
- **Application Settings tab:** Use customized HTML forms instead of the default = unchecked.
- **Bridging tab:** Redirect requests to SSL port = 443.

- **Users tab:** This rule applies to requests from the following user sets = All Authenticated Users.
- **Schedule tab:** Schedule = Always.
- **Link Translation tab:** Apply link translation to this rule = checked.

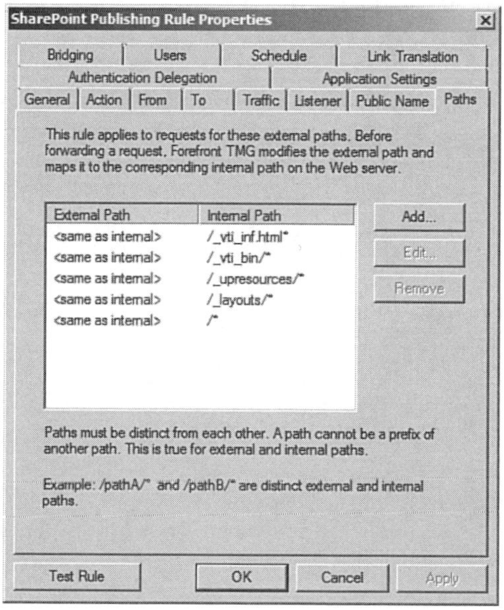

FIGURE 14.7 Viewing the tabs on a newly created SharePoint site publishing rule.

Different rules require different settings, but the settings outlined in this example are some of the more common and secure ones used to set up this scenario.

Monitoring Forefront TMG Using the Logging Feature

One of the most powerful troubleshooting tools at the disposal of SharePoint and Forefront TMG administrators is the logging mechanism, which gives live or archived views of the logs on a Forefront TMG computer and allows for quick and easy searching and indexing of Forefront TMG log information, including every packet of data that hits the Forefront TMG computer.

NOTE

Many of the advanced features of the Forefront Edge line logging are available only when using MSDE or SQL databases for the storage of the logs.

The Forefront TMG logs are accessible via the Logging tab in the details pane of the Logs & Reports node, as shown in Figure 14.8. They enable administrators to watch, in real time, what is happening to the Forefront TMG server (whether it is denying connections, for example) and what rule is being applied for each allow or deny statement.

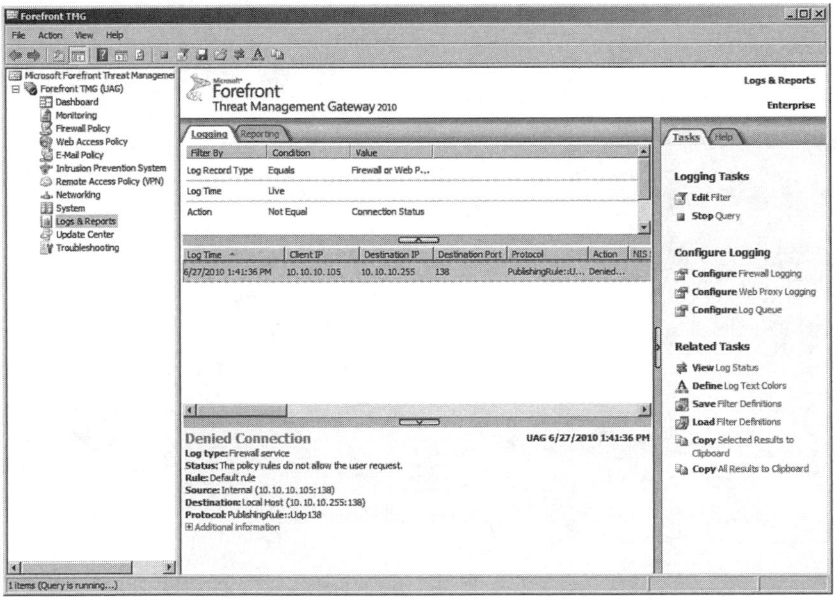

FIGURE 14.8 Examining Forefront TMG logging.

The logs include pertinent information on each packet of data, including the following key characteristics:

- **Log Time:** The exact time the packet was processed.
- **Destination IP:** The destination IP address of the packet.
- **Destination Port:** The destination TCP/IP port, such as port 80 for HTTP traffic.
- **Protocol:** The specific protocol that the packet utilized, such as HTTP, LDAP, RPC, or others.
- **Action:** What type of action the Forefront Edge line took on the traffic, such as initiating the connection or denying it.
- **Rule:** Which particular firewall policy rule applied to the traffic.
- **Client IP:** The IP address of the client that sent the packet.
- **Client Username:** The username of the requesting client. Note that this is populated only if using the firewall client.
- **Source Network:** The source network that the packet came from.
- **Destination Network:** The network where the destination of the packet is located.

- **HTTP Method:** This column displays the type of HTTP method used, such as GET or POST.
- **URL:** If HTTP is used, this column displays the exact URL that was requested.

By searching through the logs for specific criteria in these columns, such as all packets sent by a specific IP address or all URLs that match http://home.companyabc.com, advanced troubleshooting and monitoring is simplified.

NOTE

It cannot be stressed enough that this logging mechanism is quite literally the best tool for troubleshooting Forefront TMG access. For example, it can be used to tell whether traffic from clients is even hitting the Forefront TMG server, and if it is, what is happening to it (denied, accepted, and so forth).

Securing SharePoint Sites Using Forefront UAG

Microsoft's Forefront UAG tool is a full-service SSL/VPN tool that can be used to publish access to multiple services, web-based or otherwise. It can be used to strictly control what users have access to and can be very granular for granting access rights, which makes it an ideal publishing solution for SharePoint 2013, because administrators can define exactly which farms a user needs to have access to.

Architecting Forefront UAG

Forefront UAG is similar to Forefront TMG; in fact, it uses a Forefront TMG engine for the creation of all its rules. You can even access the Forefront TMG console directly from a Forefront UAG server. Subsequently, the same design criteria that applied to Forefront TMG and that are listed earlier apply to Forefront UAG.

The main difference between Forefront TMG and Forefront UAG is that Forefront UAG allows for the creation of a "trunk," which is essentially a web page that users hit first that forces them to authenticate and, when authenticated, allows them to have access to various applications through different links on that page. One user will see different applications on that page than another user, depending on their rights.

Creating a SharePoint Application within a UAG Trunk

An HTTP or (preferably) HTTPS trunk needs to be created before an application such as SharePoint can be defined. Creation of this trunk is outside the scope of this book, but more information can be found at Microsoft.com/forefront on the configuration of HTTPS trunks for Forefront UAG.

From within the trunk, shown in Figure 14.9, multiple "applications" can be created, such as one for SharePoint. To add SharePoint as an application to a trunk, follow these steps:

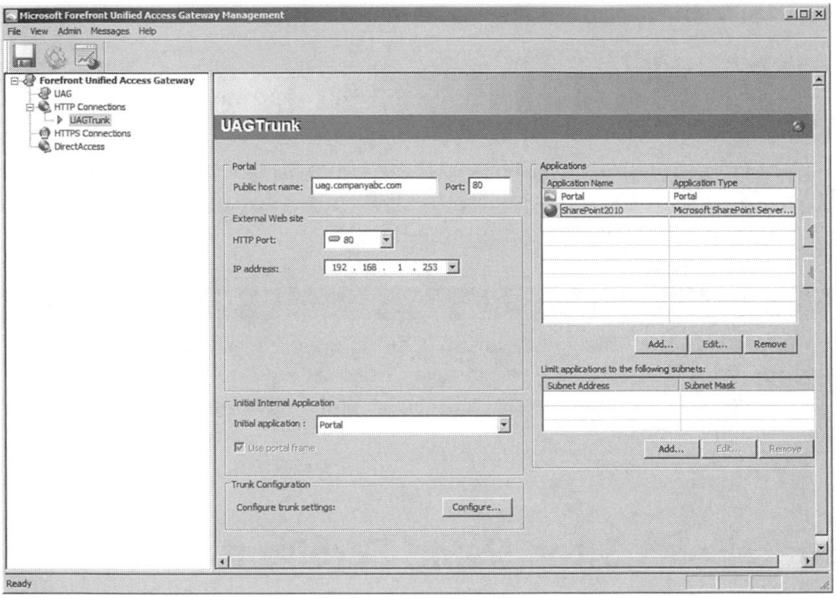

FIGURE 14.9 Viewing a Forefront UAG trunk for a SharePoint site.

1. From within the trunk, such as the one shown in Figure 14.9, click Add to add a new application.
2. Click Next at the welcome screen.
3. From the Select Application dialog box, select Microsoft SharePoint Server 2010 under the type Web. (Note that there is currently no dropdown for SharePoint 2013; you must use 2010.) Click Next to continue.
4. Give the application a name, such as **SharePoint Extranet Farm**, and click Next to continue.
5. From the EndPoint Policies screen, select what type of policies will be enabled for the application. Custom policies can be created from within Forefront UAG that allow for restriction of what types of activities are allowed on the site. Microsoft creates default policies that can be used as well, such as Microsoft SharePoint 2013 Download. Either use the default policies or custom policies, depending on the situation, and then click Next to continue.
6. Under step 4, select to configure either one published server or multiple servers, depending on how big the SharePoint farm is. For this example, we are configuring a single SharePoint server. Click Next to continue.
7. Enter the IP address of the server, plus the public hostname that the SharePoint environment is known by. (Be sure to configure AAMs for SharePoint, such as what is illustrated earlier in this chapter under the Forefront TMG publishing scenarios.) Click Next to continue.

8. Under step 6, usually leave the SSO settings at the default, unless you need to customize them. You will need to either add an authenticatic choose one that is already established (such as an AD domain control adding an authentication server, click Next to continue.

9. Select what type of link to include on the SSL/VPN page for the SharePoint application, such as what is shown in Figure 14.10. Click Next to continue.

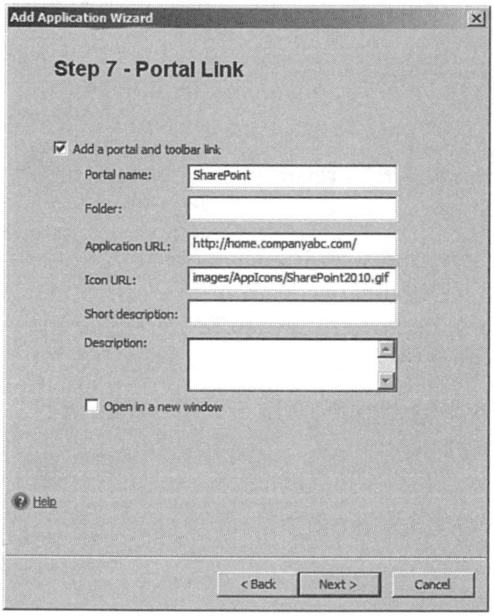

FIGURE 14.10 Creating a SharePoint application within a Forefront UAG trunk.

10. Specify which set of users will be authorized to use the specific application. This gives you the opportunity to restrict who has rights to which application. After making any necessary changes, click Next to continue.

11. Click Finish when completed.

You can create different SharePoint applications for multiple farms and then direct them at different types of users. Forefront UAG can also be set to authenticate users from multiple directory sources, allowing it to act as a meta-directory gateway for multiple platforms and environments.

Summary

The capabilities of the Forefront Edge line to secure and protect SharePoint products and technologies give it capabilities not present in other firewall solutions. In addition, the Forefront Edge line's ability to be easily deployed in the Perimeter network of existing firewalls as a dedicated security appliance further extends its capabilities and allows it to be deployed in environments of all shapes and sizes. Together, these tools allow for a higher degree of security and data integrity than would normally be possible with SharePoint 2013.

Best Practices

The following are best practices from this chapter:

- ▶ Use SSL encryption to secure the traffic to and from a SharePoint server, particularly if that traffic crosses an unsecured network, such as the Internet.
- ▶ Monitor Forefront TMG using the MSDE or SQL logging approaches to allow for the greatest level of monitoring functionality.
- ▶ Secure any edge-facing service such as SharePoint with a reverse-proxy system such as Forefront TMG or Forefront UAG.
- ▶ It is recommended to use Forefront UAG for inbound securing scenarios, but not necessarily required, as Forefront TMG also has significant reverse-proxy functionality. Because Forefront TMG is being deprecated, however, it might be necessary to deploy Forefront UAG instead for new environments.
- ▶ Deploy the Forefront Edge line of products in the existing DMZ of a firewall if it is not feasible to replace existing firewall technologies.

CHAPTER 15

Implementing and Validating SharePoint Security

IN THIS CHAPTER

- Understanding SharePoint Infrastructure Security
- Identifying Isolation Approaches to SharePoint Security
- Physically Securing SharePoint Servers
- Securing SharePoint's SQL Server Installation
- Utilizing Security Templates to Secure a SharePoint Server
- Deploying Transport-Level Security for SharePoint
- Examining Integration Points between SharePoint and Public Key Infrastructure
- Using IPsec for Internal SharePoint Encryption

Microsoft SharePoint Server 2013 was built to be a robust, capable, and scalable environment. Along with SharePoint's capabilities comes the responsibility to secure its vital components, protecting them from attacks and data loss. Fortunately, SharePoint allows for a wide range of security functionality, features, and tools to properly secure a SharePoint farm. Knowledge of these capabilities is a must for a SharePoint administrator.

This chapter focuses on the aspects of information security that an organization can implement to protect information stored in a SharePoint environment. This includes server-level security from a network operating system (OS) and web services perspective, Active Directory integration, firewall and access to intranet and extranet information, file-level security for information stored and indexed on non-SharePoint-managed data stores, file-level security for information stored within a SharePoint-managed data store, user-level security for access to SharePoint data, and administrative controls to monitor and manage user and access security.

In addition, tools and services useful for securing SharePoint such as Internet Protocol Security (IPsec), Active Directory Rights Management Services (AD RMS), and others are covered to provide for enhanced security.

Understanding SharePoint Infrastructure Security

Security in a SharePoint environment goes well beyond the simple concept of configuring who has access to what document libraries and sharing a site with users. It encompasses other layers of security, including the security of the SharePoint traffic in transport, the physical security of the servers, the security of the Authentication used, and controlling what happens to data after it has been accessed. These areas encompass the various layers of SharePoint infrastructure security and are critical components in any deployment plan.

Physical Security

The first layer of SharePoint infrastructure security deals with the physical security of the SharePoint farm environment. Physically securing the servers that house the SharePoint data might seem obvious, but is often not taken seriously. This is unfortunate as SharePoint data stored on a stolen hard drive can be easily compromised. Therefore, physically locking and securing all components of a farm is critical.

Service Account Security

SharePoint is an application that has multiple running components that operate with different security requirements. It is critical to ensure that the proper number of service accounts are used because giving too many rights to SharePoint accounts can lead to major security breaches. Table 15.1 illustrates a service account setup for fictional CompanyABC, with the various rights requirements illustrated for each account.

TABLE 15.1 Service Accounts for a Default SharePoint Install

Service Account Name	Role of Service Account	Special Permissions
COMPANYABC\SRV-SP-Setup	SharePoint installation account	Local Admin on all SP servers (for installs)
COMPANYABC\SRV-SP-SQL	SQL Service accounts—should be separate admin accounts from SP accounts	Local admin on database servers (Generally, some exceptions apply.)
COMPANYABC\SRV-SP-Farm	SharePoint farm accounts—can also be standard admin accounts	N/A
COMPANYABC\SRV-SP-Search	Search account	N/A
COMPANYABC\SRV-SP-Content	Default content access account	Read rights to any external data sources to be crawled
COMPANYABC\SRV-SP-Prof	Default profiles access account	Member of Domain Users (to be able to read attributes from users in domain) and Replicate Directory Changes rights in AD

Service Account Name	Role of Service Account	Special Permissions
COMPANYABC\SRV-SP-AP-SPCA	Application pool identity account for SharePoint Central Administration (SPCA)	DBCreator and Security Admin on SQL Create and Modify contacts rights in organizational unit (OU) used for mail Read and Read/ Execute rights on the ServerCertification.asmx file on any AD RMS servers in the environment.
COMPANYABC\SRV-SP-AP-Data	Application pool identity account for the content related app pool (portal, My Sites, and so on) Additional, as needed, for security	N/A

15

Kerberos

By default, a SharePoint web application that is using integrated Windows authentication uses NT LAN Manager (NTLM) authentication, an inherently unsecure method of authentication that relies on a user's password being encrypted in a "hash" that is sent across the wire. Kerberos uses a shared-secret approach, which is inherently more secure because it does not rely on the password being sent across the network.

Enabling Kerberos is not a complex task, but there is a great deal of confusion about how to set it up. In simple terms, the most critical step is in the creation of a service principal name (SPN) that is associated with the account that runs as the application pool identity account for the web application. That SPN should match the exact name that users use to connect to the site. For example, if your web application is home.companyabc.com and the application pool identity service account that is used for that web application is COMPANYABC\SVC_SPWA_Home, the following syntax is used to log in as a domain admin and on a domain controller, as shown in Figure 15.1:

```
Setspn.exe -A HTTP/home.companyabc.com COMPANYABC\SVC_SPWA_Home
```

Create additional SPNs for any other names that will be used for SharePoint. In Figure 15.1, the additional flat name of home is added as an SPN as well. This is by far the most critical step when enabling Kerberos.

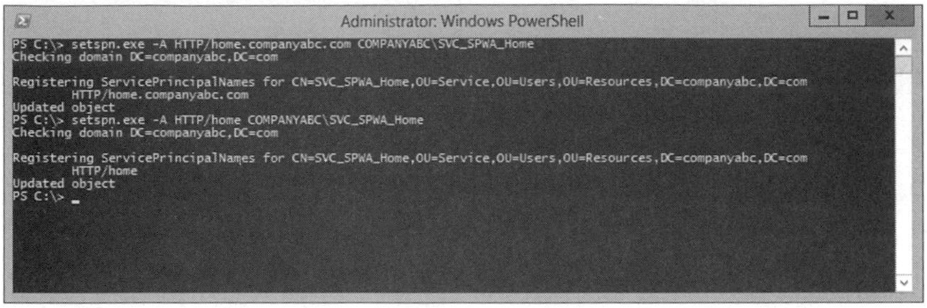

FIGURE 15.1 Creating SPNs for Kerberos authentication.

The second, and often forgotten step when enabling Kerberos, is to ensure that Kerberos is also enabled between the SharePoint web role servers and the SQL instance that runs SharePoint. To do this, create an SPN associated with the SQL Service account. For example, if your SQL instance is MSSQLSvc/spsql:1433 (the default instance running on the default port on SQL Server SPSQL) and your SQL Service account is SVC_SQL, you run the following command on a domain controller while logged in as a domain admin:

```
Setspn.exe  -A MSSQLSvc/spsql:1433 COMPANYABC\SVC_SQL
```

These first two steps (along with the final step of actually enabling the web application for Kerberos) are all that you need to do to get base Kerberos functionality up and running. For scenarios that require delegation of Kerberos to other applications like Excel Services, however, you must complete an additional step. The application pool identity account must be set to allow delegation. You can do this from within the Active Directory Users and Computers tool by right-clicking the account, choosing Properties, selecting the Delegation tab, and choosing Trust This User/Computer for Delegation to Any Service (Kerberos only), as shown in Figure 15.2.

If the web application is not already configured for Kerberos, you must now turn Kerberos on from within SharePoint Central Administration. To do so, go to Application Management, Manage Web Application, choose the web application, and then click Authentication Providers. Click the Default link under Zone, and then change to Integrated Windows Authentication—Negotiate / (Kerberos), as shown in Figure 15.3.

Role-Based Access Control

Another layer of SharePoint infrastructure security comes with role-based access control (RBAC), a concept that relies on the understanding that individual user accounts should never be given direct access to the data within an application. Rather, their specific "role" that they utilize, such as Marketing Analyst and/or Full Time Employee, should instead be given direct access. This is generally done through the creation of AD groups that correspond to the specific roles that users maintain. Those AD groups are then given rights to the data within SharePoint, rather than rights being given to the specific user accounts.

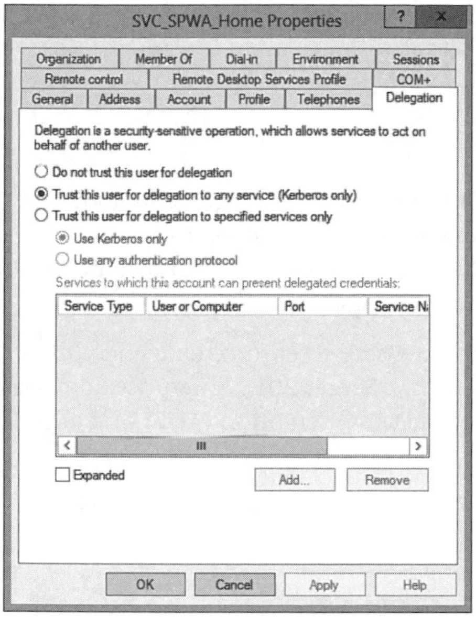

FIGURE 15.2 Enabling delegation on a service account to allow Kerberos delegation for services such as Excel Services.

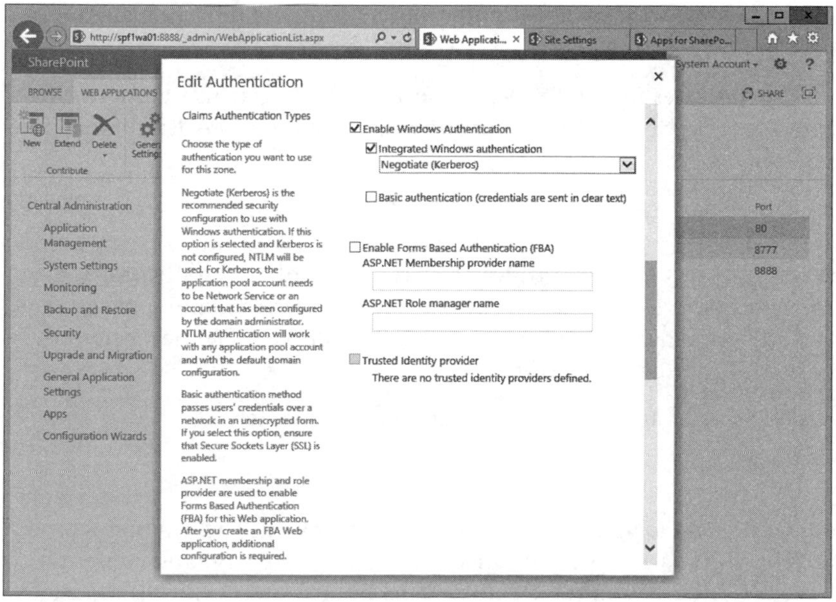

FIGURE 15.3 Enabling Kerberos authentication on the web application.

The advantage to RBAC security is that if a user changes roles, he just needs to be removed from one group and added to another. This also makes it easier to audit if someone has gone outside the boundaries of his or her role.

SQL Data Security

By default, SharePoint data is secured by access control lists (ACLs), but the data in the database itself is not encrypted in any form. If anyone were to gain access to either the SQL Server or the SQL database backups, they would be able to overwrite SharePoint security ACLs and gain access to the data in the database quite easily.

For security and compliance reasons, it may become necessary to enforce data encryption of the SQL databases. Within SQL Server 2008 R2 and SQL Server 2012 Enterprise Edition, Microsoft includes a new feature known as Transparent Data Encryption (TDE) that allows for this type of functionality.

Encryption of SharePoint databases using SQL TDE is covered in detail in Chapter 17, "Safeguarding Confidential Data in SharePoint 2013."

Secure Sockets Layer Transport Security

Protecting the packets that are sent from users to SharePoint web servers is a critical priority, especially if the transmissions take place over an unsecure network such as the Internet. Securing this traffic can be easily accomplished with the use of Secure Sockets Layer (SSL) certificates that are bound to the Internet Information Services (IIS) website used for the SharePoint web application. If you use SSL certificates and packets are intercepted, it is excessively difficult to decrypt their content.

You can purchase SSL certificates from a third-party service or autogenerate them using Active Directory Certificate Services (AD CS), a concept discussed in more detail in later sections of this chapter.

IPsec Transport Security

Even when the transport security of SSL certificates is in place, only the traffic from the user to the SharePoint farm is secured. For high-security scenarios that require all farm traffic to be secured, you can use IPsec encryption to secure the channels between SharePoint farm members and the SQL servers.

Configuring IPsec is covered in step-by-step detail later in this chapter.

Edge Security

Any time SharePoint is directly exposed to an untrusted network like the Internet, you should protect the SharePoint farms using advanced intrusion protection and content filter devices that operate at Layer 7 of the Open Systems Interconnection (OSI) model. This includes devices such as Microsoft's Forefront Unified Access Gateway (UAG) 2010 server.

Use of edge security solutions for SharePoint is covered in Chapter 14, "Protecting SharePoint with Advanced Edge Security Solutions."

Data Leak Prevention

Securing the ability to access content within SharePoint is straightforward, but when content is accessed, it can be very difficult to control what happens to that content. It can be emailed out, copied out on a thumb drive, or printed. Controlling this leakage, a concept called Data Leak Prevention (DLP), is fairly easy to configure within SharePoint with the use of a technology called AD RMS.

Use of AD RMS in a SharePoint farm is covered in detail in Chapter 17.

Identifying Isolation Approaches to SharePoint Security

Various organizations have different security needs. Some organizations, for example, require strong security and cannot tolerate even the slightest risk to their business. Other organizations have a much higher tolerance for security risks and often choose to make a system more functional at the expense of security. SharePoint scales its security well to the needs of these different organizations and provides a wide spectrum of security options that can be suited to the needs of many different organizations.

Arising from these ideas is the concept of security through isolation. SharePoint servers running on an isolated network segment, for example, are highly secure compared to those directly located on the Internet. The following section deals with approaches to isolate users via security boundaries in SharePoint. Each option further isolates users and increases the security offered. With the increased security comes decreased functionality, however. The functional needs of an organization must be weighed against the security needs.

Isolating SharePoint Data with Separate SharePoint Lists

The simplest, most straightforward approach to security through user isolation comes through the application of security on the list level in SharePoint. This model involves the entire pool of users having access to the site but then being disallowed or allowed access to SharePoint content through security set at the list level.

This model, although the most functional, is also the weakest in security. Administrators in parent sites can seize access, and users are subject to potential cross-site script attacks in this design, which limits its security.

Isolating SharePoint Through Deployment of Separate Sites or Site Collections

Granting various groups of users access to SharePoint content by organizing them into sites is a more secure approach to SharePoint design. Users are limited in the types of access they receive to other sites, and searching can be limited to specific information. Administrative overhead is increased in this example, however, as separate groups of users and permissions need to be maintained. It is also more difficult to manage because all sites must use the same content database, reducing the scalability of the system.

Deploying users into separate site collections goes even further down the path of security and scalability. Separate site collections can be more easily scaled out than separate sites because each host can theoretically host millions of sites, if required. Both of these models are still vulnerable to cross-site scripting attacks, however. If a site is vulnerable to this type of activity, a more secure model may be needed.

Isolating SharePoint with Separate Web Applications

You can address the problem of cross-site scripting attacks through the creation of multiple host headers or virtual servers in SharePoint. Host headers allow for multiple domain names to correspond to different site collections in SharePoint. As a result, you can have a single SharePoint farm correspond to http://sharepoint.companyabc.com and http://sharepoint.cco.com and have them point to separate sets of data. This allows for an increased level of security between the sites because users cannot see the data from the other site collections. This, of course, reduces the amount of collaboration that can take place between the sites and is limited in scope.

If you do this, each site collection can be associated with a separate application pool. Each application pool is logically separate from the others and is theoretically not subject to failure if another one goes down or becomes corrupt. This setup also helps to further secure the SharePoint data because users are on separate physical processes from each other.

Isolating SharePoint with Separate Physical Farms

The last, most secure, and also most expensive option for SharePoint security through isolation is by deploying each site collection on separate servers or in separate networks. By deploying on separate servers, a great deal of independence is achieved as attacks and snoops from one site are physically removed from the resources of another. This can prove to be expensive, however, because individual servers need to be purchased, configured, and maintained.

The ultimate security boundary for interconnected networks is to simply disconnect them from each other. It goes without saying that the most secure SharePoint farm is the one connected to an isolated network. Some major disadvantages apply to this, however, because access from any other location becomes impossible.

Physically Securing SharePoint Servers

One of the most overlooked but perhaps most critical components of server security is the actual physical security of the server itself. The most secure, unbreakable web server is powerless if a malicious user can simply unplug it. Worse yet, someone logging in to a SharePoint SQL database role server could potentially copy critical data or sabotage the machine directly.

Physical security is a must for any organization because it is the most common cause of security breaches. Despite this fact, many organizations have loose levels, or no levels, of physical security for their mission-critical servers. An understanding of what is required to secure the physical and login access to a server is a must.

Restricting Physical Access to Servers

Servers should be physically secured behind locked doors in a controlled-access environment. Soft-felt cubicles do not provide much in the realm of physical security, so it is unwise to place mission-critical servers at the feet of administrators or in similar, unsecure locations. Rather, a dedicated server room or server closet that is locked at all times is the most ideal environment for the purposes of server security.

Most hardware manufacturers also include mechanisms for locking out some or all the components of a server. Depending on the other layers of security deployed, it may be wise to use these mechanisms to secure a server environment.

Restricting Login Access

You should configure all servers to allow only administrators to physically log in to the console. By default, such use is restricted on systems such as AD domain controllers, but other servers such as SharePoint servers and SQL servers must specifically forbid these types of logins. To restrict login access, follow these steps:

1. Choose Start, All Programs, Administrative Tools, Local Security Policy.
2. In the left pane, navigate to Security Settings, Local Policies, User Rights Assignment.
3. Double-click Allow Log On Locally.
4. Remove any users or groups that do not need access to the server, as shown in Figure 15.4. Click OK when finished.

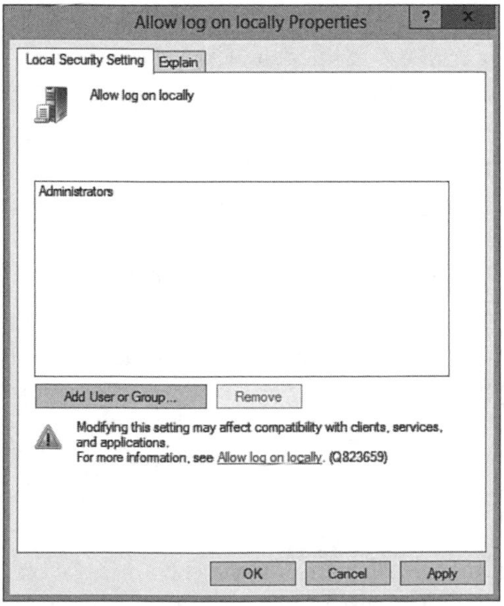

FIGURE 15.4 Restricting login access to a SharePoint server.

NOTE

A group policy set on an OU level can be applied to all SharePoint servers, simplifying the application of policies and negating the need to perform it manually on every server.

Securing SharePoint's SQL Server Installation

SQL Server has a strong relationship with SharePoint Server 2013 because it is the back-end database repository for SharePoint data. All of SharePoint configuration and content databases are stored within SQL Server, which makes it highly important and recommended to follow security best practices on SQL Server, just as one would when securing SharePoint to minimize vulnerabilities.

The enforcement of SQL Server security should be one of the most important tasks SQL Server database administrators commit themselves to. Furthermore, to properly ensure that vulnerabilities are minimized, SQL Server security should be a part of both the test and production SQL Server systems.

Equally important, as a result of continuous advancements made by Microsoft, SQL Server 2008 R2/2012 have significant enhancements to the security model of the database platform, which now provides more precise and flexible control resulting in tighter security. Some of the features that have been enhanced include the advanced security of surface area reduction, data encryption, native encryption, authentication, granular permissions, and user and schema separations. These advancements contribute to Microsoft's Trustworthy Computing initiative that defines the steps necessary to help support secure computing.

At present, numerous SQL Server security best practices are applicable when deploying SharePoint. The following sections discuss some of these best practices.

Windows Versus SQL Server Authentication

Authentication is a security measure designed to establish the validity of a user or application based on criteria such as an account, password, security token, or certificate. When the validity has been verified, the user or application is usually granted authorization to the desired object.

SQL Server continues to support two modes for validating connections and authenticating access to database resources: Windows authentication and SQL Server authentication. Both authentication methods provide the SharePoint application access to SQL Server and its resources, such as the SharePoint farm and content databases.

Windows Authentication Mode

Windows authentication mode leverages AD user accounts or groups when granting access to SQL Server. This is the default and recommended authentication mode, and it allows IT professionals to grant domain users access to the database server without creating and managing separate SQL Server accounts. In addition, if you use Windows authentication mode, user accounts are subject to enterprise-wide policies enforced in the AD domain such as complex passwords, password history, account lockouts, minimum password length, and maximum password length.

SQL Server Authentication Mode

SQL Server authentication, also referred to as mixed-mode authentication, utilizes either AD user accounts or SQL Server accounts when validating access to SQL Server. Unless some reason exists for using mixed-mode authentication, it is highly recommended not to use this with SharePoint and to instead use Windows authentication mode.

Deciding Which Authentication Mode to Use

Windows authentication works best if the SQL server is accessed from within the organization and all user accounts needing access reside in AD. For example, you can use Windows authentication when deploying SharePoint if both the SharePoint and SQL server reside in the same domain or in separate domains that are trusted. However, SQL Server mixed-mode authentication works best if users or applications require access to SQL Server and are not associated with the domain that SQL Server resides in. For example, SQL Server authentication should be leveraged if the SharePoint server is not in the same domain as the SQL server and a trust does not exist between the two environments.

Even though SQL Server can now enforce policies such as SQL Server account password complexity, password expiration, and account lockouts, Windows authentication mode is still the recommended alternative for controlling access to SQL Server. The added advantage of Windows authentication is that AD provides an additional level of protection with the Kerberos protocol, and administration is reduced by leveraging AD groups when providing access to SQL Server.

Using SQL Server Security Logs

Enabling security auditing on SQL Server monitors and tracks activity to log files that can be viewed through Windows application logs or SQL Server Management Studio. SQL Server offers four security levels with regards to security auditing, as follows:

- **None:** Disables auditing so no events are logged
- **Successful Logins Only:** Audits all successful login attempts
- **Failed Logins Only:** Audits all failed login attempts
- **Both Failed and Successful Logins:** Audits all login attempts

Security auditing is set to Failed Logins Only by default. It is a best practice to configure security auditing to capture both failed and successful logins. At the very least, security auditing should be set to Failed Logins Only. As a result, failed logins can be saved, viewed, and acted upon.

Utilizing Security Templates to Secure a SharePoint Server

Windows Server contains built-in support for security templates, which can help to standardize security settings across servers and aid in their deployment. A *security template* is simply a text file formatted in such a way that specific security settings are applied uniformly. For example, the security template could force a server to lockdown Windows firewall ports or not attempt to use down-level (and less-secure) methods of authentication across the network.

Application of a security template is straightforward and can be accomplished by applying a template directly to an OU, site, or domain via a Group Policy Object (GPO). Security templates can prove enormously useful in making sure that all servers have the proper security applied, but they come with a large caveat. Often, the settings defined in a template can be made too strict, and security templates that are too strong for a server can break application or network functionality. Therefore, you *must* test all security template settings before deploying them to production.

Deploying Transport-Level Security for SharePoint

The very nature of interconnected networks requires that all information be sent in a format that can easily be intercepted by any client on a physical network segment. The data must be organized in a structured, common way so that the destination server can translate it into the proper information. This is especially the case for SharePoint environments. This simplicity also gives rise to security problems, however, because intercepted data can easily be misused if it falls into the wrong hands.

The need to make information unusable if intercepted is the basis for all transport-level encryption. Considerable effort goes into both sides of this equation: Security specialists develop schemes to encrypt and disguise data, and hackers and other security specialists develop ways to forcefully decrypt and intercept data. The good news is that encryption technology has developed to the point that properly configured environments can secure their data with a great deal of success, as long as the proper tools are used. SharePoint's operating system, Windows Server, offers much in the realm of transport-level security, and deploying some or many of the technologies available is highly recommended to properly secure important data. This is particularly true for SharePoint content, because without transport-level security, the data sent between critical SharePoint systems, such as the communications between SharePoint web role servers and SQL database role servers, is unencrypted and can be intercepted.

Realizing Security by Deploying Multiple Layers of Defense

Because even the most secure infrastructures are subject to vulnerabilities, deploying multiple layers of security on critical network data is recommended. If a single layer of security is compromised, the intruder has to bypass the second or even third level of security to gain access to the vital data. For example, relying on a complex 128-bit "unbreakable" encryption scheme is worthless if an intruder simply uses social engineering to acquire the password or PIN from a validated user. Putting in a second or third layer of security, in addition to the first one, makes it that much more difficult for intruders to break through all layers.

Transport-level security in Windows Server uses multiple levels of authentication, encryption, and authorization to provide an enhanced degree of security on a network. The configuration capabilities supplied with Windows Server allow for the establishment of several layers of transport-level security.

Understanding Encryption Basics

Encryption, simply defined, is the process of taking intelligible information and scrambling it so as to make it unintelligible for anyone except the user or computer that is the destination of this information. Without going into too much detail on the exact methods of encrypting data, the important point to understand is that proper encryption allows this data to travel across unsecured networks, such as the Internet, and be translated only by the designated destination. If packets of properly encrypted information are intercepted, they are worthless because the information is garbled. All mechanisms described in this chapter use some form of encryption to secure the contents of the data sent.

Examining Integration Points between SharePoint and Public Key Infrastructure

The term *Public Key Infrastructure* (PKI) is often loosely thrown around but is not often thoroughly explained. PKI, in a nutshell, is the collection of digital certificates, registration authorities, and certificate authorities that verify the validity of each participant in an encrypted network. Effectively, a PKI itself is simply a concept that defines the mechanisms that ensure that the user who is communicating with another user or computer on a network is who he says he is. PKI implementations are widespread and are becoming a critical component of modern network implementations.

PKI is a useful and often critical component of a SharePoint design. The PKI concepts can be used to create certificates to encrypt traffic to and from SharePoint virtual servers to the Internet. Using SSL, encryption is a vital method of securing access to a SharePoint site and should be considered as part of any SharePoint farm that enables access from the Internet.

Understanding Private Key Versus Public Key Encryption

Encryption techniques can primarily be classified as either symmetrical or asymmetrical. Symmetrical encryption requires that each party in an encryption scheme hold a copy of a private key, which is used to encrypt and decrypt information sent between the two parties. The problem with private key encryption is that the private key must somehow be transmitted to the other party without it being intercepted and used to decrypt the information.

Public key, or asymmetrical, encryption uses a combination of two keys mathematically related to each other. The first key, the public key, is widely available and can be used to encrypt the information. The second key, the private key, is kept closely guarded and is used to decrypt the information. The integrity of the public key is ensured through certificates. The asymmetric approach to encryption ensures that the private key does not fall into the wrong hands and only the intended recipient is able to decrypt the data.

Using SSL Certificates for SharePoint 2013

A certificate is essentially a digital document issued by a trusted central authority and used by the authority to validate a user's identity. Central, trusted authorities such as VeriSign are widely used on the Internet to ensure that software from Microsoft, for example, is really from Microsoft and not from a rogue source.

Certificates are used for multiple functions, such as the following:

- Secured SharePoint site access
- Secured email
- Web-based authentication
- IPsec
- Code signing
- Certification hierarchies

Certificates are signed using information from the subject's public key, along with identifier information such as name, email address, and so on, and a digital signature of the certificate issuer, known as the certificate authority (CA).

Utilizing Active Directory Certificate Services for SharePoint Servers

Windows Server 2008, 2008 R2, and 2012 include a role that incorporates a PKI hierarchy. This role is known as AD CS. You can use AD CS to create and manage certificates; it is responsible for ensuring their validity. AD CS is often used to generate SSL certificates for SharePoint virtual servers if there is no particular need to have a third-party verify an organization's certificates. It is common practice to set up a standalone CA for network encryption that issues certificates only for internal parties. Third-party CAs such as VeriSign are also extensively used but require an investment in individual certificates.

You can install certificate services for Windows Server as one of the following CA types:

- **Enterprise root CA:** The root of a certificate chain that is also incorporated into an AD domain and can be used to automatically enroll clients and systems with certificates.
- **Enterprise subordinate CA:** Must get a CA certificate from an enterprise root CA but can then issue certificates to all users and computers in the enterprise.
- **Standalone root CA:** The root of a hierarchy that is not related to the enterprise domain information. Multiple standalone CAs can be established for particular purposes. An enterprise subordinate CA can be created from a standalone root CA,

which is often the case in security situations where the root needs to be on a workgroup system, not a domain member.

- **Standalone subordinate CA:** A standalone subordinate CA receives its certificate from a standalone root CA and can then be used to distribute certificates to users and computers associated with that standalone CA.

Examining Smartcard PKI Authentication for SharePoint

A robust solution using a PKI network can be found in the introduction of smartcard authentication for users. *Smartcards* are plastic cards that have a microchip embedded in them; this chip allows them to store unique information in each card. User login information, as well as certificates installed from a CA server, can be placed on a smartcard. When a user needs to log in to a system, she places the smartcard in a smartcard reader or simply swipes it across the reader itself. The certificate is read, and the user is prompted only for a PIN, which is uniquely assigned to each user. After the PIN and the certificate are verified, the user can log in to the domain and access resources such as SharePoint.

Smartcards have obvious advantages over standard forms of authentication. It is no longer possible to simply steal or guess someone's username and password in this scenario because the username that allows access to SharePoint can be entered only via the unique smartcard. If stolen or lost, the smartcard can be immediately deactivated and the certificate revoked. Even if a functioning smartcard were to fall into the wrong hands, the PIN would still need to be used to properly access the system. Layering security in this fashion is one reason why smartcards are fast becoming a more accepted way to integrate the security of certificates and PKI into organizations.

Using IPsec for Internal SharePoint Encryption

IPsec, mentioned briefly in previous sections, is a mechanism for establishing end-to-end encryption of all data packets sent between computers. IPsec operates at Layer 3 of the OSI model and uses encrypted packets for all traffic between members.

IPsec is often considered to be one of the best ways to secure the traffic generated in an environment and is useful for securing all SharePoint farm servers in high-risk Internet access scenarios and also in private network configurations for an enhanced layer of security. Without a technology such as IPsec, communications between farm members can be intercepted and their contents easily defined.

Reviewing the IPsec Principle

The basic principle of IPsec is as follows: All traffic between clients, whether initiated by applications, the operating system, services, and so on, is entirely encrypted by IPsec, which then puts its own header on each packet and sends the packets to the destination server to be decrypted. Because every piece of data is encrypted, this prevents electronic eavesdropping, or listening in on a network in an attempt to gain unauthorized access to data.

Several functional IPsec deployments are available, and some of the more promising ones are actually built in to the network interface cards (NICs) of each computer, performing encryption and decryption without the operating system knowing what is going on. Aside from these alternatives, Windows Server includes a robust IPsec implementation by default, which can be configured to use a PKI certificate network or the built-in Kerberos authentication provided by AD on Windows Server.

Detailing Key IPsec Functionality

IPsec in Windows Server provides for the following key functionality that, when combined, provides for one of the most secure solutions available for client/server encryption:

- **Data privacy:** All information sent from one SharePoint machine to another is thoroughly encrypted by such algorithms as 3DES, which effectively prevent the unauthorized viewing of sensitive data.
- **Data integrity:** The integrity of IPsec packets is enforced through Encapsulating Security Payload (ESP) headers, which verify that the information contained within an IPsec packet has not been tampered with.
- **Anti-replay capability:** IPsec prevents streams of captured packets from being re-sent, known as a *replay attack*, blocking such methods of obtaining unauthorized access to a system by mimicking a valid user's response to server requests.
- **Per-packet authenticity:** IPsec uses certificates or Kerberos authentication to ensure that the sender of an IPsec packet is actually an authorized user.
- **NAT transversal:** The Windows Server implementation of IPsec now allows for IPsec to be routed through current Network Address Translation (NAT) implementations, a concept defined more thoroughly in the following sections.
- **Diffie-Hellman 2048-bit key support:** Nearly unbreakable, Diffie-Hellman 2048-bit key lengths are supported in the Windows Server IPsec implementation, essentially ensuring that the IPsec key cannot be cracked.

Setting Up the Monitoring Environment for IPsec Communications

IPsec is built in to all Windows Server machines and is also available for client systems. It is a straightforward process to install and configure IPsec between SharePoint servers and should be considered as a way to further implement additional security in a SharePoint environment.

NOTE

IPsec is highly recommended, although there is a performance penalty. Assume an approximately 10% overhead to use IPsec on network communications. That said, it is extremely easy to configure and highly useful for providing for transport-level security of data between SharePoint farm servers. Transport-level security from clients to web role servers should always take the form of SSL certificate encryption.

The procedure outlined in the following sections illustrates the setup of a simple IPsec policy between two SQL servers that hold SharePoint farm databases (SQL01 and SQL02.) The OS on both servers is Windows Server 2012, but the following steps are very similar for Windows Server 2008 R2.

To view the current status of any IPsec policies, including the ones that are created in this procedure, the IPsec Security Monitor Microsoft Management Console (MMC) snap-in on SQL01 needs to be opened. The MMC snap-in can be installed and configured as follows:

1. Open PowerShell and type **mmc** into the PowerShell dialog box. Click OK when complete.
2. In MMC, choose File, Add/Remove Snap-In.
3. Scroll down and select IP Security Policy Management and click Add.
4. Select Local Computer and click Finish.
5. Scroll down and select IP Security Monitor; then click the Add button, followed by the OK button.
6. Both the IP Security Policies and the IP Security Monitor MMC snap-in should now be visible, as shown in Figure 15.5. Click OK.

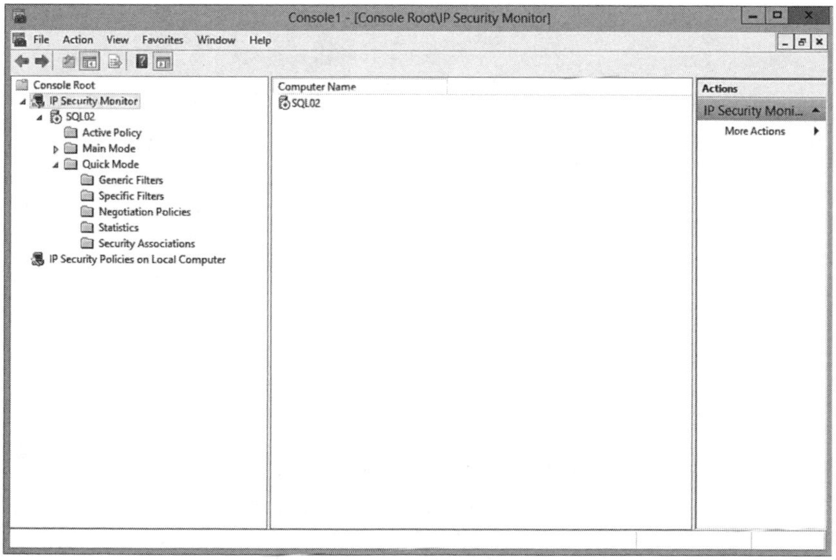

FIGURE 15.5 Configuring monitoring of IPsec transport-layer security between SharePoint servers.

7. In MMC, expand to Console Root\IP Security Monitor\SQL01.
8. Right-click SQL01 and choose Properties.

9. Change the Auto Refresh setting from 45 seconds to 5 seconds or less. Click OK when finished. You can then use the MMC IP Security Monitor console to view IPsec data.

Establishing an IPsec Policy on the SharePoint Server

Default IPsec policies must be enabled on any server in the SharePoint farm that needs to communicate over IPsec. To enable a simple IPsec policy that uses AD Kerberos (as opposed to certificates-based IPsec), complete the following steps on each server:

1. From the MMC console set up in the previous section, as shown in Figure 15.6, right-click IP Security Policies on Local Computer, and then click Create IP Security Policy.

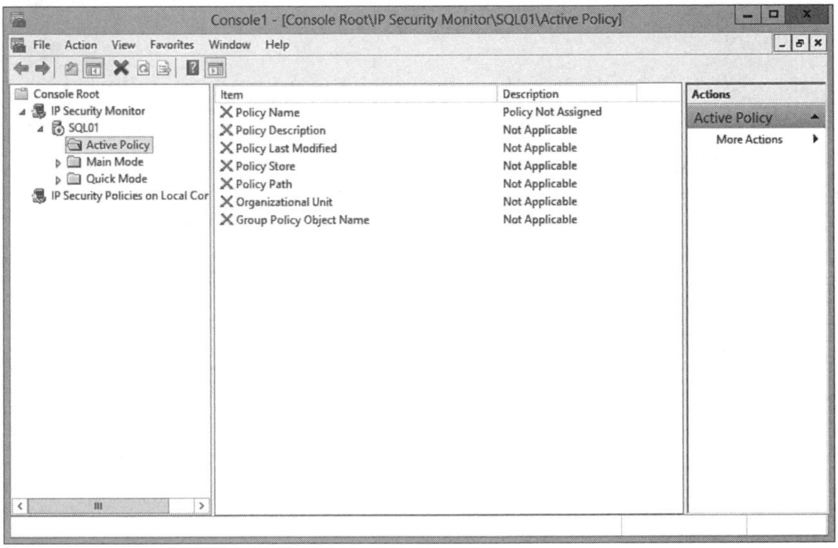

FIGURE 15.6 Creating an IP security policy.

2. Click Next at the Welcome Wizard.
3. Give a name to the IP security policy, such as **SharePoint IP Security Policy**, and click Next to continue.
4. Do *not* check the box to activate the default response rule, but do click Next to continue. The default response rule is only used for down-level systems.
5. Leave the Edit Properties check box marked and click the Finish button.
6. In the Security Rules dialog box, click Add.
7. Click Next to continue.
8. At the Tunnel Endpoint dialog box, choose that the rule does not specify a tunnel, and click Next to continue.

9. In the Network Type dialog box, choose All Network Connections and click Next to continue.
10. In the IP Filter List dialog box, click Add to add an IP filter.
11. Give a name to the IP filter, and then click Add.
12. Click Next at the Welcome Wizard.
13. Leave the Mirrored check box checked and click Next to continue.
14. For Source Address, leave the default at Any IP Address and click Next.
15. For Destination Address, leave the default at Any IP Address and click Next.
16. For Protocol, leave the default at Any, shown in Figure 15.7, and click Next.

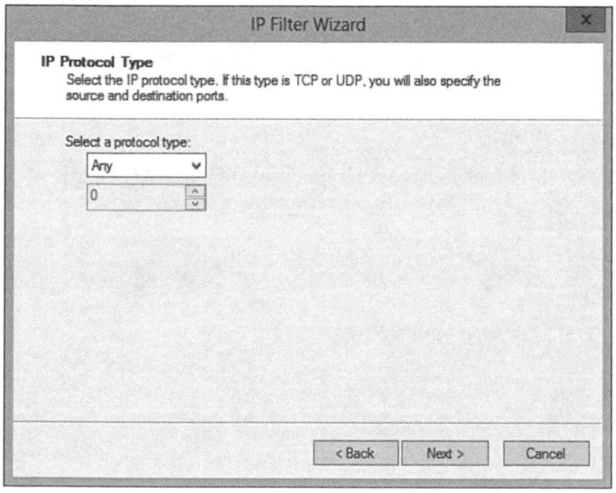

FIGURE 15.7 Creating an IP filter list.

17. Click Finish at the Completion Wizard for the IP filter.
18. Tick the circle for the filter list just created, and then click Next to continue.
19. Under Filter Action, click Add to create a filter action.
20. At the Welcome Wizard, click Next to continue.
21. Enter a name and description for the filter action and click Next.
22. Choose Negotiate Security, shown in Figure 15.8, and click Next to continue.
23. Select Do Not Allow Unsecured Communication and click Next to continue. Note that if you have servers that do not support IPsec, you may have to choose the less-secure option to allow unsecured communications in some cases.
24. In the IP Traffic Security dialog box, choose the security method of Integrity and Encryption and click Next to continue.

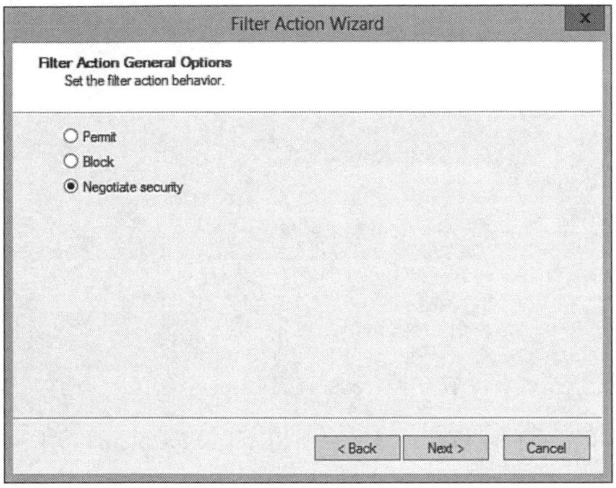

FIGURE 15.8 Selecting authentication type.

25. Click Finish.

26. Tick the circle for the filter action just created, as shown in Figure 15.9, and click Next to continue.

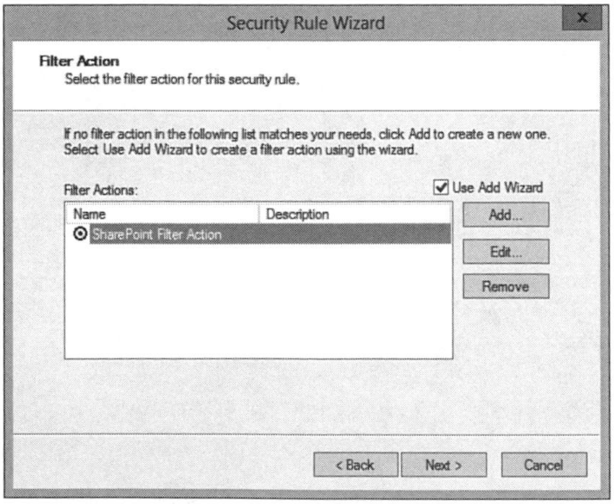

FIGURE 15.9 Selecting a filter action.

27. Select Kerberos v5 authentication and click Next to continue.

28. Click Finish to complete the wizard.

29. The Security Policy Settings should look similar to what is shown in Figure 15.10. Click OK to close the dialog box.

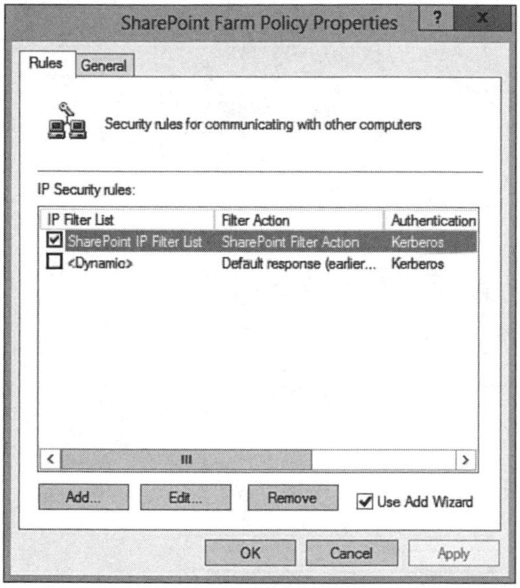

FIGURE 15.10 Finalizing security policy settings.

30. From within the IP Security Policies MMC snap-in, choose the SharePoint security policy just created, right-click it, and choose Assign.

31. Repeat on additional SharePoint servers in the farm.

Verifying IPsec Functionality in Event Viewer

After the local IPsec policies are enabled on both SQL01 and SQL02, IPsec communications can take place. To test this, either ping the server from the client desktop or perform other network tests.

A quick look at the IP security monitor that was established in MMC on SQL01 shows that IPsec traffic has been initialized and is logging itself. Traffic statistics, such as those shown in Figure 15.11, should therefore be shown. All communications between the two servers are now highly encrypted and secured.

These default IPsec policies are useful in establishing ad hoc IPsec between SharePoint clients on a network but are limited in their scope. Enterprise-wide IPsec policies can be accomplished through the use of group policies, but proper planning of an enterprise IPsec implementation is necessary to effectively secure an entire environment using custom IPsec policies.

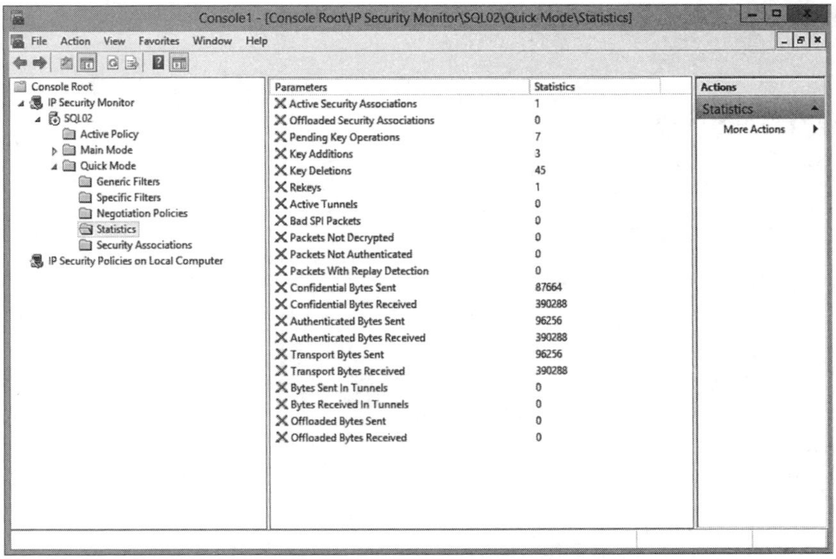

FIGURE 15.11 Viewing IPsec statistics.

Summary

SharePoint comes fully loaded with a wide variety of security mechanisms, tools, and techniques to help protect and secure data within the environment. Without a full understanding of these tools, however, it can be difficult if not impossible to properly secure a SharePoint 2013 environment.

Using a layered approach to security with SharePoint, it becomes possible to deploy multiple lines of defense against hackers, scripts, or snoops. SharePoint combines its integrated security with the security capabilities of the Windows Server operating system and the lockdown capabilities of the Baseline Security Analyzer, allowing for robust file security and physical security. All these options make SharePoint a formidable product, ready-for-enterprise deployment.

In addition, transport-level security in the form of IPsec can greatly secure interserver communications between SharePoint farm members, reducing the risk of data being intercepted and exposed.

Best Practices

The following are best practices from this chapter:

- Use a layered approach to security, with more than one mechanism in place to deter attackers.
- After validating in a prototype environment, use the latest patches and updates on SharePoint servers to further protect the server against attack.

- Use SSL certificates on any SharePoint traffic that traverses a public network such as the Internet.
- Use an internal PKI deployment with AD CS to generate SSL certificates for SharePoint if third-party certificates are not being used.
- Physically secure SharePoint servers behind locked doors and in secure locations.
- Highly consider the use of IPsec to encrypt traffic between SharePoint servers.
- Design SharePoint with isolation approaches to security in mind.
- Use Server Security templates to secure the Windows Server operating system that SharePoint runs on, but ensure that the security settings are tested in advance.
- Restrict login access to SharePoint servers.
- Consider the use of PKI smartcards for user authentication to SharePoint.
- Limit anonymous access to SharePoint farms that do not contain any proprietary information.
- Limit console logins on SharePoint servers to select administrators.
- Enable password and account lockout policies on SharePoint servers.

CHAPTER 16

Configuring Email-Enabled Content, Site Mailboxes, and Exchange Server Integration

IN THIS CHAPTER

- Enabling Incoming Email Functionality in SharePoint
- Working with Email-Enabled Content in SharePoint 2013
- Enabling Site Mailbox Functionality in SharePoint 2013
- Enabling Presence Information in SharePoint with Lync Server 2013

One of the most impressive improvements to SharePoint 2013 is the ability of the platform to directly accept email messages and place their contents into SharePoint content, such as document libraries, discussions groups, and lists. This type of functionality has been highly sought by those looking for an alternative to Exchange public folders and those who want to use SharePoint as a messaging records platform.

In addition to serving as an ideal replacement for Exchange public folders, SharePoint 2013 was built with integration with Exchange in mind, particularly with the latest version of Exchange, Exchange Server 2013. This chapter focuses on a discussion of the integration points between SharePoint 2013 and Exchange 2013, discussing in step-by-step fashion how to take advantage of email-enabled content, how to configure Site Mailbox functionality, and how to use Exchange as an outbound relay for SharePoint alerts.

In addition, this chapter focuses on how to integrate SharePoint with a Lync Server 2013 environment to provide for presence information for users in the platform.

Enabling Incoming Email Functionality in SharePoint

As previously mentioned, SharePoint 2013 can process inbound email messages and accept them and their attachments as content for SharePoint document libraries, lists, and discussion groups. Indeed, SharePoint technically does not require the use of Exchange for this component, as it utilizes its own Simple Mail Transfer Protocol (SMTP) virtual server that it can use to accept email from any SMTP server, including non-Exchange boxes.

Integration with Exchange, however, has significant advantages for SharePoint. Most notably, new email-enabled content within SharePoint can be configured to have contacts within Exchange automatically created within a specific organizational unit (OU) in Active Directory (AD). This makes it so that email administrators don't need to maintain the email addresses associated with each SharePoint list or document library in the farm.

Installing the SMTP Server Service on the SharePoint Server

The first step to setting up a SharePoint server as an inbound email platform is to install the SMTP Server service on the SharePoint server. This service is usually installed on the server or servers running the web role. To install the SMTP Server service on the server, complete the following steps. (These steps assume Windows Server 2012, though they are nearly identical for Windows Server 2008 R2.)

1. Open Server Manager.
2. Under Configure This Local Server, click Add Roles and Features.
3. Click Next in the Before You Begin dialog box.
4. Choose Role-Based or Feature-Based Installation and click Next.
5. Select the server from the server pool and click Next.
6. Click Next at the Select Roles dialog box. (Do not select anything.)
7. At the Select Features dialog box, scroll down and select SMTP Server from the list of features.
8. From the dialog box shown in Figure 16.1, choose to add the required role services.
9. Click Next to continue.
10. In the Confirm Installation dialog box, shown in Figure 16.2, click Install to install the SMTP Server feature on the server.
11. Click Close when complete. Repeat for any remaining web front ends where the incoming email feature will be supported.

FIGURE 16.1 Adding the SMTP Server feature to a SharePoint server.

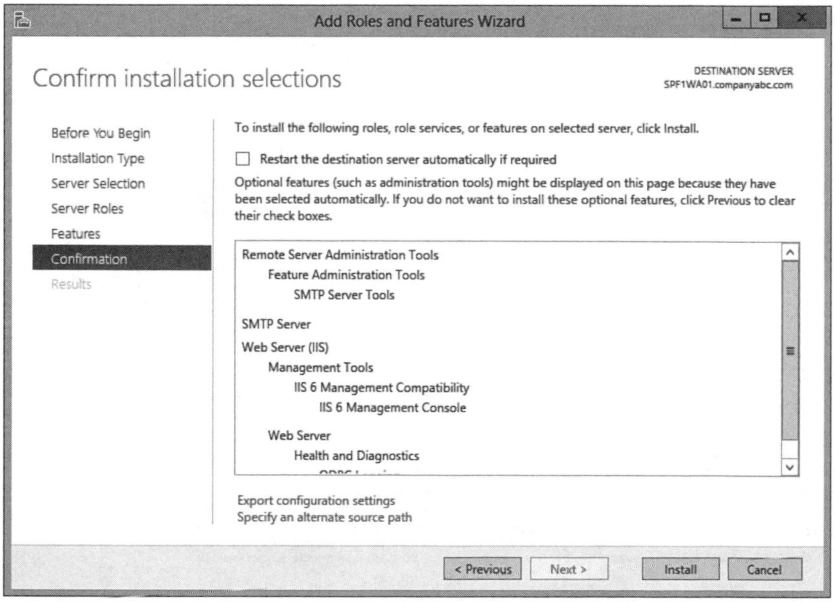

FIGURE 16.2 Finalizing the installation of the SMTP Server feature on a SharePoint server.

16

Configuring the Incoming Email Server Role on the SharePoint Server

After the SMTP Service has been installed on the server, inbound email can be enabled through the SharePoint Central Admin tool. Incoming email functionality can be configured in two ways: automatic mode or advanced mode. Automatic mode sets up inbound mail access using default settings, whereas advanced mode allows for more complex configuration to take place, but should only be used if the SMTP service is not used to receive incoming email, but rather the server is configured to point to a different SMTP server. To enable incoming email functionality in a SharePoint farm and configure it with the most ideal options, follow these steps:

1. Open the SharePoint Central Administration tool from the server console.
2. Click the System Settings link in the navigation bar.
3. Under E-Mail and Text Messages (SMS), click the Configure Incoming E-Mail Settings link.
4. In the Configure Incoming E-Mail Settings dialog box, shown in Figure 16.3, click Yes to enable sites on the server to receive email.

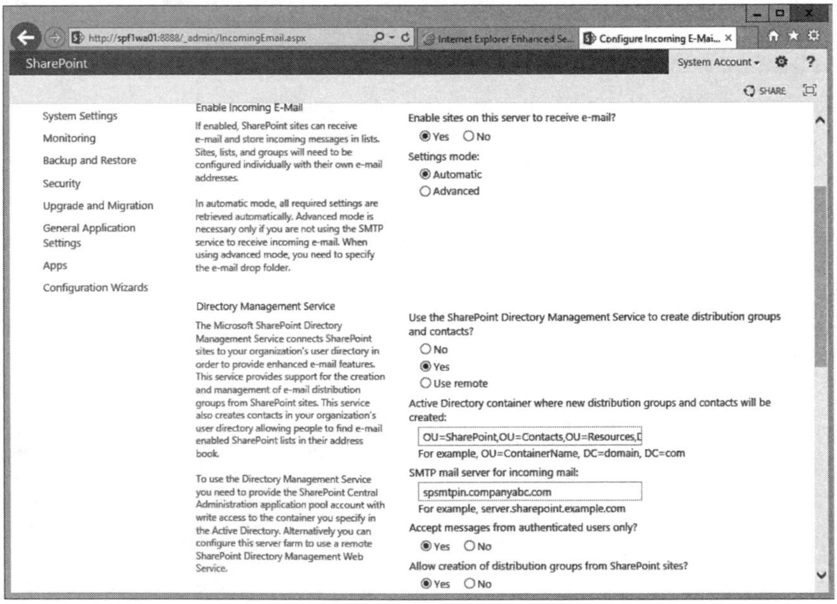

FIGURE 16.3 Enabling incoming email for a farm.

5. Set the Settings mode to Automatic.
6. Select Yes to use the SharePoint Directory Management Service.
7. Enter an AD OU where the new distribution groups and contact objects for SharePoint will be created. This OU must be created in AD in advance, and the user

account that runs as the application pool identity account for the SharePoint Central Administration web application needs to be granted the rights to create and modify user/group objects within this OU. The OU must be listed in Lightweight Directory Access Protocol (LDAP) format (for example, OU=SharePoint, OU=Contacts, OU=Resources, DC=companyabc, DC=com).

8. Enter the SMTP mail server for incoming mail, which will be the SharePoint server name in this example. This could also be an alias name, such as spsmtpin.companyabc.com that points to a load-balanced IP address that is shared by multiple SharePoint web role servers that run the SMTP service.

9. Under the setting for accepting messages from authenticated users only, click Yes, so that only authenticated domain users can send email to the server. This setting can be changed to No if you want to accept anonymous email from the Internet into the site content.

10. Scroll down in the page, and examine the settings listed in Figure 16.4. Check to allow the creation of distribution groups from SharePoint sites.

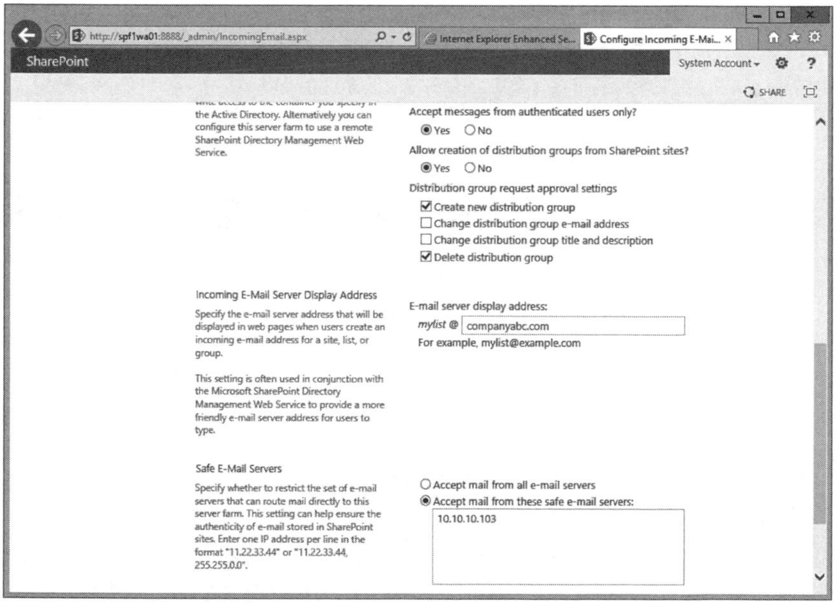

FIGURE 16.4 Finalizing incoming email settings for a farm.

11. Enter a display address for the incoming email server; it should match the domain alias of the organization. An SMTP address policy must also be created in Exchange to match this domain name if it doesn't already exist.

12. Finally, configure which email servers SharePoint will accept email from. Enter the IP address of any Exchange hub transport servers that will be relaying mail to

SharePoint. In this example, 10.10.10.103 is the IP address of the Exchange hub transport server.

13. Click OK to save the changes.

Using the Directory Management Service

The Directory Management Service in SharePoint 2013 uses a timer job within SharePoint to automate the creation of contact objects. These contacts are automatically created to allow inbound mail to document libraries or lists within SharePoint to be automatically enabled.

For example, when a document library called Companyabc-doclib is created and selected to be email-enabled, the SharePoint Directory Management Service automatically creates a contact object in AD that has a primary SMTP address of doclib@spsmtpin.companyabc.com, in this example. This contact then inherits a secondary SMTP address of doclib@companyabc.com through Exchange policies. These policies need to be set up if they are not already in place.

After the contact is automatically created, users can send email to this address and have it flow through the Exchange server, which then forwards it to the SharePoint server (the primary SMTP address). It is then accepted into the SMTP virtual server on the SharePoint server, and then imported into SharePoint via a timer job that runs on the server. In this way, all emails sent to that address appear in the companyabc-doclib document library.

NOTE

For the Directory Management Service to work, the account that runs as the SharePoint Central Admin application pool identity account needs to have add and modify rights to the OU that is specified under the Incoming Email Settings page. If this account does not have rights to the OU, automation of these contacts fails.

Working with Email-Enabled Content in SharePoint 2013

After the SharePoint server has been set up to allow inbound SMTP messages, specific SharePoint lists and document libraries can be configured to store the contents of the email messages, the attachments in the messages, or both.

Using Email-Enabled Document Libraries

To email-enable a document library in a SharePoint site, follow these steps:

1. From the document library, click the Library tab; then select the Library Settings button from the ribbon.
2. Under the Communications category, click the Incoming E-Mail Settings link.

3. From the Incoming E-Mail Settings for the document library, check to allow the doc library to receive email, as shown in Figure 16.5.

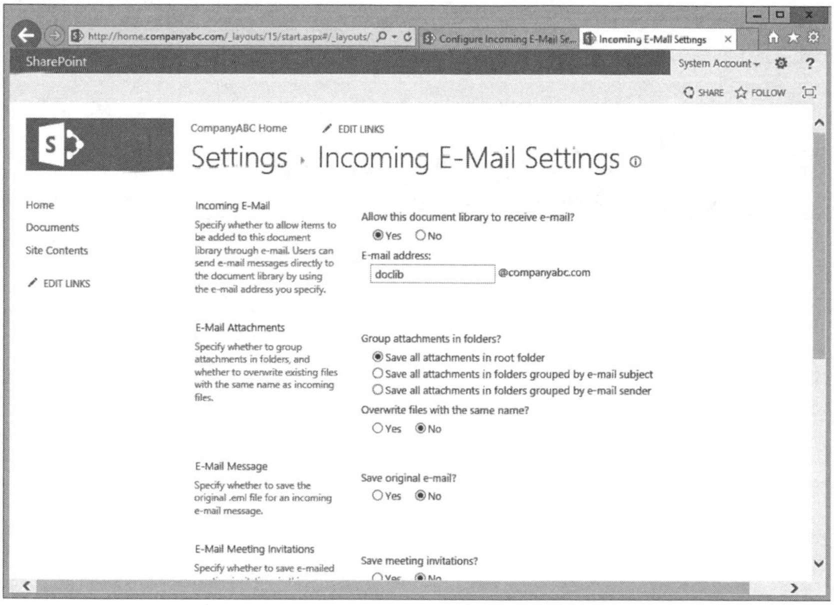

FIGURE 16.5 Enabling incoming email on a document library.

4. Enter an email address. This email address will be added to the contact object that will be created in AD.
5. Select how to handle attachments, whether to save the original .eml file, and what type of security policy you will set on the document library. If messages can be received from any sender, this may open up the document library to spam.
6. Click OK. After the contact object is created, usually within a few minutes, the document library is ready to accept messages.

You can follow this same process for any document library or list within the SharePoint farm.

Using an Exchange Server as an Outgoing Email Server for SharePoint

SharePoint needs an external SMTP server to provide for relaying alerts and reports to farm users. This server needs to be configured to allow access and relaying from the SharePoint server. To set up an outgoing email source within a SharePoint farm, complete the following steps:

1. Open the SharePoint Central Administration tool from the server console.
2. Click the System Settings link in the navigation bar.

16

3. Under E-Mail and Text Messages (SMS), click the Configure Outgoing E-Mail Settings link.

4. From the page shown in Figure 16.6, enter the fully qualified domain name (FQDN) of the Outbound SMTP Server (the Exchange server). Enter a From Address and a Reply-to Address, and leave the Character Set left at the defaults. Click OK to save the settings.

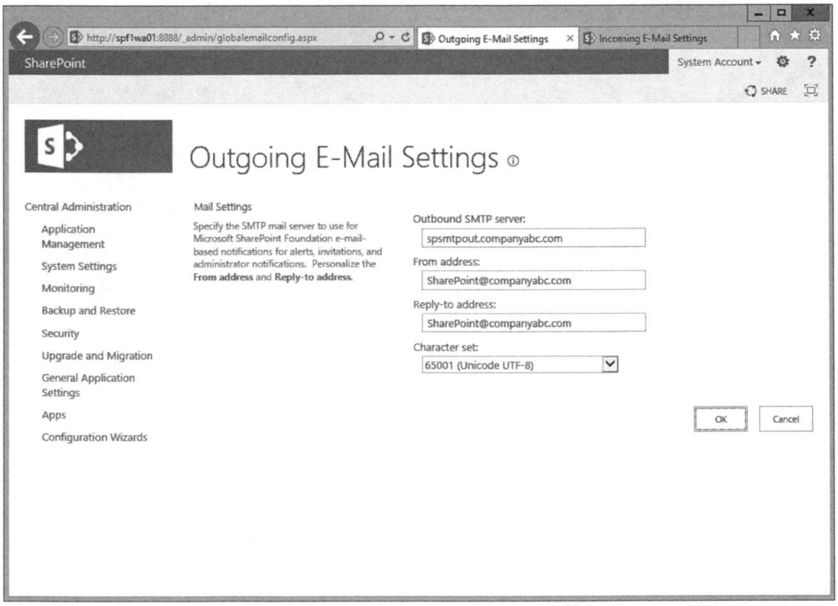

FIGURE 16.6 Enabling outbound email functionality.

Enabling Site Mailbox Functionality in SharePoint 2013

The tightest integration between Exchange Server 2013 and SharePoint 2013 comes in the form of site mailboxes, a new feature that allows a SharePoint site to serve as a repository for Exchange emails and documents. Users can simply copy the site mailbox when corresponding about a project and have all the information within that email thread saved within the site and subject to the compliance policies set on the mailbox.

From Outlook 2013, users can also simply drag and drop documents and emails directly into the shared project space, at which point they are transferred within the SharePoint content databases. New emails and documents also show up directly within Outlook 2013 as new items, just as a new email message would in a user's Inbox.

Site mailboxes can be part of eDiscovery search scopes within Exchange, and their contents can also be put under legal hold. Retention policies set on the mailbox itself are enforced on the SharePoint site itself as well.

Essentially, site mailboxes become the preferred method for a group of people that are working together on a shared set of deliverables. It allows for all messages and documents related to that project to be stored in one managed location that is subject to Exchange policies and legal requirements. In a sense, it is a replacement for common public folder usage scenarios that involve documents, as public folders do not support multi-authoring or version management like a full-blown document management platform such as SharePoint does.

Understanding the Prerequisites for Site Mailboxes

Enabling site mailbox functionality within an Exchange Server 2013 and SharePoint 2013 environment is no small task, and involves several steps around creating the trust relationship between the two environments. In addition, several prerequisites must be in place before site mailbox functionality can be enabled. This includes the following:

- Both the Exchange and SharePoint servers must be part of the same domain.
- The user running the commands must be a local administrator on the Exchange server and must also be a member of the Organization Management role in Exchange.
- There must be a root site collection setup on the SharePoint farm.
- Both the SharePoint and Exchange sites need to be using Secure Sockets Layer (SSL) certificates that are fully trusted by each other. In other words, the SharePoint servers need to trust the root certificate authority (CA) that issues the Exchange certificates, and vice versa.
- The User Profile Service Application (UPA) in SharePoint needs to be configured and working properly.
- Autodiscover in Exchange needs to be configured and working properly.
- Clients must access site mailboxes through either Outlook 2013 or through the SharePoint web interface. Outlook Web App (OWA) does *not* currently support site mailboxes.

Installing the Exchange Web Services Managed API on SharePoint Farm Members

The first step to enable site mailboxes is to install the Exchange Web Services (EWS) Managed Application Programming Interface (API) 2.0 on all SharePoint 2013 servers in your farm. To do that, complete the following steps:

1. Download the Exchange Web Services Managed API version 2.0 from Microsoft (EwsManagedApi.msi).

2. Run the Setup Wizard for the EWS Managed API 2.0 on the SharePoint server, which prompts you for a location to install the files. Alternatively, you can install the files from the command prompt by using the following syntax:

```
msiexec /i EwsManagedApi.msi
addlocal="ExchangeWebServicesApi_Feature,ExchangeWebServicesApi_Gac"
```

3. Run `iisreset /noforce` from the command prompt to reset Internet Information Services (IIS) on the SharePoint server after the installation.

Establishing SSL Trusts for Both SharePoint and Exchange

As mentioned earlier, both the SharePoint servers and the Exchange servers need to trust the root CA that issued both the Exchange SSL certificate and the SSL certificate for SharePoint (required for this configuration). If not, you need to complete the following steps on both the SharePoint and the Exchange servers:

1. Open Microsoft Internet Explorer and navigate to the SSL secured website on the other server. (That is, from SharePoint, navigate to https://e2013a.companyabc.com/owa, and from Exchange, navigate to https://sp2013a.companyabc.com, or whatever URL is used.)
2. On the Certificate Error: Navigation Blocked page, click Continue to This Website (Not Recommended), if prompted. If not prompted, the site is already trusted and the remaining steps in this list can be skipped.
3. In the Security Status bar (next to the Address bar), click Certificate Error.
4. In the Untrusted Certificate box, click View Certificates.
5. Select Install Certificate and then select Place All Certificates in the Following Store.
6. Select to show physical stores.
7. Install the certificate to Trusted Root Certification Authorities, Local Computer.

Configuring SharePoint User Profile Sync

As previously mentioned, the SharePoint UPA must be enabled for the Site Mailbox feature to work properly. Setting up UPA is a complex task and should be performed with care and with the aid of a SharePoint expert, as there are several different approaches to setting up UPA properly, and special rights such as "Replicating Directory Changes" rights are required in AD. If the UPA has already been set up, you can ignore the following steps. If not, the following process describes how to enable UPA.

To start the process of enabling UPA in SharePoint 2013 to support site mailboxes, first turn on the UPA by navigating to SharePoint Central Admin. Click System Settings, Manage Services on Server; click User Profile Synchronization Service Application, click

Start Service, and then enter the service account username and password. An IIS reset will need to be performed on the server after this step is complete.

After enabling the UPA, start a full sync by navigating to SharePoint Central Administration, Application Management, Manage Service Application, User Profile Service Application, Start Profile Synchronization, Start Full Synchronization, as shown in Figure 16.7.

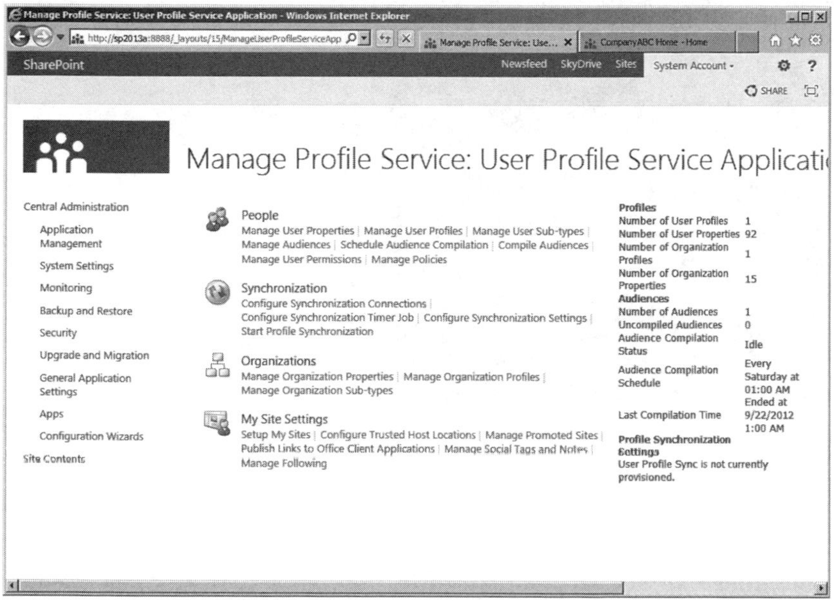

FIGURE 16.7 Starting a full sync of the UPA.

Once again, note that UPA setup is a complex thing, and this example only illustrates a sample, very simple UPA setup.

Configuring the Exchange Metadata Document as Trusted

The second step in the site mailbox process is to create a new Trusted Security Token Issuer for the Exchange Metadata document in SharePoint. To do this, type the following into the PowerShell prompt on the SharePoint server, as shown in Figure 16.8:

```
New-SPTrustedSecurityTokenIssuer -Name Exchange -MetadataEndPoint
https://e2013a.companyabc.com/autodiscover/metadata/json/1
```

(Replace the `e2013a.companyabc.com` with the name of your Exchange Client Access Server [CAS] array.)

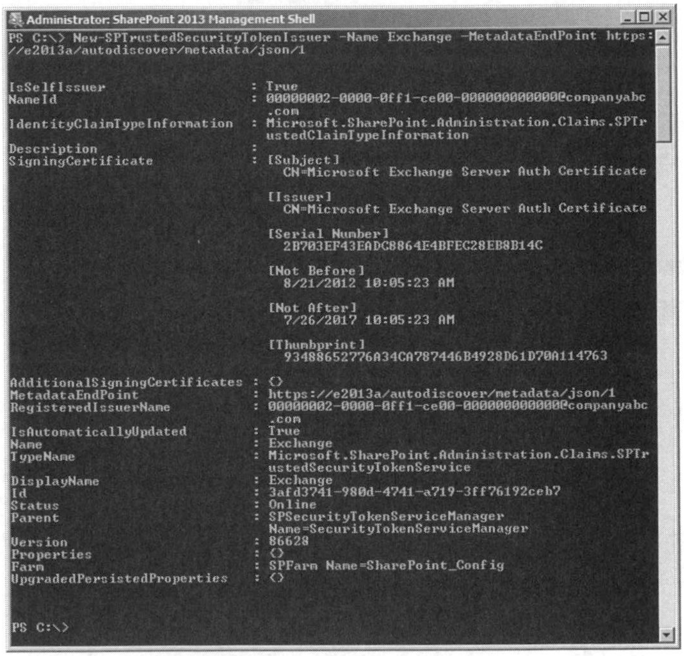

FIGURE 16.8 Configuring the Exchange Metadata document as trusted as part of a site mailbox configuration.

Granting the Exchange Service Principal Full Control to the SharePoint Site Subscription

The following PowerShell commands are required on the SharePoint server to allow the Exchange server to have full control over the SharePoint site subscription process. Perform them in order, as shown in Figure 16.9, and replace the `sp2013a.companyabc.com` parameter with the name of your SharePoint web application:

```
$exchange=Get-SPTrustedSecurityTokenIssuer
$app=Get-SPAppPrincipal -Site https://sp2013a.companyabc.com -NameIdentifier
$exchange.NameId
$site=Get-SPSite https://sp2013a.companyabc.com
Set-SPAppPrincipalPermission -AppPrincipal $app -Site $site.RootWeb -Scope
sitesubscription -Right fullcontrol -EnableAppOnlyPolicy
```

Enabling the Site Mailbox Feature on a SharePoint Web Application

Before it shows up as an installable app in SharePoint 2013, the Site Mailbox feature must first be turned on in the web application. To do this, type the following from the PowerShell prompt of the SharePoint server. It can be typed immediately after the previous PowerShell steps are complete:

```
Enable-SPFeature CollaborationMailboxFarm
```

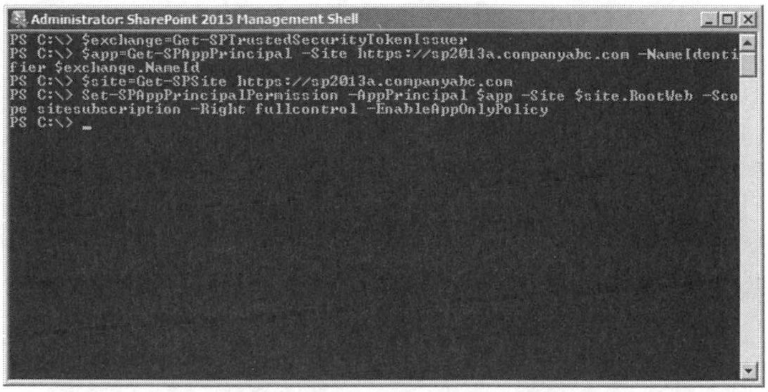

FIGURE 16.9 Granting the Exchange service principal full control to SharePoint site subscription as part of a site mailbox configuration.

Setting the Exchange Site Mailbox Target Domain for the Farm

The next step in the site mailbox process is to configure the Exchange Autodiscover domain on the SharePoint farm. Run the following commands one at a time from the command prompt of the SharePoint server, as illustrated in Figure 16.10, to accomplish these steps, replacing `sp2013a.companyabc.com` with the name of your SharePoint web application and `companyabc.com` with the Autodiscover name of your domain:

16

```
$webAppUrl=https://sp2013a.companyabc.com
$exchangeDomain="companyabc.com"
$exchangeServerName="E2013A"
$webApp=Get-SPWebApplication $webAppUrl
$webApp.Properties["ExchangeTeamMailboxDomain"] = $exchangeDomain
$webApp.Properties["ExchangeAutodiscoverDomain"] = $exchangeServerName
$webApp.Update()
```

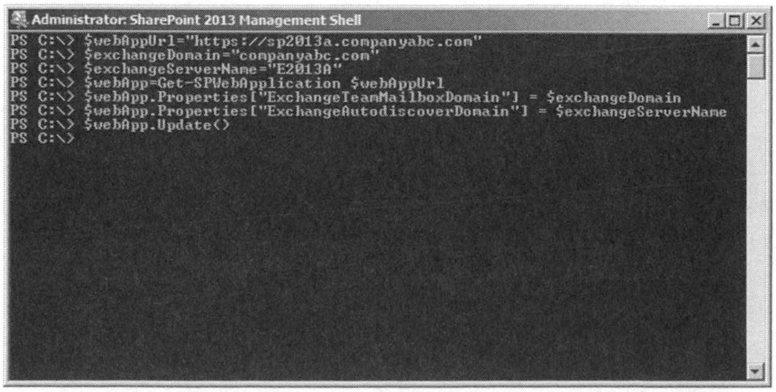

FIGURE 16.10 Setting the Exchange site mailbox target domain as part of a site mailbox configuration.

Establishing the OAuth Trust on Exchange

The final command that must be run when enabling site mailbox functionality is run on the Exchange server and involves having Exchange download a file from the SharePoint server to establish the trust relationship. Use the following syntax to enable this functionality (replacing `sp2013a.companyabc.com` with the name of your SharePoint web application). Ensure that you are in the C:\Program Files\Microsoft\Exchange Server\V15\Script directory when running this PowerShell command, as shown in Figure 16.11:

```
.\Configure-EnterprisePartnerApplication.ps1 -ApplicationType Sharepoint
-AuthMetadataUrl https://sp2013a.companyabc.com/layouts/15/metadata/json/1
```

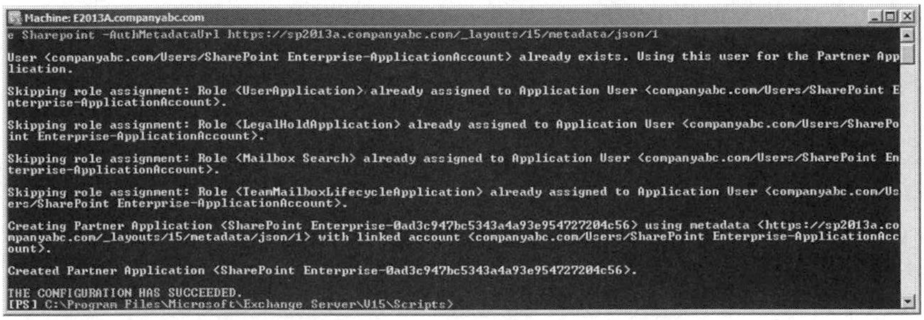

FIGURE 16.11 Creating the OAuth trust on Exchange as part of a site mailbox configuration.

Creating a Site Mailbox

After all the prerequisite steps have been performed, you can create the site mailboxes as follows:

1. Within a SharePoint site, install the Site Mailbox app by clicking the Quick Launch menu, selecting More, choosing Add an App, and selecting Site Mailbox, as shown in Figure 16.12.
2. From the Quick Launch menu in SharePoint, click Site Mailbox.
3. Sign in to Outlook Web App (OWA) with the user's credentials.
4. Enter an alias for the site mailbox and click Next.
5. Click Import to import the current users from the site.
6. Click Finish.

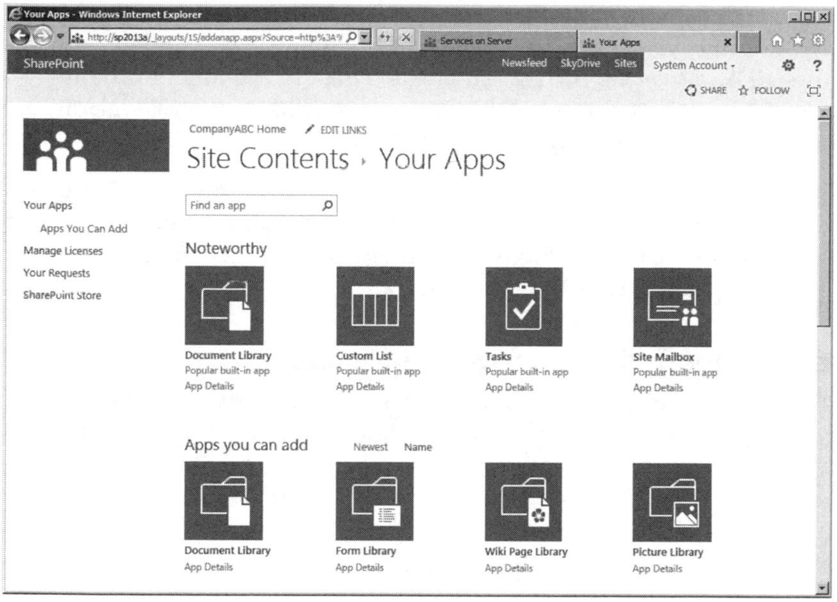

FIGURE 16.12 Adding a Site Mailbox app to a SharePoint site.

Enabling Presence Information in SharePoint with Lync Server 2013

SharePoint 2013 products and technologies give organizations unprecedented document management capabilities, allowing knowledge workers to collaborate more efficiently and share ideas more freely. In addition to its robust document management capabilities, SharePoint 2013 allows organizations to integrate with a presence management platform to help users of the platform to easily tell whether the author of a document is online and available, allowing for instant collaboration with that individual.

SharePoint integrates with this type of online presence information if used in collaboration with Microsoft's presence platform, Lync Server 2010/2013 and its predecessor, Office Communications Server. Using one of these platforms, SharePoint users can more easily collaborate with knowledge workers in real time, using an instant messaging (IM) client such as the Lync 2010/2013 client.

Configuring Presence Within SharePoint

Microsoft SharePoint Server 2013 allows for the ability to readily determine the online status of fellow coworkers and other members of a SharePoint site through the concept of online presence information, displayed to the user through a construct known as a smart tag next to the user's name.

The color of the smart tag enables a user to quickly identify if the user is available (green), busy (yellow), or not available (blank). Right-clicking these smart tags allows for a sequence of options to be displayed, such as sending an email to the user or instant messaging with them directly. This makes it easier for users to collaborate with the owners of documents, allowing for quick and easy communications.

Enabling and using presence information within a SharePoint environment requires presence to be enabled on the web application within SharePoint, and also requires the correct version of IM software on the client. In addition, for enterprise IM functionality, an enterprise IM solution such as Lync Server 2013 is required.

Enabling Presence Information on a Web Application

Online presence information is enabled by default on a SharePoint web application. In certain circumstances, however, it may be necessary to disable online presence information for troubleshooting. It is subsequently important to understand where in the SharePoint administrative hierarchy the presence information is stored and how it can be turned on and off.

To toggle online presence on or off an individual web application, follow these steps:

1. From the SharePoint Central Administration tool on a SharePoint server, navigate to the Application Management link in the navigation bar.
2. Under Web Applications, click the Manage Web Applications link.
3. Choose the web application to toggle the settings on, and then choose General Settings.
4. From the General Settings page, shown in Figure 16.13, select either Yes or No under the Enable Additional Actions and Online Status for Members, depending on whether you want to turn presence on or off.
5. Click OK to save the changes.

NOTE

Online presence info can only be turned either on or off for the entire web application. It is not possible to toggle the setting for any subcomponent of a web application.

Examining Presence Functionality Within a SharePoint Site Collection

By default, any time a user's name appears within an Office application such as SharePoint, Exchange, Word, Excel, and so on, online presence information appears next to that user via the user's smart tag. The status information must be fed to the application from an IM client, however, or else the smart tag is not able to display the status of the individual and appears blank.

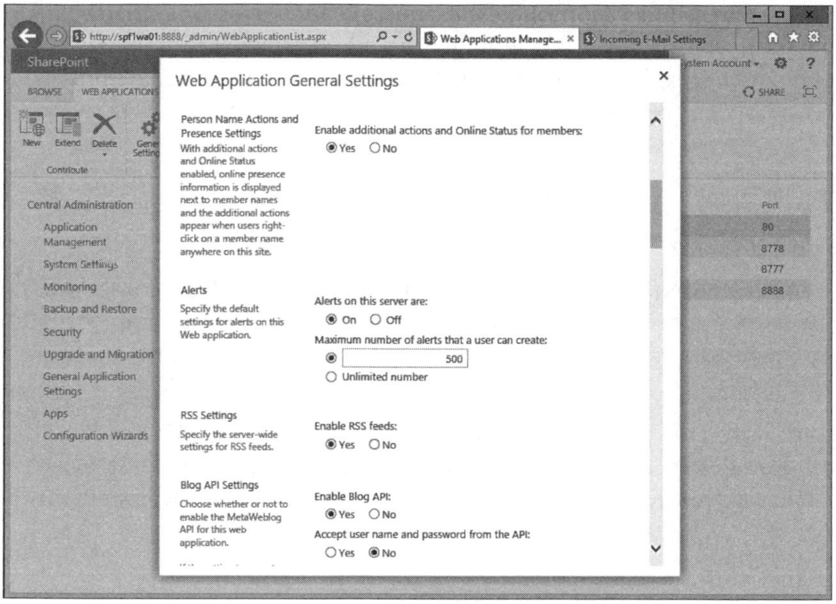

FIGURE 16.13 Toggling presence settings on a web application.

The following IM clients are supported for viewing presence information in a SharePoint 2013 site:

- Lync 2010
- Lync 2013

By default, SharePoint 2013 shows presence only for users who are members of the user's contacts within the IM client. If a user is a contributor to a SharePoint site but is not in the contact list of another user, that user's presence information is not displayed by default. To display a user's presence when he or she is not in the contact list of the other user, a centralized enterprise IM platform must be used in conjunction with SharePoint 2013.

Summary

SharePoint 2013 is the missing collaboration side of the Exchange 2013 platform, providing Exchange users with advanced document management and portal capabilities. With the ability to provide for email-enabled content, SharePoint allows administrators to receive inbound emails directly into document libraries and lists, further extending the capabilities of the platform.

In addition to email-enabled content capabilities, SharePoint 2013 has other strong integration points with Exchange 2013, including powerful Site Mailbox functionality. It is subsequently no small surprise why Exchange 2013 and SharePoint 2013 are often installed together in many environments.

Best Practices

The following are best practices from this chapter:

- Use the Directory Management Service to automate the creation of AD contacts that correspond to email-enabled content on the SharePoint server, but be cautious about allowing users to auto create groups, because this can lead to a major proliferation of distribution groups in AD.
- Enable recipient policies in Exchange to stamp the SharePoint-created contacts with secondary email addresses for the domain in which they will be accepted. If using Exchange 2010 or Exchange 2013, also configure an MX record for the SharePoint server.
- Load balance the SMTP incoming email role on multiple SharePoint servers to provide for failover and high availability of this function. Use software network load balancing if a hardware load balancer is not available. Configure a VIP name for the contacts in this scenario, such as spsmtpin.companyabc.com, so that the emails will be sent to the load-balanced SMTP servers.
- Restrict email messages to be received from only the IP addresses of Exchange servers to avoid having your SharePoint server used as a relay for spam.
- Consider deploying an enterprise corporate IM application, such as Lync Server 2013, to provide for rich presence functionality in SharePoint sites.
- Incorporate SharePoint 2013 design concepts with Exchange 2013 so that both components can fit into an overall messaging and collaboration strategy.

CHAPTER 17

Safeguarding Confidential Data in SharePoint 2013

IN THIS CHAPTER

- Understanding the Problem
- Using SQL Transparent Data Encryption (TDE)
- Enabling TDE for SharePoint Content Databases
- Using AD RMS for SharePoint Document Libraries

Protecting SharePoint data goes beyond simple backup and restore. Protection involves managing what happens to data in the event of a site outage, in the event of a major disaster, or simply what happens if someone gains unauthorized access to that data.

In today's complex data management world, administrators are increasingly being tasked with the management of the entire lifecycle of their data, from content creation, to content expiration, and the penalties for inadvertently leaking confidential data to unauthorized personnel can be substantial.

SharePoint 2013 and related database technologies using Microsoft SQL Server enable administrators to better control what happens to their data throughout its entire lifecycle. Disaster recovery (DR) and high availability (HA) of the data can be achieved through SQL Server 2012 AlwaysOn Availability Groups (AOAGs), and encryption of content in databases can be handled with SQL Transparent Data Encryption (TDE). In addition, rights protection of the content can be enabled by integration with Active Directory Rights Management Services (AD RMS).

This chapter covers these various data protection technologies related to SharePoint. With a fundamental grasp of these technologies, administrators can dramatically improve the security of their critical SharePoint data.

Understanding the Problem

A SharePoint document management and collaboration environment is a mission-critical service for many organizations. In many cases, a SharePoint environment contains the physical representation of the intellectual property of an organization, and it is therefore critical that the data in a SharePoint environment be secure and reliable.

Modern threats to SharePoint data integrity take many forms, and organizations cannot afford to ignore them. Some common issues are as follows:

- **Data redundancy:** The ability to have an up-to-date copy of data in more than one location is a critical requirement because it provides a data redundancy solution for hardware and site disaster scenarios or outages. This type of requirement is provided for SharePoint 2013 with SQL AOAGs.
- **Data high availability (HA):** The ability to eliminate single points of failure in an environment that houses mission-critical data is key. HA in SharePoint can take multiple forms, but often includes network load balancing at the web tier used together with either SQL AlwaysOn Failover Cluster Instances (FCIs) or AOAGs.
- **Data integrity:** The ability to control the integrity and security of data (in transit, at rest, and when backed up) is critical. Technologies such as SQL TDE can help to secure data in storage and when backed up, providing better overall data integrity.
- **Data leakage:** The ability to control what happens to sensitive data after it has been accessed is becoming more and more critical. Technologies such as AD RMS can be used to provide for this much needed functionality, because they restrict the ability of users to print, copy/paste, or send data outside of a company.

Each of these technologies is covered in more detail in subsequent sections of this chapter and are all highly recommended components of a SharePoint 2013 environment.

SQL Server 2012 AOAGs for SharePoint Farms

Introduced in SQL Server 2012, AOAGs are a software solution that deliver HA and database redundancy of SQL databases, including SharePoint databases. SQL AOAGs are a combination of previous database mirroring technology with clustering to provide for both HA failover with no data loss together with the multiple replica capabilities that mirroring provides.

To understand AOAGs, you must first understand the difference between an AOAG and an AlwaysOn FCI. FCI is simply a new term for traditional shared-storage clustering, which was supported in earlier versions of SQL Server. With an FCI, multiple nodes share a single copy of the content, and that storage is failed over automatically between nodes if they go down. The downside to this approach, however, is that if the storage fails or if the databases become corrupt, there is no backup copy of the content to fail over to.

SQL 2012 AOAGs, however, differ in that they allow for up to five copies of a database to be maintained across multiple independent SQL instances. Failover is allowed automatically between two of the replicas, and synchronous copies can exist on up to three replicas. This technology is highly valuable for SharePoint environments because it provides the promise of having an always-available constant replica of SharePoint databases on multiple servers and being able to fail over to at least one of those servers automatically.

Figure 17.1 illustrates the extent to which you can use AOAGs in a SharePoint environment.

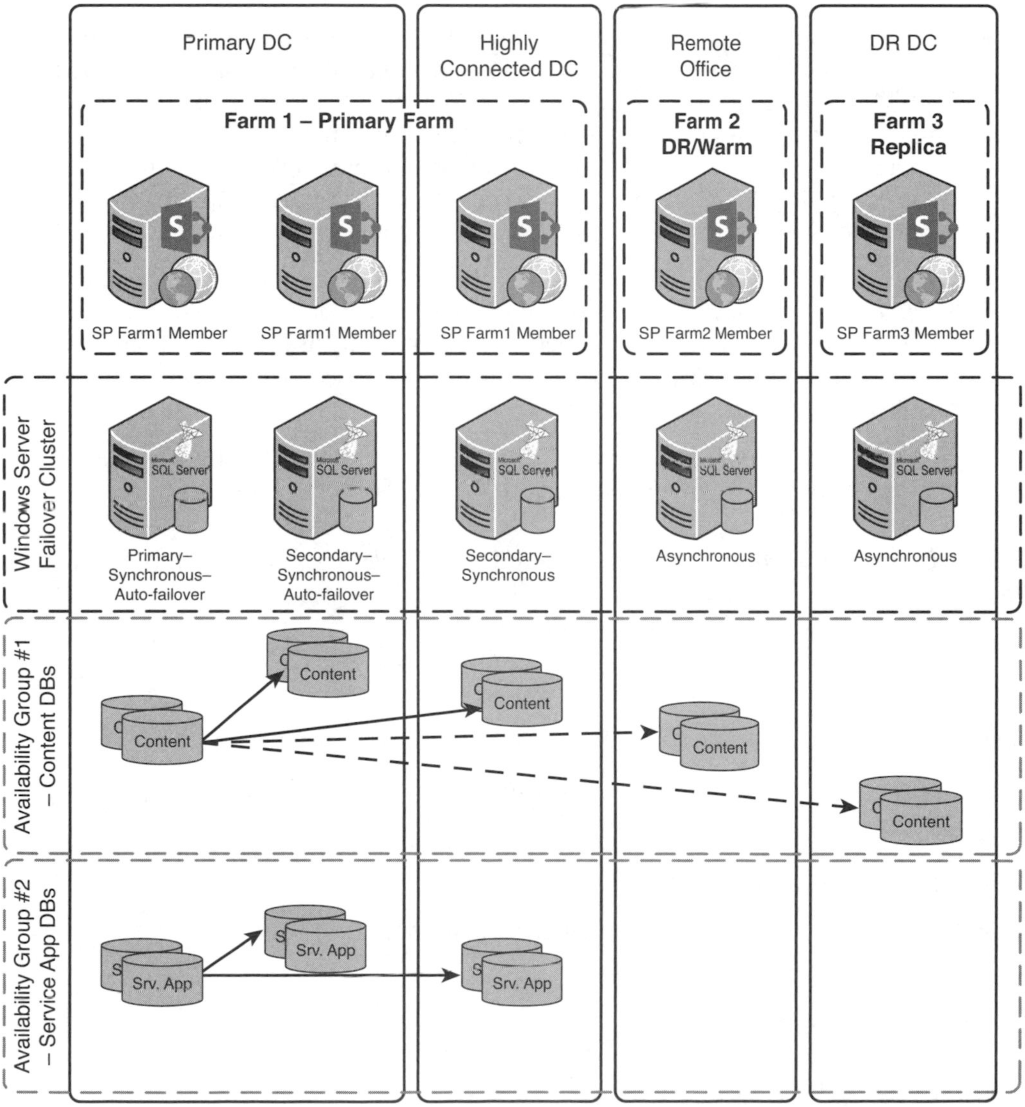

FIGURE 17.1 Examining a sample AOAG configuration for local HA and remote DR.

Note a few things about the scenario illustrated in Figure 17.1:

- SQL AOAGs require the Enterprise Edition of SQL Server 2012 to be installed on all nodes.
- Each node is installed as a standalone install of SQL Server, not a clustered install. This is true despite the fact that an AOAG works within a Windows Server failover cluster (WSFC). The cluster is only used to fail over the name of the AOAG, however, and is not used to fail over disk or network, as a traditional FCI would do.
- SharePoint databases are divided into two AOAGs in this example, the first one for content databases, which are replicated to all members of the WSFC. The second AOAG is used for all noncontent databases, including the Config and the Service Application databases. This AOAG is replicated only to those replicas that are configured for synchronous replication. The reason for this is because only content databases in SharePoint support both asynchronous and synchronous replication, whereas the other databases support only synchronous replication.
- Because only the content databases are replicated to the external sites, separate SharePoint farms must be created to attach the content databases to in the event of an outage. This also means that other strategies must be used for service application failover if there is a need to fail over specific info such as the taxonomy definitions specified in the Managed Metadata Service.
- All nodes that participate in an AOAG must be running the Enterprise Edition of SQL Server 2012; AOAGs are not supported in the Standard Edition.

The high-level steps required to create an AOAG are shown here and then explored in more detail in this chapter:

Step 1: Prepare nodes.

Step 2: Install Windows OS on both nodes.

Step 3: Patch and update with critical patches and AlwaysOn patches.

Step 4: Enable the WSFC cluster feature and .NET Framework.

Step 5: Create a WSFC cluster.

Step 6: Install SQL Server 2012 on both nodes.

Step 7: Enable AlwaysOn in SQL Configuration Manager.

Step 8: Create an AOAG.

Step 9: Test and validate.

Step 1: Prepare Nodes

Prepare servers that will act as the SQL hosts for the AOAG cluster. This includes racking the servers, cabling, and so on. Note that the storage does not need to be storage area network (SAN) storage, because SQL AOAGs do not need to utilize shared storage.

Step 2: Install Windows Server OS on Both Nodes

On all nodes, install Windows Server 2008 R2 w/SP1 Enterprise Edition or Windows Server 2012 Datacenter Edition. Following a basic installation of Windows Server, add the servers to an Active Directory (AD) domain and log in to the servers with an account that has local admin rights on all servers and that has the permission to add computer accounts to the domain.

Configure the disk locations to be identical across all servers. For example, if the data drive is D:\, Logs are L:\, and TempDB is T:\, configure that to be identical drive letters on each server.

Step 3: Patch and Update with Critical Patches and AlwaysOn Patches

Ensure that Windows is set to use Microsoft Update as opposed to Windows Update. This will allow for SQL-specific patches to be included in updates. Following this, check for updates and install all critical patches.

In addition to the patches that are provided by Microsoft Update, install patches that are specific to SQL Server AOAGs. Note that you may find that some of these patches may be superseded by newer Windows patches or unnecessary for Windows Server 2012, but it is important to try to install them in any case:

> http://support.microsoft.com/kb/976097 (Asymmetric Storage)
>
> http://support.microsoft.com/kb/2494036 (Node Weight Fix)
>
> http://support.microsoft.com/kb/2531907 (Small Computer System Interface [SCSI] Device Test Failure)
>
> http://support.microsoft.com/kb/2616514 (Unnecessary Reg Key Change Notifications)
>
> http://support.microsoft.com/kb/2654347 (Net 35 AlwaysOn Features)

Step 4: Enable the WSFC Cluster Feature and the .NET Framework

On each node, use Server Manager to install the Windows Failover Clustering component and the .NET 3.5 Framework, as shown in Figure 17.2.

Following installation, check for available patches for the .NET 3.5 Framework with Windows Update and patch if necessary.

Step 5: Create a WSFC Cluster

When all nodes have been patches and prepared, you can proceed with the creation of a WSFC that will encompass all nodes of the cluster. Create a WSFC by starting the Failover Cluster Wizard on one of the nodes.

Give the cluster a unique name that doesn't exist in AD; this becomes a computer account in AD. Remember that this step fails if the account that is logged in while running the wizard does not have Read All Properties and Create Computer Accounts rights in AD. Alternatively, if these rights cannot be granted, the computer account can be precreated.

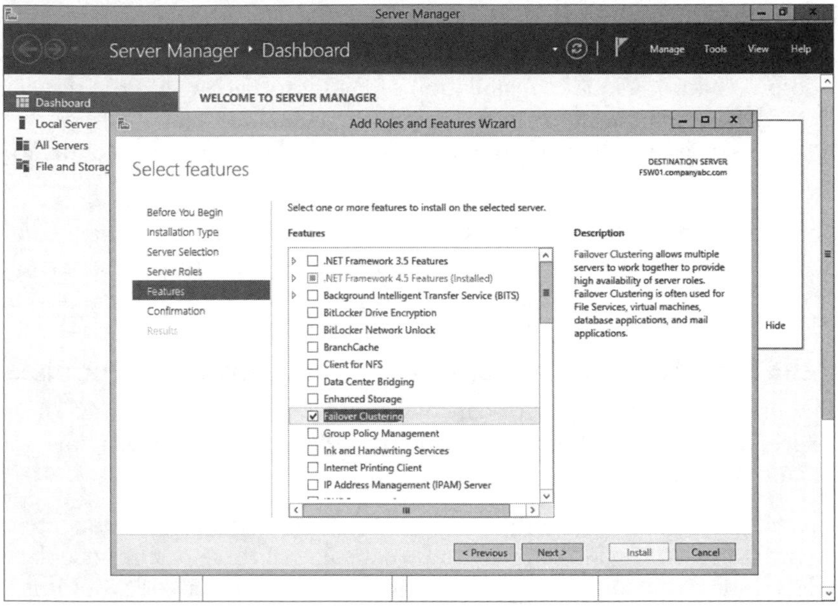

FIGURE 17.2 Adding the failover cluster feature.

Grant the Cluster computer account that was just created Read All Properties and Create Computer Accounts, which allows it to add other computers to the domain later, a requirement for AOAGs. Add all nodes into the cluster.

If automatic failover is required, there must be sufficient voting members to create a quorum of votes. In a two-server configuration, this means that a third server must act as a file share witness (FSW), which is effectively just another vote that provides for quorum. For SharePoint environments, this FSW is usually one of the SharePoint Service Application role servers. Create a share on the server designated to be the FSW and give it a name (usually just FSW); then give the cluster computer account just created full rights to the share created.

Add an FSW (one of the SharePoint app servers) using the Configure Cluster Quorum Wizard, and choose Node and File Share Majority, as illustrated in Figure 17.3.

If it fails to add the FSW, it is usually because the cluster computer account (not service account) does not have full rights to the share. At this point, the cluster should be complete and it should not be necessary to do any more configuration within the Failover Cluster tool. All remaining cluster configuration will take place within SQL Server.

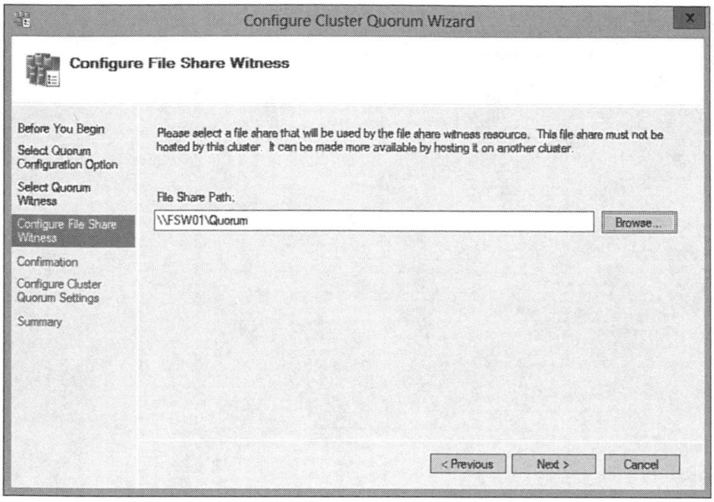

FIGURE 17.3 Configuring an FSW for the cluster.

Step 6: Install SQL Server 2012 on Both Nodes

After the WSFC is in place, you can proceed to install SQL Server 2012 Enterprise Edition on all nodes. In most environments, select only Database Services, SQL Server Agent, and SQL Management Tools—Complete. In addition, be sure to select to install only a standalone instance, illustrated in Figure 17.4, and do *not* select a cluster, regardless of the fact that an AOAG resides within a cluster. Selecting a cluster proceeds to install SQL as an FCI and not as an AOAG.

Keep the following factors in mind when installing SQL Server on each node:

- Install all defaults, with the exception of drive locations for databases; change that one to the DB drive for Databases and the Logs drive for logs. Make sure that the drive paths are consistent across all servers.
- Select the SQL Server service account, make it the same on both nodes, and ensure that it has local admin rights to each server.
- Configure the default instance of SQL (using port 1433).
- Configure the SQL Server agent using the defaults.
- Check for updates and patch SQL on each node.
- Add a firewall exception for port 1433 and port 5022 (if the Windows Firewall is enabled).
- If antivirus is enabled, put in the proper exclusions for SQL Server (http://support.microsoft.com/kb/309422). Follow the recommendations for SQL 2008 R2 in the guide listed because they also apply to SQL 2012. Follow the recommendations for a failover cluster, as well. You should contact your antivirus vendor for the proper exclusions for both a cluster node and an SQL server.

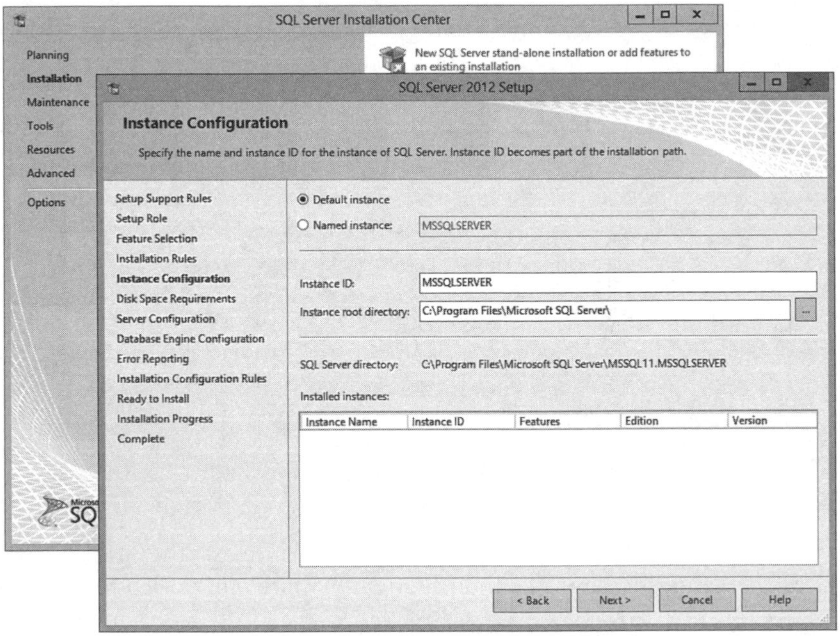

FIGURE 17.4 Installing a default standalone instance of SQL on the nodes.

Step 7: Enable AlwaysOn in SQL Configuration Manager

After SQL has been installed on all nodes, AOAG functionality can be enabled on all nodes. To do so, open SQL Server Configuration Manager and enable SQL AlwaysOn on each node, as illustrated in Figure 17.5.

Restart the SQL services on each node to finalize the configuration changes.

Step 8: Create an AOAG

To create an AOAG, there must be at least one available database to add to it. This can be an empty database that is created for the purposes of the AOAG, or it can be existing SharePoint databases. Because SharePoint would usually be pointed to the listener name, however, it's best to wait until the AOAG is created before installing SharePoint.

In this example, because two AOAGs will be created, one for Content DBs and the other for Service Application DBs, it is necessary to create two empty databases on the first node. These databases can be deleted later.

All databases that enter into an AOAG must have a full backup performed first, so ensure that you back up the newly created empty databases first. When backed up, you can then use the Create AOAG Wizard in SQL Server Management Studio to start the AOAG creation process, as illustrated in Figure 17.6.

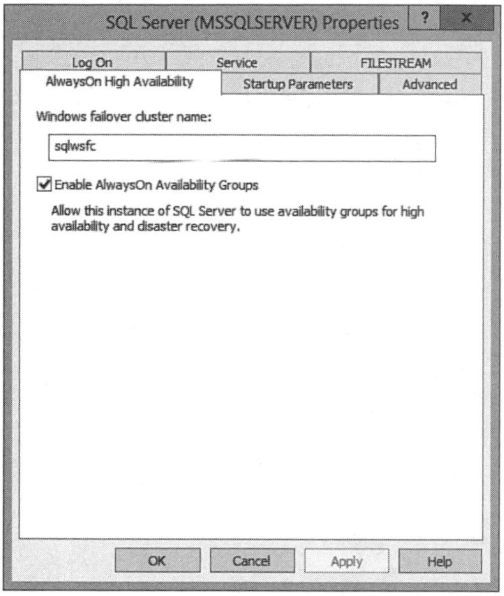

FIGURE 17.5 Enabling AOAGs within SQL Configuration Manager.

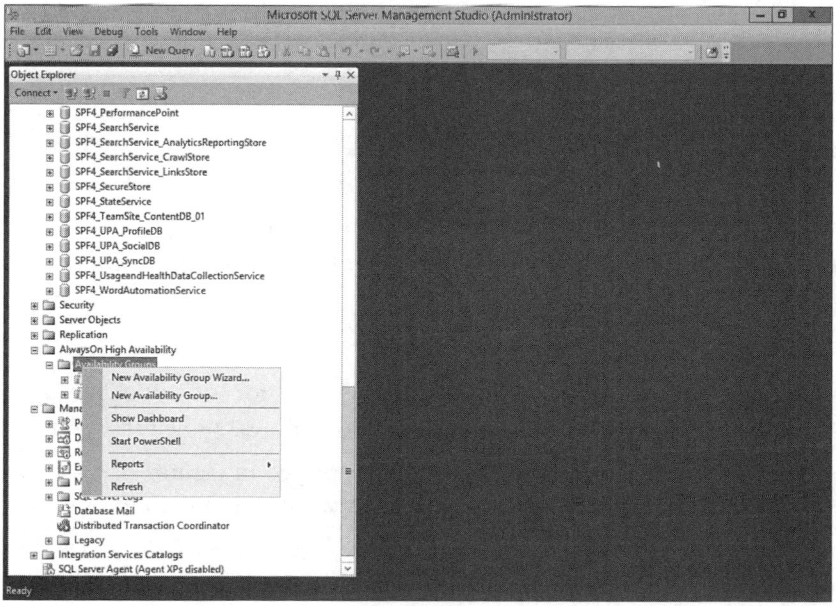

FIGURE 17.6 Running the AOAG Wizard.

Give the AOAG a name such as SPSrvApp, and then select one of the blank databases to add to the AOAG.

When prompted, add all nodes to the AOAG, as illustrated in Figure 17.7.

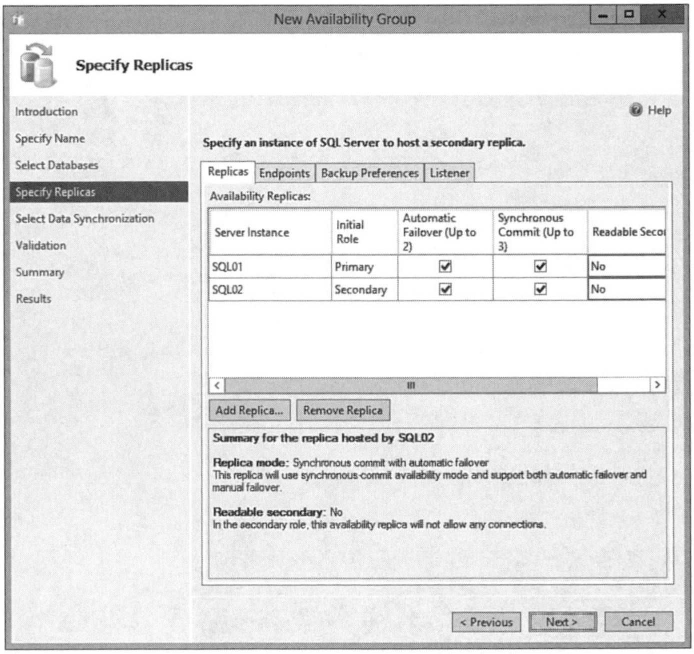

FIGURE 17.7 Adding nodes to an AOAG.

Change the nodes to Automatic Failover and Synchronous Commit (check the boxes) for both nodes, assuming that you want to configure the AOAG for synchronous commit and autofailover, typical for a SharePoint scenario.

Leave the defaults for endpoints, backup preferences, and listener.

Select a common backup location that is accessible by both servers for the initial backup. This can be an existing file share or one you create, like what is shown in Figure 17.8.

Review the settings created by the wizard, such as what is displayed in Figure 17.9. All steps should show up as green except for the listener, which is created in the next step.

After the AOAG has been created, a listener is required. This is the name that the AOAG corresponds to and the name that SharePoint connects to. To create the listener, right-click the Listener node in SQL Management Studio and select Create a New Listener.

Give it a common shared IP address and give it a name that will be used by the application connecting to the server (for example, SPSrvApp or SPContent).

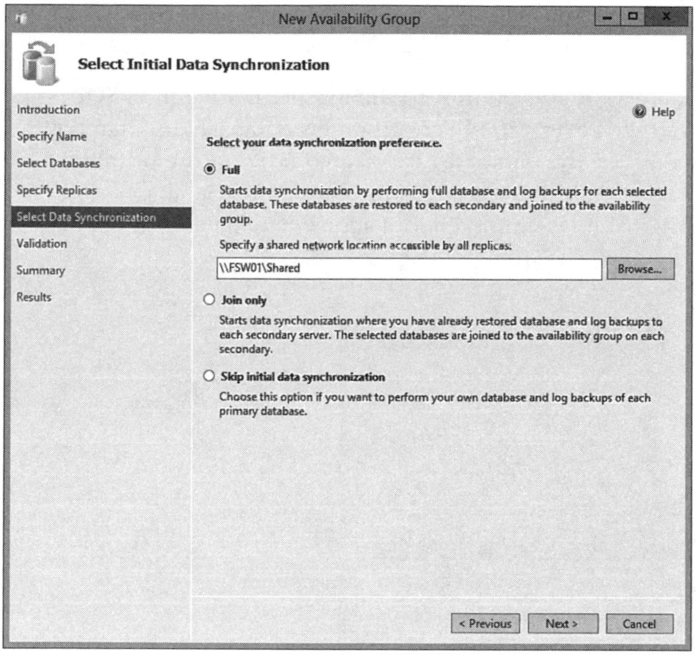

FIGURE 17.8 Specifying the AOAG shared location for the initial replication.

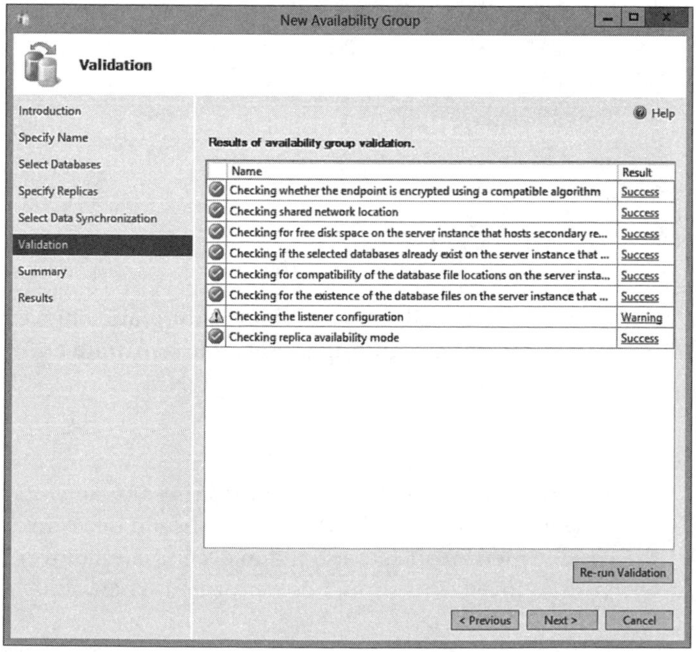

FIGURE 17.9 Validating the AOAG install.

The AOAG should be created at this point. Repeat the same steps for the second AOAG (the Content AOAG).

At this point, you can install SharePoint and point it to the listener name for its SQL server name. Note that by default, however, simply creating new databases in SharePoint does not add them to all AOAG nodes; the databases are created only on the primary replica SQL server. Add them to the AOAG by right-clicking the AOAG Databases node and selecting Add Databases, which allows you to choose additional SharePoint databases to add to the AOAG, as shown in Figure 17.10.

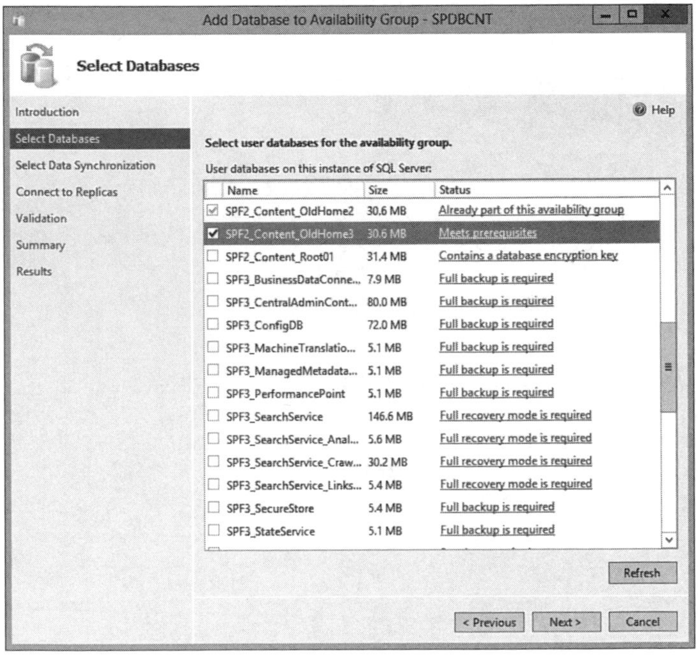

FIGURE 17.10 Adding SharePoint databases to an AOAG.

For a SharePoint environment, following these steps allows you to have automatic failover between two exact replicas of all SharePoint databases running on separate hardware and storage.

Step 9: Test and Validate

In autofailover scenarios, you can test failover of the AOAG by disconnecting the network cables on one server (or pressing the power button on the box). Failover should occur in 10 to 30 seconds, depending on the environment. You can also manually initiate failover by right-clicking the AOAG and selecting Failover. This should be performed when doing maintenance on one of the nodes.

Using SQL Transparent Data Encryption (TDE)

By default, SharePoint data is secured by access control lists (ACLs), but the data in the database itself is not encrypted in any form. If a rogue agent were to gain access to either the SQL Server or the SQL Database backups, that agent would be able to overwrite SharePoint security ACLs and gain access to the data in the database quite easily.

For security and compliance reasons, it may become necessary to enforce data encryption of the SQL databases. Within SQL Server 2008 R2 and SQL Server 2012 Enterprise Editions, Microsoft includes a new feature known as TDE that allows for this type of functionality.

Encryption Solutions

TDE is actually only one of several SQL Server encryption solutions that are available. Each encryption solution works in different ways, however, so it is important to understand first what the available encryption solutions are and how they can be utilized:

- **Cell-level encryption:** Cell-level encryption encrypts individual database cells, rather than the entire database. This type of encryption is not supported for SharePoint databases.
- **File-level encryption:** File-level encryption includes technologies such as BitLocker and the Encrypting File System (EFS). These technologies encrypt the entire hard drive and can be used with SQL. They do not, however, encrypt backups of the SQL databases that are stored on these volumes.
- **Active Directory Rights Management Services (AD RMS):** AD RMS is an encryption solution that uses encryption techniques to enforce rights protection on data, restricting what a user can and can't do with the data (for example, can't print or copy/paste content). AD RMS, covered in later sections of this chapter, do not encrypt the data at rest; it is encrypted only when it is viewed by the client.
- **Transparent Data Encryption:** TDE is the ideal solution for SharePoint content database encryption because it encrypts the entire database while in storage, while being used in the TempDB, and when backed up. In addition, the encryption is completely handled by SQL; SharePoint does not even know that the encryption is taking place.

17

NOTE

The solutions listed in this chapter are storage-level encryption solutions. To encrypt SharePoint content at the transport layer, use Secure Sockets Layer (SSL) certificate encryption from the client to the server, and use Internet Protocol Security (IPsec) encryption for the traffic between the farm members. You can find more information on setting up and using transport layer encryption in Chapter 15, "Implementing and Validating SharePoint Security."

How TDE Works

Note the following key things about TDE:

- When enabled on a database, TDE encrypts the database and its associated log file, snapshots, backups, and mirrored database instances associated with that database, if applicable.
- The TempDB for the SQL instance is also encrypted. This can affect other databases on the same instance. It is therefore recommended to create a dedicated instance for encrypted databases so that they can have their own dedicated TempDB.
- Backups cannot be restored to other servers if those servers do not have a copy of the private key used to encrypt. Stolen database files are therefore worthless to the thief.
- The overhead associated with enabling TDE is only a 3% to 5% performance penalty on the box, so there are minimal server resources required to enable.

The TDE Key Hierarchy

TDE works by establishing a hierarchy of keys. It is critical to understand what these keys are and how they are used to encrypt each other. Figure 17.11 illustrates the key hierarchy used by TDE.

At the root, the Windows Data Protection Application Programming Interface (DPAPI) is used to create and protect the service master key (SMK). The SMK is unique to each server and does not need to be backed up or recovered on any other systems. The SMK is then used to create and protect the database master key (DMK). The DMK is then used to create and protect the TDE certificate, which in turn is used to create a database encryption key (DEK), which encrypts the content DB itself.

TDE Requirements and Limitations

You need to be aware of a few requirements and limitations to TDE in advance of its deployment:

- The Enterprise Edition of SQL Server is required for TDE. This version of SQL Server is considerably more expensive than the Standard Edition.
- TDE does not encrypt the communication channel. IPsec is the solution for this.
- TDE cannot take advantage of SQL 2008 RTM/R2 backup compression.
- Replication or FILESTREAM data is not encrypted when TDE is enabled.
- The TempDB is encrypted for the entire instance, even if only one database is enabled for TDE.

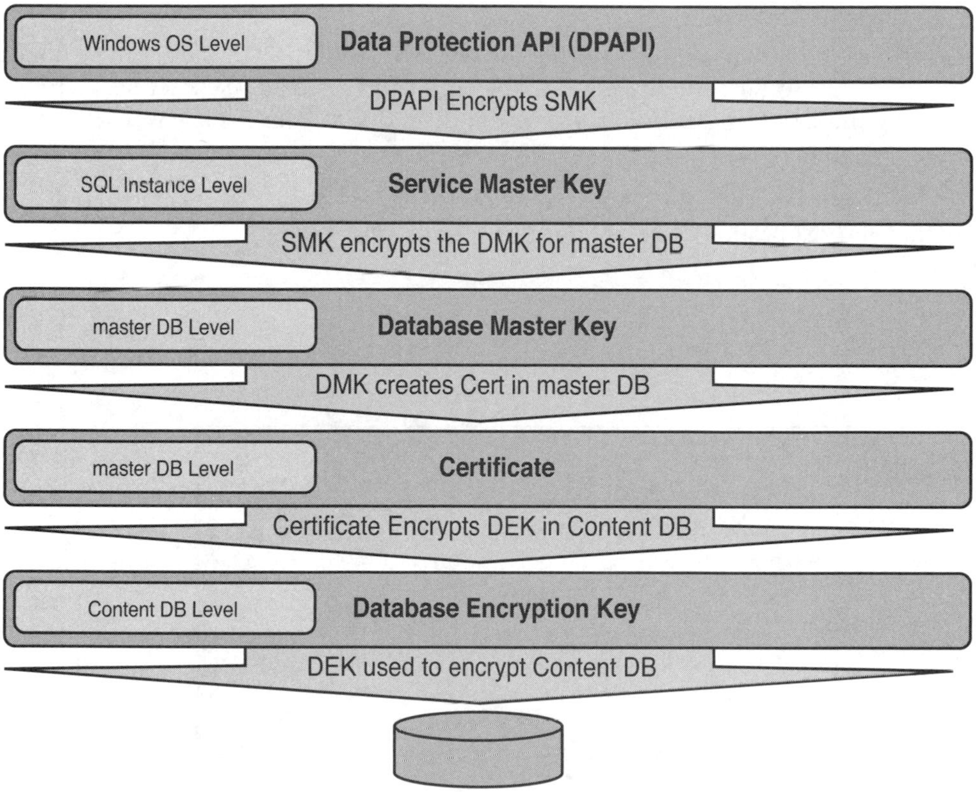

FIGURE 17.11 Understanding the TDE key hierarchy.

Enabling TDE for SharePoint Content Databases

The high-level steps for enabling TDE are as follows:

Step 1: Create the DMK.

Step 2: Create the TDE certificate.

Step 3: Back up the TDE certificate.

Step 4: Create the DEK.

Step 5: Encrypt the database.

Step 6: Monitor the progress.

Step 1: Create the DMK

The first step in the TDE process is to create the DMK. None of the TDE steps can be done from the SQL graphical user interface (GUI); they must all be run as T-SQL scripts. You should create the scripts in advance and then run them one at a time, such as what is illustrated in Figure 17.12.

The T-SQL script for creating the DMK is as follows. Change the `Password` value to one specific to your organization and store the password in a safe place.

```
USE master;
GO
CREATE MASTER KEY ENCRYPTION BY PASSWORD = 'CrypticTDEpw4CompanyABC';
```

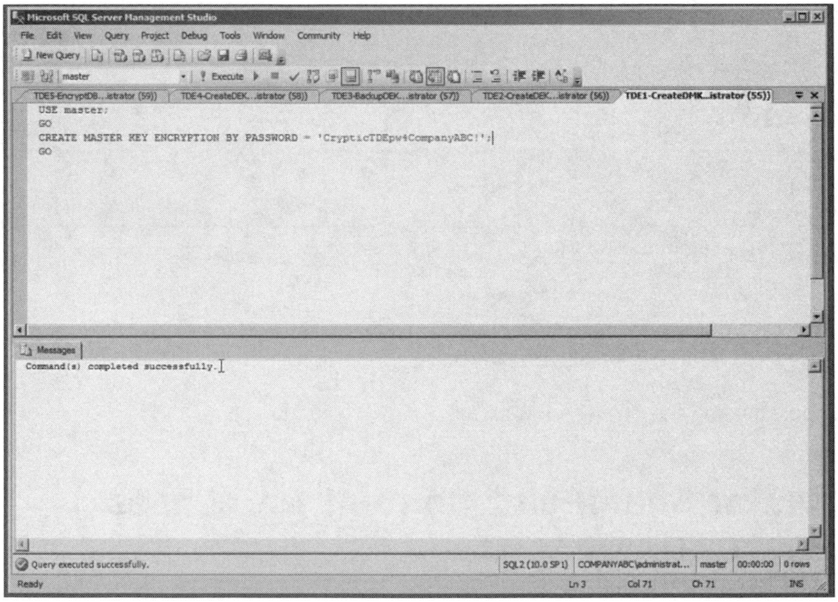

FIGURE 17.12 Creating the DMK.

When the DMK is created, it can then be used to create the TDE cert.

Step 2: Create the TDE Certificate

Using T-SQL commands again, the TDE certificate can be generated from the DMK on the server. Replace the certificate name and subject with one relevant to your organization:

```
USE master;
GO
CREATE CERTIFICATE CompanyABCtdeCert WITH SUBJECT = 'CompanyABC TDE Certificate';
GO
```

Step 3: Back Up the TDE Certificate

Upon creation of the certificate, you want to immediately back it up and store it in a safe place, away from the SQL backups for SharePoint. If this key backup is lost, the SQL backups are worthless. To back up the certificate, use T-SQL syntax similar to the following:

```
USE master;
GO
BACKUP CERTIFICATE CompanyABCtdeCert TO FILE = 'C:\Backup\CompanyABCtdeCERT.cer'
WITH PRIVATE KEY (
FILE = 'C:\Backup\CompanyABCtdeCert.pvk',
ENCRYPTION BY PASSWORD = 'CrypticTDEpw4CompanyABC!');
GO
```

CAUTION

It is extremely critical that this key is backed up and stored in a safe, fault-tolerant place. If it is lost, all SharePoint content in encrypted databases could be lost forever.

Note that the T-SQL script also specifies that the private key is backed up (CompanyABCtdeCert.pvk). This private key must be stored together with the certificate backup and restored with the TDE certificate if you want to recover TDE encrypted databases to another server. Also note that we are encrypting the certificate with a manual password. This needs to be used to restore the private key and certificate, so be sure to write it down and store it in a safe place.

Step 4: Create the DEK

The TDE certificate can then be used to create a DEK that will be used for the individual SharePoint content database that will be encrypted. Use syntax similar to the following, but substitute your SharePoint content database name for *SharePointContentDB*. A unique DEK needs to be created for each content database encrypted:

```
USE SharePointContentDB;
GO
CREATE DATABASE ENCRYPTION KEY
WITH ALGORITHM = AES_256
ENCRYPTION BY SERVER CERTIFICATE CompanyABCtdeCert
GO
```

Step 5: Encrypt the Database

Finally, use the DEK to encrypt the specific SharePoint content database. Replace the name of the database shown here with your own database. Repeat the previous step and this step for any remaining SharePoint content databases:

```
USE SharePointContentDB
GO
ALTER DATABASE SharePointContentDB
SET ENCRYPTION ON
GO
```

Step 6: Monitor the Progress

TDE immediately begins to encrypt the content database. It can do this on-the-fly as the database is being used. Depending on the size of the database, this might take a while. Progress of the encryption can be monitored with another script shown here, which returns all database with encryption state of 3. An encryption state of 1 means no encryption, and a state of 2 indicates that encryption has begun. A state of 3 means that encryption is complete. Run this command until the results show the database as having a state of 3, as shown in Figure 7.13. The TDE encryption process is then complete:

```
USE SharePointContentDB
GO
SELECT *
FROM sys.dm_database_encryption_keys
WHERE encryption_state = 3;
GO
```

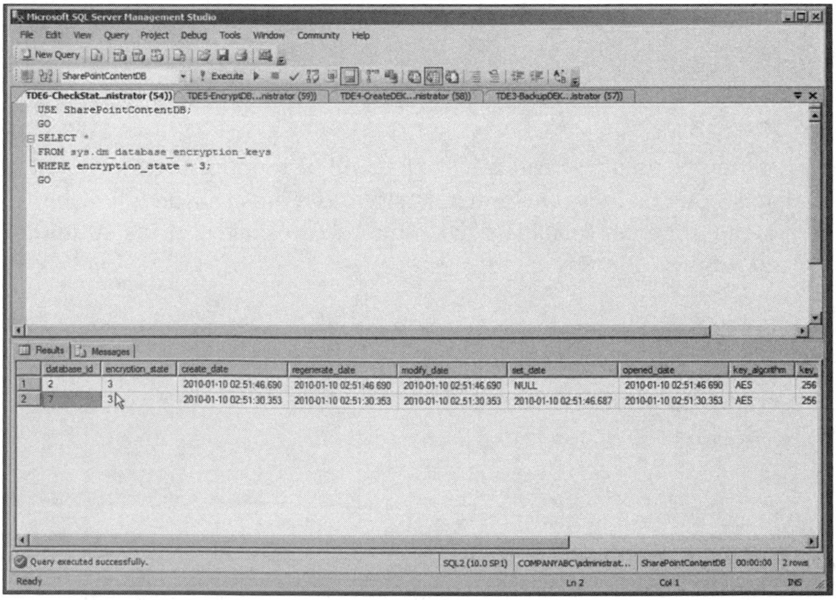

FIGURE 17.13 Monitoring TDE encryption status.

Repeat for any remaining databases.

RESTORING A TDE ENCRYPTED DATABASE TO ANOTHER SERVER

If a restore of a TDE encrypted backup file is attempted, a failure such as the one shown in Figure 17.14 occurs. To be able to restore the backup file, the target server must have the TDE certificate restored to it.

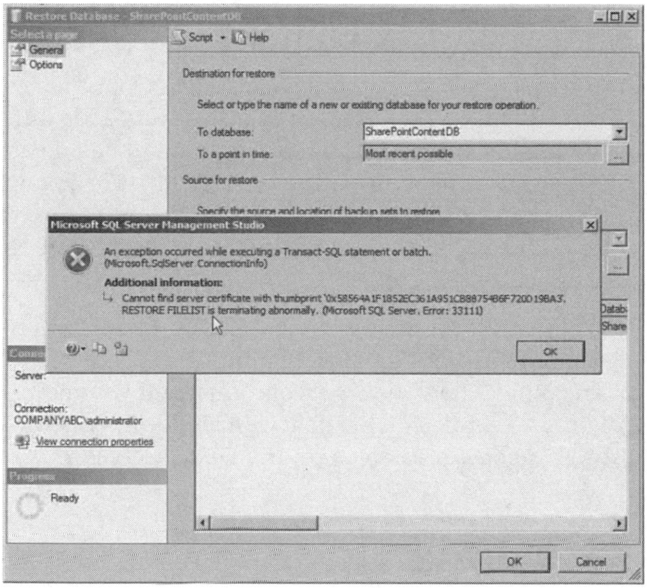

FIGURE 17.14 Viewing an error generated when attempting to restore a TDE encrypted database from backup.

The high-level steps for restoring a TDE encrypted database to another server are as follows:

1. Create a new DMK on the target server. (Each DMK is unique, so simply create a new one using the T-SQL listed in previous steps. This DMK does not need to match the one from the source server.)
2. Back up the certificate and private key from the source using the T-SQL script shown previously.
3. Restore the TDE certificate and the private key onto the target. (No need to export the DEK as it is part of the backup file.) Use similar syntax to what is shown here:

```
USE master;
GO
CREATE CERTIFICATE CompanyABCtdeCert
FROM FILE = 'C:\Restore\CompanyABCtdeCert.cer'
WITH PRIVATE KEY (
FILE = 'C:\Restore\CompanyABCtdeCert.pvk'
, DECRYPTION BY PASSWORD = 'CrypticTDEpw4CompanyABC!')
```

4. Restore the database file from the backup.

Note that the decryption password needs to match the one chosen in the previous steps.

Using this process, administrators can encrypt their critical SharePoint data, without the need for complex third-party solutions.

Using AD RMS for SharePoint Document Libraries

AD RMS is a data leak prevention (DLP) technology that uses Digital Rights Management (DRM) concepts in an attempt to prevent critical data from easily being transferred outside a company. AD RMS works by encrypting documents, then allowing them to be unencrypted only if the client application agrees to the terms of the rights policy. For example, the rights policy may dictate that the document cannot be printed, that it can't be saved in a different format, or that data from it cannot be copied/pasted. It can also dictate that the document expires after a certain period of time.

AD RMS is independent from SharePoint, and it runs as a service on a Windows Server 2008, 2008 R2, or 2012 server. Clients can encrypt files directly from their Office clients or via Outlook, with or without SharePoint. Where the SharePoint integration comes into place, however, is in SharePoint's ability to define a rights policy on all documents within a document library and have those rights policies enforced by an AD RMS server in the domain.

Prerequisites and Limitations of AD RMS

It is important to understand first what AD RMS can and cannot do in a SharePoint environment. The following key facts are important:

- AD RMS does not encrypt files in storage. Instead, the AD RMS rights policies are enforced only when the document is pulled out of the document library. This allows SharePoint indexing to be able to index the documents. If storage-level encryption is required, a technology such as SQL TDE, covered earlier in this chapter, is required.
- You can only establish one rights policy per document library, and, when established, those policies apply to all documents, both existing and new, in the library.
- The rights policies in SharePoint document libraries only define whether a user can print or programmatically access data. Other rights restrictions on documents actually depend on the SharePoint rights that a user has to the document library. If they have full Contributor rights, they can do more with the content. If they simply have Reader rights, they are fully restricted in what they can do.
- The AD RMS fully qualified domain name (FQDN) cannot be changed for existing content. Give considerable thought to what the FQDN will be and enable SSL encryption immediately on RMS. If you choose a flat name such as http://rmsserver for your URL, you would have to first change the URL before you can enable external access to RMS, which would have a big impact on existing encrypted files. Instead, consider choosing something like https://rms.companyabc.com from the beginning, even if you don't intend on turning on eternal access.

- Users using rights-protected documents or document libraries must have web-based access to the AD RMS FQDN to be able to open documents. If SharePoint is published on the outside, for example, the users need to be able to access the FQDN of the AD RMS site. In the previous example, this means being able to get to rms.companyabc.com. This means that this must be published as a site if this type of functionality is required.
- When a service connection point (SCP) is published in AD, all users can immediately use it. Consider waiting to publish the SCP until the environment has been fully tested. You can test out AD RMS by modifying the client registry to point to the AD RMS server rather than using an SCP initially.
- Add multiple AD RMS servers for redundancy and load balance them. This makes it even more critical to use an FQDN that can point to multiple servers or a load balanced virtual IP (VIP), such as rms.companyabc.com. You won't be able to add a second AD RMS server into a cluster until the SCP has been published.

Installing AD RMS

For environments that don't already have an AD RMS server in place (legacy Windows Server 2003 RMS work as well), a new Windows Server 2008 R2 AD RMS environment is required. Note that the RMS server requires a separate server from the SharePoint farm servers, and also requires a database for the AD RMS database. In many cases, the AD RMS database server is the same server as the SharePoint database server.

To install and configure AD RMS on a server, first install Windows Server 2008 R2 or Windows Server 2012 (Standard, Enterprise, or Datacenter will work) with the default installation options and then add it to the domain. Log in as an account with local admin access to the box and complete the following steps to install AD RMS:

1. On the RMS server, run the Add Roles Wizard from Server Manager.
2. Click Next to start the wizard.
3. Check the box for AD RMS.
4. Choose to add the required role services when prompted.
5. Ensure that AD RMS and Web Server are checked in the summary dialog box, shown in Figure 17.15, and choose Next to continue.
6. Click Next at the AD RMS Welcome dialog box.
7. Under Role Services, leave the default in place and click Next.
8. From the RMS Cluster dialog box, choose to create a new RMS cluster and click Next to continue.
9. From the Database dialog box, shown in Figure 17.16, choose to either use a local Windows Internal DB on the server or use a centralized SQL Server instance on another server. It is highly recommended to choose a separate SQL server for this, such as the SharePoint Database server.

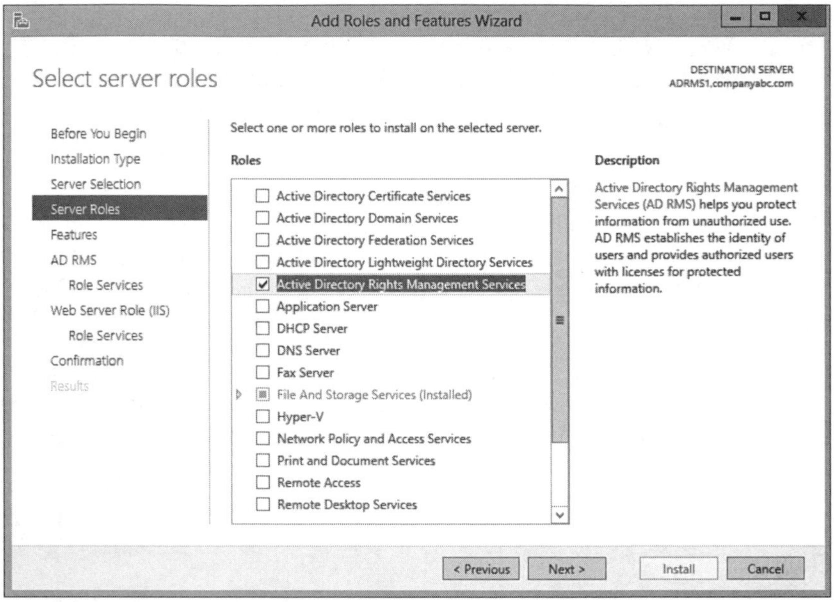

FIGURE 17.15 Installing the AD RMS role.

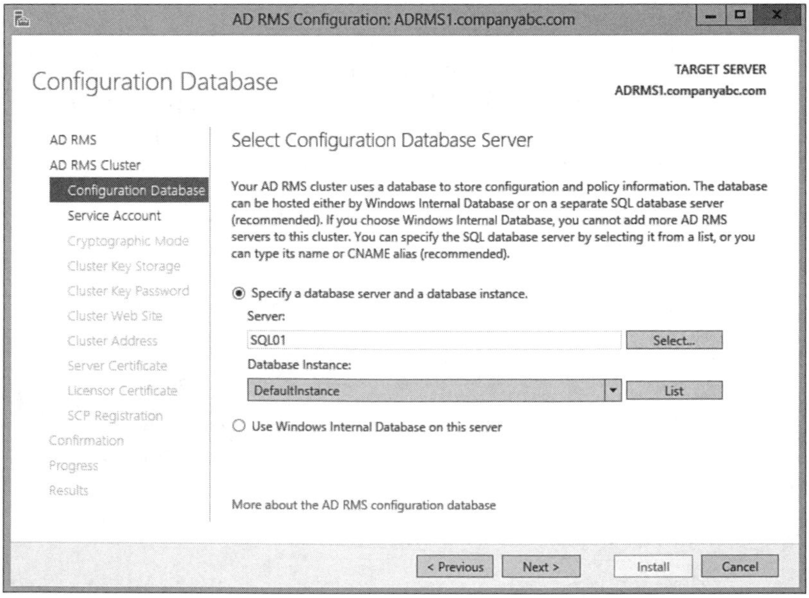

FIGURE 17.16 Selecting the database for AD RMS.

10. Specify a domain user account in the subsequent dialog box that will be used for AD RMS. This account should not have any special rights other than Domain User rights in the domain. You need to create this account in advance before proceeding. Click Next to continue.

11. In the Cluster Key Storage dialog box, choose the default AD managed key storage and click next to continue.

12. Enter a password for the cluster. Be sure to save this password; you'll need it to add additional RMS servers into the cluster in the future. Click Next to continue.

13. Use the default website and click Next to continue.

14. Select whether to use an SSL-encrypted connection to RMS or an HTTP connection, such as what is shown in Figure 17.17. It is *highly* recommended to use SSL now, because content will display this name at all times. In addition, do not use a server name for the FQDN; use a name that can be transferred to a VIP or another server in the future, such as rms.companyabc.com. Ideally, your RMS address will then always be https://rms.companyabc.com. Click Next to continue.

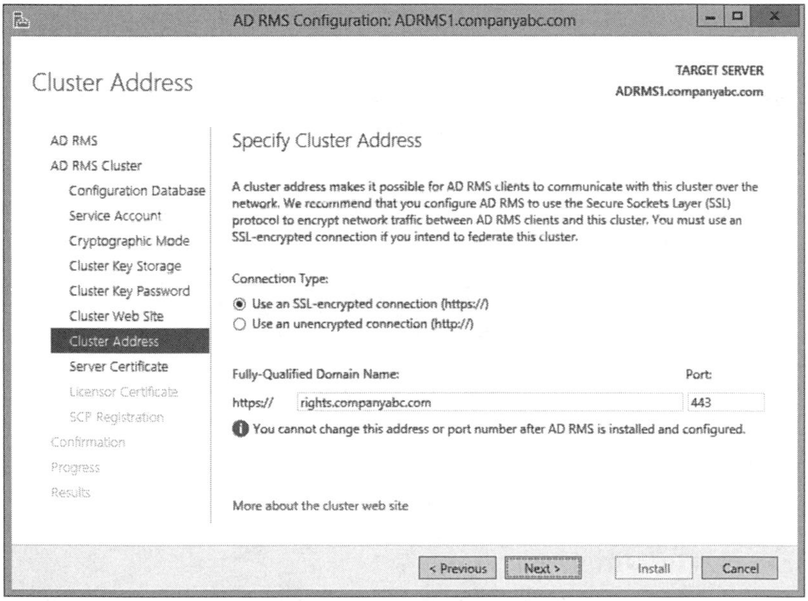

FIGURE 17.17 Specifying the FQDN for AD RMS.

15. In the subsequent dialog box, choose the SSL certificate that matches the FQDN chosen (that is, rms.companyabc.com). If it is not created yet, choose to install it later. This certificate must be installed for RMS to work properly. It is not recommended to use a self-signed certificate. Click Next to continue.

16. Choose the name of the server licensor certificate (accept the default in most cases) and click Next to continue.

17. Select whether to register the SCP now or later. Typically, the SCP is registered immediately, but be sure to understand the implications of this. When registered, all Office clients in the domain will "see" the RMS server and will be able to start encrypting content.

18. Accept the default for the Web Role Wizard (Next, then Next).

19. Review the settings, such as those shown in Figure 17.18, and click Install.

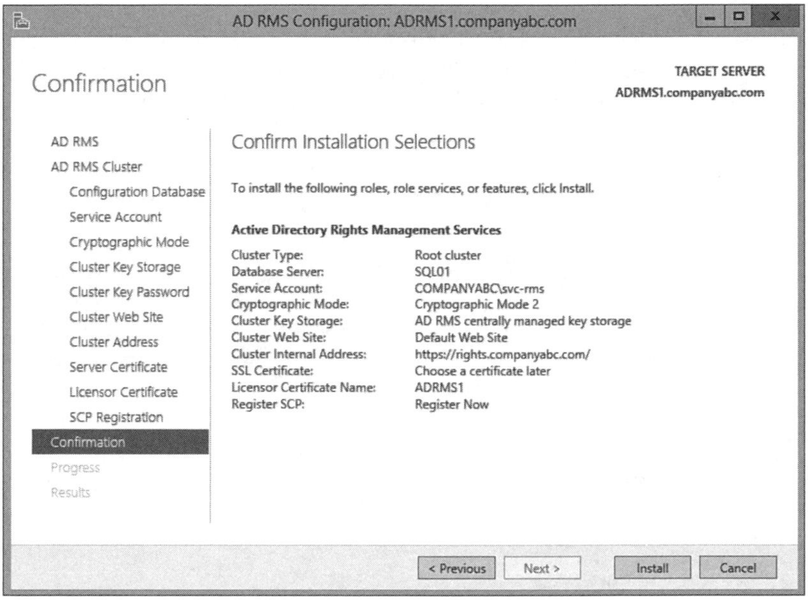

FIGURE 17.18 Reviewing AD RMS installation settings.

20. Choose Close when the wizard completes.

Modifying the RMS Certification Pipeline

When an RMS server is installed, a file on the RMS server needs to be modified to allow the SharePoint server and a local RMS group to be able to access that file. If this step is not performed, SharePoint can't make a connection to the RMS server to be able to RMS-protect document libraries. To configure this security, perform the steps while logged in as a local administrator on the RMS server:

1. On the RMS server, navigate to C:\inetpub\wwwroot_wmcs\Certification.

2. Right-click the ServerCertification.asmx file and choose Properties; then click the Security tab.

3. Click Add.

4. Click Object Types, select Computers, and then click OK.
5. Enter the name of all SharePoint web roles servers into the box, and then click OK.
6. Click Add again.
7. Select Object Types of Groups, and then click OK.
8. Type **'RMSServer\AD RMS Service Group'** (where *RMSServer* is the name of your RMS server), and then click OK.
9. Review the security settings, which should be similar to what is shown in Figure 17.19.

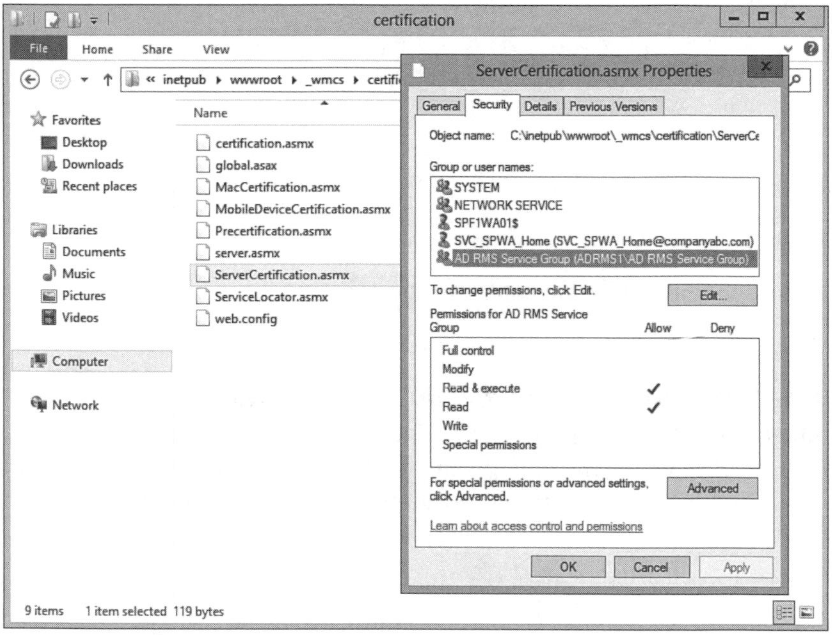

FIGURE 17.19 Modifying the security on the ServerCertification.asmx file on the RMS server.

10. Click OK to close the Security dialog box.

Enabling IRM Support in SharePoint Central Admin

After the ServerCertification.asmx file has been modified on the RMS server, switch to the SharePoint server to be able to turn on Information Rights Management (IRM) support and integrate the SharePoint servers with the AD RMS environment. To turn on this functionality, follow these steps:

1. From SharePoint Central Administration, click the Security link in the navigation pane.

2. Under Information Policy, click Configure Information Rights Management.
3. If the SCP is published in AD, choose Use the Default RMS Server Specified in AD, as shown in Figure 17.20, and then click OK.

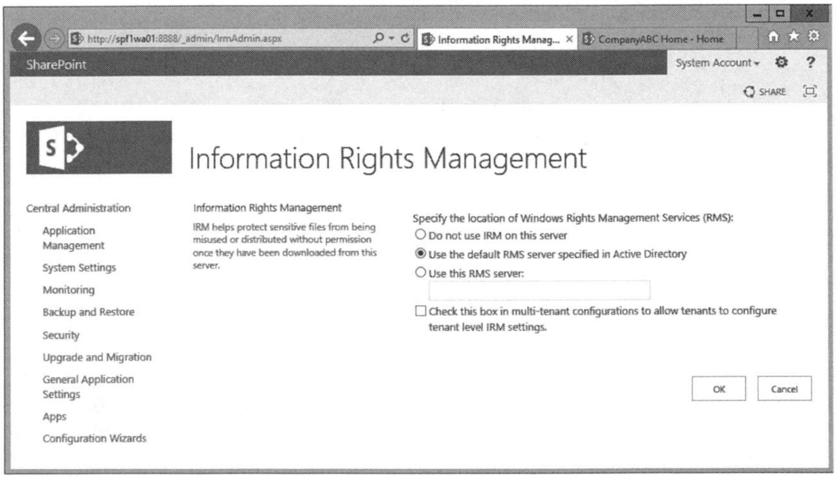

FIGURE 17.20 Enabling AD RMS support in SharePoint Central Administration.

Enabling IRM Support on an Individual Document Library

When enabled in SharePoint Central Administration, IRM protection can be enabled on individual document libraries within the farm by any site administrator who has full rights to the document library. To enable IRM protection on an individual document library, follow these steps:

1. Within a SharePoint site, select a document library.
2. From the ribbon, choose Library Tools, Library, and then click the Library Settings button.
3. Under Permissions and Management, choose IRM.
4. Check the Restrict Permission in This Library on Download check box, as shown in Figure 17.21. Enter the remaining fields depending on how the policy will be applied, whether there is expiration of policy, whether readers to the site can print or access content programmatically, and so on. Click OK.

When enabled, all current documents and future documents in that document library have the rights protection policy chosen added to them as they are viewed or modified from within the SharePoint site, such as what is illustrated in Figure 17.22. Keep in mind that the permissions are directly granted to users based on their document library permissions. So, if the user has full control over the document library, that user can copy/paste, save as, and so forth. However, if that user has only Read rights, such as what is shown in Figure 17.22, all those options are unavailable to that user from his or her client.

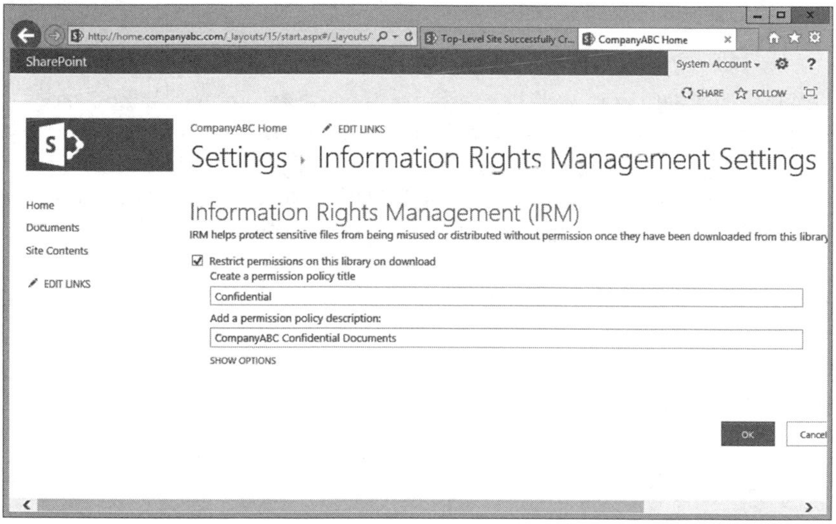

FIGURE 17.21 Enabling IRM support on a SharePoint document library.

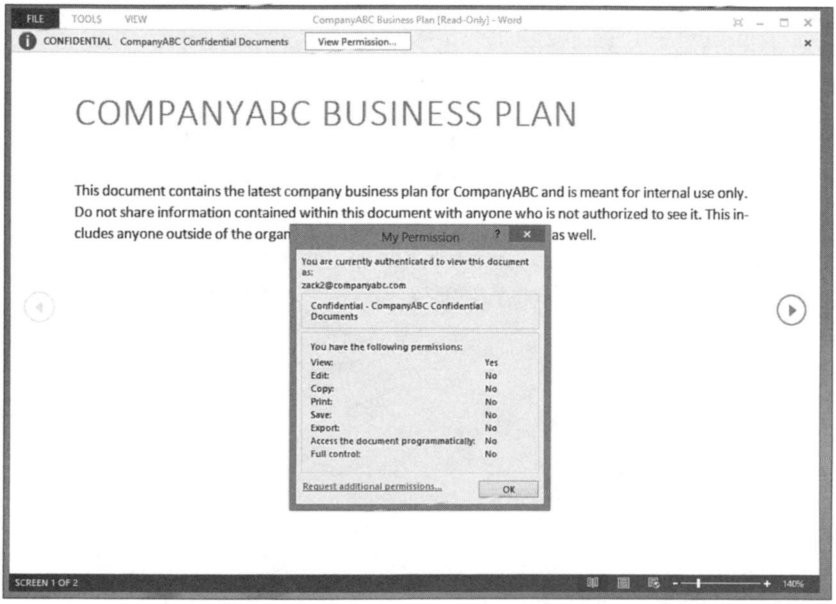

FIGURE 17.22 Viewing a document in an AD RMS-encrypted document library in SharePoint.

To turn off rights protection, simply go back into the document library settings and uncheck the box for IRM. This removes IRM protection for all documents within the library.

Summary

Protecting critical SharePoint data goes well beyond making sure to change backup tapes on the weekend. It involves identifying how to make data redundant, protect the integrity of the data, and prevent it from leaking out of an organization. By using tools discussed in this chapter such as SQL Server database mirroring, SQL TDE, and AD RMS, administrators can provide for drastically improved control over the lifecycle of their data.

Best Practices

The following are best practices from this chapter:

- Highly consider SQL AOAGs for HA and disaster recovery.
- Ensure that network links are at least 1Gb and have less than 1ms of latency if using synchronous AOAG replicas.
- Be sure that the hardware of the SQL AOAG synchronous replica servers are equivalent and ideally identical.
- For the best overall data security for a SharePoint environment, use SSL certificates for client traffic to SharePoint, use IPsec for communications between farm servers, and use SQL TDE for encryption in storage.
- Use a separate SQL instance for TDE-encrypted databases so that the encrypted TempDB from that instance won't affect the performance of other databases.
- Back up and store the TDE certificate and private key in a safe, fault-tolerant place, but ensure that that place is separate from the database backups themselves.
- Publish the AD RMS SCP in AD only after it has been fully tested, because it will be made immediately available within Office clients for client use when published.

CHAPTER 18

SharePoint Foundation Versus SharePoint Server 2013

IN THIS CHAPTER

- Clarifying the Different SharePoint Products from a High Level
- Business Applications for Different Versions of SharePoint 2013
- Feature Comparison Between SharePoint Foundation 2013 and SharePoint Server 2013 for Farm Administrators
- Reviewing the Central Administration Tools in SharePoint Foundation 2013 and SharePoint Server 2013
- Site Collection Options in SharePoint Foundation 2013 and SharePoint Server 2013

A common question when discussing SharePoint products is this: What is the difference between SharePoint Foundation 2013 and SharePoint Server 2013? As this chapter shows, this is not an easy question to answer, and there are differences across the board not only between SharePoint Foundation 2013 and SharePoint Server 2013 but also between the Standard and Enterprise Editions of SharePoint Server 2013.

This chapter gives guidelines from the authors' experience with hundreds of different clients with a wide range of business needs and software requirements, and delves more deeply into the specific tools and features offered by the three different products.

A primary goal for this chapter is to help business decision makers and SharePoint designers and architects decide which product is right for the organization. To aid in the decision-making process, a number of tables are provided that specify which tools and features each product provides.

Clarifying the Different SharePoint Products from a High Level

Nomenclature has been a challenge all the way back to the beginning of the SharePoint product line. Without recounting the various different names the different SharePoint products have carried, there have always been two different "flavors" of the SharePoint products. There has been the "free" version, which organizations can install without having to purchase SharePoint server licenses or CALs (client access licenses) from Microsoft. The "not-free" version of the product required that the organization purchase both SharePoint server licenses and end-user CALs.

The following subsections clarify the differences between the products to help you understand the pros and cons of choosing SharePoint Foundation 2013 or SharePoint Server 2013 for use in the organization.

An Overview of Licensing

SharePoint licensing has never been simple, because the organization needs to make sure the servers hosting SharePoint (which are Windows Server-based) are properly licensed (and in some cases, virtual servers are licensed differently than physical ones), the Structured Query Language (SQL) servers housing the data are properly licensed, the proper quantities of the SharePoint Server software are purchased, and the correct CALs are purchased. This can lead to quite a complex shopping list, and considerable costs, for a SharePoint implementation.

With the additional Office 365 SharePoint services available, there are even more options for organizations to consider and evaluate. These are not discussed in detail in this section. Microsoft offers a number of different licensing levels for organizations of different sizes; they also offer discounts for nonprofit and educational organizations.

NOTE

Good resources from Microsoft to help understand the current licensing landscape are the Microsoft Licensing site (www.microsoft.com/licensing/) and the Microsoft Volume Licensing site (www.microsoftvolumelicensing.com/).

In addition, the Microsoft Product Use Rights document gives granular detail on the different types of licenses available. As of this writing, the latest version is MicrosoftProductUseRights(WW)(English)(January2013)(CR).docx, which you can download from www.microsoftvolumelicensing.com.

Essentially, in the SharePoint product line, Microsoft offers a free version of SharePoint as well as not-free versions. In the SharePoint 2013 product line, the free version is officially known as SharePoint Foundation 2013. This version offers a core set of collaboration and document management tools, and is intended to meet the needs of smaller organizations and get companies that aren't ready to spend money on the more complete versions of the product started with the product line.

The more feature-rich version is called SharePoint Server 2013 and comes in Standard and Enterprise Editions. The higher-end products contain all the features offered in the entry-level products, plus many additional tools and capabilities, which are reviewed in depth later in this chapter. There is, however, only one version of the server product that can be purchased; based on the license key entered, the full set of Enterprise features are unlocked or the Standard set of features are enabled, as discussed in more detail later in this chapter.

There are two different types of CALs, and these are additive: the SharePoint 2013 Standard CAL and the SharePoint 2013 Enterprise CAL. So, users who use only the features available from SharePoint 2013 Standard just need the SharePoint Standard CAL. Users who use SharePoint 2013 Enterprise features need both the Standard and Enterprise CALs, or two CALs per user.

NOTE

SharePoint 2013 offers a number of PowerShell commandlets (cmdlets) that enable the assignment of specific types of licensing to different security groups from Active Directory. User License Enforcement needs first to be enabled for the farm, and then security groups can be given Enterprise license access. If a user does not have a license to use a particular feature, that feature is blocked at runtime for that user.

The PowerShell cmdlets offered are as follows:

```
Add-SPUserLicenseMapping
Disable-SPUserLicensing
Enable-SPUserLicensing
Get-SPUserLicense
Get-SPUserLicenseMapping
Get-SPUserLicensing
New-SPUserLicenseMapping
Remove-SPUserLicenseMapping
```

This capability is new and greatly facilitates IT's ability to ensure that only approved users are accessing Enterprise features in the SharePoint environment. Previously, organizations would either have to purchase Enterprise CALs for all employees, create separate farms for Standard and Enterprise users, or lock down the sites or site collections that used Enterprise features (such as Access Services, Excel Services, or PerformancePoint).

The free version of SharePoint (SharePoint Foundation 2013) still requires that the organization pays for the server operating system that is in use (Windows Server) and the CALs required for users to access the Windows Server, and the SQL Server software (unless an Express version is being used) and SQL Server CALs. So, the only component that is truly free with the current version of SharePoint is SharePoint Foundation 2013, not the supporting software.

Note, as well, that Microsoft has changed the licensing requirements for SharePoint 2013 Standard and Enterprise so that there is no longer a requirement for an additional license for external users. With the 2010 product line, if an organization wanted to create a SharePoint-based website that the whole world could access, it had to purchase the SharePoint Server Internet Sites license, which was quite expensive. With the SharePoint 2013 Standard and Enterprise products, however, External User Access is licensed with the server. Once again, the organization is still responsible for meeting other Microsoft licensing requirements for the Windows servers housing SharePoint and the SQL servers housing the data, but the end result is a reduction in the total cost of the SharePoint 2013-based Internet site.

Currently, the following base CALs are available for SharePoint Server 2013 on-premise:

- SharePoint Server 2013 Standard CAL
- Core CAL Suite1

- Core CAL Bridge for Windows Intune1
- Enterprise CAL Suite1
- Enterprise CAL Bridge for Windows Intune1

The following base CALs are available for Office 365 and include SharePoint use:

- Office 365 Enterprise E1-E4 User SL
- Office 365 Academic A3-A4 User SL
- Office 365 Government G1-G4 User SL
- SharePoint Online Plan 1 User SL
- SharePoint Online Plan 1G User SL
- SharePoint Online Plan 2 User SL
- SharePoint Online Plan 2A User SL
- SharePoint Online Plan 2G User SL

The following is a list of other discontinued stock keeping units (SKUs) from Microsoft that relate to SharePoint 2013:

- FAST Search for SharePoint
- Search Server
- SharePoint for Internet Sites, Standard
- SharePoint for Internet Sites, Enterprise

As with all licensing from Microsoft, at time of purchase, check with your software provider to see whether these conditions have changed.

Database Requirements of SharePoint Foundation 2013 and SharePoint Server 2013

Another variable in the architecture and installation of the SharePoint 2013 products is the choice of database. SharePoint Foundation 2013 and SharePoint Server 2013 products store data in the Express versions of SQL products (SQL Server 2008 R2 Express with SP1) when installed using the "standalone" option.

It is important to note that with the 2013 products, the SQL 2008 R2 Express maximum database size is 10GB. So, for organizations anticipating content database size exceeding 10GB, the full SQL Server products should be used; in other words, the standalone installation option is not recommended.

Experienced SharePoint administrators will quickly point out that SharePoint configurations can consist of multiple content databases, so it is possible to avoid the 10GB limit in standalone configurations where SQL 2008 Express is used by creating multiple content databases and managing growth so that no content database hits the 10GB limit. However, this is a management challenge and could potentially backfire, so is not generally recommended.

Business Applications for Different Versions of SharePoint 2013

Before moving on to a detailed comparison of the features in the different products, let's review some high-level business examples where clients decided between the SharePoint Foundation 2013 and SharePoint Server 2013 products. Because SharePoint 2013 is still a new product, examples in this section draw from decisions that clients made not only with the 2013 product but also with the 2010 products, which are quite similar to 2013 in terms of feature placement and distribution between the free version of the product and the not-free versions.

The following options represent a sampling of different configuration options based on features and cost combined with function. This is not an all-inclusive list, but is intended to help designers and decision makers categorize their requirements, and decide between the different options of SharePoint 2013 (Foundation versus Server) and between the different databases (SQL Express versus SQL Server). Specific costs can't be provided due to variables in numbers of servers, virtual versus physical servers, specifications of servers, numbers of users accessing the environment, and many types of licensing agreements offered by Microsoft.

Sample SharePoint Foundation 2013-Based Solutions

1. **Basic Features/Low Cost Team Collaboration Solution/Intranet:** SharePoint Foundation 2013 installed in standalone mode makes an excellent starter environment for simple collaboration needs in small to medium-sized organizations. It is a good choice when a budget has not been allocated for a SharePoint Server 2013 implementation. As mentioned in the previous section, SQL 2008 R2 Express has a 10GB maximum database size, so this should be taken into account. Because this is for internal use only, it is assumed that CALs have already been purchased for each user's access to Windows Server, which will house the solution.

2. **Basic Features/Low Cost Internet Site/Extranet Site:** Similar to option 1, SharePoint Foundation 2013 installed in standalone mode can make an effective platform on which to create an Internet-facing site. The organization is still responsible for purchasing the Internet license for the server operating system, but does not need to purchase CALs for SharePoint Foundation 2013. If the site is a read-only Internet site, a wide range of web parts is available to present information and documents to visitors. If the site is designed to offer extranet functionality, external users would be able to log in to the site and interact with content.

3. **Basic Features/Medium Cost Team Collaboration Solution/Intranet:** SharePoint Foundation 2013 connecting to SQL Server 2012 (or earlier) database server still saves cost when compared to using SharePoint Server 2013 with SQL Server 2012 databases, because CALs do not need to be purchased with SharePoint Foundation 2013. The organization does need to purchase SQL Server CALs or the processor-based licenses. The per-database limit does not apply, so the collaborative environment does not need to be as closely monitored or tightly controlled.

4. **Basic Features/Medium Cost Internet Site/Extranet Site:** As with option 3, SharePoint Foundation 2013 connecting to SQL Server 2012 (or earlier) database server controls the cost of the solution, while removing the content database size limitations, so is better suited to medium and large corporations, or even for smaller organizations who predict that the databases will quickly grow beyond the 10GB size limit per database. Note that the processor-based license is generally needed in this scenario for Internet sites, or extranet sites supporting large numbers, or potentially unlimited numbers of users.

Sample SharePoint Server 2013-Based Solutions

5. **Medium Features/Medium-High Cost Team Collaboration Solution/Intranet:** This solution includes SharePoint Server 2013 Standard edition installed in stand-alone mode using SQL Express, but is usually considered only for very limited use due to the limited database sizes. The organization is responsible for the CALs for the operating system and for SharePoint Server 2013, but not for SQL Express. Therefore, the costs are more than options 1 and 2, and most likely higher than options 3 and 4. Some organizations will use this configuration for a proof-of-concept or temporary configuration assuming the databases will be migrated to SQL Server 2012 in the near future.

6. **Medium Features/Medium-High Cost Internet Site/Extranet Site:** Similar to option 5, this includes SharePoint Server 2013 Standard Edition installed in stand-alone mode using SQL Express and includes similar costs, and the organization is responsible for unlimited user licenses for the Windows operating system and SharePoint Server 2013. Once again, the database size limit applies, making this a less-popular solution.

7. **Medium-High Features/High Cost Team Collaboration Solution/Intranet:** This option includes SharePoint Server 2013 Standard or Enterprise Edition connecting to SQL Server 2012 databases. The organization is responsible for CALs for the Windows OS, SharePoint Standard or Enterprise, and SQL Server, so the licensing costs accumulate. That said, this is the most popular option for organizations that are committed to the SharePoint platform, want the most scalability, and want to leverage the full range of SharePoint features. A key design decision for this option is whether to implement SharePoint Server 2013 Standard or Enterprise, because Enterprise adds cost for each CAL.

8. **Medium-High Features/High Cost Internet Site/Extranet Site:** As with option 7, this option includes SharePoint Server 2013 Standard or Enterprise Edition connecting to SQL Server 2012 databases. The organization is responsible for the same costs as in option 7, but needs the unlimited user license for the server operating system and the processor-based licensing for SQL Server. However, SharePoint Server 2013 includes external user access licensing, which reduces the overall costs from the SharePoint 2010 product line.

Feature Comparison Between SharePoint Foundation 2013 and SharePoint Server 2013 for Farm Administrators

An excellent way to gain insight into the differences between the SharePoint Foundation 2013 and SharePoint Server 2013 Standard and Enterprise products is to install all three and then walk through what features are provided with each version. This exercise is strongly recommended for organizations that want to validate which version best meets their needs and are new to the SharePoint product line or that want to perform more in-depth evaluations. Of course, not everyone has time for this level of testing, so the following information provides a top-down review of the features provided by each product by starting with the service applications provided in SharePoint Foundation 2013 and SharePoint Server 2013 Standard and Enterprise, then reviewing the management tools provided in the Central Administration site, and finally reviewing the site settings tools for a site collection in SharePoint Foundation 2013 and SharePoint Server 2013.

Service Applications Available in the Different Versions of SharePoint 2013

SharePoint 2013 products use *service applications* to provide different sets of functionality, which are available in the Central Administration Application Management page. A service application provides a set of functionalities that can be shared across sites within a farm or across multiple farms and can be enabled or disabled on a web application level.

Table 18.1 lists the service applications available in SharePoint Foundation 2013 and SharePoint Server 2013 Standard and Enterprise, and gives some insight into the range of service applications. Several subsequent sections provide more information about these service applications, so it will become clearer if and how these might be of interest to the collaboration and management needs of the organization as a whole. Figure 18.1 shows the Service Applications page for SharePoint Foundation 2013 with the New menu open, which reveals the new service applications that can be created by a farm administrator. Figure 18.2 shows the same page for SharePoint Server 2013 Enterprise version, also with the New menu open, providing a much larger range of options for the farm administrator. The links on these pages lead to additional pages where the details of the application services can be configured.

18

TABLE 18.1 Service Applications Available in SharePoint Foundation 2013 Compared to SharePoint Server 2013

Service Application	SharePoint Foundation 2013	SharePoint Server 2013 Standard	SharePoint Server 2013 Enterprise
Access Services 2010	No	No	Yes
Access Services	No	No	Yes
App Management Service	Yes	Yes	Yes

Service Application	SharePoint Foundation 2013	SharePoint Server 2013 Standard	SharePoint Server 2013 Enterprise
Application Discovery and Load Balancer Service	Yes	Yes	Yes
Business Data Connectivity Service	Yes	Yes	Yes
Excel Services Application	No	No	Yes
Machine Translation Service	No	Yes	Yes
Managed Metadata Service	No	Yes	Yes
PerformancePoint Service Application	No	No	Yes
PowerPoint Conversion Service Application	No	Yes	Yes
Search Administration Web Service for Search Service Application	Yes	Yes	Yes
Search Service Application	Yes	Yes	Yes
Secure Store Service	Yes	Yes	Yes
Security Token Service Application	Yes	Yes	Yes
State Service	Yes	Yes	Yes
Usage and Health Data Collection	Yes	Yes	Yes
User Profile Service Application	No	Yes	Yes
Visio Graphics Service	No	No	Yes
Word Automation Services	No	Yes	Yes
Work Management Service Application	No	Yes	Yes
Workflow Service Application	No	Yes	Yes

NOTE

The User Profile service application contains an important set of tools, including My Site, so it is important to note that My Site is not provided in SharePoint Foundation 2013. A number of other related tools and resources are not provided in SharePoint Foundation 2013, including the Manage User Profiles, Manage Audiences, Manage Organization Properties, and Manage Social Tags and Notes tools.

As you can see from a quick review of this table, SharePoint Foundation 2013 includes a subset of the full range of service applications. SharePoint Server 2013 Standard adds several additional service applications, including Managed Metadata Service, User Profile, and Word Automation Services. On the high end of the scale, Microsoft requires the installation of the Enterprise Edition of SharePoint Server 2013 for a number of features to be available, including Access Services, Excel Services, PerformancePoint, PowerPoint Conversion, and Visio Graphics Service.

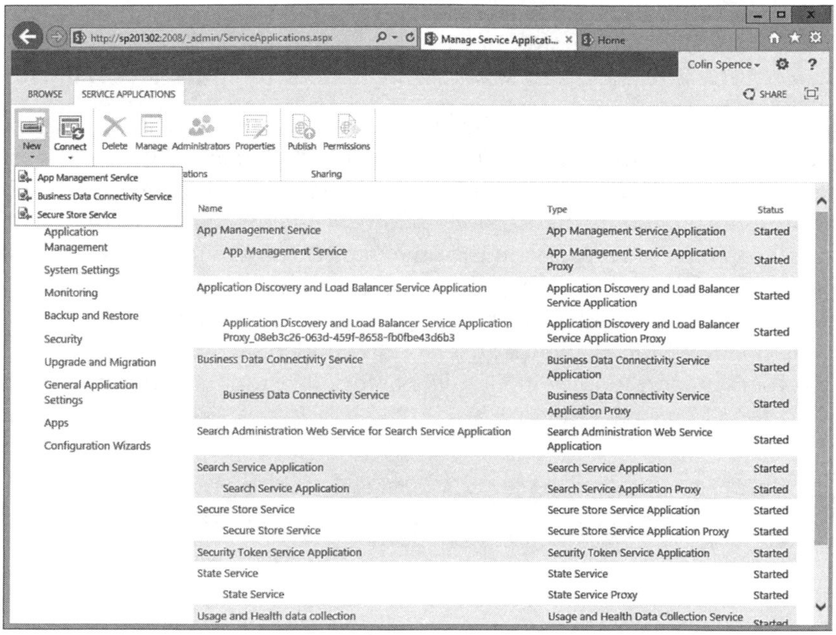

FIGURE 18.1 Service Applications page in SharePoint Foundation 2013 with New menu open.

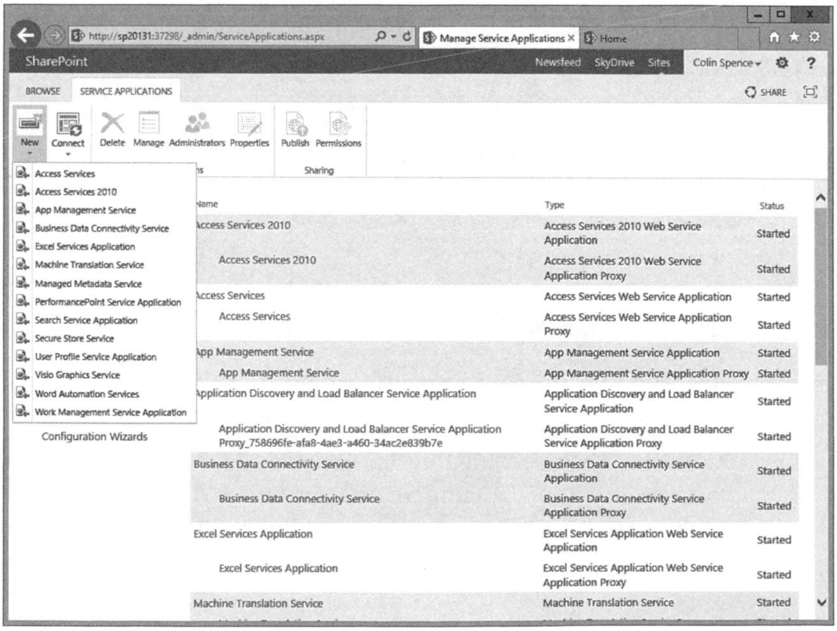

FIGURE 18.2 Service Applications page in SharePoint Server 2013 Enterprise with New menu open.

Search in SharePoint Foundation 2013 and SharePoint Server 2013

Many organizations can benefit from a powerful set of search tools, and fortunately both SharePoint Foundation 2013 and SharePoint Server 2013 provide powerful search tools.

A quick comparison of the search experience is helpful to show that the interfaces are identical, which wasn't the case with the SharePoint Foundation 2010 and SharePoint Server 2010 products. Figures 18.3 and 18.4 show the search results when the term "share-point" is searched for in document libraries with the same documents uploaded. Note that the elements of the pages are very similar, with the same refiners on the left-hand side of the screen (Result type, Author, Modified date), the same level of information displayed for the results, and the same preview window (hover panel). SharePoint Server 2013 offers the Follow link in the preview window, which SharePoint Foundation 2013 does not provide. Both search tools support more complicated searches that use the asterisk (*) as well as AND, OR, and NOT in search strings.

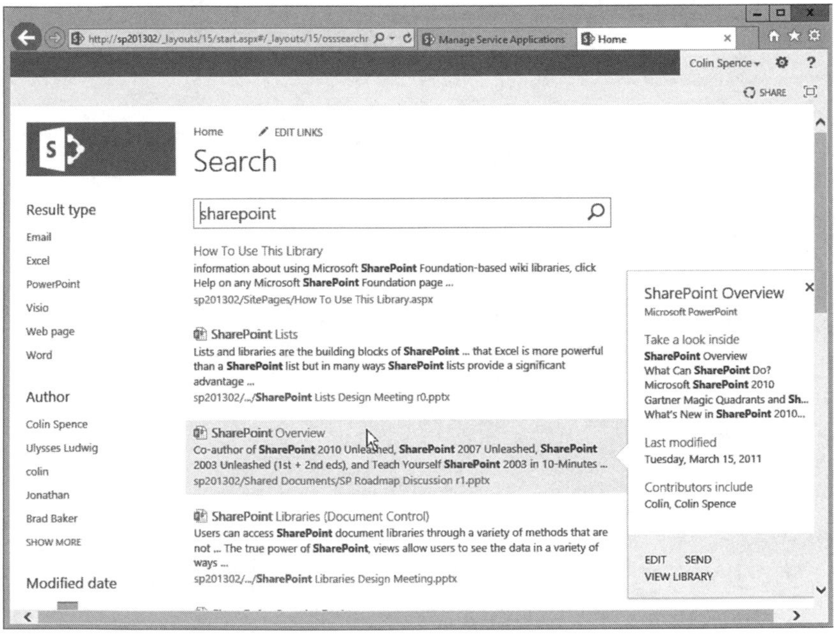

FIGURE 18.3 Search Results page in SharePoint Foundation 2013.

For site and farm administrators, the tools provided for management of the search engines are important. Both SharePoint Foundation 2013 and SharePoint Server 2013 provide the same tools from the Site Settings page for a site collection, including the following:

- Result Sources
- Result Types
- Query Rules

- Schema
- Search Settings
- Search and Offline Availability
- Configuration Import
- Configuration Export

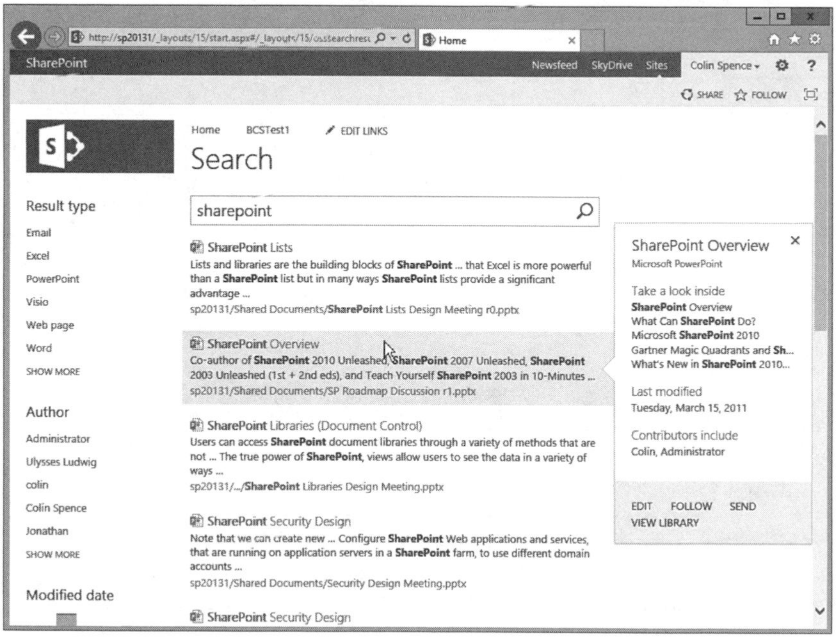

FIGURE 18.4 Search Results page in SharePoint Server 2013.

After comparing these tools, the only difference noted was that the Configure Search Navigation tool is not available in SharePoint Foundation 2013.

For farm administrators, the tools provided are also quite similar between the two product versions. Figure 18.5 shows the Search Service Application page in SharePoint Server 2013 Enterprise. The set of tools offered here allow the administrator to define additional sources of data to index, such as non-SharePoint websites, file shares, Exchange public folders, and other sources. Ranking of search results can be affected by defining most authoritative pages, second-level and third-level authoritative pages, and even sites to demote.

Note that several of the tools provided in SharePoint Server 2013 Search Administration page are not provided in SharePoint Foundation 2013. The tools not included in SharePoint Foundation 2013 are as follows:

- Usage Reports
- Query Client Types
- Search Dictionaries
- Search Results Removal

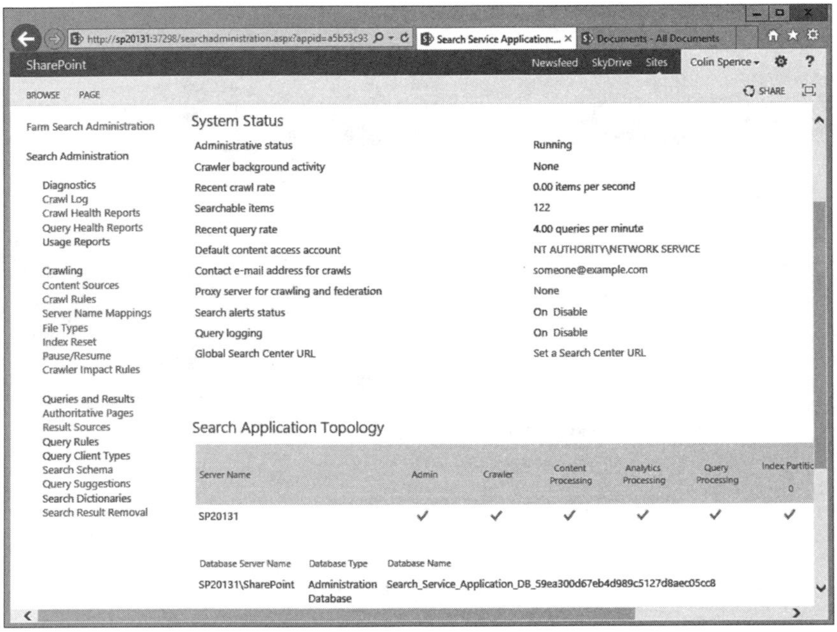

FIGURE 18.5 Search Administration for the Search Service application in SharePoint Server 2013 Enterprise.

NOTE

Without the Usage Reports tools, a SharePoint Foundation 2013 farm administrator cannot view usage reports to monitor search usage. SharePoint Server 2013 farm administrators, however, can view reports that summarize number of queries, top queries by day or top queries by month, as well as abandoned queries (searches with low click-through) and no results queries. This data is critical in helping administrators tune the search environment to make sure end users are able to find what they are looking for.

In summary, the tools provided for site administrators and farm administrators are very similar, which is a welcome change from the SharePoint 2010 product line, where there were more dramatic differences between the Foundation and Server versions of the product line. For a more detailed look at the search capabilities of SharePoint Server 2013, see Chapter 8, "Leveraging and Optimizing Search in SharePoint 2013."

Access Services, Excel Services, Visio Graphics, and Word Automation Services

As noted in Table 18.1, a number of other service applications refer to other Microsoft Office software applications: Access Services, Excel Services, Visio Graphics Services, and Word Automation Services. These service applications can prove extremely useful for organizations looking for deeper integration with the Microsoft Office applications in use such as Excel, Visio, and Access. The following list briefly describes these, and Chapter 26, "Extending SharePoint 2013 with Excel Services, Visio Graphics Services, and Access Services," delves into more detail and provides business-related examples of how these can be of benefit:

- **Access Services** allows users to create an Access app from SharePoint or publish an Access application to the SharePoint 2013 environment. SharePoint stores data in SQL database tables, but it does not provide the same level of flexibility for new or custom database design, which makes Access a valuable tool for developing more complex data-driven applications that are then managed in SharePoint 2013. Limitations apply to the complexity of the Access application that is developed, and Enterprise CALs are required for users of the Access apps in the SharePoint environment.
- **Excel Services** allows Excel users to publish worksheets or named objects in a worksheet to SharePoint Server 2013 Enterprise site collection libraries where Enterprise features are enabled. Figure 18.6 shows the results of adding the Excel Web Access web part to a SharePoint .aspx page to allow users to view and interact with a worksheet that contains data and a graph. Users can perform a variety of actions from this page, including downloading the document, downloading a snapshot of the document, printing it, or directly editing it by using the Open in Excel option. Excel Services also require a SharePoint Server 2013 Enterprise CAL to use.
- **Visio Graphics Service** allows users to share and view Microsoft Visio diagrams and supports a variety of data-connected Visio diagrams. Connecting Visio items to data sources can greatly enhance the power of the overall solution. For example, Visio objects can be connected to data sources including SQL Server 2008, 2012, and other versions, Excel workbooks (.xslx format) published to the same SharePoint farm, SharePoint server lists, and other sources. This extends Visio from "just a pretty picture" to a data-driven visual resource that is of value to the organization.
- **Word Automation Services** provides server-side automated conversion of file types that Word can open to PDF or XPS file types. The file types that can be converted include the related .docx, .doc, .rtf, .mht, and .xml.

Business Connectivity Services

Business Connectivity Services (BCS) are a set of services and features that provide a way to connect SharePoint solutions to sources of external data. Chapter 31, "Business Intelligence in SharePoint 2013 with Business Connectivity Services," provides a more in-depth review of the capabilities of BCS.

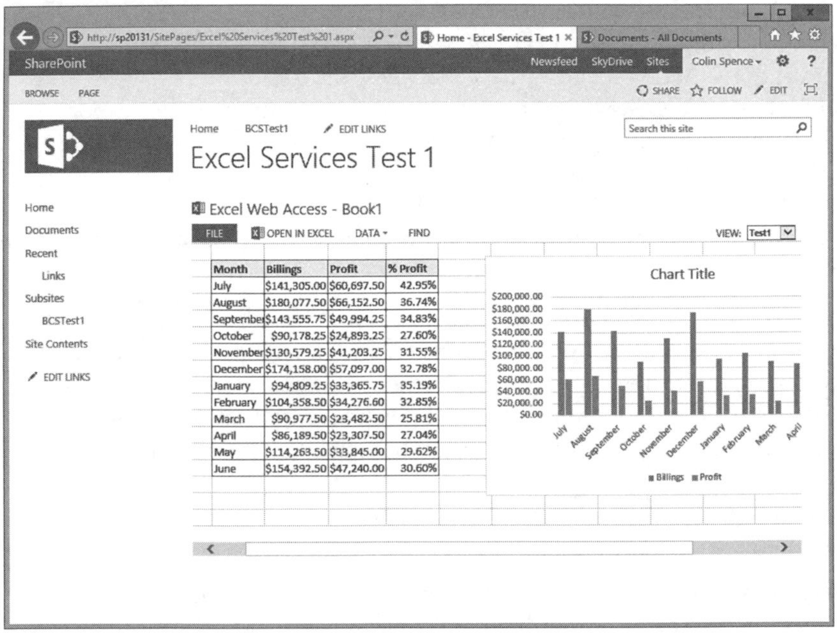

FIGURE 18.6 View of Excel worksheet published via Excel Services.

As its name implies, BCS allows connectivity to many different sources of information. This enables SharePoint administrators, developers, and power users to create dashboards that not only present data stored in SharePoint but also in other databases and sources. In addition, SharePoint-based applications (such as workflows) can take advantage of these external data sources.

A core component of BCS is the external content type, which leverages the power of SharePoint content types to connect to external data sources. External content types allow for the creation of a number of entities in SharePoint 2013, including external lists that provide access to data in the same way as standard SharePoint lists but the data is external to the SharePoint farm. External data columns can be added to standard SharePoint lists and display data from an external content type. Specific business data web parts are provided for the creation of pages or dashboards: Business Data Connectivity Filter, Business Data List, Business Data Item, Business Data Item Builder, Business Data Related List, and Business Data Actions.

An organization can also use BCS to build more complex applications that enhance SharePoint collaboration capabilities by including external business data and even modifying that external data. For example, an SQL database that contains customer information can be made accessible in a SharePoint list that displays the desired fields, and salespeople can interact directly with the data from SharePoint. This enhances SharePoint Server 2013's ability to provide full-feature applications; users don't have to leave the SharePoint environment to interact with each different business application, but instead just need to visit the appropriate site in the SharePoint environment and use the standard document library or list tools that they are used to.

Developing these solutions is not trivial and requires experienced developers and power users with Visual Studio 2012 experience to create the applications, to minimize the impact on the IT support staff, and to avoid potentially negative impact to the environment or the data being connected to.

Managed Metadata Service

Metadata is one of the key advantages of using SharePoint as a document management and collaboration tool, and is, simply put, data about data. All documents have metadata associated with them, including size of the document in bytes, date created, date modified, and other bits of data that are connected to the core file. SharePoint provides the ability to define additional metadata values for the purpose of better managing and organizing files.

For example, a metadata column titled Owner can be added to a document library, defined by the library administrator to contain People or Group information, and whenever a document is uploaded to the library, the person uploading it would define an individual or group who owns the document.

One challenge of effectively implementing SharePoint in a complex business environment is creating a taxonomy of metadata that is intuitive to users and also makes the system more effective at managing files, because otherwise, SharePoint can simply be a more expensive and complex file share. Instead of allowing users to create metadata columns "as needed," IT can offer term sets that are centrally managed in Central Administration.

With Managed Metadata Services, a "Term Store administrator" can create a group of terms that can be made available for use in site columns that can be added to any list or library. As shown in Figure 18.7, there are several default term sets, including People, Search Dictionaries, and System. The Term Store administrator has created a new term set called Subject Matter. A number of terms have been added (any of which could have subterms) to help end users define the subject matter of a document that has been uploaded. This term set can be used in any document library in any site collection in the farm. With good administration and governance of the environment, IT can then ensure that all libraries use this term set to help promote consistency, and a refiner based on this term set can be included in the Search Results page. Within a short period of time, end users will come to rely upon this Subject Matter value to quickly and easily find the documents they are looking for.

Figure 18.7 also shows the General tab highlighted on the right side of the window. Another power of managed metadata is the ability to assign a primary owner, provide an email address for that owner, and define stakeholders who should be consulted or informed in the case of major changes. In addition, a term set can be defined as closed or open. If the term set is defined as closed, only the metadata managers can add terms or delete terms, but if it is defined as open, users can add terms from the SharePoint interface.

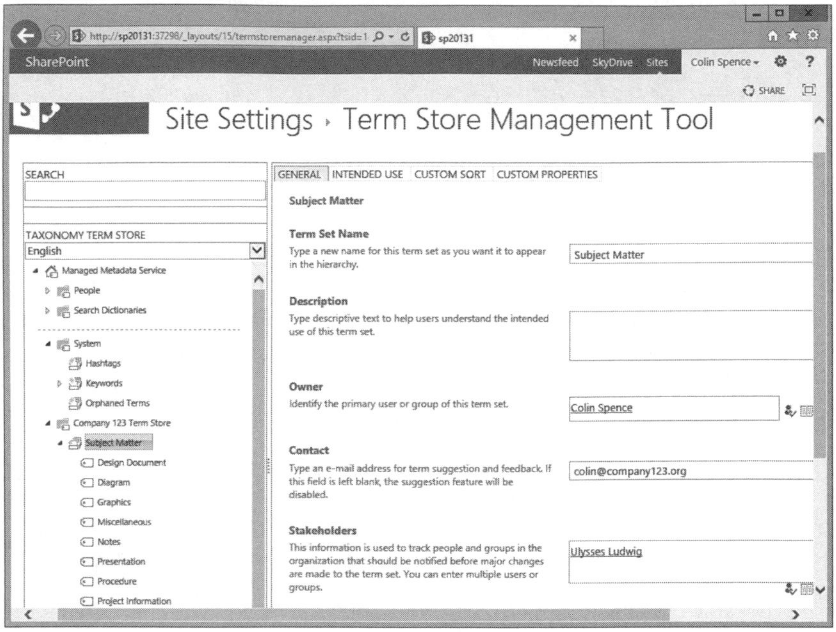

FIGURE 18.7 Term Store Management tool for creating and managing term sets.

PerformancePoint Service Application

PerformancePoint is Microsoft's high-level offering for more advanced business intelligence (BI) requirements. Historically, it was offered as a separate "for-purchase" product with SharePoint 2007 until Microsoft integrated it into SharePoint 2010 as a service application and included the rights to use it in the SharePoint Enterprise licensing. Now that PerformancePoint is a service application, it is fully integrated with SharePoint, providing better security, management, and scalability, along with ease of configuration. This integration has increased adoption among corporate clients because it's free with the SharePoint Enterprise CALs and because the cost of competing products from IBM or Oracle can be significant.

PerformancePoint doesn't operate in a vacuum, however. It is an application that needs to connect to data and then allows power users and financial analysts to create dashboards with scorecards, analytic reports, and filters. PerformancePoint can connect to data from a variety of sources, such as SharePoint lists, Excel Services, SQL Server databases, SQL Server Analysis Services, and other sources. Other features include a Visual Decomposition Tree report, Key Performance Indicator (KPI) Details report, an improved Dashboard Designer tool, and support for SQL Server and Analysis Services products.

Figure 18.8 shows the BI products from Microsoft (the basic vision for the product line). This diagram includes the Microsoft Office tools Excel and the PowerPivot Excel add-in, the SharePoint tools (including PerformancePoint, Excel Services, and Power View), and the SQL Server-based tools (including Reporting Services, Analysis Services, and Integration

Services). It can be quite a complex task putting all these moving parts together, but the end result for the organization can be incredibly valuable and can impact the agility, competitiveness, and success of the organization as a whole if used properly. Chapter 30, "Business Intelligence in SharePoint 2013 with PerformancePoint Services," delves more deeply into the capabilities of the PerformancePoint application.

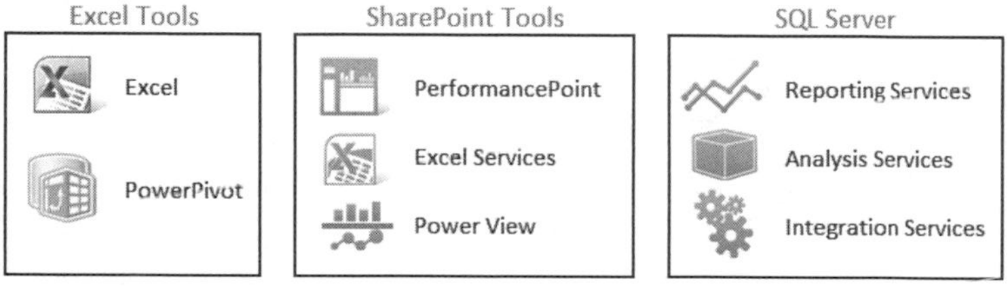

FIGURE 18.8 Diagram of BI products from Microsoft.

Reviewing the Central Administration Tools in SharePoint Foundation 2013 and SharePoint Server 2013

The previous section covered the service applications that come with SharePoint Foundation 2013 and the Standard and Enterprise Editions of SharePoint Server 2013 that directly impact the tool sets that the user community has. This section covers the administration tools that the farm administrators have access to from the home page of the Central Administration site. A simple overview is that SharePoint Server 2013 provides a larger number of management tools and, therefore, more time and training is needed to ensure that farm administrators are comfortable with the full range of tools. This is not an insignificant point because many IT resources are overburdened and might not be able to take time off to attend training and so might very well have to educate themselves on these tools.

SharePoint Foundation 2013 and SharePoint Server 2013 Enterprise Administration Tools Compared

Potential users of SharePoint 2013 products often ask what the administration differences are if the Foundation version of the product is used compared to the Server version of the product. Although there is no absolute answer comparing the differences, a general truism is that SharePoint Foundation administration is "easier" than SharePoint Server 2013 administration if more features and tools are enabled in the SharePoint Server 2013 implementation. Both products have the potential to support very complex implementations, but if the service applications and features provided in SharePoint Server 2013 Enterprise are leveraged, the environment can be considerably more complex.

Figure 18.9 shows a sample SharePoint Server 2013 Central Administration home page with Enterprise features enabled. Surprisingly, it is almost identical to the home page of SharePoint Foundation 2013 Central Administration home page. The following list summarizes the differences that can be found by comparing the tools offered in detail:

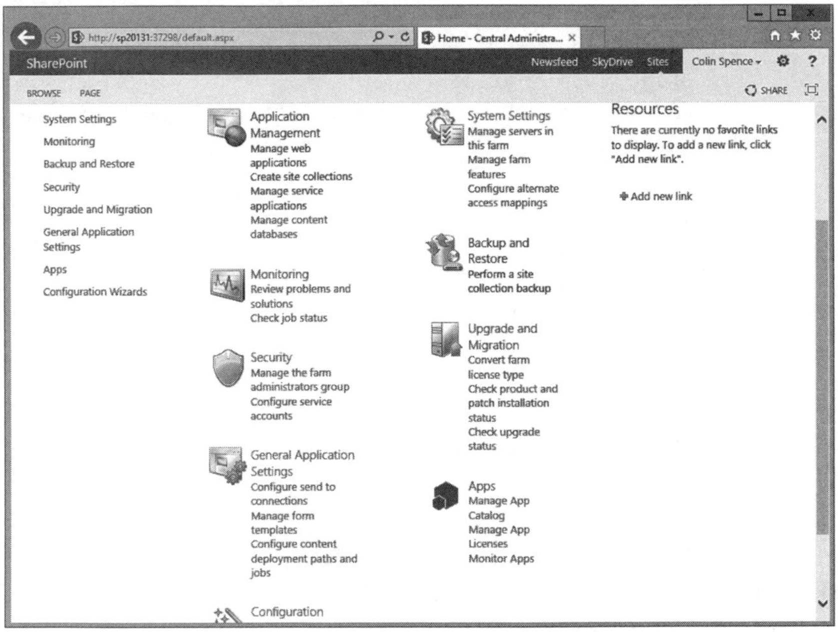

FIGURE 18.9 SharePoint Server 2013 Enterprise Central Administration site home page.

- **On the Security page:** Configure Information Rights Management Policy is not available in SharePoint Foundation 2013. This allows the farm administrator to set policies around the creation of labels, barcodes, auditing, and retention.
- **On the Upgrade and Migration page:** Enable Enterprise Features and Enable Features on Existing Sites are not available on SharePoint Foundation 2013. This is logical because SharePoint Foundation 2013 doesn't include Enterprise features.
- **On the General Application Settings page:** InfoPath Forms Services tools and Content Deployment tools are not available on SharePoint Foundation 2013. InfoPath Forms Services are only available in SharePoint Server 2013 Enterprise, so it makes sense that no management tools are provided in SharePoint Foundation 2013. Content deployment tools are very powerful because they allow the creation of paths and jobs that define the specific content that will be deployed to another location. For example, the marketing department could work on composing content and pages in a subsite and then publish to a top-level intranet home page on a nightly basis.

Site Collection Options in SharePoint Foundation 2013 and SharePoint Server 2013

Site collections are one of the fundamental building blocks in the SharePoint farm. Most organizations choose to create more than one site collection for a variety of design, management, and governance reasons. Site collections can be created from Central Administration or PowerShell, and the options differ between the SharePoint Foundation 2013 and SharePoint Server 2013 products, as reviewed in this section.

SharePoint Foundation 2013 provides a very limited number (four to be exact) of different templates for creating new site collections, as listed in Table 18.2. Team Site is usually the most widely used, but other options such as the Blog Site Collection template, Developer Site, and Basic Search Center provide the farm administrator with a chance to test the features of the different site collections.

TABLE 18.2 Templates Available in SharePoint Foundation 2013 and SharePoint Server 2013

Template Name	Available in SharePoint Foundation 2013	Available in SharePoint Server 2013 Enterprise
Team Site	Yes	Yes
Blog	Yes	Yes
Developer Site	Yes	Yes
Project Site	No	Yes
Community Site	No	Yes
Basic Search Center	Yes	Yes
Document Center	No	Yes
eDiscovery Center	No	Yes
Records Center	No	Yes
Business Intelligence Center	No	Yes
Enterprise Search Center	No	Yes
My Site Host	No	Yes
Community Portal	No	Yes
Visio Process Repository	No	Yes
Publishing Portal	No	Yes
Enterprise Wiki	No	Yes
Product Catalog	No	Yes
Select Template Later	Yes	Yes

SharePoint Server 2013 Enterprise, however, provides a number of other options that can help the organization quickly meet specific business requirements. For example, the Project Site is well suited to tracking project-related documents, the Community Site offers tools for tracking discussion threads, and the Records Center is specifically designed for organizations that need to declare documents as records for auditing and regulatory purposes. Another site collection that is of the greatest interest to most organizations is the My Site Host, which houses the My Sites that are created for SharePoint users. However, the My Site Host is not available in SharePoint Foundation 2013.

In addition, the Enterprise Search Center provides tools beyond those offered in the default basic search center in SharePoint Foundation 2013. For example, the Enterprise Search Center provides an Advanced Search Page link at the bottom of the results screen. As shown in Figure 18.10, this detailed "form" allows end users to intuitively provide detailed information on the search they'd like to execute. This level of specificity is not possible in the standard SharePoint search field unless the user is very familiar with the syntax used by SharePoint. In the example shown in Figure 18.10, the syntax is as follows:

```
%22best%20practices%22%20(DetectedLanguage%3D%22en%22)%20(FileExtension%3D%2
2doc%22%20OR%20FileExtension%3D%22docx%22%20OR%20FileExtension%3D%22dot%22%2
0OR%20FileExtension%3D%22docm%22%20OR%20FileExtension%3D%22odt%22)%20(Author
%3AColin%20OR%20Author%3AUlysses)
```

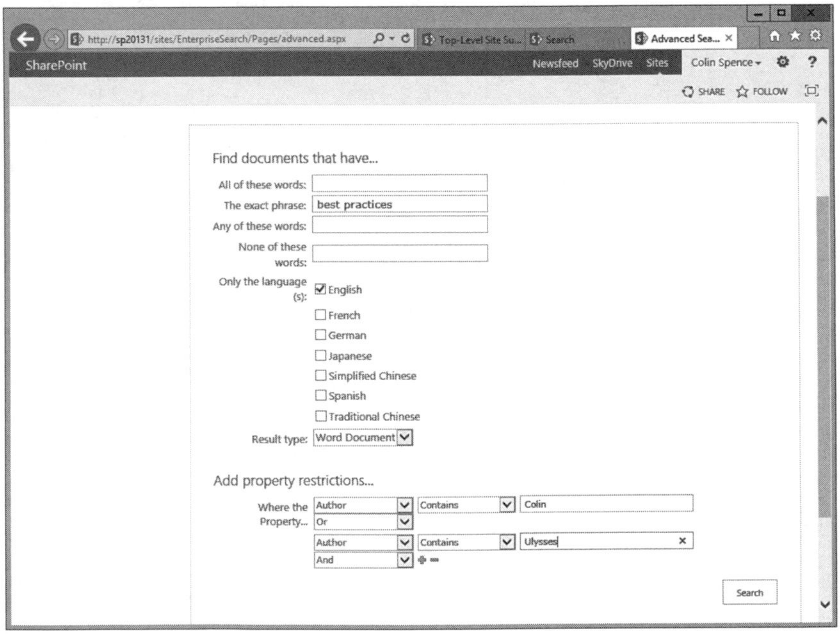

FIGURE 18.10 Advanced Search page in an Enterprise Search site collection.

It is worth mentioning that site collections can be nested; so, for example, a SharePoint Server 2013 Enterprise farm administrator can create a top-level site collection using the Team Site template, and then create nested site collections using a Records Center, Business Intelligence Center, and Community Site if needed. Also note that there might well be additional administrative overhead for more complex farm "logical" configurations, because each site collection is essentially a silo of data that is affected by a complex set of administrative tools.

NOTE

A recommended best practice, whether for farm administrators of SharePoint Foundation 2013 or SharePoint Server 2013, is to create a lab in a development environment where all the different site collection templates are used to create individual site collections, and the individuals responsible for the overall architecture of the farm gain experience with the different site collection templates. This helps key stakeholders better understand the capabilities of different site collections and to then decide which options to implement and to offer to users requesting a new site collection in the future.

Site Settings Tools Compared in SharePoint Foundation 2013 and SharePoint Server 2013

After a site collection has been created by the farm administrator, the site administrator then has a selection of tools at her disposal for configuring the features and behavior of the environment. A large number of tools are available, so they are not all covered in this section. Once again, however, the differences between SharePoint Foundation 2013 and SharePoint Server 2013 are examined.

Figure 18.11 shows a Site Settings page for a Team Site site collection created in SharePoint Foundation 2013. To access this page, click the Settings tool and select Site Settings. If this option is not offered, the account you are logged in with most likely doesn't have sufficient permissions. This page looks almost identical to the Site Settings page for a Team Site site collection created in SharePoint Server 2013 Enterprise, yet there are many differences in a couple of key areas that are discussed next.

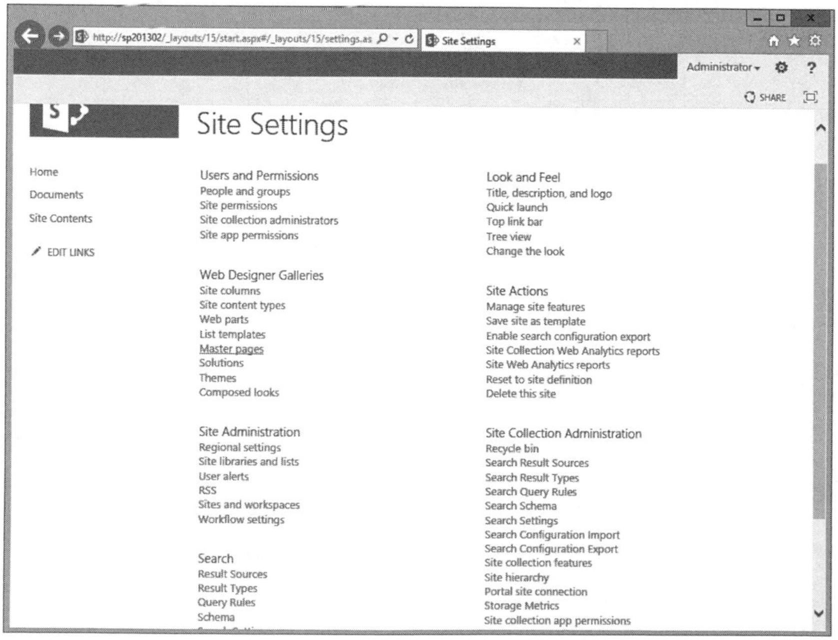

FIGURE 18.11 Site Settings page in a SharePoint Foundation 2013 team site collection.

To begin with, several tools provided in SharePoint Server 2013 Enterprise are not provided in SharePoint Foundation 2013, including the following:

- **Site Administration Tools:** Site Closure and Deletion, Term Store Management, and Popularity Trends
- **Site Collection Administration Tools:** Site Collection Audit Settings, Audit Log Reports, Site Policies, Popularity and Search Reports, Content Type Policy Templates, and Content Type Publishing

Of these, the Site Collection Audit Settings tools and the Content Type Policy tools provide powerful management and governance tools for the farm administrators and IT management and therefore merit further review.

Figure 18.12 shows the Configure Audit Settings page available to site administrators in SharePoint Server 2013 Standard or Enterprise. The audit log can audit events such as opening or downloading documents, viewing items, editing items, deleting items, searching site content, or editing users and permissions. This is a more complete list of activities that can be audited than the basic tools available in SharePoint Foundation 2013, which provides access to just the very limited Site Web Analytics Reports tool found on the Site Settings page. Note that a SharePoint Foundation 2013 farm administrator can access more complete reports from the Central Administration site, but in most organizations, the number of users allowed to access the farm-level management tools is very limited.

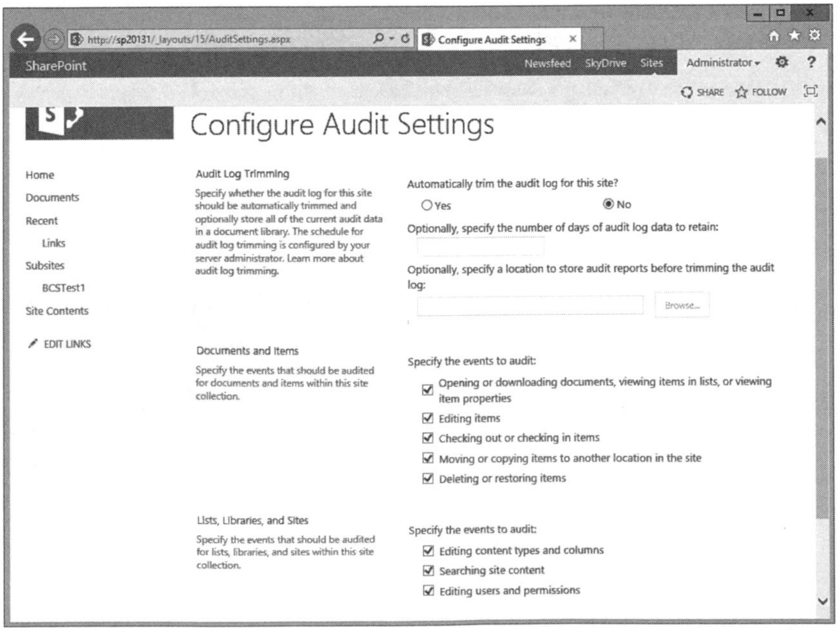

FIGURE 18.12 Configure Audit Settings page in a SharePoint Server 2013 Enterprise team site collection.

Content type policy templates can be created by a site collection administrator in SharePoint Server 2013 Standard or Enterprise or can be imported if previously created. These can include policy statements, which are displayed to end users when an item subject to the policy is opened, as well as retention policies, auditing, use of barcodes, and use of labels. These are powerful tools that can prove very valuable or even essential to more complex document management solutions. For example, a retention policy created in a site collection policy causes a stage to activate a certain amount of time after the created date, last modified, or declared record date of an item, and allows the site administrator to determine what action is triggered at that stage with the following options: Move to Recycling Bin, Permanently Delete, Transfer to Another Location, Start a Workflow, Skip to Next Stage, Declare Record, Delete Previous Drafts, and Delete All Previous Versions. A site collection policy can be a handy house-cleaning tool, enabling all earlier versions of a document to be deleted after a period of time since the last modification (for example, one year).

Comparing Features in SharePoint Foundation 2013 and SharePoint Server 2013 Enterprise

A large number of differences "under the hood" can also be found when comparing the site features and site collection features provided in SharePoint Foundation 2013 and SharePoint Server 2013 Enterprise. To access these settings, from the Site Settings page, access Manage Site Features in the Site Actions section, and then access Site Collection Features in the Site Collection Administration section.

The site collection features apply to the entire site collection, but the site features apply to the specific site that is currently being visited. If an administrator is on a subsite, the Site Settings page doesn't provide access to site collection features, but instead sees a Go to Top Level Site Settings link.

Table 18.3 shows the differences between site features available in SharePoint Foundation 2013 and SharePoint Server 2013 Enterprise. Table 18.4 shows the differences between site collection features available in SharePoint Foundation 2013 and SharePoint Server 2013 Enterprise.

NOTE

The options available from both the Manage Site Features page and the Site Collection Features links on the Site Settings page may vary depending on which service applications have been provisioned and other configuration choices. In addition, installation of third-party "bolt-on" products can add additional features, or developers can create features that will appear in these pages.

TABLE 18.3 Site Features Available in SharePoint Foundation 2013 and SharePoint Server 2013

Site Feature Name	Available in SharePoint Foundation 2013	Available in SharePoint Server 2013 Enterprise
Access App	No	Yes
BI Center Data Connections Feature	No	Yes
Class My Site Host Content	No	Yes
Class Web Types	No	Yes
Community Site Feature	No	Yes
Content Management Interoperability Services (CMIS) Producer	No	Yes
Content Organizer	No	Yes
External System Events	Yes	Yes
Following Content	No	Yes
Getting Started	Yes	Yes
Hold	No	Yes
Metadata Navigation and Filtering	No	Yes
Minimal Download Strategy	Yes	Yes
Mobile Browser View	Yes	Yes
Offline Synchronization for External Lists	Yes	Yes
Project Functionality	No	Yes
Search Config Data Content Types	Yes	Yes
Search Config Data Site Columns	Yes	Yes
Search Config List Instance Feature	Yes	Yes
Search Config Template Feature	Yes	Yes
SharePoint Server Enterprise Site Features	No	Yes
SharePoint Server Publishing	No	Yes
SharePoint Server Standard Site Features	No	Yes
Site Feed	No	Yes
Site Mailbox	No	Yes
Site Notebook	Yes	Yes
Team Collaboration Lists	Yes	Yes
Wiki Page Home Page	Yes	Yes
Workflow Task Content Type	No	Yes
Workflows can use app permissions	No	Yes

TABLE 18.4 Site Collection Features Available in SharePoint Foundation 2013 and SharePoint Server 2013

Site Collection Feature Name	Available in SharePoint Foundation 2013	Available in SharePoint Server 2013 Enterprise
Content Deployment Source Feature	No	Yes
Content Type Syndication Hub	No	Yes
Cross-Farm Site Permissions	No	Yes
Cross-Site Collection Publishing	No	Yes
Custom Site Collection Help	Yes	Yes
Disposition Approval Workflows	No	Yes
Document ID Service	No	Yes
Document Sets	No	Yes
In Place Records Management	No	Yes
Library and Folder-Based Retention	No	Yes
Limited-Access User Permission Lockdown Mode	No	Yes
Open Documents in Client Applications by Default	Yes	Yes
PerformancePoint Services Site Collection Features	No	Yes
Publishing Approval Workflow	No	Yes
Reporting	No	Yes
Reports and Data Search Support	No	Yes
Search Engine Sitemap	No	Yes
Search Server Web Parts and Templates	Yes	Yes
SharePoint 2007 Workflows	No	Yes
SharePoint Server Enterprise Site Collection features	No	Yes
SharePoint Server Publishing Infrastructure	No	Yes
SharePoint Server Standard Site Collection Features	No	Yes
Site Policy	No	Yes
Three-Start Workflow	Yes	Yes
Video and Rich Media	No	Yes
Workflows	No	Yes

Document Library Features in SharePoint Foundation 2013 and SharePoint Server 2013

This section reviews the differences in libraries between the products. Once again, this is not an exhaustive overview, but rather is intended to highlight differences in the Foundation and Server versions of the SharePoint 2013 product line.

Users interact with document libraries every day in the SharePoint environment, so the differences greatly impact end users in terms of the tools they can use and their overall experience when working with SharePoint 2013.

When users visit a document library, they usually want to interact with the documents stored within it. Assuming they have the privileges to do so, they can select one or more files in the library and then use tools from the Files tab. While the base functionality in document libraries is similar in SharePoint Foundation 2013 and SharePoint Server 2013, some differences impact the end-user experiences. The following list shows the tools that are the same in SharePoint Foundation 2013 and SharePoint Server 2013:

- New Document
- Upload Document
- New Folder
- Edit Document
- Check Out/Check In/Discard Check Out
- View Properties/Edit Properties
- Version History/Shared With/Delete Document
- Share
- Download a Copy
- Send To/Manage Copies/Go To Source
- Workflows
- Publish/Unpublish/Approve/Reject/Cancel Approval

SharePoint Server 2013 Standard and Enterprise added the following tools in a standard document library:

- Popularity Trends (only in Server)
- Follow (only in Server)
- Tags and Notes (only in Server)

A document needs to be selected for the Popularity Trends icon to be selectable, but then if it is clicked, an Excel document opens that provides a summary of hits and unique users who have viewed the document on previous days and months. The Follow tool tracks documents in the individual's My Site newsfeed. Tags and Notes options can be valuable as they allow individuals to tag items with their own metadata tags and to add notes that can be viewed by other people.

Within the document library settings for SharePoint Foundation 2013, you have a more limited selection of tools to work with, as shown in Table 18.5.

TABLE 18.5 Tools Available in a Document Library in Different Versions of SharePoint 2013

Tool Name	Available in SharePoint Foundation 2013	Available in SharePoint Server 2013 Enterprise
List Name, Description, and Navigation	Yes	Yes
Versioning Settings	Yes	Yes
Advanced Settings	Yes	Yes
Validation Settings	Yes	Yes
Common Default Value Settings	No	Yes
Rating Settings	No	Yes
Audience Targeting Settings	No	Yes
Form Settings	No	Yes
Delete This Document Library	Yes	Yes
Save Document Library as Template	Yes	Yes
Permissions for This Document Library	Yes	Yes
Manage Files Which Have No Checked In Version	Yes	Yes
Workflow Settings	Yes	Yes
Information Management Policy Settings	No	Yes
Enterprise Metadata and Keywords Settings	No	Yes
Generate File Plan Report	No	Yes
RSS Settings	Yes	Yes

Chapter 19, "Using Libraries and Lists in SharePoint 2013," covers these tools in more detail, including how they affect the day-to-day experience of document library users.

Summary

This chapter addresses many of the key differences between SharePoint Foundation 2013 and SharePoint Server 2013. Although not every possible difference between the products can be addressed in a single chapter, comparisons were provided on many different levels to help decision makers, designers, and architects make informed decisions about which product best meets their organization's requirements. For many organizations, this content will be a starting point and will lead to more in-depth conversations about the pros and cons of different approaches; hands-on testing might be required to reach a final decision.

Best Practices

The following are best practices from this chapter:

- SharePoint 2013 offers a number of PowerShell cmdlets that enable the assignment of specific types of licensing to different security groups from Active Directory. User License Enforcement needs first to be enabled for the farm, and then security groups can be given Enterprise license access. If a user does not have a license to use a particular feature, that feature is blocked at runtime for that user.
- With SharePoint Foundation 2013, it is possible to avoid the 10GB limit in configurations where SQL 2008 Express is used by creating multiple content databases and managing growth so that no content database hits the 10GB limit.
- The User Profile service application enables the use of My Sites and related functionality, but it is not provided in SharePoint Foundation 2013.
- A SharePoint Foundation 2013 farm does not provide the Usage Reports tools, so an administrator cannot view usage reports to monitor search usage. Because this data can be critical in helping administrators tune the search environment, SharePoint Foundation may not be the right product for environments where an optimized search tool is required.
- Understanding which service applications are available in the different versions of SharePoint 2013 is important in helping architects and decision makers determine which version of SharePoint meets the organization's needs. Some key service applications not offered by SharePoint Foundation 2013 include the following: Access Services, Excel Services, Managed Metadata, PerformancePoint, and User Profile Services.
- Several administration tools provided in SharePoint Server 2013 Enterprise are not provided in SharePoint Foundation 2013. Of these, the Site Collection Audit Settings tools and the Content Type Policy tools provide powerful management and governance tools for the farm administrators and IT management.
- Managed Metadata Services (only offered in SharePoint Server 2013 Standard or Enterprise) should be strongly considered by any organization interested in leveraging company-wide metadata standards across multiple site collections. Creating a taxonomy of metadata that is intuitive to users and also makes the system more effective at managing files can dramatically improve the value of a SharePoint document management system.
- If the organization is interested in Business Intelligence tools, SharePoint Server 2013 Enterprise is recommended. It provides the PerformancePoint tools that provide an extremely powerful set of tools to create dashboards, scorecards, and key performance indicators (KPIs) for analysis of data from a variety of sources. In addition, SharePoint Server 2013 provides Excel Services, which is a key component in many BI solutions.

- A recommended best practice is to create a lab in a development environment where all the different site collection templates are used to create individual site collections. This allows the individuals responsible for the overall architecture of the farm to gain experience with the different site collection templates in a safe, nonproduction environment.

CHAPTER 19

Using Libraries and Lists in SharePoint 2013

IN THIS CHAPTER

- Empowering Users Through SharePoint 2010 Libraries
- Adding Documents to a Document Library
- Working with the Other Standard Tools in a Document Library
- Working with the New Document Tools
- Using the Edit Document Tool, Check Out, Check In, and Discard Check Out Tools
- Using the Version History Tool
- Empowering Users Through SharePoint 2010 Lists

Lists and libraries are two fundamental building blocks of a SharePoint 2013 environment and offer the tools that dramatically differentiate SharePoint from a file share. They enable users to manage documents by uploading them to libraries or to manage rows of information in a list—similar to a spreadsheet in many ways—manage versions, and alert the user if anything changes; they also offer a wide range of other powerful features. This chapter presents a high-level overview of the standard tools offered in libraries and lists provided by SharePoint Server 2013 and SharePoint Foundation 2013. Examples illustrate the capabilities of the tools that are most commonly used by end users and library and list administrators.

The next three chapters cover related topics that will be of interest to information workers, architects, and managers alike. Chapter 20, "Customizing and Managing Libraries and Lists to Meet Business Requirements," builds on the content provided in this chapter to provide additional information about the standard management tasks required to customize and maintain sites and workspaces. Chapter 21, "Designing and Managing Pages and Sites for Knowledge Workers," moves beyond lists and libraries to focus on the design and management of the containers that hold them and that provide views of the data and files contained within. And then Chapter 22, "Managing Metadata and Content Types in SharePoint 2013," focuses on the complex topic of metadata for readers interested in the process of building a vibrant taxonomy for the organization.

NOTE

This chapter assumes that users are using the Windows 8 operating system, with Internet Explorer (IE) 10. For users with different environments, be sure to test the appropriate combination of operating system and browser, and be aware that the user experience may vary based on the combination of software products used. For example, the experience of a user with Windows 7, IE 9, and Office 2010 will differ from that of a user with Windows 8, IE 10, and Office 2013. Likewise, a user with a Macintosh using Safari will also have a different experience.

Empowering Users Through SharePoint 2010 Libraries

Many users wonder what the difference is between simply continuing to store their files in a file share on their network, keeping them on their local hard drives to make sure they are close at hand, or using their email inboxes as storage and management tools. They also want to understand the differences in level of effort required to use the SharePoint tools and get an inkling of the benefits they and their organization will see after investing in the new technologies presented by the SharePoint 2013 product line.

SharePoint 2013 document libraries offer a variety of features that have proven to be useful to a wide range of users and projects and empower the site administrators to customize the storage and collaborative features of the library and enhance user productivity. Advantages provided by a SharePoint document library include the following:

- The administrator of a document library has a great deal of control over who can add, modify, and delete documents, or just read them, which often is not the case if a file share on the network is being used. Therefore, a departmental manager can easily control the set of users who can read or modify documents under her control without filing a help desk ticket or needing special privileges on the network. Permissions can be modified for an individual document or folder within the document library as well.
- Versioning can be turned on for a document library that keeps a complete copy of previous versions of the document for reference or recovery purposes. Both major and minor versions can be tracked, encouraging a more formal process of determining when a document is ready for general use or still in the development cycle.
- Alerts can be set on a document within the library, a folder in the library, or for the entire library so that the user receives an email notification if a document is modified, added, or deleted. Users can also set other criteria, such as weekly summaries to minimize in-box clutter.
- Documents can be checked out, with the name of the person who has the document checked out listed in the library, so that other users can't modify the document. Checking out can be required before a user can edit a document to further ensure best practices for document editing.

- SharePoint 2013 enables users to drag and drop documents directly to the web interface. This feature is new to SharePoint 2013 and is more intuitive and easy to use when adding documents to a SharePoint 2013 document library.
- A template can be stored in the document library that can be used to create a new document that is in turn stored in the library by default. So, for example, a document library designed to hold technical specifications documents can provide a Word template document with the latest format, layout, and sections in it.
- Metadata can be added to a document library that enables users to better describe what type of document it is, based on company standards (for example, Proposal, Project Plan, Report, Procedure), which product it covers, who owns the document (as opposed to who last modified it), or pretty much any other kind of textual or numerical information. SharePoint 2013 adds more control over default settings in a document library and allows ratings to be added. Figure 19.1 shows ratings in the far-right column.

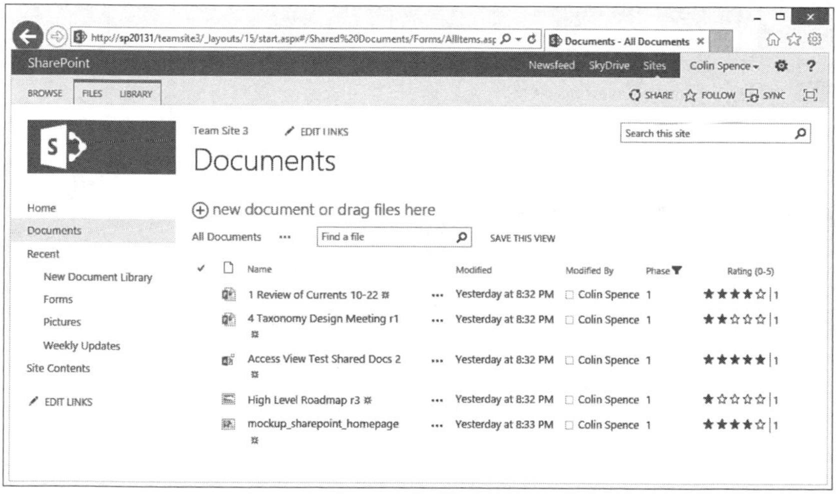

FIGURE 19.1 SharePoint 2013 document library with Ratings column.

- Views can be created that group documents by certain criteria, sort them by any of the columns in the library, or only display documents that meet certain criteria. For example, the view from the home page may well be different from the view within the document library to minimize the amount of space taken up on the home page and to only show the last ten documents modified.
- The ability to search within the library for text contained within the document is provided by SharePoint, a feature often not available on a corporate network. In addition, the ability to search the metadata associated with a document makes it easier for users to find the desired document more quickly. Entering a search term in the Search bar in a SharePoint 2013 document library defaults to the This List scope and the user can then expand and fine tune the search from the search results page.

- If the organization decides on certain standards for the customization of a document library, it can create a template that can include the content if desired and can be used in other sites. This helps promote standards for document library design and features supported.
- SharePoint 2013 libraries offer additional features such as the Follow tag, and users can add additional tags and notes to documents (which encourages comments and input from the users).
- Workflows can be created on-the-fly or predesigned for use within the document library to get feedback or approval. More advanced workflows can be designed by developers to start more complex processes that involve more complex actions and business logic. A Quick Step can be defined that appears on the ribbon to allow one-click actions that are custom designed for the library users.
- Incremental changes in the document library such as the ribbon interface and the ability to check the document or documents you are working on make it easier for administrators and end users to quickly come up to speed with the array of tools offered in the document library. Figure 19.2 shows the ribbon interface, with the Files tab active, three documents selected, and the cursor hovering over the Delete button.

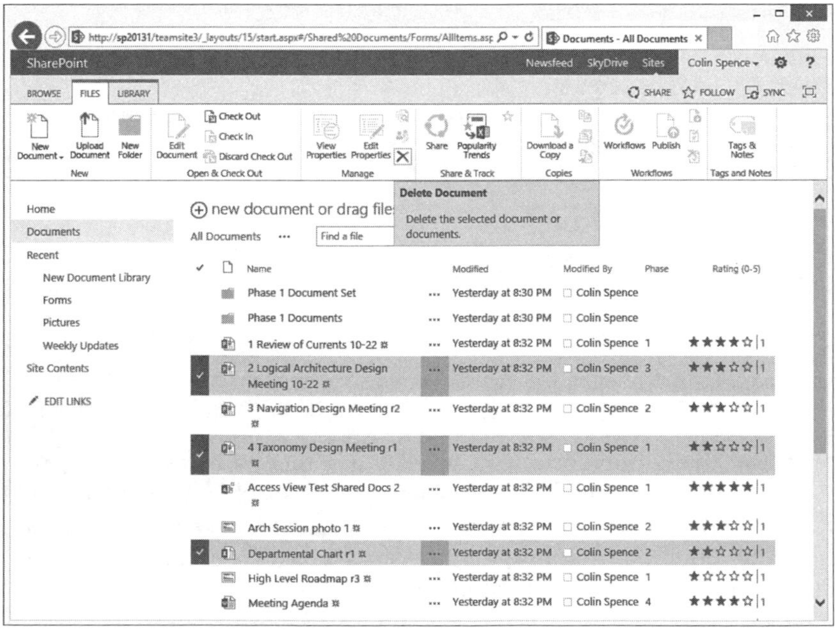

FIGURE 19.2 SharePoint 2013 document library with the Files tab on the ribbon visible and several documents selected.

- The contents of the document library can be downloaded to SharePoint Workspace or the Outlook client so that it can be accessed when the user is offline.
- A two-stage Recycle Bin is available, to rescue users' documents from the inevitable accidental deletions that occur.

NOTE

Mastering all these features can be complex for the document library administrator as well as for the users. It is important to balance the complexity of the library and the number of features leveraged with the sophistication of the typical users of the library and the type of content that is stored in the document library. Better to "start simple" with a few metadata columns, the ratings column, versioning enabled, and standard workflows than to overcomplicate the document library if users are brand new to SharePoint. However, if the document library users have been using SharePoint 2010 for several years, it can make sense to enable more complex features, such as complex metadata, document workspaces, and custom workflows.

Although a percentage of users of SharePoint document libraries may complain about learning yet a new software application, after a little training they will quickly appreciate the features that make their working day more productive. For example, one immediate benefit of having versioning enabled is that only the latest version shows up in the document library. This means that users don't have to spend extra time deciphering complex filenames or looking at modification dates to ensure that they are in fact editing the latest version. The ability to check out a document makes it easy for a user to "reserve" a document that he doesn't want anyone else modifying and knows he needs to work on over the weekend. By allowing users to rate documents, the document library takes on an added dimension of social interaction, further differentiating best-of-breed documents from mediocre and worst-of-breed documents.

Administrators will quickly come to appreciate the ability to add new columns of information to a document library that help them manage their documents and help users quickly find the exact document they are looking for, create customized views, leverage granular search, and navigate metadata. For example, by simply adding a column called Client, a sales manager can make it clear which client a document was created for. In addition, by providing a column titled Value of Opportunity, the total dollar amount of the proposal can easily be seen without opening the document. And if the Ratings column is enabled, an administrator can see over time which documents are the most popular and well received and learn about the needs of the users, as well as archive the less-useful documents if applicable.

NOTE

The ribbon interface in SharePoint 2013 offers quick access to the large number of tools available to users and admins in a tabbed interface in one place, rather than spread out among different drop-down menus, and the use of visually relevant icons truly makes a difference and speeds the learning process.

Using the Site Contents Page in SharePoint 2013

SharePoint 2013 offers a number of different libraries, which are compared later in this chapter, but it is important to understand which type of document library you are working with. You might not find this easy if you are using a SharePoint 2013 environment created by someone else, so a good place to start is by accessing the Site Contents link from the Settings (gear icon) drop-down menu or from the bottom of the quick launch area. Figure 19.3 shows the Site Contents (viewlsts.aspx) page revealing the lists and libraries (referred to as "apps" in SharePoint 2013) on the site (in this case, a SharePoint Server 2013 Enterprise team site).

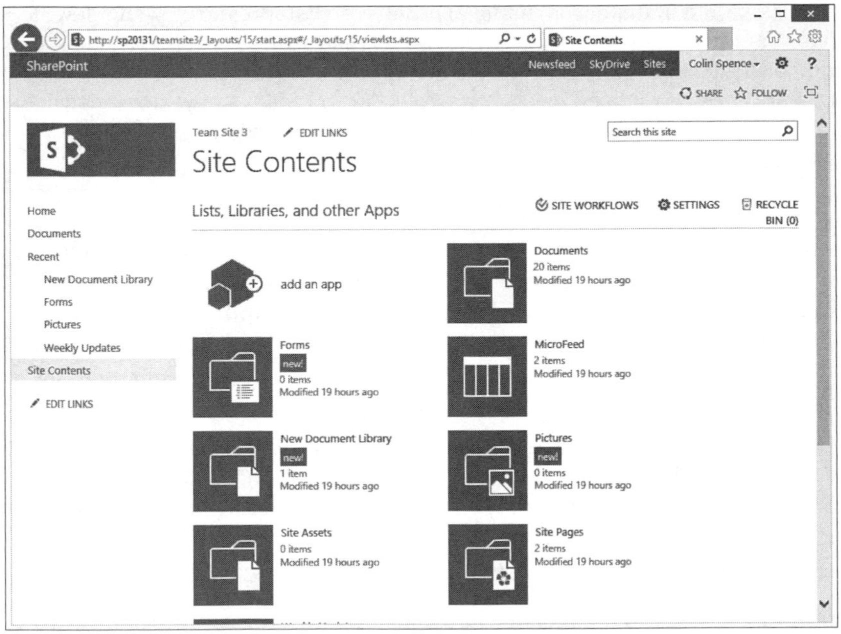

FIGURE 19.3 Site Contents page in a SharePoint Server 2013 Enterprise site.

This is a useful page to visit because it gives the visitor a summary of all the lists, libraries, and other apps that she has access to. Other information is obvious on this page, such as the names of the libraries and the lists, any notes provided about a specific library or list, the number of items in each one, and the last modified date. This gives a very quick overview of how complex the site is, which lists and libraries have been modified most recently, and how many items are in each one. If none of the lists or libraries have been modified in months, for example, this clearly indicates that no one has added, modified, or deleted content on the site in that amount of time, and it might be time to find out why.

Note that hovering over a list or library causes an ellipsis (...) to appear in the upper-right corner of the selected list or library. Clicking the ellipsis reveals additional tools and information, including descriptive text about the list or library and the tools Settings, About, and Remove.

NOTE

It is generally a bad idea to delete document libraries created by SharePoint during a site creation because they might provide functionality important to the functionality of the site.

A Brief Tour of a Document Library

This section summarizes the main features of a document library to provide an overview of the tools and features provided; the following section then drills down more deeply into more of these tools.

Figure 19.4 shows a document library titled New Documents at the root of a team site created in SharePoint Server 2013. Note that as shown in the URL, the view displayed is the AllItems.aspx page. The basic components include navigation tools in the quick launch area on the left, which includes links to libraries and lists the site administrator has chosen to include in the Quick Launch and the Site Contents links. The ribbon tools along the top include the Browse, Files, and Library tools tabs. On the right side can be found a search field. There is also a Find a File search field within the document library allowing the user to search for a file name within the document library.

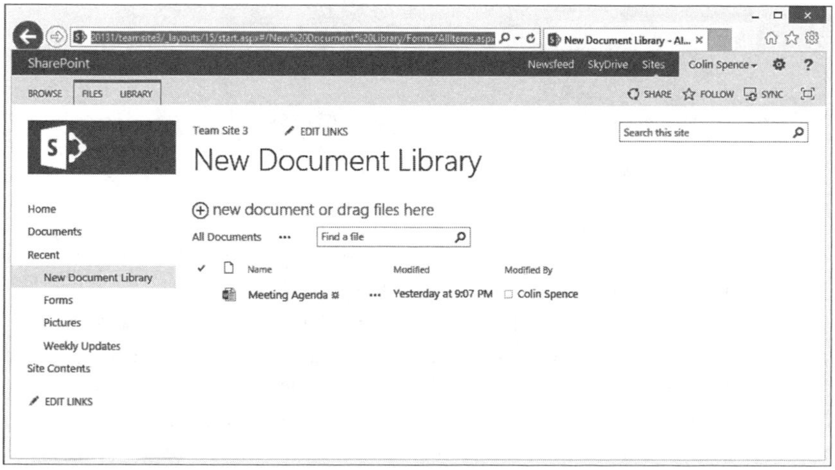

FIGURE 19.4 A document library in a team site.

In the working area, one document is visible with a Word icon in the Type column, name of the document in the Name column, modified date in the Modified column, and modified by information in the Modified By column. Note that because SharePoint 2013 is a fifth-generation product, Microsoft has worked diligently and taken end-user input to create an environment that provides a good combination of aesthetics, features, and usability, and SharePoint 2013 has an excellent balance of these components.

Adding Documents to a Document Library

The primary means of adding items to a document library is to access the new document link, which lives at the top of the working area of the document library. Figure 19.5 shows the Add a Document window that opens when this link is clicked, and this window provides the Browse button, which allows the user to browse for and select a single document for uploading, an Upload Files Using Windows Explorer Instead link, and an Overwrite Existing Files check box.

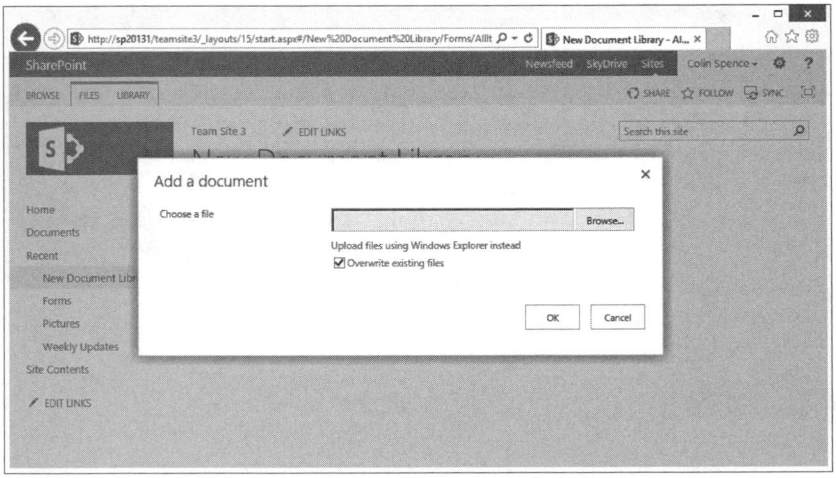

FIGURE 19.5 Add a Document window in a document library.

The Upload Files Using Windows Explorer Instead link, shown in Figure 19.6, differs dramatically from the SharePoint 2010 Upload Multiple Files, which launched another window for dragging and dropping multiple files. SharePoint 2013 opens a Windows Explorer screen and users can then drag files and folders from a Windows Explorer window to this Windows Explorer screen or click a Browse for Files Instead link. The process of dragging files and folders to the upload pane is more flexible because the user can drag over nearly any combinations of folders and files using the familiar Windows Explorer interface.

Another method that power users will find of interest is the ability to enter in the address of the document library into the Address bar of Windows Explorer in the format \\servername\site\libraryname (also referred to as Web Distributed Authoring and Versioning [WebDAV] access). Figure 19.7 shows an example where Windows Explorer was opened in Windows 8 and the address was entered as \\sp20131\teamsite3\New Document Library; as you can see, the usual Explorer tools (Open, New, Print, Cut, Copy, Delete, and Rename) are available.

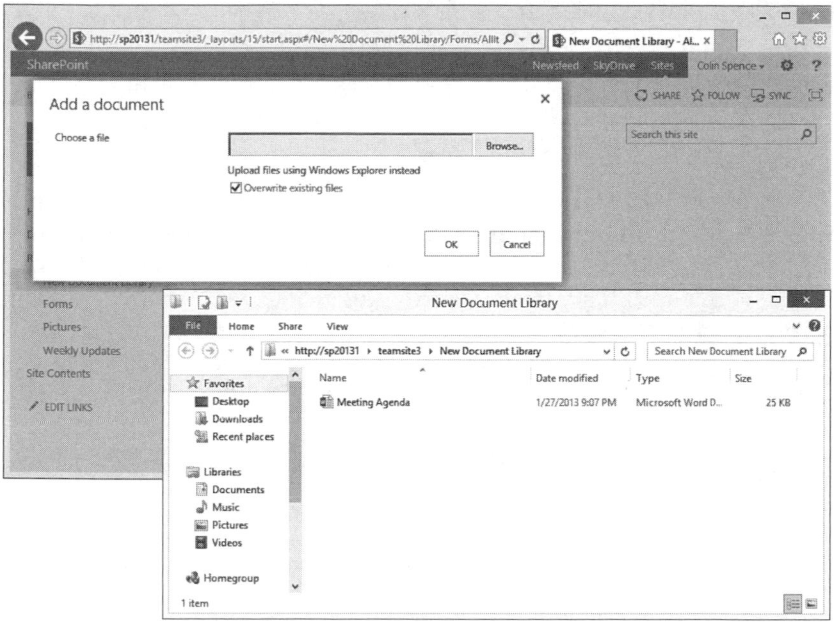

FIGURE 19.6 Uploading files to a document library using Windows Explorer.

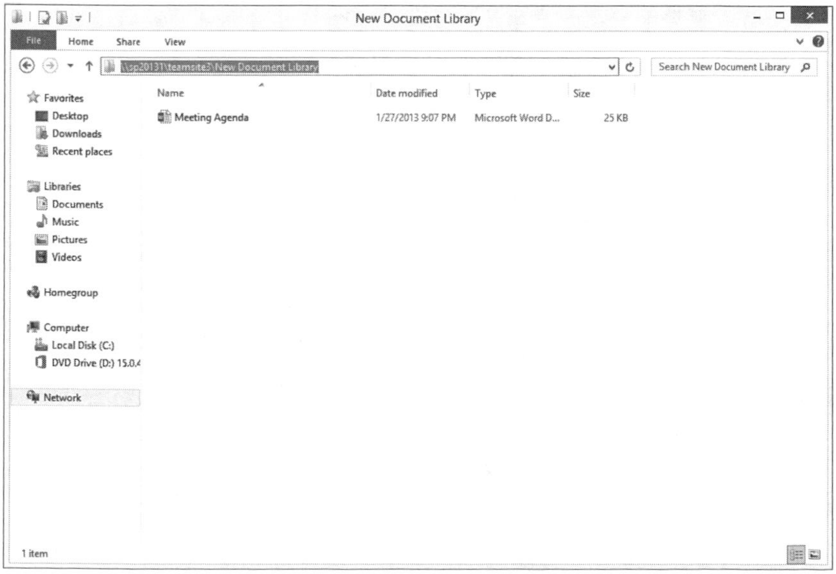

FIGURE 19.7 Accessing a SharePoint document library using WebDAV.

NOTE

Explorer view (WebDAV) access is not always available to end users on a corporate network; it might be disabled on purpose or disabled due to operating system configurations.

An additional way to add items to a document library is to use the inbound email feature for the document library. A farm administrator would need to enable inbound email from the Configure Incoming E-Mail Settings page in the Central Administration site and assign an email address to the document library from the Incoming E-Mail Settings link on the Document Library Settings page. After that is enabled, users can send emails with attachments to the document library. Chapter 16, "Configuring Email-Enabled Content, Site Mailboxes, and Exchange Server Integration," covers the configuration process.

NOTE

To determine which types of documents are allowed to be uploaded, a farm administrator needs to access the Manage Web Applications page in Central Administration, where the Blocked File Types icon provides access to all blocked file types. These include .bat, .cmd, .com, .dll, .exe, .vb, and a number of other file types.

NOTE

The default maximum upload size for a SharePoint 2013 document library is inherited from the web application that is managed in the Central Administration site. This setting is 250MB by default. Changing this setting does requires modifying the web application's Maximum Upload Size setting as well as other configuration changes (including a change to the web.config file) to ensure that the front-end SharePoint servers are able to support larger file sizes. The upload size could be theoretically as large as 2GB (2047MB), but most organizations choose to keep this in the range of 150MB to 250MB because "very large" files can take a long time to save and to open when stored in SharePoint.

Working with the Other Standard Tools in a Document Library

Now that the basic layout of a document library and the process of adding documents to a document library have been covered in the previous section, we review the additional tools available from the Documents ribbon and the drop-down menu. A number of tools are available, and the tools differ between SharePoint Foundation 2013 and SharePoint Server 2013 Standard and Enterprise, so the version of SharePoint being used in each case is clarified. Be aware that the features enabled in the document library and privileges of the user accessing the tools also affect which tools do and do not display on the ribbon and the drop-down menu, as well as which are grayed out or available for use. What you see in your environment may differ from these examples.

Figure 19.8 shows a SharePoint Server 2013 document library with several items in it. For one of these documents, the user has accessed the menu by clicking the ellipsis. This results in a checkmark being added to the left of the document signifying that the document is selected while also bringing up the menu. When one or more documents are selected, the user can access various tools from the Files tab.

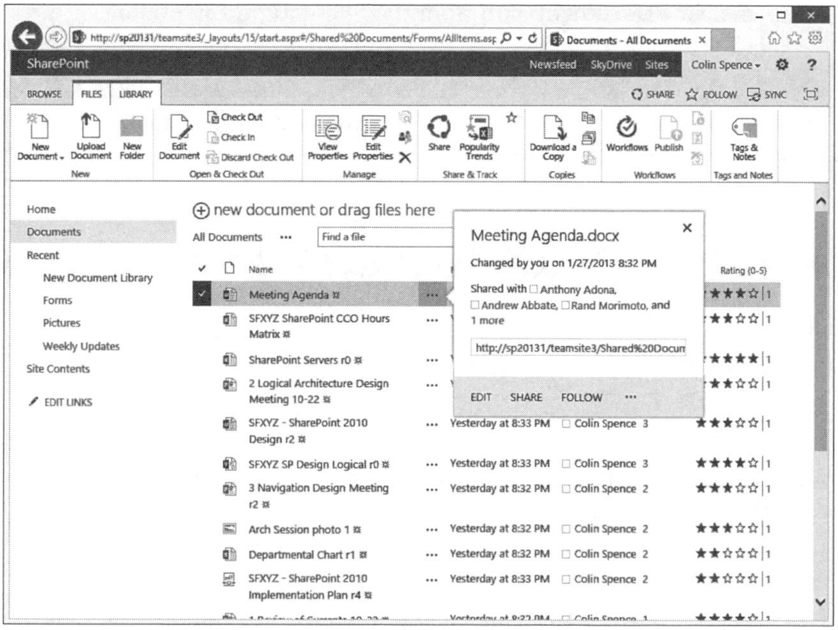

FIGURE 19.8 The Documents tab and drop-down menu for a document in a document library.

The pop-up menu offers additional information about the selected document as well as providing access to tools including Edit, Share, Follow, and another ellipsis. If the ellipsis on the pop-up menu is clicked, a number of the tools available on the Files tab of the ribbon become accessible.

The tools in the Files tab are covered in the following sections, from left to right, and include both the tools from SharePoint Foundation 2013 and SharePoint Server 2013.

Working with the New Document Tools

Located to the far left of the Documents tab on the ribbon, the New Document and Upload Document tools are often-used tools that allow a user with sufficient permissions to create a new document using the template assigned to the document library or upload documents. The Upload Document tool was discussed in detail in the earlier "Adding Documents to a Document Library" section and so is not covered in more detail in this section.

Follow these steps to use the New Document tool:

1. Create a new document library or use an existing document library for this exercise. If an existing document library is used, the steps may vary depending on how the library is configured, whether content types are enabled, and other variables.
2. From within a document library, using an account with Contributor or greater permissions, click the New Document icon from the Files tab on the ribbon.

NOTE

If the computer you are using to access the SharePoint environment is not a domain member, you are asked to log in again at this point.

NOTE

The new document link in the main body of the document library underneath the ribbon is actually a link to the Add a Document document-upload screen, and therefore can cause confusion. Logically that link should be labeled "Add a Document" or "Upload a Document."

3. Word 2013 loads and displays the template. You might need to click Enable Editing first, but then customize the template in whatever fashion desired and click the Save icon.
4. On the Save As screen, the Other Web Locations option should show the source library. Click that library on the right, and then provide the document an appropriate name. Click Save.
5. Return to the document library, refresh the page if needed, and the new document appears. The Modified information should show "A few seconds ago."
6. Select the new document by checking the box to the left of the document, and then click View Properties from the Files menu on the ribbon. As shown in Figure 19.9, this page provides access to a variety of tools on the ribbon, including Edit Item, Version History, Shared With, Delete Item, Check Out, Alert Me, Manage Copies, and Workflows, and shows the Name, Title, Created, and Last Modified information.

The document library administrator can edit the template from the Advanced Settings page, accessible from the Settings page for the document library. However, if the Allow Management of Content Types option is enabled, the Edit Template option in the Document Template section is no longer available. If content types are enabled for the library, the templates for each content type are defined and managed from the Site Content Types gallery accessible from the Site Settings page.

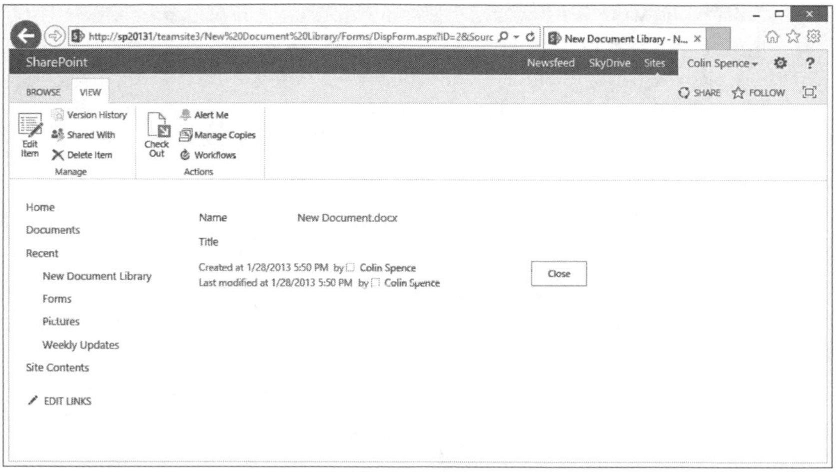

FIGURE 19.9 View Properties for a new document.

NOTE

Users can only use tools that their permission levels allow them to use. For example, if a user with Reader permissions is visiting a document library, he is not able to click the Edit Document icon. It is grayed out because he only has the ability to read documents in the library.

Pros and Cons of the New Folder Tool

An icon for the New Folder tool is available for use to the right of the Upload Document icon if the library administrator allows the creation of new folders in the document library. To allow the use of folders in a document library, the administrator needs to access the Settings page, then click the Advanced Settings link, and select Yes under the "Make New Folder" command available.

If folders are enabled, and the New Folder icon is clicked, the folder needs to be given a name; it can then be created and used to store documents or other folders. Folders are objects in the library that can be selected, just like a document, and a variety of the tools on the Files tab are active and can then be used. For example, a folder can have unique permissions assigned to it, users can create alerts based on the contents of folders, and they can be connected to Outlook, but they are not as manageable as standard items in a document library. For example, metadata columns added to a document library are not editable for a folder in that document library.

Opinions vary about the usefulness of folders in SharePoint and have been argued for years. One point of view is that folders should not be used in SharePoint because they can be seen as keeping alive old and possibly bad habits from file shares. However, folders in SharePoint are familiar to users, and comforting to less sophisticated users, and so can prove helpful to users who are just getting used to the SharePoint tool set.

An advantage of using folders in SharePoint 2013 becomes apparent if a user accesses the drop-down menu of a folder and then clicks the Connect to Outlook icon. By following the prompts that then appear, assuming the user has a current version of the Outlook client installed, he can link the folder or subfolder to Outlook and have the contents of this folder available when offline. This is a handy way to synchronize a portion of the contents of a document library with the Outlook client, rather than synchronizing the entire document library, which could be many megabytes or gigabytes in size.

The use of folders in SharePoint document libraries that contain many thousands of documents can speed up the performance of the library. For example, a document library with 20,000 documents that doesn't use folders may perform more slowly when a user is using filters to try and find the document she wants, whereas if these documents were split up among 20 folders of roughly 1,000 documents each, the performance within each folder should be faster.

NOTE

SharePoint shows an error message if the overall URL length that is created by nested folders is too long: "The specified file or folder name is too long. The URL path for all files and folders must be 260 characters or less (and no more than 128 characters for any single file or folder name in the URL). Please type a shorter file or folder name." This restriction limits the complexity of the folder structure that you can create in SharePoint.

Ultimately, the use of folders comes down to a governance issue, and different organizations handle it in different ways. Some organizations forbid their use, instead recommending metadata and customized views be used. Other organizations allow them, but limit the number of subfolders and total URL length that can be used, because long URLs can sometimes result in negative issues.

Using the Edit Document Tool, Check Out, Check In, and Discard Check Out Tools

The Edit Document, Check Out, Check In, and Discard Check Out tools are usually the most often used tools in a collaborative document library, and so time and effort should be dedicated to providing training to end users and administrators on these tools, even if they seem intuitive and everyone *should* know how to use them.

Clicking the Edit Document icon when a document is selected opens the Microsoft Office application and allows the user to edit the document, assuming she has permissions to modify the document in that library. The user may be shown the Open Document window with a warning that "Some files can harm your computer," but then can open the file in the appropriate application. Chapter 25, "Using Word, Excel, PowerPoint with SharePoint 2013," goes into more detail on best practices of using Office applications with SharePoint 2013.

The ability to check out and check in documents is widely considered one of the more important features of a document management system and differentiates SharePoint from a file share, putting it on par with other ECM (enterprise content management) products or document management products.

NOTE

If non-Microsoft file types are going to be stored in document libraries (for example, Adobe Photoshop, Autodesk AutoCAD files), IT should carefully test the behaviors of these files in SharePoint 2013 document libraries. In many cases, users may need to copy the file to their desktop, open the file for editing, save to the desktop, and finally upload back to the SharePoint 2013 document library.

A generally recommended best practice is for every user to check out a document before he is going to work on it. This lets other users of the library know that a specific user has "reserved" the document and is either working on it currently or will be in the near future.

When users check out the document, the Type icon for the document changes to include a small green arrow, as shown in Figure 19.10. The options in the document pop-up menu now include the tools Check In and Discard Check Out, also shown in Figure 19.10.

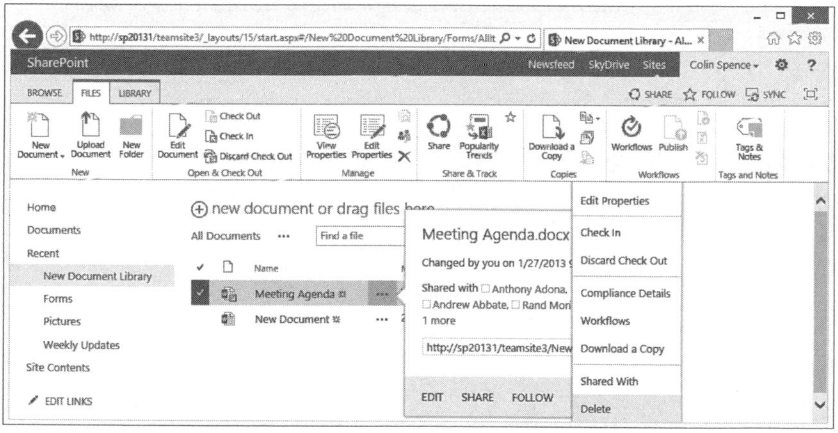

FIGURE 19.10 A checked-out document in a document library.

NOTE

Checking out a document can be made mandatory by a document library administrator: From the Settings page, click the Versioning Settings link. Then in the Require Check Out section, click Yes under Require Documents to Be Checked Out Before They Can Be Edited.

When a user has the document checked out, she can elect to then edit the document or wait until later. Other users will see from the changed icon that the document is checked out, and if the library administrator has elected to include the Checked Out To column in the view of the documents, it will be even clearer not only that the document is checked out but also to whom.

Reviewing the View Properties and Edit Properties Tools

All documents have properties, whether they are saved in SharePoint document libraries or not. Documents have filenames, created date and time, modified date and time, author, and other tags attached to the document. SharePoint allows document library administrators to define additional properties, which are metadata fields that are stored in that document library. Unlike some basic file properties, properties defined by metadata fields might get stripped from the document if it is moved to a different document library that doesn't contain the same metadata columns. The View Properties and Edit Properties tools allow users of the library to see what information about the document is available within the document library.

Figure 19.11 shows the Edit Properties window for a document stored in a document library that has been customized with the addition of a row titled Phase, a row titled Document Type, and a Document Owner row. A SharePoint Server 2013 Enterprise document library has been used for this example. The version number of the document is visible at the bottom of the window and indicates that versioning is on for the document library, and the created and last modified date, time, and user account information is also provided.

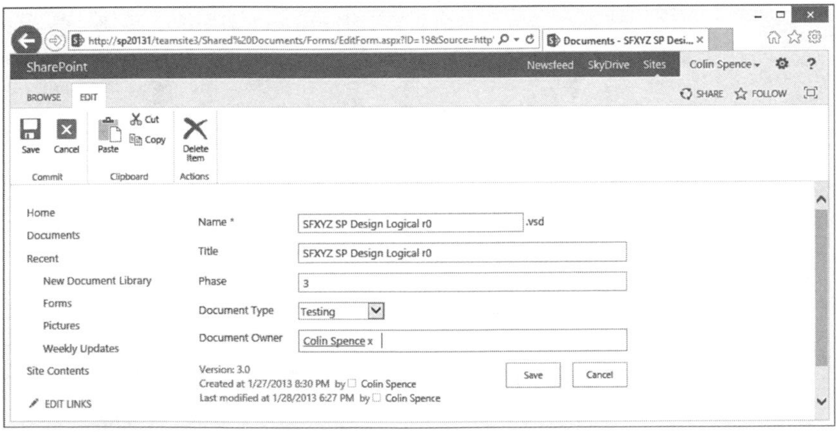

FIGURE 19.11 Edit Properties page for a document.

The document library administrator chose to add several columns to better categorize documents using metadata. By adding a row titled Document Owner that requires the entry of a domain user account name, it is clearly defined who the ultimate authority is for that specific document. Otherwise, the document library tracks who created the document (or uploaded it) and who last modified it, but neither of these people may actually be responsible for the document. By adding the Document Type row, a list of options is given to the user to choose from. This saves time and encourages users to better define the type of document, because document names can be confusing and might actually give little insight into the type of document it is.

Chapter 22 provides more information about this essential topic.

Using the Version History Tool

The next icon on the toolbar is the Version History icon. Note that Version History is not available unless versioning is enabled for the document library (accessible through the library Settings page, Versioning Settings, and then choosing either Create Major Versioning or Create Major and Minor [draft] Versions).

Version history shows the different versions of a document in the library if versioning was enabled in the library and provides information about changes that were made to the metadata of the document. Figure 19.12 shows a version history for a document with several major versions. The topmost version is indicated as being the current published major version, and the date and time modifications that took place are clearly indicated, along with the logged-in user who made the changes, the size of the document, and any comments added.

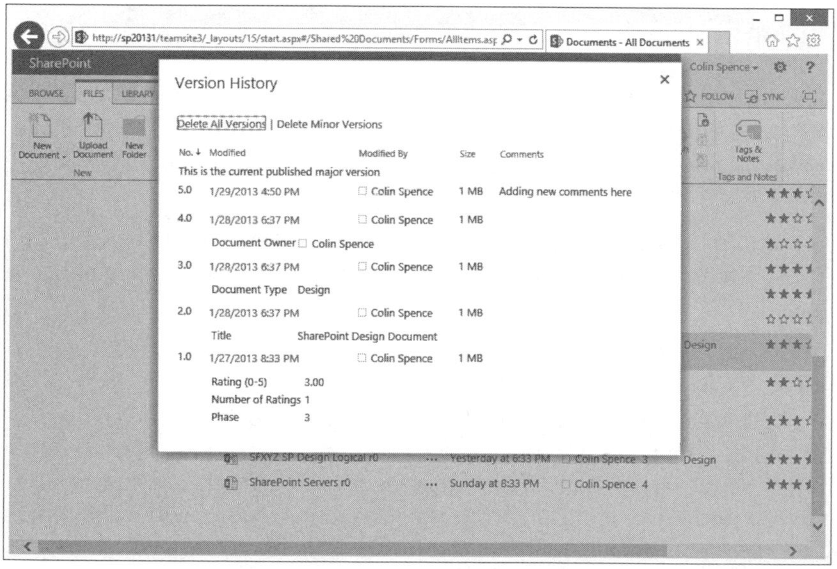

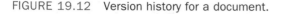

FIGURE 19.12 Version history for a document.

NOTE

Versioning is such an important feature in SharePoint 2013 that it is critical that administrators and end users feel comfortable with working with major and minor versions. They also must understand the importance of following best practices of always checking out documents before working on them, then checking them back in when complete, and deciding whether the new version should be a minor or draft version (0.1, 0.2 version) or a major or published version (1.0, 2.0 version). Comments should be added when checking a file back in to facilitate later review of previous versions as a best practice.

NOTE

The View option in the Version History window does not actually show you the document; instead, it displays the full properties of the file. So, if a user notices that the current version of a Word document is "incorrect" and wants to revert to an older version of the file, the process is somewhat complex. The user would first need to restore an older version (the one he thinks is the right version) as the current version, open it in Word, and review the actual content of the document. If this is the correct version of the document, the user then simply exits the file, as it is promoted to be the current version. If this restored version is *not* the version the user was looking for, however, he needs to then return to the library, access Version History again for the document, restore a different older version, and again review the contents of the document to determine whether that is the desired version. Most users find this is an arduous process, so the use of effective notes when checking in and publishing versions of documents is highly recommended.

Each version has a drop-down menu that provides the options to View, Restore, or Unpublish this version. The Restore tool "promotes" that version to be the latest version by making a copy of the older version and incrementing the number. Note that there are also tools to Delete All Versions and Delete Minor Versions above the version listing. Chapter 20 provides more information about the options for versioning and pros and cons of these options.

Versioning is discussed in more detail in the "How to Use the Publish, Unpublish, and Cancel Approval Tools" section later in this chapter (in the context of the Publish and Approve/Reject tools).

Using the Shared With Tool

The Shared With tool allows a user with sufficient permissions (members of the Owners group by default) to modify the permissions applied to a specific document. Figure 19.13 shows the Shared With window that loads after a document has been selected in the library and the Shared With button is clicked from the Files tab on the ribbon. (The same icon can be found on the Library tab as well, but it addresses the library as a whole, not the individual document.)

Note in the lower portion of the window shown in Figure 19.13 the options Invite People, Email Everyone, and Advanced. Figure 19.14 shows the Permissions Tools page that appears after selecting the Advanced option. Underneath the ribbon, a note reads, "This document inherits permissions from its parent," which is the default behavior. On the ribbon itself are icons to Manage Parent, Stop Inheriting Permissions, and Check Permissions.

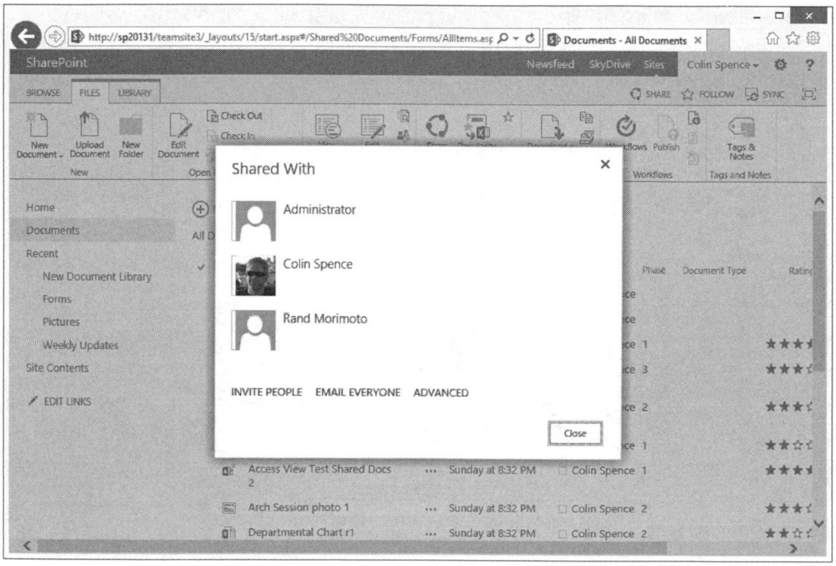

FIGURE 19.13 Shared With window of a document.

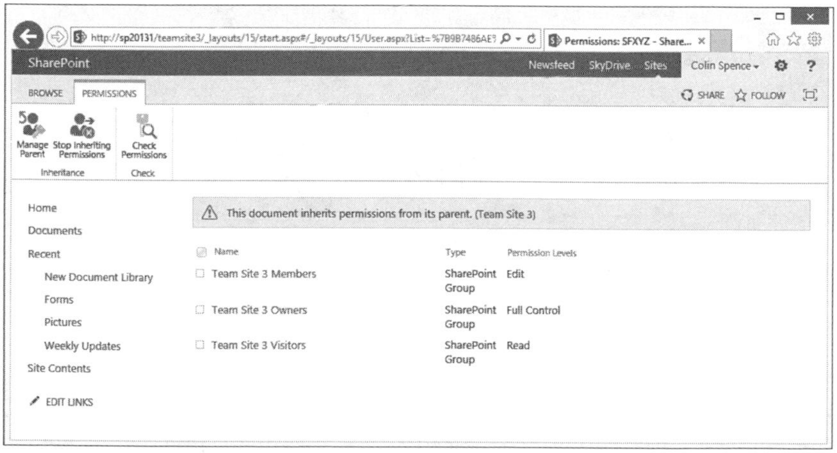

FIGURE 19.14 Permission tools for a document.

If needed, the document library administrator can grant unique permissions to this specific document by clicking the Stop Inheriting Permissions button, but this should be used only when absolutely necessary because of the added overhead and complexity of managing overly customized document libraries. That said, the Check Permissions tool is useful if unique permissions for a document are to be used.

Figure 19.15 shows the results of using the Check Permissions tool on a document with customized permissions for the SharePoint group Company123\Consultants. After the Check Now button is clicked, the tool shows the level of permissions granted to the user or group. Figure 19.15 shows that the Company123\Consultants group has no permissions, because the lowest entry on the screen after the text "Permission levels given to Company123\Consultants" reads None. If a group or user name is entered that does have permissions, this text would read Full Control, Edit, or a similar entry, and it will be clarified whether the privileges were given directly or through a group.

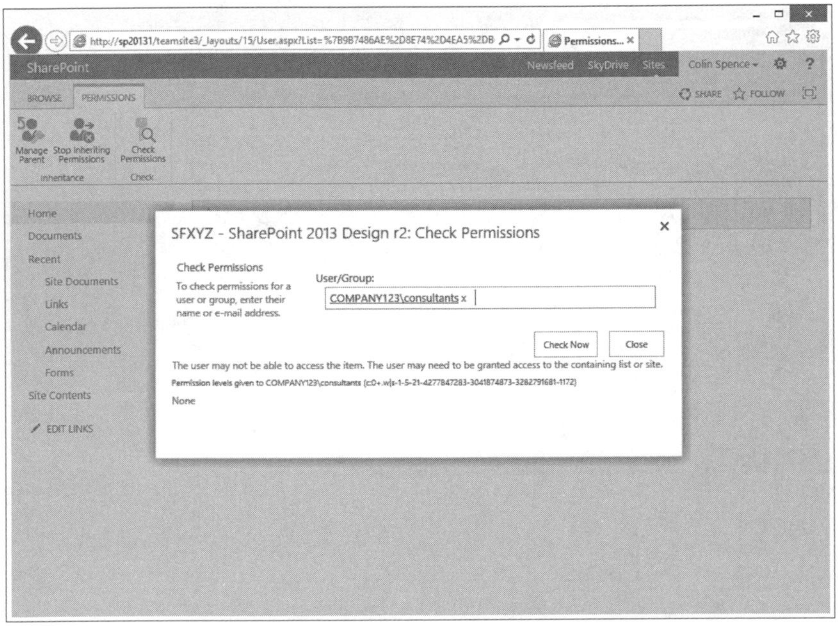

FIGURE 19.15 Check Permissions window for a document.

Using the Delete Button

The Delete button on the Documents tab sends one or more documents to the Recycle Bin for the document library. The ability in SharePoint 2013 document libraries to check one or more items as being selected allows a user who has contributor permissions or an administrator to easily delete a number of items. Note that the Delete key on the keyboard can also be used.

NOTE

In SharePoint 2013, the Recycle Bin is harder to find than in SharePoint 2010. It is no longer found on the Quick Launch menu, but can be found on the Site Contents page on the right side of the page under the Search bar. A link to the Recycle Bin could easily be added by an administrator, as follows: Access the Site Settings page and click the Navigation link in the Look and Feel section. Then, add a link to the Current Navigation options that points to */[sitename]/*_layouts/15/RecycleBin.aspx.

After items are sent to the Recycle Bin, a member with Full Control permissions can restore anyone's items, or a member with Contributor permissions can restore items he has deleted. A member with Read permissions won't have access to the Recycle Bin. An administrator with site collection administrator privileges can access the Site Collection Recycle Bin (otherwise known as the second-level Recycle Bin) that contains items deleted from the End User Recycle Bin, or to see and restore items still in the End User Recycle Bin.

Note that a farm administrator needs to determine the base settings for the Recycle Bin for the site collection in question. A farm administrator can access the Web Application General Settings interface from the Central Administration site to determine the following settings:

- Recycle Bin status on or off.
- The amount of time after which to delete items in the Recycle Bin. The default is 30 days; the number of days can be changed, or Never can be checked.
- The percentage of live site quota allocated that will be added for the second-stage deleted items, with 50 percent being the default. Note that the second-stage Recycle Bin (otherwise known as the Site Collection Recycle Bin) can be turned off.

It is an important task for site administrators and farm administrators to manage the Recycle Bins appropriately. A maximum age for retaining deleted items in the second-stage Recycle Bin should be clarified, and it should be emptied accordingly.

Understanding the Share, Popularity Trends, and Follow Tools

New to SharePoint 2013 is the grouping of tools that includes the Share, Popularity Trends, and Follow tools. The Share button is similar to the Shared With tool mentioned previously. Figure 19.16 shows the Share window, where document library administrators can enter names, email addresses, or the Everyone keyword. Then, the document library administrator can select Can Edit or Can View permissions from a drop-down, effectively granting invited people with specified access to a document.

Selecting the Popularity Trends tool opens an Excel file that contains a daily and monthly table and graph of hits for the document as well as unique users. This could be helpful in analyzing how often a document was accessed and how many users accessed this document within a certain time frame. The Follow tool allows a user to follow documents. Followed documents can be seen in their personal newsfeed.

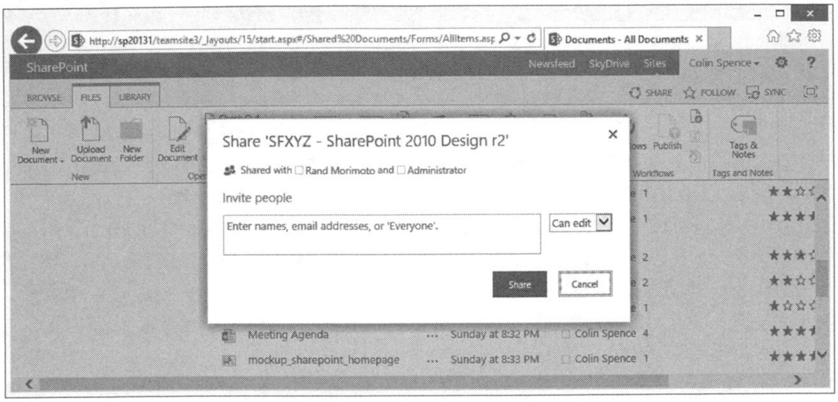

FIGURE 19.16 Using the Share tool for a document in a document library.

Reviewing the Alert Me Tool

The Alert Me tool allows the user to create an alert on a specific document, if one is checked, or to Manage My Alerts, which opens the My Alerts on This Site page. Then the user can create an alert for a list or library. Alerts are another powerful tool that sets SharePoint document libraries apart from traditional file storage solutions, because they allow SharePoint to communicate directly to end users via email alerts when existing documents change or new documents are added to a specific document library. The following example shows additional benefits of the tool set.

To create an alert for a document library, which is a common task that a user or a site or document library administrator will perform, follow these steps:

1. From within a document library, access the Files tab from the ribbon and click the drop-down arrow next to the Alert Me icon.
2. Click Manage My Alerts.
3. Click Add Alert.
4. Select a document library or list that you want to keep track of. Click the Next button.
5. Provide a title for the alert. It is a best practice to include the name of the site and the list or library in the title, such as HRSharedDocsAlert.
6. Add the users/groups the alerts will be sent to, separated by semicolons. Note that you can add whomever you like in this field, which is a power that you should not abuse! You will usually be creating the alert for your own use, but administrators and managers might put in a group name.
7. Leave the delivery method set to E-mail, unless the farm is configured to send text messages (SMS).

8. Select the Change Type to trigger the alert. This can be All Changes, New Items Are Added, Existing Items Are Modified, or Items Are Deleted.
9. Select additional criteria in the Send Alerts for These Changes section. These options are Anything Changes, Someone Else Changes a Document, Someone Else Changes a Document Created by Me, and Someone Else Changes a Document Last Modified by Me.
10. Select an option for the When to Send Alerts section. The options are Send Notification Immediately, Send a Daily Summary, or Send a Weekly Summary. For the daily summary and weekly summary options, you need to select a time or day and time. Figure 19.17 shows the Change Type, Send Alerts for These Changes, and When to Send Alerts settings for an alert.

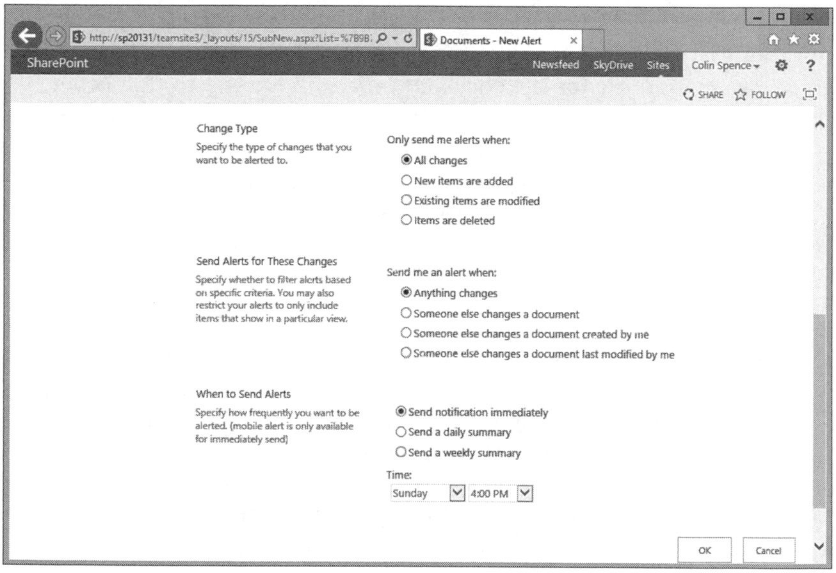

FIGURE 19.17 Creating an alert for a document library.

11. Click OK to complete the alert.
12. If the SharePoint 2013 environment is configured properly, the person or people listed in the Send Alerts To field will receive emails letting them know the alert was successfully created.

Understanding the Download a Copy, Send To, Manage Copies, and Go To Source Tools

Next on the Documents ribbon is the grouping of tools that includes Download a Copy, and then to the right, the tools Send To, Manage Copies, and Go To Source.

NOTE

The tools in this section (Download a Copy, Send To, Manage Copies, and Go To Source) should be considered advanced tools, and end users should be educated about the complexities and limitations of these tools. A criticism of these tools is that they go against one of the purposes of SharePoint, which is to centralize and consolidate documents rather than have multiple copies in different places, which these tools make possible. Sometimes, however, these tools can prove very useful, or even essential, but should still be used with caution.

The Download a Copy tool is self-explanatory and, if clicked, allows the user to save a copy of the document to another location. Ideally, this option should rarely be used, because there are a variety of ways to take content offline, including syncing a folder with Outlook or using SharePoint SkyDrive Pro 2013 or third-party tools. Sometimes, however, downloading a copy is useful. The primary situation is when a user has the document checked out and another user really needs to use the document for reference or possibly to edit it. Although a primary purpose for the checkout process is exactly so that other people don't edit the document, people sometimes forget that they have the document checked out, and the user who needs it is in a rush and doesn't want to bother an administrator or file a help desk ticket. Note that downloading a copy, editing it, and then saving back to the library when the version stored by the library has been checked in is a bad practice because the changes made in the previous version are "buried" in the previous versions.

For example, User 1 checks out a Visio and makes changes, such as adding a server icon, and then forgets to check it in. User 2 downloads a copy because he needs to make an edit and adds a printer icon to the Visio. User 2 now cannot save back to the document library as the same name, so he saves to the document library with a slightly different name (rev1). User 1 later checks in his version. Now there are two different primary documents, which is a classic problem from a file share, and this is confusing to users. A better practice is for User 2 to email User 1 and request he check the document back in, and if that fails after a reasonable amount of time, have the administrator force a check in. This way, the versioning system keeps all the versions together, and there aren't multiple primary documents in the library.

The Send To tool provides two options by default: Other Location and Create Document Workspace. If a custom Send To location is defined by the library administrator, it shows as an option as well. The Other Location can be defined on-the-fly by the user and must be a SharePoint 2013 document library that the currently logged-in user has contribute privileges in, or it can be defined by the document library administrator in document library settings, Advanced Settings page. Figure 19.18 shows the Copy window that opens when a user chooses the Send to Other Location option. The user then types in the name of the destination document library and can edit the name of the document if desired. The user has the option to ask that the author send out updates when the document is checked in and to create an alert on the source document. Although not perfect, these are both good methods of helping to ensure that the person who made the copy is aware if the source document has changed. When the process completes, a copy of the document is created in the destination library.

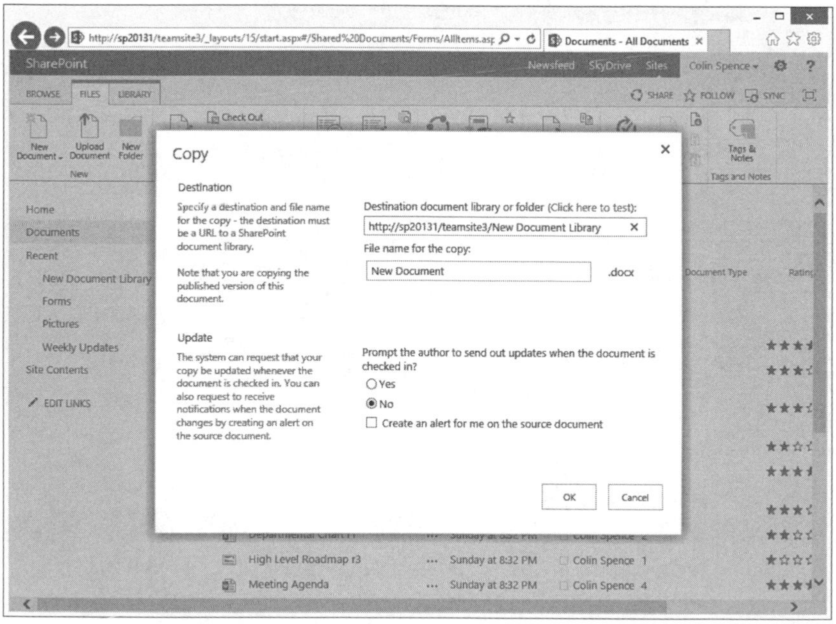

FIGURE 19.18 Copy window resulting from using the Send To tool in a document library.

An interesting feature of the Send To tool and process is that SharePoint is aware that there is another copy of the document, or even that there are multiple copies of the document. Figure 19.19 shows the Manage Copies window for the document that was just copied using the Send To command. This window allows the user to create a new copy if needed or to update copies of the document. The user can remove links to documents if desired by clicking the Edit button next to the destination URL. Note, however (and this relates to the note on the topic of document workspaces), that the document library is not aware of the copy of the document placed in the document workspace, which can cause administrative challenges.

Document workspaces are not discussed in detail here because they are covered in Chapter 21. A document workspace is actually a site that can be created by a user with sufficient privileges that contains a copy of the document as well as other lists designed for collaboration purposes. Note, however, that unlike when the Send To command is used, a document workspace copy of a document does not maintain a connection to the original, which can lead to confusion on the part of users about which is the latest and greatest version of the document (the one in the document library on the parent site or the one in the document library in the workspace).

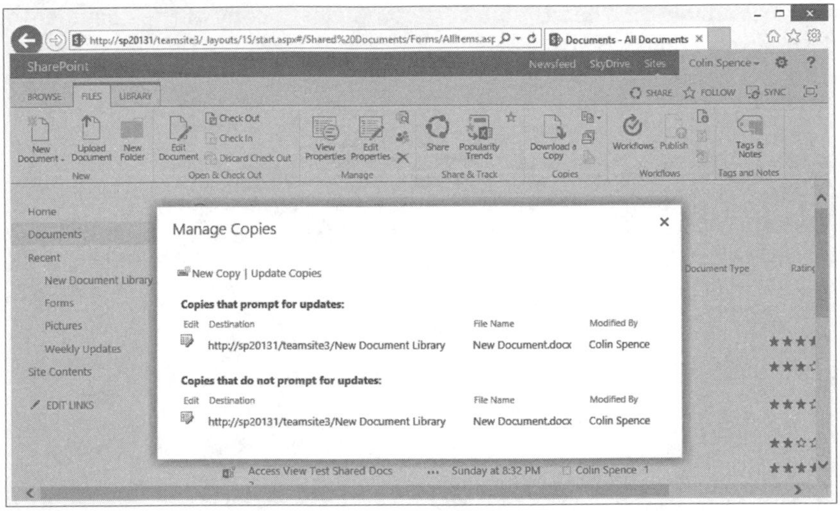

FIGURE 19.19 Manage Copies window for a document.

NOTE

Although document workspaces can be useful in some situations, creating document workspaces can be overly complex to administer, so many organizations decide to discourage their use and lock down which users have the permissions to create workspaces. For example, when a new workspace is created, the creator needs to perform the role of a site administrator and give permissions to users to allow them to access the workspace, make sure the right version of the document is being edited, and finally publish the document back to the source document library when the collaboration is complete.

The final tool in this section, Go To Source, is active if the document selected is connected to a source document. If clicked, it then shows the property information of the source document.

A High-Level Overview of Workflows

Workflows are a complex topic and have been given their own chapter, which is Chapter 28, "Out-of-the-Box Workflows and Designer 2013 Workflows," but because the Workflow tool is provided in the Documents tab on the ribbon, it is covered here at a high level.

NOTE

The Three-State Workflow is the only workflow template provided in SharePoint Foundation 2013; others are available in SharePoint Server 2010. SharePoint Server 2010 Standard and Enterprise provide the following workflow templates: Disposition Approval, Publishing Approval, Collection Signatures, Approval, and Collection Feedback.

A workflow must be created by a document library administrator for it to be available to users of the document library. The document library administrator decides whether the workflow starts automatically or if it can be started manually by users with Edit Item permissions or if users must have Manage List permissions to start the workflow. When started, the workflow communicates to participants via email, which gives instructions of what they need to do. At the same time, tasks are created in a SharePoint tasks list, which the participants interact with and update as they perform their tasks.

If more complex workflows are required, developers and administrators can use tools such as SharePoint Designer 2013, Visio 2013, Visual Studio 2013, and other tools to create more complex workflows. InfoPath 2013 can be used to create advanced forms that are used within the workflow, emails can be customized, and complex business logic can be created if needed.

To start a workflow, a user with sufficient rights follows these steps:

1. The user either selects Workflows from the drop-down menu or clicks the Workflow button in the Documents ribbon after selecting the document.
2. The Workflow.aspx opens and shows the user any workflows associated with the document library. The user clicks the desired workflow. If no workflows are available, the document library administrator needs to be contacted to create one.
3. The user then modifies the settings for the workflow entered by the document library or site administrator, which can include who is involved in the workflow, a text message, due dates for all tasks, duration per task, and other fields depending on the workflow. Figure 19.20 shows a workflow based on the out-of-the-box Collect Feedback workflow.
4. The user then clicks Start to kick off the workflow; emails are sent to the participants with instructions on the steps to take.

The next section provides an example of a Page Approval workflow, to provide a context for how an out-of-the-box workflow can be useful in an approval process.

How to Use the Publish, Unpublish, and Cancel Approval Tools

To begin with, the Publish, Unpublish, and Cancel Approval tools are active only when a document library has versioning enabled and configured to allow the creation of major and minor (draft) versions. A major version is considered the published version. Versioning is a key component of SharePoint 2013 and other document management applications because it not only keeps track of earlier versions of a document but also hides them from end users in the standard views, to make errors less likely when working with the document.

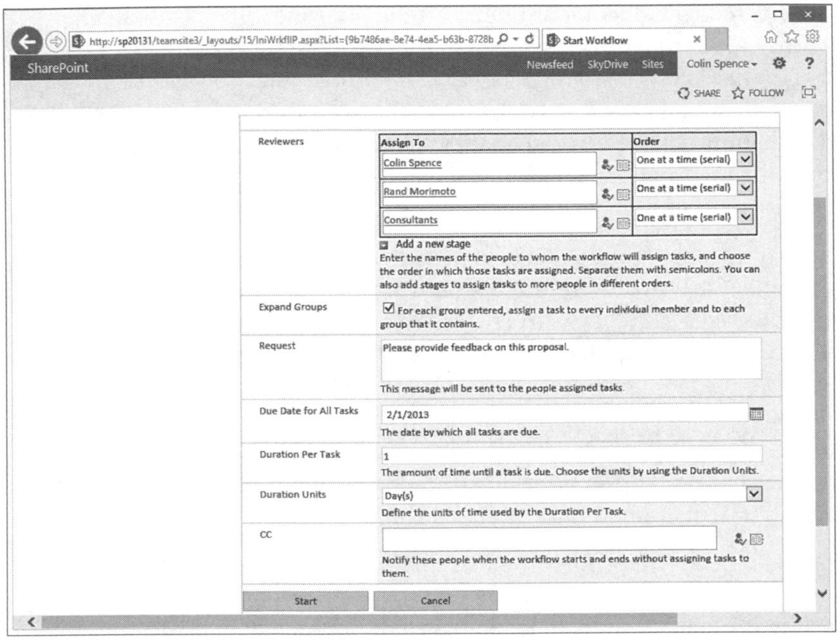

FIGURE 19.20 A Collect Feedback workflow.

NOTE

Be aware that when versioning is enabled, each version of the document adds the full document size to the Structured Query Language (SQL) content database. Versioning in SharePoint 2013 does not just track differences between the documents, but keeps a full copy. Administrators should keep this in mind when determining the policy for enabling versioning for lists and libraries.

The process of turning a draft version (for example, 0.1) into a major (for example, 1.0) version is called *publishing* in SharePoint parlance, and the Publish button is used to either start a workflow or instantly publish the document. It is up to the document library administrator whether to use a workflow for this process, which is more complex and time-consuming, or to enable instant publishing. The following example walks through the process of uploading a document to a document library with major and minor versioning enabled, scheduling enabled, and workflows enabled in SharePoint Server 2013 Enterprise.

The scheduling feature can be turned off or on for a document library by the library administrator. Scheduling determines when a document is published and available for general viewing by users of the site. Before the scheduled start date is reached, the item remains in draft status, and when that date is reached, but before the end date is reached, the document is promoted to major version published status. After the end date is reached, if there is one set, the document returns to draft status.

The Draft Item Security settings, which are set by the document library administrator and accessible from the Document Library Settings page via the Versioning Settings page, determine who can see draft (unpublished) versions of documents. The options are Any User Who Can Read Items, Only Users Who Can Edit Items, and Only Users Who Can Approve Items (and the author of the item). So, it is important for a document library administrator to determine the most appropriate combination of settings. This topic is revisited in Chapter 20.

Some document libraries that are created during the creation of a publishing site or site collection have major and minor versioning enabled, and also have Content Approval turned on, which means that a user with approver privileges needs to approve a document before it is published as a major version. And scheduling may also be enabled for the library, which determines when the item, when approved, is available for the general public. The following example helps clarify the process:

1. A user of a site collection documents library in a publishing site in SharePoint Server 2013 Enterprise uploads a document to the library. This library has major and minor versioning enabled, requires content approval for submitted items, has an Approval workflow configured, as well as scheduling enabled, and so requires a number of steps to take place before an uploaded document is available to the general public.
2. As shown in Figure 19.21, the user is prompted to verify the name and title of the document, and decide whether the scheduling start date should be immediately or a fixed date, and whether the end date should be never or a fixed date. In this example, the user wants the document to not be published to a major version until a given date, and wants it to stay published for only a few weeks. After he likes the setting, he clicks Save.

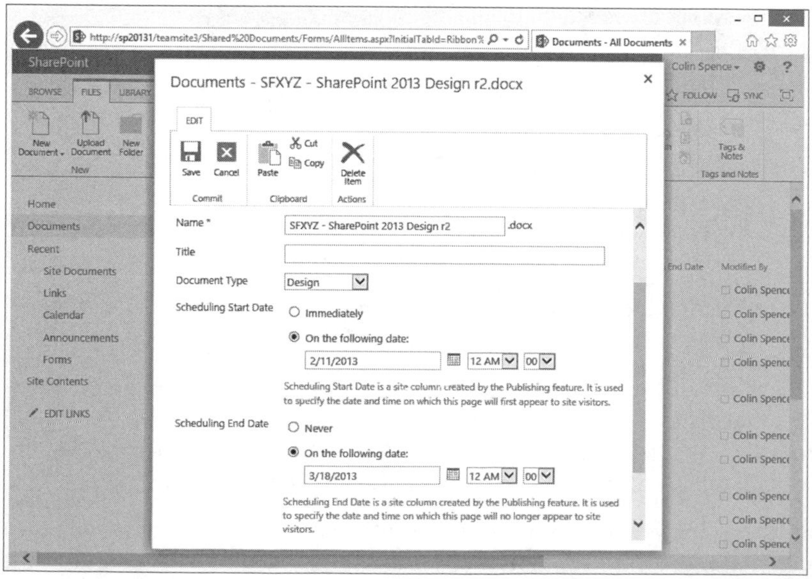

FIGURE 19.21 Finishing the upload process for a document library with Scheduling enabled.

3. The document is now saved in the document library, but is in draft status, with a version number of 0.1. Based on the settings of the document library, only users who can edit items in this document library can now see the document, which includes the user himself.

4. The user, having decided that the document is ready to be published, then accesses the drop-down menu for the item in the All Items view, and clicks the Publish button on the Documents tab of the ribbon.

5. Because the Approval workflow was configured to start this workflow to approve publishing a major version of an item, the workflow window automatically opens.

6. As shown in Figure 19.22, the user enters additional information to complete the workflow—including request text, a due date, duration for the task—and clicks Start.

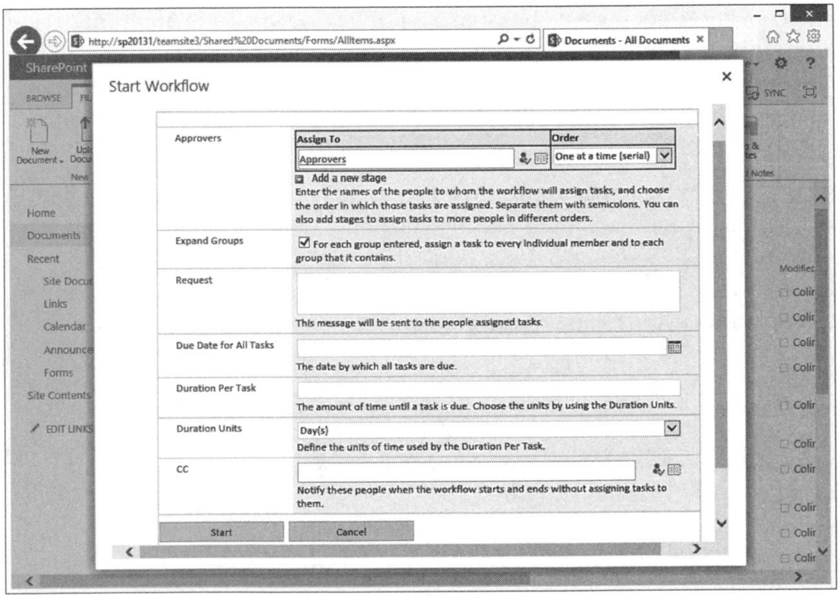

FIGURE 19.22 Starting an Approval workflow in a publishing library.

7. The approval status of the document is now set to pending and remains that way until an approver approves the document.

8. At this point, members of the approvers group on the site receive emails that a document needs approval. The approver clicks the Open This Task button in the Outlook 2013 ribbon for the email, and a form opens with the options to Approve, Reject, Cancel, Request Change, or Reassign Task. The approver clicks Approve.

9. Now the document is approved to be published on the scheduled start date. As shown in Figure 19.23, the Approval Status is set to Scheduled with the start and end dates shown in the two columns to the right. Note also in Figure 19.23 that the

Cancel Approval icon is active, so a user can choose to cancel the approval if needed and start the process over again.

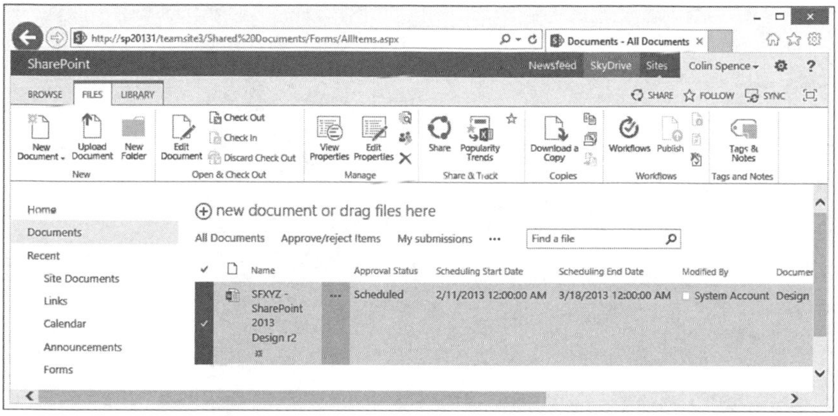

FIGURE 19.23 Document that has been approved and is scheduled to be published.

This example shows the management possibilities of enabling major and minor versioning in a document library, requiring content approval for documents, using a Page Approval workflow, as well as using Scheduling Start and End dates. Enabling the full combination of features does add overhead and complexity to the process, but it helps ensure that content is reviewed by one or more members of the approvers group for that site before the "general public" can see the document in a major published version. This complexity does require testing and training for administrators, approvers, and end users to avoid frustration during the process.

Using the Tags & Notes Tool

The Tags & Notes icon is not available from SharePoint Foundation 2013, but is available in both SharePoint Server 2013 Standard and Enterprise, and appears on the Files tab on the far-right side. These tools are discussed more in Chapter 23, "Leveraging Social Networking Tools in SharePoint 2013."

These tools are easy to use and engaging enough to end users that they will soon find themselves experimenting with them to understand the full breadth of their potential. For a specific item, such as shown in Figure 19.24, if Tags & Notes is clicked, the window for Tags and Note Board opens. In this example, a tag and a note was added by the user to this document, and recent activities are listed at the bottom of the window. This allows users to quickly create and apply their own tags and to see how others are tagging this item. Users can also set tags as Private if they don't want other users to see how they are tagging items. Clicking My Tags takes users to their My Site where they can see histories of tags they have applied. Figure 19.25 shows a My Site for a user (Colin Spence) who has been creating tags and posts recently. A tag cloud shows the frequency that tags have been used, as indicated by the size of the fonts.

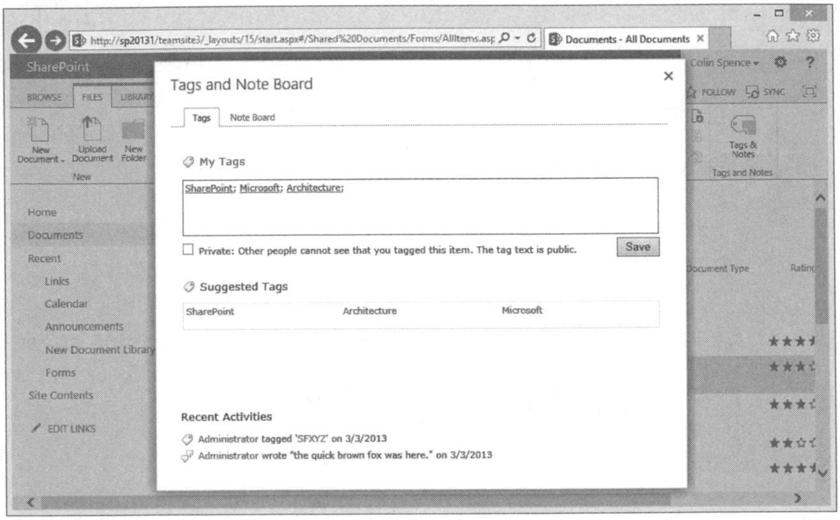

FIGURE 19.24 Tags and Note Board for an item in a document library.

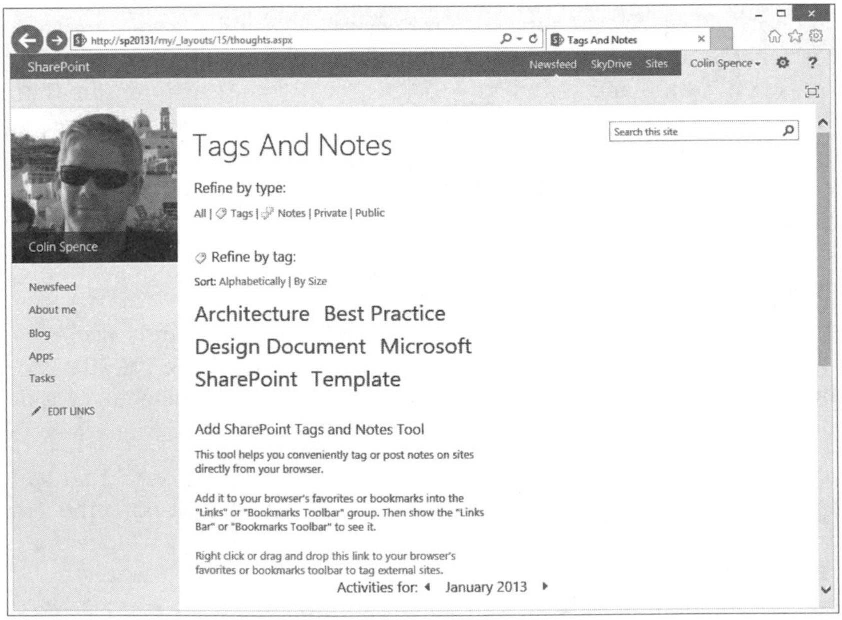

FIGURE 19.25 My Site with Tags and Notes tab selected.

As with any other tool that makes it easy to post comments, there is the possibility for abuse, but the user community should be informed of any policies surrounding inappropriate use of the tools and the repercussions of inappropriate language or use.

NOTE

The social tags and note board ribbon controls can be disabled by a farm administrator from the Central Administration site, as follows: Access the System Settings page and then click Manage Farm Features. Scroll down to the Social Tags and Note Board Ribbon Controls and click Deactivate.

Empowering Users Through SharePoint 2010 Lists

As the previous section showed, there are many very powerful features and tools provided by SharePoint libraries, and SharePoint lists provide a similar set of tools and features. Because a number of these tools and features overlap with libraries, this section concentrates on the differences between lists and libraries and gives examples that will help users and administrators grasp the differences and how to best utilize lists. Examples also show how list administrators and site administrators can customize lists to make them better suited to the needs of the users.

Differentiating Lists from Libraries

Libraries are one of the most often-used building blocks for SharePoint-based collaboration and information management systems, and lists are another. Libraries store files, whereas lists are designed to store rows of information, in much the same way as a spreadsheet stores rows of data defined by columns that are configured to support certain types of data, such as text, numbers, date and times, choices, and others.

When a user clicks the New Item link in a list, she is prompted to enter different types of information (such as text, currency value, time, and date), select an item from a list of items, or perhaps enter a user's name. This information then gets saved as a row in the list and is given a unique ID number. No document needs to be uploaded at this point, which is a fundamental difference from a library, which cannot store data without a document to attach it to.

Another revealing exercise for an administrator is to anticipate ways in which end users, especially power users, might get themselves into trouble. Earlier in the chapter, Figure 19.7 showed how a user can navigate to a SharePoint folder by using Windows Explorer (WebDAV) and entering the SharePoint server name, site name, and document library in the following format (\\servername\libraryname). In this previous example, there is no specific site name needed because the document library exists as part of the root site and the user could see the contents of the document library clearly shown as documents and even a folder. Navigating to a list in a similar fashion isn't quite as friendly a process, as shown in Figure 19.26, where there is a folder titled Announcement, one titled Attachments, and then several documents that can be seen to be ASP.NET Server Pages. Double-clicking the Announcement folder does not actually show the data that was entered into the list because the data is written to SQL databases and stored in tables. Also, data cannot be added from the Explorer interface, so there is arguably no benefit to end users of accessing a list in this fashion.

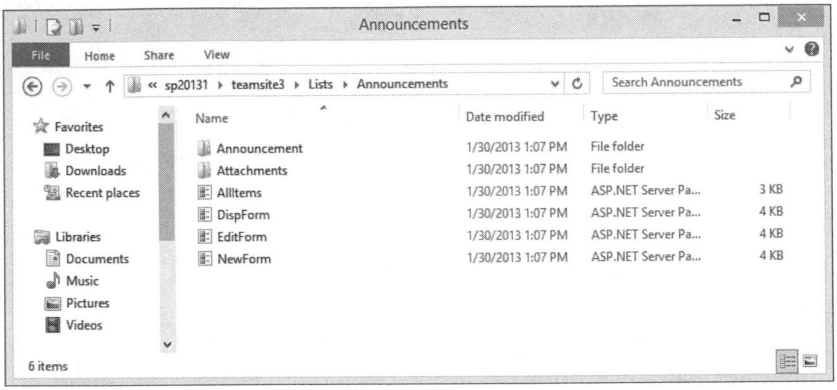

FIGURE 19.26 Explorer view of an Announcements list in SharePoint 2013.

NOTE

The organization should decide whether to allow Explorer view (WebDAV) access to SharePoint 2013 content, because the results end users see when visiting lists, in terms of the folders and ASP.NET pages end users find, may confuse them. Furthermore, an overzealous power user who deletes the folders or forms can impact the functionality of the list.

A fact that can be confusing to new users and administrators is that a SharePoint list can also add one or more attachments to a list item, so be prepared for discussions along the lines of pros and cons of using lists and libraries to store items. These attachments are stored in the Attachments folder seen via the Explorer view in Figure 19.26. Another difference between list and library functionality pertains to versioning. Even if versioning is turned on for a list, attachments do not have their versions tracked if they are changed. This can lead to potential confusion or even lost productivity if users are expecting attachments in a list to be versioned. Along these lines, a user could delete an attachment to a list item, and it will not be recoverable by just recovering an older version of the item, because the attachments aren't tracked with the versioning tool. Note that attachments that are deleted end up in the Recycle Bin for recovery if needed. An additional point on versioning is that lists offer only major versions and do not allow the saving of minor versions, making them less well suited for more intricate document review and approval processes. Possibly for these reasons, lists can be configured so that attachments to list items are disabled.

Reviewing Several Common Lists

Commonly used lists include an Announcements list, Calendar list, Links list, and Tasks list. These were included in the Team Site template in SharePoint 2010, but have been removed in SharePoint 2013. These remain popular lists, and many organizations add them to standard team site templates for collaboration purposes.

Each of these lists consists of several columns, different views, and in some cases some special functionality that has been added by Microsoft. The columns included in each list are as follows:

- The **Announcements** list stores announcements that consist of a Title, a Body section, and an Expires date. This makes it well suited as a starting point to input data that will make up an announcement on the site, which "expires" and no longer displays after a certain date.
- The **Calendar** list stores rows of data that include a number of columns of data, including: Title, Location, Start Time (and date), End Time (and date), Description, Category, whether it's an All Day Event, and whether there is Recurrence. Collected together, each row of data serves to represent an event taking place, can be displayed on a special calendar-like view, and provides different display options and navigation tools.

NOTE

SharePoint 2010 users may notice that the Calendar list no longer provides the option of creating a meeting workspace. In fact, in SharePoint 2013, all five of the Meeting Workspace site templates are no longer available. This includes the Basic Meeting Workspace, Blank Meeting Workspace, Decision Meeting Workspace, Social Meeting Workspace, and Multipage Meeting Workspace.

- The **Links** list is quite simple, and just provides a URL field, with a Description field and a Notes field. This list is designed to track URL information while displaying a friendly description instead of the whole URL.
- The **Tasks** list is also quite complex and stores data, including Task Name, Start Date and Due Date, Assigned To, % Complete, Description, Predecessors, Priority, and Task Status. This list has specially configured views to display only items that meet certain filters, such as Completed, Gantt Chart, Late Tasks, My Tasks, and Upcoming.

Chapter 18, "SharePoint Foundation Versus SharePoint Server 2013," provides additional details comparing the different lists and libraries that are available in the different versions of the SharePoint 2013 products, but this initial handful of lists gives some insight into several of the most popular lists.

Examining the Tools in an Announcements List

Figure 19.27 shows an Announcements list in SharePoint Server 2013 with an item selected in it and the Items tab on the List Tools ribbon visible. Most of these tools should look familiar, as most were covered in the earlier walk through for a library.

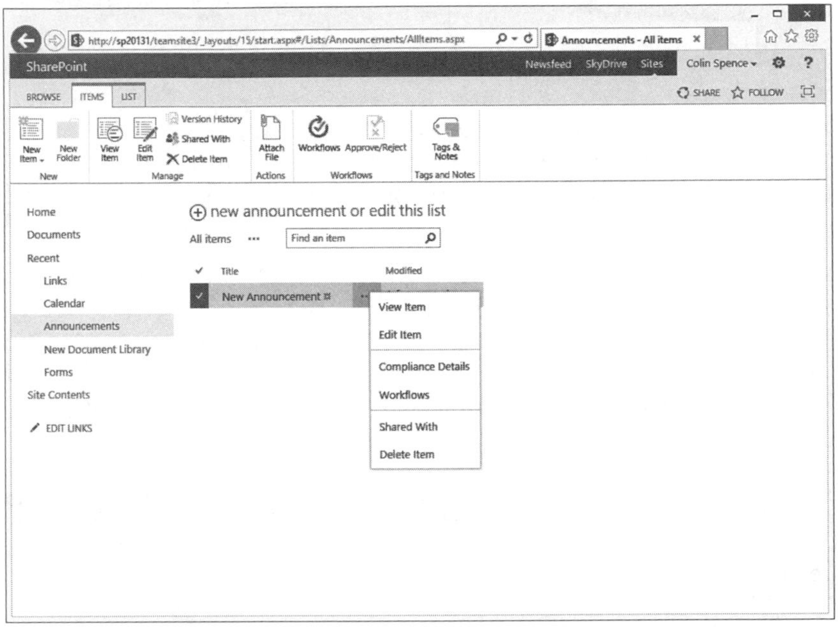

FIGURE 19.27 Items tab for an Announcements list.

One new tool offered in the list is the Attach File tool on the Items tab; this tool enables the user to browse for a single file and then save it as an attachment. Attachments are saved in the Attachments folder within the list, and although there is no published limit to the number of attachments that can be added to a list item, there are a few benefits to storing documents in this manner, as discussed earlier in this section.

The process of creating a new item in the list is simpler than in a library; the user just needs to click the New Item icon and then add content to the fields, as shown in Figure 19.28. For this example, an image was also included, which was uploaded from the user's Pictures folder, and SharePoint allows the user to simultaneously choose the picture to use and also to upload it to a desired library on the site. The text formatting tools can be seen, which are quite extensive, and the graphic image can be resized from within the editing window. These tools make it very simple and quick for users to create quite intricate postings. After the Save button is clicked, the content is saved to the list.

As with a library, an item in a list can be checked as active, and then the relevant tools become active. Figure 19.29 shows the List tab of the List Tools ribbon, as a list administrator needs to become familiar with these tools to fully realize the potential of lists. A valuable set of tools is revealed in the next section, which covers the Quick Edit (formerly called datasheet view in SharePoint 2010) from a high level, and to round out this chapter, the Create View and Create Column tools are demonstrated and discussed.

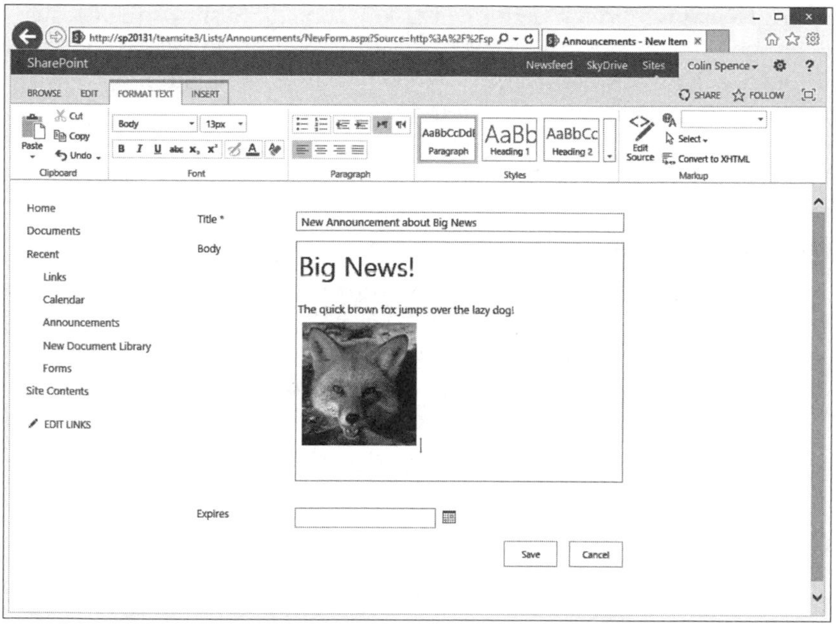

FIGURE 19.28 Creating a new announcement in a list.

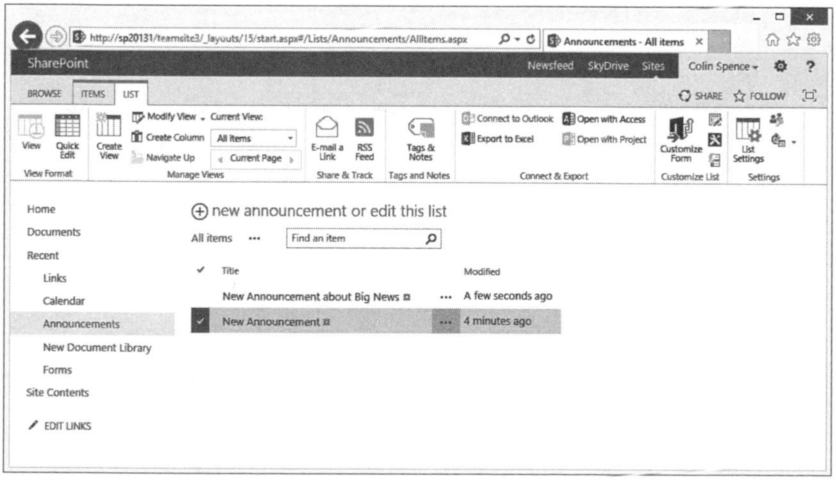

FIGURE 19.29 The List tab for an Announcements list.

Adding a Column in a List and Updating a List Item

Whereas libraries store documents, and can be extremely useful even if additional metadata columns aren't added, lists derive their value from the columns that make up the list, so adding columns to lists is an often performed task. Figure 19.30 shows the Create Column window that opens when a user with the manage lists permission clicks the Create Column button. Similar to a spreadsheet, a number of different column options are provided. In SharePoint Server 2013, these are as follows:

- Single line of text
- Multiple lines of text
- Choice (menu to choose from)
- Number
- Currency
- Date and Time
- Lookup (information already on this site)
- Yes/No (check box)
- Person or Group
- Hyperlink or Picture
- Calculated (calculation based on other columns)
- Task Outcome
- External Data
- Managed Metadata

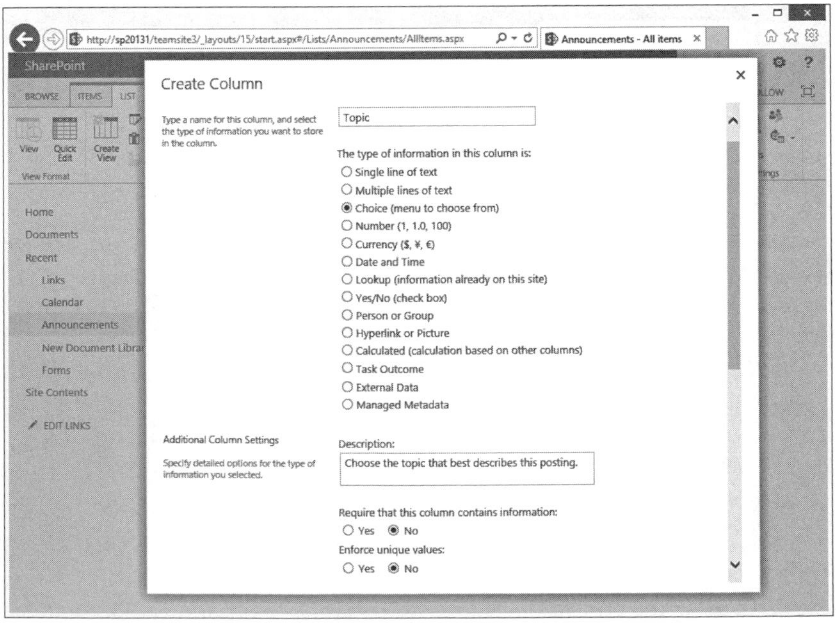

FIGURE 19.30 Create Column window in a list.

SharePoint Server 2013 Standard or Enterprise give the option of creating Managed Metadata columns in lists. Chapter 22 provides additional information about the column choices.

In this example, the Choice column is chosen, and several items that appear in the drop-down menu are provided. Radio buttons or check boxes can also be selected, and fill-in choices can be allowed, as well as a default value provided. After OK is clicked, the column is added, and if the check box is left checked to Add to Default View, the new column is added to the default view. In the earlier example, the new column named Topic can be seen on the right side of the Announcements list in Figure 19.31, because the Add to Default View check box was selected when the new column was added. The drop-down arrow next to the column header Topic is shown selected in Figure 19.31, and sorting options are provided; when there is content in this column, the different distinct values are available for selection for the filter. To populate this new column with data, several different sets of steps can be followed, as described in the following three sections.

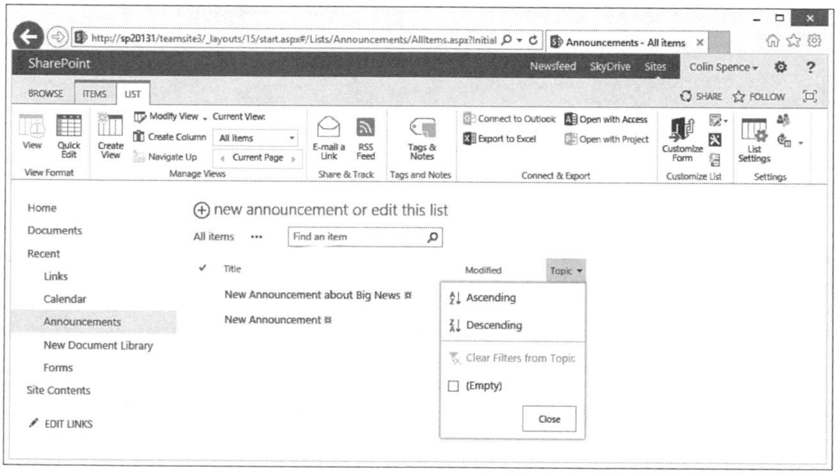

FIGURE 19.31 New column added to a list.

Clicking the Item Title to Edit Content

To edit content by clicking the title of an item in a list, follow these steps:

1. The easiest option, and most intuitive, is to simply click the title of the item (for example, New Announcement about Big News shown in Figure 19.31); the window for the item in view mode will open.
2. Then click Edit Item from the View tab, and the item changes to edit mode, as shown in Figure 19.32. Now make a change, such as clicking the drop-down arrow next to the Topic field, and select from the provided choices.
3. Then click Save to save the modification and return to the previous view of the list.

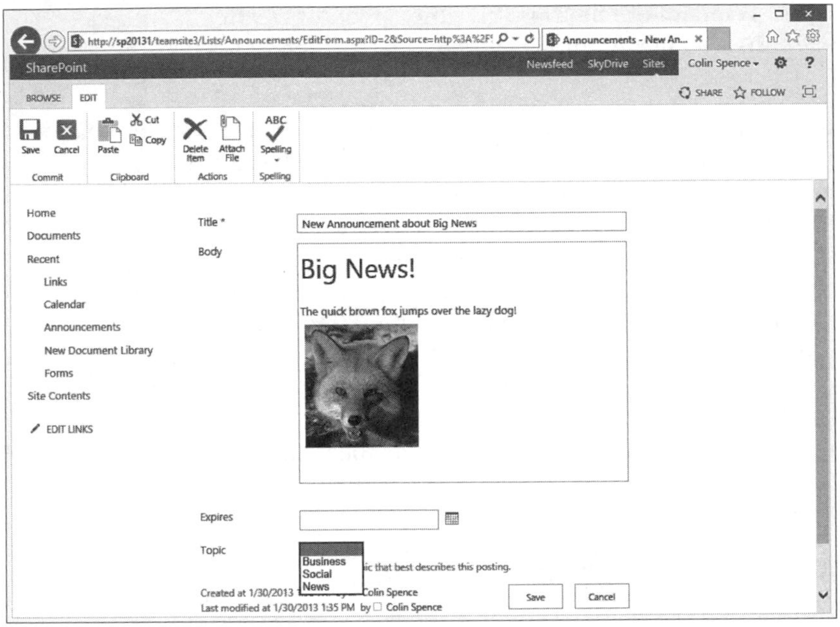

FIGURE 19.32 Edit window for a list item.

Accessing the Drop-Down Menu to Edit an Item

To edit content by accessing the drop-down menu, follow these steps:

1. As shown in Figure 19.33, hover over the Title for the list item in the list, and then access the menu by clicking the ellipsis to the right and click Edit Item.
2. The list item then opens in edit mode. Update one or more fields and click Save.

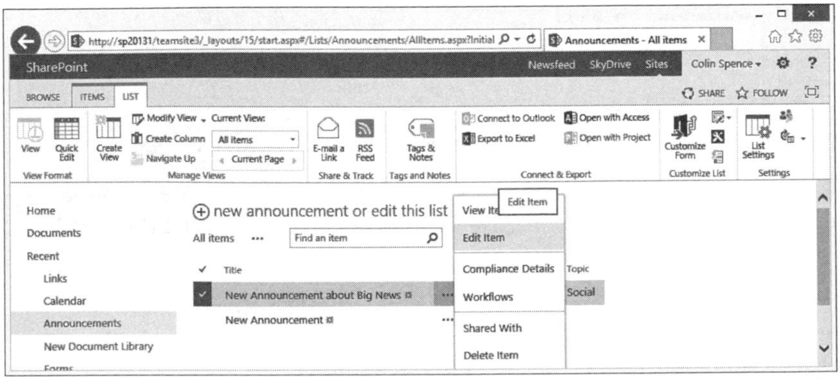

FIGURE 19.33 Drop-down menu for a list item.

Selecting the Item and Choosing Edit Item

To edit an item by first selecting it and then choosing Edit Item from the ribbon, follow these steps:

1. Hover over the list item until the box appears to the left of the title, and then check the box.
2. The Items tab under List Tools is then active. Click Edit Item, and the list item opens in edit mode. Update one or more fields and click Save.

NOTE

The check box might not always be enabled in a list or library.

Interacting with Lists Using the Quick Edit

The Quick Edit is extremely useful for quickly entering data into a list or for rapidly entering metadata for items in a library. As shown in the preceding three processes, editing a single item can involve several hovers, clicks, more mouse-work, entering the information, and then another click to save the data. Quick Edit appeals to the efficiency-conscious part of many users, and should be introduced to new users. Follow these steps to use the Quick Edit in an Announcements list (and most other lists):

1. Click the List tab under List Tools.
2. Click the Quick Edit icon in the List tab ribbon. Figure 19.34 shows an Announcements list in Quick Edit. The user clicked in an empty cell under the bottom announcement, entered a new announcement title, tabbed past the Modified cell (because this cell is populated by SharePoint automatically), and then selected Social from the drop-down menu in the Topic column. If a user tries to enter any data in the Modified column, he gets this message: "The selected cells are read-only."
3. Click Enter. The selected cell drops to the next row down, triggering a save of the data entered.

Note that the Body column is not visible in this view, so the user can't actually enter data in the body of the announcement.

In Figure 19.34, notice that there is an empty column to the right of the Topic column indicated with a +. Clicking the + icon allows the list administrator to easily and quickly add new columns. With a little experimentation, it can be seen that the Quick View allows a user to quickly enter data in lists (or libraries), cut, and paste into other cells if needed (which dramatically cuts down on the time it takes when compared to selecting items one at a time, accessing the drop-down menu, or selecting the item and then accessing the Edit Item tool on the ribbon).

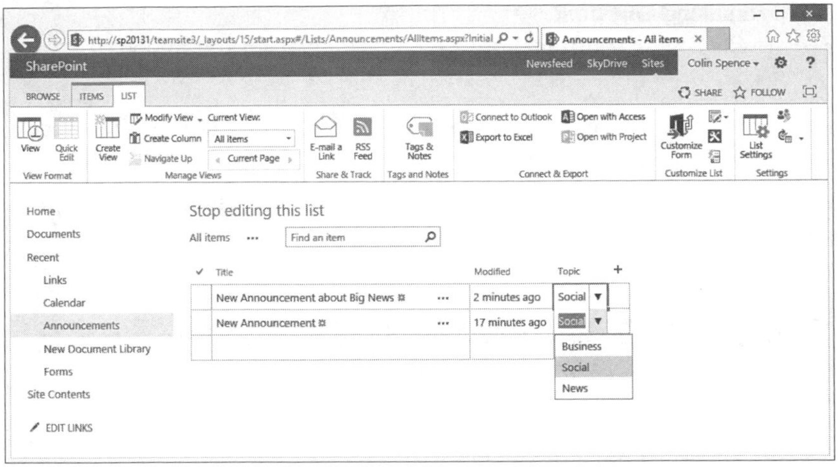

FIGURE 19.34 Using Quick Edit in an Announcements list.

NOTE

In SharePoint 2010, a Multiple Lines of Text column that is configured to allow enhanced rich text (text with pictures, tables, and hyperlinks) cannot be edited in datasheet view. However, multiple lines of text configured to allow plain text or rich text (bold, italics, text alignment, and hyperlinks) does allow editing in datasheet view. However, in SharePoint 2013, the Quick Edit option now enables you to edit multiple lines of text configured to allow enhanced rich text.

Creating a View in a List

Another important concept to understand when using SharePoint 2013 lists is that of views. When someone visits a list, the default view displays. Every list is created with a default view, and then the list administrator can either modify that view or create new views, one of which could be set to be the default. The tools required are accessed from the List tab of the ribbon toolbar and include the Create View tool, Modify View tool, and List Settings tool. The List Settings tool is the "long way" of getting to the link to modify a view.

In the following example, a user decides a new view is needed in the Announcements list that was modified in the previous example by having a new column titled Topic added. Follow these steps to create a new view in the list:

1. Click the List tab, and then click the Create View tool.
2. Several view format options are offered: Standard View, Calendar View, Access View, Datasheet View, Gantt View, and Custom View in SharePoint Designer. For this example, click Standard View.

3. The Create View page opens, as shown in Figure 19.35. Enter in a name for the view, such as **New View**, and check the Make This the Default View check box, if desired.

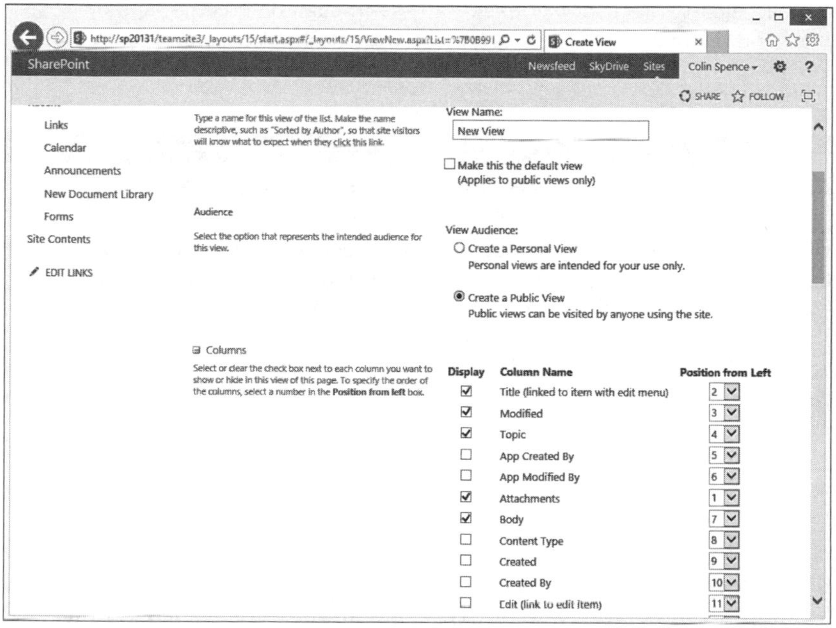

FIGURE 19.35 Creating a new view.

4. In the next section, leave Create a Public View checked, or select Create a Personal View if you intend to use only this view and you don't want to share it with other users of the list. In this example, leave Create a Public View checked.

5. In the Columns section, check any column names that you want included in the view. Change the number in the Position from Left column if needed; this often takes some trial and error to get just right. In this example, the columns titled Attachments and Body are checked because they were left out of the default view.

6. In the Sort section, determine which column to sort by. In this example, choose Title from the drop-down menu under First Sort by the Column, and check the circle next to Show Items in Ascending Order.

7. In the Filter section, choose whether to filter items and only display items that meet certain criteria. Leave the Show All Items in this View option checked for this example.

8. Feel free to experiment with the various other settings on the Create View page, such as Tabular View, Group By, Totals, Style, Folders, Items Limit, and Mobile.

9. Click OK to save the changes.

NOTE

The Group By option can be very useful for lists with numerous items as it allows the contents of one or more columns to be used to group items. Groupings can be displayed by default in collapsed mode, so a user can easily browse through different groups by expanding a header and then reviewing the contents to see whether they are of interest.

NOTE

In the Folders section for the Create View page, the option is provided to either Show Items Inside Folders or to Show All Items Without Folders. Although this might seem a fairly innocuous option, realize that the efforts to organize content in folders can be completely ignored by simply checking the circle next to Show All Items Without Folders. Any granular security settings applied to contents of folders is still honored; the view is simply flattened. With this simple option, SharePoint allows a list administrator to be freed from the constraints of folders inside of lists, even if users demand folders for peace of mind or comfort level.

Summary

Document libraries and lists are arguably the most important features of most SharePoint 2013 implementations, because they contain the documents and data that users interact with every day. Although an in-depth review of every tool and feature available from every document library and list in SharePoint is beyond the scope of this chapter, it highlights the most important and commonly used features and sets the stage for Chapter 20. SharePoint 2013 builds upon and refines the features provided by SharePoint 2010 lists and libraries in many important ways that turn SharePoint into a world-class and (just as important) easy-to-use document and data management tool.

Best Practices

The following are best practices from this chapter:

- The improvements from SharePoint 2010 to SharePoint 2013 make it easier for administrators and end users to interact with the documents and data stored in document libraries and lists and reduce the learning curve as well.
- There are a variety of ways to upload documents to SharePoint 2013 document libraries, including the Open with Explorer button on the Library tab, the Upload Multiple Documents option, and using Windows Explorer to navigate to the SharePoint server, site, and library.
- Folders can be created within a document library, and as discussed in this chapter, there are pros and cons to using folders in SharePoint document libraries. A best practice is for the organization to understand the pros and cons of using folders and make informed decisions on where they make sense (for example, document libraries with tens of thousands of documents) and where they don't (for example, smaller document libraries where the organization wants to promote the use of metadata for organization rather than folders).

- Although creating unique permissions for documents in a document library creates added overhead for administrators, the new Check Permissions tool enables administrators to determine what permission levels are given to users or groups, which allows the administrator to quickly check whether specific users or groups have any access to the document.
- Alerts can be created for items, lists, or libraries and are a very easy way to keep track of activities within a list or library or of any changes made to a document that a user is specifically interested in. Use daily and weekly summary alerts to keep the number of emails sent out to a minimum.
- Although document libraries provide tools in the toolbar that can make a copy of a document in another library (the Send To tool) and track that copy and maintain the connectivity to a certain extent by requesting updates, or can create a document workspace that contains a copy of the document, this can be a confusing and complicated process for less-experienced users and administrators. When the user base and administrators are new to SharePoint, a best practice is to recommend against using these tools unless specifically required for a business solution.
- Document library administrators can enable versioning in a document library and decide whether major and minor versions will be tracked, whether content approval is required, who can see draft versions, whether workflows are used to approve a document, and even if scheduling is used to determine when the content is published. A best practice is to make sure that the right combination of these features is applied based on the content of the document library and the sophistication of the user base. Enabling too many of these features for a user base that is new to SharePoint 2010 may steepen the learning curve and make employees hesitant to use the document libraries.
- Although the Quick Edit is available for use in both lists and libraries, it is most often used in lists for rapid data entry or bulk changes, because many users use SharePoint lists for similar tasks as they normally use spreadsheets for.
- Lists are another main building block of SharePoint collaborative environments, but they are designed primarily for storing rows of information rather than documents. As discussed in this chapter, lists can store documents as attachments, but they do not manage documents as well or as thoroughly as libraries. For example, lists do not manage versions of attachments.
- For lists to be useful, they must contain the appropriate combination of columns. A variety of lists come with SharePoint 2013 out-of-the-box, but administrators should familiarize themselves with the wide variety of columns that can be created; the usefulness of the list will increase as these are properly leveraged.
- Views are also key to the efficacy of lists, and a list administrator should become familiar with the process of creating a new view, setting it as the default, and working with sorting, filtering, and grouping within list views.
- Mobile views are created by default with any new view, and the URL is available on the Edit View page (ViewEdit.aspx) in the Mobile section at the bottom of the page.

CHAPTER 20

Customizing and Managing Libraries and Lists to Meet Business Requirements

IN THIS CHAPTER

- Planning the List and Library Ecosystem
- Understanding the Range of List and Library Options
- Creating Lists and Libraries
- Mastering the Library Tab on the Ribbon
- Creating and Managing Views
- Document Library Settings Tools Reviewed
- Permissions and Management Tools for Lists and Libraries
- Document Sets Compared to Folders as Organizational Tools in Document Libraries
- Content Organizer as a Document Routing Tool

The preceding chapter provided an overview of the wide and powerful range of tools available to SharePoint 2013 users in lists and libraries. This chapter now builds on this information to help SharePoint architects and administrators design an environment that meets the various needs of end users by focusing on the main containers of information in SharePoint 2013: lists and libraries.

This chapter concentrates on the tools available within lists and libraries, primarily from the Library tab on the ribbon, and Settings page, with the goal of exposing administrators to the range of tools they will use to initially configure lists and libraries and will access to manage them on an ongoing basis.

The chapter also covers two of the site features that can be activated by site administrators that provide tool sets pertaining specifically to the management of files and data within lists and libraries: document sets and the content organizer.

Planning the List and Library Ecosystem

The process of planning the appropriate combination of lists and libraries to meet the needs of different business units and groups can be very simple or very complex, depending on the general philosophies surrounding the SharePoint project and the needs of the organization. Some organizations spend a minimal amount of time planning, build one or more SharePoint site collections with sites defined for business units, departments, or groups, and then allow end users to customize these environments with the lists and libraries that they deem best suited to their needs. Other organizations create sites and site collections using carefully crafted templates that have specific combinations of preconfigured lists and libraries, and carefully weigh the pros and cons of the different types of lists and libraries and related features that can be provided. And then there are other permutations. For the sake of discussion, it is posited here that four primary strategies can be employed:

- Minimal planning and testing; minimal restrictions on list and library use and configuration
- Minimal planning and testing; more restrictions on list and library use and configuration
- More extensive planning and testing; minimal restrictions on list and library use and configuration
- More extensive planning and testing; more restrictions on list and library use and configuration

By using the minimal planning and testing approach, the organization shortens the time frame of the implementation, which generally controls the costs of the project. In general, the risks of "missing the mark" are higher in the minimal planning and testing approach. This can manifest, from the authors' experience, in sluggish adoption of the lists and libraries unless end users are already experienced with, and even clamoring for, SharePoint technologies or have training made readily available. Alternatively, assuming end users adopt the technology, this "blank slate" approach encourages end users to modify the tools to meet their specific needs. Combine this minimal planning approach with minimal restriction on the types of lists and libraries that can be used, and empower certain users to configure these lists to meet their needs, and the results can be positive. Tightly control the range of lists and libraries that can be used and restrict end users' ability to change the configuration of lists and libraries, and IT stays integrated in the adoption cycle, learns what the end users are requesting in terms of functionality, and can develop best practices along the way.

However, more extensive planning and testing requires more time and resource involvement and can add to the overall costs of the project. Pilots, prototypes, and proof of concepts can be executed and managed, with specific decisions made along the way of which lists and libraries will be made available and which tools enabled in the lists and libraries. Following the implementation, end users can be more or less empowered to create new libraries and lists and customize the configurations.

Every organization has its own processes and methodologies for planning and testing, so those topics are not addressed in detail here, but the topics revolving around list and library use and configuration are looked at in detail to help readers better understand the capabilities of the lists, libraries, and related tools provided by SharePoint 2013 and then decide which are appropriate for the implementations.

Understanding the Range of List and Library and App Options

Lists and libraries are key repositories in the SharePoint ecosystem, and each offers dozens of powerful features, and Microsoft offers numerous different templates for organizations to use in constructing the SharePoint environment. This section delves into more detail on the different list and library options and provides some guidance on how they should be used from a high level.

NOTE

SharePoint 2013 terminology refers to lists and libraries now as *apps* in some places, and *lists* or *libraries* in others, which can cause confusion. For example, on the Site Contents page, the top section is titled List, Libraries, and Other Apps. And there's a button to Add an App, which then displays the lists, libraries, and any other apps that are available. A general definition is that a list or library can be an app, and an app can be a list or a library but doesn't have to be.

Because of the sheer number of lists and libraries, as shown in Table 20.1, a detailed overview of each one is beyond the scope of this chapter. This table clarifies whether the template creates a list, a library, or an app and whether the template is available in SharePoint Foundation 2013 or SharePoint Server 2013 Enterprise; it also provides notes on what the list or library is designed by Microsoft to be used for.

To view which apps are available on the current site, follow these steps:

1. Click the gear icon in the upper-right corner.
2. Click Site Contents; the lists, libraries, and other apps that currently exist on the site then display.

Figure 20.1 shows a Site Contents page. Note that the permissions of the user account determine which lists, libraries, and apps display. Lists, libraries, and apps that the user account does not have permissions to at least view are not displayed.

Although this list is certainly not enough to make the final decision about which lists and libraries the organization will support and make available to specific sets of users, it can serve as a starting point, and the grid can be expanded for use during the planning process. The design team can simply review the lists and libraries, make decisions about whether to use each one, can determine whether specific lists or libraries meet the needs of a subset of users, groups, or divisions, and verify that they are all included in the version of SharePoint that the organization has chosen.

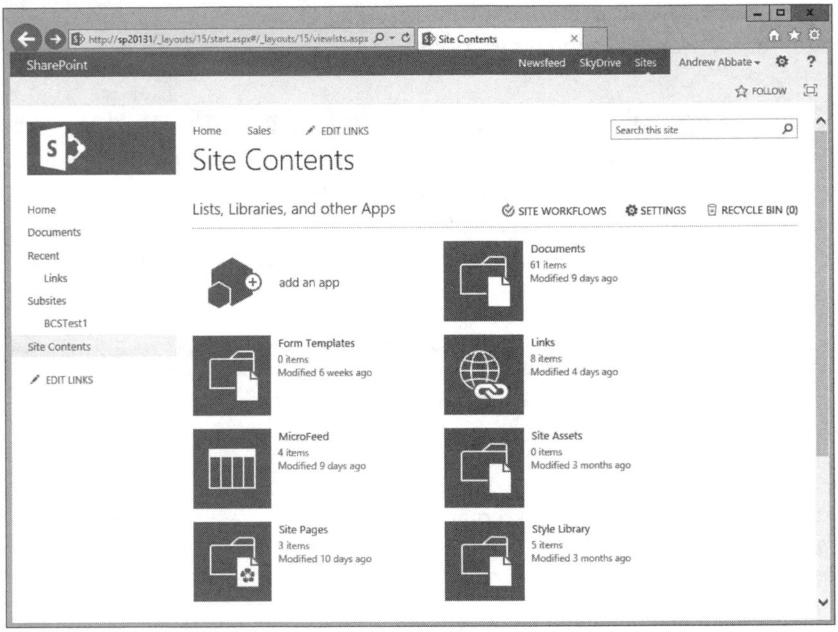

FIGURE 20.1 Site Contents page.

TABLE 20.1 Library and List Options in SharePoint Foundation 2013 and SharePoint Server 2013 Enterprise

Template Name	**List, Library, or App?**	**Available in SharePoint Foundation 2013?**	**Available in SharePoint Server 2013 Enterprise?**	**Functionality and Notes**
Access App	App	No	Yes	Allows users to create an Access app from SharePoint.
Announcements	List	Yes	Yes	Designed to store announcements with title, body, and expiration date information.
Asset Library	Library	No	Yes	Designed to store image, audio, or video files. Has image, audio, and video content types enabled by default.
Calendar	List	Yes	Yes	Designed to store items with start and end date and times.
Contacts	List	Yes	Yes	Designed to store contact information.

Template Name	List, Library, or App?	Available in SharePoint Foundation 2013?	Available in SharePoint Server 2013 Enterprise?	Functionality and Notes
Custom List	List	Yes	Yes	Blank list that contains the Title field and can be customized to add additional fields as needed.
Custom List in Datasheet View	List	Yes	Yes	Same as Custom List, but uses a datasheet view as the default. The client configuration must support datasheet view or the user won't be able to use the datasheet view.
Data Connection Library	Library	No	Yes	Store Office Data Connection (ODC) file or a Universal Data Connection (UDC) file. InfoPath 2013 is recommended for use in creating ODC or UDC files.
Discussion Board	List	Yes	Yes	Designed to store threaded discussions.
Document Library	Library	Yes	Yes	Designed for general document storage.
External List	List	Yes	Yes	This requires that an External content type has been defined by the farm administrator.
Form Library	Library	Yes	Yes	Intended for storage of InfoPath Forms.
Import Spreadsheet	List	Yes	Yes	Creates a list from an Excel spreadsheet and translates Excel columns to SharePoint columns.
Issue Tracking	List	Yes	Yes	Designed to store items assigned to a single person, and includes description, category, and other data.
Links	List	Yes	Yes	Designed to store links with URL and notes.
Picture Library	Library	Yes	Yes	Good for general graphical file management.
Promoted Links	List	Yes	Yes	Displays a set of link actions in a tile-based visual layout.

Template Name	List, Library, or App?	Available in SharePoint Foundation 2013?	Available in SharePoint Server 2013 Enterprise?	Functionality and Notes
Report Library	Library	No	Yes	Designed to store reports. Has the Report and Web Part Page with Status List content types available.
Survey	List	Yes	Yes	Designed for soliciting input from users. Input can have usernames visible or be anonymous.
Tasks	List	Yes	Yes	Designed to store task items assigned to a single person and have start and due dates assigned to them along with other data.
Wiki Page Library	Library	Yes	Yes	Manage wiki pages in one library.

NOTE

Several lists and libraries have been deprecated from SharePoint 2010, including the following:

- Status List
- Project Tasks
- Slide Library

Note that the Status List enabled you to define key performance indicators that accessed a view within a list or library and displayed red, yellow, and green icons. However, there were many limitations on how these could be configured, rendering them of limited value. This functionality has now been "moved" to Power View reports, so the Power View site collection feature needs to be enabled. Note that Structured Query Language (SQL) Server Analysis Services in SharePoint Mode needs to also be configured. Then the Power View reports in Excel can have key performance indicators added and can then be accessed via Excel Services.

Creating Lists and Libraries

After the high-level decisions have been made about which lists and libraries will be used and supported by the organization, the next step is to configure a test site with these lists and libraries and configure them to meet the expected needs of the end users and capabilities of IT to support the environment. This section gives high-level guidelines for these tasks.

A good place to start is with the team site template. The team site template contains the following lists and libraries if created in SharePoint Foundation 2013:

- Shared Documents document library
- Site Assets document library
- Site Pages wiki library

If the team site template is used to create a site in SharePoint Server 2013, there will also be a Microfeed list.

NOTE

The SharePoint 2010 team site included a number of other lists that are no longer in this template in SharePoint 2013, as follows: announcements list, calendar list, links list, tasks list, and team discussion list.

To create a team site, follow these steps:

1. From the parent site (under which the new site will be created), click the Gear icon, and then click Site Contents.
2. When on the Site Contents page, scroll down to the bottom of the page and click New Subsite. If this option isn't provided, the account you are using doesn't have sufficient permissions to create a new site.
3. From this page, enter a title for the site (such as Team Site 1) and provide a description if needed.
4. Provide a URL name in the Web Site Address section (for example, TeamSite1). By not including spaces in the title, you avoid seeing "%20" in the URL.
5. In the Template Selection section, choose the Team Site template.
6. Under User Permissions, choose Use Same Permissions as Parent Site. You can choose Use Unique Permissions, if needed, and if so will then need to provide additional information on the groups that will be used to provide access to the site.
7. In the Navigation section, choose whether to display this site on the quick launch of the parent site and whether to display this site on the top link bar of the parent site. Choosing Yes for either or both options makes it easier to navigate to the new site, but can also clutter up the quick launch or top link bar. For this exercise, choose No for both.
8. In the Navigation Inheritance section, choose whether to use the top link bar from the parent site. For this exercise, choose No.
9. Click Create. Figure 20.2 shows an example of the resulting team site.

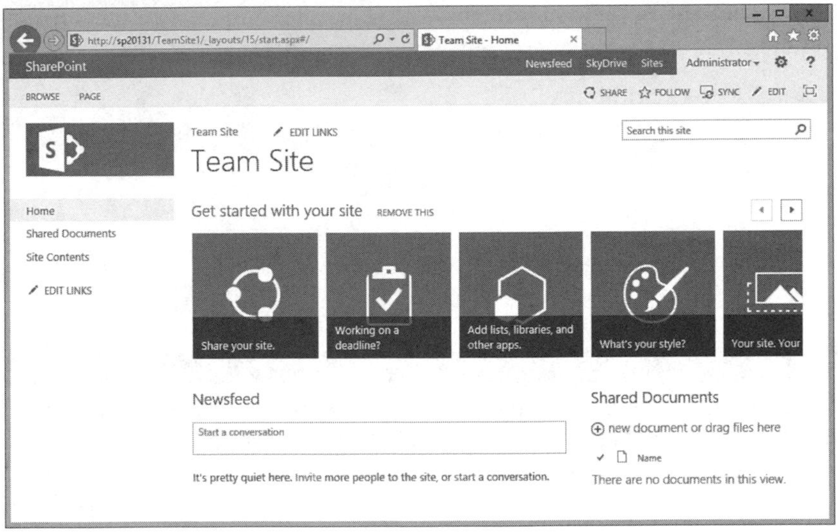

FIGURE 20.2 Team Site home page.

After the new site has been created, additional lists and libraries can be created to fully flesh out the site for testing or production purposes. Creating additional lists or libraries requires that the user have the Manage Lists permission, which permits you to create and delete lists, add or remove columns in a list, and add or remove public views of a list. This is available in the Full Control permission level and the Design permission level. To see the permission level details, follow these steps:

1. From the home page of the top-level site in the site collection, click the Gear icon, and then click Site Settings.
2. Click Site Permissions in the Users and Permissions section.
3. Click Permission Levels on the Permissions tab on the ribbon.
4. As shown in Figure 20.3, you will now see the different permission levels in place for the site collection. Note that Full Control and Limited Access permission levels cannot be deleted.
5. Click the link to a permission level, such as Design, to see the list permissions, site permissions, and personal permissions that are enabled for that level. A Copy Permission Level link appears at the bottom of the Edit Permissions Level page, which is handy if you want to create a new permission level for testing or production purposes.

NOTE

It is recommended for any site collection administrator to become very familiar with the permissions enabled for different permission levels. It is generally recommended not to change any of these default permission levels, but rather create new ones for specific purposes.

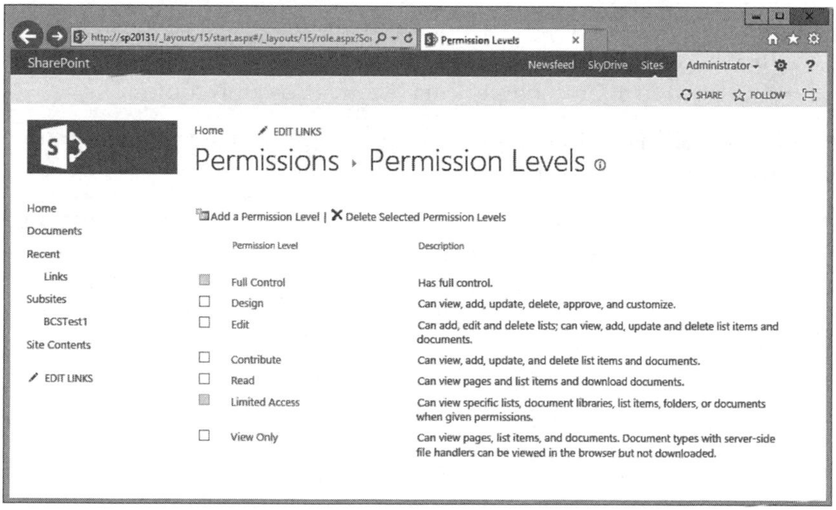

FIGURE 20.3 Permissions Level page for a site collection.

The following methods can be used to create lists and libraries from a SharePoint 2013 site:

- Access the Settings menu by clicking the Gear icon, then click Add an App, and then select the appropriate list, library, or app. Provide a name and click Create, or click Advanced Options link if needed to access additional settings.
- From the Settings menu, click Site Contents, and then from the Site Contents page, click Add an App, and then select the appropriate list, library, or application. Provide a name and click Create, or click Advanced Options link if needed to access additional settings.
- From the quick launch, click Site Contents, and then from the Site Contents page, click Add an App, and then select the appropriate list, library, or application. Provide a name and click Create, or click Advanced Options link if needed to access additional settings.
- From the Settings menu, click Site Settings, and from the Site Settings page, click the Site Libraries and Lists link in the Site Administration section. Then click Create New Content, which opens the Site Contents page, and click Add an App.

Making Basic Decisions About the List or Library

It is important to start making decisions about the configuration of the lists and libraries early in the process, certainly before hundreds of sites and possibly thousands of lists and libraries have been deployed. This section covers some of the basic configuration decisions and standards that should be clarified during the testing process.

A general tendency is to "wing it" and make decisions when the individual lists and libraries are configured, but this should be resisted, because lack of consistency makes the environment harder to manage. For example, lack of standards for a list of library names can make it more confusing for visitors to the site, and lack of standards on versioning, or whether libraries are configured to allow inbound emails, can also cause confusion.

For more managed and controlled environments, it is recommended that the organization make decisions on standards for the following items:

- **Naming lists and libraries:** Although this sounds simple, coming up with a naming scheme can actually be somewhat challenging. What might seem common sense to IT may not make sense to the end users who will be using the lists and libraries every day. From an IT standpoint, it is generally recommended that the name of the list or library include the type of list or library used. For example, creating a Picture Library and naming it Images or Graphics is not as clear to management as naming it Pictures. Ideally list or library names are unique (and the SharePoint interface states a unique name should be used in the list creation process), so adding a reference to the site that contains the list can be of help. For example, HR Pictures reveals the site that houses the library as well as the type of library template used. Finally, if there will be multiple lists or libraries of the same type, providing a number is helpful, and in some cases, lists or libraries are private as opposed to being shared with all visitors to the site. For example, HR Pictures 1 Private is a very descriptive name that should be unique. It is not unusual to see sites that have more than a handful of libraries, and it is generally easier for end users to remember to access HR Doc Library 4 than to remember a less-precise name such as New Shared Docs.

TIP

When a name is first provided to SharePoint during the list creation process, that becomes the URL, and spaces are converted to %20 in the URL. Therefore, a general recommendation is to *not* use spaces in list or library names and to edit the title of the list or library from list settings for that list or library at a later date. This can be done by accessing the Library Settings for the library, clicking the List name, description and navigation link, and simply changing the Name field. This results in a simpler and easier-to-read URL and a more standard title that is displayed on SharePoint pages.

NOTE

This default library in a Team Site is labeled as Documents on the Site Contents page and in the quick launch, yet the URL shows .../Shared%20Documents/... as the real library name. It is not usually a best practice to potentially confuse end users in this way, so a recommendation is to change the name of the library to Shared Documents to avoid confusion.

NOTE

The name chosen initially for the list or library remains in the URL even if the administrator changes the name and description by accessing the title, description, and navigation link from the settings page.

- **Choose whether to display the list or library on the quick launch:** The quick launch can get cluttered quite quickly in a site that is highly utilized and has many lists and libraries. Usually, only the most utilized lists and libraries should be included on the quick launch. Users should be reminded to use the Site Contents page to get the full listing of lists, libraries, apps, and subsites. To configure this setting, access Library Settings from the Library tab, and then click List Name, Description and Navigation, and select Yes or No in the Display This Document Library on the Quick Launch section.
- **Decide whether versioning is enabled for the document library:** This is a complex decision, and options are discussed later in the chapter. The organization should ideally set a standard for whether versioning is encouraged and supported. To configure this setting, access Library Settings from the Library tab, and then click Versioning settings and review the options.
- **Select a document template for the library:** If a user clicks New Document on the File tab in a library, the template identified for the library loads. The type of template can be chosen while creating the library by clicking the Advanced Options link, as shown in Figure 20.4. Template options are as follows:

  None

  Microsoft Word 97-2003 document

  Microsoft Excel 97-2003 spreadsheet

  Microsoft PowerPoint 97-2003 presentation

  Microsoft Word document

  Microsoft Excel spreadsheet

  Microsoft PowerPoint presentation

  Microsoft OneNote 2010 notebook

  Microsoft SharePoint Designer web page

  Basic page

  Web part page

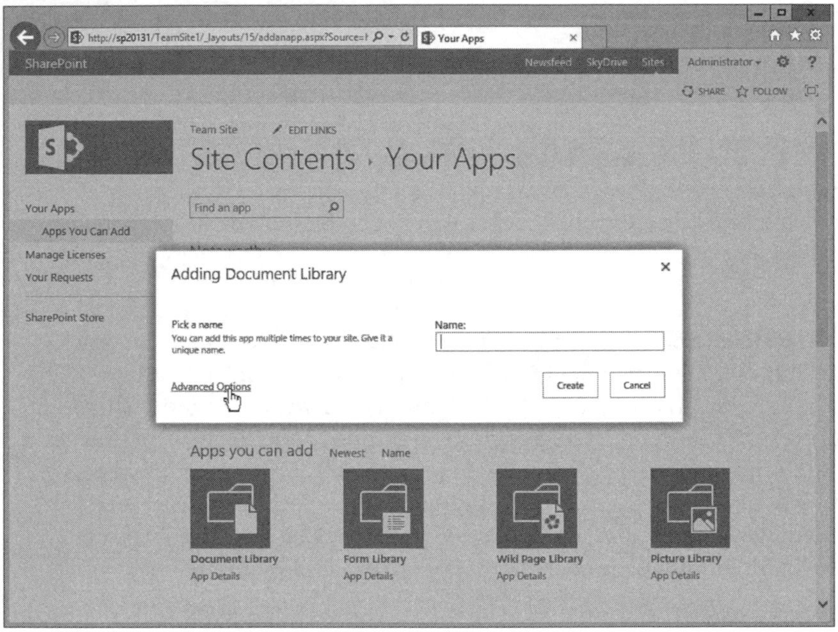

FIGURE 20.4 Advanced Options link from the Adding Document Library window.

- If the template type isn't changed, it defaults to a Word document. You can modify the template later from the Library Settings page by clicking Advanced Settings and then Edit Template in the Document Template section.

For organizations that see the value in more extensive planning and testing, it is strongly recommended that each of the lists and libraries available in the version of SharePoint 2013 that will be implemented be created and then tested to determine their relevance to the user community and goals of the project, ease of use, and anticipated support challenges.

Mastering the Library Tab on the Ribbon

Chapter 19, "Using Libraries and Lists in SharePoint 2013," covered the tools available on the Documents tab on the ribbon inside a document library. This section follows up by reviewing the tools on the Library tab, which are generally of more interest to a document library administrator and power users.

As with the Documents tab, the Library tab allows users to access only the tools that they have permissions to use and that are enabled for the list or library. For example, as shown in Figure 20.5, the user Andrew is logged in and can use only a subset of the tools, because he is a member of the Visitors group for the site and therefore has Read-level permissions.

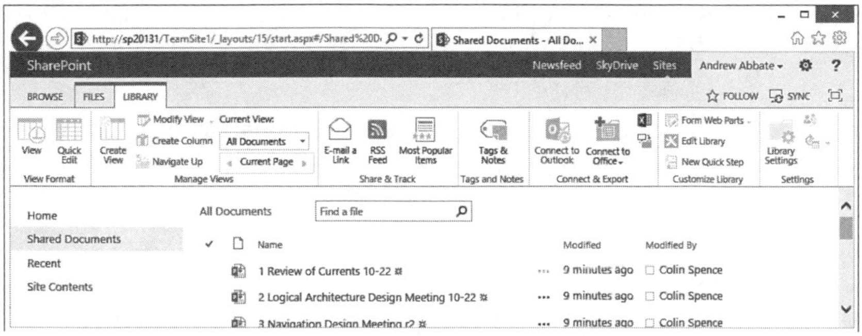

FIGURE 20.5 Limited tools available for a member of the Visitors group in a document library.

The tools on the Library tab are as described in the following bulleted list. A number of these tools are examined in more detail later in the chapter, and the appropriate sections are referenced as applicable:

- **View:** Only active when a different view, such as Quick Edit, is selected. Restores the standard view of the library.
- **Quick Edit:** Provides a view (similar to the datasheet view in previous versions of SharePoint) where metadata can be edited in a grid view. New columns can be added in this view. Figure 20.6 shows an example where the plus sign was clicked and the user chose the Number column type and then labeled it Phase, as indicated by the arrow.

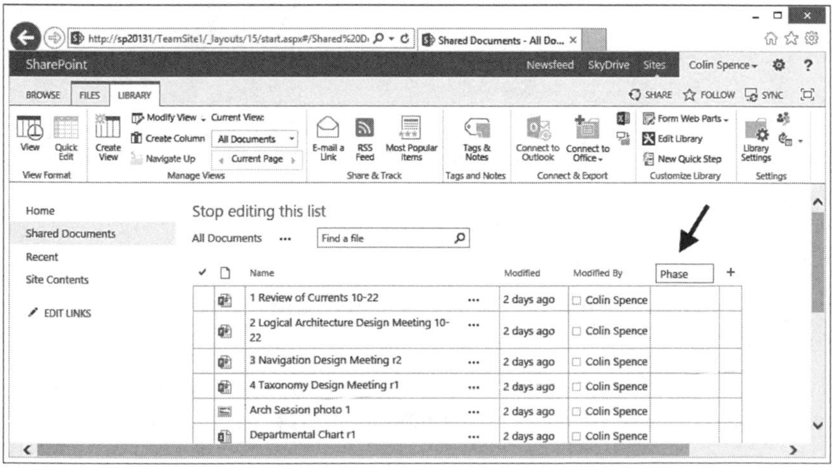

FIGURE 20.6 Adding a column in Quick Edit view.

- **Create View:** Create View gives access to a number of different types of views. The most commonly used is standard view, but several others are discussed later in this chapter in the "Creating and Managing Views" section.
- **Modify View:** Modify View offers two drop-down menu options: Modify View and Modify in SharePoint Designer. The process of modifying a view is discussed later in this chapter in the "Creating and Managing Views" section.
- **Create Column:** Provides access to the Create Column window, which provides a variety of column options, as shown in Figure 20.7. Columns in a document library are similar to columns in a spreadsheet and, with some planning, can add greatly to the value of the data stored in the library.

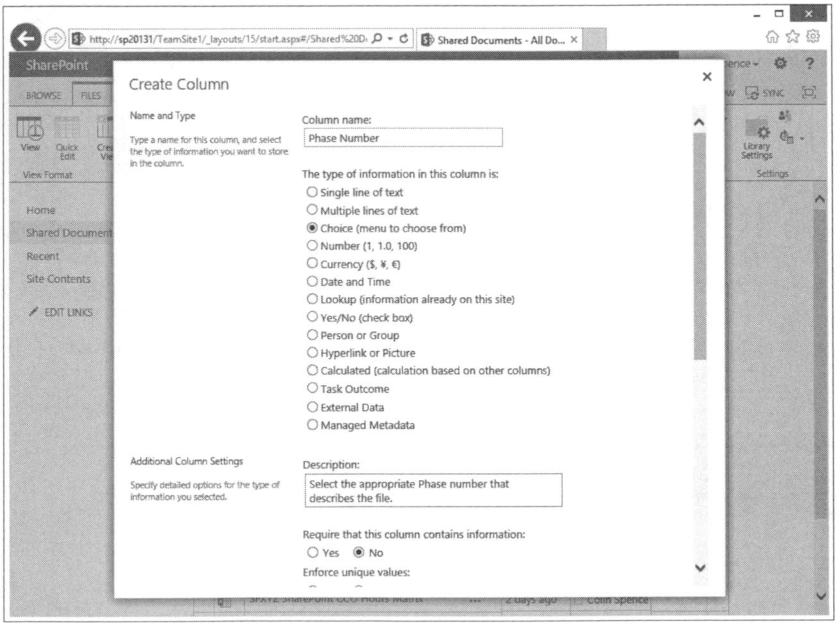

FIGURE 20.7 Column options in a document library.

- **Navigate Up:** Only active if the user has drilled into the contents of one or more folders. Navigates to the parent folder.
- **Current View:** Located below is a drop-down menu that shows the different views available to the logged-in user. Below that is a navigation tool that allows the user to page forward and backward if the library contains a large number of files.
- **E-Mail a Link:** When clicked, this provides available email options and enables the user to send an email that contains a link to the library. For example, it can provide links to Mail, Outlook, or Look for an App in the Store.

- **RSS Feed:** Opens the RSS Feed page and allows you to subscribe to it from your Outlook client. Other feed readers can be used to connect to this RSS feed if needed. This functionality can be turned off from the Settings page for the library via the RSS Settings link.
- **Most Popular Items:** Opens the Most Popular Items page, which provides data on which documents have had the most views, most views by unique users, and most recommendation clicks. This page also allows the user to refine results based on Result Type, Content Type, and Author.
- **Tags & Notes:** Allows the user to tag an item with terms or phrases, set the tags to private if desired, or post longer notes as shown in Figure 20.8. The Personal Site tracks the tags or notes posted, so it is easy to find the content later.

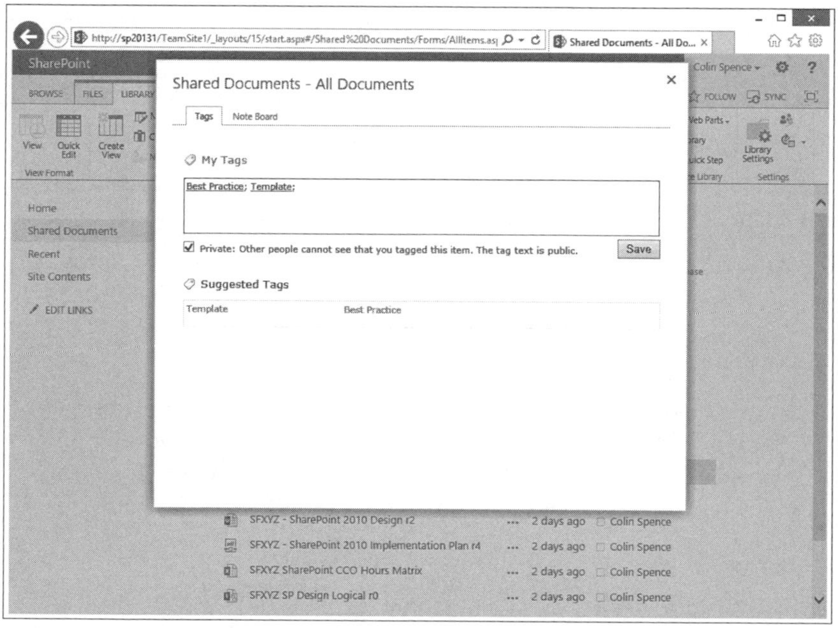

FIGURE 20.8 Tags and Notes window.

- **Connect to Outlook:** Enables you to synchronize items to an Outlook folder for offline access.
- **Connect to Office:** This provides access to several tools. Add to SharePoint Sites adds a shortcut in Microsoft Office applications, making it easy to save to this location in the future from the Office application. Remove from SharePoint Sites removes the shortcut. Manage SharePoint Sites allows you to manage the list of shortcuts.

- **Export to Excel:** Opens Excel and provides a "copy" of the library. The actual documents do not become embedded in the Excel file; instead, it provides links to the documents. Metadata provided in the active view is also exported.
- **Open with Explorer:** Open the Windows Explorer tool to allow for interaction with the files in a more familiar fashion and for access to the standard Windows Explorer tools such as Open, Cut, Copy, Delete, Rename, and Properties. This is a popular tool to allow end users to quick copy documents to the library.
- **Form Web Parts:** This tool allows the administrator to open the forms present for the list or library for editing. This is covered later in the "Modify Form Web Parts Tools" section.
- **Edit Library:** This link opens SharePoint Designer 2013 and allows the end user to edit the configuration of the library. This topic is covered later in the "Edit Library Tool" section.
- **New Quick Step:** The New Quick Step button opens SharePoint Designer 2013 and an Add a Button window, where you can start a new workflow, start an existing workflow, define the button label, and link to a button image.
- **Library Settings:** This opens the Document Library Settings page, which is discussed in more detail in the "Document Library Settings Tools Reviewed" section.
- **Shared With:** This tool shows the users who have access to the library and provides the following tools: Invite People, Email Everyone, and Advanced. Clicking the Advanced link takes you to the Permission page for the document library for complete management of access to the document library.
- **Workflow Settings:** The drop-down menu provides access to four tools: Workflow Settings, Add a Workflow, Create a Workflow in SharePoint Designer, and Create a Reusable Workflow in SharePoint Designer. This is covered in more depth later in this chapter in the "Workflow Settings" section.

Creating and Managing Views

The process of creating views was covered in Chapter 19, in the "Creating a View in a List" section, and so in this section is reviewed from the perspective of the list administrator.

One of the main concerns a list or library administrator should have pertains to the columns that are shown in the default view for a list or library (the view that shows by default when a user visits the list) and how it presents the information. It is generally an ongoing process for the list administrator to experiment with the best way to present the data stored in the list or library by manipulating the view by showing or hiding columns, using filtering, using groupings and totals, limiting the number of items shown in each view, and tuning the other options. An example is given in this section of a view that is created using a specific style to leverage the metadata that is available for documents by default (such as created date and time and created-by information).

TIP

A recommended best practice is to create a view titled Home Page View for each list or library that will have its list view web part added to the home page or other web part page. Generally, the default view can be modified and several columns hidden, which results in the list view web part taking up less space on the page that displays it, which is often the home page to the site.

When the administrator clicks the Create View button from the Library tab on the ribbon in a document library, several options are provided, as follows:

- Standard View
- Calendar View
- Datasheet View
- Gantt View
- Custom View in SharePoint Designer

A general recommendation is to experiment with the different views, but in most cases, the standard view is used. Access views are discussed later in the chapter in the "Access Views Explained" section.

Options Available When Modifying a View

If the administrator clicks the Modify View button from the Library tab on the ribbon, he has the option of changing which columns are displayed (and in which order), whether sorting is used, whether filtering is used, whether grouping is used, along with other options. Also, the administrator has the option to use tabular view, which determines whether individual item check boxes are displayed. These allow users to perform bulk operations by checking multiple items at a time. Items in the list or library can be grouped by one or more columns, and the display can default to collapsed or expanded, which can make navigating the list or library much easier. Totals can be displayed for some types of columns but not all, the Totals section shows which columns can be totaled, and the options of Count, Average, Maximum, Minimum, Sum, Std Deviation, or Variance are offered based on the type of data.

A variety of styles are offered that change the appearance of the data. For example, the shaded view style colors every other row a darker shade, making it easier for users to track metadata associated with a document as they scroll to the right.

NOTE

When you are editing or creating a view, not all columns can be totaled. For example, calculated columns cannot be totaled, which is an annoyance when tracking financial information or other numeric information where calculated columns are used.

In addition, when editing a view, the administrator can choose whether to show folders or show items without folders, and to show the view in all folders, in the top-level folder only, or in folders of a certain content type. Item limits can be set per view, and the administrator enters an integer for the number of items to display and specifies whether to display in batches of the specified size or to limit the total number of items returned to the specified amount. Finally, the administrator can determine whether the view is enabled for mobile access, if it is the default view for mobile access, and the number of items to display in web part for the view. This is important to test with any mobile devices supported because the size of the screens affects the ease of interacting with the view and how many items are displayed.

Access Views Explained

If the Access View option is chosen from the Create View page, SharePoint opens Access 2013 and asks the user to name and save (using the .accdb extension) the database that is then created. Right off the bat there is obviously more to the process than simply creating a "view," but in fact a database is created for which forms, PivotCharts, PivotTables, or reports can be created. This database remains connected to the SharePoint list, so changes in the SharePoint list are synced with this database.

NOTE

The Access "view" does not show up as an option from the Current View drop-down menu in the library, but instead creates an Access file that can be used for data analysis. The Access database must be saved either locally or to a SharePoint document library. Therefore, this "view" is better suited for data analysts than administrators.

Figure 20.9 shows the design view for a report that was created based on the data contained in a sample document library. In this example, the site administrator wanted to create a report that captured the titles of all the documents in the library, as well as some of the metadata associated with the documents, including file size, and then sorted by the file size. And the report needed to print professionally for review in a weekly meeting, a requirement that SharePoint natively does not meet.

Modify Form Web Parts Tools

The Modify Form Web Parts button on the List tab of the ribbon allows the administrator to open the forms present for the list or library for editing. The editing allowed includes inserting text, image, video and audio, web parts, or the existing list view web part. The properties of the body of the form can be edited, too, such as height, width, chrome state, layout, advanced, and miscellaneous properties. This allows the administrator a great deal of control over how the various forms (such as New, Edit, and Display forms) appear and other forms associated with content types in use in that list or library. For a simple example, an administrator could add text or even a video to the new form for a list, which provides instructions on how to fill out the form.

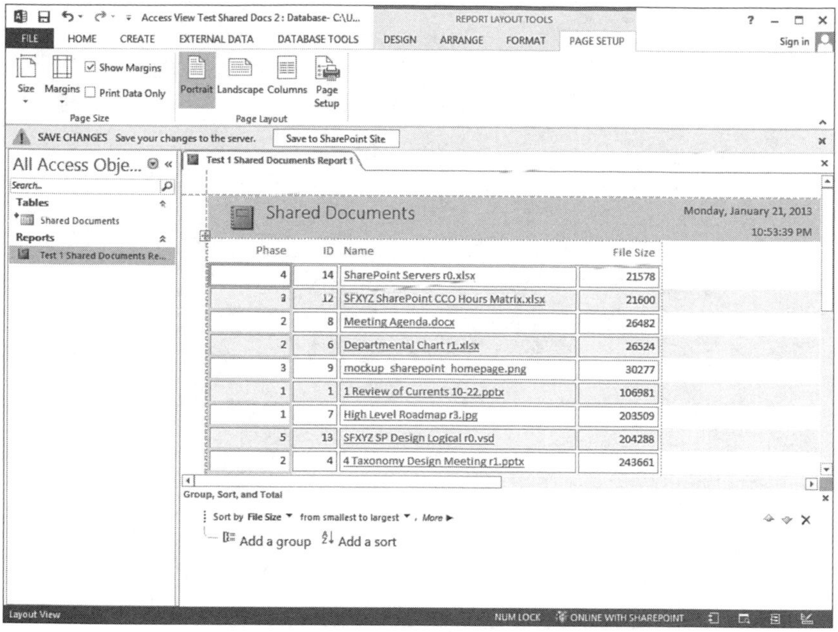

FIGURE 20.9 Creating an Access report from document library data.

Edit Library Tool

When clicked, this button opens SharePoint Designer 2013 and, as shown in Figure 20.10, provides an extensive dashboard of information about the library. This information can prove invaluable for a library administrator, as discussed briefly in this section.

From a list administrator's perspective, the dashboard of information provided by SharePoint Designer 2013 provides insight into a variety of areas:

- **List Information:** Provides the name and description of the library or list, web address, list ID, last modified, and number of items.
- **Customization:** Provides links to the Edit list columns page and Permissions page for this list.
- **Settings:** Allows the administrator to quickly change various settings, including Display this List on the Quick Launch, Hide from Browser, Display New Folder Command on the New Menu, Require Content Approval for Submitted Items, Create a Version Each Time You Edit an Item, Allow Management of Content Types, and also provides the Document Template URL.
- **Content Types:** Allows the administrator to add new content types and to view and manage settings for existing content types.
- **Views:** Allows for the creation of new views or editing of existing views.
- **Forms:** Allows for the creation of new forms or editing of existing forms.

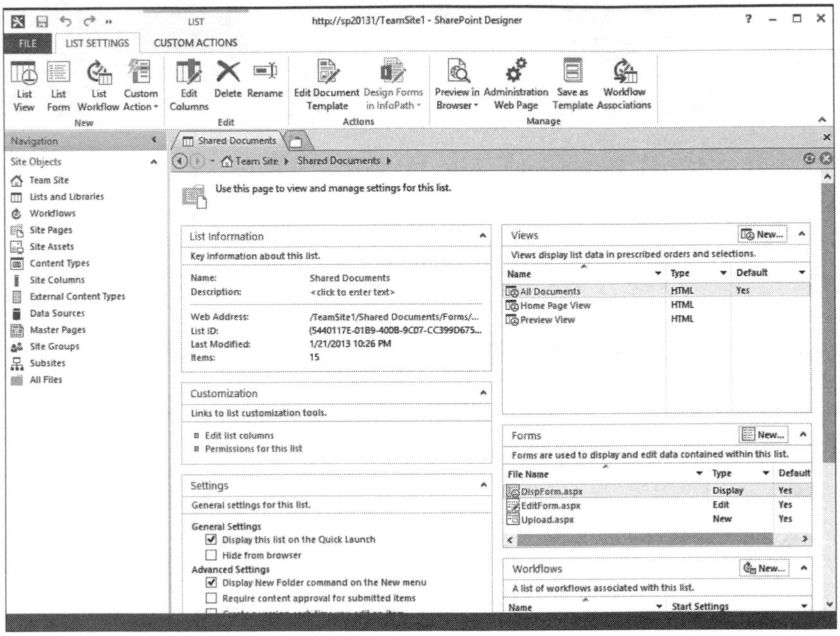

FIGURE 20.10 SharePoint Designer 2013 view of a library.

- **Workflows:** Allows for the creation of new workflows or editing of existing workflows.
- **Custom Actions:** Allows for the creation of buttons that can navigate to a form, initiate a workflow, or navigate to a URL.

Just from this quick overview of tools, you can see that SharePoint Designer 2013 offers an alternative to the administrator to the tools provided in the SharePoint 2013 user interface, as reviewed throughout this chapter. It is arguably a faster way for an experienced site administrator to navigate between sites and between lists and make changes. However, most administrators work with the tools provided through the user interface provided by SharePoint 2013, because those are integrated and meet most day-to-day needs. Be aware, however, of the capabilities of SharePoint Designer 2013 as well.

Creating a Custom Action

From SharePoint Designer 2013, with a library opened (click the Edit Library link from the Library tab of the ribbon), follow these steps to add an entry to the drop-down menu in a document library. This is a powerful way for an administrator to provide added functionality within a list or library, but should be considered an advanced and potentially dangerous process (and so should generally be done first in a lab environment):

1. Confirm that SharePoint Designer is connected to a library by looking at the active tab and the breadcrumb that shows the site and library name. For example, the tab

might be titled Shared Documents, and the breadcrumb might show Team Site > Shared Documents.

2. Click the Custom Action drop-down menu on the List Settings tab and select List Item Menu.

3. As shown in Figure 20.11, enter a name and description, and then specify either Navigate to Form, Initiate Workflow, or Navigate to URL. For this example, a link is added that simply navigates to a different website. Enter the name as **Go To Microsoft's Web Site**, set the action as Navigate to URL, and enter **www.microsoft.com**.

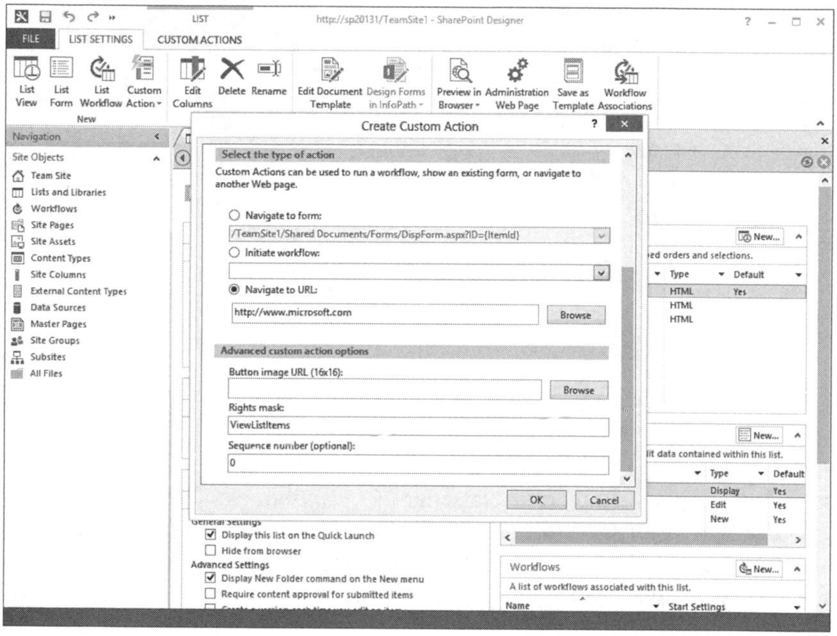

FIGURE 20.11 Create Custom Action window in Designer 2013.

4. Scroll down, and in the Rights Mask section enter **ViewListItems**. This results in this menu item only displaying to users with ViewListItems permissions.

TIP

For additional information about the options for rights masks, go to http://msdn.microsoft.com/en-us/library/microsoft.sharepoint.spbasepermissions.aspx. Some examples include EditListItems, Open, and DeleteListItems. Understanding which default groups have which permissions allows the site administrator to create menu entries that appear only for the appropriate users.

5. Click OK. This saves the new menu item to the document library. No save is needed from SharePoint Designer 2013. This new custom action displays in the Custom

Action section in the lower-right corner of SharePoint Designer 2013 when the document library is connected to.

6. Navigate to the document library that was opened in SharePoint Designer 2013. In this example, it was named Shared Documents. Access the drop-down menu for an item and confirm that the new entry appears, as shown in Figure 20.12.

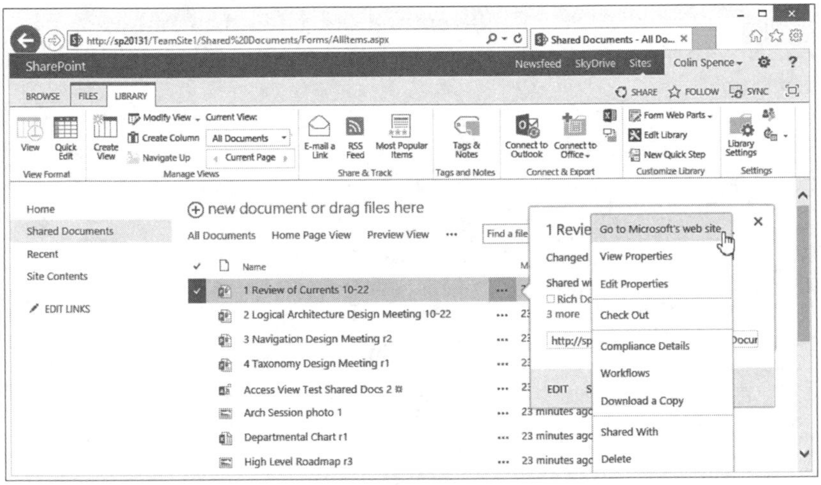

FIGURE 20.12 Viewing the new action for a library item.

New Quick Step Button

The New Quick Step button opens SharePoint Designer 2013 and an Add a Button window, which provides the options to start a new workflow or start an existing workflow and to define the button label and link to a button image. Creating workflows in SharePoint Designer 2013 is covered in Chapter 28, "Out-of-the-Box Workflows and Designer 2013 Workflows."

Document Library Settings Tools Reviewed

As one of the most commonly used libraries, the document library is a good starting point for the tools that are available for list and library administrators. The document library Settings page is reached by entering the document library, clicking the Library tab on the ribbon, and then clicking the Library Settings icon on the right side of the toolbar. The resulting array of tools varies based on whether SharePoint Foundation 2013, SharePoint Server 2013 Standard, or Enterprise is being used, and based on which site collection features and site features are enabled. Only users with the Manage Lists permission can click the Library Settings icon; it is grayed out for other users. This section reviews several of the most widely used library settings tools and explains best practices for using those tools.

Figure 20.13 shows the document library Settings page for a document library created with the Team Site template in SharePoint Foundation 2013 with a user who has Owner-level permissions logged in. Figure 20.14 shows the document library Settings page for a document library created with the Team Site template in SharePoint Server 2013 Enterprise, also with a user who has Owner-level permissions. The SharePoint Server 2013 Enterprise document library Settings page shows tools that are enabled when the SharePoint Server Publishing Infrastructure is enabled for site collection features as well as site features for the site in question.

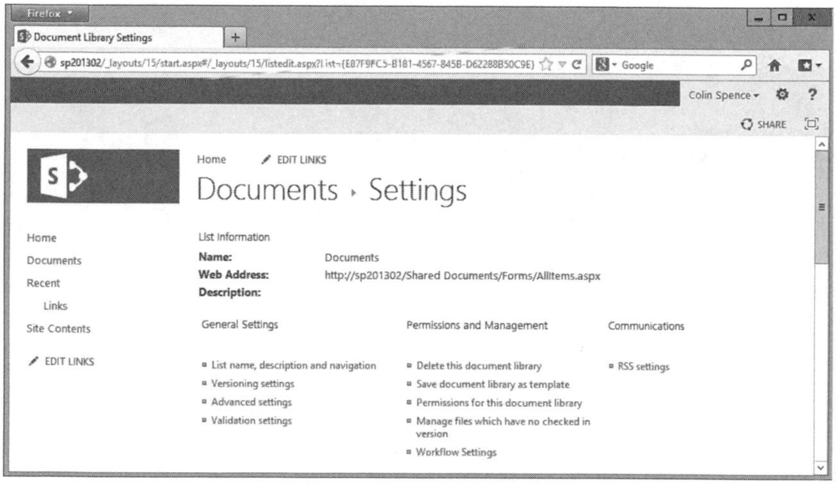

FIGURE 20.13 Document library settings for a SharePoint Foundation 2013 document library.

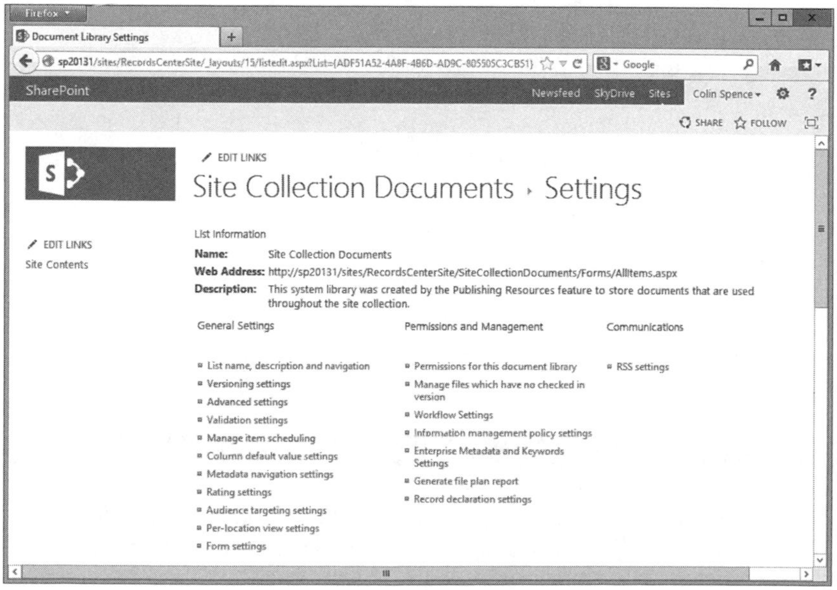

FIGURE 20.14 Document library settings for a SharePoint Server 2013 Enterprise document library.

The tools provided in SharePoint Foundation 2013 in this example and specific configuration are as follows:

- List Name, Description and Navigation
- Versioning Settings
- Advanced Settings
- Validation Settings
- Delete This Document Library
- Save Document Library as Template
- Permissions for This Document Library
- Manage Files Which Have No Checked In Version
- Workflow Settings
- RSS Settings

Additional tools provided by SharePoint Server 2013 Enterprise with SharePoint Server Publishing Infrastructure features enabled include the following:

- Manage Item Scheduling
- Column Default Value Settings
- Metadata Navigation Settings
- Rating Settings
- Audience Targeting Settings
- Per-Location View Settings
- Form Settings
- Information Management Policy Settings
- Enterprise Metadata and Keywords Settings
- Generate File Plan Report
- Record Declaration Settings

NOTE

The document library created in SharePoint Server 2013 Enterprise was created in a Records Center site collection template, as indicated in the URL. Because of this, the Delete This Document Library tool is not available. In addition, because the SharePoint Server Publishing Infrastructure is enabled, the Save Document Library as Template option is removed.

This section covers the tools provided on this page that are of most importance to document library administrators and site collection administrators. Some of the decisions of whether to enable these tools also impact overall farm governance, and therefore IT and the governance committee may need to be involved.

List Name, Description and Navigation

The first link on the document library Settings page provides access to the Name, Description, Navigation tools. Changing the name on this page does not change the library URL, but does change the display name on the Site Contents page and navigation elements, such as the Global Navigation bar. A general best practice is to have the display name and the URL name match as closely as possible, with a typical exception being the URL name should not have spaces in it, because SharePoint translates those to %20. A Description field is available, as well, and text typed in here is visible to the end user when she clicks on the *i* button to the right of the library title when inside the document library.

The other option is whether to display the library on the quick launch (also described as current navigation). This is a stylistic decision, as too many entries on the quick launch area can clutter up the page. One of the site owner's jobs is to "advertise" the lists and libraries that are of most interest to typical site users by judicious use of the entries in the quick launch.

Versioning Settings

The second link on the document library Settings page, Versioning Settings, provides access to one of the most demanded features in a document management system: major and minor versioning. This is a "basic" functionality of an enterprise content management (ECM) system that is not available with a standard file share and that allows users to save copies of the document as it evolves without having to change the actual filename of the document by adding R1, R2, or R3 to the name. You can configure a variety of different settings for document libraries, and the pros and cons of different settings are reviewed in this section.

The pros include a structured process for turning a draft document into an approved version and restrictions relating to which users can see the draft. The cons include a multistep process for posting a document to a document library and getting it approved so that other users can view or edit it.

Figure 20.15 shows the Versioning Settings page for a sample document library. It has been configured to require content approval for submitted items and has been configured to create major and minor versions. A limit has been set for how many major versions are retained and the number of major versions for which draft versions are kept. Only users who can approve items and the author of an item can see draft items. While not shown in Figure 20.15, at the bottom of the screen is the Require Documents Be Checked Out Before They Can Be Edited option, which is set to No in this example.

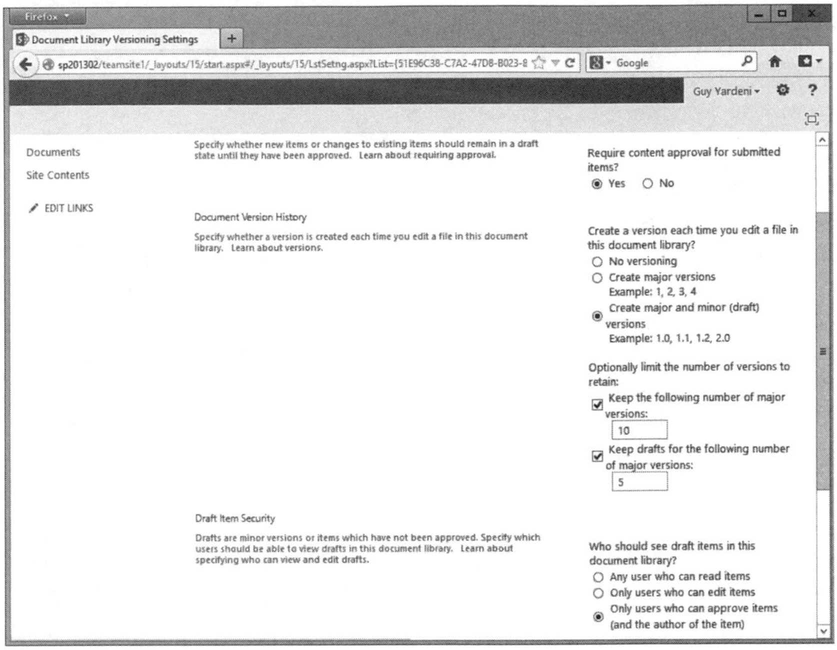

FIGURE 20.15 Versioning Settings page for a document library.

Assuming a library is configured in this fashion, the process of uploading a document to the library and it being approved is as follows:

1. A user (Guy in this example) uploads a document to the library.
2. The document is saved, but in draft status (version 0.1), and no one but users of the site with Approve Items privileges and the author (Guy) can see the document.
3. The document library administrator (Colin in this example) reviews the document, believes the document is ready for others to see it, and decides to "publish" the document, which will create a major version (version 1.0). So, Colin clicks the ellipsis next to the document title, which brings up the document menu; once again he clicks the ellipsis to bring up additional tools, as shown in Figure 20.16, and then clicks Publish a Major Version. Note that the Publish button on the Files tab of the ribbon could also be used.
4. Colin can enter comments if desired, and then clicks OK. This sets in motion the approval workflow. The approval status of the document is now set to Pending, so Guy can see that the workflow is in motion.
5. Colin (or another library administrator with Approve Items permissions) can now approve the document in one of two ways: by selecting the document and accessing the document menu and then the Approve/Reject tool, or by selecting the document

and clicking the Approve/Reject button on the Files tab on the ribbon. Either of these methods opens the Approve/Reject window shown in Figure 20.17. In this example, the document is approved, a brief comment is added, and the OK button is clicked.

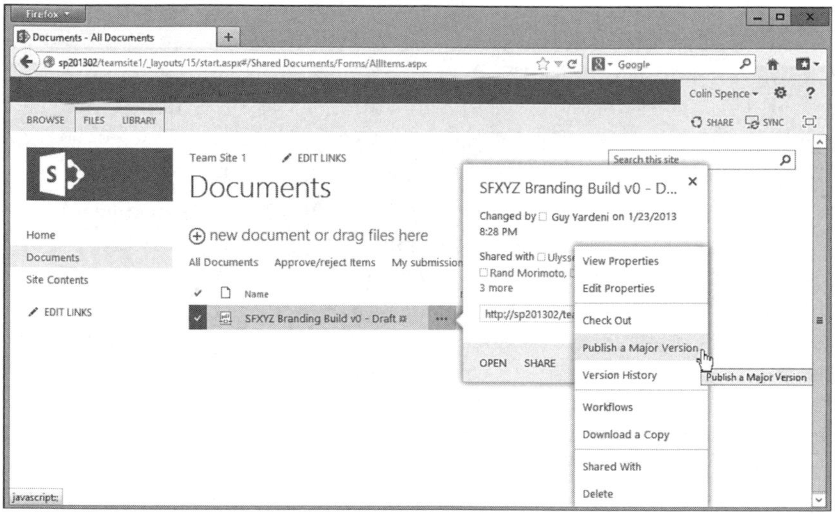

FIGURE 20.16 Accessing the Publish a Major Version tool in a document library.

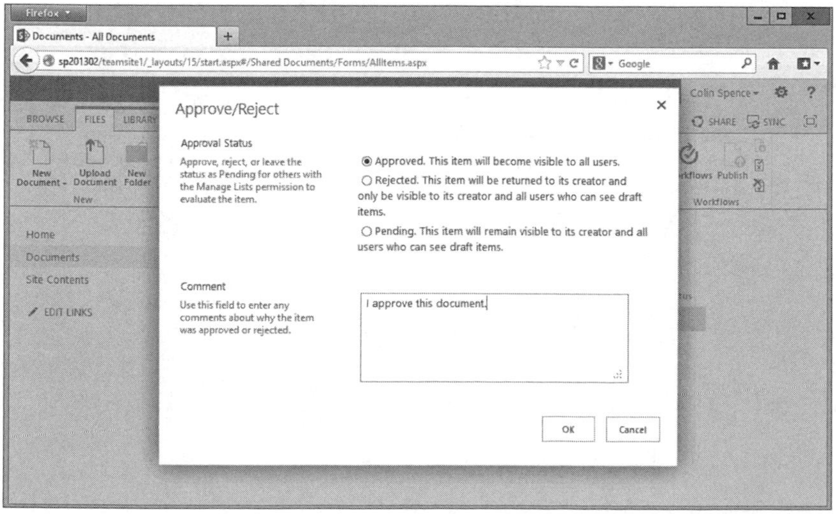

FIGURE 20.17 The Approve/Reject window in a document library.

NOTE

Another option is available from the Library tab under the Current View drop-down menu: the Approve/Reject Items view. This is a helpful view for libraries with large numbers of files because the approver doesn't need to scan down long lists of files to see what is pending approval; instead, he sees only the items pending approval in this view.

6. Guy can now can see that the approval status of the document is set to Approved; and after checking version history for the document, he sees that there is now only one version, version 1.0, because the version number was incremented at the approval stage.

Returning to the concept of planning lists and libraries, Table 20.2 provides some guidelines for when to use versioning, page approval, and content approval features. A recommendation that can be seen in this table is to enable only major versioning in environments where "basic collaboration" is required and where the users are new to SharePoint. This is a generalization, but after testing the different configuration options, most organizations realize that the process can easily become overly complex and frustrating for users who only need basic collaboration ("someplace to store my files other than the file share") and haven't used SharePoint or another document management or ECM system.

TABLE 20.2 Guidelines for Using Versioning, Page Approval Workflows, and Content Approval in Document Libraries

	Basic Collaboration (New SharePoint Users)	**Basic Collaboration (Experienced SharePoint Users)**	**Managing Content That Should Be Approved Before the "General Public" Can View It (New SharePoint Users)**	**Managing Content That Should Be Approved Before the "General Public" Can View It (Experienced SharePoint Users)**
Require Content Approval Enabled	No	No	Yes	Yes
Major Versioning Enabled	Yes	Yes	Yes	Yes
Minor Versioning Enabled	No	No	Yes	Yes
Draft Item Security Locked Down?	No	No	Maybe	Yes
Require Check Out Before a Document Can Be Edited?	No	Maybe	Maybe	Yes
Content Approval Enabled	No	No	No	Yes

Advanced Settings

The Advanced Settings link on the document library Settings page reveals additional tools of interest to the architect or administrator. In fact, these settings are so fundamental to the overall functionality of the document library that time should be spent during the design and testing phases reviewing these options and the pros and cons for the organization.

For example, the decision of whether to allow management of content types can have wide-reaching impact on the complexity of the environment and the amount of training required for users and administrators of the libraries. The ability to edit the template used by the document library may lead the architects to choose to create document libraries dedicated to the management of a single type of document (for example, resumes) and configure the template accordingly. In addition, the architects may decide that content from certain document libraries should not be able to be synced to Outlook clients or to the SharePoint Workspace product. All these settings are accessed via the Advanced Settings link:

- **Allow Management of Content Types:** The options are Yes or No. Content types can be an extremely powerful tool for more sophisticated document management in organizations that have invested time in creating a taxonomy for managing resources in SharePoint. Content types are discussed more in Chapter 22, "Managing Metadata and Content Types in SharePoint 2013."
- **Provide a Template URL:** This option is grayed out if Allow Management of Content Types is set to Yes, because, in that case, the templates are managed with each content type. If content types are not enabled for the library, the administrator can click the Edit Template link to open the document in the appropriate application (such as Word) and then edit the template. This is an easy way for the library administrator to customize the template document for the library and is most useful if the document library has been created for a specific purpose, such as containing a specific type of document (for example, proposals, resumes, diagrams, spreadsheets, or other standard Microsoft document types).

NOTE

Although it appears that the URL of "any" document stored in a SharePoint document library can be entered in the Provide a Template URL field, the template must actually exist in the Forms directory of the document library. This is accessible by using the Edit Template link on the Advanced Settings page below the URL field. If a different URL is provided, an Invalid Template URL error is given when the administrator tries to save the configuration.

- **Opening Documents in the Browser:** The options are to Open in the Client Application, Open in the Browser, or Use the Server Default (Open in the Browser). For the document to open in the browser, SharePoint 2013 must be configured to use Office Web Apps Server.

- **Define a Custom Send to Destination:** This location is visible if a user selects a document and then clicks the Send To icon in the Files tab of the ribbon along with the options Other Location or Create Document Workspace. By inputting a URL of a different document library, the library administrator makes it easy for users to send documents to a specific location. When used, this tool can also prompt the author to send out updates when the document is checked in and to create an alert on the source document. So, SharePoint can actively create "safeguards" to help avoid situations where the source document changes and the copy is not updated. In addition, when the properties of the copy of the document are viewed, a note is shown that states, "This item is a copy of http://(url of source document)" and provides links to Go To Source Item or Unlink. Figure 20.18 shows an example of this Properties page.

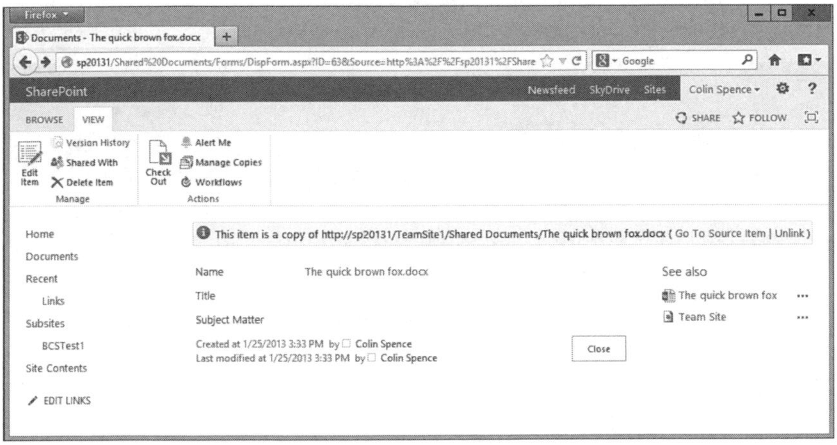

FIGURE 20.18 Properties for a copy of a document after the Send To feature is used.

- **Make New Folder Command Available:** The library administrator should decide whether to allow the use of folders within the document library, a topic discussed in detail in Chapter 19, in the "Pros and Cons of the New Folder Tool" section.

- **Allow Items from This Document Library to Appear in Search Results:** Bearing in mind that all SharePoint search results are security trimmed (that is, only users with permissions to at least view the document see its contents appear in searches), in some rare situations, the contents of a document library should *not* appear in search results. For example, a document library might be created for brainstorming; the contents of that document library should be moved to another document library (possibly by using a custom Send To destination) before being available via the search tool. This helps ensure that the results of searches are as relevant as possible.

- **Re-Index Document Library:** This ensures that all the content of the document library is fully re-indexed during the next crawl. A site administrator might use this tool if documents in the library don't appear in search results as expected or if a number of documents have just been deleted and the administrator wants to make sure that the search index is fully updated.

- **Offline Client Availability:** This applies both to using SkyDrive Pro and syncing with the Outlook client. If this option is enabled, users receive errors if they try and synchronize to Outlook or use SharePoint Workspace to sync content. The error messages are very clear. For example, the error from Skydrive Pro states, "We ran into problems syncing," and the error details state, "This library isn't available offline."
- **Site Assets Library:** If Yes is checked, this library is presented as the default location in the drop-down list for storing images or other files that users upload to their wiki pages. This does not convert the library into an assets library, nor does it add any content types to the library.
- **Quick Edit:** The Quick Edit view allows users to access the document library in a grid view where certain metadata values can quickly be edited without having to access the properties for the document. In addition, new columns can be added from this view. If enabled, this can greatly enhance the speed with which document metadata is added and can encourage the use of metadata.

WARNING

Exercise caution when using the Quick Edit view. It is relatively easy to perform large-scale edits by accident that cannot be undone with the click of a button. For example, the Name field can be selected for one document and then dragged to encompass a dozen or more, which results in the names changing for each document. There is no "undo" button after the changes are made, so many organizations shy away from allowing users to use the Quick Edit view (or enable it only during initial uploads).

- **Dialogs:** Setting this to No causes the whole page to change instead of the floating form to load. For example, if this is set to No, when a user clicks Edit Properties, the whole page changes to the editform.aspx page, rather than the floating form loading and the background dimming. This is essentially a stylistic decision, or a choice that is made if devices connecting to the SharePoint site have issues displaying the floating forms.

Validation Settings

If this link is clicked on the document library Settings page, the library administrator is taken to the Validation Settings page, as shown in Figure 20.19, where she can specify a formula to validate the data when new items are saved to the list or are edited. User message text can be entered, as well, so the end user is informed of the criteria that was not met successfully. In this example, the formula is as follows:

```
=Phase<10
```

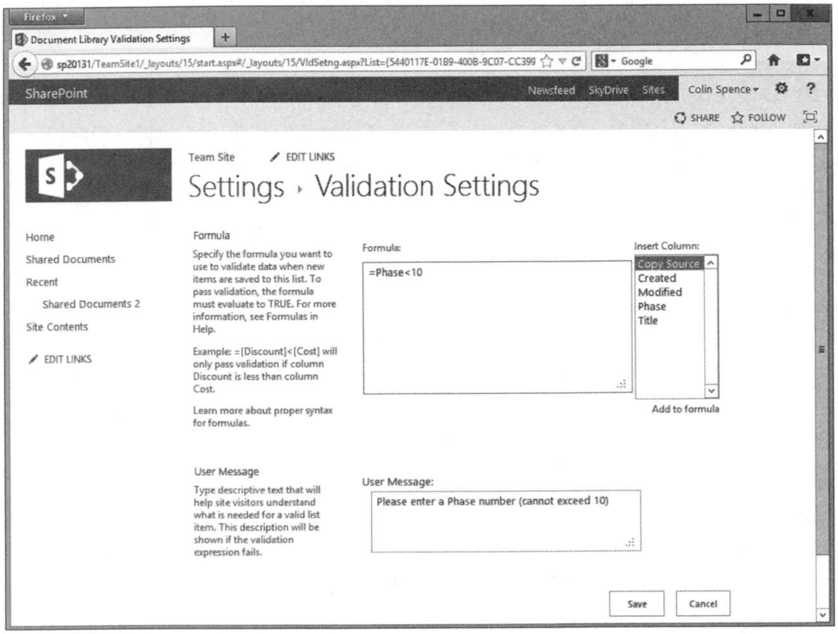

FIGURE 20.19 Validation Settings page with sample formula.

This translates as follows: The value entered in the Phase column must be less than 10 to provide a value of True. Additional information on proper formula syntax can be accessed by clicking the Learn More About Proper Syntax for Formulas link.

If the results of the equation entered do not equal a value of True, the user sees the User Message entered in the Validation Settings page, so it is important that the message be informative and help users avoid data entry errors.

Manage Item Scheduling

This feature on the Document Library Settings page is seen only in document libraries on publishing-enabled sites and is not available in SharePoint Foundation 2013. The tool is available only if the list or library has major and minor versioning enabled and content approval enabled. Assuming that the library meets these criteria, you can enable the Enable Item Scheduling option from the Manage Item Scheduling page. When enabled, any items that have content types that include start and end dates can be scheduled for publication.

Figure 20.20 shows the Properties window for a document that has just been uploaded to a document library that meets the criteria for scheduling. The content type of Page is selected, which includes a Scheduling Start Date and Scheduling End Date, as shown in Figure 20.20.

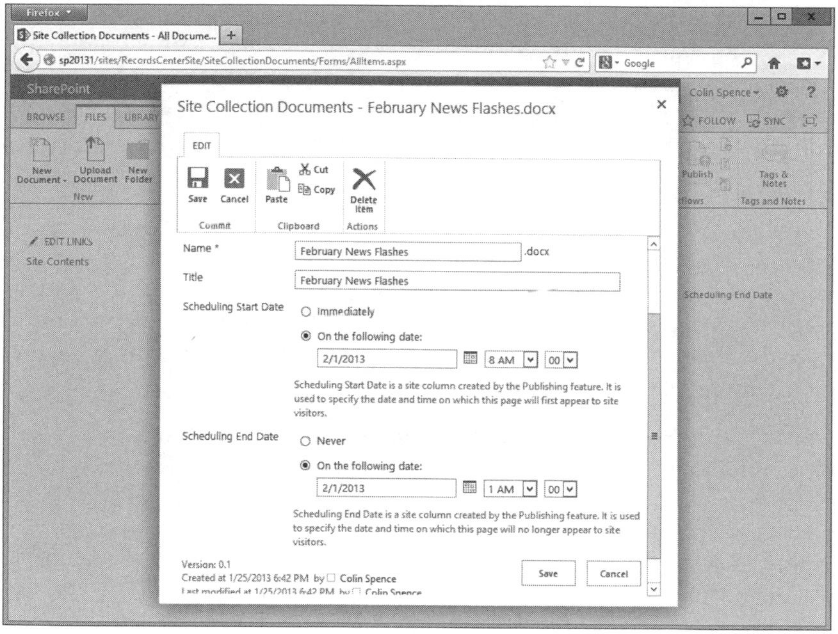

FIGURE 20.20 Entering scheduling start and end dates for a document.

Because content approval needs to be enabled, the document would need to be published to a major version and then approved by a user with Approve Items permissions in the library. Then, when the scheduling start date and time is reached, the item is available for users who could not see the draft version of the document; they can then see it and interact with it as their permissions allow.

Item scheduling is a fairly specialized tool, and because it has several dependencies that need to be configured for it to be available, as mentioned in this section, it is usually enabled only when a specific need exists to limit the time frame during which the item is available.

Column Default Value Settings

Not available in SharePoint Foundation 2013, this tool allows the library administrator to set a default value for columns in the library. This feature is covered in more detail in Chapter 22. From a list or library design standpoint, it is important to know that by using the Column Default Value Settings link from the Document Library Settings page, the administrator can set values based on folders, which can be a much more powerful and useful ability than setting default values on a column basis.

Metadata Navigation

Metadata navigation is a powerful tool available in SharePoint Server 2013 Standard or Enterprise but not in SharePoint Foundation 2013 (assuming Metadata Navigation and

Filtering is enabled as a site feature) and involves the configuration of hierarchy fields, key filters, and the management of column indexes. Essentially, the Navigation Hierarchy fields allow a user to click in a tree structure to view the content contained in folders or that meet the field criteria (such as using a specific content type). The Key Filter fields allow the user to also filter the results based on specific criteria, such as modified by a certain user. Chapter 22 covers this topic in more depth.

Rating Settings

This page allows the library administrator to decide whether items in the list or library can be rated. If Allow Items in This List to Be Rated? is set to Yes, users with Read permission level or higher can provide ratings in a list or library. Two different types of ratings can be selected: Likes or Star Ratings.

If either type of ratings is enabled for a list or library, three fields are added to the list: Rating (0-5), Number of Ratings, and Number of Likes. Enabling Likes simply adds a column to the default view titled Number of Likes, and users can click the word *Like*. If Star Ratings are selected, a Rating (0-5) column is added to the default view, with star images in that column. Users then click one of the stars to indicate their rating, and the system averages out the ratings.

Ratings is a powerful tool that encourages users to rate documents or list items on a scale of 0 to 5. Although it is impossible to enforce "responsible" use of ratings, users should be informed that SharePoint does track who rates documents how, and other users can, in fact, see what ratings a specific user applies from a My Site site from the My Newsfeed tab. So if, for example, a user chooses to rate everything as a 1, other users will see this and possibly apply social pressure on the user to be more constructive in his ratings. If enough users apply ratings, the number of ratings will make the frivolous ratings less significant through the power of averages.

The use of ratings from My Site is covered in Chapter 23, "Leveraging Social Networking Tools in SharePoint 2013."

Audience Targeting

Audience targeting can be enabled for lists and libraries by clicking this link and then clicking the Enable Audience Targeting check box. Audiences are compiled based on settings configured from Central Administration. This topic is covered in Chapter 21, "Designing and Managing Pages and Sites for Knowledge Workers," because the audience targeting process happens when web parts are configured on a SharePoint page to use audience targeting to filter the content that is displayed.

It is important for a list and library administrator to understand the topic and decide whether it should be enabled for some or all libraries/lists, because this is another metadata item that end users or list administrators need to configure to ensure that members of a specific audience are in fact seeing all the documents that should be targeted to them.

Per-Location View Settings

Per-Location View Settings are available for SharePoint Server 2013 Standard and Enterprise sites when the Metadata Navigation and Filtering site feature is enabled. Views are a fundamental tool for the list or library administrator to make the end-user experience with the list or library a productive one. SharePoint 2013 allows the list or library administrator to determine which views are available from within folders in the list or library though per-location view settings.

This is a fairly advanced tool set not often used; it can, however, be useful for libraries where there are multiple views and folders, and metadata is used to manage files in the document library because it controls which views are available to end users who navigate to the folders or use the Metadata Navigation tool.

Form Settings

SharePoint 2013 does not allow the use of this tool for all lists and libraries, and clicking the Form Settings link may simply display a message that states, "InfoPath does not support customizing the form used for this list." But if the forms are supported, the administrator can open the form in InfoPath 2013 and then edit the form to her heart's content.

This section provides an example of creating a simple modification to the form in InfoPath that should impress site administrators with the power suddenly placed in their hands by InfoPath via this tool. A good example to use is the standard Announcements list. Follow these steps to edit the form used in an Announcements list (InfoPath Designer 2013 must be installed on the computer in use):

1. Navigate to an Announcements list, click the List tab on the ribbon, and click List Settings.
2. Click Form Settings in the General Settings column.
3. The Form Settings page should display, and the circle next to Customize the Current Form Using Microsoft InfoPath should be checked. Make sure that the circle is checked and click OK.
4. A message might display that asks whether you want to allow this website to open a program on your computer. If so, click Allow.
5. InfoPath 2013 opens and displays the form.
6. Click the Expires field, also shown in Figure 20.21, and then click Add Rule from the Home tab.
7. Select Is in the Past, and then Show Validation Error from the Actions submenu, as shown in Figure 20.21. Note that in an unaltered Announcements list, a user can actually enter an expiration date in the past, as illogical as that sounds.

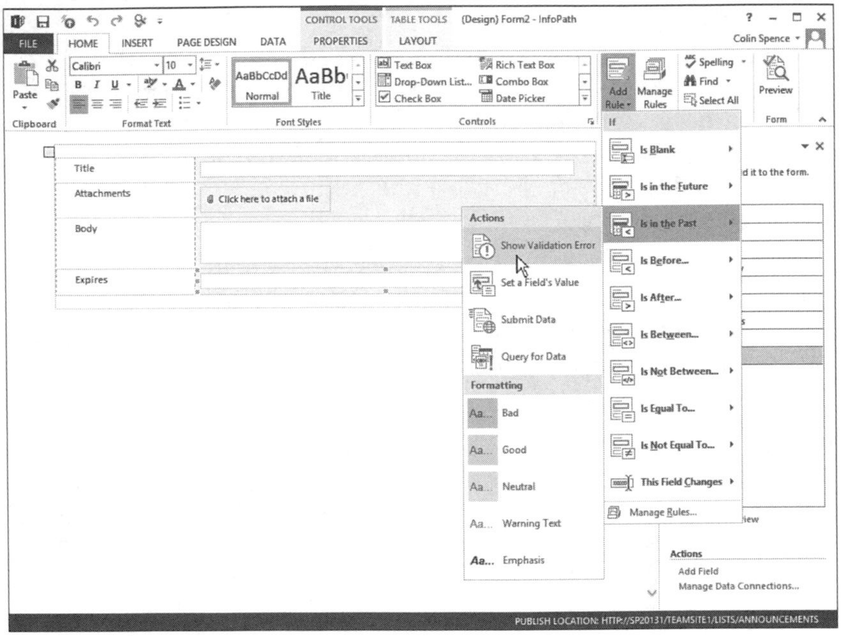

FIGURE 20.21 Editing an Announcements form in InfoPath Designer 2013.

8. Review the results in the Rules menu on the right side of the screen. Notice that a screen tip is automatically populated: Enter today's date or a date in the future. You can modify this if desired.

9. Click the File tab, then click the Publish link, and then click the tile for SharePoint List to publish the updated form to the SharePoint 2013 Announcements list.

10. A message should appear stating, "Your form was published successfully."

11. Navigate to the SharePoint 2013 Announcements list and click Add New Announcement. Enter a new announcement with a date that is in the past; when you enter that date, the error message as shown in InfoPath should display.

This simple example just scratches the surface of the power of InfoPath in the hands of experienced list and library administrators, who can easily customize the form used to add a new list item or edit a list item in a few minutes.

Permissions and Management Tools for Lists and Libraries

The Permissions and Management column on the document library Settings page provides even more tools that the list or library administrator must be familiar with. Because a number of them are covered in other chapters, this section covers just a subset of these tools.

As mentioned earlier in the "Document Library Settings Tools Reviewed" section, the tools provided to list and library administrators vary based on which version of SharePoint is being used. This section now delves into the different standard tools in the Permissions and Management Tools section of the document library Settings page.

Delete This Document Library

Every once in a while, the site administrator may need to delete a document library, and the tool executes as soon as the Delete This Document Library link is clicked. The administrator sees a message that states, "This document library will be removed and all its files will be deleted. Are you sure you want to send this document library to the site Recycle Bin?" If the administrator clicks OK, the document library and all its content are moved to the site Recycle Bin. The End User Recycle Bin now lists the document library. If deleted from the End User Recycle Bin, it is listed in the site collection Recycle Bin, so a site collection administrator can still restore it. If deleted from the Site Collection Recycle Bin, it is permanently deleted and needs to be recovered from other backups of the site collection.

Save Document Library as Template

Most organizations will customize a selection of lists and libraries and then use them as templates. This section provides an example of creating a List template from a document library and some tips pertaining to the use of these templates (as well as some of the limitations). Although these templates can be very useful, a site administrator should test them thoroughly to become familiar with the upsides as well as the downsides of using them, and might want to focus instead on using site templates for reasons provided next.

To create a List template, follow these steps:

1. From the document library Settings page for the library, click the Save Document Library as Template link.

NOTE

If there is no Save Document Library as Template link, chances are the site has SharePoint Server Publishing enabled, which removes this option.

2. Enter a filename (for example, **DocLibTemplate01**) and a template name (which can be the same as the filename). Leave the Save Content box unchecked. Click OK.
3. The Operation Completed Successfully message appears, mentioning that the template has successfully been saved to the List Template gallery. Click the List Template Gallery link visible in the body of the message; the List Template gallery for the site collection opens.

The templates are stored in the List Template gallery, accessible via the Site Settings page for the site by clicking List Templates in the Web Designer Galleries section. After a List template has been saved, it is available from the Add an App Page under Apps You Can Add.

The following list provides some tips for effectively using it:

- Create a site that contains the template lists and libraries so that they can be edited now and at later dates, and then save to the List Template gallery. Do not use this site for production purposes (for example, storing "live" files or list data) because it will be modified in the future and new templates created from it, possibly site templates as well.
- Create a logical naming scheme for the List templates that includes an identifier, such as the date it was created. For example, a name such as ProjectDocLib130126 is more useful than DocLibrary01 because it describes the type of library (a project library) and contains the date when it was created, which will be visible when creating new libraries from it.
- Although the option is given to include content when creating a template, there is a fairly small size limit of 50MB. Therefore, this is not a very powerful backup and restore tool for document libraries because most document libraries quickly exceed this limit; it could be useful for lists, though.
- List templates are shared only within a site collection. List templates can be saved locally from one List Template gallery and then uploaded to other List Template galleries for other site collections.
- Changes to the List template do not affect lists previously created with the List template. So, for example, if five lists have been created using AnnouncementsTemplate121212, each one must be visited separately to replicate the changes.
- When the List template is used to create a list at a later date, consider putting the name of the template used in the Description field of the list. This makes it easier to tell which template was used to create which list at a later date.
- If too many List templates are created, the Add an App page can become cluttered and confusing. Consider creating Site templates rather than List templates for this reason.

Armed with the preceding information, the site administrator should experiment with using List templates and determine whether they provide value for the organization or whether creating these templates clutters up the list creation options and will be confusing and whether site templates, each with customized lists, make more sense for the organization.

Permissions for This Document Library

Site administrators should be aware that list permissions can be customized and be familiar with the process. However, they should also be aware that lists and libraries with customized or "unique" permissions can be difficult to manage and that records should be kept of any changes made. No "magic" report lists all unique permissions used within a site collection or site, so a general best practice is to avoid customizing permissions for lists and libraries unless absolutely necessary.

TIP

Instead of customizing permissions on a list or library basis, consider creating a subsite with the revised permissions for that site—for example, a site (http://intranet/SiteA) is currently accessible to "everyone" (for example, Company123\domain users have read access to it) in the organization. The site administrator wants to have a few libraries and lists that are only accessible to a select group (for example, Company123\IT). Instead of modifying the permissions on those lists and libraries, he creates a subsite that houses those lists and libraries (http://intranet/SiteA/SiteAPrivate) and stops inheriting permissions for the site, and then removes Company123\domain users from access to that site, and gives Company123\IT users contribute permissions. Although this might seem like overkill initially, users can be easily taught that the subsite (SiteAPrivate) is where they upload documents that are for more restricted use, while the parent site (SiteA) is where documents that are available for anyone with a domain account to read. And the administrator now doesn't need to customize permissions for any lists or libraries on either site!

Follow these steps to customize permissions for a document library:

1. For the document library, access the Library tab and click Library Settings, and then click Permissions for This Document Library.
2. Notice whether this note appears: "This library inherits permissions from its parent." If this message appears under the ribbon, any changes to the parent will affect this document library. To change the permissions, click Stop Inheriting Permissions on the Edit tab of the ribbon.
3. A warning appears: "You are about to create unique permissions for this document library. Changes made to the parent site permissions will no longer affect this document library." Click OK. The notice now reads: "This library has unique permissions."
4. Now the user permissions can be edited. In general, it is a good idea to add the new permissions first and then remove the old permissions, to avoid excluding your own account from the list.
5. To add permissions for a group, user, or several users, click the Grant Permission link. Enter one or click the Show Options link to reveal the different permission levels available, as shown in Figure 20.22. By default, these are Full Control, Design, Edit, Contribute, Read, and View Only.
6. To remove or change user permissions, check the boxes next to the individual users or groups that are to be removed or modified. Then click Remove User Permissions or Edit User Permissions as appropriate, and repeat until the desired result is achieved.

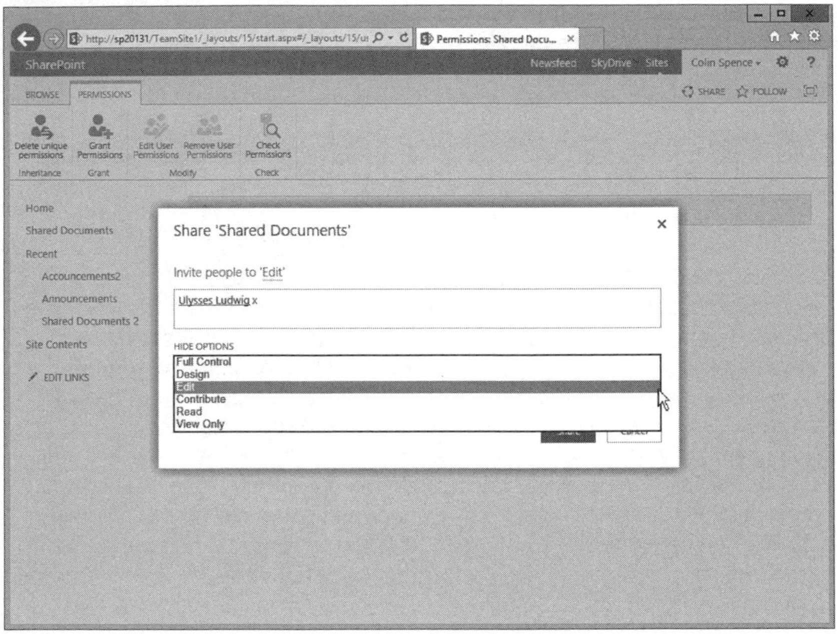

FIGURE 20.22 Granting permissions to a user in a document library.

7. Before exiting, click the Check Permissions icon and enter one or more individuals' names, and then click the Check Now button to see what permissions, if any, the users or groups have after the changes made in previous steps.

8. Finally, you can click Inherit Permissions icon to overwrite your changes with the permissions assigned at the parent site level. This is basically a "get out of jail free" tool that you can use to undo undesirable changes.

Manage Files Which Have No Checked In Version

Rarely will a file have no checked-in version, but the Manage Files Which Have No Checked In Version tool on the document library Settings page does come in handy in certain situations. This tool is not helpful if a user simply checks out a file and then forgets to check it back in, because there will be a checked-in version that exists before the file is checked out.

Where this tool is handy is when documents are uploaded to the document library but required metadata is not entered. This can happen when the Open with Explorer button on the Library tab of the ribbon is used and multiple documents are pasted into the document library; it can also happen when the Upload Multiple Documents tool is used from the Documents tab. Because many end users want to save time, it can occur that the uploaded files will end up in a checked-out status, and the list administrator will need to access this link and add the required metadata to the items and then check them in.

Workflow Settings

This page allows the administrator to see the number of workflows in progress for the list or library, or entities in the list or library, and to add or remove workflows if needed. Workflow associations can be listed for the following:

- ▶ This List
- ▶ Document
- ▶ Folder
- ▶ Basic Page
- ▶ Document Set

The Three-State Workflow is the only Workflow template provided in SharePoint Foundation 2013 by default; others are available in SharePoint Server 2013. In SharePoint Server 2013 Standard and Enterprise, additional workflows can be provisioned (assuming the Workflow Site Collection feature is enabled) as follows:

- ▶ Approval – SharePoint 2010
- ▶ Collect Feedback – SharePoint 2010
- ▶ Collect Signatures – SharePoint 2010
- ▶ Disposition Approval
- ▶ Three-State

NOTE

None of these default workflows appear to be SharePoint 2013 workflows, and that is in fact the case. To create true SharePoint 2013 workflows, the Azure components need to be installed and configured. The article "How To: Set Up and Configure SharePoint 2013 Workflows" (http://msdn.microsoft.com/en-us/library/jj163276(v=office.15).aspx) provides an overview of this process. This enables SharePoint 2013 workflows in SharePoint Designer 2013. Otherwise, SharePoint Designer 2013 is limited to SharePoint 2010-based workflows.

Workflows are examined in more detail in Chapter 28.

Additional Permissions and Management Tools

The several other tools in the Permissions and Management section on the document library Settings page are covered in other chapters. The site administrator should be familiar with these tools, too. These tools are also relevant to the topics of metadata and governance and so are covered in those chapters, as follows:

- ▶ Information Management Policy Settings are covered in Chapter 24, "Governing the SharePoint 2013 Ecosystem."

- Enterprise Metadata and Keywords Settings is covered in Chapter 22.
- Generate File Plan Report is covered in Chapter 24.
- Record Declaration Settings is covered in Chapter 24.

Document Sets Compared to Folders as Organizational Tools in Document Libraries

Document sets are a powerful tool that can be enabled for site collections that allow users to keep related documents together as a "set" to facilitate collaboration on the documents. When a user clicks a document set, all the files stored in the document set are visible. In this way, document sets are similar to folders, but as explained in this section, they have a variety of differences that are important to understand from an administrative standpoint. From a high level, folders are simpler to enable and are more limited in functionality and so make a better choice for less-advanced users or simpler collaboration requirements. But when the advantages of document sets are understood, many organizations will benefit from their capabilities.

Document sets are designed specifically to help users organize groups of files as a unit and give some special tools to users to facilitate the management of the group of documents as a whole, such as the ability to assign metadata to a document set, start a workflow on a document set, and capture a version of the entire set of documents. Following are some key technical details of document sets:

- Document sets are not available in SharePoint Foundation 2013.
- Document sets are available in SharePoint Server 2013 Standard and Enterprise Editions.
- A document set is a content type, with Document Collection Folder as the parent, and uses the Name column from the Folder content type and title from the Item content type.
- There is no hard limit on the number of documents that can exist in a document set.
- Permissions changes to a document set do affect all items within the document set.
- An alert set on a document set applies to contents of the document set.
- Deleting a document set sends the document set and all members of the document set to the Recycle Bin.
- If the Send To feature is used with a document set, the sum for all documents in a document set cannot be larger than 50MB.
- Metadata assigned to the document set is not automatically assigned to members of the document set.

NOTE

Document sets can have the Capture Version tool run to create a version of the document set, which includes the latest major or major and minor versions of documents contained within the document set. This adds another level of granularity to versioning: Not only can individual documents be versioned but also whole sets of documents, to "snapshot" the document set at a point in time.

Document sets do require some additional configuration to be available to end users, because they need to be enabled from the site collection features, which is explained later in the chapter. The document set content type then needs to be added to the document library before it can be used. Folders, however, can easily be configured from the list or library Settings page (by clicking the Advanced Settings link) to either be available or not available for a document library. Document sets can have metadata associated with the document set itself, which is different from folders, which cannot have metadata manually assigned to them. Keep in mind several other notable differences when determining whether the organization should use them:

- Document sets are not available in SharePoint Foundation 2013; folders are available.
- Document sets can be created only in document libraries; folders can be created in either libraries or lists.
- Folders are not allowed within document sets.
- Document sets cannot be nested; folders can be nested.
- Metadata can be assigned to document sets but not to folders.
- Workflows can be started on document sets but not on folders.

TIP

If a view is configured to Show All Items Without Folders, the items in a document set will be visible, just as items within a folder will be visible. Unique permissions will still be honored in both scenarios, so administrators don't need to worry about users seeing documents they shouldn't see.

Enabling Document Sets from Site Collection Features

To enable the Document Sets feature for a document library, first ensure that the feature is active for the site collection, and then add the content type to the document library by following the steps in this section. First, enable the site collection feature by following these steps:

1. Access the Site Settings page for the site collection. Under the Site Collection Administration section, click Site Collection Features.

2. On the Site Collection Features page, click Activate for Document Sets if it is not already set to Active. The Document Set content type now appears in the Content Type gallery for the site collection.

To add the content type to the document library, follow these steps:

1. Navigate to the document library that has the Document Set content type added; in this example, the document library is named Shared Documents. Click the Library tab on the ribbon, and then click Library Settings.
2. Click Advanced Settings in the General Settings section.
3. In the Content Types section, under Allow Management of Content Types, click the circle next to Yes if it is not already selected.
4. Scroll to the bottom of the page and click OK to save the change and return to the Document Library Settings page.
5. Scroll down to the Content Types section, which might not have been visible before. Click Add from Existing Site Content Types.
6. From the Add Content Types page, access the drop-down menu under Select Site Content Types From and choose Document Set Content Types. Click Document Set in the Available Site Content Types box, and then click the Add button, as shown in Figure 20.23, and then click OK.

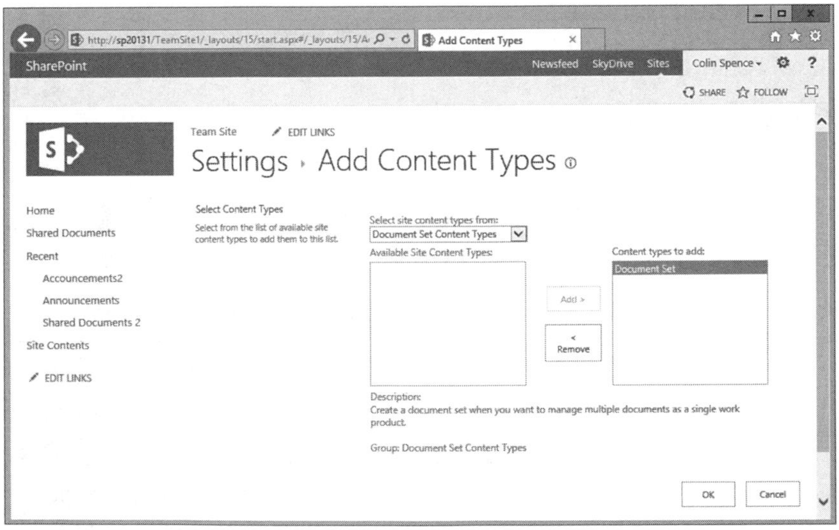

FIGURE 20.23 Adding the Document Set content type to a document library.

7. Click the document library name in the breadcrumb from Document Library Settings to return to the document library.

Now, to create a document set, follow these steps:

1. Click the Files tab on the ribbon and access the drop-down menu for New Document; there should now be an entry for Document Set. Click Document Set.
2. Enter a name for the document set, such as **Phase 1 Document Set**, and click OK. The document set is now created and appears in the default view. There are no documents within this document set yet.
3. Locate the document set you have just created and click it.
4. From this page, you can then add documents by using the New Document link, Upload Document tool from the Files tab, or drag and drop from Windows Explorer. After a few documents have been uploaded, the results will look similar to Figure 20.24. (Library columns will vary depending on how the library has been configured.) Note that in Figure 20.24, the Manage tab is open; that tab provides tools specifically for managing document sets, including the Capture Version tool.

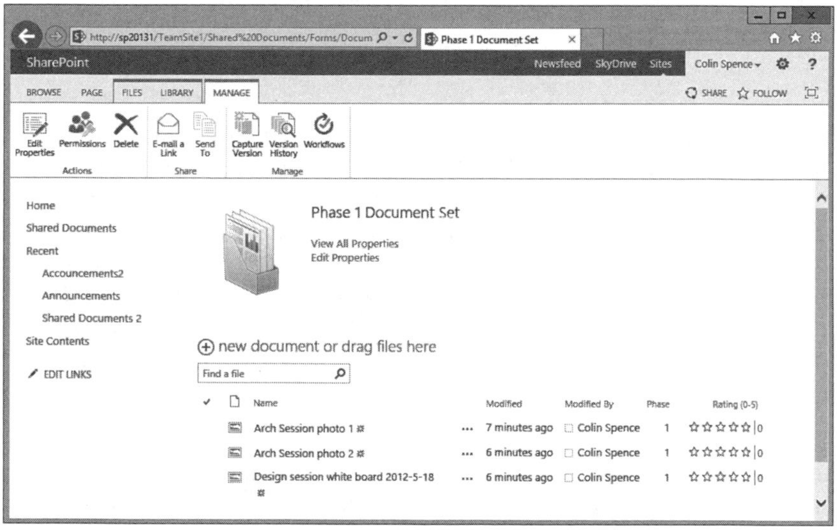

FIGURE 20.24 A document set in a document library.

Content Organizer as a Document Routing Tool

The Content Organizer is a feature in SharePoint Server 2013 Standard or Enterprise that allows content uploaded to the Drop Off library to be routed to other libraries based on the Content Organizer rules that have been created. This is an important tool to be familiar with in the context of list and library design because it can automate the task of moving content to a specific library, which affects the overall management of content.

To create a Content Organizer rule, follow these steps in SharePoint Server 2013 Standard or Enterprise. To enable or confirm that the Content Organizer feature is on and to configure the Content Organizer settings, follow these steps:

1. Confirm that the Content Organizer feature is turned on for the site in question: Access the Site Settings page and, in the Site Actions section, click Manage Site Features.
2. Check the status of the Content Organizer feature. If it is not set to Active, click the Activate button. After it has activated, click Site Settings in the breadcrumb to return to the Site Settings page. Note that a Drop Off library is created as part of the feature activation process.

NOTE

Another option on the Manage Site Features page, under Content Organizer, is E-Mail Integration with Content Organizer. This adds another option to the Content Organizer Settings page, in the Submission Points section.

3. Click the Content Organizer Settings link in the Site Administration section of the Site Settings page.
4. The first option on this page in the Redirect Users to the Drop Off Library section is Require Users to Use the Organizer When Submitting New Content to Libraries with One or More Organizer Rules Pointing to Them. If this box is checked, users will see a notice in the upload window that states, "Documents uploaded here are automatically moved to the correct library and folder after document properties are collected." Generally, this option should be enabled to ensure that the Content Organizer rules are applied to new content uploaded. Otherwise, users can bypass the rules by uploading to whichever library they choose (and thus ignoring the Drop Off library). For this example, check the Require Users to Use the Organizer check box.
5. In the Sending to Another Site section, the next decision to make is whether to check the box next to Allow Rules to Specify Another Site as a Target Location. Check this box if site quotas are in use and if IT expects the total amount of data uploaded to exceed this amount. In general, however, this complicates the management of content and can confuse end users, so leave it unchecked unless there are specific requirements for checking this box. Leave it unchecked in this example.
6. The Folder Partitioning section contains a Create Subfolders After a Target Location Has Too Many Items option, as shown in Figure 20.25. The administrator can specify the number of items allowed in a single folder and the format of the folder names that are created. Once again, it is up to IT to determine whether this is recommended as a best practice; there are pros and cons to the use of folders in SharePoint lists and libraries, but they can enhance performance when there are large numbers of items in the list or library. For this example, check the box and leave the defaults, which should be 2,500 for the number of items in a single folder and Submitted after %1 for the Format of Folder Name.

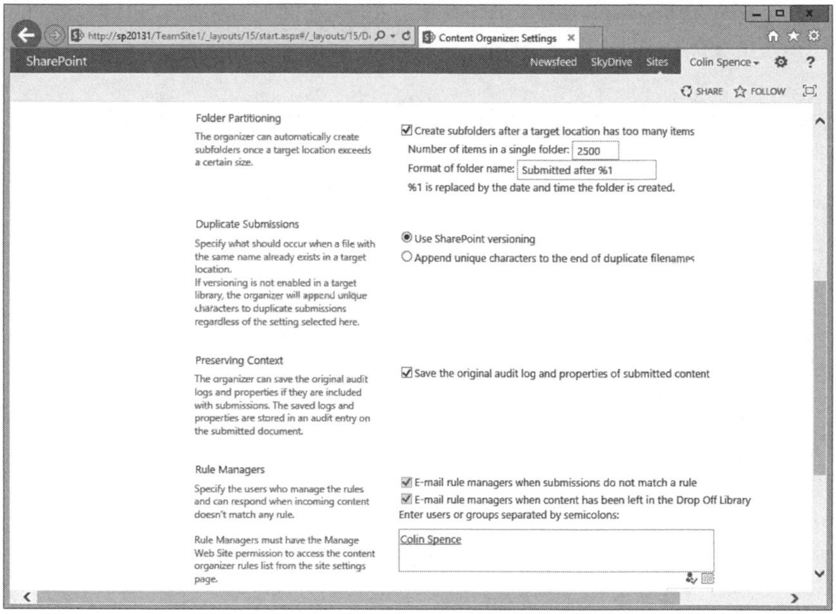

FIGURE 20.25 Content Organizer Settings page.

7. The Duplicate Submissions section has these options: Use SharePoint Versioning and Append Unique Characters to the End of Duplicate Filenames. In general, you should use SharePoint versioning because users will be familiar with its use. For this example, check the radio button next to Use SharePoint Versioning.

NOTE

If Use SharePoint Versioning is checked but the destination library does not have versioning enabled, the duplicate file or files will be appended with a string of six unique characters.

8. In the Preserving Context section, decide whether to Save the Original Audit Log and Properties of Submitted Content. For this example, check this box.

9. In the Rule Managers section, one or more users or groups who are tasked with managing the rules can be entered. These groups and/or individuals can be notified when content is left in the Drop Off Library, or when submissions do not match any rule. The default number of days to wait before sending an email is set to 3. Rule managers must have the Manage Web Site permission to access the Content Organizer Rules list from the Site Settings page.

10. The Submission Points section provides the URL to set up other sites or email messaging software to send content to this site.

11. After the settings are configured as desired, click OK to save the settings and return to the Site Settings page.

The next step in the process is to create an actual Content Organizer rule, as outlined here:

1. From the Site Settings page, in the Site Administration section, click Content Organizer Rules.
2. Click New Item to create a new rule.
3. In the Rule Name field, provide a name for the rule that will make sense to other content organizers. For this example, use the title **Audio Routing Rule 1**.
4. In the Rule Status and Priority section, select Active, and set the priority to 5 (Medium). A nice option here is to set the rule to Inactive, as opposed to having to delete the rule.
5. In the Submission's Content Type section, choose from the content types available to the site, which by default are Business Intelligence, Digital Asset Content Types, Document Content Types, Document Set Content Types, Page Layout Content Types, Publishing Content Types, and Special Content Types. For this example, choose Digital Asset Content Types, and then select Audio from the Type drop-down box. Verify the box is unchecked next to This Content Type Has Alternate Names in Other Sites.
6. In the Conditions section, choose from the Property drop-down list, and then choose an operator. For this example, select Name as the property and Contains All Of as the operator and enter a value of **Jazz**.
7. In the Target Location section, the Browse button can be clicked and the administrator can select the destination library. In this example, the library Site Collection Documents is selected, and it is added to the Destination field.

NOTE

Note that the content type associated with the rule must be available at the target location. This means that the destination document library must have Allow Management of Content Types set to Yes and the content type in question (for example, Audio in this example) added to the Content Types section on the Document Library Settings page.

8. Click OK when the rule is completed.
9. To test that the Content Organizer is working, you can visit the Drop Off library and upload a document that matches the criteria just set for the rule. In this example, an MP3 file was uploaded with the term Jazz in the document name. After you upload the file, a message should appear, as shown in Figure 20.26, telling the end user that the document was submitted successfully and saved to its final location (and the URL is provided for that location). Click OK to close the message.

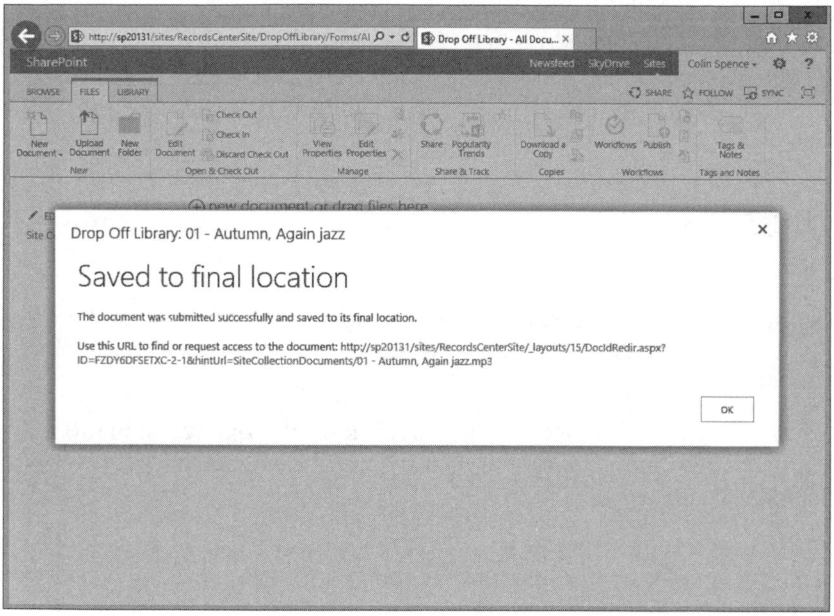

FIGURE 20.26 Content Organizer message upon successful save to final location.

10. Visit the destination location and note that the file has been assigned to the Audio content type.

Summary

Lists and libraries will most likely be the repositories that end users work with most often on a day-to-day basis. Therefore, it is critical that administrators of all levels thoroughly understand the wide range of possibilities for configuring the options in lists and libraries. This chapter covered four general philosophies for customizing and managing lists and libraries in a SharePoint 2013 environment, as follows:

- Minimal planning and testing; minimal restrictions on list and library use and configuration
- Minimal planning and testing; more restrictions on list and library use and configuration
- More extensive planning and testing; minimal restrictions on list and library use and configuration
- More extensive planning and testing; more restrictions on list and library use and configuration

Regardless of which strategy the organization takes, site administrators need to be familiar with a wide range of tools to ensure that the adoption of SharePoint 2013 lists and libraries is successful and that they meet end-user needs. This chapter covered tools on the Library tab of the ribbon, as well as most of the tools available from the Document Library Settings page, and examined document sets and the Content Organizer tool to round out the coverage of tools that SharePoint 2013 list and library administrators should fully understand.

Best Practices

The following are best practices from this chapter:

- Versioning is one of the primary capabilities of a document management system, and should be used in most situations unless storage on the database server is limited.
- Farm administrators and site architects should agree upon the right combination of content approval, versioning, draft item security, and other related tools when configuring standard collaboration sites.
- Review the features and tools available in different versions of SharePoint and decide which will have the most value for the organization.
- Using SharePoint Designer 2013 to manage lists and libraries should be investigated as another means of managing lists and libraries. SharePoint Designer 2013 provides a powerful tool set and can be a time saver for experienced administrators, and provides access to tools not available in the SharePoint 2013 user interface, such as creating SharePoint Designer workflows, creating custom actions, and editing document templates.
- The Advanced Settings page accessible from the Document Library Settings page provides access to a number of key features that can be enabled, disabled, or configured for the library. A best practice is to review these options as a group during the design phase to see which will be enabled for different document libraries and for different levels of users. For example, content types can be turned on or off here, the document template can be edited, folders can be enabled or disabled, and offline client availability can be enabled or disabled, as can the Quick Edit feature.
- Document sets offer a unique set of features that will be of interest to organizations with high-end collaboration needs and fairly sophisticated users. They differ from folders in a number of ways, as outlined in this chapter, which should be understood to help determine when folders are appropriate and when document sets are appropriate.
- Enable the Content Organizer feature for a site collection in SharePoint Server 2013 Standard or Enterprise to allow you to then create rules that define where uploaded content is eventually stored when a user uploads a document to the Drop Off Library. The Content Organizer Rule Wizard is very sophisticated, allowing the site administrator to define with great specificity where documents assigned to different content types with attributes matching certain criteria are stored when uploaded to the Drop Off Folder.

CHAPTER 21

Designing and Managing Pages and Sites for Knowledge Workers

IN THIS CHAPTER

This chapter can be considered a "survival guide" and is aimed at the site collection administrator or site administrator who is charged with creating, customizing, or managing a new or existing site collection and making it meet the needs of the organization. Depending on the size of the company, the site collection might have been created for a variety of purposes, such as for the company intranet, for an extranet to handle trusted external partners, for Internet users, or for internal only use, perhaps just by one group such as IT.

This chapter concentrates on the processes involved in creating site collections, sites, and pages, and on the wealth of tools available for managing sites and site collections from the Site Settings page. Because of the sheer number of tools, specific tools are focused on that tend to be the most used by site collection and site administrators; others are just summarized. For example, understanding the Users and Permissions tools is critical to ensure that the site administrator has a tight grasp on "who can do what" in the site collection.

Understanding Site Collection Options

It is important for the farm administrator to be conversant with the different site collection templates available and to understand when it is appropriate to create a site collection and when a site will suffice. The range of site collection templates available in the different versions of SharePoint 2013 is provided in Chapter 18, "SharePoint Foundation Versus SharePoint Server 2013," and summarized in Table 18.2 in that chapter.

This section reviews the different categories of site collections, and touches briefly on best practices for mapping out a site collection or group of site collections to meet the organization's requirements. When a farm administrator wants to create a new site collection, the Create Site Collections tool can be found under the Site Collections section on the Application Management page. These tools are categorized as Collaboration, Enterprise, Publishing, and Custom. The following section describes these templates in more detail:

- **Collaboration site collection templates:** Table 21.1 shows the lists and libraries included in each site collection, along with site collection features and site features enabled when created from SharePoint Server 2013 Enterprise. These include Team Site, Blog, Developer Site, Project Site, and Community Site. Note that if SharePoint Server 2013 Standard is used, certain features vary, because the SharePoint Server Enterprise Site Collection Features is not available as a feature, nor is the Access App.

NOTE

Users of earlier versions of SharePoint will notice that the Meetings site collection templates (Basic Meeting Workspace, Blank Meeting Workspace, Decision Meeting Workspace, Social Meeting Workspace, and Multipage Meeting Workspace) are no longer offered.

- **Enterprise site collection templates:** These include Document Center, eDiscovery Center, Records Center, Business Intelligence (BI) Center, Enterprise Search Center, My Site Host, Community Portal, Basic Search Center, and Visio Process Repository. Table 21.2 provides additional information on the lists and libraries included and notes on the purpose of each.

TABLE 21.1 Site Collection Template List and Library Components

Template Name	Lists Included	Libraries Included	Site Collection Features Enabled	Site Features Enabled
Team Site	Microfeed	Documents, Form Templates, Site Assets, Site Pages, Style Library	Disposition Approval Workflow, Document Sets, Library and Folder-Based Retention, SharePoint Server Enterprise Site Collection Features, SharePoint Server Standard Site Collection Features, Site Policy, Three-State Workflow, Video and Rich Media	Access App, Following Content, Getting Started, Minimal Download Strategy, Mobile Browser View, SharePoint Server Enterprise Site Collection Features, SharePoint Server Standard Site Collection Features, Site Feed, Team Collaboration Lists, Wiki Home Page, Workflow Task Content Type
Blog Site	Categories, Comments, Posts	Form Templates, Photos, Style Library	Disposition Approval Workflow, Document Sets, Library and Folder-Based Retention, Reporting, SharePoint Server Enterprise Site Collection Features, SharePoint Server Standard Site Collection Features, Site Policy, Three-State Workflow, Video and Rich Media	Access App, Following Content, Minimal Download Strategy, SharePoint Server Enterprise Site Collection Features, SharePoint Server Standard Site Collection Features, Site Feed, Team Collaboration Lists, Workflow Task Content Type
Developer Site	Apps in Testing, Microfeed	App Packages, Documents, Form Templates, Site Assets, Site Pages, Style Library	Disposition Approval Workflow, Document Sets, Library and Folder-Based Retention, Reporting, SharePoint Server Enterprise Site Collection Features, SharePoint Server Standard Site Collection Features, Site Policy, Three-State Workflow, Video and Rich Media	Access App, Following Content, Getting Started, Minimal Download Strategy, Mobile Browser View, SharePoint Server Enterprise Site Collection Features, SharePoint Server Standard Site Collection Features, Site Feed, Team Collaboration Lists, Wiki Home Page, Workflow Task Content Type

Template Name	Lists Included	Libraries Included	Site Collection Features Enabled	Site Features Enabled
Project Site	Calendar, Microfeed, Tasks	Documents, Form Templates, Site Assets, Style Library	Disposition Approval Workflow, Document Sets, Library and Folder-Based Retention, Reporting, SharePoint Server Enterprise Site Collection Features, SharePoint Server Standard Site Collection Features, Site Policy, Three-State Workflow, Video and Rich Media	Access App, Following Content, Getting Started, Minimal Download Strategy, Mobile Browser View, Project Functionality, SharePoint Server Enterprise Site Collection Features, SharePoint Server Standard Site Collection Features, Site Feed, Team Collaboration Lists, Workflow Task Content Type
Community Site	Categories, Community Members, Discussion List	Form Templates, Site Assets, Site Pages, Style Library	Document Sets, SharePoint Server Enterprise Site Collection Features, SharePoint Server Standard Site Collection Features, Video and Rich Media	Access App, Community Site Features, Following Content, Minimal Download Strategy, SharePoint Server Enterprise Site Collection Features, SharePoint Server Standard Site Collection Features, Team Collaboration Lists, Workflow Task Content Type

TABLE 21.2 Enterprise Site Collection Template List, Libraries, and Features

Template Name	Lists Included	Libraries Included	Site Collection Features Enabled	Site Features Enabled
Document Center	Content and Structure Reports, Reusable Content, Tasks, Workflow Tasks	Documents, Form Templates, Site Collection Documents, Site Collection Images, Style Library	Access App, Following Content, Metadata Navigation and Filtering, Mobile Browser View, SharePoint Server Enterprise Site Features, SharePoint Server Standard Site Features, Team Collaboration Lists, Workflow Task Content Type	Disposition Approval Workflow, Document ID Service, Document Sets, Library and Folder-Based Retention, Limited Access User Permission Lockdown Mode, Reporting, SharePoint Server Enterprise Site Collection Features, SharePoint Server Standard Site Collection Features, Site Policy, Three-State Workflow, Video and Rich Media
eDiscovery Center	Form Templates	Style Library	Access App, Following Content, Metadata Navigation and Filtering, SharePoint Server Enterprise Site Features, SharePoint Server Standard Site Features, Team Collaboration Lists, Workflow Task Content Type	Disposition Approval Workflow, Document Sets, Library and Folder-Based Retention, Reporting, SharePoint Server Enterprise Site Collection Features, SharePoint Server Standard Site Collection Features, Site Policy, Video and Rich Media, Workflows
Records Center		Drop Off Library, Form Templates, Record Library, Style Library	Access App, Content Organizer, Following Content, Hold, Metadata Navigation and Filtering, SharePoint Server Enterprise Site Features, SharePoint Server Standard Site Features, Team Collaboration Lists, Workflow Task Content Type	Disposition Approval Workflow, Document ID Service, Document Sets, In Place Records Management, Library and Folder-Based Retention, Reporting, SharePoint Server Enterprise Site Collection Features, SharePoint Server Standard Site Collection Features, Site Policy, Three-State Workflow, Video and Rich Media

Template Name	Lists Included	Libraries Included	Site Collection Features Enabled	Site Features Enabled
Business Intelligence (BI) Center	Content and Structure Reports, Dashboards	Data Connections, Documents, Form Templates, Images, Pages	Access App, BI Center Data Connections Feature, Following Content, PerformancePoint Services Site Feature, SharePoint Server Standard Site Features, Workflow Task Content Type	Limited Access User Permission Lockdown Mode, PerformancePoint Services Site Collection Feature, Publishing Approval Workflow, SharePoint Server Enterprise Site Collection Features, SharePoint Server Publishing Infrastructure
Enterprise Search Center	Content and Structure Reports, Reusable Content, Tabs in Search Pages, Tabs in Search Results, Workflow Tasks	Documents, Form Templates, Images, Pages, Site Collection Documents, Site Collection Images, Style Library	Access App, Following Content, SharePoint Server Enterprise Site Features, SharePoint Server Publishing, SharePoint Server Standard Site Features, Team Collaboration Lists, Workflow Task Content Type	Disposition Approval Workflow, Document Sets, Library and Folder-Based Retention, Limited-Access User Permission Lockdown Mode, Publishing Approval Workflow, Reporting, Search Server Web Parts and Templates, SharePoint Server Enterprise Site Collection Features, SharePoint Server Publishing Infrastructure, SharePoint Server Standard Site Collection Features, Site Policy, Video and Rich Media
My Site Host	Microfeed, Social	Documents, Form Templates, Style Library	Access App, Following Content, Minimal Download Strategy, Team Collaboration Lists, Workflow Task Content Type	None

Template Name	Lists Included	Libraries Included	Site Collection Features Enabled	Site Features Enabled
Community Portal	Categories, Community Members, Discussion List	Form Templates, Site Assets, Site Pages, Style Library	Access App, Community Site Feature, Following Content, Minimal Download Strategy, SharePoint Server Enterprise Site Features, SharePoint Server Standard Site Features, Team Collaboration Lists, Workflow Task Content Type	Document Sets, SharePoint Server Enterprise Site Collection Features, SharePoint Server Standard Site Collection Features, Video and Rich Media
Basic Search Center	Tabs in Search Pages, Tabs in Search Results	Form Templates, Style Library	Access App, Following Content, Team Collaboration Lists, Workflow Task Content Type	Search Server Web Parts and Templates
Visio Process Repository		Form Templates, Process Diagram, Style Library	Access App, Following Content, Getting Started, Metadata Navigation and Filtering, Minimal Download Strategy, SharePoint Server Enterprise Site Features, SharePoint Server Standard Site Features, Team Collaboration Lists, Workflow Task Content Type	Publishing Approval Workflow, SharePoint Server Enterprise Site Collection Features

- **Publishing site collection templates:** These templates include the Publishing Portal and Enterprise Wiki and Product Catalog, as shown in Table 21.3. Publishing sites are designed for sites that provide content to a large group of readers, and are better suited to that purpose. Limitations apply as to which sites can be created beneath publishing sites, so there are fewer options from a site collection design standpoint. A Publishing Portal, for example, would be a good choice for an intranet, but not if it will house departmental sites at the second level, unless they are created as site collections.

TABLE 21.3 Publishing Site Collection Template List, Libraries, and Features

Template Name	Lists Included	Libraries Included	Site Collection Features Enabled	Site Features Enabled
Publishing Portal	Content and Structure Reports, Reusable Content, Tasks, Workflow Tasks	Documents, Form Templates, Images, Pages, Site Collection Documents, Site Collection Images, Style Library	Access App, Following Content, Metadata Navigation and Filtering, SharePoint Server Publishing, Workflow Task Content Type	Disposition Approval Workflow, Document Sets, Limited-Access User Permission Lockdown Mode, Publishing Approval Workflow, Reporting, SharePoint Server Publishing Infrastructure, Video and Rich Media, Workflows
Enterprise Wiki	Content and Structure Reports, Reusable Content, Tasks, Workflow Tasks	Documents, Form Templates, Images, Pages, Site Collection Documents, Site Collection Images, Style Library	Access App, Following Content, Team Collaboration Lists, Workflow Task Content Type	Disposition Approval Workflow, Limited-Access User Permission Lockdown Mode, Publishing Approval Workflow, SharePoint Server Enterprise Site Collection Features, SharePoint Server Publishing Infrastructure, SharePoint Server Standard Site Collection Features, Workflows

Template Name	Lists Included	Libraries Included	Site Collection Features Enabled	Site Features Enabled
Product Catalog	Content and Structure Reports, Products, Reusable Content, Workflow Tasks	Documents, Form Templates, Images, Pages, Site Collection Documents, Site Collection Images, Style Library	Access App, Following Content, Metadata Navigation and Filtering, Workflow Task Content Type	Cross-Site Collection Publishing, Document Sets, Limited-Access User Permission Lockdown Mode, Reporting, SharePoint Server Publishing Infrastructure, SharePoint Server Standard Site Collection Features, Video and Rich Media, Workflows

- **Custom site collection templates:** An empty site can be created and then a template assigned at a later time.

Designing the Site and Site Collection Wireframe

A sample wireframe is provided in Figure 21.1, which is a simplified design often used for medium-sized companies (500 to 5,000 users) and includes a top-level site collection for intranet purposes, separate site collections for departments such as IT and HR, and a site collection for cross-departmental uses (such as projects).

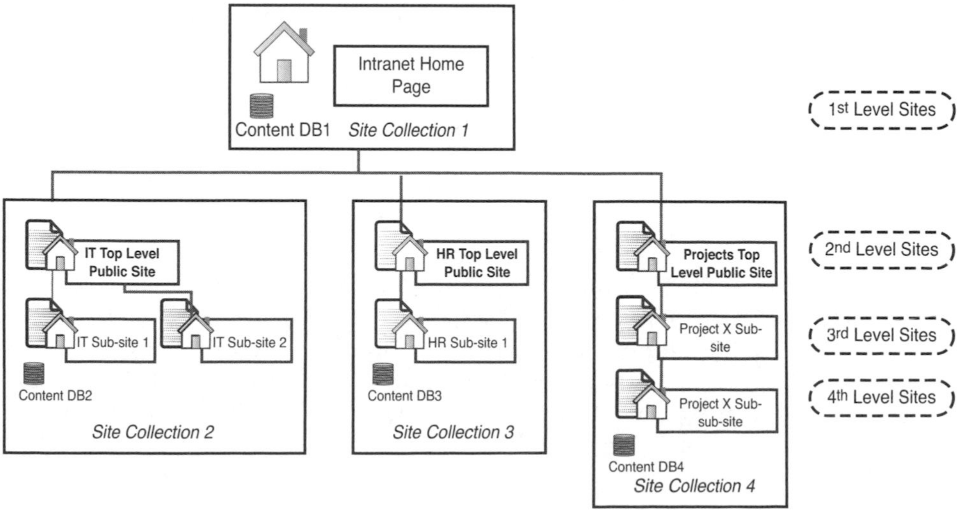

FIGURE 21.1 A site collection wireframe.

This simple example shows a ContentDB (short for content database) icon for the top-level site collection, which in this example contains intranet content, and ContentDB icons for three other site collections that are nested beneath the top-level site collection. Each organization needs to work on balancing the depth of the structure with its breadth because a structure that is too "deep" can be hard to navigate, as can a structure that is too wide. There are management complexities involved in creating too many site collections, whereas too few site collections may result in content databases that grow to "unwieldy" sizes (for example, hundreds of gigabytes or even a terabyte or more).

A tool such as this makes it easy for design committees to understand the logical design and can be expanded to include the lists and libraries that will be included in each site, and the permissions for each site, and thus become a useful management tool.

For very large organizations, a simple Visio or Excel spreadsheet most likely will not suffice, and more planning will be required in the areas of site collections and websites, along with content databases. Following are some guidelines for larger organizations from TechNet (http://technet.microsoft.com/en-us/library/cc262787(office.15).aspx):

- **Number of content databases per farm:** 500 per farm. Exceeding this limit may cause unexpected results, significant decrease in performance, or other harmful effects.
- **Content database size:** Up to 200GB per content database for "general-usage scenarios" and up to 4TB for "all-usage scenarios." 200GB is Microsoft's "strong recommendation," but up to 4TB has been tested and is listed as "supported" by Microsoft with various caveats that the native SharePoint backup and recovery tools may not meet organizational requirements for content databases larger than 200GB. Note that there is no explicit content database limit published in this article.
- **Site collections per content database:** 10,000 maximum (2,500 nonpersonal site collections and 7,500 personal sites, or 10,000 personal sites alone). 5,000 is Microsoft's strong recommendation as a limit.
- **Site collections per farm:** 750,000 (500,000 personal sites and 250,000 other sites per farm) is Microsoft's maximum recommendation. These can reside on one or more web applications.
- **Websites:** 250,000 is the maximum recommended per site collection.

Of these recommendations, the one that will usually be of the most interest and impact on overall design is that of content database size. The 200GB soft limit recommended by Microsoft is a relatively small number for many organizations and can dramatically change the design of the SharePoint environment. As a result, most organizations end up with a large number of content databases which then need to be groomed through SQL Server maintenance plans on a regular basis as well as managed by IT and the SharePoint farm administrators.

Creating a Site Collection

In many environments, the site collection administrator is also a farm administrator and needs to know how to create site collections. Although some organizations use a single site collection for all their needs, a best practice is to create separate site collections for groups that save a large amount of data (50GB to 100GB or more) and creating a content database for each of those site collections (as discussed in the previous section). Although this is not a universal rule, by creating multiple content databases, SQL Server will be managing more databases that are smaller in size, which can be advantageous when designing disaster recovery strategies and service level agreements (SLAs).

In addition, as discussed in the following sections, a large number of tools are available for each site collection; these allow customization of one site collection that won't affect other site collections. For example, Site Collection Features can be turned on for features such as Document Sets, Site Policy, or Video and Rich Media that will be available only to sites contained within the site collection.

To create a site collection from the Central Administration site, simply follow these steps:

1. From the Central Administration home page, click Create Site Collections in the Application Management section.
2. From the createsite.aspx page, enter a title for the site (**Dept X Site Collection**, for this example), optionally enter a description, and provide a URL for the site collection. (In this example, select /sites/ from the drop-down menu and enter **DeptX** for the site collection name.) Leave the Select Experience Version on 2013. Choose the Team Site template. Figure 21.2 shows an example.

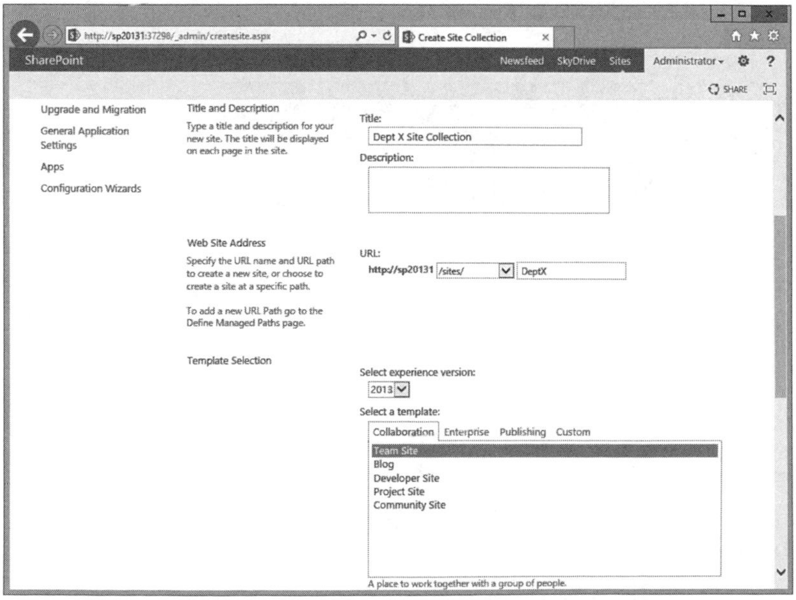

FIGURE 21.2 CreateSite.aspx page from the Central Administrator site.

3. Scroll down on the page and enter a primary site collection administrator and secondary site administrator (**company123\administrator** and **company123\colin** in this example). Click the Check Names icon next to the fields to make sure that the usernames were entered properly. Leave the quota template selection to No Quota. Click OK.

NOTE

Primary and secondary site collection administrators have additional capabilities above and beyond any site collection administrators added at a later date. The primary and secondary site collection administrators will receive administrative email alerts for the site collection. Primary and secondary site collection administrators need to be individual users, not Active Directory (AD) security groups.

These are defined during the initial site collection creation process but can be modified at a later date by visiting Central Administration, Application Management, Change Site Collection Administrators.

4. After the site has been created, a page loads indicating that the site has been created successfully. A link to the new site collection is included. Click the link to view the new site collection. Figure 21.3 shows the site created in this example.

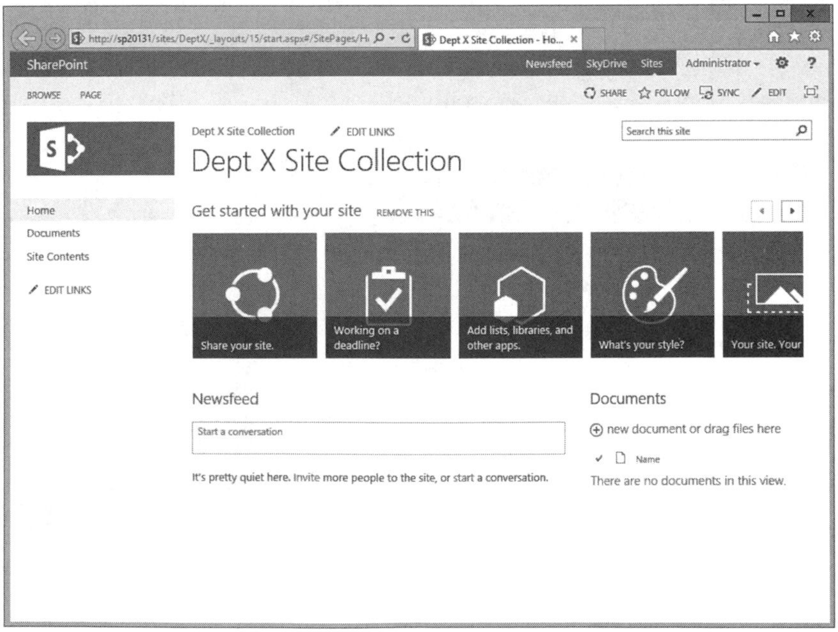

FIGURE 21.3 Home page of a New Team Site site collection.

5. Access the gear icon and click Site Settings. Figure 21.4 shows the Site Settings page for the new site collection. The various tools are covered in the following sections.

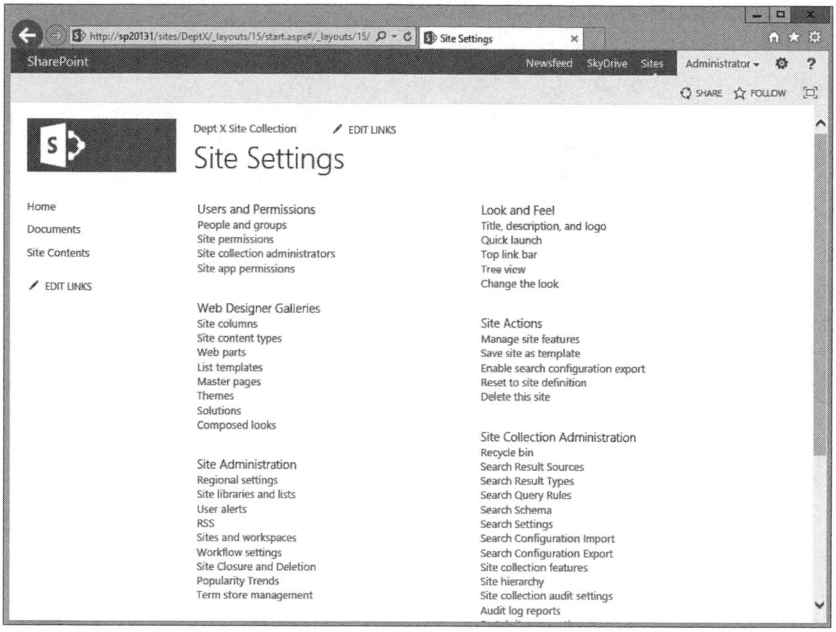

FIGURE 21.4 Site Settings page for a New Team Site site collection.

Reviewing the Scope of an Existing Site Collection

When a site collection administrator starts working with an existing site collection, it is important to determine whether additional subsites are under the existing site collection. If the site collection is new and hasn't been configured, this will most likely be an easy task, but if the administrator is taking over a site collection that has been in use for several months or years, this can be more involved.

Site collection administrators charged with taking over an existing site collection can become familiar with the site collection by visiting the Site Settings page and clicking the Sites and Workspaces link in the Site Administration section, shown in Figure 21.4. This shows the administrator whether there are any subsites beneath the existing site. However, this might not tell the full story because there may be managed paths for the web application, which may contain additional site collections, each of which may contain additional sites.

For example, a new site collection administrator should check with the farm administrator to see whether there are any managed paths such as /sites/ that contain additional subsites. Figure 21.5 shows the Sites and Workspaces page from the Site Settings page on a sample site collection (http://SP20131/). It looks like there are only five sites located beneath the top level, so the administrator may think he has a relatively easy job ahead of him. However, Figure 21.6 shows the Site Collection List page for the web application that houses the root site collection (http://SP20131/), and there are managed paths /my and /sites that each contain site collections beneath them. Suddenly, the administrator realizes he needs to review each of the site collections located under /sites to see the number of sites under each. The sites listed under /my are personal site collections that may also pose administrative challenges, but won't be addressed in this chapter.

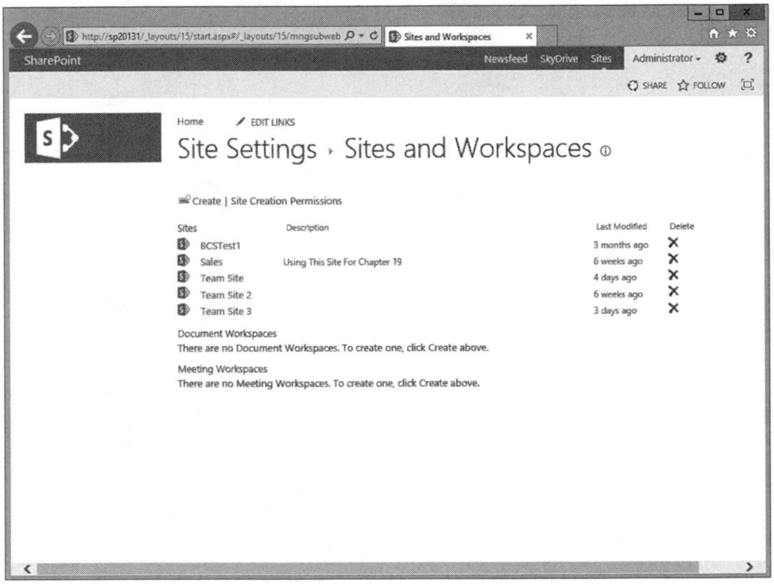

FIGURE 21.5 Sites and Workspaces page for a site collection.

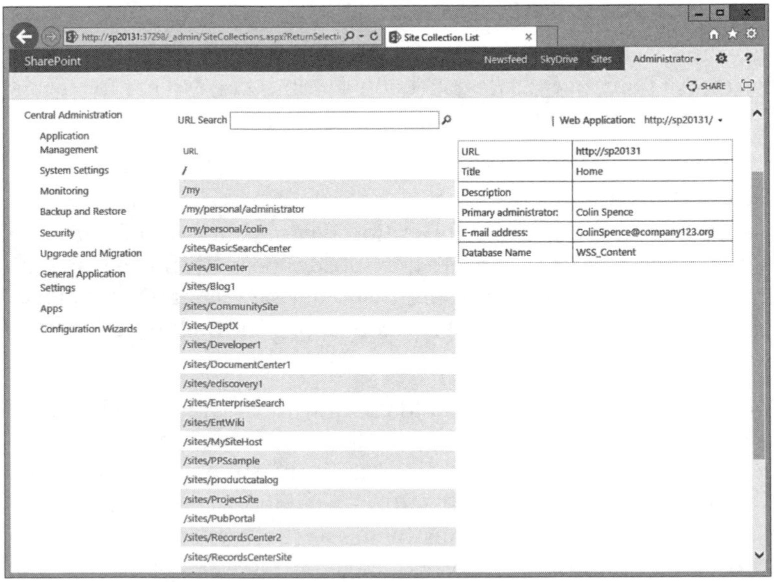

FIGURE 21.6 Site Collection List page.

Note also in Figure 21.6 that the Site Collection List page lists the URL for the site collection, the title, description, primary site collection administrator, his or her email, and the content database name on the right side.

NOTE

You can find the managed paths for a web application under Application Management, in the Web Applications section, by clicking Manage Web Applications and then locating the name of the web application that houses the site collection. Click the name of the web application, and then click Managed Paths from the Web Applications tab on the Ribbon. Figure 21.7 shows an example of the Default Managed Paths for a SharePoint 2013 Enterprise implementation. The Default Managed Paths should not be modified unless there are specific business requirements for doing so, and the farm administrator should understand the impacts of doing so.

Managed paths define the locations at which SharePoint tools should expect to find site collections. And these can be in the form of an Explicit Inclusion or Wildcard Inclusion. In Figure 21.7, the paths can be interpreted as follows: The root is explicitly included and is a site collection. Anything located under (root)/sites/ (http://sp20131/sites/ in this example) should be considered a site collection. The (root)/my/ site is a site collection, and anything located under (root)/my/personal/ is a site collection.

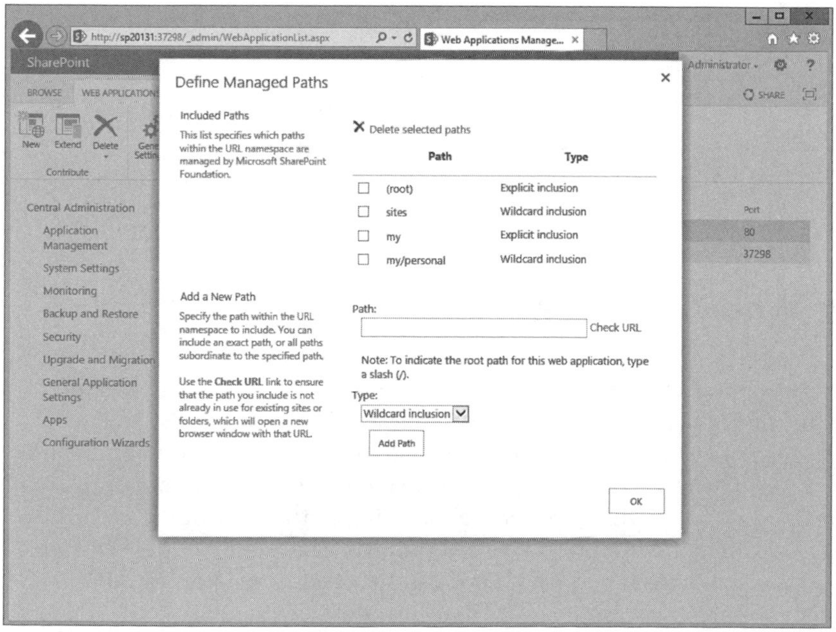

FIGURE 21.7 The Managed Paths tool for a web application.

An additional tool is available from the Site Settings page for the top-level site of the site collection: the Site Hierarchy link in the Site Collection Administration section.

This shows all websites created under the current site, as shown in Figure 21.8. This page (similar to the Sites and Workspaces page) shows the sites that exist directly below the current site, but also does not include the managed paths. The Site Hierarchy page provides the site URL, title of the site, and a Manage link that, when clicked, takes the administrator to the Site Settings page for that site.

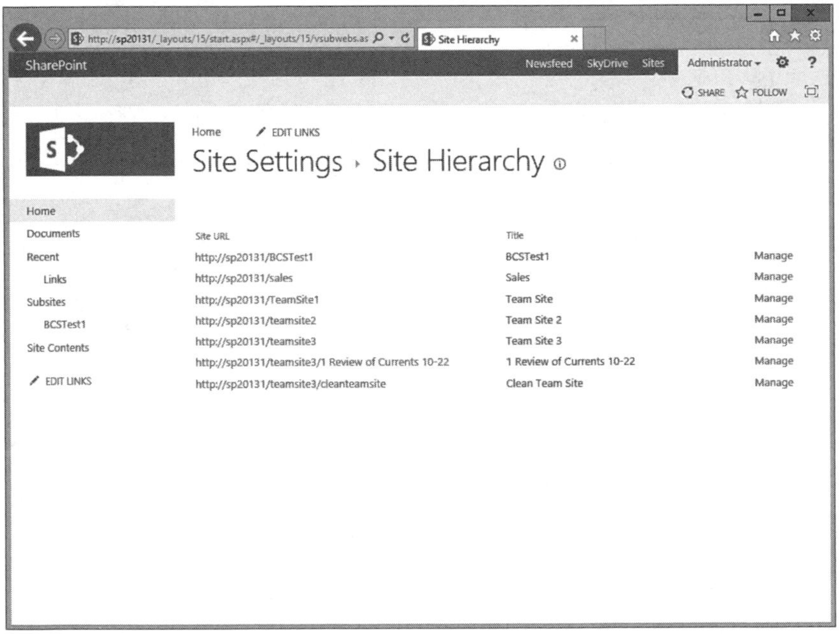

FIGURE 21.8 Site Hierarchy page.

Controlling Who Can Create Sites

Another recommended step to take for site administrators for new or existing site collections is to take a few minutes and review who has the ability to create sites. By default, only users with Full Control permissions in the site collection have the ability to create subsites (including document workspaces), which include only site collection administrators and members of the Owners group for the site collection. However, other permission levels may be able to create sites, which can be a good thing, if the organization wants to encourage the use of document workspaces and meeting workspaces and empower more users to build sites for collaboration purposes. Or it can be a bad thing and lead to an accumulation of sites and workspaces that users may abandon, or that may confuse users.

The Sites and Workspaces page discussed in the previous section (accessible from the Site Settings page) provides a link for Site Creation Permissions. By clicking this link, the administrator can provide Site and Workspace Creation Permissions to different permission levels, as shown in Figure 21.9. From this page, the administrator can check the boxes next to permission levels such as Design or Contribute, and by clicking OK adds the Create Subsites site permission for that permission level.

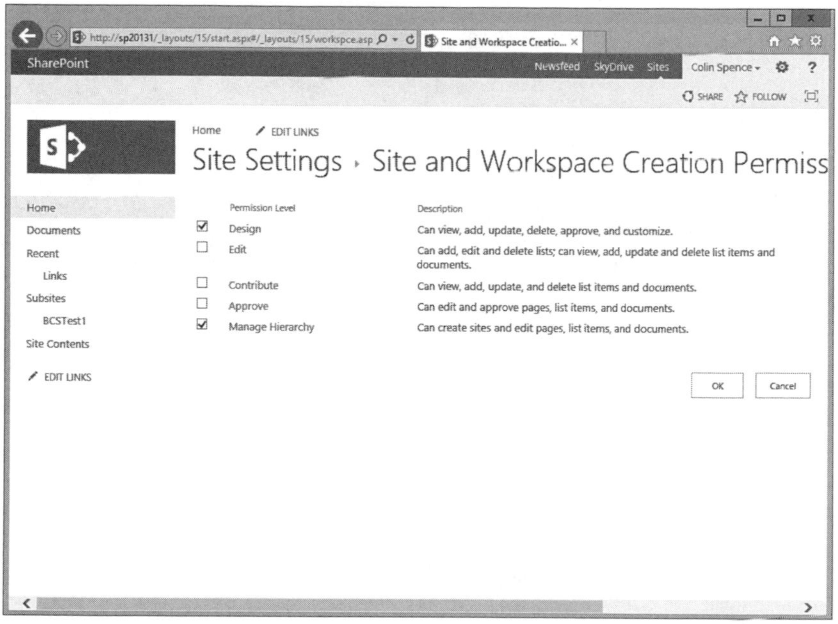

FIGURE 21.9 Site and Workspace Creation Permissions page.

Another important tool to know about is the Self-Service Site Collection Management tool. This tool is accessed from the Central Administration site by clicking the Security link in the Quick Launch area and then clicking Configure Self-Service Site Creation in the General Security section. From this page, shown in Figure 21.10, a number of options are available, as follows:

- The web application under which the sites will be created can be chosen.
- Users can be given the ability to create site collections, and if allowed, a quota template can be applied.
- The Start a Site link can be hidden, a specific managed path can be provided, any managed path can be used, or a custom form can be provided for site creation. Figure 21.10 shows the option where new sites will be created under http://sp20131/sites/[%userid%], which means the user's ID will precede the site name, making it easy to see who the originator of the site is at a later date.
- Site classifications can be hidden from users, an optional choice, or a required choice.
- A secondary contact can be required or not, and if required, this person is also a site administrator.

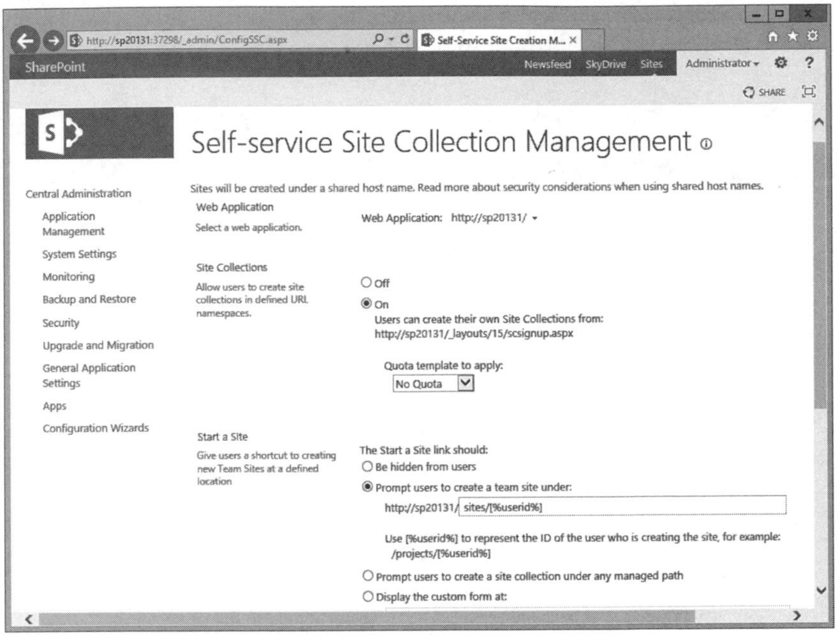

FIGURE 21.10 Self-Service Site Creation page.

NOTE

If user groups are given the ability to create sites via the Sites and Workspaces page, they will see the New Site link on the Site Contents page regardless of whether self-service site creation is enabled. The site created is a *site*, not a site collection. If self-service site creation is enabled, and a user visits the page specified by the farm administrator (for example [servername]/_layouts/15/scsignup.aspx) and creates a site, it is in fact a *site collection*. So it is very important to understand these differences and decide what is allowed in the environment.

NOTE

A general best practice is to control the number of individuals who can create sites and workspaces until users are trained about the pros and cons of site and workspace creation and the management of the sites they create. A common complaint of organizations using SharePoint products is the "sprawl" of sites, subsites, and workspaces that can grow over time if too many users are allowed to create sites and workspaces.

Creating Pages and Sites

This section provides an overview of the processes of creating pages and sites, as well as an overview of the options available for pages and sites. The previous section, "Controlling

Who Can Create Sites," gives some insight into some of the variables that determine which users can create sites, and this section discusses the topic in terms of who can create pages. In most organizations, IT chooses to limit the number of users who can create sites to site administrators or power users to ensure that those with this capability have been trained appropriately and understand the pros and cons of creating a new site as opposed to simply creating a new list or library.

The site administrator can create sites from several places. The primary tool to access is the Settings gear; then click Site Contents and scroll to the bottom and click New Subsite. Or the Site Contents link in the Quick Launch can be clicked (if available), and you can find the New Subsite link at the bottom of the page.

The Site Content and Structure link available on the Site Settings page, in the Site Administration section, also allows the administrator to create sites and lists as shown in Figure 21.11.

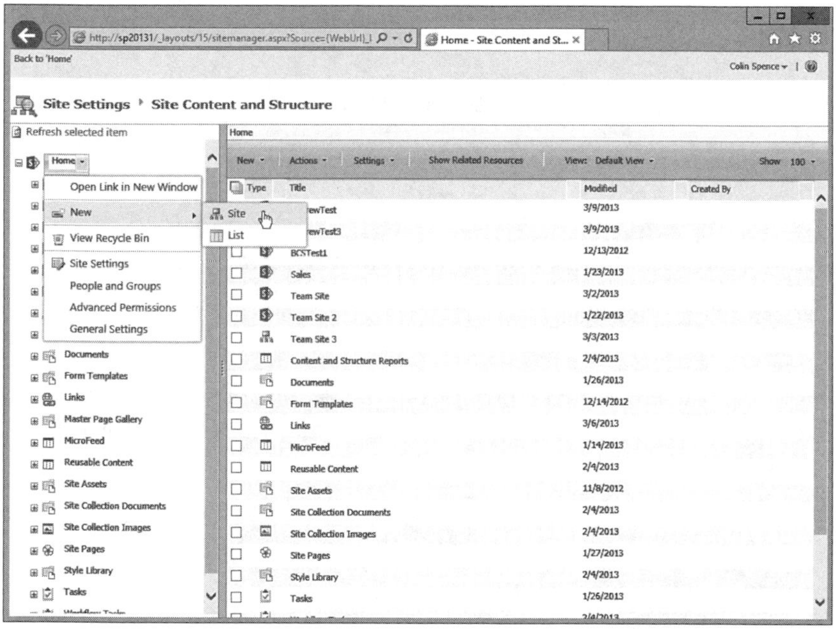

FIGURE 21.11 Create Site option from Site Content and Structure page.

Follow these steps to create a site:

1. Using an account with sufficient permissions, access the Settings gear and click Site Contents.
2. Scroll to the bottom of the page and click New Subsite.
3. Enter a title, description (optional), and URL information. A general best practice is for the URL to not contain spaces and not be too long.

4. Select a template from the Template Selection section. For this example, choose the Team Site template from the Collaboration tab. Figure 21.12 shows an example of this interface.

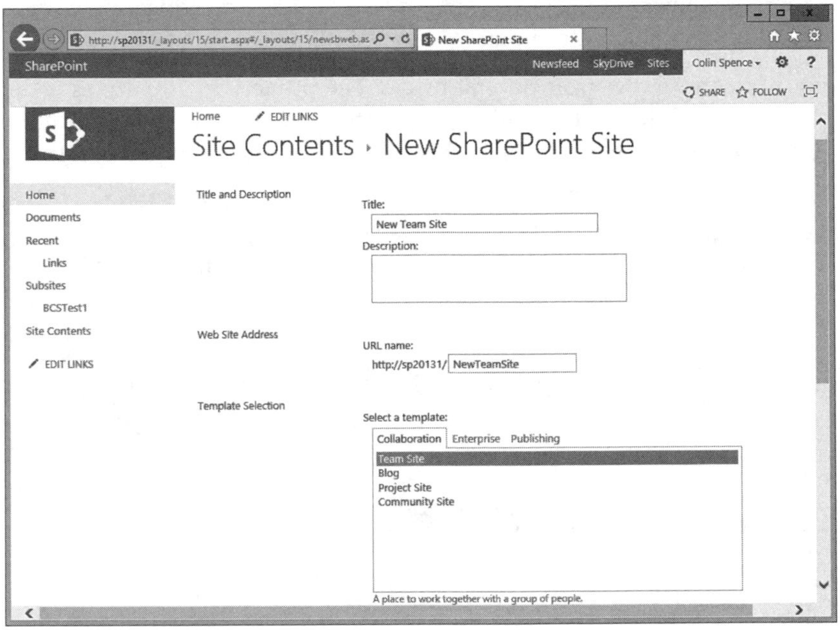

FIGURE 21.12 New SharePoint site page.

5. For this example, select Use Unique Permissions in the Permissions section. In production environments, subsites often inherit from the parent site because this eases administration.

6. In this example, select Yes to Display this site on the quick launch of the parent site, and Yes to Display this site on the top link bar of the parent site.

7. Select Yes to Use the top link bar from the parent site.

8. Click Create.

9. As shown in Figure 21.13, the Set Up Groups for this Site page displays. Leave the defaults, which in this example are Create a New Group for Visitors, Members, and Owners. Enter the domain users group (in this case, Company123\domain users) in the Visitors to this Site group and an appropriate group in Members of this Site and Owners of this site. Click OK, and the new site renders.

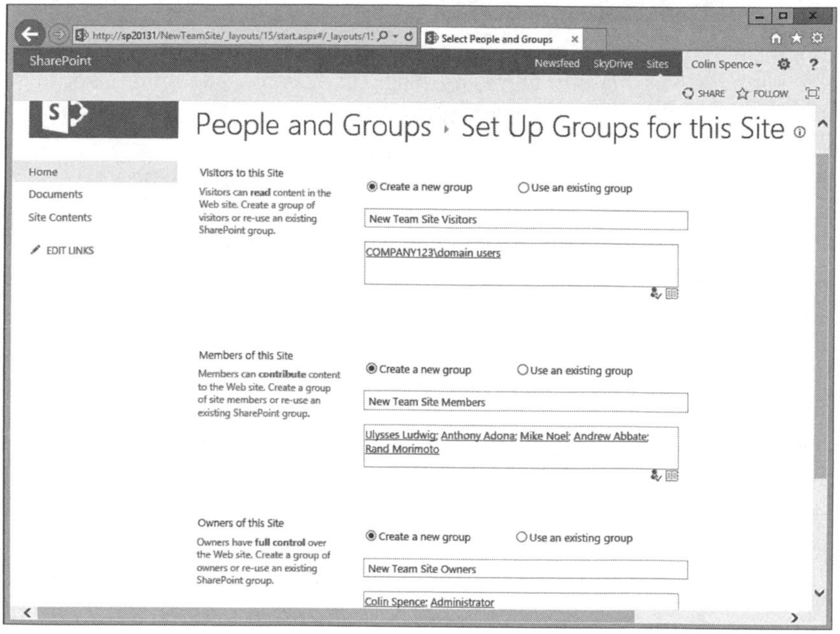

FIGURE 21.13 Set Up Groups for this Site page.

Creating Pages

Another key tool for sharing and managing information on a site are pages. Pages can be created from a number of places, and the resulting options can be used for a variety of purposes. For example, the home page for a site is in fact a page that lives in the Site Pages library and can be edited and customized. Wiki page libraries contain pages that need to be edited to contain useful content and can contain hundreds or thousands of pages if heavily used.

In addition, if Allow Management of Content Types is enabled for a document library, a variety of page content types can be added to a normal document library. And, once again, a document library can quickly house hundreds of pages. Because pages can occur in such abundance, site administrators should be very familiar with the different types of pages and how they can be used and managed.

The process of creating pages is similar to that of creating sites, but generally simpler, and like a site, when the page is created, it needs to be customized. Most organizations limit the number of users who can create or modify pages because the modification of pages or addition of pages can have serious consequences on the site that affect all users of the site. However, by default, most users of a site will have access to create and modify pages! So, it is important to understand how to control this ability. This section addresses this topic and walks through the process of creating and modifying pages.

NOTE

Site administrators should thoroughly test the capabilities of users with different permissions levels on the sites they are tasked with maintaining. For example, add a test user to the Visitors group and a test user to the Members group and then test that user's access to different tools:

- Log in as a user with Visitor privileges and see what tools are available under the gear icon.
- As a user with Visitor privileges, visit the Site Contents page and see which lists and libraries are visible.
- As a user with Visitor privileges, visit the Pages or Site Pages library and see what tools are active.
- Next, log in as a user with Member privileges and see what tools are available under the gear icon.
- As a user with Member privileges, access Site Settings and see which tools are available.
- As a user with Visitor privileges, visit the Site Contents page and see which lists and libraries are visible.
- As a user with Member privileges, visit the Pages or Site Pages library and see what tools are active.

And if other SharePoint groups are being used, test out site permissions in a similar fashion. It is typical that a site administrator will make changes to the capabilities of members of the Members group by modifying their permissions in specific libraries (such as the Pages or Site Pages library).

A good place to start when learning the options for creating pages is with the gear icon. Depending on the type of site or site collection template that has been used, and depending on the permissions of the account being used, the Add a Page tool might or might not be found here. If the user finds this tool and clicks it, a simple dialog appears that asks for a name for the page, and the URL for the library that will house the page is shown. Depending on whether the site has Publishing features enabled, the resulting page differs in properties as well.

Another way to create pages is to visit a library that has one or more page content types enabled. Most sites have a Site Pages or Pages library, which house the home page for that site (see Tables 21.1, 21.2, and 21.3 to see which site templates include them), and these libraries allow users with sufficient permissions to create new pages.

To create a new page from a Site Pages library on a default team site, follow these steps:

1. Access the Site Pages library on a team site by clicking the Site Contents link in the Quick Launch area and then click the Site Pages icon.
2. Click the New Document icon on the Files tab, and then click Web Part Page.

3. Give a name to the page. In this example, TestHomePage1 is used, as shown in Figure 21.14.

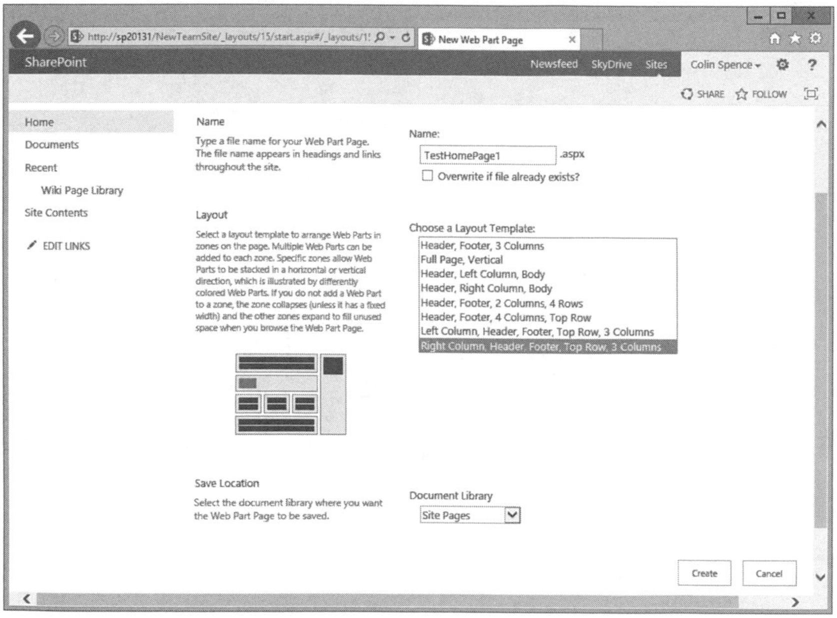

FIGURE 21.14 New Web Part page accessed from a Site Pages library.

4. Select one of the options in the Layout section. In this example, Right Column, Header, Footer, Top Row, 3 Columns are selected.
5. Confirm the Save Location is set to Site Pages.
6. Click Create.

Figure 21.15 shows the page after it has been created and after the user clicks a web part zone (Header) to activate it. The Browse, Page, and Insert tabs are visible on the ribbon, and the Insert tab is selected in Figure 21.15. From the Insert tab, the user can insert Text (a content editor web part will be inserted in the selected zone), an Image (a URL needs to be provided for the image), Video and Audio (the media web part will be inserted in the selected zone), and an App Part or Web Part. If app part or web part icons are clicked, an interface loads that allows the user to choose from available app parts or web parts.

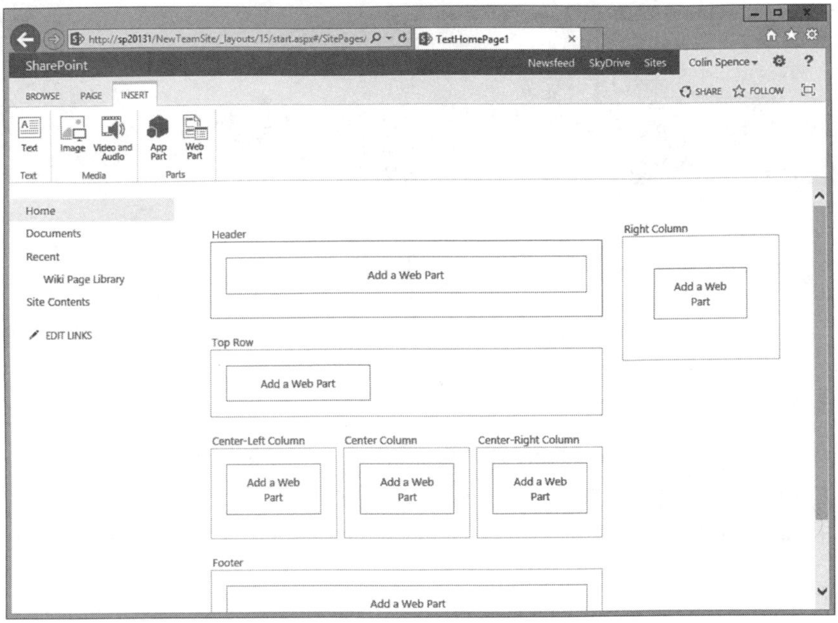

FIGURE 21.15 New web part page.

Reviewing the Pages Library on a Publishing Site Collection

One benefit of publishing sites and site collections is the inclusion of additional page types. For example, in the default Site Pages library in a nonpublishing site, such as a Team Site, the only options presented under the New Document icon are Wiki Page and Web Part Page. However, on a publishing site (such as a site created using the Publishing Portal template or other template shown in Table 21.3), additional options are provided under the New Document icon in the Pages library, as follows:

- Page
- Article Page
- Welcome Page
- Error Page

Each of these selections then allows the user to choose from the same list of page layouts, as follows:

- (Article Page) Body Only
- (Article Page) Image on Left
- (Article Page) Image on Right

- (Article Page) Summary Links
- (Catalog-Item Reuse) Blank Catalog Item
- (Catalog-Item Reuse) Catalog Item Image on Left
- (Enterprise Wiki Page) Basic Page
- (Error Page) Error
- (Project Page) Basic Project Page
- (Redirect Page) Redirect
- (Welcome Page) Blank Web Part Page
- (Welcome Page) Splash
- (Welcome Page) Summary Links

Follow these steps to create an Article page in a publishing-enabled site:

1. Access a site that was created by using the Publishing Portal template and then access the Pages library.
2. Click the New Document icon on the Files tab and select Article Page.
3. Provide a title for the page. NewArticlePage is used in this example.
4. Click the URL Name field; it should self-populate with the title provided.
5. Select (Article Page) Image on the right in the Page Layout section.
6. Click Create.
7. Click the name of the page just created to open it. A note should say that the page is checked out to you and that only you can see recent changes.
8. Click the Page tab, and then click the Edit icon.
9. Note that there are a number of fields that are displayed, including the Title already given to the page, Article Date, Byline, Page Image, Image Caption, Page Content, and Rollup Image at the bottom. Add some text into Byline and Page content, as shown in Figure 21.16, and click Save on the Page tab.

You should experiment with the wide range of different pages that you can create and with the almost limitless combinations of page layouts, web parts, and other items that you can add to pages.

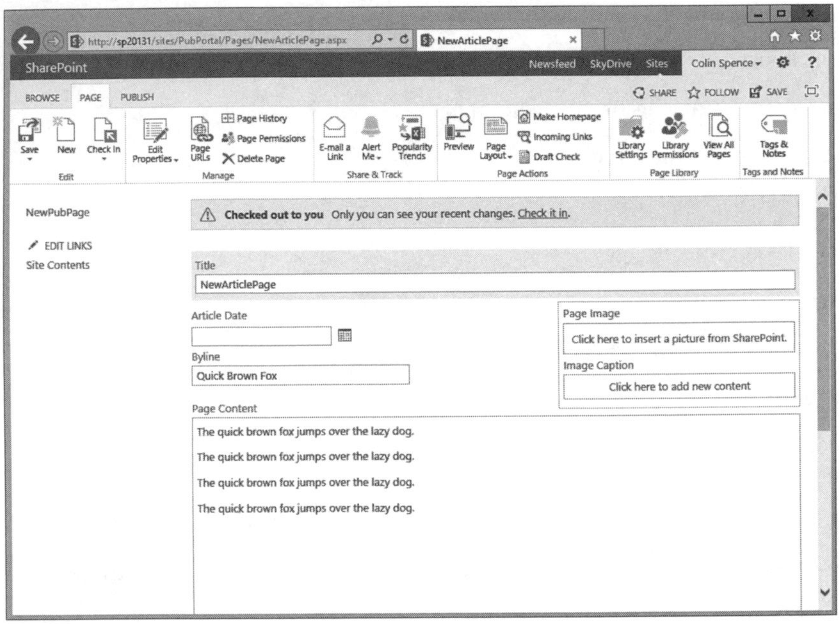

FIGURE 21.16 New article page from a publishing portal site in edit mode.

Reviewing the Users and Permissions Tools

Becoming comfortable with the users and groups that have access to the site, lists, and libraries and what level of permissions they have is one of the most important tasks for a site administrator. This section covers the tools used to do so and the best practices as to how you should use them.

When you are at the root of a site collection and using an account with Owner-level permissions, four links should be available in the Users and Permissions section on the Site Settings page:

- People and Groups
- Site Permissions
- Site Collection Administrators
- Site App Permissions

If you are on a lower-level site (subsite), you will see three options:

- People and Groups
- Site Permissions
- Site App Permissions

From the root of the site collection, it is important to review the Site Collection Administrators link to see who has been granted Full Control over the site collection and all its contents. Figure 21.17 shows an example where three individual users are present (Administrator, Colin Spence, Rand Morimoto). Although you can add AD security groups here, that is generally not recommended unless the AD group is very restrictive (to avoid giving too great a number of users complete control over the site collection). In addition, recall that during the site collection creation process, a primary site collection administrator and secondary site collection administrator were defined, and they receive email alerts pertaining to the site collection, so it is generally not recommended to remove accounts from this role without getting approval from the farm administrators.

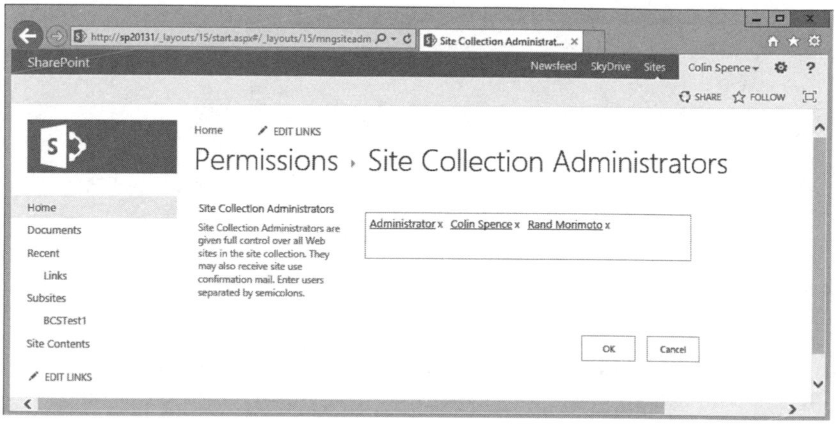

FIGURE 21.17 A Site Collection Administrators page.

Next, click the Site Permissions link from the Site Settings page, in the Users and Permissions section, to review the groups that exist for the site collection and any individual users or AD groups that have been granted direct permissions. Figure 21.18 shows the Site Permissions page (user.aspx) for a site collection. The groups that appear on this page vary based on the site collection template used, the service applications enabled, and any modifications made since it was created. This page provides a number of tools on the Permissions tab and displays information about the different groups and users that have permissions to the site collection.

The Permissions tab provides a number of tools:

- **Grant Permissions:** Add users or AD groups and grant permissions by adding to an existing SharePoint group or give direct permissions. A welcome email can be sent to the users added. Note that by default, any users or groups added here are added to the Members group (in Figure 21.18, this group is titled Home Members), and you need to click the Show Options link at the bottom of the Share window to more granularly assign permissions.

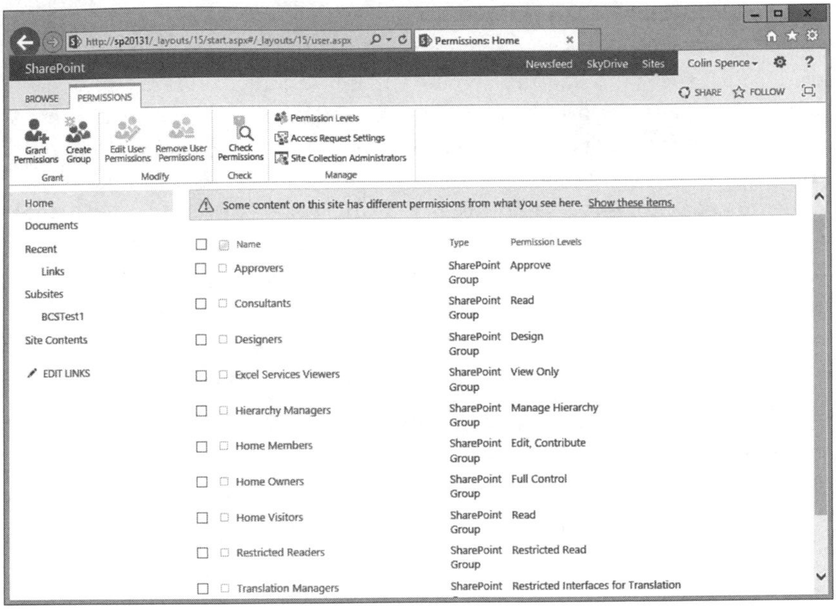

FIGURE 21.18 A Site Permissions page.

- **Create Group:** Define a new SharePoint group and description, define the group owner, and define who can view the membership of the group (Group Members, Everyone) and who can edit the membership of the group (Group Owner, Group Members). Also choose whether to allow requests to join/leave the group, auto-accept requests, and define the email address that membership requests go to. Most important, select the permission level for group members on the site, as shown in Figure 21.19.
- **Edit User Permissions:** If a group or user is selected, allows the permission level to be modified.
- **Remove User Permissions:** If a group or user is selected, clicking this button removes all permissions for the user or group to the site. A window opens asking for confirmation that you do in fact want to remove all the permissions for the user or group.
- **Check Permissions:** Allows the entry of a user or group name, and when the Check Now button is clicked, provides a summary of the permission levels given to the group or user and whether they were given directly or via a specific group.
- **Permission Levels:** Clicking this icon opens the Permission Levels page that allows the addition of a permission level, deletion of a permission level, or modification of a permission level.

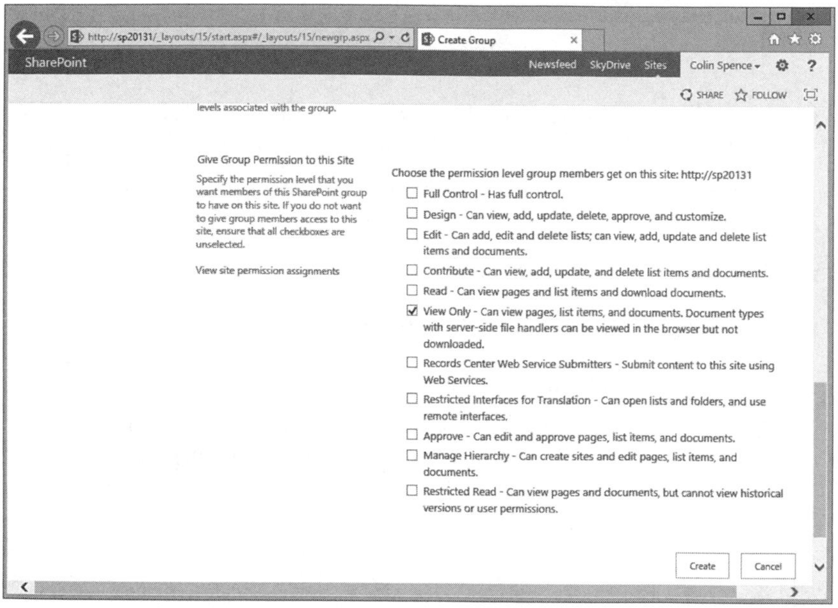

FIGURE 21.19 Create Group page.

- **Access Request Settings:** Either allows or denies requests for access and defines the email address these requests will go to.

NOTE

Double-check the email address that is defined if allowing requests for access is enabled. Often, the email is for an administration account that may not be monitored.

- **Site Collection Administrators:** This is available only when accessing this page for the root site of a site collection. Provides access to the list of users defined as site collection administrators and allows the addition of new site collection administrators or the removal of existing ones.

Clicking the name of the group from the Permissions page shows the users or AD groups that are part of the group. The administrator can also add users to the group and perform other actions, including the following:

- Add users or AD groups to the SharePoint group.
- Email users in the group.

- Call/message selected users based on the tools available (such as if Microsoft Lync is configured).
- Remove users from the group.
- Access group settings.
- View group permissions by listing the URLs to sites, lists, or items that inherit permissions from these URLs.
- Make the group the default group for the site.
- Provide access to the list settings for the User Information List.

Table 21.4 provides an overview of the permissions that Approvers, Owners, Members, Visitors, and Designers groups receive by default in a SharePoint Server 2013 Enterprise site and summarizes the privileges for each group. Table 21.5 continues to provide an overview of the privileges of Hierarchy Managers, Records Center Web Service Submitters, Restricted Readers, Style Resource Readers, and Viewers.

NOTE

A best practice recommendation is to not change the settings for these default Owners, Members, and Visitors groups. In fact, the Owners group permissions can't be changed. Although it might seem like a good idea to modify the permissions of the Members or Visitors groups to meet specific requirements (for example, to remove the ability of the Visitors group to View Versions in a list and to Create Alerts), this can lead to confusion from an administrative and end-user standpoint. Other administrators might not know about these customizations, and users may not know either and may think that, for example, their inability to create alerts is due to a SharePoint error and file a help desk ticket. The best practice is to create one or more new groups, such as Members Customized or Visitors Customized, and use those instead. This will clearly call out that the default settings have been customized. There is a Copy Permission Level button at the bottom of the Edit Permission Level page that makes it easy, for example, to copy the permissions for the standard Members group and then give it a name and add or remove permissions.

For Table 21.4 and Table 21.5, all site and site collection features have been enabled, to ensure that the full list of groups is provided.

TABLE 21.4 Default Permissions for Approvers, Members, Owners, Visitors, and Designers Groups in SharePoint Server 2013 Enterprise

	Approvers (Approve Permission Level)	Owners (Full Control Permission Level)	Members (Contribute Permission Level)	Visitors (Read Permission Level)	Designers (Design Permission Levels)
List Permissions					
Manage Lists	No	Yes	No	No	Yes
Override List Behaviors	Yes	Yes	No	No	Yes
Add Items	Yes	Yes	Yes	No	Yes
Edit Items	Yes	Yes	Yes	No	Yes
Delete Items	Yes	Yes	Yes	No	Yes
View Items	Yes	Yes	Yes	Yes	Yes
Approve Items	Yes	Yes	No	No	Yes
Open Items	Yes	Yes	Yes	Yes	Yes
View Versions	Yes	Yes	Yes	Yes	Yes
Delete Versions	Yes	Yes	Yes	No	Yes
Create Alerts	Yes	Yes	Yes	Yes	Yes
View Application Pages	Yes	Yes	Yes	Yes	Yes
Site Permissions					
Manage Permissions	No	Yes	No	No	No
View Web Analytics Data	No	Yes	No	No	No
Create Subsites	No	Yes	Yes	No	No
Manage Website	No	Yes	No	No	No
Add and Customize Pages	No	Yes	No	No	Yes
Apply Themes and Borders	No	Yes	No	No	Yes
Apply Style Sheets	No	Yes	No	No	Yes
Create Groups	No	Yes	No	No	No

21

	Approvers (Approve Permission Level)	Owners (Full Control Permission Level)	Members (Contribute Permission Level)	Visitors (Read Permission Level)	Designers (Design Permission Levels)
Browse Directories	Yes	Yes	Yes	No	Yes
Use Self-Service Site Creation (if enabled)	Yes	Yes	Yes	Yes	Yes
View Pages	Yes	Yes	Yes	Yes	Yes
Enumerate Permissions	No	Yes	No	No	No
Browse User Information	Yes	Yes	Yes	Yes	Yes
Manage Alerts	No	Yes	No	No	No
Use Remote Interfaces	Yes	Yes	Yes	Yes	Yes
Use Client Integration Features	Yes	Yes	Yes	Yes	Yes
Open	Yes	Yes	Yes	Yes	Yes
Edit Personal Information	Yes	Yes	Yes	No	Yes
Personal Permissions					
Manage Personal Views	Yes	Yes	Yes	No	Yes
Add/Remove Personal Web Parts	Yes	Yes	Yes	No	Yes
Update Personal Web Parts	Yes	Yes	Yes	No	Yes

TABLE 21.5 Default Permissions for Hierarchy Managers, Records Center Web Service Submitters, Restricted Readers, Style Resource Readers, and Viewers in SharePoint Server 2013 Enterprise

	Hierarchy Managers (Manage Hierarchy Permission Level)	Records Center Web Service Submitters (Records Center Web Service Submitters Permission Level)	Restricted Readers (Restricted Read Permission Level)	Style Resource Readers (Limited Access Permission Level)	Viewers (View Only Permission Level)
List Permissions					
Manage Lists	Yes	No	No	No	No
Override Check Out	Yes	No	No	No	No
Add Items	Yes	No	No	No	No
Edit Items	Yes	No	No	No	No
Delete Items	Yes	No	No	No	No
View Items	Yes	No	Yes	No	Yes
Approve Items	No	No	No	No	No
Open Items	Yes	No	Yes	No	No
View Versions	Yes	No	No	No	Yes
Delete Versions	Yes	No	No	No	No
Create Alerts	Yes	No	No	No	Yes
View Application Pages	Yes	No	No	No	Yes
Site Permissions					
Manage Permissions	Yes	No	No	No	No
View Web Analytics Data	Yes	No	No	No	No
Create Subsites	Yes	No	No	No	No
Manage Website	Yes	No	No	No	No
Add and Customize Pages	Yes	No	No	No	No

	Hierarchy Managers (Manage Hierarchy Permission Level)	Records Center Web Service Submitters (Records Center Web Service Submitters Permission Level)	Restricted Readers (Restricted Read Permission Level)	Style Resource Readers (Limited Access Permission Level)	Viewers (View Only Permission Level)
Apply Themes and Borders	No	No	No	No	No
Apply Style Sheets	No	No	No	No	No
Create Groups	No	No	No	No	No
Browse Directories	Yes	No	No	No	No
Use Self-Service Site Creation	Yes	No	No	No	Yes
View Pages	Yes	No	Yes	No	Yes
Enumerate Permissions	Yes	No	No	No	No
Browse User Information	Yes	No	No	Yes	Yes
Manage Alerts	Yes	No	No	No	No
Use Remote Interfaces	Yes	Yes	No	No	Yes
Use Client Integration Features	Yes	No	No	Yes	Yes
Open	Yes	Yes	Yes	Yes	Yes
Edit Personal Information	Yes	No	No	No	No
Personal Permissions					
Manage Personal Views	Yes	No	No	No	No
Add/Remove Personal Web Parts	Yes	No	No	No	No
Update Personal Web Parts	Yes	No	No	No	No

Reviewing the Galleries Tools

Beneath the Users and Permissions section on the Site Settings page is the Web Designer Galleries section, which contains links to all the galleries available for the current site, including the Site Columns, Site Content Types, Web Parts, List Templates, Master Pages, Themes, Solutions, and Composed Looks.

In general, the Site Columns and Site Content Types galleries are actively used by an organization that is seeking to leverage the metadata capabilities provided by SharePoint 2013, while the other galleries are used less often for specific purposes. Site administrators or farm administrators might want to carefully review the web parts included in the Web Parts gallery to familiarize themselves with which tools power users and administrators have access to.

Site designers will be interested in the Master Pages and Page Layout gallery and the Themes gallery. The administrator should review the List Templates gallery periodically to make sure that there aren't too many List templates accumulating, because they can clutter up the Create page that is accessed when creating new lists and libraries.

Site columns and site content types are covered in Chapter 22, "Managing Metadata and Content Types in SharePoint 2013."

NOTE

Although site galleries allow administrators to delete items from the gallery, this should be done only if the administrator is confident of what the impact will be to base site functionality. A general best practice is to leave the default items in these galleries unless there is a specific business reason to delete items.

High-level descriptions are as follows:

- **Site Columns:** A number of predefined site columns already exist and are useful to peruse and test when creating a taxonomy for the organization. Types of site columns include some or all of the following, based on the type of site and features enabled: Base Columns, Content Feedback, Core Contact and Calendar Columns, Core Document Columns, Core Task and Issue Columns, Custom Columns, Display Template Columns, Document and Record Management Columns, Enterprise Keywords Group, Extended Columns, JavaScript Display Template Columns, Page Layout Columns, Publishing Columns, Reports, Status Indicators, and Translation Columns. New site columns can be created from this gallery as well.
- **Site Content Types:** A number of content types are in this gallery by default, which should be reviewed and tested so that the administrator becomes familiar with their use and capabilities. Types of content types include some or all of the following, based on the type of site and features enabled: Business Intelligence (BI), Community Content Types, Digital Asset Content Types, Display Template Content Types, Document Content Types, Document Set Content Types, Folder Content Types, Group Work Content Types, List Content Types, Page Layout Content Types, Publishing Content Types, and Special Content Types.

- **Web Parts:** This gallery contains the web parts available to administrators and designers on this site. There can be 75 or more web parts in this gallery with .webpart and .dwp extensions. The names tend to be explanatory, but it is not always easy to know the capabilities of different web parts, so the Recommendation Settings column provides information on recommended usage. If you click the Edit icon next to a web part, more information about that web part displays, as shown in Figure 21.20. Note that the tools available include an Export tool that allows a copy of the web part to be downloaded and then edited with a tool such as SharePoint Designer or Visual Studio. Also, recommendations can be added or modified that help users understand where the web part should be used.

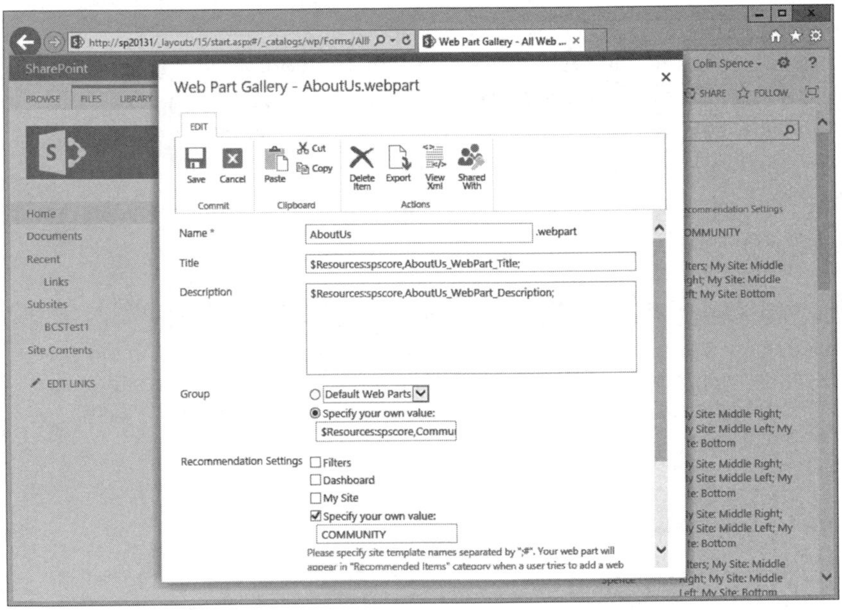

FIGURE 21.20 Web part properties screen.

- **List Templates:** This gallery is empty for new sites and site collections, but shows any List templates created for the site collection. These List templates (with the .stp extension) are available to use for creating new lists and libraries within the site collection. Note that if selected, an .stp file can be downloaded from this gallery (by clicking Download a Copy from the Files tab on the ribbon) or uploaded to the gallery (by clicking Upload Document on the Files tab on the ribbon). This makes it possible to "export" and then "import" templates in other site collections.

- **Master Pages and Page Layouts:** This gallery contains a variety of .xml, .aspx, and .master files and pages. SharePoint Designer 2013 is the tool of choice for editing the .aspx page layouts and the .master pages. A column lists the Compatible User Interface (UI) versions, usually 15 (the current SharePoint 2013 products) or four (SharePoint 2010 products). It is definitely *not* recommended to experiment with master pages and page layouts on production environments; instead, create a development environment. You should also make copies of existing files rather than alter the originals.

- **Themes:** A number of themes (which consist of .spfont and .spcolor file types) are provided that can be applied to the site to change the basic look and feel of the site. Custom themes can be added by creating additional color palettes and font schemes and uploading them to the Theme Gallery.
- **Solutions:** If any solutions have been deployed to the site collection by third-party providers or developers, they appear here. By default, a quota of 300 server resources are allowed for solutions, and this page shows Current Usage and Average Usage.
- **Composed Looks:** Composed looks are collections of Master Pages, Themes, Images, and Font Schemes and can be accessed by using the Change the Look tool on the Site Settings page in the Look and Feel section. URLs are provided for these different elements, which can be seen stored in the following locations:

  Masterpages: /_catalogs/masterpage/

  Themes: /_catalogs/theme/15/

  Images: /_layouts/15/images

  Font Scheme: /_catalogs/theme/15/

NOTE

With the introduction of apps, some confusion can occur between apps and solutions. A solution has a .wsp extension (but is really a .cab file) and can be created as either a farm solution (deploys to the farm's solution store) or a sandboxed solution (deploys to a site collection solution store). Farm solutions generally run with "full trust," whereas sandboxed solutions have code-execution and resource-access restrictions. Apps are the next iteration of sandboxed solutions in SharePoint 2013, and although sandboxed solutions are deprecated, they can, in most cases, still be installed in SharePoint 2013. Therefore, apps are really lightweight solutions, with a variety of restrictions, and a key functionality of apps is that they can be hosted in SharePoint 2013 on premises or in the cloud. This functionality is provided by SharePoint REST/OData services to access SharePoint sites, lists, and other data, and SharePoint data can be accessed through the SharePoint JavaScript, Silverlight, or .NET Framework client object models.

Reviewing the Site Administration Tools

On the Site Settings page in the Site Administration section are a number of links to additional tools that the site collection administrator should be familiar with. The links that show vary based on the version of SharePoint 2013 in use and on the features enabled for the site and site collection. The tools in the Site Administration section allow site collection and site administrators to gain a thorough understanding of the settings that apply to a specific site, view and manage libraries and lists, see workflows that are available, access managed metadata through the term store (without having to go to Central Administration), and manage content and the overall structure of the site.

Logically, these tools should be thoroughly investigated and understood for effective site management. These tools are available to site administrators that are "downstream" and have Owner-level privileges on lower level sites but aren't site collection administrators, so IT usually needs to provide training to lower-level site administrators, or power users, on this set of tools.

A summary of these tools is as follows:

- **Regional Settings:** Allows the administrator to set locale, sort order (for lists and libraries), time zone, calendar type, alternate calendar, days in the work week, first day of the week (which affects how calendars in that site display the week), start time, first week of the year, end time, and time format (12 versus 24 hour).
- **Site Libraries and Lists:** Shows all lists and libraries in the current site. Clicking a link opens the Settings page for the list or library. Allows creation of new lists and libraries, apps, and sites.
- **User Alerts:** Shows any existing alerts on the site and allows their deletion. This can be useful to simply see whether users are taking advantage of alerts, but also to delete alerts after a user changes roles or positions or leaves the company.
- **RSS:** Defines whether RSS feeds are allowed in this site collection, and whether they are allowed in the site itself, and if copyright information is attached to RSS feeds, who the managing editor and webmaster are, and defines the time to live in minutes.
- **Sites and Workspaces:** Shows sites, document workspaces, and meeting workspaces that exist below the current site. Clicking a link opens the home page for the site or workspace. This was discussed earlier in the chapter in the section "Reviewing the Scope of an Existing Site Collection."

NOTE

Meeting workspaces have been deprecated in SharePoint 2013, so the list for Meeting Workspaces on the Site and Workspaces page is most likely to show Meeting Workspaces that may have been migrated from an earlier version of SharePoint to SharePoint 2013.

- **Workflow Settings:** Lists workflows associated with the site.
- **Site Output Cache:** This page provides several options for the use of caching page output for anonymous and authenticated users. For the Anonymous Cache Profile, the options are to Inherit or Select a page output cache profile. (The options are Public Internet, Extranet, or Intranet.) For the Authenticated Cache Profile, the options are Inherit or Select a page output cache profile. (The options are Extranet or Intranet.) There is also the option to apply these settings to all subsites.

- **Site Closure and Deletion:** Offers tools for Site Closure, Site Deletion, and allows the selection of a site policy if any have been defined.
- **Popularity Trends:** Provides access to a usage report (Excel format) that downloads and opens when clicked, as shown in Figure 21.21, if Excel is loaded on the local machine.

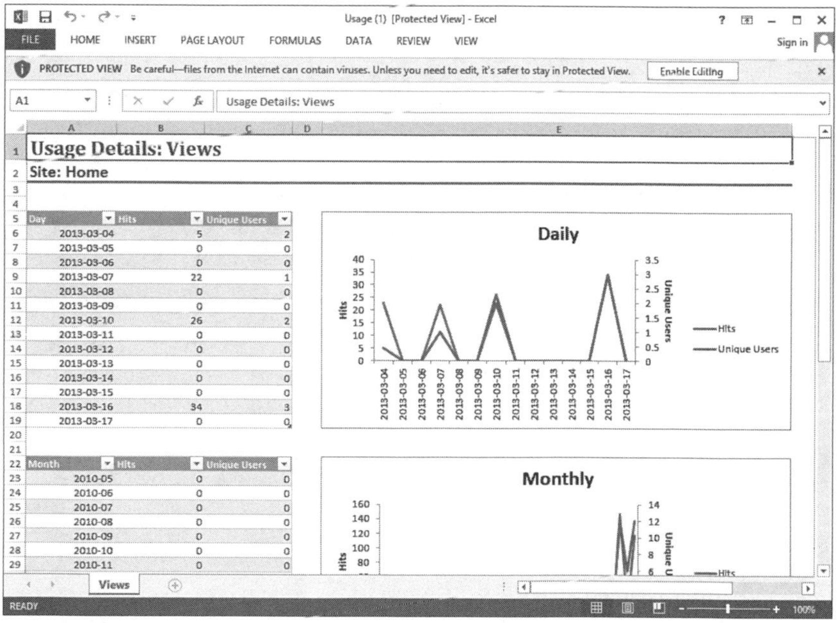

FIGURE 21.21 Usage report example.

- **Term Store Management:** Allows the administrator to review the keywords available to use for tagging items in the site collection and to add or remove keywords. Giving site administrators access to this tool from the Site Settings tools instead of having to access it from Central Administration allows site collection and site administrators to more effectively leverage these tools. Note that the individuals need to be given appropriate permissions in Central Administration to the Managed Metadata service application to manage term sets. This is covered in more detail in Chapter 22, in the "Creating and Using Managed Metadata" section.
- **Manage Catalog Connections:** Allows the connection of a publishing site collection to a library or list that is shared as a catalog.
- **Content and Structure:** This page provides a tree view of all lists, libraries, and sites underneath the current site collection and allows a wide range of interaction with these entities (as discussed earlier in this chapter and shown in Figure 21.11). New sites, lists, or pages can be created beneath the top-level site, new items can be created in lists or libraries, list settings can be modified, and individual items can be edited, copied, deleted, and managed.

- **Content and Structure Logs:** Active if the site is a publishing site or if publishing features are enabled, these logs provide information about final status, source and target, errors, and recovery instructions.
- **Translation Status:** If publishing sites are using variations, this list tracks the progress of these activities.

Understanding the Search Tools

Chapter 8, "Leveraging and Optimizing Search in SharePoint 2013," discusses the capabilities of the search tools in SharePoint 2013, which combine some of the capabilities of SharePoint Search in the 2010 version with capabilities from the FAST Search add-on to SharePoint 2010. This section summarizes the basic tools provided to an administrator on the Site Settings page in the Search section, to clarify what can be managed from a site collection and site perspective without resorting to Central Administration tools.

As will be evident, these are not tools that you will master quickly. In general, you should experiment with them in a development environment before modifying default settings in a production environment. But if the organization truly wants to optimize the use of the search tools, it is important for IT to have a good understanding of the capabilities of the tool set.

The tools offered in SharePoint 2013 Foundation, Standard, or Enterprise in Site Settings are as follows:

- **Result Sources:** In SharePoint 2010, these were referred to as *search scopes*, which are now deprecated and are now called *result sources*. A number of built-in result sources are included: Documents, Items Matching a Content Type, Items Related to Current User, Local People Results, Pages, Pictures, and Wiki. New result sources can be defined in this tool and provide a choice of protocols that can be used, including Local SharePoint, Remote SharePoint, OpenSearch 1.0/1.1, or Exchange. A query builder is also available that provides a wide range of keyword filters and property filters and enables you to test the query immediately and see what results are returned.
- **Result Types:** SharePoint 2013 provides a much more granular set of tools to dictate how certain results are rendered. Figure 21.22 shows the Manage Results Type page, which lists the standard result types. As shown in Figure 21.22, these include Person, Microsoft Access, Microsoft Excel, Microsoft OneNote, and more. Copies can be made of existing default result types and then modified. Result Conditions are shown, along with Result Actions, as shown in Figure 21.22. New result types can be created from this page, and if the links to the display template is clicked, the admin is taken to the Design Manager: Edit Display Templates page (covered in the "Reviewing the Look and Feel Tools" section).
- **Query Rules:** These can be defined to conditionally promote specific results, show blocks of additional results, and tune rankings. Query rules can be created for a site, a site collection from the Site Settings interface, or for a Search service application

via the Search service application in Central Administration. Query rules allow administrators to define conditions and actions. Several conditions are provided, including Query Matches Keyword Exactly, Query Contains Action Keyword, Query Matches Dictionary Exactly, and several others. The actions provided are Add Promoted Result (and URL needs to be provided), Add Result Block (complex queries can be created), and Change Ranked Results by Changing the Query.

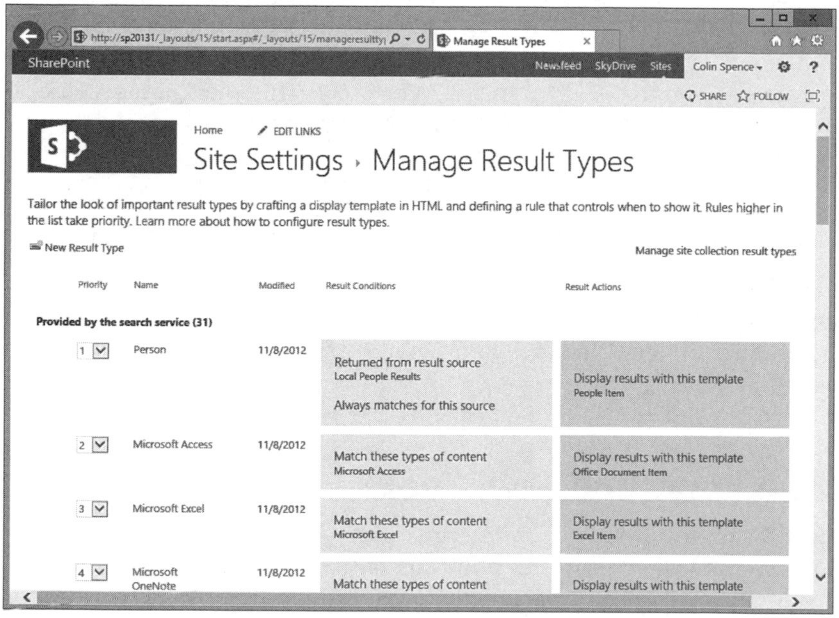

FIGURE 21.22 Manage Result Types page.

- **Schema:** This page allows the administrator to view the managed properties, crawled properties, and categories. The search schema is essentially the detailed mapping of "how SharePoint search works." For example, the Managed Properties view shows the roughly 650 different property names in batches of 50. It also defines the mapping between crawled properties and managed properties; only managed properties are written to the search index. In addition, it defines the type of property (text, integer, decimal, date and time, and other choices); whether the items are queryable, searchable, retrievable, refinable, and sortable; and whether multiple values are allowed. Note that new managed properties need to be defined from the Search Service Application: Search Administration page in Central Administration.
- **Search Settings:** This page allows the configuration of the Search Center URL, which adds a message to all users offering them the ability to try their search again from that Search Center. In addition, the results page can be configured to be the same as the parent or a custom results page, or a search navigation node can be used as the destination results page.

- **Searchable Columns:** Columns can be selected here that will be *excluded* from search indexing so that their contents do not appear in search results.
- **Search and Offline Availability:** This page allows the administrator to determine whether the site will appear in search results and whether items from the site can be downloaded to offline clients and enables the administrator to mark the site for re-indexing. An important option also available on this page is the treatment of .aspx pages if the site contains fine-grained permissions. This simply means that if the site does not inherit permissions from the parent, and the permissions have been further customized, the site will be treated differently in terms of what is indexed on the .aspx page. The options are Do Not Index Web Parts If This Site Contains Fine-Grained Permissions, Always Index All Web Parts on This Site, and Never Index Any Web Parts on This Site.
- **Configuration Import:** Allows the import of an exported search configuration Extensible Markup Language (XML) file. This can be a great time saver due to the possible complexity of search customizations.
- **Configuration Export:** Allows the administrator to save the current search configuration to an XML file. This can then be imported using the Configuration Import tool.

Reviewing the Look and Feel Tools

The tools that appear in this section of the Site Settings page vary based on the version of SharePoint 2013 in use and the type of site collection created. For example, the Design Manager and Welcome Page links are available only in publishing sites.

This section of tools is a mixture of "harmless" and easy-to-use tools and "dangerous" tools, so the farm administrators should be aware of the capabilities of the different tools and train site collection and site administrators accordingly. For example, the Title, Description, and Logo tools allow the user to change the title of the site, provide a description, and add or modify the logo being used, which are all "safe" changes. Tree view allows an administrator to display or hide the quick launch and display or hide the tree view, again very simple and safe changes. But other tools allow the administrator to change master pages, specify a custom Cascading Style Sheet (CSS) file that should be used, import design packages, or make other changes that could cause dramatic changes or actually stop the site from rendering. Of special interest is the Design Manager "tool," which is actually more of a collection of tools that provide access to some new master page and page layout editing tools that will be very valuable to organizations wanting to customize the look, feel, and functionality of SharePoint 2013.

Following is a summary of the tools provided:

- **Design Manager:** Design Manager is a publishing feature available in publishing sites in SharePoint Server 2013 and provides access to a selection of eight pages, or a wizard of sorts, as shown in Figure 21.23. The user can choose any of the options desired and learn more about the particular component of SharePoint branding:

Device Channels, Design Files, Master Pages, Display Templates, Page Layouts, and other components. These tools allow the user to create new device channels from the Manage Device Channels link or create new master pages (or edit existing ones) using the Edit Master Pages link. Likewise, new page layouts can be created, and a design package can be created containing multiple elements.

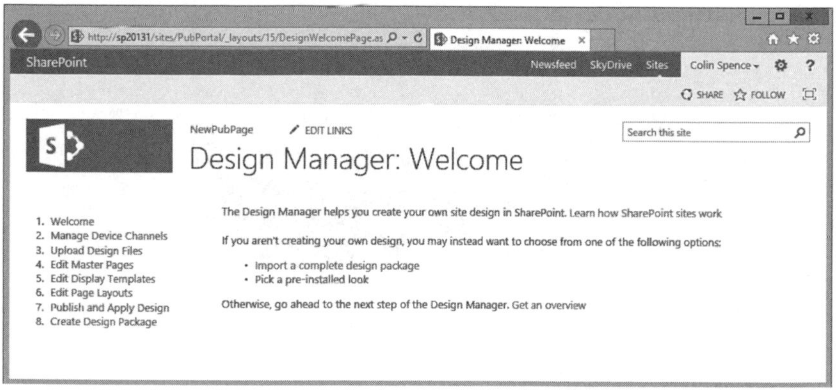

FIGURE 21.23 Design Manager welcome page.

NOTE

Design Manager is also available from the gear icon to users with sufficient permissions.

NOTE

SharePoint branding is a complex process, and although the Design Manager may be of some value to experienced or novice branding resources, there are still many risks involved with attempting to dramatically alter the look and feel of the SharePoint environment. Microsoft has put a lot of effort into making SharePoint branding easier, and SharePoint Designer is no longer the only tool that is recommended. Tools such as Visual Studio, Dreamweaver, and others can now be used. By accessing the Snippet Gallery, as shown in Figure 21.24, different master page components (such as Top Navigation, Vertical Navigation, and Search Box) can be customized in the Customization section on the right of the screen. The Hypertext Markup Language (HTML) snippet and the preview image are updated accordingly, and this makes the testing process easy to experiment with. You can see the results immediately; they are often not as expected. The HTML snippets can then be pasted into a different editing tool set, such as Dreamweaver. Figure 21.24 shows an example of where the search box component was edited by accessing the Appearance section in the Customization area.

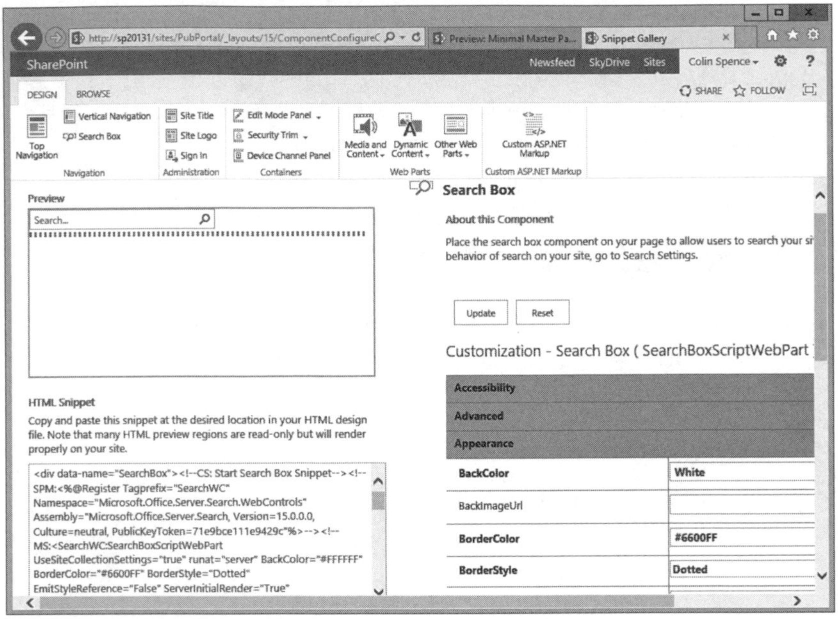

FIGURE 21.24 Snippet Gallery used to edit a search box on a master page.

- **Master Page:** This page allows the administrator to determine site master page settings, system master page settings, theme, and alternate CSS URL. The site master page and system master page can be inherited from the parent (assuming the site is not the top level site, in which case there is no parent), or a master page can be chosen from the drop-down list (which provides choices from the master page and Page Layout gallery). The default master pages available are Seattle and Oslo. Under the Theme section, a check box allows the administrator to determine whether the site inherits the theme from the parent of this site (if there is a parent). Under the Alternate CSS URL section, the administrator can choose to Inherit Alternate CSS URL from Parent of This Site, Use Default Styles and Any CSS Files Associated with Your Master Page, or to Specify a CSS File to Be Used by This Site and All Sites That Inherit from It. If the third option is chosen, a Browse button allows the administrator to select from the Style library.

NOTE

Specifying a CSS file is a relatively "safe" way to overwrite settings determined by the current master page and page layouts, because they can easily be managed as separate entities and attached or removed very simply, making it easy to undo any undesirable effects on the site.

- **Title, Description, and Logo:** Allows the administrator to quickly change the title of the site (no effect on the actual URL) and add comments (that appear if the *i* button next to the name of the site is clicked). Also, if a custom logo is desired (which it will be in every instance except perhaps in basic development labs), it can be modified by uploading a graphic image from the user's computer or a SharePoint library. The image is uploaded to the Site Assets library.
- **Page Layouts and Site Templates:** This tool allows administrator to determine which site templates, page layouts, and default page layout for new pages will be used when administrators or users create subsites and pages. This can be very useful in limiting the range of site templates and page layouts that can be used, which can make training and support easier for IT. Note there is now an option to convert blank spaces in the page name to –; so, instead of %20, a dash is used to represent a space in page names, which shortens the URL and makes it easier to read.
- **Welcome Page:** In publishing-enabled sites, this allows the administrator to select a different page that is presented when a user navigates to the site. In a publishing site, the default page is titled default.aspx and is located in the Pages library.
- **Device Channels:** In SharePoint 2010, there was only one default mobile page, but device channels in SharePoint 2013 can be used to provide different renditions of content for multiple different types of devices. Device channels are available only on publishing sites, and there is only one (titled default) to start with, but others can be created from this page by clicking the New Item link. Organizations that are tasked with supporting multiple devices such as Windows phones, iPhones, and tablets will find this useful. There can be a maximum of 10 device channels (including the default).
- **Tree View:** This page allows the administrator to enable quick launch and enable tree view, or disable either. Note that some organizations feel that the quick launch takes up valuable real estate on the screen or is simply distracting and not useful and choose to hide it. However, the Site Contents link will still be on the left side of the screen, so the horizontal space will still be taken up. Figure 21.25 shows an example where the tree view is enabled, and it appears underneath the quick launch content in the lower-left part of the screen.
- **Change the Look:** A number of predesigned themes can be selected from this page. You can find the details of each theme by accessing the Composed Looks link in the Web Designer Galleries section of the Site Settings page.
- **Import Design Package:** Design Packages can be created in the Design Manager or in tools that can create .wsp files (SharePoint solution files). When imported, the .wsp is stored in the Solutions gallery and automatically activated.

- **Navigation:** These tools allow the administrator to define how the global navigation works (which is shown near the top of the page on most pages) and the local navigation works (shown in the quick launch on most pages). For global and current navigation, if the site is a lower-level (not top-level) subsite, the option Display the Same Navigation Items as the Parent Site is provided. In addition, for global and current navigation, the options Managed Navigation (navigation items are represented using a managed metadata term set) and Structural Navigation (displays the navigation items below the current site) are provided. There is an additional option for current navigation, which is Structural Navigation (displays the current site, the navigation items below the current site, and the current site's siblings). New to SharePoint 2013 is the ability to connect to a term set for navigation items. In addition, options are provided to add new pages to navigation automatically, to create friendly URLs for new pages automatically, and to make Show Ribbon and Hide Ribbon commands available.

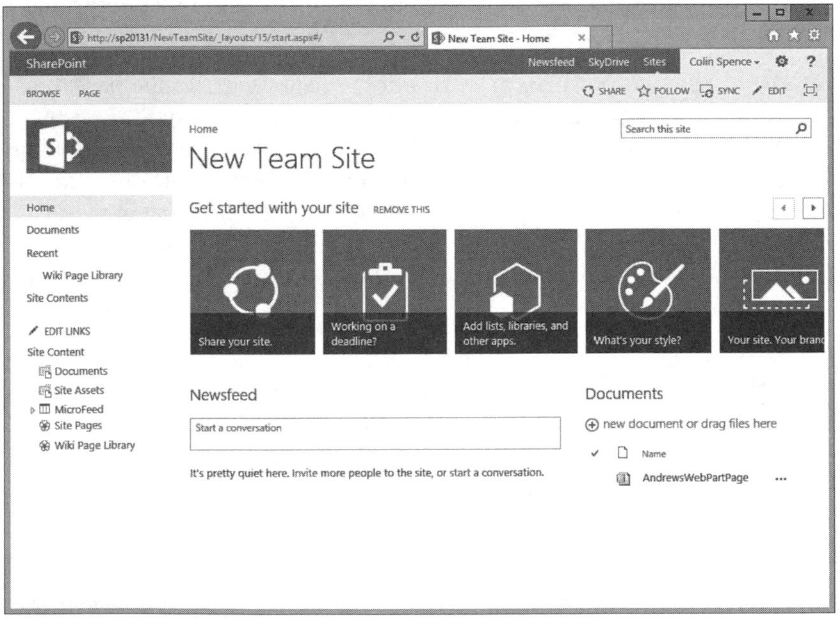

FIGURE 21.25 Team site home page with tree view enabled.

NOTE

Figure 21.26 shows the Managed Navigation: Term Set section, which is a powerful new tool that enables administrators to define the key navigation items as part of a managed metadata term set. This makes it easier to enforce a standard navigation structure, and if changes are made to the term set, they are propagated to any navigation elements that connect to the term set. Note that there is a link to Open the Term Store Management Tool to Edit Term Sets for complete access to the members of the term set.

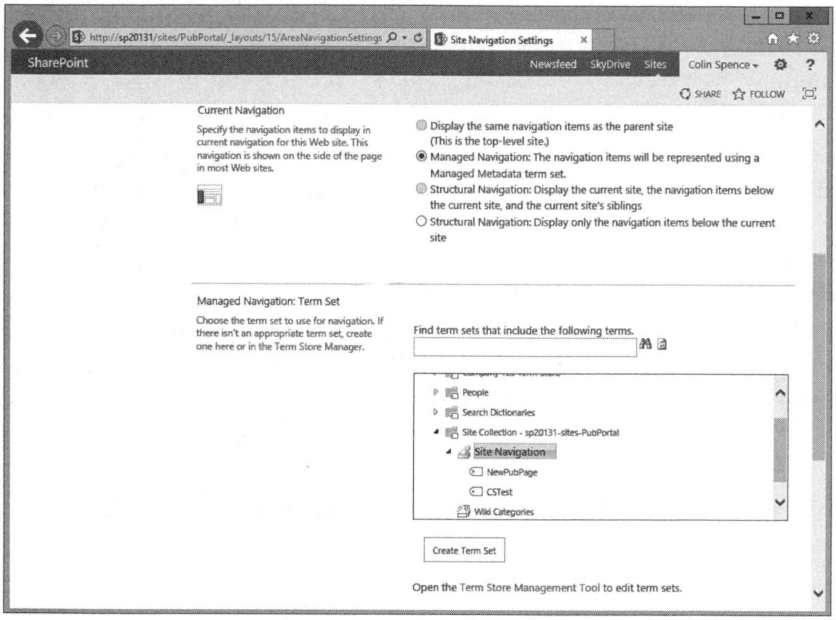

FIGURE 21.26 Navigation Settings page showing the Managed Navigation section.

Reviewing the Site Actions Tools

The Site Actions section of the Site Settings page provides tools that enable the administrator to manage site features, enable search configuration export, reset to a site definition, or delete the site. On a subsite, the Site Collection Administration tools are not available, so site administrators and site collection administrators want to be comfortable with the Site Actions tools.

Site features are reviewed in more detail later in this section, but (in brief) enable the site collection administrator to control which tool sets are available to site collection and site users.

The Site Actions section contains the following tools:

- **Manage Site Features:** These are discussed in more detail in the "Reviewing Site Features and Site Collection Features" section in this chapter.
- **Save Site as Template:** Not available for publishing sites, this tool is very useful for saving sites that have been customized for specific uses, such as for specific types of groups of users such as Departmental Public site, Departmental Private site, Project X site, and so on. A check box is available that enables the saving of content with the template.

- **Enable Search Configuration Export:** If this is clicked, Search Configuration Export is enabled. This can be valuable if the search customization tools are going to be used, because the search configuration details can be very intricate and can be time-consuming to reproduce.
- **Reset to Site Definition:** This tool is generally used only when the site or a page on the site is damaged. Using this tool removes all customizations from a page or all pages on the site, including web part zones, custom controls, and inline text. The options include Make "Show Ribbon" and "Hide Ribbon" Commands Available and Reset All Pages in this Site to Site Definition Version.
- **Delete This Site:** If the link is clicked, additional information is provided on the items that will be deleted and sent to the Recycle Bin. The administrator then needs to confirm the action by again clicking the Delete button.

An Overview of Site Collection Administration Tools

These tools are visible only to a site collection administrator and only from the top-level site of the site collection. Lower-level sites have a link in this section of the page labeled Go to Top Level Site Settings. These tools affect the full range of sites in the site collection and can affect search settings, site collection features, auditing, policies, content types, the use of SharePoint Designer, and numerous other features.

The tools included in this section vary based on the type of site in use, so this section covers the most common tools, as follows:

- **Recycle Bin:** Displays the End User Recycle Bin and gives a link to Deleted from End User Recycle Bin (otherwise known as the Second-Level Recycle Bin). The administrator can restore sites, lists, libraries, or individual items that have been deleted. Individual items can be deleted from the First- or Second-Level Recycle Bins, or the First-Level Recycle Bin can be emptied.
- **Search Result Sources:** This provides the same capabilities as the Result Sources link under the Search heading on the Site Settings page, with the exception that these apply to the full site collection, not just to a specific site. This is covered earlier in this chapter in the "Understanding the Search Tools" section.
- **Search Result Types:** This provides the same capabilities as the Result Types link under the Search heading on the Site Settings page, with the exception that these apply to the full site collection, not just to a specific site. This is covered earlier in this chapter in the "Understanding the Search Tools" section.
- **Search Query Rules:** This provides the same capabilities as the Query Rules link under the Search heading on the Site Settings page, with the exception that these apply to the full site collection, not just to a specific site. This is covered earlier in this chapter in the "Understanding the Search Tools" section.

- **Search Schema:** This provides the same capabilities as the Schema link under the Search heading on the Site Settings page, with the exception that these apply to the full site collection, not just to a specific site. This is covered earlier in this chapter in the "Understanding the Search Tools" section.
- **Search Settings:** This provides the same capabilities as the Search Settings link under the Search heading on the Site Settings page, with the exception that these apply to the full site collection, not just to a specific site. This is covered earlier in this chapter in the "Understanding the Search Tools" section.
- **Search Configuration Import:** This provides the same capabilities as the Configuration Import link under the Search heading on the Site Settings page, with the exception that these apply to the full site collection, not just to a specific site. This is covered earlier in this chapter in the "Understanding the Search Tools" section.
- **Search Configuration Export:** This provides the same capabilities as the Configuration Export link under the Search heading on the Site Settings page, as covered earlier in this chapter in the "Understanding the Search Tools" section.
- **Site Collection Features:** These are discussed later in this chapter in the "Reviewing Site Features and Site Collection Features" section.
- **Site Hierarchy:** Shows all websites that have been created under the current site. This was discussed earlier in this chapter in the "Reviewing the Scope of an Existing Site Collection" section.
- **Search Engine Optimization Settings:** This page provides the ability to include meta tags on pages that verify ownership of the site, and to provide filter link parameters for search engines that track link popularity for multiple URLs separately.
- **Site Collection Navigation:** Enabled by default, navigation links can be disabled from this page. If this is disabled, the navigations are hidden. Security trimming on navigation is also on by default, but you can turn it off. If this is turned off, users will see links even if they don't have permissions to access the URLs the links connect to. Audience targeting, also on by default, can be turned off for navigation links.
- **Site Collection Audit Settings:** Provides access to a number of settings pertaining to audit logs, such as automatic trimming of audit logs and specifying the events that will be audited on documents and items, as well as on lists, libraries, and sites. Figure 21.27 shows a configuration example where the site collection administrator wants to track certain events that apply to documents or items (Moving or Copying Items to Another Location in the Site and Deleting or Restoring Items) as well as certain events that apply to lists, libraries, and sites (Editing Content Types and Columns, Searching Site Content, and Editing Users and Permissions).

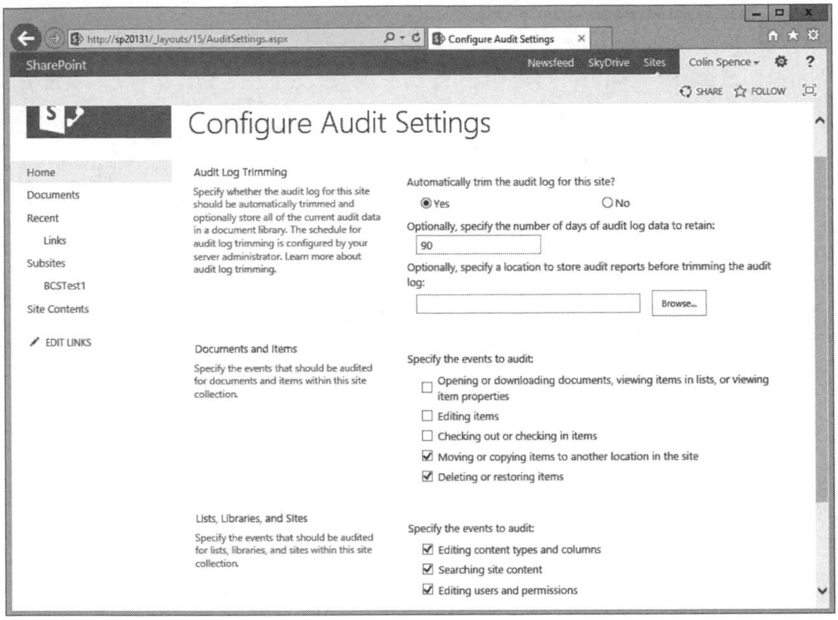

FIGURE 21.27 Configure Audit Settings page for a site collection.

- **Audit Log Reports:** This page provides access to several categories of reports: Content Activity Reports, Custom Reports, Information Management Policy Reports, and Security and Site Settings Reports. The Run a Custom Report link allows the administrator to define the specific events to report on such as deleting or restoring items or searching site content for the entire site collection or a particular site or list in the site collection. These reports are generated when selected, and the administrator simply needs to enter a destination for the report and it is generated and can be opened immediately. A people picker field is available to specify which user this report should be restricted to. Figure 21.28 shows a custom report that was generated to show any Editing Users and Permissions activities that took place for an entire site collection. The first tab (not shown) provides a summary of total activities, and the second (shown in Figure 21.28) provides the details of the activity, including the item type, user ID who made the change, date and time, and type of event. Because the report is in Excel format, it is easy for most users to filter, sort, or format the information as needed.

- **Portal Site Connection:** A portal site connection can be used to link one site collection to another site collection. For example, if you have a main site collection that you want to provide a link to, you can configure a portal site connection that points to the main site collection. The portal site is added to the global breadcrumb navigation for the current site collection. When site collection users click the up folder, the portal site is listed as the parent of the site collection. This enables users to navigate to the portal site more easily.

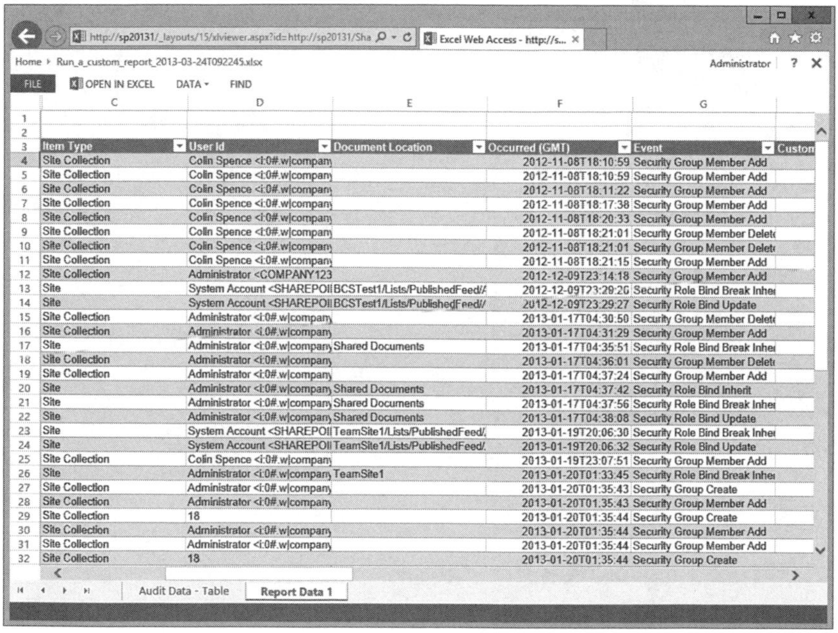

FIGURE 21.28 A custom report for a site collection that shows editing users and permissions activities.

- **Content Type Policy Templates:** This tool provides the ability to create policies for the site collection. Policies can include policy statements that display to end users when an item subject to this policy is opened; then retention, auditing, barcodes, and labels can be enabled. Only certain events can be audited in this tool, and those are opening or downloading documents, viewing items in a list, viewing item properties, editing items, checking out or checking in items, moving or copying items to another location in the site, and deleting or restoring items. Figure 21.29 shows the Stage Properties window that appears when the Add a Retention Stage link is clicked. This allows the administrator to determine what date property of the item triggers a specific retention activity, as follows: Move to Recycle Bin, Permanently Delete, Transfer to Another Location, Start a Workflow, Skip to Next Stage, Declare Record, Delete Previous Drafts, and Delete All Previous Versions. When defined, these can be applied from lists and libraries in the List Settings page, under the Information Management Policy Settings link.
- **Storage Metrics:** Provides a list of SharePoint objects, including lists, libraries, .aspx pages, and sites and documents, as well as the total size of the object, % of parent, and last modified date. An administrator can drill down into lists, libraries, or subsites to investigate the contents in more detail. There is no built-in export capability, however.

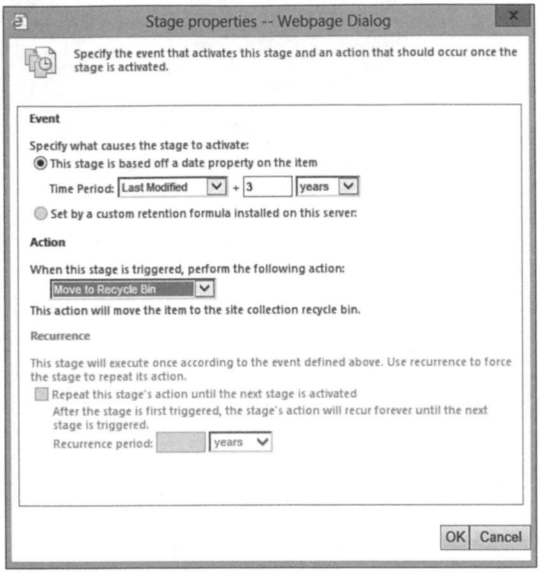

FIGURE 21.29 Creating a new retention stage in a policy template.

- **Site Collection App Permissions:** This page shows apps that have access to the content within the site collection.
- **Site Policies:** This allows the administrator to configure how sites under the policy are closed/deleted automatically. "Closing" a site simply removes the site from places that aggregate sites (Outlook, Office Web Apps [OWA], project server), but users with access to the sites can still access and modify content. There is also an option to set the site collection to read only after it is closed. Administrators can define after what period of time the site is deleted, can schedule email notifications to be sent, and can even allow owners to postpone deletion for a period of days, months, or years.
- **Content Type Publishing:** The first entry on the page allows the administrator to refresh all published content types on next update. A link to the content type publishing error log is provided. The Managed Metadata Service hub, if one is defined, is displayed, along with any subscribed content types.
- **Popularity and Search Reports:** This link provides access to a wide variety of reports, including Usage, Top Queries by Month, Abandoned Queries by Day, Query Rules Usage by Day, and others. By regularly reviewing these reports, an administrator can get a sense for how well search is configured to meet end-user requirements and whether modifications or changes are needed.
- **HTML Field Security:** Allows the administrator to specify whether users can insert external iframes in HTML fields on pages or not, and if allowed, whether iframes from any external domain can be inserted or only iframes from certain domains (such as youtube.com, bing.com, and so on).

- **Help Settings:** The administrator can enable any or all available help collections; for example, Central Administration, SharePoint Help, Student Help, and Teacher Help.
- **SharePoint Designer Settings:** This link allows the administrator to enable or disable the following settings: Enable SharePoint Designer, Enable Detaching Pages from the Site Definition, Enable Customizing Master Pages and Page Layouts, and Enable Managing of the Web Site URL Structure.
- **Site Collection Health Checks:** This allows the administrator to run an automated site collection health check by clicking the Start Checks button. A report then shows whether any issues exist in a number of categories, such as conflicting content types, customized files, missing galleries, missing parent content types, missing site templates, and others. This is designed to be used if the site collection is from a SharePoint 2010 farm or has been migrated to a 2013 farm but is running in SharePoint 2010 mode. It can also prove useful for a basic health check to be run on a regular basis, especially for customized site collections.
- **Site Collection Upgrade:** This applies if the site collection was migrated from a SharePoint 2010 farm and was then upgraded to 2013 mode. To see whether a site has been migrated, simply click the Review Site Collection Upgrade Status link.

NOTE

Site variations are designed for organizations that support users who speak a number of different languages and expect to see sites in the language they use on their computer. More specifically, when site variations are defined, users are redirected based on the language their browser is set to, assuming a site is defined and the prerequisites are configured.

SharePoint 2013, unfortunately, does not do any translation, so the organization will be responsible for performing the translations of the content. The Translatable Columns link from the Site Settings page provides access to the full list of columns used in the site collection and allows the site administrator to select columns that are "translatable" and will be flagged as requiring translation.

Note also that variations can be used only on sites that are created with one of the Publishing site templates, or on sites for where the SharePoint Server Publishing Infrastructure feature has been enabled. Also, it is important to point out that by default the variations feature copies only publishing pages from the Pages library of the source variation site and does not copy content from lists or document libraries.

Reviewing Site Features and Site Collection Features

Site features and site collection features allow the site collection administrator to turn on and off a wide variety of features that enable different combinations of tools to be used on the site or site collection. Tables 21.1, 21.2, and 21.3 provided earlier in this chapter list the site features and site collection features in the standard templates that are provided out-of-the-box. These tables can help an architect or farm administrator get a sense for which site and site collection features are required for certain templates, and it is a good idea to not turn off features that are on by default.

These pages are fairly intimidating if SharePoint Server 2013 Enterprise is installed, so the site collection administrator should carefully consider which, if any, of these features to enable above and beyond the features that are enabled by default when the site collection is created. Some site features require that site collection features are enabled, and error messages will indicate when a prerequisite has not been met.

This section provides a high-level overview of site features provided by SharePoint Server 2013 Enterprise. You can access these by clicking the Manage Site Features link in the Site Actions section on the Site Settings page.

Standard site features in SharePoint Foundation 2013 are as follows:

- **External System Events:** This feature enables Alerts and Event Receivers on the External List and External Content Types. This is a new feature in SharePoint 2013 Business Data Connectivity Services (BCS) that enables SharePoint to receive events from external systems, to let a SharePoint REST endpoint know that an event has occurred.
- **Getting Started:** Provides a tile view experience for common SharePoint site actions. This is enabled by default in most SharePoint sites, but administrators may want to turn it off for more advanced user groups.
- **Minimal Download Strategy (MDS):** MDS delivers a faster page-rendering experience and is enabled by default on a number of sites. When MDS is enabled, pages are rendered through the /_layouts/15/start.aspx page. Essentially, it downloads and renders only those portions of a page that are changing. Publishing site templates do not use MDS by default, and it is recommended that it be left inactive on publishing sites.
- **Mobile Browser View:** Provides the document library and other lists in the team site with a mobile view optimized for smartphone browsers that is accessible by accessing a /mobile version of the site. Figure 21.30 shows a view of a document library accessed under the /mobile path. (In this example, the path is http://sp201302/_layouts/15/mobile/viewa.aspx?List=e87f9fc5%2Db181%2D4567%2D845b%2Dd62288b50c9e&View=37302d80%2D319e%2D42bd%2D83c8%2Dbf3f698681ea.) The gear icon for a mobile page gives the user access to a very limited set of tools, such as Site Contents, Details View, Switch to PC View, and Sign Out.
- **Offline Synchronization for External Lists:** Enables offline synchronization between external lists and Outlook. This enables the use of the Connect to Outlook button on the Library tab on the Ribbon; it also enables the configuration of certain external content types.
- **Search Config Data Content Types:** Installs content types designed to manage search configuration. Note that this must be enabled before you export a design package from the Design Manager.

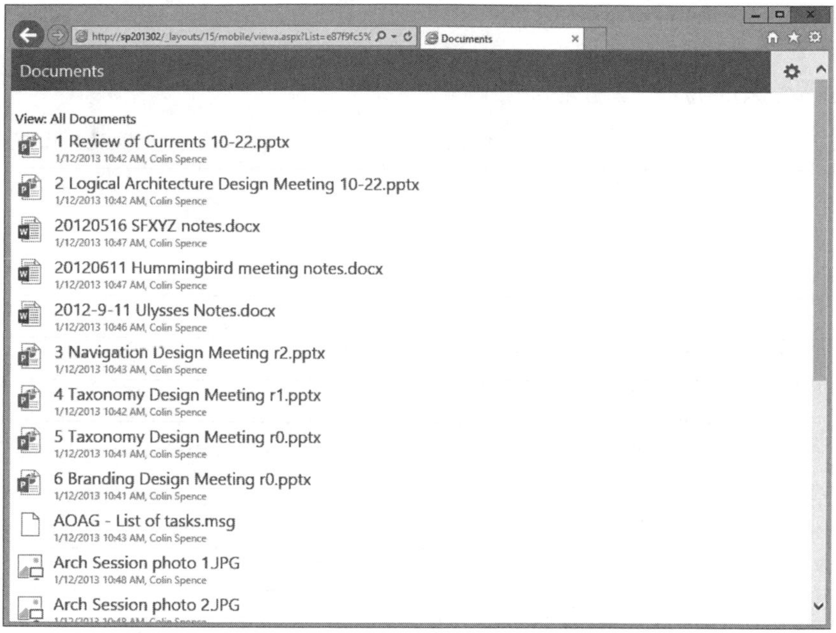

FIGURE 21.30 A mobile browser view of a document library.

- **Search Config Data Site Columns:** Installs columns designed to manage information about search configurations. Note that this must be enabled before you export a design package from the Design Manager.
- **Search Config List Instance Feature:** Provisions a list to enable the import and export of search configurations. Note that this must be enabled before you export a design package from the Design Manager.
- **Search Config Template Feature:** Creates a Search Config Template for the Search Config List to enable the import and export of search configurations. Note that this must be enabled before you export a design package from the Design Manager.
- **Site Notebook:** Creates a Microsoft OneNote 2010 notebook in the Shared Documents library and places a link to it on the quick launch. This feature requires a properly configured WOPI (Web Application Open Platform Interface) application server (such as OWA Server 2013) to create OneNote 2010 notebooks.
- **Team Collaboration Lists:** Provides team collaboration capabilities for a site by making standard lists, such as document libraries and issues, available.
- **Wiki Page Home Page:** This site feature will create a wiki page and set it as your site home page.

Standard site features in a SharePoint Enterprise 2013 team site add the following to the previous list:

- **Access App:** Adds the Access web application.
- **BI Center Data Connections Feature:** One of the features required for full BI functionality in SharePoint 2013 Enterprise.
- **Class My Site Host Content:** Adds class and group content to SharePoint My Site Host site collection.
- **Class Web Types:** Adds required content types to the SharePoint Class web.
- **Community Site Feature:** This feature adds community functionality such as discussion categories, content and people reputation, and the members list. It also provisions community site pages, which contain these lists and features. This is on by default in site collections created using the Community Site template.
- **Content Management Interoperability (CMIS) Producer:** Makes the data stored in the SharePoint site available using the CMIS standard. This connector was originally available in SharePoint 2010 Administration Toolkit and has been redesigned for SharePoint 2013. It allows users to interact with content that is stored in any repository that has implemented the CMIS standard and makes SharePoint content available to any application that has implemented the CMIS standard. Basic document-management operations are supported, such as creating, updating, deleting, checking in and checking out, and managing the versions of documents and document metadata.
- **Content Organizer:** Enabling the Content Organizer feature will add the Content Organizer Settings and Content Organizer Rules that were covered in Chapter 20, "Customizing and Managing Libraries and Lists to Meet Business Requirements."
- **Following Content:** Enables users to follow documents or sites. If users choose to follow documents, sites, or tags, conversations on sites, notifications of tag use, and other information will show up in their newsfeeds.
- **Hold:** This enhanced eDiscovery feature is used to track external actions like litigations, investigations, or audits that require the suspension of the disposition of documents. In-place holds can be placed on SharePoint sites or mailboxes, and if content is modified or deleted, a copy of the unmodified data is made and moved to a library that is invisible to end users.
- **Metadata Navigation and Filtering:** This allows the use of metadata tree view hierarchies and filter controls to enhance navigation within lists and libraries. This topic is covered in Chapter 22.
- **Performance Point Services Site Features:** This site feature depends on the Site Collection feature. If both are active, the PerformancePoint Services list and document library templates are enabled. These include the Dashboards Library, DataConnections Library for PerformancePoint, and PerformancePoint Content list.

- **Project Functionality:** This feature adds project management functionality to a site. It includes tasks, a calendar, and web parts on the home page of the site (such as the Project Summary timeline).
- **SharePoint Server Enterprise Site Features:** Features included only in the Enterprise license are enabled via this feature for the site, including Visio Services, Access Services, and Excel Services Application.
- **SharePoint Server Publishing:** This powerful feature is simplistically described on the Site Features page as providing the ability to create a web page library and supporting libraries to create and publish pages based on page layouts. This is only the tip of the iceberg, because a publishing site is very different, in many ways, from a "nonpublishing" site. Publishing sites are created using Publishing Portal, Enterprise Wiki, or Product Catalog site collection templates, or a nonpublishing site can have the SharePoint Server Publishing feature enabled. It is strongly recommended that the organization evaluate whether publishing site collections or nonpublishing site collections (or a combination) best meet the goals for the SharePoint implementation.
- **SharePoint Server Standard Site Features:** Features such as user profiles and search, included in the SharePoint Server Standard License. Note that this feature is not part of SharePoint Foundation 2013, so it includes features that are added on top of SharePoint Foundation 2013.
- **Site Feed:** Enables the use of site feeds, which provide newsfeed functionality to a specific group of users and are available on a variety of sites by default. The sites must consume the same User Profile Service application as My Sites.
- **Site Mailbox:** The Site Mailbox app connects the site to an Exchange mailbox. This enables users to view their email on SharePoint and view site documents in Outlook. A number of prerequisites are required, however: Exchange Server 2013 is required, the Exchange Web Services application programming interface (API) must be installed on the SharePoint server, user profile synchronization must be configured in the farm, the app management service application must be configured in the farm, and Secure Sockets Layer (SSL) must be configured for the default zone.
- **Workflow Task Content Type:** Adds the SharePoint 2013 Workflow Task content type to the site.
- **Workflows can use app permissions:** Allow workflows to read from and to write to all items in this site. This feature does not activate unless the SharePoint 2013 Workflow platform and apps for SharePoint are properly configured.

The following are the standard site collection features provided with SharePoint Foundation 2013:

- **Custom Site Collection Help:** Creates a Help library that can be used to store custom help for this site collection.

- **Open Documents in Client Application:** Configures links to documents so that they open in client applications instead of web applications, by default.
- **Search Server Web Parts and Templates:** This feature adds the Search Server Web Parts and Display Templates to your site. Search works on most sites without this feature being activated. If a message about missing templates when searching appears, activating this feature may resolve the issue.
- **Three-State Workflow:** When active, enables the three-state workflow for use in the site collection. A list must have a column that has at least three different "states" (such as Active, Ready for Review, Complete) for the workflow to function properly.

The following are the standard site collection features added with SharePoint Enterprise 2013:

- **Content Deployment Source Feature:** Enables content deployment specific checks on source site collection and enables setting up content deployment from the site collection to a target site collection. When enabled, a link for Content Deployment Source Status is added in the Site Collection Administration section on the Site Settings page. Clicking this link shows the errors that will prevent successful content deployment from the site collection, as shown in Figure 21.31. These errors must be rectified to ensure a successful content deployment.

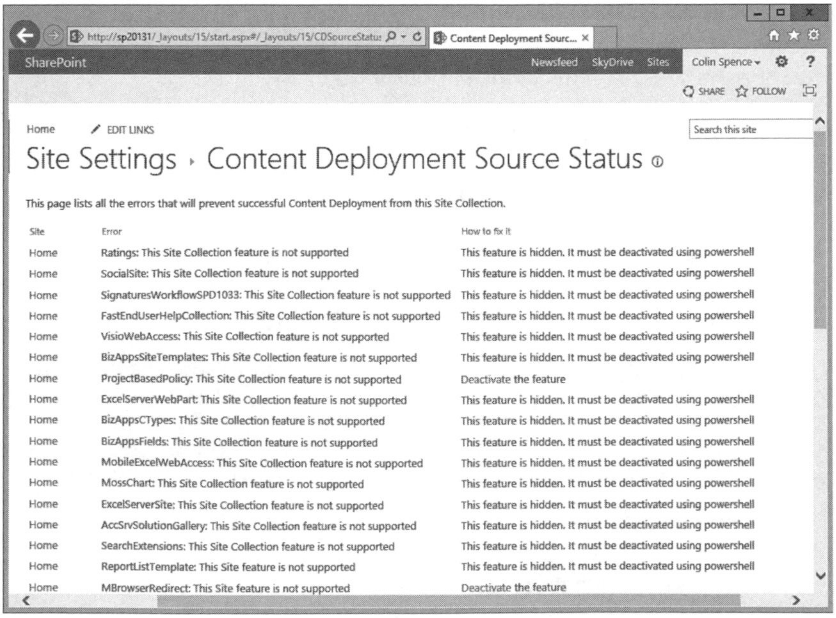

FIGURE 21.31 Content Deployment Source Status page.

- **Content Type Syndication Hub:** Provisions a site to be an enterprise metadata hub site, as covered in Chapter 22.
- **Cross-Farm Site Permissions:** Allows internal SharePoint applications to access websites across farms.
- **Cross-Site Collection Publishing:** Enables site collection to designate lists and document libraries as catalog sources for cross-site collection publishing. Because content will be reused across site collections, there must be at least two site collections (one for authoring content and one for publishing content). The Cross-Site Collection Publishing feature must be enabled on the authoring site collection. If the Product Catalog Site Collection template is used to create the site collection, the Cross-Site Collection Publishing feature will already be active.
- **Disposition Approval Workflow:** Enables the disposition approval workflow, which manages document expiration and retention by allowing participants to decide whether to retain or delete expired documents.
- **Document ID Service:** Assigns IDs to documents in the site collection, which can be used to retrieve items independent of their current location. When enabled, this adds a Document ID Settings link under the Site Collection Administration section. This provides access to several settings, where assign document IDs can be turned on or off, and a field lets the administrator define the prefix (4–12 characters) that will be used for document IDs in the site collection. A check box allows administrators to reset all document IDs in this site collection to begin with these characters. It is generally recommended that the document ID prefix be linked to the name or the site collection to enable tracking of documents that might be moved in the future.
- **Document Sets:** When active, this enables document sets to be used, as covered in Chapter 20, in the "Document Sets Compared to Folders as Organizational Tools in Document Libraries" section.
- **In Place Records Management:** Enables the definition and declaration of records in place. When configured, a link for Record Declaration Settings is added in the Site Collection Administration section of the Site Settings page. This provides settings in the areas of Record Restrictions, Record Declaration Availability, and Declaration Roles, as shown in Figure 21.32. For example, the administrator may choose the option where records Cannot Be Edited or Deleted and that record declaration is Available in All Locations by Default.
- **Library and Folder-Based Retention:** Allows list administrators to override content type retention schedules and set schedules on libraries and folders.
- **Limited-Access User Permission Lockdown Mode:** When this feature is enabled, permissions for users in the "limited access" permissions level (such as anonymous users) are reduced, preventing access to application pages.
- **PerformancePoint Services Site Collection Features:** Enables the PerformancePoint Services site, including content types and site definitions for this site collection.

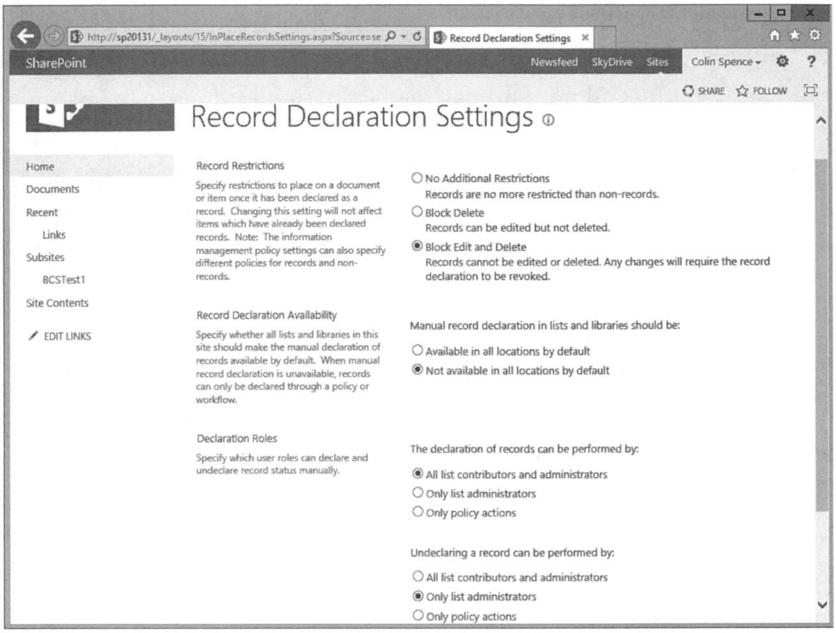

FIGURE 21.32 Record Declaration Settings page.

- **Publishing Approval Workflow:** A key component of a publishing site collection, this workflow routes pages for approval. Approvers can approve or reject the page, reassign the approval task, or request changes to the page. This is enabled by default on the publishing site collection templates as well as BI Center, Enterprise Search, and Visio Process Repository.
- **Reporting:** Creates reports about information in Microsoft SharePoint Foundation.
- **Reports and Data Search Support:** Provides content types, site columns, and library templates required to support Reports and Data Search in the Enterprise Search Center.
- **Search Engine Sitemap:** This feature automatically generates a search engine sitemap on a recurring basis that contains all valid URLs in a SharePoint website. Anonymous access must be enabled to use this feature.
- **SharePoint 2007 Workflows:** This enables a set of out-of-the-box workflow features provided by SharePoint 2007, which is usually only needed for backward compatibility purposes.
- **SharePoint Server Enterprise Site Collection Features:** Features only included in the Enterprise license are enabled via this feature for the site collection, including Visio Services, Access Services, and Excel Services Application.

- **SharePoint Server Publishing Infrastructure:** Provides centralized libraries, content types, master pages, and page layouts, and enables page scheduling and other publishing functionality for a site collection. See the description earlier for SharePoint Server Publishing under Site Features.
- **SharePoint Server Standard Site Collection features:** See the description earlier for SharePoint Server Standard Site Features under Site Features.
- **Site Policy:** Allows site collection administrators to define retention schedules that apply to a site and all its content. See the Site Policies bullet earlier in the "An Overview of Site Collection Administration Tools" section.
- **Video and Rich Media:** Provides libraries, content types, and web parts for storing, managing, and viewing rich media assets such as images, sound clips, and videos.
- **Workflows:** Aggregated set of out-of-the-box workflow features provided by SharePoint.

Summary

This chapter took on the challenging task of covering the tools that site collection administrators and site administrators need to be comfortable with if they are to effectively plan, design, build, and support site collections. The process of creating a site collection was reviewed briefly, and recommendations were given on how the administrator can review the scope of the site collection to thoroughly understand the scope of the administrative challenge. One of these challenges involves controlling who can create sites within the site collection. Then the process of creating pages and sites was discussed and demonstrated, and a full list of the site template options in the full range of the SharePoint 2013 product was provided; this included notes on the functionality and distinguishing features of each item. The wide range of tools available on the Site Settings page was reviewed; but because of the sheer number of items, in many cases, only high-level descriptions were given. Site features and site collection features were covered, as well, once again from a high level.

Best Practices

The following are best practices from this chapter:

- The site collection administrator needs to understand the differences between creating a site collection, which is done from the Central Administration site, creating sites, which can be done in a variety of ways from within the site collection, and creating pages, which can also be done in a variety of ways from within sites and libraries.
- The Site Settings page contains myriad tools that the site collection and site administrators should be conversant with. The tools shown vary based on the site collection features, site features enabled, and the version of SharePoint 2013 installed.

- A site collection administrator taking over an existing site collection should thoroughly review the subsites that exist in the site collection and any managed paths that contain additional site collections. The Site Settings page offers the Sites and Workspaces link that shows subsites, document workspaces, and meeting workspaces; it also provides the Site Hierarchy link that shows all subsites. However, the Site Collection List should be visited from the Central Administration site to see whether managed paths exist, which can contain additional site collections, each of which can have any number of subsites.
- Administrators should review which permission levels have the ability to create sites and workspaces in the environment. This is done by accessing Site Settings, Sites and Workspaces, and then clicking Site Creation Permissions. Also, Self-Service Site Creation settings should be checked from the Central Administration site, Security page, by clicking Configure Self-Service Site Creation.
- Another area a site collection administrator needs to be familiar with is the Users and Permissions section in the Site Settings page, and especially the Site Permissions interface and the permissions that are granted by default to the standard SharePoint Groups, especially Owners, Members, and Visitors, because these are the most widely used groups.

CHAPTER 22

Managing Metadata and Content Types in SharePoint 2013

IN THIS CHAPTER

- Effectively Using Metadata in Lists and Libraries
- Working with Metadata in a Word Document and Document Libraries
- Reviewing the Column Choices in SharePoint 2013
- Differences in Multiple Lines of Text Columns in Libraries and Lists
- Working with Lookup Columns in Document Libraries
- Setting Metadata Standards with Default Values
- Site Columns Practical Applications
- Content Types Practical Applications
- Creating and Using Managed Metadata
- Content Type Syndication Hubs
- Metadata as a Navigation Aid

Metadata has been mentioned many times in this book in previous chapters. This chapter provides a thorough overview of the different ways that metadata can be created and managed, starting with the creation of columns in lists and libraries and then to site columns and content types. Finally, managed metadata is discussed, along with ways in which it facilitates the metadata management process.

Instead of spending a lot of time on the theory of metadata and creating taxonomies that involve metadata, a hands-on approach is taken in this chapter. A number of step-by-step exercises are provided, and going through these steps is a key component in the learning process. The sections in this chapter build upon each other, so it is strongly recommended that the exercises be done in order for the latter exercises to make sense for new SharePoint administrators.

Effectively Using Metadata in Lists and Libraries

Essentially, metadata is "data about data," and even users who don't use SharePoint have experience with it every day. Any file created has some metadata associated with it. For example, a simple Microsoft Word document needs to have a filename, which is a key piece of metadata. In addition, it has a creation date and last modified date, and then Microsoft Word allows users to add additional metadata to the document. SharePoint 2013 exposes this basic metadata that is embedded in the document and allows administrators to add new metadata columns in document libraries that store the files.

Lists are essentially nothing but metadata, unless one or more attachments are added to an item in a list. Administrators and power users will very quickly become accustomed to adding metadata columns when working with lists.

This section starts with an investigation into the interaction between metadata stored in a Word 2010 document and the library that ends up housing that document. Following this, a high-level walkthrough is provided, covering the column choices included in SharePoint 2013. The chapter then provides tips and notes on certain column types, and then a number of exercises help administrators and power users gain hands-on experience with metadata.

Working with Metadata in a Word Document and Document Libraries

The following section and step-by-step exercises provide a thought-provoking introduction to the functionality of metadata in SharePoint 2013 and the interaction of SharePoint with the embedded metadata in a Word document. By following these steps, an administrator will gain a better understanding of the interaction between SharePoint 2013 document libraries and the documents that will be stored in them, and will probably want to perform additional testing to further master the topic.

This exercise walks an administrator through the process of creating two different document libraries that contain different metadata columns and the process of accessing the properties for a Word 2010 document, populating metadata within the document, and then uploading the document and adding additional metadata. The document is then moved to the second document library, where some of the metadata appears to be lost but is, in fact, still contained within the Word document.

NOTE

Microsoft Word 2010 was used for this example since more organizations use the Office 2010 products than the Office 2013 products at the time this was written. Other versions of Word may be used for this exercise, whether older or newer, but the steps will vary slightly.

To complete the exercise, follow these steps:

1. Create a new document library on a SharePoint 2013 site. Leave the settings at their defaults. Title it **Metadata Test 1**. Steps for creating a new document library are provided in Chapter 20, "Customizing and Managing Libraries and Lists to Meet Business Requirements," in the "Creating Lists and Libraries" section.
2. Click the Library tab, and click the Create Column icon.
3. Name the column **Subject**, choose Single Line of Text, leave the rest of the settings at their defaults, and click OK.
4. Click the Library tab, and click the Create Column icon again.

5. This time, name the column **Project Name**, and choose Choice (menu to choose from) as the column type. In the Type Each Choice on a Separate Line box, delete the default entries and add **Project ABC**, **Project DEF**, and **Project GHI**, as shown in Figure 22.1. Clear the Default Value field, leave the other fields at their defaults, and click OK.

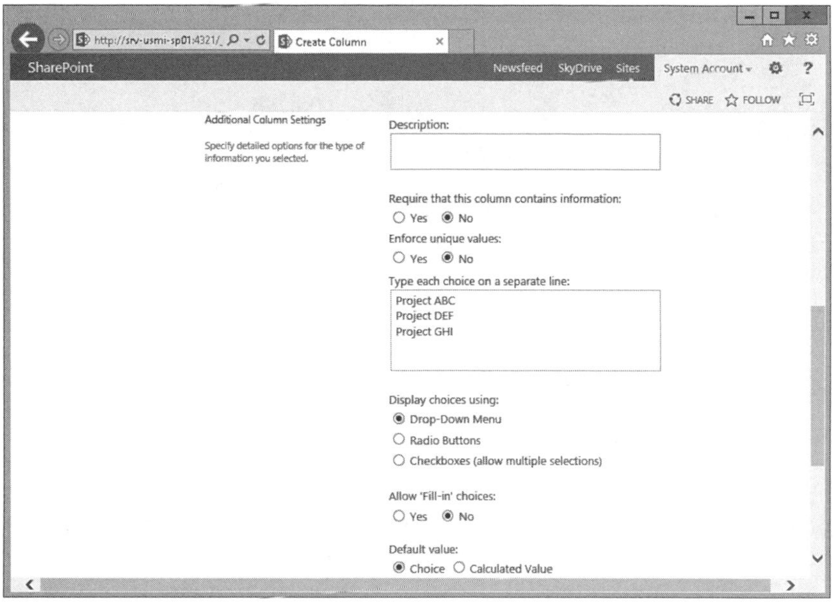

FIGURE 22.1 Creating a choice column.

6. Create a second document library, title it **Metadata Test 2**, and add the column titled **Subject** to it, as well, but do not add the Project Name column.

7. Next, create a new Word 2010 document and enter some sample text.

8. Click the File tab, click the Info link on the left side, and then click the Properties drop-down menu on the right side and select Show Document Panel.

9. The Document Panel now appears for the document. Enter a value into the Subject field (for example, **Mission Statement**), and the results will look like Figure 22.2.

10. Now click the Save icon, save the document locally to My Documents, and close the document. For this example, the document is saved as **Mission_Statement_for_Project_ABC**.

11. Navigate to the Metadata Test 1 document library and upload the document by clicking the Upload Document button on the File tab of the ribbon, then the Browse button, and locating the document, click Open, and then click OK. Alternatively, the New Document link underneath the ribbon can be used.

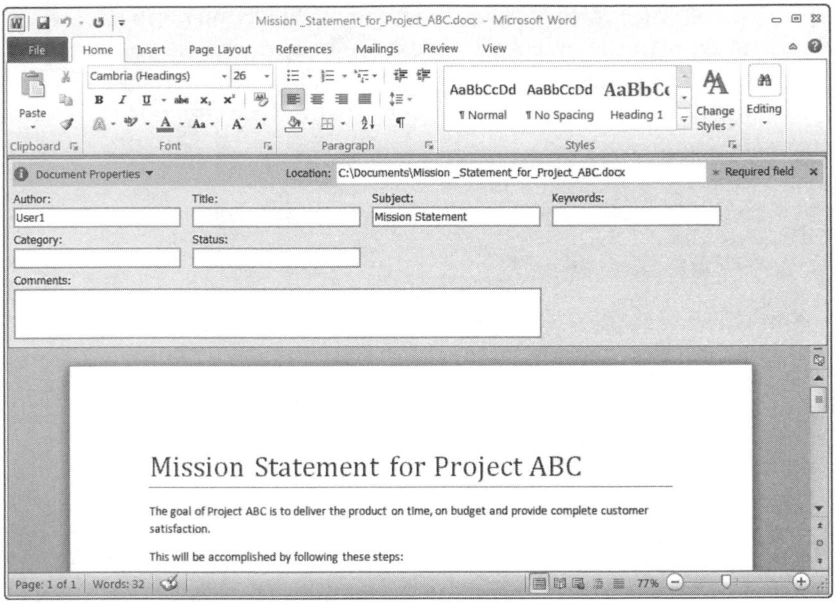

FIGURE 22.2 Entering metadata in Word 2010.

12. As shown in Figure 22.3, the upload window prompts for additional metadata, including the Title field, Subject field, and Project Name drop-down list. Recall that Subject and Project Name were added in steps 3 to 5. Note that content is already populated in the Subject field. This is because the Word document has a metadata field defined within the document named Subject in which text was entered from Word in step 9. Select Project ABC in the drop-down menu next to Project Name. Click Save.

13. The document now appears in the document library Metadata Test 1 with several metadata columns populated: the Name column, which contains the filename of the document; the Modified column, which contains the date and time the file was last modified (the date and time it was uploaded to the document library) and modified by information; and the Subject and Project Name metadata columns that were added in this exercise.

14. Next, the document is moved to the second document library that was created. To accomplish this, click the Library tab, click the Open with Explorer button, and a new window opens, showing the contents of Metadata Test 1 document library.

NOTE

The Open with Explorer button might be grayed out if a 64-bit version of Internet Explorer (IE) is being used. The control might also be unavailable in non-IE browsers.

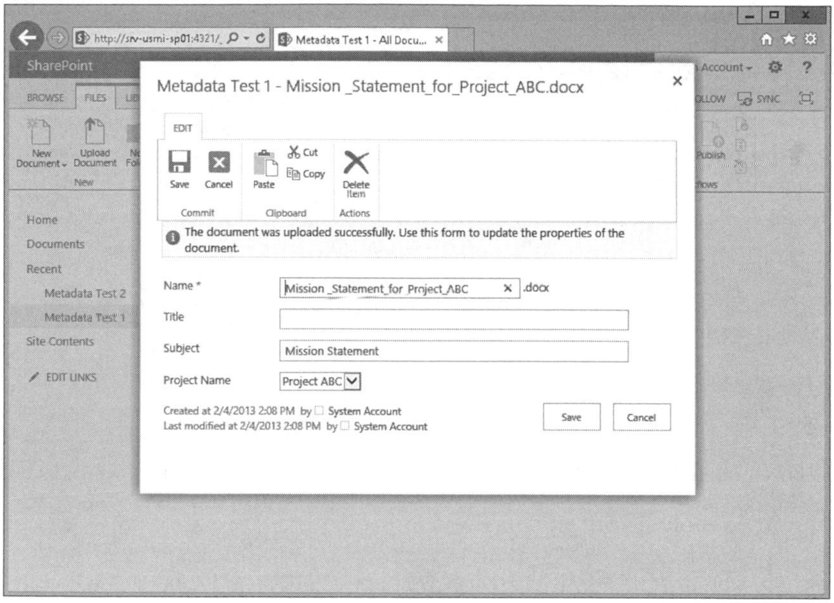

FIGURE 22.3 Adding metadata to the document on upload.

15. Return to SharePoint and navigate to Metadata Test 2 library that was created in step 6, click the Library tab, and click the Open with Explorer button.

16. Click the document in the Explorer window for Metadata Test 1 and drag it to the Explorer window for Metadata Test 2. This moves the document from Metadata Test 1 library to Metadata Test 2.

17. Navigate to the Metadata Test 2 library and the document appears as shown in Figure 22.4. The Subject column is populated, but there is no Project Name column. A valid question to ask at this point is this: What happened to the metadata in the Project Name column?

18. To answer this question, select the document from the Metadata Test 2 library and click the ellipsis to open the menu, click Edit, and it opens in Word.

19. Click the File tab, click the Info link on the left side, and then click the Properties drop-down menu on the right side and select Show Document Panel.

20. This time, the Document Panel displays the Server properties information by default because the document is being opened from a SharePoint document library. Notice that the Subject field is populated, but there is no Project Name field visible because that metadata column does not exist in the document library (Metadata Test 2) it was opened from.

21. To find the Project Name metadata, click the drop-down menu next to Document Properties – Server and choose Advanced Properties from the list. The Advanced Properties window opens.

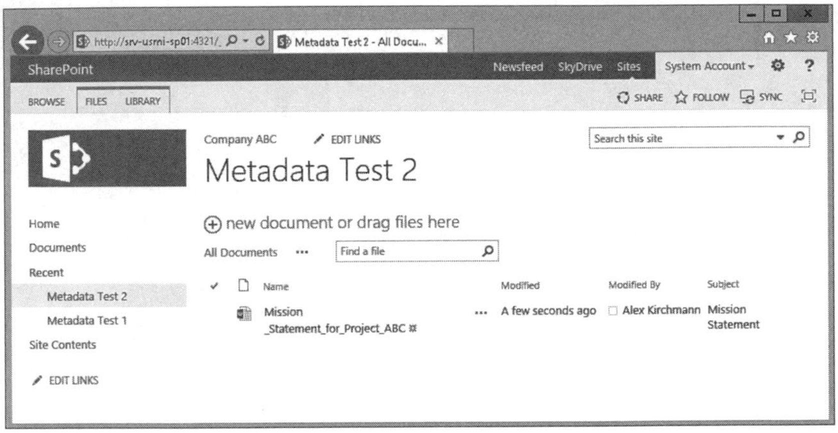

FIGURE 22.4 Document copied to second document library without the Project Name metadata field.

22. Click the Custom tab, and note that Project Name appears in the Properties window, with the value Company ABC (as shown in Figure 22.5), which was added to the document in step 12.

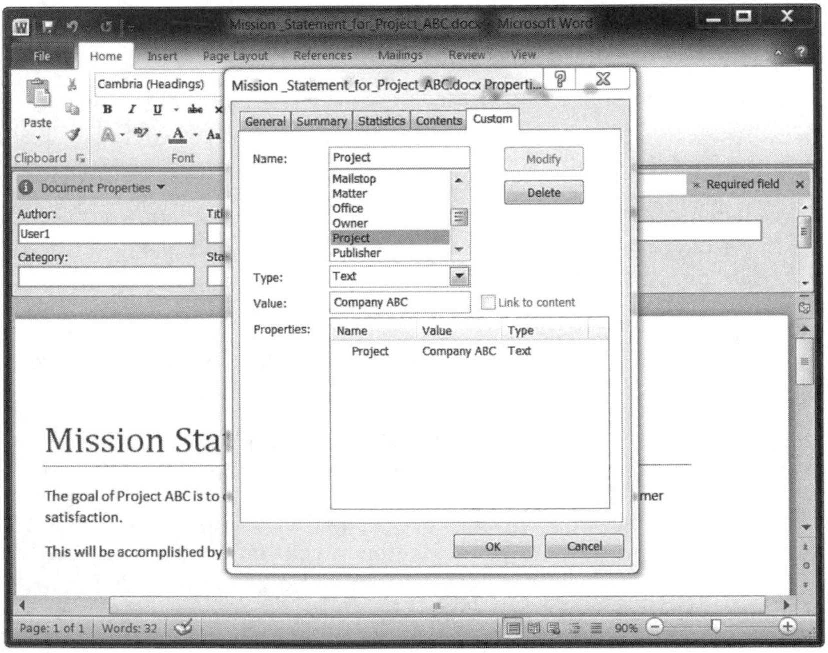

FIGURE 22.5 Advanced Properties, Custom tab showing metadata exists in the Word document.

A natural question at this point is this: How do non-Microsoft Office documents behave in similar tests? The administrator should experiment with different types of files, such as a PDF file, for example.

Reviewing the Column Choices in SharePoint 2013

A powerful feature of SharePoint 2013 lists and libraries is the ability for an administrator to customize the list or library in many ways, one of which is to add columns, similar to the process of adding a column in Excel. This is accomplished from the Document Library Settings page, which is reached by entering the document library, clicking the Library tab on the ribbon, and then clicking the Library Settings icon on the right side of the toolbar. Only users with the manage lists permission are able to click the Library Settings icon; it is grayed out for other users. By default, members of the Owners, Designers, and Hierarchy Managers groups have the "manage lists" permissions.

On the document library Settings page, the Columns section is found midway down the page, and provides the options of Create Column, Add from Existing Site Columns, Column Ordering, and Indexed Columns. If Create Column is clicked, the administrator has a selection of columns to choose from, which vary slightly based on the version of SharePoint 2013 in use because SharePoint Foundation 2013 does not offer the Managed Metadata option. Descriptions of these columns are as follows:

- **Single line of text:** Has the following options: Description (text), Require That This Column Contains Information (Yes or No), Enforce Unique Values (Yes or No), Maximum Number of Characters, Default Value (Text or Calculated Value), Add to All Content Types (Yes or No), and Add to Default View (Yes or No).
- **Multiple lines of text:** Has the following options: Description (text), Require That This Column Contains Information (Yes or No), Allow Unlimited Length in Document Libraries (Yes or No), Number of Lines for Editing (Integer), Add to All Content Types (Yes or No), and Add to Default View (Yes or No).
- **Choice (menu to choose from):** Has the following options: Description (text), Require That This Column Contains Information (Yes or No), Enforce Unique Values (Yes or No), Type Each Choice on a Separate Line, Display Choices Using (Drop-Down Menu, Radio Buttons, Checkboxes [Allow Multiple Selections]), Allow Fill-in Choices (Yes or No), Default Value (Text or Calculated Value), Add to All Content Types (Yes or No), and Add to Default View (Yes or No).
- **Number:** Has the following options: Description (text), Require That This Column Contains Information (Yes or No), Enforce Unique Values (Yes or No), Specify a Minimum and Maximum Allowed Value (Two Integers), Number of Decimal Places (Integer), Default Value (Number or Calculated Value), Show as a Percentage (for example, 50%), Add to All Content Types (Yes or No), and Add to Default View (Yes or No).
- **Currency:** Has the following options: Description (text), Require That This Column Contains Information (Yes or No), Enforce Unique Values (Yes or No), Specify a Minimum and Maximum Allowed Value (Two Integers), Number of Decimal Places

(Integer), Default Value (Currency or Calculated Value), Currency Format (for example, United States), Add to All Content Types (Yes or No), and Add to Default View (Yes or No).

- **Date and Time:** Has the following options: Description (text), Require That This Column Contains Information (Yes or No), Enforce Unique Values (Yes or No), Date and Time Format (Date Only, Date & Time), Default Value (None, Today's Date, Date in M/D/YYYY format) or Calculated Value, Add to All Content Types (Yes or No), and Add to Default View (Yes or No).
- **Lookup (information already on this site):** Has the following options: Description (text), Require That This Column Contains Information (Yes or No), Enforce Unique Values (Yes or No), Get Information From (drop-down menu to select list or library), In This Column (drop-down menu to select the column), Allow Multiple Values (Yes, No), Allow Unlimited Length in Document Libraries (Yes, No), Add a Column to Show Each of These Additional Fields (Title, Expires, ID, Modified, Created, Version, Title [linked to item]), Add to All Content Types (Yes or No), Add to Default View (Yes or No), and Enforce Relationship Behavior (Restrict Delete, Cascade Delete).
- **Yes/No (check box):** Has the following options: Description (text), Default Value (Yes or No), Add to All Content Types (Yes or No), and Add to Default View (Yes or No).
- **Person or Group:** Has the following options: Description (text), Default Value (Yes or No), Require That This Column Contains Information (Yes or No), Allow Multiple Selections (Yes or No), Allow Selection Of (People Only, People, and Groups), Choose From (All Users, SharePoint Group), Show Field (ID, Name, Modified, Created, Account, Email, Mobile Number, SIP Address, Department, Job Title, Name [with Presence], Name [with Picture], Name [with Picture and Details], Content Type), Add to All Content Types (Yes or No), and Add to Default View (Yes or No).
- **Hyperlink or Picture:** Has the following options: Description (text), Require That This Column Contains Information (Yes or No), Format URL As (Hyperlink, Picture), Add to All Content Types (Yes or No), and Add to Default View (Yes or No).
- **Calculated (calculation based on other columns):** Has the following options: Description (text), Formula, Insert Column (shows valid columns to add to the formula), The Data Returned from This Formula Is (Single Line of Text, Number, Currency, Date and Time, Yes/No), Add to All Content Types (Yes or No), and Add to Default View (Yes or No).
- **Task Outcome:** Has the following options: Description (text), Require That This Column Contains Information (Yes or No), Enforce Unique Values (Yes or No), Type Each Choice on a Separate Line, Default Value (Text or Calculated Value), and Add to Default View (Yes or No).
- **External Data:** Has the following options: Description (text), Require That This Column Contains Information (Yes or No), External Content Type, Select the Field

to Be Shown on This Column, Display the Actions Menu (Yes or No), Link This Column to the Default Action of the External Content Type (Yes or No), Add to All Content Types (Yes or No), and Add to Default View (Yes or No).

NOTE

External data is discussed in Chapter 31, "Business Intelligence in SharePoint 2013 with Business Connectivity Services," and an example is given of creating an External Content type to connect to an AdventureWorks database using SharePoint Designer 2013 as well as using the External Data column type. After the External Content type is created, it can be selected from the External Data column settings. Note that a number of steps are required that are also discussed in Chapter 31, including installing the AdventureWorks database. The main difference between an external list and a regular SharePoint list is that the actual contents of the external list live outside SharePoint lists or libraries.

- **Managed Metadata:** Has the following options: Description (text), Require That This Column Contains Information (Yes or No), Enforce Unique Values (Yes or No), Add to All Content Types (Yes or No), Add to Default View (Yes or No), Allow Multiple Values (Yes or No), Display Value (Display Term Label in the Field or Display the Entire Path to the Term in the Field), Use a Managed Term Set (Find and Reset buttons) or Customize Your Term Set, Allow Fill-in Choices (Yes or No), and Default Value (Browse button). (Managed metadata is covered later in this chapter in more depth.)

With this wide range of choices, it should be obvious that an incredible number of combinations can be created to meet business needs. This chapter provides examples of several different column types, but an administrator should become familiar with the capabilities of the different columns through personal experience, trial and error, and by taking the effort to meet specific end-user and business requirements through lists and libraries.

NOTE

Restraint should be used when creating more complex lists and libraries that involve dozens or even hundreds of columns as SharePoint lists and libraries have limits on how many of each type of column can be supported in any given list or library. TechNet offers an overview of column limits in the article titled "Software Boundaries and Limits for SharePoint 2013" in the "Column Limits" section (http://technet.microsoft.com/en-us/library/cc262787.aspx#Column). A table clearly lists the type of column (such as Single Line of Text), the maximum value (for example, 276 for number of Single Line of Text columns), and provides additional descriptive information.

For example, it is not unusual for an organization to want to move away from a very complex Excel spreadsheet and leverage a SharePoint 2013 list instead. Some spreadsheets have hundreds of columns in one worksheet, and although a SharePoint 2013 list can replicate this design, this can result in the SQL database requiring multiple rows to store the data and a slowdown in performance.

An Introduction and Practical Application of Calculated Columns

Calculated columns are enticing and powerful, but can be frustrating to use without some background. A starting rule of thumb is this: If it works in Excel, it probably works in SharePoint. SharePoint, unfortunately, has a wide range of restrictions when compared to Excel, so this rule should be understood with a dose of healthy skepticism.

Some important rules and guidelines are as follows:

- Arithmetic operators supported include + (addition), – (subtraction), * (multiplication), / (division), % (percent), and ^ (exponentiation).
- Parentheses are supported in equations.
- Comparison operators supported include = (equal to), > (greater than), < (less than), >= (greater than or equal to), <= (less than or equal to), and <> (not equal to).
- & (ampersand) connects two values to produce one continuous text value.
- Lists and libraries do not support the RAND and NOW functions.
- The TODAY and ME functions are not supported in calculated columns but are supported in the default value setting of a column.
- You cannot reference a value in a row other than the current row.
- You cannot reference a value in another list or library.
- Many Excel functions are supported in SharePoint calculated columns, but testing should be performed to verify functionality.

This is an example that adds a calculated column to see whether the profit on an item exceeds the goal of a 10% profit. A new list is created and several columns added to it, one of which is a calculated column. Then some sample items are added to the list and the calculated column works its magic to determine whether the Sell Price exceeds a 10% profit:

1. Create a new list using the Custom List template and name it **CalculatedColumnTest**. Steps for creating a new list are provided in Chapter 20, in the "Creating Lists and Libraries" section.
2. From the CalculatedColumnTest list, click the List tab, and then click List Settings.
3. Scroll down and click the Create Column link.
4. Name the new column **Cost** and check Currency; leave the other settings and click OK.
5. Scroll down and click the Create Column link once more.
6. Name the new column **Sell Price** and check Currency; leave the other settings and click OK.
7. Scroll down and click the Create Column link a third time.

8. Name the new column **Meets Profit Goal** and check Calculated.
9. Scroll down to the Additional Column Settings section, and enter the following formula:

```
=IF(Cost>([Sell Price]-(Cost*(10/100))),"No","Yes")
```

   The `IF` function is described in more detail in Excel 2010 Help, and the syntax is the same in a SharePoint 2013 calculated column. A translation of the syntax is "IF(logical_test, [value_if_true], [value_if_false])." In the case of the formula used in this example, this translates to "If the cost is greater than the sell price minus 10% of the cost, display the value No; if not, display the value Yes."
10. Verify that Single Line of Text is checked below the formula; then leave the other settings at their defaults. Click OK.
11. Click CalculatedColumnTest from the breadcrumb to return to the All Items view of the list.
12. Click the New Item link on the Items tab of the ribbon.
13. Enter a title for the entry, such as **Widget**, enter **20** in the Cost field, enter **22** in the Sell Price field, and click OK.
14. Click the New Item link a second time.
15. Enter a title for the entry, such as **Gadget**, enter **40** in the Cost field, enter **43.99** in the Sell Price field, and click OK.
16. Click the New Item link a third time.
17. Enter a title for the entry, such as **Mousetrap**, enter **60** in the Cost field, enter **66** in the Sell Price field, and click OK.
18. The results will look like Figure 22.6. This makes it easy for a manager to glance at the list and see whether items are being sold at an acceptable level of profit.

TIP

Additional guidance and information is available by accessing SharePoint Help, then entering **introduction to data calculations** in the Search field, and then clicking the Introduction to Data Calculations article title.

Leveraging Validation Settings

Another means of ensuring that the correct data is entered into columns in a list and library is through the use of validation settings, which can be added to the list or library on the List Settings or Library Settings page, or to an individual column. The equations that can be used are more limited, as the result of the equation must equal the value True or the user won't be able to save the entry.

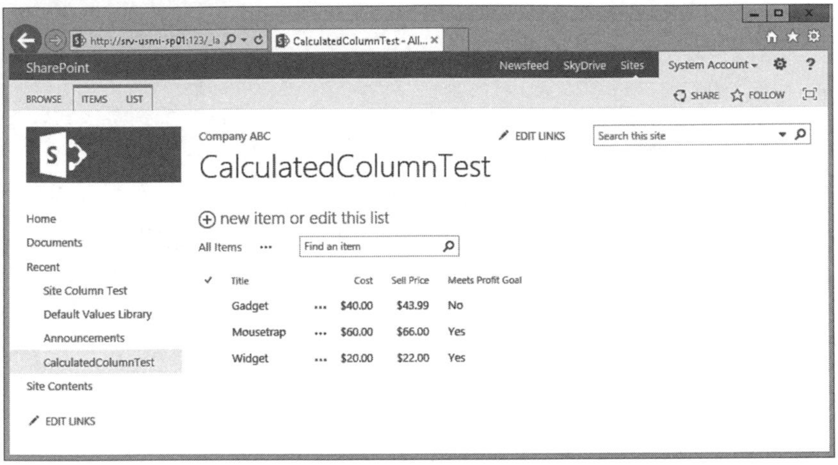

FIGURE 22.6 Example of a list with a calculated column to determine whether a Sell Price meets a profit goal.

A simple example is as follows:

```
=[ColumnA]>[ColumnB]
```

Assuming the value in ColumnA is greater than ColumnB, the formula generates the value True and therefore passes the validation test.

Building on the list created in the previous section, follow these steps to add validation to the CalculatedColumnTest list:

1. Navigate to the CalculatedColumnTest list created in the previous section that contains the columns Title, Cost, and Sell Price, as described in the example, as well as sample data, as shown in Figure 22.6.
2. Click the List tab on the ribbon, and then click Create Column.
3. Enter **Invoice Number** as the column name, and then choose Single Line of Text.
4. Scroll down to the Description field and enter **Enter a valid invoice number starting with "2010-" and then up to 4 digits**.
5. Click "Yes" for Enforce Unique Values.
6. Enter **9** for Maximum Number of Characters.
7. Expand the Column Validation section by clicking the + and enter the following in the Formula field:

```
=FIND("2010-",[Invoice Number], 1)
```

The `FIND` function is also defined in Excel 2010 Help, and the syntax translates to "FIND(find_text, within_text, [start_num])," or in this example to "Find the string 2010- in the column Invoice Number, starting with the first character in the string and the value is True." This logic is pretty hard for a careless or even malicious user to beat because there is a limit of nine characters that can be entered in the field and it must include the string 2010-. Furthermore, the entry must be unique.

8. Finally, enter the following in the User Message field: **Enter a valid invoice number starting with "2010-" and then up to 4 digits** (see Figure 22.7). Click OK to save.

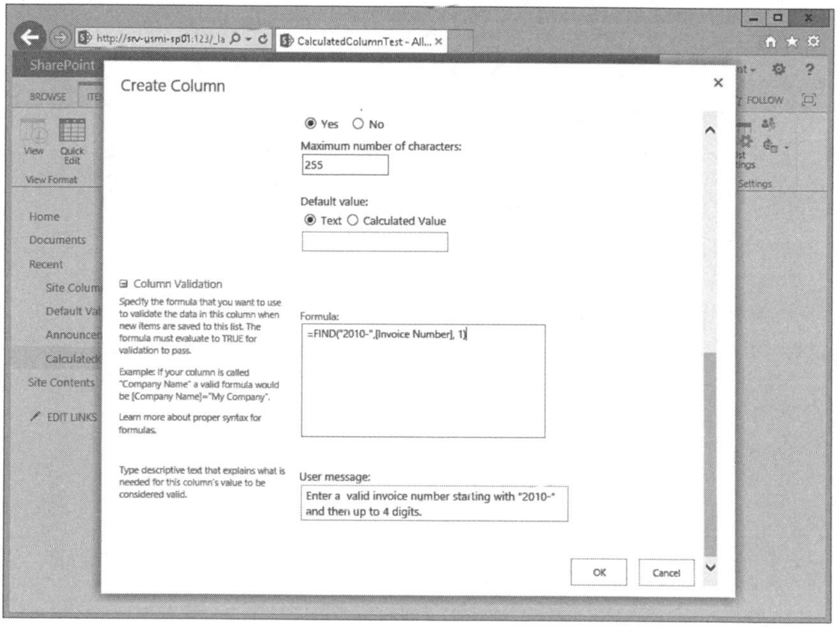

FIGURE 22.7 Column settings for a column using column validation.

9. Click OK to the message stating, "This column must be indexed to enforce unique values. Do you want to index this column?"

10. Click the New Item link and enter the title as **Whoozit**, the Cost as **100**, the Sell Price as **150**, and Invoice Number as **123456789**. Click Save. A red error message displays stating, "The validation formula has evaluated to an error," and then gives additional information as shown in Figure 22.8, because this invoice number doesn't meet the validation.

11. Re-enter the invoice number as **2010-123** and click Save; this time the entry succeeds because it meets the validation requirements.

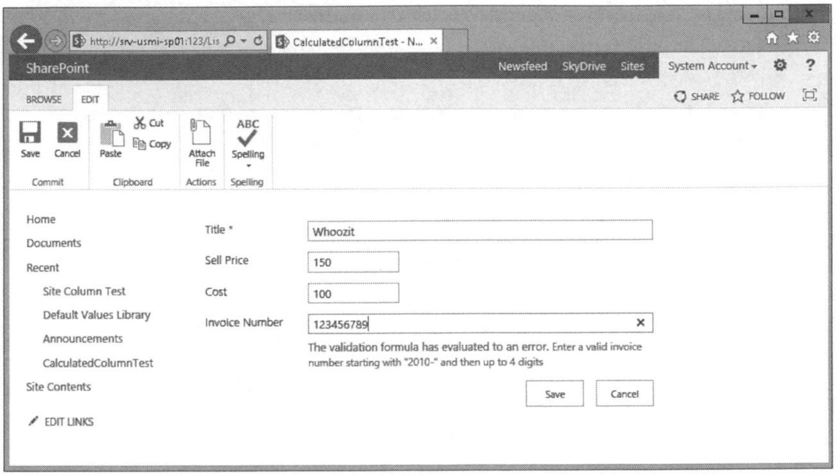

FIGURE 22.8 Validation formula error for a New List item.

Enforcing Unique Values in Columns

Certain column types offer the option to Enforce Unique Values for the column (in the Additional Column Settings portion of the Create Column page). This is a capability that has been requested by many clients over the years, and various workarounds were developed using workflows or leveraging the ID value of the list item. For example, a list that tracks serial numbers, employee IDs, invoices, or many other values is less valuable if data entry errors can lead to nonunique numbers.

Table 22.1 summarizes what column types can and cannot be used to create unique columns.

TABLE 22.1 Unique Column Options

Supported Unique Column Types	Unsupported Unique Column Types
Single line of text	Multiple lines of text
Choice (single value)	Choice (multivalued)
Number	Lookup (multivalued)
Currency	Hyperlink or Picture
Date and Time	Calculated
Lookup (single value)	External Data
Person or Group	Yes/No
Task Outcome	
Managed Metadata	

CAUTION

If Content Approval is enabled for a document library and then unique values are enabled, a warning note displays: "This list or document library has content approval enabled. A column that enforces unique values may let users determine information about a list item or document even if they do not have permission to view it." This is logical because when a user sees an error about the item not being a unique value, she can deduce that there already exists a list item with that value.

Differences in Multiple Lines of Text Columns in Libraries and Lists

An interesting difference exists in the capabilities of the Multiple Lines of Text column when it is used in a library as opposed to when it is used in a list. When a Multiple Lines of Text column is added to a document library, there is an option to Allow Unlimited Length in Document Libraries. If this option is selected, a message displays that states, "Columns with long text are not supported by most applications for editing documents and could result in loss of data. Only remove this limit if users will be uploading documents through the website, and not saving directly from the application." Otherwise, the column configuration is straightforward.

TIP

A major irritation, if unlimited length is not allowed in a document library, is that the end user doesn't know how many characters have been entered because SharePoint does not provide a character counter. Nor is any warning provided until the user clicks Save. So, a user could type his life's story in the text box and click Save only to be told, "This field can have no more than 255 characters." So, a best practice is to add a note about the limitation of 255 characters in the Description field when a Multiple Lines of Text column is added to a document library, and in addition, provide a second Multiple Lines of Text column for document libraries where it is expected that more lengthy descriptions might be needed.

If a Multiple Lines of Text column is created in a list, however, the options are quite different. As shown in Figure 22.9, a Multiple Lines of Text column in a list offers additional options:

- Plain Text
- Enhanced Rich Text (rich text with pictures, tables, and hyperlinks)
- Append Changes to Existing Text

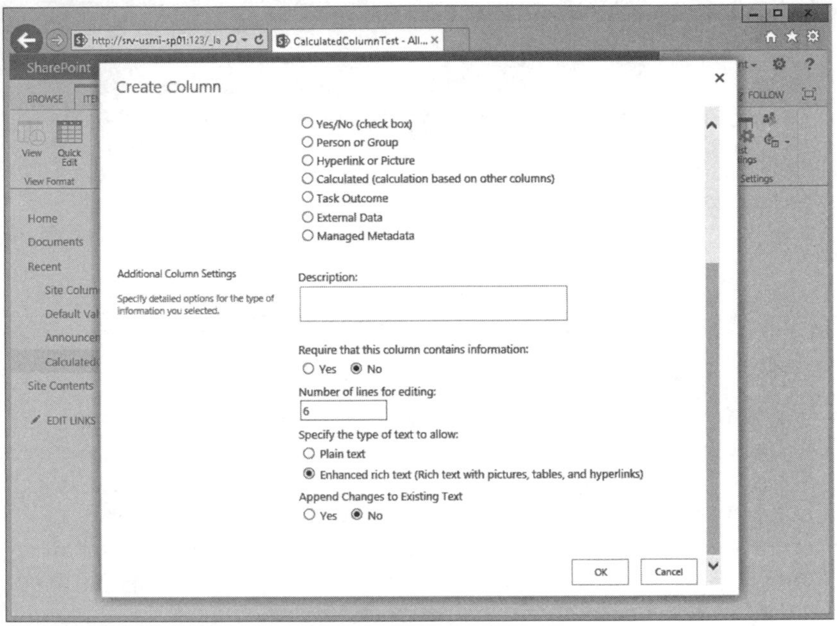

FIGURE 22.9 Additional options for Multiple Lines of Text column in a list.

The options for Multiple Lines of Text columns in lists, which are not available in libraries, clarify a key difference between the two. The metadata attached to documents added to document libraries is meant to be purely informational and textual, whereas the metadata added to lists can be rich text and include pictures, tables, and hyperlinks and therefore is well suited for providing visually complex information and images on a SharePoint page. It is recommended for administrators and power users to experiment with the differences between these different types of Multiple Lines of Text columns, especially to determine the differences between rich text and enhanced rich text.

With regards to the Append Changes to Existing Text option for a Multiple Lines of Text column, versioning must be turned on for the list before it can be enabled. After it is enabled, the changes to the content are tracked and visible to users who view the list item. Figure 22.10 shows an example of an item in an Announcements list (which has versioning enabled) that has been edited by two users. Most likely, this is not the best setting to apply to an Announcements list because what most likely should be behind the scenes editing will become visible to readers.

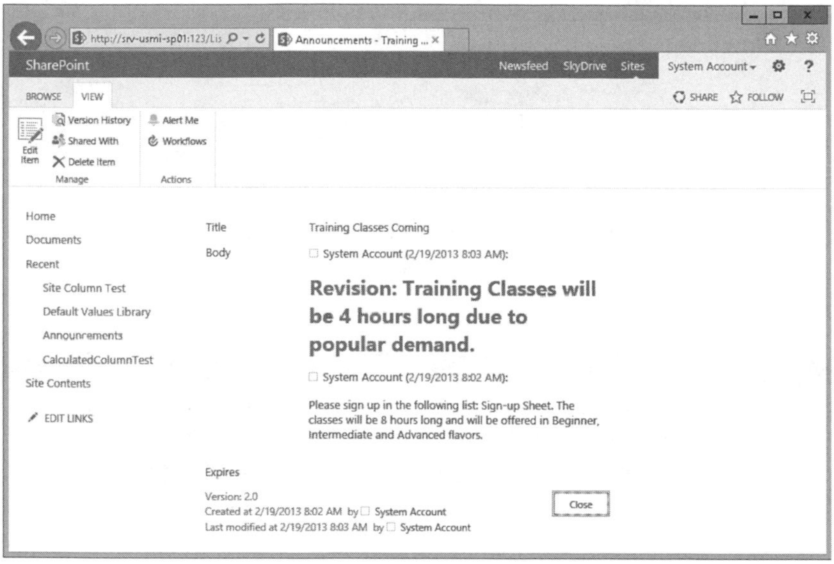

FIGURE 22.10 Example of Append Changes to Existing Text setting for a Multiple Lines of Text column in a list.

Working with Lookup Columns in Document Libraries

This next exercise uses two standard lists in a SharePoint 2013 team site: the Calendar list and the Tasks list. The goal of this example is to show the basic capabilities of the lookup column using a business example where a department tracks tasks using a Tasks list, and has weekly meetings that are managed in the Calendar list. The manager wants to use SharePoint to make the meeting more productive and wants to use the lookup column to pull additional information from the Tasks list into the Calendar list.

Consider the possibility that the Tasks list might have different permissions configured than the Calendar list. For example, on this site, the administrator may only allow project managers to edit the Calendar list, whereas all departmental employees can add to the Tasks list.

Before jumping into the example, some information about the functionality and limitations of the lookup column should be provided. To begin with, only certain column types are available to lookup columns. The following list shows the supported column types:

- Choice (single value)
- Currency
- Date and Time

- External Data
- Lookup (single value)
- Number
- Single Line of Text

If other column types exist in the list that is being connected to with the lookup column, they are not available for selection. This limitation should be kept in mind when planning for the use of lookup columns.

CAUTION

Exceeding eight lookup columns per list view consumes a large amount of SQL resources, which can result in performance degradation when the view is rendered. Although there can be more than eight lookup columns in the list, make sure to limit the number that are included in specific views.

Follow these steps to learn more about the lookup column's functionality:

1. Create a new site using the Team Site template. Instructions for creating a site are provided in Chapter 21, "Designing and Managing Pages and Sites for Knowledge Workers," in the "Creating Pages and Sites" section.
2. Click the Tasks tile with the text Working on a deadline? and this will bring up a window stating that a Tasks list and a Calendar list will be added. Click the Add Them button.
3. Click the Edit link on the new Project Summary web part that has been added to the site home page.
4. Click the List tab on the ribbon, and click the Create Column icon.
5. Title the column **Flags**, and select Single Line of Text as the column type. Leave the other fields on their default values and click OK to save.
6. From the Tasks tab on the ribbon, click New Item. On the New Item page, click the Show More link at the bottom to display all columns where you can enter information, then enter the following content in the appropriate fields:

   Task Name: Enter the text **Lookup Task 1**.

   Start Date: Enter a sample start date in the future.

   End Date: Enter a sample end date that is after the start date.

   Assigned To: Enter a sample username.

   % Complete: Enter 0%.

   Task Status: Not Started.

   Flags: Enter the text **Scope of work not clear**.

Leave the other fields with the default values. Click Save when the data has been entered.

7. After the task is added, click New Item again. Click Show More, and then enter the following content in the appropriate fields:

   Title: Enter the text **Lookup Task 2**.

   Start Date: Enter a sample start date in the past.

   End Date: Enter a sample end date in the future.

   Assigned To: Enter a sample username.

   % Complete: Enter the text 10%.

   Task Status: In Progress.

   Flags: Enter the text **Team lead is on vacation**.

   Leave the other fields with the default values. Click Save when the data has been entered.

8. The task list should look similar to Figure 22.11.

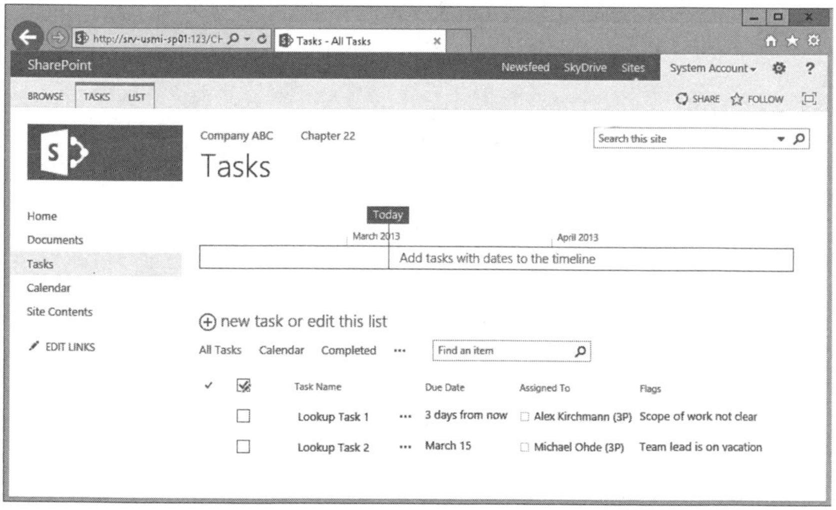

FIGURE 22.11 Tasks list with sample tasks to use in a lookup column.

9. Now click the link to Calendar from the quick launch.
10. Click the Calendar tab on the ribbon, and then click List Settings.
11. Scroll down until the link to Create Column appears, and then click Create Column.
12. Enter **Task Lookup** as the title of the column, and then click Lookup (information already on this site).

13. Scroll down to the Additional Column Settings section, click the drop-down menu under Get Information From, and select Tasks. The page updates to now show the columns that are valid lookup columns.
14. Select Task Name (linked to item) from the list.
15. Check the box next to Allow Multiple Values.
16. Then check the boxes next to % Complete, Start Date, Due Date, and Flags. Leave the other values at their defaults, as shown in Figure 22.12, and click OK.

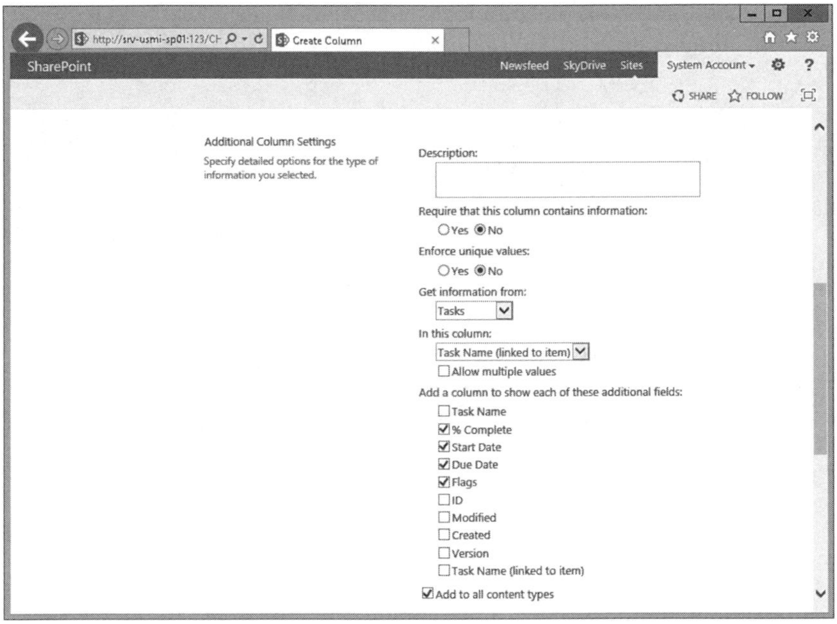

FIGURE 22.12 Settings for the lookup column in the Calendar list.

17. Click Calendar from the breadcrumb trail to return to the Calendar list.
18. Click the Events tab, and then click New Event from the ribbon.
19. Enter the following values in the new event:

    Title: Enter the text **Status Meeting**.

    Location: Enter the text **Meeting Room A**.

    Start Time: Enter a date and time in the next week.

    End Time: Enter a date and time 1 hour after the start time.

    Task Lookup: Click Lookup Task 1 and click the Add button; then click Lookup Task 2 and click the Add button.

    Leave the other fields at their defaults and click Save.

20. The event now appears on the calendar on the date specified. Click the name of the event to see the event details; it should be similar to Figure 22.13. Note that even though only the tasks names were selected, the list item is populated with additional values from the Tasks list: % Complete, Start Date, Due Date, and Flags information is populated. The links to Lookup Task 1 and Lookup Task 2 can be clicked on from this screen to open the tasks to see additional information.

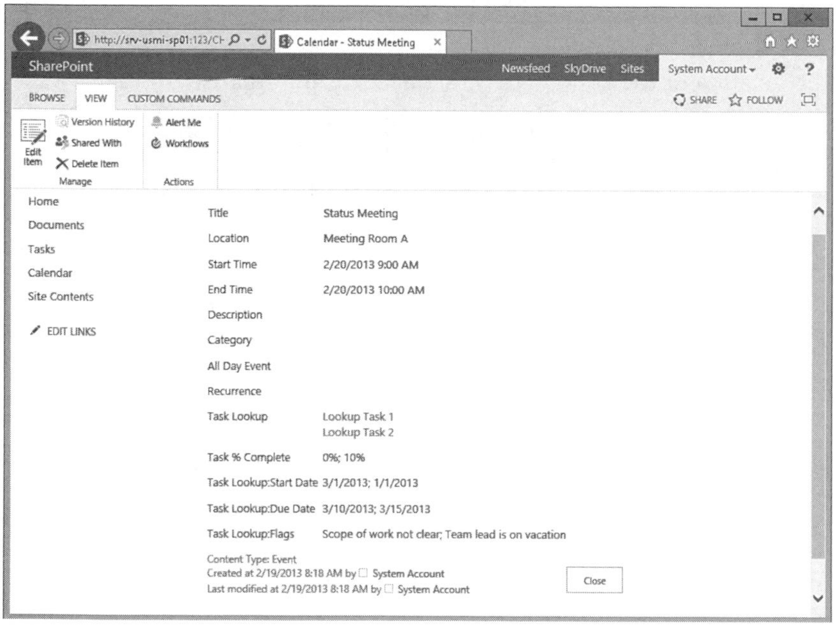

FIGURE 22.13 Calendar event with lookup data values.

21. Close the Calendar item window by clicking Close.

22. From the Calendar, click the Calendar tab, and then click List Settings.

23. Locate the Task Lookup:% Complete column and click it. Change the column name to **Task % Complete** and click OK. Note that the name of the column is now changed without breaking the functionality of the column. So, the administrator can make these lookup column titles more user-friendly than the default names that are assigned.

An additional option provided in a lookup column is Enforce Relationship Behavior. While experimenting with this functionality, it is not unusual to see a message display that states, "This lookup field cannot enforce a relationship behavior because this list contains incompatible fields." The following example provides a case where Enforce Relationship Behavior can be tested.

Testing Enforce Relationship Behavior

To continue the process of understanding lookup columns, the Enforce Relationship Behavior setting needs to be experienced. The example provided in this section leverages an Announcements list and a lookup column to connect to a list of donated items, which makes it easy for an organization to create an announcement when someone offers an item of value to other employees. The Restrict Delete setting is applied to ensure that when the announcement has gone out, the details of the donated item are still available. Restrict Delete means that the child item cannot be deleted because it is related to an item in the "parent" list. Following that configuration, the Cascade Delete option is configured, and in that case, the deletion of the child item causes a deletion of the parent item.

This example scratches the surface of what's possible in enforced relationships between lists but provides a real-world example that can be leveraged in numerous ways within the organization. Database developers will immediately see the similarities between this capability and the types of joins and other interactions possible between database tables and will no doubt be able to leverage lookup columns in many creative ways.

Follow these steps to create two lists and leverage the Enforce Relationship Behavior setting:

1. Create a new site using the Team Site template. Instructions for creating a site are provided in Chapter 21, in the section titled "Creating Pages and Sites."
2. Create a new list using the Custom List template and name it **Donations**. Steps for creating a new list are provided in Chapter 20, in the "Creating Lists and Libraries" section.
3. From the Donations list, click the List tab, and then click List Settings.
4. Scroll down and click the Create Column link.
5. Name the new column **Item Description** and check Single Line of Text; leave the other settings as default and click OK.
6. Return to the list all items view by clicking the list name in the breadcrumb.
7. Click New Item on the Item tab on the ribbon.
8. Enter a title for the entry, such as **Kodak z7590 Camera**, and enter text in the Item Description field such as **5.0 Megapixels, 10x zoom, very portable, works great**.
9. Click Site Contents from the quick launch, and click add an app in the Lists, Libraries, and other Apps section of the page.
10. Select the Announcements tile and then Name the list, **Announcements**.
11. Navigate to the Announcements list, click the List tab, and then click List Settings.
12. Scroll down and click Create Column.
13. Title the column **Donation Lookup** and select the Lookup type of column.

14. In the Additional Column Settings section of the screen, click the drop-down menu under Get Information From, and select Donations. Verify that Title appears in the drop-down menu under In This Column. Check the box next to Item Description in the next section down, as shown in Figure 22.14.

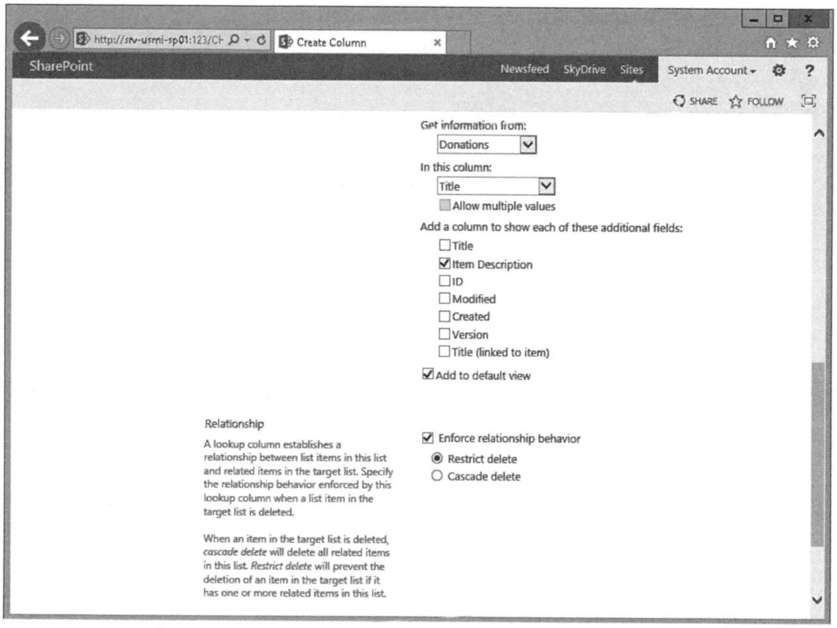

FIGURE 22.14 Selecting the Enforce Relationship Behavior option for a lookup column.

15. Check the box next to Enforce Relationship Behavior, and then select the radio button next to Restrict Delete, as is also shown in Figure 22.14.

16. Click OK. Click OK for the message, "This column must be indexed to enforce a relationship behavior. Do you want to index this column?"

17. Click the Announcements link from the breadcrumb to return to the list.

18. Click the New Announcement link.

19. Enter a title for the announcement (for example, **Generous Donation**). Click the drop-down list in the Donations Lookup field and select Kodak z7590 Camera. Click OK. The result should look like Figure 22.15.

20. Return to the Donation list by clicking its link in the quick launch.

21. Select the list item entered in steps 7 and 8, and then click Delete Item on the ribbon. Click OK to confirm the deletion. An error message appears stating, "Sorry, something went wrong... This item cannot be deleted because an item in the 'Announcements' list is related to an item in the 'Donations' list."

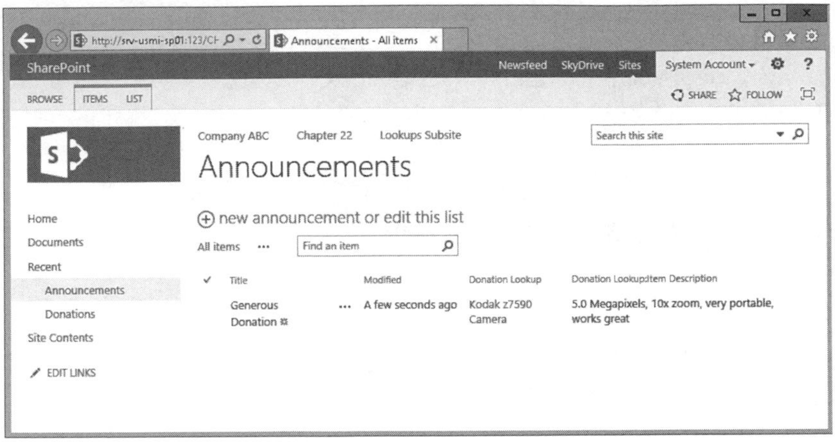

FIGURE 22.15 Announcement with lookup information.

TIP

Use lookup columns with the Enforce Relationship Behavior option and Restrict Delete to ensure that the target item of the lookup can't be deleted if it is referenced by an item in the "parent" list.

22. Next, the lookup column is set to Cascade Delete. Navigate back to the Announcements list.
23. Click the List tab, and then click List Settings.
24. Scroll down to the Columns section and click Donations Lookup column.
25. Scroll down to the Relationship section, and this time select Cascade Delete. Click OK.
26. Navigate to the Donations list.
27. Select the list item entered in steps 7 and 8, and then click Delete Item on the ribbon. Click OK to confirm the deletion. An error message appears stating, "Sending this item to the site Recycle Bin will also send any related items in the following lists to the site Recycle Bin: [Announcements]. Are you sure you want to send the item(s) to the site Recycle Bin?" Click OK.
28. Navigate to the Announcement list to verify that the announcement is also deleted.

TIP

When related items are deleted in a Cascade Delete enforced relationship, restoring the child item from the Recycle Bin also restores the related item.

Setting Metadata Standards with Default Values

For the metadata entered to be useful in searches and filters, it is important that it be accurate. List and library administrators can use a variety of methods to control the entries that users provide.

List or library administrators can set default values for metadata when the column is being created, or can return to the list settings page at a later date to change the default values. Setting a default value may not be advisable in some cases because end users who are in a rush, or feeling lazy, may simply leave the default setting when uploading a document. So, consideration should be given to the pros and cons of using default values.

Figure 22.16 shows a section of the settings available for a choice column in a document library. In the Default Value section, the administrator can choose to set one of the choices in the list above as the default value, or can have a Calculated Value. In this figure, the default value is Enter Choice #1. If the field is cleared of text, the default value is left empty. If Calculated Value is chosen, the administrator needs to enter an equation in the field provided.

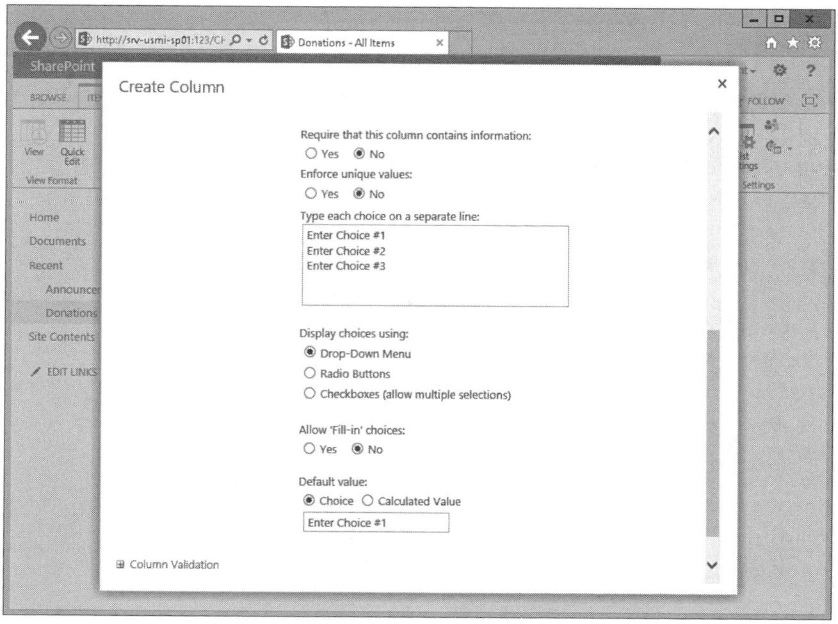

FIGURE 22.16 Default Value field for a choice column.

Note also that there is the option to Allow Fill-In Choices for the choice column, which may be a good option if strict control over the metadata entries is not critical for this column and library.

Setting Default Values from the Settings Page

By accessing the Column Default Value Settings link from the Document Library Settings page, the administrator can set values based on folders, which can be a much more powerful and useful ability than setting default values on a column basis. The following section provides an example of using the Column Default Value Settings for folders within a document library:

1. Create a new document library, create two or more folders in it, and add two or more new columns. In this example, the document library contains folders titled Folder 1 and Folder 2, a column titled Subject (single line of text column), and one titled Choice Column (choice menu to choose from column). It is important to include these items for the following steps.
2. From the document library, click the Library tab on the ribbon, and then click Library Settings.
3. Click Column Default Value Settings link in the General Settings section.
4. From the Change Default Column Values page, click one of the folders in the left pane. In this example, Folder 2 is selected.
5. Click the column name to change. In this example, the Choice Column link was selected.
6. In the Edit Default Value window, select the radio button next to Use This Default Value and enter the desired default value in the field. An error message displays if you enter an invalid choice. In this example, Choice #2 is entered, as shown in Figure 22.17. Click OK.

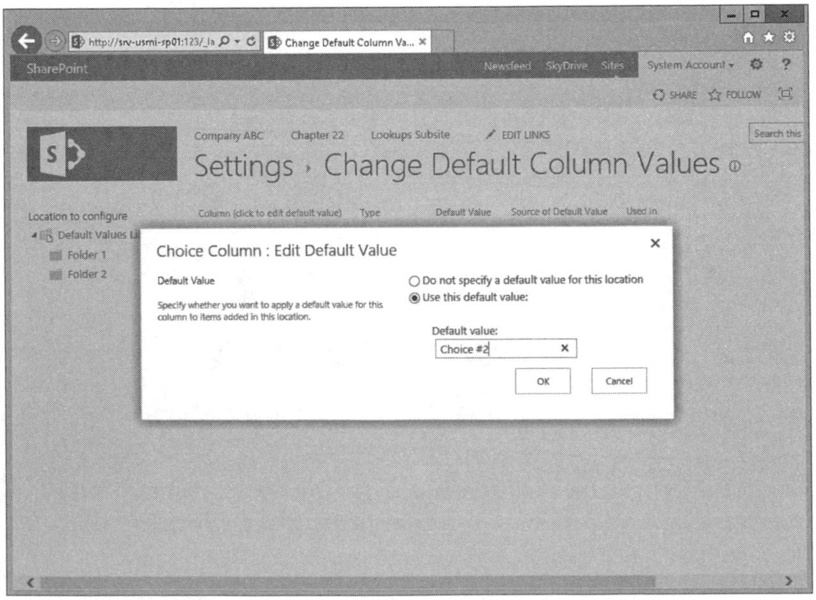

FIGURE 22.17 Assign default column values for folder contents in a document library.

7. As shown in Figure 22.18, the Change Default Column Values page now shows what the default value is by column and by folder. A folder with a gear icon on it has a default value assigned to it. Other folders without specific default values assigned and documents not stored in a folder are assigned the document library default.

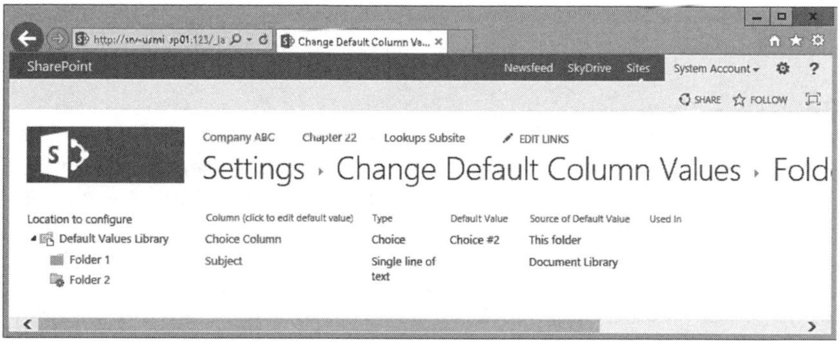

FIGURE 22.18 Change Default Column Values page.

While at first glance this feature seems of limited use, if the document library uses folders or is designed to hold a specific type of document that shares default settings, the default values can be a great time saver and help ensure that the proper values are set for documents. This is especially true for organizations where end users are "addicted" to folder structures and are reluctant to give them up. The administrator can create a column titled Folder Name and then assign default values to this column on a folder-by-folder basis that mirrors the names of the folders. Then views can be created that ignore the folder structure for more advanced users, but the documents will be tagged with the folder name so that information is still captured. This also solves the problem of users knowing which folder items "live" in when they are using a view that is set to ignore the folder structure.

NOTE

If the default column value is changed, it does not affect documents already uploaded to the document library; only documents that are uploaded after the default value are changed.

Site Columns Practical Applications

Previously in this chapter, a variety of columns have been created for the examples. Each of these columns exists in only one place: inside the list where they were created. For example, in one example, a column was created that was named Project Name and used the Choice variety of column, and had several values added to it: Project ABC, Project DEF, and Project GHI. This is fine if that column needs to be used in only one list or library, but if the administrator suddenly finds that this column needs to be used in multiple lists and libraries by the project managers, for example, several things can be done:

- The administrator can manually create the same column in the other lists and libraries that need it. If changes are needed to the settings of the column, the administrator needs to manually make the changes in each list and library.
- The administrator can create a template of the entire document library or list and then use that template to create a new list or library and it will contain the Project Name column and choice values. If changes are needed to the settings of the column, the administrator needs to manually make the changes in each list and library.
- The administrator can create a site column that can be referenced by different lists and libraries and even different sites within the site collection. Changes can be made to the site column that are immediately reflected in the locations where this column is used. The column can also be modified from the libraries and lists where it is used.
- The administrator can create a site column, and also create a content type that uses the site column. This allows the benefits of the site column's capabilities and leverages the content type's capabilities.

Follow these steps to create a site column called Project Name, then add it to a list, and then experiment with making changes to the site column from the list to verify these changes do not go "upstream":

1. Access the Site Settings page for the top-level site of a site collection where the site column will be used using an account that is a member of the Site Collection Owners group.
2. Click Site Columns in the Web Designer Galleries section.
3. The Site Columns page displays. Note that there are a large number of site columns already in existence for the site collection, many of which are self-explanatory. Click the Create link.
4. Enter the title **Project Name** and choose the Choice column type. Note that there are several columns types that may be new to the administrator. These include Full Hypertext Markup Language (HTML) Content with Formatting and Constraints for Publishing, Image with Formatting and Constraints for Publishing, Hyperlink with Formatting and Constraints for Publishing, Summary Links Data, and Rich Media Data for Publishing.
5. Scroll down to the Group section, click the circle next to New Group, and enter the name **Company ABC Columns**.
6. Scroll down to the Additional Column Settings section and enter in several choices for the project names in the box under Type Each Choice on a Separate Line. In this example, enter **Project ABC**, **Project DEF**, **Project GHI**. Select Yes under Allow Fill-In Choices, and clear the text in the Default Value field.

7. Expand the Column Validation section, and enter the following formula, as shown in Figure 22.19:

```
=FIND("Project",[Project Name], 1)
```

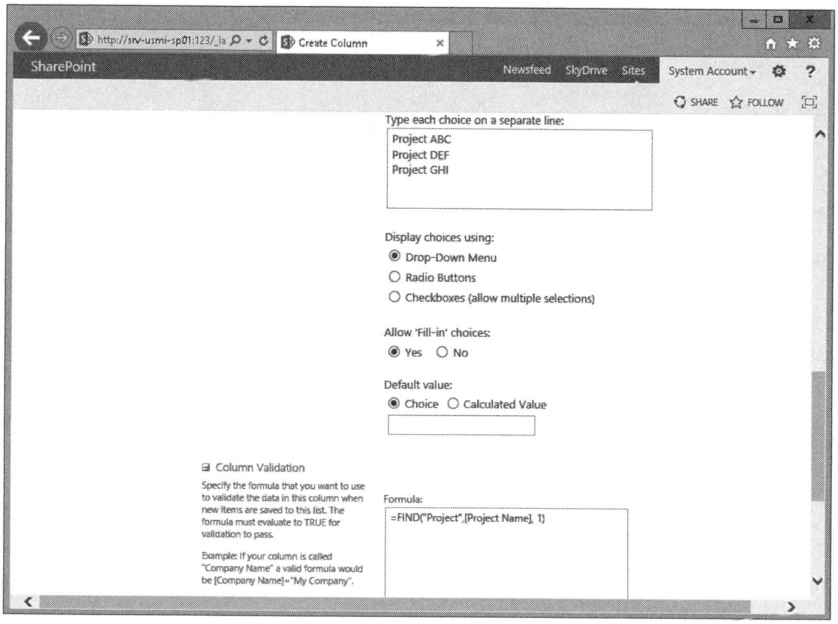

FIGURE 22.19 Creating a site column with choices and column validation settings visible.

8. Enter text in the User Message section: **Value must include the word "Project."**

9. Click OK to save. The Site Columns page now shows the new site column in a section titled Company ABC Columns. If needed, the name of the site column can be clicked and the settings modified.

Now that the site column has been created, it can be used in a list or library. Follow these steps to use the site column in a list and to test the addition of values:

1. Create a Tasks list and title it **Site Column Test**. Steps for creating a new list are provided in Chapter 20, in the "Creating Lists and Libraries" section.

2. Click List Settings from the List tab on the ribbon.

3. Click Add from Existing Site Columns in the Columns section.

4. On the Add Columns from Site Columns page, select Company ABC Columns from the Select Site Columns From drop-down menu. Click Project Name in the Available Site Columns pane and click the Add button. Leave the Add to All Content Types and Add to Default View selected as shown in Figure 22.20. Click OK to save.

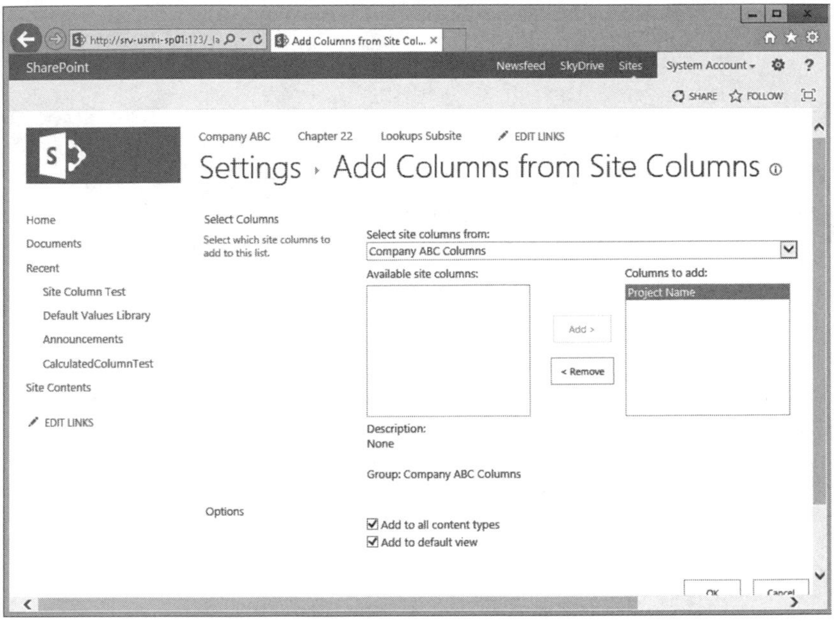

FIGURE 22.20 Adding a site column to a list.

5. Click the name of the list in the breadcrumb to return to the list and click the new task link.

6. Create a new task with the title of **Task 1.** Click the Show More tool. Leave the default values and scroll down to where the field Project Name is visible. Note that there is a drop-down list with the field values defined in the previous exercise. Verify that Project ABC, Project DEF, and Project GHI appear.

7. Click the circle next to Specify Your Own Value, enter the text **Project JKLMNOP**, and click Save.

8. Now see whether the new value added modifies the site column by navigating to the Site Settings page by accessing Site Settings from the Settings gear drop-down menu. Click Site Columns in the Web Designer Galleries section.

9. Click Project Name in the Company ABC Columns section and verify that the new project name was not added to the site column. Project ABC, Project DEF, and Project GHI should be the only entries. The value Project JKLMNOP was not added.

Now that the site column has been created and it is referenced in a list, the administrator can experiment with further modifications to get a better sense for the connectivity between the site column and the list. For example, the following tests will be revealing:

- Modify the title of the column in the list where it is used. Note that this doesn't change the site column settings in the Site Column Gallery.

- Modify the type of column (for example, change it from Choice to Single Line of Text) and verify this doesn't change the site column settings in the Site Column Gallery.
- Add a new value to the site column in the Site Column Gallery and verify that it populates to the instance of the site column in the test list.
- Remove a value from the site column choice fields that is actually used in the list, and verify that the value in the list still remains even after the site column has been modified.

NOTE

When pushing down site column changes, the entire list column definition is overwritten with the current site column definition. Therefore, any changes you make to the list column are overwritten. If errors are encountered, the process moves on to the next use of the site column and report errors.

Content Types Practical Applications

Now that metadata has been reviewed in detail, the initially confusing concept of content types should make more sense. Just as site columns were accessed from the Site Settings page, Site Column link in the Web Designer Galleries section, Content Types are accessed from the Site Content Types link in the same section of the page. Each content type can contain the following settings and components:

- Name, description, and group.
- Advanced settings, including the URL of an existing document template or a new document template that can be uploaded. The option to set the content type as Read Only is provided, and the option to update all content types inheriting from this content type is provided.
- Workflow settings allow the addition of a workflow to the content type. Workflows available in SharePoint Server 2013 are affected by site collection features enabled, but can include Disposition Approval, Three-State, Approval, Collect Signatures, Publishing Approval, and Collect Feedback.
- Information management policy settings provide options including the following: policy statement that displays when the item is opened, enabling retention and definition of retention stage, enabling auditing of interactions between end users and the documents, enabling barcodes, and enabling labels.
- Document Information panel settings: These settings allow the administrator to use the existing template, point to an existing .xsn template to use (which can be created in InfoPath), or upload a new .xsn template. In addition, the Document Information panel can be set to always show on document open and initial save.

- The Columns section shows the columns currently associated with the content type, the type of column, whether the column is Required or Optional, and the source, if any, of the column from another content type.
- Columns can be added from existing site columns, or a new site column can be created for the content type. And Column order can be modified if needed.
- When creating a new content type, a parent content type can be defined to which additions or changes are made.

As with site columns, there are a large number of content types already in place to include the following groupings:

- Business Intelligence
- Community Content Types
- Digital Asset Content Types
- Display Template Content Types
- Document Content Types
- Document Set Content Types
- Folder Content Types
- Group Work Content Types
- List Content Types
- Special Content Types

This list may vary based on the version of SharePoint 2013 in place and the site collection features enabled.

These content types can be associated with lists or libraries, and when this has taken place, the content type is available for selection from the New menu. If a content type is added after content already exists in the list or library, it can then be assigned to items.

Follow these steps to add the site column created in the previous section to an existing content type:

1. Navigate to the Site Content Types page by accessing Site Settings for the top-level site of the site collection as a site collection administrator and clicking Site Content Types in the Web Designer Galleries section.
2. Click Create.
3. Enter a name for the content type (in this example, **Company ABC Task**), select List Content Types from the Select Parent Content Type From drop-down, and select Task from the Parent Content Type drop-down menu.
4. Select Custom Content Types from the Put This Site Content Type into the Existing Group drop-down menu, as shown in Figure 22.21. Click OK to save.

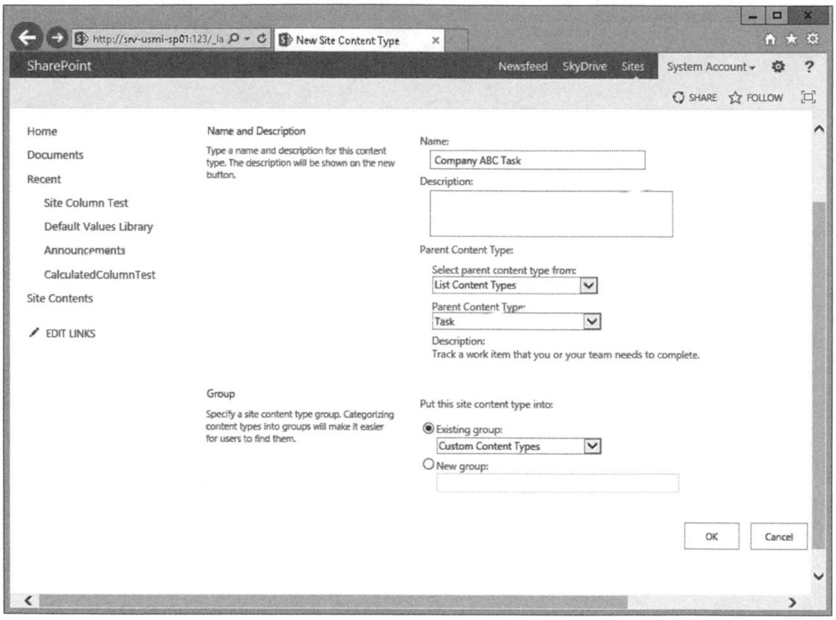

FIGURE 22.21 Creating a new content type based on a parent content type.

5. The Site Content Type page then opens for the new content type. This page shows the settings inherited from the parent and allows the administrator to make changes that only affect this new content type and future content types that inherit from it. In this example, the administrator wants to add the site column Project Name created previously.

6. Click Add from Existing Site Columns under the Columns list. The Add Columns page opens.

7. In the Select Columns From drop-down, select Company ABC Columns, then select Project Name from the Available Columns pane, and click the Add button. Click OK to save.

8. As shown in Figure 22.22, the Site Content Type page now shows the new column in the Columns table, and unlike the other columns, it has no listing under Source, indicating that it was added directly to this content type.

9. To validate that this content type is functional, create a new Tasks list titled **New Tasks List**.

10. From the new Tasks list, access List Settings for the list and click Add from Existing Site Content Types in the Content Types section.

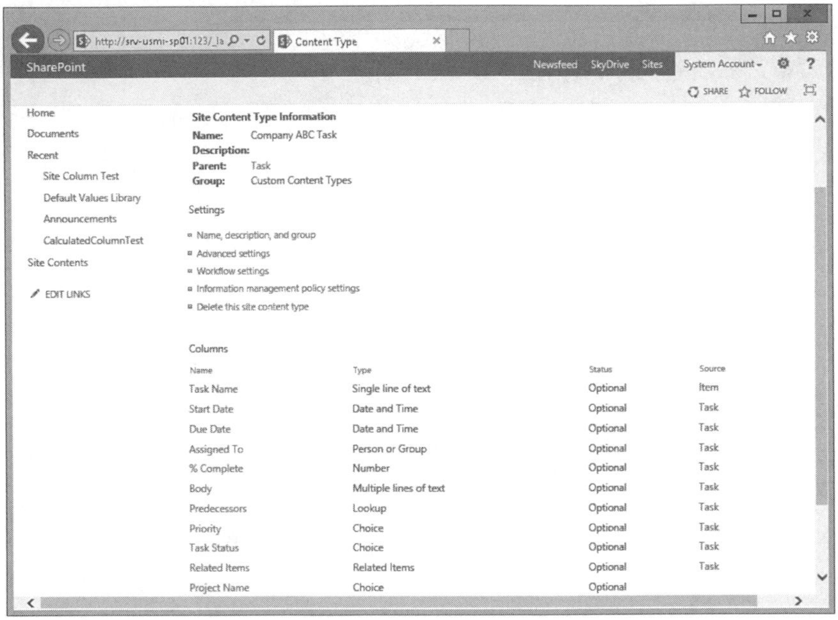

FIGURE 22.22 New Content Type Management page showing added site column.

TIP

If there is no Content Types section, click the Advanced Settings link on the List Settings page, then select Yes in the Content Types section under Allow Management of Content Types, and then click OK to save the changes.

---

11. Select Custom Content Types from the drop-down menu under Select Site Content Types From, and then click Company ABC Task in the Available Site Content Types section and click the Add button. Now the Company ABC Task content type should appear in the Content Types list.
12. Return to the list by clicking the list name in the breadcrumb. Click the New Item drop-down from the Tasks tab and click Company ABC Task.
13. Give the item a title such as **Task Testing New Content Type** and click the Show More link to show the Project Name field and verify that the expected choices from the site column are shown (in this example, Project ABC, Project DEF, and Project GHI), as shown in Figure 22.23. Select one of these values and click OK.
14. Note that in the main view of the list, the Project Name column isn't shown since it hasn't been added to the default view, so click the List tab and then the Modify View button.
15. From the Edit View page, find the Project Name entry in the Columns section, and check the box in the Display column. Click OK, and now the Project Name column should display in the default view, on the right-hand side.

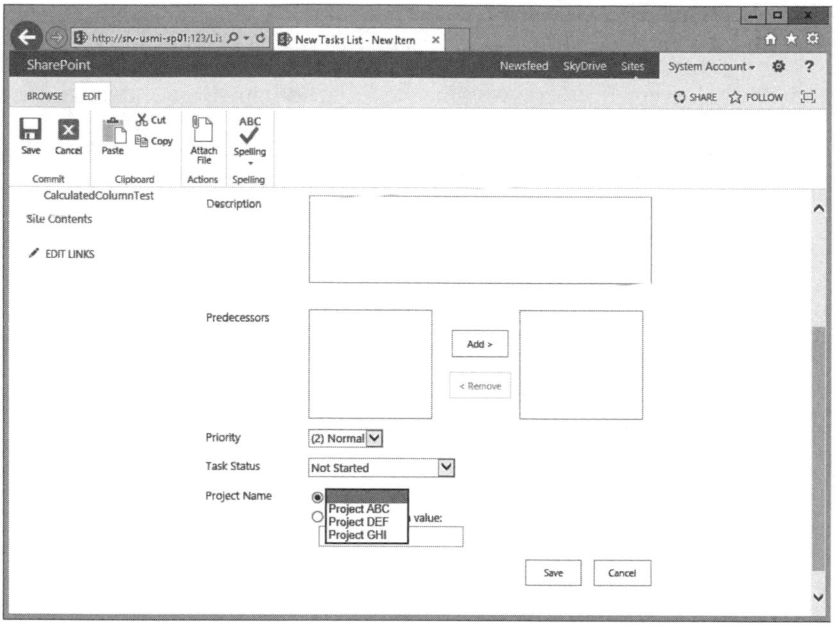

FIGURE 22.23 Adding a new item to a Tasks list that uses the new content type.

Considering the Dublin Core Content for Taxonomy Inspiration

Neatly tucked away in the Site Content Types gallery, in the Document Content Types section, is an entry titled the Dublin Core Columns. Spending some time with this content type is a great way to gain insight into a full set of columns that can be used to describe the elements of a document to enable it to fit into an overall taxonomy or structure.

The Dublin Core metadata element set contains descriptors designed to make it easy for users to easily understand the content described by the metadata elements regardless of the type of content managed. This element set has been widely accepted as documented by the National Information Standards Organization (NISO) in their document titled "The Dublin Core Metadata Element Set" (ISSN: 1041-5653).

The elements are as follows and some description of the value of the fields is given where appropriate:

- **Name:** This is the standard filename field.
- **Contributor:** One or more people or organizations that contributed to the resource.
- **Coverage:** The extent or scope of the document.
- **Creator:** The primary author who may be different from the individual or account uploading the document.

- **Date Created:** This is different from the automatic metadata value tracked by the system. A date and time for when the item was actually created can be entered.
- **Date Modified:** Also different from the system tracked modified value; a date and time can be added here.
- **Description:** A standard multiple lines of text column where descriptive text can be entered.
- **Format:** Media type, file format, or dimensions can be entered as appropriate.
- **Resource Identifier:** An identifying string or number, usually conforming to a formal identification system.
- **Language:** Language in which the item is recorded or written.
- **Publisher:** The person, organization, or service that published this resource.
- **Relation:** References to related resources.
- **Rights Management:** Information about rights held in or over this resource.
- **Source:** References to resources from which this resource was derived.
- **Keywords:** Standard multiple lines of text to enter in keywords.
- **Subject:** Single line of text field for the subject.
- **Title:** Single line of text.
- **Resource Type:** A set of categories, functions, genres, or aggregation levels.

This may be "overkill" in terms of complexity for most organizations, but there may be items in this content type that can be adopted for the organization. For example, the concept of adding the creator information to an item is a powerful one, because the person who created the document might be different from the person who uploaded it. Tagging the item with format metadata is also helpful in many cases because SharePoint can make it hard to see the file extension, and adding paper sizes for Visio or computer-aided design (CAD) documents can be useful.

Creating and Using Managed Metadata

Managed metadata was described from a high level in Chapter 18, "SharePoint Foundation Versus SharePoint Server 2013," in the section titled "Service Applications Available in the Different Versions of SharePoint 2013." This section builds on the basic concepts presented in that section and gives an example of creating managed metadata and how it can be used to make centrally managed metadata available to multiple site collections.

Managed Metadata Service is a service application managed and accessed from the Central Administration site. For testing purposes, it is generally a good idea to create a new service application, by completing the following steps. The first step is to set a content type, then create the service application, and then define the term sets:

1. Access a site collection that will be used as the content type syndication hub and access site settings from the top-level site. Click Site Collection Features in the Site Collection Administration section.
2. Locate the Content Type Syndication Hub and click Activate. Make sure the Active box shows up before proceeding to the next step.
3. Next, access the Central Administrator site and click Manage Service Applications under the Application Management section.
4. Click the New drop-down menu on the ribbon and select Managed Metadata Service.
5. Give a title to the service application (for example, **Test Managed Metadata Service App**).
6. Scroll down and verify that the Database server name is correct and provide a name for the database that will be created (for example, **TestManagedMetadataServiceApp**).
7. In the Application Pool section, click Use Existing Application Pool, and select SharePoint Web Services Default.
8. In the Content Type Hub field, enter the URL for the site collection that was activated in step 2, as shown in Figure 22.24.

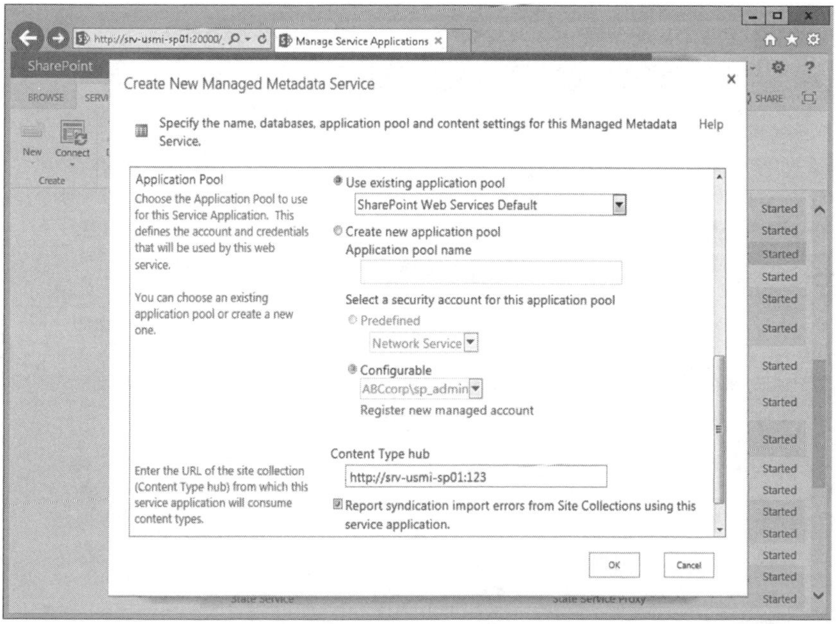

FIGURE 22.24 Creating a new Managed Metadata Service.

9. Leave the other settings at their defaults and click OK. The service application is created along with the database, and it then shows on the ServiceApplications.aspx page.

10. Click the top line of the new service application so that the line is selected (do not click the active hyperlink), and then click the Properties button on the ribbon. This page lists the settings that were just entered. Click Cancel to return to the ServiceApplications.aspx page.

11. Now click the actual link to the service application in the top line (Test Managed Metadata Service App, in this example); the Term Store Management Tool page opens.

12. Click the top-level node in the left Taxonomy Term Store area and then select New Group from the drop-down menu on the right side of the top-level node.

13. A new node appears. Click the new node, give it a title such as **Company ABC Terms**, and press Enter.

NOTE

Enterprise keywords can also be added to the Managed Metadata Service application, as shown in Figure 22.25. After being added, these words or phrases can then be used by tagging tools in SharePoint 2013 site collections. Enterprise keywords are part of a single, nonhierarchical term set called the *keyword set*.

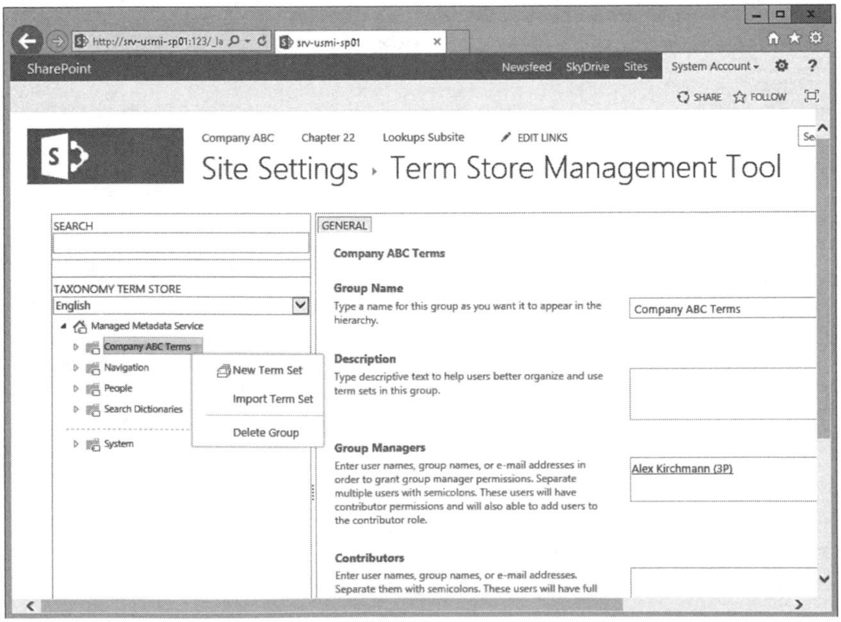

FIGURE 22.25 Creating a new term set.

14. Click New Term Set from the drop-down menu on the new node (Company ABC Terms in this example), as shown in Figure 22.25. Title this node **Client Codes** and press Enter.
15. Next access the drop-down menu for Client Codes node and click Create Term.
16. Title the term **Company DEF Codes** and press Enter.
17. Click the node for Company DEF, access the drop-down menu for it, and click Create Term.
18. Title the term below as **Company DEF USA**, which would correspond to a division of Company DEF with offices in the United States, and then press Enter.

TIP

When creating a term, the option exists to provide other labels to the term, which are also called synonyms. For example, when the term Company DEF USA is defined, a synonym might be DEFCo New York, which is another way to refer to Company DEF USA branch. Another might be DEFCo LA (if there is also an office in Los Angeles). The farm administrator did not want to create individual terms underneath the Company DEF USA term because that is "too granular," and for the organization's requirements, having end users differentiate between the different international branches of Company DEF is sufficient.

19. Repeat step 17 to create additional nodes under Company DEF (Company DEF EMEA, Company DEF Asia), as shown in Figure 22.26.

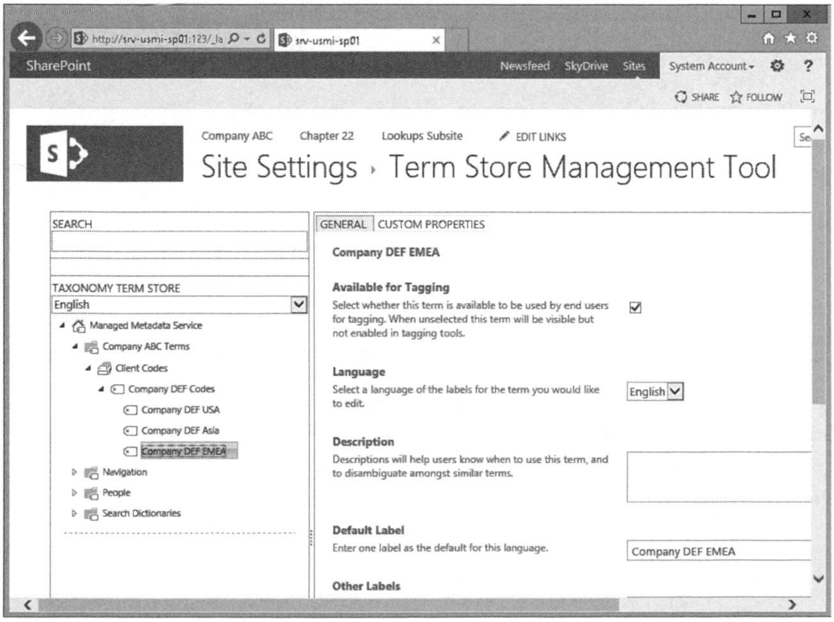

FIGURE 22.26 Adding additional terms to the Company ABC term set.

20. Click the node Company DEF Codes, and the right pane should show additional settings for the term. Uncheck the box next to Available for Tagging because this is an organizational term rather than a term the administrator wants end users to use as metadata. Click Save to save the changes to the term.

21. Click the node Client Codes and review the settings in the right pane. Note that there are fields for Description, Owner, Contact, Stakeholders, a choice to leave the term set Open or Closed, and a check box to allow the term set to be used for tagging or not.

These terms are now available for use from SharePoint lists and libraries. As briefly reviewed earlier, a number of configuration options are available for each term. In the following section, this managed metadata is accessed from a list to show the power of the tool.

NOTE

A *term* is a word or phrase that can be associated with an item in SharePoint Server 2013. A *term set* is a collection of related terms. *Local* term sets are created within the context of a site collection. For example, if you add a column to a list in a document library, and create a new term set to bind the column to, the new term set is local to the site collection that contains the document library. *Global* term sets are created outside the context of a site collection.

Adding Managed Metadata in a List

After the managed metadata term set has been created, as demonstrated in the previous section, it can be used in lists and libraries, as shown in the following steps:

1. Access the site collection used in the previous exercise, where the content type syndication hub site collection feature was enabled. Create a new list using the Discussion Board List template. Title the list **ManagedMetadataTestDiscussion** and click Create.

2. From the list, click List Settings from the List tab.

3. Click Create Column in the Columns section.

4. Title the column **Client Codes** and check the circle next to Managed Metadata.

5. Scroll down to the Term Set Settings section, enter the text **Company DEF** in the field under Find Term Sets that Include the Following Terms, and click the binoculars button. As shown in Figure 22.27, the term set created in the previous section should be returned.

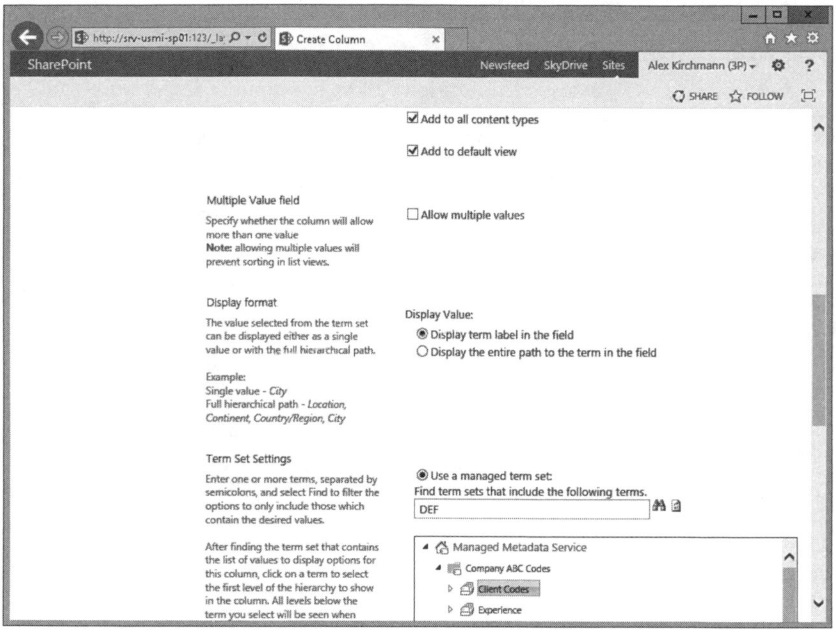

FIGURE 22.27 Adding a managed metadata column to a list.

6. Click the Client Codes node in the results from the search. This will be the “anchor point” for the options that are shown to users of this list. Leave the other settings at their defaults. Click OK to save the settings. Note in the Columns section of the Settings page that this column is listed as managed metadata in the Type column.

7. Return to the discussions list view by clicking the list name in the breadcrumb and click the new discussion link.

8. Provide a title for the discussion item (for example, **Company DEF not paying bills!**), then scroll down to the Client Codes field, and click the Browse for a Valid Choice icon to the right of the field.

9. The Select: Client Codes window opens. Drill down under Company DEF codes and select Company DEF USA, as shown in Figure 22.28. Then click the Select button to select the term. Click OK.

10. Click Save to save the list item and return to the AllItems.aspx page.

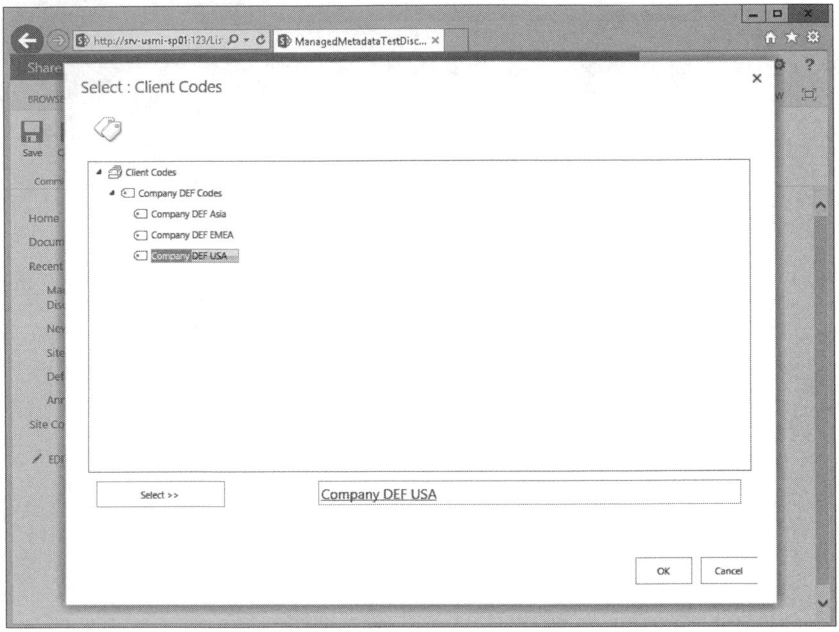

FIGURE 22.28 Choosing a managed metadata term from a list.

Content Type Syndication Hubs

A site collection feature that can be enabled is the Content Type Syndication Hub; this provisions a site to be an enterprise metadata hub site. When a content type is created in a content type hub, the content type is available to other site collections that are part of web applications associated with that Managed Metadata Service instance. The Content Type Hub and Content Type Subscriber jobs need to run for the content type to be synchronized and logs to be updated. Note that in Site Settings for the Content Type Syndication Hub site collection, the tool Content Type Publishing provides a check box to Refresh All Published Content Types on Next Update.

Metadata as a Navigation Aid

One of the primary reasons that organizations put time and effort into creating taxonomies and enforcing their use is to help knowledge workers quickly and precisely locate the documents they are looking for.

Metadata navigation is a powerful tool available in SharePoint Server 2013 Standard or Enterprise, and involves the configuration of hierarchy fields, key filters, and the management of column indices to facilitate browsing for specific types of content within a document library and creating filters to limit the results.

The terminology is a bit confusing, so the best way to understand how it works is to experiment with it. The following example walks through the process of creating a new document library, enabling content types, adding a content type to a document library, and then configuring the metadata navigation settings:

NOTE

The Metadata Navigation and Filtering feature must be active in order to see the Metadata Navigation Settings on the Settings page. To verify that this is active for the site being used, navigate to site settings, click Manage Site Features link in the Site Actions section, and then click Activate next to the Metadata Navigation and Filtering feature.

1. Create a new document library by accessing the Site Actions drop-down menu and clicking New Document Library. Title the library **Metadata Navigation Library**.
2. After the document library is created, navigate to the library and click Library Settings from the Library tab on the ribbon.
3. Next click Advanced Settings in the General Settings section. Click Yes under Allow Management of Content Types. Click OK to save this setting and return to the Document Library Settings page.
4. Scroll down to the Content Types section and click Add from Existing Site Content Types.
5. From the Add Content Types page, as shown in Figure 22.29, change the content types to Document Content Types in the Select Site Content Types From drop-down menu. Select Basic Page and click the Add button. Click OK to add this content type and return to the Document Library Settings page.
6. Click the Metadata Navigation Settings link in the General Settings section. See the note at the beginning of this section if the Metadata Navigation Settings links isn't there.
7. Content Type should be highlighted in the Available Hierarchy Fields area, so click the Add button to add it to selected hierarchy fields.

NOTE

Other fields can be selected in the Available Hierarchy Fields section. Besides Content Type, Single-Value Choice Field and Managed Metadata Field can also be selected.

8. In the Configure Key Filters section, in the Available Key Filter fields, click Modified By, and then click the Add button. The screen should now match Figure 22.30.

NOTE

A variety of fields can be used as key filters. These include Content Type, Choice field, Managed Metadata field, Person or Group field, Date and Time field, and Number field.

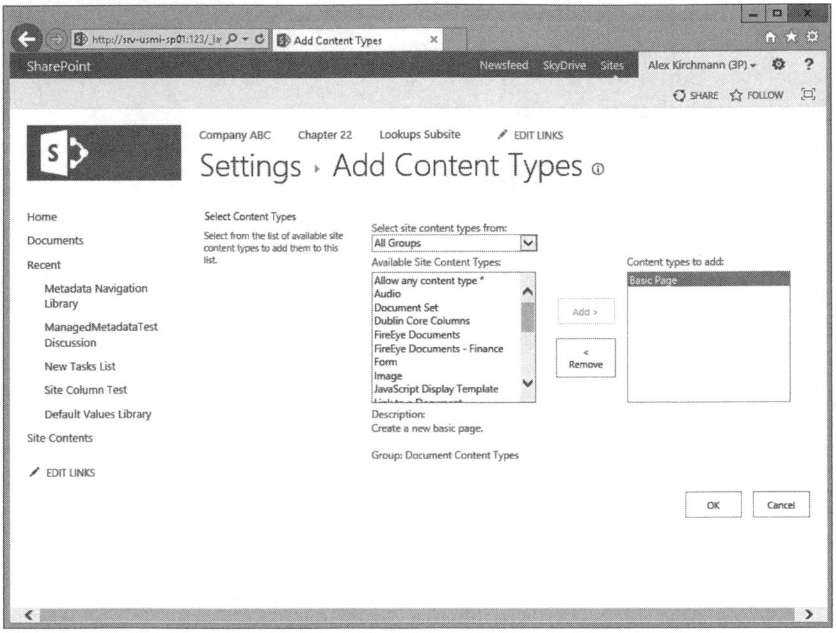

FIGURE 22.29 Adding a content type to a document library.

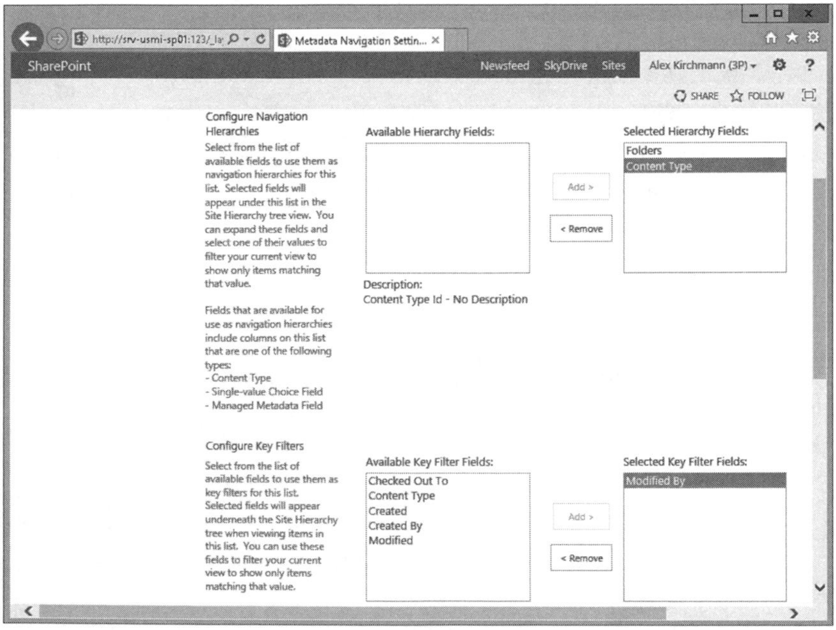

FIGURE 22.30 Selecting hierarchy fields and key filter fields.

9. Leave Automatically Manage Column Indices on This List checked. Click OK to save the changes and return to the Document Library Settings page.

NOTE

Leaving Automatically Manage Column Indices on This List selected will improve the performance of queries when the Navigation Hierarchy and Key Filter tools are used. There are a maximum of 20 columns that can be indexed in a list or library, so on rare occasions, the administrator might need to decide which 20 are indexed.

10. Click the name of the document library in the breadcrumb to return to the default view of the library. The library should now have the hierarchy fields in the quick launch area on the left, and below it the key filter fields. (You might need to scroll down to see the key filter fields.) Test these tools by creating several folders and uploading several documents to the library and assigning them to the Document and Basic Page content types during the upload process.

Figure 22.31 shows the navigation hierarchy after several folders have been created, and where the user has clicked the Basic Page content type, as well as the key filter section where the user has entered **Alex Kirchmann** and the filtering criteria for the Modified By field of metadata. This very intuitive navigation tool enables users to quickly navigate to folders and subfolders and to see only certain content types or other fields, such as managed metadata fields.

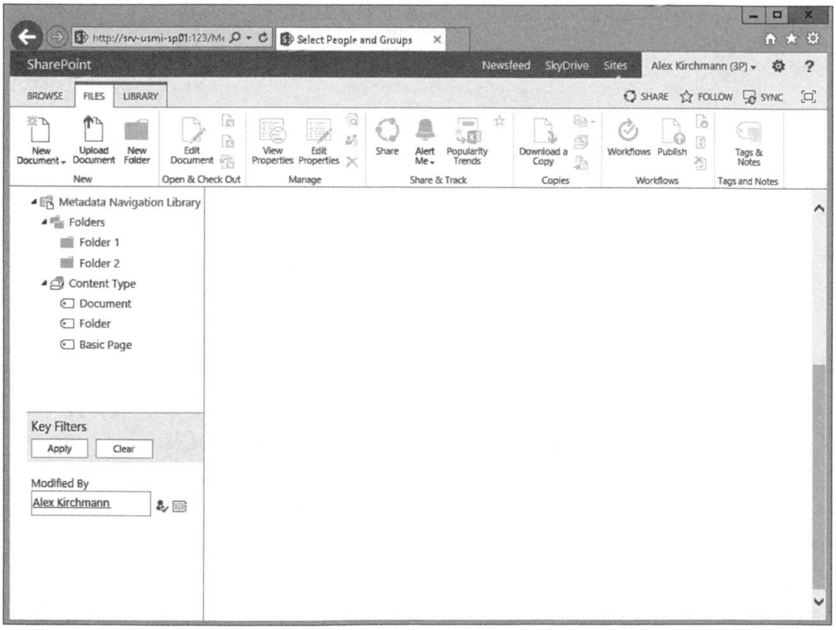

FIGURE 22.31 Navigation hierarchy and key filters in a document library.

Summary

This chapter provided a thorough overview of the wide range of applications of metadata in SharePoint 2013 by using hands-on exercises as well as feature discussions and examples. Because of the ways that metadata is enmeshed with SharePoint 2013, administrators must "get their hands dirty" to set standards for how metadata will be used and which SharePoint 2013 metadata-related features will be used.

In this chapter, a summary of the different types of columns available from lists and libraries was provided, along with examples of how metadata is populated to documents. Exercises involving the calculated column and lookup column types were provided, and features such as validation settings and enforcing unique values in columns were discussed and practical applications were covered. Default values and the enforce relationship behavior were also discussed. The chapter then moved on to cover site columns and content types when the "basics" of metadata had been covered, because effective use of site columns and content types requires a familiarity with the capabilities of metadata columns used in lists and libraries. Finally, managed metadata and using metadata as a navigation aid was discussed and exercises were provided.

Best Practices

The following are best practices from this chapter:

- A recommended best practice for a farm or site collection administrator is to become familiar with the process of creating metadata columns in lists and libraries and the range and options available for the different column types.
- Set standards for document libraries and lists in terms of the standard metadata columns added to ensure consistency across libraries in one site or across multiple sites.
- Calculated columns support a wide range of mathematical functions, and Excel users can leverage their skills creating complex formulas in SharePoint 2013. Be sure to test the Excel formulae in SharePoint because not all Excel functions are supported and there are other restrictions, some of which are pointed out in this chapter.
- Column validations and validation settings for a list or library help IT ensure that users are entering valid values in lists and libraries, and also leverage Excel equations, which generate the results of true or false.
- Lookup columns are very powerful, but also have limitations in terms of which columns can be connected to. Also understanding the capabilities of the Restrict Delete and Cascade Delete options in the Enforce Relationship Behavior section for a lookup column is important and can lead to powerful applications built on relationships between lists.
- Site columns allow an administrator to create a column once that can be added to any list or library in the site collection. Changes push down only, so changes to the site column from the list level do not affect the site column itself, which is stored in the Site Column gallery.

- Content types provide additional features and settings that make them effective and powerful tools, and can leverage site columns. They are defined in content type galleries.
- Managed metadata is defined at the Central Administrator site level, and multiple Managed Metadata Service applications can be created. The term sets created within the service applications can then be managed centrally and made available to lists and libraries throughout the farm.
- Not only does metadata allow for effective management of documents and list items, but it can also be used to facilitate navigation within lists and libraries.

CHAPTER 23

Leveraging Social Networking Tools in SharePoint 2013

IN THIS CHAPTER

- Creating and Exploring Personal Sites
- Modifying Your Profile
- Reviewing Relevant Central Administration Tools
- Reviewing Relevant User Profile Tools
- Reviewing the My Site Settings Section
- Following Sites
- Managing Social Notes and Tags
- Advantages of Using a Dedicated Web Application for My Sites
- Restricting User Access to and Creation of My Site Sites
- Community Sites Explored

When discussing SharePoint 2013 designs (and earlier versions of SharePoint) with clients, the issue of My Site sites and social networking invariably involves discussions of whether they are "good" or "bad" for the organization, and IT decision makers tend to have strong opinions one way or the other. Those in favor of My Site sites (also referred to as personal sites) see them as having the potential to get users more involved with SharePoint 2013 implementations, and a way to not only make the implementation more successful from an adoption standpoint but to also provide social collaboration tools that can enhance the productivity of users. This stance has gotten more popular over the past handful of years due to the rampant success of sites such as Facebook and tools such as Twitter. Those against My Site sites tend to see the sites as potential time wasters, are afraid that the users are not sophisticated enough to understand how to use them, or are afraid that users will use them as "dumping grounds" for personal documents.

Both stances are valid, and after all, IT management tends to have good insight into the types of users who will be interacting with the SharePoint environment, and their concerns are most likely justified. That said, the SharePoint 2013 My Site tools and capabilities (available in SharePoint Server 2013 Standard or Enterprise) are dramatically improved and different from My Sites in SharePoint 2010. Therefore, it makes sense for IT to test and evaluate My Site capabilities to see the tools in action before a firm choice is made.

These tools also rely on the User Profile service application in Central Administration, so understanding how My Sites can be managed and the "moving parts" behind the capabilities of these sites is valuable. SharePoint 2013 also adds Communities to the social networking offerings (which can be created using the Community Site and Community Portal site templates) and these are also discussed in this chapter.

Because the personal sites are so intertwined with Central Administration tools such as the User Profile Service and web applications and site collections, a number of Central Administration tools are touched on to help administrators gain a full understanding of how My Sites can and should be managed.

Creating and Exploring Personal Sites

A good place to start when either taking over the management of an existing SharePoint Server 2013 Standard or Enterprise environment or putting the finishing touches on a new installation is to test My Site creation and the tools provided in a personal site, to gain a better understanding of the components and tools (and to see whether everything is working properly). The installation process of SharePoint 2013 Standard or Enterprise generally results in a functional User Profile Service in Central Administration, assuming the farm configuration wizard is used and the box to configure User Profile Service is checked during the configuration process. This allows for the creation of My Sites, but you want to verify that the process is functioning properly.

NOTE

There are many reasons why My Site creation may not work. A number of these are discussed throughout this chapter. These may include improper configuration of the environment or features that have been disabled on purpose by IT.

Assuming the User Profile Service has been properly configured, either through the wizard during configuration or manually if the wizard was not used, to create a personal site for a user, follow these steps in a SharePoint 2013 Standard or Enterprise environment:

1. Log in to the SharePoint 2013 Standard or Enterprise environment with a test account that hasn't created a My Site yet but that has access to the SharePoint environment. In this example, the user TestUser1 is used.
2. From the site home page, click the Sites link at the top of the page. In a default installation, a Getting the Most Out of SharePoint window appears, with a Let's Get Social check box with the description, "Use recommended settings to allow others to see certain activities in the newsfeed." Click OK.
3. The page then displays the text, "We're almost ready!" on it, as shown in Figure 23.1. In this example, the URL is http://sp20131/my/_layouts/15/start.aspx#/default.aspx. Note that the page only has the About Me and People links under the picture

placeholder on the left. A note on the screen states, "It could take us a while, but once we're done, here's what you'll get" and then mentions Newsfeed, SkyDrive Pro, and Sites. But these aren't available yet. That is because the site collection for the individual needs to be created in the background.

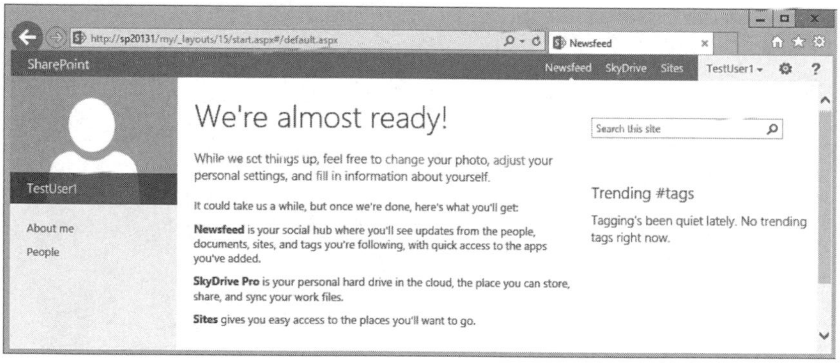

FIGURE 23.1 New My Site home page immediately after initial creation.

4. However, in a few minutes, refresh the screen, and the look and feel changes, which shows that the site collection has been created for the user. As shown in Figure 23.2, additional links appear under the picture placeholder. A number of web parts appear on the screen, including a web part to start a conversation, links (Following, Everyone, Mentions), the I'm Following web part, and Trending #tags. Note that this is in fact the Newsfeed site for the user, as shown by the active tab at the top of the screen, but the URL remains http://sp20131/my/_layouts/15/start.aspx#/default.aspx.

NOTE

It is interesting to visit Central Administration after starting the personal site creation process. Immediately after clicking the Sites link for a user who doesn't have a personal site, visit Central Administration, click Application Management, click View All Site Collections in the Site Collections section, and then look for the new site collection. In the current example, TestUser1 is the user, and there should be a corresponding site collection under the /my/personal path, as shown in Figure 23.3.

However, if the site does *not* appear, something is stopping the creation of the site. Most likely, self-service site creation is not turned on for the web application hosting the personal sites. Visit the Application Management page in Central Administration and click Manage Web Applications in the Web Applications section, highlight the web application that houses the personal sites, and click the Self-Service Site Creation icon on the ribbon. Make sure that the On option is selected for Allow Users to Create Site Collections in Defined URL Namespaces.

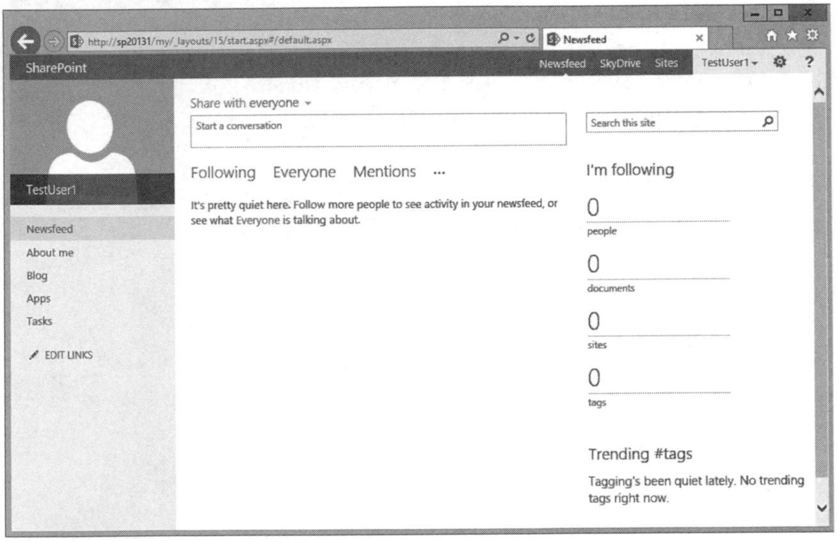

FIGURE 23.2 New My Site Newsfeed page after site collection has been created.

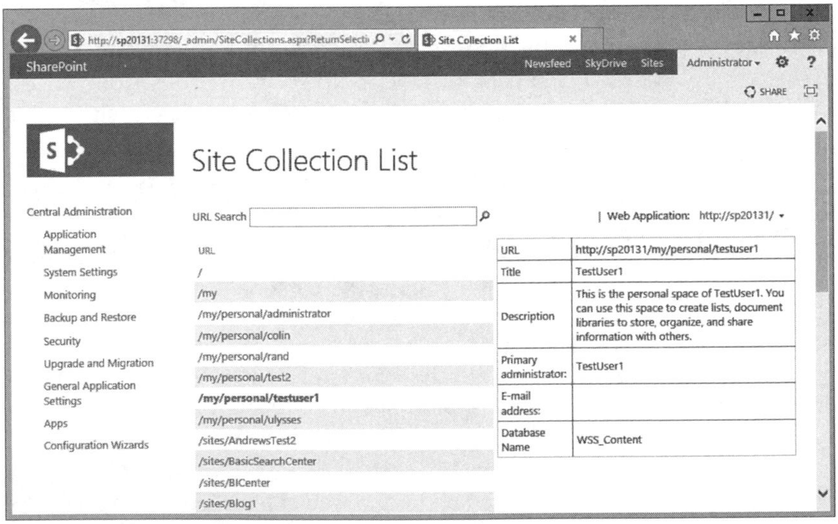

FIGURE 23.3 Central Administration Site Collection List page showing new personal site collection.

5. Click the different links to get a sense for the other tools available. These should include the following: About Me, Blog, Apps, and Tasks. Following sections look at these different tool sets in more detail.

Modifying Your Profile

One of the first tasks most users should do, to add value to their My Site, is to edit their profile. This information is critical to the foundation of a useful social networking solution in SharePoint. While some information comes over from Active Directory (AD), which varies based on the information that the AD account contains and the settings in the User Profile Service, there are a number of fields where the user can enter information that will help coworkers know his or her background, skills, projects worked on, and other information.

Follow these steps to modify the profile for the logged-in user. The assumption is that the user has already created the base My Site including the site collection:

1. Click the Newsfeed link at the top of the page to access the logged-in user's Sites page. In this example, the user is TestUser1.
2. From the Newsfeed page, click the About Me link under the photo placeholder.
3. Click the Edit link to the right of the photo.
4. As shown in Figure 23.4, the Edit Details page opens. In this case, AD contained some information that was imported when the My Site was created. The Name, Work Phone, and Department fields were filled during the My Site creation process.
5. Note that the Name, Work Phone, and Department fields are read only and can't be edited.
6. Click Upload Picture, click the Browse button, and upload a picture.
7. In the About Me field, enter in some sample descriptive text about the experience of the user. Note that the ribbon provides a number of text formatting tools to allow the user to personalize the description and have certain pieces of information stand out.
8. In the Ask Me About field, enter in a topic. In this example, the user started typing and was given some suggestions, also shown in Figure 23.4. In this example, the user typed s and was offered several managed metadata terms that start with the letter *S*. When a handful of entries have been entered, click Save All and close. You'll receive this message: "Your changes have been saved, but they may take some time to take effect." Click OK.

NOTE

In a new environment, there might not be any managed metadata term sets, but this illustrates how setting up term sets in advance can make it easier for users to choose terms to describe themselves and their abilities in their My Site profiles, as well as ensure consistency and reduce typos.

9. The Newsfeed My Site page now displays the uploaded photo and the text entered in the About Me field, and an activity shows up for each of the Ask Me About items that were entered, as shown in Figure 23.5. In this example, three terms were added in the Ask Me About field, so three activities are now listed.

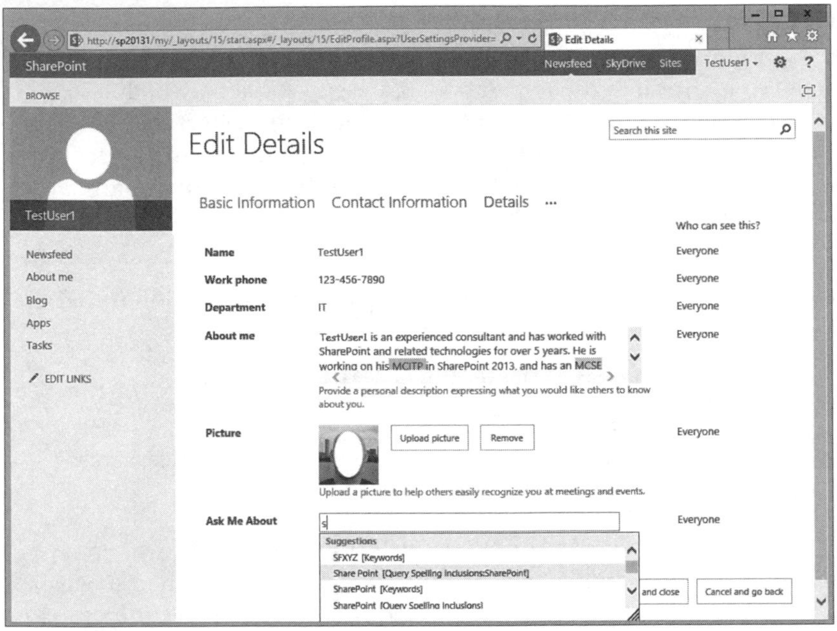

FIGURE 23.4 Edit Details page for a user profile.

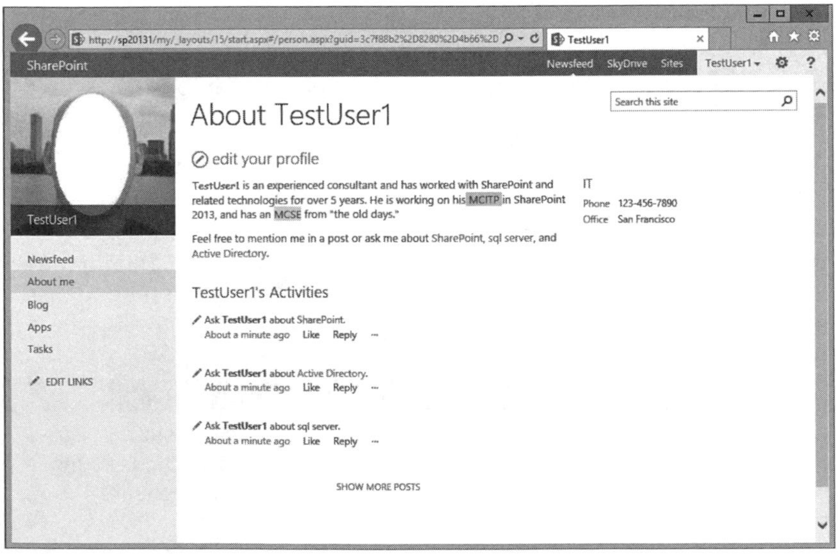

FIGURE 23.5 Newsfeed page after updating a user's profile.

NOTE

In SharePoint Server 2013, a new feature known as the Distributed Cache (which uses AppFabric for Windows Server) maintains the newsfeed. This infrastructure better supports the read and write operations generated by users' activities and participation in microblogging. The new microblogging functionality enables users to do the following:

- Participate in conversations by posting comments and replies
- Post pictures and links
- Use tags (starting with the # symbol) to define keywords that users can follow and search for
- Use mentions (starting with the @ symbol) to tag users in posts and replies
- Indicate agreement with comments and replies by clicking Like
- Follow people, documents, sites, and tags to customize their feed

Reviewing Relevant Central Administration Tools

Now that a new user My Site has been created, and some basic customizations have been made in the previous section, a visit to Central Administration is helpful to get a better understanding of the tools that the farm administrators have at their fingertips.

The following list provides a high-level overview of several key tools that farm administrators should be familiar with when managing My Sites:

- **Application Management page, View All Site Collections tool:** This tool allows the farm administrator to see all the My Site site collections that have been created. As shown in Figure 23.3, when a My Site is highlighted, information about that site is shown in the table on the right side of the page. It shows the database name that stores the My Site site collection and the primary administrator.
- **Application Management page, Change Site Collections Administrators tool:** Farm administrators are not by default site collection administrators to the site collections created as My Sites. Figure 23.6 shows the result of clicking Change Site Collection Administrators on the Application Management page and then selecting a My Site (for TestUser1 in this example). Note that the only default site administrator for this site collection is the user himself. The impact of this is that a farm administrator won't be able to perform certain commands from the Manage Profile Service page for the User Profile service application.
- **System Settings page, Manage Services on Server tool:** Shows the status of the User Profile Service and User Profile Synchronization Service. If the User Profile Synchronization Service has not been configured in the User Profile service application, it will most likely show as Stopped.
- **Monitoring page, Review Job Definitions tool:** This tool shows the different SharePoint jobs and when they are configured to run. The farm administrator may want to tune these settings based on which components of user profiles are going to be used. The relevant jobs for user profiles are as follows:

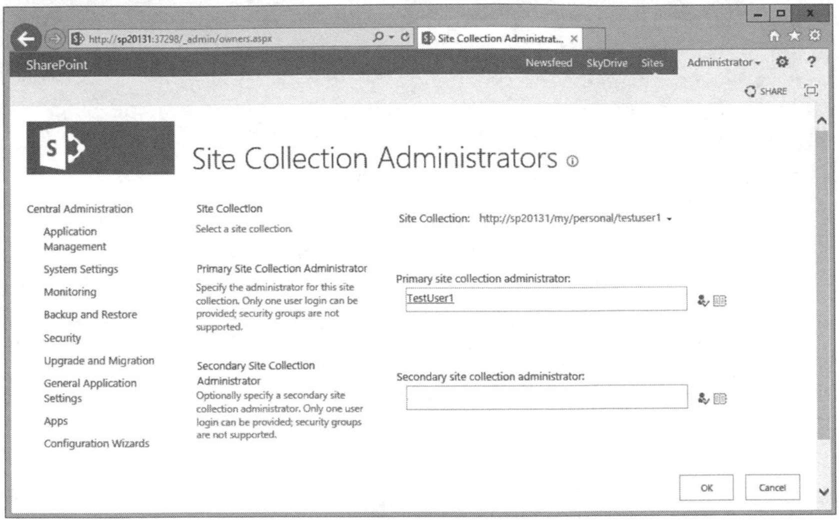

FIGURE 23.6 Site Collection Administrators page for a My Site site collection.

User Profile Service Application—Activity Feed Cleanup Job (set to Daily by default)

User Profile Service Application—Activity Feed Job (set to Minutes by default)

User Profile Service Application—Audience Compilation Job (set to Weekly by default)

User Profile Service Application—Feed Cache Repopulation Job (set to Minutes by default)

User Profile Service Application—My Site Suggestions Email Job (set to Monthly by default)

User Profile Service Application—Social Data Maintenance Job (set to Hourly by default)

User Profile Service Application—Social Rating Synchronization Job (set to Hourly by default)

User Profile Service Application—System Job to Manage User Profile Synchronization (set to Minutes by default)

User Profile Service Application—User Profile Change Cleanup Job (set to Daily by default)

User Profile Service Application—User Profile Change Job (set to Hourly by default)

User Profile Service Application—User Profile Incremental Synchronization (set to Daily by default)

User Profile Service Application—User Profile Language Synchronization Job (set to Hourly by default)

User Profile Service Application—User Profile to SharePoint Full Synchronization (set to Hourly by default)

User Profile Service Application—User Profile to SharePoint Language and Region Synchronization (set to Minutes by default)

User Profile Service Application—User Profile to SharePoint Quick Synchronization (set to Minutes by default)

Reviewing Relevant User Profile Tools

This section focuses on demystifying the user profile tools and giving the farm administrator a better sense of the capabilities of the tools. A user profile is a collection of properties that describes a SharePoint user and is used in tools such as My Sites and People Search, and they can be created by importing data from directory services, such as AD. The User Profile Service Application page provides access for the farm administrator to a range of tools to manage user profiles, synchronize with AD or other directory services, and configure My Site settings.

Most organizations do not need to customize or modify these settings to any great degree, and leaving them as close to out-of-the-box as possible is recommended for smaller organizations and organizations new to SharePoint products. As discussed in this section, SharePoint 2013 should connect automatically to the AD domain the farm is attached to, which will be a welcome change from SharePoint 2010 synchronization issues.

It is important to understand that Microsoft Forefront Identity Manager (FIM), formerly known as Microsoft Identity Integration Server (MIIS), is used to facilitate the synchronization process. FIM is automatically installed as part of the SharePoint 2013 installation, but it won't show up in Programs and Features in Windows Server 2012. It is not a full installation of FIM 2010 R2 either, and is a much more limited implementation, designed primarily for profile synchronization with AD.

NOTE

A new feature in SharePoint 2013 is called Direct Active Directory Import. This is designed to allow "basic" import of user information from AD without requiring the configuration and use of the Profile Synchronization Tools. The tool has limitations when compared with the profile synchronization tools, but in many cases is sufficient for basic synchronization with AD.

NOTE

SharePoint Server 2013 can create connections to the following directory services to synchronize users. Groups can only be synchronized with Active Directory Domain Services (AD DS):

- AD DS 2003 SP2 and AD DS 2008
- Sun Java System Directory Server version 5.2
- Novell eDirectory version 8.7.3
- IBM Tivoli version 5.2

Accessible by clicking the Manage Service Applications link on the Application Management page in Central Administration, and then clicking the appropriate service application (by default named User Profile), the Manage Profile Service: User Profile Service Application page provides access to a number of tools that a farm administrator should be familiar with when managing My Sites. An example of the Manage Profile Service: User Profile Service Application page is shown in Figure 23.7. Although it is not required that a farm administrator master all the settings on this page, a number of tools are important for day-to-day operations and management of user profiles and My Site Settings and so are covered in this section:

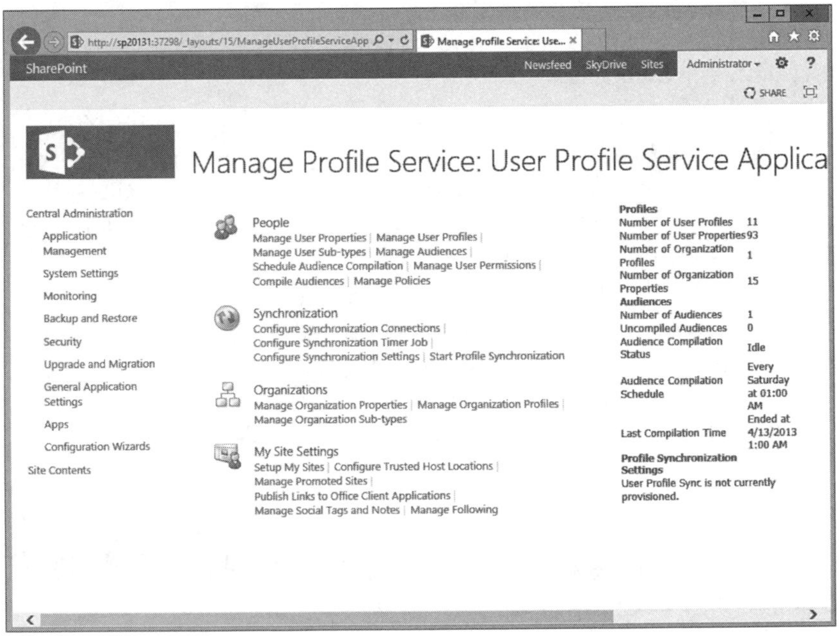

FIGURE 23.7 Manage Profile Service: User Profile Service Application page.

- **People:** Tools are provided to Manage User Properties as well as to Manage User Profiles, Manage User Sub-Types, Manage Audiences, Schedule Audience Compilation, Manage User Permissions, Compile Audiences, and Manage Policies. Of primary importance for an administrator in charge of managing My Sites is to understand user properties. Figure 23.8 shows a sample Manage User Properties page, which lists the Property Name, Property Type, Mapped Attribute, Multivalue, and Alias columns. Tools are provided to create a New Property, New Section, Manage Sub-Types, and to Select a Sub-Type to Filter the List of Properties. If a property name is clicked, a drop-down menu appears, and an Edit tool can be clicked. If the Edit tool is clicked, additional details of the settings for this property can be accessed. For example, settings such as default privacy settings, editing settings, display settings, and search settings can be configured here. By reviewing the properties and their individual settings, the administrator will gain a better understanding of how properties are used by SharePoint and how they can be customized if needed. This is important if the organization wants to modify the default settings, which isn't generally recommended, or add new properties. The Manage User Profiles is also a very powerful and useful tool, and it is discussed later in the chapter in the "Restricting User Access to and Creation of My Site Sites" section.

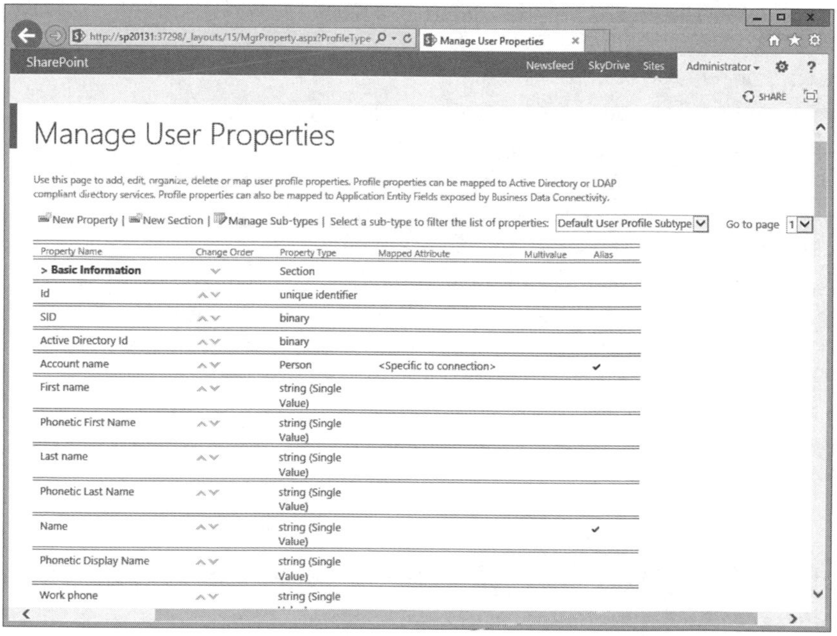

FIGURE 23.8 Manage User Properties page.

NOTE

An alias property is treated as equivalent to the username and account name by SharePoint when searching for items authored by a user, targeting items to a user, or displaying items in the Documents web part of the personal site for a user. Aliased properties must be public. Default aliased properties are Account Name, Name, User Name, and Work Email.

- **Synchronization:** Tools provided include Configure Synchronization Connections, Configure Synchronization Timer Job, Configure Synchronization Settings, and Start Profile Synchronization. These tools may actually *not* be needed at all for many implementations, because the Direct Active Directory Import tool automatically (in most cases) ensures that "basic" AD synchronization occurs with the domain to which the SharePoint farm is connected. Note in Figure 23.7 a message in the lower-right corner: "User Profile Sync is not currently provisioned." Yet the Direct Active Directory Import tool has imported a variety of AD field values, as demonstrated earlier in this chapter and shown in Figure 23.4, where work phone and department information was imported from AD.

NOTE

If the full FIM-based profile synchronization process is to be used, a number of configuration changes might be needed before it will work properly (depending on how the farm was provisioned and configured). SharePoint users familiar with SharePoint 2010 may have experienced this "pain" previously in SharePoint 2010.

Some configuration requirements are as follows:

- You must have a full installation of SQL Server, not the Express Edition.
- The synchronization account for a connection to AD DS must have the Replicate Directory Changes permissions on the domain being synchronized with.
- Generally, the Farm Configuration Wizard should not be used, or if it was used, a new User Profile service application should be provisioned.

Recommended steps to ensure proper functionality also include creating a dedicated web application to host the My Sites, a managed path for My Sites, a My Site Host site collection, a new User Profile service application, enabling NetBIOS domain names for user profile synchronization via PowerShell, and then starting the User Profile Service.

When the basic functionality is working, there are additional configuration steps required, including configuring the synchronization connections and thorough testing to ensure the tool is working properly.

NOTE

When troubleshooting synchronization issues, check the services running on the server housing the User Profile services application and verify that the following services are running when the synchronization process is running. These services may show as disabled until a profile synchronization is started:

- FIM Service
- FIM Synchronization Service

- **Organizations:** Tools include Manage Organization Properties, Manage Organization Profiles, and Manage Organization Sub-Types. For large organizations that want to leverage My Sites to their fullest, organization profiles and subtypes can be defined and the properties and settings for those properties customized for different groups of users.
- **My Site settings:** Setup My Sites, Configure Trusted Host Locations, Manage Promoted Sites, Publish Links to Office Client Applications, Manage Social Tags and Notes, Manage Following—these tools are very important for all My Site administrators to understand and are addressed in more detail in the "Reviewing the My Site Settings Section" section.

Reviewing the My Site Settings Section

Available on the Manage Profile Service page for the User Profile service application, as shown in Figure 23.7, the Setup My Sites link in the My Site Settings section provides access to several tools that should be familiar to the farm administrator for effective My Site management. These include the following:

- **Preferred Search Center:** The farm administrator should decide whether to use the default search center when users execute a search from their My Site or to map to a different search center, and which scopes to configure as the people scope and the documents scope.
- **My Site Host:** This can be changed if needed for the service application. However, any existing sites on the previous host will need to be manually transferred (that is, backed up and restored) to the new host, which can be a time-consuming process.
- **My Site Host URL in Active Directory:** This URL is returned through Exchange Auto Discovery.
- **Personal Site Location:** Usually set to my/personal; this can be changed if needed. A wildcard inclusion managed path matching this setting needs to exist on the web application hosting the My Site.
- **Site Naming Format:** Changing this setting will affect any future personal sites created, and will not affect existing personal sites. The farm administrator can choose between several options:

  User Name (Do Not Resolve Conflicts)

  User Name (Resolve Conflicts by Using domain_username)

  Domain and User Name (Will Not Have Conflicts)
- **Language:** Users can be allowed to set the language of their My Site.
- **Read Permission Levels:** These accounts are given read permissions when new personal sites are created.
- **Security Trimming Options:** Activity feeds, ratings, social tags, and notes may contain links. If the organization wants to hide links that the user doesn't have access to, all links can be checked for permission. This is a general best practice because it can be seen as a security risk to show users links they shouldn't have access to. However, the process of checking permissions does take time and therefore might slow down the rate at which the items appear on the user's page. The options are as follows:

  Check All Links for Permissions

  Check Only Specified Links for Permissions (URL hierarchies can be entered to specify which links need to be checked, and URL hierarchies can be specified that should be displayed without checking.)

  Show All Links Regardless of Permissions

- **Newsfeed:** Activities on My Site newsfeeds can be enabled or disabled here. Legacy SharePoint 2010 activity migration can be enabled or disabled here as well.
- **Email Notifications:** An email string should be entered here, and it is used when SharePoint sends out certain email notifications. Newsfeed email notifications can be enabled or disabled as well.
- **My Site Cleanup:** If a user's profile has been deleted, that user's My Site is flagged for deletion after 14 days. Access can be granted to the user's manager if Enable Access Delegation is enabled, or a secondary owner can be defined to manage all such activities.
- **Privacy Settings:** My Sites are private by default, but the option to Make My Sites Public can be selected, which overrides policies set in People and Privacy in the Manage Policies page.

Reviewing Other Configuration Tools in the My Sites Settings Section

Configure Trusted Host Locations, Manage Promoted Sites, Publish Links to Office Client Applications, Manage Social Tags and Notes, and Manage Following are other important tools for the My Site administrator to be familiar with:

- **Configure Trusted Host Locations:** Configuring trusted host locations can be of specific interest to larger organizations with thousands of users who want to leverage My Site sites, because the idea of putting all users in one "basket" (that is, managed by one service application and stored in one My Site Host site collection) may be unappealing. A large organization (for example, with 10,000 users) may want to create multiple User Profile service applications, each of which has a My Site Host site collection, and then split up where individuals' My Site sites are created based on which branch office they are in. Several audiences would need to be created for this purpose, which look at the value of the Office field in AD, and if it matches a specific value, the user becomes a member of that audience when it is compiled. The audiences would then be used to determine where the users' My Site personal sites are created.
- **Manage Promoted Sites:** Promoted sites are sites that can be defined by a farm administrator and that appear on a user's Sites page on their My Site.
- **Publish Links to Office Client Applications:** The Publish Links to Office Client Applications settings enable a farm administrator to define links and push them to the My SharePoints tab when opening or saving documents. Audiences can be used in both of these cases to determine which users receive these links.
- **Manage Social Tags and Notes:** This is covered in the "Managing Social Notes and Tags" section.
- **Manage Following:** This tool enables farm administrators to set limits for maximum number of followed people (default value 1,000), maximum number of followed documents (default value 500), and maximum number of followed sites (default value 500).

Following Sites

A user who has successfully created a new My Site site collection is able to click the Sites link at the top of the screen and go to his Sites.aspx page, as shown in Figure 23.9. This will be a common occurrence due to the location of the link at the top of the page.

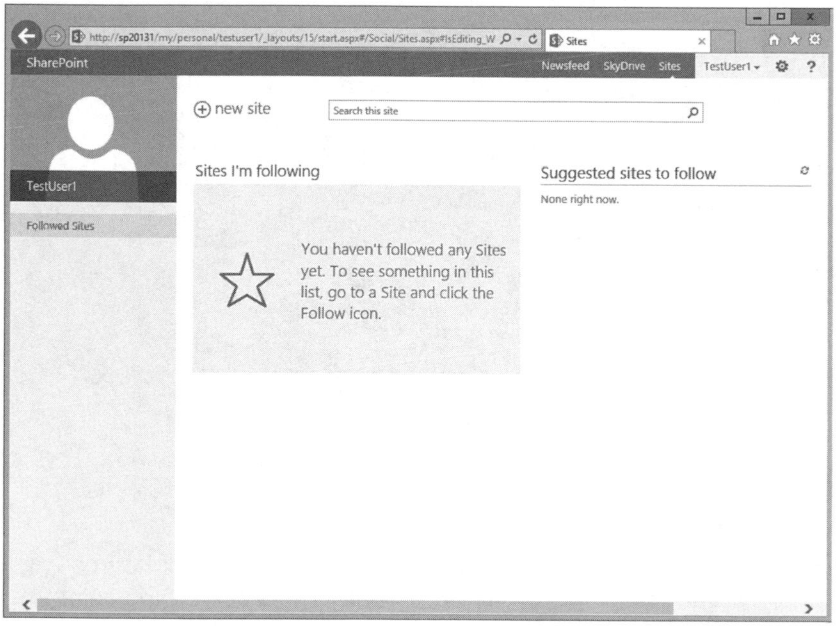

FIGURE 23.9 Sites page in a newly created My Site.

The process for adding a site to the Sites page is quite simple. The user simply visits a site and clicks the Follow link in the upper-right part of the screen. A link to that site is then added to the Sites page. If the user tries to follow a list or library contained in that site, he receives a message: "You're already following this site."

Now if items are added to a Site Feed web part on the site that is now being followed, it then appears immediately in the newsfeed on the user's My Site. An example is shown in Figure 23.10, where the administrator posted notes about the availability of free pizza.

NOTE

For this Follow tool to be enabled on a site, the Following Content site feature needs to be enabled, and the Site Feed site feature also needs to be enabled.

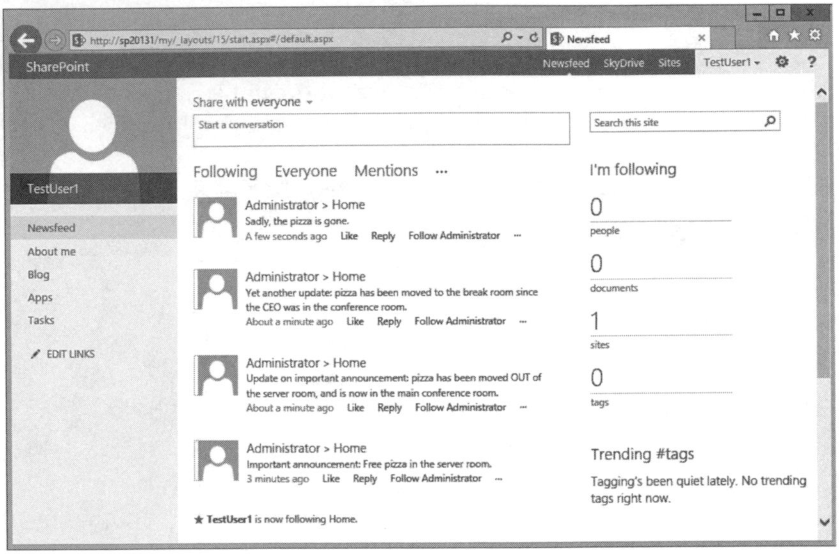

FIGURE 23.10 Newsfeed page showing site feeds in a My Site.

Managing Social Notes and Tags

You can find this tool on the Manage Profile Service: User Profile Service Application page, in the My Site Settings section, and it will assuage many of the fears of the farm administrator, who may well be concerned about allowing users to post "whatever they want" in a forum that other users can see. The nature of posting a note tends to encourage off-the-cuff comments, and the farm administrator may want to do periodic searches for certain words to make sure they aren't appearing. Or an employee may leave the company, and IT decides that his tags should be removed.

This tool is not self-explanatory and can appear to "not work," so a quick review of how to use it will be beneficial to administrators. In the following example, the user Test1 entered a comment that offended a user, who complained to a manager. The farm administrator now needs to do a general search and see whether he can locate and remove the comment. Follow these steps to learn more about the process of managing social tags and notes:

1. Click the User Profile service application from the Manage Services Applications page, and then click Manage Social Tags and Notes in the My Site Settings section.
2. From the Type drop-down menu, select Tags or Notes. In this example, the farm administrator was told it was an offensive note.
3. Either enter a username and click the Check Names button to resolve, or use the Browse tool to find the username required. Multiple names cannot be entered. In this example, **Test1** is entered in the User field, and Check Names is clicked.

4. A URL can also be entered to narrow down the search. In this example, this field is left blank because the farm administrator doesn't know which list or library the comment was made in.

NOTE

When searching from the Manage Social Tags and Notes page, either a valid username or a valid URL must be entered. Note that the URL needs to be the exact view where the tag or note was added. So in this example, the URL must be entered as follows: http://sp20131/sitecollectiondocuments/forms/allitems.aspx. This can be confusing and time-consuming, so it is generally better to search by username and see all of a user's posts.

5. A date range can be entered. The farm administrator doesn't know the date and so leaves these fields blank.
6. The Tag/Note Contains field can be filled out, and in this example, the farm administrator is looking for a specific word to search for and so he enters the term **stupid**.
7. The farm administrator clicks Find to see what Test1 has been posting over the past week. A number of results appear, as shown in Figure 23.11.

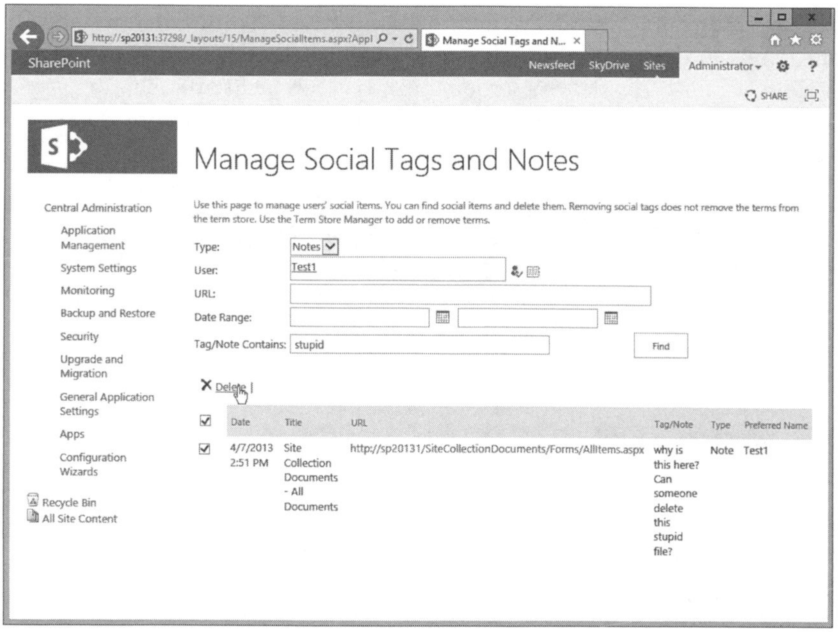

FIGURE 23.11 Using the Manage Social Tags and Notes feature.

8. The farm administrator checks the box next to the one comment that returns, because he agrees it could be offensive, and clicks the Delete button. He clicks the OK button to confirm the deletion, and the note is deleted immediately.

NOTE

A site collection administrator can also delete notes directly from the document library or list by clicking Tags & Notes in the list or library and visiting the Note Board and clicking the Delete button. Other users can edit their own comments at a later date if needed.

Advantages of Using a Dedicated Web Application for My Sites

If the Farm Configuration Wizard was used during the configuration of the SharePoint 2013 Standard or Enterprise environment, the My Sites site collection is provisioned on the default web application. Although this may be acceptable to smaller organizations (for example, under 500 people), larger organizations may have more-complex requirements for the creation and management of My Sites. This section reviews some of these advantages that IT may want to consider before using the standard out-of-the-box configuration.

There can be advantages to using a dedicated web application for the creation of personal sites, especially if the full FIM Profile Synchronization capabilities are to be leveraged. One main advantage is that a web application is a "module" in the SharePoint environment that can be managed and configured in numerous ways. The Manage Web Applications page, as shown in Figure 23.12, provides numerous tools that can be used, including Authentication Providers, Blocked File Types, User Permissions, Web Part Security, User Policy, Anonymous Policy, and Permission Policy.

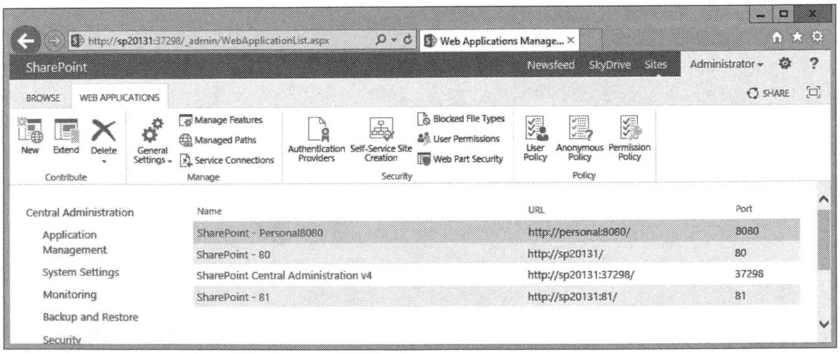

FIGURE 23.12 Manage Web Applications page.

NOTE

Microsoft recommends limiting the total number of web applications in a farm to 20. This is a "supported" limit, which means that exceeding this number of web applications may cause unexpected results, decrease in performance, or other effects.

In addition, every time a user creates a My Site site, a site collection is created, so from a management standpoint, having these organized in a separate web application has its advantages, since a larger organization may have thousands of site collections to manage.

Another advantage is that the farm administrator can control a large number of basic settings for the web application that will house the My Sites, such as the following:

- **Quota Template:** A personal site quota template is provided by default that limits storage to 100MB for each site collection.
- **Recycle Bin:** The amount of time after items are deleted can be reduced, or the second-stage Recycle Bin can be turned off if the organization wants to limit the amount of storage space that "personal" information is taking up.
- **Maximum Upload Size:** This can be reduced, once again to control the total amount of data that needs to be backed up.
- **Blocked File Types:** Blocked file types can be customized for the web application, which allows IT to be more (or less) restrictive over which file types can be uploaded.
- **Permission Policy:** Policies can be created to limit users' abilities to customize their sites (for example, such as Edit Personal Information or Create Subsites).

The process can be quite complex because a new web application needs to be created, and then the My Site Host site collection template needs to be used, and settings in the User Profile service application then need to be modified. So, the full process is not covered in this chapter. Note that audiences can be defined in Central Administration (from the User Profile Service Application management page, Configure Trusted Host Locations) so that users in different audiences can have their personal sites created in different locations.

Restricting User Access to and Creation of My Site Sites

Some administrators want to restrict the use of My Site sites because they may want to pilot the use of these sites with a limited number of users, in the short term, or permanently exclude certain groups of users for a variety of business reasons. This section reviews several ways of controlling access to and creation of My Sites.

An initial requirement for My Sites is that Self-Service Site Creation needs to be activated for the site collection that houses the My Site host and also needs to be available for the web application that hosts the My Site host. If this isn't configured, the full My Site deployment does not complete.

Assuming that My Sites are in use and are deploying successfully, the Manage User Profiles tool in the People section of the User Profile Service Application page provides a way to manage individual My Sites. So, for example, if IT wants to control access to TestUser1's My Site, this is a good place to start. However, My Sites are "secure" by default, so even a farm administrator doesn't have the privileges needed to manage this personal site!

However, the farm administrator can gain access to the My Site site collection without having to ask the owner (TestUser1) by following these steps:

1. Access the Application Management page on the Central Administration site and click Change Site Collection Administrators.
2. Click the drop-down arrow next to the site collection indicated and choose Change Site Collection. Select the desired site. In this example, the site is my/personal/testuser1. Click OK.
3. As shown in Figure 23.13, only the user (TestUser1) is a site collection administrator by default. Click inside the Secondary Site Collection Administrator field, type in the domain and username of the desired secondary site collection administrator (**company123\administrator** in this example), click the Check Names icon, and the name should resolve. Click OK to save.

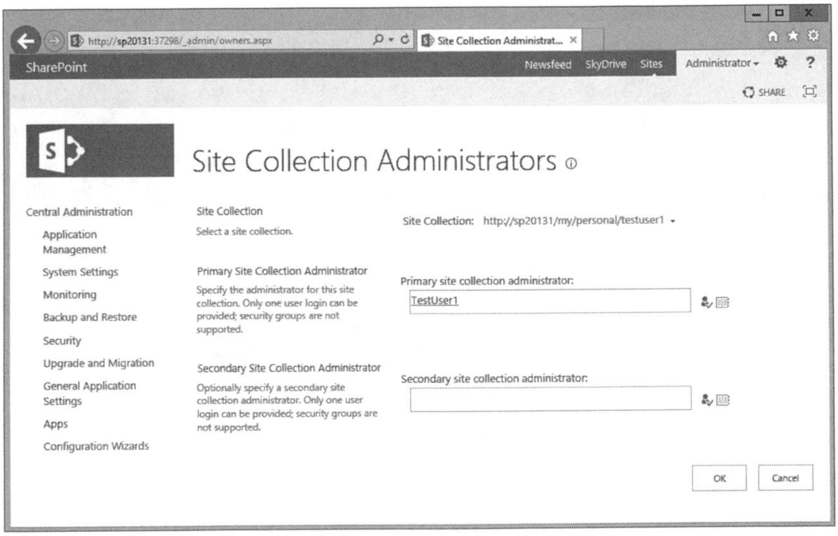

FIGURE 23.13 Site Collection Administrators page for a My Site site collection.

4. Now that the administrator has site collection administrator rights on the user's My Site, he can navigate to the Manage Service Applications page, click User Profile Service Application, and then click Manage User Profiles.
5. Here, enter the user's name (**TestUser1** in this example) in the Find Profiles field and click Find.
6. The user should show up in the results section of the page. Now click the drop-down arrow next to the user and select Manage Personal Site.
7. The familiar Site Settings page appears, and the farm administrator can now tweak permissions to the user's My Site by accessing the Site Permissions page.

Another method is to create a user policy for the web application. This affects access to the entire web application, so this should *not* be used to restrict access to My Site sites if they are housed on the same web application that houses the intranet or portal site collection. The assumption here is that a separate web application was created for My Site and that the user policy will stop certain users from accessing that web application. Follow these steps to create a policy denying access to a My Site dedicated web application to the AD group External Partners:

1. Access the Central Administrator site, click Application Management, and then click Manage Web Applications.
2. Select the My Site web application (in this example, Personal) and click the User Policy button from the Web Applications tab on the ribbon.
3. Click Add Users.
4. Keep All Zones selected. Click Next.
5. From the Add Users window, add the username or AD group name to the Choose Users field (**COMPANY123\external partners** in this example), and click the Check Names button, or use the Browse button to add the users or groups. Figure 23.14 shows the results when the group is validated.

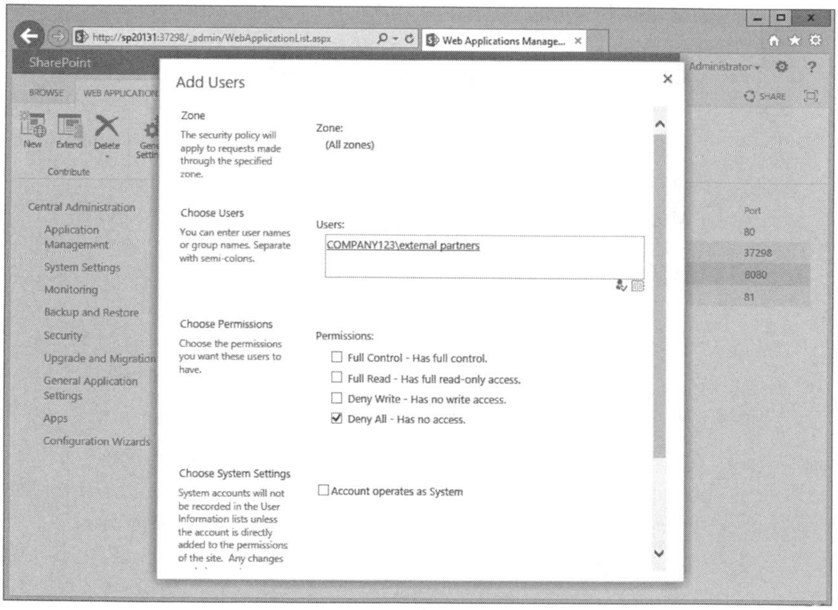

FIGURE 23.14 Creating a policy for a My Site web application to deny an AD group all access.

6. Check the box next to Deny All–Has No Access. Click Finish.
7. Then log in to SharePoint using the account that is a member of the AD group that the policy applies to and try to access My Site. In this example, the user Contractor1, who is a member of the Contractors group, gets a "Let us know why you need access to this site" message when trying to access her My Site.

TIP

Web application policies "win" over site collection policies, and web application deny policies win over web application allow policies. For example, in the previous exercise, a policy was created for the My Site Host web application that denies all access to members of the Contractors group. If a site collection administrator gives direct permissions to the Contractors group to the My Site Host site collection, any member of the group still gets an "Access Denied" error. This is useful to know when troubleshooting these types of errors.

Community Sites Explored

Community sites in SharePoint 2013 provide a number of tools and capabilities to create "forums" where users can post ideas and comment on other topics to generate content on one or multiple topics. Key components of a community are the topics that are defined as managing tools that can be used to categorize posts on the site. Moderators need to then manage posts and interactions on the site and define categories, set different levels of achievement that users can achieve by defining "badges" for the community, and perform other duties.

As with My Sites, community sites may not be for every organization and be relevant to every SharePoint 2013 implementation. To begin with, they should generally be used in conjunction with My Sites to fully leverage the capabilities of My Site newsfeeds and other My Site tools. In addition, community sites require time and effort from IT to set up, and then of moderators to monitor and manage the configuration of the communities, behavior, and posts of the members. Unregulated communities can easily get out of control and, if users report issues and no one responds, can lead to HR issues.

As with My Sites and many other SharePoint 2013 features, the general best practice recommendation is to test the capabilities of the community sites and make a decision from both a technology and governance standpoint on the value of the tools to the overall SharePoint project and act accordingly. Because community sites are usually rolled out as site collections or subsites, it is easy to control access to a test community during a pilot or prototype.

You can create communities within the SharePoint 2013 environment in several different ways:

- **Create a community at the site collection level:** This creates the community in a site collection "silo" and allows very granular management of the configuration of the environment and the storage of community data in a dedicated content database if needed. This is a good option if the community is used by many users and offers specific benefits to the SharePoint project. For example, a company that works in the entertainment space might benefit from a community that allows employees to share thoughts and ideas in a free-form forum type of environment.

- **Create a community at the site level (for example, as a subsite beneath an intranet or departmental root site):** This is less of a commitment in terms of resources and administration and is a good option for SharePoint environments where there might be many communities with compartmentalized user bases. For example, a manufacturer might create a community with each departmental site to promote sharing of ideas within each department or group.
- **Community features can simply be activated on an existing site:** Doing so provides the core community site pages, moderation, membership, and reputation functionality without creating a community itself. This is potentially less overhead than creating a dedicated site, but might confuse users about the true "purpose" of the site because many of the community site features might be seen as more "social" and less "business-like."

NOTE

A number of customized web parts are available on community site collections and sites with special capabilities designed for the community site. These include the following:

- **What's Happening:** Displays how many members, discussions, and replies the community has
- **Top Contributors:** Displays the members who contribute most to the community
- **My Membership:** Displays information about a user's membership in the community, such as the number of posts and replies
- **Manage:** Provides site owners and community moderators tools to manage discussions, categories, members, reputation settings, and community settings

Follow these steps to create a unity site:

1. From Central Administration, click Create Site Collection from the Application Management page.
2. Select the web application that will house the Community Site, enter a title in the Title field (in this example, **Having Fun Community**), provide a URL in the URL field (in this example, **http://sp20131/sites/Fun**), choose Community Site from the Collaboration tab in the Select a Template section, identify primary and secondary site collection administrators, and click OK.
3. When the community site collection has been created, visit it by clicking the link provided. The results should look like Figure 23.15.

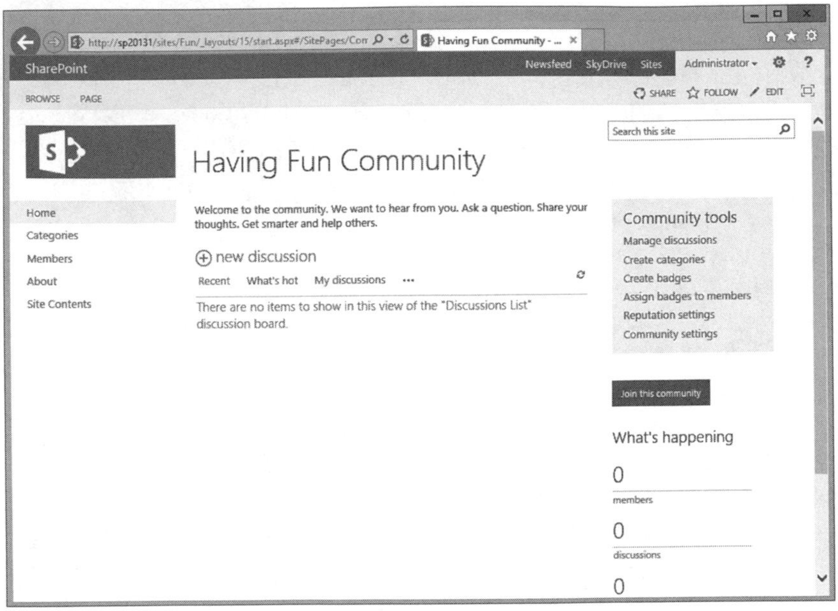

FIGURE 23.15 A new community site.

4. Click the Join This Community button. A welcome message should appear. Refresh the screen and the Member counter in the What's Happening section should increment to 1.

5. From the home page, click the Community Settings link in the Community Tools section on the right side of the page.

6. Check the Enable Auto-Approval check box, and check Enable Reporting of Offensive Content check box. Click OK.

7. From the home page, click the Reputation settings link in the Community Tools section on the right side of the page.

8. Note that Allow Items in This List to Be Rated is set to Yes and that the Likes option is selected. Note the Member Achievements Point System, as shown in Figure 23.16. Leave these settings set to their defaults.

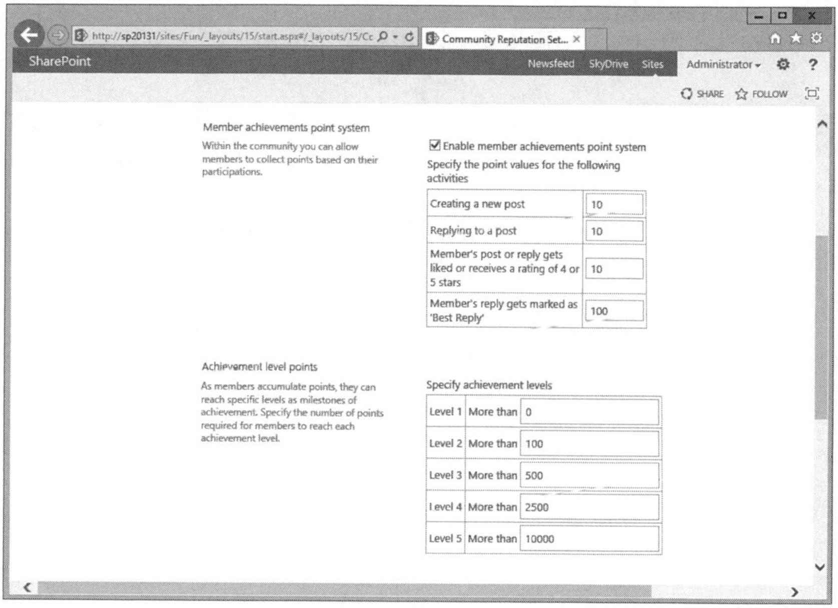

FIGURE 23.16 Community Reputation Settings page.

9. In the Achievement Level Representation section, select Display Achievement as Text. Note that the fields are populated with the text Level 1, Level 2, Level 3, Level 4, and Level 5. Click OK.

10. From the home page, click the Create categories link in the Community Tools section on the right side of the page.

11. Click New Item and enter a category name (for this example, **Restaurants**). In real-world situations, it is worth finding, editing, and uploading images that will be used for the category for a more visually rewarding end-user experience. In this example, leave the Category Picture fields empty. Click Save.

12. Return to the home page and click the New Discussion link; a form will load. Enter in a sample subject, sample body text, select Restaurants from the Category drop-down list, and click Save. The home page will look similar to Figure 23.17.

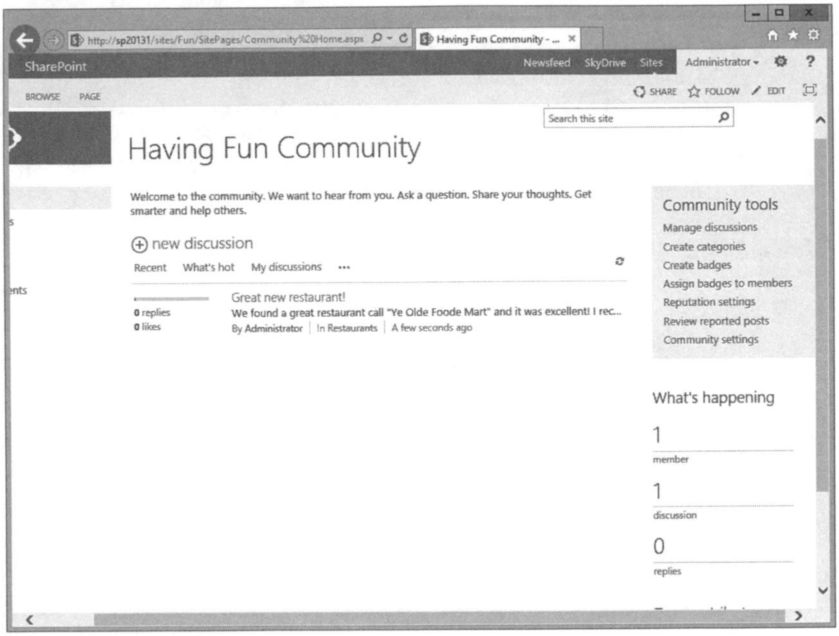

FIGURE 23.17 Community home page with discussion item.

Summary

My Sites in SharePoint 2013 are dramatically improved and seem to hit the mark when it comes to providing a suite of tools that allows organizations to easily deploy My Sites, create Community template-based site collections, and allow users to start following sites and activities of other users. The Newsfeed page quickly becomes a Facebook-like page to check regularly and see what's going on. As this chapter showed, there are many interesting and powerful features available in My Sites, and also many tools in Central Administration for the farm administrator to become familiar with to be able to thoroughly understand the "moving parts" of the My Site environment. For end users to have a positive experience, it is important to carefully test the tools that will be rolled out and to ensure that policies around the use of these tools be established and enforced.

Best Practices

The following are best practices from this chapter:

- Before actively enlisting users to create My Site sites, the farm administrator should verify that all the Central Administration components are properly configured and meet the needs of the organization and that AD synchronization is functional.

- A new feature in SharePoint 2013 is called Direct Active Directory Import. It allows "basic" import of user information from AD *without* requiring the configuration and use of the FIM-based Profile Synchronization tools. The tool has limitations when compared with the Profile Synchronization tools, but in many cases is sufficient for basic synchronization with AD.
- For organizations with more-complex synchronization requirements, where the full Profile Synchronization features are required, a recommended best practice is to create a new web application and My Sites Host site collection and a User Profile service application. The full configuration process varies based on the details of the environment and isn't covered in this chapter. Although it is generally quite involved, it is often required for larger organizations with more-complex needs.
- By default, only the creator of the My Site (such as TestUser1) is a site collection administrator of that site collection. Therefore, farm administrators should be familiar with how to add themselves as My Site administrators where necessary, as covered in this chapter.
- Managed metadata, along with audiences, can be leveraged in many places in the My Site environment and should be considered as vital tools to the success of a well-thought-out My Site strategy.
- Numerous tools important to the successful management of My Sites are found in Central Administration on the Manage Profile Service: User Profile Service Application page. As reviewed in this chapter, the farm administrator should become thoroughly familiar with these tools to understand the fields in user profiles and how to manage user profiles, configure My Sites, and perform other management functions.
- Communities can be deployed as site collections, and subsites or community features can be enabled on existing sites. In general, it is recommended to create community sites as site collections or subsites rather than mixing community features with a departmental or collaboration site to keep more formal business documents and procedures separate from the less structured "forum-like" community environment where end users earn points and badges based on activities and contributions and are prone to off-the-cuff posts and comments.

CHAPTER 24

Governing the SharePoint 2013 Ecosystem

IN THIS CHAPTER

Managing any software product takes time and energy, but few software products provide the number of tools and allow for the same range of interactivity with end users and their data and ideas as the SharePoint product line. With many software products, the work is mostly done when the servers are built and the software installed and working. But with SharePoint 2013 (and previous versions), it can be said that the work is just beginning when the environment is configured and in use.

Of course, SharePoint 2013 can be locked down so that a very limited number of users can add documents, use My Site sites, or add items to lists, but then the value of what is at the heart of a set of collaboration tools diminishes. At the other end of the spectrum, allowing complete freedom to all users to create sites, delete sites, and leverage every tool in the SharePoint 2013 arsenal would most likely lead to a state of anarchy where users would have little faith in security and stability of the environment.

The term *governance* in the context of SharePoint 2013 includes concepts of maintenance of the hardware and software that supports the tools, but is more focused on creating and enforcing policies, rules of conduct, and the process of understanding "what's going on" in the environment. This chapter discusses governance from a conceptual and process-oriented level, while giving examples of specific SharePoint 2013 tools and components that should be included in the governance plan, many of which are covered in other chapters of this book in greater detail.

Ultimately, this chapter shares strategies and tools to consider for defining a governance plan for a SharePoint 2013 environment that any sized or shaped company should consider and helps provide impetus to get started on the road to effective governance.

The Importance of Governance

Is governance something that needs to be implemented with SharePoint, or should the SharePoint environment be a place for creativity and freedom? Although cases can be made for lack of structure, most organizations don't need to think for too long before they can come up with examples of IT projects that could have gone better and produced better results, and of technologies that failed to deliver the functionality that was expected. A governance plan must carefully balance user innovation and freedom versus manageability and support.

An almost universal experience is that of data repositories that have not had the proper governance, whether it be paper-based files, file shares, or the email environment, and these generally tend to be inefficient and sources of contention. There are many strong reasons for putting governance in place for any applications, three of which follow:

- Although maintenance costs of "unmanaged applications" seem low initially, the impact on the organization can be significant in the long term in less-tangible ways. User complaints about not being able to find anything, not understanding the purpose of different applications through lack of training, or not being able to get support when issues are encountered, erode the level of confidence in the application and ultimately in IT.
- Unmanaged applications over time either become abandoned or fail to garner user adoption. Consider a poorly managed intranet. It may have cost a considerable amount of time and money to create, and there may be recurring software costs and resources dedicated to keeping it running, but without appropriate governance, it can become disorganized, the content stale, and users unhappy with levels of support provided.
- Unmanaged applications are difficult to secure. If policies for entitlement and rights are not well defined from the beginning, securing vital corporate assets can be difficult later on. It is usually harder to take away user privileges and tools than just to control what is provided to begin with.

SharePoint is a powerful tool with tremendous potential. By spending time prior to or during the implementation of SharePoint 2013 on the governance plan, IT can help ensure that the project is initially perceived as a success, that the environment offers a well-defined set of tools to end users, and that it will be managed over time as it evolves.

A final thought for this section is that the governance plan does not need to fall into place all at once. There can certainly be phases to a governance plan, as there are phases to technology implementation projects.

Creating the Governance Plan

Governance is the process of governing, or managing, the SharePoint environment, which consists of hardware, software, data, processes, and people. Determining the right level of governance for the organization requires an understanding of the goals of the SharePoint 2013 infrastructure and related projects. If the SharePoint environment is being built to simply provide My Site sites for employees to get to know each other better, the goals are quite different from an implementation where SharePoint houses the corporate Internet site and allows customers to conduct monetary transactions. Therefore, a key step is defining the governance plan from a high level that takes into account the goals for the SharePoint implementation and sets forth a plan of action for ensuring that those goals continue to be met after the "go live" of the SharePoint environment.

This section discusses the importance of having vision and scope of work documents in place before diving into the governance plan, provides recommendations on a starting point for the governance plan creation process through a visualization tool, and then moves into the components of the governance plan.

Reviewing the Vision and Scope Documents

Before beginning the governance plan, the vision and scope of work documents should be dusted off. If they don't yet exist, you need to define these elements. Even for the smallest implementation, documenting the vision and the scope of work are critical factors for success, even if each is made up of a few bullets on a Post-It. The vision document should provide high-level goals and objectives for the project, whereas the scope of work document should describe the tasks to take place, timeline, roles and responsibilities, communications plan, training, and support. These two documents provide the foundation for the governance plan.

NOTE

An important variable in the process of creating the governance plan is the current state of the SharePoint 2013 environment. If the environment has not been built yet, the process is different from if there is already a SharePoint 2013 environment in place and the organization finally has time to take a breath and devote attention to the governance plan. The process is also different for an organization that has SharePoint 2010 in place, has been using it for years, and is planning an upgrade to SharePoint 2013.

It is understood that the temptation to skip the documentation process is very strong, but to show how simple this can really be, here is a simple vision and scope of a work statement that provides enough basic guidance to develop a governance plan:

- **Vision statement:** The goal of SharePoint 2013 at Company 123 is to provide a better alternative to our current intranet and file share while providing enhanced collaboration tools.

- **Scope of work summary:** SharePoint 2013 will be implemented by internal IT resources, with assistance from subject matter experts in a phased approach. The phases will be proof of concept (POC), pilot, implementation/migration, and finally governance and support. Best-of-breed backup, management, and add-on web parts will be identified in the POC phase. Documentation of server builds and recommended best practices for maintenance will be included, as will knowledge transfer to internal IT resources.

Guiding principles and steps such as these provide direction to the project and define basic milestones. Without at least a basic and agreed-upon foundation of vision and scope, the chances of a successful project are reduced; in fact, even determining whether the project was or was not successful will be difficult, because the success criteria and milestones were never set.

Visually Mapping the Governance Strategy

To prepare for the more formal documentation step, it is useful to visualize the overall plan, which will help provide shape to the plan of action and map the logical components of hardware, software, people, and processes to the different areas of functionality that will be implemented in the project. Figure 24.1 shows an example of a visualization tool for a governance plan for Company 123.

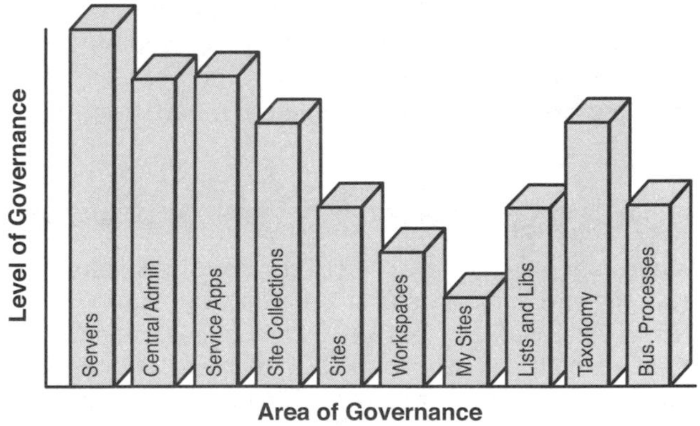

FIGURE 24.1 Governance diagram example for a company.

One way to define this diagram is to call it an *equalizer chart,* referring to the piece of audio hardware. This brings to mind the process of determining different settings for the components that comprise the SharePoint 2013 environment and then adjusting the individual settings as time goes by to tune the overall levels of governance. A distinction to make at this point in the governance process (brainstorming) is that the chart is driving the output rather than data driving the chart. For example, if the IT department is locked in a room working on this chart together, the CIO might simply say, "We don't have budget for new staff or any additional software and we're not supporting My Sites."

That would immediately result in the removal of the My Site component from the chart and "shorten" the bars across the board because the component of support resources is reduced.

To further understand how this chart can be useful, review Figure 24.1 in more detail. It is suggested that on the far left, the bar that represents governance of the servers that support the SharePoint environment (for example, Windows 2012 servers, one or more Structured Query Language [SQL] servers, and one or more SharePoint 2013 servers) represents a maximal level of governance. Company 123 governs these servers very carefully, fully realizing that if they aren't stable, the entire environment suffers. Therefore, the bar takes up the full height (or ranks an 8 of 8 in governance). To be more specific, there are standards for the operating system configuration in place, as well as for which version of Windows Server will be installed, how patches are applied, and antivirus use. Standards are also in place for backup software, maintenance plans for the SQL databases, as well as strict controls over which Active Directory (AD) groups and users have permissions to manage these servers.

Moving to the right in Figure 24.1, the Central Administration site will also be tightly controlled in terms of the configuration of the various components, such as web applications, jobs, reporting, and groups and accounts, that can make changes, and ranks a 7 out of 8. The service applications will be governed at a similar level. Site collections will be slightly less controlled and governed (6 of 8), sites still less (4 of 8), workspaces still less (3 of 8), and My Site sites the least (2 of 8). The lists and libraries will be governed to a medium degree, while the overall taxonomy more highly managed, and business processes (which include workflows) in the medium range.

NOTE

The level of governance for each area on this chart carries with it an element of cost and level of effort, both one-time (such as purchasing third-party software or hiring administrators) and over the long term (time to use the software, update policies, and enforce procedures). The level of risk in each area grows inversely to the level of governance. Consider, for example, a SharePoint 2013 environment where the servers that house SQL Server and the SharePoint 2013 software are not managed, not backed up, and open for many users to modify the settings. Most people would agree that is a riskier configuration than the alternative.

Continuing with this visualization, each bar on the chart can be broken down into components, including the following:

- **Resources involved in the governance process:** This should include full-time and part-time resources as well as consultants and contractors.
- **Level of security and privilege constraints implemented:** A higher level of security translates to added governance, or control over the specific area that generally requires more time to manage than "looser" controls.

- **Templates used for creating the site collection, site, list, workflow, and other components:** Templates take time to create, manage, and update, as well as time to verify they are in fact being used.
- **Reporting and auditing to track events and activities:** This includes the built-in tools in the operating system, Internet Information Services (IIS), and SharePoint 2013, and can include third-party tools such as Microsoft System Center Operations Manager and products from AvePoint, Axceler, Metalogix, Quest, or other third party.
- **Policies and procedures to define acceptable usage of the resources:** These can be enforced to a certain degree by the tools in place (SharePoint and third party, group policies, and so forth), but these also need to be documented and communicated to the user community and at some level enforced.
- **Third-party tools to add functionality:** Besides the possibilities mentioned previously, third-party tools can be used to add functionality to SharePoint 2013 in every conceivable area, or tools (such as new web parts) can be created internally.

Figure 24.2 gives an example of what generates the height of several sections of the chart, which should be translated as cost and level of effort. In this example, starting at the right, the My Site environment will be minimally governed at Company 123. Support staff is a fixed number, but no additional training will be provided to them on My Site support; the basic out-of-the-box templates will be provided, but no new ones created; and policies and procedures on My Site usage will be loosely defined, to essentially clarify that users can do what they want within the constraints of the software. Moving to the left, workspaces will be allowed, which translates to users having self-service site creation privileges, and the regular templates for meetings and document workspaces will be provided. The policies and procedures for using the sites will be loosely defined, and out-of-the-box auditing and reporting will be in place. However, IT will not be responsible for policing or cleaning up idle or abandoned workspaces. Moving to the Sites column shows a higher level of governance where the governance items security constraints and third-party tools have been added, increasing the level of governance. IT wants to strictly control privileges for the sites themselves that house the workspaces, lists, and libraries that users will be using. Finally, to the far left, the site collections will have additional constraints and auditing tools in place. IT will track carefully the different levels of usage of the site collections (as opposed to the sites themselves, which won't be as carefully managed) and have tools in place to manage the site collections.

Defining Governance Roles and Responsibilities

One of the more important things to ensure success in SharePoint 2013 governance is to ensure that the roles and responsibilities of the parties involved are well defined not only in the rollout, but in the day-to-day processes in a SharePoint deployment and its maintenance. It is often underestimated what the day-to-day maintenance is for the "steady-state" deployment of SharePoint.

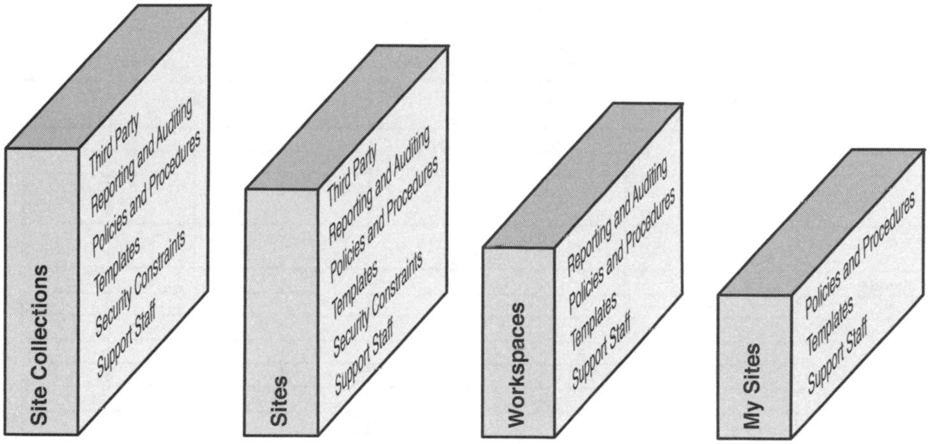

FIGURE 24.2 Detail of several components of the governance diagram.

Often, the emphasis is placed on the IT administrator, whereas little emphasis is placed on necessary business roles, designer roles, or even IT support structures. It's common to find entire roles undefined and failures can definitely happen as a result.

To start with, the organization should define the SharePoint farm administrator and site collection administrators. Key stakeholders, project managers, and business analysts can also add value to the governance process. For example, defining a "SharePoint steering committee chairperson" and "taxonomy czar" can enhance the involvement of individuals in specific areas of the ongoing maintenance of the SharePoint 2013 environment. Members of the SharePoint steering committee might not be technical in nature, but they will bring their individual perspectives to the process and help drive adoption of the technologies (and often, funding for specific initiatives).

Many organizations use a RACI charting strategy, which stands for responsible, accountable, consulted, and informed. A RACI chart is a simple and powerful vehicle for communication. It is used for defining and documenting responsibility. For each aspect of the project, both the initial rollout and the day-to-day management should have the people and their roles identified as well as the level of their involvement. This helps keep resources focused on their tasks and levels of involvement and usually enhances communications paths. Often, roles and responsibilities cross group and team lines. Figure 24.3 shows a RACI table example for Company 123.

SharePoint Governance	IT Mgmnt	Steering Committee	Business Analyst	Farm Admin	Site Collection Admin	Site-Admin	Operations	Help Desk	Trainers
Governance Documentation, Policies and Procedures	A	C, I	C, I	R	R	C, I	C, I	C	
Hardware and OS Maintenance	A			I			R		
SQL Server Management	A			I			R		
Central Admin Site Management	A	I		R	C		I	I	
Service Applications Management	A	C	C	R	C		I	I	
Site Collection Management	A	I		C, I	R	I	I	I	
Site Management	A	I		C	R	R		I	
List, Library Management	A	I		C	C, I	R		I	
Taxonomy Management	A	C	R	C	C, I	C, I		I	
Business Process Design	I	C	R	C	C, I	C			
Change Control	A	C		C	C, I	I	R		
End User Support	A		C		C	R		R	
End User Training	A		C		C	R		C	R
Administrator Training	A		C		C	I			R
Communications	A	C	I	C, I	C, I	I		I	

FIGURE 24.3 RACI table for roles and responsibilities.

Governing the Farm

This section concentrates on the tools provided in the Central Administration site to provide an overview of the areas the governance plan should include. References are made to other chapters in the book that provide additional detail on specific areas, because each topic can be complex. For the purposes of this chapter, governing the farm can be seen to include the Central Administration site tools, settings combined with PowerShell and `stsadm` command-line tools, and any third-party tools from companies such as AvePoint or Quest that assist the farm administrators with their jobs. The service application tools are embedded in the Central Administration site, and these settings should be clarified in this process.

To begin, the organization should work through the different components of Central Administration. Chapter 6, "Managing and Administering SharePoint 2013 Infrastructure," gives a thorough walkthrough of the basic management categories that are broken out in Central Administration, as follows:

- Application Management
- System Settings
- Monitoring
- Backup and Restore
- Security

- Upgrade and Migration
- General Application Settings
- Configuration Wizards

The following is a partial list of important topics for which systemwide policies and standards should be defined:

- **Site collection creation standards:** Important items to cover in governance include which templates will be used, the use of managed paths, and the creation of different content databases for site collections. In addition, the use of site quotas, and their settings, is included. The site collection administrators need to be defined for each site collection and whether self-service site creation will be allowed.
- **"Standard" service application standards:** For the required service applications, the settings should be reviewed. For example, the Search Service application has a number of settings that need to be configured, such as Content Sources, Crawl Rules, File Types, Authoritative Pages, Query Rules, and other settings. The User Profile Storage Service application performs a vital role in syncing with AD, and has numerous other capabilities that can be configured, such as compiling audiences. Usage and Health Data Collection is generally considered a vital component for IT to manage and monitor farm usage. Some less-familiar service applications like the Secure Store Service application and Managed Metadata Service application should also be reviewed and tested to see whether and how they will be used in the farm.
- **"Optional" service application standards:** If SharePoint Server 2013 Enterprise is being used, a number of additional service applications can be rolled out, including Access Service application, Excel Services Service application, PerformancePoint Service application, PowerPoint Service application, Visio Graphics Service application, and the Word Viewing Service application. The organization needs to decide which of these will be deployed, to which users, and at what point in the project. Rolling out "everything" during the initial phases of a project is generally considered ill-advised unless both the user community and IT are fairly advanced in their SharePoint skills and training is provided for resources who will be managing these tools. Figure 24.4 illustrates a portion of service applications available in the Enterprise edition of SharePoint 2013.

NOTE

Chapter 22, "Managing Metadata and Content Types in SharePoint 2013," provides insight into the power of using managed metadata in SharePoint 2013. Chapter 26, "Extending SharePoint 2013 with Excel Services, Visio Graphics Services, and Access Services," and Chapter 27, "Office Web Apps 2013 Integration with SharePoint 2013," provide additional information about the configuration options for these service applications. Chapter 30, "Business Intelligence in SharePoint 2013 with PerformancePoint Services," provides information about and examples of PerformancePoint capabilities.

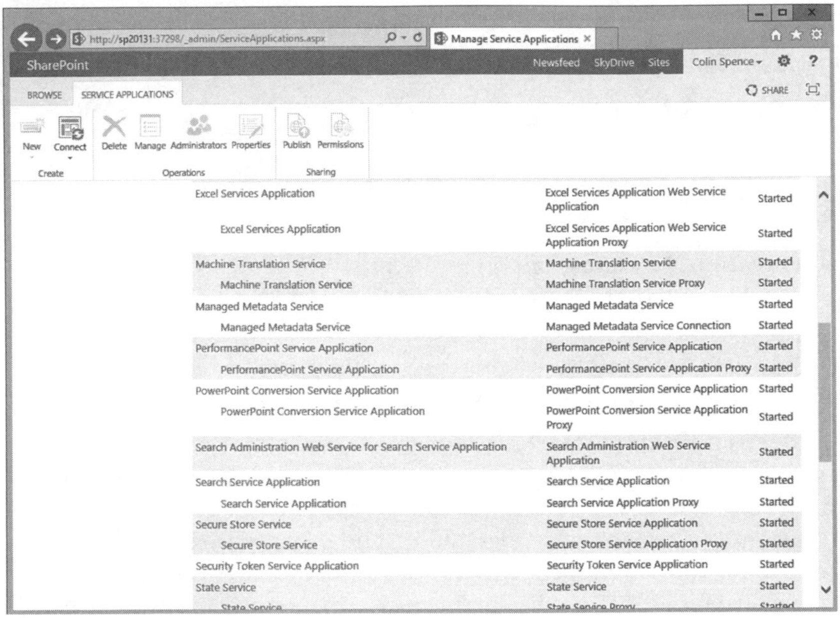

FIGURE 24.4 Service applications in Central Administration.

- **Managing services on servers:** For multiserver implementations, decisions should be made concerning which services will run on which server. This can impact performance and the user experience, since overloading servers will impact their responsiveness.

- **Monitoring settings:** Pay special attention to the tools in this section of the Central Administration site because they allow the farm administrators to review problems and solutions, review rule definitions, review job definitions and job status, view administrative reports, configure diagnostic logging, review information management policy usage reports, view health reports, configure usage and health data collection, and view web analytics reports. Chapter 11, "Monitoring a SharePoint 2013 Environment," provides more information about these built-in tools and provides information about Microsoft's System Center Operations Manager (SCOM).

- **Backup and restore:** A high-level decision to be made here is whether the native SharePoint backup and restore tools will be used or if third-party backup tools from Symantec, Commvault, AvePoint, or others will be used. If the native SharePoint tools will be used, the farm administrators need to become familiar with the use of these tools and understand their strengths and weaknesses. Although a basic service level agreement (SLA) may be separate from the governance plan, the capabilities of the tools will affect the farm administrators' ability to meet end-user requests. Chapter 10, "Backing Up and Restoring a SharePoint Environment," provides additional information about this topic, including using PowerShell for backup and restore and backing up IIS configurations.

- **Security:** This page provides access to tools such as the farm administrators group and its members, web application security policies, managed accounts, service accounts, blocked file types, web part security, information rights management, and whether labels, barcodes, auditing, and retention will be available for use. Chapter 15, "Implementing and Validating SharePoint Security," gives additional information about this topic.
- **General application settings:** As shown in Figure 24.5, these settings include tools such as External Service Connections, InfoPath Forms Services, Site Directory, SharePoint Designer, Search, Reporting Services, and Content Deployment. Each of these tools should be reviewed and decisions made about their configurations.

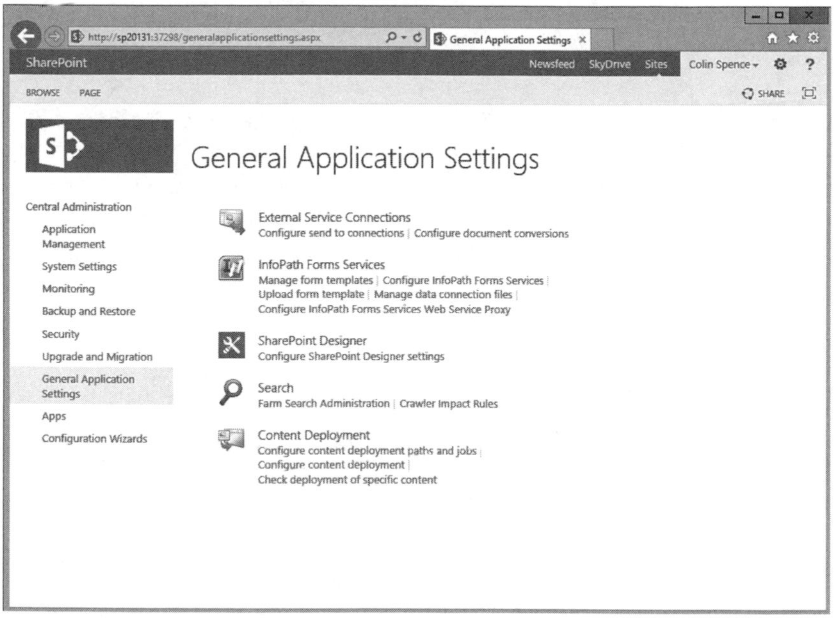

FIGURE 24.5 General Application Settings page in Central Administration.

Having reviewed this list, you might think it sounds like an overwhelming task to define how each and every component will be configured. However, it might suffice, based on the organizational needs, to just create a grid of which features and tools will be made available during the initial phase and not delve too deeply into the individual configurations of the tools.

Chapter 18, "SharePoint Foundation Versus SharePoint Server 2013," provides a number of charts that can easily be adapted for use in the governance plan, to provide a summary of high-level organizational decisions about which tools and features will be used and supported. For example, Table 24.1 provides a grid that could be used to define the decisions that are made in the area of service applications with a minimal investment of time, and without delving too deeply into the details of the configuration of each service application.

TABLE 24.1 Governance Plan for Service Applications for Company 123

Service Application	Provided in Phase 1	Provided in Future Phases	Notes
Access Services 2010	No	No	
Access Services 2013	No	Maybe	If it can be justified.
App Management Services	Yes	Yes	
Application Discovery and Load Balancer Service application	Yes	Yes	
Business Data Connectivity Service	No	Maybe	If Business Intelligence (BI) project is approved.
Excel Services application	Yes	Yes	Finance department only.
Managed Metadata Service	Yes	Yes	This is key to the success of our SharePoint project.
PerformancePoint Service application	No	Maybe	If BI project is approved.
PowerPoint Conversion Service application	No	No	Not in scope.
Search Service application	Yes	Yes	Key requirement for the project.
Secure Store Service	Yes	Yes	
Security Token Service application	Yes	Yes	
State Service	Yes	Yes	
Usage and Health Data Collection	Yes	Yes	Need to clearly define who will manage this.
User Profile Service application (including My Site)	Yes	Yes	My Sites are important to success of the project.
Visio Graphics Service	Yes	Yes	
Word Automation Services	No	No	Not in scope.
Work Management Service application	Yes	Yes	Important for task management across projects.
Workflow Service application	Yes	Yes	

TIP

A recommended best practice for the development of governance documentation is to have a lab environment available where team members can gain experience with the Enterprise version of SharePoint 2013, where all service applications are enabled and configured. This can also be used when reviewing the site collection and site features that will be supported and also the list and library features and tools.

As mentioned previously, other chapters in this book review features at this level and can help designers and planners determine which features offer the most value to the organization and should therefore be governed.

For some organizations, the activity of reviewing the functionality can be done in the scope of a few hours; in others, this process might take months. In either case, the end result is a list of functionality that helps give shape to the governance plan in terms of which tools and features will be supported by IT and therefore need to be governed.

Another key element of the governance plan is defining the scope for which functionality will be governed. Whereas some settings are global to the farm, others are specific to the web application or the service application, and therefore can be made available to limited groups of users. This can, of course, complicate the governance process, but in most organizations, there is a demographic of users who are highly advanced and can be trusted to use more advanced functions, whereas a majority of users would simply get confused or not be interested. Being able to cater to the more advanced group is often where innovation and improvements come from. For additional granularity, features can be activated/deactivated at the site, site collection, web application, or farm level. Depending on how your organization decides to develop its taxonomy or information architecture, activate the features at the appropriate scope to simplify management. The web application and site collection level are usually a better place to manage most functions.

Governing Site Collections and Sites

Site collections and sites require more governance than the Central Administration tools and environment because usually some of the day-to-day management of the site collections and sites is distributed to a wider group of IT staff and end users. Although some organizations do retain complete control over site and site collection settings, this is often seen to be overly heavy-handed, and users, especially users with significant SharePoint experience, will push back. Furthermore, the workload will increase over time for the help desk performing menial tasks such as modifying views, tweaking .aspx pages, and changing user permissions.

Chapter 21, "Designing and Managing Pages and Sites for Knowledge Workers," provides a thorough exploration of the different tools available to the site collection administrator and the subsets available to the site administrator. Figure 24.6 shows the Site Settings page when a site collection administrator logs in to a site collection where most of the site collection features have been enabled, which enables additional management tools. Not all the tools need to be included in a governance plan, but the governance plan should address several key areas:

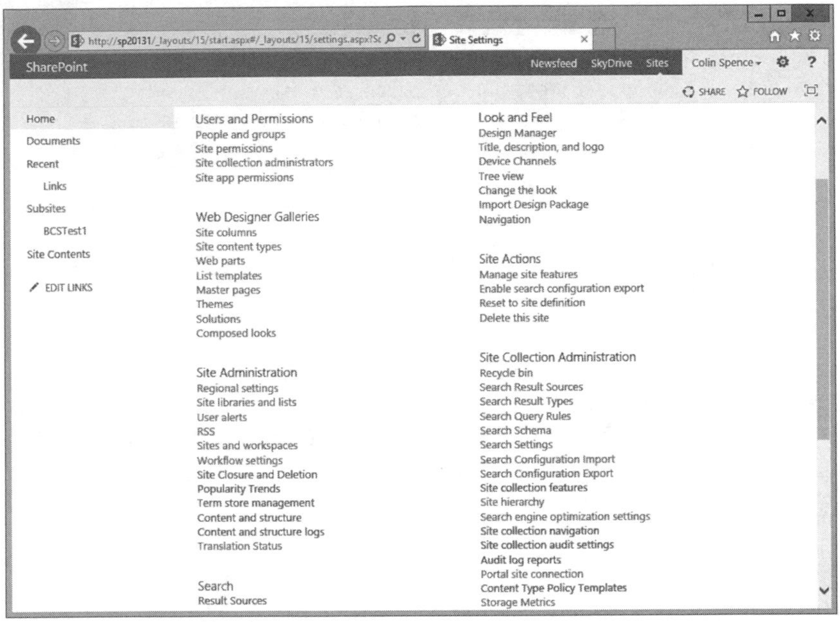

FIGURE 24.6 Site Settings page as seen by a site collection administrator.

- To begin, the question of which **site collection features and site features** should be enabled needs to be addressed. For example, IT may not want end users to use the legacy SharePoint 2007 workflows, PerformancePoint site collection features, Document ID Service, and In Place Records Management site collection features. IT might also want to make sure that SharePoint Server Publishing Infrastructure site and site collection features are not enabled.

  Managing the site columns and content types in use can be critically important if the organization is serious about taking advantage of the metadata-oriented tools in SharePoint 2013. Ensuring that the different site collections stay in sync can be a challenge and often requires the use of custom scripts or third-party management tools.

- Providing an approved set of **list and library templates** can greatly facilitate governance because it allows site collection and site administrators to simply choose an approved template and set a couple of settings, and it can be used immediately. For example, this helps ensure that required columns are in place, managed metadata is properly leveraged, and versioning settings are consistent.

- **Look and feel tools** can dramatically affect the user experience and should also be governed to a certain extent. Approved master pages and page layouts should be set, as well as themes, navigation standards, and related standards.

- **Site collection audit settings and report settings** should be governed to ensure the appropriate events are tracked, audited, and can be analyzed. Figure 24.7 shows the Configure Audit Settings page for the site collection. In this example, IT wants "everything on" so that user usage patterns can be analyzed, but they only need to retain the data for 90 days.

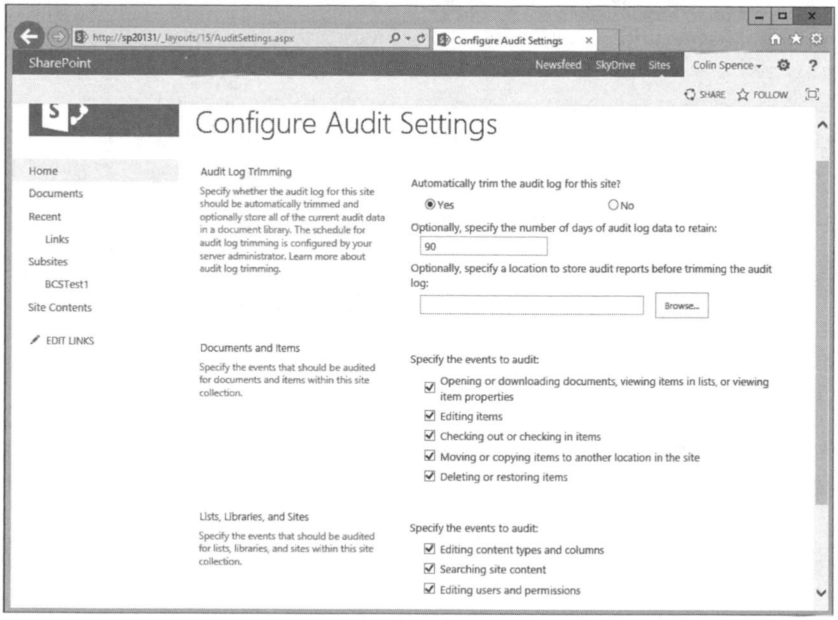

FIGURE 24.7 Configure Audit Settings page for the site collection.

- **Site collection policies** provide options for enabling retention and retention stages, enabling auditing of opening or downloading documents, editing items, and checking out, moving, or deleting items. Barcodes and labels can also be enabled if used by some or all groups that use SharePoint.
- **Record declaration settings** can be important to define, as well. When an item has been declared a record, additional restrictions and retention policies can be applied. The ability to manually declare a record can be enabled or disabled, and the declaration of records and undeclaration of records can be set to be performed by members of specific SharePoint groups.
- **SharePoint Designer settings** are used to enable SharePoint Designer 2013 use, enable detaching pages from the site definition, and enable customizing master pages and page layouts. IT might want to disable some or all these tools.

These bullets give some suggestions as to areas that should be governed for sites and site collections, but this list is by no means exhaustive. Each project differs, and each SharePoint 2013 environment has unique purposes, so the governance plans should focus on the components and tools that are most important in the overall vision and scope of the project. Once again, without a defined vision and scope for the project, it becomes very difficult, if not impossible, to adequately govern the environment.

Records Management in SharePoint

Records management can be executed in a number of different ways. SharePoint has continued to advance records management capabilities since the last release. Records management must truly begin at the business level and be carefully governed. Before determining how to use the Records Center, workflow, and notifications, you should answer the following questions:

- What is (and often more important, what is not) a record?
- What are the stages and life cycle of the record?
- What are the critical requirements for the proper management of the record?

Only after these basic questions are understood at a detailed level can technology begin to enable records management within an organization. That said, after those questions have been answered, SharePoint can provide valuable tools to simplify and improve the management of business-critical records within the organization.

TIP

A useful exercise is to use a SharePoint list to build out a file plan that documents the types of records, life cycle, access, and archive. Having a central file plan for key records is a proactive and strategic way to begin using SharePoint as part of a records management solution.

Records Declarations

With a new records management strategy, often a challenge for records that are not formally being managed is the declaration of when something becomes a record. The optimal situation is for the system to "know" when something is a record and then have a way to execute the proper requirements on that record. Whenever possible, look to automate the declaration of a record. Following are a few strategies for the automated, semi-automated, and manual declaration with SharePoint's records management capabilities.

Content types with associated workflows are the most flexible and likely to fit a specific requirement. The downside with this approach is that it is practical only when the declaration is something triggered in SharePoint, such as an approval or change in a metadata field. Also, this approach is complex particularly if it requires integration with the systems initially generating the files that become records. Think of an enterprise resource planning (ERP) system that generates invoices. This method is particularly effective when there is not a person responsible for gathering, classifying, and stewarding records.

The Records Center is a site template that provides a way for users to declare records by uploading directly to the site and identifying the type of record. This method is good when a user or group of users is trained specifically on the record types and has a basic understanding of records management. The Records Center also provides a hold capability to facilitate eDiscovery.

eDiscovery can be a hugely resource-intensive activity for organizations, particularly if litigation is common for the organization. In addition to the hold capabilities with SharePoint, consider using SharePoint's search engine to search all repositories and enable select staff to then access these search results.

CAUTION

Indexing content of non-SharePoint content may not be able to properly prune results based on security. For eDiscovery, this might actually be beneficial because the organization is legally responsible to provide "everything," but when architecting your search environment, make sure to partition these search scopes so that they are available to only select members of the team who are gathering discoverable information.

The Governance Cycle

In the United States, Congress and the Supreme Court are constantly changing laws and passing bills in an attempt to improve the country. The government is constantly striving to improve how they govern our country. The best governance plan is one that changes and adjusts itself to the growing needs and pains. Figure 24.8 shows the cyclical nature of governance and suggests that each "component" of the plan should be regularly reviewed. A component might be taxonomy governance, for example, or site management, or service applications governance.

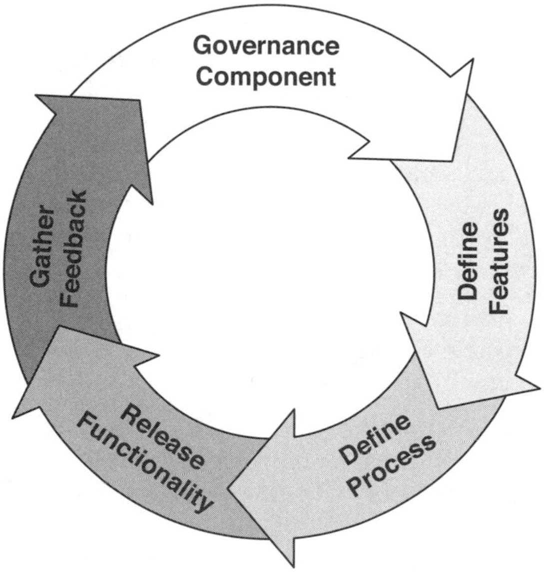

FIGURE 24.8 Cycle of governance.

Developing a mechanism to solicit user feedback and make refinements to the plan is a great way to proactively manage the application. Developing a governing board that includes application/system administrators and end users is a good way to discuss issues, requests, and build out new templates or expand features.

To be able to really take advantage of a governing board, an agenda needs to get built, and materials should be brought together. A good starting point for these meetings is a review of the usage trends, user feedback, and any issues that have arisen since the last meeting. Consider using a meeting workspace to capture agendas as well as tasks or takeaways.

Summary

A governance plan must carefully balance user innovation and freedom versus manageability and support. This requires that the organization "right size" the governance plan based on resources available to participate in the governance cycle and the vision and goals for the SharePoint 2013 project. Just configuring SharePoint initially is usually not sufficient. People need to review reports, gather input from end users, and perform spot checks to ensure that the rules and regulations are being followed and that they continue to map to end-user requirements. For example, the governance plan may require that IT make all changes to lists, libraries, and sites, but then find that this is stifling effective use of the SharePoint tools and so change the governance policy. And in closing, it is important to remember that taking away privileges and tools is generally more damaging than being restrictive to start with and just adding tools and capabilities over time.

Best Practices

The following are best practices from this chapter:

- Governance includes maintenance of the SharePoint 2013 environment but extends to include policies and procedures, roles and responsibilities, and periodic review to ensure that the myriad SharePoint tools are being used in productive ways that meet the needs of management and end users.
- Any sized organization should have a SharePoint governance plan in place. It doesn't have to be hundreds of pages long, but should at least be defined from a high level, as suggested in this chapter, with specific roles and responsibilities defined for the tasks that should be performed.
- One key component of the governance plan should focus on the Central Administration site settings that will impact the tools and features made available to the site collection administrators, site administrators, and end users.
- An important subset of the Central Administration site settings are those that apply to the web applications that house the site collections and the service applications that IT chooses to provide to the user community.

- In addition, specific settings for site collections and sites should be governed, to ensure that the right combination of tools is provided to the user community. Just "turning everything on" is generally not an actionable governance plan, because many of the tools are complex to use and administer.
- If SharePoint is to be used for records management, the tools and processes made available by SharePoint should be governed closely.
- The governance plan should be reviewed periodically to ensure that it continues to meet the organization's requirements and those of the end-user community.

CHAPTER 25

Using Word, Excel, PowerPoint with SharePoint 2013

IN THIS CHAPTER

- Support for Earlier Versions of Office with SharePoint 2013
- Using Word 2013 with SharePoint 2013
- Working with the Protect Document Tools in Word 2013
- Working with Document Versions in Word 2013
- Creating Shortcuts to SharePoint 2013
- Coauthoring Word 2013 Documents Stored in SharePoint 2013
- Administering Coauthoring in SharePoint 2013
- Using Microsoft SkyDrive Pro with SharePoint 2013
- Connecting SharePoint 2013 Content to Outlook 2013

This chapter examines key features and integration points when Office 2013 products are used with SharePoint 2013. The intention of this chapter is to build upon "the basics" covered in previous chapters that will be of special interest to SharePoint administrators, power users, and administrators.

Chapter 19, "Using Libraries and Lists in SharePoint 2013," covers many of the standard skills end users need when working with Office 2013 documents and SharePoint 2013. Chapter 26, "Extending SharePoint 2013 with Excel Services, Visio Graphics Services, and Access Services," covers integration points among Excel 2013, Visio 2013, and Access 2013 from the same point of view of interaction with SharePoint 2013 sites. Chapter 27, "Office Web Apps 2013 Integration with SharePoint 2013," provides additional information on integration points between Office applications and SharePoint via the Office Web Apps (OWA) feature.

This chapter focuses on new and powerful collaboration features in the Office 2013 suite such as the SkyDrive Pro tools, coauthoring of documents, working with document versions, and using the Protect Document tools in Word 2013. Having a familiarity with the tools covered in this chapter will help IT, SharePoint administrators, and power users best leverage the synergy between Office 2013 and SharePoint 2013.

Support for Earlier Versions of Office with SharePoint 2013

Microsoft has greatly enhanced the functionality and tools offered in SharePoint 2013, and it makes sense that the latest version of Office provides the best level of integration with SharePoint 2013. This said, numerous organizations still use older versions of the Office products. This chapter provides examples of select Office 2010 product integration with SharePoint 2013 for reference purposes, but won't go further backward to older versions of the Office products (such as Office 2007/2003) because of space limitations. And in keeping with its general practices, Microsoft offers the highest level of support for the latest version of Office (Office 2013), and lesser levels for support for older products such as Office 2010 and Office 2007. This level of support and integration degrades as the version of Office gets older, so users of Office 2010 and earlier should test integration thoroughly with SharePoint 2013. This should also be said of support for non-Microsoft operating systems, such as the Mac OS, when using Office products.

The end-user experience with SharePoint 2013 will, of course, also be affected by the operating system in use and the browser in use. So not only is the version of Office in use important to test, but the standard build the typical end user uses. Microsoft provides a detailed overview of browser support on the following page: http://technet.microsoft.com/en-us/library/cc263526.aspx. This should be reviewed to ensure that IT understands the pros and cons of using browsers other than Internet Explorer.

Using Word 2013 with SharePoint 2013

Users and administrators alike will want to become very familiar with the process of using Word in conjunction with SharePoint 2013 document libraries since it is one of the most commonly used applications in most organizations that use the Microsoft Office line of products. This section builds upon information provided in previous chapters and provides information and examples specific to Word 2013 that are important for IT and power users to be familiar with.

Chapter 19 covers a number of the tools available in document libraries that will be of interest to IT and end users alike when uploading documents to SharePoint document libraries and interacting with these documents. Specifically, the following topics are covered on a step-by-step basis in Chapter 19 that are relevant here.

The "Adding Documents to a Document Library" section covers the main methods of uploading documents to a document library, which include the following:

- Using the Upload Document icon on the Files tab
- Using the Upload Files Using Windows Explorer Instead link in the Add a Document window
- Using WebDAV (Web Distributed Authoring and Versioning) to access the library directly
- Using the inbound email feature

Creating a Word 2013 Document from a SharePoint 2013 Document Library

This section adds to content from Chapter 19 by covering the basic steps a user needs to follow to create a new document in a document library, populate the metadata fields, and save the document.

An assumption for the following exercise is that the document library used in this example has had several columns added to it that will provide the metadata and has a Word document as a template for the document library. To create a new document in a document library, populate the metadata fields, and save the document, follow these steps:

1. Click the New Document icon from the File tab in a document library that has had one or more choice columns added and one or more managed metadata columns added. The assumption is that the document library uses a Word template.
2. When the new document opens, enter some text in the document, as shown in Figure 25.1. Note that in this example, the Document Properties – Server data displays under the ribbon.

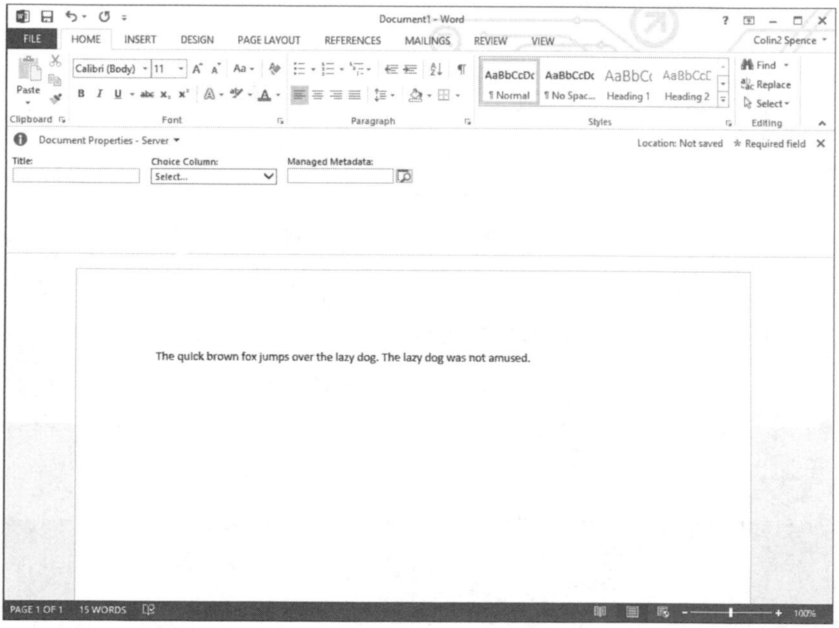

FIGURE 25.1 New Word document created from a SharePoint 2013 document library.

NOTE

If the Document Properties panel isn't visible, click the File tab, make sure that the Info tab is active, access the Properties drop-down menu, and click Show Document Panel; the Home tab opens with the Document Panel now visible.

3. Enter some metadata into the fields visible in the Document Properties panel. Steps will vary based on the configuration of the parent list. In this example, as shown in Figure 25.1, there is a Choice column and a Managed Metadata column. Select appropriate values to populate these fields. Click the Save icon.
4. The Save As tab on the File tab opens, and the source SharePoint document library should appear in the Other Web Locations section to the right of the screen, as shown in Figure 25.2. In this example, the source document library is http://sp20131/sites/TeamSite25/Shared Documents.

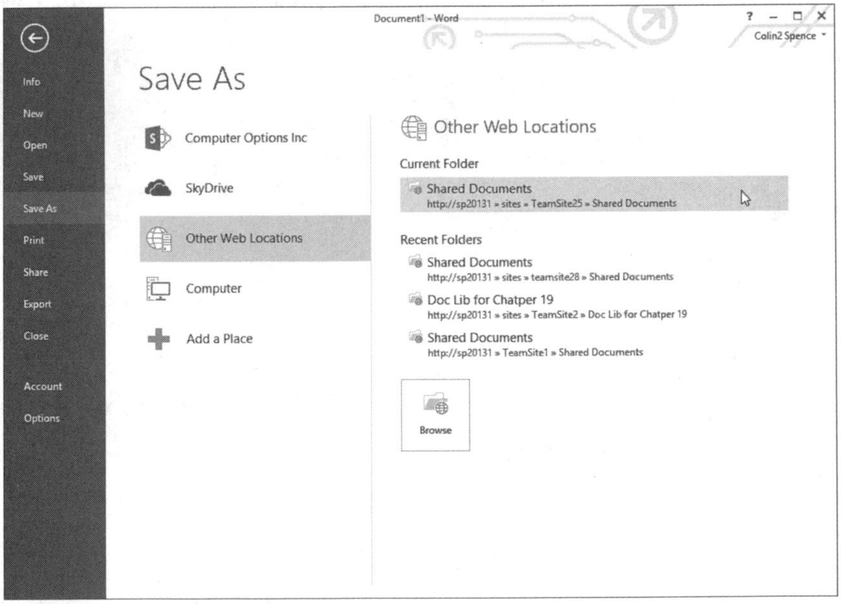

FIGURE 25.2 Saving to the source SharePoint document library from Word 2013.

5. Click the desired location to save to; the Save As window opens. Enter an appropriate filename and click Save.
6. When saved, the save location populates in the Document Properties tab. This helps end users be clear on where the file they are working on is stored.
7. Return to the document library and note that the document has successfully been saved and the metadata values are visible in the library.

Working with the Protect Document Tools in Word 2013

IT and site administrators often need to tackle the complex topic of protecting data that is stored in SharePoint 2013. The primary methods for document access control are typically permissions applied to the lists and libraries that house the documents, and in many cases, these inherit permissions from the sites that house the lists and libraries. Folders and document sets in document libraries can have unique permissions applied to them, and even individual documents can have unique permissions applied!

It is easy to see how this can lead to confusion for end users who may lose track of who has access to their documents. Fortunately, SharePoint offers the Shared With and Check Permissions tools (covered in Chapter 19, in the "Using the Shared With Tool" section) to help clarify who has access.

It is also important for IT to understand what can be done in Word 2013 with regard to protecting documents in SharePoint 2013 document libraries and to educate users on the pros and cons of different options.

In the following exercise, the document created in the previous section is reused, so it is assumed the previous exercise was completed. Follow these steps to become familiar with the Protect Document tools available from the Info tab on the File tab in Word 2013:

1. Click the ellipsis to access the hover panel for the newly created document (in this case, titled Quick Brown Fox Article) and click Edit to open the document once more in Word 2013.
2. Click the File tab, and the Info tab should be active. Click the Protect Document icon to see the tools available. These tools include Mark as Final, Encrypt with Password, Restrict Editing, Restrict Access (requires a Microsoft Rights Management Server be available), and Add a Digital Signature (requires a digital ID).
3. For this example, click Mark as Final, as shown in Figure 25.3. A message appears stating, "This document will be marked as final and then saved." Click OK. An additional lengthy message appears explaining that the status of the document is set to Final and typing and editing commands are turned off. Click OK again.
4. Exit the document and return to the document library that contains the document (using the same account in SharePoint is fine). Click the refresh button in the browser.
5. Access the hover panel for the document (in this case, titled Quick Brown Fox Article) and click Edit to open the document once more in Word 2013. The document now has a message under the ribbon stating, "Marked as Final. An author has marked this document as final to discourage editing." An Edit Anyway button is available. Click the Edit Anyway button, and the user is able to edit the document.

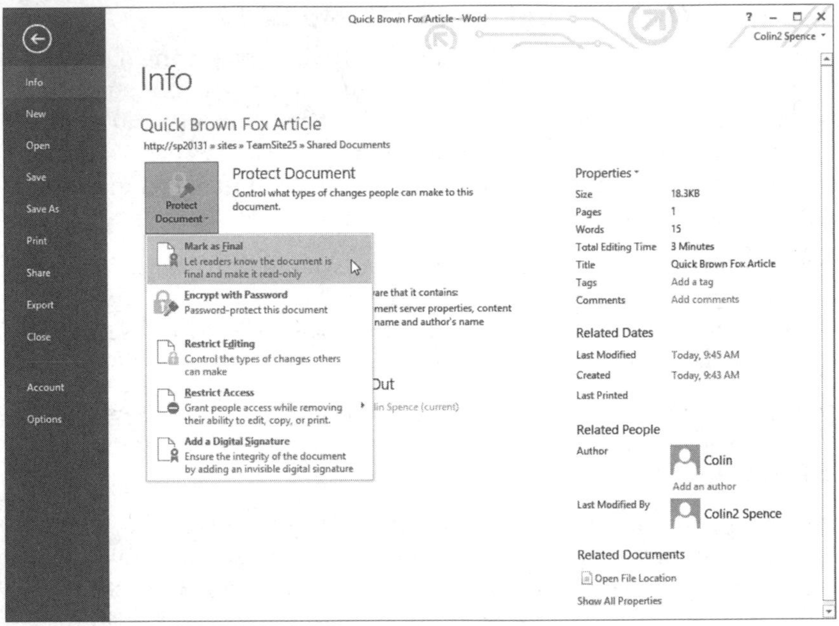

FIGURE 25.3 Marking a Word 2013 document as Final.

NOTE

The Mark as Final tool available from the Info tab on the File tab (Backstage) in Word 2013 does not protect a document from editing; it merely alerts users to the status of the document as "final." To better protect a Word document from editing, use the Restrict Editing tool or Restrict Access which requires Microsoft Rights Management Server be configured.

6. Access the File tab, Info tab and once again click the drop-down menu for Restrict Editing. A Restrict Editing panel opens on the Home tab, as shown in Figure 25.4.
7. In the Restrict Editing panel, check the Allow Only This Type of Editing check box, where No Changes (Read only) is selected in the drop-down list. Click the Yes, Start Enforcing Protection button.
8. The Start Enforcing Protection window opens. Enter a password and then re-enter the password. Click OK.
9. Click Save and exit the document.
10. Return to the document library, refresh the page, and click Edit from the hover panel for the document.
11. Word opens, and the document displays in a minimal view, with only the File, Tools, and View tabs visible. Click the View tab, and click Edit Document.

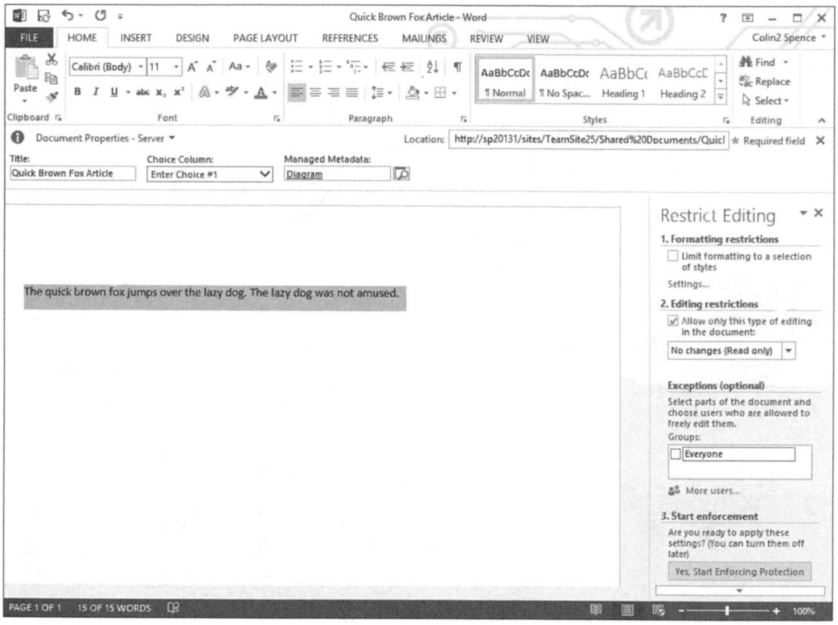

FIGURE 25.4 Restrict Editing for a Word 2013 document.

12. Note that the text cannot be edited. Click the Review tab, and verify that Restrict Editing is enabled. The Restrict Editing panel displays, as shown in Figure 25.5. If specific regions were set to allow editing, they can be viewed by clicking the Find Next Region I Can Edit button or the Show All Regions I Can Edit button.

13. Click the Stop Protection button and enter the password entered in step 8. Note that the document can now be edited.

14. Click Save and exit the document.

NOTE

The Check for Issues menu on the Info tab under the File tab offers three tools that IT and power users should be familiar with: Inspect Document, Check Accessibility, and Check Compatibility tools. The Inspect Document tool checks for hidden properties or hidden information (which might be important for documents that are delivered to external parties), Check Accessibility looks for content that might be hard for a person with disabilities to read, and Check Compatibility checks for features not supported by earlier versions of Word. Check Compatibility proves especially useful in environments that support multiple different versions of Office products.

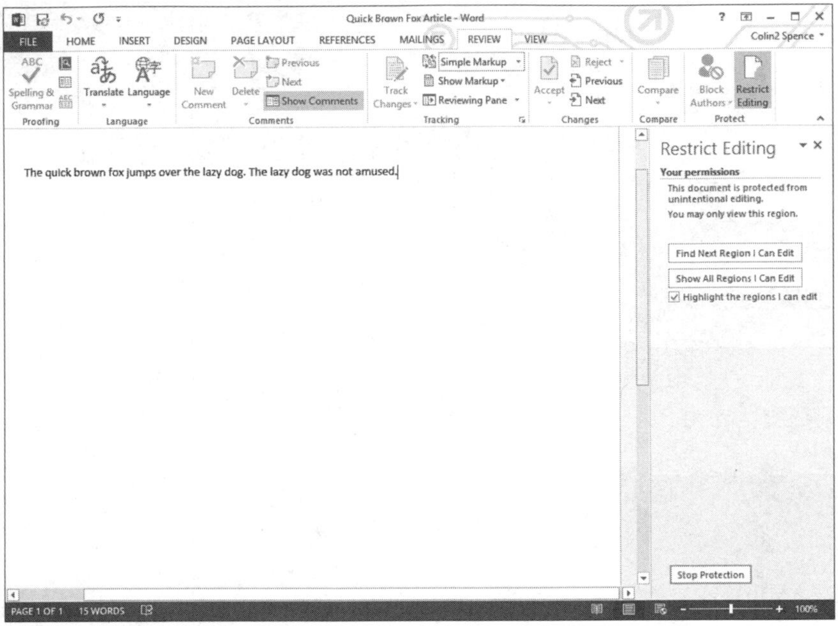

FIGURE 25.5 Viewing the Restrict Editing panel for a Word 2013 document where Restrict Editing was enabled.

Working with Document Versions in Word 2013

SharePoint's ability to track different major and minor versions of documents in document libraries is a key feature that can provide huge benefits to organizations with sophisticated document tracking needs. Versioning is discussed in numerous places in Chapter 19, notably in the "Using the Version History Tool" and the "How to Use the Publish, Unpublish, and Cancel Approval Tools" sections.

Yet versions can be confusing to end users. Fortunately, Word 2013 offers tools to help end users work with versions from the Word 2013 application. Figure 25.6 shows an example of the Info tab under the File tab for a Word document opened in Word 2013 from a document library that has both major and minor versions enabled. In Figure 25.6, the Manage Versions icon was clicked and several tools are visible:

- Refresh Server Versions List
- Check Out
- Compare with Major Version
- Compare with Last Version
- Recover Unsaved Documents

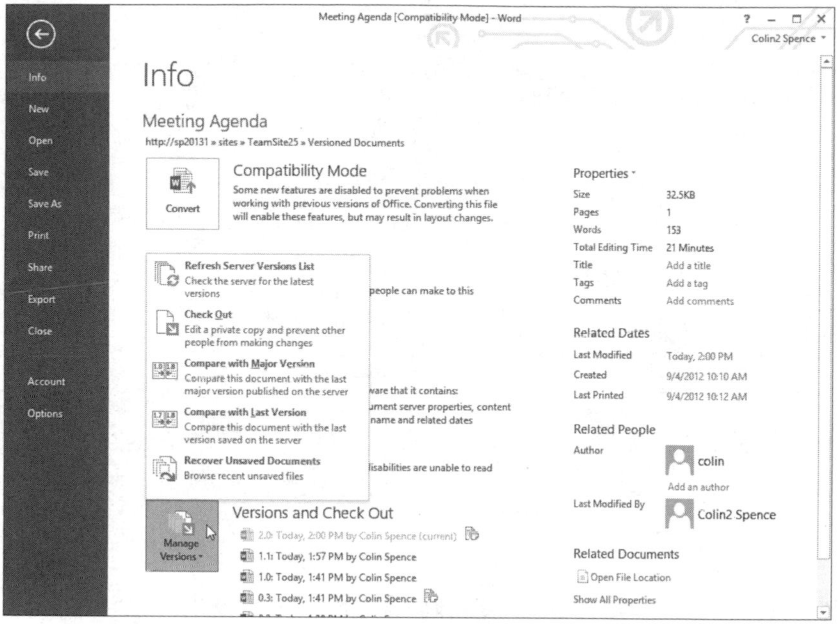

FIGURE 25.6 Viewing the Manage Versions tools on the BackOffice tab.

These tools enable the user to perform a variety of tasks, starting with refreshing the versions list to ensure that they are seeing the most current list of versions, to checking out the document, which creates a private copy and prevents other people from making changes. The next two tools, Compare with Major Version and Compare with Last Version, are selectable only if other major versions or minor versions are available.

A Compare tool on the Review tab of the ribbon adds a key tool to the ones available in the BackOffice Info tab:

- Specific Version
- The Compare with Major Version, Compare with Last Version, and the Specific Version tools are important for end users to be able to work effectively with documents that have multiple major and minor versions. Without these tools, end users have to rely on comments added by users after edits, changes to metadata tags on the document which are tracked, or view the different versions from the Version History window available from the hover panel for the document. These are laborious ways of simply trying to see what is different between versions of documents in a library. Figure 25.7 shows an example of the Specific Version compare of two versions of a sample meeting agenda. Note that the results are intuitive and easy to interpret: The pane on the left shows the specific Revisions, the middle pane shows a Compared Document (red-lined), and the two panes on the right show the Original Document and below it the Revised Document.

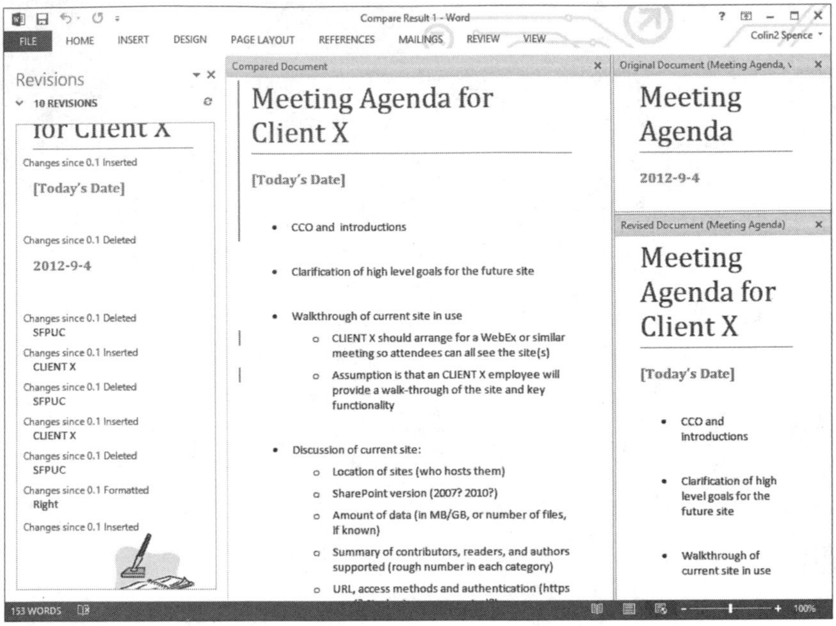

FIGURE 25.7 An example of using the Compare Specific Version tool in Word 2013.

Creating Shortcuts to SharePoint 2013

New users will be very happy if they find the process of saving documents to SharePoint easy and intuitive. And generally, users don't like always having to open a browser, find their bookmark to get to SharePoint, navigate to the site they're using, find the document library, and then have to upload a document after saving it locally.

There are several ways to facilitate the process of saving documents to SharePoint by creating favorites and shortcuts. This first set of steps that follows shows how to create a shortcut by using the Connect to Office button in a document library, and the section that follows that describes how to manually create the shortcut from Windows Explorer.

Another way to create shortcuts, which you can use on computers not using Office 2013, is to simply create a shortcut under Network Places, which is useful to know about if the SharePoint Sites folder isn't available for certain users.

NOTE

This section assumes Windows 8 is installed along with Office 2013.

Using the Connect to Office Tool to Create Shortcuts

The Connect to Office tool available on the Library tab in a document library is the easiest way to create shortcuts from Office 2013 applications via the Save As interface.

Follow these steps to use the Connect to Office feature in a SharePoint document library:

NOTE

This exercise assumes that User Profile Service and My Sites have been properly configured.

1. Visit a SharePoint document library using a computer with Office 2013 installed and an account with at least Read permissions to the library.
2. Click the Connect to Office button from the Library tab, and then select Add to SharePoint sites. A message appears that states, "To connect libraries in this site to Microsoft Office, your machine must register the user profile service application used by this site." Click Yes; the SharePoint folder is created under Favorites for the user, and the shortcut is added.

NOTE

If Office 2007 or a previous version of Office is installed, the Connect to Office button is inactive.

3. Click the Connect to Office button again, but this time click Manage SharePoint Sites; the MyQuickLinks page displays, showing the links available, as shown in Figure 25.8. Note that additional tools are available, including Add Link, Edit Link, Delete, and Create Tag from Link.

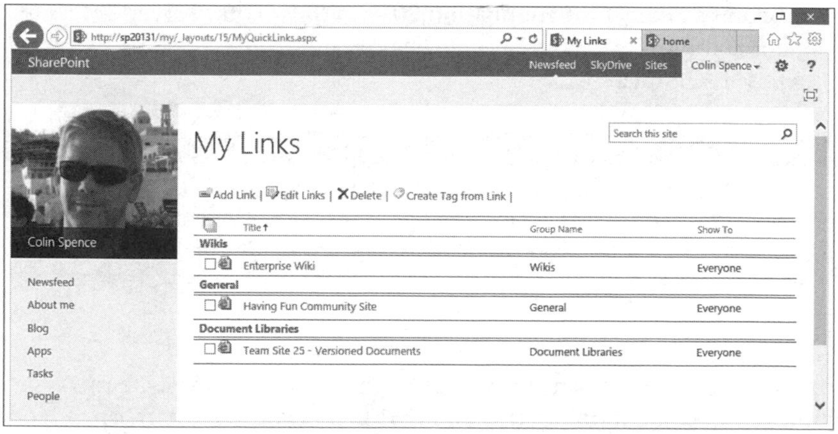

FIGURE 25.8 The MyQuickLinks page in SharePoint 2013.

4. Verify that the new link appears in Word 2013 by opening Word 2013, and click the Save As button from the File tab.

Coauthoring Word 2013 Documents Stored in SharePoint 2013

A common request for a collaboration feature is to enable more than one user to work on a document at the same time, or "coauthor" a document. As discussed in Chapter 27, OWA make it possible for multiple users to coauthor Excel, Word, PowerPoint, and OneNote documents using the browser-based Web Apps. The "Testing Excel Access via Office Web Apps" and "Testing Word Access via OWA 2013" sections provide examples. For this to work, however, OWA 2013 must be installed and configured on the SharePoint 2013 farm and the organization must have the appropriate OWA 2013 licensing in place. Word 2013, PowerPoint 2013, Visio 2013, and OneNote 2013 also support coauthoring on documents stored in SharePoint 2013 document libraries without OWA 2013 being installed.

NOTE

SharePoint 2013 coauthoring functionality requires *no* additional server setup and is the default state for documents stored in SharePoint 2013 and SharePoint Online. SharePoint 2013 Standard, Enterprise, and Foundation support this functionality. File synchronization is accomplished via Simple Object Access Protocol (SOAP) over Hypertext Transport Protocol (HTTP) (MS-FSSHTTP), which allows incremental upload or download of file changes and metadata changes.

In the following example, Word 2013 is used by two users to simultaneously edit and save changes to a document that is stored on a SharePoint 2013 server. To test coauthoring, two computers or virtual images with Word 2013 installed are required along with a document library housed in a SharePoint Foundation 2013 or SharePoint Server 2013 site collection. Enable major and minor versioning to review the number of versions that were created when the exercise is complete.

NOTE

Make sure that Require Documents to Be Checked Out Before They Can Be Edited is *not* enabled in Document Library settings Versioning Settings, because documents that are checked out are locked and Word 2013 cannot therefore take advantage of coauthoring.

Follow these steps to test coauthoring using Word 2013:

1. From Computer A (used by Company123\Colin in this example), navigate to the SharePoint 2013 document library (http://sp201302/_layouts/15/start.aspx#/Shared%20Documents/Forms/AllItems.aspx in this example). Click the ellipsis to open the hover panel for the document and click Edit.
2. After the document opens in Word, click the Enable Editing button under the ribbon if needed.

3. From Computer B (used by Company123\Rand in this example), navigate to the same SharePoint document library, click the ellipsis to open the hover panel for the same document, and click Edit.

4. When the document opens on Computer B, a message at the bottom of the Word application should notify the user that another user is currently editing the same document. In addition, the status bar at the bottom of the screen shows an icon with two torsos with the number 2 next to it. When clicked, as shown in Figure 25.9, it displays the authors editing the document.

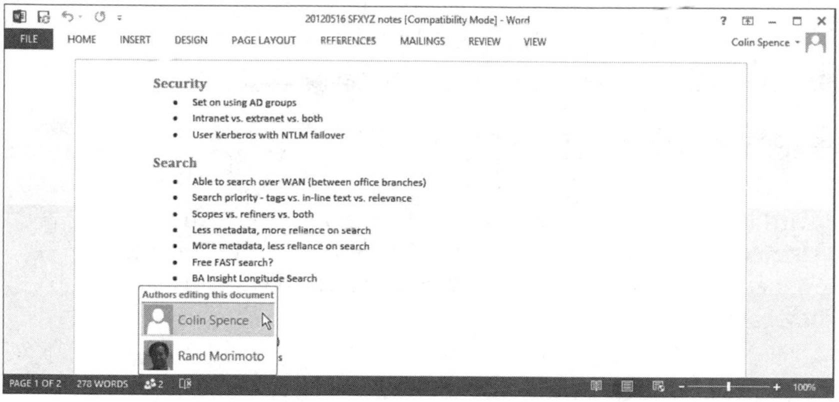

FIGURE 25.9 Viewing the identities of coauthors in Word 2013.

5. Start editing the document from Computer A (for example, perform a find and replace of a word that appears multiple times in the document to make a number of changes) and notice that a dotted gray bracket appears to the left of the line being edited.

6. Switch over to Computer B and note that the sections that were changed by the other user are marked with the username (in this example, Colin Spence, as shown in Figure 25.10).

7. Switch back to Computer A and click the Save button in the upper left, or if not available, click the File tab and click Save.

8. Switch to Computer B, and a message should appear in the bottom status bar that updates are available. Click the message, and the file updates. A window appears that states, "When you save, Word updates your document with the changes made by others. You can easily find the new content by looking for a green overlay." Click OK.

   Note that the modified sections now have a light green highlight applied.

9. Close both documents.

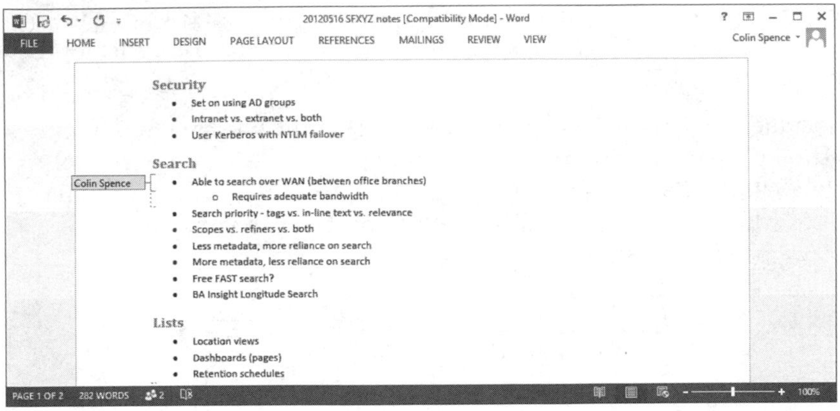

FIGURE 25.10 Tags on changes while coauthoring Word 2013.

Additional testing with multiple users is recommended, for both Word 2013 and PowerPoint 2013. Users will soon learn that they need to perform a Save frequently to make sure that they share their edits with their coauthors and allow their coauthors to edit the sections they have changed.

Administering Coauthoring in SharePoint 2013

Administrators should be aware that there are a number of settings that can be made with PowerShell that determine several variables in the coauthoring process. The following bullets provide an overview of the PowerShell code. (You can find additional information on TechNet at http://technet.microsoft.com/en-us/library/ff718235.aspx.)

- **Configure the Coauthoring Versioning Period:** The `CoauthoringVersionPeriod` property determines how often SharePoint stores a version of a document that is being edited on a specific server. This is measured in minutes, and if set to zero, every change made by a new user in a different version of the document results in a new version of the document. If the value is set to a number that exceeds the amount of editing time by a user, SharePoint Server creates just one version for the editing session.
- **Configure the Maximum Number of Coauthoring Authors:** The `CoauthoringMaxAuthors` property limits the maximum number of authors that can coauthor a Word or PowerPoint file at the same time on a specific server.
- **Disable Coauthoring:** The `DisableCoauthoring` server property disables coauthoring for Word and PowerPoint documents on a specific server. Group policies can also be used to disable coauthoring.

If the organization plans on training end users on coauthoring, and to then support issues that might arise, decisions should be made on each of these settings. For example, IT may choose to configure the maximum number of coauthoring authors to two or three to avoid possible scenarios where a large number of users are working on the same document at the same time. Alternatively, if the organization decides to not support coauthoring, IT may want to explicitly turn it off by using the `DisableCoauthoring` server property.

Using Microsoft SkyDrive Pro with SharePoint 2013

Microsoft has struggled over the years with providing a client-based application that effectively enables users to sync SharePoint content with their local computer. A number of years ago, Microsoft purchased Groove and leveraged their technologies to create the SharePoint Workspace product. That product has been deprecated with SharePoint 2013, and the new solution is branded SkyDrive, but more accurately (as this section discusses) is the SkyDrive Pro sync client. The current SkyDrive "product line" is confusing because there is both a consumer-oriented SkyDrive client and service offered by Microsoft, as well as use of the term *SkyDrive* in SharePoint 2013 that isn't necessarily accurate, and a SkyDrive Pro sync client that allows documents to be synced to user computers. This section clarifies how the SkyDrive components work in a SharePoint 2013 context to better help end users use the tools and IT support the tools.

To summarize, in a SharePoint 2013 context, SkyDrive Pro can be defined as the following:

- A link on a SharePoint 2013 Standard or Enterprise page that takes users to their My Site document library. Oddly, it is labeled SkyDrive, not SkyDrive Pro.
- A sync component that allows SharePoint 2013 Standard or Enterprise users to sync content to their local computer when they click the Sync button on a SharePoint 2013 Standard or Enterprise site. This uses the SkyDrive Pro sync client, which is included with Office 2013 products or can be downloaded separately as noted in this section.
- One or more entries in the user's Favorites folder in Windows Explorer where the user can access files stored in a SharePoint environment. These entries can be labeled SkyDrive Pro or SharePoint, but both may use the SkyDrive Pro sync client tool.

NOTE

Microsoft also offers a consumer level product called SkyDrive. You can download it from http://windows.microsoft.com/en-us/skydrive/download. This is *different* from the SkyDrive Pro sync client application that can be downloaded from http://www.microsoft.com/en-US/download/details.aspx?id=39050. This is useful for organizations not yet using Office 2013, because it can be installed side by side with previous versions of Office, such as Office 2010 or Office 2007.

NOTE

The SkyDrive Pro sync client has the following system requirements:

- Windows 7, Windows 8, Windows Server 2008 R2, Windows Server 2012
- Computer and processor 1 gigahertz (GHz) or faster, x86- or x64-bit processor with SSE2 instruction set
- Memory: 1 gigabyte (GB) RAM (32 bit); 2GB RAM (64 bit)
- Hard disk 3.0GB available
- Display graphics hardware acceleration requires a DirectX10 graphics card and 1024 x 576 resolution.
- Browser: Microsoft Internet Explorer 8, 9, or 10; Mozilla Firefox 10.x or a later version; Apple Safari 5; or Google Chrome 17.x
- .NET version 3.5, 4.0, or 4.5
- Multitouch: A touch-enabled device is required to use any multitouch functionality. However, all features and functionality are always available by using a keyboard, mouse, or other standard or accessible input device. Note that new touch features are optimized for use with Windows 8.

Any user accessing a SharePoint 2013 Standard- or Enterprise-based site will notice the SkyDrive tab prominently displayed at the top of the browser screen. This tab is not present on a SharePoint 2013 Foundation site because My Sites are not included with that version of the product. Clicking the SkyDrive tab takes users to their personal site and to their own library (simply labeled Documents). Figure 25.11 shows an example of this. There is a Shared with Everyone default folder in what appears to be a standard document library. On the left, the My Documents tab shows as active, and beneath it is a Followed Documents tab. Essentially, this is a private document library that allows the user to upload documents to the Shared with Everyone folder or to the root of the library, which by default is accessible only by that user.

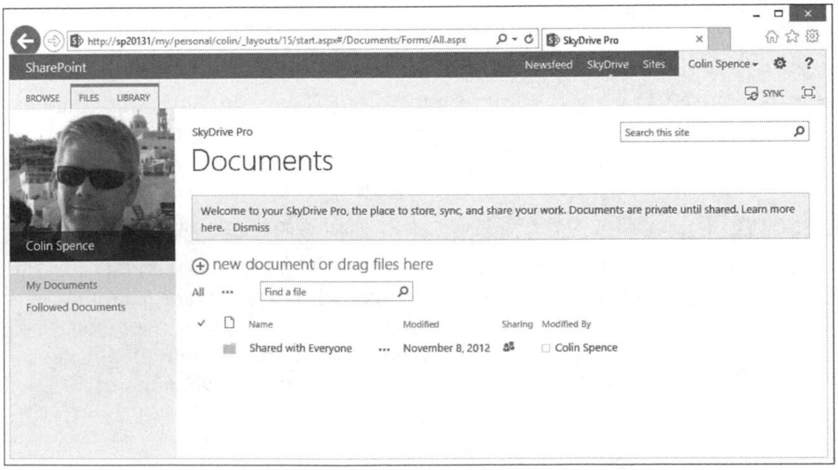

FIGURE 25.11 My Site Documents library accessed by using the SkyDrive link in SharePoint 2013.

These documents are not yet available on the user's computer because they have not been synced. They can be synced, but the SkyDrive Pro client sync application must be used for that to occur.

Follow these steps to synchronize a SkyDrive (My Sites) document library to the computer:

1. From a SharePoint 2013 Standard or Enterprise environment where My Sites have been properly configured and are working, click the SkyDrive link at the top of the screen.
2. Click the Sync icon in the upper-right corner of the screen (visible in Figure 25.11).
3. The Microsoft SkyDrive Pro window opens. The URL for the My Site document library should be correctly listed. A note states, "You'll find your documents under Favorites in Windows Explorer." The location of the library is also shown (for example, C:\Users*username*). Click Sync Now to begin synchronizing the library.
4. A new window opens with this message: "Your files are syncing as we speak." The location where the files can be found is shown in this window (for example, C:\Users\[*username*]\SkyDrive Pro). Click the Show My Files button to view the destination folder.
5. Figure 25.12 shows the results in Windows Explorer. The Shared with Everyone folder is visible, and any additional files that are added to the My Site document library will be synced in the future to this local folder.

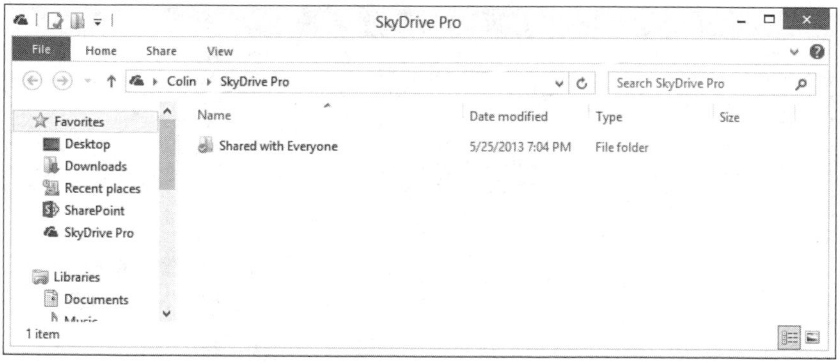

FIGURE 25.12 Windows Explorer view of a SkyDrive Pro folder after syncing with a My Site document library.

NOTE

SkyDrive Pro 2013, unlike SharePoint Workspace 2010, only supports list and library synchronization. Site synchronization is not currently supported.

This next exercise shows the process for syncing a specific SharePoint document library using the SkyDrive Pro client sync application. This exercise assumes the previous one has been completed:

1. From the same computer used in the previous exercise, access the Windows system tray. If using Windows 8, access the desktop first. Click the cloud-shaped icon, which then provides a selection of tools. Select Sync a New Library.
2. Enter the URL of the SharePoint 2013 site and click Sync Now. In this example, **SP20131** is entered. Click Sync Now.
3. The next window asks you to select the library you want to sync and show the document libraries found. In this example, the library Documents is chosen. Note that no lists are shown, only libraries. Click Sync Selected to start the synching process.
4. In the next window that opens, click Show My Files. Figure 25.13 shows the results where a number of files are syncing to the local computer. A green check mark in the document icon shows a successful and completed sync.

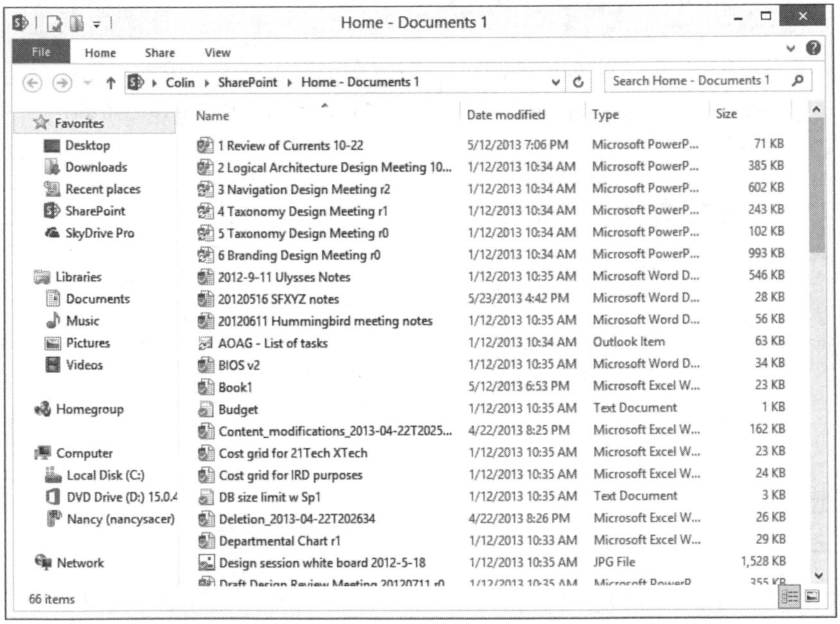

FIGURE 25.13 Windows Explorer showing the SkyDrive Pro sync client in action.

5. Figure 25.14 shows the contents of the Favorites folder for the user after both the syncing of the My Site document library and another SharePoint library using the SkyDrive Pro application.

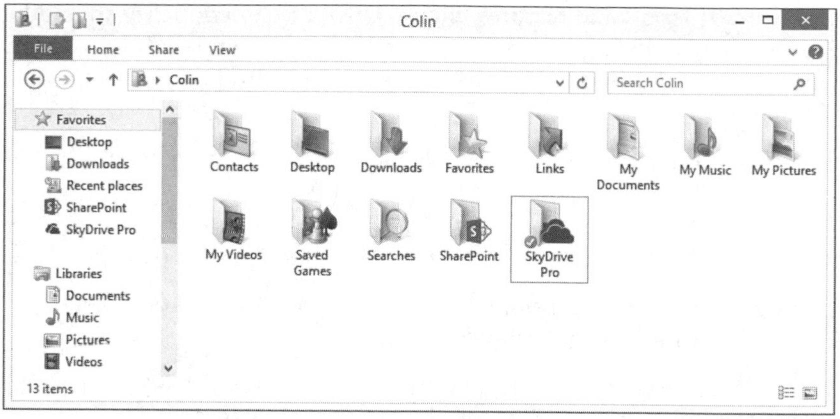

FIGURE 25.14 Windows Explorer showing the SharePoint and SkyDrive Pro folders.

Although there aren't a host of tools specific to SkyDrive Pro that are added in the Windows Explorer interface, right-clicking a document shows the SkyDrive Pro entry, which has several options:

- **Go to Browser:** This opens a browser to the library that contains the document, which is a nice, quick way to interact with the full set of SharePoint tools and the original source library and documents.
- **Copy Link:** Copies the full link to the document in its SharePoint document library location. This can then be sent to other users as a shortcut instead of emailing the document as an attachment.
- **Share:** If active, this opens the SharePoint 2013 Share window, which shows who the current document or folder is shared with and allows the user to enter user or group names and choose whether they can edit or just read.
- **View Sync Problems:** If active, this provides information on sync issues.

In addition, the SkyDrive Pro cloud icon in the system tray provides access to several tools when clicked:

- Open Your SkyDrive Pro Folder
- Sync a New Library
- Sync Now
- Pause Syncing
- Stop Syncing a Folder
- Help
- Exit

As with other SharePoint 2013 tools and features, the SkyDrive Pro functionality should be tested thoroughly with different desktop configurations the organization needs to support. With the fear of laptop theft and cybercrime increasing, many organizations may choose to disable this functionality.

Follow these steps using an account with site collection administration privileges:

1. Access the Site Settings page.
2. Click the Search and Offline Availability link in the Search section of the page.
3. In the Offline Client Availability section, select the No option under Allow Items from This Site to Be Downloaded to Offline Clients.
4. Then test by attempting to sync using the SkyDrive Pro sync client. To do this, click the SkyDrive Pro icon in the system tray, and then click Sync Now.
5. The content won't sync. To verify that it hasn't, again click the SkyDrive Pro icon in the system tray and click View sync problems. A window opens that provides additional information, as shown in Figure 25.15. Note that at the top of the window, it shows the status as Not Permitted, and at the bottom of this window, you see this: This Library Isn't Available Offline.

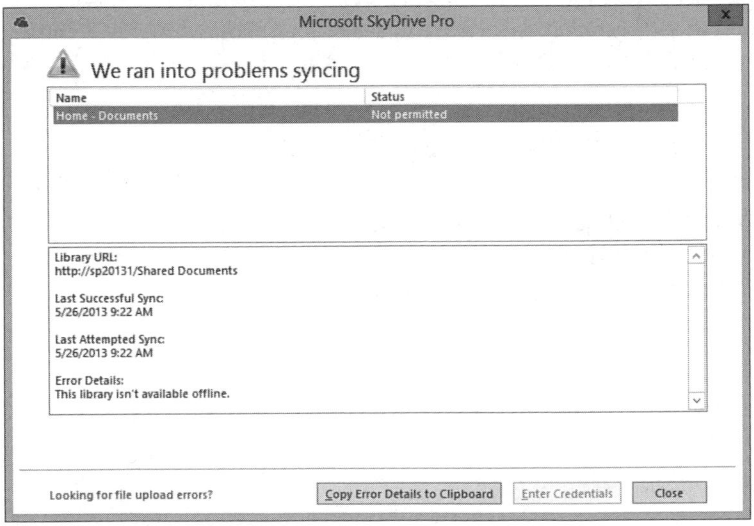

FIGURE 25.15 Viewing sync problems after Allow Items from This Site to Be Downloaded to Offline Clients has been turned off in Site Settings.

In addition, the standard library configurations the organization supports should be tested to ensure that the tool functions properly with checkout requirements, approval workflows, managed metadata, and other configuration options.

Connecting SharePoint 2013 Content to Outlook 2013

Another option for taking content offline for mobile users is to synchronize with Outlook 2013. This section reviews the process for syncing with Outlook 2013 initially for document libraries and then for task lists and calendars. An assumption for this section is that the connectivity between the SharePoint farm and the Exchange server is working properly; this topic is covered in detail in Chapter 16, "Configuring Email-Enabled Content, Site Mailboxes, and Exchange Server Integration." A quick way to make sure that this functionality is working (if IT isn't readily available) is to create an alert in a library and test to ensure that the email alert is in fact delivered.

The SharePoint administrator should understand the differences between the SkyDrive Pro tools and connecting content to Outlook, and the example shown here will help make these differences clear. For example, files downloaded to Outlook 2013 are "read only," but can still be edited by following the steps listed here. New files can't be added to Outlook folders synchronized with SharePoint document libraries, although tasks and calendar items can be added from Outlook.

To begin, follow these steps to take a library offline in Outlook 2013:

1. Navigate to a document library in SharePoint 2013 that contains one or more Word documents using an account with at least Contributor-level permissions and access the Library tab.
2. Click the Connect to Outlook button.

NOTE

Note that in numerous cases with the release to manufacturing (RTM) version of SharePoint 2013, the Connect to Outlook button is grayed out and that simply pressing F5 to refresh the browser results in the Connect to Outlook button suddenly appearing.

3. A message appears, asking whether you want to allow this website to open a program on your computer. Click Allow.
4. Outlook 2013 opens (if not open already), and a message appears, asking for confirmation to connect this SharePoint document library to Outlook. Click Yes.

NOTE

An Advanced button is available from the confirmation window. If clicked, it allows the user to change the folder name or add a description to the folder. Another option is Display This List on Other Computers with the Account: *username*, and there is an option to update this subscription with the publisher's recommendation. These settings are usually left on their defaults.

5. The folder is then created in Outlook 2013 under the SharePoint lists node, and the content synchronizes. Assuming the documents are standard Office documents, previews are available in the preview pane, as shown in Figure 25.16.

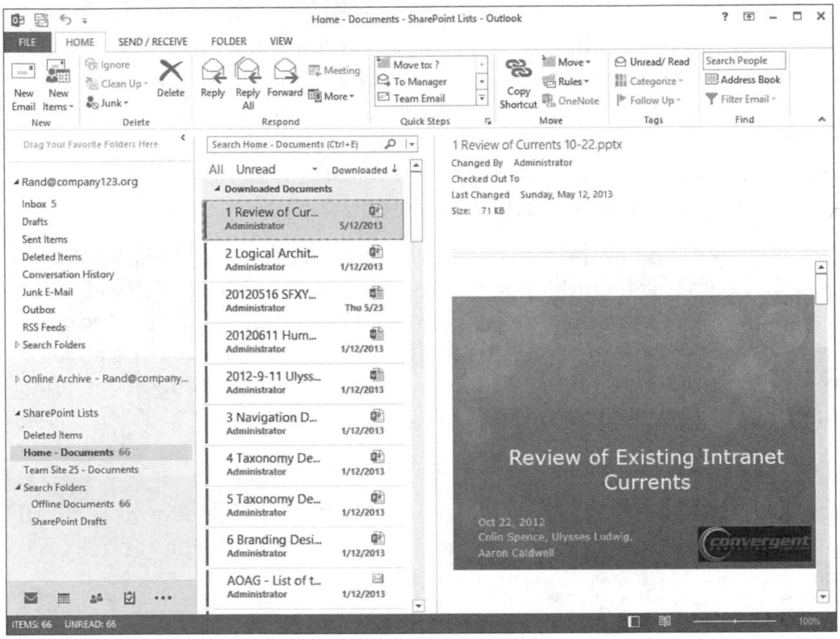

FIGURE 25.16 Results of using the Connect to Outlook tool from a document library in Outlook 2013.

NOTE

Outlook 2010 provides similar functionality with document library synchronization to SharePoint 2013.

6. Double-click one of the Word documents, and it opens in Word 2013 with this message at the top of the Word application: "Offline Server Document. To modify this document, edit it offline and save it to the server later." Click the Edit Offline button.
7. A window opens, informing the user that the document will be stored in the SharePoint Drafts folder. Click OK.
8. Make some edits to the document, and then click Save.
9. Access the File menu and click Close.
10. Return to the document library in SharePoint 2013 and open the document (or view it using OWA if configured). Note that the changes were saved to the document library.

11. Return to Outlook 2013, and with the SharePoint folder still active, click an item, and then click Delete. A message appears: "This SharePoint list is read-only in Outlook."
12. Right-click the same document and select Remove Offline Copy.
13. The document then appears in a group titled Available for Download in Outlook. After the next synchronization, the documents are synchronized, so this is a temporary setting.
14. Try to drag and drop a document from a local folder to the Outlook 2013 folder, and note that it does not complete.
15. Try right-clicking the item on the local computer and clicking Copy, and then try right-clicking in the SharePoint connected folder, and note that the option to Paste is not provided. This illustrates that even if the account in use has Owner-level permissions in the document library, items cannot be created in the connected Outlook folder.

Connecting Task Lists to Outlook 2013

Assuming that the user has completed the previous section, the process of taking content offline from a SharePoint document library should be clear. It is encouraged that the administrator or end user also test taking a Tasks list offline by following the previous steps, but on a Tasks list that has items in it.

SharePoint 2013 adds a new level of functionality, which is that Microsoft Outlook tasks will also show up under Newsfeed (SharePoint 2013 Standard or Enterprise).

As shown in Figure 25.17, the list shows up in the Other Tasks node. The user can interact with tasks, whether to Mark Complete, Remove from List, or change the data associated with the tasks. Tasks can also be dragged from the SharePoint Tasks list to the individual's Tasks list in Outlook and vice versa, which makes a copy of the task in the other task folder, and results in the task being added to the SharePoint Tasks list if a personal task is dragged to the SharePoint Tasks list in Outlook 2013.

Connecting Calendars to Outlook 2013

Assuming that the user has completed the previous sections, the process of taking content offline from a SharePoint list should be clear, and as with Tasks lists, the administrator or end user should also gain experience with the process of connecting Calendar lists to Outlook 2013. The steps are similar to a Tasks list, and the ability of end users to drag a SharePoint calendar item to their personal calendar is the same, and to drag a personal event to the SharePoint calendar. This is an extremely useful capability because it enables end users to connect to SharePoint calendars and drag and drop their personal events, such as vacations, to a shared SharePoint calendar so that the whole team will know about it. Likewise, users can drag events from the SharePoint calendar to their personal calendar so that they can set reminders on those events and have them show up on personal calendars and mobile devices.

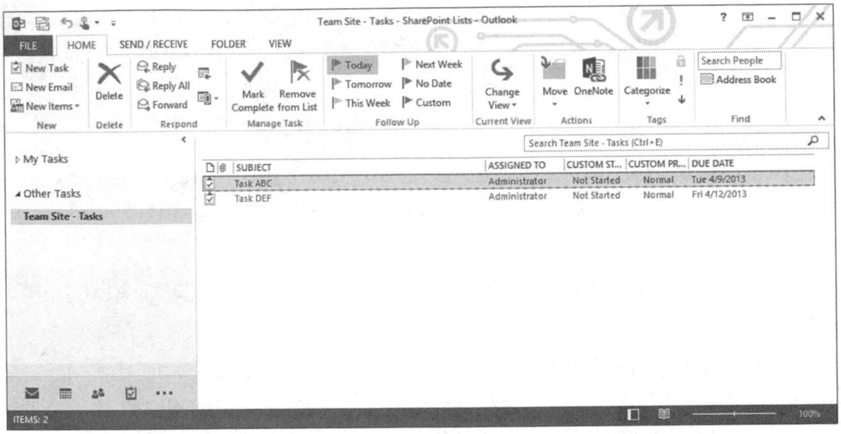

FIGURE 25.17 Results of syncing a SharePoint Tasks list in Outlook 2013.

NOTE

Full functionality between Outlook and SharePoint requires disabling the Minimal Download Strategy feature in Site Features.

Summary

This chapter covered a number of the key integration points between Office 2013 and SharePoint 2013. Not every feature could be covered in the space of one chapter, but a number of key topics were covered, such as the basics of using Word 2013 and SharePoint 2013 and key tools from the Office 2013 Backstage tool. In addition, the coauthoring capabilities of Word 2013 and PowerPoint 2013 were covered, and the different "moving parts" of the SkyDrive Pro products demystified. Finally, the basics of connecting Outlook 2013- to SharePoint 2013-based libraries, task lists, and calendars were covered.

Best Practices

The following are best practices from this chapter:

- Some key tools available in Office 2013 products are important for IT and SharePoint administrators to be familiar with because they can cause confusion for end users. If understood properly, though, they can enhance users' ability to effectively collaborate in SharePoint 2013. These include several tools on the Info tab on the File tab (also called Backstage): Mark as Final, Restrict Editing tool, Refresh Server Versions List, Compare with Major Version, Compare with Last Version, and the Compare tool available from the ribbon.

e 2013 products that allow multiple users
me: Word 2013, PowerPoint 2013, Visio
possible by OWA 2013 for several apps:
T and SharePoint administrators should
ities of coauthoring in the Office applica-
3.

thoring, as well. For example, if a Word
n't function, so checkouts can't be required
provided on PowerShell commands that
of simultaneous coauthors, how often
sable coauthoring.

and features are reviewed, in an attempt to
they can do. Note that the SkyDrive link in
nerely brings the user to their My Site docu-
ble on SharePoint sites invokes the SkyDrive
aries to local computers accessible through

client can be downloaded separately for
d in this chapter.

SkyDrive Pro sync client should and can be
specific sites or site collections, as covered in

Point 2013 in a number of ways. First,
utlook when a user is accessing the list or
n addition, Tasks lists and Calendars can be
lity appreciated by many end users.

CHAPTER 26

Extending SharePoint 2013 with Excel Services, Visio Graphics Services, and Access Services

IN THIS CHAPTER

- Working with Excel Data in SharePoint 2013
- Getting to Know the Excel Services Service Application
- Managing the Excel Service Application
- Publishing to Excel Services
- Allowing Parameter Input in Excel Web Access
- Visio Graphics Service Overview
- Access Services Overview

The service applications covered in this chapter are available only in the SharePoint Server 2013 Enterprise Edition, but provide a variety of tools and capabilities that may be of interest to organizations that are already familiar with the SharePoint "basics" and want to understand some more advanced tools in the product line.

The capabilities of Excel Services are covered in the most depth, due largely to its popularity and the proliferation of Excel spreadsheets in almost every type of organization. Visio Graphics Services and Access Services are more specialized and appeal to a smaller subset of users and organizations.

All these service applications can be leveraged by developers within the organization to create sophisticated applications, and this chapter touches on some of those capabilities from a high level.

Note that this chapter focuses on the Microsoft Office 2013 products, including Excel 2013, Access 2013, and Visio 2013, but not earlier versions. Therefore, if organizations have earlier versions of these Office products, they should test the capabilities of these products with SharePoint 2013 to ensure that they function properly.

Working with Excel Data in SharePoint 2013

Integration between Excel spreadsheets and SharePoint has been a hot topic for years, and Microsoft has provided a number of methods to integrate the two products. This section reviews some basic methods of working with Excel data in SharePoint from a high level to provide some background on different ways Excel data can be integrated with the SharePoint 2013 environment and to prepare for additional discussions around Excel Services.

To begin with, users can simply upload Excel spreadsheets to SharePoint libraries (without using the Excel Services publishing process described later in this chapter). Users gain the many benefits and tools provided by the document library, but are still working with the same Excel spreadsheets. These spreadsheets are still highly portable, difficult to manage when they leave the SharePoint library. Many organizations want to better manage the data contained in the spreadsheets and control the proliferation of versions of the spreadsheet.

A SharePoint list has many similarities with an Excel spreadsheet. Both allow the creators of the documents to define the columns that are part of the entity, define what type of content is stored in each column (text, currency, date/time, numeric, and so on), and control the format of the data. Excel provides many more tools to format the data than SharePoint does, but SharePoint lists still provide an excellent alternative to "emailing spreadsheets to the whole company" by centralizing the data in a secure location, allowing multiple users to edit the list at the same time, tracking versions of row data, and providing features such as alerts, workflows, custom views, and many other features. There are many more differences between a SharePoint list and an Excel spreadsheet that are not detailed here, but through some trial and error an organization can quickly learn where a SharePoint list is better suited to their requirements and where an Excel spreadsheet still needs to be used.

SharePoint also offers an Import Spreadsheet list template, which pulls in select data from a spreadsheet and creates a SharePoint list based on that data. The administrator or power user simply chooses the Import Spreadsheet list template (also called an app in SharePoint 2013 parlance), then specifies the spreadsheet to import, and then selects the range of cells. SharePoint then creates a list and does its best to choose column types to match the columns in the spreadsheet. Although not always perfect (the administrator or power user should verify the column settings to make sure that they do in fact match the type of content in the columns), this is a quick way to pull Excel content into SharePoint and then allow users to collaborate on the data.

When the Import Spreadsheet list template is used, no connectivity exists between the SharePoint list and the source spreadsheet. Therefore, if the source data changes, there is no effect on the SharePoint list, and likewise if the SharePoint list data changes, there is no impact on the source spreadsheet. In some cases, this is perfectly acceptable, but in others the users or administrators want to preserve connectivity between the source and the "clone."

SharePoint lists allow users to export content out to Excel using the Export to Excel tool on the List tab of the ribbon. This process is "sticky" because a connection is established between the SharePoint list and Excel 2013, but it is a one-way connection. The content in the spreadsheet can be updated by clicking Refresh All on the Design tab, and any changes in the SharePoint list are synced to the local copy of the spreadsheet.

Each of these processes has pros and cons, and the administrator or power users involved with managing and migrating content to SharePoint 2013 should be familiar with the different processes and the capabilities of Excel Services, as covered in the sections to follow in this chapter.

Getting to Know the Excel Services Service Application

From a high level, Excel Services is a service application in SharePoint 2013 Enterprise that provides a number of powerful tools used for "business intelligence (BI)" applications in the enterprise. It is designed for sharing, securing, managing, and using Excel 2013 workbooks in a browser to enable the organization to better manage key data and better leverage this data. Real-world experience has shown that many organizations can realize benefits on a less grandiose scale, and all levels of employees and knowledge workers can—and do—benefit from Excel Services in many other ways.

Fundamentally, Excel Services provides the following capabilities:

- Sharing workbooks
- Building BI dashboards
- Reuse of logic encapsulated in Excel workbooks in custom applications
- Report building

From a functional standpoint, Excel Services consists of three main components:

- **Excel Calculation Services:** A service that can be enabled on one or more SharePoint 2013 Enterprise servers
- **The Excel Web Access Web Part:** A web part that can be added to SharePoint web pages
- **Excel Services Application:** A service application that is managed through Central Administration

These components are discussed in more detail later in the chapter.

A primary capability is that Excel Services enables users to "publish" Excel workbooks to a document library. This is not meant to replace the other means of making Excel data available in SharePoint 2013 as outlined in the previous section, but is meant as a means of managing and securing the workbooks and publishing content through the SharePoint interface. For example, if Company 123 wants to make their Product Sales spreadsheet available to all users in the organization so that they can input their personal sales information, Excel Services would *not* be the best way to do this. Rather, the manager, who wants to leverage SharePoint technologies, would ask users to update a SharePoint list (such as a Product Sales list) and then review the information to ensure it is accurate. The manager would then export this content to create a spreadsheet, add graphs for ease of analysis, and *then* publish it using Excel Services. This example is shown in action later in this chapter.

NOTE

Excel Services can open workbooks from SharePoint libraries as well as from Universal Naming Convention (UNC) paths and Hypertext Transport Protocol (HTTP) websites. For initial testing purposes, it is generally recommended to start with SharePoint library-based workbooks and then extend to other sources.

Before the process of publishing using Excel Services is reviewed, the Excel Services service application will be reviewed from a high level because it is important for the farm administrator to understand the different tools available for configuring and managing the Excel Services service application before opening it up to users for testing purposes.

A Brief History of the Evolution of Excel Services

Excel Services was introduced in SharePoint 2007, where it was part of the shared services provider and created the foundation for the product as it exists today. It served as a key component in Microsoft's BI strategy, as Microsoft realized that Excel spreadsheets contained an incredible amount of data in the average organization, as well as equations, macros, scripts, and even usernames and passwords that connected to data sources and other spreadsheets. SharePoint was a natural platform to use to allow organizations to better manage their valuable data.

A number of new features were then added to the product for the SharePoint 2010 version, including the following:

- Excel Services became a service application, and as such became more manageable and customizable than it was in SharePoint 2007, where it was part of the shared services provider.
- Excel Services provided the rendering engine that Office Web Apps for SharePoint 2010 used to allow users to read, edit, and collaborate on spreadsheets stored in SharePoint libraries via their browsers.
- PowerShell commandlets (cmdlets) for Excel Services management were provided.
- Representational State Transfer (REST) application programming interface (API) support was added. The REST API is a client/server software architecture/protocol that uses hyperlinks and lets the user access entities (such as ranges and charts) in workbooks using Excel Services through HTTP and also provides a method for users to set values in these ranges, including single cells.

Excel Services in SharePoint 2013 has continued to evolve and provides additional functionality, such as the following:

- Code can be written using the JavaScript Object Model (JSOM). There are two supported scenarios where this code can run: The code can live on a SharePoint 2013 page or on a host web page that contains an embedded workbook that is stored on SkyDrive.
- JavaScript user-defined functions (UDFs) enable developers to add JavaScript to a web page and then reference the code from a spreadsheet. This allows functionality that Excel may not provide natively, such as getting the stock price of a current stock from a website.
- Excel Interactive View allows developers to add some Hypertext Markup Language (HTML) code to a page that contains an HTML to add a clickable Excel icon above the table. If a user clicks the icon, an Excel table and chart is generated, in the browser, providing more options for interacting with the data. Excel Interactive View uses HTML, JavaScript, and Excel Services to generate these Excel tables and chart views on-the-fly.
- Excel Services can now access data using the Open Data Protocol (OData), which builds upon the capabilities of the existing Excel Services REST API. OData can be used to get information about tables in a workbook that is stored in a SharePoint library, which is returned in the Extensible Markup Language (XML) Atom format.

Managing the Excel Service Application

Most SharePoint Server 2013 Enterprise installations contain an Excel Services service application. If a new service application is needed, you can create it from the Manage Service Applications page on the Central Administration site. The details of each configuration will vary based on the needs of the organization, and the settings for the service application are discussed here from a high level.

A number of tools allow farm administrators to manage the instance of Excel Services, as shown in Figure 26.1. Each of these tools is important for more complex Excel Services configurations, but the farm administrator can most likely leave them at their default settings for simpler implementations where the workbooks are stored in SharePoint libraries and don't contain connections to external content.

The Global Settings tool provides access to a number of settings that are essential to configure properly if content not stored in SharePoint libraries is being accessed. The configuration details will vary based on a number of factors, such as whether there is a dedicated Excel Services front-end server (in which case, more resources can be dedicated to the Excel Services service application) or if Excel Services is sharing a front-end server with numerous other services applications. Also, the location of the data being connected to will affect these settings. For reference purposes, here are the items that you can configure:

- **Security settings:** File Access Method (Impersonation or Process Account), Connection Encryption (Not Required or Required), and Allow Cross Domain Access (Yes/No). File Access Method settings have no effect when users try to access content stored in SharePoint 2013 libraries, only when the workbooks are stored in UNC or HTTP locations. Connection encryption supports Secure Sockets Layer (SSL) and IPsec.

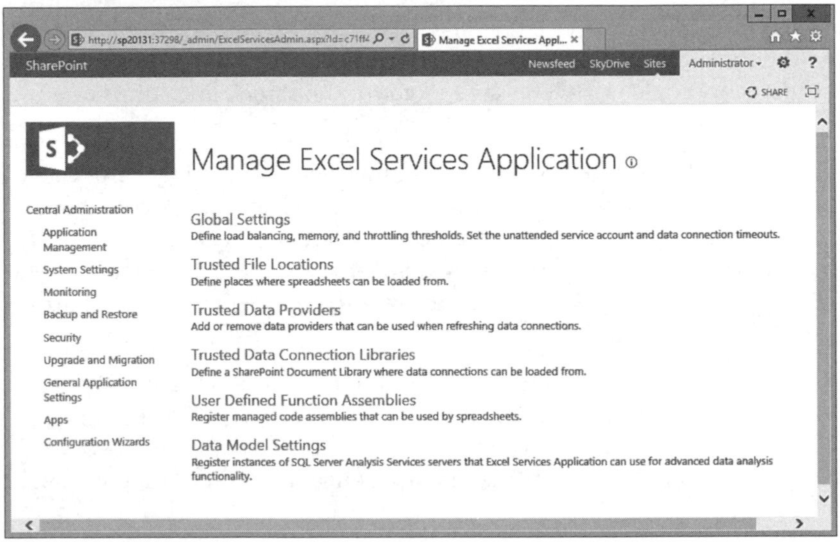

FIGURE 26.1 Excel Services service application management tools.

NOTE

In most SharePoint 2013 deployments where front-end servers and Excel Calculation Services application servers run on different computers, impersonation requires Kerberos delegation.

- **Load-balancing options:** Workbook URL, Round Robin with Health Check, or Local.
- **Session management:** Maximum Sessions per User (default setting 25).
- **Memory utilization:** Maximum Private Bytes (set to 50% of physical memory on the machine by default), Memory Cache Threshold (set to 90% by default), and Maximum Unused Object Age (set to no maximum by default).
- **Workbook cache:** Location (by default stored in the system temporary directory), Maximum Size of Workbook Cache (by default set to 40,960MB), and Caching of Unused Files (enabled by default).
- **External data settings:** Connection Lifetime (set to 1,800 seconds by default), Analysis Services EffectiveUserName (disabled by default), and Unattended Service Account. (Secure Store Service Association can be provided or a new Unattended Service Account can be defined.)

NOTE

The Unattended Service Account option allows the farm administrator to specify the application ID of a target application ID that needs to be configured in the Secure Store service application. The target application ID is provided with credentials and a password, administrators are configured, and a key is generated for it. This target application ID is then used as a "get data" type of account when a workbook is loaded that contains a data connection for the unattended account, and it is required when a workbook connection specifies None for authentication.

Additional tools available from the Manage Excel Services Application page include the following:

- **Trusted File Locations:** These are the file locations (SharePoint Foundation-based, UNC, or HTTP) that are considered "trustworthy," and Excel workbooks can be published to these locations. Child libraries and directories can also be trusted; Session Timeouts, Maximum Workbook Size, and Maximum Chart Size can be defined; and external data connections can be configured here. By default, the address http:// is considered trusted along with children sites, but you can change this (for example, to only include the Finance Department's site or other site or site collection). Figure 26.2 shows an example where the URL http://sp20131/sites/Finance is the only trusted location.

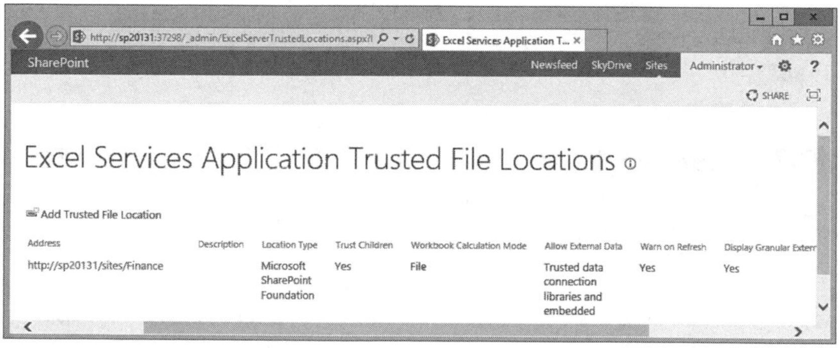

FIGURE 26.2 Excel Services Application Trusted File Locations page.

- **Trusted Data Providers:** A number of data providers that can be used for external data sources in Excel workbooks are already provided, and new ones can be defined using the data provider types OLE DB, ODBC, or ODBC DSN. Figure 26.3 shows the full list.

- **Trusted Data Connection Libraries:** By default, there aren't any trusted data connection libraries, so a farm administrator needs to add them. First, use the Data Connection Library template to create the library in the desired site collection, then click Add Trusted Data Connection Library, and then enter the URL of the library.

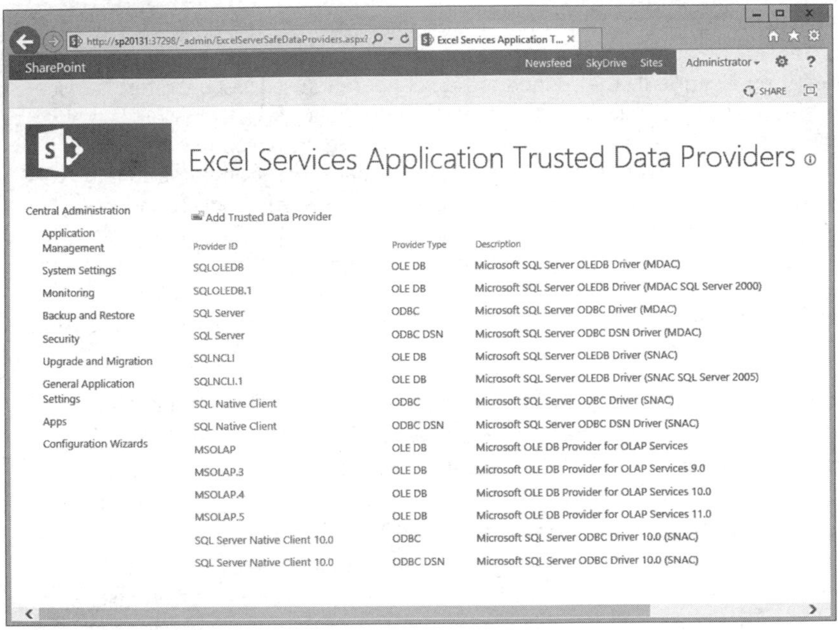

FIGURE 26.3 Excel Services Application Trusted Data Providers page.

- **User-Defined Function Assemblies:** None are provided by default, so a farm administrator must provide the strong name or full path of the assembly.

NOTE

STSADM commands (such as `Add-ecsfiletrustedlocation`, `Add-ecssafedataprovider`) are no longer supported against Excel Services in SharePoint 2013. Fortunately, an error is displayed in the command prompt if an administrator tries to run one of these commands. The error states: "Error. This stsadm command is no longer supported. Use PowerShell to modify Excel Services Application settings from the command line." The cmdlets are listed in full on TechNet at http://technet.microsoft.com/en-us/library/ee906545.aspx.

Publishing to Excel Services

This section provides a walkthrough of exporting a SharePoint list to an Excel 2013 spreadsheet and then publishing that content using Excel Services. This example walks through a process where a manager at Company 123 asks his employees to update a SharePoint list with sales data, then he exports this to Excel 2013, edits it, and then publishes back to SharePoint 2013 using Excel Services. The home page for the site is then edited to include an Excel Web Access web part that links to the published content.

This example helps to clarify the full process of publishing using Excel Services and then exposing the data using the Excel Web Access web part, so administrators and power users can get a sense for what is and isn't possible using Excel Services. This is just "scratching the surface," and administrators and power users should feel free to experiment with publishing other Excel workbooks using Excel Services and learning what is and isn't supported in the publishing process.

Prerequisites for this example include the following:

- SharePoint 2013 Enterprise must be installed, and an Excel Services service application must be configured and working for the site where the lists live.
- A PC or image with Excel 2013 must be available.

The site that will be used needs to have a custom list (described next), as well as a document library that doesn't need any special configuration settings. The site used in this example is http://sp20131/salestest and is built using the Team Site template.

Assuming these prerequisites are met, follow these steps to walk through this example:

1. Create a list called **Product Sales** using the Custom List template, and then configure the list so that it contains the columns and settings described in Table 26.1.

TABLE 26.1 Product Sales List Columns and Settings

Column	Data Type	Require That This Column Contains Information
Title (change the name of the column to Invoice Number)	Single Line of Text (already present) Set Enforce Unique Values to Yes	Yes
Salesperson	Person or Group	Yes
Product	Choice (enter choices of Widget and Gadget)	Yes
Quantity Sold	Number	Yes
Month of Sale	Choice (enter choices of January and February)	Yes

2. Add several items to this list so that there is enough data to create charts from (for example, data for several different salespeople for different products sold in different months). An example of the resulting list is shown in Figure 26.4. This simulates a simplified tracking tool that salespeople use to enter their sales into a list that the manager then verifies, analyzes, and publishes in Excel Services.

3. From the Product Sales list, click the List tab on the Ribbon and select Export to Excel button.

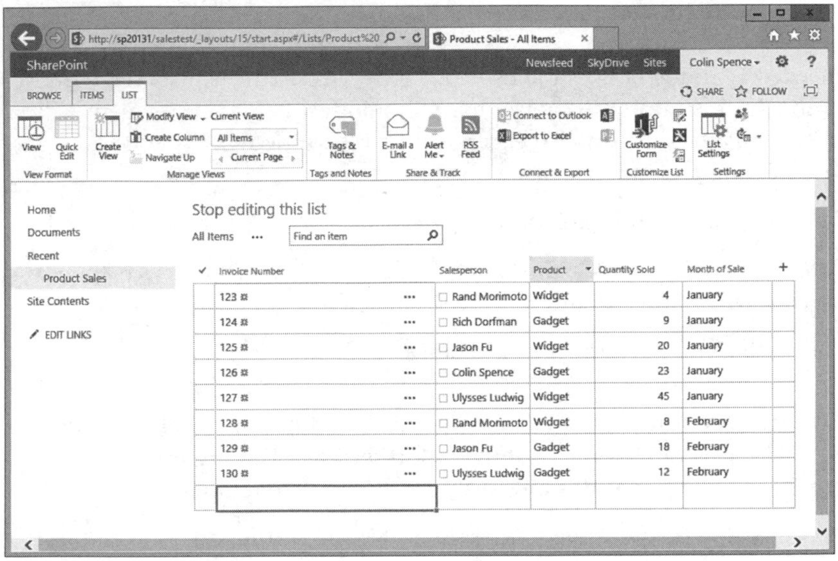

FIGURE 26.4 Custom list to use for Excel Services test.

4. Click Open when the File Download window opens.

5. Click Enable when the Microsoft Excel Security Notice window opens. This enables data connections between the computer and SharePoint 2013, which are required to update the content of the workbook at a later time.

6. An Import Data appears. Verify the options Table and New Workbook are checked. Click OK.

7. Excel opens and displays the content similar to what is shown in Figure 26.5. Actual values will vary based on what was entered in the SharePoint Product Sales list. At this point, there is still connectivity between the SharePoint list and the Excel workbook, as you can see on the Design tab on the ribbon, which shows the Refresh button that will refresh the content from the SharePoint 2013 list.

8. Click the File tab in Excel, then Save As, and save the workbook to a local folder on the computer as **Product Sales Local Copy** and click Save. This reflects the manager's desire to save the workbook locally so that he can edit it before he publishes it using Excel Services.

9. Navigate back to the Product Sales list in SharePoint and change a value, such as the product sold for a specific entry. This simulates the manager spotting an error in the spreadsheet and fixing it in the list.

10. Return to the spreadsheet, make sure the Data tab is active, click the drop-down arrow under the Refresh All icon, and select Refresh All. Verify that the value in the spreadsheet changes to reflect the change made in the SharePoint list.

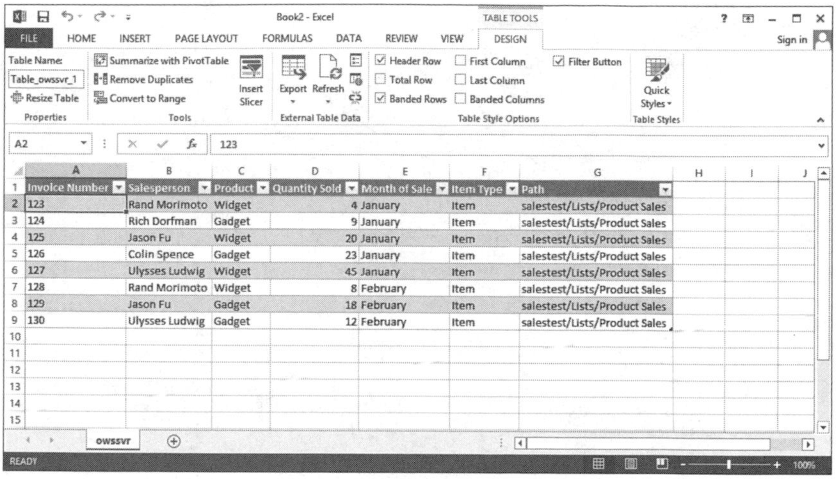

FIGURE 26.5 Product Sales list exported to Excel 2013.

11. Still in Excel, click the Design tab (if not visible, click any cell that contains data in the table) and check the value of the table name in the Table Name field in the Properties section of the Ribbon on the left. It will be something similar to Table_owssvr_1. Change this value to **Table1** and press Enter to save the value.

12. Right-click the tab at the bottom of the screen and rename the active tab to **Sales Numbers.** These small changes make the workbook easier to deal with when it is published using Excel Services.

13. Next, a PivotChart is added for more interactive analysis of the data. Click the Insert tab on the ribbon and then the PivotChart icon.

14. The Create PivotChart window opens. The Table/Range field should be active and have the blinking text entry cursor in it. Click and drag on the worksheet to select the range of cells that includes the content under the Salesperson, Product, Quantity Sold, Month of Sale, and Item Type columns (but not the header rows), as shown in Figure 26.6. This selects a subset of the data contained in the table but leaves out the Invoice Number column, as well as the Path column.

15. Verify that New Worksheet is selected in the Choose Where You Want the PivotChart to Be Placed section. Click OK.

16. A new worksheet opens, and the PivotTable Field List tool pane is open on the right side of the screen. Check the Salesperson, Product, Quantity Sold, Month of Sale, and Item Type check boxes in the Choose Fields to Add to Report field, as shown in Figure 26.7.

17. Close the PivotChart Fields list pane.

18. Click the Save button to save the changes locally.

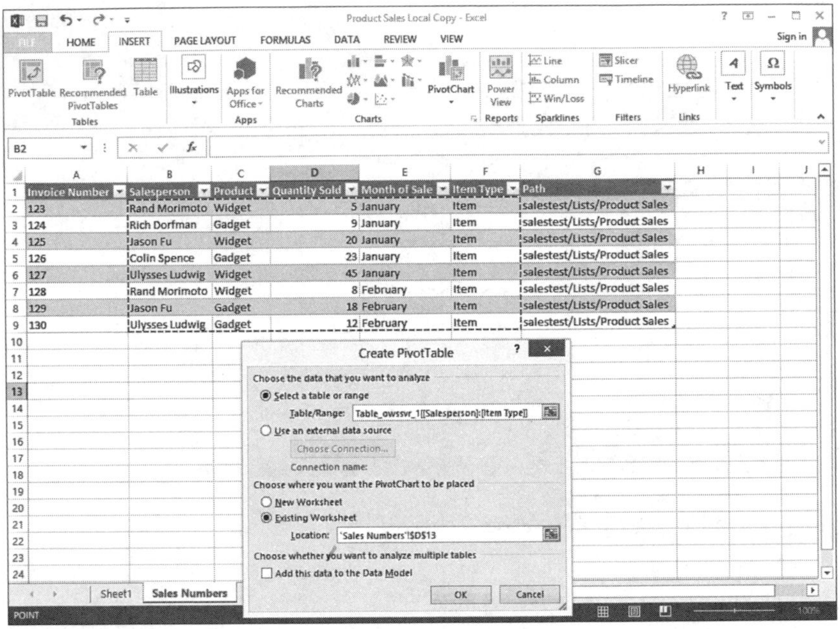

FIGURE 26.6 Selecting a data range for a PivotChart in Excel 2010.

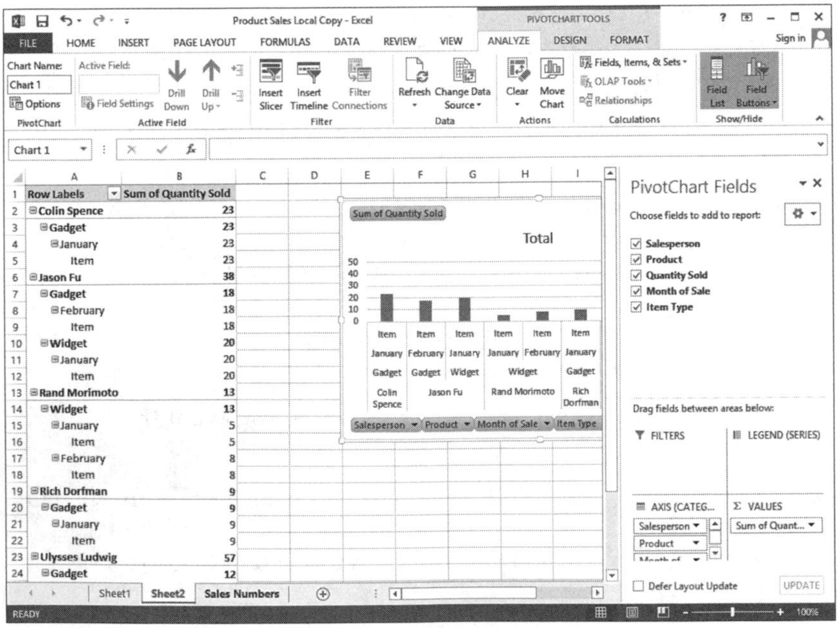

FIGURE 26.7 Selecting fields to add to the report.

19. Now the manager is ready to publish the workbook to a SharePoint document library using Excel Services. To accomplish this, click the File tab on the ribbon, and then click Save As.

20. Click Other Web Locations and the Browse button.

21. From the Save As window, type in the URL of the site where the spreadsheet is to be saved at the top of the window (in this example, http://sp20131/salestest/shared documents is entered), and then click Enter. Give the document an appropriate filename, such as **Product Sales Shared**. Figure 26.8 shows an example. Click Save.

FIGURE 26.8 Save As window in Excel 2013.

At this point in the example, the workbook has been saved to the document library. The manager, who happens to also manage the SharePoint 2013 site, now wants to display this content on the home page of the site, and so performs the following steps:

1. Assuming the previous steps have been completed successfully, return to the home page of the site that houses the document and list (http://sp20131/salestest/_layouts/15/start.aspx/ in this example) and access the Edit icon.

2. Click the Insert tab on the ribbon and click the Web Part button.

3. Click the Business Data folder in the Categories list of items, and then click Excel Web Access in the Web Parts section. Click Add, and the Excel Web Access web part is added to the page, as shown in Figure 26.9.

4. Next, the Excel Web Access web part needs to be edited to display data. Click the link inside the Excel Web Access web part that reads Click Here to Open the Tool Pane; the tool pane opens on the right.

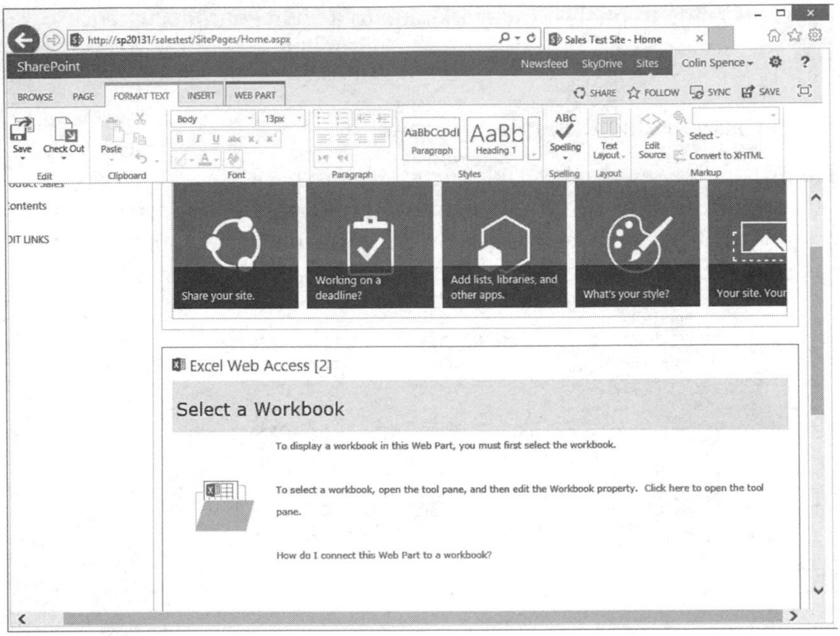

FIGURE 26.9 Excel Web Access web part added to a home page.

5. Scroll to the right to expose the tool pane if needed, and click the ellipsis next to Workbook at the top. Then from the Select as Asset window, navigate to the document library that the Excel workbook was published to and select the workbook (Product Sales Shared.xlsx in this example), and click Insert.

6. Click OK, and the page should look like Figure 26.10. In this example, Sheet 2 is displayed, which includes the PivotTable, but other tabs can be displayed by clicking the tab in the web part.

NOTE

If there is an error displaying content in the web part, go to Central Administration and make sure Excel Calculation Services is started under System Settings, Manage Services on Server.

7. Click the Save button to save changes.

8. Finally, collapse the nodes in the PivotTable view and note that the table reflects the changes and now only displays a single column per salesperson, as opposed to multiple columns per salesperson, when the PivotTable nodes are expanded. Note that none of the cells can be edited in the Excel Web Access web part.

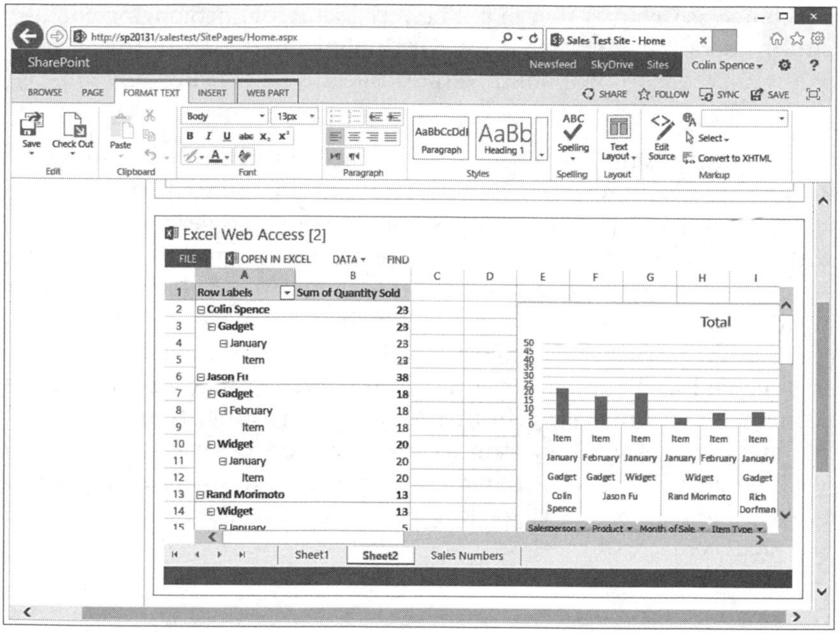

FIGURE 26.10 Excel Web Access web part after connection to the workbook.

NOTE

The Excel Web Access web part offers a handy tool in the File tab: the Reload Workbook tool. This reloads the workbook to Excel Services, which may sometimes be needed because content is cached and the version being viewed might not reflect all the most recent changes.

This exercise shows an example of how a manager can use Excel Services to publish certain items from a workbook to a document library, and then the Excel Web Access web part can be added to a page to allow users to interact with a PivotTable and PivotChart.

Additional experimentation with the different tools provided in the Excel Web Access web part is encouraged, as well as additional modifications to the data in the SharePoint list, which is still connected to the spreadsheet and can, therefore, be refreshed when the SharePoint 2013 list changes and then republished to the SharePoint document library via Excel Services.

Allowing Parameter Input in Excel Web Access

Another feature to be familiar with is the ability to name a cell in Excel 2013 and publish it using Excel Services, enabling users to input a value through the Excel Web Access interface. Although somewhat time-consuming to configure, it can allow for interactivity through the Excel Web Access web part that might be very useful for encouraging end users to interact with the data. Remember that any data input by end users in the Excel Web Access web part is not saved to the published spreadsheet, so it is really only for "what if" scenarios.

The following example reflects a situation where an IT manager wants to show senior management the impact of total number of help desk resources on average time to resolve the help desk tickets that come in based on numbers from the previous year. She creates a base spreadsheet with the months and number of help desk tickets per month, and then creates an equation for the Average Time to Resolve (Hrs) column that divides the total number of tickets by the variable that will be input by the Excel Web Access web part users. This allows users of the published worksheet to enter in different numbers in the Number of Resources cell and see the results over the course of the year. She is hoping this will enable her to convince senior management that the organization needs more help desk staff at certain times of the year if they want to meet their service level agreement (SLA) of no more than 4 hours average time to resolve help desk tickets. This example also allows the IT manager to show off her Excel Services skills to show senior management another capability of SharePoint 2013.

Follow these steps to test the process:

1. Create a new spreadsheet in Excel 2013.
2. Provide the heading **Month** to column A in cell A1.
3. Enter the text **January** in cell A2. Grab the lower-right corner of the cell, while highlighting cell A2, and drag downward until all the fields are populated with the months up to December.
4. Enter **Help Desk Tickets** as the header in cell B1. Enter random numbers between 0 and 200 for cells B2 through B13.
5. Enter **Average Time to Resolve** as the header in cell C1.
6. Enter the text **Number of Resources** in cell A15.
7. Select cell B15 and access the Formulas tab.
8. Click Define Name in the Defined Names section of the ribbon. Enter a name of **NumberofResources** and click OK. The results should look like Figure 26.11, with the exception of the actual values entered in cells B2 through B13. Note in Figure 26.11 that the name of the named cell (NumberofResources) appears in the name box to the left below the Ribbon where the cell name is normally displayed.
9. Select cell C2 and enter the following formula, which divides the number of tickets by the number of resources multiplied by four:

   ```
   =B2/(NumberofResources*4)
   ```

   Click Enter to save the equation. This equation assumes that each resource can resolve four help desk tickets in an hour.

   The error #Div/0 error displays because there is no value in cell B15.

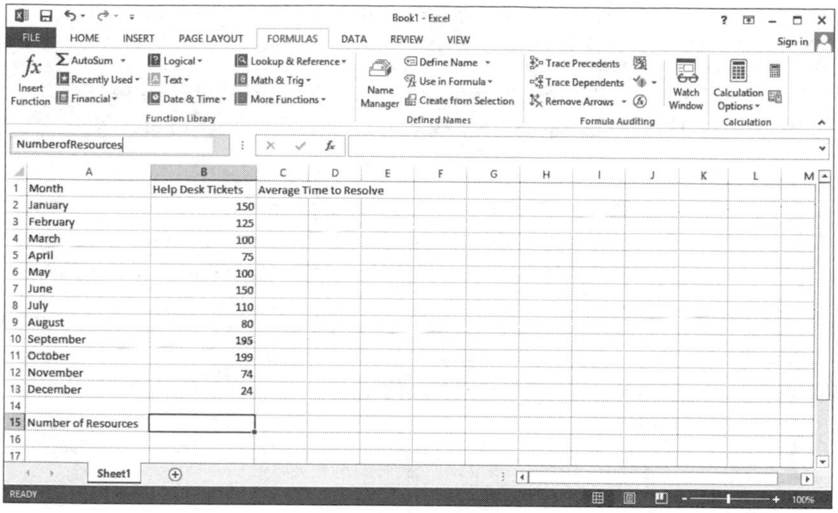

FIGURE 26.11 Naming a cell in an Excel 2010 worksheet.

10. Click cell C2 and drag down to cell C13; all cells should display the #Div/0 error.

11. Click the File tab, click Save As, and click Other Web Locations. Click the Browse button.

12. Click the Browser View Options button in the lower-left corner of the Save As window, click the Parameters tab, click the Add button, and check the box next to NumberofResources; then click OK. The results should match Figure 26.12.

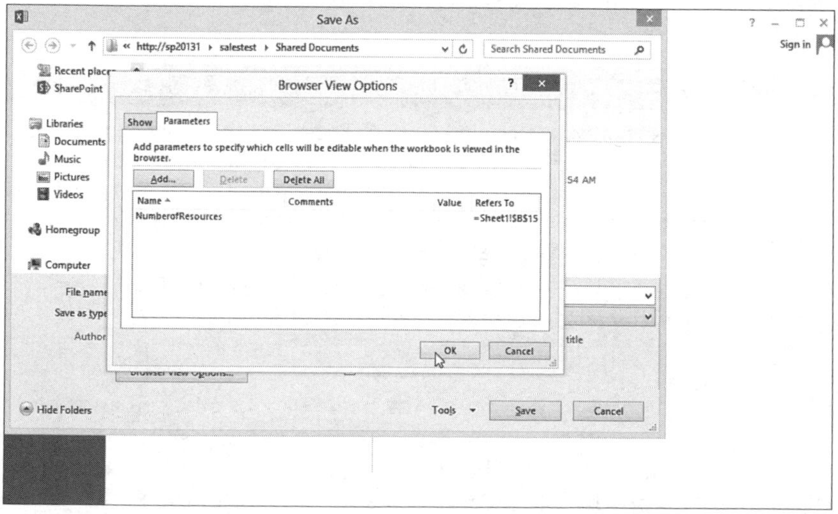

FIGURE 26.12 Using the Parameters tab in the Browser View Options windows when saving an Excel file to SharePoint.

13. Click OK again to close the Browser View Options window.

14. In the Save As window, enter the full path for the SharePoint site and document library in the Filename field and enter the filename **HelpDeskTickets** (so in this example, it is http://sp20131/salestest/shared documents/HelpDeskTickets). Click Save.

15. Navigate to the document library where the document was stored and click the document filename. The document should display in the browser. Enter a whole number in the Parameters pane to the right and click Apply; the results should be similar to Figure 26.13.

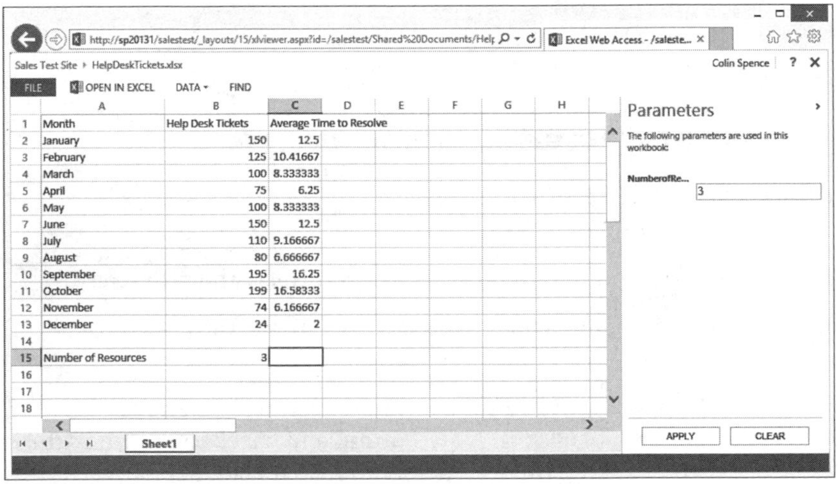

FIGURE 26.13 Results of entering a parameter value in the browser.

NOTE

If the document does not open in the browser using Excel Services, as mentioned in step 15, a number of factors could be involved. Check the Library Settings, Advanced Settings link, and verify that Open in the Browser or Use the Server Default (Open in the Browser) are selected. Also make sure that Excel Calculation Service is started. Check under Central Administration, System Settings, Manage Services on Server.

If this doesn't resolve the problem, there may be other problems with Excel Services, or the site or library containing the spreadsheet isn't trusted by Excel Services.

This example shows the steps involved with defining the name of a specific cell and then including that cell in the publishing process using Excel Services, as well as showing the interface that results. Multiple named cells can be defined in a workbook, which can then essentially be used as variables in the resulting content that is surfaced in the Excel Web Access web part. Combine this with tools such as charts, PivotTables, and conditional formatting, and the results can be very powerful.

Visio Graphics Service Overview

Visio Graphics Service is somewhat similar to Excel Services. For example, it enables users to view a Visio diagram (saved in .vsdx format) directly in their browser without having to open it locally. In addition, SharePoint 2013 Enterprise offers a Visio Web Access web part that enables administrators and developers to add the web part to a page and connect to a Visio document. There are also tools provided for developers to connect to external data sources, such as a SharePoint list or a variety of other data sources, and the JSOM provides tools for developers to create interactive mashups and applications based on Visio diagrams.

Visio Graphics Service in SharePoint 2013 has improved since the SharePoint 2010 version; a new type of Visio file (.vsdx) allows users to save files directly to SharePoint where they can be viewed in the browser using Visio Services. In SharePoint 2010, the Visio files had to be published in Visio Web Drawing (.vdw) format to be viewed in Visio Services, and only Visio Professional 2010 or Visio Premium 2010 could publish to those formats. Visio Services can still render the .vdw formats in SharePoint 2013.

The following list summarizes some other key improvements in Visio 2013 and Visio Services 2013:

- Visio Professional 2013 supports coauthoring on documents stored in SharePoint 2013 or SkyDrive so that multiple users can work on Visio diagrams simultaneously.
- Comments can be attached to shapes in Visio 2013, and users without Visio on their desktops can access comments and add their own through the browser if Visio Services is installed.
- Visio 2013 diagrams can be connected to external lists created using SharePoint Business Connectivity Services (BCS) on SharePoint Server 2013.
- Visio 2013 includes a framework for adding comments, which can be associated with a particular shape or page.
- Users can now configure their data-connected diagrams directly from the Visio client, which allows data sources to be refreshed in Visio Services.
- The JSOM in Visio Services provides programmatic access to Visio drawings displayed in the Visio Web Access web part so that developers can create mashups or applications that access data stored in shapes interactively.

Figure 26.14 shows an example of a Visio 2013 drawing saved to a SharePoint 2013 Enterprise document library in a farm where Visio Services is enabled. In this example, the Library Settings for the library have been configured so that the Default open behavior setting (accessible under Advanced Settings) for browser-enabled documents set to Open in the browser or Use the server default (Open in the browser). In this example, a user simply clicks the document filename in the document library, and Visio Services renders the drawing in the browser. At the top of the screen, the breadcrumb is listed, and Visio Web Access is shown to the right. Beneath that information are several links: Open in

Visio, Refresh, Share Information, and Comments. A drop-down menu lists any additional pages contained in the Visio file. A zoom-in/out slider bar is provided in the lower-right corner.

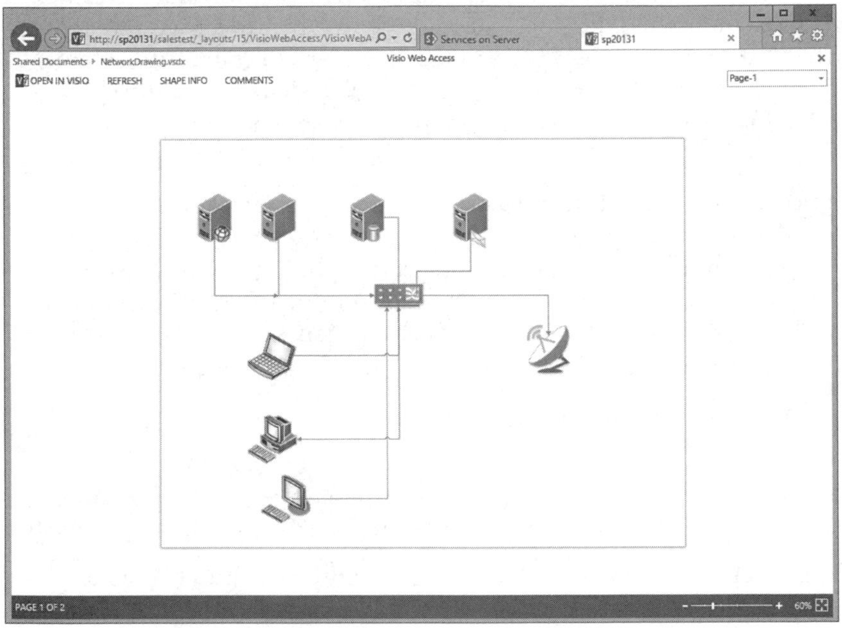

FIGURE 26.14 Example of a Visio 2013 file viewed in the browser.

Figure 26.15 shows the results in this example where a shape was selected, then the Shape Info was clicked, and the Comments link was clicked. In this example, the author of the drawing added data to the server shape—as shown in Figure 26.15—including the asset number, serial number, location, and other default data fields associated with the shape in Visio 2013. By clicking Comments, an end user (who doesn't need Visio on his desktop) can add comments that other users can respond to.

While Visio Graphics Service might not be one of the most widely used tools in the SharePoint toolbox, it does provide features than can enhance the collaborative use of SharePoint by the organization, especially where graphically detailed documents are required. Basic examples include network diagrams, flow charts for business processes, maps, floor plans, and the like. A developer can then add functionality to these files that can make them much more useful to the user population. For example, a map of the United States in Visio 2013 could show shapes for each office around the country, connect to additional information about each office, and provide a hyperlink to the SharePoint site for each office.

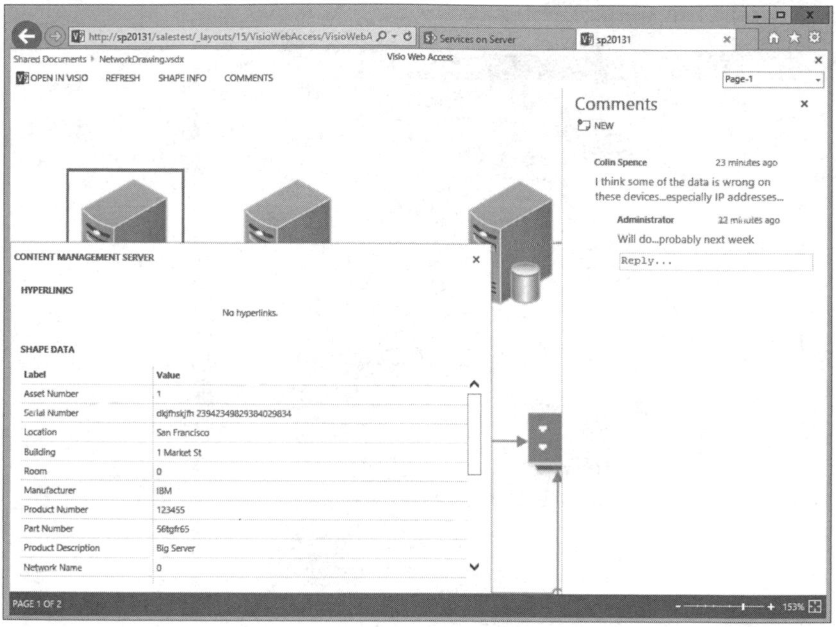

FIGURE 26.15 Visio 2013 file viewed in the browser with Shape Information and Comments visible.

Reviewing the Visio Graphics Service Service Application

As with the Excel Services service application, the Visio Graphics Service service application is created by default in SharePoint Server 2013 Enterprise via the wizard in most cases. If a new service application is needed, you can create it from the Manage Service Applications page on the Central Administration site.

The settings for the Visio Graphics Service service application are as follows:

- **Global Settings:** Include Maximum Web Drawing Size (25MB is the default, with 50MB being the supported limit), Minimum Cache Age (5 minutes is the default number of minutes and 34,560 the maximum), Maximum Cache Age (60 minutes is the default number of minutes and 34,560 the maximum), Maximum Recalc Duration (60 seconds is the default and 120 seconds the maximum), and Unattended Service Account Application ID.
- **Trusted Data Providers:** A number of data providers are already provided as shown in Figure 26.16, and new ones can be added.

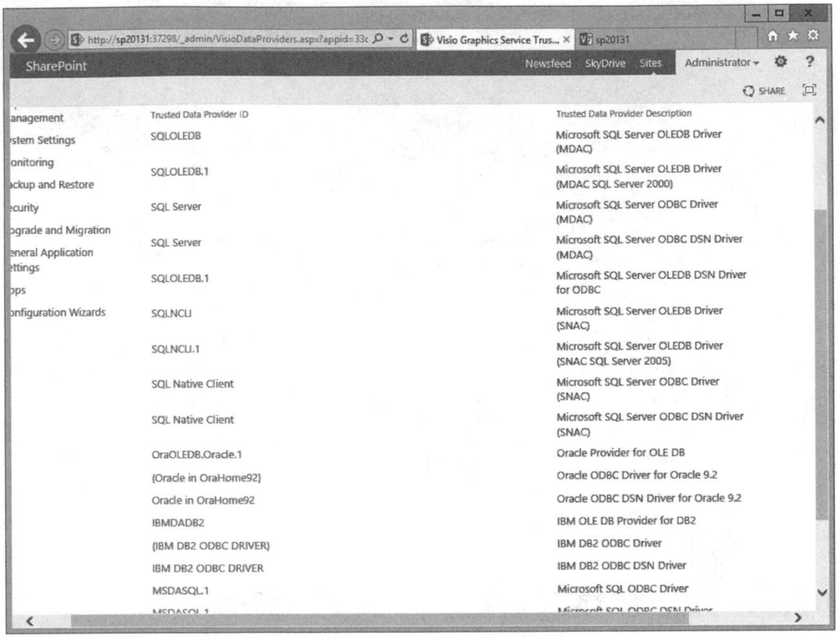

FIGURE 26.16 Visio Graphics Service trusted data providers.

Access Services Overview

Microsoft Access is a very powerful and easy-to-use database, form and report creation tool. From an IT perspective, however, it can be seen as a tool set that encourages users to create databases and even applications to meet their needs and that IT has no control over. For example, an employee may have used Access to create a custom database, complete with several reports, customized forms for data entry and macros to perform calculations on data entered, that stores and reports on key sales information. The database could be saved to a file share, the employee's local computer, or be copied as needed to other devices such as a laptop or home computer. And although this is very handy to the employee, it becomes difficult if not impossible for IT to back up the data or ensure that it won't accidentally—or otherwise—end up in a competitor's hands. If the database contains healthcare information about patients or personal data, it is likewise a source of concern for IT (and the legal department).

In addition, Access was designed by Microsoft to be a "lightweight" database tool, for less-sophisticated users, and therefore had a number of limitations. For example, Access 2010 has a limit of 2GB for an Access database (.accdb file), including all database objects and data. There are workarounds, such as linking multiple tables, but as end users and developers pushed the limits of what Access was capable of, IT was forced to look for alternatives, one of which is to move the databases to Structured Query Language (SQL) Server, and another of which is to move the databases to SharePoint Access Services.

Access Services in SharePoint 2010 was designed as an alternative to the "rogue" databases and applications, as it allowed IT to migrate Access databases, forms, and reports to the SharePoint environment, which was more effectively controlled by IT. Access Services also allowed users to create sites using out-of-the-box site templates (including Assets Web Database, Charitable Contributions Web Database, and Contacts Web Database), which could be modified much as Access databases could be, and end users could create forms and reports to meet their precise needs, without using the standalone Access products.

Access Services in SharePoint 2013 still supports Access Services from SharePoint 2010, but also provides a new incarnation of the tools, which have been modified significantly.

Assuming SharePoint Server 2013 Enterprise is installed and the wizard was used to configure the farm, the default service applications will include both Access Services 2010 and Access Services (which is really Access Services 2013). When a new Access application is created, Access Services creates a new database that stores the data, view, queries, and macros contained in the app. A key difference between Access Services 2010 and Access Services 2013 is that Access Services 2013 can take advantage of isolated app domains and can create the new databases on a different SQL 2012 server. This allows IT the option of separating the Access data and related components on a different SQL instance or a different server.

Summary

This chapter covered the integration of Excel and SharePoint, especially using the Excel Services tools, because this is such an important capability of SharePoint 2013. Many knowledge workers and managers still "live" in Excel and manage much of the most critical information in workbooks, so understanding what Excel Services can and cannot do is important for SharePoint power users and administrators. A brief overview of Visio Graphics Services and Access Services was provided to suggest some use cases for these tools. Access Services can be used for a wide range of database requirements and supports both legacy Access Services 2010 databases and the new Access Services 2013 apps, but coverage of this topic in depth is beyond the scope of this chapter.

Best Practices

The following are best practices from this chapter:

- There are numerous ways to move content from Excel spreadsheets and workbooks into SharePoint 2013. IT should understand the different options, including the following: creating a new list and cutting/pasting content into it, using the Import Spreadsheet list template to import data from an Excel spreadsheet, exporting list data to an Excel spreadsheet, or using Excel Services to publish a spreadsheet to a SharePoint 2013 library.

- Excel Services allows Excel 2013 users to save a workbook to a SharePoint library, and then the Excel Web Access web part can be used to connect to a published Excel workbook and display tables, charts, and other items in the web part, usually on a read-only basis.

- Many users want to interact with the data presented by Excel Web Access web part, so the different tools available from the File tab in the Excel Web Access web part (Open in Excel, Download a Snapshot, and Download a Copy) should be demonstrated to users. In addition, the section in this chapter titled "Allowing Parameter Input in Excel Web Access" shows how a cell can be named and then published via Excel Services to allow input to the Excel Web Access web part.
- Visio Graphics Service allows users to save Visio 2013 documents in the new .vsdx format, which can be rendered in the browser if Visio Graphics Service is properly configured.
- Visio 2013 also offers coauthoring, comments, and other powerful application development tools that can allow the creation of graphically driven mashups and applications for collaborative purposes.
- Access Services 2010 and 2013 service applications are provided in SharePoint 2013 Enterprise. These should be considered development tools, and the organization should carefully test these tools and determine whether they should be made available to the general user population.
- A generally recommended best practice with Access Services 2013 is to create an isolated app domain where the Access Services databases are created on a separate SQL Server 2012 instance.

CHAPTER 27

Office Web Apps 2013 Integration with SharePoint 2013

IN THIS CHAPTER

- Planning for Office Web Apps 2013 Use
- Key Differences Between Excel Services and Excel Web App
- Server Prerequisites for OWA 2013 Overview
- Browser Support of Office Web Apps
- Licensing Requirements for OWA 2013
- Installing and Configuring Office Web Apps 2013
- Verifying the Settings in the Document Library
- Testing OWA 2013 Functionality

Office Web Apps 2013 (OWA 2013) provides a browser-based viewing and editing experience for SharePoint 2013 users who need to collaborate on Word, Excel, PowerPoint, or OneNote documents. This is the second version of this product, and Microsoft has changed it from a SharePoint service application in SharePoint 2010 to a standalone product for use with SharePoint 2013 (and, of course, improved it in many respects, as covered in this chapter). OWA 2013 also provides functionality that Exchange Server 2013 and Lync Server 2013 can use, but this chapter focuses on the SharePoint 2013 features.

The browser-based viewing and editing of document capabilities has become more popular since other companies such as Google started offering products like Google Docs, and more knowledge workers needed access from a variety of devices such as smartphones and tablets, which often do not have the full Microsoft Office applications installed.

OWA 2013 also "powers" a large portion of the thumbnail previewing capabilities in SharePoint 2013 (in search results and in document libraries), and for that reason is also an important component for most enterprise implementations of SharePoint 2013.

This chapter provides an overview of the capabilities of the tool set and the configuration process, and walks through the user interface to clarify how the product might be of value to different types of organizations.

Planning for Office Web Apps 2013 Use

This section provides some "food for thought" for organizations interested in implementing the OWA 2013 functionality to allow end users another method of collaborating on Word, Excel, and PowerPoint documents. Prerequisites, licensing issues, and limitations by browsers are covered in this section, albeit from a fairly high level because of the wealth of information provided by Microsoft on these topics (for which links are given).

Fundamentally, it is important to be familiar with the different file types OWA 2013 can display. Fortunately, OWA 2013 displays the most common Microsoft Office file types, as summarized in the following list:

- Word documents (.doc, .docx, .dotx, .dot, .dotm extensions)
- Excel documents (.xls, .xlsx, .xlsm, .xlm, .xlsb extensions)
- PowerPoint documents (.ppt, .pptx, .pps, .ppsx, .potx, .pot, .pptm, .potm, .ppsm extensions)

NOTE

PowerPoint Broadcast was provided in SharePoint 2010 but is removed from SharePoint 2013. It is available through SkyDrive and Lync Server 2013. This feature broadcasts PowerPoint slides and provides an embedded PowerPoint viewer that provides an optimal viewing experience, but is available only on the Windows platform.

Unlike its predecessor, which was a service application in SharePoint 2010, OWA 2013 provides functionality that can be used by a number of other popular Microsoft products. Figure 27.1 provides a visual summary of the connectivity points between OWA 2013 and other key Microsoft products (namely Exchange 2013, Lync 2013, and SharePoint 2013).

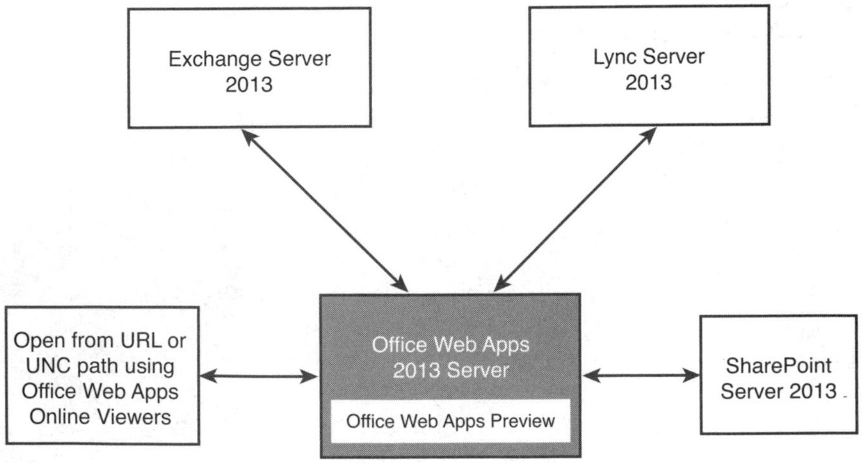

FIGURE 27.1 OWA 2013 interacts with other Microsoft products.

Key Differences Between Excel Services and Excel Web App

As discussed in detail in Chapter 26, "Extending SharePoint 2013 with Excel Services, Visio Graphics Services, and Access Services," Excel Services provides a number of features that can be seen to overlap with OWA 2013. First of all, Excel Services allows users to view Excel files in their browsers and, to a very limited degree, interact with them. But Excel Services is not intended to allow users to edit content directly in the browser, whereas Excel Web App in OWA 2013 is specifically designed for editing content in the browser. Table 27.1 provides additional information about the differences between the products.

TABLE 27.1 Comparing Excel Services to Excel Web App

Task	Supported in Excel Services?	Supported in Excel Web App?
Create or edit a workbook in a browser window	No	Yes
View and interact with a workbook that contains a data model	Yes	No
View and interact with a workbook that contains Power View views	Yes	No
View and interact with items, such as PivotChart reports, PivotTable reports, timeline controls, and slicers	Yes	Yes (assuming a data model is not used as the data source)
View and interact with a workbook that contains calculated items (such as calculated fields, calculated measures, or calculated members)	Yes	Partially: Calculated fields are not supported. Calculated measures and calculated members are supported for viewing.
Display a single item (PivotChart, worksheet, range of data) from a workbook in its own web part	Yes	Yes

NOTE

It can be confusing to determine which product (Excel Services or Excel Web App) is rendering content, but the URL can help. If the URL contains the term *WopiFrame*, Excel Web App is involved; if the URL contains the term *xlviewer*, however, Excel Services is rendering the page.

Server Prerequisites for OWA 2013 Overview

OWA 2013 has a number of prerequisites, as covered in this section, to ensure a successful configuration. There are a number of recommendations on how *not* to configure the server that are important for the architect or administrator to understand to avoid unnecessary troubleshooting efforts.

Server prerequisites are listed in Table 27.2 along with other key notes on server configuration to keep in mind.

TABLE 27.2 Server Prerequisites

System Requirements	Details
Supported operating systems	The 64-bit edition of Windows Server 2008 R2 Service Pack 1 (SP1) Standard, Enterprise, or Datacenter with KB2592525 installed.
	The 64-bit edition of Windows Server 2012 Standard or Datacenter.
Hardware	Processor: 64-bit, 4 cores
	RAM: 8GB or more RAM
	Hard disk: 80GB
Unsupported configurations	Do not install Office Web Apps Server on a domain controller (a Windows Server running Active Directory Domain Service).
	Servers that run Office Web Apps Server must not run any other server application. This includes Exchange Server, SharePoint Server, Lync Server, and SQL Server.
	Do not install any services or roles that depend on the Web Server (Internet Information Services [IIS]) role on port 80, 443, or 809 because Office Web Apps Server periodically removes web applications on these ports.
	Do not install any version of Office. You must uninstall Office before you install Office Web Apps Server.
Ports that must be available and not blocked by firewalls	Port 443 for Hypertext Transport Protocol Secure (HTTPS) traffic.
	Port 80 for HTTP traffic.
	Port 809 for private traffic between the servers that run Office Web Apps Server (in a multiserver farm).

Specific Server 2008 R2 Prerequisites

As an older operating system, Windows Server 2008 R2 requires more downloads to be installed than Windows Server 2012, as summarized in the following list:

- Office Web Apps Server 2013
- .NET Framework 4.5
- KB2592525 (An application that uses DirectWrite does not start in a restricted security context in Windows 7 or in Windows Server 2008 R2.)
- Windows PowerShell 3.0

For Windows Server 2008 R2, the following list describes the minimum role services that are required for the web server (IIS) server role:

- Common HTTP features

  Static content

  Default document

- Application development

  ASP.NET

  .NET Extensibility

  Internet Server Application Programming Interface (ISAPI) extensions

  ISAPI filters

Server-side includes

- Security

  Windows authentication

  Request filtering

- Management tools

  IIS Management Console

- Ink and handwriting services

  Ink support

The following are recommended but not required for Windows Server 2008 R2:

- Performance

  Static content compression

  Dynamic content compression

Specific Windows Server 2012 Prerequisites

As a newer operating system, Windows Server 2012 already includes .NET Framework 4.5, KB2592525, and Windows PowerShell 3.0. However, the OWA Server 2013 software does still need to be downloaded as with Windows Server 2008 R2.

For Windows Server 2012, the following list describes the minimum role services that are required for the web server (IIS) server role:

- Management tools

  IIS Management Console

- Web server

  Common HTTP features

  Default document

  Static content

- Security

  Request filtering

  Windows authentication

- Application Development

  .NET Extensibility 4.5

  ASP.NET 4.5

  ISAPI extensions

  ISAPI filters

  Server-side includes

In addition, the following are recommended but not required for Windows Server 2012:

- Performance

  Static Content Compression

  Dynamic Content Compression

NOTE

Additional guidance and information is available from TechNet: http://technet.microsoft.com/en-us/library/jj219435.aspx. This includes guidance on load balancers, domain name server (DNS) requirements, planning language packs, topology planning, security planning, and design recommendations for larger OWA 2013 farms.

NOTE

Note that applying Office Web Apps Server updates by using the Microsoft automatic updates process isn't supported with OWA 2013. First, the OWA 2013 Server must be removed from the farm by using the PowerShell commandlet (cmdlet) `Remove-OfficeWebAppsMachine`, and then Office Web Apps Server must be uninstalled by using Add or Remove Programs, the software update installed, and then the Office Web Apps Server farm can be re-created. This process is more complicated with multi-server farms and is described in detail on TechNet: http://technet.microsoft.com/en-us/library/jj966220.aspx. Microsoft recommends that organizations manage updates by using Windows Server Update Services (WSUS) or by using System Center Configuration Manager (SCCM), which uses WSUS.

Browser Support of Office Web Apps

For organizations that decide to support Office Web Apps, it is important to test the various browsers in use because the browser will become a primary tool used for editing documents. Simply stated, browser support for OWA 2013 is the same as for SharePoint 2013, so here is quick reminder of browsers supported by SharePoint 2013:

- **Internet Explorer (IE) 10:** Supported
- **IE 9:** Supported
- **IE 8:** Supported
- **IE 7:** Not Supported
- **IE 6:** Not Supported
- **Google Chrome (latest released version):** Supported
- **Mozilla Firefox (latest released version):** Supported
- **Apple Safari (latest released version):** Supported

Mobile browser support is shown in Table 27.3. Because there is such a proliferation of mobile devices, not all devices are officially supported by Microsoft and therefore not included in this table. The organization should test any devices not "officially" supported by Microsoft to determine the level of interaction possible when using these devices.

TABLE 27.3 Mobile Device and Browser Support

Mobile Device Operating System	Operating System Version	Browser	Smartphone Device	Slate or Tablet Device
Windows Phone	Windows Phone 7.5 or later versions	IE Mobile	Supported	Not applicable
Windows	Windows 7 or later versions	Internet Explorer	Not applicable	Supported
iOS	5.0 or later versions	Safari	Supported	Fully supported on iPad 2 or 3 with iOS 6.0 or later, partially supported on older versions
Android	4.0 or later versions	Android Browser	Supported	Supported

27

NOTE

Some functionality in SharePoint 2013 requires ActiveX controls, and currently only 32-bit versions of Internet Explorer support this functionality. You can find more information about the features that won't be supported by browsers that don't support ActiveX controls at http://technet.microsoft.com/en-us/library/cc263526.aspx#activex.

Licensing Requirements for OWA 2013

Organizations interested in using Office Web Apps in their environments still need to comply with Microsoft licensing policies. View-only functionality in OWA 2013 is free, but the ability to edit Office files in the browser requires an editing license.

SharePoint 2013 provides new license enforcement capabilities that are controlled through PowerShell, and which work with OWA 2013. This new licensing needs to be enabled, also via PowerShell, and then only users who have the appropriate license, or belong to Active Directory (AD) groups that have been approved, can edit Office files in their browsers using OWA 2013.

Office Web Apps licensing offers two options:

- **View-only:** By default, OWA 2013 is view-only. View-only functionality is provided for free.
- **Edit and view:** An editing license is required to use the editing features of OWA 2013 with SharePoint 2013. Editing can be enabled when you create the OWA 2013 Server farm.

  Enterprise customers who are licensed for Office 2013 through a Volume Licensing program can enable OWA 2013 editing for SharePoint 2013 on-premises.

  Refer to the Microsoft Software License Terms shown when Office Web Apps Server is installed for more details on licensing.

As always, consult with a qualified Microsoft software vendor for more complete details, because there are many ways OWA 2013 can be used. For example, there are additional capabilities when OWA 2013 is used in conjunction with Lync 2013.

Installing and Configuring Office Web Apps 2013

This section gives instructions for installing OWA 2013 on a single Windows Server 2012 server, and then shows how to connect to a SharePoint Server 2013 enterprise farm over HTTP. Many organizations might have more complex configurations, but this process provides an overview of the process involved with establishing basic functionality for testing purposes, or for smaller environments where a single OWA 2013 server may suffice.

Microsoft provides detailed instructions for a number of other different configurations at http://technet.microsoft.com/en-us/library/jj219455.aspx. It includes the following scenarios:

- Deploy a single-server Office Web Apps Server farm in a test environment
- Deploy a single-server Office Web Apps Server farm that uses HTTPS
- Deploy a multiserver, load-balanced Office Web Apps Server farm that uses HTTPS

The following steps apply to the first scenario, that of deploying a single-server OWA 2013 Server farm in a test environment. The prerequisites for the server that are needed for this exercise are covered previously in this chapter in the section titled "Server Prerequisites for OWA 2013 Overview" in the Windows Server 2012 column. The items in the subsection titled "Specific Windows Server 2012 Prerequisites" are installed in the exercise steps that follow, so those do not need to be preinstalled.

Assuming you have a server that meets those requirements, and is connected to the same domain as your SharePoint 2013 farm, complete the following steps to configure Office Web Apps:

1. A PowerShell script will be run first to prepare the server for the OWA 2013 installation. If it isn't run, you will receive an error message when trying to install OWA 2013.

2. Open Windows PowerShell on the Windows Server 2012 server (named OOWA201301 in this example). Paste in the following script and press Enter:

   ```
   Add-WindowsFeature Web-Server,Web-Mgmt-Tools,Web-Mgmt-Console,Web-
   WebServer,Web-Common-Http,Web-Default-Doc,Web-Static-Content,Web-
   Performance,Web-Stat-Compression,Web-Dyn-Compression,Web-Security,Web-
   Filtering,Web-Windows-Auth,Web-App-Dev,Web-Net-Ext45,Web-Asp-Net45,Web-
   ISAPI-Ext,Web-ISAPI-Filter,Web-Includes,InkandHandwritingServices
   ```

   This character maps to American Standard Code for Information Interchange (ASCII) 45; to see the character, hold down the ALT key, type 45 on the numeric keypad, and then let go of the ALT key.

NOTE

A number of things can go wrong when using PowerShell and pasting in code. A general best practice is to paste code into Notepad first to clear any unneeded formatting, and then paste it into PowerShell. PowerShell also needs to run with sufficient permissions to execute the code, which can require additional steps, depending on the server configuration.

The results should be similar to those shown in Figure 27.2.

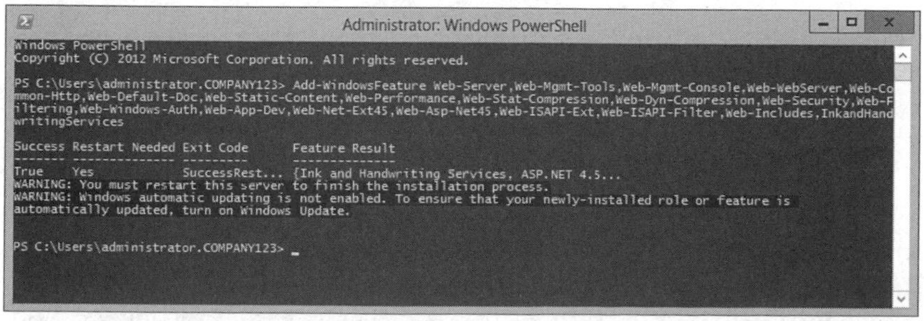

FIGURE 27.2 Results of `Add-WindowsFeature` preparation for installation of OWA 2013.

3. Reboot the server to complete the installation process.
4. When the server reboots, log in and download the Office Web Apps Server software, or locate the DVD with the software on it. The file used in this example is en_office_web_apps_2013_x64_dvd_1123682.iso.
5. Mount the ISO file so that it can be used, or insert the DVD; a message box should appear allowing you to tap to choose what happens with this disc. Click the link and click Run Setup.exe. If this message does not come up automatically, browse to the installation media and click Setup.exe.
6. Check the box next to I Accept the Terms of This Agreement, and click Continue.
7. On the Choose a File Location page, leave the defaults unless there is a specific reason for changing the file locations. 2.23GB is required for the installation, so verify that you have plenty of drive space available for the installation. Click Install Now.
8. When the installation completes, click Close to close the Microsoft Office Web Apps Server 2013 window.
9. Open Internet Explorer, and enter the following URL to locate and then download KB2810007: **http://support.microsoft.com/kb/2810007**. Then press Enter. Locate the link to download the 64-bit update package and click it.
10. When the download page opens, verify that English is the selected language and click the Download button. Answer any prompts to save the download in the appropriate location. The file wacserver2013-kb2810007-fullfile-x64-glb.exe will download.
11. Locate the file and click it to start the installation of KB2810007.
12. Check the box next to Click Here to Accept the Microsoft Software License Terms. Click Continue.
13. When the installation has completed, click OK to close the Update window.
14. Next, the OWA 2013 server farm is created. Open Windows PowerShell and enter the following code, replacing *`servername`* with the name of your server:

    ```
    New-OfficeWebAppsFarm -InternalURL "http://servername" -AllowHttp -
    EditingEnabled
    ```

    In this case, the *`servername`* is http://owa201301. Note that Secure Sockets Layer (SSL) is not being used in this example.
15. When the script completes, as shown in Figure 27.3, you are prompted to enable editing. If you are confident that your environment is properly licensed, type **Y** and press Enter.
16. When the process completes, a list of configuration details is provided, as shown in Figure 27.4. This is a good time to take a screen capture of these settings or use PowerShell commands to export the settings to a text file. Note that the log location is listed here, which is important to know if you need to troubleshoot in the future.

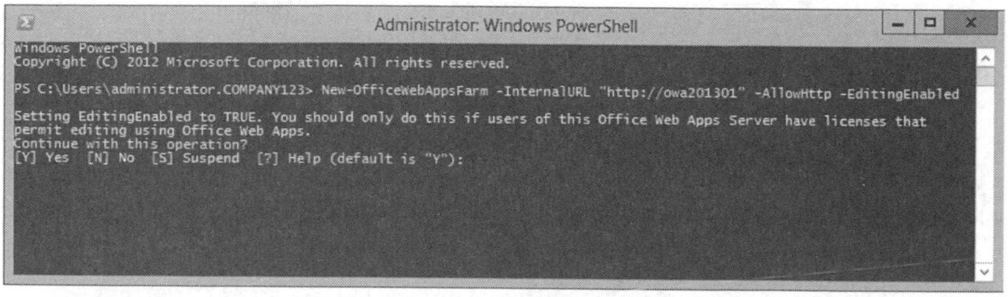

FIGURE 27.3 Results of `New-OfficeWebAppsFarm` PowerShell script.

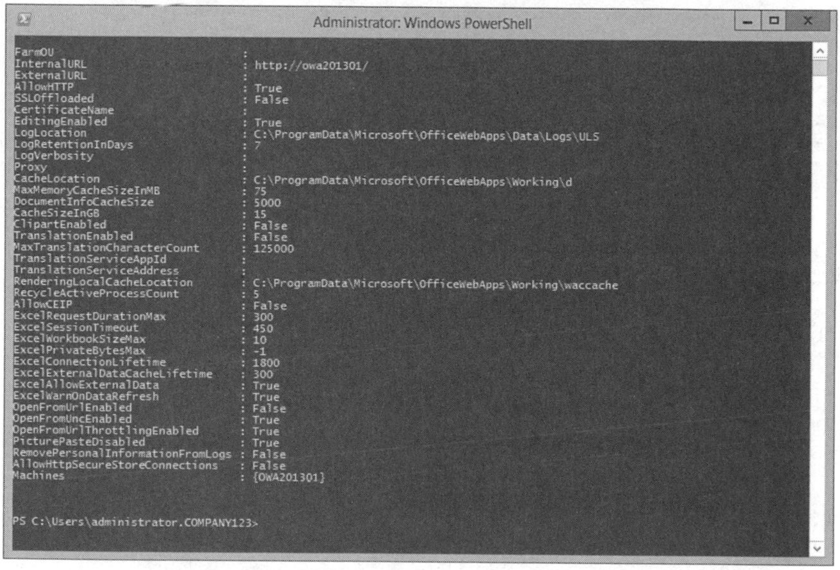

FIGURE 27.4 Settings after the completion of the `New-OfficeWebAppsFarm` PowerShell script.

17. Next, verify that the Office Web Apps server farm was created successfully by browsing to the .../hosting/discovery website on the OWA 2013 server. In this example, the URL http://owa201301/hosting/discovery is entered into the Address bar, and the results are shown in Figure 27.5.

Now that the OWA 2013 server has been configured, the SharePoint 2013 "host" needs to be configured. You can find additional information about the host configuration process at http://technet.microsoft.com/en-us/library/ff431687.aspx.

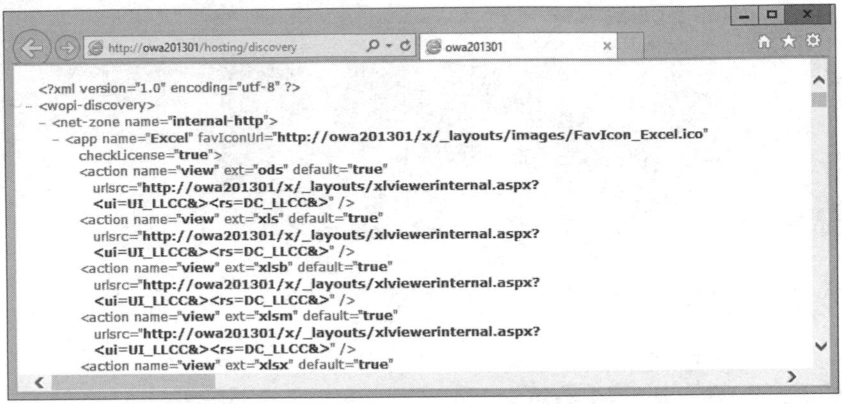

FIGURE 27.5 Results of browsing to the .../hosting/discovery website after a successful OWA 2013 farm creation.

NOTE

Office Web Apps can be used only by SharePoint 2013 web applications that use claims-based authentication. Office Web Apps rendering and editing do not work on SharePoint 2013 web applications that use classic mode authentication. To verify the setting for the web application in question, access Central Administration, click Application Management, Manage Web Applications, select the web application in question (for example, SharePoint - 80), and click Authentication Providers on the ribbon. The Authentication Providers window should show claims-based authentication. If it doesn't, OWA 2013 won't support connectivity to the web application.

If you completed the steps in the previous section successfully, perform the following steps to configure the SharePoint 2013 host and test functionality:

1. From the SharePoint 2013 host server, open SharePoint 2013 Management Shell.

2. Next, you create the binding between SharePoint 2013 and the OWA 2013 server. Enter the following code into the Management Shell and press Enter:

   ```
   New-SPWOPIBinding -ServerName servername -AllowHTTP
   ```

   In this example, *`servername`* is replaced by `"owa201301.company123.org"` (with quotations included), which is the fully qualified domain name (FQDN) for the OWA 2013 server.

   A long list of settings displays, as shown in Figure 27.6.

3. Next, the Web application Open Platform Interface (WOPI) zones for the SharePoint bindings need to be set. OWA 2013 uses the concept of zones to determine which URL (internal or external) and which protocol (HTTP or HTTPS) to use when it communicates with the host. Enter the following code in the Management Shell:

   ```
   Set-SPWOPIZone -zone "internal-http"
   ```

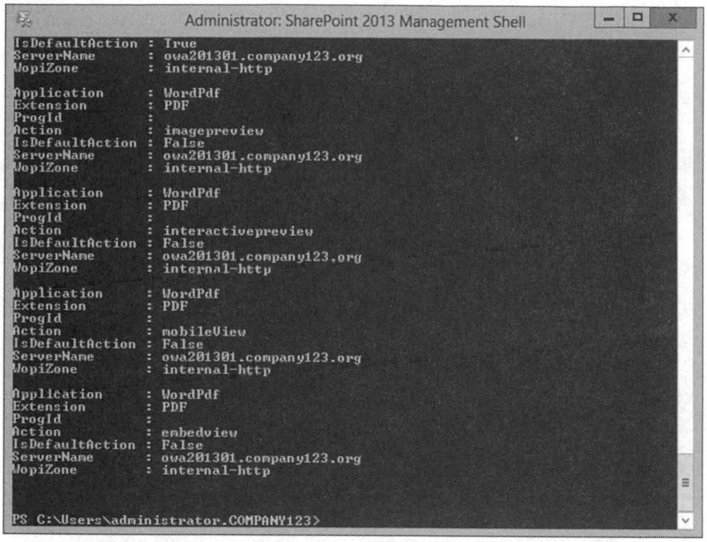
Administrator: SharePoint 2013 Management Shell
IsDefaultAction : True
ServerName : owa201301.company123.org
WopiZone : internal-http
Application : WordPdf
Extension : PDF
ProgId :
Action : imagepreview
IsDefaultAction : False
ServerName : owa201301.company123.org
WopiZone : internal-http
Application : WordPdf
Extension : PDF
ProgId :
Action : interactivepreview
IsDefaultAction : False
ServerName : owa201301.company123.org
WopiZone : internal-http
Application : WordPdf
Extension : PDF
ProgId :
Action : mobileView
IsDefaultAction : False
ServerName : owa201301.company123.org
WopiZone : internal-http
Application : WordPdf
Extension : PDF
ProgId :
Action : embedview
IsDefaultAction : False
ServerName : owa201301.company123.org
WopiZone : internal-http
PS C:\Users\administrator.COMPANY123>

FIGURE 27.6 Results of `New-SPWOPIBinding` PowerShell command from the SharePoint 2013 host server.

4. To verify the setting, enter the following code in the Management Shell:

```
Get-SPWOPIZone
```

The results should look like Figure 27.7, where the `SPWopiZone` displays as `internal-http`.

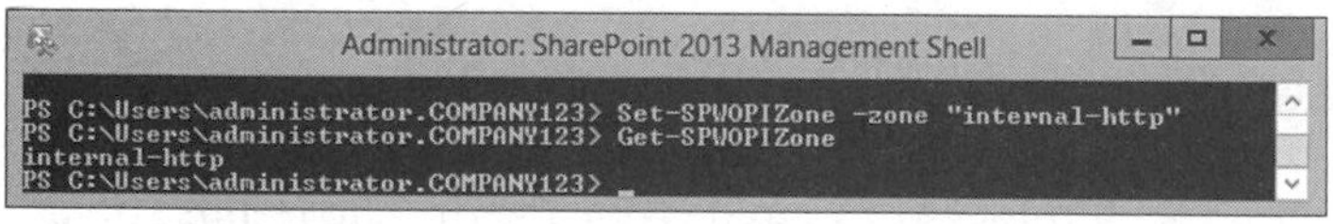
Administrator: SharePoint 2013 Management Shell
PS C:\Users\administrator.COMPANY123> Set-SPWOPIZone -zone "internal-http"
PS C:\Users\administrator.COMPANY123> Get-SPWOPIZone
internal-http
PS C:\Users\administrator.COMPANY123>

FIGURE 27.7 Results of `Get-SPWopiZone` command.

NOTE

The application programming interface (API) that OWA 2013 uses to communicate with hosts is called WOPI (Web application Open Platform Interface). Office Web Apps Server accesses and manipulates files using the WOPI API. WOPI is a RESTful API that uses HTTP/HTTPS, which means that, as much as possible, Office Web Apps Server is stateless. This makes it more resilient to failures such as network outages to hardware failure.

5. Next, the AllowOAuthOverHttp setting in SharePoint 2013 needs to be set to True. Enter the following code in the Management Shell:

```
$config = (Get-SPSecurityTokenServiceConfig)
```

6. Then, enter the following code:

```
$config.AllowOAuthOverHttp = $true
```

7. Next, enter the following code:

```
$config.Update()
```

8. To verify the settings have applied, enter the following code:

```
(Get-SPSecurityTokenServiceConfig).AllowOAuthOverHttp
```

Figure 27.8 shows the results of these PowerShell commands. Note that the value of `True` should appear after the last `Get` command is entered. This means that `AllowOAuthOverHttp` is set to `True`.

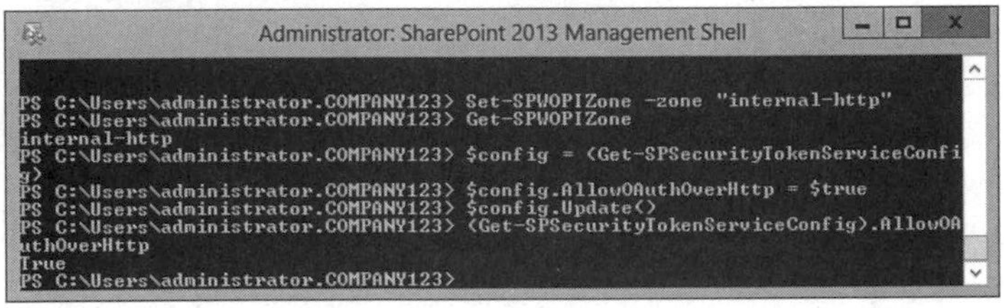
Administrator: SharePoint 2013 Management Shell
PS C:\Users\administrator.COMPANY123> Set-SPWOPIZone -zone "internal-http"
PS C:\Users\administrator.COMPANY123> Get-SPWOPIZone
internal-http
PS C:\Users\administrator.COMPANY123> $config = (Get-SPSecurityTokenServiceConfi
g)
PS C:\Users\administrator.COMPANY123> $config.AllowOAuthOverHttp = $true
PS C:\Users\administrator.COMPANY123> $config.Update()
PS C:\Users\administrator.COMPANY123> (Get-SPSecurityTokenServiceConfig).AllowOA
uthOverHttp
True
PS C:\Users\administrator.COMPANY123>

FIGURE 27.8 Results of `AllowOAuthOverHttp` commands.

9. Now it is time to verify that Office Web Apps is working. Navigate to the SharePoint 2013 site collection on the host that has been configured in this exercise. Access a document library and click the ellipsis next to a Word document. The results should look like Figure 27.9, where the hover panel displays a thumbnail of the first page of the Word document.

NOTE

There are many reasons why OWA 2013 might not work even if all the previous steps have been followed. Some tips are as follows:

- Make sure that the library containing the files is configured to allow OWA 2013 viewing (see the next section, "Verifying the Settings in the Document Library").
- Verify that claims authentication is enabled for the web application housing the site collection that houses the documents being tested.
- Verify that the Site Collection Feature Open Documents in Client Applications by default is *not* activated.
- A full crawl may be required for thumbnails to function properly.

- Make sure that you are not logged in as System Account. Whenever the currently logged-in username appears as sharepoint\system, that user cannot edit or view the document. Log in as a different user and try to access Office Web Apps again.
- Make sure that the document doesn't exceed 10MB, which is the default limit.

You can find additional troubleshooting tips at http://technet.microsoft.com/en-us/library/ff431687.aspx.

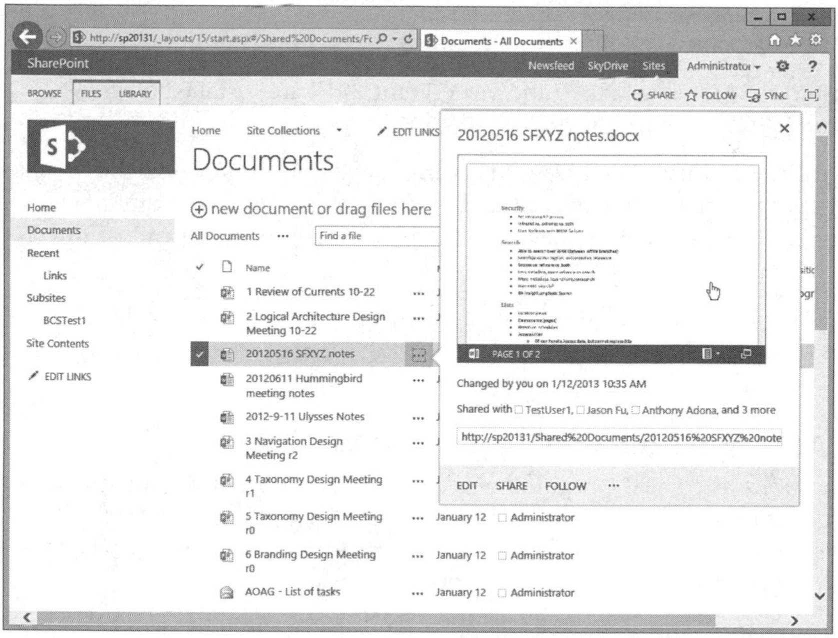

FIGURE 27.9 Testing OWA 2013 for a Word document in the SharePoint 2013 host.

Verifying the Settings in the Document Library

An additional step to take in an existing SharePoint 2013 environment is to validate the settings of the document library or libraries that house the documents that the administrator wants to support the OWA 2013 access method. Follow these steps to ensure that the document library is configured to support OWA 2013 use:

1. Navigate to the document library with an account that has owner-level permissions on the site and click the Library tab on the ribbon; then click the Library Settings button.
2. Click Advanced Settings in the General Settings section.
3. In the Opening Documents in the Browser section, select the option next to Open in the Browser or Use the Server Default (Open in the Browser). Click OK.

4. Test that viewing Word, Excel, or PowerPoint documents in the browser and editing in the browser is functioning properly.

Testing OWA 2013 Functionality

Now that the service applications are configured and the configurations for the site collection, library, and Central Administration have been reviewed, it is time to test the functionality of OWA 2013 by accessing and editing documents in the browser.

The following sections assume the following:

- **On the PC:** Word 2013, Excel 2013, and PowerPoint 2013 are installed on the PC, which is using Windows 8 and IE 10.
- **For the document library:** The Advanced Settings page is set to Open in the Browser in the Opening Documents in the Browser section. Documents are not required to be checked out before they are edited, nor is content approval required for submitted items.
- **For the site collection:** In Site Collection Features, the Open Documents in Client Applications by default is *not* activated.

Testing Word Access via OWA 2013

Assuming the conditions listed at the beginning of the "Testing OWA 2013 Functionality" section are met, follow these steps to test Office Web Apps with a Microsoft Word 2010 document. These steps are high level, and additional testing from different browsers, operating systems, and versions of Office should be performed:

1. Using an account with contribute-level permissions, navigate to the document library that meets the prerequisites listed in the previous section and that contains one or more files created in Word 2013.
2. Hover over the Name field of a Word document and click it. The file should open in the same browser session, as shown in Figure 27.10. Note that the toolbar provides a File tab, Edit Document, Share, Find, and Comment icons, and a Zoom drop-down menu in the lower-right corner.
3. Click the Edit Document icon, and select the Edit in Word Web App option; the Word Web App re-renders and adds a ribbon to allow for editing of the document.
4. A limited Word ribbon now appears, which provides File, Home, Insert, Page Layout, and View tabs. Review the tools available to get a sense for the functionality supported.

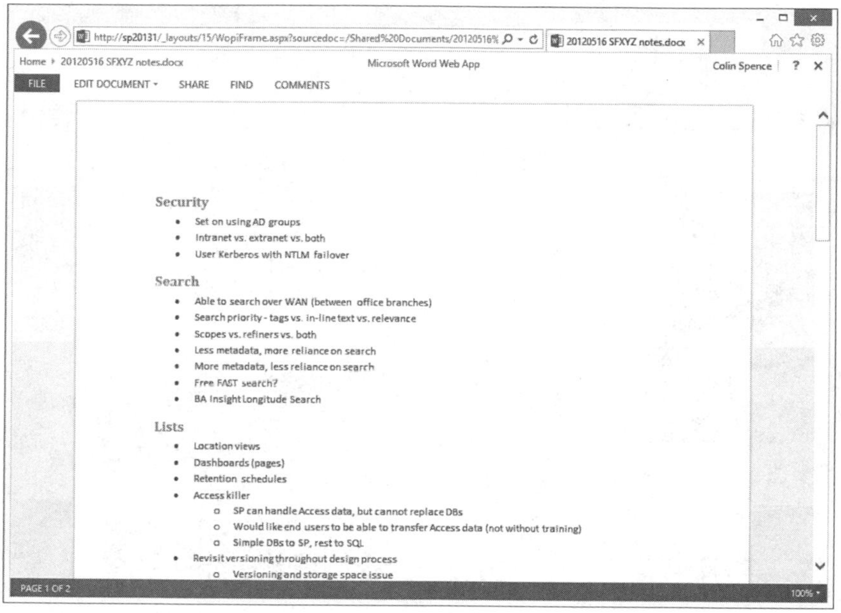

FIGURE 27.10 Word document viewed in the browser.

NOTE

Multiple users can now edit a Word document via OWA 2013, a feature not available with OWA in SharePoint 2010. To test this, with the Word document open for editing as one user (User1), access the same document using another PC and different user account (User2) so that it opens in the browser, and click Edit in Browser. Make changes using the different user accounts, and save from both accounts; then exit, reopen, and review the changes. If multiple users are editing the same document, OWA 2013 displays a message that another user is also editing the document and highlights changes in a different color after they are saved.

5. Add an image to the document, as shown in Figure 27.11. Note that a new tab appears when the image is added and selected that provides limited image-editing tools.
6. Click the Save button to save the changes.
7. Click the Close button; the browser returns to the document library.

This simple testing can be used as training for users new to the OWA 2013 products and can help them gain confidence editing documents in the browser.

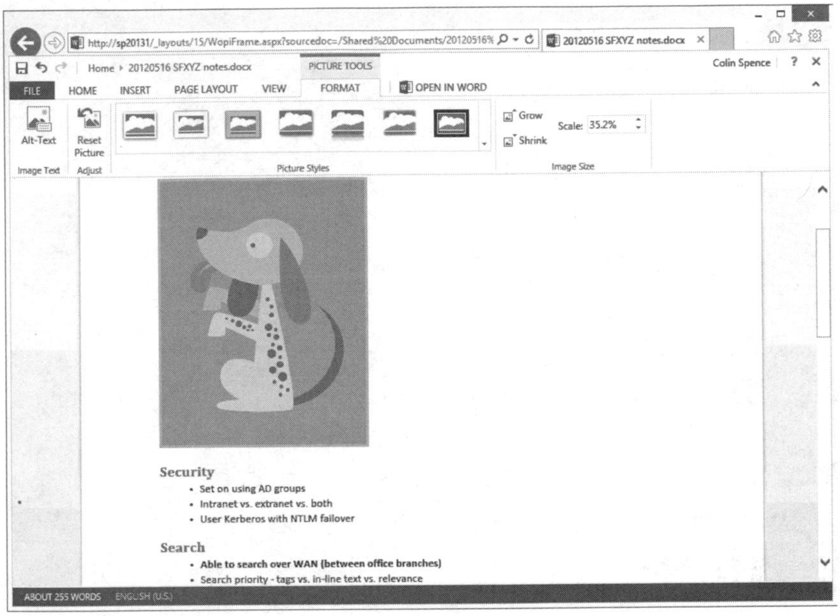

FIGURE 27.11 Word document edited in the browser.

Testing Excel Access via Office Web Apps

If the organization has both Excel Services and OWA 2013 installed, it is important for IT, site administrators, and end users to understand the differences in capabilities between the products. The differences between Excel Services and Excel Web Apps were discussed earlier in this chapter in the section titled "Key Differences Between Excel Services and Excel Web App," but IT should ideally provide training to users to ensure that they understand the capabilities and the pros and cons of each solution.

Assuming the conditions listed at the beginning of the "Testing OWA 2013 Functionality" section are met, Excel document access via Office Web Apps should be functional. This section reviews a sampling of features available when a user chooses to edit an Excel spreadsheet in SharePoint 2013, and also tests two users accessing and editing the same spreadsheet in OWA 2013.

Follow these steps to test the Excel services application:

1. Using an account with contribute-level permissions, navigate to the document library that meets the prerequisites listed at the beginning of this section and that contains one or more files created in Excel. The Excel file should have some equations and at least one graph in it ideally.
2. Hover over the Name field of an Excel document and click it. The file should open in the same browser session.

3. Access the Edit Workbook drop-down menu, and select Edit in Excel Web App. Note that the tools offered for Excel differ subtly from those for Word (as covered in the previous section). The toolbar provides a File tab, Home tab, Insert tab, View tab, and Open in Excel icon, as shown in Figure 27.12. Note that the URL contains the page WopiFrame.aspx, which informs us that OWA 2013 is rendering the current content.

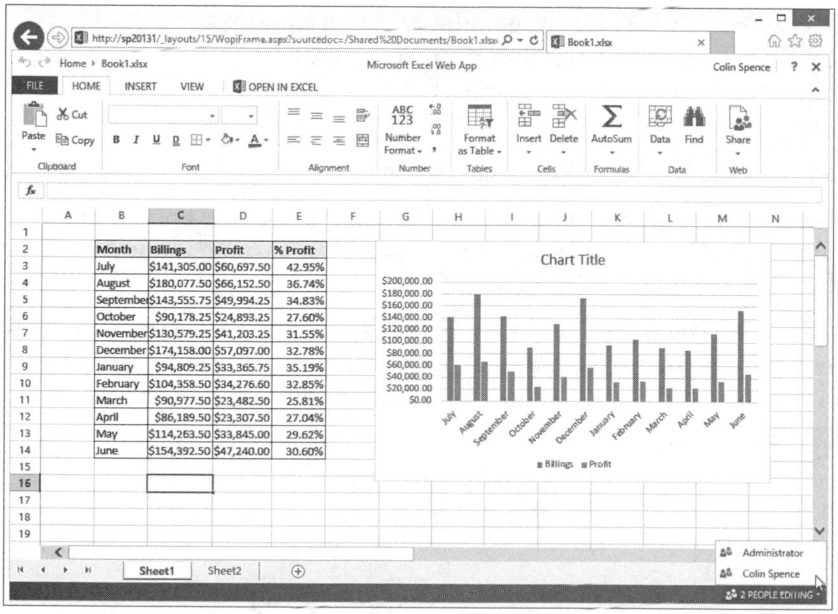

FIGURE 27.12 Excel document edited in the browser using OWA 2013.

NOTE

There is no Save button when Excel is edited in the browser. Instead, all changes are saved when they are made.

4. Test multiple people editing the spreadsheet in the browser by logging in to the same SharePoint site with a different user from a different PC or image and access the Edit Workbook drop-down menu; then select Edit in Excel Web App. As shown in Figure 27.12, in the lower-right corner, the different users editing the spreadsheet are tracked.

5. Test modifying the spreadsheet with two users simultaneously to see the results.

CAUTION

If two or more people edit a spreadsheet in the browser, none of the users can click Open in Excel; instead, a message displays stating, "You are currently collaborating on this workbook with other people. You cannot edit this workbook in Excel while other People are also editing it in the browser or filling out a survey from this workbook."

Testing PowerPoint Access via Office Web Apps

Assuming that the conditions listed at the beginning of the "Testing OWA 2013 Functionality" section are met, PowerPoint document access via Office Web Apps should be functional. This section reviews a sampling of features available when a user wants to access a PowerPoint document via Office Web Apps.

Follow these steps to test the PowerPoint services application:

1. Using an account with contribute-level permissions, navigate to the document library that meets the prerequisites listed previously and that contains one or more files created in PowerPoint.
2. Click the name of the PowerPoint file; it opens in the browser. A File tab is visible, as are Edit Presentation, Share, Start Slide Show, and Comments tabs. Slide navigation arrows are available at the bottom, as well as a Notes button, Editing View button, Reading View button, and Slide Show button.
3. Access the Edit in Presentation drop-down menu and click Edit in PowerPoint Web App. As shown in Figure 27.13, the tabs available are: File, Home, Insert, Design, Animations, Transitions, and View.

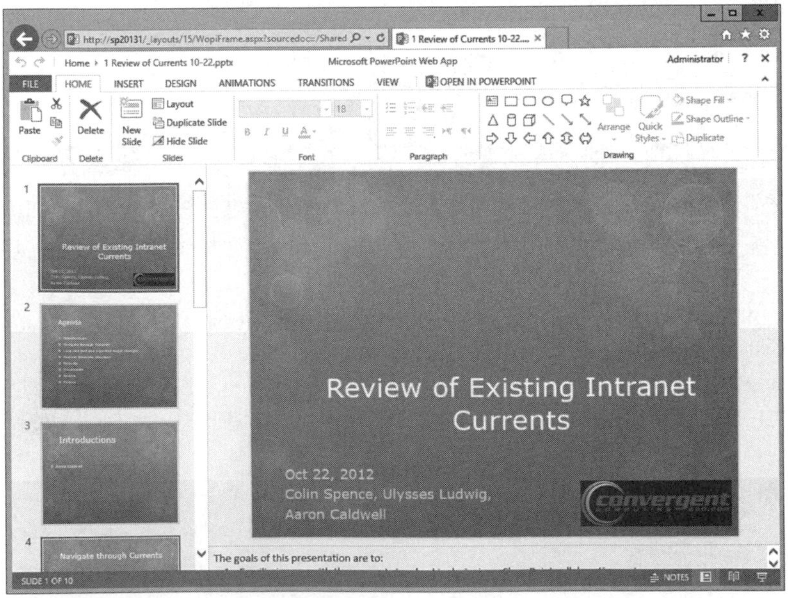

FIGURE 27.13 PowerPoint document edited in a browser.

Summary

This chapter covers the new iteration of Office Web Apps that is a separate application from the SharePoint product line. The general consensus is that this is a good thing, because the previous version of Office Web Apps as a service application had some issues. It is also an appropriate change since OWA 2013 provides functionality to other Microsoft applications other than SharePoint. Prerequisites are covered along with the installation and configuration process of OWA 2013 on a single server that connects via HTTP to a SharePoint host. Numerous notes are provided that further expand on the capabilities, limitations, and troubleshooting the product. Examples of interacting with OWA 2013 are provided for Word, Excel, and PowerPoint documents. In summary, Office Web Apps provide some valuable tools for organizations wanting to provide viewing and editing of Word, Excel, and PowerPoint content to users through supported browsers, but caveats and limitations also apply to the editing and collaboration tools made available in the browser.

Best Practices

The following are best practices from this chapter:

- OWA 2013 enables end users to view and edit Word, Excel, and PowerPoint documents in supported browsers when properly configured. It also renders thumbnail images in document libraries and the SharePoint 2013 search engine. Most organizations find these are highly valuable features and save end users time by allowing them to see the documents before opening them, as well as editing them in supported browsers if needed.
- Organizations interested in using OWA 2013 in their environments still need to comply with Microsoft licensing policies, as discussed from a high level in this chapter.
- There are a number of differences between the capabilities of Excel Services and Excel Web App, both of which allow end users to interact with Excel documents in their browsers, that are summarized in this chapter.
- OWA 2013 now allows multiple users to edit Word, Excel, and PowerPoint documents simultaneously.
- Even when OWA 2013 is properly configured, troubleshooting may be required, and there are many prerequisites that need to be met in terms of the configuration of the OWA 2013 servers, the web application, and the document library that houses the documents. These were covered throughout the chapter.

CHAPTER 28

Out-of-the-Box Workflows and Designer 2013 Workflows

IN THIS CHAPTER

- Defining Workflows in the Business Environment
- Considering Alerts as Basic Workflows
- Reviewing the Workflow-Related Settings in Central Administration and Site Settings
- Testing the Three-State Workflow
- An Overview of Other Standard Workflows
- Verifying the Web Application Settings for SharePoint Designer 2013 Use
- Downloading and Installing SharePoint Designer 2013
- Creating a Reusable Workflow from SharePoint Designer 2013

SharePoint 2013 offers a variety of different types of workflows that can be used to enhance business processes and replace legacy business workflows that involve time-consuming manual processes and may not be well defined. This chapter provides information on a number of different workflows available in the SharePoint 2013 product line out-of-the-box. It is intended to whet the appetite of users and administrators alike to delve deeper into the out-of-the-box workflows as well as capabilities of SharePoint Designer 2013 to create powerful workflows to meet everyday user requirements.

Alerts are discussed briefly as an introduction to the concept of workflows in SharePoint 2013 products, and then a detailed look at a three-state workflow in action is provided, which is a complex enough process to give a solid introduction to the processes involved with starting and interacting with a workflow in SharePoint 2013. An overview of the other standard workflows is given from a high level, as well as the process of installing and using SharePoint Designer 2013 to create a custom workflow. Along the way, tips are given for farm administrators and site collection administrators about the tools and settings available to manage workflows and the use of SharePoint Designer 2013.

SharePoint 2013 has a host of new features in the realm of workflows; however, a number of complex configuration steps need to be completed to use the new workflow platform. This chapter focuses on the SharePoint 2010 workflows supported out-of-the-box by SharePoint 2013 because those are immediately available to users of the 2013 environment. SharePoint 2010 workflows in a SharePoint 2013 farm still run on top of Microsoft's Windows Workflow Foundation, whereas the SharePoint platform 2013 workflows utilize the Azure-based workflow engine, which is installed and configured independently of SharePoint itself.

Defining Workflows in the Business Environment

In a business environment, workflows exist throughout the organization in formal and informal incarnations, and organizations of all sizes are increasingly concerned with formalizing and streamlining processes critical to the business. A key challenge in workflows is the combination of forms, the human element, time, and lack of defined processes. Consider the prototypical workflow involving an expense report form filled out by hand by User5, who then puts it in the mail slot of User2, who signs it, and puts it into the HR mail slot for processing. Consider then that User5 doesn't get the reimbursement and the steps that need to be taken by him to try and figure out what happened.

The combination of all elements, actors, tasks, and timing is often summarized as business process management or BPM. BPM is an endeavor to automate or enhance a process within an organization to see an increased return on investment or a lower total cost of ownership. SharePoint 2013 has moved closer to a more seamless BPM solution with full integration of the core business components, including forms, email, tasks, document control, alerting, and timing. This BPM effort is supported under the hood by built-in workflows and alerts, SharePoint Designer workflows, Windows Workflow Foundation workflows, and Azure-based workflows, which are new in SharePoint 2013.

SharePoint-based workflow is one of the enterprise-level features that many users began to adopt in the SharePoint 2007 and 2010 product lines, and continues to leverage in SharePoint 2013 products. This is especially true as users come to embrace the SharePoint storage modules of libraries and lists, where the ability to leverage workflows is immediately available. Furthermore, the ability to harness the hybrid cloud and increased integration features with Active Directory and external data sources has furthered the platform's reach and subsequent capabilities.

The several advantages of creating and managing workflows in a SharePoint 2013 environment include the following:

- An easy-to-use design interface in SharePoint 2013 that quickly enables site administrators and power users to translate informal processes into well-defined, automated, and audited processes
- A structure that contains and manages the workflow engines, leveraging the hardware and software investment already made in SharePoint
- Interaction with SharePoint lists such as the Tasks list to facilitate the use and management of workflows and reduce the learning curve for end users

- The option of using SharePoint Designer 2013 rather than the SharePoint interface to create different types of workflows that offer more options, flexibility, and intelligence
- The option to use Visio 2013 to make the workflow design process more intuitive for less-technical users
- Seamless integration with InfoPath forms and forms libraries providing a rich forms development and hosting environment

Considering Alerts as Basic Workflows

As discussed in Chapter 19, "Using Libraries and Lists in SharePoint 2013," and specifically in the "Reviewing the Alert Me Tool" section, alerts are powerful and simple to use and can be seen to provide a type of workflow functionality. Alerts are triggered by certain activities or changes, and they result in an email being sent immediately, or at a later time, to one or more end users. The end users can then take action based on the alert as they see fit.

To create a workflow in a document library, follow these steps:

1. Select the document by clicking to the left of the document icon; a check mark appears. Note that if two or more documents are selected, an alert cannot be created.

> **TIP**
>
> If the alert button is not visible in the ribbon, the Simple Mail Transfer Protocol (SMTP) Server Feature is most likely not configured on the SharePoint front-end server or the Outgoing E-mail Settings are not set up in Central Administration for the farm.

2. Click the Alert Me icon on the Files tab on the ribbon. Click Set alert on this document. The New Alert window opens.
3. Configure the desired options and click OK.

This is a form of workflow because an automated process is pushing information to end users via email, which is similar to one component of the workflows that are discussed in this chapter such as the three-state workflow. Although alerts are very limited in terms of configuration options, they do provide a number of options, as shown in Figure 28.1. Note that the user in this case (because he has Full Control permissions in the library) is able to enter additional names in the Send Alerts To field. Alerts options include the following:

- When anything changes
- When someone else changes a document
- When someone else changes a document created by me
- When someone else changes a document last modified by me

- Send notification immediately
- Send a daily summary
- Send a weekly summary

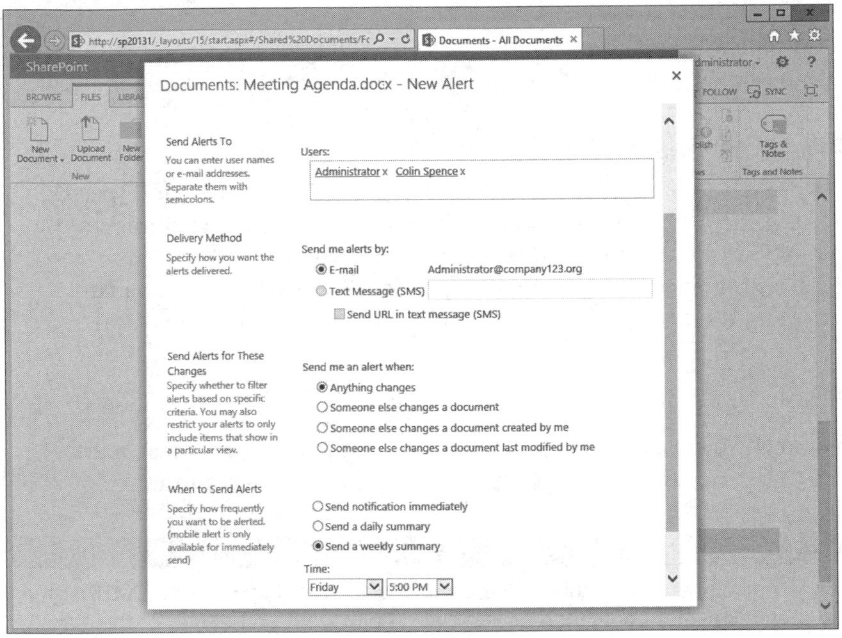

FIGURE 28.1 Alert options for a document for a user with Full Control permissions in a library.

Certain lists add customized alerts to the list of what's available. For example, in an Issues list, an alert option is added in the Send Alerts for These Changes section: Someone changes an item that appears in the following view. As shown in Figure 28.2, an alert in this type of list can be triggered by a change in a specific view. Because views are extremely customizable, and could, for example, just include items where the column values match certain criteria, this capability can be very powerful. For example, a view could be created in an Issues list called My Active High Priority Issues that only displays items where the Assigned To value equals [Me], the Priority is set to (1) High, and where the Issue Status is set to Active. Then if any changes happen in this very specific view, the user is notified.

TIP

Review the different Alert options available in lists such as Calendar, Tasks, and Issues to see the unique alerts provided and think about how they might be leveraged to enhance the usefulness of the alerts for users of the lists.

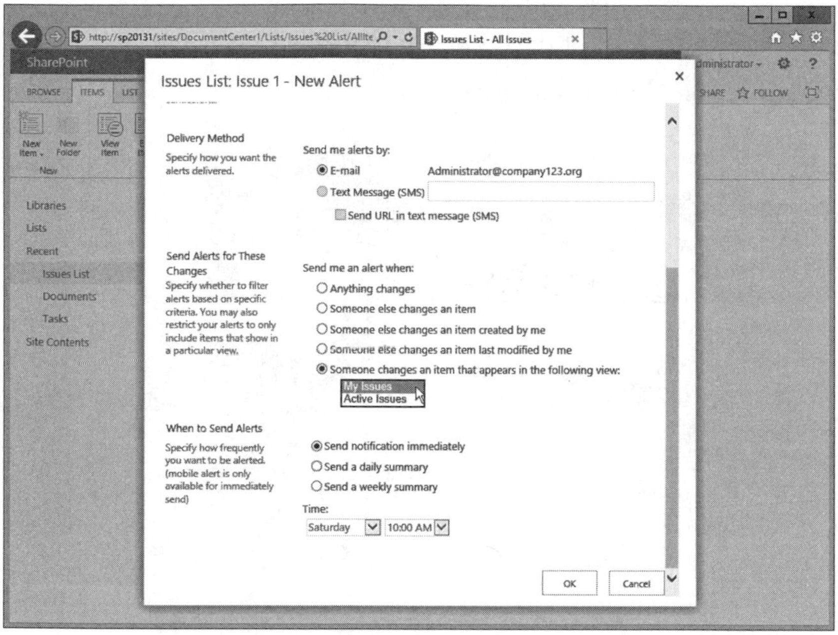

FIGURE 28.2 Alert options for an item in an Issues list.

Reviewing the Workflow-Related Settings in Central Administration and Site Settings

Workflows are configured on a variety of SharePoint components, including the web application, site collection, site, list, or content type level. In the case of web application and site collection workflow manipulation, the configuration will likely be completed by a SharePoint administrator. For lists and content types, users can use the ribbon to manage workflows and may activate or deactivate some of the built-in SharePoint workflows in Site Features.

Each web application has workflow-related settings that should be reviewed. Follow these steps to review the workflow settings for a web application:

1. Click the Application Management link from the Central Administration home page, and then click Manage Web Applications.
2. Select the web application of interest (for example, SharePoint – 80) so that the row is highlighted, and then click General Settings on the Web Applications tab on the ribbon. Select Workflow from the drop-down list, and the Workflow Settings window opens, as shown in Figure 28.3. These determine whether user-defined workflows are enabled for all sites on the web application, whether internal users

who do not have site access will be alerted if assigned a workflow task, and whether external users will be sent a copy of the document to participate in workflows.

3. Click OK after any required changes have been made.

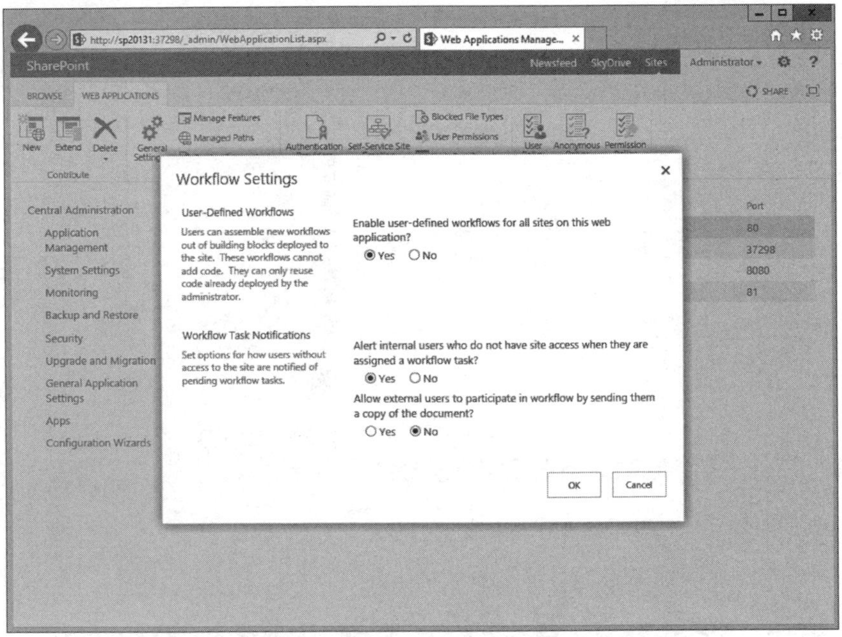

FIGURE 28.3 Workflow settings options for a web application.

It is important to understand the impact of these settings and make decisions on what will be supported by IT. If Enable User-Defined Workflows for All Sites on This Web Application is set to No, site users can still use out-of-the-box workflows, but they can't create workflows from SharePoint Designer 2013. If a developer or power user tries to create a workflow on a web application where Enable User-Defined Workflows for All Sites on this Web Application is set to No, they will receive an error message: "User-defined workflows have been disabled by the Administrator. User-defined workflows will be unable to run."

The Allow External Users to Participate in Workflow by Sending Them a Copy of the Document option could be used to circumvent security settings applied to a document library and allows User A to send a document to User B via a workflow. But it could also be argued that User A could simply download a copy of the document to his local PC and then send it as an email attachment to User B.

NOTE

If nonsite members are to be included in workflows, each of those users needs a minimum of Contribute-level permissions to the task list that is used by the workflow. Otherwise, they won't be able to interact with the tasks that are assigned to them, limiting the usefulness of the workflow.

NOTE

PowerShell commandlets (cmdlets) are available to complete these tasks: `Get-SPWorkflowConfig` returns workflow settings for the specified web application, and `Set-SPWorkflowConfig` configures the workflow settings for the specified web application.

There are also workflow-related jobs that can be found by clicking the Monitoring link from the Central Administration site and then clicking Job Definitions, as follows:

- **Bulk Workflow Task Processing:** This job processes bulk workflow tasks, and by default is set to occur once a day.
- **Workflow:** This job processes workflow events and by default is set to occur every 5 minutes.
- **Workflow Auto Cleanup:** By default set to occur daily, this deletes tasks and workflow instances that have been marked complete longer than the expiration specified in the workflow association.
- **Workflow Failover:** By default, set to occur every 15 minutes. This processes events for workflows that have failed and are marked to be retried.

NOTE

SharePoint workflows are "long running," meaning that they take longer than typical server operations, which complete in milliseconds. Workflows *dehydrate* (turn into a string and are stored to the database) and *rehydrate* (made active and returned to memory) as servers are rebooted. Workflow states are preserved during server reboots, and time-sensitive operations pick up when the server is back online.

Reviewing the Settings Tools for Workflows at the Site and List Levels

In addition to configuring some workflow behavior for the web application that hosts the site collection where workflows will be used, it is important for the farm administrator or site collection administrator to be familiar with the settings that affect the use of workflows in site collections under their management. The workflow settings will differ based on the site collection template that is used and if anyone has made modifications to the site collection features for the site collection.

Site collection features should be reviewed to see what is currently enabled by default for the specific site collection, and then to make changes if needed. For a site collection created using the Team Site site collection template, the default site collection features related to workflows are configured as follows:

- **Disposition approval workflow:** Active
- **Publishing approval workflow:** Inactive
- **SharePoint 2007 workflows:** Inactive
- **Three-state workflow:** Active
- **Workflows:** Inactive

The workflows available from a library in a site collection created by using the Team Site site collection template when the Add a Workflow Page is accessed are as follows:

- Disposition approval
- Three-state

For a publishing site collection built off the Publishing Portal site collection template, the default site collection features related to workflows are configured slightly differently, as follows:

- **Disposition approval workflow:** Active
- **Publishing approval workflow:** Active
- **SharePoint 2007 workflows:** Inactive
- **Three-state workflow:** Inactive
- **Workflows:** Active

Therefore, the workflows available from a library in a publishing site collection with default settings when the Add a Workflow page is accessed are more numerous:

- Approval – SharePoint 2010
- Collect Feedback – SharePoint 2010
- Collect Signatures – SharePoint 2010
- Disposition Approval
- Publishing Approval

A general best practice is to not change the workflows feature settings for a site collection unless there is a specific reason to do so. Some reasons can include a specific need to support workflows that are migrated from a SharePoint 2007 environment. The publishing approval workflow should only be enabled in sites where content approval is going to be used in document libraries. (This is turned on from Document Library Settings, Versioning Settings page.) This workflow then triggers when documents are saved as major versions in document libraries with Content Approval enabled, which can annoy end users if they don't see specific value in it and are not trained in the process.

A quick place for a site administrator to check on which workflows are associated with a site is from the Site Settings page in the Site Administration section by clicking the Workflow Settings link. This displays any workflows associated with the site, for example, created in SharePoint Designer 2013 and published to the site. Figure 28.4 shows an example where one workflow was created in SharePoint Designer 2013 and published to the site. The administrator can click the Remove, Block, or Restore a Workflow links to further manage the workflows associated with that site.

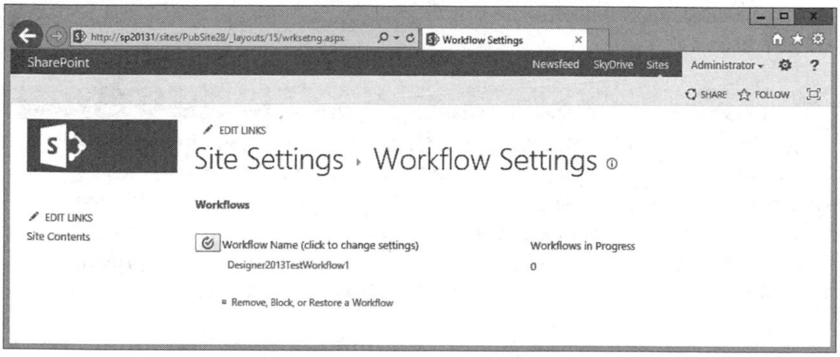

FIGURE 28.4 Workflow Settings page accessed from Site Settings.

NOTE

Note that the workflows shown in the Workflow Settings page for a site are only the workflows that have been associated with that specific site. Workflows associated with subsites do not show up on the parent site, nor do the child sites show workflows associated with the parent.

To see the workflows associated with or running on a list or library, an administrator can access the Library tab on the ribbon and click the Workflow Settings icon on the far right. Or the administrator can access the List or Library Settings page and then click Workflow Settings from the Permissions and Management section. Figure 28.5 shows an example where a workflow was started within a list. Note that additional workflows can be added from the Workflow Settings page by clicking Add a Workflow, or additional information can be accessed about the workflow's configuration by clicking the workflow name.

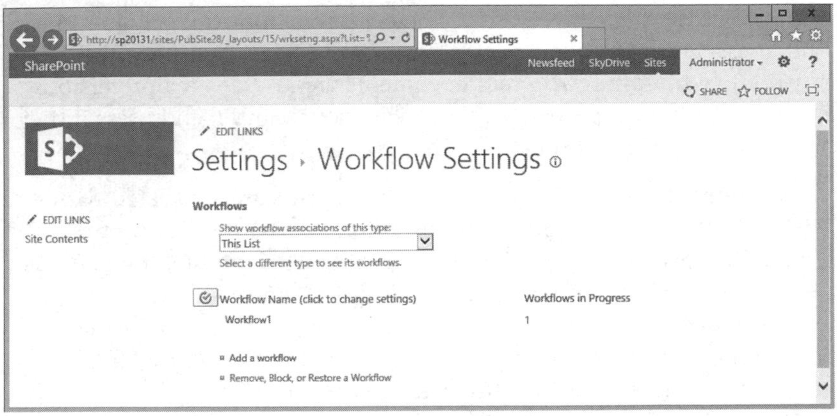

FIGURE 28.5 Workflow Settings page accessed from the Library Settings page.

NOTE

A useful hidden page that is still available but no longer directly accessible in SharePoint 2013 is the Workflow Manager page. To open this page, go to http://*<ServerName>*/*<SiteName>*/_layouts/wrkmng.aspx. As shown in Figure 28.6, this page gives a full list of the out-of-the-box workflows, the status of each, any associations, and in-progress workflows for the whole site collection. One problem with this page is that it doesn't provide any drill-down capabilities, so there is no way to know which site a particular workflow is running on.

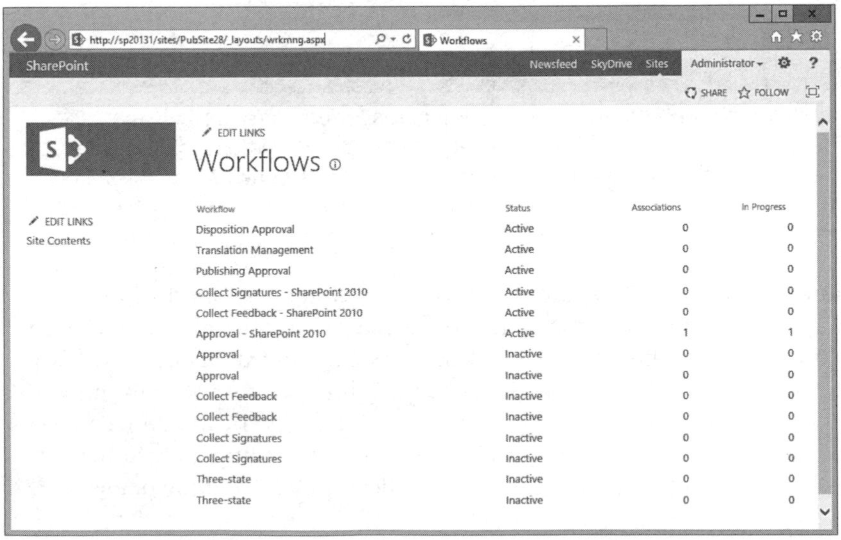

FIGURE 28.6 Wrkmng.aspx page in SharePoint 2013 showing workflow status and activity for a site collection.

Testing the Three-State Workflow

The three-state workflow is a good choice for initial testing and to get more familiar with the "moving parts" of a workflow in SharePoint 2013. It is a somewhat complex workflow and takes a number of steps and at least two user accounts to test to completion. The main steps involved with this workflow are as follows:

1. An issue is created in an Issues list by a manager (Rand), where an assignee is specified (Colin) and the issue saved.
2. The workflow is manually started by the manager (Rand).
3. When the workflow starts, it notifies Rand and Colin with a brief email, then creates a new task in thc Tasks list, which is assigned to Colin.
4. The assignee (Colin) gets a more detailed email 1 to 5 minutes later that gives instructions on what to do. These instructions tell the assignee to review the issue and then update the task.
5. When the assignee (Colin) updates the task and sets it to Completed, the state of the issue changes to Resolved and the manager/initiator (Rand) is assigned a new task.
6. The manager (Rand) receives an email with instructions to review the issue and then update the task.
7. When Rand sets the task to Completed, the state of the issue changes to Closed.

There are several key concepts to understand in this process. One is that this workflow is associated to a specific list and won't be available from other lists in the site or site collection unless explicitly associated with that list. Another key concept is that tasks are generated in a separate Tasks list by the workflow, first when the workflow is started, and then when the first task is marked as Completed, which then changes the value of a column in the list and creates a second task. Each of these actions makes entries into the History list, which is visible on the workflow status page and provides an audit history of the workflow.

It is also important to realize that there are multiple points of interaction with the issue and the task items, and that users can change more than just the minimal fields discussed in the example. So, in other words, there is margin for error, and users need to be clear which fields they should and shouldn't modify.

The prerequisites for this testing are as follows:

- The three-state workflow is enabled for the site collection. A site collection created using the Team Site site collection template has the three-state workflow site collection feature enabled by default.
- Two accounts are available for testing, each with an active email account in Outlook, and preferably Outlook 2010 or 2013. While this workflow can be completed by using just one account, it is harder to interpret the activities taking place and less useful as a training exercise.

- The account that creates the workflow should be a site owner; the other account can just be a site member.

Follow these steps to test the workflow:

1. Create a new list using the Issue Tracking application template and name it **Issues List**.
2. Click the List tab from within the Issue Tracking list, and then click List Settings.
3. Click the Issue Status link in the Columns section. Scroll down on the Edit Column page to the choices and note that there are three choices for this column: Active, Resolved, and Closed. These are the "states" that are modified during the three-state workflow.
4. Click Cancel to return to the List Settings page. Click Workflow Settings in the Permissions and Management section.
5. The Workflow Settings page opens. Click the Add a Workflow link.
6. The Add a Workflow page loads. Select Three-State from the list of workflows.
7. Name the workflow **Issues-ThreeStateTest1**.
8. Verify that the Task List is set to Tasks (New) and that the History List is set to Workflow History (New). These settings indicate that a new tasks list will be created to track tasks associated with this workflow and that a new workflow history list will be created to track workflow auditing information.
9. In the Start Options section, verify that the Allow This Workflow to Be Manually Started by an Authenticated User with Edit Item Permissions option is selected. Click Next.
10. The Customize the Three-State Workflow page opens. Verify that the Select a 'Choice' field is set to Issue Status, the Initial State is set to Active, the Middle State is set to Resolved, and the Final State is set to Closed, as shown in Figure 28.7.
11. Scroll down to the next section, Task Details, and review these settings. Leave these settings at their defaults, but review the different components of this section. Add some custom text in the two Body fields provided. In this example, the text added to the first (which is included in the email that is sent when the workflow is initiated) is "The quick brown fox jumps over the lazy dog." And the second includes the text, "A rolling stone gathers no moss."
12. Click OK to complete the workflow definition process and return to the Issue Tracking list.

To create an issue and assign it to a user for completion, follow these steps:

1. Verify that you are logged in to the SharePoint site as a user who will be considered to be the manager for this test (Rand in this example). This user will create the issue and then assign it to another user for completion.

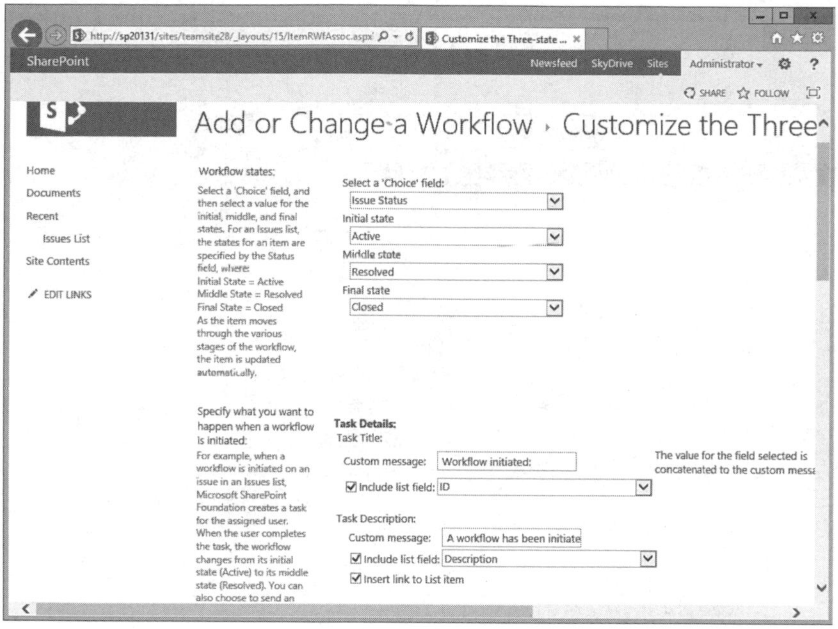

FIGURE 28.7 The Customize the Three-State Workflow page.

2. From the Issues list, click the New Item link, create a new issue called **Test Issue 1**, and assign it to a test user who will be charged with completing the task (Colin in this case). Leave the Issue Status to Active, Priority to (2) Normal. Enter a brief description for the issue, such as **Test issue for workflow testing**. Leave the other settings on the page at their defaults and click Save.

3. Navigate to the Tasks list that was defined in step 8 of the previous exercise (in this case, Tasks) and note that no tasks have been created at this point. This is because the workflow has not been started.

4. The manager (Rand) needs to manually start the workflow that will assign it to the user in the Assigned To column (Colin in this example). To do this, return to the Issues list, select the issue by clicking to the left of the Issue ID for the Item to select the item, and then from the Items tab on the ribbon, click Workflows.

5. The Workflow.aspx page opens. Click the Issues-ThreeStateTest1 link in the Start a New Workflow section.

6. The workflow starts, and the user (Rand) is returned to the Issue Tracking list, as shown in Figure 28.8. Note that a new column is visible that is titled Issue-ThreeStateTest1 and shows the In Progress status for the workflow. The initiator and the assignee each receive an email with a subject that reads, "Workflow initiated" with the ID number of the workflow included. This email also provides a link to the issue in the Issues list. This helps remind the manager that he did in fact start the

workflow. Note that the text entered while creating the workflow ("The quick brown fox jumps over the lazy dog") in included in this email, as shown in Figure 28.9.

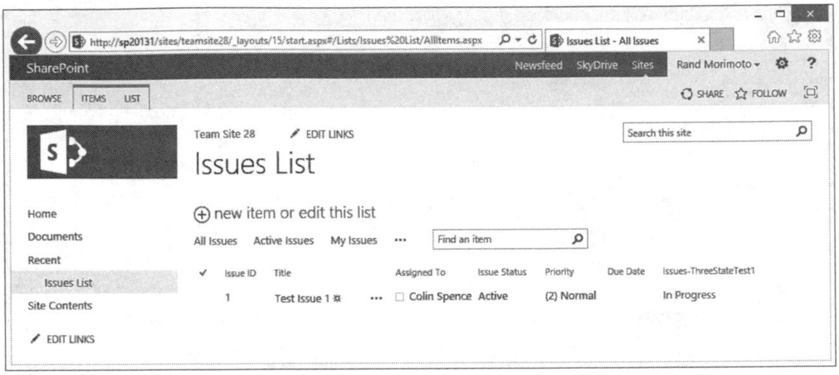

FIGURE 28.8 Issues list after the three-state workflow is started.

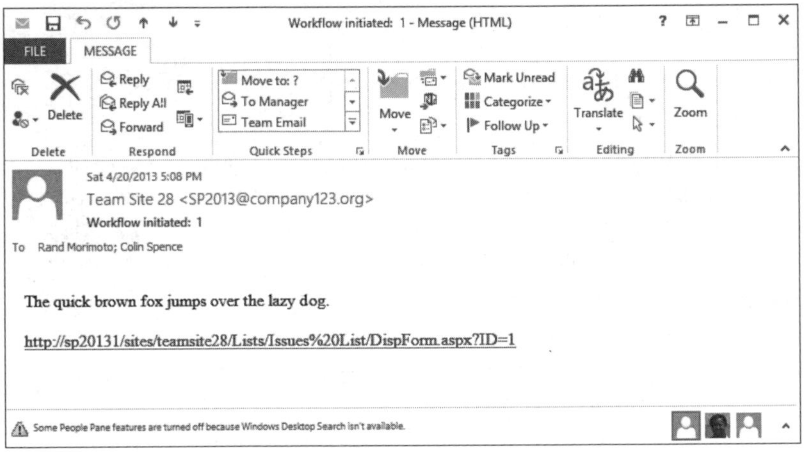

FIGURE 28.9 Email sent after initiation of workflow with custom text added.

7. Log out as the manager (Rand in this example), log in as the assignee (Colin in this example), and open Outlook. This user should have received both a copy of the "Workflow initiated" email and shortly thereafter an email that informs him that he has been assigned a task; he is also given other information about the task, as shown in Figure 28.10. The email clearly informs the assignee that a task has been assigned by the initiator. A URL is given to the issue in the Issue Tracking list, as well as instructions on how to complete the task: Review the issue, perform specific activities required for this task, edit the task, and then mark it as Completed.

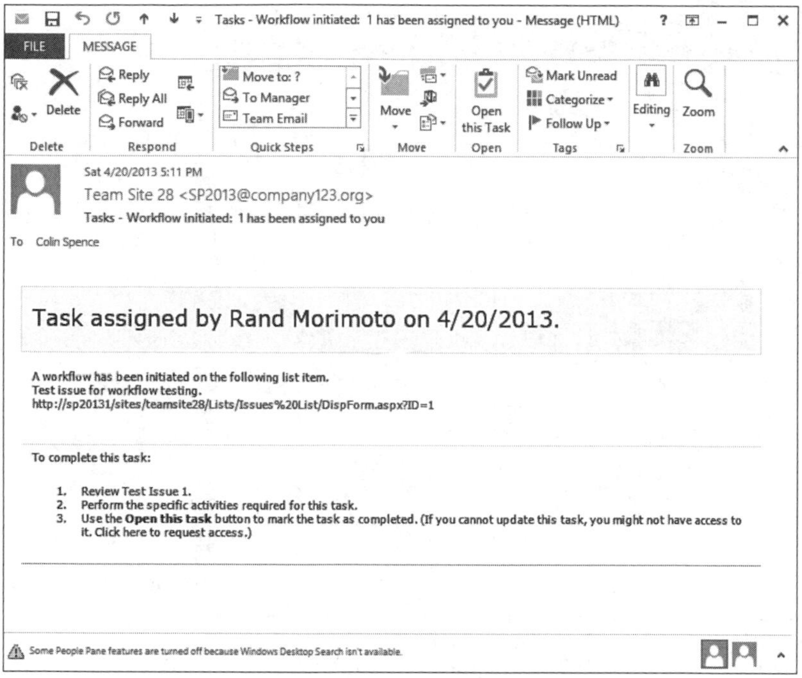

FIGURE 28.10 Email received by issue assignee when the three-state workflow is started.

CAUTION

This is a key point in the workflow where users forget to edit the task! They click the link to the issue, update the issue, and then think they are done. So, the training process should emphasize the importance of updating the task as well as the issue.

8. At this point in the process, the assignee (Colin) now knows he has an issue to work on, and he clicks the URL to open the issue and get to work on it and updates the issue (for example, by clicking Edit Item and adding comments such as "I fixed the problem" and then clicking Save).

9. After the issue has been resolved, this user still needs to edit the task to indicate the issue has been resolved. To do this, the assignee (Colin) returns to the email and clicks the Open This Task button on the ribbon to edit the task that was created by the workflow.

10. The task opens. Click the Show More link at the bottom of the screen. Then scroll down and set the status to Completed, as shown in Figure 28.11. Then click Save.

11. The assignee (Colin) is then returned to the Tasks list and will see in a moment (may require a page refresh) that a new task has been created which is assigned to the initiator (Rand).

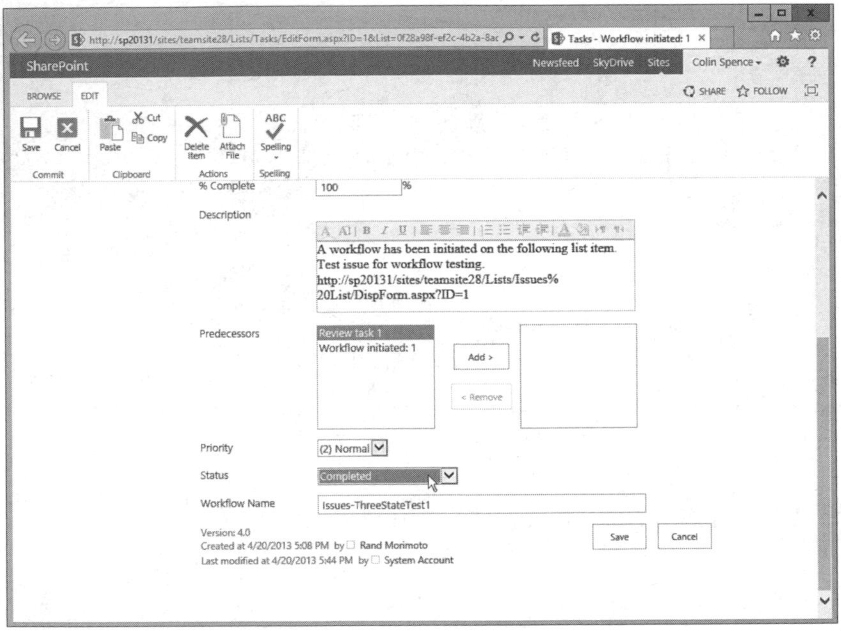

FIGURE 28.11 Editing the task assigned by the three-state workflow.

12. Log back in as the manager/initiator (Rand in this example) and open Outlook. Two emails should have been received, the first with the second custom set of text entered in step 11 of the previous section ("A rolling stone gathers no moss" in this example) and the second assigning the user his own task. In the second email, click the URL to review the issue, which the assignee (Colin) claims to have completed. Then click the Open This Task icon on the ribbon of the email to set the task status to Completed.

13. The Tasks list is now visible, as shown in Figure 28.12, and shows both the original task, where the assignee (Colin) was assigned a task and marked it as Completed, and the second task, where the initiator (Rand) was assigned a task.

14. Still logged in as the manager (Rand), navigate to the Issue Tracking list and verify that the status of the issue is now set to Closed and that the field under the column titled Issues-ThreeStateTest1 shows the value of Completed.

15. Click the Completed link in the Issues-ThreeStateTest1 column to view more details about the workflow, as shown in Figure 28.13. This page shows detailed information about the Tasks created in the workflow process (two tasks were created) as well as the Workflow History, which consisted of the following steps: Workflow Initiated, Task Completed, Task Completed, and Workflow Completed. It can be seen that the Issues List Status changed to Resolved and then to Closed in the Description column.

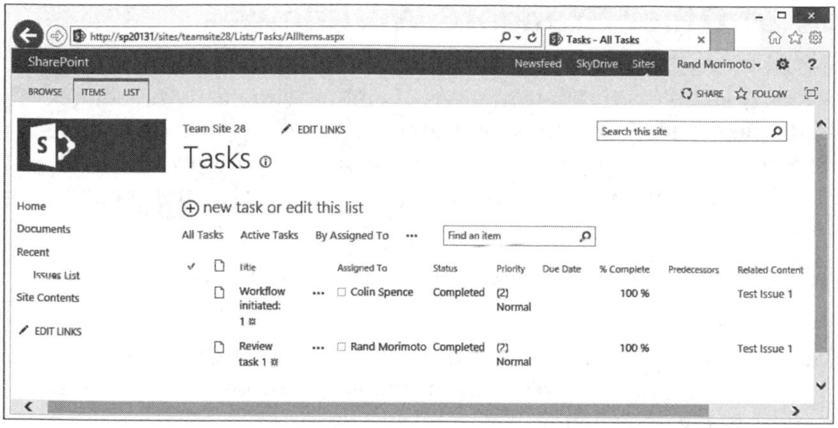

FIGURE 28.12 Viewing the tasks created by the three-state workflow.

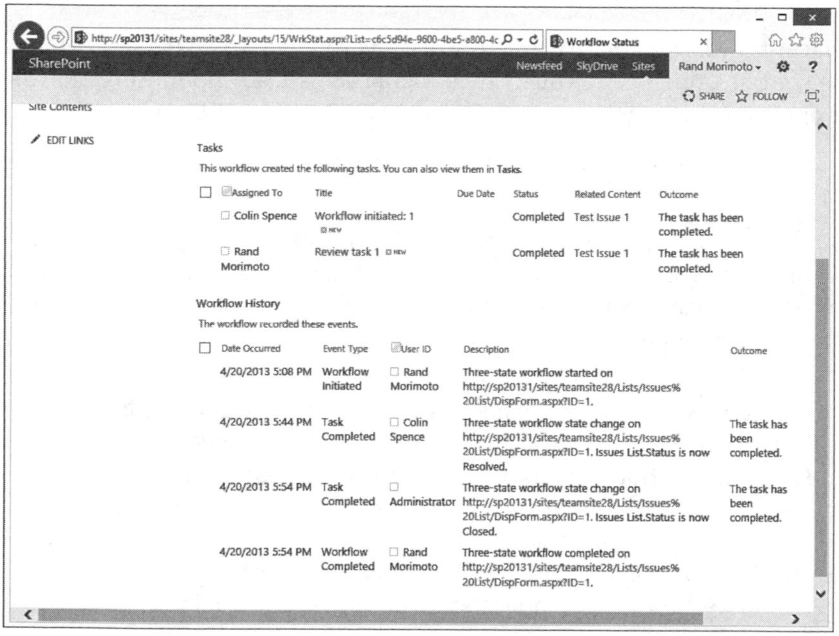

FIGURE 28.13 Viewing the workflow information for the three-state workflow.

An Overview of Other Standard Workflows

The previous example of the three-state workflow could be considered a form of "tough love" because it is a fairly complex workflow in terms of end-user interactivity requirements. It could also be suggested by a savvy administrator that instead of using a three-state workflow, the manager could simply create an alert that notifies him via email if anything in the Issues list changes, which would save time and effort but not use the whole workflow engine.

Other standard workflows available in SharePoint 2013 Standard and Enterprise include the following:

- **Approval – SharePoint 2010:** An approval workflow routes a document for approval. Approvers can approve or reject the document, reassign the approval task, or request changes to the document.
- **Collect feedback – SharePoint 2010:** This SharePoint 2010 workflow routes a document for review to reviewers who can provide feedback, which is compiled and sent to the person who initiated the workflow.
- **Collect signatures – SharePoint 2010:** This workflow routes a Microsoft Office document to a group of people to collect their digital signatures and must be started in an Office application that is part of the Office 2007, 2010, or 2013 family.
- **Disposition approval:** This manages document expiration and retention by allowing participants to decide whether to retain or delete expired documents.
- **Publishing approval:** This allows for approval of list and library submissions where the content approval advanced feature is enabled. When used properly, the publishing approval workflow can allow contributors to author content that is only visible to readers after explicit approval from an administrator.

The approval, collect feedback, and collect signatures workflows are available for editing when Designer 2013 is used to open a site and are listed in the Globally Reusable Workflow section. Figure 28.14 shows the settings page for the collect feedback workflow. Note that there is an Edit Workflow link available in the ribbon, as well as the ability to disable different Start Options, and note that the actual InfoPath Forms can be accessed and edited. Using SharePoint Designer 2013 with SharePoint 2010 workflows is covered later in this chapter and in Chapter 29, "Application Development with SharePoint Designer 2013 and Visual Studio."

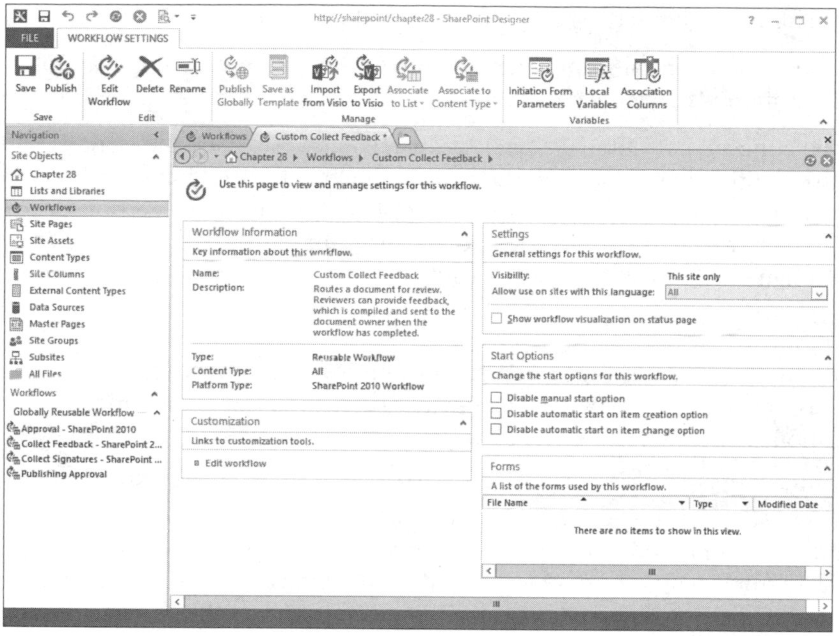

FIGURE 28.14 Modifying a collect feedback workflow in Designer 2010.

Verifying the Web Application Settings for SharePoint Designer 2013 Use

Organizations often find that the standard out-of-the-box workflows simply do not provide enough flexibility to meet their requirements and want to be able to access additional tools to create these workflows and the logic that drives them. SharePoint Designer 2013 can be used to create a wide variety of workflows, including list workflows, reusable workflows, and site workflows. SharePoint Designer 2013 also allows users to leverage Visio 2013, InfoPath 2013, and a host of other tools to facilitate the overall design and implementation process.

Power users and developers who will be using SharePoint Designer 2013 should verify that it is supported by IT, even though the software can be downloaded for free, to ensure that it will function properly. It is not unusual for SharePoint Designer 2013 to not function properly if IT is not prepared to "officially" support it, due to configurations in SharePoint or on the desktop.

In addition, the farm administrator may have chosen to not allow the use of SharePoint Designer from the Central Administration site. This should be verified to avoid possible confusion or issues during the development process.

To configure SharePoint Designer settings for a web application, follow these steps:

1. Open SharePoint 2013 Central Administration and click Manage Web Applications from the Application Management Section.
2. Select the web application to manage (such as SharePoint – 80), click the General Settings button on the ribbon bar, and then choose SharePoint Designer from the drop-down menu that appears. The Configure SharePoint Designer Settings are usually all checked. If one or more are not enabled, that limits the number of SharePoint Designer 2013 customizations possible.

   The options are as follows:

   - **Allow SharePoint Designer to Be Used in This Web Application:** If this option is not checked (enabled), SharePoint Designer can't be used in the web application.
   - **Allow Site Collection Administrators to Detach Pages from the Site Definition:** If pages are detached from the site definition using SharePoint Designer 2013 and modified, they are not updated when the site definition is updated, for example by a server upgrade, or applying a solution upgrade. "Old timers" in the SharePoint world will remember this as the "unghosting" process, which can cause complexities in supporting sites.
   - **Allow Site Collection Administrators to Customize Master Pages and Layout Pages:** Master pages and page layouts define how SharePoint renders and displays content. By allowing site collection administrators to customize these items using SharePoint Designer 2013, they may unintentionally break from organizational branding standards or even damage functionality of the site collection.
   - **Allow Site Collection Administrators to See the URL Structure of Their Website:** This allows site collection administrators to manage the URL structure of their site using SharePoint Designer 2013, by accessing the All Files icon in the Navigation pane. However, modifying the structure of the site, or deleting forms or folders, can damage the site's functionality, and therefore can have negative side effects.
3. Click OK when finished.

Downloading and Installing SharePoint Designer 2013

SharePoint Designer is available free of charge from Microsoft, who wants to encourage power users and developers to customize the SharePoint 2013 environment to meet a wide variety of business needs. The workstation or server needs to have .NET 4.0 installed, and as discussed in the previous section, the web application needs to be configured to allow the use of SharePoint Designer 2013.

SharePoint Designer 2013 is available in both 32-bit and 64-bit versions, so users should be sure to download the version that corresponds to their workstation's operating system version. SharePoint Designer 2013 is supported on Windows 7, Windows 8, Windows Server 2008 R2, and Windows Server 2012.

To install SharePoint Designer 2013, follow these steps:

1. If it is not already installed on the workstation that will house SharePoint Designer 2013, install .NET 4.0 from www.microsoft.com/en-us/download/details.aspx?id=17851.
2. Download the 32- or 64-bit version of SharePoint Designer from www.microsoft.com/en-us/download/details.aspx?id=35491.
3. Run the SharePointDesigner.exe and complete the install by selecting either the Standard or Custom option.

With SharePoint Designer 2013 downloaded and installed, development can begin immediately as long as the user has a minimum of Designer-level rights to a SharePoint 2013 site.

Creating a Reusable Workflow from SharePoint Designer 2013

A reusable workflow is technically a workflow associated with a content type instead of being associated directly to a SharePoint list. Content types not only contain columns and policies but also behavior that comes in the form of workflows. By associating a workflow with a content type, the user is causing that workflow to be available for reuse within any list or library that contains that content type.

To create a reusable workflow, the site that will house the workflow must be opened from SharePoint Designer 2013, and then the workflow is designed, tested, and published to the site. It can then be added to a list or library on that site and is then ready for use. The following example creates a reusable workflow that is triggered whenever the word *rush* is found in the title field of a document. The application in this example is a collaboration site where managers (User1 and User2) need to review and provide feedback on documents in different libraries before they can be released to marketing. Complaints had occurred before when User1 and User2 weren't responsive enough, so the workflow was created. If a user believes her document deserves "rush" status, she just needs to add that text to the title field, and the workflow initiates, and User1 is informed of the task, and when he or she completes it, User2 is assigned a task. Auditing information tracks the responsiveness of both users.

This workflow takes advantage of the Start Feedback Process action in SharePoint Designer, which contains the logic and functionality of the collect feedback workflow that is a standard workflow in SharePoint Server 2013 that uses the SharePoint 2010 workflow platform. So this is an example of a workflow within a workflow, which enables even relatively novice workflow designers to take advantage of the standard workflows provided out-of-the-box.

Follow these steps to open a SharePoint 2013 site and create this site workflow:

1. Open SharePoint Designer 2013 (method will vary based on the operating system in use).
2. From the File tab, the Sites node should be open; if it does not open, click Sites. Then click the Open Site icon.
3. Type the URL of the site (for example, **http://sharepoint/Chapter28**) or select the site from the list of available sites if it has been accessed before. Note: Do not include a page name such as default.aspx or /pages/home.aspx.
4. Click Workflows from the Site Objects list in the Navigation pane.
5. Click Reusable Workflow from the Workflows tab; the Create Reusable Workflow window opens, as shown in Figure 28.15.

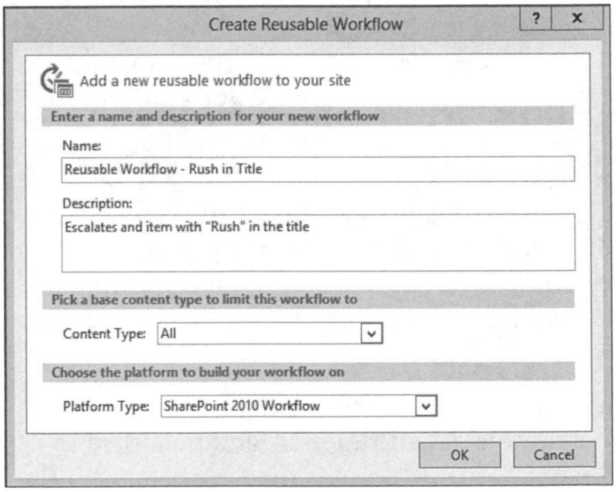

FIGURE 28.15 Naming the reusable workflow in Designer 2013.

6. Provide a title for the workflow such as **Reusable Workflow – Rush in Title**, and a description if desired. In this case, the description reads **Escalates any item with "Rush" in the title**. Leave Content Type set to All, and under Platform Type, choose SharePoint 2010 Workflow and click OK.
7. Click the flashing line in the Step 1 canvas: type **if** and then press Enter. A dialog box pops up with several conditions that contain the word *if*. Choose If Any Value Equals Value. Alternatively, you can click the Condition button and choose Title Field Contains Keywords.

8. Click the Value link in the Step 1 box, and then click the Function button, which opens the Define Workflow Lookup dialog. Leave the Data Source set to Current Item and choose Title from the Current Item drop-down list. Click OK to save.
9. Click the Equals link in the Step 1 box, and select Contains from the drop-down menu.
10. Click the Value link in the Step 1 box, and then type **rush** and press Enter. The results will look like Figure 28.16.

NOTE

Workflows built using the SharePoint 2013 workflow platform type cannot call a workflow built on the SharePoint 2010 platform type.

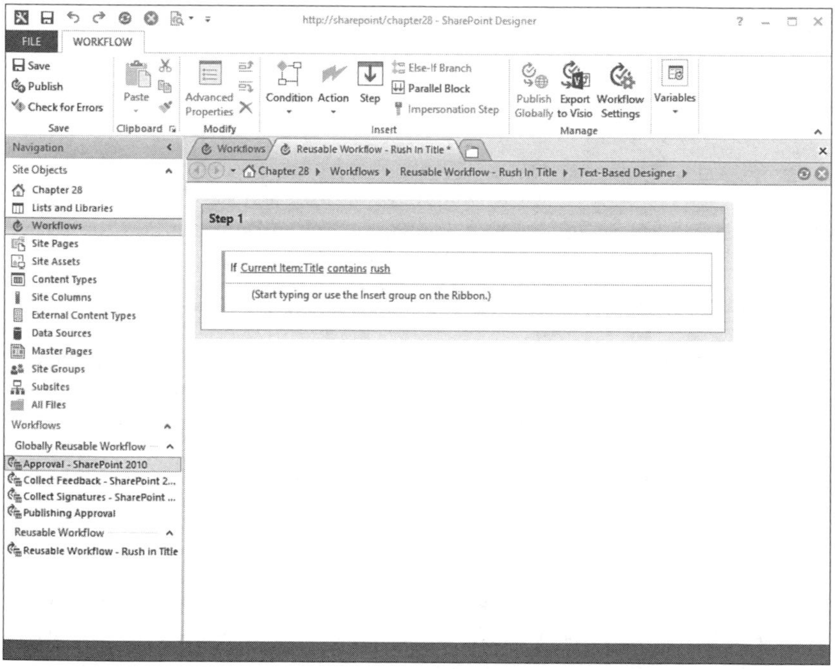

FIGURE 28.16 Setting conditions for the workflow in Designer 2013.

11. Click the area directly below the line where data was just entered and type **Start** and press Enter. Designer 2013 provides several actions that contain the word Start including Start a Site Workflow or Start Feedback Process, as shown in Figure 28.17. This action effectively imbeds a Collect Feedback workflow within this Reusable Workflow, which provides significant functionality within the workflow as is demonstrated upon completion of the workflow.

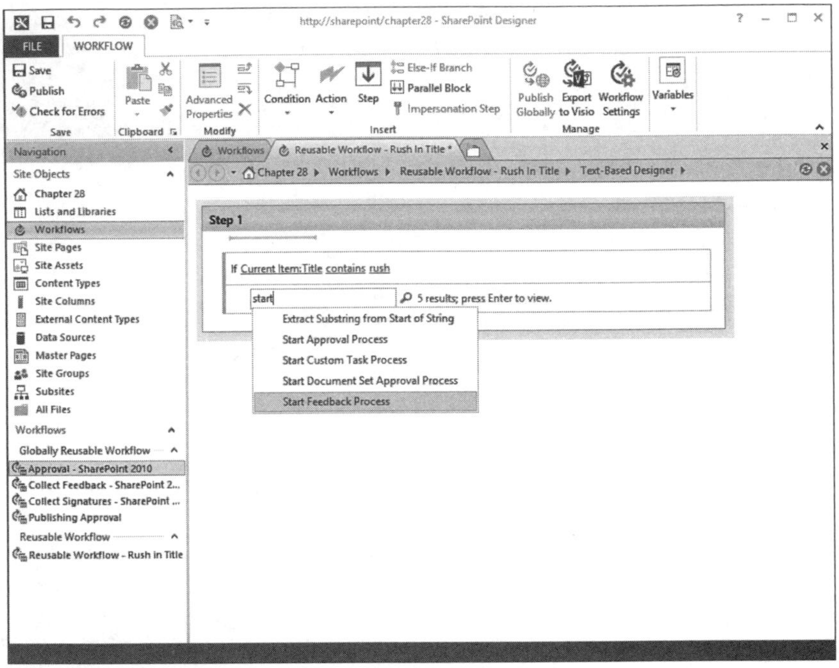

FIGURE 28.17 Adding Start Feedback Process to a workflow action in Designer 2013.

12. Click the These Users link; the Select Task Participants window opens.
13. In the Participants field, use the address book dialog to enter two valid usernames separated by a semicolon (;). User1;User2 is used in this example. Leave Serial (one at a time) selected in the field to the right of Participants.
14. In the CC field, click the Select Users icon on the right, click User Who Created Current Item, and then click the Add>> button. Click OK.
15. In the Title field, enter the text **Rush item escalated**.
16. In the Instructions field, enter text describing the activity, such as: **This item's title contained the word "rush" and so it has been escalated for review and processing.** The window should look like Figure 28.18.
17. In the Duration per Task field, enter **1** and verify that Day(s) is selected to the right. Click OK.
18. Click the Check for Errors button on the ribbon; a message that the workflow contains no errors should display.
19. Click the Publish button on the ribbon to publish the workflow to the site.

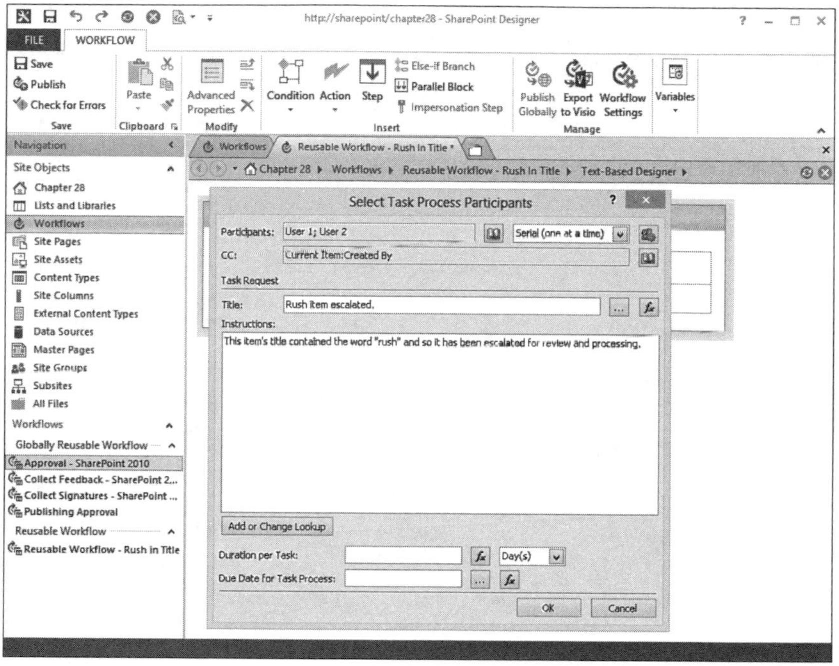

FIGURE 28.18 Defining participants in the Start Feedback Process action in Designer 2013.

In this next section, the workflow is initiated, and started, to display the functionality without completing the entire workflow. To test the workflow, follow these steps:

1. Log in to the site as an account with Owner-level permissions (http://sharepoint/Chapter28 in this example).

2. Navigate to the document library, and add the reusable workflow to the library by accessing Library Settings and clicking the Workflow Settings link in the Permissions and Management section.

3. The reusable workflow should appear in the Select a Workflow Template list, as shown in Figure 28.19. Click the workflow.

4. Enter a name for the workflow in the Name section (for example, **Rush in Title Workflow**).

5. Leave the Task List and History List settings at their defaults.

6. Under Start Options, verify that the Allow This Workflow to Be Manually Started by an Authenticated User with Edit Item Permissions check box is checked, and check the Creating a New Item Will Start This Workflow and Changing an Item Will Start This Workflow boxes. Click OK.

7. Now, log in as a user who is not involved in the feedback process but has Contributor-level permissions in the library (for example, User3).

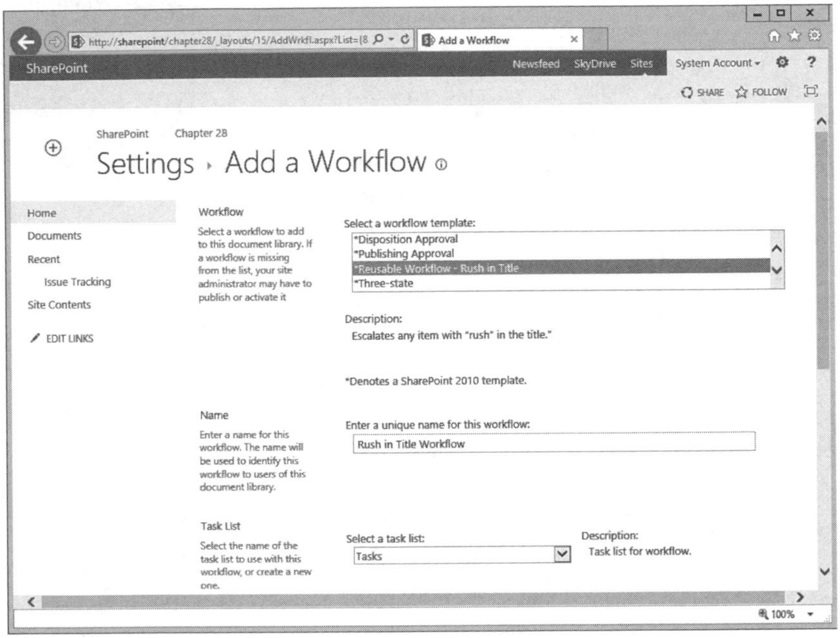

FIGURE 28.19 Choosing and configuring the workflow from Library Settings.

8. Access the document library on the site and upload a sample document. For this example, the document title is User3's super important document.docx.
9. Edit the properties of the document and add the word **Rush** to the Title field, and then save.
10. The column titled Rush in Title Workflow appears, and the document should be set to a status of In Progress.
11. Open Outlook for this user (User3), and an email is there announcing the start of the feedback workflow.
12. Log out, and then log back in as the first approver (User1 in this example). Open Outlook and note that an email has been received.

The rest of the workflow is not covered here, but it gives User1 a chance to provide feedback on the document, and then when approved, a task is created for User2 and that user is given a chance to provide feedback.

Summary

This chapter touched on the different types of workflows provided out-of-the-box in the SharePoint 2013 product line, and gave two detailed examples to familiarize readers with the process of creating and using workflows. Information was also provided pertaining to the management of workflows and for controlling SharePoint Designer 2013 use. Testing workflows can be challenging due to the requirements of having multiple user accounts involved in the process, but it is the best way for an administrator to get comfortable with the "moving parts" of the workflow process. Having a solid foundation on the out-of-the-box workflows will lead to a better understanding of where SharePoint Designer 2013 can come into play and where it can extend upon basic workflows.

Best Practices

The following are best practices from this chapter:

- SharePoint 2010 workflows are the most common platform for general workflow development on SharePoint 2013. SharePoint 2013 workflows do support additional features such as For-Each loops, but there is significant setup and configuration effort required to take advantage of SharePoint 2013 workflows.
- As a starting point for encouraging end users to use SharePoint workflows, train them on the range of capabilities of list and library alerts, and educate users about some of the unique alerts available in lists such as the Calendar, Issues, and Tasks lists. This is a good starting place before more-complex workflows are implemented.
- Before testing workflows in the organization, verify that the settings outlined in this chapter in the Central Administration site, as well as for the site collection where they will be used, to ensure that the settings meet the organization's needs and that the appropriate workflows are enabled.
- As a general rule, don't enable the SharePoint 2007 workflows unless they are specifically required.
- The three-state workflow is available in both SharePoint Foundation 2013 and SharePoint Server 2013 and is useful for testing and training purposes because there are multiple tasks generated and several points of interaction for end users.
- Other standard workflows should be tested, and IT should decide which, if any, of the additional workflows will be available for use by end users.
- IT should decide whether to allow the use of SharePoint Designer 2013 to create or modify workflows and can control its use on a per web application basis in the Central Administration site.
- SharePoint Designer 2013 allows the creation of new workflows and for the modification of out-of-the-box workflows and provides access to many powerful conditions and actions that can create complex workflows, as shown in this chapter.
- In SharePoint 2013, users may use SharePoint Designer 2013 to create workflows on SharePoint 2010 platform by default. To enable SharePoint 2013 workflows, IT must configure a Windows Azure farm and join SharePoint 2013 to that farm.

CHAPTER 29

Application Development with SharePoint Designer 2013 and Visual Studio 2012

IN THIS CHAPTER

Application development is a weighty topic, and this chapter seeks to communicate to architects, administrators, and developers some of the new and exciting features in terms of developing for SharePoint 2013 using Designer 2013 or Visual Studio 2012. This chapter also includes exercises that provide users of varying levels of expertise experience with Designer 2013 application design and that create a Visual Studio 2012 Visual web part.

SharePoint Designer 2013 will be used to create a workflow that interacts with several SharePoint lists and is meant to serve as the foundation for an "application" that could be created by a power user within the organization. This workflow allows a user to convert a sales lead into a customer by executing a workflow that creates a new item in a different list, and leverages lookup columns to populate the new list.

The example using Visual Studio 2012 demonstrates the development of a Visual web part that utilizes many new development features that SharePoint 2013 supports, including the JavaScript Object Model (JSOM).

Deciding If Development Is Required to Meet Business Needs

When embarking on a development project in Microsoft SharePoint 2013, you want to consider several important criteria so that you have the proper tools to complete the task at hand. An initial question to ask is whether SharePoint 2013 offers tools out-of-the-box that might provide the functionality required. Some investigation in this area might save the developer many hours of needless labor.

For example, some of the lesser-known web parts (such as the Content Query web part, Content Editor web part, or Page Viewer web part) provide functionality that can be leveraged and extended to meet more-complex business needs. Many tips exist for pasting JavaScript into the Content Editor web part to perform a wide variety of tasks.

SharePoint web parts can be connected to each other, allowing one list to filter the contents of another list. Connected web parts allow a selection in one list to filter the contents of another list. Although the functionality is limited to single column joins, the relative ease of connecting web parts should not be overlooked as a possible solution and is leveraged in many "dashboard" configurations to allow a user to interact with the data displayed.

In SharePoint 2013, to support the connected web part features, the underlying lists and libraries continue to maintain enforced relationships between each other using the lookup column, as covered in Chapter 22, "Managing Metadata and Content Types in SharePoint 2013." Lookup columns can spawn additional columns from the source list into the host list that contains the lookup column. Calculated columns allow SharePoint administrators and developers alike to complete many of the same calculations that Excel supports, including advanced string, date, and number operations. The functionality is fairly limited, but this just might satisfy the business owner's requirements.

Content types are another overlooked and often misunderstood feature in SharePoint that, when used properly, can reduce the need for custom programming. Content types are in use throughout SharePoint from lists and libraries to article pages and are heavily used "under the hood" by InfoPath Forms Services. Creative use of content types is a very powerful way of providing enhanced behavior through the use of metadata and workflows, ultimately providing the user with a rich and intuitive experience.

There are also many development possibilities provided by features such as alerts, tasks, project tasks, or out-of-the-box workflows that push information to users of the SharePoint environment. SharePoint administrators can also solve business process needs by employing SharePoint 2013 alerts as simple workflows, because they push a limited amount of information to end users based on changes that take place in lists and libraries.

TIP

As well as out-of-the-box SharePoint tools, features, and capabilities, make sure to research whether third-party retail products might provide the required functionality. No developer wants to explain why they have spent weeks developing a web part that could be purchased for $500 from a reputable vendor and comes with updates, technical support, and other benefits.

Assuming this due diligence has been performed, and the desired functionality was not readily attainable, it is time to look into SharePoint Designer 2013 or Visual Studio 2012. This chapter demonstrates several different methods to harness the features provided by the two very different applications.

Planning the Development Project

A recommended best practice is always to document the goals for the application development project to ensure that the scope of work is clearly defined and there are clear milestones for the development process. Simply writing up a list of bullets of the reasons for the project, and the success criteria that will prove that the project has been successfully completed, can prove extremely valuable at a later date.

A simple development project (for example, a workflow for an expense report or the creation of a web part that displays data from a website on the Internet) might only require a few minutes to summarize, but a more complex project (for example, a purchase order application development project) can require several days and numerous meetings to thoroughly define.

SharePoint development projects usually involve out-of-the-box SharePoint components, as well as the creation of workflows in SharePoint Designer 2013, forms in InfoPath 2013, and solutions in Visual Studio 2012. Putting together a list of the components that are expected from the final project can help guide the development process. The following list provides a number of high-level tasks that should not be overlooked when planning a more complex development project:

- Define the statement of work (SOW).
- Configure/update the development environment.
- Configure the base SharePoint 2013 site/sites/site collection.
- Configure required lists and libraries to support the application.
- Create mock-ups of forms and visual components.
- Develop the required components and functionality in Designer 2013 / Visual Studio 2012.
- Ensure that auditing functionality is in place as needed.
- Ensure that security for the objects involved in the application (lists, libraries, forms, and so on) is in place.
- Ensure that the application is fault tolerant and scalable enough to meet the needs of the organization.
- Ensure that exception handling and logging is in place.
- Document key steps in the development process.
- Test functionality and “prove the concept” of the application.

- Make sure that the application is portable and can be moved from the development environment to the staging or production environments.
- Allow time for user acceptance testing (UAT) and pilot phases before a full rollout.
- Allow time for end users and administrator training to use and support the application.
- Include signoffs along the way to ensure management approval of progress.
- Establish change control practices for changes after the application is being used in production.

Following these steps for even simpler projects will enhance the success, and sometimes even more importantly, the perception of success, by managers and stakeholders who may not be technically savvy enough to appreciate the elegance of stable code.

Evolution in the SharePoint Platform for Developers

SharePoint 2010 grew in leaps and bounds over SharePoint 2003 and SharePoint 2007 and became recognized as a versatile and powerful development platform, but there were still limitations in the areas of security, portability, performance, reliability, and features. With SharePoint 2013, the bar has been raised yet again. The latest iteration of the SharePoint platform has too many enhancements to cover in a single chapter, but some of the highlights are covered in this section, as well as a summary of enhancements in Designer 2013 and Visual Studio 2012.

New in SharePoint 2013 are several client object models allowing interaction with SharePoint objects, methods, lists, libraries, and even service applications. The client object models come in two flavors, the first is the Client-Side Object Model (CSOM) dynamic link library (DLL)-based client library, which allows for the development of rich client applications using the familiar IntelliSense that developers have grown used to and the immediacy of synchronous calls. The second object model is the JSOM, which allows for browser-hosted, AJAX rich application development without the overhead of .NET.

From a list, library, and service application perspective, under the hood, SharePoint 2013 is very similar to SharePoint 2010. In fact, most solutions developed for SharePoint 2010 will continue to function, and upgraded code often only needs minor updates before successfully compiling for SharePoint 2013.

The largest change in SharePoint 2013 from a programmatic perspective other than the addition of the new object models is the addition of the SharePoint 2013 Workflow Manager. The Azure-based Workflow Manager is a cloud-enabled workflow engine that works side by side with the SharePoint 2010 Windows Workflow Foundation engine, which is still delivered with SharePoint 2013. Developers now have the choice to develop against the SharePoint 2010 Workflow Engine or SharePoint 2013 Workflow Manager.

In addition to the base features of the .NET Framework, SharePoint 2013 also leverages Windows Workflow Foundation, a powerful business process management engine that is seamlessly integrated into SharePoint for the development of advanced state applications. Visual Studio 2012 provides the project templates necessary to create sequential and state machine workflows and now supports their full development lifecycle from development, to testing, deployment, and packaging.

NOTE

A state machine workflow is a workflow associated with a SharePoint list item or document that can enter different states in any order. For example, a purchase order may have five states (such as Not Submitted, Submitted, Pending, Approved, and Completed). A state machine workflow, unlike a sequential workflow, allows the item to be routed and rerouted to each state as needed.

To make the development process more seamless and intuitive, Visual Studio 2012 contains a variety of templates available for SharePoint 2013. These templates are available after installing Microsoft Office Developer Tools for Visual Studio 2012 from http://msdn.microsoft.com/en-US/office/apps/fp123627. Some of the templates include site definitions, business data connectivity model, event receivers, and modules. Coupled with the new deployment features, developers are provided with the entire framework and are simply required to produce the code for the desired solution.

SharePoint 2013 continues to support a variety of deployment and debugging scenarios. Developers can develop sandboxed solutions, GAC-deployed assemblies that support fully integrated applications, and, now, a variety of application (app) programs. Unlike SharePoint 2007 and SharePoint 2013, these apps can be deployed and debugged directly from Visual Studio 2012 and even support deployment and debugging on Office 365.

Designer 2013 Enhancements

Designer 2013 has gone somewhat unchanged from Designer 2010. The notable enhancements include the Office 2013 look and feel, enhanced Visio 2013 integration, and better support for external content types. However, power users and nondevelopers will be surprised to find that the visual editor that they heavily relied on for visual layouts is no longer available. Some of the highlights of SharePoint Designer 2013 include the following:

- **Support for SharePoint 2013 platform workflows:** The 2013 workflows use the new Workflow Manager Azure-based workflow engine and come with a completely new set of actions.
- **Impersonation steps:** These allow workflows to run under the context of another user other than that of the executing user. This allows a user with lesser privileges to start a workflow that can then perform actions that the author of the workflow has permissions to perform. This eliminates a major challenge in workflow design where the initiator's privileges often limit the tasks that can be performed.
- **Reusable and exportable workflows:** A workflow created at the top level of a site collection can be used by any subsite, and a workflow created in a specific subsite

can be reused within that subsite. Workflows can also be exported from one site collection and then uploaded to and activated in another site collection.

- **Association columns:** If the reusable workflow requires certain columns to exist in the list or library that it is associated with, those columns can be added as association columns and they will get added automatically to a list or library when a reusable workflow is associated with that list or library.
- **Associate workflows with content types:** Reusable workflows can be filtered to a specific content type and be associated either with that specific content type or with any content type that inherits from that content type. If a workflow is associated with a site content type, that workflow becomes available for all items of that content type in every list and library to which that site content type has been added.
- **Site workflows are associated to a site, rather than to a list, library, or content type:** Clicking Site Workflows on the Site Actions menu will show the status of these types of workflows.
- **Edit the workflows included with SharePoint Server:** Approval, Collect Feedback, and Collect Signatures workflows are now "declarative workflows," which means they are customizable in SharePoint Designer 2013.

Visual Studio 2012 Enhancements

Visual Studio offers many enhancements in Visual Basic, Visual C#, Visual C++ and Visual F#, Office system development, and it leverages improvements in .NET Framework 4.5 that are beyond the scope of this chapter. For developers familiar with Visual Studio 2012 or other integrated development environments that might access SharePoint, some highlights are as follows:

- A new app catalog allowing for developers to develop, package, and deploy apps that integrate with SharePoint, both directly and remotely. Apps can also directly access SharePoint hosted content through permission manifests that allow SharePoint administrators to enable communication between the app catalog's domain and that of SharePoint 2013 itself.
- A new C# and JavaScript client object model allowing for code to be run on a client that was once relegated to only running on the SharePoint server itself.
- REST application programming interfaces (APIs) allowing for standards-based Extensible Markup Language (XML) over HTTP communication with SharePoint.
- Enhanced client object models that allow for both C#-based and JavaScript-based applications and solutions.
- LINQ support allowing for integrated, object-like access to SharePoint data from familiar .NET languages such as C# and VB.NET.
- Sandboxed solutions are solutions that are safely deployed to a SharePoint site and are limited from doing harm to the farm through code access security (CAS).

- Improved monitoring through timer jobs, which can be scheduled to run as often as every minute for a specified time span.
- New service application framework designed to support applications that were once reserved only for the components of the shared service provider (SSP).
- Import, modify, and extend solution packages (.wsp).
- Develop SharePoint solutions with SharePoint project type templates and SharePoint project item templates.
- Design association and initiation forms for sequential and state workflows.
- Aggregate and integrate back-end data by using Business Data Connectivity (BDC) models.
- Create web parts and application pages for a SharePoint site.

Considering SharePoint Designer 2013 for Development

SharePoint Designer has evolved from SharePoint FrontPage 2003 to its latest manifestation as SharePoint Designer 2013, and Microsoft has continued to make it available free of charge to encourage its use by SharePoint power users and developers.

SharePoint Designer 2013 provides a wide range of tools for power users, site administrators, farm administrators, and developers, which become immediately obvious when opening a website, as shown in Figure 29.1. Similar to SharePoint Designer 2010, SharePoint Designer 2013 has a streamlined look and feel, a customizable ribbon, and broad access to functionality that was reserved to the browser in SharePoint 2007. The most notable change in functionality includes a larger repertoire of workflow actions and conditions, looping actions, and reduced page design capabilities.

Common Development Tasks

SharePoint Designer 2013 supports a variety of development tasks, including the following items:

- Extending upon the basic workflows provided out-of-the-box with SharePoint 2013. These were covered in more detail in Chapter 28, "Out-of-the-Box Workflows and Designer 2013 Workflows."
- While basic branding can be done with the standard browser interface in SharePoint 2013, more extensive branding in SharePoint 2013 requires SharePoint Designer 2013. In SharePoint 2013, the WYSIWYG editor is no longer available, and administrators are now limited to CSS- and HTML-based branding efforts.
- Custom ASPX and .NET pages extend the functionality of SharePoint and allow the development of custom .NET web pages within SharePoint that take advantage of powerful components such as the DataView.

- Custom forms to extend the functionality of the built-in SharePoint 2013 forms.
- Basic web parts can be developed using SharePoint Designer 2013, but not all the features supported by Visual Studio 2012 are available.

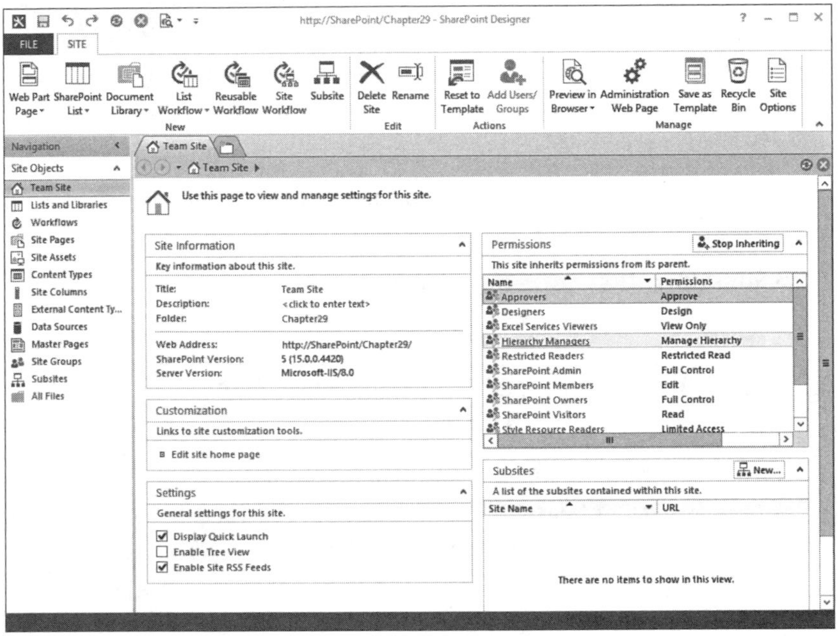

FIGURE 29.1 A site opened in SharePoint Designer 2013.

Creating a Workflow-Based Application in SharePoint Designer 2013

Chapter 28 provides an introduction to the basic types of workflows available in SharePoint 2013 and covers some of the capabilities of SharePoint Designer 2013 when working with workflows. This section now takes the process further and covers the creation of a basic application that involves multiple lists and a customized workflow that creates a new item in a new list and leverages lookup columns.

The following instructions describe how to create a workflow that interacts with multiple SharePoint lists when items are created and modified. The workflow is based on three lists: a Region list, a Sales Lead list, and a Customer list. When a user marks a Sales Lead as SaleClosed, a manager can trigger the workflow and create a customer based on the data in the Sales Lead list. This workflow also demonstrates how to work with SharePoint lookup columns by copying the Salesperson from the Region list and adding the value to the Customer list.

Although limited, this example demonstrates the steps necessary to develop a relatively simple application using SharePoint Designer. The functionality is limited because the processes are asynchronous, and the lists can be joined by only a single column, but the general concept could be reused for a variety of business purposes. Generally, a quickly developed application built in SharePoint is an easier sell to business owners than a stand-alone .NET application that requires everything from an Internet Information Services (IIS) site, security, documentation, and even its own database. Furthermore, the following example can be extended with list item security, custom views, custom forms, and email notifications to make the application more fully featured.

Follow these steps to create the application using SharePoint Designer 2013:

1. In a nonproduction site collection, create three SharePoint lists with a standard view (do not use datasheet view) using the Custom List template with the columns and data types as shown in Tables 29.1, 29.2, and 29.3. Unless specified in these tables, leave the other settings for the columns and the list on their defaults. Table 29.1 provides the columns needed for the Region list, Table 29.2 provides the columns needed for the Sales Leads list, and Table 29.3 provides the columns needed for the Customer list. Several of the columns are specified as Required to maintain data integrity within the application. If fields are allowed to be left blank, the application might not function properly.

TABLE 29.1 Region List Columns and Settings

Column	Data Type	Require That This Column Contains Information
Title	Single Line of Text (already present)	Yes
Salesperson	Person or Group	Yes

TABLE 29.2 Sales Leads List Columns and Settings

Column	Data Type	Require That This Column Contains Information
Title	Single Line of Text (already present)	Yes
Region	Lookup Column – Link to Region list's Title column	Yes
SaleClosed	Yes/No with Default Value set to "No"	No

TABLE 29.3 Customer List Columns and Settings

Column	Data Type	Require That This Column Contains Information
Title	Single Line of Text (already present)	Yes
Region	Lookup Column – Link to Region list's Title column	Yes
Salesperson	Person or Group	No
Customer ID	Single Line of Text	No

NOTE

Leave the lists blank at this point. They will be populated after the workflow is created; full instructions are provided later.

2. Open SharePoint Designer 2013, select Open Site, and enter the URL for the site that houses these lists (such as http://SharePoint/Chapter29/). Provide credentials if asked.

3. Select the Workflows entry from the navigation pane, Site Objects section, on the left side of SharePoint Designer. Then select the drop-down menu under List Workflow in the Workflows tab, which should be active. Click the Sales Leads list, as shown in Figure 29.2.

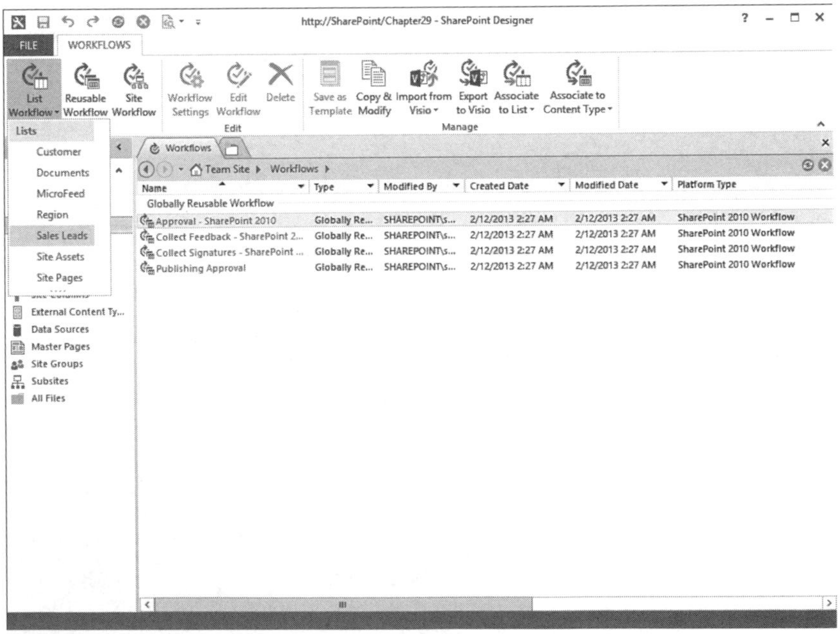

FIGURE 29.2 Creating a workflow for the Sales Leads list.

4. Name the workflow **Sales Leads – On Change** and specify the platform type as SharePoint 2010 Workflow. Click OK.

TIP

When creating a workflow, it is good practice to provide a name that identifies the underlying list and whether the workflow is triggered on change, manually, or on create.

5. Upon creation of a new workflow, the workflow editor screen appears with a blank canvas containing a single step named Step 1. Click within the Step 1 editor box in the section under the title bar to ensure that it is active, and then click the Condition button on the Workflow ribbon and choose the condition If Current Item Field Equals Value. Step 1 will now reflect this change and display If Current Item Field Equals Value.
6. Click the field link that now appears in Step 1 and select SaleClosed from the drop-down list.
7. Then, click the value link and select Yes from the drop-down list. Figure 29.3 shows the contents of the step at this point.

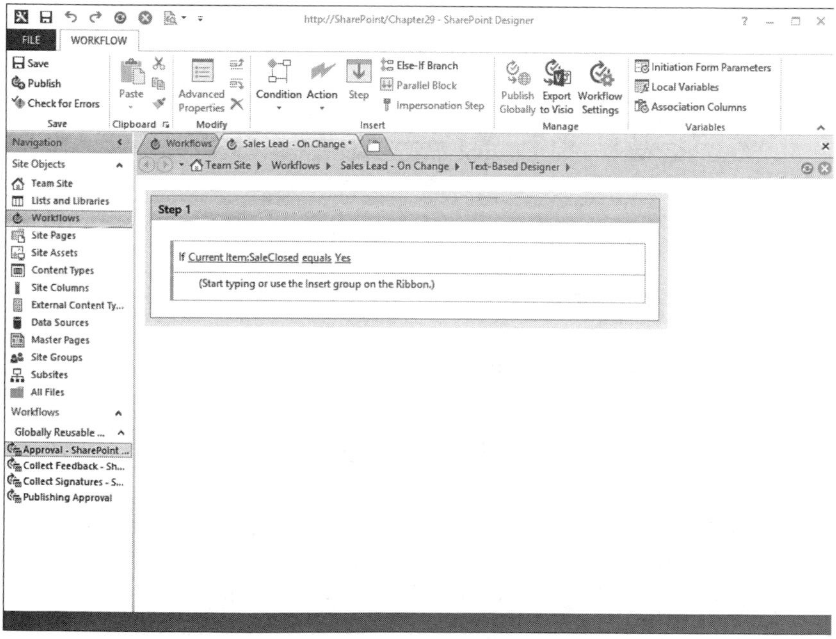

FIGURE 29.3 Creating a workflow condition.

8. Add an action just below the condition created. Click in the Step 1 box below the row where the condition was just defined. Type **Create**,press Enter, and choose Create List Item from the options.

9. Click the Create List Item link that will now be visible to open the Create New List Item window.

10. Choose Customer from the drop-down menu List field at the top of the window. Figure 29.4 shows the results.

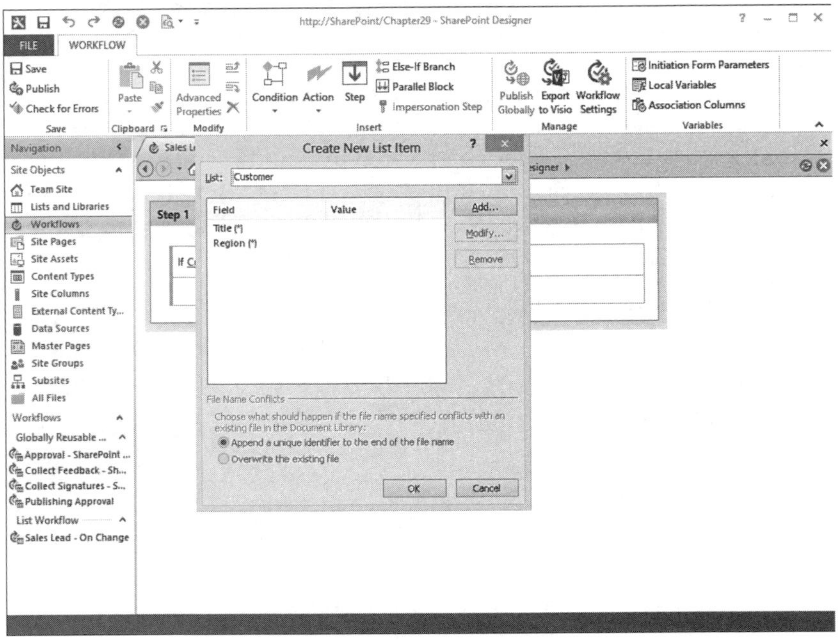

FIGURE 29.4 Create a New List Item window.

11. In the Create New List Item window, double-click the Title field to open the Value Assignment window.

12. In the Value Assignment window, click the fx button; the Lookup for Single Line of Text window will open.

13. In the Lookup for Single Line of Text window, select Title in the Field from Source field, as shown in Figure 29.5.

14. Click OK to close the Lookup for Single Line of Text window, and click OK to close the Value Assignment window. The Create New List Item window should be active. The Title (*) entry in the Field column will now have a Value entry of Current Item:Title.

15. In the Create New List Item window, double-click the Region field to open the Value Assignment window.

16. In the Value Assignment window, click the fx button to open the Lookup for Integer window. Verify that the Data Source field has Current Item in it.

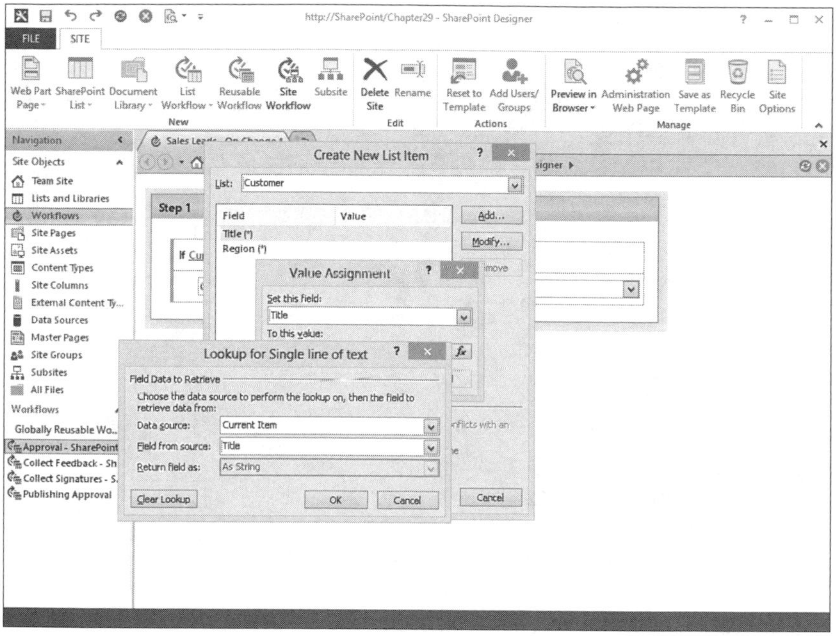

FIGURE 29.5 Completing the Lookup for Single Line of Text window.

17. Change the value for the field from Source to Region.

18. Choose Lookup Id (as Integer) for the Return Field As field. The completed Lookup for Integer window will look like Figure 29.6.

19. Click OK in the Lookup for Integer window and again in the Value Assignment window to return to the Create New List Item window. Now the Create New List Item window will have a value assigned to the Region (*) field of Current Item:Region.

20. In the Create New List Item window, click the Add button to open the Value Assignment window.

21. In the Value Assignment window, specify Salesperson for the Set This Field drop-down list.

22. Click the fx button to open the Lookup for Person or Group window.

23. Change the value in the Data Source field to Region, and additional fields will appear.

24. In the Field from Source field, select Salesperson from the drop-down menu.

25. In the Return Field As drop-down menu, verify that User ID Number String is selected.

26. In the Find the List Item section of the Lookup for Person or Group window, select Title in the Field drop-down list, as shown in Figure 29.7.

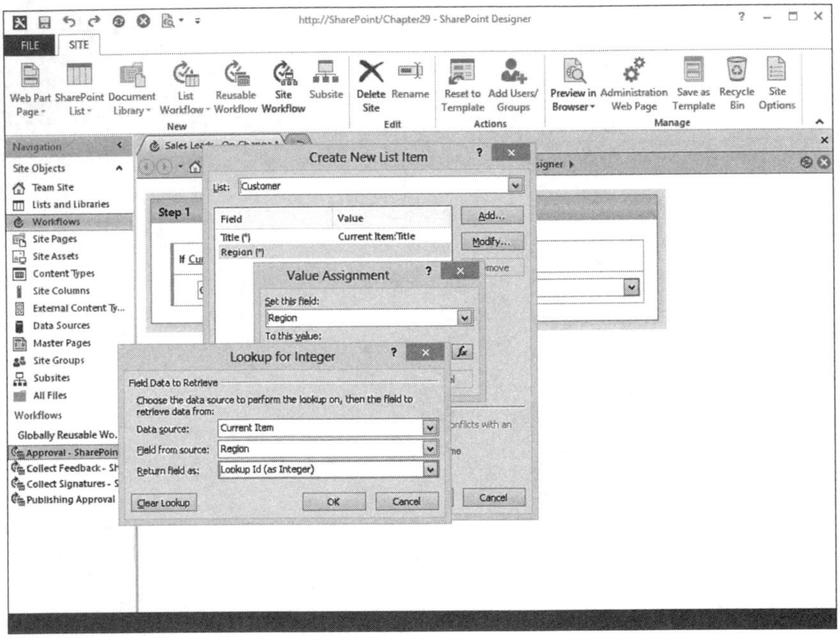

FIGURE 29.6 Lookup for Integer window.

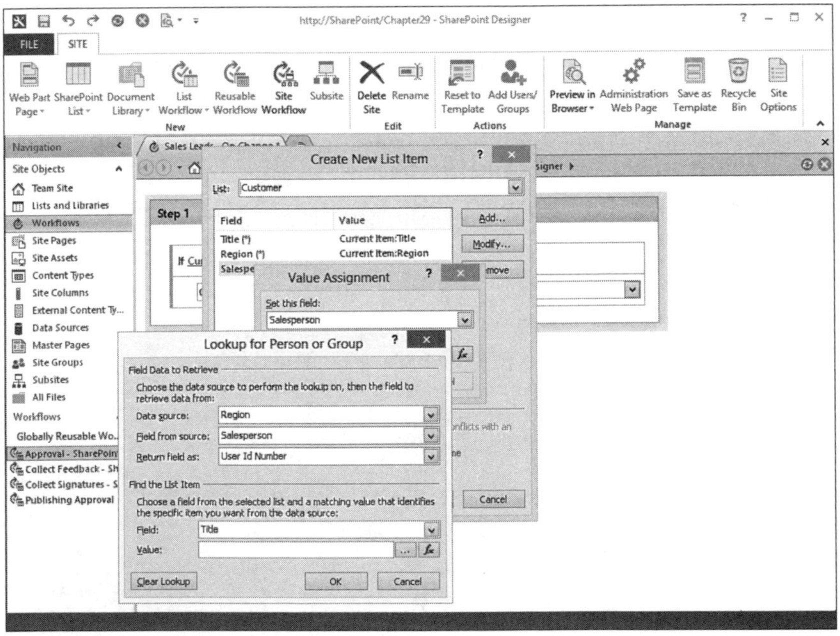

FIGURE 29.7 Partial Lookup for Person or Group window configuration.

27. To complete the Lookup for Integer window, click the fx button for the Value field to open the Lookup for Person or Group window.

28. In the Data Source field, leave Region selected.

29. In the Field from Source field, choose Salesperson from the drop-down menu.

30. In the Return Field As drop-down, choose User ID Number from the drop-down menu. Click OK.

31. The Lookup for Person or Group window will now be complete and look like Figure 29.8.

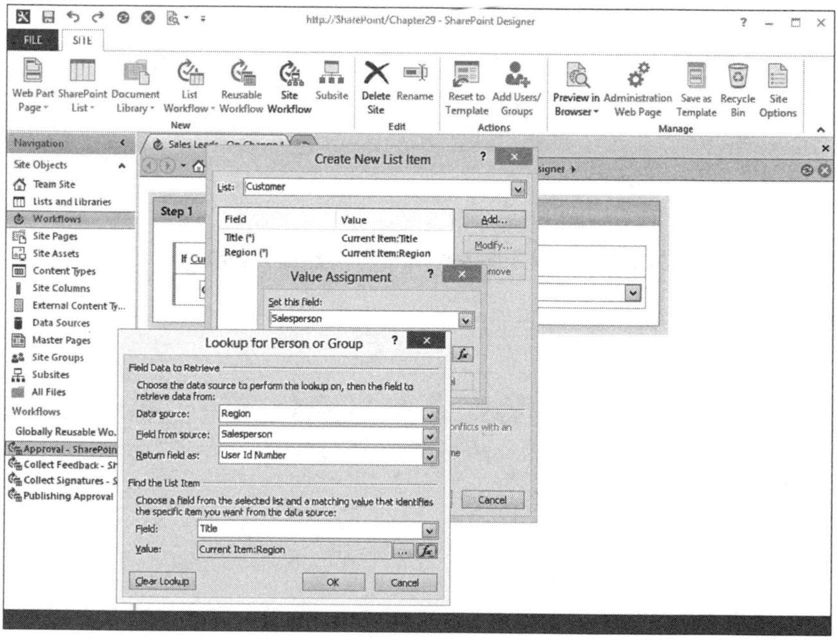

FIGURE 29.8 Completed Lookup for Person or Group window configuration.

32. Click OK to close the Lookup for Person or Group window, and click Yes when the message "The lookup you defined is not guaranteed to return a single value" appears. Click OK to close the Value Assignment window.

33. The Create New List Item window should now look like Figure 29.9 and include a Salesperson field with a value of Region:Salesperson.

34. Click OK to close the Create New List Item window.

35. Save the workflow by clicking the Save button on the SharePoint Designer ribbon.

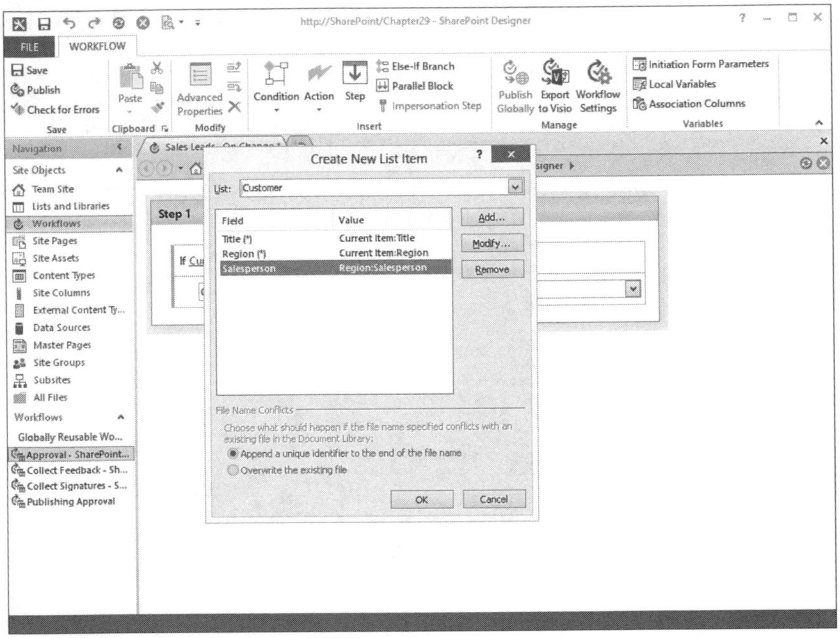

FIGURE 29.9 Completed Create New List Item window.

NOTE

Unlike SharePoint 2007 workflows, which were immediately active upon save, SharePoint 2013 and 2010 workflows are available for use only after they are published. To publish a SharePoint Designer workflow, follow these steps:

1. Click the Workflow Settings tool on the ribbon. The display will change to show the workflow settings.
2. Verify that Allow This Workflow to be Manually Started is selected from the Start Options section on the lower-right side.

   The workflow can be configured to start automatically, but the logic in this example is that the list item may be changed many times, and a user might accidentally set the item to closed, so a manager should be the only one starting the workflow, after the manager has confirmed that the lead is in fact closed.
3. Click the Publish button on the ribbon to deploy and activate the workflow on the list.

TIP

A form will be visible on the Workflow Settings page that should be titled Sales Leads – On Change.xsn. Clicking this link will open InfoPath 2013 if installed on the computer and allow customization of the initiation form.

Testing the Workflow

Immediately after you save and publish the workflow, it's ready for testing. To test the Sales Lead workflow, follow these steps to populate the necessary lists and start a workflow:

1. Return to the SharePoint site where the workflow was published; the three custom lists are present. (In this example, the site is http://SharePoint/Chapter29/.)
2. Access the Region list and add two items. The first item should be titled **Region A** and have a Salesperson assigned who is a valid Active Directory (AD) user account (User1 in this example). The second item should be titled **Region B** and have a different Salesperson (User2 in this example).
3. Access the Sales Leads list on the SharePoint site. Click New Item and fill in the title with **Customer ABC** and select Region A. Click Save. This simulates the process of a field being created for a sales prospect in a specific region. In a production situation, additional fields could be added to track conversations with the client or upload proposals and other documents to the list item.
4. Edit the Sales Lead item created in the previous step and check the SaleClosed check box, and then click Save. This simulates the event where the sale is closed and the lead ready to be converted to a customer.
5. Access the ellipsis menu for the item and click Workflows.
6. The Sales Leads – On Change workflow should appear next to the workflow icon as shown in Figure 29.10. Click the link next to the workflow icon to access the initiation page.
7. The IniWrkflIP.aspx page will load. Click the Start button.

NOTE

If State Service is not installed, the user will receive the following error: "The form cannot be rendered. This may be due to a misconfiguration of the Microsoft SharePoint Server State Service. For more information, contact your server administrator."

A likely solution is to create the State Service Application through PowerShell (there is no UI option available in SharePoint 2013). And then associate the service application with the web application from Central Administration.

8. You will return to the Sales Leads list, and a Sales Leads – On Change column will appear and indicate that the workflow is In Process and then Completed.
9. Navigate to the Customer list and verify that a new item has been created, as shown in Figure 29.11.
10. Return to the Sales Leads list and click the value that appears in the Sales Leads – On Change column to view the workflow history for that particular list item. The Workflow History window will open and display the status for the latest instance of the workflow.

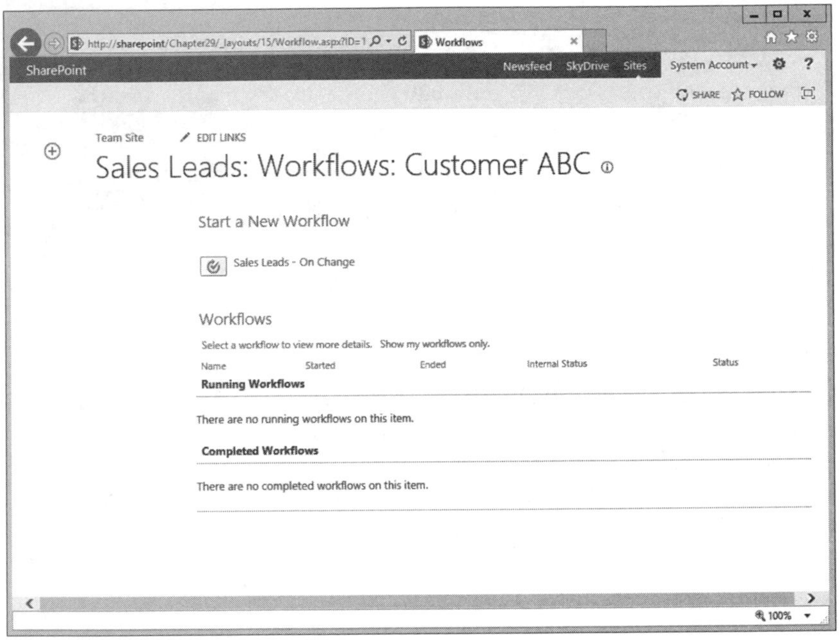

FIGURE 29.10 Initiating the workflow from the Sales Leads list item.

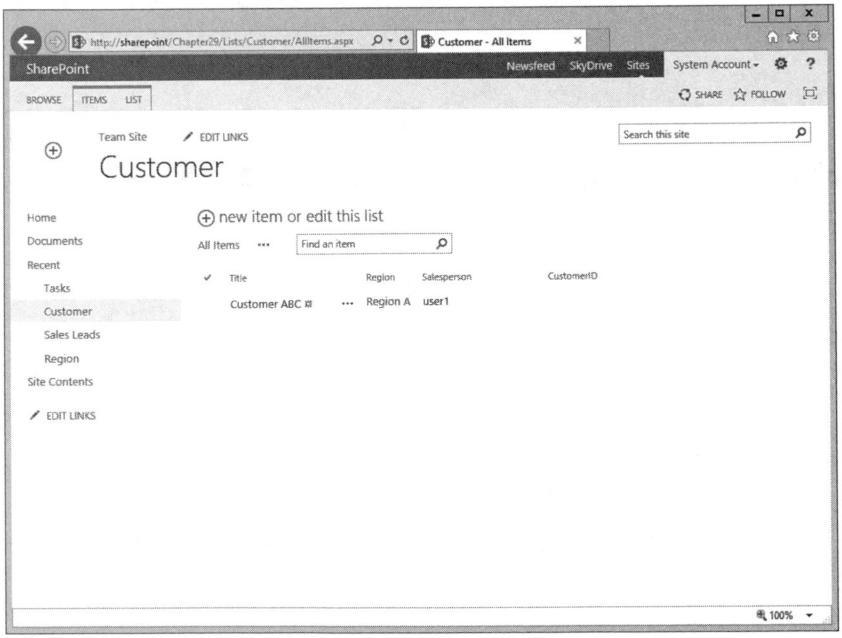

FIGURE 29.11 New item created in the Customer list as a result of the workflow.

Extending the Capabilities of the Application

While the workflow outlined previously will function properly, it is just a starting point and would not generally be considered to be "enterprise ready." Here are some items to consider as ways of enhancing the functionality of the application:

- Create custom list views to show and hide the sales leads depending on whether the lead is actually closed.
- Create an alert in the Sales Leads list that alerts a manager when an item is set to SaleClosed equals Yes.
- Create a new workflow that starts when an item is added to the Customer list and sends an email to the assigned Salesperson to alert him or her that they have a new client.
- For testing purposes, add the workflow action Log to History List to output debug or informational messages to the workflow history screen.
- Logically, the application has flaws due to the fact that if a Sales Lead were reopened and then marked as Closed again, the workflow would trigger and create a duplicate customer. Therefore, a condition should be added to Step 1 that checks for the existence of the customer through the use of a lookup on the customer's title column.

Using Visual Studio 2012 with SharePoint 2013

Development for SharePoint 2013 using Visual Studio 2012 requires the developer to take caution and adhere to more stringent standards for the project to be a success. Although an aggressive approach may allow the developer to make great strides in a short period of time, .NET and SharePoint 2013 development is both a science and an art. Code can still cause memory leaks, applications can enter near-endless loops, and simple mistakes may drastically affect SharePoint 2013's performance. However, the resulting applications can meet a great range of business requirements, making Visual Studio 2012 the choice of many developers.

Visual Studio 2012 is the de facto standard for development on the Windows platforms and was first released in 1995. While developers can take advantage of Visual Studio 2012 to develop C++ applications and other applications that are compiled down to machine code, the typical developer creates applications on top of the .NET Framework, the same framework that SharePoint is built upon. SharePoint's use of the .NET Framework is apparent in the ASP.NET controls, layout pages, master pages, .ascx controls, and .aspx pages that are visible throughout the system's C:\Program Files\Common Files\Microsoft Shared\Web Server Extensions\15\ directory.

When developing applications for SharePoint 2013, developers usually code using familiar languages such as VB.NET or C#. Although the syntax of these two languages differs, Visual Studio 2012 compiles the code down to an intermediate language called MSIL, where the code, regardless of the originating syntax, behaves roughly the same. Furthermore, code developed in different .NET projects using different languages can reference code developed in another .NET language. For more information about the .NET Framework, see http://www.microsoft.com/net/.

Visual Studio 2012 has standardized and streamlined packaging and deployment of solution packages and applications, an area where the preceding versions of Visual Studio fell short. A solution package and an application are cabinet files with a .wsp or .app extension, respectively, which contain the application code, a manifest, and one or more directories containing application specific files. Visual Studio 2012 can deploy, activate, deactivate, and retract solutions and applications without requiring the developer to open a command prompt or PowerShell. New in Visual Studio 2012 and SharePoint 2013 is the ability to publish and debug an Office 365 hosted application.

NOTE

Before starting development in SharePoint 2013 with Visual Studio 2012, a developer should understand the Microsoft.NET framework and VB or C# because most code samples available on the web are provided in one or both of these common languages.

Getting Started with Visual Studio 2012

This section introduces some basics in getting Visual Studio installed and the basics of creating a new project. Experienced users might want to skip this section and move on to the next section that covers creating a web part.

You can download Visual Studio Professional, Premium, or Ultimate from Microsoft at http://www.microsoft.com/visualstudio/ for a 90-day trial, if needed. The Professional, Premium, and Ultimate versions of Visual Studio 2012 can all be used to develop for SharePoint when the Microsoft Office Developer Tools are installed from http://msdn.microsoft.com/en-US/office/apps/fp123627. Visual Studio 2012 supports development and deployment of SharePoint components on a remote server, but most templates cannot be developed or deployed unless SharePoint is installed on the same system as Visual Studio 2012.

Downloading and Installing Visual Studio 2012

Follow these steps to download and install Visual Studio Professional. These steps may vary slightly on different system configurations. Note that the full installation requires at least 7.5GB of space.

1. Access the Microsoft Downloads site (http://www.microsoft.com/visualstudio/eng/downloads) (or search on "Microsoft Visual Studio 2012 Professional Trial" on Microsoft's website) and click Install Now.

NOTE

You may need to install KB 2781514 which improves the stability of Visual Studio 2012 and KB 2799752 which is a Cumulative Update that defines new states for queue, topic, and subscription and contains a number of bug fixes for Service Bus 1.0.

2. Click Run to run the downloader application vs_professional.exe.
3. Click Run when this application downloads.
4. The Installation Wizard opens and starts. If desired, uncheck the box next to Yes, Send Information About My Setup Experiences to Microsoft Corporation. Click the box next to I Have Read and Accept the License Terms, and then click Next.
5. The wizard then informs that it will install: Blend for Visual Studio, LightSwitch, Microsoft Foundation Classes for C++, Microsoft Office Developer Tools, Microsoft SharePoint Developer Tools, Microsoft SQL Server Data Tools, Silverlight Development Kits, and Microsoft Web Developer Tools. For SharePoint development, ensure that the Microsoft Office Developer Tools and Microsoft SharePoint Developer Tools are checked. Click Install.
6. The items mentioned in step 5 will then download and install. This process will take a while, but the wizard lists which step it is on and the download speed, which is more helpful then the average progress bar.
7. Once the installation is complete, a reboot is required, so click Restart Now.
8. Upon reboot, the installation process will complete, which again takes a while.
9. After the setup completes, the option is provided to Install Documentation, which is recommended for less-experienced users of Visual Studio. Click Install Documentation to start the process.
10. Accept the default library location or enter a new one. Click OK.
11. The Help Library Manager window then provides a directory of content to choose from. For example, click Add next to SharePoint Development in the Visual Studio 2012 section and click Update.
12. Click Finish and then click Exit to exit the Help Library Manager.
13. Click Finish to close the Visual Studio installation wizard.

Developing a SharePoint 2013 App

The newest and most exciting feature of SharePoint 2013 is the ability to develop apps that support on premise and hosted SharePoint 2013, such as Office 365. Visual Studio 2012 contains project templates that contain all the functionality that supports the immediate deployment of a variety of objects, including apps, workflows, event receivers, web parts, BDC objects, and even list definitions. Developers will be pleased to note that the packaging of these components as a SharePoint solution (.wsp) is automatic and applications (.app) will automatically be created for solutions that utilize the application template.

Follow the steps listed here to create an app that renders a SharePoint announcements list in a custom format using the JavaScript Client Object Model (JCOM). To show some of the more recent advancements of both .NET and SharePoint 2013, this example uses the JavaScript Object Model and AJAX to dynamically render content in a web page.

Apps in SharePoint 2013 run in an independent application domain that is separated from the core SharePoint applications; this is furthered by the fact that apps reside in a different URL, such as apps.sharepoint.com rather than sharepoint.com/apps. By providing an independent application domain, apps run with a virtual separation of concerns between themselves and production SharePoint components. Because of this separation, app development is relatively easy unless the app needs to communicate directly with the host SharePoint sites. The example in this chapter demonstrates how to create an app using the cross-domain library, which allows the app to communicate from its host site.

To create an app for SharePoint, follow these steps on a system with SharePoint Server 2013 Standard or Enterprise installed, along with Visual Studio 2012 Professional or Ultimate:

1. Open Central Administration and click Application Management. Click the Create Site Collections link.
2. On the Create Site Collections screen, enter the title **Chapter 29 Development** and select /sites/ managed path in the URL drop-down. In the URL text box enter **Chapter29Dev**, as shown in Figure 29.12. In this example, the developer site collection's URL will be http://SharePoint/Sites/Chapter29Dev/.

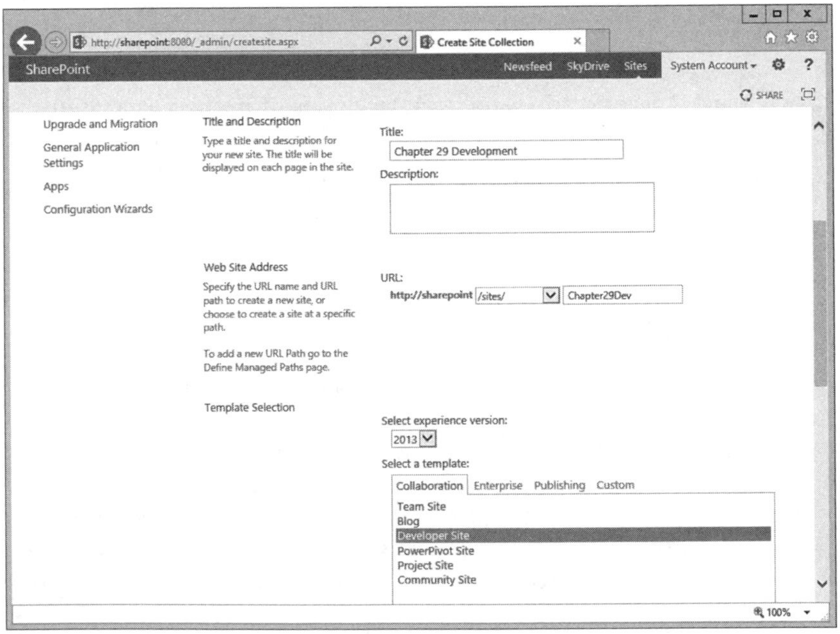

FIGURE 29.12 Creating the Developer site collection.

3. Once the developer site is created, access the site via the URL, such as http://SharePoint/Sites/Chapter29Dev/.

4. Click the Site Contents link and click Add an App. Create an Announcements app and a Picture Library app. If these do not exist, they will need to be created. The Announcements app will need to be named **Announcements** for the code included in this exercise to work. The Picture Library app can be named anything because it is not directly addressed in the code. For this exercise, the Picture Library app is named **Pictures**.

   The Announcements list needs to have several columns added; otherwise, settings should be left at their default. Table 29.4 shows the columns that need to be added and relevant settings.

TABLE 29.4 Add These Columns to the Announcements List

Column	Data Type
Author	Person or Group
Start Date	Date and Time
Picture	Hyperlink or Picture (Choose the Picture option under Format URL As.)

The Picture Library app should have an image uploaded to it. Once the image is uploaded, capture the URL for the image, and then create an announcement and paste the URL for the image in the Picture field. Figure 29.13 shows the Announcements list with an entry in it that references a picture.

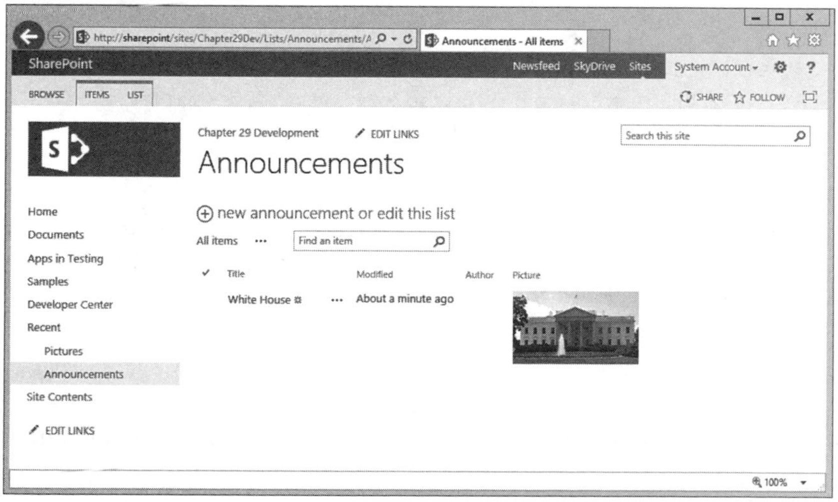

FIGURE 29.13 Preparing an Announcements list prior to the creation of the app.

NOTE

The files that support the JavaScript object model (.js) are located in %ProgramFiles%\Common Files\Microsoft Shared\web server extensions\15\TEMPLATE\LAYOUTS. These files are delivered to each server when SharePoint is installed, and it is recommended that they *not* be modified.

Before continuing with the web part development, verify that the account being used to run Visual Studio 2012 has the following rights:

- The account is not the SharePoint system account. In most cases, the application pool and system account are the same.
- Local administrator rights to the development machine.
- Farm administrator rights (not necessary if a sandboxed solution is being created, but always helpful to have if possible).
- Site collection administrator rights to the developer site collection where the solution will be deployed during debugging.

CAUTION

SharePoint 2013 does not allow the system account to deploy apps or solutions.

To create a project in Visual Studio 2012, which will be used in the following exercise, follow these steps:

1. Open Visual Studio 2012 by clicking the Start button. Click All Programs, then click Microsoft Visual Studio 2012.
2. The first time it is opened, the default environment settings need to be set. Different developers will have their preferences, but for the exercises in this chapter, the first setting (General Development Settings) is sufficient.
3. Once Visual Studio is open, access the File menu and click New, Project.
4. In the New Project window, choose Visual C# and choose the Office/SharePoint node from the list of choices in the pane on the left. Expand the Office/SharePoint node and click the Apps node. Click the app for SharePoint 2013, as shown in Figure 29.14.
5. Then select the App for SharePoint 2013 template from the center pane. Name the app **EventApp**, and it will be auto-populated in the Solution Name field. Verify the location where Visual Studio 2012 will create the project folder structure is suitable. Click OK.

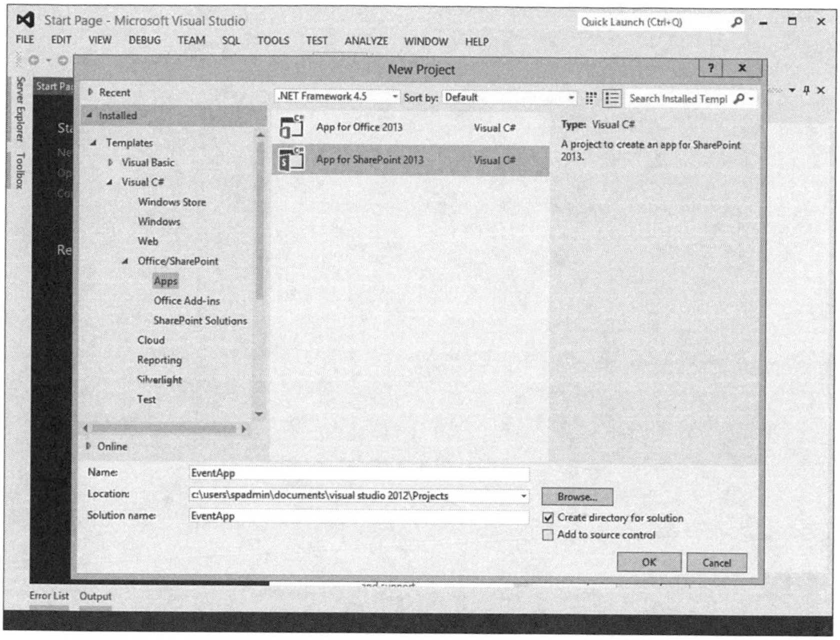

FIGURE 29.14 Creating an app for SharePoint using Visual Studio 2012.

CAUTION

If the account being used does not have sufficient permissions, an error message appears. You might need to restart Visual Studio 2012 by right-clicking it from the Start menu and choosing Run as Administrator.

NOTE

Attempting to deploy an app to a SharePoint site collection that is not configured using the Developer Site template will receive the following error: "Error occurred in deployment step 'Install app for SharePoint': Sideloading of apps is not enabled on this site."

6. The Specify the App for SharePoint Settings window opens. Provide the name **EventApp** for the application, and then enter the URL for the target SharePoint site. Be sure to specify the site that contains the Announcements list. In this example, the URL is http://SharePoint/Sites/Chapter29Dev/. Click the Validate button, and Visual Studio 2012 will verify that the URL responds properly and is running the appropriate version of SharePoint 2013 and should display a Connection Successful message. Click OK to close the message. Select SharePoint-Hosted in the How Do You Want to Host Your App for SharePoint drop-down list, as shown in Figure 29.15, and click Finish. The resulting view should be similar to Figure 29.16.

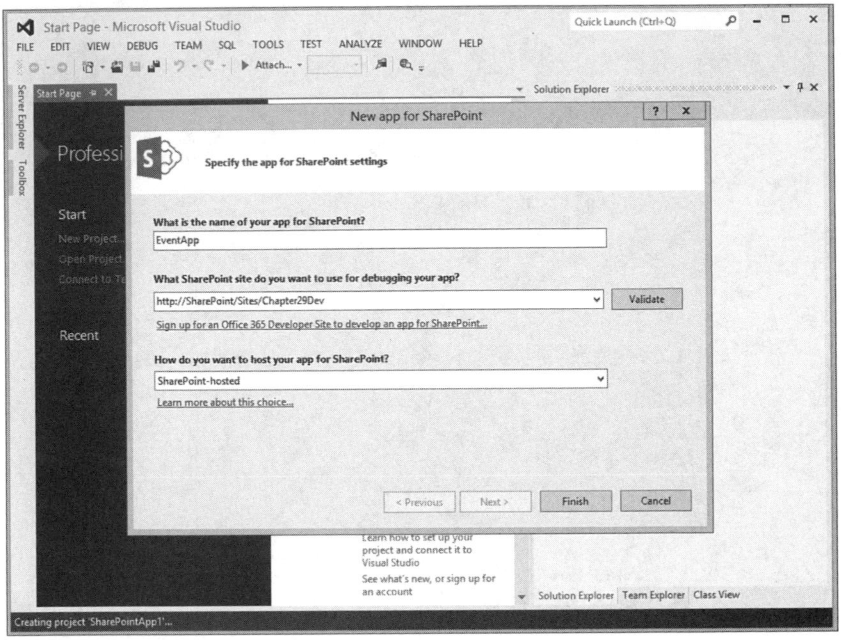

FIGURE 29.15 Choosing the local site that will be used for debugging.

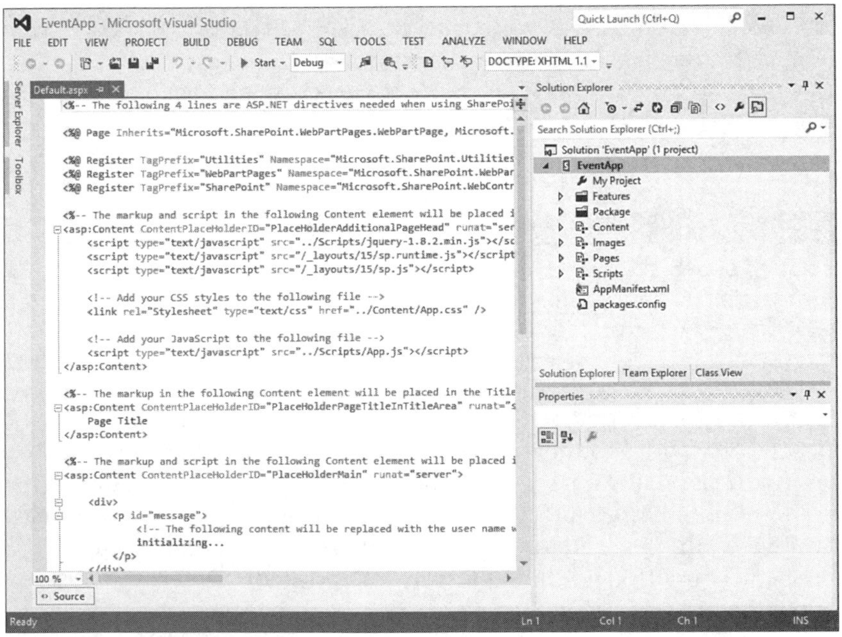

FIGURE 29.16 The new EventApp with the default components configured automatically.

NOTE

Visual Studio 2012 supports development and deployment of apps targeted at Office 365. Developers can sign up for a trial developer site on Office 365 at http://msdn.microsoft.com/en-us/library/fp179924.aspx.

7. Before adding any code or display components to the EventApp, debug the app. Just click the Debug menu, and then click Start Debugging. Alternatively, click the green start arrow. Debugging the app before adding code or UI components allows the developer to verify that the project and development environment are working as expected.

NOTE

An error message may appear after Start Debugging is clicked. This message states "ErrorDetail: Apps are disabled on this site." If this message appears, ensure that apps are enabled on the SharePoint 2013 environment by creating an app catalog site (http://technet.microsoft.com/en-us/library/fp161236.aspx).

8. A browser window will open to the SharePoint site as part of the debugging process. The current user's name should replace the word *Initializing* when the page finishes loading, as shown in Figure 29.17.

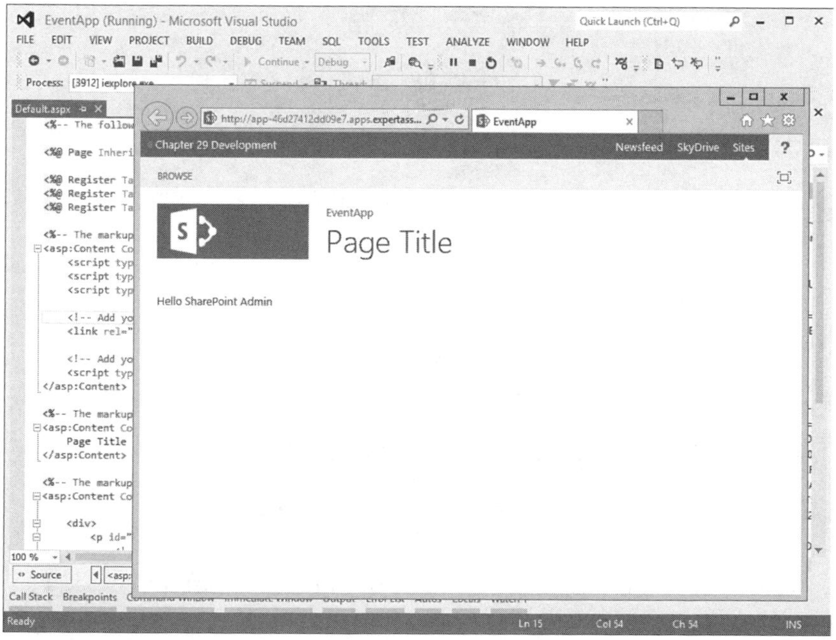

FIGURE 29.17 The default app displaying the current user's name.

9. Close Internet Explorer, and in Visual Studio the debug process will complete. Unlike development in SharePoint 2010, where the solutions were retracted after exiting debug mode, apps remain deployed to SharePoint until explicitly retracted by the developer by choosing Retract from the Build menu.

NOTE

For JavaScript and some .aspx or HTML pages, developers can now make changes in Visual Studio and see the changes in the app after refreshing the page. This time saver allows the developer to continue testing without having to restart the debugging process.

10. To create a page component to display the events, edit the Default.aspx page and add the following HTML within the body. When opened, the EventApp will replace the Loading Events text and replace it with the announcements dynamically pulled from the host site. Figure 29.18 shows the resulting contents of default.aspx:

```
<p id="events">Loading Events...</p>
```

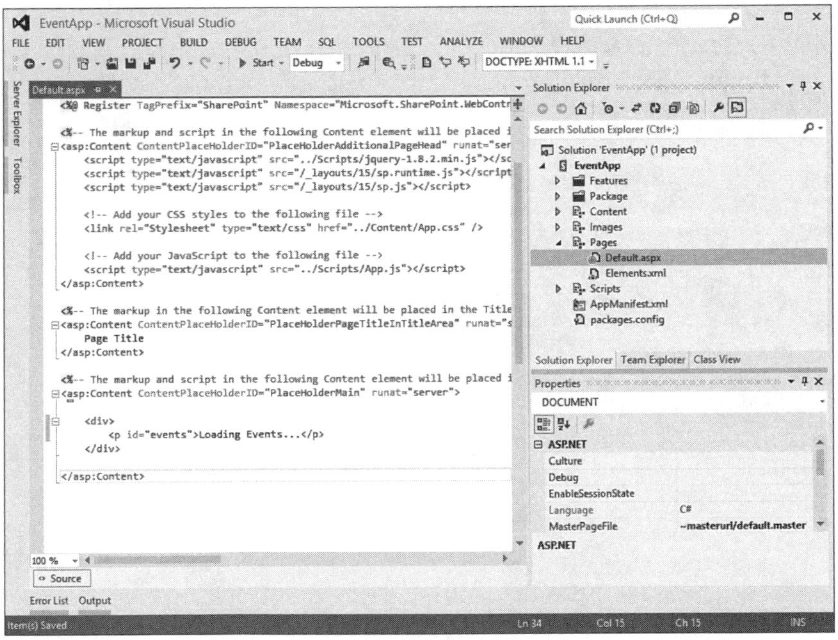

FIGURE 29.18 The default.aspx page of EventApp with an Events placeholder.

11. Delete the portion of the default.aspx that was responsible for displaying the user's name in Figure 29.17. This code is no longer necessary.

```
<p id="message">
        <!-- The following content will be replaced with the user name when you
run the app - see App.js -->
        initializing...
    </p>
```

12. Save Default.aspx, and then from the tree view that appears in the Solution Explorer, click Scripts and open the file App.js.

13. Replace the entire contents of the App.js file with the following code. This JavaScript code is the basis for the EventApp that pulls information from the host site and displays it on the app's Default.aspx page. Save the App.js file when done editing the file. The resulting contents of App.js should appear similar to Figure 29.19:

```
// jQuery function that runs when the document completes loading
$(document).ready(function () {

        // Get the URL for the host SharePoint site
        hostweburl = decodeURIComponent(getURLParameter("SPHostUrl"));
        // Get the URL for the app
        appweburl = decodeURIComponent(getURLParameter("SPAppWebUrl"));
        // Load the library that allows for cross-domain scripting
        $.getScript("/_layouts/15/SP.RequestExecutor.js", getAnnouncements);
});
// Get the announcements from the host site
function getAnnouncements() {
        // Get the app's context
        context = new SP.ClientContext(appweburl);

        // Load the content of the host site
        factory = new SP.ProxyWebRequestExecutorFactory(appweburl);
        context.set_webRequestExecutorFactory(factory);
        appContextSite = new SP.AppContextSite(context, hostweburl);
        web = appContextSite.get_web();

       // Get the announcements list from the host web
       list = web.get_lists().getByTitle("Announcements");
       camlQuery = new SP.CamlQuery();
       camlQuery.set_viewXml(
              '<View><Query><Where><Geq><FieldRef Name=\'ID\'/>' +
              '<Value Type=\'Number\'>1</Value></Geq></Where></Query>' +
              '<RowLimit>10</RowLimit></View>'
       );
       listItems = list.getItems(camlQuery);
```

```
        // Identify the objects to request from the query
        context.load(listItems);

        // Execute the query
        context.executeQueryAsync(
              Function.createDelegate(this, successHandler),
              Function.createDelegate(this, errorHandler)
        );


        function successHandler() {
              var eventHTML = "";
              listEnum = listItems.getEnumerator();
              while (listEnum.moveNext()) {
                    var listItem;
                    listItem = listEnum.get_current();
                          eventHTML += //"ID: " + listItem.get_id() + "<br/>" +
                          "<h1 style='margin-bottom:-15px'>" + listItem.get_
  item("Title") + "</h1><br/>" +
                          "<h3>By " + listItem.get_item("Author") .get_
  lookupValue()    + ", " + listItem.get_item("Modified").toString().substring(0,
  10) + "</h3><br/>" +
                          "<img style='float:left;padding-right:10px' src='" +
  listItem.get_item("Picture").get_url() + "'>" +
                          listItem.get_item("Body") + "<br/>";
              }
              events.innerHTML = eventHTML;
        }

        // Prints the error message to the page.
        function errorHandler(data, errorCode, errorMessage) {
              events.innerHTML = "Unable to load announcements" + errorMessage;
        }
  }

  // Function to get the URL parameters
  function getURLParameter(name) {
        return decodeURI(
              (RegExp(name + '=' + '(.+?)(&|$)').exec(location.search) || [,
  null])[1]
        );
  }
```

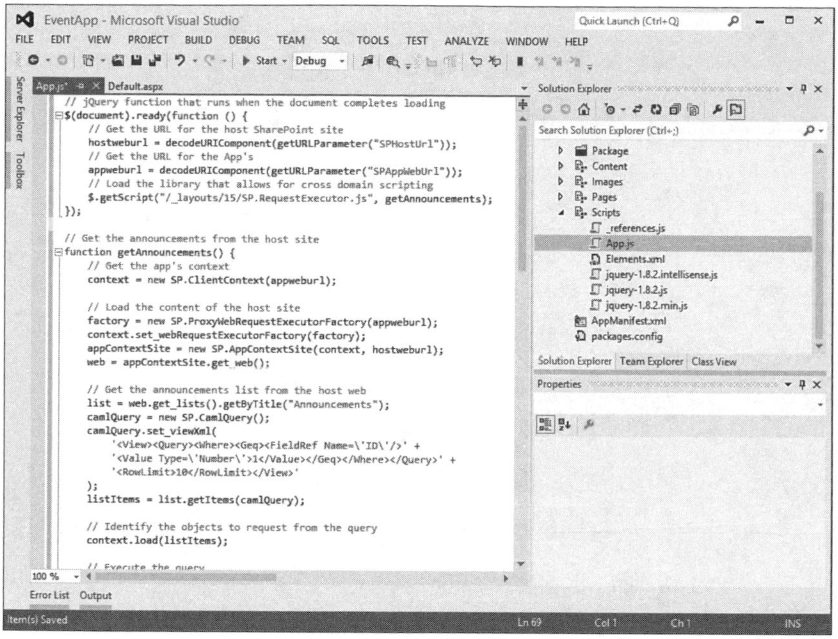

FIGURE 29.19 The code for the EventApp visible in the App.js scripts file.

14. For a SharePoint 2013 app to function in a SharePoint farm, the person responsible for installing the app must grant the app permissions to the host SharePoint 2013 environment. These required permissions are defined by the application developer by identifying different scopes and associated permissions that are required for the app to function. To specify the EventApp's required permissions, open the AppManifest.xml file from Solution Explorer.

15. Click the Permissions tab shown in Figure 29.20 to see the permissions the app will require to run.

CAUTION

For the purposes of this example, the JavaScript directive "use strict" has been omitted from the App.js. This allows for variables to be created and used without first declaring the variable, which makes code files much shorter and faster to write. However, it is not best practice for proper development. After becoming familiar with coding in JavaScript and Visual Studio 2012, be sure to take advantage of the "use strict" feature to ensure proper coding techniques are followed.

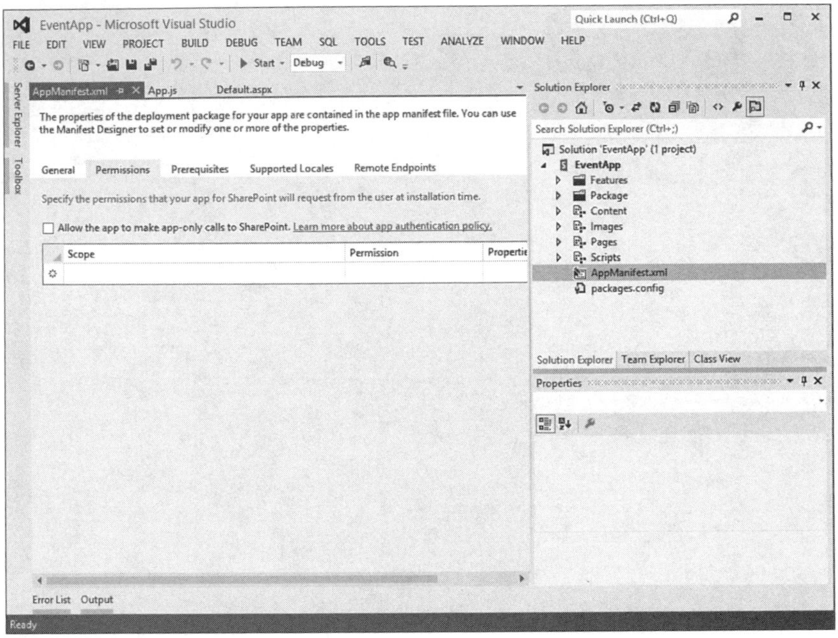

FIGURE 29.20 The AppManifest.xml Permissions tab.

NOTE

Note that Visual Studio 2012 will immediately attempt to compile and validate the code. Any code that Visual Studio 2012 flags as problematic will appear with a red underline. Before debugging or testing the app, these issues must first be addressed.

16. On the AppManifest.xml permissions page, click in the first row of the Scope column and choose Web from the drop-down list that appears. In the Permission column, choose Read, as shown in Figure 29.21.

17. Now test EventApp by clicking the Debug menu and choosing Start Debugging. If errors appear in the output window, attempt to address the errors, which usually specify the offending file and, in some cases, the line number where the error exists.

18. When debugging starts successfully and Internet Explorer opens, a screen appears, as shown in Figure 29.22, asking the user to trust the application. Click the Trust It button; the application will appear as shown in Figure 29.23.

NOTE

Note that an app only needs to be trusted one time when debugging. The screen that asks the user to trust the application will not reappear for subsequent debugging sessions. However, the trust page will appear if the application is deployed by clicking the Build menu and choosing Deploy.

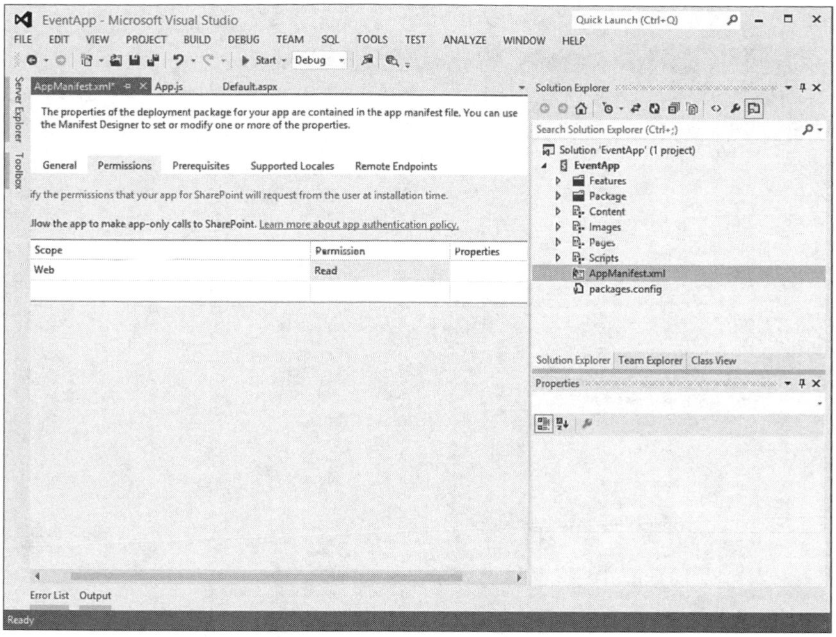

FIGURE 29.21 Applying AppManifest.xml permissions.

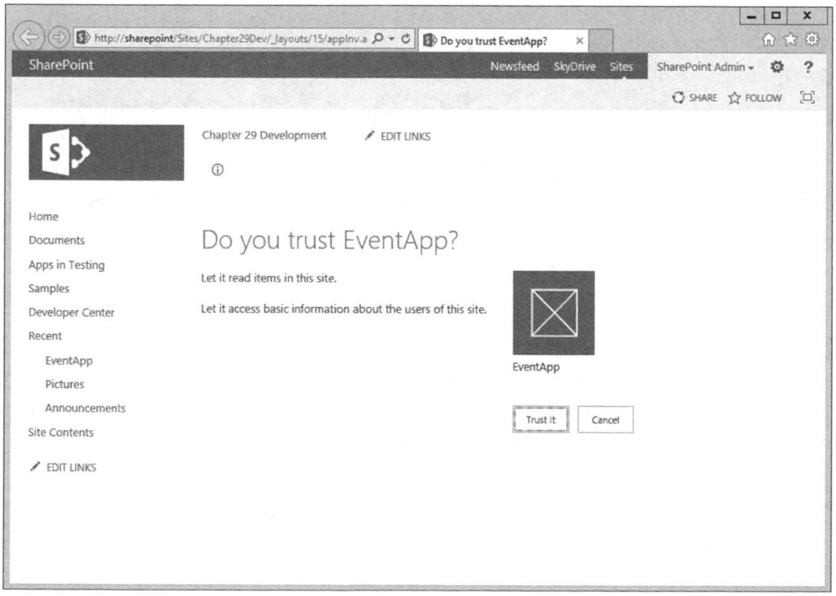

FIGURE 29.22 Approval page to trust an app before use.

29

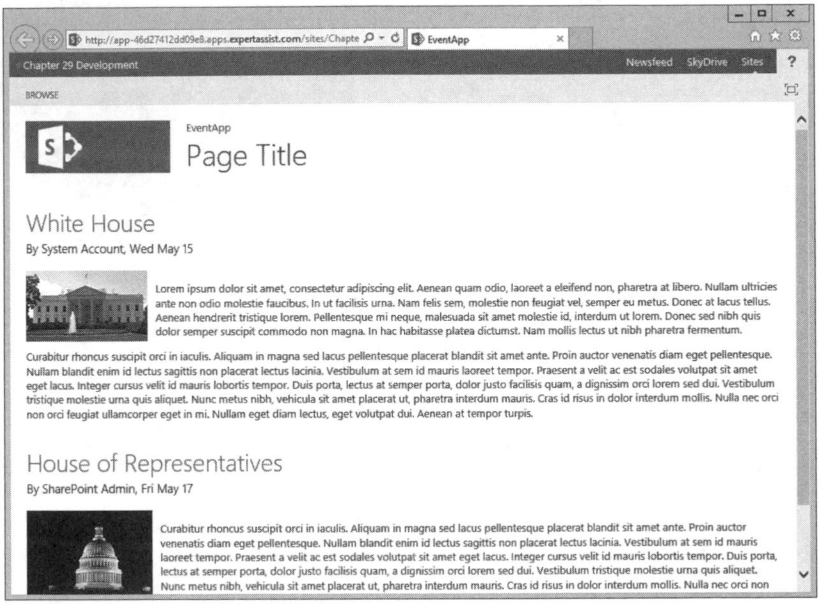

FIGURE 29.23 The EventApp showing events from the host SharePoint site's Announcements list.

19. Without closing the browser window, leave EventApp in debug mode and switch to Visual Studio 2012. Open the App.js from the Scripts node in Solution Explorer if it is not already open and scroll down to the line that starts with `eventHTML+=`. Modify the `eventHTML` code by changing `float:left` to `float:right` in the style property of the `Img` tag. Click Save, and then switch back to the EventApp in Internet Explorer and refresh the page. Figure 29.24 shows the EventApp with the image aligned to the right side of the content. This demonstrates how JavaScript code can be modified without requiring a redeployment of the application.

20. Switch back to Visual Studio 2012 and double-click the margin to the left of the line `events.InnerHTML = eventHTML`. A red dot will appear in the margin signifying a debug breakpoint. Switch back to Internet Explorer and refresh the page. The breakpoint will trigger, and when the cursor is positioned over `eventHTML`, the contents of the variable will be visible, as shown in Figure 29.25. Click the Continue button next to the green arrow in the ribbon to allow the page to continue loading. The Continue button may require multiple clicks before the page completes loading, because the breakpoint is in the middle of a `while` loop that iterates through each event stored in the list.

NOTE

Debugging is a useful method for quickly identifying issues with code. In Visual Studio 2012 and SharePoint 2013, the debugging process is steamlined, with faster deployment and automatic redeployment of client-side code.

FIGURE 29.24 Image alignment changed without redeploying the EventApp.

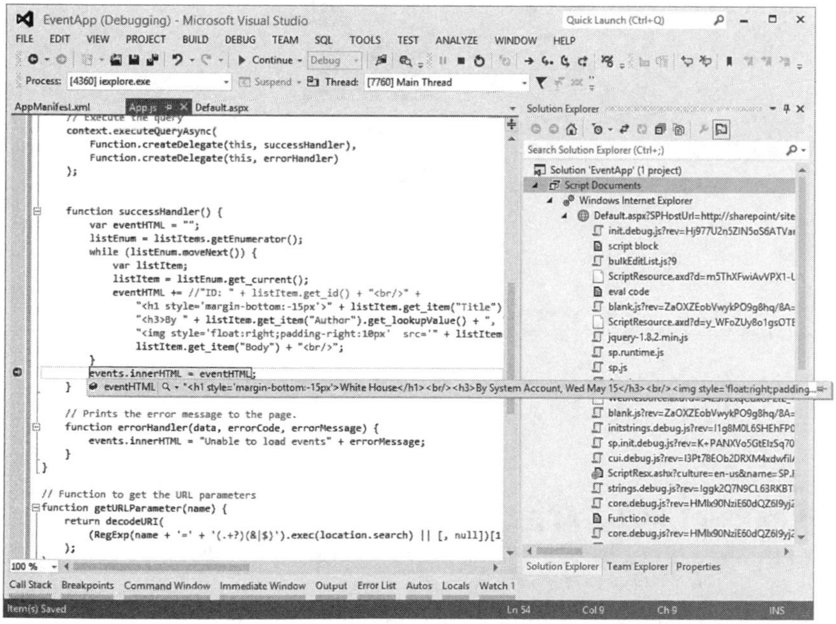

FIGURE 29.25 Debugging the EventApp JavaScript.

21. To stop debugging, choose Stop Debugging from the Debug menu. The Internet Explorer window that displayed the EventApp will close when debugging is stopped. Likewise, if Internet Explorer is closed while debugging, Visual Studio will recognize the change in state and will automatically stop debugging.

The EventApp may not appear to be "earth shattering" in its complexity, but this app displays Announcements in a format that differs significantly from a normal list view web part, an example of which is shown in Figure 29.26. In this regular list view, the column headers cannot be removed, nor can the chrome font sizes be changed, all changes that were accomplished in the App.js code. Also note in Figure 29.23 that the column headers are not included, making the announcements appear more aesthetically pleasing. This is a common request and an example of making a page look "less SharePoint-y."

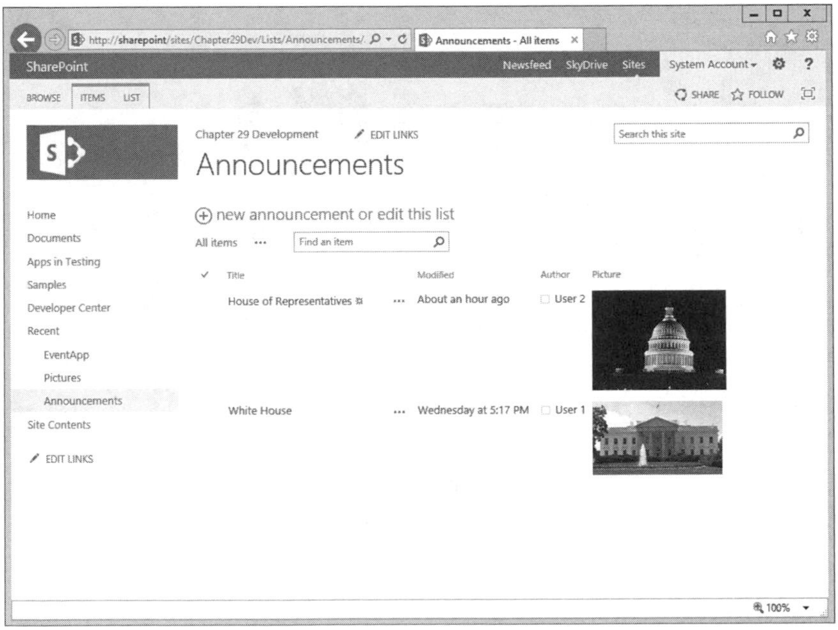

FIGURE 29.26 The original Announcements list as displayed in SharePoint 2013, with additional columns for Author and Picture.

Packaging a SharePoint 2013 App

This section assumes that the previous section was completed successfully and that EventApp displayed as shown in Figure 29.23 (with the exception that most likely a different image was displayed). To deploy the solution to a staging or production machine, follow these steps:

1. With the EventApp solution open in Visual Studio 2012, access the Solution Configuration drop-down menu on the standard toolbar, as shown in Figure 29.27,

visible just beneath the top menu bar. Change the configuration to Release. The next time the project is built, Visual Studio 2012 will generate each project's binaries (DLLs) without the debug symbols, making them optimized for deployment to production environments.

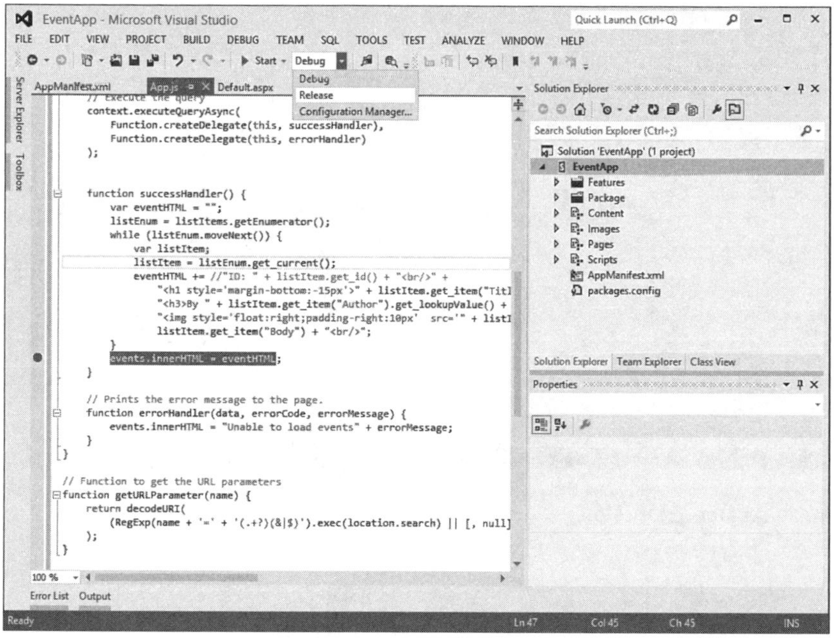

FIGURE 29.27 Changing the project to release configuration for production-ready code.

2. Rebuild the solution by choosing Rebuild Solution from the Build menu.

3. In Solution Explorer, highlight the EventApp project, and then choose Publish from the Build menu, as shown in Figure 29.28. Publishing the app creates a SharePoint application file with the .app extension. The published app file is a compressed .cab file that contains the web part's DLL, its visual components, and a manifest.

4. In the Publish apps for Office and SharePoint window, leave the Open Output Folder after Successful Packaging check box checked, as shown in Figure 29.29. Click Finish.

5. A Windows Explorer window will open upon successful publishing of the app, as shown in Figure 29.30. The file with the .app extension is similar to a SharePoint 2010 solution file that had the .wsp extension, but has a manifest and files that support deployment to the SharePoint 2013 app catalog.

29

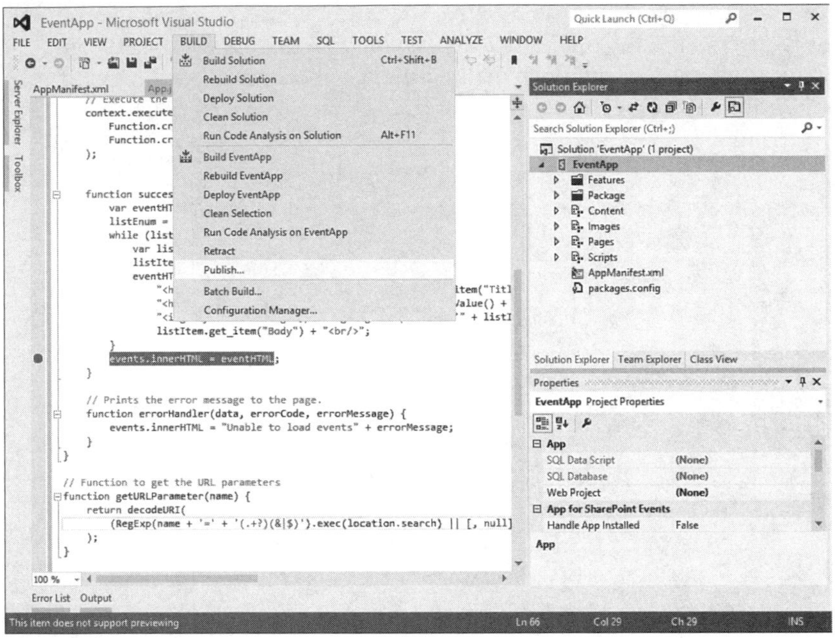

FIGURE 29.28 Publishing the EventApp.

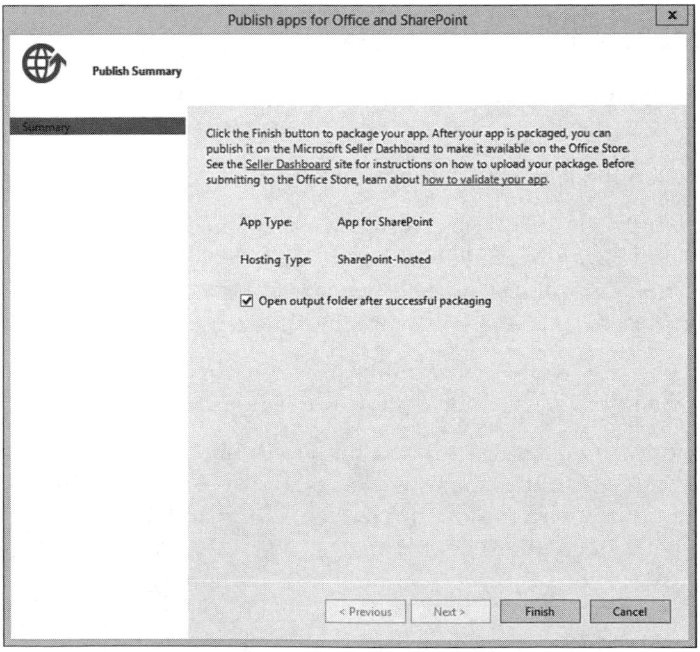

FIGURE 29.29 The Publish Apps for Office and SharePoint dialog.

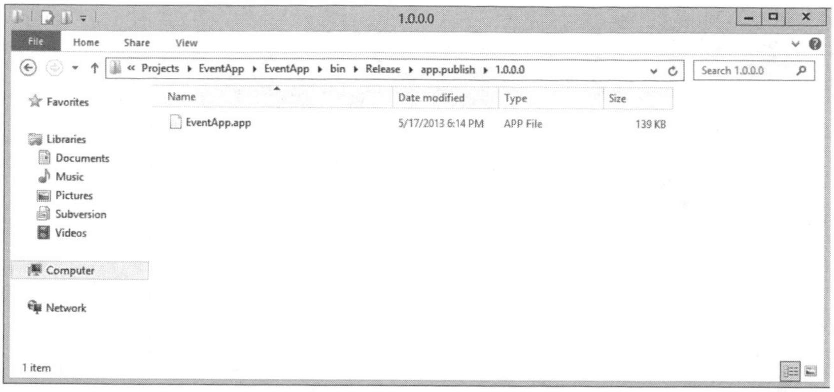

FIGURE 29.30 The .app appears in the project's bin folder after publishing.

CAUTION

The menus that appear on the top of Visual Studio are dynamic and change based on the node that is selected in Solution Explorer. The Publish menu item appears only if the project is highlighted in Solution Explorer and disappears if the Solution node is highlighted.

6. Return to Visual Studio 2012 and retract the debugged version of the EventApp from SharePoint by choosing Retract from the Build menu. This will allow for a clean install of the published app.

7. Open the Developer, which has the URL http://SharePoint/Sites/Chapter29Dev/, and click the Apps in Testing link that appears on the left side. If the EventApp appears in the Apps in Testing link, click the ellipsis and delete the app manually.

8. In the Apps in Testing list, click the New App to Deploy link. Click the Upload link that appears in the If the App Is Stored on the Local Machine, Then Upload it to the Developer Site. As shown in Figure 29.31, in the Upload App dialog, click the browse icon, locate the EventApp.app file and click OK.

9. The Deploy App dialog will again be active with the message "EventApp.app has been successfully uploaded." Verify the site URL, and then click Deploy. Trust the app when the Trust this App window appears.

CAUTION

The SharePoint System account cannot deploy apps.

10. Refresh the Apps in Testing page; EventApp's title will turn into a hyperlink after SharePoint 2013 has successfully installed the app (see Figure 29.32). Click the EventApp title to launch the app.

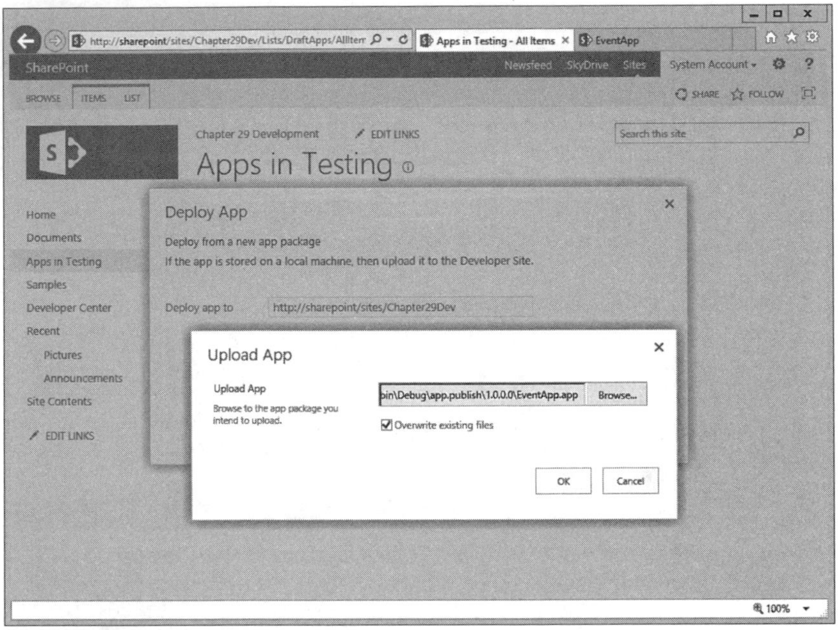

FIGURE 29.31 Uploading an app to the developer site's Apps in Testing list.

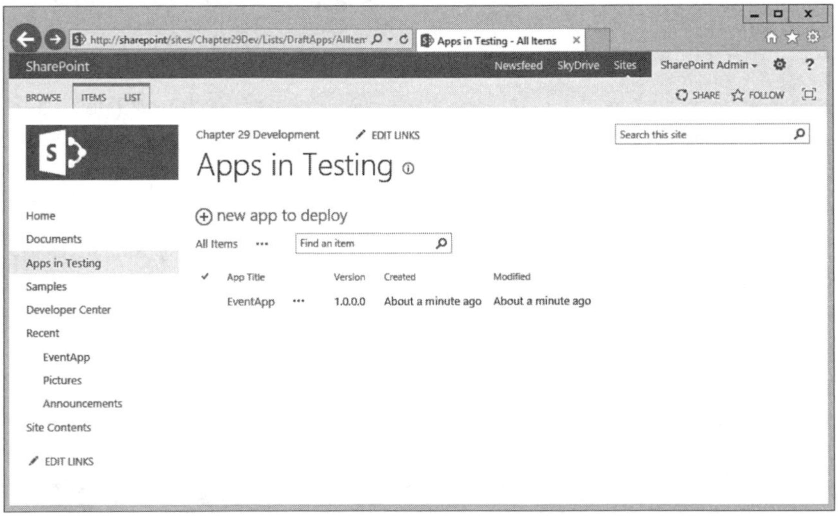

FIGURE 29.32 The EventApp successfully uploaded to the Developer Site's Apps in Testing list.

Summary

This chapter started with some cautionary information about taking time to understand what SharePoint 2013 can do out-of-the-box before deciding to use SharePoint Designer 2013 or Visual Studio 2012 to develop Windows SharePoint 2013 apps, web parts, event handlers, and workflows. In addition, developers should have experience with the .NET platform and preferably C# or VB.NET before delving into Visual Studio 2012 development.

An example of creating a workflow-based application in Designer 2013 was provided that showed how to create a workflow that interacts with several SharePoint lists. The workflow, while demonstrating basic functionality, shows how a power user can quickly develop SharePoint workflows supporting basic needs using a variety of predefined actions and conditions.

The example using Visual Studio 2012 demonstrated the development of the SharePoint 2013 app. The app utilizes many new development features that SharePoint 2013 supports, including the JavaScript Object Model and real-time debugging. The chapter also demonstrated the packaging and deployment of the app.

Best Practices

The following are best practices from this chapter:

- Before delving into Designer 2013 or Visual Studio 2012, confirm whether out-of-the-box SharePoint 2013 features provide capabilities that can meet end-user requests. This is no easy task, because SharePoint 2013, as shown throughout this book, has many new and powerful features such as calculated columns, lookup columns, external data, workflows, alerts, and other tools that might be "good enough" for end users to start with, rather than overbuilding a solution.
- When working with Designer 2013, you should not install Designer 2013 on production servers. Instead, install it on a workstation or on a development or test SharePoint 2013 server.
- Always use a nonproduction server to develop and test code. When a development server is not available, use sandboxed solutions in a nonproduction web application or site collection.
- When installing Visual Studio 2013, check the box that installs Microsoft SharePoint Developer Tools. If the Microsoft SharePoint Developer Tools are not installed, download and install them from http://msdn.microsoft.com/en-US/office/apps/fp123627.
- When possible, utilize a development, staging, and production deployment scenario to minimize the impact on the production environment.
- When developing code for SharePoint 2013 solutions using Visual Studio 2012, you need both Visual Studio 2012 and SharePoint 2013 installed on the same machine.

- When developing code for SharePoint 2013 apps using Visual Studio 2012, you need both Visual Studio 2012 and SharePoint 2013 installed on the same machine or an Office 365 developer site for deploying and testing SharePoint 2013 apps.
- JavaScript code developed using Visual Studio 2012 should begin with a "use strict" directive to ensure developers adhere to coding best practices.
- Many new features in SharePoint 2013 make it better suited to use as a development platform, including the sandboxed solution deployments, client object model, LINQ integration, and enhanced development environments. However, not all projects require direct integration with SharePoint. Take care to evaluate all contingencies, because SharePoint might not be the optimal platform to support the desired solution for many reasons, including licensing, storage requirements, throughput, record count, and security (to list a few).

CHAPTER 30

Business Intelligence in SharePoint 2013 with PerformancePoint Services

IN THIS CHAPTER

- PerformancePoint Services Overview
- What's New in PerformancePoint 2013
- Getting Started with a PerformancePoint Service Application
- Understanding Dashboard Designer
- Creating Dashboards in Dashboard Designer
- Building a Dashboard

Business intelligence (BI) can be thought of in broad terms as the key pieces of information that are used to support business decisions. BI can take many forms—analytical, measurable data, anecdotal information, or factual details. It can be used by people at many different levels of an organization. Senior executives may use high-level analytical sales data to make key decisions about hiring. Mid-level managers may make budget allocation decisions based on available budget and departmental objectives. And project managers may shift project resources based on project-specific factors. Different types of decisions can be made at many distinct times. Regional sales information may be used mid-year to support an increase or decrease in advertising dollars for a particular region. Year-end performance metrics can be used to justify disbursements of end-of-year bonuses. And a customer service agent may utilize customer or product history information during a customer service call.

For information consumers to make the correct decisions, the information they utilize must fulfill three criteria. First, it must be the correct information. Second, it must be current information. Having either inaccurate or out-of-date information leads to bad decisions. Third, it must be available to the people who need the information.

In short, the making of informed decisions is all about the right information being available to the right people at the right time. While a number of systems exist to produce, store, consolidate, or aggregate data, the set of tools available for "surfacing" the information—making it readily available to the information consumer—are historically lacking. SharePoint provides a rich suite of tools whose intended purposes are to bring the information out of their discrete systems and into the hands of the decision makers.

The next two chapters focus on two key BI components of SharePoint 2013. PerformancePoint Services is intended more for top-down views of information; it starts with high-level enterprise metrics, but provides the ability to break numbers down by region, county, product line, time period, and other key dimensions. Tools are provided for building dashboards, scorecards, and key performance indicators (KPIs). Business Connectivity Services, which is covered in the next chapter, is intended for bottom-up views of information, such as details on a product or an order.

PerformancePoint Services Overview

The 2010 version of SharePoint was the first to include PerformancePoint Services as a base part of the installation. The product was born from a merger of Microsoft's Business Scorecard Manager and products acquired from ProClarity. The first version of PerformancePoint was launched in 2007 and was initially sold under a separate license.

In early 2009, Microsoft announced plans to roll it into the SharePoint product. Effective in 2009, owners of the SharePoint Enterprise Client Access License (CAL) became licensed for PerformancePoint; however, it remained a separate installation file. With SharePoint 2010 and now SharePoint 2013, PerformancePoint Services is rolled into the SharePoint 2010 Enterprise installation.

PerformancePoint Services helps provide key decision makers with the ability to measure business performance in real time. This is due primarily to its ability to place rich report creation capabilities into the hands of power users. Users who are interested in seeing real-time analytical metrics will be able to create reports that they can see updated whenever the data changes. No longer will they have to wait on a reporting tool or another department to generate a monthly or quarterly report. In addition, some reports provide interaction for report consumers, which allows them to more deeply analyze specific metrics that are of greater interest. Therefore, they are no longer limited to the information they can glean from predefined report formats. Following are three example scenarios:

- A company's advertising department is trying to target their advertising based on a number of factors. One objective is to help the company achieve its regional and product sales goals. At the same time, a limited advertising budget requires them to make appropriate decisions on where to place advertisements. Every month, advertising dollars are designated to specific television spots with all the major networks. To make the right decisions, the brand managers need to be able to determine which product lines are on track to sell above their target levels and which ones are falling short. By having sales data available immediately, they can make more rapid decisions about where to and how often to place advertisements.

- A sales executive is reviewing sales data for the last quarter. In reviewing a graph of sales, he notices that one product line had lower sales during the period. With one click of the mouse, he can re-form the chart by drilling down into that one product line to view individual products within the product line. He then notices that sales of most products within the product line remained steady during the quarter; however, one specific stock-keeping unit (SKU) underperformed. He could also see how the same data looks on a regional basis. With no individual region standing out as a problem area, he can return to the previous graph. From there, he can once again drill down to see sales for the one product, broken down by monthly or weekly timely periods. Having this power to regenerate graphs on demand will allow people to isolate a problem area, which in turn will let them make the decisions necessary to correct the problem.
- A product manufacturing company has several plants that have been producing below target levels. Several factors could help drive this, including frequency of safety incidents, capacity utilization, availability of just-in-time materials, and several other components. At the same time, other plants may be producing above their target levels. By having the appropriate metrics available to them, executives can strategically shift resources as appropriate to help the plants that are underachieving.

In the coming sections of this chapter, we look at some examples of how the various reports are built and distributed to help drive some of these decisions. We also explore examples of the types of dashboards users might create with the tools available.

What's New in PerformancePoint 2013

The core functionality of PerformancePoint hasn't changed significantly since the 2010 version, but a number of improvements are important to call out because they can affect the implementation and adoption process. The key improvements are as follows:

- **Dashboard migration:** This was a challenge in the 2010 product line, which many organizations complained about. With the 2013 product line, users with sufficient rights can copy complete dashboards and dependencies to other site collections or servers from the SharePoint ribbon. This helps address some of the challenges of moving content from development environments, to staging/quality assurance (QA) or production tiers.
- **Filter enhancements:** Filters are critical in allowing designers and users to change the scope of the data displayed. PerformancePoint 2013 contains new filters, including: show subselections in tree filters, dynamically size the tree filter height, create a filter based off a measure, select different tree filter actions by selecting all, clearing all, and other options.
- **Filter search:** Filter search enables the user to search among filter members. For example, a user can search within certain tree filters, search Analysis Services and PowerPivot data sources, as well as certain other filters.

- **New and improved themes:** Since one of the primary goals of using a BI tool is to communicate information effectively, the overall look and feel of the pages needs to be "cutting edge." Improvements in this area enable more contemporary and dramatic use of SharePoint 2013 themes and branding.
- **EffectiveUsername:** PerformancePoint can now be configured to use the EffectiveUsername property and will add it to the connection string that is passed to analysis services, and the data that is returned is security trimmed to that user. Previously, Kerberos constrained delegation would need to be set up, so this is a welcome feature.
- **New BI Center site:** The look and feel of the BI Center site is updated and simplified, and dashboard components such as PowerPivot and Excel Services are highlighted.

Getting Started with a PerformancePoint Service Application

Before building a PerformancePoint service application, you need to complete a few initial setup steps. The first step of setting up is to configure the web application to use PerformancePoint Services. SharePoint Central Administration utilizes the service-oriented architecture, where service applications can be shared across multiple web applications. One of these service applications is PerformancePoint Services.

NOTE

To configure a PerformancePoint service application, you must have SharePoint Server 2013 Enterprise installed and configured. Neither SharePoint Foundation 2013 nor SharePoint Server 2013 Standard offers the PerformancePoint service application.

Before getting started with a PerformancePoint Services site, you need to have a service established for PerformancePoint Services. It is recommended that a new service application be created for testing purposes, which is done by following these steps:

1. Open SharePoint Central Administration by opening the Start menu and typing **SharePoint**. Click the SharePoint 2013 Central Administration tile.
2. Under Application Management, click Manage Service Applications.
3. In the Service Applications ribbon, select New and then PerformancePoint Service Application from the list. The New PerformancePoint Service Application dialog opens.
4. Enter a name for the service application, which is the name of the PerformancePoint service application itself and needs to be unique. It is helpful to start the name with **PerformancePoint** so that it appears at a logical place in the list of other service applications on the ServiceApplications.aspx page and it is immediately clear what

the purpose of this service application is in the future. Figure 30.1 shows a dialog box example.

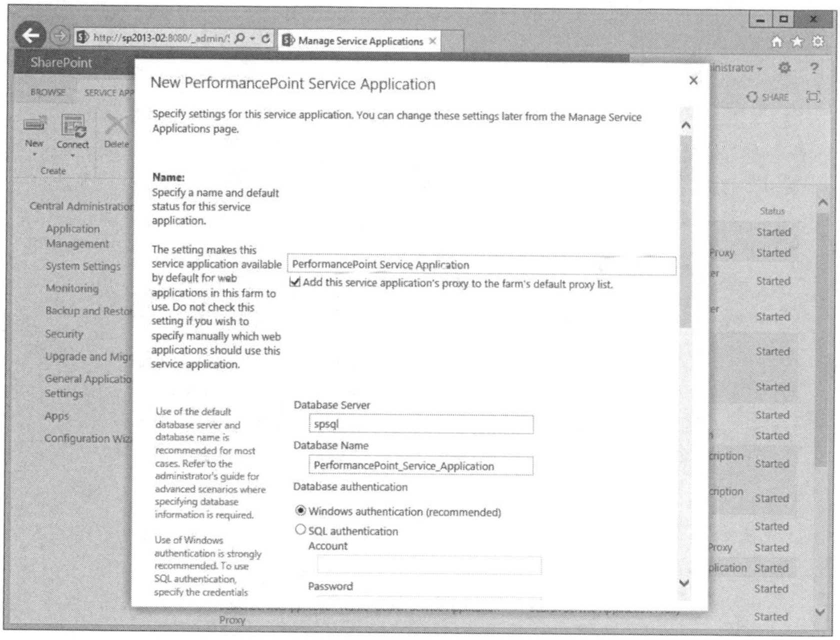

FIGURE 30.1 The New PerformancePoint Service Application Wizard.

You can optionally choose to make this service application part of the Default settings for all future web applications. If you later create additional SharePoint web applications on your SharePoint farm—for example, for additional URLs, such as http://external.mycompany.com and http://projects.mycompany.com—the default set of service applications can be shared among those web applications.

5. Next, enter a database name. The database name will default to have a prefix of PerformancePoint Service Application_, with a unique globally unique identifier (GUID) appended to the end. It is recommended that spaces be removed from the database name and the GUID be replaced with a friendlier name or removed.

6. After you configure the database settings, a reminder indicates that a Secure Store Service application and proxy is also required, as is an unattended service account for the PerformancePoint service application.

7. Choose to use an existing application pool or create a new one. A general best practice is to create a new application pool, bearing in mind that server performance can degrade if there are too many application pools running at once. Then, determine whether to use one of the existing managed accounts or register a new managed account.

8. After applying all the settings, click Create to create the new service application.

The next step is to create a new Secure Store service application, as follows:

1. From Central Administration, on the Manage Service Applications page, on the Service Applications ribbon, click New and select Secure Store Service.
2. Give the new service application a name, such as **Secure Store Service**. Figure 30.2 shows the dialog box for creating a new Secure Store Service application.

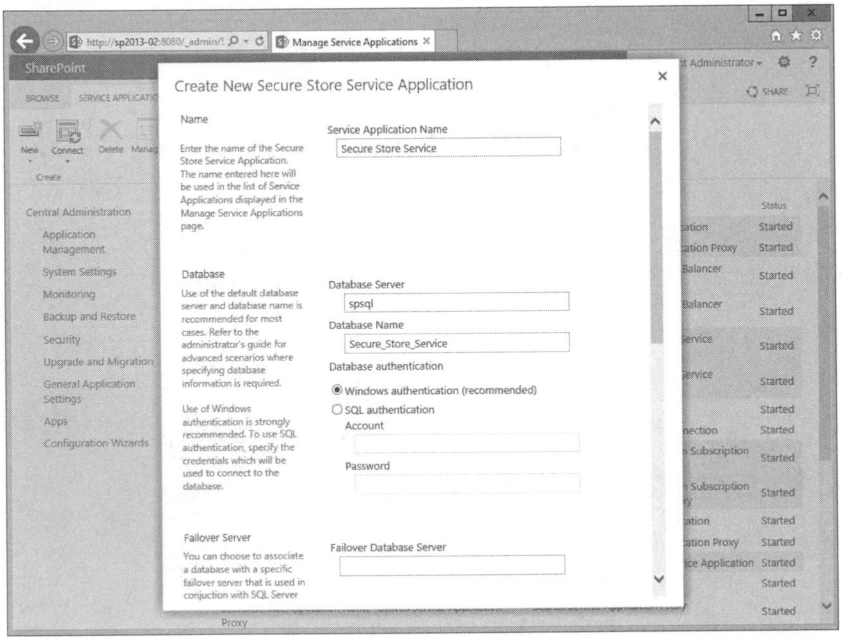

FIGURE 30.2 The New Secure Store Service Application Wizard.

3. The default database name will include a GUID appended to the end of the name, which is recommended to be removed or replaced with a friendlier distinction.
4. Create a new application pool for the service application or use an existing application pool. Remember that too many application pools running simultaneously can degrade server performance significantly. Choose an existing managed account, or register a new managed account.
5. Click OK to create the service application.
6. After the service application has successfully created, refresh the Manage Service Applications page and click the name of the Secure Store Service application that was just created. A message appears: Before creating a new Secure Store Target Application, you must first generate a new key for this Secure Store Service Application from the ribbon.
7. On the Edit ribbon, click Generate New Key.

8. Enter a passphrase for database encryption. This passphrase will be required when adding new Secure Store Service servers and restoring backed-up Secure Store databases. However, this passphrase will not be recorded by SharePoint, so save the passphrase in a safe location for future reference.
9. Click OK to generate a new key.

To configure PerformancePoint and its unattended service account, follow these steps:

1. On the Manage Service Application page, click the name of the PerformancePoint service application. Alternatively, select the PerformancePoint service application item and click Manage on the Service Applications ribbon.
2. Click PerformancePoint Service Application Settings.
3. The Secure Store Service Application field should automatically recognize the Secure Store Service application on the server. Input the credentials to be used for the unattended service account and click OK to finish.

Following completion of the service application creation and configuration, create a new site collection using the BI Center site template. To do so, follow these steps:

1. On the SharePoint 2013 server, return to the home page of Central Administration.
2. Under the Application Management section, click Create Site Collections.
3. On the Create Site Collection page, verify that the web application is the one where you want your PerformancePoint site to be located. Any existing web application can be used. If the desired one is not already selected, click the down arrow in the Web Application box and select Change Web Application. Then change the web application to the correct one.
4. In the Title box of the Create Site Collection page, enter **PPS Sample Site**.
5. In the URL section, select the /sites/ option in the drop-down box, and enter **PPSSample** in the text box.
6. In the Template Selection section, select 2013 under Select Experience Version.
7. In the Template Selection section, click the Enterprise tab, and choose the Business Intelligence Center site template, as shown in Figure 30.3.
8. Enter one or two login accounts to serve as the site collection administrators.
9. Select No Quota in the Quota Template section, because this is for testing purposes.
10. Click OK to create the site collection.

After creating this site, you can begin building a PerformancePoint Services dashboard.

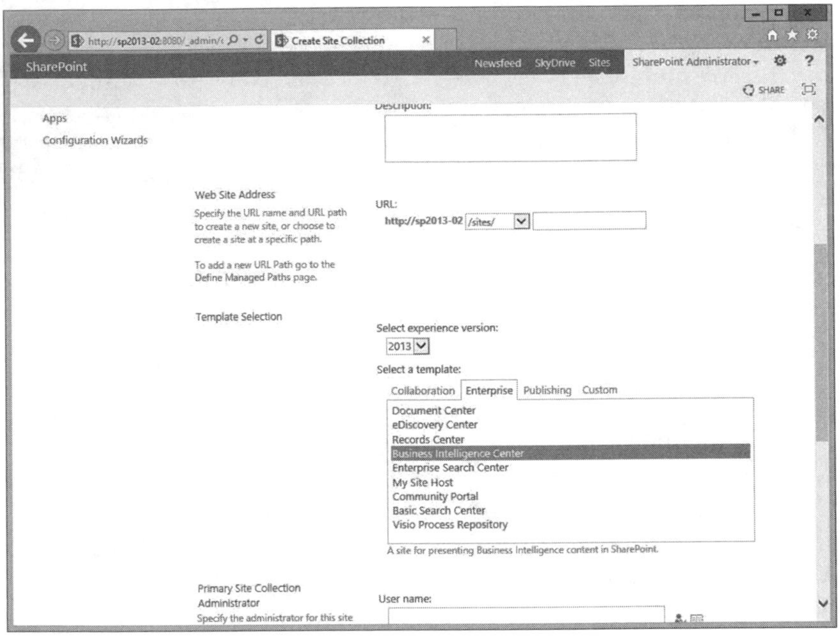

FIGURE 30.3 Create a BI Center site collection.

Understanding Dashboard Designer

A key to understanding PerformancePoint Services (PPS) is to know how to use Dashboard Designer. Dashboard Designer is the client interface for building PerformancePoint reports and scorecards. It provides a drag-and-drop interface for creating the dashboards, scorecards, reports, and KPIs that bring a company's BI and analytical metrics to life. Equally significant is that it allows business users to build reports without having to do any programming.

Many veterans of SharePoint are familiar with SharePoint Designer as one of the tools that allow power users to create SharePoint sites. Dashboard Designer can be thought of as the SharePoint Designer of the PerformancePoint world. However, unlike SharePoint Designer, which is not required for creating and setting up SharePoint sites, Dashboard Designer is a necessary component to creating PerformancePoint dashboards.

Dashboard Designer can be launched as follows:

1. On the SharePoint server, go to the SharePoint site built from the BI Center site template in the previous section. The URL should be http://servername:portnumber/sites/PPSSample/.

2. Click the PerformancePoint Content link on the left sidebar.

3. From this page, click the PerformancePoint ribbon, shown in Figure 30.4, and then click the Dashboard Designer icon. When prompted, click the button to run the executable. The executable downloads and runs.

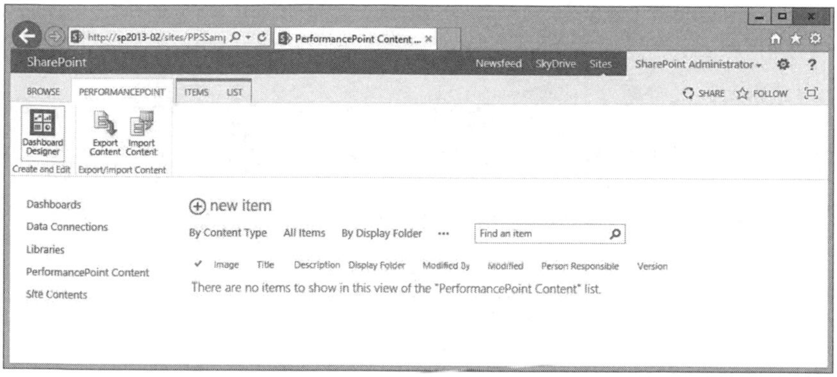

FIGURE 30.4 Launching Dashboard Designer.

After running Dashboard Designer for the first time, a menu option for PerformancePoint Dashboard Designer is added to the Programs menu on the local desktop, in a Programs group called SharePoint. So, all future designing sessions can be launched from the desktop. However, note that no application is actually stored on the desktop, as the shortcut that is added to the Programs menu actually points to the executable that lives on the SharePoint 2013 server.

It is helpful to understand the four main components of Dashboard Designer, which are the Office button, the Office ribbon, the workspace browser, and the working area as shown in Figure 30.5:

- **Office button:** Just like the other products in the Office suites, Dashboard Designer contains the Office button in the upper left. This button contains the usual menu options for New, Open, Save, and Close. There is also a button at the bottom to set specific Designer options.
- **Dashboard Designer ribbon:** Also like all other Office products, Dashboard Designer contains the ribbon interface across the top, as shown in Figure 30.5. Ribbon options include Home, Edit, and Create.

  The Home ribbon allows for operations such as cut/copy/paste, adding items and lists from the SharePoint server to the workspace, and a Delete button to remove items from the server and workspace. There are also a few buttons for comparing server and workspace versions of components. The Home ribbon also contains an Import button that allows for pulling items from one workspace into a new SharePoint site.

  The Edit ribbon provides the ability to apply bulk changes to several items simultaneously.

  The Create ribbon contains icons to instantiate each of the different PPS components that make up a PerformancePoint dashboard. Each of these components is discussed in more detail later.

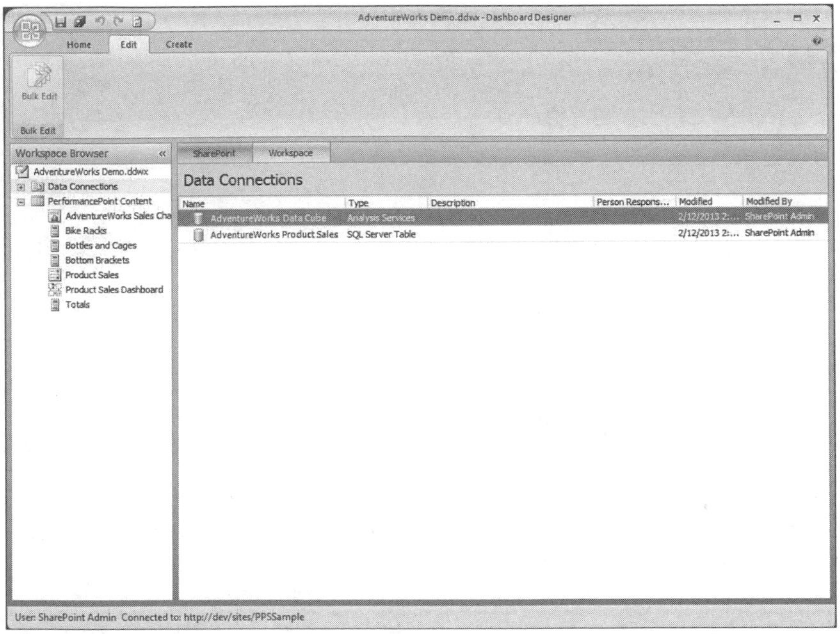

FIGURE 30.5 Dashboard Designer with AdventureWorks Data Connections.

- **Workspace browser:** The workspace browser, displayed along the left sidebar of Dashboard Designer, shows all the components in use in the current workspace. The workspace browser is divided into two groupings. In the Data Connections grouping are the different sources of data that determine how the visuals are displayed. PerformancePoint Content, the second grouping, lists the various visual elements that are being used by the workspace.
- **Working area:** The last section of Dashboard Designer is the working area, which consumes the majority of the Dashboard Designer window. The working area displays two different views: SharePoint and Workspace. As you create new components, copies are stored on both the local computer and the SharePoint Server.

The local, or workspace, versions are bundled together and saved to a local file with a .ddwx extension. The server components are stored in a SharePoint site in a list called PerformancePoint Content.

As you browse through Dashboard Designer, notice a pair of tabs in the PerformancePoint Content section labeled SharePoint and Workspace, as shown in Figure 30.6. The SharePoint tab lists all the content currently stored in the linked SharePoint site. The Workspace tab shows the items that are utilized in the current workspace.

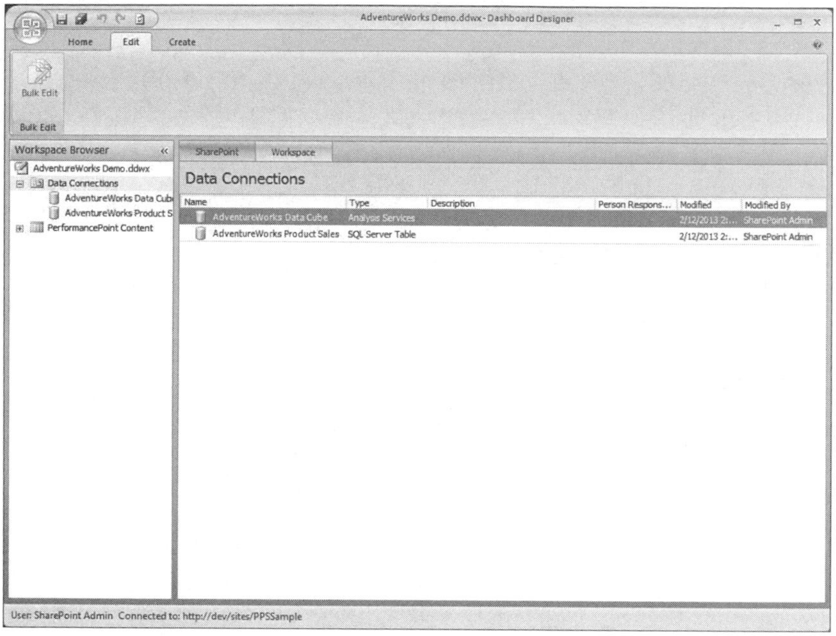

FIGURE 30.6 Dashboard Designer showing data connections for the SharePoint tab.

The reason for having both a local and a server copy of the various PPS components is that multiple individuals or departments may use some common KPIs but would be interested in seeing the data grouped together in many different ways. This fits into the notion of PerformancePoint Server providing a framework where individuals and teams can easily build the reports that are of interest to them.

Consider, for example, shoe sales based on both brand and region, where there are four different geographic regions and six unique brands. Factoring in both brand and region, there are 24 unique combinations of measurements. A brand manager may be interested in seeing just the four KPIs derived from his brand. The manager of the East region, however, may be interested in all six brands, but only how they sold within the East region. While the same figures are being measured, they each have their own set of measurements that they want to monitor. Having the components stored on the server enables reuse of commonly used items, while having the workspace copies for individuals to consume prevents the clutter of unwanted components.

In addition, storing PerformancePoint content in a central SharePoint list allows for many of the same benefits offered by other SharePoint lists. Approval routing, categorization based on metadata, and the application of security to various components are all standard functionality provided to PerformancePoint content.

NOTE

If there is a server component, such as a KPI, that you want to include in your workspace, simply locate it under the Server tab and double-click it. Switch back to the Workspace tab, and you will notice that it has been added to the workspace components. This saves the designer the time of having to otherwise re-create an existing component.

Creating Dashboards in Dashboard Designer

When you have loaded Dashboard Designer, as described in the previous section, you are ready to start creating dashboards in your local workspace.

To begin adding components to be stored on the SharePoint server, a connection to a specific SharePoint site needs to be established. To do so, follow these steps:

1. Click the Office button, and then click the Designer Options button.
2. In the Options dialog box, click the tab for Server.
3. The Server settings tab prompts for a URL, as shown in Figure 30.7. Enter the URL of the SharePoint site where you intend to store your dashboard components.

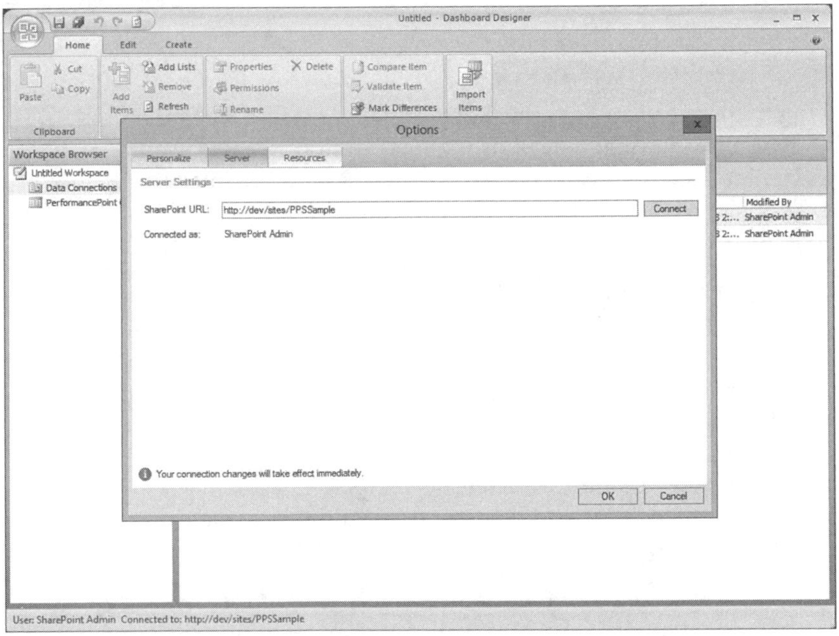

FIGURE 30.7 Set the URL for the SharePoint site in Dashboard Designer Options.

NOTE

The SharePoint site to which you connect does not necessarily have to be based on the BI Center site template. As long as the site to which you connect has the feature titled PerformancePoint Services Site Features activated, you can use this site in the SharePoint URL box of Dashboard Designer.

In the coming sections, you learn about the different components available to create dashboards.

Data Connections Defined

The first thing to design and plan out when building dashboards in PerformancePoint is which data connections to use. The data connections are links to any externally generated and maintained set of data on which the dashboard components will be based. Data can come from any of the following types of sources:

- SQL Server Analysis Services
- Excel components from either Excel Services or Excel Workbooks
- SharePoint lists
- SQL Server tables

Recall that BI in SharePoint is not about creating data or determining how to organize it. SharePoint's focal point is about surfacing the data—making it available, presentable, and consumable for those who need to make key business decisions. Therefore, a key prerequisite to doing anything with PerformancePoint Services is to have the right data repositories already in place.

In Dashboard Designer, you can create all new components from either of two places. The Create ribbon contains a series of icons for the various components. In addition, from the workspace browser, you can right-click the Data Connections grouping and select the appropriate option.

Key Performance Indicators (KPIs)

A KPI is a measurement against a specific, measurable objective. It is one specific numeric measurement, comparing an actual result to a target result.

When creating a new KPI, the subsequent KPI Details screen presents two rows—an actual and a target value. Both fields can be input manually in this screen. Alternatively, the values for these items will come from one or more of the predefined external data sources.

For example, consider a multidimensional data source Annual Shoe Sales. The data source may have dimensions for product line, region, and size, as well as measures for dollar sales and unit sales. Results from this data source can be used as the actual value.

Consider also a SharePoint list that contains a set of target values for each product line in the various regions. Each KPI can be configured to point to items in the SharePoint list as their target values.

As either the target or the actual value changes in the data source, the resulting KPI is automatically updated.

Indicators

KPIs are usually presented in a graphical fashion, using visual indicators. An indicator can be any type of visual display that represents the degree to which the target measurement has been achieved or exceeded. Examples of indicators include fuel gauges, thermometers, stop lights, and many others.

Each indicator is divided into multiple levels, each of which displays differently. A stop-light indicator, for example, might have three indicators—red, yellow, and green. A green level would visually demonstrate that the target measurement has been achieved or exceeded. A yellow indicator would show that the actual result is slightly off-target. And a red indicator would mean that the actual is farther off-target.

They say a picture is worth a thousand words, and KPIs make this adage a reality. When viewing multiple KPIs on a single scorecard, a manager can very quickly scan through the KPIs to quickly identify and root out those that are off-target, and focus on those that warrant additional investigation.

When creating a new indicator, a number of different visual indicators are available, as shown in Figure 30.8.

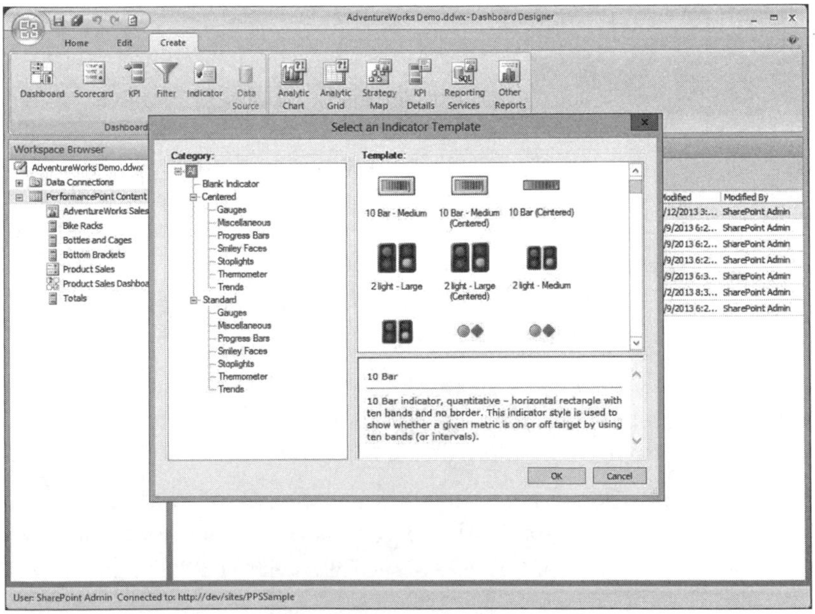

FIGURE 30.8 Different indicator template styles available for KPIs.

Different indicators serve different purposes and visually convey different messages. For example:

- The various "trending" indicators display arrows in various colors: red, yellow, and green—and pointing in various directions. These indicators would be useful for KPIs that compare the results of a previous period to the current one.
- Some indicators—Stoplights and Smiley Faces, for example—are helpful in demonstrating targets versus actuals at the end of a measurable period of time. Use these indicators to show how sales figures at the end of a year or quarter compare to their corresponding target measurements.
- The set of Bar, Cylinder, Gradient, and Gauge indicators might be appropriate for showing progress during the middle of a measurable period of time. They might be appropriate in scenarios where you want to present things like amount of budget exhausted, month-to-date or year-to-date figures versus the corresponding targets for the month or year. Because the measure would continue to change over the course of the measurable period, this set of indicators would convey the amount of progress toward a specific goal. Halfway through the month or quarter, you would expect to see progress of halfway (or better) toward the goal.

Besides the display style for indicators, there are a couple of other settings that you can apply to make the indicator set unique. KPIs can have both positive and negative measurements. With targets such as sales volumes, the more the better. Thus, with a positive KPI, exceeding the target result is good. However, for a measurement such as number of safety incidents, the fewer the better. Thus, staying at or below the target level is preferable. When defining indicators, designers can specify whether more is better or less is better.

In addition, for each level within a set of indicators, you can specify the percentage toward the actual goal that applies to each level. For some goals, 75% of the total may be considered "slightly off target," whereas for other measurements, 75% would be considered "way off target."

Scorecards

KPIs are the individual measurable goals. A number of KPIs are grouped together to form a scorecard. For example, on a Capacity Utilization scorecard, each factory could represent a unique KPI. All the company's factories could be grouped together to display a single scorecard. In this example, a similar measurement would show in each KPI on the scorecard, where only the dimension changes in each row. Another type of scorecard might focus on different measurements for the same dimension. For example, a scorecard for a single factory could have KPIs for number of safety incidents in the current and recent quarters, total amount of down time per time period, and units produced per time period.

A scorecard is an example of a report about the achievement of measurable goals. The scorecard will show a series of measurements, along with the target amount, and the degree to which the target has been reached. The scorecard can provide either a visual or numeric indication to show to what degree the goal has been attained.

In the PerformancePoint world, a scorecard represents the same thing: a set of measurable goals and their corresponding levels to which those goals have been attained. Ultimately, a scorecard is displayed as a web part on a SharePoint page.

Each scorecard will contain a set of KPIs. Scorecard examples include the following:

- Sales volumes, with specific KPIs for each region
- Capacity utilization, with factories making up the individual KPIs
- Number of safety incidents, with per-plant line items
- Customer service complaints, based on product line

Alternatively, a plant manager's scorecard might show a number of disparate measurements that demonstrate the overall performance of his plant. The following KPIs, when grouped together on a scorecard, might be useful in determining the plant manager's compensation:

- Number of safety incidents
- Capacity utilization
- Units manufactured

When provisioning a new scorecard, you have three categories of scorecards from which to choose, as follows:

- **Microsoft:** This category allows for a scorecard based on Analysis Services, which requires that you have a corresponding data source based on SQL Server Analysis Services.
- **Standard:** This category allows you to create either a blank or fixed value scorecard. These two options allow you to add KPIs created and manually added to your workspace.
- **Tabular:** This category contains several options for creating KPIs based on various table-centric data sources. Like the Analysis Services scorecard, selection of any of the scorecards in this category requires you to have a data source based on the corresponding KPI type.

Some of the scorecard types allow you to define additional KPI measurements as part of the creation process. In addition, when the scorecard is created, you can drag additional KPIs onto the scorecard.

Figure 30.9 shows a scorecard for sales per product line. Notice that some KPIs are on-target, while one is slightly off-target. Notice also that KPIs on a scorecard can be rolled up into a parent KPI (All Products), to show how the grouping as a whole is performing.

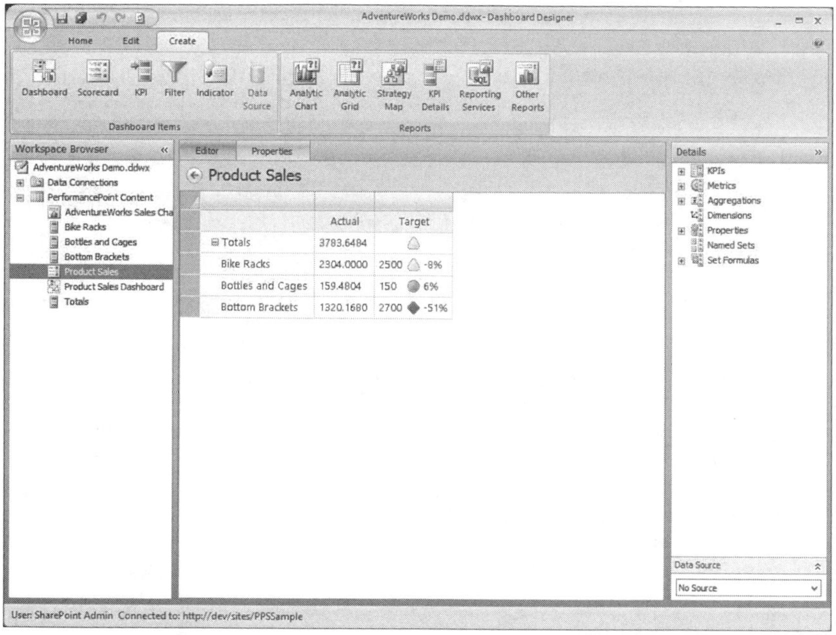

FIGURE 30.9 Sample Product Sales scorecard.

Reports

Like scorecards, reports in PerformancePoint are ultimately displayed as a web part on a SharePoint page. Reports can be of several different varieties, each of which requires you to have a corresponding data source of the same type:

- **Analytic Chart:** Interactive charts, based on online analytical processing (OLAP) cube data, such as SQL Server Analysis Services, can be in bar, line, and pie chart format
- **Analytic Grid:** Also based on data from OLAP cubes, analytic grids display rows and columns of processed data
- **Excel Services:** Allows for views of any components from Excel Services
- **KPI Details:** View detailed information about any KPI line item
- **Reporting Services:** Display an existing SQL Services Reporting Services report
- **Strategy Map:** Visually connect shapes from a Microsoft Visio diagram to a scorecard
- **Web Page:** Reference an existing web page

One popular report type is the Strategy Map, which allows dashboard designers to create heat maps, such as a map of the United States, where individual states change colors based on performance.

Of all the report types, the Analytic Chart is one of the most interesting and most often used by organizations. When connecting to a well-defined Analysis Services OLAP data source, you can drag any combination of relevant measures and dimensions to the series and Axis sections to quickly spin up various charts.

Even more interesting, however, is the ability to click any data point within the chart and drill down to see how the chart changes based on the selected factor. Imagine the power of an executive viewing corporate sales data to be able to re-create the chart, on-the-fly, based on any of the following:

- Salesperson
- Region
- Product line
- Year, month, quarter, week, or day
- Customer

Figure 30.10 shows a simple report showing the progression of sales on a quarterly basis. Notice that the user, when viewing the chart, has several options. He can drill down to view the chart based on one of the other dimensions. In addition, he can sort, filter, pivot, and perform a number of other additional actions.

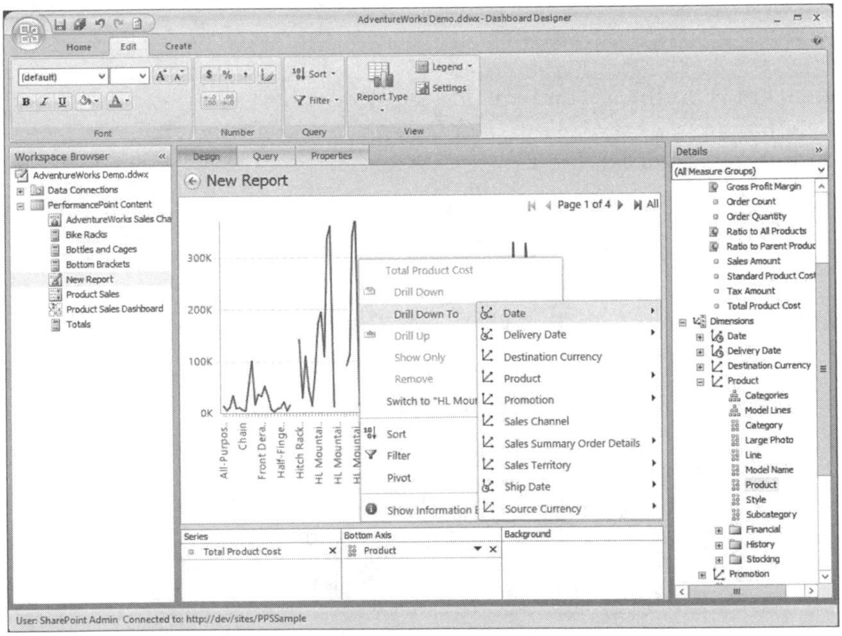

FIGURE 30.10 Drilling into information data using key data dimensions.

Dashboards

A dashboard is loosely defined as having a lot of visual information, displayed in a number of different ways, on a screen for a user to quickly assess the current state of affairs. A car's dashboard, for example, provides the driver with important information about the current state of the car—how fast the car is going, the current engine temperature, the amount of fuel in the tank, and many other things.

Similarly, a web dashboard provides a manager with several key pieces of information about the current state of affairs. The previous sections discussed how reports and scorecards are ultimately displayed as web parts on SharePoint pages. In the SharePoint and PerformancePoint world, a dashboard can also be thought of as a web part page. In fact, when creating a new dashboard in PerformancePoint Server, a new page is added to the SharePoint Pages library, which, when published, can be viewed by authorized users.

Like all the other PerformancePoint components discussed previously, a new dashboard page can be created from one of two places: the Create ribbon or the workspace browser. If you're accustomed to creating new pages in SharePoint from the various layout pages available, the first screen of the New Dashboard interface should be pretty familiar. On this screen, you are presented with a set of dashboard page templates, each of which provides a unique combination of web part zones. Select the zone that is right for you for the data you want to display.

NOTE

Users are not ultimately tied to the page layout that was initially selected. If the user right-clicks any existing dashboard page zone, she can add new zones, split a zone into two, delete the zone, or change the existing zone's settings. Using these options, she can essentially change the whole layout of the page she started with.

After selecting a template, a Details pane is displayed on the right side of Dashboard Designer (as shown in Figure 30.10). As you create scorecards and reports, or grab existing ones from your SharePoint site, those elements become available for you to drag—essentially as web parts—onto your dashboard page. Simply drag the appropriate ones to the various zones available.

Building a Dashboard

Now that each of the components of Dashboard Designer has been presented, we're ready to walk through setting up a dashboard. The first step in this exercise is to download and install the AdventureWorks sample databases, as follows:

NOTE

You need a server running SQL Server 2012 and SQL Server Analysis Services to proceed with this exercise.

1. To get started, you need a couple of data sources to work with. Download and install the AdventureWorks sample databases from CodePlex.
2. Click Download the SQL Server 2012 DW and SQL Server 2012 LT product sample databases from http://msftdbprodsamples.codeplex.com/releases/view/55330. Save the file to a machine running SQL Server 2012.
3. When the files have finished downloading, extract the files.
4. Attach the databases to SQL Server 2012 Database Engine.

Preparing the Data Sources

Next, compile and build the AdventureWorks data warehouse by completing the following steps:

1. On the SQL Server 2012 machine, download AdventureWorks Multidimensional Models for SQL Server 2012 from http://msftdbprodsamples.codeplex.com/downloads/get/258486.
2. Unzip the file and double-click AdventureWorksDW2012Multidimensional-EE.sln from the Enterprise folder. Open the solution file with Visual Studio 2012.
3. From the Solutions Explorer, right-click the solution name and select Deploy.

Next, create a new view in the AdventureWorksLT database, as follows:

1. Launch SQL Server Management Studio from the Programs area.
2. Connect to the SQL Server instance where you installed the AdventureWorksLT2012 database.
3. In the Object Explorer, expand the databases node, and then the AdventureWorksLT2012 node.
4. Right-click the Views node and select New View.
5. Close the Add Table dialog box, and enter the following directly in the text box, as shown in Figure 30.11:

```
SELECT PC.Name AS ProductCategory, SOD.UnitPrice, SOD.OrderQty, SOD.UnitPrice
* SOD.OrderQty as TotalSales, SOH.OrderDate
FROM SalesLT.SalesOrderDetail AS SOD
INNER JOIN SalesLT.Product AS P ON SOD.ProductID = P.ProductID
INNER JOIN SalesLT.ProductCategory AS PC ON PC.ProductCategoryID =
P.ProductCategoryID
Inner JOIN SalesLT.SalesOrderHeader SOH on SOH.SalesOrderID = SOD.SalesOrderID
```

6. Save the view with the name **vw_ProductCategorySales**.

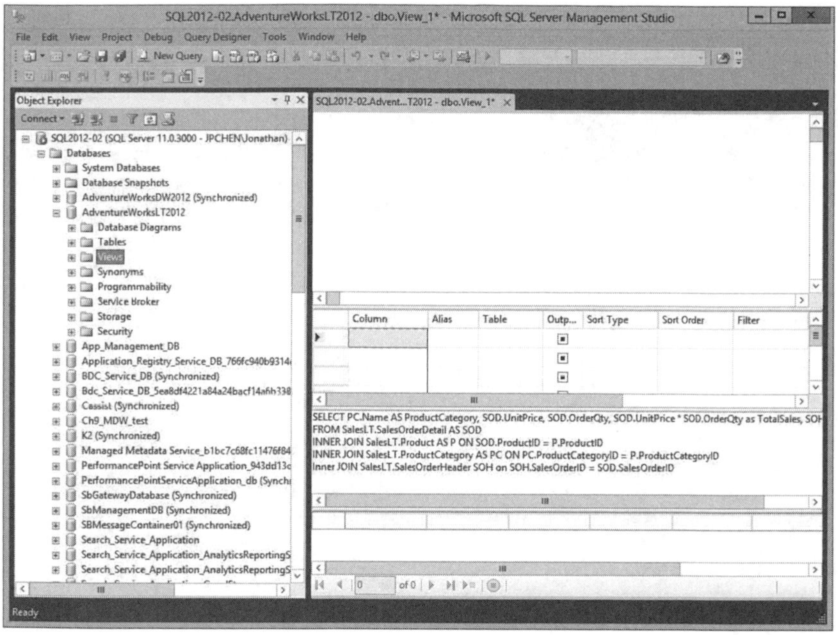

FIGURE 30.11 Create a new view on the AdventureWorksLT database.

Creating Data Connections

At this point, a lot of the initial plumbing is in place, and you are ready to start building a dashboard.

Start by creating at least two data sources to be used by the PerformancePoint Content. To create these, follow these steps:

1. In the Workspace Browser of Dashboard Designer, click Data Connections.
2. On the Create ribbon, click Data Source, as shown in Figure 30.12. Note that when Data Connections is selected in the workspace browser on the left pane, Data Source is enabled and all other items disabled. When PerformancePoint Content is selected, Data Source is disabled, and all other items enabled.
3. In the Select a Data Source Template dialog box, select SQL Server table and click OK.
4. In the Editor tab of the data source settings, configure the data source. In the Server text box, enter the name of your SQL Server instance where you installed the AdventureWorksLT database, as shown in Figure 30.13. For example, enter **sql2012-02**.
5. After you enter the server name, the Databases list box is enabled. Click the down arrow for the Databases list box. A list of databases on the server loads. Select AdventureWorksLT2012.

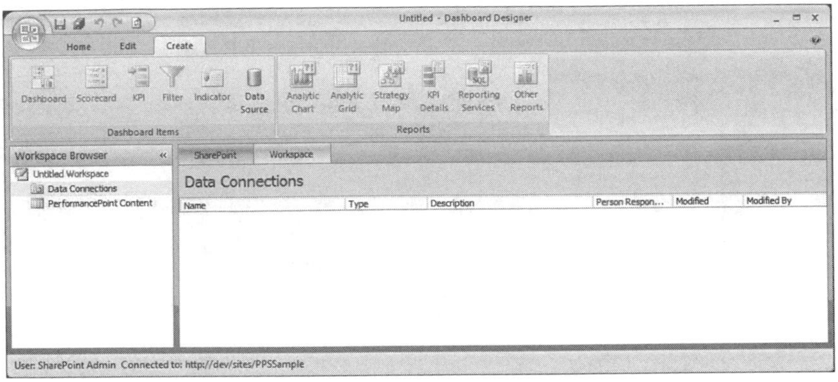

FIGURE 30.12 Create tab on the ribbon for Dashboard Designer.

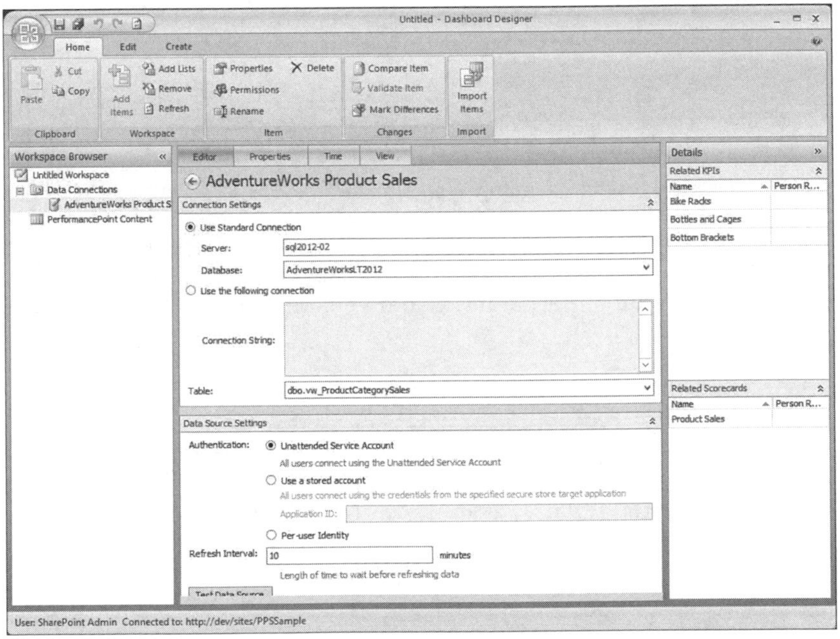

FIGURE 30.13 Connection settings for the AdventureWorks Product Sales data connection.

6. Click the down arrow for the Tables list box. Note that both SQL Server tables and views appear in this list, sorted alphabetically. Select dbo.vw_ProductCategorySales.

7. Click the Test Data Source Connection button.

8. Switch to the Properties tab in Dashboard Designer, and change the Name of the Data Source to **AdventureWorks Product Sales**. Click the Save icon (located in the top-left corner of Dashboard Designer, next to the Office button) to add the new data source to your SharePoint site.

9. Preview the data by selecting the View tab of the data source properties, as shown in Figure 30.14. Click the Preview Data button, and the data loads in five columns: ProductCategory, Unit Price, OrderQty, TotalSales, and OrderDate.

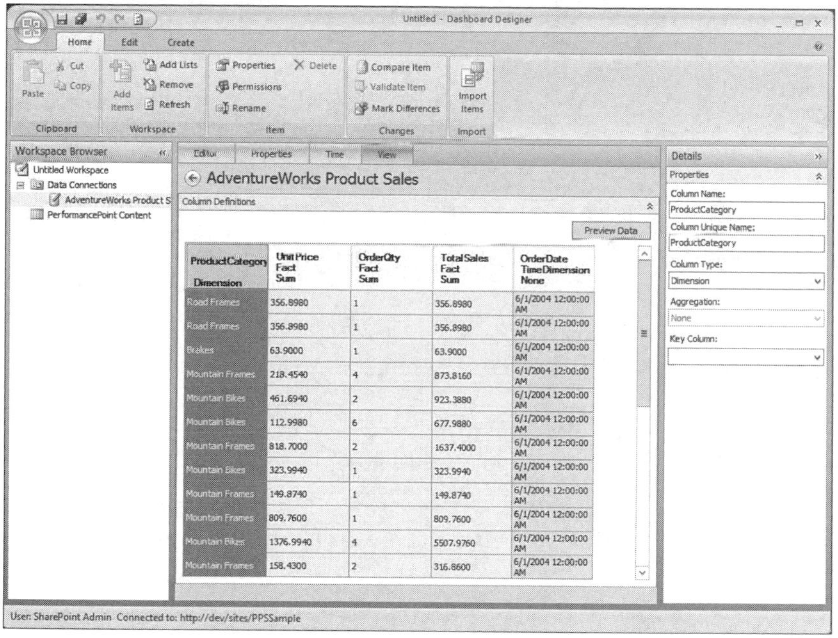

FIGURE 30.14 Preview of data in the AdventureWorks Product Sales Data Connection.

Next, you need to create a second data source, this time connecting to an SQL Server Analysis Services data cube. To do so, follow these steps:

1. On the Create ribbon, click the Data Source icon.
2. In the Select a Data Source Template dialog box, this time select Analysis Services.
3. In the connection settings, in the Server text box, enter the name of the SQL Server Analysis Services server where you installed the AdventureWorks DW cube, as shown in Figure 30.15. In this example, the database server is SQL2012-02.
4. In the Database list box, select AdventureWorksDW2012Multidimensional-EE.
5. In the Cube list box, select Sales Summary.
6. Click the Properties tab, and change the Name to **Adventure Works Data Cube**.

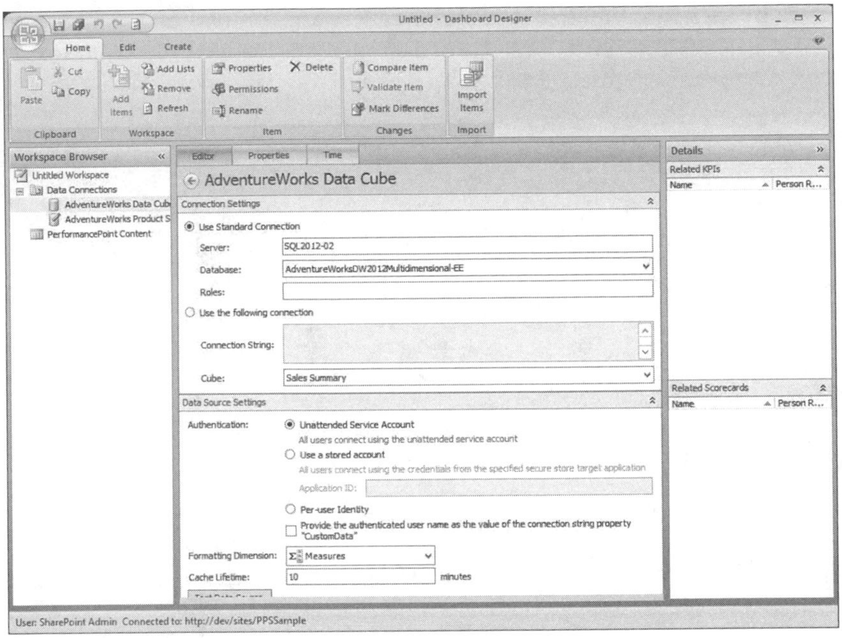

FIGURE 30.15 Creating a data connection to the AdventureWorks Data Warehouse.

Creating KPIs

Now that the data connections are in place, the next step is to begin creating a few KPIs. To do so, follow these steps:

1. In the Workspace Browser, click PerformancePoint Content.
2. On the Create ribbon, click KPI.
3. In the Select a KPI Template dialog box, select Blank KPI and click OK.
4. In the Workspace Browser, rename the KPI to **Bike Racks**.
5. Next, configure the actual value for the KPI to use the database. In the Actual row, click 1 (Fixed Values) under the Data Mappings column. In the Dimensional Data Source Mappings dialog box, click the Change Source button. In the Select a Data Source dialog box shown in Figure 30.16, click AdventureWorks Product Sales, and then click OK.
6. In the Dimensional Data Source Mapping dialog box, click the arrow for the Select a Measure list box and select TotalSales.
7. In the Select a Dimension section, click the New Dimension Filter icon.

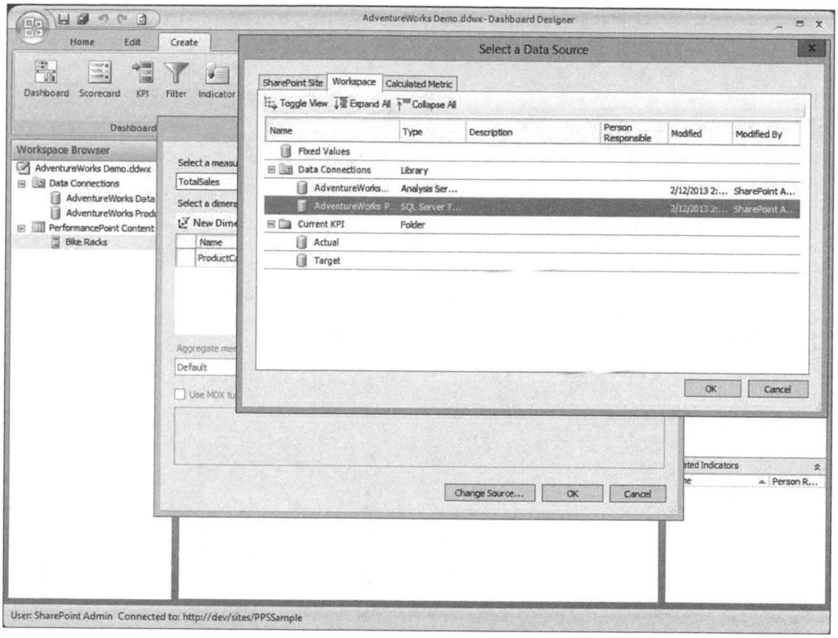

FIGURE 30.16 Configuring the Bike Racks KPI.

8. In the Select a Dimension dialog box, select ProductCategory and click OK.
9. In the Default column, click the Default link, and select Bike Racks in the Select Members dialog box. Click OK.
10. Next, configure the target value against which the KPI will be measured. In the Target row for the KPI, click 1 (Fixed Values), enter **2500** for the Value, and click OK. When complete, your KPI settings should look like Figure 30.17.
11. When selecting the Target row of the KPI settings, in the bottom half of the KPI settings, you can optionally select a different indicator by clicking on the Set Scoring Pattern and Indicator button. Step through the wizard, but do not make any changes.
12. Repeat steps 1 through 10 for a second KPI. For the KPI name, use **Bottles and Cages**. For the KPI Actual value, again use **Bottles and Cages** as the selected member in the dimension filter. For the target value, use **150**.
13. Repeat steps 1 through 10 for a third KPI. For the KPI name and for the dimension filter select member, use **Bottom Brackets**. For the target value, use **2700**.

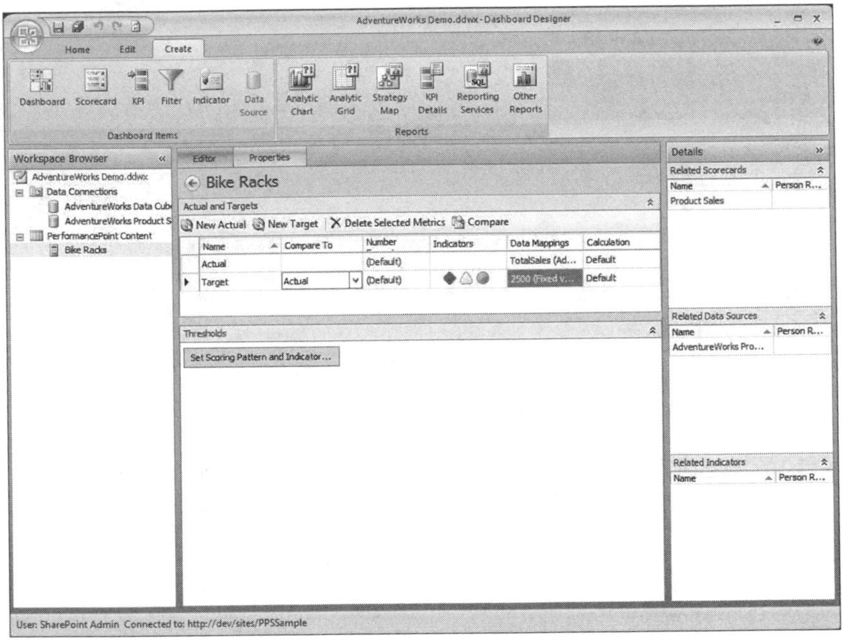

FIGURE 30.17 Configuration for the Bike Racks KPI.

Lastly, you need to create a rollup KPI, which will use the aggregate of the three previous KPIs by following these steps:

1. Create a new KPI, but this time in the Select a KPI Template dialog box, select Objective.
2. Rename the KPI to **Totals**.
3. In the Calculation column of the KPI settings for Actual and Target rows, click No Value.
4. Select the Sum of Children option. Apply this setting for both the Target and the Actual values. Figure 30.18 shows the Totals KPI.

Creating a Scorecard

Now that the KPIs have all been created, you can combine them into a single scorecard. To do so, follow these steps:

1. On the Create ribbon of Dashboard Designer, click Scorecard.
2. In the Select a Scorecard Template dialog box, select the Standard category, and select Blank Scorecard.

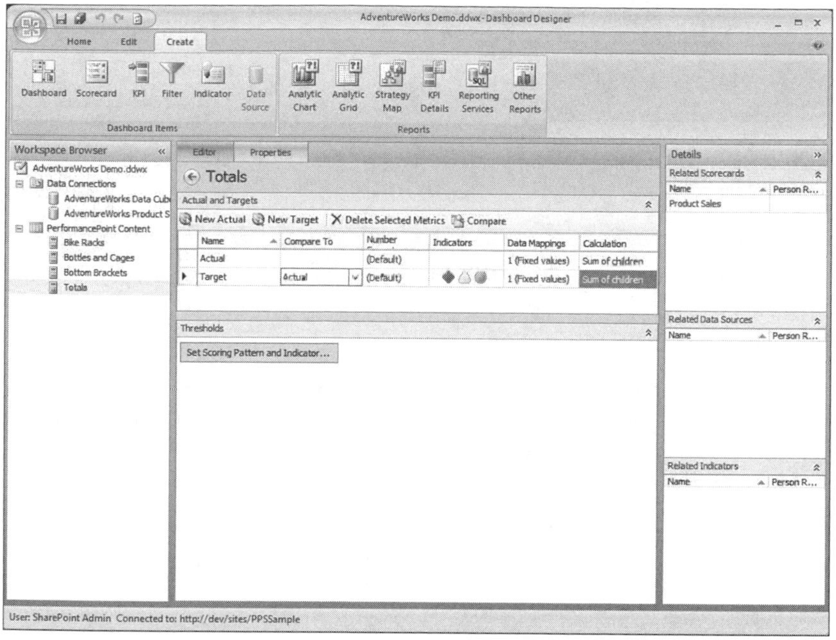

FIGURE 30.18 KPI using the Sum of Children calculation, to be used for aggregation.

3. Click the Properties tab, and change the name for the scorecard to **Product Sales**.
4. In the Details pane on the right side of Dashboard Designer, expand KPI, and expand PerformancePoint Content.
5. Drag the Totals KPI to the left working pane over the Drop Items Here label.
6. Drag the Bike Racks KPI to the working pane. While holding the left mouse key, drag the Bike Racks KPI to the right edge of the label for the Totals label. You should see the Total KPI highlighted, with gray borders on the left, top, and bottom edges. The right edge of the Totals KPI should be blue. In addition, a blue arrow should be pointing at the right edge of the Totals KPI. Release the mouse key, and the Bike Racks KPI should display beneath the Totals KPI, slightly indented. This is shown in Figure 30.19.
7. Repeat step 6 for the Bottles and Cages KPI, and again for the Bottom Brackets KPI. Bike Racks, Bottles and Cages, and Bottom Brackets should all display on the scorecard beneath the Totals KPI, and all three should be indented.

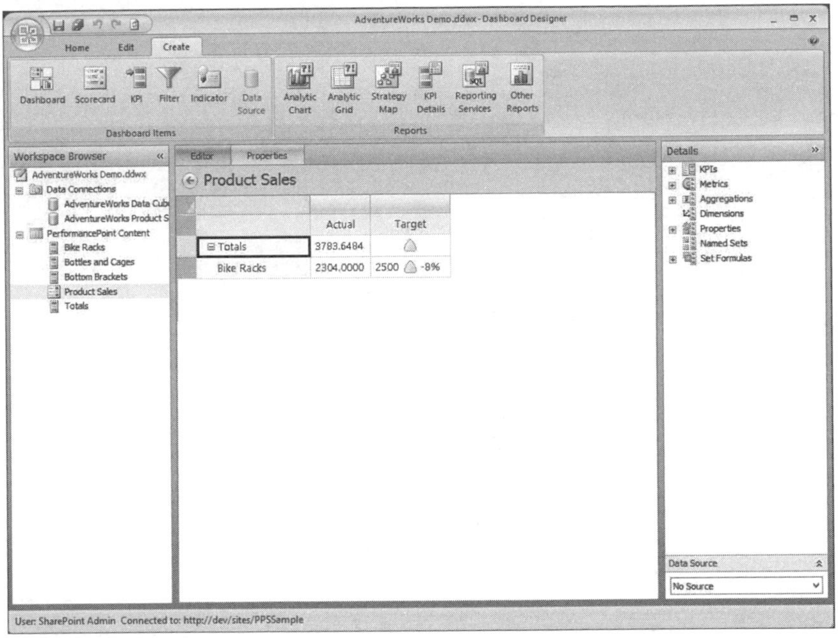

FIGURE 30.19 Adding a child KPI to a scorecard.

Creating a Report

Reports are the life blood of many companies, and Dashboard Designer provides a variety of chart options to facilitate the process. The following steps walk through the process of creating an analytic chart:

1. On the Create ribbon, select Analytic Chart.
2. In the Select a Data Source dialog box, select AdventureWorks Data Cube.
3. In the workspace browser, the new report is selected, with the name highlighted. Change the name to **Adventure Works Sales Chart**. Alternatively, you can change the name by clicking the Properties tab in the working area.
4. The report Details pane loads on the right side of Dashboard Designer. Expand the Measure grouping, and drag Sales Amount to the Series pane.
5. Expand the Dimensions grouping, the Date subgrouping, and the Calendar subgrouping. Drag the Calendar Quarter of Year dimension to the Bottom Axis section.
6. Expand the Named Sets grouping and the Sets subgrouping. Drag the Core Product Group Named Set to the Bottom Axis section. The report should look like Figure 30.20.
7. Click the Save All icon (or press Ctrl+Shift+S) to save all items.

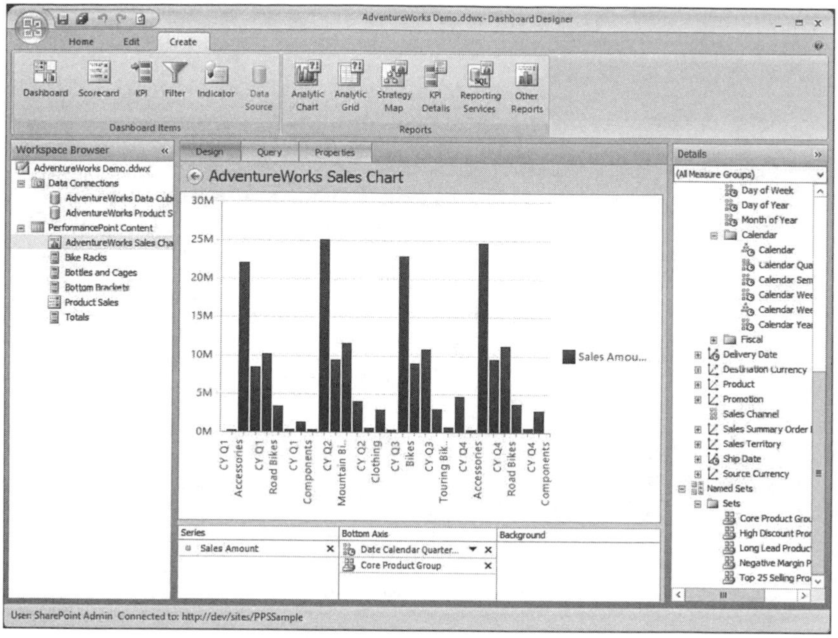

FIGURE 30.20 Completed analytical chart of sales amounts by quarter for each core product group.

Creating a Dashboard

The previous sections walked through the process of creating KPIs, scorecards, and reports. As noted earlier in the chapter, scorecards and reports are examples of web parts that appear on dashboard web pages. The final steps of the process demonstrate how to make these contents viewable on dashboard pages in SharePoint:

1. On the Create ribbon, select Dashboard. You can select any of the dashboard page templates.
2. In the Workspace Browser, rename the dashboard to **Product Sales Dashboard**.
3. In the Pages section of the working area, click Page 1, and rename it to **Product Sales**.
4. In the Details pane, expand Scorecards, and expand PerformancePoint Content. Drag the Product Sales scorecard into one of the dashboard zones.
5. In the Details pane, expand Reports, and expand PerformancePoint Content. Drag AdventureWorks Sales Chart onto the other zone.
6. In the Workspace Browser, right-click Product Sales Dashboard and select Deploy to SharePoint.
7. Select one of the master page options and click OK.

8. After the deployment is complete, the dashboard page launches in Internet Explorer, as shown in Figure 30.21.

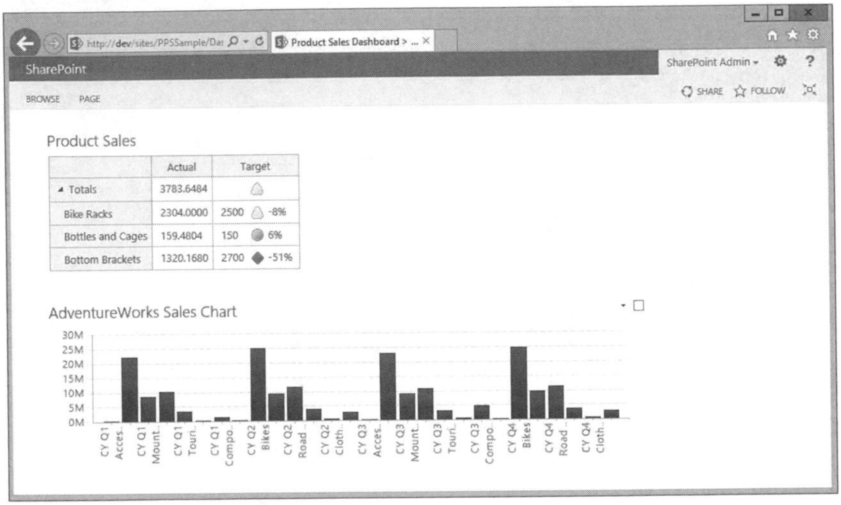

FIGURE 30.21 PerformancePoint dashboard page, as viewed in SharePoint.

Summary

The age of waiting for periodic reports to be generated by IT is over. The day has arrived where reports no longer need to be predefined and preformatted before delivering them to the person who needs to see them. With PerformancePoint Services, included in the Enterprise version of SharePoint Server 2010, and in particular with the power of the analytical reports, the right BI is truly placed in the hands of the right people at the right time.

This chapter walked through the process of configuring a PerformancePoint service application, working with Dashboard Designer and creating a dashboard, using data connections, KPIs, indicators, scorecards, reports, and dashboards. It also walked through the process of creating a dashboard so that the PerformancePoint tools are no longer mysterious and the process of creating a dashboard is less intimidating.

Best Practices

The following are best practices from this chapter:

- Review the new features in PerformancePoint 2013 to see how they can enhance preexisting dashboards and the user experience. Of particular interest is the ability to move any or all of your PerformancePoint content from one site or one server to another.

- When connecting to a data source, use the Unattended Service Account option for authentication. If using the Per-User Identity option, you might find that the dashboard components that utilize the data source load when you log in but fail to connect for other users visiting your page.
- With PerformancePoint Services, the quality of the dashboard is all about the data. To that end, some additional planning needs to go into the types of data sources you want to leverage. Well-designed transactional databases and data cubes are key to a successful BI implementation.
- Give some thought to which indicator sets you want to use for each KPI. Different image sets convey different messages. Comparisons of metrics from one time period to those from another warrant use of one of the trending indicators. Some indicators are appropriate to show at the end of a measurable time period, whereas others make more sense in the middle of a measurable time period.
- If starting a new Dashboard Designer workspace, check the SharePoint tab of Dashboard Designer to see which dashboard components have already been defined. If one exists that you want to utilize, simply double-click the component to include it in your workspace.
- It is not necessary to create a site using the BI Center site template to use PerformancePoint Services. Just activating the feature PerformancePoint Site Features will suffice.

CHAPTER 31

Business Intelligence in SharePoint 2013 with Business Connectivity Services

IN THIS CHAPTER

Business Connectivity Services (BCS) provides an interface for surfacing detailed information about an entity in SharePoint. As noted in Chapter 30, "Business Intelligence in SharePoint 2013 with PerformancePoint Services," business intelligence (BI) in SharePoint is about bringing the right information to the right people at the right time. Chapter 30 focused on PerformancePoint Services, which emphasizes the presentation of analytical data—numbers that can be totaled, averaged, or analyzed in other mathematical ways. With BCS, the information that is being surfaced is usually more anecdotal, presenting detailed information about a specific entity, such as a customer, a product, or an individual sale.

Consider, for example, a customer service department for an online retailer. The company receives an average of 200 calls and online chats per hour. With recent staff cuts, the customer service agents are under increasing pressure to address calls as quickly as possible, without sacrificing the quality of the customer service. For the various types of customer interactions, the customer service representative needs to quickly and easily access information about the customer, the order, and the products included in the order.

The company has a variety of applications that serve various business functions. There is an order-fulfillment system based on an SQL Server database. A customer database, owned by the marketing department, contains information about previous customers and is used for direct marketing initiatives. Lastly, the customer service department has started using a SharePoint team site and a SharePoint issues list to track customer service issues.

Using the BCS features of SharePoint 2013, the company can tie all this information together so that their customer service representatives can quickly and easily be able to access key information about orders and customers when handling calls. The department's goal is to provide one single, seamless user interface. The vision is to create a "customer service dashboard," where anyone in the department can quickly record, view, and address customer service issues in the shortest amount of time.

A Brief Introduction to BCS Development

SharePoint 2007 introduced the Business Data Catalog (BDC), which then evolved in SharePoint 2010 to be known as the Business Connectivity Services (BCS) and is still known as BCS with SharePoint 2013. The BDC in SharePoint 2007 was designed to provide a set of services and features that provided a way to connect solutions based on SharePoint Server to sources of external data. In the SharePoint 2007 BDC, definitions of entities required third-party tools. A few competing tools were available, but they only provided functionality for building BDC entities. Two such products that were commonly used were BDC Metaman from Lightning Tools and MOSS BDC Design Studio from Simego.

Now with SharePoint 2013 BCS, Visual Studio 2012 and SharePoint Designer 2013, both of which provide functionality for developing a wide range of other SharePoint features, introduce built-in BCS design and development tools. This enables easy definition of external content types for later consumption in SharePoint. The ability to build BCS functionality using the SharePoint tools that are already used for other SharePoint extensions is one improvement in the capabilities offered by the 2013 suite of products.

Key components to the BCS tools include the following:

- **The Business Data Connectivity (BDC) Service:** This service application stores BCS entities including BDC models, external systems, and external content types.
- **Secure Store Service:** The Secure Store Service provides the capability of securely storing credential sets and associating them to identities or groups of identities.

Developing external content types in Visual Studio 2012 requires a machine running SharePoint 2013. This can be either a Windows Server machine running SharePoint 2013 or a Windows 7 machine capable of running a development version of SharePoint. It is generally recommended that Windows Server be used, and the basic server options are as follows:

- The 64-bit edition of Windows Server 2008 R2 Service Pack 1 (SP1) Standard, Enterprise, or Datacenter.
- Or, the 64-bit edition of Windows Server 2012 Standard or Datacenter.

- Other standard prerequisites as covered previously in this book are also required for SharePoint 2013 installation.

CHANGES IN BCS 2013

Although there are a number of changes in the 2013 version of BCS, they are mostly "under the covers" and are not discussed in great detail in this chapter. Some key changes include the addition of OData BDC connections, which adds to the previous data connections for Windows Communication Foundation (WCF), SQL Server, and .NET assemblies. OData is an industry standard protocol for accessing data through URLs.

Apps for SharePoint are now supported in BCS, and BDC models can be packaged as apps for SharePoint. These are self-contained and do not make any changes to the SharePoint servers running the code, which minimizes risk and eases administration of the apps.

External lists have been enhanced in a number of ways, including the following:

- Performance improvements in external lists
- Limiting number of records returned by the external system
- Data source filtering
- Sorting external lists
- Export external lists to Excel

BCS in SharePoint 2013 exposes the Representational State Transfer (REST) application programming interfaces (APIs) for web and mobile app developers to use.

A detailed description is available on TechNet: http://technet.microsoft.com/en-us/library/fp161238.aspx.

External Content Types

SharePoint 2010 added the notion of external content types, and these are key components in developing BCS solutions. The content type, first introduced in SharePoint 2007, is a way of describing an entity of information stored in SharePoint. Document content types can be items like contracts, policies, and forms. Non-document content types can be items like announcements, tasks, or contacts. All of these are content types whose information is physically stored within the SharePoint taxonomy. Each would have its respective set of attributes, also known as columns, properties, or metadata.

An external content type is just what it sounds like—an entity whose underlying data exists external to SharePoint. Just like a SharePoint content type, an external content type also has its set of attributes or columns. Using BCS, external content types can be defined and made available for consumption within SharePoint.

Installing SharePoint Designer

SharePoint Designer 2013 also includes built-in capabilities for developing external content types. SharePoint Designer 2013 is a free tool that can be used to extend and customize SharePoint sites.

NOTE

At the time of this writing, SharePoint Designer 2013 encountered errors when used with SharePoint 2013; so in some cases, SharePoint Designer 2010 was used instead in this chapter. Make sure to download any updates of patches to SharePoint Designer 2013 when using it with SharePoint 2013.

To download and install SharePoint Designer 2013, follow these steps:

1. In Internet Explorer, go to www.microsoft.com/downloads.
2. In the Search box on the Downloads page, enter the phrase **SharePoint Designer 2013**.
3. Select either Microsoft SharePoint Designer 2013 (32-bit) or Microsoft SharePoint Designer 2013 (64-bit), depending on your desktop operating system.
4. On the following page, click the Download button. When prompted with "Do you want to run or save this file?" select Save, and save the file to your Desktop.
5. When the download is complete, double-click the SharePointDesigner.exe file on your desktop. This begins the installation process.
6. After the file extraction process completes, read the Microsoft software license terms, accept the terms of the agreement, and click OK. Click the Install Now button. When the installation completes, you are ready to start using SharePoint Designer.

Preparing to Build External Content Types

Prior to building external content types in SharePoint Designer, a few preparation steps are necessary. First, the SharePoint farm needs to be configured to receive connections, as follows:

1. On the SharePoint 2013 server, select Start and SharePoint 2013 Central Administration.
2. Under Application Management, click Manage Service Applications.
3. On the Service Application ribbon, click New and select Business Data Connectivity Service.
4. Give the service application a name, such as **Business Data Connectivity Service**.
5. Input the database server and remove or replace the globally unique identifier (GUID) that is appended to the database name. In this example, the database server name is spsql, as shown in Figure 31.1.
6. Select a preexisting application pool or create a new application pool for the service application, keeping in mind that running too many application pools simultaneously can result in diminished server performance. In this example, a new application pool, BDCAppPool, was created. Choose to use an existing managed account or to register a new managed account.

7. Click Create to finish.

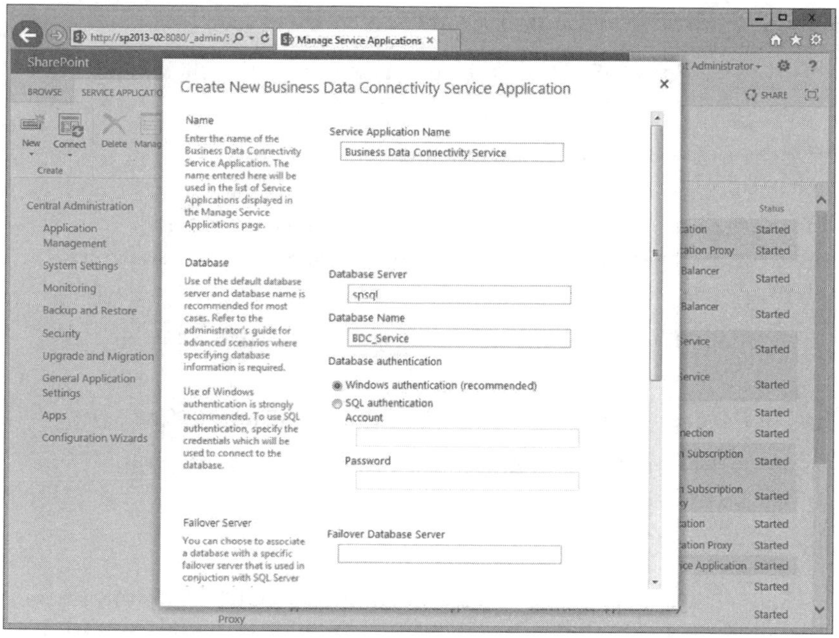

FIGURE 31.1 Create the BDC service application.

8. After the service application has successfully created, hover over the service application name until it turns into a hyperlink. In this example, the name Business Data Connectivity Service turned into a hyperlink. Click the link to manage the service application.

9. On the Edit ribbon, click Set Metadata Store Permissions.

10. Grant the necessary service accounts access permissions.

11. Click OK to finish.

Next, the appropriate services and features should be started on in the farm, on the site collection, and on the site itself. Follow these steps to start the services and features on the farm:

1. In Central Administration, under Application Management, click Manage Services on Server.

2. Start the BDC service.

3. Navigate to the BCSSample site collection and click the gear icon in the upper right. Select Site Settings. In this example, the site collection URL is http://sp2013-02/sites/BCSSample/.

4. On the Site Settings page for the site collection, under Site Collection Administration, click Site Collection Features.
5. Locate PerformancePoint Site Collection Features and click Activate.
6. Navigate back to Site Settings, and under the Site Actions heading, click Manage Site Features.
7. Locate the BICenter Data Connections Feature and click Activate.

Finally, a SharePoint site collection or site is required. In general, creating a new site collection is preferable for testing of this nature. To create a new SharePoint site collection, follow these steps:

1. In Central Administration, under Application Management, click Create Site Collections.
2. In the Title box of the Create Site Collection page, enter **BCS Sample Site**.
3. In the URL section, select the /sites/ option in the drop-down box, and enter **BCSSample** in the text box.
4. In the Template Selection section, choose Team Site.
5. Enter one or two login accounts to serve as the site collection administrators, as shown in Figure 31.2. In this example, the SharePoint Administrator (SPAdmin) account was set as the primary administrator. Click OK.

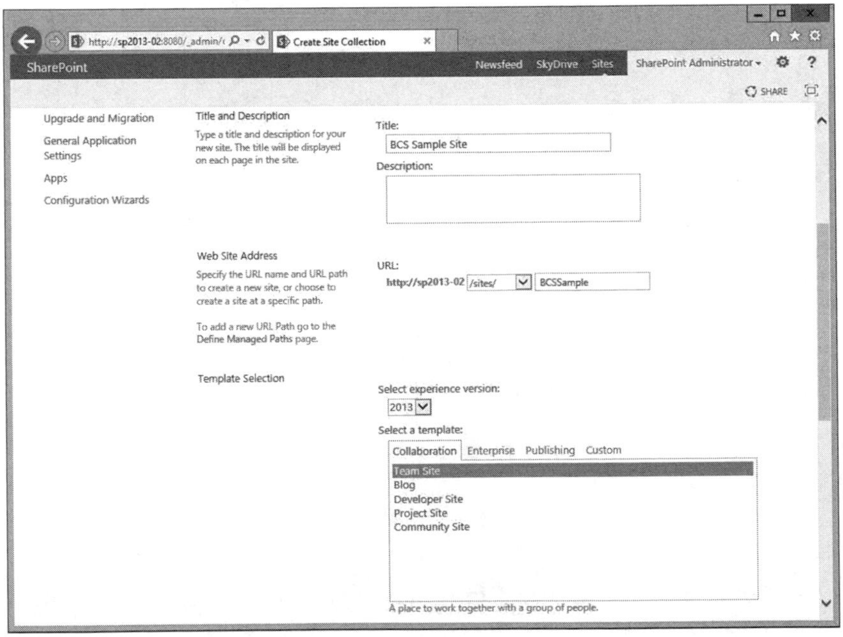

FIGURE 31.2 Create a blank SharePoint site.

In addition, external content types require an SQL Server database to connect to. Chapter 30 includes a set of steps to install the AdventureWorksLT database. If you completed those steps in the previous chapter, you do not have to do so again. If not, here are the steps:

NOTE

You need a server running SQL Server 2012 and SQL Analysis Services to proceed with this exercise.

1. Download and install the AdventureWorks samples databases by visiting http://msftdbprodsamples.codeplex.com/.
2. Click the link to the SQL Server 2012 product sample databases (http://msftdbprodsamples.codeplex.com/releases/view/55330), and then click the AdventureWorksLT2012_Data link to download. Save the installation file to a machine running SQL Server 2012. To avoid hassle in later steps, save the file to C:\Program Files\Microsoft SQL Server\MSSQL11.MSSQLSERVER\MSSQL\DATA or copy the file to that location when it finishes downloading.
3. When the file (AdventureWorksLT2012_Data.mdf) has finished downloading, the database needs to be attached to the SQL Server 2012 database engine instance. Open SQL Server Management Studio from the Start menu.
4. Connect to the database engine on the appropriate database server.
5. Right-click Databases and select Attach.
6. Click the Add button and navigate to the Save location. Select the database file and click OK to finish.
7. In the Database Details pane, select the LOG file type and click Remove.
8. Click OK to attach the database.

Defining the External Content Type

The next set of exercises step through the example of creating a basic external content type. The example utilizes the Customers table of the AdventureWorks database.

There are several operations available for an external content type; however, two specific ones—Read List and Read Item—are required before it can be consumed by SharePoint.

A Read List operation provides all the rows of the table that meet the criteria defined in the operation. In the Customer example, a Read List operation enables viewing of all the records from the Customers table in one SharePoint list, with it looking and acting like a SharePoint list. Although the data continues to live in the AdventureWorksLT database on SQL Server, it can be consumed in SharePoint, with the benefit of SharePoint views, as well as column sorting and filtering.

A Read Item operation allows for the isolation of an individual record from the list, based on some unique identifier, such as a Customer ID. The Read Item operation also allows you to join together a regular SharePoint list with the records of the Customer table. In the forthcoming examples, a Customer Service Issues list, stored in SharePoint, captures data about calls fielded by the Customer Service department. The list contains a mixture of SharePoint data and external data.

There are other operations available as well for external content types, including the following:

- **Create:** Add a new record to a table.
- **Update:** Modify an existing record.
- **Delete:** Remove a record from a table.
- **Association:** Define a relationship between two related tables.

Each of these operations is discussed in later sections of this chapter.

To begin building the external content types, follow these steps:

1. Open SharePoint Designer 2013. Following installation, the application should be added to a SharePoint grouping on your computer's Programs menu.
2. In SharePoint Designer 2013, click the Open Site button from the File menu. Enter the web address for the site created in the previous section. For example, enter http://sp2013-02/sites/BCSSample/.
3. Open the navigation pane on the left side if it is not already expanded.
4. In the Site Objects pane, shown on the left sidebar in Figure 31.3, select External Content Types.
5. In the External Content Types ribbon at the top of the screen, select External Content Type.
6. In the External Content Type Information section, click the link next to Name that says New External Content Type. The link is replaced with a text box to enter the name. Enter **BCS Customer**. Repeat with the Display Name field.
7. Next to the External System header, click the Click Here to Discover New External Data Sources and Define External Content Types link.
8. In the data source explorer view, click the Add Connection button.
9. In the External Data Source Type Selection dialog box, select SQL Server as the data source type and click the OK button.

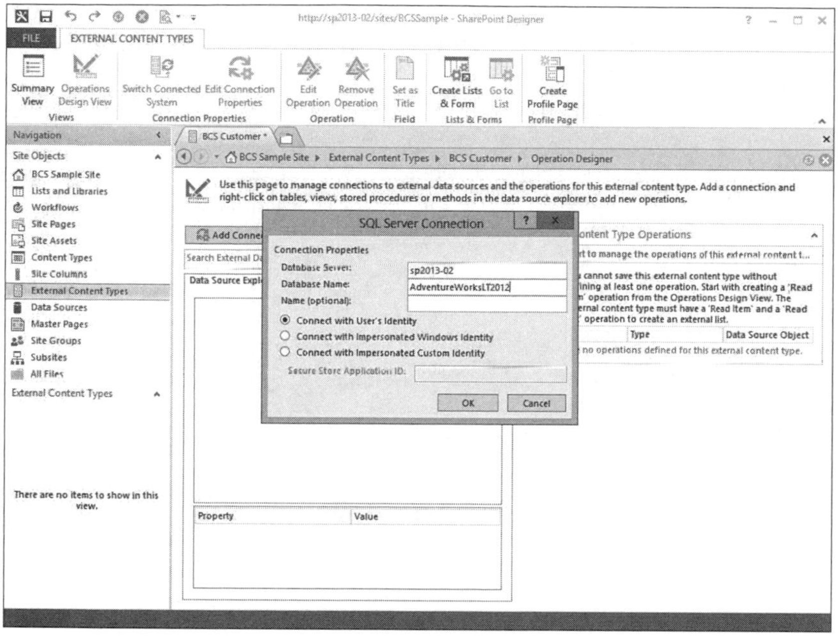

FIGURE 31.3 Connect to the AdventureWorksLT database.

10. In the SQL Server Connection dialog box, enter the SQL Server connection information. The Database Server should be the name of the SQL Server name and instance where you installed the AdventureWorks LT database. For example, enter **sp2013-02**. For the Database Name, enter **AdventureWorksLT2012**. For the connection options, select Connect with User's Identity, as shown in Figure 31.3. Click the OK button.

11. After a connection to the AdventureWorksLT database is established, the database schema loads under the Data Source Explorer. Expand the AdventureWorksLT node. Note that tables, views, and routines (SQL Server stored procedures) are all available for use. Expand the Tables node, as well.

12. Right-click the Customer table, and a list of available operations loads. Begin by selecting New Read Item Operation.

13. The Read Item Wizard is divided into three parts. In the first part—Operation Properties—enter **Customer Read Item** as both the operation name and the operation display name. Click the Next button.

14. In the Input Parameters, the CustomerID field, by virtue of it being defined as a unique identifier for the table in the database, is automatically recognized as the identifier for the external content type. Notice when the CustomerID field is selected, the Map to Identifier box is selected. No changes are necessary on this screen. Click the Next button.

15. The last portion of the wizard—Return Parameters—defines which columns from the database will be available for consumption and is shown in Figure 31.4. No changes are necessary on this screen. Click the Finish button.

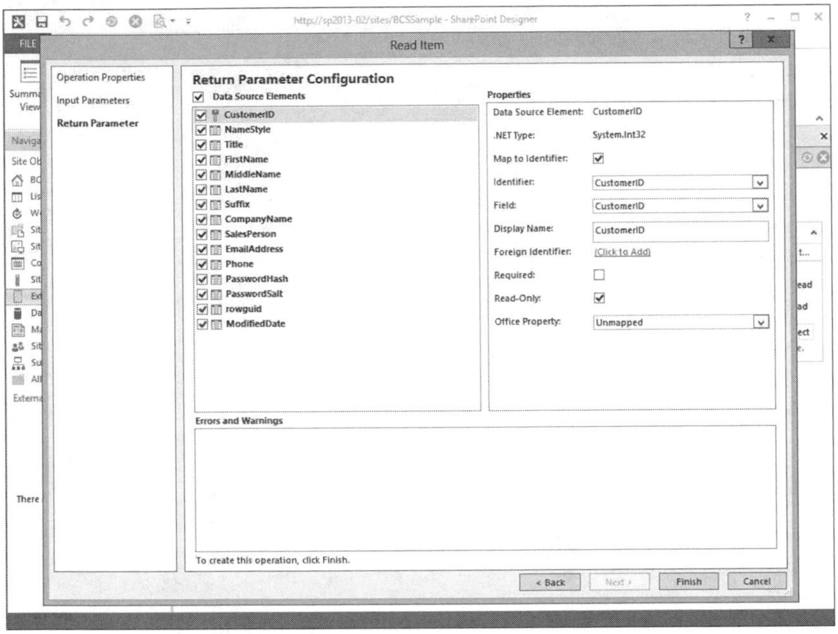

FIGURE 31.4 Creating the External Content Type Read Item Operation.

16. In the Data Source Explorer of SharePoint Designer, right-click the Customer table and select New Read List Operation.

17. In the Operation Properties portion of the wizard, enter **Customer Read List** as the operation name and the operation display name. Click Next.

18. In the Filter Parameters section, no changes are necessary. Click Next.

19. In the Return Parameters section, select CustomerID field in the Data Source Elements section, and select the Show in Picker box in the Properties section. Repeat this for the FirstName, LastName, EmailAddress, and Phone fields. Click Finish.

20. Click the Save icon in the upper-left corner of SharePoint Designer (or press Ctrl+S) to save the external content type.

NOTE

Saving the external content type uploads the information to the BDC service application in SharePoint Central Administration. The external content type can later be removed or modified by going to Central Administration, Application Management, Manage Service Applications, Business Data Connectivity.

Creating an External Content Type for a Related Item

Most normalized databases have several tables with relationships to other tables, which are models for real-world information. A customer, for example, will place one or more orders with a company. An order will contain one or more products. And a single order might be delivered in one or more shipments.

A normalized database, to accurately model this information, will define relationships between these tables. A one-to-many relationship would exist between a Customers table and an Orders table. Both tables would contain a field called CustomerID. In the Customers table, each individual record would have a unique CustomerID. In the Orders table, there might be several records with the same CustomerID. This represents that one customer has placed multiple orders.

The AdventureWorksLT database contains this exact relationship between the Customers and Orders tables. With BDC, an extra step is involved with defining an external content type with this type of relationship.

The following exercise addresses how to create an external content type for orders, where a relationship to another content type exists:

1. In SharePoint Designer, in the Site Objects pane on the left side, click the External Content Types option.
2. On the External Content Types ribbon, click the External Content Type button.
3. In the External Content Type Information section, enter **BCS Order** for both the name and the display name.
4. In the External System field, click the Click Here to Discover External Data Sources and Define External Content Types link.
5. The AdventureWorksLT data source should already be available from having completed the previous set of exercises. Expand the AdventureWorksLT node, and then the Tables node. Expand the SalesOrderHeader node and the Columns node to view the columns in the SalesOrderHeader table. Notice the CustomerID column.
6. Right-click SalesOrderHeader, and select New Read Item Operation.
7. In the first part of the Read Item wizard—Operation Properties—enter **Sales Order Read Item** as both the operation name and the operation display name. Click the Next button.
8. As with the CustomerID field for the Customer external content type, the SalesOrderID field is automatically recognized as the identifier for the external content type. No changes are necessary on this screen. Click the Next button.
9. The last portion of the wizard—Return Parameters—defines which columns from the database will be available for consumption. No changes are necessary on this screen. Click the Finish button.
10. Right-click SalesOrderHeader, and select New Association. This is the operation necessary to establish the relationship between a customer and an order.

11. The Association Creation Wizard is divided into four sections, as shown in Figure 31.5. In the first—Association Properties—enter **SalesOrder Customer Association** as both the name and the display name.

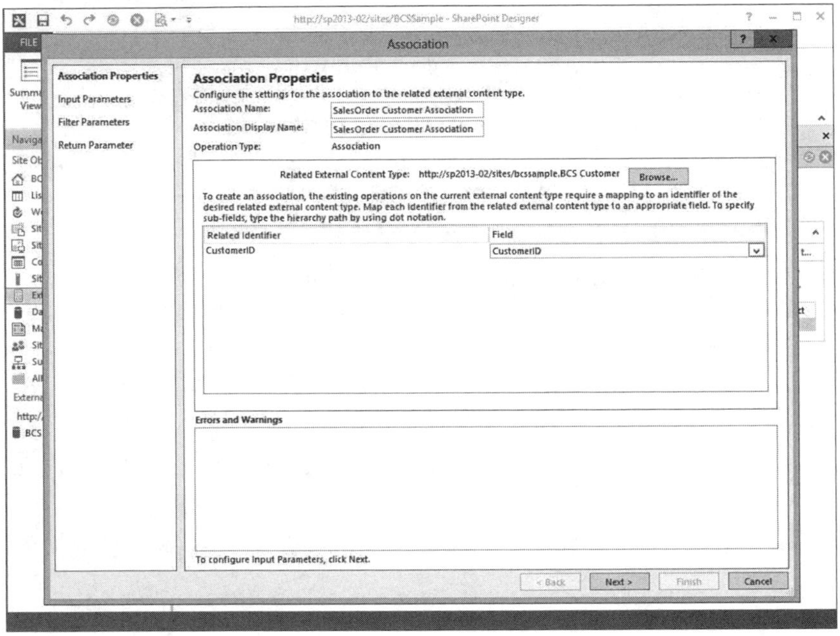

FIGURE 31.5 Create an association between related external content types.

12. Next to Related External Content Type, click the Browse button. The BCS Order (the current one) and BCS Customer (created earlier) external content types should both be available. Select BCS Customer and click the OK button. Below, the field CustomerID is automatically selected because both tables have the field with the same name. SharePoint Designer recognizes that this is the likely field on which to establish the relationship. Click Next.

13. In the second part of the wizard—Input Parameters—click the CustomerID field under Data Source Elements. Then check the box to the right labeled Map to Identifier and click Next.

14. In the Filter Parameters section, no changes are necessary. Click Next.

15. In the Return Parameters section, no changes are necessary. Click Finish.

16. In the Data Source Explorer of SharePoint Designer, right-click the SalesOrderHeader table and select New Read List Operation.

17. In the Operation Properties portion of the wizard, enter **SalesOrder Read List** as the operation name and the operation display name. Click Next.

18. In the Filter Parameters section, click the Add Filter Parameter button. In the Properties section for the new filter, change the Data Source Element to CustomerID. For the Filter parameter, click the Click to Add link. Make no changes in the Filter Configuration dialog box, and click OK. For the Default Value property, enter 1. Click Next.

19. In the Return Parameters section, select SalesOrderID field in the Data Source Elements section, and select the box in the Properties section labeled Show in Picker. Repeat this for the OrderDate, ShipDate, and TotalDue fields. Click Finish.

20. Click the Save icon in the upper-left corner of SharePoint Designer (or press Ctrl+S) to save the external content type.

At this point, there are now two external content types in the BDC Metadata Store in SharePoint Central Administration. These external content types are now available for use in the SharePoint sites.

Consuming External Content Types

After all the heavy lifting is complete, and the external content type has been built and saved into SharePoint, it is ready for consumption. There are three main ways that you can leverage the external content type in SharePoint: external lists, external data, and BCS web parts.

Creating an External List

An external list looks and acts just like a SharePoint list. Contents are displayed in rows and columns. You can also leverage the columns by sorting and filtering on them, as well as by creating custom views. The main difference between an external list and a regular SharePoint list is that the actual contents of the external list live outside of SharePoint, hence the name.

To create an external list, follow these steps:

1. In Internet Explorer, open the SharePoint site created earlier in the chapter. The URL will be something like http://sp2013-02/sites/BCSSample/.

2. Click the gear icon in the upper right and select Add an App.

3. In the Find an App search box, enter **External List** and click the search icon.

4. In the search results, click the External List app icon.

5. In the Adding External List dialog box, enter **Customers** as the list name.

6. For the External Content Type field, an External Content Type picker is available. Click the icon for Select External Content Type. Select BCS Customer, as shown in Figure 31.6, and click OK. BCS Customer (AdventureWorksLT2012) should display as underlined. Click the Create button.

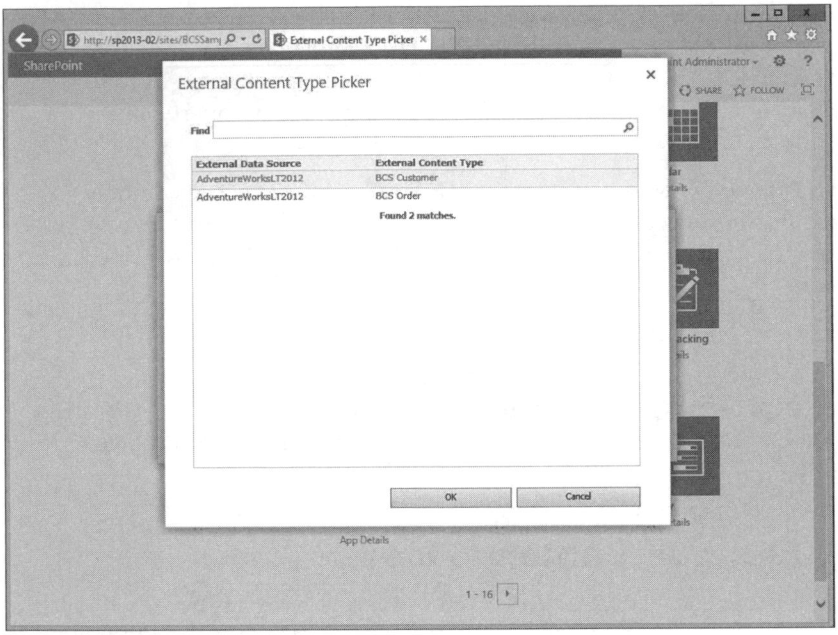

FIGURE 31.6 Settings for creating a new external list.

The resulting display is the entire Customers table from the AdventureWorksLT database, looking and acting like a standard SharePoint list as shown in Figure 31.7. Notice that the following capabilities are available on the list:

- **Sorting:** Hover over any of the column headers to sort the list in either ascending or descending order.
- **Filtering:** Any column (for instance, SalesPerson) can be used for refining the number of records shown in the list.
- **Views:** As with any other SharePoint list, site owners can create custom views.

Leveraging External Data

The second means by which external content types can be consumed in SharePoint sites is through external data columns. An external data column basically provides a hybrid between a SharePoint list and an external list. External data starts with any basic SharePoint list. The example that follows uses the SharePoint issues list with an external column to connect each issue to one of Adventure Works' customers:

1. In the SharePoint site, select the Add an App option from the Settings gear icon.
2. In the Find an App search box, enter **Issue** and click the search icon.

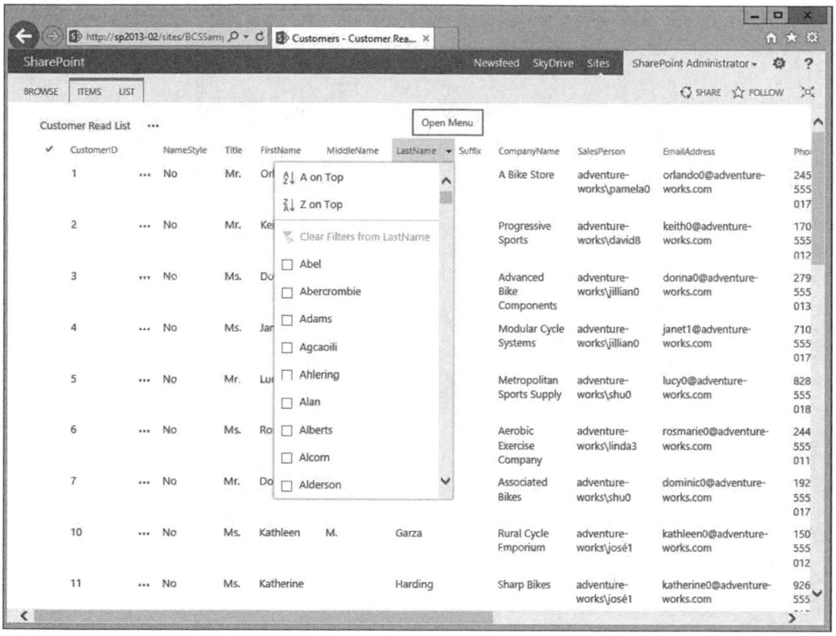

FIGURE 31.7 Sorting and filtering columns on an external list.

3. Click the Issue Tracking icon. In the Name box, enter **Customer Complaints** and click the Create button.

4. When the list is created, click the Customer Complaints list in the navigation on the left side of the page.

5. In the List ribbon, click Create Column.

6. Enter **Customer** as the column name, and select External Data as the column type.

7. In the External Content Type picker, type the word **Customer** into the text box and click the checkmark icon for Check If External Content Type Exists. BCS Customer (AdventureWorksLT2012) should display as underlined, as shown in Figure 31.8.

8. Select CustomerID from the Select the Field to be Shown on This Column drop-down menu.

9. Under Add a Column to Show Each of These Additional Fields, select CompanyName, EmailAddress, FirstName, LastName, Phone, and SalesPerson. After you make these selections, all the fields selected are dynamically added to the custom SharePoint list. Click OK.

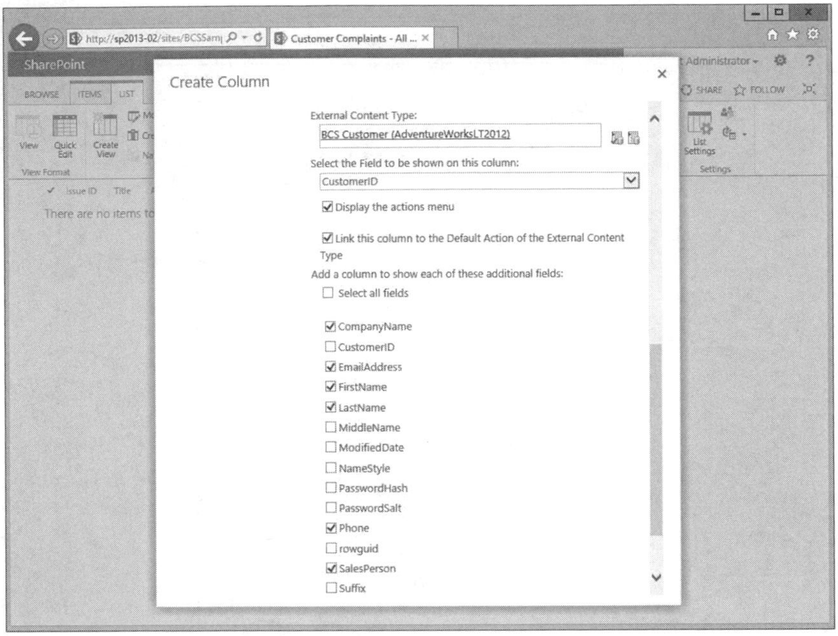

FIGURE 31.8 Applying the external data column settings.

When all of this is complete, you can begin entering data into the Customer Complaints list, as follows:

1. In the Customer Complaints list, click the New Item link.
2. Enter **Order received was incomplete** as the title.
3. The Customer field, displayed at the bottom of the New Item form, provides an External Item picker utility. Click the icon for Select External Item (the second icon). Select the record with CustomerID of 3, Donna Carreras, and click OK.

NOTE

Recall that, earlier in the chapter, when creating the Read List operation on the Customers table, the Return Parameters portion of the wizard included a Show in Picker check box for each field listed. The exercise called for checking this box for the CustomerID, FirstName, LastName, EmailAddress, and Phone fields. These are the fields that are displayed in the Choose BCS Customer lookup.

4. Click Save to commit the new item to the Customer Complaints list.
5. Repeat steps 1–4 to add a second record. Enter **Order included broken parts** as the title. Select the record with a CustomerID of 4, Janet Gates.

6. Repeat steps 1–4 to add a third record. Enter **Order is three weeks overdue** as the title. Select the record with a CustomerID of 2, Keith Harris.

Figure 31.9 shows a view of the Customer Complaints list that has the three records entered in the preceding exercises. Notice that in addition to the traditional issue tracking columns there is also the Customer (external data) column.

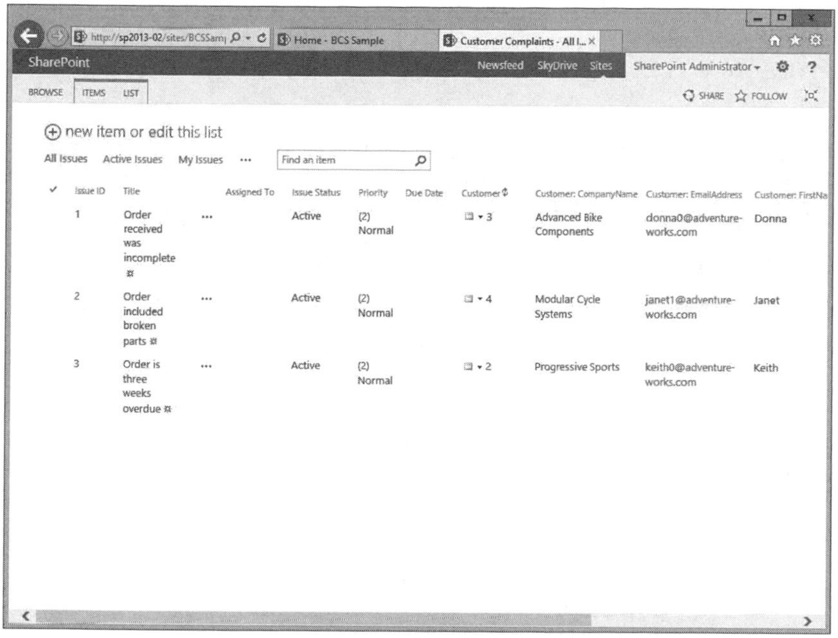

FIGURE 31.9 View of a SharePoint list with an external data column.

The view also includes several additional columns relating to the customer. These columns are prefixed with Customer:, which indicates that they are columns based on the Customer external content type.

Periodically, data in the source SQL Server database might change. The BCS database contains cached versions of this data. In Figure 31.9, the Customer column header is highlighted, the result of hovering the mouse over this header. The column includes a double-arrow icon next to it. Clicking this arrow initiates a refresh of the data stored in SQL Server. If using external data columns, periodically click this icon to ensure that the most current data is displayed in your SharePoint lists.

Writing to External Content Types

Just like in SharePoint 2010, with BCS in SharePoint 2013, external content types can be defined with full CRUD (create, read, update, and delete) capabilities.

For many scenarios, writing to an external content type is going to be beyond the scope of what you can do within the confines of SharePoint Designer. It's likely that the database to which you are connecting will have columns with more sophisticated data requirements. For example, many database tables will have some internal fields whose values are generated by the code in whatever application the database connects to.

The following examples walk through the process of creating these operations, and subsequently demonstrate why there are limitations to using SharePoint Designer for write-back operations:

1. Open SharePoint Designer 2013 from the SharePoint grouping on your computer's Programs menu.
2. In SharePoint Designer 2013, click the Open Site button from the File menu. Enter the web address for the site created in the early parts of this chapter. For example, enter http://sp2013-02/sites/BCSSample/.
3. In the Site Objects window, select External Content Types.
4. BCS Customer and BCS Order should be listed in the External Content Types pane in the bottom-left corner of SharePoint Designer. Click BCS Customer.
5. On the External Content Types ribbon, click the Operations Design View icon.
6. In the Data Source Explorer, right-click the Customer table and select New Create Operation, as shown in Figure 31.10.

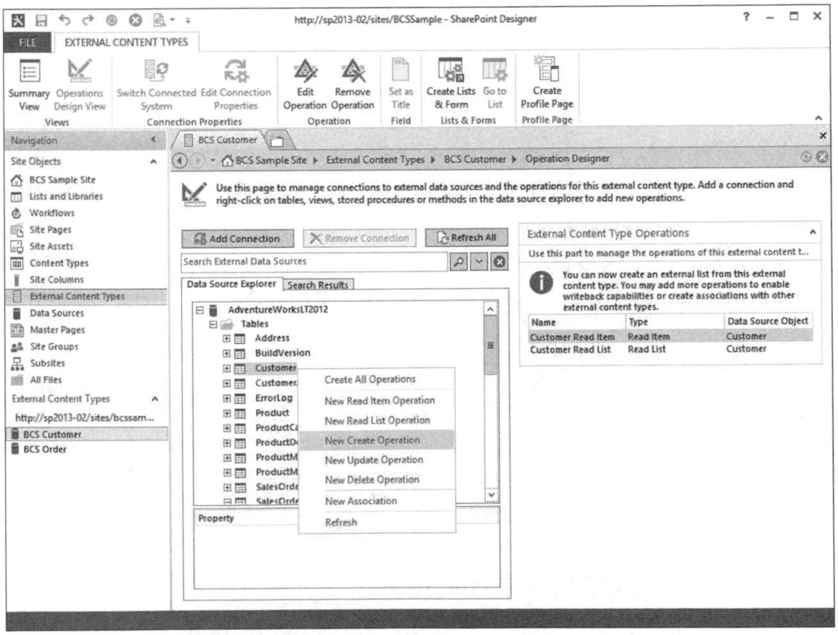

FIGURE 31.10 Building a create operation for an external content type.

7. In the Operation Properties section of the Create Wizard, enter **Create Customer** as both the operation name and the operation display name. Click Next.
8. In the Input Parameters section, no changes are necessary. However, notice that there are several fields—PasswordHash, PasswordSalt, and ModifiedDate, which are discussed in more detail shortly. Also, notice the opportunity to enter a default value for each of the fields below. Lastly, observe that each field can be unchecked; however, doing so results in an error message being added to Errors and Warnings, which will block instantiation of the create operation. Click Next.
9. In the Return Parameter portion of the wizard, no changes are necessary. Click Next.
10. Click the Save icon, or press Ctrl+S, to save the changes.

While this exercise provided a simple set of steps to build a create operation on the Customers table, some of the fields mentioned—PasswordHash, PasswordSalt, and ModifiedDate—present specific problems.

These fields are all ones that perform important functions on the database. Yet, at the same time, they aren't the types of fields that are meant to be provided by end users. The PasswordHash and PasswordSalt fields, for example, are managed by other applications and provide encryption on the actual password entered by a system user. Lastly, the ModifiedDate field, also intended to be system-generated, is used to capture when the field was actually entered.

For fields such as these, SharePoint Designer is only sophisticated enough to allow you the following options: ignore the fields on write operations, specify a default value, or leave it up to the user to enter a value. The resulting outcomes of these options would be that a) the field was left blank on the new entry, b) useless data was entered, or c) an invalid entry resulted in an error that prevented the entire record from being added.

So, while BCS provides the capability to write back to SQL Server from SharePoint, and although this can be a very powerful business tool, it is only realistic for small, simple databases. For most line-of-business database systems, this is most likely going to be a practice best left to a more advanced BCS authoring tool, such as Visual Studio 2013.

Delete operations can pose similar problems on many database applications. A well-designed normalized database is likely going to have records in one table that depend on records in another table. An Orders table, for example, might have a CustomerID foreign key field, which depends on a related record in the Customers table. On the database, if you try to delete a Customer record when there are dependent records in the Orders table, SQL Server might issue an error message and block the deletion. The error message would be returned to the user and indicate the existence of such a dependency.

A simple delete operation, however, can be created with the following steps:

1. In the Data Source Explorer of SharePoint Designer, right-click the Customer table and select New Delete Operation.

2. In the Operation Properties section of the Create Wizard, enter **Delete Customer** as both the operation name and the operation display name. Click Next.
3. In the Input Parameters section, no changes are necessary. Note that the CustomerID field is automatically selected, with the Map to Identifier check box automatically checked. Click Finish.
4. Click the Save icon, or press Ctrl+S, to save the changes.

To see how these additional operations would be used in SharePoint, as well as how the problems previously described manifest themselves, follow these steps:

1. In Internet Explorer, open the SharePoint site used by all previous examples in this chapter. The URL, for example, would be http://sp2013-02/sites/BCSSample/.
2. Click the Customers list from the Quick Launch bar on the left side.
3. Click the List ribbon, and click the List Settings icon.
4. Click Delete this List, and confirm the deletion.

NOTE

When including create or update operations on an external content type, it is important to create these operations before creating the external list in SharePoint. The reason the operations need to be defined first is that, when SharePoint creates a new list, it creates the form pages as needed for Edit Item and New Item. If no operation is defined, no corresponding form pages are created when the list is instantiated. If the list is created first, and operations for create or update are then retroactively defined, the Add/Edit options show up on the item's actions menu. However, selecting one of these options on the external list results in an error message. This is corrected by deleting and re-creating the external list.

5. Select Settings, Add an App.
6. In the Find an App search box, enter **External List** and click the search icon.
7. In the app search results, click the External List icon.
8. In the new list page, enter **Customers** as the list name.
9. For the External Content Type field, an External Content Type picker is available. Click the icon for Select External Content Type. Select BCS Customer, and click OK. BCS Customer (AdventureWorksLT2012) should display as underlined. Click the Create button.
10. After the list is re-created, click the Item ribbon, and click the New Item link.
11. Fill in the New Item record as shown in Figure 31.11 and click Save.

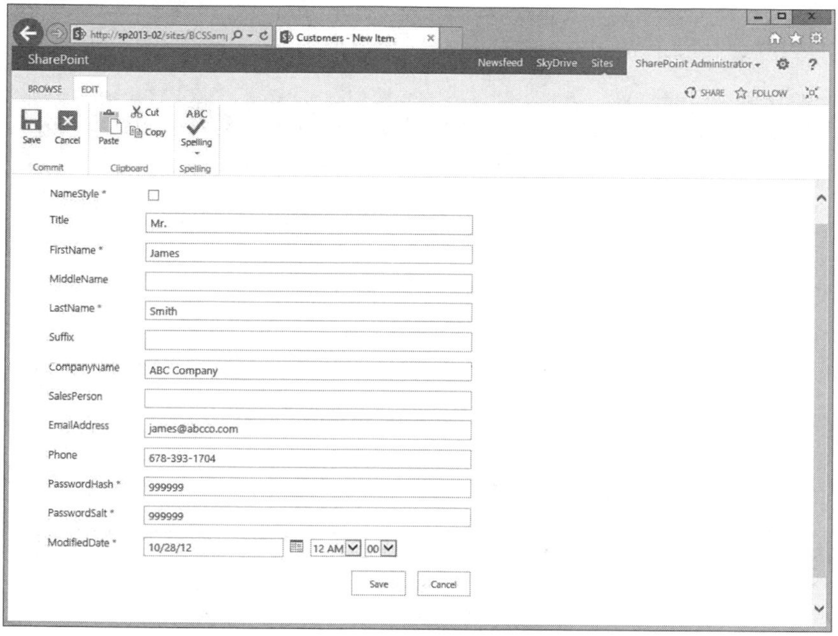

FIGURE 31.11 New Item screen for the Customers external list.

Notice a few things about the New Item screen. First, the PasswordHash and PasswordSalt fields provide no guidance to the user completing the form on how to fill in the fields. In addition, the fields are required because they are required in the AdventureWorksLT2012 database. Therefore, leaving the fields blank is not an option for the user. Also, the ModifiedDate field allows the user to directly input a date, even though it is intended to be controlled by the system.

Business Connectivity Services Web Parts

Up until this point, all the functionality covered in this chapter is available with SharePoint Foundation 2013, the nonlicensed version of SharePoint. The Enterprise version of Microsoft SharePoint Server offers some additional functionality.

Specifically, a set of Business Data web parts are available. These web parts provide a third way that BCS external content can be consumed in SharePoint and can be useful for building dashboard pages.

Consider, for example, a Customer Details page which would show profile information—Name, Phone Number, Company, and Email Address—about the customer in one web part. Another web part could show recent orders—including Order Date, Total Amount, and Order Status. A last one would list a set of recent customer service calls. Having all this information available in one screen would make it easier for a Customer Service Representative to quickly access all relevant information, without having to go from one application to another. It doesn't even matter that all this information would live in a series of different SharePoint lists and database tables, or even in separate databases. The power of BCS is the ability to pull it all together into one location.

Before using these web parts, however, SharePoint Server Enterprise Site Collection Features needs to be activated. Activating this feature adds the web parts described previously to the site collection's web part gallery. Follow these steps:

1. In Internet Explorer, open the SharePoint site used throughout this chapter. The URL will be something like http://sp2013-02/sites/BCSSample/.
2. From the Settings gear icon, select Site Settings.
3. Under the Site Collection Administration heading, click the Site Collection Features link.
4. Locate the feature labeled SharePoint Server Enterprise Site Collection Features, and then click the corresponding Activate button.

NOTE

If this feature is not listed, navigate to Central Administration. Under Upgrade and Migration, verify that Enable Enterprise Features is available. This feature should already be enabled if SharePoint 2013 Enterprise is installed. Then, click the link for Enable Features on Existing Sites, check the box to enable features, click OK, and wait for the features to propagate. After completing this, SharePoint Server Enterprise Site Collection features should be visible in Site Collection Features.

The following sets of examples show how to use three main web parts to build this dashboard: the Business Data Item, Business Data Related List, and the Query String (URL) Filter web parts.

Business Data Item Web Part

The first web part of interest is the Business Data Item web part, which can be used to show the details of a single BCS record. The example that follows uses this web part to show the main profile information about a customer—Name, Phone Number, Email Address, and so on:

1. In Internet Explorer, return to the home page of the SharePoint site used throughout this chapter.
2. From the Page ribbon, select Edit Page. The web page should show Left and Right web part zones.
3. In the Left Zone, click the Web Part button in the Insert ribbon.
4. In the Categories section, select the Business Data category. In the Web Parts section, select the Business Data Item web part. Click the Add button.
5. The Business Data Item web part should display in the Left web part zone. Click the link Open the Tool Pane in the web part to modify the web part settings.

6. For the Business Data Item section of the settings, enter the word **Customer** in the Type field, and check the checkmark icon to locate the BCS Customer external content type. After the external content type is located, it should display in the Type box as underlined.
7. In the View list box, select Default (Customer Read Item).
8. In the Item field, enter the number **2**, and click the checkmark icon to locate the record with CustomerID of 2. When the record is located, it should also display in the box as underlined.
9. Click the OK button in the web part settings to save the changes to the web part. When the page reloads, the record for Keith Harris should be displayed, as shown in Figure 31.12.

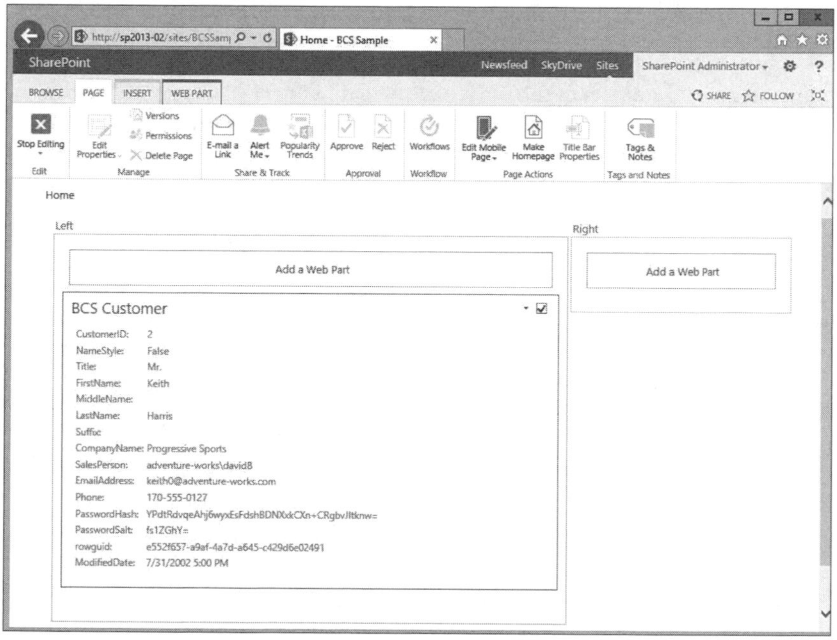

FIGURE 31.12 Configured Business Data Item web part.

Business Data Related List Web Part

Another important component of the Customer dashboard page is the Recent Orders web part. As the name implies, this web part shows recent orders associated with the given customer. This web part utilizes the Business Data Related List web part.

The Business Data Related List web part utilizes associations defined between two external content types. Recall the earlier set of exercises to create the BCS Order external content type, which included an association to the BCS Customer external content type. The

Business Data Related List web part leverages this association to display only the orders that relate to a selected customer:

1. From the Page ribbon, select Edit Page.
2. In the left zone, click the Add a Web Part link.
3. In the Categories section, select the Business Data category. In the Web Parts section, select the Business Data Related List web part. Click the Add button.
4. The Business Data Related List web part should display in the Left web part zone, just above the BCS Customer web part. Move the new web part below the BCS Customer web part by clicking on the Business Data Related List header, holding the mouse button down, and dragging it beneath the BCS Customer web part. Release the left mouse button.
5. Click the link Open the Tool Pane in the web part to modify the web part settings.
6. In the Type box, click the Select an External Content Type icon. Notice that only the BCS Order content type appears in the selection list. This is because BCS Order was the only external content type for which an association was defined. Select BCS Order and click OK.
7. In the Relationship list box, select Default (Sales Order Customer Association), which should be the only option in the list. Click the OK button to save the web part settings.
8. All the columns from the Sales Order table should display. To reduce the columns displayed, use Internet Explorer's horizontal scrollbar to move to the right. Click the Edit View link, which appears just above the rightmost column.
9. In the Columns section of the view settings page, deselect all *except* the following columns: OrderDate, ShipDate, SalesOrderNumber, CustomerID, SubTotal, TaxAmt, and TotalDue. Click OK.
10. Next, a connection must be established between the two web parts, so that the value used in the BCS Customer web part (Business Data Item web part) is passed to the Sales Orders List web part (Business Data Related list web part).
11. From the Page ribbon, select Edit Page.
12. Hover over the BCS Customer web part header. Click the down arrow that appears at the right of the web part header. Click Connections, select Send Selected Item To, and then select BCS Order List, as shown in Figure 31.13.

Query String Filter Web Part

Recall that the operations assigned to both the Customer and SalesOrderHeader operations contain filters for CustomerID. Rather than try to view all customers and all sales orders on one web page, the orders information is most usable when viewing it one customer at a time. To isolate the records to just those for a single customer, a filter can be used.

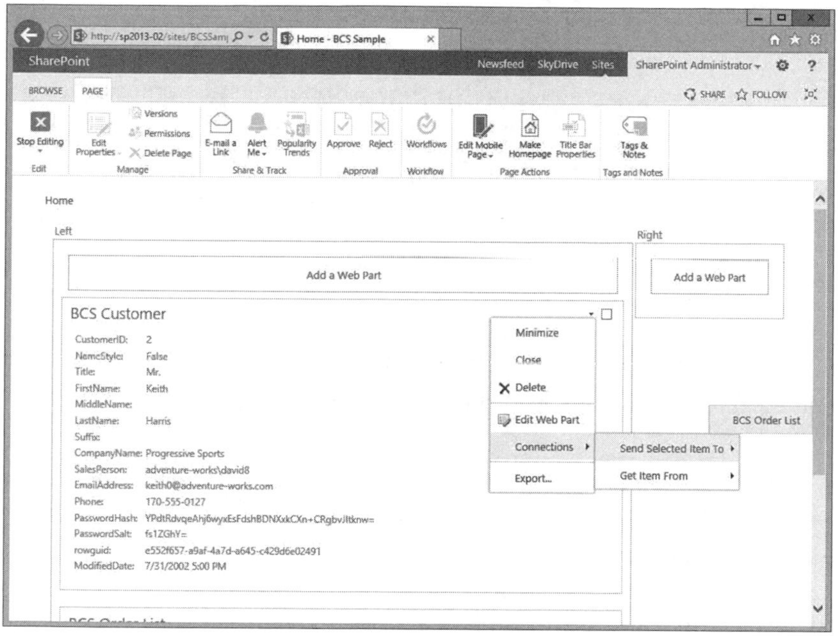

FIGURE 31.13 Establishing a connection between two web parts.

Furthermore, it would be very inefficient to create a separate page for every single customer in the database and have to design it the exact same way each time, changing only the CustomerID in each web part. Instead, it obviously makes much more sense to create a single page and simply differentiate between customers via a single parameter.

A query string parameter provides this very capability. A query string parameter is the portion of a website address that appears after the question mark. For example, a query string parameter might be something like CustomerID. The web address to a page might look something like http://mss2010.abcco.com/Pages/CustomerDashboard.aspx?CustomerID=227. This URL will pull up the page called CustomerDashboard.aspx and will reference the customer whose ID is 227.

The Query String Filter web part is designed to read the designated query string parameter and then send that value to connected web parts. To see this web part in action, follow these steps:

1. From the Page ribbon, select Edit Page.
2. In the left zone, click the Add a Web Part link.
3. Select the Filters category and the Query String (URL) Filter web part. Click the Add button.
4. Click the Open the Tool Pane link to edit the web part settings.
5. In the Filter Name property, enter **CustomerID**.

6. For the query string parameter name, enter **CustomerID**.
7. Lastly, assign **2** as the default value. This last parameter is not critical, but will assign an ID to be used if the user lands on the page without the CustomerID being specified.
8. Under the Appearance heading, change the web part title to **CustomerID Query String Filter**.
9. Click OK to save the web part settings.
10. Finally, connect the web part to the BCS Customer web part. To do so, hover over the CustomerID Query String Filter web part header. To the right, click the arrow, select Connections, select Send Filter Values To, and select BCS Customer.
11. In the Configure Connection dialog box, select BCS Customer and click the Finish button.
12. In the Page ribbon at the top of the SharePoint page, click the Stop Editing button to complete all changes.
13. In the address bar of Internet Explorer, change the address, removing everything that appears after default.aspx. In its place, type **?CustomerID=2** and press the Enter key. Notice that the page shows the default data for Keith Harris and any related orders.
14. Repeat step 13, but use **61** for the CustomerID. Notice that the data changes to show the customer details and orders for Jeffrey Kurtz, as shown in Figure 31.14.

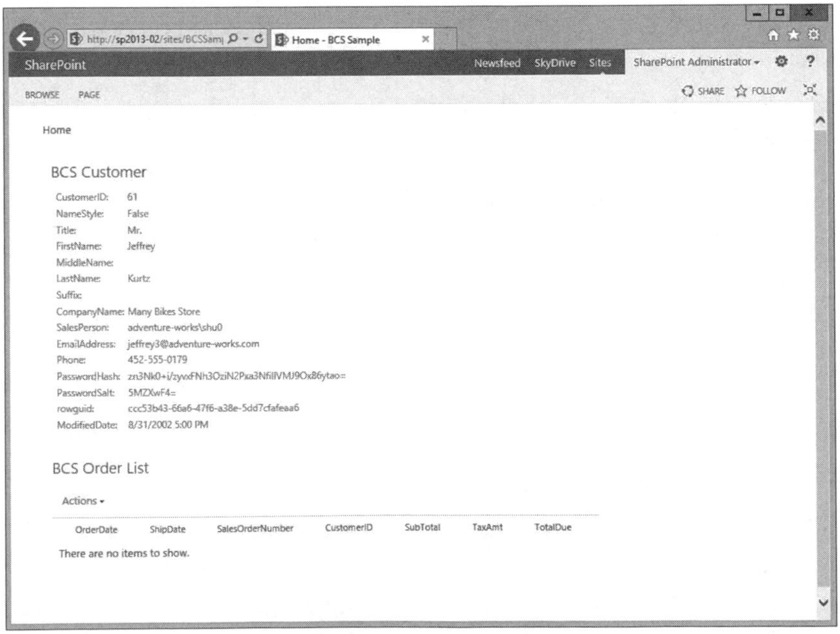

FIGURE 31.14 Customer dashboard for Jeffrey Kurtz.

15. Repeat step 13, and instead use **151**. Observe how the data changes again, this time showing the records for Walter Brian.

Summary

BCS provides a unique way of making information available for widespread consumption. A successful implementation is all about the data. However, assuming that the proper data repositories are available, the tool provides a means of quickly and easily presenting the data for consumers to access the information.

For years, powerful tools have made it possible to generate reports based on large volumes of data. Nevertheless, the traditional problems have been related to making the reports available to the right people and having the reports available at the time that they were most useful.

Like PerformancePoint Services in the previous chapter, BCS solves these problems in several ways. First, the ability to publish information to pages in SharePoint brings the information to the fingertips of anyone who might need it. Second, the client tools in SharePoint Designer make it possible for nondevelopers to build relevant, meaningful reports and to establish their own connections to the data. Lastly, having a single location to where the information is published means that only one version of the truth is available for consumption.

For all these reasons, SharePoint 2013's enhanced BCS functionality helps make the right information available to the right people at the right time.

Best Practices

The following are best practices from this chapter:

- Although there are a number of changes, improvements, and updates in SharePoint BCS 2013, the underlying architecture has remained largely the same, so the changes will be of most interest to more experienced BCS developers.
- External content types are one of the key components in SharePoint 2013 BCS, and this chapter reviews the process of creating these by connecting to the Microsoft AdventureWorksLT database.
- There are three main ways that you can leverage the external content type in SharePoint: external lists, external data, and BCS web parts.
- Define associations for external content types that have relationships with others, such as the relationship between customers and orders.
- If using external data columns in SharePoint lists, periodically click the refresh icon to ensure that the most current data is displayed in your SharePoint lists.

- For simple databases with little or no logic on various columns or tables, SharePoint Designer may be a useful tool for creating write-back operations. However, for larger or more complex databases, use a more advanced tool, such as Visual Studio 2013.
- When including create or update operations on an external content type, it is important to create these operations before creating the external list in SharePoint.

Index

Symbols & Numerics

A

B

C

D

E

F

G

H

I

J

K

L

M

N

O

P

Q

R

S

T

U

V

W-X-Y-Z

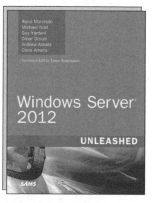

informIT.com THE TRUSTED TECHNOLOGY LEARNING SOURCE

PEARSON

Addison-Wesley | Cisco Press | EXAM/CRAM | IBM Press | QUE | PRENTICE HALL | SAMS | Safari Books Online